THE CAMBRIDGE HISTORY OF
THE AMERICAN ESSAY

From the country's beginning, essayists in the United States have used their prose to articulate the many ways their individuality has been shaped by the politics, social life, and culture of this place. *The Cambridge History of the American Essay* offers the fullest account to date of this diverse and complex history. From Puritan writings to essays by Indigenous authors, from Transcendentalist and Pragmatist texts to Harlem Renaissance essays, from New Criticism to New Journalism: The story of the American essay is told here, beginning in the early eighteenth century and ending with the vibrant, heterogeneous scene of contemporary essayistic writing. The essay in the United States has taken many forms: nature writing, travel writing, the genteel tradition, literary criticism, and hybrid genres such as the essay film and the photo essay. Across genres and identities, this volume offers a stirring account of American essayism into the twenty-first century.

CHRISTY WAMPOLE is an essayist and professor at Princeton University. She has published two scholarly books, *Degenerative Realism: Novel and Nation in Twenty-First-Century France* (2020) and *Rootedness: The Ramifications of a Metaphor* (2016), and a collection of essays titled *The Other Serious: Essays for the New American Generation* (2015).

JASON CHILDS is a writer and independent scholar based in Berlin and Dijon. He has published research on the essay in *The Cambridge Companion to the Essay* (2022), *The Edinburgh Companion to the Essay* (2022), and *The Essay at the Limits: Poetics, Politics and Form* (2021).

THE CAMBRIDGE HISTORY OF THE AMERICAN ESSAY

*

Edited by
CHRISTY WAMPOLE
Princeton University, New Jersey

JASON CHILDS
Independent Scholar

Shaftesbury Road, Cambridge CB2 8EA, United Kingdom

One Liberty Plaza, 20th Floor, New York, NY 10006, USA

477 Williamstown Road, Port Melbourne, VIC 3207, Australia

314–321, 3rd Floor, Plot 3, Splendor Forum, Jasola District Centre,
New Delhi – 110025, India

103 Penang Road, #05–06/07, Visioncrest Commercial, Singapore 238467

Cambridge University Press is part of Cambridge University Press & Assessment,
a department of the University of Cambridge.

We share the University's mission to contribute to society through the pursuit of
education, learning and research at the highest international levels of excellence.

www.cambridge.org
Information on this title: www.cambridge.org/9781316512708

DOI: 10.1017/9781009070041

© Cambridge University Press & Assessment 2024

This publication is in copyright. Subject to statutory exception and to the provisions
of relevant collective licensing agreements, no reproduction of any part may take
place without the written permission of Cambridge University Press & Assessment.

First published 2024

Printed in the United Kingdom by TJ Books Limited, Padstow, Cornwall 2024

A catalogue record for this publication is available from the British Library.

Library of Congress Cataloging-in-Publication Data
NAMES: Wampole, Christy, 1977– editor. | Childs, Jason (Independent scholar), editor.
TITLE: The Cambridge history of the American essay / edited by Christy Wampole,
Jason Childs.
DESCRIPTION: Cambridge ; New York, NY : Cambridge University Press, 2024. | Includes
bibliographical references.
IDENTIFIERS: LCCN 2023027898 (print) | LCCN 2023027899 (ebook) | ISBN 9781316512708
(hardback) | ISBN 9781009069021 (paperback) | ISBN 9781009070041 (ebook)
SUBJECTS: LCSH: American essays – History and criticism.
CLASSIFICATION: LCC PS420 .C36 2024 (print) | LCC PS420 (ebook) | DDC 814.009–dc23/eng/
20230919
LC record available at https://lccn.loc.gov/2023027898
LC ebook record available at https://lccn.loc.gov/2023027899

ISBN 978-1-316-51270-8 Hardback

Cambridge University Press & Assessment has no responsibility for the persistence
or accuracy of URLs for external or third-party internet websites referred to in this
publication and does not guarantee that any content on such websites is, or will
remain, accurate or appropriate.

Contents

Acknowledgments page ix
Notes on Contributors xi

Introduction 1
CHRISTY WAMPOLE

PART I
THE EMERGENCE OF THE AMERICAN ESSAY
(1710–1865)

1 · Essays to Do Good: Puritanism and the Birth of the American Essay 15
JAN STIEVERMANN

2 · Prattlers, Meddlers, Bachelors, Busy-Bodies: The Periodical Essay in the Eighteenth Century 32
RICHARD SQUIBBS

3 · *The Federalist* and the Founders 46
MATTHEW GARRETT

4 · American Nature Writing: 1700–1900 61
NOAH RAWLINGS

5 · The Essay and Transcendentalism 81
LAURA DASSOW WALLS

6 · Old World Shadows in the New: Europe and the Nineteenth-Century American Essay 96
PHILIP COLEMAN

Contents

7 · Poet-Essayists and Magazine Culture in the Nineteenth Century   114
JOHN MICHAEL

8 · Antebellum Women Essayists   129
CHARLENE AVALLONE

PART II
VOICING THE AMERICAN EXPERIMENT
(1865–1945)

9 · Writing Freedom before and after Emancipation   149
KINOHI NISHIKAWA

10 · Social Justice and the American Essay   166
CHRISTY WAMPOLE

11 · "Zones of Contention" in the Genteel Essay   182
JENNY SPINNER

12 · The American Comic Essay   197
DAVID E. E. SLOANE

13 · Nineteenth-Century American Travel Essays: Aesthetics, Modernity, and National Identity   218
BRIGITTE BAILEY

14 · American Pragmatism: An Essayistic Conception of Truth   235
JONATHAN LEVIN

15 · The Essay in the Harlem Renaissance   250
SHAWN ANTHONY CHRISTIAN

16 · The Southern Agrarians and the New Criticism   265
SARAH E. GARDNER

17 · Subjective and Objective: Newspaper Columns   280
WILLIAM E. DOW

18 · The Experience of Art: The Essay in Visual Culture   300
TOM HUHN

Contents

19 · The Essay in American Music *314*
KYLE GANN

PART III
POSTWAR ESSAYS AND ESSAYISM (1945–2000)

20 · The Essay and the Twentieth-Century Literary Magazine *337*
ELENI THEODOROPOULOS

21 · Germans in Amerika: Written Possibility, Uninhabitable Reality *361*
FLORIAN FUCHS

22 · The Essay and the American Left *378*
ANDREA CAPRA

23 · The Native American Essay *395*
HERTHA D. SWEET WONG

24 · Conservatism and the Essay *410*
JEFFREY R. DUDAS

25 · Opinions and Decisions: Legal Essays *425*
PETER GOODRICH

26 · World War Two to #MeToo: The Personal and the Political in the American Feminist Essay *441*
ELLENA SAVAGE

27 · Self-Portraits in a Convex Mirror: The Essay in American Poetry *460*
LUCY ALFORD

28 · The American Essay and (Social) Science *477*
TED ANTON

29 · Philosophy as a Kind of Writing *490*
PAUL JENNER

30 · The Essay and Literary Postmodernism: Seriousness and Exhaustion *509*
STEFANO ERCOLINO

Contents

PART IV
TOWARD THE CONTEMPORARY AMERICAN ESSAY
(2000–2020)

31 · The American Essay Film: A Neglected Genre   527
NORA M. ALTER

32 · Literary Theory, Criticism, and the Essay   545
CAROLINA IRIBARREN

33 · Gender, Queerness, and the American Essay   565
DAVID LAZAR

34 · Disability and the American Essay   582
ANNE FINGER

35 · The Radical Hybridity of the Lyric Essay   597
MICHAEL ASKEW

36 · Writing Migration: Multiculturalism, Democracy, and the Essay Form   612
CYRUS R. K. PATELL

37 · Latinx Culture and the Essay   627
YOLANDA PADILLA

38 · Black Experience through the Essay   643
WALTON MUYUMBA

39 · The Essay and the Anthropocene   668
DAVID CARLIN

Recommendations for Further Reading   683
Index   697

Acknowledgments

First, we'd like to thank all of the contributors to this volume, who did much of the writing and research for their chapters under the challenging circumstances brought by the pandemic. Their perseverance in the face of those difficulties is commendable, and we appreciate all of the efforts they made to get their contributions to us and work alongside us through the various phases of editing.

Ray Ryan at Cambridge University Press has been a wonderful interlocutor and editor as we tackled this intimidating project. Thank you, Ray, for your sharp editorial eye and your guidance as this book of such enormity came together. We'd also like to thank Edgar Mendez at the press for his help with the project logistics.

Joseph Tabbi and Thomas Karshan offered helpful and encouraging feedback on the project in its earliest stages. Pierre Azou, Carolina Iribarren, and Hannah Grunow did incredible work on the Recommendations for Further Reading section, for which we are very grateful. Their thoroughness, determination, and many hours of work are much appreciated. We are also grateful for the attentive copy-editing done by Anne Sussmann, Hannah Grunow, Cecelia Ramsey, Pierre Azou, and Molly O'Brien, which put the finishing touches on the volume. Special credit is owed to Hannah Grunow, who went above and beyond on the many chapters she worked on.

We would like to thank our friends, family, and colleagues who supported us over the years this volume took to come together. Their encouragement was especially important during the most challenging phases of the project, which we might not have completed without their moral support. In particular, Jason Childs would like to thank Marion Childs and Noah Childs for their love, generosity, and patience. Christy Wampole would like to thank Florian, her loved ones and colleagues in Texas, Florida, California, New Jersey, Germany, and France, and the students at Princeton in her graduate seminars and creative writing courses on the essay for their thoughtfulness, originality, and the inspiration they provided.

Finally, we wanted to honor the rich contributions to the field of essay studies of two tremendous scholars who, sadly, passed away recently. The first is Cheryl A. Wall (Rutgers University), whose book *On Freedom and the Will to Adorn: The Art of the African American Essay* (2019) showed the vast impact of Black writing on expanding the possibilities of what the essay can do. We'd also like to honor Ned Stuckey-French (Florida State University), whose many interventions on the essay were read and appreciated by essay lovers across the country, and who had pledged a chapter to this volume that his passing regrettably prevented him from writing. His book *The American Essay in the American Century* (2011) was an important model and inspiration for our own volume.

Notes on Contributors

LUCY ALFORD is Assistant Professor of Literature at Wake Forest University, specializing in twentieth- and twenty-first-century American and comparative poetry and poetics. Her book *Forms of Poetic Attention* (2020) examines the modes of attention poems both require and produce, drawing examples from a range of historical and linguistic settings. She holds a PhD in Comparative Literature from Stanford University and a PhD in Modern Thought from the University of Aberdeen. Her poems have been published in the *Warwick Review*, *Literary Matters*, *Streetlight*, *Harpur Palate*, *Mantis*, *Atelier*, *Action*, *Spectacle*, and *Fence*.

NORA M. ALTER is a scholar of comparative film and media arts and Professor at Temple University in Philadelphia. She has published numerous essays on cultural and visual studies, contemporary art, and sound studies. She is author of *Vietnam Protest Theatre: The Television War on Stage* (1996), *Sound Matters* (2004), *Chris Marker* (2006), and *The Essay Film after Fact and Fiction* (2018). She has a forthcoming monograph on Harun Farocki.

TED ANTON is Professor of English specializing in nonfiction and science writing at Chicago's DePaul University. He is the author of five books, including *Programmable Planet: The Synthetic Biology Revolution* (2023). His articles have appeared in *Nautilus*, the *Chicago Tribune*, *Publishers Weekly*, and other magazines. He is a winner of a Carl Sandburg Award for nonfiction from the Chicago Public Library and a finalist for a National Magazine Award.

MICHAEL ASKEW is an independent scholar and Eric Gregory Award–winning poet based in Gloucestershire, UK. He was recently awarded his PhD from the University of East Anglia for his thesis, entitled "The Lyric Essay: A Contemporary Mode of Reading and Writing." He has also published research on the essayist Eliot Weinberger.

CHARLENE AVALLONE works as an independent scholar, having served on the faculties of the University of Hawai'i and the University of Notre Dame, where she was a cofounder of the Gender Studies Program. Her essays on nineteenth-century literary culture appear in such venues as *ESQ: A Journal of the American Renaissance*, *George Sand Studies*, *Legacy*, *Nineteenth-Century Literature*, *PMLA*, *Reception*, and in numerous critical anthologies. She was president of the Margaret Fuller Society from 2017 to 2020.

Notes on Contributors

BRIGITTE BAILEY is Professor of English at the University of New Hampshire. She is the author of *American Travel Literature, Gendered Aesthetics, and the Italian Tour, 1824–1862* (2018), has coedited two books – *Transatlantic Women: Nineteenth-Century American Women Writers and Great Britain* (2012) and *Margaret Fuller and Her Circles* (2013) – and has edited a special issue of *Nineteenth-Century Prose* on Margaret Fuller (2015). She is coediting the Library of America volume *Margaret Fuller: Collected Writing* (forthcoming). Her current book project examines periodical depictions of metropolitan spaces, especially of New York, from 1830 to 1860.

ANDREA CAPRA holds a PhD in Italian from Stanford University and is a Cotsen postdoctoral fellow at Princeton's Society of Fellows. His current book project analyzes horror's phenomenology in modernity and its representation in literary texts beyond the horror genre. He also writes for academic audiences on the storytelling surrounding computational technologies and for more public-facing venues on internet-centered fringe political movements. Some of his most recent work has appeared in the *Los Angeles Review of Books*, *il verri*, *Neue Zürcher Zeitung*, and *Angelaki: Journal of the Theoretical Humanities*.

DAVID CARLIN is Professor of Creative Writing at the Royal Melbourne Institute of Technology University in Australia. His books include the collaboratively authored *The After-Normal* (2019) and *100 Atmospheres: Studies in Scale and Wonder* (2019), as well as *Our Father Who Wasn't There* (2010) and *The Abyssinian Contortionist* (2015). He has coedited volumes including *A to Z of Creative Writing Methods* (2023), *The Near and the Far*, volumes 1 and 2 (2016 and 2019), and *Performing Digital* (2015) and made award-winning works for radio, film, theater, and circus. David is a copresident of the NonfictioNOW Conference and cofounder of the WrICE Asia-Pacific Collaborative Residency program and the non/ fictionLab research group.

JASON CHILDS is a writer and independent scholar based in Berlin and Dijon. He coedited *The Cambridge History of the British Essay* (forthcoming) and has published research on the essay in *The Cambridge Companion to the Essay* (2022), *The Edinburgh Companion to the Essay* (2022), and *The Essay at the Limits: Poetics, Politics and Form* (2021). His writing has also appeared in the *Sydney Review of Books* and *American Book Review*, among others. He received his PhD from the University of Technology, Sydney, and trained as a psychotherapist at Deakin University in Melbourne. He maintains a small private counseling practice.

SHAWN ANTHONY CHRISTIAN is Associate Professor and Chairperson of English at Florida International University. He is the author of *The Harlem Renaissance and the Idea of a New Negro Reader* (2016). His other writings on the Harlem Renaissance and African American literary and print culture have appeared in several journals and volumes, including *The Harlem Renaissance Revisited* (2010), *Editing the Harlem Renaissance* (2021), and *African American Literature in Transition, 1930–1940* (2022).

PHILIP COLEMAN is Professor in the School of English, Trinity College Dublin, where he is a fellow. With Calista McRae, he coedited *The Selected Letters of John Berryman* (2020), and he has published *John Berryman's Public Vision* (2014). He has coedited several essay collections, including *"After thirty Falls": New Essays on John Berryman* (2007), *Critical Insights: David Foster Wallace* (2015), *John Berryman: Centenary Essays* (2017), *George Saunders: Critical Essays* (2017), and *Robert Lowell and Irish Poetry* (2020). He contributed an essay entitled "Transatlantic Essayism" to *The Cambridge History of the British Essay*, edited by Jason Childs and Denise Gigante (forthcoming).

WILLIAM E. DOW is Professor of American Literature at the Université Gustave Eiffel (Paris-Est) and Professor of English at The American University of Paris. He is an associate editor of *Literary Journalism Studies* (Northwestern University Press) and has published articles in such journals as *Publications of the Modern Language Association*, *Twentieth-Century Literature*, *ESQ: A Journal of the American Renaissance*, and *MELUS*. He is the author of the book *Narrating Class in American Fiction* (2009) and coeditor of *Richard Wright: New Readings in the 21st Century* (2011), *Richard Wright in a Post-Racial Imaginary* (2014), *Latitudes Unknown: James Baldwin's Radical Imagination* (2019), and *The Routledge Companion to American Literary Journalism* (2020).

JEFFREY R. DUDAS is Professor of Political Science at the University of Connecticut, where he also serves on the American Studies Executive Committee. He is cofounder and co-coordinator of UConn's MA program in Politics and Popular Culture. He is author of *The Cultivation of Resentment: Treaty Rights and the New Right* (2008) and *Raised Right: Fatherhood in Modern American Conservatism* (2017). His essays appear in numerous venues, including *Law and Society Review*, *Law, Culture, and the Humanities*, *Law and Social Inquiry*, *Studies in Law, Politics, and Society*, and *Perspectives on Politics*.

STEFANO ERCOLINO is Associate Professor of Comparative Literature at Ca' Foscari University of Venice. His work has appeared in *Comparative Literature*, *Novel*, and *Historical Materialism*, among others. He is the author of *The Maximalist Novel: From Thomas Pynchon's "Gravity's Rainbow" to Roberto Bolaño's "2666"* (2014), *The Novel-Essay, 1884–1947* (2014), and, with Massimo Fusillo, of *Empatia negativa: Il punto di vista del male* (Negative empathy: The point of view of evil) (2022). He taught at Yonsei University's Underwood International College and has been a visiting professor at the University of Manchester, postdoctoral fellow at Freie Universität Berlin, and Fulbright Scholar at Stanford University. He co-edited the volume *Critica sperimentale: Franco Moretti e la letteratura* (Experimental Criticism: Franco Moretti and Literature) (2021), to be translated into English by Verso.

ANNE FINGER is a memoirist, novelist, and short story writer. Her most recent novel is *A Woman, in Bed* (2018). Her short story collection *Call Me Ahab* (2009), which won the Prairie Schooner Award, takes iconic disability stories such as *Moby-Dick* and "crips" them, rewriting them from a disabled perspective. She has also written two memoirs, two short story collections, and a novel, *Bone Truth* (1994). She is the recipient of a Creative Capital Grant and the Berlin Prize (2019), and she has held residencies at MacDowell, Djerassi, Yaddo, and Hedgebrook.

FLORIAN FUCHS is a postdoctoral researcher in Comparative Literature and Media Studies in the EXC 2020 "Temporal Communities" at Freie Universität Berlin. He received his PhD from Yale University in 2017 and was a postdoctoral researcher at

Princeton University from 2018 to 2021. His first book, entitled *Civic Storytelling: The Rise of Short Forms and the Agency of Literature*, was published with Zone Books in 2023. He coedited and cotranslated *History, Metaphors, Fables: A Hans Blumenberg Reader*, published in 2020 with Cornell University Press.

KYLE GANN is a composer and the author of seven books, including *The Arithmetic of Listening: Tuning Theory and History for the Impractical Musician* (2019) and *Charles Ives's Concord: Essays after a Sonata* (2017), as well as books on Robert Ashley, Conlon Nancarrow, and John Cage's *4'33"*. From 1986 to 2005, he was new-music critic for the *Village Voice* in New York City. Since 1997, he has taught at Bard College, where he is Hawver Professor of Music. His musical magnum opus is *Hyperchromatica* (2015–2021), a three-hour-plus work for retuned, computerized pianos.

SARAH E. GARDNER is Distinguished University Professor and Professor of History at Mercer University. She is author most recently of *Reviewing the South: The Literary Marketplace and the Southern Renaissance, 1920–1941* (2017) and coeditor of *The Lost Lectures of C. Vann Woodward* (2020) and *Insiders/Outsiders: Toward a New History of Southern Thought* (2021). She has written extensively on mid-nineteenth- and early twentieth-century literary culture. She is currently writing a book on reading during the American Civil War.

MATTHEW GARRETT is Associate Professor of English and American Studies at Wesleyan University. His work concerns the relationship between literary form and social history. He is the author of *Episodic Poetics: Politics and Literary Form after the Constitution* (2014) and editor of *The Cambridge Companion to Narrative Theory* (2018), and his essays have appeared in *American Literary History*, *American Quarterly*, *Critical Inquiry*, *ELH*, the *Journal of Cultural Economy*, *Radical History Review*, and other venues.

PETER GOODRICH is Professor of Law and Director of the Program in Law and Humanities at Cardozo School of Law and Visiting Professor in the School of Social Science, NYU Abu Dhabi. He is an ardent advocate of argute alliterations and of the silent *p*, as in raspberry or psittacist. Chef, filmmaker, and essayist, his most recent book, *Judicial Uses of Images: Vision in Decision*, was published in 2023.

TOM HUHN is Chair of the Art History and Visual and Critical Studies departments at the School of Visual Arts in New York City. He wrote *Imitation and Society: The Persistence of Mimesis in the Aesthetics of Burke, Hogarth, and Kant* (2004) and has edited or coedited *The Cambridge Companion to Adorno* (2004), *The Wake of Art: Criticism, Philosophy, and the Ends of Taste* (1998), and *The Semblance of Subjectivity: Essays in Adorno's Aesthetic Theory* (1997). His essays have appeared in *Art in America*, *The Oxford Encyclopedia of Aesthetics*, *New German Critique*, *British Journal of Aesthetics*, and *Eighteenth-Century Studies*.

CAROLINA IRIBARREN is a PhD candidate in French at Princeton University. Her areas of focus are twentieth-century literature and film, with a special interest in Marxism and feminist theory. She has forthcoming and published articles on Simone Weil and ecology, Virginia Woolf and communication, and Anne Carson's translations of ancient Greek plays. Her present research concerns experimental fiction and film after May 1968 and the interplay of realist-utopian impulses therein.

PAUL JENNER is a lecturer in English at Loughborough University. His primary research areas are literature and the philosophy of literature. He has published, among others, on Marilynne Robinson, Stanley Cavell, Thomas Kuhn, George Santayana, and Richard Rorty. He is currently writing a monograph on Stanley Cavell and Marilynne Robinson.

DAVID LAZAR'S most recent books are *Celeste Holm Syndrome: On Character Actors* (2020) and the anthology *Don't Look Now: Writers on What They Wish They Hadn't Seen* (2020). His other essay collections include *I'll Be Your Mirror: Essays and Aphorisms* (2017), *Occasional Desire* (2013), *The Body of Brooklyn* (2012), and two prose poem collections, including *Who's Afraid of Helen of Troy* (2016). Ten of his essays were named Notable Essays of the Year by *Best American Essays*. Lazar was awarded a Guggenheim Foundation Fellowship in Nonfiction in 2016. He is the coeditor of Ohio State University's 21st Century Essays imprint. Lazar created the undergraduate and graduate nonfiction programs at Ohio University and Columbia College Chicago.

JONATHAN LEVIN is Professor of English at the University of Mary Washington. He is the author of *The Poetics of Transition: Emerson, Pragmatism, and American Literary Modernism* (1999), as well as numerous essays and reviews on American literature and culture. He has edited editions of Thoreau's *Walden* and *"Civil Disobedience"* and Gertrude Stein's *Three Lives*, as well as a children's illustrated *Walt Whitman*. He has taught at Columbia and Fordham Universities, served as Dean at SUNY-Purchase and at Drew University, and served as Provost at Mary Washington, where he presently teaches and chairs the Department of English and Linguistics.

JOHN MICHAEL is John Hall Deane Professor of English and of Visual and Cultural Studies at the University of Rochester. He is the author of *Emerson and Skepticism: The Cipher of the World* (1988), *Anxious Intellects: Academic Professionals, Public Intellectuals, and Enlightenment Values* (2000), *Identity and the Failure of America from Thomas Jefferson to the War on Terror* (2008), and *Secular Lyric: The Modernization of the Poem in Poe, Whitman and Dickinson* (2018). He has published many articles on American literature, cultural studies, and critical theory, most recently on the novel epistemology of Amitav Ghosh and on history as lyric. He is finishing a book on globalization and the humanities.

WALTON MUYUMBA is Ruth N. Halls Associate Professor at Indiana University Bloomington. He teaches literary studies and creative writing. Muyumba's essays have appeared in the *Atlantic*, the *Believer*, *Film Quarterly*, *liquid blackness*, the *New York Review of Books*, and *Oxford American*, among other outlets. He has produced scholarship for *The Cambridge History of American Poetry*, *The Oxford Handbook of Critical Improvisational Studies*, *The Princeton Encyclopedia of Poetry and Poetics*, and *Trained Capacities: John Dewey, Rhetoric, and Democratic Practice*. Muyumba is the author of *The Shadow and the Act: Black Intellectual Practice, Jazz Improvisation, and Philosophical Pragmatism* (2009).

Notes on Contributors

KINOHI NISHIKAWA is Associate Professor of English and African American Studies at Princeton University. He is the author of *Street Players: Black Pulp Fiction and the Making of a Literary Underground* (2018), and he is currently writing "Black Paratext," a history of modern African American literature and book design. Nishikawa's essays have appeared in *PMLA*, *American Literary History*, *MELUS*, *Chicago Review*, and other journals.

YOLANDA PADILLA is Associate Professor in the School of Interdisciplinary Arts and Sciences at the University of Washington, Bothell. She is coeditor of three volumes: *Latina Histories and Cultures: Feminist Readings and Recoveries of Archival Knowledge* (2023), *Bridges, Borders, and Breaks: History, Narrative, and Nation in Twenty-First-Century Chicana/o Literary Criticism* (2016), and *The Plays of Josefina Niggli: Recovered Landmarks of Latina Literature* (2007). She is currently working on a book on early twentieth-century borderlands literature and print culture, and has published work related to this project in journals such as *New Centennial Review*, *Women's Studies Quarterly*, *English Language Notes*, and *Aztlan*.

CYRUS R. K. PATELL is Professor of English at New York University and the author of *Emergent U.S. Literatures: From Multiculturalism to Cosmopolitanism in the Late Twentieth Century* (2014), *Cosmopolitanism and the Literary Imagination* (2015), and, most recently, *Lucasfilm: Filmmaking, Philosophy, and the Star Wars Universe* (2021). He is the coeditor (with Deborah Lindsay Williams) of the *Oxford History of the Novel in English*, volume 8, *American Fiction since 1940* and is presently at work on a study of the global spread of Shakespeare's *Hamlet* and a personal narrative about the importance of cosmopolitanism.

NOAH RAWLINGS is a writer from North Carolina and a doctoral student in Princeton University's Department of French and Italian. His criticism, reporting, and creative writing have appeared in *Art Papers*, *Burnaway*, *Joyland*, and elsewhere; he also copyedits for the *Los Angeles Review of Books*. His research concerns the history of environmental thought and its manifestations in literature, philosophy, visual art, and material practices (agriculture, horticulture) in the long nineteenth century.

ELLENA SAVAGE is an early career scholar in creative writing with an interest in the essay; life writing; queer, feminist, and activist literatures; and experimental textual practices. Her debut essay collection, *Blueberries* (2020), was shortlisted for the Victorian Premier's Literary Award and longlisted for the Stella Prize. She was a Marten Bequest traveling scholar in 2019–21 and a teaching fellow at the University of Birmingham in 2022–23. She is currently working on a novel with support from the Australia Council for the Arts.

DAVID E. E. SLOANE is Professor Emeritus, University of New Haven. He earned his PhD at Duke University in 1970. Among the books he has authored are *Mark Twain as a Literary Comedian* (1979), *The Literary Humor of the Urban Northeast, 1830–1890* (1983), *American Humor Magazines and Comic Periodicals* (1987), *Adventures of Huckleberry Finn: American Comic Vision* (1988), and *Student Companion to Mark Twain* (2001). He is the editor of *Mark Twain's Humor: Critical Essays* (1993) and *New Directions in American Humor* (1998); he also contributed "Huckleberry Finn and Race:

A Teacher's Toolbox" to Victor Doyno's CD *Huck Finn: The Complete Buffalo and Erie County Public Library Manuscript* (2003).

JENNY SPINNER is Professor of English at Saint Joseph's University in Philadelphia. She is the author of creative essays as well as numerous works on the history of women essayists, including *Of Women and the Essay: An Anthology from 1655 to 2000* (2018). She serves as a senior editor of *Assay: A Journal of Nonfiction Studies*.

RICHARD SQUIBBS is Associate Professor of English at DePaul University in Chicago and author of *Urban Enlightenment and the Eighteenth-Century Periodical Essay* (2014), as well as more recent articles and chapters on British and early American periodicals. He is currently writing a monograph that explores the messy entanglements of picaresque fiction and the early English novel, portions of which have appeared in *Eighteenth-Century Fiction* (2018) and *The Eighteenth Century: Theory and Interpretation* (2019).

JAN STIEVERMANN is Professor of the History of Christianity in the United States at Heidelberg University. His publications include book-length studies of Emerson's theology and aesthetics (2007), as well as of Cotton Mather's *Biblia Americana* (2016). For the scholarly edition of the *Biblia*, he has edited volumes 5 and 10 (2015 and 2022), and he serves as the executive editor of the whole project. Among other multiauthored volumes, he coedited *A Peculiar Mixture: German-Language Cultures and Identities in Eighteenth-Century North America* (2013), *The Oxford Handbook of Jonathan Edwards* (2021), and *The Bible in Early Transatlantic Pietism and Evangelicalism* (2022).

ELENI THEODOROPOULOS is a PhD student in comparative thought and literature at Johns Hopkins University, where she works on the essay and twentieth-century essayistic fiction.

LAURA DASSOW WALLS is Professor Emerita at the University of Notre Dame, where she taught American literature and the history and theory of ecological thought; previously she taught at Lafayette College and the University of South Carolina. Her book *Henry David Thoreau: A Life* (2017) received Phi Beta Kappa's Christian Gauss Award and the *Los Angeles Times* Book Award for Biography. Her other books include the award-winning *Passage to Cosmos: Alexander von Humboldt and the Shaping of America* (2009), *Emerson's Life in Science: The Culture of Truth* (2003), and *Seeing New Worlds: Henry David Thoreau and Nineteenth-Century Natural Science* (1995). Currently she is working on a literary biography of the American writer Barry Lopez.

CHRISTY WAMPOLE is an essayist and professor at Princeton University. In addition to her two scholarly books, *Degenerative Realism: Novel and Nation in Twenty-First-Century France* (2020) and *Rootedness: The Ramifications of a Metaphor* (2016), she has published a collection of essays titled *The Other Serious: Essays for the New American Generation* (2015). Her work has appeared in the *New York Times*, the *New Yorker*, *Aeon Magazine*, the *European Review of Books*, *Public Books*, and the *Los Angeles Review of Books*.

Notes on Contributors

HERTHA D. SWEET WONG, Professor of the Graduate School at the University of California, Berkeley, teaches and writes about autobiography, visual culture, and American literature, particularly Indigenous literatures. She is author of *Picturing Identity: Contemporary American Autobiography in Image and Text* and *Sending My Heart Back across the Years: Tradition and Innovation in Native American Autobiography* and numerous essays on Indigenous literatures, as well as editor or coeditor of three anthologies of Native American literatures.

Introduction

CHRISTY WAMPOLE

In a photo essay called *America and the Americans* (1966), which pairs John Steinbeck's writing with striking images taken by forty American photographers, the reader encounters this description of the country's gestation:

> America did not exist. Four centuries of work, of bloodshed, of loneliness and fear created this land. We built America and the process made us Americans – a new breed, rooted in all races, stained and tinted with all colors, a seeming ethnic anarchy. Then in a little, little time, we became more alike than we were different – a new society; not great, but fitted by our very faults for greatness. *E Pluribus Unum*.[1]

The distinctiveness of this passage comes from its blunt rendering of America's chaotic, less than glorious inauguration, but it is also remarkable how stealthily Steinbeck draws parallels – maybe unconsciously – between the singular country he describes and the anomalous literary form in which he writes. Three of his words make this connection. The first is *process*. The essayist is a person who transcribes their thought processes, tracking the swerves and outgrowths of a brain in motion. Rather than presenting what has already been fully conceived, the essay shows its work and consists of its own unfolding. The second is *anarchy*. The essayist is sometimes an unruly writer, dispensing with more ordered types of writing and choosing instead a wilder, looser form of expression. Literary disobedience is its vocation. The third is *faults*. From its inception, the essay featured the essayist's flaws. We find, for example, in Montaigne's famous preface to his essays an accommodation – even a celebration – of the author's many defects and imperfections. The essayist is an imperfect human, and these imperfections make ideal fodder for the genre's ruminations. The United States, in its striving to

---

[1] John Steinbeck, *America and the Americans* (New York: Bantam Books, 1968), 12–13.

become a more perfect nation, tacitly admits that it has not yet achieved perfection.

What we the editors hope will be clear in this volume is that a natural compatibility exists between the essay form and the unusual experiment called the United States. A diversity of form and content, a certain insubordinate spirit, a striving for things to come: A country might never have been more suited to tell itself through a particular literary genre. Although the essay existed long before the United States became a country – the genre having been officially christened by Montaigne in 1580 upon the publication of his first edition of the *Essais*, but existing already in a nameless, prototypical form since antiquity – the affinity between the two is hard to deny. The essay thrives today in the United States and has given Americans an ever-renewing literary-scientific tool for studying the self. This self might be an individual or the member of a social group; it might turn its attentions outward or inward, preoccupied with life as it was, as it is, or as it might soon be. This volume attests to the richness of the American essay, assuming such a thing can be said confidently to exist; both the United States and the essay are elusive objects.

Telling the history of the American essay – and we use the shorthand "American" in place of the bulkier "US American" throughout the volume – is no small task. There are surely a few glaring omissions, but given that the volume spans roughly 310 years and over 3,000,000 square miles, this was hard to avoid. That said, the essayists and essays featured by our contributors do quite a good job of illustrating the depth and breadth of American essay writing, and the patterns that emerge offer a compelling portrait of a country trying to figure itself out. As every book on the essay points out, to try (*essayer*) is the essay's main task. What exactly are the essayists profiled here trying to do? It varies from essay to essay. This edited volume offers a whole taxonomy of trying, an almanac of attempts.

Even the most schematic list of important American essays that have been anthologized, widely taught, or rewarded with prizes or critical acclaim demonstrates the vast range of styles and themes Americans have embraced in their writing. If one were to read one by one the following pieces, a general sense of the sprawling, polychromatic United States would begin to take shape: Judith Sargent Murray's "On the Equality of the Sexes" (1790), William Apess's "An Indian's Looking-Glass for the White Man" (1833), Ralph Waldo Emerson's "Self-Reliance" (1841), Henry David Thoreau's "Where I Lived, and What I Lived For" (1854), Sui Sin Far's "Leaves from the Mental Portfolio of an Eurasian" (1890), Mark Twain's "The Turning Point in My Life" (1910),

Introduction

Hannah Arendt's "We Refugees" (1943), Aldo Leopold's "The Land Ethic" (1949), Richard Hofstadter's "The Paranoid Style in American Politics" (1964), Susan Sontag's "Notes on Camp" (1964), William H. Gass's "On Talking to Oneself" (1979), Audre Lorde's "The Master's Tools Will Never Dismantle the Master's House" (1984), Nancy Mairs's "On Being a Cripple" (1986), Richard Rodriguez's "Hispanic" (2002), or collections like W. E. B. Du Bois's *The Souls of Black Folk* (1903), James Baldwin's *Notes of a Native Son* (1955), Joan Didion's *Slouching towards Bethlehem* (1968), or Alexander Chee's *How to Write an Autobiographical Novel: Essays* (2018). American writers have used the essay's literary in-betweenness to explore other forms of the in-between. For example, Gloria Anzaldúa's *Borderlands/La Frontera: The New Mestiza* (1987) explores the ambivalence of border spaces, smudging the line between Texas and Mexico, colonizer and colonized, men and women, straight and gay. Fascinating formal experimentations, such as James Agee and Walker Evans's photo-essay collaboration *Let Us Now Praise Famous Men* (1941), Orson Welles's documentary essay film *Filming Othello* (1978), or Claudia Rankine's multigenre instant classic *Citizen* (2014), show that the essay need not remain a purely textual object; it is capable of using whatever is at hand – music, images moving or still – to divulge its meaning. American essayists have treated every subject, in every style, through every medium.

There have been a few modest attempts to tell parts of the history of the American essay – these have informed our own work – but the scale of *The Cambridge History of the American Essay* is unprecedented. Ned Stuckey-French's *The American Essay in the American Century* (2014) and Cheryl A. Wall's *On Freedom and the Will to Adorn: The African American Essay* (2019) were important models for us. Anthologies by Philip Lopate, Jenny Spinner, Garrett Kaoru Hongo, and John D'Agata, as well as Robert Atwan's *The Best American Essays* series, helped us craft a list of writers whose work has become part of the essayistic canon and introduced us to lesser-known writers who have brought important innovations to the form. Several *Cambridge Histories* were also indispensable as this project came together.[2] In the Recommendations for

---

2 These include *The Cambridge Companion to the Essay* (eds. Kara Wittman and Evan Kindley), *The Cambridge History of African American Literature* (eds. Maryemma Graham and Jerry W. Ward Jr.), *The Cambridge History of American Literature* (ed. Sacvan Bercovitch), *The Cambridge History of American Women's Literature* (ed. Dale M. Bauer), *The Cambridge History of Asian American Literature* (eds. Rajini Srikanth and Min Hyoung Song), *The Cambridge History of Gay and Lesbian Literature* (eds. E. L. McCallum and Mikko Tuhkanen), *The Cambridge History of Latina/o American Literature* (eds. John Morán González and Laura Lomas), and *The Cambridge History of Native American Literature* (ed. Melanie Benson Taylor).

Further Reading section at the end of this book, readers will find an extensive list of monographs, edited volumes, articles, and anthologies, all of which offer important insights on the history and theory of the essay form.

Our definition of the essay is – like the genre – quite open ended. We've included short prose works that call themselves essays and others that do not bear this name but retain the essay's qualities: brevity, attentiveness to a specific field of contemplation, a translucence that allows the writer's subjectivity to shine through. In addition, readers will also find essayistic writing that borrows from other genres like sermons, memoirs, confessions, manifestos, speeches, meditations, dialogues, portraits, epistolary writing, and polemical texts. Composite forms such as the photo essay, the essay film, the essayistic novel, essayistic poetry, and other transmedial artifacts are also explored throughout. The essay is and always has been a hybrid entity. Our contributors have embraced the paradox of the essay: namely, that for such a small-scale type of writing, it hungrily absorbs into it all possible themes and neighboring literary forms. The essay's simultaneous smallness and largeness are celebrated in the following pages.

How to organize the vast history of the American essay? Chronologically? By subgenre or theme? We've decided that the best approach was all of these combined; in other words, we decided not to decide. The volume follows a loose chronological flow, with chapters clustered into four eras: The Emergence of the American Essay (1710–1865), Voicing the American Experiment (1865–1945), Postwar Essays and Essayism (1945–2000), and Toward the Contemporary American Essay (2000–2020). These dates provide an architecture around which the contributors could freely build the histories of certain subgenres (the lyric essay, the nature essay, the travel essay), important figures (Cotton Mather, Margaret Fuller, James Baldwin), philosophical tendencies (Transcendentalism, Pragmatism), themes (the environment, music, law, art, science), or literary movements, critical schools, or aesthetic tendencies (the Harlem Renaissance, the Southern Agrarians and New Criticism, New Journalism, the New York Intellectuals). In some chapters, it was necessary for contributors to reach beyond the assigned time frame to offer earlier context or later updates to the developments they lay out in detail. Our ambitions were far greater than what was possible in the time allotted for the project, but we hope that scholars of the essay will be inspired by what we've tried to do here and continue the work we've begun, recognizing promising sites for expansion throughout these pages.

Part 1: The Emergence of the American Essay (1710–1865) shows that many of the earliest American essays sought answers to spiritual, political, philosophical, and moral questions. Puritan writings of the early eighteenth century were pedagogical at their core, offering guidance on theological problems or delivering religious instruction. These writings had a special relationship with the sermon, a feature that endures in American writing even today. In early political writings like *The Federalist* (1787–88), one perceives the gravity of the task before the Founders: to codify a fresh, tyranny-resistant politics. The inherent paradox of this scene – namely, that slaveholders were championing liberty in their writings – would not be fully acknowledged until much later, particularly in essays by Black Americans whose ancestors had been enslaved by whites. Later, starting in the 1820s and '30s, the Transcendentalists crafted a spiritually inflected philosophy centered on the self-reliant individual. The pondering of questions on responsibility, service to one's community, and how one should live characterizes the compact, contemplative prose of Transcendentalism. In the years leading up to the Civil War, many American essays debating the ethics of slavery or the rights of women became a fixture of public writing. In the antebellum period, it was often white women who were first able to take up the pen to counter the assumption of a universal subject who could speak on behalf of everyone. The seeds of liberation were planted at this time, germinating too slowly for many of those who'd called for freedom in their writing to experience it themselves. And it was only later that Native Americans began to offer a fuller record via the essay form of the many ways their lives were convulsed by settler colonialism. The earliest American essays also attempted to capture the enormity and strangeness of the landscape, flora, and fauna of this new continent. This scientific and aesthetic attention to nature would initiate a rich tradition of nature writing in the decades to follow, expressed in various modes: the purely descriptive, the idealized, the elegiac. For the recent arrivals, this wild setting offered the possibility of a rupture with the past and with Europe. One perceives in American essays of the eighteenth and nineteenth century an anxiety about this break. Essayists of the time were clearly pulled between a respect and sense of indebtedness toward European tastes and traditions and a desire to produce something truly new and tailored to measure for a populace that had less and less in common with those on the old continent. For example, many American periodical essays of the eighteenth century followed conventions of their British equivalents – such as the use of a bachelor persona disguised behind an often humorous pseudonym – yet they also caricatured their European counterparts and sought to describe new social types that only existed in the United States. As a specifically American magazine industry burgeoned and the survival rate of its publications increased, a new poetics emerged along with a new critical language for talking about literature and the arts. Literary magazines of the nineteenth century published criticism of fiction and poetry, seeking mass audiences not only for the magazines themselves but to promote a growing body of writing by American novelists and poets. The history of American essayism has been one of increasing access, an opening up of channels of expression to more and more kinds of people whose destinies could barely be compared. As more people began to tell their lives through the essay, the genre took on new features, broached new subjects, and expanded the record of human experience.

Part 2: Voicing the American Experiment (1865–1945) follows the developments in the essay from the end of the Civil War to the end of World War II, a period of sweeping social and technological change. After emancipation, Black Americans could finally give a fuller account of their experiences, aspirations, and fears in an age in which, though liberated from slavery, they still faced cruelties and injustices at every turn. The language of social justice, whose roots can be found at the crux of Christianity and worker-centered politics, began to coalesce in this period. Over the subsequent decades, it morphed into a more expansive notion, embracing racial, gender, and environmental justice. Among the more significant groups to have turned to the essay as the primary means of expression were the Pragmatists, who, beginning in the late 1870s, sought to craft a down-to-earth philosophy tailored to Americans by articulating the practical ways that thought might affect the actual world. The concrete was privileged over the abstract, action over theory or empty conceptualizing. Some of the most canonical American essays emerged from the Pragmatist movement and illustrated once again the constant striving in American writing to become something separate from – albeit influenced by – Europe. Writers continued to refine and "update" certain kinds of essayistic writing for a growing American readership: travel writing, the genteel essay, the comic essay, criticism, journalistic writing. Advancements in transportation gave certain Americans access to new parts of the country and the world, which resulted in an explosion of travel essays during this time. Faraway places were brought home to people who didn't have the privilege of traveling. These essays provide interesting documentary evidence but are also impressionistic and often marked by the preconceptions or prejudices of their authors. Taken as an ensemble, American travel essays of the late nineteenth and early twentieth centuries prefigure the acceleration of globalization, which would explode as the new millennium loomed on the horizon. Genteel essays –

which had a distinctly European flair and offered commentary on contemporary manners and morals – waned and then largely vanished by the 1930s, perhaps because of their perceived mustiness and elitism. A looser, less conservative style would gain prominence and, one could argue, it has maintained its stronghold in American letters even up to today. This loosening up can be seen in American comic essays, which, since the nineteenth century, have sought out new targets of humor, especially in the realm of politics and social life. Through regional humor or humor based on other aspects of identity such as social class, gender, or race, American essayists often tested the limits of decorum and freedom of speech with their provocations. Among other forms, comic essays were and continue to be a site for critique of the traditions and behaviors of a given social milieu. In the years between the Civil War and the end of World War II, another form of critique gained more momentum in the United States, namely, literary criticism. In the 1920s and '30s, writers and critics who were part of the Harlem Renaissance critiqued racist and white supremacist ideologies embedded not just in the politics and social life of the time but in American arts and letters of the first quarter of the twentieth century, while beginning in the early 1940s, the New Critics (whose genealogy intertwines with that of the Fugitive Poets and the Southern Agrarians in sometimes complicated ways) attempted to develop an objective system of close reading that privileged a text's form rather than external factors such as its historical context or the life of its author. Modernity brought a new experimental frame of mind and a more sophisticated language for writing about art, music, and literature, which would prefigure the rise of critical theory and postmodernism later in the century. With a growing newspaper landscape and more venues for essayistic writing, the early twentieth century was a particularly rich period for the genre. The American readership at the turn of the century and moving toward and through the World Wars became more cosmopolitan, more interested in writing that was both thought-provoking and entertaining, and more hungry for a mix of hard news and subjective reflection.

Part 3: Postwar Essays and Essayism (1945–2000) shows how the era after World War II opened up new fields of exploration for the essay. While the essay form is generally associated with the ruminations of a single, contemplative individual, it is also a space for the mulling over of life collectively lived. The appeal for an expansion of civil rights became a central theme of many essays in those years. Black Americans simultaneously processed and protested against the horrors of Jim Crow and celebrated the richness and variety of artistic, musical, and literary innovations by a population that, just one to two generations earlier, had been virtually excluded from American arts and letters. Various waves of feminism swept in and then away in the essayistic writing of the time, in which women debated what the priorities of the movement should be despite its fragmentation by race, class, region, and generation, among other tribalizing factors. Indeed, in more general political writing of this era, the Left and Right churned out critiques of the other side and generated writings presenting their own plan for how the country could be made better. In comparing these political visions, one has the impression that those on either side of the partisan divide are truly living in two separate worlds, each studying a different set of civic objects and using these as evidence to support their claims. The tensions between two other categories were being confronted through the essay form: the indigenous and the foreign. Paradoxically, both native peoples and many immigrants faced discrimination based on their imagined deviation from ever-changing norms whose contours were not easily discernible. Time and again, Indigenous writers have turned to the essay form to articulate the brutalities of life since the Europeans' arrival, to vindicate their rights, to celebrate the richness and diversity of their traditions, and to eulogize nature. During the postwar period, Jews and others fleeing the horrors of World War in Europe came to the United States, bringing their stories of refuge seeking, loss, trauma, adaptation, and hope that their descendants might thrive in this new place. As cultures blended and novel ways of thinking became necessary for addressing the realities of postwar America, essayistic writing absorbed new methodologies and put a fresh twist on older themes of philosophical inquiry: media's role in shaping reality, the role of identity in a stratified society, the instabilities of written and spoken language, the problematic nature of binary thinking. Moving past modernism toward the postmodern period beginning in the late 1960s and peaking in the '90s, the prose of ideas underwent drastic upheaval as theory and philosophy began to meld in elaborate ways. Beginning already in the 1930s but thriving particularly strongly in the '60s, '70s, and '80s, a group of mainly Jewish writers and critics known as the New York Intellectuals mixed politics, criticism, and creative expression in their incisive, left-wing, anti-Stalinist essays. Around the same time, the first whispers of poststructuralism (and all neighboring forms of a burgeoning critical theory) were heard on American campuses and in writing by Europhile public intellectuals. Poststructuralism's new vocabularies and critical techniques were coproductions between Europe (especially France and Germany) and the United States, which both traded ideas across the Atlantic, receiving them sometimes with enthusiasm, sometimes with skepticism. This seems to have permanently altered the style and method of essays written by American scholars and public intellectuals. The line between scholarship and personal essay began to blur, as did the line between poetry and prose (see the lyric prose and essayistic poetry of the period), literature and journalism (see the long-form pieces by New Journalists of the 1960s and '70s), and literature and philosophy (see the thriving literary magazine scene of the late twentieth century, which featured these side by side or increasingly superimposed, or academic writing of the 1980s and '90s, which reads at times like hermetic poetry). Interdisciplinary writing thrived alongside more specialized essays on themes like law or the sciences, which alternated between a highly specialized idiom addressed to other experts and a more accessible, public-friendly prose meant to persuade or instruct readers on complex issues of these fields. In this period, various forms of authority were challenged through the essay. Targets included everything from patriarchy and empire to scientific objectivity and literary canons. This hybrid, anarchic form seemed the perfect medium through which to express the confusion, rage, disenchantment, paranoia, and melancholy that characterized the turn of the new millennium.

Part 4: Toward the Contemporary American Essay (2000–2020) acknowledges already in its short time frame the acceleration of essayistic production in the twenty-first century. This section spans only twenty years – the other sections cover far vaster temporal terrain – but is nonetheless densely packed for many reasons: the changed media landscape, the new writing channels for more people (especially people whose stories had not yet been told), and a certain hunger in the reading public for more essays all the time, perhaps because of the ways they conjugate the personal and the political in compact, digestible bites. In this period, more and more American writers have tried to make sense of the essay, theorizing it and testing out what happens when it is combined with photography, poetry, cinema, or other media. Its sphere has become more particularist; a major objective of contemporary essayists is to flesh out the record of human experience, interrogating how identity acts as an existential filter. As evinced by this section's chapters, the body's limitations, its color, gender, shape, desires, and effect on others is a central preoccupation of contemporary American essayism. More than in any period in history, essayists of the twenty-first century have used their writing to delve into their identities. As a land of immigration, the United States was bound to use the essay as a tool for studying cultural difference, belonging, exclusion, homesickness, and the whole range of feelings produced by the immigrant experience. Alienation is perhaps one of the most pervasive themes in contemporary American essays. This feeling might be produced by rapid technological change, social discord, changing cultural norms, or humanity's self-excision from nature. Indeed, a mournful tone infuses much American writing on the natural world. The naming of the Anthropocene has given essayists the opportunity to reflect on the extractive logic of modernity and its injuries to the planet. They recognize in their writing that since the Earth is the necessary precondition for all human action and thought, its demise will mean the end of all reflection, all literature, all meaning-making; in short, the end of the essayist's vocation.

These are the broad strokes of the history of the American essay, but which overarching patterns can be discerned in this chronology? How has its form and content changed? The essay has naturally responded to the novelties brought by time. With each new technology (television, the atom bomb, the Internet), social or political movement (hippy culture, compassionate conservatism, Black Lives Matter), generational cohort (Boomers, Gen X, Millennials), or significant event (the Vietnam War, 9/11, the coronavirus pandemic), there are essays that respond to it, giving it substance and duration simply by reflecting on it. In this sense, the essay has often been a form of Zeitgeist literature, tracking American history as it happens, portraying the country's mood with only a slight delay.

Certain cultural novelties have altered the essay's course. One general shift that has greatly impacted the essay form is a certain vulgarization of the language. The bulk of early American essays were written by white men who, through the privilege of a long and involved humanities education, produced writing with a rich vocabulary (informed by etymological knowledge or proficiency in several languages), a sometimes elaborate syntax, and a reliance on a set of fixed rhetorical maneuvers to persuade or divert readers. There is great variety in any group of essays published at a given time, but in comparing the average essay from the nineteenth century to the average contemporary essay, one will immediately note a tendency now toward the colloquial, the straightforward, the accessible, the personal, a writing based as much on feeling as on thought and representing a broader range of experiences. In many cases, the form has become a mere mode of transportation for the content (often social or political in nature), not something tended to with slower attention. These changes reflect the new priorities of the contemporary education system, which puts less emphasis on the formation of well-rounded, well-read citizens and more emphasis on the creation of workers in increasingly technocratic fields.

Furthermore, there is no longer the assumption of a universal subject; the particular is emphasized instead. This was to be expected in a place of such extraordinary diversity. When people of many backgrounds encounter each other in one space, the universal begins to seem, in the best case, an impossible utopian dream, and, in the worst case, a nightmare of cultural hegemony. In the particularizing context of the contemporary United States, the "we" pronoun no longer holds up, at least not as a marker of ubiquity. It signals instead one's belonging to a smaller community, sometimes pitted against those who aren't part of it. The "we" of the essay now cannot even attempt to include everyone. In other words, the essay has segmented itself according to cohorts, or, perhaps more cynically put, to markets.

The essay's commodification, which increased greatly in the latter half of the twentieth century and into the twenty-first, has been one of the most substantial changes to the form. Once a literary form acquiesces to the logic of markets, it will begin to yearn for mass appeal and be reduced to a success-seeking formula. It will seek out an audience to whom it can administer a satisfying dopamine boost, readying readers for the next essay put online or the next collection published in paperback. Essayists always sought to appeal to readers, but it was only relatively recently that the essay or essay collection became a product *first* and a work of literature second. Dysfunction, polemics, sex, grievance, sickness, injustice, addiction, environmental catastrophe: This is the stuff of modern mediatized life, and, yes, the sustenance of essay-as-commodity. More ruminative, slow, unspectacular prose whose urgency is not immediately apparent seems like a luxury in a world ablaze.

In the pages that follow, a much more nuanced account of the history of the essay in the United States is delivered scene by scene, with important figures making appearances across chapters and unexpected cross-pollination being shown between various traditions and movements. It is our hope that scholars of the essay will discover the work of essayists unknown to them and will pursue new avenues of research related to the essay's history. Another hope of equal importance is that essayists, too, will be inspired by our contributors' findings and will use them as stimuli for new pieces that might be folded into a future history of the American essay. Contemporary prose writers might see promise in blending the aesthetics of past movements to create something new, in absorbing the rhythms or lexicons of excellent writers past, or filtering their old themes – human nature, the meaning of life – through a twenty-first-century subjectivity. This book is for those who are drawn to the essay, a site of possibility, conviction, and beauty, for any of its countless fascinations. The essay is a place where people may be themselves. In it, they show what their mind is made of, pouring out its contents on pages meant to receive them. It is fortunate that such a vessel exists and that its contents are freely available to us, offering an alternative history of the United States told through one of its most robust literary traditions.

PART I

★

THE EMERGENCE OF THE
AMERICAN ESSAY (1710–1865)

I

Essays to Do Good: Puritanism and the Birth of the American Essay

JAN STIEVERMANN

Consisting mostly of Congregational clergymen in the Puritan tradition, the intellectual elite of post-Restoration New England inherited and further developed several forms of early modern English essay writing. While some of the respective texts actually carried "essay" in their title, many others appeared as "discourses," "dissertations," "observations," or "attempts" – rubrics not (yet) sharply delineated from the essay either in terms of style or matters treated. What these texts had in common, besides their relative brevity and pragmatic intentions, was that their authors were making a self-conscious intervention in an ongoing transatlantic debate. By publishing something as an "essay," "attempt," or the like, writers signaled to their audiences on both sides of the ocean that they did not expect their deliberations or propositions to be the final word, but rather an "inquiry" or "offering" (two other related rubrics), which would likely be augmented, complemented, or even revised. Often these texts appealed to personal experience and observation in making their case and were concerned with practical applications and improvements.

Most popular were essays (often derived from sermons) that treated specific theological subjects (e.g., a dogmatic issue or exegetical problem) or advanced lessons for religious instruction. Examples would be *A Brief essay to the resolution of that question, viz whether the English custom of laying the hand upon the Bible in swearing be lawful?* (1689) by the prominent Boston minister Samuel Willard (1640–1707), or the posthumously published *Discourse on the Trinity* and *Treatise on Grace* that Jonathan Edwards (1703–1758) wrote in the 1730s and '40s. Reflecting the involvement of New England's intelligentsia with the early Enlightenment, the essay form was also widely used in the fields of natural philosophy and history, or for projects in the practical sciences. For instance, the Harvard almanacks regularly contained brief descriptive discourses on comets and other astronomical phenomena observed in the American sky. Some graduates of that college even had their essays printed in the proceedings of the Royal Society. Furthermore, ministers in New as well as in Old England blended religious inquiries and empirical investigation, as evinced, for example, by Increase Mather's (1639–1723) collection of supernatural occurrences, *An essay for the recording of illustrious providences* (1684). It was Increase's son Cotton Mather (1663–1728), however, who became New England's most prolific and versatile essayist.

This chapter will focus on Cotton Mather's *Bonifacius: An Essay upon the Good* (1710), in which he makes a series of proposals for how Christians might advance the gospel cause and exercise social benevolence. For this purpose, Mather creatively amalgamated different variants of the genre. First published anonymously in 1710 but quickly associated with Mather's name, *Bonifacius* has often been considered an aesthetically and intellectually inferior predecessor of the American essay tradition, rather than its first full instantiation. Even so, the work enjoyed great popularity in the United States and Britain throughout the eighteenth and nineteenth centuries. Instrumental to this success was the stylistically modernized English edition with the altered title *Essays to Do Good* prepared by George Burder in 1807.

Moreover, the Burder edition helped cement the connection with Benjamin Franklin (1706–1790), already established in the latter's *Autobiography*. Here Franklin had praised the role of *Bonifacius* for his early moral formation.[1] In his introduction, Burder cited a letter by Franklin to Cotton Mather's son Samuel, saying that "If I have been a useful citizen, as you seem to think, the public owes the advantage to that book."[2] Franklin's various schemes for social improvements might indeed have been inspired, to some degree, by Mather's suggestions for "Doing Good." Yet the relation between the Deist freethinker and the Calvinist theologian was anything but unambiguous, and involved at least as much criticism and ridicule as it did appreciation and appropriation.[3] The persona of "Mrs. Silence Dogood" that Franklin adopted for his early

---

[1] Benjamin Franklin, *The Autobiography of Benjamin Franklin*, ed. Edmund S. Morgan (New Haven, CT: Yale University Press, 1964), 58.

[2] George Burder, "Preface," in *Essays to Do Good*, by Cotton Mather (London: J. Dennett, 1807). The letter, from 12 May 1787, can be found here: www.masshist.org/database/533.

[3] See, for instance, G. D. McEwan, "'A Turn of Thinking': Benjamin Franklin, Cotton Mather and Daniel Defoe on 'Doing Good,'" in *The Dress of Words: Essays on Restoration and Eighteenth Century Literature in Honor of Richmond P. Bond*, ed. Robert B. White Jr. (Lawrence, KS: University of Kansas Press, 1978), and Mitchell Robert Breitwieser, *Cotton Mather and Benjamin Franklin: The Price of Redemptive Personality* (New York: Cambridge University Press, 1984).

satirical essays was a spoof on Mather, "counting on his Bostonian readers to know that the author of *Essays to Do Good* was rarely silent," as David Levin puts it.[4] Franklin thus prepared the ground for later critics who represented *Bonifacius* as a stepping stone on the way to more fully developed literary works, such as Franklin's mature essays, and, more generally, paint Mather as a transitional figure in the evolution of early American culture from colonial preparations to national fulfillment, from the Puritan era to the Age of Enlightenment.

Usually seen through the lens of secularization theories, the Franklin connection has also colored the perception of *Bonifacius*'s religious content. Perry Miller, for one, made Mather's – to his modernist sensibilities insufferable – *Essays to Do Good* a key exhibit for a grandiose declension narrative.[5] This narrative told of the creeping tendency away from Calvinism and toward an Arminian theology of free will. It also told of a shattering of the Puritan synthesis of piety and reason through the increasing bifurcation between the anti-intellectualism and enthusiasm of evangelical religion, on the one hand, and the rationalism and moral utilitarianism embodied by Franklin's schemes of self-improvement, on the other. The end result, according to Miller, was the shallow materialism and conformity of America's increasingly secular middle class. For others, *Bonifacius* illustrated how the original Puritan communitarianism was being transformed by a new democratic ethos but also "economic individualism" that inadvertently undermined any commitment to the common good.[6]

In what follows, I seek to offer a corrective to these two teleological interpretations of *Bonifacius* as protonational precursor of a more fullfledged, genuinely American essay-writing tradition and as a text symptomatic of secularizing and rationalizing tendencies. For this purpose, the chapter will first situate *Bonifacius* in its relevant transatlantic religious-intellectual contexts. A second section then puts *Bonifacius* in conversation with diverse practical divinity writers, but also subgenres and authors of the British essay tradition during the Augustan Age, notably the project essay. This will then enable a fresh view of *Bonifacius*'s theology of experimental piety.

---

4 David Levin, "Introduction," in Cotton Mather, *Bonifacius: An Essay Upon the Good*, ed. David Levin (Cambridge, MA: Belknap Press of Harvard University Press, 1966), vii–xxviii, viii. In the following discussion, parenthetical references will be made to this edition.
5 See his widely influential *The New England Mind: From Colony to Province* (Cambridge, MA: Harvard University Press, 1953), 395–416.
6 Virginia Bernhard, "Cotton Mather and the Doing of Good: A Puritan Gospel of Wealth," *New England Quarterly* 49, no. 2 (1976): 225–51, 229.

Cotton Mather, the Early Enlightenment, and the Protestant Awakening

Cotton Mather lived in a period of dramatic transformations. Puritanism as a comprehensive social order was fading as the colonies became more fully integrated into the British Empire. In this situation, Mather worked from his Boston ministry to exert godly influence on an increasingly pluralistic and commercially oriented society. Through his practical activities but also through more than 400 publications, the Congregational clergyman promoted religious renewal and missionary work, as well as social and educational reform. At the same time, Mather was a very active scholar-theologian.[7] He entertained a vast epistolary network with intellectuals across the Atlantic world, and was recognized in the wider British Empire and beyond. Reflecting his close ties with British and Scottish Dissenters, Mather received an honorary doctor of divinity from the University of Glasgow in 1710. Three years later, he was elected a fellow of the Royal Society of London. In Halle, the center of German Lutheran Pietism, his works – notably the great New England church history *Magnalia Christi Americana* (1702) – were well received by August Hermann Francke and his associates, with whom he exchanged letters for many years.

These connections reflect Mather's involvement with two larger movements. First, Mather embodies the kind of moderate, self-proclaimed Christian Enlightenment ethos prevalent with many British clergymen as well as the gentlemen philosophers of the Royal Society, such as John Woodward, Hans Sloane, Isaac Newton, and especially Robert Boyle. In many of his own works Mather similarly sought to demonstrate that the new philosophy, with its rationalism and empiricism, were not enemies but allies of faith, which could contribute much to the necessary further reformation of Protestantism and the practical application of Christian ethics. Notable in this context is Mather's *The Christian Philosopher* (1720/21), the first substantial work of "physico-theology" in America.[8]

The second movement in which Mather was fully immersed by the time he wrote *Bonifacius* was that of a revivalist pan-Protestantism, which soon

---

7 On Mather as a biblical scholar, see Jan Stievermann, *Prophecy, Piety, and the Problem of Historicity: Interpreting the Hebrew Scriptures in Cotton Mather's Biblia Americana* (Tübingen: Mohr Siebeck, 2016).

8 Winton U. Solberg, "Introduction," in *The Christian Philosopher*, by Cotton Mather, ed. Winton U. Solberg (Urbana, IL: University of Illinois Press, 1994), xix–cxxxiv; Reiner Smolinski, "Editor's Introduction," in *Biblia Americana*, vol. 1, *Genesis*, by Cotton Mather, ed. Reiner Smolinski (Tübingen: Mohr Siebeck, 2010), 1–210.

after his death would erupt in the transatlantic awakenings of the mid-eighteenth century. Mather advocated inner-Protestant toleration and for years continued to work on a platform of doctrinally minimalistic, experiential, and practically oriented "maxims of Piety." These were to serve as the basis for reconciliation and cooperation between pious British Dissenters and Anglicans, but also with Continental Protestants.[9] In this spirit, Mather became involved with several transdenominational societies aiming to renew Protestant culture from within and to propagate the gospel abroad. Important to mention here are the Society for the Reformation of Manners (founded in 1691) and the Society for Promoting Christian Knowledge (SPCK; founded in 1699). Mather was in touch with some of the SPCK's most prominent members, including Josiah Woodward, Henry Newman, Thomas Reynolds, and Daniel Defoe. The SPCK also served as an important link with the Francke Foundation at Halle, the central hub of German Pietist educational, philanthropic, and missionary endeavors. Mather was greatly inspired by Francke and, as Mark Peterson points out, the "interlocking array of issues and subjects for pious reform" that Mather sketched out in *Bonifacius* constituted his own "developing vision of an ideal society that Boston could come to represent – a vision shaped by the transatlantic conversation with German Pietism."[10]

Singled out for special praise in *Bonifacius*, Halle's India missions were closely bound up with the SPCK, and both were associated with the New England Company, founded in 1649 to gospelize the region's natives. Significantly, Mather dedicated *Bonifacius* to Sir William Ashurst, an English banker and Whig politician. During Ashurst's governorship of the Company, Mather had become a local commissioner in 1698 and energetically worked to revive the missions after the Anglo-Native wars. While *Bonifacius*, like much of Mather's oeuvre, in some ways reflects a British provincial identity, it thus also reveals his aspirations to contribute to an international Protestant cause and republic of letters.

---

9 On Mather's pan-Protestantism and his connection to German Pietism, see Jan Stievermann, "A 'Syncretism of Piety': Imagining Global Protestantism in Early Eighteenth-Century Boston, Tranquebar, and Halle," *Church History: Studies in Christianity and Culture* 89, no. 4 (December 2020): 829–56.

10 Mark Peterson, *The City-State of Boston: The Rise and Fall of an Atlantic Power, 1630–1865* (Princeton, NJ: Princeton University Press, 2019), 237–38. On Mather's theological affinities with Halle Pietism, see Richard Lovelace, *The American Pietism of Cotton Mather: Origins of American Evangelicalism* (Grand Rapids, MI: Wm. B. Eerdmans, 1979).

Bonifacius and the British Essay Tradition in the Augustan Age

Mather worked in a great variety of literary genres, from sermons, devotional writings, and history, to biography, political fables, and religious poetry, as well as in different types of essayistic texts. He was more versatile and more self-conscious in his stylistic choices than any other colonial author. Over the decades, his prolific pen also caught him in the middle of the debates over the changing literary fashion that characterized the Augustan Age. Some of Mather's major works are written in a highly ornate and erudite style, at every turn digressing into curious asides, anecdotes, and learned allusions.

In the early eighteenth century, this baroque style was quickly falling out of favor in the cosmopolitan center. Augustan literati, such as Joseph Addison, Richard Steele, and Jonathan Swift, were advocating new standards of neoclassical elegance. In his *Letter to a Young Gentleman Lately Entered into Holy Orders* (1721), Swift advised that a writer as well as a preacher ought to strive for clarity, directness, and a simple grace and ease, as well as a freshness of expression. Consequently, some of Mather's writings began to appear outmoded to like-minded English critics, and they have frequently been attacked as fervent and pedantic ever since. In a chapter entitled "Of Poetry and Style," included in his handbook for candidates of the ministry, Mather answered his detractors, arguing that "Every man will have his own *Style*, which will distinguish him as much as his *Gate*." And, at least in most of his major works, Mather's was the "Massy *Way*" that packed as much wit and learning into each sentence as possible, and whose every paragraph was "embellished with *Profitable References*" for the benefit of the reader.[11] However, most of Mather's shorter religious and scientific works, like his extensive correspondence, is written in a more direct, if never artless, manner.

Even though it now and then tilts toward the "Massy *Way*," Mather's prose in *Bonifacius* is actually, for the most part, precise, forceful, and straightforward. The occasional English and ancient language citations are not just ornamental, but effectively add emphasis or serve to make a further point. Mather quotes from a great variety of sources – ranging from the Church Fathers and various classical authors, to contemporary naturalists. For instance, in chapter 7, on the role of "Magistrates," he highlights how much good rulers could do, while in reality the lives of most of them "are not

---

[11] Cotton Mather, *Manuductio ad Ministerium* (Boston: [Thomas Hancock], 1726), 44–46.

worth a *prayer*, nor their *deaths* worth a *tear*." Mather then hammers home his point with a reference from the *Quaestiones* of Anastasius Nicaenus: "Thus when a *Phocas* was made Emperor, a religious man complained unto Heaven, *Cur fecisti eum Imperatorem*? Heaven gave to the complaint that answer, *Non inveni pejorem*."[12] These examples also show Mather's love for classical rhetorical devices such as chiasmus and parallelism, but also witty puns and anagrams. However, compared to other works by Mather, especially the *Magnalia*, the rhetoricity and intertextuality of *Bonifacius* appears relatively restrained.

The book's propositional format and hortatory rhetoric are strongly influenced by two complex traditions that also informed similar writings by Mather's New England colleagues. The first is that of British practical divinity writing. Famous examples of this genre that certainly influenced *Bonifacius* were Richard Baxter's *How to Do Good to Many; or the Public Good Is the Christian's Life* (1682), and his massive *Christian Directory* (1673), which guided its readers on "How to Improve all Helps and Means" toward a holy life in the world. Toward the end of Mather's life, William Law, to cite another example, published *A Practical Treatise Upon Christian Perfection* (1726). Mather himself wrote a great deal in this vein, including numerous publications that carry the moniker "essay" in their title, such as *Corderius Americanus: An Essay upon the Good Education of Children* (1708) or *The Sacrificer: An Essay upon the Sacrifices, Wherewith a Christian, Laying a Claim to an Holy Priesthood, Endeavours to Glorify God* (1714).[13] The second influence is that of the new types of "utilitarian" prose employing the essay form.

Mather was certainly familiar with the more literary essay tradition, too, and frequently referred to classical authors of the genre such as Plutarch. Indeed, Mather's lives of eminent New England divines and politicians in the *Magnalia* are adaptations of the Plutarchian biographical essay. He greatly admired the English pioneer Francis Bacon for his *Essayes or Counsels, Civill and Morall* (1597) and *Advancement of Learning* (1605). In chapter 8, on "Physicians," *Bonifacius* also alludes to Thomas Browne's famous essays of

---

12 "Why did you elect him Emperor? ... I could not find a worse [man]." Mather, *Bonifacius*, 92.

13 Mather also frequently used the subtitle "An essay" or "essays on" in other sub-genres of theology, such as apologetics, polemics, and even funeral orations. See, for instance, his *A servant of the Lord, not ashamed of his Lord: a short essay to fortify the minds of all persons, ... against the discouragements of piety* (Boston: [Timothy Green], 1704); *The Christian Temple. Or, an Essay upon a Christian Considered as a Temple* (Boston: [Bartholomew Green], 1706); or *Awakening Thoughts on the Sleep of Death. A Short Essay on the Sleep, Which by Death, All Men Must Fall Into* (Boston: [Timothy Green], 1712).

1642/43, where Mather writes that *"Religio Medici . . .* has the least reason of any under Heaven, to be an *irreligion."*[14] The Boston cleric was well aware, too, of the latest London fashion in essay writing. He read a great deal in the rising number of journal publications and gazettes that his age produced, scientific and otherwise. However, Mather disliked the tone and purpose of the kind of coffeehouse essays published in the *Tatler* (1709–11) and the *Spectator* (1711–), which cultivated the perspective of a detached, even skeptical observer (embodied in Swift's persona Isaac Bickerstaff, Esq.) reflecting and critically, but never passionately, commenting on the changing ways of the world. Still, Mather could very well satirize the *Spectator* style and does so with much glee in his chapter on "Of Poetry and Style," which, ironically, sometimes gets included in anthologies of the American essay for that reason.[15]

Bonifacius has more in common with the straightforward propositional character, descriptive exactness, and learned gravitas of the kind of scientific but also antiquarian essays penned by the gentleman of the Royal Society, such as John Woodward's *An Essay toward a Natural History of the Earth and Terrestrial Bodies* (1695). As noted earlier, some New England worthies, including Leonard Hoar, John Winthrop Jr., or Paul Dudley, sent briefer texts of this nature to the Society. Winthrop and Dudley also had epistolary essays on American fauna and flora published in the *Philosophical Transactions*. Mather achieved the same with some of the "Curiosa Americana" letters he submitted to the Society. An even more significant scientific essay published in London and dedicated to Hans Sloane is Mather's *An Account of the Method and Success of Inoculating the Small-Pox in Boston in New England* (1722), which defended his controversial advocacy of "variolation" during the Boston epidemic of 1720 and '21, and helped to establish that medical procedure in England.[16]

Mather's most polished essays combining natural philosophy with pious reflections are to be found in the *Christian Philosopher* and his *Thoughts for the Day of Rain. In Two Essay's* [sic] (1712). The manner in which *Bonifacius* blends scientific essay writing with the aims of a practical divinity piece was, of course, not without parallel at the time. Some of the abovementioned

---

[14] Mather, *Bonifacius*, 98.
[15] Most recently in Philip Lopate, ed., *The Glorious American Essay: One Hundred Essays from Colonial Times to the Present* (New York: Pantheon, 2020), 3–9.
[16] See Raymond Phineas Stearns, *Science in the British Colonies of America* (Urbana, IL: University of Illinois Press, 1970); and George L. Kittredge, "Cotton Mather's Scientific Communications to the Royal Society," *Proceedings of the American Antiquarian Society* 26 (April 1916): 18–57.

religious reformers did something similar when advocating specific projects, as did Josiah Woodward in his *An Account of the Rise and Progress of the Religious Societies in the City of London* (1698).

A projector, in early eighteenth-century parlance, was someone who proposed, initiated, and promoted activities that frequently combined elements of public and private gain. Boston's Paul Dudley, to cite a colonial example, published essays on the method of "Making Sugar from the Juice of the Maple Tree" and "For Discovering Where the Bees Hive in the Woods," both promising revenue and larger benefits for the common weal.[17] The best-known author of such project essays was Daniel Defoe, another Dissenting correspondent of Mather. Defoe's usage of the term "essays," as in his *An Essay upon Publick Credit* (1710) or *An Essay on the Late Storm* (1704), very closely resembles that of Mather: Its primary meaning "is an experimental or initial attempt to treat a subject, only secondarily referring to the resulting text."[18] Thus, Defoe writes in the introduction to *An Essay upon Projects* (1697) that "If I have given an Essay towards any thing New, or made Discovery to advantage of any Contrivance now on foot, all Men are at liberty to make use of the Improvement." This was very much what Mather had in mind with his *Essay Upon the Good*, just as he also would have appreciated Defoe's remarks on the essay as a kind of text defined by a "Free and Familiar" language unconcerned with "Exactness of Style."[19]

Both Defoe's *Essay on Projects* and Mather's *Bonifacius* seek to advance public welfare and morality, proposing, among other things, "Friendly Societies" for several kinds of life and medical insurance. There are also striking family resemblances with Jonathan Swift's *A Project for the Advancement of Religion* (1709), whose ideas and language echo in several parts of *Bonifacius*, especially chapter 7, on "Magistrates." Mather, no doubt, detested Swift's High Church and Tory proclivities, but would have agreed with the Dublin cleric that "in this projecting Age," there was need to make better proposal "for the Improvement of Religion and Morals," which, besides winning souls for Christ, offer "the best natural Means for advancing the Publick Felicity of the State, as well as the present Happyness of every

---

17 Paul Dudley, "Making Sugar from the Juice of the Maple Tree," *Philosophical Transactions* 31, no. 364 (1720): 27–28; "For Discovering Where the Bees Hive in the Woods," *Philosophical Transactions* 31, no. 367 (1720): 148–50.
18 Stephen M. Adams, "Defoe, Daniel," in *The Encyclopedia of the Essay*, ed. Tracy Chevalier (London: Routledge, 2012), 445–48, 445.
19 Daniel Defoe, *An Essay upon Projects* (London: [Thomas Cockerill], 1697), 10, 336.

Individual."[20] Among his New England contemporaries, similar reform proposals were put forth by, among others, Mather's rival for the Harvard presidency, Benjamin Wadsworth, in his *An Essay to Do Good* (1710). Thus, we understand much about *Bonifacius* if we look at it as a religious project essay in dialogue with those of Defoe, Swift, or Wadsworth, but of a rather different piety.

Bonifacius and Mather's Theology of Experimental Piety

Like Defoe, and the Baconian essay tradition behind him, Mather regarded his concrete proposals for doing good as preliminary and open to further additions. "We will not propose, that our *essays to do good*, should ever come to an end," he quipped in his conclusion. "But we will now put an end unto this, of tendering Proposals for it."[21] At the same time, Mather made sure to let his readers know right from the beginning of *Bonifacius* that the basic beliefs underlying his undertaking were anything but provisional and that he, all modesty aside, needed

> to be very *positive* in asserting, that the only *wisdom* of man lies in conversing with the great GOD, and his glorious CHRIST; and in engaging as many others as we can, to join us in this our blessedness; thereby promoting His *Kingdom* among the children of men; and in studying to *do good* unto all about us; to be blessings in our several relations; to heal the disorders, and help the distress of a miserable world, as far as ever we can extend our influence.[22]

Theologically, Mather here extends three major Reformation impulses into the age of Enlightenment and early evangelicalism. The primary impulse is that of living each individual life wholly unto God, from which grows the notion of an inner-worldly vocation that, in turn, is closely connected to the second impulse: realizing the priesthood of all believers. The third impulse consists in the completion and worldwide triumph of the Reformation itself. *Bonifacius* is therefore inspired by, and a concretization of, Mather's vision of pan-Protestantism: The work of the Reformers will be finished by moving from the restoration of biblical teachings to a *reformatio vitae*, by transcending confessionalism and spreading an "experimental" piety – a key term of his mature theology. It signified a heartfelt, vital faith

---

20 Jonathan Swift, *A Project for the Advancement of Religion, and the Reformation of Manners* (London: [Benjamin Tooke], 1709), 7.
21 Mather, *Bonifacius*, 138.   22 Mather, *Bonifacius*, 6.

that was at once practically oriented and rooted in the individual's personal experience of the gospel's saving truths. Giving a spiritual twist to Baconian experimentalism, Mather presents *Bonifacius* as the quasi-empirical trial of such a faith, which tries out new opportunities for application and, in so doing, confirms what the Bible teaches.

Bonifacius begins by asserting that humans had been created for the sole purpose of living for the glory of God. This general Christian belief was nowhere more strongly emphasized than in the Reformed Puritan tradition, as evinced by the opening lines of the *Westminster Catechism*. By searching out ways for "Doing Good" in every situation, Mather avowed, a Christian was seizing opportunities "directly to answer the great END of his being."[23] "Doing Good" meant glorifying and praising God through one's actions, expressing one's love and thankfulness, and seeing to it that His revealed will might prevail on earth. That Mather pushed this agenda under rapidly changing circumstances of a more materialistic and individualistic society does not mean, as Miller and others have claimed, that his project was in essence symptomatic of or complicit with these tendencies.[24]

If read on its own terms rather than in the service of some grand narrative about American culture, *Bonifacius* does not anticipate a middle-class ethos of shallow moral conformity and materialism. We should take seriously Mather's insistence that, when undertaken in earnest, "Doing Good" is a form of *kenosis*, an emptying out of the self to make room for the love of God and our fellow human being, which requires "a consent to be made *nothing*."[25] It starts and ends with humility and, as he emphasizes, often with outright humiliation. Even if God sometimes chooses to bestow temporal blessings on his servants, all Christians, ultimately, had to accept their cross and be ready to suffer as they followed in the footsteps of their master. For Mather, charity had to be embraced as an end in itself without any hope of recompense other than the pleasure of serving God.

Charitable enterprises will help to improve society and thus, as a side effect, a state might profit from it politically and even commercially, as Mather points out. But the individual undertaking them often will not. And herein lies a significant difference between Mather, Defoe, and Swift. Whereas other religious project essays of the age assumed a natural reciprocity between private and public gain, Mather thought individuals had to

---

23 Mather, *Bonifacius*, 19.
24 See Miller, *New England Mind*, 402; and Bernhard, "Cotton Mather and the Doing of Good," 235.
25 Mather, *Bonifacius*, 143.

be willing to sacrifice their interests on the altar of God. "What God gives us," he writes in the chapter on "Rich Men," is not given us for ourselves, but *for the Lord.*" There is only one passage in that chapter where Mather suggests material reward for doing good, quoting Thomas Gouge to the effect that those who give generously are often "rewarded with a strange success, and increase of their estate; even in this world."[26] Overall, however, *Bonifacius* consistently foregrounds the spiritual reward of doing good and in many other places emphasizes that the most pious Christians are frequently burdened with opposition, temporal afflictions, losses, and poverty. A Christian ought to accept these strictures as well as any temporal blessings from God's hand, trusting that they are providential means both to prove and to deepen one's faith.

While Mather calls upon individuals in an increasingly dynamic and commercial culture to busy themselves and even do business in the service of God, his was no gospel of wealth. His aims are resolutely God-centered and communitarian. Mather's ethos of doing good was based on a concept of universal relatedness, from which grew mutual responsibilities of all Christians toward one another.[27] True, Mather did by no means condemn commercialism per se. Like other New England ministers of his cohort, as Mark Valeri has shown, Mather internalized the emergent imperial ideology "that promoted trade as an instrument of English hegemony," and condoned business practices, including the exchange of credit in the transatlantic market, that his Puritan forefathers had condemned as usury and oppression. In *Bonifacius* and other works such as *Durable Riches* (1695), he taught that the new economic ambitions and tactics of profit making were acceptable before the Lord if large portions of the revenues were given to the common good.[28] As much as Mather sanctified the political economy of the Empire, however, he also criticized in no uncertain terms any extravagant accumulation of wealth for private purposes, as well as inhumane business practices, including excessive interest rates or "the *slave-trade*," which in *Bonifacius* he calls "a spectacle that shocks humanity."[29]

In Swift's and also Defoe's projects, there is an unmistakable accent on free human agency. Most explicitly in his prefatory chapter, "Essays to Do Good,"

---

26 Mather, *Bonifacius*, 108, 110.
27 Robert Middlekauff, *The Mathers: Three Generations of Puritan Intellectuals, 1596–1728* (New York: Oxford University Press, 1971, 1999), 269.
28 Mark Valeri, *Heavenly Merchandize: How Religion Shaped Commerce in Puritan America* (Princeton, NJ: Princeton University Press, 2010), 126, 112.
29 Mather, *Bonifacius*, 54.

Mather sought to counter such Arminian tendencies. He repeatedly emphasizes that no one can even begin to do any real good out of their own power, but only after being made anew in faith by the "sovereign grace" of God. But neither good works nor "faith itself, either as doing of good works, or as being itself one of them, ... entitles us to the *justifying righteousness* of our Savior." Commitment to *sola fide*, to Mather, demanded a complete "renouncing of our own righteousness," and all "attempts at good works will come to nothing, till a *justifying faith* in your Saviour, shall carry you forth unto them." At the same time, Mather warned of what Bonhoeffer would call "cheap grace," and stressed that "[a] *workless faith* is a *worthless faith*." Vital religion must necessarily bring forth fruits of charity. Still, Mather ascribed any growth in holiness to the power of God through the indwelling of the Holy Spirit. As Christians are doing good, they are receiving the blessings of the Spirit and vice versa, and thus, as Mather wittily puts it, "my BONIFACIUS [the doer of good] anon comes to wear the name of BENEDICTUS [the blessed one] also."[30]

Expanding upon the Reformers' notion of an inner-worldly calling, Mather held that every station, trade, or activity provided occasions to become a "BONIFACIUS." As the second part of the original subtitle indicates, the book follows a series of widening circles, starting with general advice "unto all CHRISTIANS, in a PERSONAL Capacity, or in a RELATIVE," to then proceed to more specific proposal for various professions and institutions. While all of *Bonifacius* carries a personal stamp, the two chapters on "The Duty to Oneself" and "Relative to Home and Neighborhood," as well as the chapters on "Ministers," "Schoolmasters," and "Churches," are most immediately drawn from Mather's own life and work as pastor, teacher, and reformer. They are drenched in firsthand experience and often correspond with journal passages.

"The grand Intention of my Life," Mather committed to his journal in 1713, "is, *to Do Good*."[31] Almost every week since 1709, Mather jotted down items under the rubric "G.D.," meaning "Good Devised," and filled page after page documenting his tireless efforts to "live more perfectly, more watchfully, more fruitfully before the glorious Lord."[32] From these personal attempts – very much in the mode of empiricism – he endeavored to derive some

---

30 Mather, *Bonifacius*, 28–29, 150.
31 Cotton Mather, *The Diary of Cotton Mather*, ed. W. C. Ford, Massachusetts Historical Society Collections, 7th ser., vol. 7–8, 2 vols. (Boston: Massachusetts Historical Society, 1911–1912), 2:263.
32 Mather, *Bonifacius*, 35.

general rules for cultivating individual habits of devotion (such as Bible reading, constant prayers, fast days, and the "spiritualizing" of daily events) and organizing family religion as well as neighborhood groups and charity schools. Based on his own experimentation with English models in Boston, Mather especially recommends "Young Men's Associations," as well as religious societies particularly for the poor, servants, "Indians," and "Negroes." To help the needy in their communities, whether widows, orphans, or the sick, Christians, led by their ministers, ought to give generously, and extend other forms of practical and spiritual support. Mather himself tirelessly visited the distressed, suffering, and dying, bringing them provisions and spiritual comfort, and, by his own estimation, donated above one-seventh of his own income.

From Mather's perspective, evangelization was the primary form of doing good, and every act of charity ought to be made a vehicle for this purpose as well. What chapter 4, on "Ministers," proposes about the importance of catechizing the young and uneducated, about promoting female piety, about better forms of preaching to instigate awakenings, and about mass distributing simple works of practical divinity, he practiced with great energy as pastor. Likewise, his call to reform Protestant churches (chapter 6), including the organization of a treasury for donations to make them more effective as engines of evangelization and welfare institutions, was based on his successes and frustrations with Boston's North Church.

However, the priesthood of all believers ultimately made spreading the gospel the sacred obligation and privilege of all lay Christians. Among those working "in more *public* circumstances,"[33] Mather first singles out teachers and physicians, as these callings provided special opportunities. While the former should combine general education with the teaching of biblical literacy and Christian principles (while using progressive pedagogy and eschewing corporal punishment), the latter ought to take a more holistic approach that pays attention to spiritual as well as physical causes of their patients' suffering and will not neglect the soul in curing the body. Mather then devotes separate chapters to "Magistrates," "Rich Men," and "Official and Lawyers." These reveal some interesting differences from Swift and other religious project writers at the time, who assigned key roles to the powerful and wealthy. Their schemes to reform society were decidedly top down, emphasizing the need to start with a moral regeneration of society's upper echelons. They imagined a trickling down of influence that emanated from the royal family and the nobility and continued with the church

---

33 Mather, *Bonifacius*, 69.

hierarchy, government officials, and militaries, while making the lower ranks more or less passive objects of social disciplining and improvement.

In contrast to "other English writings on charity in the eighteenth century," that tended to "assume a great social distance between doers of good and the recipients of it," Mather's *Essays to Do Good*, as Bernhard rightly observes, provide "a manual of practical charity intended not for one class but for the whole community." Reflecting a very different social situation in New England, Mather's project adopts more of a bottom-up approach, in which an ordinary person "could do as much in his way as the rich."[34] This approach also colors his suggestions for setting up more "Reforming Societies" (chapter 11) of the kind that he had been organizing in Boston since the turn of the century. To some extent Mather follows the model of the English Society for the Reformation of Manners, which aimed to suppress public immoralities, such as prostitution, drunkenness, and profanity, by lobbying for new laws and creating a system of social control to maintain them. But Mather's plan neither includes a hierarchy of class associations nor the kind of paid informers and enforcers that Swift so vocally criticized. Instead *Bonifacius* proposes voluntary neighborhood associations that would work "towards the execution of wholesome *laws*, whereby *vice* is to be discouraged."[35] With their heavy involvement of ministers and civil officials, these societies, in some ways, aimed to create a new alliance between state and religion on a broader Protestant basis. But their main thrust was toward encouraging religion and morality by means of what the nineteenth century would call moral suasion.

As laid down in the concluding "Desiderata," the end goal of all these activities was the global triumph of the Reformation, which, from a Puritan perspective, required the *"reviving of primitive Christianity."*[36] Freed from the last vestiges of Antichristian corruption, a renewed Protestantism would, with the help of a new outpouring of the Spirit, spread across the world. Protestants ought to put aside their minor differences, focus on the essentials of their faith, and make every possible effort to advance interior and foreign missions. Some laudable forays had already been made in that direction, including those that Mather documented in his "Appendix" on the activities of the New England Company. But so much more needed to be done to Christianize large swaths of Europe and the East and West Indies and to bring back Catholics, Orthodox Greeks, Armenians, and "Muscovites" into the true Church of Christ.

---

34 Bernhard, "Cotton Mather and the Doing of Good," 237.   35 Mather, *Bonifacius*, 133.
36 Mather, *Bonifacius*, 142.

All of this is given the greatest urgency by the "pervasive millennial expectations" that, as Bercovitch rightly points out,[37] characterize *Bonifacius* as much as any work by Mather. Millennialism was very widespread among all stripes of revivalist Protestants of the period, but Mather was a particularly ardent kind. He expected the imminent and personal return of Christ. Very soon, everyone would have to personally answer to Christ for what they did and did not do. Significantly, a premillennialist eschatology here does not lead to indifferentism toward the world. Instead Mather invokes the parable of the talent ("Our *opportunities to do good* are our Talents") to jolt his audience into action, reminding them of the "awful account [that] must be rendered unto the great GOD, concerning our use of the Talents,"[38] even if it was Christ alone who could and would perfect his kingdom on earth during the thousand-year reign.

Conclusion

Bonifacius undoubtedly lacks certain characteristics that, in our prevalent modern understanding, are routinely associated with the essay: succinctness, a personal, even subject-centered quality, as well as a provisional, open-ended approach. By contrast, Mather's *Essay Upon the Good* is a book-length exercise in religious pedagogy that is resolutely theocentric rather than focused on the individual's perspective. *Bonifacius*, however, shares many of its features with various forms of essayistic writing popular in Mather's day, especially the project essay. Even though definitive, even dogmatic, in its theological assertions and goals, Mather's writing also reflects his personal experience and has an experimental quality in that it explores different possibilities of being active as a Christian in this world, at the same time that it emphasizes the preliminary nature of its concrete propositions. With regard to its significance for the development of American Protestantism and the larger culture, this chapter has argued against the still prevalent perception of *Bonifacius* as a work that, as Emory Elliott authoritatively pronounced, "displays the liminality of Mather's intellectual situation as he slipped into an eighteenth-century mentality, recommending good works for their practical worldly value and proposing common sense as the way to salvation

---

37 Sacvan Bercovitch, "Cotton Mather and the Vision of America," in *The Rites of Assent: Transformations in the Symbolic Construction of America* (New York: Routledge, 1993), 90–146, 121. However, Bercovitch misconstrues the nature of that expectation as being focused on an American New Jerusalem.

38 Mather, *Bonifacius*, 31.

and wealth."[39] Such a symptomatic reading has to ignore, or dismiss as self-deception, a great deal of what the text is actually and very explicitly saying. And it depends almost entirely on preconceived generalizations of the early eighteenth century as an age of transition and declining piety, where people like Mather were sliding down the slippery slope of secularization while foolishly believing that the new sciences and commercial culture could be made subservient to the Christian faith.

But if we, for a moment, put aside our critic's love for historical ironies and unintended consequences, a much simpler, and arguably more valid, connection becomes visible. *Bonifacius* marks the arrival of a revivalist, reformist, and missionary-oriented type of Protestantism that, as recent studies have demonstrated, partly intersected with more moderate, Christian strands of the Enlightenment. As such it was appreciated by early evangelicals across the British Empire and German Pietists alike. In the *longue durée*, Mather's work anticipates in many ways the Second Great Awakening with its theologies of holiness and its complex of Bible, tract, and temperance societies and the rise of the foreign mission movement – all of which continued to be intensely transatlantic. It is no coincidence that George Burder was an English Congregational minister, influential in the foundation of the London Missionary Society in 1795, the Religious Tract Society in 1799, the British and Foreign Bible Society in 1804, and editor of the *Evangelical Magazine*. Franklin's appropriation of Mather notwithstanding, it was evangelical readers who, as Currie has shown, had most use for *Bonifacius* and kept it in print through no less than sixteen further editions – English, Scottish, and American – during the nineteenth century, making it Mather's most popular and enduring work.[40]

---

39 To be fair, Elliott, unlike Miller, does acknowledge that a closer reading of *Bonifacius* reveals how deeply Mather, in many ways, was still "steeped in the traditional Puritan theology that privileged grace and conversion as the only means of salvation and that commended the spiritual over the material world." Ultimately, however, Mather is interpreted as having engaged in a kind of doublespeak, "using his words in ways that permits both a conservative doctrinal reading and a more practical moral application." Emory Elliott, "New England Puritan Literature," in *The Cambridge History of American Literature*, vol. 1, *1590–1820*, ed. Sacvan Bercovitch (Cambridge, UK: Cambridge University Press, 1994), 169–306, 277–78.

40 David A. Currie, "Cotton Mather's *Bonifacius* in Britain and America," in *Evangelicalism: Comparative Studies of Popular Protestantism in North America, the British Isles, and Beyond, 1700–1990*, ed. Mark A. Noll, David W. Bebbington, and George A. Rawlyk (New York: Oxford University Press, 1994), 71–89, 86. Overall, a total of eighteen editions of *Bonifacius* appeared between 1710 and 1940. See Thomas J. Holmes, *Cotton Mather: A Bibliography of His Works* (Cambridge, MA: Harvard University Press, 1940), 1:90, 324–38.

2

Prattlers, Meddlers, Bachelors, Busy-Bodies: The Periodical Essay in the Eighteenth Century

RICHARD SQUIBBS

Benjamin Franklin (1706–1790) explains in his *Autobiography* how he found his writing voice by imitating the *Spectator* (1711–14), which was then (as now) the most famous and widely read English periodical essay series. This teenaged Bostonian already loved to debate, and an argument between him and his friend John Collins about the propriety of women's education led him to realize that even when he had the better part of a dispute, his writing let him down. As a printer's apprentice, Franklin easily bests Collins in spelling and punctuation, yet Franklin's father points out that his prose falls short in "elegance of Expression ... Method and ... Perspicuity."[1] After finding "an odd Volume of the Spectator" in a shop, Franklin pores over it, determining to imitate its stylistic graces. Ingeniously, he makes "short Hints" of the "Sentiment in each Sentence" in a *Spectator* essay, sets them aside for a few days, and then uses the hints to rewrite each sentence from memory, replicating its core sentiment "in any suitable Words that should come to hand."[2] By doing this repeatedly, and comparing his versions with the originals, he starts to recognize and correct his shortcomings and bad habits on the page. The young Franklin's writing then begins to catch up to his thinking; not only that, but he "sometimes had the Pleasure of Fancying that in certain Particulars of small Import, [he] had been lucky enough to improve the Method or the Language" of the *Spectator*.[3]

Nearly one hundred years later, an insouciant young New Yorker, Washington Irving (1783–1859), registers in "The Letters of Jonathan Oldstyle" (1802–03) and *Salmagundi* (1807–08) the abiding influence of the *Spectator* on a new American literati determined not to praise the polite society that the first

---

1 Benjamin Franklin, *Autobiography, Poor Richard, and Later Writings*, ed. J. A. Leo Lemay (New York: Library of America, 1987), 11.
2 Franklin, *Autobiography*, 11.   3 Franklin, *Autobiography*, 12.

periodical essays had helped create, but to lampoon it. These two writers – one a proud American colonial striving to better his English models, the other a citizen of the new Republic markedly ambivalent about early national society and culture – bookend the story of how the *Spectator* and other popular British serials helped essayists in North American cities imagine the kinds of local communities and citizens they either wanted to encourage or hoped to dispel. Flexible in topic and tone, relatively informal and inherently cosmopolitan, the periodical essay proved an attractive medium for aspiring provincial writers.

So what was the periodical essay? Those British series canonized at the end of the century by collections like *The British Classicks* (1793) and *The British Essayists* (1803) presented themselves as the periodic musings of fictional personae – sometimes assisted by friends, correspondents, and/or members of their clubs – who live in cities. The persona (almost always male) wanders about town, reflecting on what he observes and overhears in the coffee-houses, streets, theaters, and other places of business or leisure. He's often diverted and sometimes frustrated by his fellow citizens; he also strives to enlighten with casual criticism of the arts or musings on the relevance of religion and history to everyday life. The topics are occasional, though a series will sometimes pursue a theme over the course of two or three essays. The periodical essay is highly sociable, without the sternness of didactic or political essay serials; the persona banters with readers instead of lecturing from on high (a quality that William Hazlitt and Charles Lamb, among others, later used to great success).[4] A pervasive, low-level irony is common. Next to the bare fact of periodical publication (normally twice per week in London, though the *Spectator* kept up a run of six days per week for almost two years), this kind of voluble, good-humored, and self-ironizing persona is the genre's characteristic feature.

The periodical essay initially established itself in opposition to newspapers. England's first series, the *Tatler* (1709–11), debuted as an antidote to the distractions of news. In the guise of Isaac Bickerstaff, Esq., Richard Steele (1672–1729) offered a thrice-weekly series of essays designed to make readers more thoughtful, and less contentious, citizens. The genial tone of the essays modeled polite manners and conversation; reflections on fashion, literature, civility, and other familiar topics offered light social and cultural criticism. With the *Tatler*, then, Steele created a distinctive new popular genre, defined (in part) by defying the modes and expectations of news reading. The fact that

---

4 William Hazlitt, "The Round Table," in *The Collected Works of William Hazlitt*, ed. A. R. Waller and Arnold Glover (London: J. M. Dent, 1902), 1:1–164; Charles Lamb, *The Essays of Elia* (London: Chapman and Hall, 1920).

he edited the Whig ministry's polemical newspaper, the *London Gazette* (1675–present), when he launched the *Tatler* made him aware of the potent impact of newswriting: Steele's understanding of how to fan the flames of political controversy with the *Gazette* showed him how he might also use the press to nudge readers toward consensus around moral and cultural issues of the day.[5]

The story of the periodical essay's rise and fall in popularity and critical esteem across the eighteenth century can, in fact, be told in terms of its formal relations with other serial media. The first British series, like the *Tatler*, the *Spectator*, and the *Guardian* (1713), were printed on single folio half sheets, just like the newspapers they contended with. But as early as the *Censor* (1715–17), which appeared thrice weekly in *Mist's Journal*, periodical essays were absorbed into newspapers and magazines as daily or weekly columns. In 1750, Samuel Johnson published the *Rambler* (1750–52) on half sheets in an effort to draw renewed attention to the genre, spurring a revival of the half-sheet essay that lasted a decade. But aside from the *Mirror* (1779–80) and the *Lounger* (1785–86) in Edinburgh, and the *Looker-On* (1792–93) in London, periodical essays after the 1750s were mostly reabsorbed into magazines and newspapers, thereby losing (again) their once prominent status in British literary culture.

The most popular British half-sheet series were issued afterward in collected, bound editions, and this is how the first British-American periodical essayists encountered them, as books imported from London and Dublin. But American essay serials from the start appeared in newspapers and magazines, and it would take almost a century before an American series (*Salmagundi*) circulated proudly alone as a short duodecimo pamphlet. This was necessary because even the largest colonial cities had nowhere near the population or wealth of London and had trouble enough sustaining monthly magazines for more than a few issues, never mind weekly essays. It wasn't until after Independence that an American magazine lasted more than a year, and even then few ran longer than three years.[6] These material constraints

---

5 This bifurcation was not always easy to maintain, however, and Steele's strident Whig politics often erupted into the *Tatler*, especially in times of political crisis. See Brian Cowan, "Mr. Spectator and the Coffeehouse Public Sphere," *Eighteenth-Century Studies* 37, no. 3 (Spring 2004): 345–66; and Rachel Scarborough King, "The *Gazette*, the *Tatler*, and the Making of the Periodical Essay: Form and Genre in Eighteenth-Century News," *Papers of the Bibliographical Society of America* 114, no. 1 (March 2020): 45–70.

6 Not until the Columbian Magazine (Philadelphia, 1786–90) did an American magazine last more than three years. The *Massachusetts Magazine* (1789–96) and the *New-York Magazine* (1790–97) were the first to make it beyond five years. See Heather A. Haveman, *Magazines and the Making of America: Modernization, Community, and Print Culture, 1741–1860* (Princeton, NJ: Princeton University Press, 2015); and Lyon N. Richardson, *A History of Early American Magazines* (New York: Thomas Nelson and Sons, 1931).

might have hindered colonial acolytes of Addison and Steele from finding, and/or creating, their polite publics. Yet the compromises they were forced to accept in publishing their musings monthly, amid the miscellaneous stuff of magazines, helped some British-American periodical essayists see new literary potential in what was already a venerable genre by the mid-1750s.

This is not to say that colonial cities teemed with original, or distinctly "American," takes on their English inspirations. Most are merely imitative, and even those that most pretended to originality would soon fall back into old, received habits. "The Friend" (1786) is a case in point, made more striking by its status as one of the earliest post-Revolutionary series. In its first number, "James Littlejohn, Esq." points to the limited appeal British serials had for American readers. While acknowledging how "many of the truths contained in [British collections] are capable of universal application," he notes that "many others are immediately directed to that state of society, and those circumstances of life, by which the writers saw themselves surrounded."[7] Thus, "part of the pleasure and instruction, which a British reader, in the age of Queen Anne, derived from perusing the Spectator, is lost to an American reader of the present age, [for the] state of society in London is widely different from the state of society in an American village."[8] The problem, Littlejohn says, is that American essayists have generally ignored "the entire novelty of [American] circumstances," drawing "their remarks [not] so much from life, as from books and speculation."[9] "The Friend" aims to remedy this, bringing American life and manners into a genre so readily equipped to illuminate them.

In the event, Littlejohn fails. "The Friend," like "The Nursery" and "The Competitor" (in the *Boston Magazine* [1785–86]), and "The General Observer" (in the *Massachusetts Magazine* [1789–96]), mostly imitates the sober moralism of Johnson's *Rambler*.[10] The promised close observations of novel American manners never materialize, while three numbers near the end are taken up by a sonorous, interminable poem, "The Trial of Faith." Other colonial and early national serials that strove to introduce specifically American subjects, like "The Hermit," "The Planter," and "The Watchman" (all in the *American Magazine and Monthly Chronicle* [1757–58]), or "The Philanthropist" and "The

---

7 "The Friend," *New-Haven Gazette, and the Connecticut Magazine* (March–October 1786): 42–43.
8 "Friend," 42.   9 "Friend," 43.
10 See, for instance, no. 6 (on candor and liberality versus prejudice and contraction [89–90]); no. 9 (on the inconveniences of second marriages [137–38]); and nos. 11 and 12 (on aesthetic and moral taste, respectively [145–46, 161–63]), all of which might have appeared in any essay series on the Johnsonian model on either side of the Atlantic.

Reformer" (in the *Massachusetts Magazine* [1789]), were repetitively topical and didactic, without the wry personae of the periodical essay proper.[11] So a series like Franklin's "Silence Dogood" (1722), which plays with and transforms conventions inherited from its English models, stands out.

"Silence" is the first British-American persona with a distinctive voice. Female personae were not unheard of in periodical essays: Phoebe Crackenthorpe and Jenny Distaff had held forth over a decade earlier in the *Female Tatler* (1709) and the *Tatler* (1709), respectively. But Silence was unique in colonial America. Neither a spinster nor a yenta, Silence exemplifies an incipient form of what Mary Beth Norton has called "the feminine private," an Enlightenment discourse that licensed woman publicly to criticize only domestic concerns and matters of female conduct.[12] Yet, as Norton notes, Franklin wrote "Silence Dogood" before the gendered public/private distinction had fully hardened in American (or British) civic life, and hence Silence opines across a wider field of concern. In a series of letters to the *New-England Courant* (Franklin's brother James's paper), she introduces herself to readers on a similar rhetorical footing as Mr. Spectator: Everyone, she contends in the first number, decides to read something based on "whether [the author] be *poor* or *rich*, *old* or *young*, a *Schollar* or a *Leather Apron Man*, &c."[13] Silence falls somewhere in the middle: She's a widowed mother, orphaned young but apprenticed to a country minister who had instilled her with a love of reading, and who now enjoys a fair amount of simple leisure in the country with her son. This backstory distinguishes her from Crackenthorpe and Distaff, who had engaged in the sharp, knowing banter of habitués of London's fashionable places. Silence is instead studious and self-critical, though capable of inveighing against religious hypocrisy and excessive tippling, among other foibles.[14] Her

---

11 This is also the case with the handful of serials published in the Southern colonies. See Bruce Granger, *American Essay Serials from Franklin to Irving* (Knoxville, TN: University of Tennessee Press, 1978), 70–96.
12 Mary Beth Norton, *Separated by Their Sex: Women in Public and Private in the Colonial Atlantic World* (Ithaca, NY: Cornell University Press, 2011), 144.
13 Benjamin Franklin, *Silence Dogood, The Busy-Body, and Early Writings*, ed. J. A. Leo Lemay (New York: Library of America, 2005), 5. Compare with the opening of the *Spectator*: "I have observed, that a Reader seldom peruses a Book with Pleasure 'till he knows whether the Writer of it be a black or a fair Man, of a mild or cholerick Disposition, Married or a Batchelor" (*Spectator*, ed. Donald F. Bond [Oxford: Oxford University Press, 1965], 1:1).
14 See Sarah Prescott and Jane Spenser, "Prattling, Tattling and Knowing Everything: Public Authority and the Female Editorial Persona in the Early Essay-Periodical," *British Journal for Eighteenth-Century Studies* 23, no. 1 (March 2000): 43–57.

sojourn in Boston (numbers 6 to 14) then allows Franklin to revise the trope of the naïve observer in an unfamiliar environment to prompt his urban readers to see themselves through the eyes of a sober, literate, rational woman of sense.

Nearly seventy years would pass before another Boston essayist created a comparably original persona; in the meantime, Philadelphia essayists stepped into the breach. While New York City was known mainly as a commercial hub and Boston as a haughtily provincial town, Philadelphians took pride in their learned societies and reputation as the most enlightened and cosmopolitan citizens of colonial, and then early national, America. It's not surprising, then, that six of the eight colonial-era essay serials on the British model originated in Philadelphia. Most, like Franklin's first Philadelphia venture, "The Busy Body" (1729–30), offered faithful versions of their London-based forerunners (by "erect[ing] [him] Self into a Kind of *Censor Morum*," the Busy Body follows directly in the footsteps of Isaac Bickerstaff, self-appointed "Censor" of "a Nation of Liberty" in the *Tatler*).[15] But some of the most creative revisions of the genre in post-Revolutionary America were published there as well.

"The Prattler," which ran in William Bradford's *American Magazine and Monthly Chronicle* (1757–58), is colonial America's first stab at revising the *Spectator*'s formula from the ground up. Presented as the monthly musings of Timothy Timbertoe, "The Prattler" (like Silence Dogood) explicitly invokes Mr. Spectator's self-introduction, promising to entertain and enlighten readers with reporting from "tea-tables, . . . the coffee-house, or adventures in private life."[16] But where Mr. Spectator's dispassionate anonymity had made him what Michael Warner deems "almost an allegorized literalized embodiment of [the] supervision" at the heart of republican print culture, striving to infuse coffeehouse and tea-table conversation with elevating "Philosophy,"[17] Timbertoe is sneakier and his motives more suspect.[18] In the first "Prattler," he adopts the traditional stance of the periodical persona, averring a disinterested desire "to hold the *Glass to folly*, wherein she may . . . perceive what it would otherwise be difficult to persuade her of."[19] Professing

---

15 Franklin, *Silence Dogood*, 100; *Tatler*, ed. Donald F. Bond (Oxford: Clarendon Press, 1985), 2:318.
16 "The Prattler," *American Magazine and Monthly Chronicle*, 76. Mr. Spectator had aimed to bring "Philosophy out of Closets and Libraries, Schools and Colleges, to dwell in Clubs and Assemblies, at Tea-Tables, and in Coffee-houses" (*Spectator*, vol. 1, 44).
17 *Spectator*, vol. 1, 44.
18 Michael Warner, *The Letters of the Republic: Publication and the Public Sphere in Eighteenth-Century America* (Cambridge, MA: Harvard University Press, 1990), 66.
19 "Prattler," 76.

to be too humble to detail his own personal qualities (the customary mode of introduction for personae since the *Spectator*), he solicits a letter from a friend to supply this portrait. His friend demurs, but sends a long letter to the magazine's publishers, warning that Timbertoe is an imperious and self-absorbed failed poet who publishes private conversations solely to make his acquaintances, and even friends, look ridiculous. The letter's author – Dick Dimple – is hardly a disinterested party: Timbertoe had once embarrassed him by repeating in company an account of Dimple's nightly skin-care ritual, as originally told to a cooing Miss Patty Prim. Timbertoe's decision to publish the letter (defying Dimple's injunction not to read it) then compounds the original offense by publicizing Dimple's embarrassment to a wider audience, while bearing out Dimple's charge that Timbertoe is not to be trusted. No one comes off looking good. In its first number, then, "The Prattler" satirizes the periodical essay's pretensions to civic disinterestedness even more thoroughly than had its popular London contemporaries the *World* (1753–56) and the *Connoisseur* (1754–56), whose comic laments over their failure to reform the public were part of their appeal.[20] For "The Prattler," the genre's conventional concern with public reform appears as little more than a rote rhetorical gesture.

Where "The Prattler" takes aim at the *Spectator*, "The Old Bachelor" (which appeared for ten numbers in the *Pennsylvania Magazine* in 1775, some of which have been attributed to Thomas Paine) sets its sights on the *Rambler*.[21] Johnson's essays were notorious for what one contemporary deemed their "affected appearance of pomposity" (which made them "greatly inferior to the easy and natural *Spectator*"), a reputation the Bachelor invokes in hailing Johnson as "the prince of ill-nature" whom he's so determined to emulate that he hangs a print of Johnson over his writing desk to inspire his surliness.[22] Nothing could be further from the *Rambler*'s chaste sententiousness, however, than the Bachelor's boasts about having "been as great a benefactor to the province of Pennsylvania, (you understand me,) as any man" despite being single, with his various progeny dispersed far and wide throughout the colony.[23] Most of the "Old Bachelor" essays

---

20 For an account of this ironic turn in midcentury London serials, see Richard Squibbs, *Urban Enlightenment and the Eighteenth-Century Periodical Essay: Transatlantic Retrospects* (Basingstoke, UK: Palgrave, 2014), 72–93.
21 For attributions of particular essays to Paine, see Granger, *American Essay*, 246n39.
22 Vicesimus Knox, "On the Periodical Essayists," in *Essays, Moral and Literary*, vol. 1 (London, 1786), 132–38, 136; "The Old Bachelor," in *Pennsylvania Magazine* 1 (1775): 111–13, 455–57, 111.
23 "Old Bachelor," 113.

vacillate between such un-Johnsonian ribaldry (as when the Bachelor catches one of his maids undressed on her way to, or from, an assignation with another servant [number 3]) and rank misogyny (he wishes he'd been born an oyster so that he'd "have propagated [his] species in a numerous offspring, without the help, without the plagues, without the expence [sic] of a female assistant."[24] Other Philadelphia series like "Atticus" and "The Visitant" (in the *Pennsylvania Chronicle* [1767–69]) had imitated the *Rambler*'s moral sobriety as faithfully as "The Busy Body" had the *Tatler*'s public censoriousness. But "The Old Bachelor" plays Johnsonian pessimism strictly for laughs.

The last Philadelphia series to do something original with the periodical persona ran in the *Columbian Magazine, or Monthly Miscellany* at the end of the 1780s. "The Retailer" (1788–90) and "The Rhapsodist" (1789) each transform the terms of the persona's engagement with readers in ways specifically tailored to postcolonial American life. Like "The Prattler," "The Retailer" dismisses the periodical essay's usefulness as a vehicle for moral reform. To try to justify his essays in those terms, he contends, "would argue the want of an implicit confidence in the judgment of an Addison, Steele, Johnson" and others, for if the public still needs reforming after having had access to the *Tatler*, the *Spectator*, and the *Rambler* for so many decades, then perhaps effective reform isn't the periodical essay's strong suit.[25] What essays like these can offer instead is "the history of the fashionable world," which may prove at least fascinating or amusing (if not wholly enlightening) to readers in the future.[26] With this mission in mind, it's striking how the Retailer identifies himself primarily with the mercantile, rather than the narrative, connotation of his title. He thus glosses the rationale for the essayist's pseudonymity not in the traditional terms of republican supervision but in commercial ones: to indulge in the "egotism" of making himself the subject of an essay would distract from the "*wares*" he means to display monthly for "the observation of his customers." One of his associates likewise jibes that the series will serve as a "chapman for the *dry goods*" and "*low priced*" wit" the Retailer has "on hand."[27] This commercial conceit reaches its apogee in number three, where the spirit of Addison leads the Retailer in a dream, as Virgil had led Dante, through the "*city of literature*," where writers from Martial to Pope to Hume display their works as vendible foodstuffs (for, the Retailer notes, "Literature [is] the food of *the mind*"[28]). While Londoners may have seen themselves as a "polite and commercial people," this former

24 "Old Bachelor," 455,
25 "The Retailer," *Columbian Magazine, or Monthly Miscellany* (1788): 83–85, 202–206, 85.
26 "Retailer," 85.   27 "Retailer," 84.   28 "Retailer," 203.

colonial subject subordinates the polite to the commercial to introduce a new, distinctly American vein of ironic humor to the periodical essay.[29]

The innovations of "The Rhapsodist" run in a different direction. Across these four essays, Charles Brockden Brown turns the conventional periodical persona around and around, like clay on a wheel, without resolving it into a definite shape. As with the Prattler, everything for the Rhapsodist springs from idiosyncratic, personal motives. His deep aversion to business, for instance, prevents him from enjoying what he otherwise recognizes as the sparkling "wit and ingenuity" of the "'Retailer,'" merely on account of the persona's name.[30] Readers of the first number learn only what the Rhapsodist is not: He's unsociable, unable to contribute "more than [an] ordinary share of amusement or instruction" to the public, and no better a man, morally, than anyone else.[31] As for his age, station in life, or any of the traditional markers of a persona's character, he'll only "from time to time, as occasion requires, give such useful hints."[32] More than just amplifying the persona's customary anonymity, the Rhapsodist's reticence expresses a deep self-absorption at odds with the civic disinterestedness that had been the modus operandi of the periodical essay since the *Tatler*. He's "an enemy to conversation" who prefers talking to himself and to his imaginative creations,[33] and a stranger to "[l]ove and friendship, and all the social passions."[34] His ideal citizens reject society altogether in favor of a "visionary happiness in a world of their own creation," into which no one from the outside is allowed.[35] While the Rhapsodist's aversion to commercial business and indulgence in solitary imaginings have been read as evidence of a nascent strain of American Romanticism, the series' relentless negation of the conventional periodical persona seems too tied to what it rejects to allow its alienated individualism to attain coherent form.[36] The abandonment by Brockden Brown (1771–1810) of the series after just four numbers, during which his persona never achieves real definition, suggests that reformulating the periodical essay according to social and imaginative virtues so at odds with the genre's traditional civic orientation was beyond his capacities.

---

29 The phrase first appears in Blackstone's *Commentaries* (1765–69). See Paul Langford, *A Polite and Commercial People: England 1720–1783* (Oxford: Oxford University Press, 1989), 1.
30 "Retailer," 466–67.
31 "The Rhapsodist," *Columbian Magazine, or Monthly Miscellany* (1789): 464–67, 537–41, 465.
32 "Rhapsodist," 464.   33 "Rhapsodist," 537.   34 "Rhapsodist," 538.   35 "Rhapsodist," 539.
36 See Steve Hamilton, "Rhapsodist in the Wilderness: Brown's Romantic Quest in *Edgar Huntly*," *Studies in American Fiction* 21, no. 2 (Autumn 1993): 171–90.

While "The Retailer" and "The Rhapsodist" challenged the expectations of Philadelphia's readers with their nascent modernism, "The Dreamer" (1789) and "The Gleaner" (1792–94) tentatively asserted themselves among the more conservatively minded public of Boston. Both appeared in the *Massachusetts Magazine*, home as well to sober, pro forma series in the *Rambler* mode like "The General Observer" (1789–91), "The Philanthropist" (1789–90), and "Philo" (1789–90). "The Dreamer" is, in most respects, a conventional moralistic series. Its concern with women's education and fashion-mindedness, for instance, echoes that of many English and colonial American predecessors, as do its accounts of dreams that point up the morals of its essays. But there are enough specifically American inflections to its Dreamer persona, and to the eccentricities of the would-be members of the Dreamers Club he proposes, to make it stand out from the pack.

Dreamers are no mere idealists. True, some follow the absent-minded example of Cardinal Richelieu, who once ran "to church without breeches" and others have repeatedly "been *fooled by hope*, in any *love affair*."[37] But most dreamers just aspire to distinction while lacking the requisite means: "merchants without credit, writers without wit, beauties without affectation, travellers without lies, mechanicks without industry, or politicians without money."[38] In a new nation where, as "The Friend" had put it, "equal division of property [*sic*], universal diffusion of knowledge . . . [and] absolute personal independence . . . furnish [essayists] with as fair a field of reflection, as was perhaps ever furnished,"[39] such bereft strivers were legion, and the Dreamer welcomes them to his club. But he's not as ecumenical as he initially seems. Of the eleven letters from putative readers seeking admission, the Dreamer approves only two requests: one from a stern moralist whose intention "to separate the *sweet from the useful* in his endeavours for reformation" make him "a Vain Dreamer,"[40] and the other from a man determined to dwell in his hopes for blissful, pastoral love affair (number 12). The rest he dismisses either as insufficiently misanthropic, or as "Insurgent Critick[s]" whose "IDEAS OF GOODNESS" proceed from mistaken assumptions that value judgments are anything but relative and subjective.[41] The public, such as it exists for "The Dreamer," is at best too self-absorbed (like the Dreamer himself) to hang together as a sociable group. At worst, its concerns are simply too trifling to matter to the essayist.

---

37 "The Dreamer," *Massachusetts Magazine* (1789): 32–36, 152–55, 153.   38 "Dreamer," 153.
39 "Friend," 43.   40 "Dreamer," 155.   41 "Dreamer," 34.

"The Gleaner," by Judith Sargent Murray (1751–1820), appeals to readers of a more serious and sentimental bent. In the roster of serials from the *Massachusetts Magazine* that Murray cites as inspirations, "The Dreamer" is conspicuously absent.[42] "The Gleaner's" male persona, Vigillius, professes a calm, Universalist piety that sometimes clashes with his high-toned Federalism (he calls for "the political Hercules" of virtual representation to "crush the Hydra faction," for instance[43]). "The Gleaner" thus often reads more like a topical serial in "The Reformer" and "Atticus" mode, with few flashes of "The Prattler's" or "The Retailer's" acerbic wit. Yet unlike those irascible bachelors, Vigillius is happily married, a domestic situation that accounts for the unusually deep vein of sentiment running through the series. Where "The Dreamer" had ridiculed the fashion for sentimental fiction, Vigillius devotes twelve of the thirty-two numbers originally published in the *Massachusetts Magazine* to the story of Margaretta, a novelistic account of this sensible, thoughtful young woman's near-seduction by the caddish Sinisterius Courtland and ultimate marriage to a proper young minister.

While "The Gleaner" doesn't print as much reader correspondence as had earlier American series, the letters it does (which, Murray frankly avows in the *Gleaner*'s final number, she'd "written to [her]self"[44]) periodically demand that Margaretta's tale (introduced in the second number) be continued. When, after the *Massachusetts Magazine* had temporarily folded at the end of 1794 and Murray continued to write what would become the three-volume *Gleaner* collection published in 1798, Margaretta's tale expanded to a further seventeen numbers. Because of this, "The Gleaner" features regularly in studies of the early American novel; equally significant, though, it was the first American serial to have been reissued in book form.[45] With the *Gleaner* (whose subscription list included George and Martha Washington, John Adams, and John Hancock), the American periodical essay made its first serious bid for historical recognition.

Along with modeling a sentimental American public in its pages, "The Gleaner" prophesied that America would soon challenge the international

---

42 "The General Observer," "Philo," and "The Philanthropist," however, earn pride of place (Judith Sargent Murray, *The Gleaner*, ed. Nina Byam [1798; repr. Schenectady, NY: Union College Press, 1992], 16). I cite *The Gleaner* when referring to those that Murray published only in the original three-volume book version, and "The Gleaner" when referring to essays from the original periodical run.

43 Murray, *Gleaner*, 212.   44 Murray, *Gleaner*, 807.

45 See Cathy Davidson, *Revolution and the Word: The Rise of the Novel in America* (New York: Oxford University Press, 1986), 129–31; and Marion Rust, *Prodigal Daughters: Susanna Rowson's Early American Women* (Chapel Hill, NC: University of North Carolina Press, 2008), 98–100.

While "The Retailer" and "The Rhapsodist" challenged the expectations of Philadelphia's readers with their nascent modernism, "The Dreamer" (1789) and "The Gleaner" (1792–94) tentatively asserted themselves among the more conservatively minded public of Boston. Both appeared in the *Massachusetts Magazine*, home as well to sober, pro forma series in the *Rambler* mode like "The General Observer" (1789–91), "The Philanthropist" (1789–90), and "Philo" (1789–90). "The Dreamer" is, in most respects, a conventional moralistic series. Its concern with women's education and fashion-mindedness, for instance, echoes that of many English and colonial American predecessors, as do its accounts of dreams that point up the morals of its essays. But there are enough specifically American inflections to its Dreamer persona, and to the eccentricities of the would-be members of the Dreamers Club he proposes, to make it stand out from the pack.

Dreamers are no mere idealists. True, some follow the absent-minded example of Cardinal Richelieu, who once ran "to church without breeches" and others have repeatedly "been *fooled by hope*, in any *love affair*."[37] But most dreamers just aspire to distinction while lacking the requisite means: "merchants without credit, writers without wit, beauties without affectation, travellers without lies, mechanicks without industry, or politicians without money."[38] In a new nation where, as "The Friend" had put it, "equal division of property [*sic*], universal diffusion of knowledge ... [and] absolute personal independence ... furnish [essayists] with as fair a field of reflection, as was perhaps ever furnished,"[39] such bereft strivers were legion, and the Dreamer welcomes them to his club. But he's not as ecumenical as he initially seems. Of the eleven letters from putative readers seeking admission, the Dreamer approves only two requests: one from a stern moralist whose intention "to separate the *sweet from the useful* in his endeavours for reformation" make him "a *Vain Dreamer*,"[40] and the other from a man determined to dwell in his hopes for blissful, pastoral love affair (number 12). The rest he dismisses either as insufficiently misanthropic, or as "Insurgent Critick[s]" whose "IDEAS OF GOODNESS" proceed from mistaken assumptions that value judgments are anything but relative and subjective.[41] The public, such as it exists for "The Dreamer," is at best too self-absorbed (like the Dreamer himself) to hang together as a sociable group. At worst, its concerns are simply too trifling to matter to the essayist.

---

37 "The Dreamer," *Massachusetts Magazine* (1789): 32–36, 152–55, 153. 38 "Dreamer," 153.
39 "Friend," 43.   40 "Dreamer," 155.   41 "Dreamer," 34.

"The Gleaner," by Judith Sargent Murray (1751–1820), appeals to readers of a more serious and sentimental bent. In the roster of serials from the *Massachusetts Magazine* that Murray cites as inspirations, "The Dreamer" is conspicuously absent.[42] "The Gleaner's" male persona, Vigillius, professes a calm, Universalist piety that sometimes clashes with his high-toned Federalism (he calls for "the political Hercules" of virtual representation to "crush the Hydra faction," for instance[43]). "The Gleaner" thus often reads more like a topical serial in "The Reformer" and "Atticus" mode, with few flashes of "The Prattler's" or "The Retailer's" acerbic wit. Yet unlike those irascible bachelors, Vigillius is happily married, a domestic situation that accounts for the unusually deep vein of sentiment running through the series. Where "The Dreamer" had ridiculed the fashion for sentimental fiction, Vigillius devotes twelve of the thirty-two numbers originally published in the *Massachusetts Magazine* to the story of Margaretta, a novelistic account of this sensible, thoughtful young woman's near-seduction by the caddish Sinisterius Courtland and ultimate marriage to a proper young minister.

While "The Gleaner" doesn't print as much reader correspondence as had earlier American series, the letters it does (which, Murray frankly avows in the *Gleaner*'s final number, she'd "written to [her]self"[44]) periodically demand that Margaretta's tale (introduced in the second number) be continued. When, after the *Massachusetts Magazine* had temporarily folded at the end of 1794 and Murray continued to write what would become the three-volume *Gleaner* collection published in 1798, Margaretta's tale expanded to a further seventeen numbers. Because of this, "The Gleaner" features regularly in studies of the early American novel; equally significant, though, it was the first American serial to have been reissued in book form.[45] With the *Gleaner* (whose subscription list included George and Martha Washington, John Adams, and John Hancock), the American periodical essay made its first serious bid for historical recognition.

Along with modeling a sentimental American public in its pages, "The Gleaner" prophesied that America would soon challenge the international

---

42 "The General Observer," "Philo," and "The Philanthropist," however, earn pride of place (Judith Sargent Murray, *The Gleaner*, ed. Nina Byam [1798; repr. Schenectady, NY: Union College Press, 1992], 16). I cite *The Gleaner* when referring to those that Murray published only in the original three-volume book version, and "The Gleaner" when referring to essays from the original periodical run.

43 Murray, *Gleaner*, 212.   44 Murray, *Gleaner*, 807.

45 See Cathy Davidson, *Revolution and the Word: The Rise of the Novel in America* (New York: Oxford University Press, 1986), 129–31; and Marion Rust, *Prodigal Daughters: Susanna Rowson's Early American Women* (Chapel Hill, NC: University of North Carolina Press, 2008), 98–100.

"empire of arts" with its new, democratic "mental *Commonwealth*."[46] Yet just 200 miles to the south, Washington Irving sought to check such nationalistic optimism with his cynical reconception of the periodical essay. Unlike Philadelphia and Boston, New York had not been distinguished for its essay serials. The city's first substantial literary monthly, the *New-York Magazine* (1790–97), featured a number of short-lived ones like "Juvenis," "The Scribbler," and "The Club," all of which read as rote imitations of their English models. A few years before, the *American Magazine* (1787–88) had published six numbers of "The Life and Amusements of Isaac Bickerstaffe Junior," an incomplete, witless stab at a *Tristram Shandy*–like serial novella that, despite its title, shares little with the periodical essay.[47] So the "Oldstyle" letters were the city's first substantial contribution to the genre. Recalling Franklin's debut as an essayist, Irving published these nine letter-essays in his brother Peter's newspaper, the *Morning Chronicle*. But where Dogood had tweaked Boston's pretensions with wry common sense, a cranky, exasperated Oldstyle lashes out at New York's cultural scene. His attitudes belong to an earlier era (the switch from Old Style to the New Style calendar occurred in the colonies in 1752); but unlike his closest literary predecessor, the *Spectator*'s genial old bachelor Sir Roger de Coverley, Oldstyle finds the present jarring and disorienting, much as Rip Van Winkle would over a decade later.

Oldstyle's anachronistic grousing is prompted by the late arrival of polite society in New York. Six of the nine essays focus on the scene at the New Theatre, which in 1798 had replaced the John Street Theatre, America's second permanent playhouse (established in 1767). The other three decry modern fashion, courtship, and recent antidueling legislation. Spruce attire has given way to "slovenliness," and chivalric devotion to the "ladies" sunk into the torpid self-absorption of "the modern beau," a "sluggish animal" given to "affecting the helplessness of an invalid."[48] Oldstyle's young creator appears to share his complaints about rudeness at the theater, foppish attire, and the barbarity of gentlemen who settle disagreements with pistols rather than "the *small sword*"[49] – to a degree. The letter on dueling ends with Oldstyle's friends Mr. Quoz and Jack Stylish recommending that disputants might draw lots to see which gets to drop

---

46 Murray, *Gleaner*, 126.
47 The essays in New York's first magazine, the *Independent Reflector* (1752–53), were exclusively political and informative (concerning agriculture, civic improvements, and other practical topics).
48 Washington Irving, *History, Tales and Sketches*, ed. James W. Tuttleton (New York: Library of America, 1983), 5–6.
49 Irving, *History, Tales and Sketches*, 40.

a brick from a window on the other's head. Failing this, they could apply at a proposed institution, the *"Blood and Thunder Office,"* for a license to hold public combat – with "two or three weeks notice ... in the newspapers" – to add to "our refined amusements."[50] Oldstyle favors the second option because, he reasons, since duelists "fight to please the world" by way of preserving their honor, crowds should be "permitted to attend and judge of their conduct" as the ancient Romans did their gladiators.[51] In this final letter in the *Oldstyle* series, the past (with its genteel traditions of bloodshed) looks no better than the present. And the present, with its newspaper-fed mass culture, seems incapable of generating much beyond ever more debased forms of entertainment. All that's left to do, for Irving, is to laugh at the sorry spectacle.

With *Salmagundi*, Irving pushes "Oldstyle's" ironic reformulation of the genre to its terminus. Spurred to publish by the appearance of the *Town*, a short-lived thrice-weekly series that had the temerity to identity itself as an American *Spectator*, Irving joined with his brother William and brother-in-law James Kirke Paulding to publish a series devoted to pulling the rug out from under New York's aspirant polite set.[52] *Salmagundi*'s ostensible conductors are a group of three bachelors modeled on the Spectator Club, each tasked with a different area of inquiry: Launcelot Langstaff, Esq., handles general topics, Anthony Evergreen (like the *Spectator*'s aged beau Will Honeycomb) writes on matters of fashion, and Will Wizard is the resident critic. Their aggressive dedication to bachelorhood exceeds anything professed by earlier bachelor personae, reflecting a newfound civic irresponsibility; for in a new nation given to fetishizing republican motherhood and public-spirited men, and driven ever westward to expand its territory, to opt out of raising families could look downright unpatriotic.[53] Nonetheless, these "eccentric, whim-whamsical" gentlemen[54] say they want "to instruct the young, reform the old, correct the town and castigate the age" – so long as it doesn't put them out too much.[55] Their material choices likewise work at cross-purposes with their professed aims: While the "small neat duodecimo" pamphlets are designed, like the original London half-sheet essay serials, to be circulated easily throughout town, *Salmagundi* is also helpfully "printed on

---

50 Irving, *History, Tales and Sketches*, 42.   51 Irving, *History, Tales and Sketches*, 43.
52 The first number of the *Town* appeared on 1 January 1807; the last on 12 January 1807.
53 For later manifestations of the problematic bachelor figure in American literature, see Katherine V. Snyder, *Bachelors, Manhood, and the Novel, 1850–1925* (Cambridge, UK: Cambridge University Press, 2009).
54 Irving, *History, Tales and Sketches*, 198.   55 Irving, *History, Tales and Sketches*, 49.

hot-prest vellum paper," which is best "for buckling-up young ladies' hair – a purpose to which similar works are usually appropriated".[56] And where the "Oldstyle" letters were thematically anachronistic, *Salmagundi* defies the conventional temporality of the periodical essay altogether, declaring in its first number that subsequent issues "will not come out at stated periods" but instead whenever the essayists feel like publishing them (on average, a little over two weeks for each number during the series' year-long run).[57] In *Salmagundi*, the ostensible needs of the public are subordinated to the whims of its conductors.

A few decades later the English poet Samuel Rogers reportedly sniffed that Irving's essays were just "Addison and Water."[58] This mild insult is not without insight. The British periodical essay didn't make its way across the Atlantic without getting roughed up in the voyage. But to imply that the water merely diluted the *Spectator's* original potency misses what the salty new cocktail had to offer literary history. Here and there amid the merely imitative series, colonial and early national American writers – some well known to literary history, others lost to anonymity – used the cultural chasm between the dense, cosmopolitan scenes of urbane London and their sparser, rawer towns to sharpen the edges of the periodical essay's normally genial persona. The result is a vein of essay writing that makes civic improvement and the cultivation of polite society subjects of sport, and forges a new kind of literary affect out of the social alienation of its personae, one for which civic disengagement becomes a cultural imperative.[59] In forswearing any power to change how their readers behave, these non-civic-minded essayists compel them instead to see their societies as amusing, and sometimes outrageous, spectacles. This is not yet the full modern alienation of the *flâneur*.[60] But the most original early American essay series sketch in their personae a knowing independence of mind amid a distracted and unreflective urban crowd, a rhetorical standpoint that – paradoxically – would come to define a newly nationalistic body of literature in the nineteenth century.

---

56 Irving, *History, Tales and Sketches*, 50–51.   57 Irving, *History, Tales and Sketches*, 51.
58 Quoted in Joseph J. Firebaugh, "Samuel Rogers and American Men of Letters," *American Literature* 13, no. 4 (January 1942): 331–45, 336.
59 For a related impulse in the Philadelphia *Port Folio* magazine, see William C. Dowling, *Literary Federalism in the Age of Jefferson: Joseph Dennie and* The Port Folio, *1801–1811* (Columbia, SC: University of South Carolina Press, 1999).
60 For a history of the relationship between early periodicals and the *flâneur*, see Dana Brand, *Spectator and the City in Nineteenth-Century American Literature* (Cambridge, UK: Cambridge University Press, 1991), 1–7.

3
The Federalist and the Founders

MATTHEW GARRETT

"In every human society, there is an essay continually tending to confer on one part the height of power and happiness, and to reduce the other to the extreme of weakness and misery."[1] On 21 June 1788, Melancton Smith (1744–1798) quoted this sentence from the English translation of Cesare Beccaria's (1738–1794) *Essay on Crimes and Punishments* (1774) in his response to Alexander Hamilton during the New York Ratification Convention. Smith uses the word *essay* in accordance with standard late eighteenth-century semantics: "effort," or more precisely, "hostile attempt."[2] He does not seem to intend any reference to the literary form. But *essay* opens, even in this seemingly divergent context, toward the question of genre: specifically, the relationship between the essay as a form of writing and the styles of power and persuasion with which it is linked during the agon of US state formation. In order to grasp the mediating role of the essay as a public mode of political expression in this period, we must also understand how the sense of the term shuttled between literary form and political ambition. The US Constitution had created a novel condition of speech and writing due to the direct invocation of "the People" in its preamble, a textual innovation that was the result of the Constitution's reach to act directly on individual citizens rather than merely on federated states (as had the Articles of Confederation). That aim was itself determined by the new national ruling class's drive to extinguish the residual egalitarian energies of the American Revolution and to establish a unified

---

[1] "Convention Debates, 21 June 1788," *The Documentary History of the Ratification of the Constitution Digital Edition*, ed. John P. Kaminski et al. (Charlottesville, VA: University of Virginia Press, 2009). Smith himself cites the phrase in reference to the Continental Congress's effort, in 1775, to persuade Quebec to join the American Revolutionary cause. The *Documentary History*, which is the indispensable resource for primary materials related to ratification, is hereafter abbreviated *DHRC*.

[2] *Oxford English Dictionary*, s.v. "essay."

commercial and merchant capitalist republic, setting the stage for what they envisioned as a US "empire" of commodity production.[3] The new speech context was one in which the possessing class – merchants, landed men, slaveholders – was obliged to use a language of social reference to a people that it did not and could not represent politically. Such was the representational condition within which the essay as form was refashioned in the ratification period.

During the previous day's debate, Smith had argued that the Constitution's logic of representation was both flawed and unjust. Not only did the low proportions in the House of Representatives (30,000 inhabitants per representative) artificially concentrate power (and thus deny representational agency to the mass of the people, whom Smith identified as the "middling class" of "respectable yeomanry"), but in addition the very construction of the unit of representation was flawed at its heart.[4] Smith reserved his most acid commentary for the notorious "three-fifths" clause of article 1, section 3:

> In the first place the rule of apportionment of the representatives is to be according to the whole number of the white inhabitants, with three fifths of all others, that is in plain English, each state is to send Representatives in proportion to the number of freemen, and three fifths of the slaves it contains. He [Smith] could not see any rule by which slaves are to be included in the ratio of representation: The principle of a representation, being that every free agent should be concerned in governing himself, it was absurd to give that power to a man who could not exercise it – slaves have no will of their own: The very operation of it was to give certain privileges to those people who were so wicked as to keep slaves.[5]

As often happened during the ratification debate, here Smith's commentary moves between levels of "representation." What appears first as a question of

---

[3] The enduring, lapidary encapsulation of this move to "separate the people from power over their own economic life" remains Karl Polanyi, *The Great Transformation: The Political and Economic Origins of Our Time* (Boston: Beacon Press, 2001), 234. For its literary-historical consequences beyond the genre of the essay, see Matthew Garrett, *Episodic Poetics: Politics and Literary Form after the Constitution* (New York: Oxford University Press, 2014). *The Federalist* opens with an invocation of an American empire, in *Federalist* 1, and the vision of an empire of production is consolidated by Alexander Hamilton's *Report on Manufactures* (1791), itself edging the genre of the essay.

[4] Saul Cornell locates Smith within the tradition of "middling Anti-Federalists" (Saul Cornell, *The Other Founders: Anti-Federalism and the Dissenting Tradition in America, 1788–1828* [Chapel Hill, NC: University of North Carolina Press, 1999], 83–84), while Gordon Wood labels him a "socially inferior politician" (*The Creation of the American Republic, 1776–1787* [Chapel Hill, NC: University of North Carolina Press, 1969], 487).

[5] "Convention Debates, 20 June 1788," *DHRC*, n.p. In the record of the debates, speakers are referred to in the third person.

political ratio (how many representatives per unit of population?) emerges as a matter of representation as such – of the capacities of an agent to govern itself, and therefore of the nature and tendency of agents and governing alike.[6] Politically, Smith argues, enslaved people have "no will of their own" because they are not "free" but rather agents of the master class; the three-fifths clause is a distribution of power to that class and therefore both a political and a moral solecism.

Beccaria thus supplies Smith with an axiom about the class struggle in history. "Every society," Smith avers, "naturally divides itself into classes," and the task of a federal constitution should be to control that natural division, bending it toward a just distribution of political power (which for Smith was toward the "middle" fraction of smallholders).[7] Such a position is consistent with the period's use of the word *government*, which denoted a largely negative function of constraint.[8] What is therefore at stake in the ratification debate, for Smith, is the direction of such government. Could there be an essay – a concerted effort – striving toward just representation?

Federalists versus Anti-Federalists

To pursue the question, let's adjust the terms of the Beccaria quotation. In what kind of society, in which historical conditions, does an *essay* – a text of moderate length and restricted scope, especially "a loose sally of the mind; an irregular undigested piece; not a regular and orderly composition," as Samuel Johnson had put it three decades earlier[9] – continually tend to confer power on the few and misery on the many? The pun is proper to the moment. On New Year's Eve 1787, the Connecticut *Middlesex Gazette* printed a Federalist dialogue satire attacking the Anti-Federalists John Lamb and James Wadsworth (named "Wronghead" in the poem), entitled "The Forc'd Alliance." Working with the Federalist image of anarchic and incoherent enemies of the Constitution, the poem envisions a coalition of self-interest born out of political chaos: "Tho' foes by instinct; yet their private ends / And common danger taught them to be friends."[10] Central to the poem's conceit

---

6 On competing theories of representation during the Constitutional Convention and ratification debate, see Eric Slauter, *The State as a Work of Art: The Cultural Origins of the Constitution* (Chicago: University of Chicago Press, 2009), 123–66.
7 "Convention Debates, 21 June 1788," DHRC, n.p.
8 *Oxford English Dictionary*, s.v. "government."
9 Samuel Johnson, *A Dictionary of the English Language* (London: 1755), 1: n.p. (sig. 8H).
10 "The Forc'd Alliance: A DIALOGUE. Or, the News-Boys Shift for January 1, 1788," *Middlesex Gazette* (31 December 1787), DHRC, n.p. The poem was reprinted in

is the production of bad writing, specifically in the form of the essay, which represents a damaging, unprincipled solvent on rational politics:

WRONGHEAD.
What then remains? shall men of sense and note,
Who scorn my counsels and give me no vote,
Shall laws, shall government, shall foederal power,
Rise from the dust, and rule the peaceful shore?

LAMB.
Nor yet despair – for trite *Objections* rise,
Where Mason gains, and Gerry, full supplies.
See the loud Lees eke out their scribbling trade,
And all York wits afford their feeble aid;
No day elapses, but essays a score
Come out from men, who ne'er essay'd before.

WRONGHEAD.
Had my good fire but taught this hand to write,
That Constitution ne'er had seen the light.
My sinking glory I'd revive amain,
And vile *Detectors* should detect in vain.

LAMB.
This load of sly-wrote Pamphlets, small and great,
Distribute gratis – they'll distract your State.
In them you'll find the hopeful scheme we form,
To save our cause, and ward the gathering storm;
In this let all your friends with us embark,
And seek their safety in the chosen ark.¹¹

The essay form here is a flawed genre of *essaying*, the congelation of bad thought scribbled to the moment, contributing to a cacophony of distracted (and distracting) argument. "This Constitution," says Wronghead earlier in the poem, "haunts my turbid brain," and this Federalist poem identifies muddled thought with striving yet directionless form. An essay is the product of scribblers who merely essay; the essay is the literary form of their striving, and amounts to nothing more than a *scheme*. In the movement from verb to noun, the concept of essay assumes a certain monstrosity. Indeed, using the language Immanuel Kant develops in the philosophical aesthetics he was

---

Connecticut and Massachusetts newspapers, and later issued as a stand-alone broadside. Most likely it was authored by Lemuel Hopkins, known as one of the Connecticut Wits.

11 "Forc'd Alliance," *DHRC*, n.p.

composing at the same moment, the essay in the Federalist view is a "monstrous" object that "by its magnitude ... annihilates the end which its concept constitutes."[12] Another way to say this, in relation to the concrete situation of 1787–88, is that as a form, the essay has no concept; it is a mere conjuration, an opportunistic ark – a shipwreck of state in preparation – set against the sea of "sense," "government," and "foederal power."

But in articulating the nexus of genre and politics in this way, "The Forc'd Alliance" also points, negatively, toward the period's equally common view of the value of the verb *essay* and its salutary relation to literary expression. According to this seemingly opposite position, to essay is to endeavor *toward* improvement rather than to fancy a state of realized perfection. This notion was integral to the Federalist worldview, in the specific sense that Federalist arguments in favor of the new Constitution – like the logic behind the Constitutional Convention itself – were based on incremental improvements within a firm but amendable framework; the radical intervention, seen as the precondition for practical refinement (in James Madison's [1751–1836] word), was the Constitution itself. It is according to a version of that model that the future president James Monroe (1758–1831), deeply ambivalent about the Constitution, composed his pamphlet *Some Observations on the Constitution* in 1788. Monroe deploys the same lurid imagery as "The Forc'd Alliance" but reassigns its valences:

> We have struggled long to bring about this revolution, we have fought and bled freely to accomplish it, and in other respects braved difficulties almost without a parallel. Why then this precipitation, why this hurry upon a subject so momentous, and equally interesting to us all? Is it to be supposed that unless we immediately adopt this plan, in its fullest extent, we shall forever loose [sic] the opportunity of forming for ourselves a good government? That some wild phrensy or delirium of the brain will seize upon us, and losing all recollection of things past, and abandoning the social ties that bind mankind together, we shall fall into some strange and irritrievable [sic] disorder? Or is it not more natural to suppose that perfection in any science, if attainable at all, is to be approached by slow and gradual advances, and that the plan of government now presented for your inspection, though a powerful effort of the human mind, is yet to be improved by a second essay?[13]

---

12 Immanuel Kant, *Critique of the Power of Judgment*, ed. Paul Guyer, trans. Guyer and Eric Matthews (Cambridge, UK: Cambridge University Press, 2000), 136.
13 James Monroe, *Some Observations on the Constitution* (Petersburgh, VA.: 1788), DHRC, n.p.

Against the notion of the Constitution as a bulwark against disorder, Monroe offers a more moderate view of amendable politics. Monroe too speaks the language of bound and unbound energies, but he locates peril on the side of the rush toward a fantasy of political perfection, which for him is the Federalist flaw. Whereas the Federalist author of "The Forc'd Alliance" sees in Anti-Federalists nothing but delirium, Monroe redirects the accusation toward the Federalist frenzy for consolidation. For both the poet and the ambivalent statesman, *essay* is on the Anti-Federalist's side. The instability of the term is evident in the Anti-Federalist Smith's association of the partial quality of *essay* with iniquitous actors, against Monroe's celebration of the "slow and gradual advances" of scientific knowledge; but the link between political effort and partial writing is clear.

Writing in which the parts do not cohere into a whole: If there was a Federalist definition of a *literary* enemy, this was it. Late in 1788, the *Pennsylvania Gazette* lampooned anticonstitutional form in the anonymously authored "A Receipt for an Antifederalist Essay." Working in the vein of Alexander Pope's "Receipt to Make an Epic Poem" (1727), it insists upon the formulaic incoherence of Anti-Federalist writing:

> WELL-BORN, nine times – *Aristocracy*, eighteen times – *Liberty of the Press*, thirteen times repeated – *Liberty of Conscience*, once – *Negroe* [sic] *slavery*, once mentioned – *Trial by jury*, seven times – *Great Men*, six times repeated – Mr. WILSON, forty times – and lastly, GEORGE MASON's *Right Hand in a Cutting-box*, nineteen times – put them altogether, and dish them up at pleasure. These *words* will bear boiling, roasting, or frying – and, what is remarkable of them, they will bear being served, after being used once, a dozen times to the same table and palate.[14]

What is the essay form in a text like this? The emerging answer during the ratification debate is that the essay as a literary form is the dialectical opposite of the Constitution itself. Whereas the Constitution supplies a solid, permanent, and *containing* structure within which a multiplicity of dynamic parts has limited freedom of movement, the essay is nothing more than the moving parts. The essay is the literary form – the stylistic Kantian monstrosity – in which "the laws of the whole are in danger of being contravened by the laws

---

14 "A Receipt for an Antifederalist Essay," *Pennsylvania Gazette* (14 November 1787), DHRC, n.p. George Mason had promised, during debate in the Philadelphia Convention, that he would "sooner chop off his right hand than put it to the Constitution as it now stands." Max Farrand, ed., *The Records of the Federal Convention*, 3rd ed. (New Haven, CT: Yale University Press, 1927), 2:479.

of the parts," as Alexander Hamilton put it in *Federalist* 22.[15] The essay is in this view always the "feeble essay," as one "L.S." wrote in a letter to the New York *Daily Advertiser* in early 1788. Significantly, as the "Receipt" already suggests, Federalist argument linked the Anti-Federalist essay with the figure of the enslaved person, such that a roughly abolitionist (or simply propertied but nonslaveholding class fraction) interest was metonymically identified with the nonsubject position of the enslaved. Following the racist chute of this logic, the monstrosity and incoherence of the essay as a form was itself crudely racialized:

> Many of your readers, through the channel of your paper, beg leave to request the author or authors of the *Centinel*, published at Philadelphia, would desist from pestering the good people of these states with any more of their *antifederal* productions; they had better wipe their pens in clean, rather than in dirty cotton. The convention of Massachusetts has ratified the Constitution of the United States, and it being expected that there will not be a dissenting state in the union, the effect of their feeble essays therefore ought to convince them of their laboring in vain, as much as their attempting to wash the Blackamoor white.[16]

L.S. is not a logically rigorous writer, but the very incoherence of the reasoning brings the argument's symbolic infrastructure to the surface. Political futility joins with lack of formal cohesion: From the pro-Constitution vantage, Anti-Federalist writing fails the tests of aesthetics and strength alike. Melancton Smith's argument against article 1, section 3, articulated a broadly democratic politics with a strictly resigned antislavery but nonabolitionist position; for Smith, moral "wickedness" has no relation to political possibility, and the subtraction of proper agency ("will of their own") from enslaved people subordinates the question of free will to the execution of social power. The "Receipt" seizes upon the partial quality of such reasoning (of which Smith is emblematic) to suggest that Anti-Federalists opportunistically invoke the figure of the enslaved as an inert element within their writing. In L.S.'s letter, the metonymical slide is complete, as Anti-Federalism is distilled into a *practice of writing* in which a certain politically devalued "ink" (the political vocabulary itemized in the

---

15 James Madison, Alexander Hamilton, and John Jay, *The Federalist Papers*, ed. Isaac Kramnick (London: Penguin, 1987), 182. In this passage, Hamilton specifically addresses the argument for a national supreme court.
16 Letter from "L.S.," *New York Daily Advertiser* (16 February 1788), DHRC, n.p.

"Receipt") produces only scrawled and racially absurd stains. In short, from this virulent Federalist point of view, the Anti-Federalist essay is not *writing* at all.[17]

The Federalist

We are now in a position to recognize the structuring difference between Anti-Federalist argument and what we might call Federalist formalism: Federalists were, both politically and stylistically, warriors of the whole against the parts.[18] The most famous and influential text to emerge from the ratification debate, *The Federalist*, enacts this principle while simultaneously elevating it to the level of an achieved literary device. Its literary triumph is somewhat surprising, if retrospectively self-evident, since the text's material conditions were the very definition of the piecemeal. It was first serialized in eighty-four numbers in New York newspapers between 27 October 1787 and 15 August 1788, then gathered in somewhat shuffled order into a two-volume book of eighty-five (number 31 having been in the meantime split in two). *The Federalist* also iteratively constructs the personality of the pseudonym "Publius" from its three individual authors, Alexander Hamilton (ca. 1755–1804), James Madison (1751–1836), and John Jay (1745–1829). (Hamilton authored two-thirds of the pieces, Jay just five of them.) The pseudonym was itself a striking device, ensuring continuity of presentation in a crowded and often confusing barrage of newspaper print.[19]

---

17 In terms of aesthetics, it is worth noting that the *Centinel* series, the object of L.S.'s ire, was one of the most sustained and coherent sequences of anti-Constitution writing during the ratification debate. In terms of strength, the L.S. letter fits into the narrative of exclusionary citizenships outlined by Derrick Spires: "Even as federalists and antifederalists debated the nature of the bonds between citizens in a republic, the role of human interests in maintaining and/or disrupting those bonds, and the kinds of institutions best suited to managing those (particularly economic) interests, black citizens were forming citizenship practices based on their own experiences and understandings of political and religious texts" (Derrick R. Spires, *The Practice of Citizenship: Black Politics and Print Culture in the Early United States* [Philadelphia: University of Pennsylvania Press, 2019], 35). Contemporary Black "civic schematics" based on an "ethic of neighborliness" in the 1780s and '90s are categorically omitted from the ratification debate on both counts (Blackness and neighborliness) (Spires, *Practice*, 35).
18 The difference is also registered in the historical labels of these two factions. The Federalist position came to be associated with a consolidated national government, which was precisely the opposite of the term's common meaning in the 1780s. As a result, the so-called Anti-Federalists were relegated to a permanently negative position: piecemeal arguments against "federalism." See Jackson Turner Main, *Antifederalists: Critics of the Constitution, 1781–1788*, new ed. (Chapel Hill, NC: University of North Carolina Press, 2004).
19 In this sense the Publius pseudonym was both an extension and a specifically political deployment of the collective *eidolon* of eighteenth-century periodical essays such as Joseph Addison and Richard Steele's *Spectator*.

The text has endured as both the preeminent literary work of the ratification debate and the period's primary interpretative artifact within constitutional law largely because of its formal and material coherence: One *book* rises out of the constitutional moment, and it does so both through and against the essay as a form.

The word *essay* is not used in *The Federalist*, only in its paratexts: on the title pages of its two-volume book appearance (volume one in October 1787, volume two in early spring of the next year) and in a footnote citation of David Hume's *Essays and Treatises on Several Subjects* (London and Edinburgh, 1753). (The term was most likely chosen for the book title by the printers, Archibald and James McLean, rather than by the authors, though Hamilton was the major architect of the publishing plan.) *Paper* is Publius's preferred designator, and the one that has appended itself to the book's title in common memory: *The Federalist Papers*. Suspending together the multiplicity of the text (its cascade of installments) and its consolidation into a single, overarching project (the physical two-volume book and the institution of juridical interpretation for which it stands), *papers* indexes the materiality of the publishing project but says nothing about its rhetorical or literary form.[20] On the one hand, as Trish Loughran has shown, the "language of parts and partialness is disdained" throughout the multiple pieces constituting the text.[21] We have already seen Hamilton address, emblematically, the contradictory rather than synthetic relation of whole to parts, and that derision for the partial is doubled in Federalist contempt for both the Anti-Federalist essay as a form and mere essaying as an enterprise. Yet, as its movement from newspaper serialization to book suggests, *The Federalist*'s allergy to the parts and to partialness is only the first moment of its formal and rhetorical strategy. After all, as the title page gives it, the book is *The Federalist: A Collection of Essays, Written in Favour of the New Constitution*. As with the Federalist view of the Constitution, with *The Federalist* the whole enacts its comprehension of the parts. It is through this dialectic that *The Federalist* actualizes a shift in the literary history of the essay.

---

20 Given the flux of the concept of the essay in the period, as we have seen, it is noteworthy that *paper* is often the first recourse for authors of these kinds of text. For instance, the Anti-Federalist "Brutus" suggests that the history of European tax duties "may be essayed in some future paper." The juxtaposition of the two terms illustrates what we may call the partial concretization of the formal category of essay, situated very much between action (effort) and outcome (text). See "Brutus VI," *New York Journal* (27 December 1787), *DHRC*, n.p.

21 Trish Loughran, *The Republic in Print: Print Culture in the Age of U.S. Nation Building, 1770–1870* (New York: Columbia University Press, 2007), 125.

The distinction between disdain and dialectic is subtle but significant, since the logic of Federalism depended, crucially, upon the coordination of a new politics of national consolidation with a language of federalist (regional, state-driven) latitude. Hamilton's comment on the courts, cited above, is an illustrative reference point more precisely in this context, since the pro-Constitutional case innovated upon the relations among state law, national legislature, and juridical review. Specifically, during the Convention James Madison unsuccessfully had proposed a national legislative negative over local state laws, such that Congress would be empowered to review and reject local legislation. In place of the Madisonian negative, the Constitution provided for the Supreme Court's constitutional review of all laws in line with the so-called "Supremacy Clause" of article 6, which indicated that the Constitution "shall be the supreme Law of the Land; and the Judges in every State shall be bound thereby." This constitutional outcome was, as Allison LaCroix has argued, an idiosyncratic but epochal formation:

> The radical concept of multiplicity that undergirded Revolutionary challenges to unitary authority had demanded robust new structures to replace the tentative efforts of the Articles of Confederation. In this way, the new ideology of multiplicity had both created and required new institutions, setting the scene for the convention's confrontation between the negative and the Supremacy Clause. With the culmination of those debates in the adoption of the Supremacy Clause and a notion (albeit sketchy) of judicial review, the idea of multiplicity found an institutional mooring in the judiciary. This coupling of multiplicity as an idea with courts as a mode of mediating among multiple levels of government in turn created a new ideology: federalism.[22]

Such unity-within-multiplicity demanded not only juridical innovation, but also a transformation of writing: of the means of representing, and giving rhetorical force to, a circumstance that Hamilton constructs for his reader in terms of mathematical axioms, "that the whole is greater than its parts" and of the "INFINITE divisibility of a FINITE thing."[23] That is, the complex mediations described by LaCroix were anything but innately persuasive before the doubled audiences of 1787–88: on the one hand, the propertied class of state ratifiers (both New York and in the other states to which Hamilton wished to send copies of *The Federalist* to serve "as a debater's handbook"); on the other, the disenfranchised and amorphous "people" in whose name the state itself was being remade. *The Federalist* is effectively forced, by the political novelty of

---

22 Allison L. LaCroix, *The Ideological Origins of American Federalism* (Cambridge, MA: Harvard University Press, 2010), 172.
23 Madison, Hamilton, and Jay, *Federalist Papers*, 216–17.

its conditions, to supply a more complex representation of part-whole relations than was hitherto available within political polemic.

Federalist Style and the Antinomies of the Political Essay

But to speak in terms of polemic is already to rush ahead of *The Federalist*'s literary style. Unlike the Anti-Federalist texts we have examined, and in a wholly different mood from the degraded manner of an L.S., *The Federalist* speaks that Hamiltonian discourse of the axiomatic. It either avoids polemical statement or embeds its diatribe within a coolly rational frame. For example, in the final number Hamilton exudes feeling, but he does so inside the bounds of reason: "A NATION without a NATIONAL GOVERNMENT is, in my view, an awful spectacle. The establishment of a Constitution, in time of profound peace, by the voluntary consent of a whole people, is a PRODIGY, to the completion of which I look forward with trembling anxiety."[24] Rhetorically, Hamilton positions Publius as both the medium of reasoned argument and the emotive spectator of that argument's outcome. Sentiment is the product of reason's efficacy. With stealthy care throughout the text, Publius sustains that tension while locating the Constitution's enemies on the opposite side of the rational frontier:

> A torrent of angry and malignant passions will be let loose. To judge from the conduct of the opposite parties, we shall be led to conclude that they will mutually hope to evince the justness of their opinions, and to increase the number of their converts by the loudness of their declamations and by the bitterness of their invectives. An enlightened zeal for the energy and efficiency of government will be stigmatized as the offspring of a temper fond of despotic power and hostile to the principles of liberty. ... [A] dangerous ambition more often lurks behind the specious mask of zeal for the rights of the people than under the forbidding appearance of zeal for the firmness and efficiency of government.[25]

Publius's prescient framing of the ratification debate here in *Federalist* 1 locates the text in a uniquely commanding position, capable (as in *Federalist* 85) of a critically spectatorial view of the totality of argument, including reflexive attention to his own motivations. "My motives must remain within the depository of my own breast," he writes. "My arguments will be open to

---

24 Madison, Hamilton, and Jay, *Federalist Papers*, 487.
25 Madison, Hamilton, and Jay, *Federalist Papers*, 88–89.

all and may be judged of by all."[26] What matters within the ratification debate is, in this regard, less the substance of Publius's claims than the ethics of writing through which they are made. Like the Constitution itself, *The Federalist* formally encircles all objections to it.

Ethically, Publius captures opposing arguments by capturing himself: Moral sentiment is enclosed by reason. More mechanically, *The Federalist* also insists upon its completeness: "In the progress of this discussion I shall endeavor to give a satisfactory answer to all the objections which shall have made their appearance, that may seem to have any claim on your attention."[27] The deployment of the future perfect tense ("shall have made") ensures that the debate is doubly governed by Publius, since the sentence digests all forthcoming contributions *and* evaluates them in advance. The papers will answer all objections that will be made *if* Publius (lightly hidden behind the passive construction) deems them worthy of "your" attention. It is a sophisticated rhetorical maneuver, far more complex (formally and conceptually) than any other text in the debate, Federalist and Anti-Federalist alike. One might begin here to note a certain hypertrophy of devices that scatter and recontain components in this text, as though it is working excessively to enclose politics within its abstracted, self-referential bounds. *The Federalist* is thus in an important way the ultimate "essay" in the specific sense of the term as we have seen it in 1787–88: an extraordinary, disproportionate exertion of effort, tending as much toward the concavity of its own activity as to a referential engagement with the world.

At the same time, no other text in the ratification debate claims the comprehensiveness of answering all objections. The language of completeness is the rhetoric of the book, not of the newspaper essay. *The Federalist*, of course, already speaks this language in its newspaper instantiation; it is, as it were, written in the rhetorical form of the book even prior to its organization in that format. Yet as *The Federalist* accents its consolidating ambitions it also foregrounds the teeming multiplicity of the parts, both the formal papers that constitute the text and the social components – the mass of people across class divisions – that are *not* unified within an organic or mechanical whole. Dynamically, *The Federalist* represents that multiplicity and then represents its containment in a rhetorical two-step. This is the formal process enacted in the gathering of the individual, piecemeal papers into the book; it is the ethical

---

26 Madison, Hamilton, and Jay, *Federalist Papers*, 89.
27 Madison, Hamilton, and Jay, *Federalist Papers*, 90.

grammar that enables Publius to split and recombine himself as both a composite author and a unity of feeling and reason.

Opponents of the Constitution were unpersuaded and even especially provoked by the Publius pose, seeing it as one more example of Federalist usurpation of authority. Thus, writing under the pseudonym of "Interrogator" in late 1787 or early 1788, the Anti-Federalist Hugh Hughes authored a manuscript entitled "To Publius or the Pseudo-Federalist," in which he attempted to explode *The Federalist's* representational pretense by returning to the basics of social class. Who, he asks in a bombardment of questions, authorized the Convention not only to form a new government but to do so on the backs of enslaved people and modest "Plebians"? The new US state was, indeed, "founded in Fraud, Violence Murder [sic] and Slavery" and its only hope would be full social renovation, not a mere rearrangement of existing powers. But in addition to being a critical student of colonial and early national history, Interrogator had a keen eye for literary form, and he attempts to short-circuit the very ethical splitting and recombining we have identified above:

> Only reflect on how little you know of your own mental and corporeal Composition, as well as of what daily and momently [sic] contributes to your support and Existence or, that many of the most simple Plebians, or Mechanicks, can teach you some of the first principles of Philosophy. Or how very little you know of any Thing, when compared with what is unknow [sic] to you and Thousands who are much wiser, & you will not find much Cause to value yourself on your Omniscience.[28]

If, as we have seen, Publius summons writerly authority through his separation from the mass of the people (reading *for* us so that he may also *argue* for us), Interrogator attempts to resituate that separation within the force field of class antagonisms. For the tactic to achieve its radical ambition, "the people" – the slaves, mechanics, and plebeians – would have to *read* Interrogator's text, itself an all but impossible aspiration. Appropriately enough, in the event the return to conflictual basics would be deferred by even more materialist limitations: Despite the efforts of Hughes and his well-placed friends, the essay manuscript was never published.

What is enacted at the formal and ethical levels to which Interrogator responded is also notably thematized within *The Federalist's* political arguments, as in the dramatic episode of *Federalist* 51, in Madison's infamous theory of the federal system's block on the tyranny of the majority: "Whilst

---

28 "Interrogator: To Publius or the Pseudo-Federalist," *DHRC*, n.p.

all authority in it [the federal republic] will be derived from and dependent on the society, the society itself will be broken into so many parts, interests and classes of citizens, that the rights of individuals, or of the minority, will be in little danger from interested combinations of the majority." The security of "civil rights" and "religious rights" consists, he continues, "in the one case in the multiplicity of interests, and in the other in the multiplicity of sects. The degree of security in both cases will depend on the number of interests and sects; and this may be presumed to depend on the extent of country and number of people comprehended under the same government."[29] In the Madisonian axiom, "Ambition must be made to counteract ambition," but that celebrated watchword must be read against the phrase "multiplicity of interests."[30] For Madison's ordered social diorama is itself like a printed copy struck off from the constitutional plates: The dynamism of the parts is contained by the structure of the whole through the "exquisite balance of a complex system of antagonisms."[31] Complexity, then, is only a first moment whose sequel is consolidation; the parts shift and collide, chaotically, within the framework of order. Madison's is not only a political theory of constitutional government, but a literary theory of the new US essay in the age of constitutional consolidation. Its template is *The Federalist*.[32]

During the ratification debate, the essay was a highly fraught political-literary form. It is impossible to separate this form from its political occasion because, as we have seen, the two aspects are mutually constitutive. More pointedly, the essay in this context differs from its English and European forebears; references to Beccaria and Hume in the material we have examined (not to mention Montaigne, Locke, and Rousseau elsewhere in this culture) indicate clearly that there is nothing especially vexing about the category as such. But what had been seemingly settled as a matter of heuristics – that the essay was either a relatively short prose piece of indeterminate finish or a prose argument of especially exploratory ambition – is reagitated in the moment of constitutional consolidation. The essay in this

---

29 Madison, Hamilton, and Jay, *Federalist Papers*, 321.
30 Madison, Hamilton, and Jay, *Federalist Papers*, 319.   31 Garrett, *Episodic Poetics*, 40.
32 Paul Downes has productively accented Madison's metaphor of refined representation in *Federalist* 10, in order to contrast its seemingly Lockean basis with Hobbesian artifice. Reading *The Federalist*'s more dominant concern with multiplication and consolidation (not least in *Federalist* 10) allows us to see that Hobbes's artificial sovereign – Downes calls it the "sovereign supplement" – is already present within Federalist argument, enacted and even theorized as a political practice of writing, though no Federalist would ever have said so through the dangerous reference to Hobbes himself. See Paul Downes, *Hobbes, Sovereignty, and Early American Literature* (New York: Cambridge University Press, 2015), 157–64.

representational ecology is rhetorically risky, a literary form ill suited to handling the questions of formal stability, social conflict, and quantitative overload that were forced by the Constitution. *The Federalist* surfaces from the literature of ratification both as and because of its distinctive position as an essay *collection*, uniquely unified in multiplicity. Understood within the formal and conceptual field we have examined, the texts of the ratification debate manifest a two-term opposition, a set of antinomies across whose oscillations we can finally locate the emergent form of the political essay itself:

Statecraft versus Politics
Whole versus Part
One versus Many
Representation versus People
Consolidation versus Complexity
Book versus Papers
Commentary versus Political Philosophy
Explication versus Polemic
Achievement versus Effort

Shuttling between the two sides of this opposition and uniting them, dialectically, in their difference, *The Federalist* serves a precise literary-historical function. Diverting political argument from the substance of a "people" invoked, spectrally, by the preamble to the Constitution, *The Federalist* version of the essay refounds the United States in literary form.

4
American Nature Writing: 1700–1900

NOAH RAWLINGS

"Nature writing," a loose literary genre that crystallized in the eighteenth and nineteenth centuries, may be the most distinctly American contribution to the essay as form. The phrase "nature writing" is not particularly idiomatic; theoretically, it should not be difficult to translate. And yet it has been adopted wholesale by numerous tongues – an indication of the outsize role that American (and British) writers had in its initial formation. French: *le nature writing*; Spanish: *el nature writing*; German: *das Nature Writing*; Italian: *il nature writing*.

It is not that nature writing lacked continental practitioners (Jean-Jacques Rousseau, Alexander von Humboldt). It is not that it was without historical precedents (the pastoral poetry of antiquity, in which technical explanations of natural phenomena comingled with lyrical description; or the works of natural historians, in which philosophical ruminations and scientific observations mixed and merged). It is certainly not that it is in want of British analogues (Gilbert White, John Ray, Thomas Bewick, John Ruskin, Alfred Russel Wallace – writers who are surely also responsible for "nature writing" becoming a widespread loanword). But it was American writers – Thoreau and Emerson, Muir and Burroughs, King and Powell – who would make of nature writing a distinct, if elastic, literary species.

This is due in no small part to the unique historical situation of the North American landscape in the era under consideration. There and then, nature – conceptually and physically – was particularly foregrounded in a land that was both less familiar and considered less "tame" than that of the Old World. European Americans saw American nature as more "natural," more "wild" than that of Europe.[1] This view, which rested upon a partially legitimate material basis, was only exaggerated by those who sought to identify something that distinguished America from other nations, something that was without a foreign equivalent. For many, it was American nature that became a distinctive source of national pride.[2] "There are new lands, new men, new thoughts," Emerson (1803–1882) writes in *Nature* (1836), urging his readers to cast off the weight of the past in order to "demand our own works...."[3] The essayistic form that is nature writing was one means of expressing all this alleged newness.

American nature writing as an essayistic subgenre – as opposed to the larger category of "writing about nature," which extends much further back – emerged simultaneously with the politico-geographic entity that is the United States. The subgenre congealed throughout the centuries in which the United States became a nation (1776), acquired the Louisiana Territory (1803), annexed Texas (1845), signed the treaties of Oregon (1846) and Guadeloupe Hidalgo (1848), and made the Alaska Purchase (1867). Those were the political preconditions for the Lewis and Clark Expedition (1803–1807), the Geological Exploration of the Fortieth Parallel (1867–72) led by Clarence King, the geological surveys of John Wesley Powell (1867–72), and John Muir's move to Northern California (1868) – all of which generated canonical works of nature writing.

Like the essay in general, nature writing is a hybrid form. It is omnivorous, incorporating elements of travel writing, natural philosophy, ethnography, diarism, and epistolary writing. One literary scholar defines the nature writer as "one who sees the environment as a scientist but who describes it as a humanist."[4] The definition is apt. Nature writing of this period is filled with technical information on plants and animals, agricultural practices, and methods for hunting or navigating, but it also abounds with metaphysical speculations, theological pronouncements, elaborate landscape descriptions, and dramatic accounts of practices like hiking, camping, fishing, and farming. Unsurprisingly for a form whose practitioners have often had professional ties to disciplines like geology, botany, and forestry, nature writing of this period maximally exploits the "undifferentiated unity with science, ethics,

---

1 Roderick Nash, *Wilderness and the American Mind* (New Haven, CT: Yale University Press, 1973), 49.
2 Nash, *Wilderness*, 67.
3 Ralph Waldo Emerson, "Nature," in *The Complete Essays and Other Writings*, ed. Brooks Atkinson (New York: Modern Library, 1950), 1–42, 3.
4 Lee Schweninger, "Writing Nature: Silko and Native Americans as Nature Writers," *MELUS* 18, no. 2 (Summer 1993): 47–60, 47.

and art" that György Lukács (1885–1971) identifies with essayistic writing in general.⁵

Different nature writers brought different sensibilities, forms, and rhetoric to the genre. Often these corresponded to their professional or educational backgrounds. The nature encountered by a settled farmer like St. John de Crèvecœur (1735–1813) necessarily diverged from that of an explorer like Meriwether Lewis (1774–1809), and a rather secular geologist like John Wesley Powell (1834–1902) had habits of thought distinct from a spiritually driven writer like John Muir (1838–1914). With this in mind, the present chapter proceeds both thematically and chronologically, tracing nature writing through the eighteenth and nineteenth centuries by attending both to historical change and the evolution of ideas.

Writing Agrarian America: Crèvecœur and Cooper

We begin our history of American nature writing with a Frenchman, a Frenchman who wrote as an American. "The following letters are the genuine production of the American farmer whose name they bear," begins the half-honest preface to the original 1782 edition of *Letters from an American Farmer; Describing Certain Provincial Situations, Manners, and Customs Not Generally Known; and Conveying Some Idea of the Late and Present Interior Circumstances of the British Colonies in North America* by Hector St. John de Crèvecœur.⁶

Born in Normandy in 1735, dying in the suburbs of Paris in 1813, Crèvecœur spent over two of the nearly eight decades between in North America, first in Canada as a soldier in the French Army, then as a land surveyor throughout the United States and a farmer in Chester, New York. It was this last stint that furnished the material for the *Letters*. This lengthy essayistic work was not the first to describe America's flora and fauna, but it develops many of the techniques and concerns that would thenceforth prove foundational to American nature writing.⁷ Indeed, its importance in the formation of the genre was recognized as early as 1912, when one critic called Crèvecœur "the eighteenth-century Thoreau."⁸

---

5 George Lukács, *Soul and Form*, trans. Anna Bostock (Cambridge, MA: MIT Press, 1974), 13.
6 Hector St. John de Crèvecœur, *Letters from an American Farmer* (London: J. M. Dent and Sons, 1951), 3.
7 The journals of William Byrd II, for instance, are plentiful with descriptions of plants, animals, and landscapes, and predate the *Letters* by almost a half century.
8 Warren Barton Blake, "Some Eighteenth Century Travelers in America," *Dial* 52 (1 January 1912): 5–9, 8.

Written in the form of letters from a fictitious farmer to a fictious English friend, the *Letters* exploit epistolary conventions to essayistic ends. Since its origins with Montaigne, the essay has been productively embroiled with the epistle, a form allowing for both intimate address and discursive structure. In Crèvecœur's hands, it permits the easy exposition of anecdotal material. "As I was one day sitting ...," "One day my eldest son ...": Several of his illustrative tales begin thus. "One anecdote I must relate," he tells his reader in a letter titled "On Snakes; and On the Humming Bird."[9] In the ensuing paragraph, Crèvecœur bubbles with enthusiasm for the titular birds: "On this little bird Nature has profusely lavished her most splendid colours; the most perfect azure, the most beautiful gold."[10] This loving description becomes something more, namely, a chance to relay zoological information: "Nature has taught it to find out in the calyx of flowers and blossoms those mellifluous particles that service it for sufficient food."[11] This tendency to mingle anecdotally the technical and the aesthetic becomes a hallmark of most subsequent nature writing.

Although Crèvecœur finds the complex workings of the natural world worthy of admiration, beauty and wonder are not his chief concerns. For him, nature's ideal form is not the unspoiled wilderness of later writers like John Muir. Nor is it the vast frontier of Lewis and Clark. Rather, it is the property of a farmer, and Crèvecœur clearly embodies the proprietor's perspective. Just prior to the hummingbird anecdote cited above, Crèvecœur tells his reader: "One of my constant walks when I am at leisure is my lowlands, where I have the pleasure of seeing my cattle, horses, and colts. Exuberant grass replenishes all my fields, the best representative of our wealth."[12] Crèvecœur's "exuberant grass" is a welcome sign of economic prosperity, not, in this instance, a symbol of nature's formal splendor or technical ingenuity.

Related to Crèvecœur's economic vision is a political and social one. The most famous letter in the work is "What Is an American?," which ostensibly takes as its central object neither landscapes nor creatures but a nationality, a citizenry. Nonetheless, essential to Crèvecœur's formulation of this question is the dialogue the citizenry has with its natural setting. In this letter, Crèvecœur makes an extended analogy of enduring importance: "Men are like plants; the goodness and flavour of the fruit proceeds from the peculiar soil and exposition in which they grow. We are nothing but what we derive

---

9 Crèvecœur, *Letters*, 178.   10 Crèvecœur, *Letters*, 178.   11 Crèvecœur, *Letters*, 179.
12 Crèvecœur, *Letters*, 178.

from the air we breathe, the climate we inhabit, the government we obey, the system of religion we profess, and the nature of our employment."[13] Americans, therefore, are part and parcel of their environment. Here are early intimations of the consequential idea that American nature is constitutive of American national identity.

The daughter of the novelist James Fenimore Cooper (1789–1851) and an important influence on Henry David Thoreau (1817–1862), Susan Fenimore Cooper (1813–1894) has been called the first American woman to publish nature writing.[14] In her *Rural Hours* (1850), she develops a temporally sustained, locally concerned attention to nature that anticipates Thoreau's *Walden* (1854). Beginning in March and ending in February, the book scrupulously documents a year of weather, flora, fauna, and farming in Cooperstown, New York.

Like Crèvecœur's *Letters*, Cooper's *Rural Hours* is intimate in its form. But instead of the epistolary mode, Cooper opts for the diary, an approach that nature writers from John Wesley Powell to Aldo Leopold (1887–1948) would exploit for more than its rhetorical strengths. The diary form answers needs peculiar to place-based nature writing in a temperate climate. It is particularly convenient for depicting the gradual (or sudden) transitions between or within seasons: the dipping or rising of temperature, the arrival or disappearance of a given species, the spectacle of storm or snow or sun.

Like many a diary, the entries of *Rural Hours* are irregular in length; they can contract to a single line or dilate to several pages. "Friday, 21st [of April 1848]. – Fresh lettuce from the hot-beds," reads the entirety of one entry that, while unusually laconic, is typical in conveying an essentially seasonal fact.[15] Ten days later, Cooper opens in much the same way: "Thursday, 4th. – Potatoes planted in the garden to-day. First mess of asparagus. . . . The chimney-swallows have come in their usual large numbers, and our summer flock of swallows is now complete."[16] But this last detail, about the arrival of swallows, expands into a six-paragraph excursus on local ornithology, in which Cooper describes the appearance, behavior, and geographic distribution of not only the chimney swallow but five related species.

---

13 Crèvecœur, *Letters*, 44–45.
14 Susan Fennimore Cooper, *Rural Hours*, eds. Rochelle Johnson and Daniel Patterson (Athens, GA: University of Georgia Press, 1998), ix. The claim is contestable. After all, in 1844, Margaret Fuller published a generically hybrid account of her travels through the Great Lakes region, *Summer on the Lakes, in 1843*.
15 Cooper, *Rural Hours*, 27.   16 Cooper, *Rural Hours*, 34.

Much inspired by English naturalists like Gilbert White (1720–1793) and John Leonard Knapp (1767–1845) as well as continental botanists like Augustin de Candolle (1778–1841), Cooper's work brims with scientific information. The place of nature within art and society is no less great a theme. On Wednesday, 11 October 1848, Cooper does not furnish us with her customary notes on the weather or the latest harvest. Instead, she pens what we might (anachronistically) call a work of ecocriticism, rhapsodizing about different affective responses to the season of autumn across English, French, German, and Italian poetry. Not unlike Raymond Williams's (1921–1988) turning to poetry to discover shifting attitudes toward the English countryside in *The Country and the City* (1973), Cooper reads a historically unprecedented shift in her contemporaries' perception of nature: "English writers . . . seem suddenly to have discovered Autumn under a new character," a beautiful, joyous character out of keeping with earlier poetic representation, she argues.[17]

Thus we witness in *Rural Hours* the dual satisfactions of the scientist and humanist, both spurred on by the natural world. A third form of delight in nature, a more utilitarian one, also pervades Cooper's pages. This is the pleasure of the new world settler at seeing "wild" land cultivated. "A stranger moving along the highway looks in vain for any striking signs of a new country," she writes on 27 June. "[A]s he passes from farm to farm in unbroken succession, the aspect of the whole region is smiling and fruitful."[18]

"Smiling and *fruitful*."[19] We are a far cry from the John Muirs and Clarence Kings who will venerate landscapes unspoiled by humans. Like Crèvecœur, Cooper does not see nature's ideal form as the wilderness, and the fact that most "striking signs of a new country" have been erased by agricultural production is less cause for lamentation than celebration.

Exploring the Early Nation: Bartram, Lewis and Clark, and Audubon

Differing from the sustained, place-based works of nature writers like Crèvecœur and Cooper is the travel journal. In the former, time moves while space is constant. In the latter, both writer and seasons are in motion; not one but many landscapes unfold diachronically. Novel natures are explored rather than observed from a single vantage point.

The land such writers ventured out into was unknown – and wild by European standards. Yet, while travel writers might perceive this land as

---

17 Cooper, *Rural Hours*, 208.   18 Cooper, *Rural Hours*, 88–89.   19 My emphasis.

undeveloped, most were not under the illusion that it was uninhabited. Early European American nature writers devoted significant attention to the Indigenous people they encountered, whom they tended to consider as coextensive with "nature" itself. As Roderick Nash argues in *Wilderness and the American Mind*, "Indians were regarded as a form of [wilderness] whose savageness was consistent with the character of wild country."[20] At times, nature writers merely reflect the condescending attitude of the colonizer: "We made [the Indians] sensible of their dependance on the will of our government," Meriwether Lewis writes in the journal he kept during the Lewis and Clark Expedition.[21] At other times, nature writers convey interest in or respect for Native Americans, as when John James Audubon (1785–1851) bemoans the settler-driven decline of Indigenous communities in the Ohio River Valley, or when William Bartram (1739–1823) writes, "[A]s moral men they certainly stand in no need of European civilization."[22] Reading such writers, it becomes impossible to sustain the pernicious myth of a "natural history ... devoid of people."[23]

William Bartram was the son of John Bartram, a man who was esteemed by the greatest living botanist in the world (Carl Linnaeus) to be the greatest living botanist in the world. Accompanying his father on travels near and far from their home of Philadelphia, Pennsylvania, William developed quickly into an exceptionally able naturalist. From an early age, he corresponded with famous naturalists like John Latham and Linnaeus, and he had identified several previously unknown species of American birds by the age of seventeen.

In 1773, William Bartram embarked upon a four-year journey throughout the American South that would result in his most influential written work. He did so out of his own naturalistic interests and on behalf of the English botanist John Fothergill, who wished Bartram to collect and send him native plant specimens.[24] The breadth and depth of Bartram's travels were made manifest in the title of the hugely popular book that grew out of them: *Travels through North and South Carolina, Georgia, East and West Florida, the Cherokee*

20 Nash, *Wilderness*, 7.
21 Meriwether Lewis and William Clark, *The Journals of Lewis and Clark*, ed. Frank Bergon (New York: Viking, 1989), 239–40.
22 William Bartram, *Travels through North and South Carolina, Georgia, East and West Florida, the Cherokee Country [...]* (Dublin: Moore, Jones, McAllister, and Rice, 1793), 487.
23 Debbie Lee, "Travelling in Wilderness," in *The Cambridge History of Travel Writing*, ed. Nandini Das and Tim Youngs (Cambridge, UK: Cambridge University Press, 2019), 376–90, 385.
24 Ernest Earnest, *John and William Bartram* (Philadelphia: University of Pennsylvania Press, 1940), 110–11.

Country, the Extensive Territories of the Muscogulges or Creek Confederacy, and the Country of the Chactaws. Containing an Account of the Soil and Natural Productions of Those Regions; Together with Observations on the Manners of the Indians (1791).

Bartram's *Travels* is the work of a writer as artful as he was scientific. Nowhere is its artistry more evident than in Bartram's dramatic encounter with alligators in Florida. The passage begins with Bartram setting up camp along the St. Johns River, beside a live oak. It is late, and he has just realized he lacks sufficient provisions for supper, so he decides to venture out to catch some fish. No sooner is Bartram on his boat than he spots an alligator, which he summons vividly before us: "Behold him rushing forth from the flags and reeds.... Clouds of smoke issue from his dilated nostrils. The earth trembles with his thunder."[25] Shortly after this dramatic description, Bartram witnesses a fight between this first alligator and a "rival," remarking,

> My apprehensions were highly alarmed after being a spectator of so dreadful a battle. It was obvious that every delay would but tend to increase my dangers and difficulties, as the sun was near setting, and the alligators gathered around my harbour from all quarters. From these considerations I concluded to be expeditious in my trip to the lagoon, in order to take some fish. Not thinking it prudent to take my [musket] with me, lest I might lose it overboard in case of a battle, which I had every reason to dread before my return, I therefore furnished myself with a club for my defence.[26]

Generating suspense through something like dramatic irony, the Bartram who narrates makes his reader wide-eyed at the choices of the Bartram who acts: The sun is setting? He can't wait until tomorrow to catch some fish? He purposefully leaves his gun in case there is a ... battle?! Bartram often shrewdly frames his experience of the natural world through the conventions of eighteenth-century travel writing, portraying a natural world rife with misadventure and thereby creating narrative tension.[27]

Coexisting with the travel writer's narrative prowess is also the scientist's eye. This latter perspective is made explicit in the *Travels* through Bartram's citations of eminent naturalist like Linnaeus, Hans Sloane, and George Edwards, as well as in the lengthy ornithological catalogue he inserts in the middle of the book. But it also takes subtler forms. It is in fact incorporated into the very texture of Bartram's prose, as when he anecdotally describes

---

25 Bartram, *Travels*, 116.   26 Bartram, *Travels*, 117.
27 On the importance of misadventure and danger in eighteenth- and nineteenth-century travel writing, see Carl Thompson, *The Suffering Traveller and the Romantic Imagination* (Oxford: Oxford University Press, 2007), 1–30.

a young alligator as having *"transverse* waved clouds or blotches" on its back, availing himself of a word – "transverse" – that was endemic to geometric, anatomical, and zoological discourse.[28] But partway through Bartram's famous encounter with Florida alligators, both scientific and melodramatic description meet their limits, giving way to a trope that runs rampant throughout later American nature writing: the performative display of an author's floundering before the grandeur or magnificence of the natural world. In short, aporia: "How shall I express myself so as to convey an adequate idea of it to the reader, and at the same time avoid raising suspicions of my veracity?"[29] Bartram, like his successors, will occasionally find that the best way to write a novel nature is to describe one's inability to do so.

Thirty years after Bartram began his famous travels through America's southern reaches, the nascent nation doubled in size with the Louisiana Purchase of 1803. The following year, Meriwether Lewis and William Clark (1770–1838) set out on their expedition to explore this vast territory west of the Mississippi. While commercial, political, and scientific interests drove the Corps of Discovery onward – from Camp Dubois, Illinois, to Fort Clatsop, Oregon – the expedition's main architect, Thomas Jefferson, also regarded it as a fundamentally "literary pursuit."[30] Indeed, Jefferson had Bartram's *Travels* explicitly in mind when he conceived of the trip: Lewis and Clark were to write nature as well as explore it. The literary product that emerged from this voyage of some 8,000 miles and 1,228 days is a strange one, a collection of journals kept jointly by Lewis and Clark in which verbal expression "itself seems stretched," as Robert Finch and John Elder have observed; for the explorers were attempting to describe animals, plants, peoples, and geographics for which the English language as yet had no vocabulary.[31]

The language of the *Journals of Lewis and Clark* is often unpolished, and unconventional spelling and punctuation abound. "'This country has a romantick appearance river inclosed between high and steep hills cuts to pices by revines but little timber and that confined to the Rivers & creek," writes Clark in Montana on 25 June 1805. He omits periods and commas and verbs, running the landscape's parts together in one breathless sentence.[32]

---

28 Bartram, *Travels*, 124. My emphasis. 29 Bartram, *Travels*, 120–21.
30 The words are Jefferson's own. See Frank Bergon, "Introduction," in Lewis and Clark, *Journals*, ix–xix, xv.
31 Robert Finch and John Elder, "Meriwether Lewis," in *The Norton Book of Nature Writing* (New York: W. W. Norton, 2002), 95–104, 96.
32 Lewis and Clark, *Journals*, 178.

"This morning was very cold," writes Lewis on 21 August of the same year, "The ink freizes in my pen." Here nature writing is almost halted in its tracks by nature itself. In describing the near impossibility of taking notes due to the elements, Lewis relays their very intensity, more forcefully even than his earlier mention of "ice ¼ of an inch thick on the water" or "deerskins that ... are stiffly frozen."[33] If a certain rawness or roughness characterizes the *Journals*, well-established literary conventions still mediate the explorers' depiction of the Louisiana Territory, as Clark's use of the phrase "romantick appearance" indicates. Lewis deploys this same term elsewhere to describe the White Cliffs of Choteau County, Montana, writing that "the hills and river Clifts ... exhibit a most romantic appearance." He then proceeds to render this landscape through picturesque and romantic tropes, seeing in the cliffs "a thousand grotesque figures" as well as "the remains or ruins of eligant buildings."[34] We are yet a ways away from the vision of John Muir, who will extol untamed wilderness, or that of Clarence King (1842–1901), who will conscientiously eradicate associations between nature and culture from his mind, the better to apprehend nature itself. We are yet with a romanticism-inflected subjectivity that delights in imagining traces of dilapidated antiquity, that revels in finding "parapets," "collumns," and "long galleries" in nature.[35]

In a way, such passages, with their sweeping literary descriptions of the country's new landscapes, are not typical: The *Journals* are mostly filled with the daily challenges of traversing rough and unfamiliar terrain, careful measurements of animals, estimates of geographic sizes or distances, and detailed ethnographic information on the diet, rituals, and material practices of various Indigenous communities. Yet it is precisely passages such as those cited above that were most widely circulated in nineteenth-century periodicals, where the greatest number of contemporary readers could access excerpts from the *Journals*.[36] They represent the *Journals*' "dramatic and exciting moments," moments that would provide source material for fiction writers like Washington Irving, James Fenimore Cooper, and Edgar Allan Poe.[37]

---

33 Lewis and Clark, *Journals*, 251.   34 Lewis and Clark, *Journals*, 143–44.
35 Lewis and Clark, *Journals*, 144.
36 Comprising over a dozen notebooks, the first official publication of the journal was done in 1814 by Nicholas Biddle. This edition was the definitive one until an eight-volume version was published in 1904.
37 Spencer Snow, "Maps and Myths: Consuming Lewis and Clark in the Early Republic," *Early American Literature* 48, no. 3 (2013): 671–708, 693.

Like the expedition itself, the *Journals of Lewis and Clark* today have a complicated legacy. They recorded scientific data. They generated national pride in the natural features of the United States, informing a potent picture of "American identity," as Spencer Snow notes.[38] They also contributed to the imperialist belief that would eventually become known as Manifest Destiny, which served as ideological justification for dispossessing Indigenous people of their land.[39] Like Bartram's *Travels*, the *Journals* bear witness to the obvious but underemphasized fact that early American nature writing was never about a nature devoid of humankind.

In 1803, the same year Thomas Jefferson commissioned Lewis and Clark's Corps of Discovery, a Frenchman by the name of John James Audubon set out from Nantes to the United States. Born in Haiti, raised in France under the birthname Jean-Jacques, Audubon immigrated to the United States at the behest of his father, who wanted him to avoid conscription in the Napoleonic Wars. After several years in Pennsylvania, where Audubon (enthusiastically) honed his birding skills and (unenthusiastically) pursued mining ventures, he moved to Louisville, Kentucky. There he ran a general store along the Ohio River and maintained a serious hobby of observing and drawing birds, creatures to which he had been attached since childhood. When his business failed with the financial panic of 1819, his birding avocation became a vocation: The following year, Audubon conceived the scientific-artistic project for which he would become famous: *The Birds of America* (1827–1838), a multivolume work of over 400 color plates depicting hundreds of life-size birds.

This work has its textual counterpart in the *Ornithological Biography* (1831–39), in which Audubon relays information about the habitat, morphology, and behavior of various birds represented in *The Birds of America*. The bulk of *Ornithological Biography* is devoted to succinct descriptions of bird behavior (their geographic distribution, diet, and interactions with other animals). Nevertheless, Audubon does not write about birds solely from the disinterested perspective of science; he also considers them vis-à-vis humanity's pragmatic concerns. He regularly notes whether a bird's flesh is "palatable" or "tolerable," and he documents various groups' relationship to given species: "The Creoles make *gumbo* of [the Barred Owl]"; white ibises "are frequently eaten by the Indians"; "Good dogs scent the [wild] Turkeys, when

---

38 Snow, "Maps and Myths," 701.
39 See Robert J. Miller, *Native America Discovered and Conquered: Thomas Jefferson, Lewis and Clark, and Manifest Destiny* (Westport, CT: Praeger, 2006), 106–12.

in large flocks, at extraordinary distances.... This is of great advantage to the hunter."[40]

Although Audubon received assistance from other artists, hunters, and ornithologists in gathering material for *Birds of America* as well as *Ornithological Biography*, both books developed significantly out of his own birding expeditions throughout the American Southeast. As such, they are deeply rooted in travel, in naturalistic journeys. They may lack the linear structure of Lewis and Clark's *Journals* or Bartram's *Travels*, which receive their essential outline from the various stops of their epic journeys, but the points of Audubon's itineraries are simply dispersed unevenly across the various bird biographies in *Ornithological Biography*, culled from this or that expedition.

In this sense, one might also say that the author of *Ornithological Biography* considers the birds in question vis-à-vis the concerns of one man in particular: John James Audubon. The individual bird biographies of the book, when taken together, constitute a hazy biography of Audubon himself. Known by some contemporaries as "The American Woodsman" (an appellation of his own invention), Audubon was crafty in constructing his authorial identity. Juxtaposing himself with more gentlemanly European scientists, Audubon forcefully asserts his role as field researcher and eyewitness throughout the *Ornithological Biography*. "I have seen," "I have witnessed," "I have watched," and "I have found" all feature as regular, proud refrains. When Audubon contests the Comte de Buffon's suggestion that "Woodpeckers are miserable beings" by writing, "to one who might have lived long in the woods [he] would seem to have lived only in [his] libraries," we are to understand that the "one" in question is Audubon himself.[41] When Audubon asserts that the hiss of young barred owls is "to a person lost in a swamp ... extremely dismal," we are likewise to intuit that the author has indeed found himself in such a position, brave traveler that he is.[42]

Audubon rightly remains most known for his masterful illustrations in *The Birds of America*, but he may also be seen as a pioneer in the construction of a certain kind of heroic persona in nature writing. Salient in Audubon, as in later nature writers like Edward Abbey (1927–1989) or Wallace Stegner (1909–1993), is the way in which the literary representation of nature is also the representation of self.

---

40 John James Audubon, *The Audubon Reader*, ed. Richard Rhodes (New York: Knopf, 2006), 142, 366, 267.
41 Audubon, *Audubon Reader*, 140.   42 Audubon, *Audubon Reader*, 142.

Surveying Nature: King and Powell

The latter half of the nineteenth century saw the establishment of numerous federal agencies to assess, exploit, and manage the natural resources of the United States: the Department of the Interior (1849), the Department of Agriculture (1862), the United States Fish Commission (1871), and the United States Geological Survey (1879). Along with them, a distinct body of nature writing emerged, embodied by the works of writers like Clarence King and John Wesley Powell, both of whom directed the Geological Survey (King from 1879 to 1881, Powell from 1881 to 1894). Despite the strictly professional goals of their explorations, both writers produced popular literary works in which nature is experienced as a site of adventure and aesthetic wonder.[43]

Unlike an earlier generation of autodidactic nature writers (Audubon, Bartram, Lewis, Clark), Clarence King received an elite education. From Yale's Sheffield Scientific School he obtained a degree in chemistry, though after graduating in 1862 his interests gravitated rapidly toward geology. Enraptured by stories of the California Geological Survey of Josiah Whitney (1819–1896), King eventually decided to venture west to this enticing new state. As the first transcontinental railroad was not yet finished, King set out in 1863 on horseback, a testament, perhaps, to a spirit characterized by "optimism [and] self-confidence."[44]

Once in California, King found work with Whitney's Geological Survey exploring the heights of the Sierra Nevada mountain range. As a member of a team that included the botanist William Henry Brewer (1828–1910) and the topographer Charles Frederick Hoffman (1838–1913), King surveyed and named several now famous peaks of the range, including Mount Whitney and Mount Tyndall, and he conducted the first scientific expeditions of regions such as Kings Canyon. King wrote about these experiences in essays published in the *Atlantic Monthly* and *Overland Monthly*, which he subsequently reworked into his renowned book *Mountaineering in the Sierra Nevada* (1872).

Mountaineering is written in an assured, refined tone reflective of King's education in the arts and sciences. A devotee of the Victorian polymath John Ruskin (1819–1900), King developed a literary style that is romantic, allusive, and sometimes pompous. He is fond of Gallicisms – *en rapport, comme il faut, dénouement, après-dîner* – and calls a mountaineer's relationship to his pack

---

[43] John Wesley Powell, *The Colorado River and Its Canyons* (New York: Dover, 1961), iii.
[44] James M. Shebl, "Introduction," in *Mountaineering in the Sierra Nevada*, by Clarence King (Lincoln, NE: University of Nebraska Press, 1970), vii–xiii, vii.

mule an *entente cordiale*.[45] He references Virgil, Longfellow, and Shakespeare in a single chapter on Mount Shasta.[46] And he describes the natural history of the Sierra Nevada by analogy to Mozart's *Magic Flute*: "As the characters of the *Zauberflöte* passed safely through the trial of fire and the desperate ordeal of water, so, through the terror of volcanic fires and the chilling empire of ice, had the great Sierra come into the present age of tranquil grandeur."[47] European high culture constantly frames King's experience of the mountains of California.

Lofty ideals animate this work as much as cultural allusions. In King, we find a love for uninhabited, uncultivated wilderness, as well as an aversion to aspects of modern civilization. Chapter 11 of *Mountaineering* begins with an invective against agricultural mechanization: "I try to believe all [farming's] poetry is not forever immolated under ... the stream-reaper."[48] And in the book's opening chapter, observing the Sierras from Pacheco Pass (a part of the California Coast Ranges near Santa Clara), King recounts seeing, or imagining he sees, the lights of "mining towns planted in its rusty ravines."[49] This is unsavory to him – "a suggestion I was glad to repel." So he looks farther, higher, "to that cool realm where the pines stand, green-roofed, in infinite colonnade. Lifted above the bustling industry of the plains and the melodramatic mining theatre of the foothills, it has a grand, silent life of its own, refreshing to contemplate even from a hundred miles away."[50] He willfully avoids the "suggestion" of habitation. He *wants* to apprehend a wilderness untainted by human activities. In doing so, King conveys an early, if underdeveloped, form of environmental consciousness, a consciousness disconcerted by the deleterious effects of industry upon the natural world.[51]

Nonetheless, *Mountaineering* is no ideal environmental text. King's reflections on the Chinese immigrants, Native Americans, and poor white laborers that he encountered during his travels often reek of arrogance and condescension. Moreover, his proto-environmental consciousness rests upon an unproductive dichotomy: a stark conceptual division between nature and culture.[52] In turning his gaze away from the mining towns in the foothills to

---

45 King, *Mountaineering*, 14.   46 King, *Mountaineering*, 223, 241.
47 King, *Mountaineering*, 4–5.   48 King, *Mountaineering*, 223.
49 King, *Mountaineering*, 23–24.   50 King, *Mountaineering*, 24.
51 This said, after serving for several years as the first director of the United States Geological Survey, King would go on to direct several private mining enterprises in the West and Southwest.
52 One classic critique of this dichotomy comes from William Cronon, "The Trouble with Wilderness: Or, Getting Back to the Wrong Nature," *Environmental History* 1, no. 1 (January 1996): 7–28.

the sublime peaks of the mountains, King effectively avoids a more substantial consideration of how nature and culture might better coexist.

In the summer of 1869, while Clarence King was leading the government-backed Geological Exploration of the Fortieth Parallel, another ambitious scientific survey was underway: a three-month exploration of the Green and Colorado Rivers. Its leader, John Wesley Powell, was as passionate about geology as King; he was, however, the product of drastically different circumstances. The son of poor Welsh immigrants who eventually settled in Illinois, Powell never obtained a degree from any of the three universities he intermittently attended, largely for want of funds.[53] While King had decided not to fight in the Civil War, Powell enlisted five days after Abraham Lincoln issued a call for volunteers, losing his right arm in the Battle of Shiloh.[54] After the war, he obtained a position teaching at Illinois Wesleyan University and curating the museum of natural history at Illinois State Normal University. In 1867, with his interest in the landscape and intellectual climate of Illinois diminishing, Powell began planning the first of several expeditions to the American West, garnering support from several universities and the federal government.[55]

The most famous of these trips would be the expeditions of 1869 and 1871, in which Powell and his team ventured by boat down the Colorado River and through the Grand Canyon – the first recorded travelers to do so. Like King, Powell wrote about these excursions in articles for magazines such as *Popular Science Monthly* and *Scribner's* before compiling them into a book: *The Exploration of the Colorado River and Its Canyons* (1895).[56] Despite Powell's insistence in the book's preface that he had no real interest in publishing "an adventure, but was interested only in the scientific results," he proves an adept dramatizer of the surveys.[57] "There is a descent of perhaps 75 or 80 feet in a third of mile, and the rushing waters break into great waves on the rocks, and lash themselves into a mad, white foam," Powell writes in a chapter titled "From the Little Colorado to the Foot of the Grand Canyon." Despite this great danger, these all-or-nothing stakes, the author and his crew act

---

53 Donald Worster, *A River Running West: The Life of John Wesley Powell* (Oxford: Oxford University Press, 2001), 37–85.
54 Worster, *River Running West*, 85, 94.   55 Worster, *River Running West*, 117.
56 Worster, *River Running West*, 330. An earlier version of the book was published in 1875 by the Smithsonian as *Report of the Exploration of the Colorado River of the West and Its Tributaries*.
57 John Wesley Powell, *The Exploration of the Colorado River and Its Canyons* (New York: Dover, 1961), iv.

decisively: "[W]e must run the rapid or abandon the river. There is no hesitation. We step into our boats, push off, and away we go."[58]

The authorial voice in the *Exploration* is a deliberately heroic one, and Powell projects a courageous, adventuresome persona not unlike that cultivated by Theodore Roosevelt. The nature writer is heroic by virtue of his vigilance, his triumphing over a wild landscape, which Powell often represents in elaborate prose packed with alliteration and rhythmic repetitions:

> Down in these grand, gloomy depths we glide, ever listening, for the mad waters keep up their roar; ever watching, ever peering ahead, for the narrow canyon is winding and the river is closed in so that we can see but a few hundred yards, and what there may be below we know not; so we listen for falls and watch for rocks.[59]

Powell finds grandeur in the West's physical features and in the history of its rivers and canyons, but he does not perceive it as benign. He is not one with nature; rather, he *braves* it. In this regard, he differs sharply from Emerson and his later acolytes like John Muir and John Burroughs (1837–1921). As Donald Worster writes of Powell, "[W]ilderness for him was ... a condition to be overcome."[60]

Extending Transcendentalism: Burroughs and Muir

Longtime friends John Burroughs and John Muir expressed a delight in the natural world more unqualified than that of government-employed adventurers like King or Powell. In this regard, both bear the profound influence of Ralph Waldo Emerson, who in *Nature* (1836) wrote, "Nature never wears a mean appearance."[61] Burroughs read Emerson "in a sort of ecstasy" as a young man;[62] and when Muir met Emerson in 1871, he fondly described him as being "serene as a sequoia, his head in the empyrean."[63] While they differed in how they processed the Transcendentalist's work and developed their own particular ideas, both writers articulated a spiritual, even religious appreciation for nature. In Burroughs, this spiritual vision is often temperate,

---

58 Powell, *Exploration of the Colorado River*, 250–51.
59 Powell, *Exploration of the Colorado River*, 251–53.   60 Worster, *River Running West*, 471.
61 Ralph Waldo Emerson, *Nature* in *Essays and Poems* (New York: Library of America, 1996), 9.
62 Clara Barrus, *The Life and Letters of John Burroughs* (Boston: Houghton Mifflin, 1925), 41.
63 John Muir, "Forests of Yosemite Park," in *Selected Essays*, ed. William Cronon (New York: Library of America, 1997), 767–89, 786.

intermittent. In Muir, it is omnipresent; everywhere in nature, he detected divine benevolence.

Deeply influenced by Ralph Waldo Emerson and Walt Whitman (1819–1892), John Burroughs is perhaps less noteworthy as an original thinker than as a popularizer of American interest in the recreational and aesthetic enjoyment of the natural world. Through manifold essays and over thirty books of nature writing – from *Wake Robin* (1871) to *Ways of Nature* (1905) to *Under the Maples* (1921) – Burroughs sought to transmit the majesty and pleasure of places like the Alaskan coast, the Hawaiian Islands, and – above all else – the Catskill Mountains, where he spent most of his life. This pleasure sometimes shaded into something greater, a kind of hazy pantheism. However, the philosophy Burroughs most frequently espoused was a domesticated, "garden-style nature appreciation."[64] As he announced early in his career, he was not a deep ethical thinker like such Transcendental predecessors as Emerson or Thoreau. "My own aim ... is entirely artistic," he declared.[65]

Unlike Powell or King, both of whom published little, Burroughs yearned for literary success from an early age, but in many ways he is less writerly, less deftly poetic than those unprolific geologists. Here are a few paragraph openers from one of Burroughs's popular works, an essay about Mammoth Cave in Kentucky: "No part of Mammoth cave was to me more impressive than its entrance"; "Another very interesting feature to me was the behavior of the cool air"; "Probably the prettiest thing they have to show you in Mammoth Cave is the Star Chamber."[66] His style of exposition is journalistic, deliberate, and at times heavy-handed. But it was digestible to a broad public, a public that even came to include industrialists like Henry Ford, Andrew Carnegie, and Harvey Firestone, all of whom Burroughs befriended.

As that roster of friends might indicate, Burroughs was not the fiercest conservationist or most vocal critic of the status quo. Insofar as he had political or environmental commitments, they were mildly expressed: a gentle praising of the virtues of agrarianism; skepticism toward "the vast system of artificial things" produced by civilization.[67] He promoted interest and attention toward the natural world, but compared to another one of his friends, John Muir, Burroughs can appear rather tame. As Edward Renehan,

---

64 Edward J. Renehan, *John Burroughs: An American Naturalist* (Post Mills, VT: Chelsea Green, 1992), 4.
65 Barrus, *Life and Letters*, 212.
66 John Burroughs, "In Mammoth Cave," in *The Complete Nature Writings of John Burroughs* (New York: Wm. H. Wise, 1904), 261–72, 269, 270, 265.
67 Renehan, *John Burroughs*, 302.

one of Burroughs's biographers, writes: "Muir and others of his school believed a firm line had to be drawn to protect the lands of the West against exploitation by timber, oil, and coal interests. They were the first environmental activists. And Burroughs was not one of their number."[68]

Before John Muir, most American nature writers perceived the sublime features of the natural world with alloyed emotion. Standing before the edge of a precipice or witnessing the tumult of a thunderstorm, their awe was mixed with anxiety. In Muir's work, however, we repeatedly encounter an unprecedented sentiment: unadulterated love for nature in even its most violent states. Indeed, fear of nature is almost entirely absent; he sees nature as ever goodly, ever godly. John Burroughs, a self-professed nature lover, could still see the aftermath of a storm as constituting a "desolate scene."[69] With Muir, it is otherwise. He experiences a flood in the Yosemite Valley as "liberated waters [holding] jubilee."[70] He sees "marvelous lavishness" in a snowstorm on Mount Shasta.[71] And, after a powerful rainstorm in the Sierra Nevada, Muir "saunter[s] down through the dripping bushes, reveling in the universal vigor and freshness with which all the life about me was inspired," thinking, "How clean and unworn and immortal the world seem[s] to be!"[72]

Muir derives his environmental ethic from his overflowing belief in nature's holiness. His essays advocating for environmental protections brim with religious rhetoric. In an 1876 article on "the practical importance of the preservation of our forests," he conferred on them the title of "God's First Temples."[73] In the posthumously published essay "Save the Redwoods," Muir refers to forest conservation as "a righteous uprising in defense of God's trees."[74] And in "Hetch Hetchy Valley," he claims that those who support damming the valley deliver "arguments . . . curiously like those of the devil, devised for the destruction of the first garden."[75] Belief in nature's sacredness convinced Muir of the need to defend it resolutely.

Thanks to his energetic defense of wilderness, Muir has long been venerated as a charismatic cornerstone of modern environmental thought. Through his impassioned essays as well as the Sierra Club he founded in 1892, Muir contributed to the establishment of the National Park System and the conservation of regions like Yosemite Valley and Mount Rainier. In

---

68 Renehan, *John Burroughs*, 253.
69 John Burroughs, "From London to New York," in *The Writings of John Burroughs with Portraits and Many Illustrations*, vol. 2, *Winter Sunshine* (Boston: Houghton Mifflin, 1904), 221–56, 252–53.
70 Muir, "Forests of Yosemite Park," 588.
71 Muir, "Forests of Yosemite Park," 664.
72 Muir, "Forests of Yosemite Park," 614.
73 Muir, "Forests of Yosemite Park," 629.
74 Muir, "Forests of Yosemite Park," 828.
75 Muir, "Forests of Yosemite Park," 816.

recent years, however, scholars have subjected him to a more critical eye. Environmental historian William Cronon identifies Muir as a key contributor to the fetishization of "sublime" spaces to the detriment of less sensational ones.[76] The historian Mark David Spence also notes that Muir regularly disregarded or disparaged the role of the Indigenous people who had long inhabited the places he naïvely revered as pristine wilderness.[77] (That said, later in life Muir held the view that Native Americans had been "robbed of their lands and pushed ruthlessly back into narrower and narrower limits by alien races."[78]) Muir thus marks a complicated turning point in the history of nature writing. He infused the genre with a political urgency absent from many of his literary predecessors. But at times, he neglected what writers like Thoreau, Audubon, and Bartram knew clearly: North America was not an unpeopled Eden prior to the arrival of European settlers; long had Native Americans lived in, studied, and managed these lands.

Conclusion: Beyond Nature Writing

This chapter has focused on "nature writing" as a loose nonfiction genre that emerges from a tradition of European naturalism and essayism, with all the limitations thereby entailed. But it should be asked: What is the ultimate utility of this classification? What is lost by omitting nonessayistic works that nonetheless deal with nature? What is lost by excluding oral works? Though a thorough deconstruction of the genre is beyond the scope of this chapter, it is worth interrogating the boundaries of "nature writing" as it has been historically understood to consider, in turn, other literary traditions for which nature is likewise a key concern.

In his article "Writing Nature," scholar Lee Schweninger notes that "whereas the Euro-American tradition considers nature writing as a special genre," Native American oral literature had reflected deep practical and spiritual engagement with the natural world long prior to the genre's formation.[79] Nature also occupies an important place in many Native American written works, even when nature itself is not the principal subject. In the 1829 autobiography of William Apess (1798–1839), a Pequot writer and activist, he declares that "the forests . . . are vocal with the praises of God" and

---

76 See Cronon, "Trouble with Wilderness."
77 Mark David Spence, *Dispossessing the Wild: Indian Removal and the Making of the National Parks* (Oxford: Oxford University Press, 1999), 109.
78 John Muir, "Lessons of the Wilderness," *Atlantic Monthly* III, no. 1 (1913): 81–92, 88.
79 Schweninger, "Writing Nature," 49.

describes going "into the woods [where] all nature seemed to smile and rejoice in the freshness and beauty of spring."[80] In *The Traditional History and Characteristic Sketches of the Ojibway Nation* (1850), the Mississauga writer George Copway (1818–1869) writes that "the mountains, rivers, lakes, cliffs, and caverns of the Ojibway country, impress one with the thought that Nature has there built a home for Nature's children."[81] And in *Life among the Piutes* (1883), Sarah Winnemucca (1844–1891) records the social and ethical rules governing Northern Paiute hunting practices.[82] Although not exclusively focused on particular natural features or "outdoor activities," all such works express important religious, pragmatic, and epistemological attitudes toward nature, much like the Euro-American texts explored in this chapter.

One of the most prominent literary engagements with the natural world by a nineteenth-century Indigenous writer comes from the Yankton Dakota pan-Indian activist Zitkála-Šá (1876–1938). Writing for some of the same magazines as John Muir, Susan Fenimore Cooper, Clarence King, and John Burroughs, Zitkála-Šá published memoirs, critiques of Euro-American values and institutions, and essays on Indigenous thought. Her essay "Why I Am a Pagan" may be her most nature-oriented work. Originally published in the December 1902 issue of the *Atlantic*, the essay is an articulation of Zitkála-Šá's spiritual beliefs as well as a rebuke of Christian evangelism. It is also an expression of her relationship to the natural world. "Drifting clouds and tinkling waters, together with the warmth of a genial summer day, bespeak with eloquence the loving Mystery round about us," reads a sentence in the opening paragraph.[83] "I prefer to ... dogma my excursions into the natural gardens where the voice of the Great Spirit is heard in the twittering of birds, the rippling of mighty waters, and the sweet breathing of flowers," reads the essay's penultimate sentence.[84] Here, in a work that both is and is not "nature writing," Zitkála-Šá communicates a sense of radical immanence and a profoundly relational worldview: She voices "a kinship to any and all parts of this vast universe" and perceives all life as "symbols of omnipotent thought."[85] Under this expansive conception of the natural world, the boundaries between the human and nonhuman, nature and culture, dissolve.

---

80 William Apess, *A Son of the Forest* (New York: Apess, 1829), 72–73.
81 George Copway, *The Traditional History and Characteristic Sketches of the Ojibway Nation* (Boston: Sanborn, Carter, Bazin, 1850), 14.
82 Sarah Winnemucca, *Life Among the Piutes* (Boston: Cupples, Upham, 1883), 50–51.
83 Zitkála-Šá, "Why I Am a Pagan," *Atlantic Monthly* 90 (December 1902): 801–803, 801.
84 Zitkála-Šá, "Why I Am a Pagan," 803.   85 Zitkála-Šá, "Why I Am a Pagan," 802.

5
The Essay and Transcendentalism
LAURA DASSOW WALLS

What one notices first are the voices: "A foolish consistency is the hobgoblin of little minds"; "Let them be sea-captains, if you will"; "I went to the woods because I wished to live deliberately."[1] Each of these voices represents an innovation on the essay, from Ralph Waldo Emerson's (1803–1882) imperial, world-creating self, to Margaret Fuller's (1810–1850) searching exploration of female identity, to Henry David Thoreau's (1817–1862) quest for meaning that joins inner self with outer nature. Had the essay not already existed, the Transcendentalists would have had to invent it. They used it to write themselves, and thus Transcendentalism as a movement, into being, creating a flexible, open-ended, and experimental instrument for the radical self-fashioning of an emergent sensibility: the American individual as a freestanding soul, entire in (him)self, capable of encompassing all the potential of the cosmos. The resulting works forever stamped this most antinomian of genres with the Transcendentalist's indelible signature.

The "I" striving for union with the divine, the "I" striving to build and serve the human community: Both versions of the Transcendentalist self drew from the evolving role of the New England minister, as liberalizing Protestant churches adapted the traditional public sermon to a more private, intimate form verging on the essayistic. One hears this in the voice of Jonathan Edwards (1703–1758), the great pre-Revolutionary Puritan minister who moved the public to salvation through words that made them feel the

---

[1] Ralph Waldo Emerson, "Self-Reliance," in *Essays and Lectures*, ed. Joel Porte (New York: Library of America, 1983), 257–82, 265; Margaret Fuller, *Woman in the Nineteenth Century*, in *The Essential Margaret Fuller*, ed. Jeffrey Steele (New Brunswick, NJ: Rutgers University Press, 1992), 243–78, 345; Henry David Thoreau, *Walden*, ed. J. Lyndon Shanley (Princeton, NJ: Princeton University Press, 1971), 90.

fire of God on their very nerve endings, even as his "Personal Narrative" walked through agonies of doubt and ecstasies of grace – a solitary "I" terrorized by every lapse and failure. But one also hears this in the garrulous voice of Edwards's contemporary, Benjamin Franklin (1706–1790), whose essays invented a modest, rambling, conversational self whose self-skeptical "I" exemplified both normative reasonableness and the limits of reason itself, while shapeshifting across a range of narrative voices from the feisty "Constance Dogood" to the sententious "Poor Richard" to the public-spirited Ben Franklin himself, conscientious corrector of his life's many "errata." Edwards's painstaking sincerity lingers on in the American Transcendentalists, leavened, here and there, by Franklinian drollery – and, in Thoreau, by the flexible personae of a narrating self who can be, by turns, preacher, instructor, polemicist, poet, humorist, and mystic.

The American essay was formalized at Harvard College, where Professor William Tyrell Channing (1790–1856) taught his students – including both Emerson and Thoreau – how to compensate for the erosion of the Bible's once privileged status by inculcating a formal, didactic, moralistic "I" as a depersonalized authority. The results were stilted at best – as Lawrence Buell remarks, "it took Thoreau and Emerson ten years to begin to outgrow" Channing's abstract and conventionalized prose – but on the other hand, as Sandra Gustafson argues, Channing's articulation of calm, "deliberative" values recognized that "a self-governing people must go beyond superficial emotional appeals and embrace the hard work of political understanding."[2] Only the earned authority of such a careful and deliberative "I" could have empowered Emerson to explain so calmly, in 1832, why he was refusing to administer the Eucharist, or ritual of communion: "It is my own objection. This mode of commemorating Christ is not suitable to me. That is reason enough why I should abandon it." As Emerson went on to assert, Christianity, which he felt free to redefine as "a moral system" suited for the wants of men, can live or die only if such poet-preachers as himself can breathe life back into it – life carried not in any old book, but only in the living word of the living writer.[3]

---

[2] Lawrence Buell, *Literary Transcendentalism* (Ithaca, NY: Cornell University Press, 1973), 99; Sandra Gustafson, *Imagining Deliberative Democracy in the Early American Republic* (Chicago: University of Chicago Press, 2011), 23.

[3] Ralph Waldo Emerson, "Sermon CLXII" ["The Lord's Supper"] 9 September 1832, in *Transcendentalism: A Reader*, ed. Joel Myerson (Oxford: Oxford University Press, 2000), 68–78, 75, 76.

Inheritances

For Emerson and his generation, the heart and soul of liberal faith was the Rev. William Ellery Channing (1780–1842), the great architect and defender of New England Unitarianism, whom Emerson called "our Pope." Channing entered Harvard in 1794, in the era when the French Revolution, abetted by Thomas Paine's *Age of Reason*, was thought to be spreading an infidel and irreligious spirit. Channing's own wavering faith was renewed by a conversion experience that revealed the human soul, while fallen and prey to evil, was yet capable of infinite moral perfection in a universe of progressive order and beauty. The key was to destroy the notion that private interest was at odds with the public good, and to put in its place a conviction that all creatures are united by mutual dependencies; as Channing said in an early sermon, "No man is unnecessary; no man stands alone."[4] The challenge he faced was how to cultivate individual self-reliance, thereby giving each person the agency to develop and express their own conscience, while resisting American notions of individualist autonomy.

Channing had a profound effect on progressive thought, both through his personal influence and through his popular sermons and high-minded essays. The controlled passion of his writings appealed, soul to soul, to the best in his readers, as when he told them that the hallmark of the human is not our weakness or worthlessness, but our innate greatness – a divinity within every human being, a spark that we can unfold through self-knowledge. As Channing wrote in his influential sermon "Likeness to God" (1828), "God becomes a real being to us, in proportion as his own nature is unfolded within us." His summation (which sounds very like the future Emerson) reflects Channing's deep reading in post-Kantian Romanticism: "The Infinite Light would be forever hidden from us, did not kindred rays dawn and brighten with us. God is another name for human intelligence, raised above all error and imperfection, and extended to all possible truth."[5] This Christian principle of "likeness to God" became Transcendentalism's foundational tenet, one that Emerson would use to defend his authority to resign from the ministry and embark on his secular career as a lecturer and writer. "The whole secret is in one word, '*Likeness*,'" he wrote in 1831; "The way to perceive a spirit is to become like it. What is unlike us, we cannot perceive.

---

[4] William Henry Channing, *The Life of William Ellery Channing, D.D.* (Boston: American Unitarian Association, 1880), 32, 142.
[5] William Ellery Channing, "Likeness to God," in Myerson, *Transcendentalism*, 3–20, 4–5, 7.

We cannot perceive the spirit of purity without being pure; of justice, without being just; of wisdom, without being wise."[6] Thus the cure for diseases of the soul can only lie *within*: it is up to us to work out our own salvation, an interior work that none can do for us. But how? In 1838, Channing showed the way in his great essay "Self-Culture," which he defined as "the care which every man owes to himself, to the unfolding and perfecting of his nature."[7]

The most obvious means of self-culture is, of course, reading, study, and education – literally, the *educing*, or unfolding, of the divinity that slumbers within each of us – but Channing hardly confined this culture to books alone: "We are told, that the education of the multitude is necessary to the support of a republic; but it is equally true, that a republic is a powerful means of educating the multitude. It is the people's University." Self-culture requires everyone: the community, the nation, foreign lands and literatures, the public spirit directed to "the general weal"; it reaches from schools and books – fiction, history, biography, nature, travels, and poetry – to lectures, meetings, and discussion groups, to every means of reaching and cultivating the minds of the people, for only informed and enlightened political engagement can protect democracy against the perils of despotism or authoritarian rule.[8] Self-culture also requires the natural world, as Amos Bronson Alcott (1799–1888) recognized: "Man's mission is to subdue Nature; to hold dominion over his own body; and use both these, and the ministries of Life, for the growth, renewal, and perfection of his Being."[9] Alcott's friend Thoreau, in following this path to Walden Pond, would come to redefine "man's mission" from dominion to companionship, innovating on the essay form by shifting, in Lawrence Buell's formulation, from Transcendental "egocentrism" to a radical new "ecocentrism." By granting independent agency to nature, Thoreau initiated a new kind of essay centered on the nonhuman world, founding the American tradition of nature writing.[10]

All of Transcendentalism, from its high religious tone, to the honor it gives to the beauty of nature, to its passionate engagement with politics – even to the defense of civil disobedience, lest the individual be recruited to evil by

---

6 William Ellery Channing, "Sermon CLXII," in Myerson, *Transcendentalism*, 63.
7 William Ellery Channing, *The Works of William E. Channing, D.D.* (Boston: George G. Channing, 1849), 2:354.
8 Channing, *Works*, 2:386.
9 Bronson Alcott, "The Doctrine and Discipline of Human Culture," in Myerson, *Transcendentalism*, 167–81, 178–79.
10 Lawrence Buell, *The Environmental Imagination* (Cambridge, MA: Harvard University Press, 1995), 155.

conforming to the majority – is present in Channing's prolific writings. Transcendentalism may have been born in the meetings Emerson and his friends held, starting in 1837, to discuss their new philosophy, but it gestated years earlier in Channing's home, where most of the original Transcendentalists first met each other, and whence they took up their various projects in the wider world. Two of them, George and Sarah Ripley, went on to found the Utopian community Brook Farm, trying to work out by example a just union of individual and community; one of the original "Brook Farmers" was Nathaniel Hawthorne (1804–1864). The Ripleys' friend Orestes Brownson (1803–1876), a Utopian socialist and spiritual seeker who credited Channing's "Likeness to God" with saving him from atheism, even moved his family to Boston to be near Channing – who, in turn, helped Brownson found his radical church for the working classes, bringing religion from the churches of the elite to the pulse of the people. In this heady environment, Brownson refined his oratorical and literary skills, laying the foundations for a long career as a political and religious controversialist. He founded the *Boston Quarterly Review*, then *Brownson's Quarterly Review*, whose pages he filled with his strenuous and high-minded essays on contemporary literature, politics, and religion. After a disillusioned Brownson converted to Catholicism in 1844, he went on to become nineteenth-century America's greatest and most prolific Catholic intellectual.

Perhaps most significantly, in 1834 Channing encouraged his close friend and amanuensis, Elizabeth Peabody (1804–1894), to join forces with Bronson Alcott to found their experimental Temple School, dedicated to putting the principles of self-culture to work in the American classroom. Peabody's account of their experiment, *Record of a School* (1836), details the innovative role of writing in their classroom, in which children would begin to keep journals "as soon as they can join letters," not only for the purpose of "self-inspection," but more, to enable "the writers to give unity to their own being, by bringing all outward facts into some relation with their individuality, and gathering up fragments which would otherwise be lost."[11] After Peabody moved on, Alcott sought the assistance of Margaret Fuller (1810–1850), yet another member of Channing's circle, who joined him in the classroom for a time before herself moving on to become the editor of the *Dial*, the Transcendentalists' own periodical (of which more below), and the author of a range of essays dedicated to improving American intellectual culture and defending the rights of women.

11 Myerson, *Transcendentalism*, 105, 116.

Although controversy soon forced Alcott to close his school, his educational methods were adapted by Horace Mann (1796–1859), the husband of Peabody's sister Mary Peabody Mann, into a program for American mass education. Despite Horace Mann's Transcendentalist principles, this set in motion a process of standardization that would turn American education from the cultivation of freethinking individuals to a stratified system of hierarchy and social control – yet the original Transcendentalist impulse would live on as a counter-tradition of progressive education.[12] For her part, Elizabeth Peabody went on to promote a novel German educational experiment, "Kindergarten," in which exercises of structured play and experiential learning would inculcate the principles of Transcendentalist self-culture starting with childhood's earliest years – principles that Bronson Alcott's daughter Louisa May Alcott would dramatize in her wildly popular novel *Little Women* (1868) and its sequels *Little Men* (1871) and *Jo's Boy's* (1886), in which homeschooling for girls mutates into a private school for wayward boys and then into a radically inventive coeducational college. Generations of Alcott's young readers, then and now, would grow up imagining themselves the authors of their own lives – many, like Jo herself, taking up the pen to write themselves into voices and futures all their own.

Emerson Reinvents the American Essay and the Essay Reinvents America

The expansive Romantic ego that Channing distrusted became the hallmark of his friend and associate Ralph Waldo Emerson, who merged sermon, oratory, conversation, and journal keeping with philosophy, science, and poetic lyricism to forge the essay into a new form, one in which the narrative "I" does not merely *approach* God in Channingesque "likeness," but literally *becomes* God – the divine creative faculty born anew, in human form, self-creating a world on paper as a way to build a new world for all humanity. Even the sermons of the young Emerson read not as biblical exegesis but as uplifting moral essays; like Channing, he sought not to instruct his congregation but to inspire them. After Emerson resigned from the ministry, he abandoned theological argument altogether to celebrate the world-making power of the creative, poetic soul. But merely making life into art for art's sake was never his aim. From youth onward, he steeped himself in the essays

---

12 Martin Bickman, *Minding American Education* (New York: Teachers College Press, 2003), 5–19.

of Francis Bacon, imagining himself as an American Bacon who would articulate anew the first principles of truth for a new nation. Accordingly, Emerson honed his prose into balanced Baconian aphorisms: "Nature always wears the colors of the spirit"; "The invariable mark of wisdom is to see the miraculous in the common"; "The corruption of man is followed by the corruption of language"; "In every work of genius we recognize our own rejected thoughts: they come back to us with a certain alienated majesty."[13]

It is no accident that these aphorisms have the ring of conversational bon mots, for before the Transcendentalists published, they met and talked, formally and informally, in dining halls, salons, and Victorian parlors. They relished fine conversation as an art in itself, elevated by deftly turned phrases, sallies of wit, and clever puns.[14] Emerson hammered out his aphorisms in his journal, aired them in conversations, and refined them on the lecture circuit, judging their effect on his audiences before publishing them in his essays. His lectures, too, have the tone of fine conversation, loosely structured, reflective, full of digressions and explorations. When Emerson moved his material from lectures to polished essays, he refined his freely associated turns of thought into virtuoso oratorios, challenging to follow, impossible to paraphrase, but intoxicating in their sheer dynamism. Take, for example, this passage from one of his finest essays, "Experience":

> It is very unhappy, but too late to be helped, the discovery we have made, that we exist. That discovery is called the Fall of Man. Ever afterwards, we suspect our instruments. We have learned that we do not see directly, but mediately, and that we have no means of correcting these colored and distorting lenses which we are, or of computing the amount of their errors. Perhaps these subject-lenses have a creative power; perhaps there are no objects. Once we lived in what we saw; now, the rapaciousness of this new power, which threatens to absorb all things, engages us. Nature, art, persons, letters, religions, – objects, successively tumble in, and God is but one of its ideas.[15]

And on he goes for another page, dazzling his reader into admiring silence. "A man is a method," he once remarked, and Emerson trusted his mind to be all the method he needed. As he admonished the Harvard graduates of 1837 in his address "The American Scholar," the duty of the scholar is self-trust: "In self-trust, all the virtues are comprehended. Free should the scholar be, – free

---

13 Emerson, *Essays*, 11, 47, 22, 259. For Emerson's engagement with Bacon, see Laura Dassow Walls, *Emerson's Life in Science: The Culture of Truth* (Ithaca, NY: Cornell University Press, 2003), particularly 33–42.
14 Buell, *Literary Transcendentalism*, 88–91.   15 Emerson, *Essays*, 487.

and brave. Free even to the definitions of freedom, 'without any hindrance that does not arise out of his own constitution.' Brave; for fear is a thing, which a scholar by his very function puts behind him" – and off he goes again, baffling and irresistible. A few years later, in "Self-Reliance," Emerson polished this sequence into a single gem: "Trust thyself: every heart vibrates to that iron string."[16]

No other Transcendentalist wrote like Emerson, but the more writerly among them took hold of the same impulse to follow the track of one's thought wherever it led, composing oneself into being on the page. Bronson Alcott, famed for his elevated conversations, tried to reproduce their elevating effect in his published prose, but the sententious, abstract, "Orphic" paragraphs that resulted earned him much ridicule. Typical, if shorter than most, is "Obituary": "Things are memoirs of ideas; ideas the body of laws; laws the breath of God. All nature is the sepulchre of the risen soul, life her epitaph, and scripture her obituary."[17] The same impulse drew the young Thoreau, who, after graduating from Harvard in 1837 and founding his own experimental school, apprenticed himself to Emerson. For several years Thoreau lived with the Emerson family, helping around the house, raiding the library, and striving to become a writer on the Emerson model. It was tough going. Thoreau's stilted and moralistic early essays, written under the red pencil of Harvard's Professor Channing, show no promise of the feisty, trickster fluidity of the artist to come, and his earliest Transcendental writings are almost as constipated as Alcott's. Fuller rejected outright Thoreau's first submissions to the *Dial*. As she wrote him in a magnificently brutal rejection letter, "I cannot read it through without *pain*. I never once feel myself in a stream of thought, but seem to hear the grating of tools on the mosaic."[18]

This careful editorial scrutiny by one of America's first great literary critics suggests how important the *Dial* was for sharpening and circulating the distinctive style and tone of the Transcendentalist essay. Founded in 1840 as a vehicle to announce themselves and their writing to the world, the *Dial* lasted for four years, the first two under Fuller's editorship and the second two under Emerson's, with Thoreau's assistance. Their mission was not merely to self-publish the productions of their tight coterie, but to reach out to the world and encourage all those who have "no external organization, no badge, no creed, no name" to cultivate their inner life, then contribute

16 Emerson, *Essays*, 260.
17 Bronson Alcott, "Orphic Sayings," *Dial* 1, no. 3 (January 1841): 351–61, 361.
18 Henry David Thoreau, *The Correspondence*, vol. 1, *1834–1848* (Princeton, NJ: Princeton University Press, 2013), 70.

their discoveries to its pages. As this suggests, the *Dial* was less about providing educational content than establishing a principle – namely, as Ripley said of Brownson, "the sincere expression of a human voice."[19] True to their words, the *Dial* published the full range of Transcendentalist voices: Emerson, of course, but also Fuller's "Great Lawsuit" and Thoreau's breakthrough essay "The Natural History of Massachusetts," as well as hundreds of essays and poems by lesser-known writers – including women, then excluded from the literary establishment by its patriarchal overseers, such as Sarah Anne Freeman Clarke, Elizabeth Peabody, Sophia Ripley, and Ellen Sturgis Hooper. None achieved the fame of Emerson, Fuller, or Thoreau, but for Thoreau in particular, the *Dial* was instrumental. It gave him room to grow and a place to experiment with his own distinctive voice; it trained him in the realities of the publishing marketplace; and it gave him the confidence to shop his work around to the best and most widely circulated periodicals of the day.

Emerson, Fuller, Thoreau: Three Paths to the Transcendentalist Essay

Remarkably enough, the *Dial*'s three editors – Emerson, Fuller, and Thoreau – were the same three Transcendentalists to become literary classics, representing dozens of other writers and intellectuals who today remain known only to specialists. To briefly consider each of them in turn is to explore the resources of the Transcendentalist essay overall, and see how each turned these resources in a distinctive direction.

Emerson's most original leap came after he had quit the ministry and set about finding a new ground for truth. The Bible was too fallible, history was too inconstant, but God's Creation was eternal and law-bound: Emerson named it Nature, launching a new tradition in American writing. As he announced in the opening of his watershed essay *Nature* (1836), "The foregoing generations beheld God and nature face to face; we, through their eyes. Why should not we also enjoy an original relation to the universe?" By "Nature" he meant not natural history – that would be Thoreau's terrain – but "the integrity of impression made by manifold natural objects" as seen by the eye of the poet: he whose eye, or "I," is alone capable of integrating all the parts of the world into a harmonious whole, in which nature is realized as the

---

19 "The Editors to the Reader," *Dial* 1, no. 1 (July 1840): 2; George Ripley, "Brownson's Writings," *Dial* 1, no. 1 (July 1840): 23.

embodiment of divine Idea, and hence a symbolic gateway into understanding humanity.[20]

This vision moved Emerson's essayism away from inquisitive Montaignian ramblings and toward an imperial "I" with the power to "build your own world," connecting directly to the creative power that generates, and endlessly regenerates, the cosmos. Yet Emerson still honored Montaigne as the writer who showed him "the terms of admission" to this great spectacle of the cosmos: "a certain solid and intelligible way of living of his own," the stoutness of character that entitles the author "to fellowship and trust," wise moderation, vigorous originality.[21] To these qualities Emerson added the key Transcendentalist ingredient, borrowed from Kant via the essays of Samuel Taylor Coleridge (1772–1834). As his friend Frederic Henry Hedge (1804–1890) put it, whereas philosophers used to assume that what we can know is determined by what our limited senses can reveal of the material world, Coleridge (paraphrasing Kant) shows the reverse: "Let us therefore try whether ... we may not succeed better by assuming that the objects without us are determined by our cognitions." This is sometimes called Kant's Copernican turn: Whereas Copernicus revolutionized our world by showing that the earth-bound observer revolves around the sun, Kant revolutionized it again by showing that the mind is a sun around which revolves the earth. "The world without us depends on the nature of our intuitions," said Hedge; or, as Channing put it, "the beauty and glory of God's works are revealed to the mind by a light beaming from itself."[22] That is, the world does not present itself to us through the eye; rather, it is the eye, or "I," that radiates meaning into the world. This is "the transcendental method" for which "Transcendentalism" was named.

Thus, at the heart of every Transcendentalist lies a Christian idealist. Their theological commitment – their certainty that the relation between mind and matter "is not fancied by some poet, but stands in the will of God" – is what allows Emerson to declare that the poet "unfixes the land and the sea, makes them revolve around the axis of his primary thought, and disposes them anew .... The sensual man conforms thoughts to things; the poet conforms things to his thoughts."[23] This absolute centrality of the shaping eye of the writer, who looks form and meaning into a universe fluid and responsive to

---

20 Emerson, *Essays*, 7.   21 Emerson, *Essays*, 48, 696.
22 Frederic Henry Hedge, "Coleridge's Literary Character," in Myerson, *Transcendentalism*, 78–97, 91–92; William Ellery Channing, "Likeness to God," in Myerson, *Transcendentalism*, 3–20, 8.
23 Emerson, *Essays*, 34.

thought, allows Emerson to sermonize nature into faith while establishing textuality itself as the privileged site of world creation. Whatever appears sundered and broken to the merely sensual, or materialist, mind, the transcendental vision of the poet will rejoin into harmony; in his eyes, "the universe becomes transparent, and the light of higher laws than its own, shines through it."[24] Nature and soul become organs of each other, each passing into the other through the voice of the liberating poet – "the sayer, the namer" – who stands at the center and shows us the generative Idea of which all materiality is the multiform, fluid precipitate in which we must learn how to stay afloat. As Emerson states in "Montaigne," "The philosophy we want is one of fluxions and mobility . . . . We want a ship, in these billows we inhabit," for we are "golden averages, volitant stabilities, compensated or periodic errors, houses founded on the sea."[25]

This is heady stuff. Emerson's eye is infinitely expandable, free to be whatever it wants, free to defy history and call the recalcitrant universe to heel. As John Snyder observes, in Emerson the author's eye becomes the reader's eye, a node of vision in a cosmos in which everything is symbolic of everything else – a vision that calls the reader to keep reading, impelled by the sheer exhilaration of this endless voyage through discursivity. As Snyder adds, "No writer in English is more readable and less subject to précis" than Emerson.[26] His essays become self-enclosed, designed less to communicate than to provoke: restless, improvised, always ready to incorporate pain and defeat into yet another act of self-regeneration. In short, Emerson made himself inimitable – except for Walt Whitman, whose "Song of Myself" reinvented Emerson's essays in a new American poetry that, like Emerson's circular all-seeing "kosmic" enclosure, is endlessly liberating yet finally unapproachable. In Snyder's words, "the tyrannizing self, like the 'kosmos' of Whitman, gorges itself on the world's metamorphic associations, confident they are all reducible to self."[27] The endpoint of the Emerson essay turns out to be not the moralizing philosopher, but the lyric poet.

In her 1843 essay "The Great Lawsuit," Margaret Fuller paid tribute to her mentor, William Ellery Channing, "whose enlarged and tender and religious nature shared every onward impulse of his time." Above all Channing's high qualities, wrote Fuller, was the great honor he gave women by regarding them "as souls, each of which had a destiny of its own, incalculable to other minds, and whose leading it must follow, guided by the light of a private

[24] Emerson, *Essays*, 25.   [25] Emerson, *Essays*, 449, 696.
[26] John Snyder, *Prospects of Power* (Lexington, KY: University Press of Kentucky, 1991), 195.
[27] Snyder, *Prospects of Power*, 196.

conscience.... The young and unknown, the woman and the child, all felt themselves regarded with an infinite expectation," which demanded of them only what Channing called "great truths."[28] Fuller's own self-trust enabled her to argue openly with Emerson, her friend and interlocutor, whose eponymous 1840 essay offered "Self-Reliance" as the self-constituting ground for both essay and essayist: "I would write on the lintels of the door-post, *Whim*."[29] But Fuller, as a woman, found this door closed – a weakness (from Emerson's perspective) that she leveraged into a strength. Women, asserts Fuller, are never isolates, but always relationally constituted. The key to recovering women's full humanity is to resist the relations forced upon her as daughter or wife and create a space of deliberation from which she may freely choose her relations herself: "We would have every arbitrary barrier thrown down. We would have every path laid open to woman as freely as to man" – including the path of equal partnership, should that be her choice.[30]

Fuller's concept of relationality ran deeper than gender politics, too: In a *Dial* essay on literary criticism, she argued that the true, or "comprehensive," literary critic must "enter into the nature of another being and judge his work by its own law," "walk around the work ... stand above it ... uplift it, and try its weight." Only then is he worthy "to judge it."[31] In this way, her argument with Emerson presses the essay into a form of historical evaluation – instead of jettisoning history, like Emerson, Fuller leans into it: Who we are, as women, becomes legible only by reading who have we been through history, and who are we today in our many multifarious and individual forms. Fuller's respect for the uniqueness of each individual being is closer to the natural historian's love of the particular than to Emerson's embrace of the abstract whole. That is, for Fuller, history is not nullified but constitutive; the other is not transparentized, but gathered and dignified: "Woman, self-centred, would never be absorbed by any relation; it would be only an experience to her as to a man." And what, then, shall we call this new woman? The answer awaits her, for "she herself must teach us to give her the fitting name."[32]

Fuller experimented with the essay form in her first book, *Summer on the Lakes* (1844), a loosely structured narrative of her excursion through the Great Lakes region that combined descriptive reportage and literary reviews with

---

28 Margaret Fuller, "The Great Lawsuit. Man versus Men. Woman versus Women," in Myerson, *Transcendentalism*, 383–427, 416–17.
29 Emerson, *Essays*, 262.   30 Fuller, "Great Lawsuit," 394.
31 Margaret Fuller, "Essay on Critics," *Dial* 1, no. 1 (July 1840): 6–7.
32 Margaret Fuller, "Great Lawsuit," 422.

essayistic reflections. Reviewers found her lack of method incoherent, but Thoreau used it as the model for his own first book, *A Week on the Concord and Merrimack Rivers* (1849). Fuller's emphasis on becoming the "comprehensive" critic meant going forth into the world, weighing it sympathetically, and bringing back to the reader whatever one saw and felt, transmuted through the mind of the writer. She continued to explore her writerly method as a feature reporter for the *New-York Tribune*, and then as America's first wartime foreign correspondent, writing dispatches from Italy during the Revolution of 1848. In Fuller, the essay mutates into nonfiction journalism. Tragically, her meteoric career was cut short in 1850, when the ship returning her to America was wrecked off the shore of Fire Island, killing her along with her husband and their son. Lost in the wreckage was her manuscript history of the Italian Revolution, whose publication she planned to oversee in person – not trusting another to be true to the "great truth" she had to tell the world.

The most important writerly advice Thoreau ever received came from Margaret Fuller: Don't say "too constantly of nature She is mine," she warned him; "She is not yours till you have been more hers."[33] Fuller's sympathetic yet critical insights gave Thoreau the counterbalance he needed to break open Emerson's dynamic self-enclosure, enabling him, drawn as he was to the nonhuman world, not to see it as a cipher of spirit, but to embrace it as spirit's living embodiment – an embrace that had to be mutual. The Thoreau who first built his house at Walden Pond imagined nature as a stage for spiritual epiphany, but his very act of building swiftly transformed their relationship, as the wild, uncontrolled, uncontainable life of the land interpenetrated both house and self, remaking Thoreau in an ongoing process of regeneration. This, of course, is a sacramental vision, a conversion to nature that enacts the same incarnational, Eucharistic ceremony that Emerson had begun his mature career by rejecting. In this opening of attention to life by communion was born the classic American nature essay, which, as Mark Tredinnick observes, engages all that goes beyond yet contains the human world: "It writes ecologies, not just societies." Where theory asserts, in the Emersonian way, that it is men and women who make meaning in the world, "nature writing senses that it is the land that gives rise to all meaning."[34]

Thus in Thoreau, the Transcendentalist essay's source in the American sermon returns, through nature, to the realm of the sacred, not via traditional

---

33 Thoreau, *Correspondence*, 94.
34 Mark Tredinnick, *The Land's Wild Music* (San Antonio, TX: Trinity University Press, 2005), 23, 25.

Christianity (which Thoreau folds into pre-Christian, Buddhist, and Hindu scriptures), but through what Buell calls "the American environmental imagination," or what Tredinnick names the "ecological imagination"[35] – a participatory model closer to Montaigne (whom Thoreau never cites) than to Emerson. Thoreau developed his own distinctive voice while at Walden Pond, steeped in wind, weather, and birdsong: The first step was his excursion away from the human. But the second was his turn back to writing: Thoreau spent his first months at the Pond studying the essays of Thomas Carlyle, who showed Thoreau how to release his voice from the hold of Harvard's stilted academic formalism, and infuse it with extravagant hyperbole, rhapsodic lyricism, and a Yankee drollery he honed by delivering his rough drafts in lecture form.[36] Finally, and most distinctively, Thoreau gained authority for his emergent voice by integrating into it what Buell calls a "dual accountability to matter and to discursive mentation," a willingness to give the ultimate authority not to the mind, not even to the science, but to the world "out there" – the world beyond the human, in which failure or inaccuracy threatens not just the quality of the prose, but the possibility of survival.[37] Thoreau's narrative structure – the outward quest beyond the horizon of the known, the return bearing the gift of language – works by engaging the reader as a proxy participant in the journey, thus literally bringing the story home to us. In this way, though Thoreau's New England nature may resemble nothing in your own world, to the degree that your world resonates with Thoreau's, the ceremony enacted by his sacred journey will move you, too, to a higher awareness – not by rendering the observed details of pond or loon or Irish workers as bare facts, or symbols of some higher truth, but as beacons by which we can navigate our shared, but mutually inaccessible, mind-worlds. What, this writing asks, is it like where you stand? If here is my Walden, then where might yours be?

The act of coming to voice, then, is also an act of convocation, assembling those who are susceptible to that voice. This bonding across duality – the inner self, the outer otherworld – is fundamental to the genre called "nature writing," which attempts to triangulate across minds by sharing a narrative that orients us, standing together, not to look into each other's eyes but to look, together, out on the land. This is the I/eye that Scott Russell Sanders

---

35 Buell, *Environmental Imagination*, 2; Tredinnick, *Land's Wild Music*, 7.
36 For more on the importance of Thoreau's study of Carlyle while at Walden Pond, see Laura Dassow Walls, *Henry David Thoreau: A Life* (Chicago: University of Chicago Press, 2017), 243–44.
37 Buell, *Environmental Imagination*, 92–94, 108.

seeks to open in his essay "The Singular First Person": "I choose to write about my experience not because it is mine, but because it seems to me a door through which others might pass." It is also why Barry Lopez holds that truth cannot be stated, only evoked: "Neither can truth be reduced to aphorisms or formulas. It is something alive and unpronounceable. Story creates an atmosphere in which it becomes discernible as a pattern," a pattern so intricate and complex that even the writer cannot contain it.[38]

A voice, weighing the world and offering its deliberations to us: We are back to the essay's origins in Montaigne. Is it true, as Tredinnick suggests, that nature writing "carried on what Montaigne had begun"?[39] I am inclined to agree, for that would put the Transcendentalist essay at the heart of the American essay writ large, from Emerson's expansive mental gymnastics, to Fuller's language of self-realization, to Thoreau's quest for meaning in nonhuman nature in which writing becomes a middle voice, tending to the wild, not entirely humanized, yet embedded in Emersonian paradoxes of seduction and resistance. In their train come so many more: John Muir, Aldo Leopold, Loren Eiseley, Rachel Carson, Scott Russell Sanders, Annie Dillard, Barry Lopez, Rebecca Solnit – voices that don't reflect on the world as given, but that ask what worlds the practice of the essay might materialize, and ask, with Lopez, how walking this horizon between the human and the wider world can turn boundaries into possibilities.

---

38 Scott Russell Sanders, "The Singular First Person," *Sewanee Review* 96, no. 4 (Fall 1988): 667; Barry Lopez, "Landscape and Narrative," in *Crossing Open Ground* (New York: Charles Scribner's Sons, 1988), 69; Annie Dillard, *Living by Fiction* (New York: Harper Perennial, 1988), 105.
39 Tredinnick, *Land's Wild Music*, 4.

6

Old World Shadows in the New: Europe and the Nineteenth-Century American Essay

PHILIP COLEMAN

Europe as Shadow

"The identity of 'Europe' has always been uncertain and imprecise," the historian and political scientist Anthony Pagden has written, describing it as "a source of pride for some and hatred and contempt for others."[1] The point applies very well to perceptions and constructions of the continent among nineteenth-century American essayists, for whom "Europe" represented both a goad and a guide, a source of deep critical conflict and, at the same time, a model of enduring cultural sustenance. These opposing views were often held at the same time and expressed in the same essay. In "The Author's Account of Himself" in *The Sketch Book of Geoffrey Crayon, Gent.* (1819–20), Washington Irving (1783–1859) imagined a "great man of Europe ... as superior to a great man of America, as a peak of the Alps to a highland of the Hudson."[2] Irving wanted to distinguish himself as an "American" man of letters in *The Sketch Book*, as an author whom readers in England or Germany would be willing to read and enjoy, but his essays are full of doubt and self-deprecation. He may celebrate "the charms of nature" that have been "prodigally lavished" on his own country and insist that "never need an American look beyond his own country for the sublime and beautiful of natural scenery."[3] However, he also argues that "Europe held forth all the

---

[1] Anthony Pagden, ed., *The Idea of Europe: From Antiquity to the European Union* (Washington, DC, and Cambridge, UK: Woodrow Wilson Center Press and Cambridge University Press, 2002), 33.

[2] Washington Irving, "The Author's Account of Himself," in *The Sketch Book of Geoffrey Crayon, Gent.*, in *Washington Irving: History, Tales and Sketches*, ed. James W. Tuttleton (New York: Library of America, 1983), 743–45, 744.

[3] Irving, "Author's Account," 744.

charms of storied and poetical association" for him as a young man: "My native country was full of youthful promise; Europe was rich in the accumulated treasures of age."[4]

Irving's *Sketch Book* contains some of the clearest examples of essays in which Europe's shadow over the United States is presented as a source of concern for the nineteenth-century American writer. The point is reinforced in "English Writers on America," where he writes that it "is with feelings of deep regret that I observe the literary animosity daily growing up between England and America."[5] For Irving, the relationship between Europe and the United States was far from straightforward, but neither "Europe" nor "America" had clear meanings either. One of the aims of *The Sketch Book* was to explore and explain each culture to the other through a series of essays and tales, but Irving was also writing at a time when American literary culture was in its infancy. What we call "Europe" in the twenty-first century was a very different place and idea in the 1800s. However, its presence is palpable not just in Irving's writings but as a major theme in the work of many of the most significant American essayists of the long nineteenth century.

In his poem "Europe, The 72d and 73d Years of These States," first published in 1850, Walt Whitman (1819–1892) writes of "a shape, / Vague as the night, draped interminably, head, front and form, in scarlet folds, / Whose face and eyes none may see . . . ."[6] The poem is a reflection on the uprisings that swept across Europe in 1848, and the poet sympathizes with the fallen rebels whom he identifies with the casualties of the colonial wars in America seven decades earlier. Whitman describes a powerful vision of "Europe" as site of revolutionary conflict where "the ferocity of kings" constantly threatens democracy.[7] There are other writers, however, for whom the institutions of Europe are often presented as exemplary in political and cultural terms, and whose work gives voice to a kind of Europhilic nostalgia that tempers Whitman's democratic radicalism and American exceptionalism.[8] In his book-length essay on Nathaniel Hawthorne (1804–1864), first published in 1879, for example, Henry

---

4 Irving, "Author's Account," 744.
5 Irving, "English Writers on America," in *Sketch Book*, 786–94, 786.
6 Walt Whitman, "Europe, The 72d and 73d Years of These States," in *Leaves of Grass and Other Writings*, ed. Michael Moon (New York and London: W. W. Norton, 2002), 223–25, 224.
7 Whitman, "Europe," 224.
8 For an account of Whitman (and other nineteenth-century American writers) and exceptionalism, see Deborah L. Madsen, *American Exceptionalism* (Edinburgh: Edinburgh University Press, 1998), 70–99.

James (1843–1916) bemoaned the fact that so many aspects of English culture are absent from American life:

> No State, in the European sense of the word, and indeed barely a specific national name. No sovereign, no court, no personal loyalty, no aristocracy, no church, no clergy, no army, no diplomatic service, no country gentlemen, no palaces, no castles, nor manors, nor old country-houses, nor parsonages, nor thatched cottages nor ivied ruins; no cathedrals, nor abbeys, nor little Norman churches; no great Universities nor public schools – no Oxford, nor Eton, nor Harrow; no literature, no novels, no museums, no pictures, no political society, no sporting class – no Epsom nor Ascot![9]

While he goes on to grant that writers in the United States have the "national gift" of "American humour," James nonetheless presents England – and the Old World more broadly – as a cultural and historical backdrop against which the United States is marked by a profound and pervasive sense of absence and "terrible denudation."[10]

Margaret Fuller (1810–1850), in a verse epigraph to *Summer on the Lakes* (1843), describes "Summer days of busy leisure, / Long summer days of dear-bought pleasure," but her speaker's meditations are troubled by "shadows" that "pass" over her "new-world":

> Had the scholar means to tell
> How grew the vine of bitter-sweet,
> What made the path for truant feet,
> Winter nights would quickly pass,
> Gazing on the magic glass
> O'er which the new-world shadows pass . . . .[11]

What are these "shadows"? In a sense, they represent all that the "scholar" – an Emersonian construct so central to the development of the essay and the activity of essaying in the United States in the nineteenth century[12] – must get beyond before they can "tell" the truth of America's sense of its distinctive, exceptional "magic." Fuller, like Ralph Waldo Emerson (1803–1882), Henry David Thoreau (1817–1862), and others at midcentury, needed to find a way to

---

9 Interestingly, James's book on Hawthorne, which he describes in the opening sentence as a "critical essay," was published as part of a series entitled "English Men of Letters." See Henry James, *Hawthorne* (London: Macmillan, 1879), 1, 44.
10 James, *Hawthorne*, 44.
11 Margaret Fuller, *Summer on the Lakes, during 1843*, in *The Portable Margaret Fuller*, ed. Mary Kelley (New York: Viking, 1994), 69–227, 70.
12 See Ralph Waldo Emerson, "The American Scholar," in *Emerson's Prose and Poetry*, ed. Joel Porte and Saundra Morris (New York: W. W. Norton, 2001), 56–69.

overcome the charms of the "courtly muses of Europe" before they would be able to write in a voice that was entirely their own.[13] In the hands of these writers, the essay became a space where the idea of Europe as an overwhelming source of cultural pressure could be resisted. Through their essaying, they signaled new alternatives for American culture to the imported cultural examples from the Old World. In *The Sketch Book*, Irving wrote that Americans "are a young people, necessarily an imitative one, and must take our examples and models, in a great degree, from the existing nations of Europe."[14] It was not long, however, before American writers started to reject this view to create new possibilities for literary expression not just in poetry and fiction, in the examples of Whitman, Nathaniel Hawthorne, and Herman Melville (1819–1891), for example, but also within the field of the essay. The writers considered here made new claims for the essay's place in the nineteenth-century creation of distinctly American versions of traditional European genres.

If Europe overshadows a great deal of American literary and cultural production in the first half of the nineteenth century, then, the place of the essay in helping the nation's writers develop strategies to reject European influence should not be underestimated. In what follows, I survey the work of several key nineteenth-century American authors in a way that reinforces this point, beginning with the Early National Period (1789–1830) before moving on to some of the central players in the American Renaissance.[15] I then consider the ways that certain American essayists engaged with the idea of Europe in the second half of the nineteenth century, revealing the theme's complexity and recurring significance into the twentieth century and beyond. In *The Communist Manifesto* (1848), Karl Marx and Friedrich Engels wrote that a "spectre is haunting Europe – the spectre of Communism."[16] For the nineteenth-century American essayists discussed here, many of whom were also prolific authors in other forms, it was "Europe" itself that often

---

13 Emerson, "American Scholar," 68.   14 Irving, "English Writers," 792.
15 The term "American Renaissance" is used here, but it is important to note the complexity of its emergence as a literary historical concept and construct. See Christopher N. Phillips, "Introduction: The Very Idea of an American Renaissance," in *The Cambridge Companion to the Literature of the American Renaissance*, ed. Christopher N. Phillips (Cambridge, UK: Cambridge University Press, 2018): 1–10.
16 Karl Marx and Friedrich Engels, *The Communist Manifesto*, trans. Samuel Moore (London: Penguin Books, 2015). If the "spectre of Communism" is difficult to discern in the nineteenth-century American essay, it is certainly present in the work of several important twentieth-century American essayists, including Richard Wright and James Baldwin.

overshadowed and, indeed, threatened their creative and cultural efforts. The work they did to exorcise the European specter, however, was central in preparing the ground for those who came after them not just in the field of the essay but across the range of American literary and cultural production.

The Early National Period

One of the most immediately recognizable things about Irving's essays and tales is the author's fondness for name-play. Writing in the guise of Diedrich Knickerbocker – more persona than pseudonym – he published *A History of New York* in 1809, but as early as 1802 he was publishing in New York's *Morning Chronicle* under the name "Jonathan Oldstyle, Gent." The character of Knickerbocker was reprised in 1819 in *The Sketch Book of Geoffrey Crayon, Gent.*, initially in periodical installments and then in two volumes in 1820 by the London publisher John Miller. *The Sketch Book* made Irving's name. On the strength of it, he became friendly with some of the most significant literary luminaries of the time, but the fictional names it popularized, including Crayon, Knickerbocker, and others such as Ichabod Crane and Rip Van Winkle, revealed Irving's cultural and artistic sense of the important connections and tensions that persisted in the United States throughout the early decades of the nineteenth century. While there is something delightfully playful about Irving's work, almost all of his earliest creations dwell between the Old World and the New. Neither European nor American exactly, they are caught, like Rip Van Winkle, on a threshold of uncertainty that reflects Irving's conflicted feelings about how best to handle the specter of Europe that overshadowed his emergence as "the first American man of letters with an international reputation."[17]

Irving's approach can often appear lighthearted, and his work influenced the later genteel and Fireside writers of the nineteenth century.[18] However, his essaying on the topics of European and, specifically, English identity also sought to challenge the criticisms of Sydney Smith (1771–1845) and others regarding the cultural inferiority of the United States in the Early National Period. As Smith famously put it in 1820, "In the four quarters of the globe, who reads an American book? or goes to an American play? or looks at an

---

17 The description is James W. Tuttleton's, in his edition of Irving's *History, Tales and Sketches*, 1101.
18 Ned Stuckey-French affirms Irving's importance (over Emerson) in *The American Essay in the American Century* (Columbia, MO: University of Missouri Press, 2011), 24–30.

American picture or statue?"[19] After the publication of Irving's *Sketch Book*, Smith had his answer in the form of a collection largely made up of essays on aspects of popular life and lore on both sides of the Atlantic. Irving's essaying in *The Sketch Book* succeeded in providing entertainment for the literate public, but it also made an important cultural statement that marked the arrival of the new nation's first literary celebrity, one who sought to expose the follies and shortcomings of transatlantic rivalry through humor and satire. Unlike some later authors, Irving is not entirely dismissive of European examples; on the contrary, his work is positively Europhilic in its fond recollections and descriptions of the customs of the Old World. At the same time, his depictions of American landscape and character convey an awakening sense of cultural distinctiveness in the United States that is matched in the creation of a style and voice that is often jocular and informal – exactly what one might expect from narrators named Oldstyle, Knickerbocker, and Crayon.

Throughout the texts gathered in *The Sketch Book*, there is also an interest in the supernatural that is rooted in a sense of the persistence of Europe in the United States in the early decades of the nation's formation. The nightly visit of the headless horseman in "The Legend of Sleepy Hollow," on this reading, represents the return of the European repressed, a community's inability to fully forget the trauma of the recent Revolutionary War.[20] "The Legend of Sleepy Hollow" offers an important counterpoint to Irving's more sentimental musings on England in essays such as "The County Church," "The Inn Kitchen," "Westminster Abbey," and the several pieces on Christmas that have been seasonal favorites since they first appeared in print. Irving's *Sketch Book* therefore establishes the basis for a kind of literary *entente cordiale* between the United States and Europe in the so-called Era of Good Feelings, but the fear of Europe, coupled with the "animosity" Irving perceived in contemporary British critical responses to American writers, is not laid to rest here. It persists, for example, in the work of Edgar Allan Poe (1809–1849).

---

19 See Smith's review of Adam Seybert's Statistical Annals of the United States of America (1818) collected in Sydney Smith, *The Works of the Rev. Sydney Smith* (New York: Edward G. Taylor, 1844), 93–96.
20 "The Legend of Sleepy Hollow" is a well-known tale, but it was presented by Irving as a historical "paper"; in a way, it is a work of fiction passing as nonfiction, a short story written in the margins of a research essay.

Poe also used the essay to challenge the view that American literary culture was inferior to its European counterpart. He puts it as follows in "Letter to B—" (1836):

> You are aware of the great barrier in the path of an American writer. He is read, if at all, in preference to the combined and established wit of the world. I say established; for it is with literature as with law or empire – an established name is an estate in tenure, or a throne in possession. Besides, one might suppose that books, like their authors, improve by travel – their having crossed the sea is, with us, so great a distinction. Our antiquaries abandon time for distance; our very fops glance from the binding to the bottom of the title-page, where the mystic characters which spell London, Paris, or Genoa, are precisely so many letters of recommendation.[21]

In light of Poe's comment, the fact that Irving's *Sketch Book* was first published in London may have played a role in vouchsafing its early commercial success. Poe's essay, however, is a reminder that the problem of transatlantic cultural prejudice persisted well into the nineteenth century. In his preface to *Tales of the Grotesque and Arabesque* (1840), he famously stated that "terror is not of Germany, but of the soul," suggesting that his work's ostensibly European settings were not to be confused with any particular place but were the product, rather, of his imagination.[22] While this claim is worth keeping in mind in relation to his tales, Poe shows a great deal of interest in contemporary European (mainly British) culture and ideas in his essays, from the poems of Elizabeth Barrett Browning to the novels of Charles Dickens. This complicates our understanding of Poe's engagement with Europe, revealing a critical sensibility that was alert to the latest developments in literature on both sides of the Atlantic, but which also sought to develop and promote the idea of originality as an essential concept in relation to his own work and that of other American writers. In his best-known essays, including "The Philosophy of Composition" (1846) and "The Poetic Principle" (published posthumously in 1850), as well his critical responses to the work of Hawthorne (1842, 1846) and other contemporaries in the United States, Poe affirms the importance of originality as a key driver in American literary and cultural progress in the early decades of the nineteenth century.[23] In the first of his pieces on

---

21 Edgar Allan Poe, "Letter to B—," in *Edgar Allan Poe: Essays and Reviews*, ed. G. R. Thompson (New York: Library of America, 1984), 5–12, 5.
22 Edgar Allan Poe, "Preface," in *Edgar Allan Poe: Poetry and Tales*, ed. Patrick F. Quinn (New York: Library of America, 1984), 129–30, 129.
23 Poe's separate reviews of Hawthorne's *Twice-Told Tales* (1842) and *Mosses from an Old Manse* (1846) were published together under the title "Hawthorne" in *Godey's Lady's Book* (1847). See Edgar Allan Poe, "Nathaniel Hawthorne," in *The Selected Writings of*

Hawthorne, he says that American culture has seen "no . . . tales of high merit" apart from Irving's "Tales of a Traveller" – collected in *Tales of a Traveller, by Geoffrey Crayon, Gent.* (1824), a sequel to the earlier *Sketch Book* – but it seems that Poe was more deeply troubled by the problem of European influence than was Irving, who often took a more magnanimous view.[24] Between them, however, their work represents important early nineteenth-century responses to the problem of how to negotiate the shadow of Europe by writers in the United States and, in this regard, they helped to prepare the way for what would become known as the American Renaissance.[25]

Essaying the American Renaissance

It is not possible to discuss the American Renaissance without acknowledging the central place of essayists to its formation: Ralph Waldo Emerson, in particular, closely followed by Margaret Fuller and Henry David Thoreau, but even those writers who are best known for their work in fiction or poetry, such as Herman Melville and Walt Whitman, made important contributions to the genre. Melville's essay on Hawthorne's *Mosses from an Old Manse* (1846), "Hawthorne and His Mosses" (1850), is an essayistic masterpiece that combines critical insight with revealing contextual detail.[26] Likewise, Whitman's "Preface" to the 1855 edition of *Leaves of Grass* may be read as an important nineteenth-century experiment in the formal and syntactical possibilities available to the essayist, and it was included in Brander Matthews's *Oxford Book of the American Essay* (1914) as an example of what had been achieved by American essayists in the nineteenth century.[27] Emerson, however, is the central figure in the development of the American essay in the nineteenth century. His work raised the stakes for future generations of essayists not only in terms of their philosophical

---

Edgar Allan Poe, ed. G. R. Thompson (New York: W. W. Norton, 2004): 685–93. Poe's essays on nineteenth-century American literature include pieces on Henry Wadsworth Longfellow, James Russell Lowell, Walt Whitman, and many others.

24 Edgar Allan Poe, "Nathaniel Hawthorne" (1842), in Thompson, *Edgar Allan Poe: Essays and Reviews*, 568–88, 568.

25 As Russell Sbriglia has shown, Poe's position in relation to the American Renaissance is complicated and he has often been excluded from studies of the Renaissance. See Russell Sbriglia, "The Trouble with the Gothic: Poe, Lippard, and the Poetics of Critique," in Phillips, *The Cambridge Companion to the Literature of the American Renaissance*, 38–51.

26 Herman Melville, "Hawthorne and His Mosses," in *Nathaniel Hawthorne's Tales*, ed. James McIntosh (New York: W. W. Norton., 1987), 337–50.

27 See Walt Whitman, "Preface to 'Leaves of Grass,'" in *The Oxford Book of American Essays*, ed. Brander Matthews (New York: Oxford University Press, 1914), 194–212.

expansiveness but also for the way that they complicate traditional ideas about the difference between poetry and prose. In a letter to Lydia Jackson in 1835, Emerson wrote:

> Under this morning's severe but beautiful light I thought dear friend that hardly should I get away from Concord. I must win you to love it. I am born a poet, of a low class without doubt yet a poet. That is my nature & vocation. My singing be sure is very "husky," & is for the most part in prose. Still am I a poet in the sense of a perceiver & dear lover of the harmonies that are in the soul & in matter, & specially in the correspondence between these & those.[28]

Emerson's insistence on the poetic character of his prose is carried over into his essays, where he developed forms of essaying the American self that inspired the aesthetic and ideological work for which several of his younger contemporaries, including Whitman, Thoreau, and Fuller, became known and celebrated. This work was centered on the question of what it would mean for American writers to strike out on their own: to learn "to walk on [their] own feet ... work with [their] own hands [and] speak [their] own minds," as Emerson put it in "The American Scholar" (1837).[29]

"The American Scholar" was delivered as a lecture before the Phi Beta Kappa Society at Harvard in 1837, and it reminds us of the important connection between speech and the written word in Emerson's essays.[30] Many early readers of his works first encountered them in the lecture hall, and his earlier career as a Unitarian pastor informed his sense of the essay as a space for the trialing of ideas, where he could explore a wide range of topics from many different, often conflicting perspectives. This clearly had an impact on Whitman, for whom the idea of embracing multiplicity would become a central aspect of his poetic (and political) reinvention of the American self in the nineteenth century, but it also informed the thought and essay-writing practice of Henry David Thoreau. Thoreau was present when Emerson delivered his "American Scholar" address at Harvard in 1837 and, like Whitman, he was influenced deeply by the older figure's ideas. In the work of Thoreau, Emerson's celebration of the local American environment was taken to a new level in pieces such as "Autumnal Tints" (1862),

---

28 Ralph Waldo Emerson, letter to Lydia Jackson, 1 February 1835, in Porte and Morris, *Emerson's Prose and Poetry*, 540–41.
29 Ralph Waldo Emerson, "The American Scholar," in Porte and Morris, *Emerson's Poetry and Prose*, 69.
30 For a consideration of the importance of Emerson's sermons to his other work as a writer, see Wesley T. Mott, *"The Strains of Eloquence": Emerson and His Sermons* (University Park, PA: Pennsylvania State University Press, 1988).

where he wrote, "Europeans coming to America are surprised by the brilliancy of our autumnal foliage. There is no account of such a phenomenon in English poetry, because the trees acquire but few bright colors there.... The autumnal change of our woods has not made a deep impression on our poetry yet. October has hardly tinged our poetry."[31] Thoreau's appreciation of the American landscape aligns with Emerson's sense of the inferiority of European examples when compared with native phenomena on the other side of the Atlantic.

For Thoreau, as for Emerson, the problem of how to get out from under the shadow of Europe necessitated a new envisioning of American space that was to be accompanied by a wholesale reimagining of language and the forms of literary expression by the nation's writers. He frames it as follows in "Autumnal Tints":

> Shall the names of so many of our colors continue to be derived from those of obscure foreign localities, as Naples yellow, Prussian blue, raw Sienna, burnt Umber, Gamboge? – (surely the Tyrian purple must have faded by this time), – or from comparatively trivial articles of commerce, – chocolate, lemon, coffee, cinnamon, claret? – (shall we compare our Hickory to a lemon, or a lemon to a Hickory?) – or from ores and oxides which few ever see? Shall we so often, when describing to our neighbors the color of something we have seen, refer them, not to some natural object in our neighborhood, but perchance to a bit of earth fetched from the other side of the planet, which possibly they may find at the apothecary's, but which probably neither they nor we ever saw? Have we not an *earth* under our feet, – ay, and a sky over our heads? ... I do not see why, since America and her autumn woods have been discovered, our leaves should not compete with the precious stones in giving names to colors; and, indeed, I believe that in course of time the names of some of our trees and shrubs, as well as flowers, will get into our popular chromatic nomenclature.[32]

Thoreau's emphasis on the third-person plural in this passage – "our leaves," "our trees and shrubs" – is crucial to his ideological project. What he is proposing, taking his cue from Emerson, is nothing less than a radical reimagination of American identity; his essays insist that the United States be represented and spoken about henceforth in a language unique to the literal ground of the nation's own historical and cultural experience. The essay is used by these writers as a space where formal and thematic questions

---

31 Henry David Thoreau, "Autumnal Tints," in *Collected Essays and Poems*, ed. Elizabeth Hall Witherell (New York: Library of America, 2001), 367–95, 367.
32 Thoreau, "Autumnal Tints," 384.

can be teased out and explored, but their work also anticipates the aesthetic procedures that are so important to the work of Whitman, for example, and Herman Melville.[33]

Even when they were arguing for greater literary and cultural independence, however, the Old World was always in view, and it often afforded lines of direct engagement and influence for writers of the American Renaissance such as Emerson and Thoreau. This is clearly the case with Emerson, whose volume *Representative Men* (1849), for example, includes no Americans.[34] His essay on Montaigne in that volume, indeed, establishes an important sense of continuity between his own work as an essayist and that of his French precursor, but it ends with a clear reference to the Transcendentalist context within which Emerson was operating in the 1840s: "Let a man learn to look for the permanent in the mutable and fleeting . . . let him learn that he is here not to work, but to be worked upon, and that, though abyss open under abyss, and opinion displace opinion, all are at last contained in the eternal Cause."[35] In Emerson, in other words, we find Europe acknowledged in ways that are not always combative or dismissive, but are in fact essential to the new discoveries and possibilities that he believed were possible for the American writer. It could even be said that Emerson's essaying of American exceptionalism began in Europe: His time there in the early 1830s was formative and led to the publication of *Nature* (1836), which was followed by major pieces such as "The American Scholar" (1837) and "Self-Reliance" (included in *Essays: First Series* in 1841). Emerson's insistence on the importance of originality to the development of American culture in these essays is prompted by a desire to sever ties with the Old World, certainly, but his work draws sustenance from Europe, too. Whitman gave voice to this idea in the "Preface" to *Leaves of Grass* (1855), and it is a theme that was also developed by Margaret Fuller in her essays.[36]

---

33 The importance of Emerson's essays to the development of Whitman's poetics is widely acknowledged, but the significance of the essay as a form – and essaying as a distinct mode of literary inquiry – can also be discerned in works of fiction such as Melville's *Moby-Dick* (1851).
34 Emerson's "Representative Men" are Plato, Emanuel Swedenborg, Michel de Montaigne, William Shakespeare, Napoléon Bonaparte, and Johann Wolfgang von Goethe.
35 Ralph Waldo Emerson, "Montaigne, or the Skeptic," in Porte and Morris, *Emerson's Prose and Poetry*, 234–46, 247.
36 In the "Preface" to *Leaves of Grass* (1855), Whitman says that "America does not repel the past or what it has produced under its forms or amid other politics or the idea of castes or the old religions . . . accepts the lesson with calmness." See Walt Whitman, "Preface 1855," in *Leaves of Grass and Other Writings*, ed. Michael Moon (New York: W. W. Norton, 2002), 616–35, 616.

In a review of Emerson's *Essays: Second Series* published in 1844, Fuller anticipates that his works "will lead to great and complete poems – somewhere."[37] In other words, she recognizes a propaedeutic impulse that is evident throughout Emerson's essays and that accounts for their generative influence throughout subsequent American writing.[38] However, Fuller also acknowledges that Americans up to this point in their history have been "necessarily occupied in these first stages by bringing out the material resources of the land" and that they have "not generally been prepared by early training for the enjoyment of books that require attention and reflection," but her own contributions to the development of American literary culture are of great importance especially with regard to the emergence of the essay as a significant mode of literary and cultural expression.[39] Her *New-York Daily Tribune* columns and dispatches made an enormous contribution to the development of American literary culture in the nineteenth century not just because of the quality of the essays in themselves, but also in terms of the way that they addressed the major political and social questions of the day, from the idea of cultural independence to poverty, the role of women in society, and the evils of slavery. "American Literature: Its Position in the Present Time, and Prospects for the Future," collected in her *Papers on Literature and Art* (1846), offers one of the most succinct accounts we have of the dilemma facing the American writer in the middle decades of the nineteenth century in terms of how to engage with the shadow of Europe. "Some thinkers may object to this essay," she begins, "that we are about to write of that which has, as yet, no existence":

> For it does not follow because many books are written by persons born in America that there exists an American literature. Books which imitate or represent the thoughts and life of Europe do not constitute an American literature. Before such can exist, an original idea must animate this nation and fresh currents of life must call into life fresh thoughts along its shores.[40]

Fuller draws attention to writers she believes are worth noting among her contemporaries. Emerson – the "Sage of Concord" – is preeminent, but she is not afraid to question the success of some she believes were overpraised by

---

37 Margaret Fuller, "Emerson's Essays: Second Series [December 7, 1844]," in *Portable Margaret Fuller*, ed. Mary Kelley (New York: Viking, 1994), 364–70, 370.
38 Laurence Buell explores this idea in detail in *Emerson* (Cambridge, MA: The Belknap Press of Harvard University Press, 2003), 142–57.
39 Fuller, "Emerson's Essays," 364.
40 Margaret Fuller, "American Literature: Its Position in the Present Time, and Prospects for the Future," in *Margaret Fuller: Essays on American Life and Letters*, ed. Joel Myerson (Oxford: Rowman and Littlefield., 2003), 381.

earlier readers.[41] Of Irving, for example, she observes that he "has his niche," while "[t]he first enthusiasm about [James Fenimore] Cooper having subsided," she says, "we remember more his faults than his merits."[42]

Notwithstanding her acknowledgment of these and other literary success stories in the literature of the early Republic, however, Fuller argues that true literary and cultural independence will not be achieved by the United States "until the fusion of races among us is more complete"; until then, she says, "all attempts to construct a national literature must end in abortions like the monster of Frankenstein, things with forms, and the instincts of forms, but soulless, and therefore revolting."[43] The frankness of Fuller's language is a far cry from the genteel overtures toward English writers made by Irving a few decades earlier, but it is a sign, too, that by the middle decades of the nineteenth century the cultural weather was changing in the United States. Fuller's essays express real impatience with the lack of literary and cultural progress in the nation, but they also recognize the dark underbelly of American democracy, especially where the questions of race, gender, and class were concerned. In essays such as "What fits a Man to be a Voter?" and "Mistress of herself, though china fall," she articulates a kind of radicalism that is closer to the work of Frederick Douglass (c. 1817–1895), whose work and cause she also championed, than the more abstract Emerson. While she is very much associated with the writers of what has also been called the "New England" Renaissance (Emerson and Thoreau in particular), the political work of Fuller's essays anticipates many of the important social and cultural changes that would occur in the United States in the second half of the nineteenth century and after.

European Returns

When Margaret Fuller died in 1850, while on a return trip from Europe to the United States, Emerson wrote in his journal that he had "lost in her [his] audience."[44] For a number of years before her death, Fuller lived in Italy and England, where she worked as the first female foreign correspondent for the *New-York Daily Tribune*. Her sense of Europe, then, especially in her later writings, was informed by the experience of living there, and she is an

---

41 Fuller uses this epithet to describe Emerson in the same essay, "American Literature," 386.
42 Fuller, "American Literature," 387.   43 Fuller, "American Literature," 383.
44 Emerson's journal entry is quoted in Porte and Morris, *Emerson's Prose and Poetry*, 372n1.

important nineteenth-century example of the American expatriate writer for whom the Old World provided both context and stimulus for her work's development.[45] In this regard, Fuller's sense of democracy – and the inadequacies of American political institutions, especially in the period before the Civil War (1861–65) – was very much shaped by her encounters with figures such as Giuseppe Mazzini and Giovanni Angelo Ossoli during her time in Italy. (She is said to have married Ossoli, with whom she had a son, in 1848.[46]) Quite apart from these biographical details, however, it can be seen that Fuller found in Europe, and especially in Italy, a model for a more radical form of democratic politics than she had previously encountered in the United States. In this, she may be fruitfully compared with Douglass, whose *Narrative of the Life of Frederick Douglass, an American Slave* (1845) she also promoted in her *New-York Daily Tribune* columns. In the same year that Douglass first traveled to Europe to gain support for the Abolitionist movement (1845), Fuller wrote that "we have never read [a narrative] more simple, true, coherent, and warm with genuine feeling." "It is an excellent piece of writing," she continued, "and on that score prized as a specimen of the powers of the Black Race, which prejudice persists in disputing. We prize highly all evidence of this kind, and it is becoming more abundant."[47] Douglass provided further "evidence" of the kind of writing sought by Fuller in the speeches and lectures he delivered across Britain and Ireland in 1845 and 1846, many of which were later published as essays in Abolitionist periodicals in the United States as well as in publications sympathetic to the cause in Europe.[48]

Europe – and Ireland, in particular – provided a crucial context for the development of Douglass's work in the 1840s.[49] His essays are not preoccupied with the idea of Europe as a cultural shadow or specter, even if some of

---

45 While it is common to think of American modernist writers in an expatriate context – Ezra Pound, Gertrude Stein, Ernest Hemingway, for example – the issue also pertains to studies of earlier periods. For more detailed considerations see, for example, Yvon Bizardel, *The First Expatriates: Americans in Paris during the French Revolution*, trans. June P. Wilson and Cornelia Higginson (New York: Holt, Rinehart and Winston, 1975).
46 As Joan Von Mehren puts it, "The ambiguity of Margaret Fuller's marriage has challenged Fuller's biographers for over 150 years." See Joan Von Mehren, "Margaret Fuller, the Marchese Giovanni Ossoli, and the Marriage Question: Considering the research of Dr Roberto Colzi," *Resources for American Literary Study* 30 (2005): 104–43, 104.
47 Margaret Fuller "Narrative of the Life of Frederick Douglass: An American Slave, Written by Himself [June 10, 1845]," in Kelley, *Portable Margaret Fuller*, 379–81, 379.
48 Examples of Douglass's key essays in this respect range from "What, to the Slave, Is the Fourth of July?" (1852) to "My Escape from Slavery" (1881).
49 See Christine Kinealy, ed., *Frederick Douglass in Ireland* (London: Routledge, 2018).

the cities he visited during his European travels, such as Liverpool, played central roles in the slave trade until well into the nineteenth century. Instead, Douglass's travels in Europe mark the former slave's return to the home of the historical oppressor – an attempt by him to remind European readers of the consequences of decisions taken by traders and merchants on the other side of the Atlantic, and which continued to inform aspects of transatlantic trade and commerce until well into the nineteenth century. At the same time, he sought to make connections between forms of oppression he perceived in Ireland, for example, in relation to the persecution of Roman Catholics, and the situation in the United States for members of the Black American community. In the years following the Civil War and through the decades of so-called Reconstruction, Douglass's essays helped to keep the issue of racism in the United States in the minds of readers at home and abroad, and this was accomplished, in part, through the strategies of identification he established when he first visited Ireland and Great Britain in the 1840s.

The case of Henry James could not be more dissimilar, though he lived through the same decades and helped to establish the so-called "international theme" in late nineteenth- and early twentieth-century American literature. While James does engage to a certain extent with the issue of slavery in his fiction, he never wrote about race in his essays.[50] However, his essays engage extensively with several aspects of European literary culture, and they helped bring the latest developments in British and French fiction and drama, in particular, to the attention of readers in the United States into the early years of the twentieth century. Their popularity is reflected, for example, by the inclusion of James's essay "The Théâtre Français" (1876) in Matthews's *Oxford Book of American Essays*.[51] James's statement that "Mademoiselle Sarah Bernhardt ... is simply, at present, in Paris, one of the great figures of the day" has as much significance in the second decade of the twentieth century, in Matthews's view, as it had for readers nearly forty years earlier.[52] In James's essays, then, whether he is writing about French theater, British towns and cities, or travels on the Continent, Europe appears as a perennially significant presence in the life of the American writer himself, and, given his prominent place in the literature of the nation at the turn of the twentieth

---

50 Elsa Nettels claims that "James wrote no essay on race" though he did engage with the topic in his fiction. See Elsa Nettels, "Henry James and the Idea of Race," *English Studies* 59, no. 1 (1978): 35–47, 35.
51 See Henry James, "The Théâtre Français," in *The Oxford Book of American Essays*, ed. Brander Matthews (New York: Oxford University Press, 1914), 368–93.
52 James, "Théâtre Français," 393.

century, he helped to maintain the European shadow and give it strength long after the writers of the midcentury Renaissance had sought to overcome its influence.

The persistence of the European shadow in late nineteenth-century American cultural life is acknowledged by Agnes Repplier (1855–1950) in her essay "Americanism," which appeared in the *Atlantic* magazine in 1916. There Repplier writes:

> There must be an interpretation of Americanism which will express for all of us a patriotism at once practical and emotional, an understanding of our place in the world and of the work we are best fitted to do in it, a sentiment which we can hold as we hold nothing else – in common, and which will be forever remote from personal solicitude and resentment. Those of us whose memories stretch back over a half a century recall too plainly a certain uneasiness which for years pervaded American politics and American letters, which made us unduly apprehensive, and, as a consequence, unduly sensitive and arrogant.[53]

For Repplier – described by Edward Wagenknecht in 1946 as "our dean of essayists"[54] – the sense of inferiority in relation to Europe that was felt among American writers, as described by Irving in the 1820s, persisted not just into the middle decades of the nineteenth century but well into the next century also. In "Americanism," she calls for a new form of "patriotism" that would not fall foul of the kind of cultural arrogance that many later critics have seen in the work of Whitman, Emerson, and Thoreau.[55] For Repplier, then, as for James and Douglass in very different ways before her, the problem of how to negotiate Europe's persistent return in the American literary imaginary occasioned the production of works that showed distinct signs of cultural maturation among the writers of the United States, but their very different identities as writers were formed in important ways by their awareness of and engagement with European contexts.

One of the most influential articulations of the problem of the European shadow on American literary consciousness by a nineteenth-century American essayist is "Americanism in Literature" (1871) by Thomas Wentworth Higginson

---

53 Agnes Repplier, "Americanism," *Atlantic* (March 1916): 289, www.theatlantic.com/magazine/archive/1916/03/americanism/305935/.
54 Henry Wagenknecht, cited in Nancy Walker and Zita Dresner, eds., *Redressing the Balance: American Women's Literary Humor from Colonial Times to the 1980s* (Jackson, MS: University Press of Mississippi, 1988), 207.
55 For example, Denis Donoghue critiques this aspect of the writers of the American Renaissance, and others, in *The American Classics: A Personal Essay* (New Haven, CT: Yale University Press, 2005).

(1823–1911). Higginson begins by imagining a "voyager from Europe" arriving in the United States who "perceives a difference in the sky above his head."[56] Higginson regrets that American writers have not taken up the challenge of describing and affirming this traveler's sense of "difference." He writes: "It is but a few years since we have dared to be American in even the details and accessories of our literary work; to make our allusions to natural objects real and not conventional; to ignore the nightingale and skylark, and look for the classic and romantic on our own soil."[57] Henry James clearly did not agree with Higginson's position, but the originality and importance of James's achievement is not lessened by its engagements with Europe. Higginson overstates the case, perhaps, when he says that "Americans have hardly begun to think of the details of execution in any art" – the examples of Emerson, Fuller, Douglass, and Thoreau in relation to the essay present a clear challenge to his position.[58] His view was reinforced, however, by another prominent nineteenth-century American man of letters, Edward Everett Hale (1822–1909), in the introduction to his anthology *American Essays* (1902). Reflecting on the work of British essayists from Joseph Addison to Charles Lamb, Hale states:

> Of such essays the literature of our own country has comparatively little. It may be for many reasons. Perhaps Americans, as a nation, are too practical to take pleasure in what might be called intellectual idling; it may be that they feel the necessity of accomplishing something, or, to put the matter in another way, it may be that they have not leisure enough either to write anything of such an idle character as the essay, or to read it. Whatever be the reason, we have on our side of the water not many collections like those by English writers which may be easily found.[59]

Subsequent generations of writers and critics have corrected Hale's view. However, its persistence as a form of pervasive Europeanism is present throughout the history of the nineteenth-century American essay, and it frames discussions until well into the next century.

While it is presented as a project that celebrates the American essay on its own terms, Matthews's *Oxford Book of American Essays* begins and ends with essays written within a European frame of reference. The first essay in the volume is Benjamin Franklin's (1706–1790) "The Ephemera: An Emblem of

---

56 Thomas Wentworth Higginson, "Americanism in Literature," in Matthews, *Oxford Book of American Essays*, 213–28, 213.
57 Higginson, "Americanism in Literature," 216.
58 Higginson, "Americanism in Literature," 217.
59 Edward Everett Hale, ed., "Introduction," in *American Essays* (New York: Globe School Book Company, 1902), vii–xii, vii.

Human Life," which is addressed to the French noblewoman Madame Brillon de Jouy, while the concluding piece is William Peterfield Trent's (1862–1939) "On Translating the Odes of Horace."[60] Although it includes important examples by many of the essayists considered in this survey – including Irving, Emerson, Poe, Thoreau, and James – Matthews's volume also contains examples by writers who have long since been neglected by critics and literary historians, such as Trent, Francis Hopkinson, George William Curtis, Hamilton Wright Mabie, and others. As he was compiling his book of exemplary American essayists from the late eighteenth to the early twentieth centuries, Matthews was aware of the problem of European influence and inheritance, but he overlooked the extent to which many figures not included in his anthology, such as Fuller and Douglass, responded to the issue of the shadow of Europe in unique and important ways. In the decades after his anthology appeared, the American essay came into its own. It did so, to a large degree, because of advances made by nineteenth-century authors who showed that there was more than one way to write about what it meant to be American and, in the process, to reject the models and examples that had been imported by earlier generations from the other side of the Atlantic. From the essays of expatriate modernists such as T. S. Eliot and Ernest Hemingway to later writers including James Baldwin and Susan Sontag, Europe continued to provide a crucial context – home and inspiration – for some of the greatest American essayists of the twentieth century.

---

60 Benjamin Franklin, "The Ephemera: An Emblem of Human Life," in Matthews, *The Oxford Book of American Essays*, 1–3; William Peterfield Trent, "On Translating the Odes of Horace," in Matthews, *The Oxford Book of American Essays*, 497–508.

7

Poet-Essayists and Magazine Culture in the Nineteenth Century

JOHN MICHAEL

The Poet Essay in a Changing World

In the nineteenth century, with the ascendency of the popular magazine in capitalist print culture, the essay achieved new prominence as well as a somewhat altered function as a marketable vehicle for literary criticism aimed at a popular audience. While literary artists as different and otherwise familiar as Lydia Maria Child (1802–1880), Ralph Waldo Emerson (1803–1882), Nathaniel Hawthorne (1804–1864), Margaret Fuller (1810–1850), Harriet Beecher Stowe (1811–1896), Frederick Douglass (c. 1818–1895), and Walt Whitman (1819–1892) exemplified the scores of writers who turned their hand to innovative work in what one might call the philosophical, political, or ruminative essay, Edgar Allan Poe (1809–1849) worked assiduously to found his literary reputation not only on his poetry but on an innovative form of the magazine essay as an exercise in expert aesthetic criticism. Poe's work as a literary critic publishing in and often editing commercial magazines helped reshape both the popular and the critical sense of the nature and potentials of literary art, especially poetry, in the modern world in ways that remain vital, if controversial, to both poets and critics today.

In the nineteenth century, literature assumed a still familiar form as a commodity confronting the large, anonymous readership that was emerging as a mass market for professional writers. This entailed changes in both poetry and fiction and in the critical literary essay as both became forms addressed to popular audiences. Edgar Allan Poe was at the forefront of both these developments, yet he has seldom received credit for the ways in which he explored and exploited the capacity of the critical magazine review to be both a specialized and a popular genre, though his work as an essayist represents a significant inflexion point in the history of the American essay.

The professionalization of authorship in the United States advanced rapidly during the decades preceding the Civil War. In 1825, William Cullen Bryant (1794–1878) could still tell writers that literature should not become a trade: "Let the avocation of literature be a recreation of an opposite character of one's business or profession."[1] Ten years later, this advice could only be lost on a writer like Edgar Allan Poe, struggling to make a living by writing essays, fiction, and poetry for publications like the *Messenger* in Richmond, Virginia. Soon he would write for and edit popular journals, the most prominent new form of publication, in Philadelphia and New York City. Poe was certainly among the era's most gifted poets and fiction writers, but it was as an essayist and editor for the new mass market magazines that he dedicated his talent to shaping the expanding demand for literary entertainment into a market where professional writers might sell their works. If Poe was, as Gero Guttzeit puts it, "the paradigmatic case for antebellum print culture," he also represented a paradigm shift in the culture of literature in the nineteenth century.[2] His innovative and original exploitation of the literary critical essay both differentiates him from his contemporaries and indicates the future of the form.

Writing in these competitive markets could be a rough business. Poe's notorious distaste for his more genteel colleagues in Boston – for example, his insistence on calling them Frog Pondians and his libeling of Professor Longfellow of Harvard College by accusing him of plagiarism and incompetence – bespoke a regional and class antagonism between an itinerant literary laborer exposed to the discipline of the marketplace and a ministerial, legal, and professorial elite who enjoyed a settled aura of Brahmin authority.[3] What Leon Jackson diagnoses as Poe's "status incongruity," his anxiety about the precariousness of his social and economic position in the world of letters, was more than a personal neurosis.[4] It was a symptom of rapid changes in the field

---

[1] Quoted in Thomas Bender, *New York Intellect: A History of Intellectual Life in New York City from 1750 to the Beginnings of Our Own Time* (Baltimore: Johns Hopkins University Press, 1987), 133.

[2] Gero Guttzeit, *The Figures of Edgar Allan Poe: Authorship, Antebellum Literature, and Transatlantic Rhetoric* (Berlin: De Gruyter, 2017), 9. See also Terence Whalen, *Edgar Allan Poe and the Masses: The Political Economy of Literature in the Antebellum America* (Princeton, NJ: Princeton University Press, 1999).

[3] Sidney Moss, *Poe's Literary Battles: The Critic in the Context of His Literary Milieu* (Durham, NC: Duke University Press, 1963).

[4] On Poe's status worries, see Leon Jackson, "'The Rage for Lions': Edgar Allan Poe and the Culture of Celebrity," in *Poe and the Remapping of Antebellum Print Culture*, ed.

of literature as literature became a profession. In J. Gerald Kennedy's words, Poe was a "shrewd, peripatetic, author-journalist, whose circulation in what he called 'Literary America' epitomized the ploys and practices of a horizontal culture of letters."[5] Poe's significance for the new culture of literary professionalism is most evident in his critical essays and in the hybrid genre of essay fiction that he was crucial in popularizing.

Changes in print culture marked by the ascendency of popular magazines were apparent to other essayists as well. In 1846, Margaret Fuller, the *New-York Tribune*'s first full-time reviewer, would write, "The life of intellect" is becoming more and more determined by "the weekly and daily papers," and in the "condensed essay, narrative, criticism" they published.[6] The addition of "criticism" to the list of literary products marks the establishment of the reviewer as a critical essayist with the "right of aesthetic pronouncement," as Thomas Bender describes the critic's new function.[7] Poe was an early master of the art of critical writing for the general reader, however much he manifested an artist's ambivalence toward his audience. He could draw readers with provocative, even outrageous, polemics and personal attacks, and he was willing to risk alienating or antagonizing them by a combination of hoaxing and pedantry that can seem at times aggressive and baffling. None of this, however, can obscure his serious innovations in literary criticism as a topic for American essayists.[8] What Coleridge (1772–1834) had been in Great Britain and what Baudelaire (1821–1867) would be in France, Poe was in the United States.

In the United States, as in Europe, prominent among the first practitioners of the literary-critical essay were poets. Who better to expound upon the craft of literature than its practitioners? For the first time, artistic skill and sophisticated taste came to be understood as professional specialties. As Thomas

---

    J. Gerald Kennedy and Jerome McGann (Baton Rouge, LA: Louisiana University Press, 2012), 37–61.
5 J. Gerald Kennedy, "Introduction," in Kennedy and McGann, *Poe and the Remapping of Antebellum Print Culture*, 1–12, 2.
6 Margaret Fuller, *Papers on Literature and Art* (London: Wiley and Putnam, 1846), 138; cited in Bender, *New York Intellect*, 160.
7 Levin Schücking, *The Sociology of Literary Taste*, rev. ed. (London: Routledge and Kegan Paul, 1966), 62–63; cited in Bender, *New York Intellect*, 121–22. Robert J. Scholnick notes that substantial space devoted to literary discussion was a new phenomenon in the antebellum journal. See Robert J. Scholnick, "'The Ultraism of the Day': Green's 'Boston Post,' Hawthorne, Fuller, Melville, Stowe, and Literary Journalism in Antebellum America," *American Periodicals* 18, no. 2 (2008): 163–91.
8 Gero Guttzeit gives a condensed account of the ways in which Poe's adherence to the teachable rhetorics of pre-Romantic periods in texts like "The Philosophy of Composition" becomes integral to academic departments of literature in the United States. See Guttzeit, *Figures of Edgar Allan Poe*, 54–86.

Bender explains, "In the eighteenth century, ... culture did not imply some special realm. Culture and society were not sharply distinguished. In the nineteenth century ... they have been torn asunder. Indeed, contention and conflict came to define their relations – art and culture became oppositional to society."[9] For Poe, contention and conflict were part of the critical field. Whether art opposes the bourgeoisie or becomes one of its preferred ornaments and marks of distinction, for Poe, the emergence of a mass audience, mostly middle class, literate but largely unschooled in art or connoisseurship, was a challenge and an opportunity that he met in his essays.

Poe's critical debts to and his differences from Coleridge are instructive. As Alexander Schlutz has demonstrated, many of Poe's poetic principles were "purloined" from the Romantic sage, including the principle that poetry's proper province is not truth but pleasure, especially the pleasure beauty affords.[10] But, as Schlutz also points out, Poe resisted Coleridge's attempt to link poetry to divine revelation and rejected the role Coleridge imagined that writers might play as a member of a "clerisy," a sort of intellectual priesthood reunifying society under the sign of culture.[11] Poe showed no interest in becoming, as Shelley would have it, an "unacknowledged legislator" of the world.[12] Instead, in his essays, Poe specifies a limited area of professional expertise that an artist or a critic might legitimately claim. He knew how to make works that attracted readers and subscribers, both those who sought only diversion and those interested in the experience of that elevation of spirit Poe called beauty and identified as the sole virtue art can possess. He rigorously refused to reduce his sense of art's specificity by suturing it to truth, morality, or political reform, and he created an intense symbiosis between art and the critical essay by explaining for the untutored reader how art works.

For instance, Poe refused to celebrate the importance of literature to the formation and maintenance of the nation, as did most other literary essayists of the time. Writing in *The United States Literary Gazette* for 1 April 1824, Henry Wadsworth Longfellow (1807–1882) celebrated a "national talent [that] is gradually developed in the walks of literature, and unfolds itself with greater

---

9   Bender, *New York Intellect*, 121.
10 See Samuel Taylor Coleridge, "Chapter XIV," in *Biographia Literaria*, ed. Adam Roberts (Edinburgh: Edinburgh University Press, 2014), 53–66; and Alexander Schlutz, "Purloined Voices: Edgar Allan Poe Reading Samuel Taylor Coleridge," *Studies in Romanticism* 47, no. 2 (Summer 2008): 195–224.
11 See Samuel Taylor Coleridge, *On the Constitution of the Church and State*, ed. John Colmer (London: Routledge, 1976); and Schlutz, "Purloined Voices," 196–97.
12 Percy Bysshe Shelley, *A Defense of Poetry* (Indianapolis, IN: Bobbs-Merrill, 1904), 90.

vigor and richness as day after day a national literature will be formed."[13] Poe rejected such Romantic ideas of national literary cultures altogether. In an essay he wrote in 1845 as editor of the *Broadway Journal*, he decried the popular fascination with achieving "a proper *nationality* in American Letters," which, he charged, showed no understanding of "what this nationality *is*, or what is to be gained by it." Nationalism, in Poe's estimation, is "rather a political than a literary idea – and at best a questionable point."[14] As Meredith L. McGill has argued, Poe's resistance to nationalism in literature was grounded in his working knowledge of fiction, poetry, and essays as commodities in a decidedly international marketplace for print.[15] As today's professors of literature continue to reassess the founding disciplinary assumptions of academic literary studies, still rooted in Romantic ideas of national languages and cultures, Poe's more critical, cosmopolitan ideal of literature assumes new and somewhat surprising relevance.

The Essay as Criticism

As Edgar Allan Poe saw it, "magazine literature," designed explicitly for the new, usually short-lived journals springing up in New York, Philadelphia, and other US cities, was "a sign of the times, an indication of an era in which men are forced upon the curt, the condensed, the well-digested in place of the voluminous – in a word, upon journalism in lieu of dissertation."[16] Poe recognized that literature, and above all the literary essay, must assume a broader and more heterogenous readership, an audience without reliably educated taste or sophistication, one requiring introductions to the fine points of poetry, fiction, and aesthetics. As a virtuoso "magazinist," as he

---

13 Henry Wadsworth Longfellow, "The Literary Spirit of Our Country," in *Longfellow: Poems and Other Writings*, ed. J. D. McClatchy (New York: Library of America, 2000), 791–95. Such appeals for a national literature were common in essays and speeches of the day. Familiar examples can be found in Emerson, Whitman, and others. See Benjamin Spencer, *The Quest for Nationality* (Syracuse, NY: Syracuse University Press, 1957).
14 Edgar Allan Poe, "Editorial Miscellanies," in *Edgar Allan Poe: Essays and Reviews*, ed. G. R. Thompson (New York: Library of America, 1984), 1067–117, 1076. In the realm of the critical essay, however, Poe had little patience for the authority of British examples: "There is not a more disgusting spectacle under the sun," he continues the thought above, "than our subserviency to British criticism."
15 See Meredith L. McGill, *American Literature and the Culture of Reprinting, 1834–1853* (Philadelphia: University of Pennsylvania Press, 2003), esp. 187–217.
16 Edgar Allan Poe, "Marginal Notes," *Godey's Lady's Book* (September 1845), in Thompson, *Edgar Allan Poe: Essays and Reviews*, 1309–1472, 1377, quoted in Bender, *New York Intellect*, 157. On the emergence of modern conceptions of literature after Poe, see Guttzeit, *Figures of Edgar Allan Poe*, 1–86.

called himself, Poe wrote poems, stories, and reviews for the literary journals he also came to edit. In his essays, he often attempted to provide a literary education for his readers to make them better able to appreciate his literary output.[17]

As an essayist, Poe restricted his subject matter in ways that predecessors like Montaigne or Bacon or contemporaries like Emerson, Fuller, or Child did not. They felt free to explore philosophy, morals, politics, and nature, among other topics. Poe as a critic maintained a rigorous focus on critical analysis of and theoretical statements about form, for form – distinct from truth or politics – was for him the only topic worthy of a poet's attention. In his occasional essays, such as "Mazel's Chess-Player" or "A Few Words on Secret Writing," he does explore more general topics, but it is in his many literary essays and reviews that he develops a form of commentary appropriate to the altered character and context of literary work. For Poe, the poet and critic are both practitioners and theoreticians of literary form. While in his poetry he adopts a version of the Sapphic suffering popularized by the poetesses he often published, in his essays he presents himself as a detached and masterful analyst of literary technique.[18] Poe's innovation was to make literature the exclusive area of the critical essayist's expertise. He separated the criticism of art from considerations of social utility or moral efficacy. As Nina Baym notes, among antebellum American reviewers only Poe "stated that in principle the morality of the books he wrote about was not his business."[19] His business, as he advertised it, was to offer lessons in the appreciation of literary form, not moral uplift or political provocation. He

---

17 See Poe's letter to Charles Anthon in *The Collected Letters of Edgar Allan Poe*, ed. John Ward Ostrom (New York: Gordian Press, 1966), 1:270. See Kay Ellen McKamy, "Poe as Magazinist" (PhD dissertation, University of South Florida, 2011), http://scholarcommons.usf.edu/etd/3242.

18 For a rich account of the Sapphic suffering – bittersweet physical and emotional torments of desire and melancholy – that becomes a stock in trade for nineteenth-century poetesses, see Yopie Prins, *Victorian Sappho* (Princeton, NJ: Princeton University Press, 1999); Eliza Richards, *Gender and the Poetics of Reception in Poe's Circle* (New York: Cambridge University Press, 2004); and Virginia Jackson, *Dickinson's Misery: A Theory of Lyric Reading* (Princeton, NJ: Princeton University Press, 2005), esp. 204–40.

19 Nina Baym, *Novels, Readers, and Reviewers: Responses to Fiction in Antebellum America* (Ithaca, NY: Cornell University Press, 1984), 173ff. It was for this reason, no doubt, that James Russell Lowell, writing in *Graham's Magazine* in February of 1845, took Poe to task for lacking "in the faculty of perceiving the profounder ethics of art" and for the "coldness of his mathematical demonstrations," though he credits them as novel and "strikingly refreshing." James Russell Lowell, "Edgar A. Poe," in *The Function of the Poet and Other Essays*, ed. Albert Mordell (Boston: Houghton Mifflin, 1920), 150–63, 163. Margaret Fuller similarly, in 1845 in Graham's Magazine, criticized Poe for letting the "cold, hard, and self-sufficient critic" take precedent over the sentiments of the poet.

attempted to teach his readers how to enjoy the literary entertainments he purveyed, proffering an education in taste and, as a bonus, a glimpse into the creative and editorial processes that shape a poem or story calculated to appeal to the critical and popular taste and to sell magazines. This was no merely crass or philistine ploy. It was an innovation in the popular literary essay that has had enduring effects, for good and ill, even on students and professors of literature today.

As a professor without a post, Poe offered instruction to anyone willing to pay for his lessons.[20] To today's reader, his essays appear both familiar and strange – as his detective, August Dupin, himself skilled in literary analysis (he solves the "Murders in the Rue Morgue" by analyzing newspaper stories, and he writes poetry) would say, they are both "simple and odd."[21] They combine aesthetic analysis and commercial calculation, especially in Poe's most popular efforts, like "The Literati of New York City," "Fifty Suggestions," "Marginalia," and of course, "The Philosophy of Composition."

Poe's critical method resembles the methodical ratiocination that Dupin explains in "The Purloined Letter." For Dupin, thinking involves a play of doubles in which the detective emerges as a master of hermeneutics, an embodiment of what Emerson called "the fundamental law of criticism," which he borrowed from the higher criticism: "Every scripture is to be interpreted by the same spirit which gave it forth."[22] In Poe's reinterpretation of this principle, fundamental both to biblical and literary exegesis, it becomes an agon of doubling and a struggle for ascendency between an author and a reader, the goal of which is not exactly truth but victory. Thus, in "The Purloined Letter" (with its famous game of odds and evens where success depends on the estimation and imitation of an antagonist's intelligence and intention), Dupin distills thought into a simple formula as "merely ... an identification of the reasoner's intellect with that of his opponent."[23] This game of ratiocination – this agon of thinking with and

---

Margaret Fuller, Critic: Writings from the New-York Tribune, 1844–1846, ed. Judith Mattson Bean and Joel Meyerson (New York: Columbia University Press, 2000), 45.

20 Poe represents an early, literary version of the professionalization that was redefining middle class life. See Burton J. Beldstein, *The Culture of Professionalism: The Middle Class and the Development of Higher Education in America* (New York: W. W. Norton, 1976), ix–x.

21 Edgar Allan Poe, "The Purloined Letter," in *Edgar Allan Poe: Poetry, Tales, and Selected Essays*, ed. Patrick F. Quinn and G. R. Thompson (New York: Library of America, 1984), 680–98, 681.

22 Ralph Waldo Emerson, "Language," in *Nature in Ralph Waldo Emerson: Essays and Lectures*, ed. Joel Porte (New York: Library of America, 1983), 20–25, 25.

23 Poe, "Purloined Letter," 689.

through another – leads in Poe's formulation not to a neutral or timeless truth, but to the satisfaction of a desire to get the best of an argument, to be one up on another, to win an audience or to win them over, to have, or to play at having, the last word on a topic, to impress a reader with one's acumen. And yet Poe also knew that this game of reflective doubling cannot finally be won. Victory is always subject to reversal, and there can be no last word when reading a consciousness or intention that is simultaneously reading and interpreting one's own or when reading a text that another can and will eventually reread differently. This is a principle of thinking as conversation or discourse with another, an agonistic working through that can be loving or hostile but can never end. It is often – in its provisional nature – characteristic of critical thinking and of the critical essay as exemplified in Poe. In his practice as an essayist, however commercial his aims may be, he offers a model for critical discourse in literary studies and in the academic humanities more generally, as forms of tentative thinking with and through another that may furnish moments of elevation and a beauty of its own.

The Essay as Performance

Poe nonetheless played the critical game with his essays' readers as if he might win it. As a writer, Poe could not count on an audience with taste or leisure for serious considerations of art or criticism. In his essays, he tries to form a readership capable of appreciating the art of poetry generally and his own poetry in particular. He had a knack for making his lessons in prosody and judgment entertaining, often including dazzling demonstrations of analytical skill and sometimes descending to scandalous displays of outrageous snark. Teachers have always known that a little showmanship helps maintain students' interest, but Poe does sometimes go to extremes.

For example, in "The Philosophy of Composition," he describes his own versification as follows: "Of course, I pretend to no originality in either the rhythm or metre of the 'Raven.' The former is trochaic – the latter is octameter acatalectic, alternating with heptameter catalectic repeated in the *refrain* of the fifth verse, and terminating with tetrameter catalectic."[24] As if remembering himself and estimating the limitations of his reader (who, we may assume, is unversed in the technicalities of prosody), Poe then offers

---

24 Edgar Allan Poe, "The Philosophy of Composition," in Quinn and Thompson, *Edgar Allan Poe: Poetry, Tales, and Selected Essays*, 1373–85, 1381.

a lay translation of his description. "[L]ess pedantically," he writes, "the feet employed throughout (trochees) consist of a long syllable followed by a short: the first line of the stanza consists of eight of these feet – the second of seven and a half (in effect two-thirds) – the third of eight – the fourth of seven and a half – the fifth the same – the sixth three and a half.[25] This metrical tour de force might easily make a reader (especially one for whom the word *trochee* is Greek) dizzy. Someone sufficiently moved by "The Raven" (moved perhaps to tears) to want an explanation of how the poem works might well agree with James Russell Lowell's (1819–1891) well-known accusation in *A Fable for Critics* (1848) that Poe "talks like a book of iambs and pentameters, / In a way to make people of common-sense damn metres."[26] Poe's reviewers often complained that he was all head and no heart, and here he seems intent to embrace and perhaps to parody that characterization, seasoning his impersonation of a virtuoso versifier with a suggestion of the mad genius. Yet the pedagogical impulse behind this performance is serious and the information conveyed is accurate. Poe wants readers better prepared to appreciate poetry as an art.

Poe's performances in his essays assume an intelligent reader who desires instruction in the appreciation of literature as art. His persona is neither Byronic hero nor inspired demiurge; even less does he dress the poet as a democratic Orpheus and national bard, as will Emerson or Whitman. Poe's persona in his essays is a skillful practitioner of literary arts and critical sciences, a man of letters and a virtuoso artist and analyst willing to reveal the tricks of his trade without needing to make further claims for himself or his art. Like the modern professor of literature, Poe adopts the guise of professional expertise, though his role in shaping the contours of the modern professor's performance is seldom acknowledged.[27]

The most serious point in Poe's pedagogical performance is his performance of pedagogy itself. He claims the authority of expertise to act as a popular professor of literature and a critical arbiter of taste. Poe begins "The Philosophy of Composition" in character: "I have often thought how interesting a magazine paper might be written by any author who would – that is to say, who could – detail, step by step, the processes by which any of

---

25 Poe, "Philosophy of Composition," 1381.
26 James Russell Lowell, *A Fable for Critics* (New York: G. P. Putnam, 1848), 78.
27 Scott Peebles notes that in Poe's essays, "the image of the pedant or the detached intellectual competed with the image of the passionate, out-of-control romantic artist. Those competing images actually complement each other." Scott Peebles, *The Afterlife of Edgar Allan Poe* (Rochester, NY: Camden House, 2004), 15.

his compositions attained its ultimate point of completion"[28] Poe not only rejects any "species of fine frenzy" or "ecstatic intuition" as an explanatory scheme for poetry, he also minimizes the impact of lived experience on the poet and the poem.[29] It is not the actual death of a beautiful woman but the material needed to write something "that should suit at once the popular and the critical taste" that inspires the professional poet.[30] In its dispassionate expertise, Poe's essay harkens back to pre-Romantic traditions that viewed art as a craft that the poet-rhetorician could be hired to teach and looks forward to the twenty-first-century creative writing workshop. Poe demonstrates how prosody, if properly understood, can shape a performance that will be attractive to a mass readership by creating a simulacrum of emotion and that will appeal to the savvy critic or common reader who is equipped to appreciate the artifice of the work.

In an instructive sense, Poe echoes Denis Diderot's (1713–1784) postulate about acting in "Le Paradoxe sur le comédien." Art conveys an intensity of emotion the artist cannot afford to feel. The artist, seeking to move an audience, estimates the effectiveness of each gesture in the creation of an imitation of affect, a semblance of passion. The educated critical reader knows that artistic creation is primarily an affair of the head and not the heart.[31] Poe, like the philosophe, does not mean to disillusion his audience but to enhance their pleasure. To mistake the imitation of nature for nature obscures the most intense and elevated pleasure that art affords, the appreciation of the beauty of the artist's artifice. It is this that, in Poe's analysis, an artwork purveys. The "beautiful woman" whose death Poe famously deployed to delimit the proper province of poetry only becomes artistically beautiful in the poem the poet writes about her loss. The reader Poe wants to educate in an essay like "The Philosophy of Composition" will learn to embody that "critical taste" to which Poe hopes to appeal.

---

28 Poe, "Philosophy of Composition," 1374. Poe began to formulate these ideas and the character of the artist as calculating craftsperson in a piece called "Chapter of Suggestions," which he published the previous year in the *Opal*; see Thompson, *Edgar Allan Poe: Essays and Reviews*, 1292–96, 1293.
29 Poe, "Philosophy of Composition," 1374.   30 Poe, "Philosophy of Composition," 1375.
31 As Diderot put it, "[T]ous les grands imitateurs de la nature ... sont trop occupés à regarder, à reconnaître et à imiter, pour être vivement affectés au dedans d'eux-mêmes" (all those who create great representations of nature ... are too preoccupied with observing, with analyzing, with imitating to be themselves strongly moved [my translation]). Denis Diderot, *Oeuvres esthétiques* (Paris: Garnier Frères, 1968), 289–381, 310.

Many of Poe's interventions belong to aesthetic philosophy or to literary theory. His quarrel with Coleridge's influential distinction between imagination and fancy, which appears in a pedantic note he appends to his discussion of N. P. Willis, one of the literati of New York Poe presented to the readers of *Godey's Lady's Book*, is especially suggestive. "'[F]ancy,'" Poe writes, "[according to Coleridge] 'combines – imagination creates.' This was intended and has been received as a distinction, but it is a distinction without a difference – without a difference even of degree. The fancy as nearly creates as the imagination, and neither at all."[32] However aggressively pointed this passage may be, Poe makes a point worth pondering. If there is, in fact, nothing new under the sun, then what the naïve call original and new appears to the discernment of the educated critical reader as an effect of the recombination of preexisting and often familiar elements into new and surprising arrangements, like a griffin or centaur. This is a point he will make again with reference to the composition of his own stanzas in "The Raven."

Essay Fiction

An example of Poe's own originality in the essay form appears in his distinctive employment of a hybrid genre one might call essay fiction, a precursor to the genre Stefano Ercolino calls the "novel essay" and sees emerging in Europe decades after Poe's death, though certainly Melville's (1819–1891) *Moby-Dick* (1851), with its long disquisitions on whaling and philosophy, psychology, and politics, belongs in any genealogy of this genre.[33] Poe's "The Purloined Letter," to take a well-known example, offers memorable commentary on the affinities of mathematical analysis and poetic creation and on ratiocination or thinking as a game or agon. These interludes, often presented in the detective's voice, constitute short essays that have had large implications for fields like aesthetics, hermeneutics, and psychoanalysis. The critical history of these tales and their influence in these and other fields is well known.[34] This sort of generic crossing characterizes many of Poe's

---

32 Edgar Allan Poe, "The Literati of New York City," in Thompson, *Edgar Allan Poe: Essays and Reviews*, 1118–222, 1126n.
33 See Stefano Ercolino, *The Novel-Essay, 1884–1947* (New York: Palgrave McMillan, 2014).
34 See, for example, John P. Muller and William J. Richardson, eds., *The Purloined Poe: Lacan, Derrida, and Psychoanalytic Reading* (Baltimore: Johns Hopkins University Press, 1988); and especially Barbara Jordan, "The Frame of Reference: Poe, Lacan, Derrida," in Muller and Richardson, *Purloined Poe*, 213–51. See as well John T. Irwin, *The Mystery to a Solution: Poe, Borges, and the Analytic Detective Story* (Baltimore: Johns Hopkins University Press, 1994), esp. 1–12; John T. Irwin, *American Hieroglyphics: The Symbol of the Egyptian Hieroglyphics in the American Renaissance* (New Haven, CT: Yale University

best-known texts and has inspired acknowledged imitators from A. C. Doyle to Jorge Louis Borges, Paul Auster, Umberto Eco, and others. Less well known but suggestive in the present discussion is the strange horror story cum literary essay called "How to Write a Blackwood Article," which lays bare the conventions of the Gothic that *Blackwood's Magazine* so successfully marketed and at which Poe himself exceled. Here, one might say, the reader is admitted not to the poet's but to the editor's workshop. In this story, which recounts Psyche Zenobia's interview with *Blackwood's* editor, Poe presents a telling rhetorical analysis of a popular genre and gives advice, tongue-in-cheek but nonetheless sound, for aspiring writers hoping to win a readership. The story's two halves first appeared separately, but in *Tales of the Grotesque and Arabesque* (1840) Poe combined them and thus foregrounded their utility as an instructional packet, a parodic but accurate statement of theory followed by a burlesque but also practical demonstration.

In the first part, Psyche Zenobia, "corresponding secretary" to an amalgam of provincial literary periodicals incorporated with the acronym "P.R.E.T.T. Y.B.L.U.E.B.A.T.C.H.," appears in Blackwood's office seeking his advice. He obliges, she says, with "a clear explanation of the whole process."[35] First, he tells his epigone to identify a subject fit for the intense treatment the Gothic demands, perhaps a first-person account of an unusual fate like falling out of a balloon, or being swallowed up by an earthquake, or self-poisoning. Zenobia promises to hang herself with her own garters and he commends her choice.[36] The story's second half in fact tells the grisly tale of how Zenobia is slowly beheaded when she catches her head beneath the minute hand of a tower clock. Most memorable is the moment when her eye, under pressure from the clock hand, pops out of her head and rolls to the roof edge from where it stares back at her in her predicament.

In Poe, the difference between parodic silliness and serious art can be difficult to trace. Blackwood continues, "Having determined upon your subject, you must next consider the tone," and he offers a comical menu including "the tone didactic, the tone enthusiastic, the tone natural," along with the "tone laconic," which, as he says, "has lately come much into use."[37] This goes on for several paragraphs and – as in "The Philosophy of Composition" a decade later – tone is given primacy of place.

Press, 1980); and Joan [Colin] Dayan, *Fables of Mind: An Inquiry into Poe's Fiction* (New York: Oxford University Press, 1987).
35 Edgar Allan Poe, "How to Write a Blackwood Article," in Quinn and Thompson, *Edgar Allan Poe: Poetry, Tales, and Selected Essays*, 278–97, 279–80.
36 Poe, "How to Write," 282–83.   37 Poe, "How to Write," 282.

Amid the buffoonery of this earlier work, Poe makes a point that he takes very seriously. He teaches his readers that art is technique and that technique can be taught. As a corollary, art should be appreciated as skillful artifice rather than mistaken for unmediated or vicarious experience. Despite the Byronic self-torment he often incorporates into his own persona, Poe is a classicist. For him, art depends not on deep feeling but on the artist's mastery of rhetorical devices calculated to attract and move an audience. Poe's contemporary critics, who took him to task for a lack of heart and an excess of head in his work, were not completely wrong. In contrast to Margaret Fuller (1810–1850) or Lydia Maria Child (1802–1880), innovators who took the nineteenth-century magazine essay in directions that would become the contemporary editorial and the journalistic exposé and who made sensation and sentiment serve their vision of public morality and practical reform, Poe kept his literary essays, like his poems and tales, within the narrow precincts of what he considered literature's sole legitimate province: beauty and affect.

Poe's Lessons

In modern terms, Poe was a disciplinary specialist. In response to those who would confuse criticism with "a sermon, an oration, a chapter in history, a philosophical speculation," all areas in which writers of reviews commonly worked, Poe insists that criticism "can be nothing in the world but criticism," nothing but an analysis and assessment of literary form. "It is against this frantic spirit of *generalization* that we protest," Poe adds.[38] In one sense, Poe was uncannily attuned to his time and to the transformation of literature's place in it. The emotional responses that Poe places at the center of his aesthetics were by his definition ephemeral (in "The Philosophy of Composition," he specifies that aesthetic effects are necessarily short in duration) and therefore well suited to the new mass-market periodical and its often hard-pressed audience. If the eighteenth-century periodical essay had furnished a forum for reasoned exchanges among equals, the nineteenth-century journals purveyed ephemeral diversions to a mass, often distracted readership.[39] Poe is not only among the first serious writers to accept this shift in the public sphere, however conflicted about popular taste he might have

---

[38] Edgar Allan Poe, "Exordium to Critical Notices," in Thompson, *Edgar Allan Poe: Essays and Reviews*, 1027–32, 1030–31.
[39] Jared Gardner, *The Rise and Fall of Early American Magazine Culture* (Urbana, IL: University of Illinois Press, 2012), ix–30.

been, but he seeks to capitalize on it. In his essays, he manages not only to instruct his readers in the criteria for aesthetic judgment but also to enhance his own marketable reputation for genius. Poe modernizes the classical ideal of literary art, familiar to readers of Horace and Aristotle, or Addison and Steele, by proffering delight and instruction limited to his readers' taste and ignoring their morals. He embraced the new journals as popular entertainment, but he acted as if they could be classrooms as well, open to anyone with a dollar or three for a subscription.

Poe knew that while taste may not be disputed, it can be improved. Then as now, "good" taste was believed to be the sign of an educated sensibility and to help maintain orderly hierarchies in bourgeois society.[40] Essays like those comprising "The Literati of New York City" and "A Chapter on Autography" that Poe wrote as editor of *Grahams Magazine* combined gossipy sniping with serious literary criticism and shrewd assessments of the competition, even if he sometimes dabbled in carnival tricks like handwriting analysis and phrenology.[41] He demonstrates a shrewd eye for the business side of the literary enterprise. For example, in "The Literati of New York City," he analyzes the failure of "Sargent's Magazine," a monthly magazine edited by Epes Sargent, as the unfortunate result "of falling between two stools, never having been able to make its mind whether to be popular with the three or dignified with the five dollar journals."[42] Unlike his failed colleague, Poe knew how to estimate his market. And he knew how to write for it. In his well-known review of *Twice-Told Tales* and *Mosses from an Old Manse* in the November 1847 number of *Godey's Lady's Book*, Poe advises Hawthorne that he limits his popular appeal by failing to include the market's desire for novelty in his calculations. The characteristically calm irony of Hawthorne's narrative voice and tone makes the artist seem "peculiar," Poe says, rather than "original."[43] This lesson regarding the calculated adjustment of aesthetic effect to popular taste characterizes Poe and his professional judgments in his essays.

---

40 Julia Straub compares the literary scene Poe reflected on and helped produce, and which he graphed for the readers of *Godey's Lady's Book* in "The Literati of New York," to Bordieu's mapping of Paris in *Distinction* and the function of establishing hierarchies of taste in establishing and maintaining social order. Julia Straub, *The Rise of New Media: 1750–1850: Transatlantic Discourses and American Memory* (New York: Palgrave, 2017), 138–39.
41 Edgar Allan Poe, "A Chapter on Autography [part I]," *Graham's Magazine* 19 (November 1841): 224–34.
42 Poe, "Literati of New York City," 1186.
43 Edgar Allan Poe, "Nathaniel Hawthorne," in Thompson, *Edgar Allan Poe: Essays and Reviews*, 577–88, esp. 580–81.

Jared Gardner points out that modern critics tend to forget "how very short the reign of the novel, the author, and the critic has been."[44] Poe looms large as both author and critic at the beginning of what Michael Newbury describes as "a newly arranged hierarchy of labor [... in an] increasingly complex literary profession."[45] In many ways, his greatest originality lies in his critical essays. The emergence of literature as a modern phenomenon was abetted by a new expert, the literary critic, whose essays became vehicles for literary judgments and interpretations designed for readers anxious to become, or to seem, more expert themselves. This new critic, of whom Poe was the prime example, found a ready niche in the rapidly expanding world of the magazine essay.

44 Gardner, *Rise and Fall*, 40. That the elevation of these newly refurbished characters was meant to be a profitable ploy in an expanding literary market should surprise no one.
45 Michael Newbury, *Figuring Authorship in Antebellum America* (Stanford, CA: Stanford University Press, 1997), 5.

8

Antebellum Women Essayists

CHARLENE AVALLONE

But for cultural androcentrism, American women writing between 1810 and 1860 could have located their essays in a women's tradition commencing with Marie Le Jars de Gournay (1565–1645), Montaigne's editor and commentator, generally recognized as the first female essayist. As it was, their allusions signaled generic affiliation with later writers, often men, while, given constructions of the otherness of "woman" ongoing from the seventeenth century, their essays share some of her formal deviance from men's traditions and engage many of her subjects: female character and capacities, education, the woman writer, equality of the sexes, and denial of freedoms, property, and public authority to women.[1]

Antebellum women exploited the essay's openness to write in formats that conformed approximately to conventions of men's writings, but might take shape in host genres, frequently letters, or in generic hybrids as they negotiated gender prescriptions. Conduct manuals, schooling, and published lecture-essays advised on composing essays, yet encouraged cultivation in cognate genres of conversation and the familiar letter, social "accomplishments" ceded as the sole literary "arts" in which women might excel.[2] Such tutoring developed a literary decorum suited to the essay's familiar relation with an addressee, colloquial style, and avoidance of contention. Conversational culture also spawned associations in which women circulated manuscripts and could offer access to periodical publishers in need of materials for audiences growing as literacy spread. Publishing compositions

---

[1] See Marie Le Jars de Gournay, *Apology for the Woman Writing and Other Works*, ed. and trans. R. Hillman and C. Quesnel (Chicago: University of Chicago Press, 2002).
[2] See Almira H. Lincoln Phelps, *Lectures to Young Ladies* (Boston: Carter and Hendee, 1833); Lydia Huntley Sigourney, *Moral Pieces in Prose and Verse* (Hartford, CT: Sheldon and Goodwin, 1815).

became almost "a rite of passage" for middle-class white women.[3] Poverty and racist practices posed obstacles to education, publication, and fame for other women who nonetheless composed essays in societies[4] and published outside mainstream venues. They figure among those who produced an extensive body of essays whose range, merit, and impact remain inadequately acknowledged.

The essay not only provided admission to authorship in a genre then commanding greater literary status than the novel, but also afforded participation in crucial discussions denied women in discourses coded more public. It served to conceive identities divergent from prevailing ideology, as it variously served social reform or conservativism. A conservative strand of essayists reinforced religious and social orthodoxy, promulgated in serial antebellum evangelical awakenings. While even conservatives might promote moderate reforms, other essayists stressed progressive, even radical, change, often employing an Enlightenment discourse of equality. Some women published polemical essays, writing anonymously as if men and in service to men's politics, while journalists evolved idealist and commercial essays.

A Conservative Line

Sarah Ewing Hall (1761–1830), taught by her father (a Presbyterian minister and university provost), gained distinction as an "eloquent" conversationalist in Joseph Dennie's coterie and published in his *Port Folio* "some of [its] most sprightly essays, and pointed criticisms."[5] Her son's collection of her writing praises her "innate delicacy," which made her "withhold the expression of every thought and feeling which concerned only herself," suggesting the constraint on women publishing personal essays.[6] Hall instead wrote informed essays of biblical criticism, reviews of moral fiction, and pieces attempting to reconcile female education with the conservative ideology of domesticity, such as "On the Extent of Female Influence, and the Importance

---

3 Nicole Tonkovich, "Writing in Circles: Harriet Beecher Stowe, the Semi-Colon Club, and the Construction of Women's Authorship," in *Nineteenth-Century Women Learn to Write*, ed. Catherine Hobbs (Charlottesville, VA: University of Virginia Press, 1995), 145–75, 156.
4 Elizabeth McHenry, *Forgotten Readers: Recovering the Lost History of African American Literary Societies* (Durham, NC: Duke University Press, 2002).
5 Sarah Hall, *Selections from the Writings of Mrs. Sarah Hall, Author of Conversations on the Bible, with a Memoir of Her Life* (Philadelphia: Harrison Hall, 1833), xvii.
6 Harrison Hall, "Preface," in Hall, *Selections*, xvii.

of Exerting It in Favour of Christianity." "Defence of American Women" countered a claim that all but laboring-class women were ignorant of domestic economy with praise of extended learning that equipped some for household management. Remarking on tensions between women's domestic duties and authorship, Hall justified writing as religious duty on the model of British Bluestockings: "Why should not our females emulate such examples" as Hannah More's "religious and moral" essays, Hall asked, and, write tracts to Christianize the West?[7] Hall commended "the female style – simple and unpretending" as "adapted to the comprehension of all classes."[8]

Less intellectual evangelical essayists later advanced several of Hall's interests, and, like her, wrote against gender equality. Lydia Huntley Sigourney (1791–1865), privileged to receive private schooling thanks to the employer of her laborer father, pushed to extend education on a model of social control to inculcate obedience, piousness, order, and self-discipline. Her collection *Moral Pieces* (1815) recommended reading the Bible rather than novels and features such essays as "On the Government of the Passions." *Letters to Young Ladies* (1833), conduct essays signaling generic affiliation with citations of Bacon and More and such typical topics as friendship and conversation, promoted the Prussian ideal of education, "'the means of patient usefulness and contentment with the lot which Heaven has appointed.'"[9] "On Domestic Employments" attempted to reconcile domesticity with "the modern system of female education" by charging mothers to model ways that "intellectual pursuits and household cares" might "relieve each other."[10] Sigourney, celebrated for her verses, encouraged women to write to keep "vivid in the heart, the lessons taught by the discipline of Heaven"[11] rather than for publication. Her essays were widely reprinted, and her *Girl's Reading Book* (1837) and *Boy's Reading Book* (1839) were used in the common schools. Her praise of woman's limited "'sphere'" and call to mothers to agree that their "rights [are] sufficiently extensive," however, met with criticism.[12]

Although Ann Plato's (c. 1824–unknown) race is uncertain, her *Essays* (1841) is claimed as the first book of essays by a Black writer and the first by an Indigenous one. Like the child in "Lessons from Nature," the young author desired "moral and intellectual views" that give meaning to

---

7 Hall, *Selections*, 16.   8 Hall, *Selections*, 16.
9 Lydia Huntley Sigourney, *Letters to Young Ladies*, rev. ed. (London: Jackson and Walford, 1841), 263.
10 Sigourney, *Letters to Young Ladies*, 77.   11 Sigourney, *Letters to Young Ladies*, 18.
12 Mary F. Love, "Mrs. Sigourney on Women's Rights," *Una* 2, no. 6 (June 1854): 282.

experience.[13] Her moral, occasional, biographical, and nature essays endorsed religion; education; values of discipline, industriousness, service, and economy; and an agrarian ideal, while also stressing mutability, death, and immortality. Her allusiveness, pronounced "[d]erivative" of Sigourney,[14] may reflect instruction given apprentice writers to learn "original composition" by copying or paraphrasing passages from model essays, emulating styles, and interweaving their own reflections with citations. That Plato's quotations come predominantly from the Bible and moral essays in five popular school readers whose design, topoi, and even titles echo in her collection suggests her possible intent to compose a school text. If her allusions are not "belletristic,"[15] Plato's style often approaches the literary, as she weaves prose from biblical quotes, paraphrases, diction, and figures more than do other essayists.

Sarah Josepha Hale (1788–1879) stretched the conservative essay beyond Sigourney and Plato. Tutored by her mother and college-educated brother, she taught and then participated with her husband in a literary society publishing in their hometown paper.[16] Widowed, Hale edited and wrote for the *Ladies Magazine*, the first US magazine for women, becoming editor of the most widely circulated women's magazine when it merged into *Godey's Lady's Book* (1837). While she published in several genres, essayistic ones predominate. *Woman's Record* (1853) alone contains hundreds of biographical-critical essays. Hale avoided personal essays, however, hesitating to "obtrude our own doings or experiences" as "egotism."[17] She did not hesitate to obtrude her conservative beliefs, promoting the ideology of woman's moral influence based in a gender binary she regarded as established in nature and the Bible, where "the Creator marked [woman's] destiny" and made it "idle to talk of the 'Rights of Woman.'"[18] Hale ceded all but moral power to men and rationalized reform proposals on religious grounds. "The foundation" of women's "learning must be the Gospel," she insisted in urging expanded education.[19] Her essays envisioned ways to extend female moral

---

13 Ann Plato, *Essays: Including Biographical and Miscellaneous Pieces, in Prose and Poetry*, ed. K. J. Williams (Oxford: Oxford University Press, 1988), 57.
14 Ron Welburn, *Hartford's Ann Plato and the Native Borders of Identity* (Albany, NY: SUNY Press, 2015), 171.
15 Welburn, *Hartford's Ann Plato*, 172.
16 Nicole Tonkovich, *Domesticity with a Difference* (Jackson, MS: University Press of Mississippi, 1997), 30–32.
17 Sarah Hale, "Editor's Table," *Godey's Magazine and Lady's Book* 34 (January–June 1847): 50–53, 51.
18 Sarah Hale, "Sketches of American Character," *Ladies' Magazine* 1 (1828): 202–219, 204.
19 Hale, "Editor's Table," 51.

influence into public reforms. Advising essaying as one means of exerting influence, she recommended reading Bacon and More to form style, urged participation in improvement circles, published other women's essays, and sought to establish her own conservative model as paradigmatic. Credited with contributing to the professionalization of American authorship[20] and recognized for advocating women's education, teaching roles, and property entitlements, Hale aimed higher: She exhorted women writers to advance "Christian principles" so "literature" would "claim kindred to the holy office of religion."[21]

Textile workers gained attention for magazines begun in one improvement circle organized by their minister and edited by the daughter of another from bygone "gentry,"[22] Harriet Farley (c. 1813–1907). In the best known magazine, the *Lowell Offering*, "factory girls" wrote little about their workplaces, twelve-hour day, or wages. Their essays instead represented operatives as respectable youths engaged in self-culture and paid labor for self- and family support in the interval between school and marriage; they often recalled agrarian ideals or aimed to disarm public prejudice against female factory labor. After European criticism recognized the *Lowell Offering*, Farley claimed its unique "contribution to American literature,"[23] and she achieved sufficient status to publish essays in *Godey's* and in her collection, *Shells from the Strand of the Sea of Genius* (1847), which treated such topics as "The Romance of Factory Life."[24] Betsey Chamberlain (1797–1886), the "most original" and "'noted'" Lowell writer, however, departed from conservative tradition in essays including "protests against Indian persecution" and dream visions that Judith Ranta sees inspired by tribal traditions.[25] Chamberlain, a widow of Indigenous ancestry with little education, contributed epistolary, humorous, and satiric essays, and visionary reveries of an animated nature. "A New Society," one of few *Offering* interventions in labor reform, stages a reverie far from Charles Lamb's (1775–1834) sentimental model, envisioning an eight-hour workday, equal wages for women, and boycott of writers not doing manual labor or public service.[26]

---

20 See Patricia Okker, *Our Sister Editors: Sarah J. Hale and the Tradition of Nineteenth-Century American Women Editors* (Athens, GA: University of Georgia Press, 2008), 84–109.
21 Sarah Hale, "Editor's Table," *Godey's Lady's Book* 16 (1838): 144–43, 144.
22 John S. Hart, *Female Prose Writers of America*, rev. ed. (Philadelphia: Butler, 1855), 245.
23 Harriet Farley, "Editor's Table," *New England Offering* 1 (April 1848): 22–24, 23.
24 Harriet Farley, *Shells from the Strand of the Sea of Genius* (Boston: James Munroe, 1847).
25 Judith A. Ranta, *The Life and Writings of Betsey Chamberlain, Native American Mill Worker* (Boston: Northeastern University Press, 2003), 4; see 82, 10.
26 Tabitha [Betsey Chamberlain], "A New Society," *Lowell Offering* 1 (1841): 191–92.

More Learned Essaying

Educator and publisher Elizabeth Palmer Peabody (1804–1894) extended the more intellectual essaying begun in Hall. Peabody reviewed books, art, and social movements in the Transcendentalist coterie journal the *Dial*, and published extensively on history and education, initiating the kindergarten movement in 1859.[27] Wide reading in history and contemporaneous European criticism informs her more elaborate essays, including biblical criticism in the *Christian Examiner* and her "aesthetic" model of reform in "The Dorian Measure." This essay, inspired by discussion of Spartan social harmony in her history conversation classes, advocates ongoing revelation and interpretation – "ever-progressing truth" – against fundamentalist Christianity and authoritarianism.[28] Sparta, which prioritized education above "government," serves as standard by which to critique the American overemphasis on politics, failure to practice professed Christian ideals, and religion's "perversion of thought concerning everything pertaining to the body."[29] Peabody envisioned reforms that would realize religious principles, center the arts, and turn resources from warfare to civic "universities" for adult "universal culture."[30]

Learned allusions in *Rural Hours* (1850) by Susan Fenimore Cooper (1813–1894) display Cooper's European education. Remarked by contemporary naturalists, then recovered in the environmental movement of the 1960s, *Rural Hours* earned appreciation for Cooper's detailed descriptions of plant and animal life and seasonal and historical change. These four hybrid essays, written "for the writer's amusement"[31] from the pose of a leisure-class amateur naturalist and structured loosely by the shifting seasons, combine diary records of Cooper's reflections with observations drawn from forays into the Cooperstown countryside and Cooper's own reading. Depictions of the manners of villagers and farmers draw on moral-essay tradition to commend temperance, industry, piety, and benevolence. While conservatism informs Cooper's interpretation of "nature" to reinforce class hierarchy and a gender binary, it importantly informs her promotion of protective game laws and forest conservation. Several lengthy passages might stand alone as essays: the holiday themes, reflections on autumnal poetry, and

---

27 Elizabeth Palmer Peabody, "Kindergärten of Germany," *Christian Examiner* 67 (September 1859): 313–39.
28 Elizabeth Palmer Peabody, "The Dorian Measure, with a Modern Application," *Aesthetic Papers* (1849): 64–110, 110.
29 Peabody, "Dorian Measure," 85, 100. 30 Peabody, "Dorian Measure," 110.
31 Susan Fenimore Cooper, *Rural Hours* (London: Putnam, 1850), v.

a rumination on "Indians," which registers Cooper's pain regarding "how little has been done for the Indian" since settler contact.[32] Cooper saw that "something more may justly be required of us ... who have taken their country," but imagined as reparations only "improvement" through "civilization" and "the blessings of Christianity."[33]

Radical Writers

Women's essays appeared in the radical and abolitionist press not long after Hall's publications. Scottish immigrant Frances Wright (1795–1852) wrote, lectured, and edited three newspapers with the aim of prompting the nation toward a social system that realized its founding ideals of freedom and equality. Her "exertions in every style possible to [her] invention" challenged conventional *"nonsense"* with dissenting thought, often in hybrid forms she called "heterodox essays."[34] "I seek truth wherever I can find it," she wrote in one article that claimed Jesus as a radical whose censure of clerical hypocrisy preceded hers.[35] While Wright's lectures circulated as essays on many themes that preoccupied other women, her interrogative stance as "an enquirer, not a teacher" ran counter to their assumption of received beliefs.[36] Her opinions – on free inquiry and speech, amalgamation, anticlericalism, universal education, workers' and women's rights, marriage law, and sexual freedom – threatened established society. Clergymen represented her as the personification of infidelity, and journalists warned she reawakened the anarchy of the French Revolution. But activists later credited her "'Herculean'" essaying "'on the equality of the sexes'" as the first "'agitation [that] shook the time-hardened crust of conservatism and prepared the soil'" for their labors.[37]

Maria Stewart (1803–1879), whose essays initiated African American women's "use of this genre" for "sociopolitical purposes,"[38] left indentured service at fifteen, educated herself through Sunday school, and began writing when "knowledge of the truth, as it is in Jesus" inspired a "spirit of

---

32 Cooper, *Rural Hours*, 182.   33 Cooper, *Rural Hours*, 181–82.
34 Frances Wright, *Free Enquirer* (29 October 1828): 7. Emphasis in original.
35 Frances Wright, "Jesus," *Free Enquirer* (1 July 1829): 286.
36 Frances Wright, "Course of Popular Lectures," in *Women and Radicalism in the Nineteenth Century*, ed. Mike Sanders, vol. 2, *Frances Wright* (London: Routledge, 2001), 29–119, 33.
37 Ernestine Rose, quoted in Bonnie S. Anderson, *The Rabbi's Atheist Daughter: Ernestine Rose, International Feminist Pioneer* (Oxford: Oxford University Press, 2017), 53.
38 Jacqueline J. Royster, *Traces of a Stream: Literacy and Social Change among African American Women* (Pittsburgh, PA: University of Pittsburgh Press, 2000), 174–75.

independence."[39] Her essays interpreted that truth to support activism. Stewart avowed that spiritual equality revealed in the gospel and preached by Christians should extend to equality of political, social, and economic opportunity. She reflected on her experience to redefine spirituality as she refocused racial justice from slavery to the "powerful force of prejudice,"[40] which she perceived affected her community nearly as much as slavery did the South. She encouraged her readers to escape internalized racism and identity predetermined by "color" and caste; "what makes the man," she observed, "is the principles formed within the soul."[41] Stewart's understanding of the "soul" and its "energies" extended beyond conventional religious spirituality to the fire of ambition and aspiration to knowledge, rights, and privileges.[42] She stretched contemporary discourse of individual spiritual awakening to social application as she advised white men "to awake" and invest in colleges for Blacks, not in colonization,[43] and addressed the "daughters of Africa," perhaps for the first time publicly by any essayist, urging them to "awake! Awake!" to the influence they might exert.[44]

Others who challenged the status quo found themselves, like Stewart, closed out of the mainstream press. After clergymen rebuked Sarah Grimké (1792–1873) and Angelina Grimké (1805–1879) for abolitionist lecturing, Sarah answered indirectly with open letters in the *New England Spectator* to her "Dear Friend," president of the Boston Female Anti-Slavery Society. Grimké distanced her epistolary essays from theological and political polemics as her personal "search of truth" shared, as if privately, with another woman who asked her "views on the Province of Woman."[45] Grimké's youth in a slaveholding family, advanced study with a brother, and Quaker conversion equipped her to compose the essays collected as *Letters on the Equality of the Sexes, and the Condition of Woman* (1838). Grounding her sophisticated, (proto) feminist biblical exegesis in the Protestant "duty of every individual to search Scriptures for themselves,"[46] Grimké revealed mistranslations and misinterpretations. Understanding gender itself as a changing set of interpretive conventions defining sexual difference, she challenged "prejudices" distorting

---

39 Maria W. Stewart, *Maria W. Stewart, America's First Black Woman Political Writer: Essays and Speeches*, ed. Marilyn Richardson (Bloomington, IN: Indiana University Press, 1987), 29.
40 Stewart, *Maria W. Stewart*, 46.   41 Stewart, *Maria W. Stewart*, 29.
42 Stewart, *Maria W. Stewart*, 47.   43 Stewart, *Maria W. Stewart*, 63.
44 Stewart, *Maria W. Stewart*, 30.
45 Sarah Grimké, *Letters on the Equality of the Sexes, and the Condition of Woman* (Boston: Isaac Knapp, 1838; New York: Burt Franklin, 1970), 3. Citations refer to the Burt Franklin edition.
46 Grimké, *Letters*, 4.

scripture.[47] Grimké found no biblical authority for ecclesiastical dogma of female inferiority, but everywhere "the Scripture doctrine of the perfect equality of man and woman."[48] Her consideration of institutions that dogma sustained exposed sexual abuse of enslaved women and annulment of women's rights under coverture law. Grimké's essays ranged over women's oppression worldwide, female exemplars, marriage, and women's intellectual and moral equality. Abjuring "*man's* rights, or *woman's* rights," the *Letters* claimed equal "human rights,"[49] and became foundational to the women's movement.

Unitarian philanthropist Elizabeth Elkins Sanders (1762–1851) engaged in religious and political controversy through anonymous self-publications. Her *Tract on Missions* (1844) brought extensive reading on world civilizations to urge that funds spent to convert "the Heathen," an ineffective enterprise without scriptural "foundation," be redirected to needs of "the poor and unfortunate" at home.[50] Sanders proposed Americans "atone for the rank offences which have so long marred our national fame" by emancipating enslaved "Africans, who for centuries have been deprived of their birthrights" and granting property and citizenship rights to compensate for "wrongs" against "the Aborigines."[51] Finding only one (unnamed) journal "independent" enough to publish her critique of a missionary account of the Hawaiian islands,[52] Sanders reprinted it in her self-published *Remarks on the "Tour around Hawaii"* (1848). Extensive allusions to scripture, precolonization travels in Pacific Island cultures, contemporary periodicals, and missionaries' chronicles lend authority to her protest against missionary interventions in Hawaiians' religion and government. Sanders appreciated the Indigenous social organization that missionaries had worked to eradicate, including precontact "equality which prevailed between the sexes."[53] Rather than "forcing our creeds and artificial systems on foreigners," she proposed "we adopt such of their customs as will meliorate ... Christendom."[54]

Popular Polemicists

Polemical writers Jane McManus Storm Cazneau (1807–1878), daughter of a lawyer, and Louisa S. McCord (1810–1879), daughter of the director of the national bank, also chose anonymity but found welcome in popular journalism

---

47 Grimké, *Letters*, 91.   48 Grimké, *Letters*, 98.   49 Grimké, *Letters*, 117.
50 Elizabeth Elkins Sanders, *A Tract on Missions* (self-pub., 1844), 14, 21.
51 Sanders, *Tract on Missions*, 20.
52 Elizabeth Elkins Sanders, *Remarks on the "Tour around Hawaii"* (self-pub., 1848), iii.
53 Sanders, *Remarks on the "Tour*," 1.   54 Sanders, *Remarks on the "Tour*," 12–13, 27.

for essays supporting the imperialism and slavery Sanders condemned. Few antebellum essayists wrote under more pen names than Cazneau. Few published more or in more venues. None pushed more for American annexation of Texas, Mexico, and Cuba, even, her biographer claims, inventing the slogan "manifest destiny."[55] An established writer and foreign correspondent for the *New-Yorker*, Cazneau published in the *Democratic Review* and became a political editor at the New York *Sun*, "the world's largest penny" paper.[56] Her essays imposed political interpretations on geographical descriptions to read "the unequivocal finger of Providence" pointing out the path of American "empire" and "the sovereign sisters of the Union" bound together around slavery by "unrestrained profit."[57] Cazneau alleged "principle" as ground for her arguments yet argued from personal "interest" – "the governing wheel" of "Man"[58] – to support her land investments. Although she termed Indian dispossession and slavery "sin"[59] and contested "extermination" of Native Americans, Cazneau promoted organizing a "militia" of "tribes" "friendly" to her against others[60] and became an apologist for racist theory and slavery. She reported "laughing, dancing slaves" that would make "resolute abolitionists" question if the "undeveloped race, still in the imbecility of its unprepared animal dependence, did not require the social polity that gives him a master."[61]

Louisa McCord argued even more forcefully in support of slavery and free trade. Although late esteemed an intellectual, she relied on reactionary French economic theory, which she translated from periodicals such as the *Journal des Economistes*, and race theory from such fellow slaveholders as Josiah Nott. Her originality seems limited to premiering the word *feminist* in one attack on women writers who overlooked "the great law" of *"duty"* in abandoning their God-given, natural "position."[62] Her review essays (signed L. S. M.), served to invoke natural and divine law against progressive movements. They aspersed socialism and defended "the God-established

---

55 Linda S. Hudson, *Mistress of Manifest Destiny: A Biography of Jane McManus Storm Cazneau, 1807–1878* (College Station, TX: Texas A&M University Press, 2001), 45–46.
56 Hudson, *Mistress of Manifest Destiny*, 64.
57 "The Texas Question: A Letter from Alexander H. Everett," *U.S. Magazine and Democratic Review* 14, no. 75 (September 1844): 250–69, 252; Cora Montgomery, *The Queen of Islands, and The King of Rivers* (New York: C. Wood, 1850), 29.
58 Montgomery, *Queen of Islands*, 40.   59 Montgomery, *Queen of Islands*, 31.
60 Montgomery, *Eagle Pass; or, Life on the Border* (New York: George Putnam, 1852), v; Hudson, *Mistress of Manifest Destiny*, 135.
61 Montgomery, *Queen of Islands*, 33.
62 L. S. M., "Woman and Her Needs," *DeBow's Review* 13 (September 1852): 267–90, 269, 272.

system of slavery, which our Southern States are beautifully developing to perfection," as the "only safeguard of our morals and manners" and best provision for a race "incapable of civilization."[63] The women's movement, "but a piece with negro emancipation," would lead to "extinction" of "all law, human and divine" or "worse."[64] McCord's polemics do not speak with the voice of the "true woman" she championed, whose "duty" was "to civilize by love!"[65]

Schools of Idealist and Commercial Journalism

The careers of two progressive essayists, Lydia Maria Child (1802–1880) and Margaret Fuller (1810–1850), led from Transcendentalist New England to popular journalism in New York. Child, shunned in Boston after her *Appeal in Favor of That Class of Americans Called Africans* (1833) endorsed immediate emancipation, devoted herself to abolition and later moved to edit the *National Anti-Slavery Standard*. Aiming to make it a "family newspaper,"[66] she penned conversational editorials and a column of epistolary journalistic essays about her experience of the city. The popularity of this column and another in the *Boston Courier* led to mainstream republication in *Letters from New-York* (1843, 1845).

These hybrid essays trace shifting moods of her persona as Child exploits the genre's freedom of form, intimate relation with a reader, and deep value of amity. Child calls these miscellanies "letters" for want of a "better name," and she notes their digressive nature as she writes in them of "whatever my mind is full."[67] Together with her idealistic perspective on the city, this subjective wandering provides the essays' unity. Child acknowledges the need to temper her idealism to reach a market, yet repeatedly moves readers from material facts to spiritual ones, principles, and the possibilities of humanity. The essays' construction of an allied reader, curious to know more about the city and the narrator through their epistolary conversation, avoids polemic and gains an ear for criticism – of the war profiteering of Wall

---

63 L. S. M., "Uncle Tom's Cabin," *Southern Quarterly Review* 24 (January 1853): 81–129, 109; "Diversity of Races, Its Bearing upon Negro Slavery" *Southern Quarterly Review* 3, no. 6 (April 1851): 392–419, 410, 413.
64 L. S. M., "Enfranchisement of Woman," *Southern Quarterly Review* 5, no. 10 (April 1852): 322–41, 323, 327.
65 L. S. M., "Enfranchisement of Woman," 325.
66 Carolyn L. Karcher, *The First Woman of the Republic: A Cultural Biography of Lydia Maria Child* (Durham, NC: Duke University Press, 1994), 273.
67 Lydia Maria Child, *Letters from New York. Second Series* (New York: C. S. Francis, 1845), 120.

Street, slavery, economic and gender inequalities, crime, proliferation of guns, houselessness, capital punishment, animal cruelty, and political corruption – and praise of reforms. Child's essayistic approach allowed her, on the one hand, to confront mainstream readers with disquieting breaches between national and religious ideals they celebrated ritualistically and, on the other hand, their daily practices and institutions. The essays also entertain with details of the sights and sounds of the new urban landscape, bringing to life the city's inhabitants through fictional devices of narrative and dialogue; their wide allusiveness and mix of colloquial with figurative language further enhance their literary character. Critics, including Fuller, as editor of the *Dial* and then culture critic at the *New-York Tribune*, admired them.

Extraordinary education and social connections furthered Fuller's own uncommon essaying. As the *Dial*'s first editor, Fuller produced essays to fill issues. Some are considered her best literary criticism; several reappear in *Papers on Literature and Art* (1846), which established Fuller as a leading critic. Another proved the most impactful of anything she wrote. "The Great Lawsuit: MAN *versus* MEN. WOMAN *versus* WOMEN," revised as the pamphlet *Woman in the Nineteenth Century* (1845), extended Fuller's essaying toward a new idea of "woman" begun in her composition for a Unitarian literary society and developed in her Conversations, classes for women's mutual cultivation. Her title signals claims of Transcendental ideals against the way men and women actually live. The essay, positioning itself in the contemporaneous discussion of better interpretations of "the principle of liberty" on "behalf of woman,"[68] takes form as a free-ranging, high-toned conversation that reviews current and historical wisdom on gender. It pointedly negotiates debate over antislavery reformers' call for political and social privileges for women and distances itself from Mary Wollstonecraft's and George Sand's radical "interpretation of rights."[69] Fuller argued liberty rather as a spiritual, moral ideal – "one law for all souls" – requiring clarification in America.[70] The essay centrally develops her theory of gender fluidity: that universal feminine and masculine energies are not "incarnated pure in any form" but always "are passing into one another."[71] Revisions in the pamphlet show her growing engagement with reform in New York.

At the *Tribune*, Fuller's style grew more direct and colloquial, her idealism more specifically progressive. Her reviews evaluated contemporary culture,

---

68 Margaret Fuller, "The Great Lawsuit: MAN *versus* MEN. WOMAN *versus* WOMEN," *Dial* 4, no. 1 (July 1843): 1–47, 7.
69 Fuller, "Great Lawsuit," 29.   70 Fuller, "Great Lawsuit," 14.
71 Fuller, "Great Lawsuit," 43.

condemned capital punishment, and endorsed Black men's voting rights and the spirit of socialism. Personal essays reported visiting the city's emerging institutions. Holiday essays critiqued shortfalls of the nation from its stated ideals. Before embarking as European correspondent, Fuller pronounced journalism to be the "most important" US writing; leading intellectual life and open to "great excellence in condensed essay," journalism worked toward the "fusion of races" necessary for any expressly "American" literature.[72] Her travel dispatches exceeded convention in conversing diversely on cultural, social, and political issues, most dramatically the Roman Revolution. Subjective "reflections" often interpret her experience in terms of ideals, especially what she called "genuine Democracy," regarding "rights" as "holy."[73] Despite failed political revolution, Fuller expressed "faith" that a new era of "radical" social "revolution" would realize that ideal.[74]

Fuller and Child, alongside Grace Greenwood, were credited with creating a "modern school of newspaper correspondence," a distinctively feminine essay with "something of the charm of women's private letters," wherein "description preponderates over argument" and "fancy and enthusiasm" displace "statistics."[75] Critics located Greenwood alternatively in another "new school of literature" founded by Fanny Fern and free from "scholastic refinements, and big dictionary words."[76] This school of pathos and humor might more justly be traced to Fanny Forester, who introduced the commercial form of popular essay that made all three celebrities.

Although poverty put Emily Chubbuck (1817–1854) to work at eleven in a textile mill, she made her way through a district school and a female seminary to become "Fanny Forester," author of popular periodical collections, *Alderbrook* (1846) and *Trippings in Author-Land* (1846). Her artful inquiry into the possibility of being paid enough to buy a new dress for contributing to the popular *New - Mirror* had famously initiated an epistolary exchange with editor Nathaniel P. Willis (1806–1867) in the paper. There she posed as a literary ingenue to write "money-and-praiseworthy articles" some

---

72 Margaret Fuller, "American Literature; Its Position in the Present Time, and Prospects for the Future," in *Papers on Literature and Art* (New York: Wiley & Putnam, 1846), 122–43, 139, 137, 124, 124.

73 Margaret Fuller, *"These Sad but Glorious Days": Dispatches from Europe, 1846–50*, ed. Larry J. Reynolds and Susan Belasco Smith (New Haven, CT: Yale University Press, 1991), 161, 163.

74 Fuller, *These Sad but Glorious Days*, 321.

75 Thomas Wentworth Higginson, "Lydia Maria Child," in *The Writings of Thomas Wentworth Higginson* (Boston: Houghton Mifflin, 1900), 2:108–41, 127.

76 "Literary Notices," *Harper's New Monthly Magazine* 9, no. 49 (June 1854): 276–80, 277.

compared favorably to those in the *Spectator*.[77] Her writing often addresses class and female roles and takes hybrid form as narrative or character sketches in essay or conversational frames. Forester frequently drew subjects from rural life, which she represents as the archetypal American experience. Except in treating temperance or abstract topics such as "Genius," she tempers conventional moralism with wit. Willis praised Forester's "genius" for "the only style salable," the "off-hand piquancy" that achieved "the most difficult kind of writing, the *careless* finish."[78] Her chatty familiarity and artlessness set a pattern for later journalists.

Sara Jane Clarke Lippincott (1823–1904) honed her "piquant, racy" style from her first schoolgirl newspaper publications,[79] then brought the widest reading and intellectual range to this line of vernacular journalism as "Grace Greenwood." Leaving teaching to pursue a career in the magazines, in open-letter essays in the *New Mirror*, *Home Journal*, and *Saturday Evening Post*, Greenwood posed as "a simple country girl," not a knowledgeable *"blue."*[80] A self-aware essayist, however, she signals her evasions of becoming overly serious or personal, while reflections on the *Spectator*, Irving, and especially Lamb, situate her work in essay tradition. Her letter essays and tales, collected in *Greenwood Leaves* (1850, 1851), made her penname a household word.

Greenwood's stance of spontaneity and humor allowed her cultural, social, and political criticism occasional expressions of "ultra sentiments."[81] She appreciated readers who did not regard her as "a mere incarnation of light literature" and proclaimed, "[W]hile my soul is my own, it shall speak its own language in the freedom which is its priceless and inalienable birthright."[82] In impassioned rhetoric, Greenwood promoted prison and asylum reforms, urged provisions for the poor, and protested capital punishment and the war against Mexico, while also deploying puns, suggestive elisions, irony, and sharp satire to mock men and laws that violated her sense of justice. Forced to resign from the editorial staff of *Godey's* after Southerners objected to her publishing in the antislavery *National Era*, Greenwood was

---

77 *New Mirror* 3, no. 19 (10 August 1844): 304; see "Copyrights: American and Foreign Literature," *New-York Daily Tribune* 5, no. 202 (2 December 1845): n.p.
78 *New Mirror*, 304.
79 Joseph B. Lyman, "Grace Greenwood," in *Eminent Women of the Age* (Hartford, CT: S. M. Betts, 1868), 147–68, 151.
80 Grace Greenwood, *Greenwood Leaves* (Boston: Ticknor, Reed, and Fields, 1850), 327, 359.
81 Greenwood, *Greenwood Leaves*, 376.   82 Greenwood, *Greenwood Leaves*, 400.

hired there, giving her a platform to critique politicians and the church's "time-serving expediency."[83] She also gained access to congressional press galleries, enabling her to publish a series, Letters from the Capitol, in the *Washington Post*. By the 1850s, noting that she had "become impatient and indignant for my sex" being "lectured to, preached at, and satirized eternally," Greenwood acknowledged the "great truth involved in this question of 'Woman's Rights.'"[84] Although some of her later journalism served as "propaganda" for western settlement, heedless of Indigenous peoples,[85] much of her antebellum writing – including European correspondence with personal reflections on her travel that reappeared in the most popular of her essay collections, *Haps and Mishaps of a Tour in Europe* (1854) – advocated the "justice and freedom" that she identified as "the great principles of the age."[86]

While Sara Payson Willis Parton (1811–1872) cannot, as her biographer proposes, be credited with having "invented the form" of the essay,[87] as Fanny Fern she capitalized on it more than any earlier woman. Fern might be said to be born to her vocation: Her grandfather, father, and two brothers – Nathaniel P. Willis, who tried to hinder her career, and Richard Storrs Willis, who promoted it at the *Musical World* – were newspapermen. Within five years of her 1851 professional debut she became the most famous of essayists as she transferred from the Boston press, established "Fanny Fern's Column" at the *Musical World*, reprinted articles in *Fern Leaves* (1853, 1854), and, as columnist at the weekly *New York Ledger* in 1856, commanded the highest salary of any newspaper journalist. In becoming a phenomenon, Fern had help from the exchange system of reprinting uncopyrighted materials from newspapers,[88] from the revelation that she authored the scandalous novel *Ruth Hall*, from the mystery of her identity, and from her publishers' and editors' extraordinary publicity.

Fern made the newspaper essay more an entertaining form than a reflective one. She aimed to amuse, stimulate tears or laughter, and

---

[83] Greenwood, *Greenwood Leaves, Second Series* (Boston: Ticknor, Reed, and Fields, 1852), 380.
[84] Greenwood, *Greenwood Leaves, Second Series*, 289.
[85] Margaret Farrand Tharp, *Female Persuasion: Six Strong-Minded Women* (New Haven, CT: Yale University Press, 1949; repr. Hamden, CT: Archon, 1971), 173.
[86] Greenwood, *Greenwood Leaves, Second Series*, 117.
[87] Joyce W. Warren, "Fanny Fern's Rose Clark," *Legacy* 8, no. 2 (1991): 92–103, 102.
[88] See Melissa J. Homestead, *American Women Authors and Literary Property, 1822–1869* (Cambridge, UK: Cambridge University Press, 2005), 152–57, 164.

provoke. She might say of herself (as of one character), "'[I]f I had to stop to reflect, I should never be saucy.'"[89] The journalistic essay became more colloquial and urban in her columns. She concentrated its characteristic wit into pointed satire and irony, with an emphatic style featuring strong emotions, wordplay, dashes, and exclamation points. Her tightly focused, compressed articles were called "models of style," said to be "read to schools as models of composition."[90] Fern adapted the character in a series of moral and satirical "models" and soliloquies, some reworking traditional thematics of old maids, bachelors, and good wives. She further manipulated essay formulae to offer conduct advice on parenting, education, and marriage and to satirize conventional advice to women.

Much scholarship depicts Fern's writing as "feminist," subversive, or radical, but in the context of her contemporaries, she appears less a bellwether than a gauge of shifting popular opinion. More interested to criticize conservatism than to promote progressive causes, Fern retained a conventional religious perspective and appealed to philanthropy, rather than imagined institutional change. Her double-edged irony advised "policy," "cunning" submission to the "lords of creation," as more effective than agitation for rights.[91] Her antebellum essays focused on personal freedoms more than on rights and maintained solidarity not so much with the rights movement as with women writers, challenging stereotypes and defending others from the personal and patronizing criticism that depreciated her.

Paulina Wright Davis (1813–1876), editor of the woman's rights paper the *Una*, reprinted Fern's open-letter essay protesting critics' view that the popularity of women's writing was antithetical to "genius."[92] Yet the woman's movement, as one of Davis's own strong editorial essays argued, aspired to greater "justice" through "radical, thorough reorganization of society."[93] To that end, Davis, one of the earliest and most active organizers,

---

[89] Fanny Fern, "What to Do When You Are Angry," in William Moulton, *The Life and Beauties of Fanny Fern* (New York: H. Long and Brother, 1855), 303.

[90] John S. Hart, "Fanny Fern," in *Female Prose Writers of America*, 470–75, 472; O. D., *The Musical World and the New Musical Times* 5, no. 12 (19 March 1853): 178.

[91] Fanny Fern, "A Little Good Advice – from Fanny Fern," in Moulton, *Life and Beauties*, 276.

[92] Fanny Fern, "Very Good for a *Lady's* Book!," in *The Radical Women's Press of the 1850s*, ed. Cheris Kramarae and Ann Russo (London: Routledge, 1990), 58–60, 59.

[93] P[aulina] W[right] D[avis], "The Re-Organization of Society," *Una* 3, no. 2 February 1855): 24.

published (proto)feminist essayists who provided "stronger nourishment" than "Ladies Magazines"[94] or even Fern.

New scholarly interest in essays will no doubt attend more to these and other antebellum women who speak to our time as well as our history. Greater consideration of their essays would expand understanding of the genre and its significance in American culture.

---

94 P[aulina] W[right] D[avis], "The Introduction," *Una* 1, no. 1 (1 February 1853): 4.

PART II

★

VOICING THE AMERICAN EXPERIMENT (1865–1945)

9
Writing Freedom before and after Emancipation

KINOHI NISHIKAWA

"No subject has engaged African American essayists more than freedom."[1] So writes the late Cheryl A. Wall in her study of the African American essay, *On Freedom and the Will to Adorn* (2018). While that statement seems self-evident, in fact Black writers have long wrestled with defining and debating the terms of freedom itself. Before the abolition of slavery in the United States, freedom was tightly associated with emancipation and the world-historical struggle to recognize Black people as rights-bearing citizens, not chattel or property. However, after the Emancipation Proclamation, which took effect on 1 January 1863, and after the end of the Civil War in 1865, freedom came to be thought of along other axes – collective, still, but intertwined with notions of Black personhood and racial identity. While principled protest against white supremacy continued in the postbellum era, other voices urged self-reliance and introspection in a context in which Southern forces suppressed and Northern interests retreated from African American civil rights. Freedom meant something different to these writers than it had to those fighting for abolition.

The period from the lead up to the Civil War to the end of the nineteenth century shows particularly well the shifts in how Black essayists engaged the question of freedom. It is salient because it encompasses pre- and postemancipation American history, a time of tremendous flux in how freedom was defined and debated not just between whites and Blacks but within the Black community itself. The period is salient, too, because it sees the rise of a vibrant Black press and periodical culture, a sociocultural development that helps cultivate the self-expression that is a hallmark of the essay form.

---

[1] Cheryl A. Wall, *On Freedom and the Will to Adorn: The Art of the African American Essay* (Chapel Hill, NC: University of North Carolina Press, 2018), 10.

While a number of Black newspapers and journals were based in the Northeast, the South also hosted its share of periodicals. In all cases, as scholars of Black social and educational history have shown, Black people achieved literacy and exercised literate practices at rates more numerous and in ways more creative than the prohibition on enslaved people's literacy might lead one to expect.[2] Against this backdrop, the early Black press, with its emphasis on Black ownership of the means of literary expression, may be understood as a vibrant medium of community formation and social advancement. The periodical culture of this moment thus supported the composition and circulation of trenchant and searching essays exploring Black freedom in the age of emancipation.

In the sections that follow, a capacious understanding of the essay form is used to group nonfiction prose by Black writers who published in the Black press. Like Ralph Waldo Emerson's (1803–1882) "The American Scholar" (1837), which was originally delivered as a speech to the Phi Beta Kappa Society of Harvard College, many early African American essays were orations that the press documented and recirculated in print. As Cheryl Wall notes of this period in Black essay writing, the "line between spoken and written was blurred by nineteenth-century conventions."[3] Yet insofar as these works helped shore up the literate voice that had long been denied to enslaved people, they shed light on the various determinations of freedom in pre-emancipation essay writing. Proceeding from this basis, the chapter shows how the century's standout Black orator, Frederick Douglass, became a print phenomenon in his own right, advancing a strong first-person voice that seemed to speak for the conscience of the nation.

Douglass lived long enough to witness the failure of Reconstruction and the codification of white supremacy in the social, political, and economic structures of the South. However, it was left to younger writers to tackle the meaning of freedom at a time when emancipation seemed like a hollow promise. Activist journalist Ida B. Wells is the subject of the third section, which highlights the synergy between investigative reporting and essay writing during the period. The chapter concludes with a comparison of prose works by two towering figures of

---

2 Heather Andrea Williams, *Self-Taught: African American Education in Slavery and Freedom* (Chapel Hill, NC: University of North Carolina Press, 2005); Christopher Hagar, *Word by Word: Emancipation and the Act of Writing* (Cambridge, MA: Harvard University Press, 2013); Beth Barton Schweiger, *A Literate South: Reading before Emancipation* (New Haven, CT: Yale University Press, 2019).

3 Wall, *On Freedom*, 36.

turn-of-the-century race leadership: Booker T. Washington and W. E. B. Du Bois. The ideological split in their views on civil rights is registered in their different styles of writing, with Washington stressing action and advocacy and Du Bois embracing introspection and contemplation. Between them, these figures register the suite of oratorical, journalistic, and literary resources that will be bequeathed to twentieth-century practitioners of the African American essay.

Freedom's Journal and the *Colored American*: Debating the Terms of Emancipation

The first African American–owned newspaper was established in New York City in 1827. Free Black religious and civic leaders started *Freedom's Journal* to advocate on behalf of the Black community in the North. The newspaper's approach was two-pronged: to counteract misrepresentations of Black people in the mainstream press and to cultivate Black virtue through education and uplift. In cultural historian Benjamin Fagan's terms, the publication's middle-class orientation aimed to "show white readers a complete picture of black life, countering distortions that cast all blacks as ignorant and vicious." At the same time, *Freedom's Journal* addressed Black readers directly, emphasizing the importance of respectability as a pillar of social activism: "In order to be free, black Americans had to learn how to act right."[4] These editorial goals were to be applied across the country, including in the slaveholding South, but it had a particular resonance in Northern states like New York, whose final act of emancipation occurred on the Fourth of July in 1827, four months after the first issue of *Freedom's Journal* had appeared.

The newspaper's mission was realized by two editors who viewed themselves as leaders of the race. The newspaper's senior editor was Samuel Cornish (1795–1858). Born to free Black parents in Delaware, Cornish grew up in Philadelphia, where he trained as a Presbyterian minister, and later moved to New York, where he founded the city's first Black Presbyterian church. The newspaper's junior editor was John Brown Russwurm (1799–1851). Born to an enslaved Black woman and a white merchant in Jamaica, Russwurm was raised in Maine and graduated from Bowdoin College before he became a civil rights activist in New York. The first issue's editorial by

---

4 Benjamin Fagan, *The Black Newspaper and the Chosen Nation* (Athens, GA: University of Georgia Press, 2016), 27, 28.

Cornish and Russwurm advances the corrective discourse they intended to foster:

> We wish to plead our own cause. Too long have others spoken for us. Too long has the publick been deceived by misrepresentations, in things which concern us dearly, though in the estimation of some mere trifles; for though there are many in society who exercise towards us benevolent feelings; still (with sorrow we confess it) there are others who make it their business to enlarge upon the least trifle, which tends to the discredit of any person of colour; and pronounce anathemas and denounce our whole body for the misconduct of this guilty one.[5]

The editors' statement of intent claims self-representation as the periodical's goal. Yet Cornish and Russwurm have respectable free Blacks like themselves in mind as those likeliest to suffer from white "misrepresentations." Their effort to correct white attitudes is affirmatively pursued yet defensively staged.

The elite politics of free Black society imbued *Freedom's Journal*. Abolitionist appeals were strong, but they were printed alongside equally passionate calls for the migration of formerly enslaved people to Liberia on the coast of West Africa. Liberia had been used as a settlement by the Society for the Colonization of Free People of Color (later the American Colonization Society) since 1827. Acting under the assumption that emancipated slaves and even freeborn Blacks would struggle to integrate into American society, the organization promoted their migration. Russwurm supported colonization, but Cornish did not. The rift led the latter to leave the newspaper. Under Russwurm's editorship, the newspaper gave space to voices that framed resettlement as a way for the enslaved to gain manumission and for the formerly enslaved to rebuild their lives. Yet *Freedom's Journal* printed dissents to the plan, too, reflecting the diverse opinions of its readership. In an 1828 piece, for example, a group of Black Philadelphians protest a local, unnamed white newspaper editor's support for colonization. After skewering the philanthropic and religious rationales used to justify resettlement, the authors identify what they take to be its baseline motive: racism. The editor balks at the fact that some Blacks "live here in peace and plenty enjoying all the luxuries of life in the same degree with the whites." The authors reply by facing up to such hostility: "Some live in peace, we are happy to say – if they live in plenty, no praise whatever is due to the editor or any

---

[5] Samuel Cornish and John Brown Russwurm, "To Our Patrons," *Freedom's Journal* (16 March 1827).

man possessing his tyrannical opinion."[6] That Russwurm was willing to publish this objection reveals the value he placed on fostering debate about what emancipation entailed for a free Black community.

When Russwurm himself migrated to Liberia in 1829, Cornish returned to the newspaper, reversed editorial support for colonization, and called it the *Rights of All*. The periodical continued under that masthead until 1830. Although this reorientation was short-lived, Cornish's position was ascendant among abolitionist and elite Black circles. In 1837, he cofounded with Philip Alexander Bell (1808–1889) and Charles Bennett Ray (1807–1886) the *Weekly Advocate*, a newspaper committed to the struggle not only for emancipation but also for the recognition of Blacks' civil rights on American soil. Bell was born in New York City and educated at the African Free School, an institution founded to educate Black children whether born free or previously enslaved. He joined the city's abolitionist networks and came to learn the newspaper business by working at the *Liberator*, the newspaper run by white abolitionist William Lloyd Garrison (1805–1879). Ray was born in Falmouth, Massachusetts, and studied theology before moving to New York and taking up pastoral positions in the city. As a community leader, Ray became a fervent supporter of the antislavery cause as well as allied religious pushes for temperance and moral education. Cornish had the backing of these men when he helmed the newspaper, which was renamed the *Colored American* after a couple of months.

Cornish's new platform allowed him to foreground essays that rejected plans for colonization. In the unsigned front-page piece "Declaration of Sentiments, on the Sin of Slavery," for example, it is noted that "immediate emancipation" does not mean "that slaves ... shall be deprived of employment and turned loose to roam as vagabonds," or "that they shall be expelled from their native country, as the price and condition of their freedom." Instead, the essay proclaims a vision of freedom that is premised on the recognition of Blacks' inherent, natural rights:

> We maintain that the slaves belong to themselves; that they have a right to their own bodies and minds, and to their own earnings; that husbands have a right to their wives, and wives to their husbands; that parents have a right to their children, and children to their parents; and that he who plunders them of these rights, commits high-handed robbery, and is sacredly bound at once and utterly to cease.[7]

---

6 "Philadelphia Report," *Freedom's Journal* (18 July 1828).
7 "Declaration of Sentiments, on the Sin of Slavery," *Colored American* (17 June 1837).

The essay, which may be a Black-voiced version of the American Anti-Slavery Society's 1833 Declaration of Sentiments, endorses a capacious view of emancipation as the securing of Black personhood, property, and family ties. In its defense of classical liberal ideals of self-possession, the *Colored American* staked its vision of freedom on what was then a radical Enlightenment commitment to equality.

To be sure, rights were not simply a matter of the law. As abolitionists gained momentum in the years leading up to the Civil War (1861–65), their drive to put an end to slavery was imagined as the only true path to salvation. In one entry of the running column "Prejudice in the Church," Cornish laments, "The American Church, more favored of God than any other, is the STRONG HOLD of an unholy prejudice against color, more *oppressive* and *fatal* in its results than any other sin. It is not only a generator of the darkness, but it is an extinguisher of *the light*." Against this hypocrisy, Cornish offers a collective protest: "God hath assigned to his ambassadors, different departments in his Church, and we feel that ours is, to warn the people of *this sin*, lest the sword come, and they fall by the hand of the sword, and their blood be required at our hands."[8] As Fagan notes of this passage, Cornish "paraphrases the prophet Isaiah, who, like his successor Jeremiah, preached during a time when the Israelites faced grave threats from powerful enemies."[9] By deploying the rhetoric of prophesy and assigning it to the "we" of the *Colored American*'s readers, Cornish casts free Black people as uniquely positioned to speak out against the prejudice that justifies slavery in the South and shapes race relations in the North.

Frederick Douglass: Emancipation of the Self

Cornish left his editorial post in 1840, but it would not be long before Frederick Douglass (ca. 1818–1895) took up his charge. Born into slavery in the Chesapeake Bay region of Maryland, Douglass spent his formative years working for the Auld family in Baltimore. While living in the city with the patriarch's brother and sister-in-law, Douglass taught himself how to read and write in secret. As an adolescent, he was returned to plantation slavery and hired out to farmers. One of them, Edward Covey, routinely beat him until Douglass physically resisted the assault. Before he turned twenty, Douglass fell in love with a free Black woman, Anna Murray. Within

---

8 [Samuel Cornish], "Prejudice in the Church," *Colored American* (11 March 1837).
9 Fagan, *Black Newspaper*, 49.

a year of their meeting, Douglass escaped from slavery by traveling on a northbound train out of Baltimore in disguise, aided by Murray. The couple settled in Massachusetts. In the North, Douglass's firsthand experiences and eloquent intellect brought him to the attention of Garrison's American Anti-Slavery Society. With support from this abolitionist network, Douglass published his celebrated autobiography, *The Narrative of the Life of Frederick Douglass, an American Slave* (1845), and toured Ireland and Great Britain on a transatlantic antislavery campaign. Upon returning to the United States in 1847, he used funds from supporters to start his own newspaper, the *North Star*, named for the constellation that enslaved people took to be a symbol of and guide to freedom. In this periodical and its successors – *Frederick Douglass' Paper*, *Douglass' Monthly*, and the *New National Era* – the man who would become the country's most prominent abolitionist at once covered and shaped the national debate over slavery and freedom.

Although he was known primarily as an orator, Douglass contributed writing to newspapers that laid the groundwork for the modern African American essay. An 1848 issue of the *Liberator*, for example, contains an open letter to Thomas Auld, Douglass's former enslaver. The letter's beginning merits attention for its audaciousness:

> The long and intimate, though by no means friendly relation which unhappily subsisted between you and myself, leads me to hope that you will easily account for the great liberty which I now take in addressing you in this open and public manner. The same fact may possibly remove any disagreeable surprise which you may experience on again finding your name coupled with mine, in any other way than in an advertisement, accurately describing my person, and offering a large sum for my arrest.[10]

This wry, controlled performance contrasts with parts of the letter where Douglass condemns his treatment under Auld's ownership. For instance, Douglass refers to his own family as that which he seeks to defend from the horrors of slavery, but then he turns the screw and asks Auld how he would like having his daughter subjected to similar treatment: "[C]ompel her to work, and I take her wages – place her name on my ledger as property ... feed her coarsely – clothe her scantily, and whip her naked on the back occasionally."[11] As graphic as this section is, Douglass pulls back to say he holds nothing personally against Auld – only that he wishes to emphasize the

---

10 Frederick Douglass, "To My Old Master," *Liberator* (22 September 1848).
11 Douglass, "To My Old Master."

brutality of a system that lies behind the kind of polite affectation with which he begins his letter.

Douglass exercises a different mode of address in his open letter to enslaved people published in the *North Star*. Speaking for a group of "runaway slaves" who now find themselves living and working in the North, Douglass aims to undercut the culture of fear that masters, whom he calls "pirates," instill among the enslaved. "When they told us, that the abolitionists, could they lay hands upon us would buy and sell us, and we could not certainly know, that they spoke falsely," he writes, "and when they told us, that abolitionists are in the habit of skinning the black man for leather, and of regaling their cannibalism on his flesh, even such enormities seemed to us to be possible."[12] Although not every white person in the North has been hospitable, Douglass reassures readers that Black people have been able to earn modest wages, gain an education, and enjoy the support of antislavery organizations. In dispelling the myths that Southern slaveholders propagate, he aims not only to encourage those in bondage to make their escape toward freedom but also to underscore their fundamental humanity in the very act of reading his words. Here Douglass's mode of address accounts for the varieties of literacy enslaved Black people would have exercised in hearing his prose through both individual and collective acts of reading.[13]

That sense of optimism was dashed when Congress passed the Fugitive Slave Act on 18 September 1850. As part of a compromise between slaveholding and free state interests, the act required that those who had escaped from bondage be returned to their owners, and that Northerners cooperate in retrieving fugitives. The resulting extension of the culture of fear into the North radicalized Douglass's views on Black participation in abolitionism, which had for a time encouraged nonviolent resistance. Now, though, Douglass was unequivocal. "Such submission," he writes in *Frederick Douglass' Paper* in 1854, "instead of being set to the credit of the poor sable ones, only creates contempt for them in the public mind, and becomes an argument in the mouths of the community, that Negroes are, by nature, only

---

12 Frederick Douglass, "A Letter to the American Slaves from Those Who Have Fled from American Slavery," *North Star* (5 September 1850).

13 On Douglass's periodical writings and their relationship to Black reading networks, see Elizabeth McHenry, *Forgotten Readers: Recovering the History of African American Literary Societies* (Durham, NC: Duke University Press, 2002); Derrick R. Spires; *The Practice of Citizenship: Black Politics and Print Culture in the Early United States* (Philadelphia: University of Pennsylvania Press, 2019); and Benjamin Fagan, "Journalism," in *Frederick Douglass in Context*, ed. Michaël Roy (Cambridge, UK: Cambridge University Press, 2021), 108–20.

fit for slavery; that slavery is their normal condition." The man who, from the confrontation with Auld to his fugitive trip North, created a mythos of liberating himself, states flatly: "This reproach must be wiped out, and nothing short of resistance on the part of colored men, can wipe it out. Every slavehunter who meets a bloody death in his infernal business, is an argument in favor of the manhood of our race. Resistance is, therefore, wise as well as just."[14] In response to the essay title's question, "Is it right and wise to kill a kidnapper?," Douglass's answer is a resounding yes.

The martial tone of Douglass's essays gathered force in the years leading up to secession and reached a fever pitch during wartime. One month after the Battle of Fort Sumter in April 1861, Douglass announced a call to arms: "Freedom to the slave should now be proclaimed from the Capitol, and should be seen above the smoke and fire of every battle field, waving from every loyal flag! ... The weak point must be found, and when found should be stuck with the utmost vigor."[15] Over the next several years, the newspaper advanced a steady drumbeat of support for the Union and, in essays like "Why Should a Colored Man Enlist?" and "Another Word to Colored Men" (both 1863), addressed the men who now put their bodies on the line in the fight for Black freedom. While these essays are blunter in address and style than Douglass's earlier writings, they celebrate a militant racial self-determination that future activists would use as a template in their own essays.

Douglass' Monthly wound down in 1863, leaving Douglass to explore other venues to comment on the assassination of President Abraham Lincoln, the Union's victory over the Confederacy, and the onset of Reconstruction (1865–77). By using federal powers to enforce the law in Southern society, the Reconstruction effort was able to accord equal rights to African Americans through the passage of the Thirteenth, Fourteenth, and Fifteenth Amendments to the US Constitution. At least that was the nominal outcome. When Douglass returned to journalism in 1870 with his *New National Era* newspaper, he sounded a note of skepticism about the whole enterprise. "The pen is often mightier than the sword and the settled habits of a nation mightier than a statute," he intones, further observing, "It has been said that no people are better than their laws. Many have been found worse than their laws. It is no unreasonable impeachment to say that the American people, and even the American churches, are far in the rear of American law in

14 Frederick Douglass, "Is It Right and Wise to Kill a Kidnapper?," *Frederick Douglass' Paper* (2 June 1854).
15 Frederick Douglass, "How to End the War," *Douglass' Monthly* (May 1861).

respect to the Negro."[16] As resistance to Reconstruction set in, Douglass could see that Black people's freedom had not been secured by formal emancipation. His writing during this period revives the circumspection of his earlier prose, suggesting that the project of upholding white supremacy lies behind North-South reconciliation. His view was prescient, for in 1877 Reconstruction collapsed after another political compromise was struck between white interests on opposite sides of the Mason-Dixon line. As federal troops and investment left the South, freedmen and freedwomen were left to fend for themselves.

Ida B. Wells: Reporting on Freedom Denied

The demise of Reconstruction put African American citizenship at the very center of national debate. At stake was no longer the legal declaration of emancipation but the practical well-being of emancipated Black life. Although nominally granted citizenship, Black people witnessed their rights trampled on by revanchist Southern elements and their economic fates bound up with regimes of debt peonage. For the masses of Black sharecroppers, life after Reconstruction did not look appreciably better than life under slavery. Black writers, intellectuals, and political leaders took note and began guiding the debate toward the cause of racial uplift. What was required of a nation in which the institution of slavery had been abolished yet slavery's vestiges could be seen and felt everywhere? What did it mean to push for Black people's advancement in a society that, by most accounts, consigned them to second-class citizenship? Essayists took up these and related questions in tackling the problem of persistent racial inequality.

The most forceful voice of protest to emerge during this era was Ida B. Wells (1862–1931). Born into slavery in Mississippi, Wells realized freedom as a child in the wake of the Emancipation Proclamation. Tragically, both of her parents and a sibling were killed during the yellow fever epidemic that hit the country in 1878. Faced with the risk of having the remaining siblings separated, Wells kept the family together and relocated to Memphis, Tennessee. There she began teaching elementary school and pursuing her studies in her free time. Her activist spirit was kindled in 1884 when a train conductor ordered her to give up her seat in the ladies' first-class car and move to the smoking car. After refusing to do so, Wells had to be physically dragged out. She subsequently sued the railroad company for damages and,

---

16 Frederick Douglass, "Seeming and Real," *New National Era* (6 October 1870).

having won at the local circuit court level, wrote an article about her experience for the *Living Way*, a local Black church weekly. She ultimately lost her case on appeal at the Tennessee Supreme Court. However, Wells, who continued writing for the *Living Way*, had discovered the value not only of protesting Southern segregation but of publicizing that protest through the Black press. Soon she became co-owner of the *Free Speech and Headlight* newspaper and took to decrying injustice in those pages.

Although Wells is perhaps best described as an investigative journalist, the articles she produced amid the rising tide of white violence against Black people constitute an important precedent for the modern African American protest essay.[17] In the early 1890s, Wells trained her attention on the scourge of lynching, which mobs often justified in the name of avenging white women who presumably had been assaulted by Black men. Wells picked apart that justification through eyewitness interviews and, at any rate, denounced the spread of vigilante violence across the country. In the 21 May 1892 issue of the *Free Speech*, after a series of lynchings stretching from Arkansas to Georgia, Wells folds her voice into journalism: "Nobody in this section of the country believes the old thread-bare lie that Negro men rape white women. If Southern white men are not careful, they will overreach themselves and public sentiment will have a reaction; a conclusion will then be reached which will be very damaging to the moral reputation of their women."[18] Not only does Wells dare to name the lie that is used to justify lynching, but she also dares to tell white men to exercise caution: Their rectitude is bound to be discredited when facts on the ground contradict the cover story. Wells's outspokenness provoked a reaction when, several days after the publication of this article, a white mob destroyed the *Free Speech* office and all its contents.

Wells's early journalism survives only in mentions from contemporary Black newspapers and in summary form in *Southern Horrors: Lynch Law in All Its Phases*, a pamphlet published by the Black-owned *New York Age* in October 1892. After the destruction of *Free Speech*, Wells left Memphis to work at the *New York Age*. As a reconstructed archive of her protest writing, *Southern Horrors* combines trenchant criticism with rhetorical flourishes. In addition to debunking the myth of the Black rapist, Wells takes a hammer to

---

17 For a similar assessment of Wells's newspaper writing, see Cara Caddoo, "Black Newspapers, Real Property, and Mobility in Memphis after Emancipation," *Journal of African American History* 102, no. 4 (2017): 468–91.
18 Ida B. Wells, *Southern Horrors: Lynch Law in All Its Phases* (New York: New York Age Print, 1892), n.p., www.gutenberg.org/ebooks/14975.

Northern states reneging on their commitment to Black civil rights. Ku Klux Klan raids and other white supremacist subversions of Reconstruction were tacitly "excused" by Northerners as "the natural resentment of intelligence against government by ignorance." But that overly benign view "did not remove the trouble, nor move the South to justice." Instead, Wells writes, "One by one the Southern States have legally (?) [sic] disenfranchised the Afro-American, and since the repeal of the Civil Rights Bill nearly every Southern State has passed separate car laws with a penalty against their infringement."[19] This last indignity, of course, is something Wells directly experienced, and she rightly connects vigilante violence to segregationist policies.

Wells's most daring statement comes near the end of the pamphlet. Addressing a predominantly African American readership, she asserts, "The world looks on with wonder that we have conceded so much and remain law-abiding under such great outrage and provocation." But the world will wonder no more, she predicts, for in two cases where lynchings were prevented in the past year, the reason for deterrence is clear: A Black man "had a gun and used it in self-defense." Moving from diagnosis to prescription, she continues, "The lesson this teaches and which every Afro-American should ponder well, is that a Winchester rifle should have a place of honor in every black home, and it should be used for that protection which the law refuses to give."[20] This call for armed self-defense would have been highly unusual for a Black person or a woman, much less a Black woman, to make at the time. Regardless, Wells refuses to let social and journalistic conventions determine an adequate response to unchecked racial violence. For her, Black self-defense is a matter of physical survival and moral conscience. As such, there is no room for compromise, rhetorical or otherwise.

Booker T. Washington: Freedom and Self-Reliance

Wells's fiery protest stood in contrast to the conciliatory persona of the most prominent African American social leader in the decades after emancipation: Booker T. Washington (1856–1915). Born into slavery in Virginia, Washington did not know his biological father, a white man from the plantation neighboring the one where his mother toiled. His mother moved him to West Virginia in an effort to reunite with her husband, a man who had escaped from slavery during the Civil War. After spending his formative years in West

---

19 Wells, *Southern Horrors*, n.p.   20 Wells, *Southern Horrors*, n.p.

Virginia, Washington moved back to Virginia to attend Hampton Institute, a school established to educate freedmen and their descendants. He continued his studies at Wayland Seminary in Washington, DC. Then, at the comparatively young age of twenty-five, Washington shot to prominence when Hampton's president recommended that he lead the newly established Tuskegee Normal and Industrial Institute in Alabama. Washington oversaw the opening of the school on the Fourth of July, 1881, and would helm what came to be known as Tuskegee Institute for the next thirty years.

In his role as director, Washington advanced a social, political, and educational program that emphasized vocational training, self-reliance, and entrepreneurship. His outlook was motivated by realpolitik: Recognizing the intransigence of white Southern attitudes, Washington believed Blacks should aim to provide for themselves and succeed in business, the one area where he thought Blacks could cut through discriminatory intent. Tuskegee's message found a welcome reception not only among white philanthropists and politicians but also among the Black elite, including church leaders. In the essay "Taking Advantage of Our Disadvantages," published in the *A.M.E. Church Review* in April 1894, Washington describes how a Jewish man, "only a few months from Europe," came to Tuskegee with hardly anything and lifted himself up from poverty through hard work, land subleasing, and store ownership.[21] Within four years, the man had become a pillar of the community: a landowner, a contractor of cotton, and a businessman. To the question of whether a Black man could succeed in the same ways a Jewish man did, Washington confidently responds, "Yes; this is just what I mean to say. . . . When it comes to business, pure and simple, stripped of all sentiment, I am constantly surprised to see how little prejudice is exhibited."[22] Marshaling a plainspoken Yankee style, Washington offers a model for self-reliance that he insists is applicable to the Black situation in the South.

To be sure, Washington's readers would have been well aware of the ills and prejudices against which Wells protested so passionately. What the Wizard of Tuskegee (as he came to be called) gave them, though, was a sense of responsibility over their own fate. He captures this sense in another anecdote from the essay, this one adapted from a speech by the Black educator Hugh Mason Browne (1851–1923). A ship lost at sea comes within sight of another ship. The first sends out an emergency signal for water.

---

21 Booker T. Washington, "An Article in the *A.M.E. Church Review*," in *Booker T. Washington Papers*, vol. 3., 1889–95, ed. Louis R. Harlan, Stuart B. Kaufman, and Raymond W. Smock (Champaign, IL: University of Illinois Press, 1974), 408–12, 408.

22 Washington, "Article in the *A.M.E. Church Review*," 409.

The second responds, "Cast down your buckets where you are." In disbelief, the first repeats its distress three more times; the other ship maintains its advice. Finally, the captain of the first ship casts a bucket over the side and brings up "pure, fresh, sparkling water from the Amazon river." Framing the story like a parable, Washington contends that the lesson here is for Black people not to "secure every right that is ours at once" but to discover "the opportunities that are right about us," even in seemingly inhospitable and unwelcome circumstances.[23] For Washington, genuine Black freedom lies in economic advancement, and since land is cheap and skilled labor is available in the South, that is where such freedom may be realized.

Washington perfected his message in a speech he delivered at the Cotton States and International Exposition in Atlanta, Georgia, on 18 September 1895. Known as the Atlanta Compromise, the address retreated on civil rights, accepting as it did the terms of racial segregation, in order to make the case for Black self-reliance. Although the speech draws on language from the *A.M.E. Church Review* essay, including the "cast down your buckets" parable, it seeks to curry favor with a privileged white audience. An infamous passage reads:

> As we have proved our loyalty to you in the past, in nursing your children, watching by the sick-bed of your mothers and fathers, and often following them with tear-dimmed eyes to their graves, so in the future, in our humble way, we shall stand by you with a devotion that no foreigner can approach, ready to lay down our lives, if need be, in defense of yours, interlacing our industrial, commercial, civil, and religious life with yours in a way that shall make the interests of both races one. In all things that are purely social we can be as separate as the fingers, yet one as the hand in all things essential to mutual progress.[24]

Washington may have felt he had earned the right to speak for (Southern) Black people, but his "we" rings hollow as a rhetorical device. Part of that has to do with the slippage between the "we" who are Black people to the "we" who are "as separate as the fingers." Washington's status as spokesman is, finally, lost in his effort to appeal to whites.

The Washington who went on to publish the celebrated autobiography *Up from Slavery* (1901) recalibrated his prose style in essays he published after the address.[25] Take "The Awakening of the Negro," which appeared in the *Atlantic*

---

23 Washington, "Article in the *A.M.E. Church Review*," 410.
24 Booker T. Washington, "The Standard Printed Version of the Atlanta Exposition Address," in Harlan, Kaufman, and Smock, *Booker T. Washington Papers*, 583–87, 585.
25 For a similar assessment of post–Atlanta Exposition works, see Laura R. Fisher, "Head and Hands Together: Booker T. Washington's Vocational Realism," *American Literature* 87, no. 4 (2015): 709–37.

Monthly in 1896. Washington turns conventional wisdom about moral and intellectual life on its head, stressing that material conditions are the basis for any high-minded pursuit. "When a mere boy," he begins disarmingly, "I saw a young colored man, who had spent several years in school, sitting in a common cabin in the South, studying a French grammar. I noted the poverty, the untidiness, the want of system and thrift, that existed about the cabin, notwithstanding his knowledge of French and other academic subjects."[26] At Tuskegee, however, Washington watches young men literally build the infrastructure necessary for their communities' well-being. An illustrative example is the new chapel, the materials and foundation for which were made and constructed by students. Only through technical know-how and hard work, Washington suggests, can Black people "become a centre of influence and light" – that is, figures of racial uplift.[27] In positing this form of practical enlightenment, Washington finds his first-person singular voice in the unmistakably American grain of individual pluck and advancement.

W. E. B. Du Bois: Emancipation Refracted

Washington's commentary on race relations for the mainstream press did not go unchallenged. Among the essayists who advocated for Black people's civil rights, none was more eloquent than W. E. B. Du Bois (1868–1963). By the mid-1890s, Du Bois had earned his undergraduate degree from Harvard, studied in Berlin, and become the first African American to earn his PhD from Harvard. Du Bois sharpened his commitment to civil rights through extensive study in the fields of sociology, history, and economics. After teaching stints at Wilberforce University in Ohio and the University of Pennsylvania, he assumed a professorship at Atlanta University in 1897. While he pursued his academic research, Du Bois synthesized his reflections on the status of African Americans in the postemancipation years in a series of essays he published in mainstream periodicals. He was drawn to the *Atlantic Monthly*, where he placed four essays between 1897 and 1902, broadening the reach of his work at a historically Black institution in the South.

If Washington's writing sought to assure a white readership that his example, if followed, would lead formerly enslaved people to the land of milk and honey, Du Bois's writing reflected deeply on the conflicted nature of being a racial spokesman for such an audience. His first essay, "Strivings of

---

26 Booker T. Washington, "The Awakening of the Negro," *Atlantic Monthly* (September 1896): 322–38, 322.
27 Washington, "Awakening of the Negro," 324.

the Negro People," which appeared in the August 1897 issue of the magazine, stands out for its rhetorical flair and social perspicacity. Consider the opening paragraph:

> Between me and the other world there is ever an unasked question: unasked by some through feelings of delicacy; by others through the difficulty of rightly framing it. All, nevertheless, flutter round it. They approach me in a half-hesitant sort of way, eye me curiously or compassionately, and then, instead of saying directly, How does it feel to be a problem? they say, I know an excellent colored man in my town; or, I found at Mechanicsville; or, Do not these Southern outrages make your blood boil? At these I smile, or am interested, or reduce the boiling to a simmer, as the occasion may require. To the real question, How does it feel to be a problem? I answer seldom a word.[28]

Du Bois captures the personal impersonality of his encounters with white people not through objection or protest but through reflection and measurement. In this restaging, the uttered questions signify a kind of evasion, a refusal to address what is actually on the speaker's mind. The interlocutors' politeness serves the purpose of projecting a tremendous burden onto him. The coolness of the prose matches the fact that this is a conversation between a Black man and his ostensible allies.

"Strivings of the Negro People" goes on to turn the mirror on these interlocutors, the very readers of the *Atlantic*. The problem of persistent racial inequality, Du Bois argues, cannot be laid at the feet of Black people. It must be understood as a terrible consequence of the country's collective failure to reckon with the legacy of slavery. Du Bois lists the human consequences of this failure: "The holocaust of war, the terrors of the Kuklux [sic] Klan, the lies of carpet-baggers, the disorganization of industry, and the contradictory advice of friends and foes left the bewildered serf with no new watchword beyond the old cry for freedom."[29] In other words, emancipation alone did not resolve the conflict between race and citizenship, enslavement and national belonging, that had defined the Black experience for so long. Black people are still fighting to be free. That struggle is not only political and economic in nature. It also embeds itself in the split or refracted interior lives of Black people: "One ever feels his two-ness, – an American, a Negro; two souls, two thoughts, two unreconciled strivings; two warring ideals in one dark body, whose dogged strength alone keeps it from being

---

28 W. E. B. Du Bois, "Strivings of the Negro People," *Atlantic Monthly* (August 1897): 194–98, 194.
29 Du Bois, "Strivings of the Negro People," 196.

torn asunder."[30] Du Bois terms this dualism "double-consciousness," and it is an alienation of racial identity from national belonging that came about because of the unfulfilled promises of emancipation.

Du Bois's essay is better known as "Of Our Spiritual Strivings," the first chapter of his classic book *The Souls of Black Folk* (1903). Three other essays he wrote for the *Atlantic Monthly* also appear in the collection ("The Freedman's Bureau," revised as "Of the Dawn of Freedom"; "A Negro Schoolmaster in the New South," revised as "Of the Meaning of Progress; and "Of the Training of Black Men"), as do four that had been published in other venues and were reworked into five chapters. Five pieces, including "Of the Passing of the First-Born," a meditation on the loss of his newborn son, and "Of the Coming of John," a story about the different life trajectories that separate white from Black Americans of the same background, were composed specifically for the volume.[31] Although the fourteen chapters are wide-ranging in genre and style, *The Souls of Black Folk* is definitively anchored by "Of Our Spiritual Strivings." The essay not only identifies the dualism that becomes a thematic thread connecting pieces in the collection, it also underscores the *unfreedom* that continues to circumscribe Black life fifty years since the Emancipation Proclamation.

That Du Bois made this point forcefully to a predominantly white readership, first for *Atlantic Monthly* and then through his book, indicates a new phase in the history of the African American essay. Over the next century, writing about freedom would exceed the terms of formal emancipation. In a move that continues to inspire the rhetoric and substance of Black writing, Du Bois identifies the lingering effects of slavery not just in the social fabric but in the collective psyche of the nation. No amount of Washingtonian self-reliance could repair the shattered dreams of freedmen and freedwomen. Deeper insight is needed to confront the problems of the twentieth century. The brilliance of Du Bois's notion of double-consciousness, then, and the reason that it has influenced the argument and shape of so many essays since, is that it is both a curse and a gift. It is a way of seeing the world that emerged from the failure of Reconstruction. But it is also a strategy for overcoming obstacles the world throws up, an insistence that Black people are stronger for having strived.

---

30 Du Bois, "Strivings of the Negro People," 194.
31 For an astute publishing history of the essays that went into the composition of *The Souls of Black Folk*, see Lucas Dietrich, "'At the Dawning of the Twentieth Century': W.E.B. Du Bois, A.C. McClurg & Co., and the Early Circulation of *The Souls of Black Folk*," *Book History* 20 (2017): 307–29.

10

Social Justice and the American Essay

CHRISTY WAMPOLE

Today, the term *social justice* summons a constellation of figures to mind, including people as varied as Martin Luther King Jr., Gustavo Gutiérrez, Bernie Sanders, Angela Davis, and Alexandria Ocasio-Cortez. A number of living and historical civil rights leaders, activists, liberation theologians, and progressive thinkers who've inspired a young generation of Americans to fight for prison and policing reform, economic and housing equality, or environmental justice could also be included. While the term has become a catchall to describe the main objective of various strands of left-leaning activism, this chapter reveals a somewhat neglected historical account of the term *social justice* and tracks the way a particular set of essayists has deployed it. All five of the thinkers whose work is explored here – Eugene Debs, Helen Keller, Peter Maurin, Dorothy Day, and Cornel West – have produced an abundance of essays that underscore the original mid-nineteenth-century meaning of the term *social justice*. It is important to provide an earlier history of a term used so widely in the contemporary United States because it gets to the heart of a persistent tension in American politics, namely, between Christianity and working-class interests. Historically, many in the United States have defined the country as a Christian nation, a belief that still holds sway in many places. At the same time, there is a chronic allergy in the United States toward socialism, Marxism, communism, and other belief systems structured around the interests of the working class. In returning to the origins of the term *social justice*, an untaken historical path becomes visible, one where Christianity and worker-centered thought might have merged more thoroughly and become a more significant force in American political consciousness.

While other chapters in this volume deal with specific social justice–related themes such as slavery and abolition, racial and gender justice, and climate justice, this chapter returns to the origins of the term *social justice* and the two most prominent discourses attached to these words in their early use, namely, Christian discourses and socialist discourses. In other words, I will explore here the writings of those whom Vanessa Cook has called "spiritual Socialists."[1] Among prominent American spiritual socialists are many figures, some more and some less well known today. Though it would be impossible to name them all here, a list might include Sherwood Eddy, A. J. Muste, Myles Horton, Staughton Lynd, Eugene Debs, George Washington Woodbey, Helen Keller, Dorothy Day, Peter Maurin (a French expatriate), Henry Wallace, Martin Luther King Jr., Mary Daly, Rosemary Radford Ruether, Letty Mandeville Russell, James H. Cone, Pauli Murray, Cornel West, and William Barber.

Although the first prominent uses of the term *social justice (giustizia sociale)* were found in Italy in the 1840s in the work of the Jesuit thinker Luigi Taparelli, and the dissemination of it started in the 1850s through the Jesuit journal *Civiltà cattolica*, the term has had sustained resonance far beyond Catholic circles in the United States since the late nineteenth century and has become a key motivating force in contemporary American progressive politics. The term and its frequent synonym *distributive justice* have been used widely in the fields of law (in the cases and theories of progressive legal thinkers such as Louis Brandeis and Roscoe Pound or in the legal work of the NAACP, founded in 1909); in political philosophy (in Westel Woodbury Willoughby's *Social Justice: A Critical Essay* [1900], for example, or in John Rawls's *A Theory of Justice* [1971] and "Justice as Fairness" [1985]); economics (in Thomas Nixon Carver's *Essays in Social Justice* [1915]); and theology (John A. Ryan's *Distributive Justice: The Right and Wrong of Our Present Distribution of Wealth* [1916]). An early influential text for those involved in Catholic-worker organizations and Catholic social teaching more broadly was Pope Leo XIII's 1891 encyclical *Rerum Novarum*, which makes the case for distributive justice:

> To the State the interests of all are equal whether high or low. The poor are members of the national community equally with the rich; they are real component parts, living parts, which make up, through the family, the living body; and it need hardly be said that they are by far the majority. It would be irrational to neglect one portion of the citizens and to favor another; and

---

[1] See Vanessa Cook, *Spiritual Socialists: Religion and the American Left* (Philadelphia: University of Pennsylvania Press, 2019).

therefore the public administration must duly and solicitously provide for the welfare and the comfort of the working people, or else that law of justice will be violated which ordains that each shall have his due. To cite the wise words of St. Thomas of Aquin: "As the part and the whole are in a certain sense identical, the part may in some sense claim what belongs to the whole." Among the many and grave duties of rulers who would do their best for their people, the first and chief is to act with strict justice – with that justice which is called in the Schools *distributive* – towards each and every class.[2]

While the term originated in Catholicism, many Christians who situate themselves within the Protestant tradition have understood social justice as a key motivation for faith-based political action as well. This chapter explores the essayistic writing of those who saw common cause between Christianity and workers' movements. Because of its plasticity, the essay form allows for a seamless blending of these discourses, processed through the writerly subjectivity of thinkers and activists drawn to the utopian thinking of Christian and socialist thought. What did the essay allow these reformers to do that other forms could not? By triangulating these three elements – Christian thought, socialist thought, and essayism – this chapter offers subtle revelations on America's political origins, its untaken paths, and its potential future trajectories. It will focus on those thinkers who produced an abundance of essayistic writings that celebrate the alliance of Christian and socially progressive thought.

Eugene Debs's Impassioned Essayism

Eugene V. Debs (1855–1926) is most remembered today as a founding member of several political parties, including Social Democracy of America, the Social Democratic Party of America, and the Socialist Party of America. He was also a prolific writer and orator. Bernard J. Brommel estimates that Debs "delivered over six thousand speeches and wrote approximately three thousand items for publication in newspapers, journals, and books."[3] The topics he covers in his short prose writings for various labor publications included alcoholism, tramping, elections, boycotting, child labor, nationalism, political parties, strikes, and federations.

---

2 Pope Leo XIII, *Rerum Novarum: Encyclical Letter of Pope Leo XIII on the Condition of Labor* (New York: Paulist Press, 1939), 20–21.
3 Bernard J. Brommel, quoted in Eugene V. Debs, *Walls and Bars* (Chicago: Charles H. Kerr, 1973), 20.

At times, his writing bears a manifesto-like quality, at other times an almost elegiac tone, mourning the suffering of humanity. His was a politics of passion. The convention of titling an essay "How I Became a Socialist" became a fixture in twentieth-century labor magazines and radical newspapers like *Comrade* or *Labor Leader* or in the autobiographies or memoirs of writers who wanted to narrate their political conversions. Among these are William Morris, Jack London, Helen Keller, Caroline Hollingsworth Pemberton, Margaret McMillan, J. Stitt Wilson, Job Harriman, and Fanny Bixby Spencer, just to name a fraction. In his own "How I Became a Socialist" essay (1902), describing the spark of his worker's consciousness provoked by laboring alongside railroad men, Debs writes:

> Through all these years I was nourished at Fountain Proletaire. I drank deeply of its waters and every particle of my tissue became saturated with the spirit of the working class. I had fired an engine and been stung by the exposure and hardship of the rail. I was with the boys in their weary watches, at the broken engine's side and often helped to bear their bruised and bleeding bodies back to wife and child again. How could I but feel the burden of their wrongs? How the seed of agitation fail to take deep root in my heart?[4]

Even though he expressed suspicion toward organized religion in some of his personal exchanges, much of Debs's writing turns the worker into a subjugated Christlike figure locked in an eternal *Pietà*. An example can be found in *The Cry for Justice: An Anthology of Social Protest* (1915), edited by Upton Sinclair, introduced by Jack London, and described on its cover page as containing "the writings of philosophers, poets, novelists, social reformers, and others who have voiced the struggle against social injustice."[5] This important collection includes a short piece Debs wrote on Jesus:

> The martyred Christ of the working class, the inspired evangel of the downtrodden masses, the world's supreme revolutionary leader, whose love for the poor and the children of the poor hallowed all the days of his consecrated life, lighted up and made forever holy the dark tragedy of his death, and gave to the ages his divine inspiration and his deathless name.[6]

---

4 Eugene V. Debs, *Debs: His Life, Writings, and Speeches* (Chicago: Charles H. Kerr, 1908), 81.
5 Upton Sinclair, ed., *The Cry for Justice: An Anthology of the Literature of Social Protest* (New York: Upton Sinclair, 1915), n.p.
6 Debs, in Sinclair, *Cry for Justice*, 345.

In *Walls and Bars* (1927) – which is part carceral autobiography, part vociferous call for reform – Debs dedicates the book to the impoverished prisoners who populated America's prisons, men and women he came to know during the times he himself spent behind bars in Chicago (for participating in a strike despite a court's injunction against it) and in Woodstock (for mail obstruction):

> To the countless thousands of my brothers and sisters who have suffered the cruel and pitiless torture and degradation of imprisonment in the jails, penitentiaries and other barbarous and brutalizing penal institutions of capitalism under our much-vaunted Christian civilization, and who in consequence now bear the ineffaceable brand of convicts and criminals, this volume is dedicated with affection and devotion by one of their number.[7]

Debs was sensitive to the Christian hypocrisy he saw in the punitive social practices both in and outside the jailhouse. For him, prison was not a redemptive place but rather a generator of more social dysfunction and wretchedness. He wrote, "The prison problem is directly correlated with poverty, and poverty as we see it today is essentially a social disease. It is a cancerous growth in a vulnerable spot of the social system. There should be no poverty among hard-working people."[8] The style of Debs's essays could be described as impassioned, accusatory, empathetic, and action oriented. His shorter pieces were attached to specific objects of concern, and the brevity of the essay form allowed him to address piecemeal each aspect of the workers' struggle in units of text small enough to be consumed quickly and painlessly by his working-class readership. He achieves a balance between pithiness and ardor, communicating powerful sentiments in the space of a page or two. He leaned on tropes of fervent Christian writing because he understood perhaps that politics is its own form of religion.

Helen Keller's Social Vision

Helen Keller (1880–1968) also wrote extensively about her faith and her commitment to social justice. Blind and deaf from the age of two, she described the arrival of her teacher, Anne Sullivan, as the birthday of her soul because this woman was the single figure who helped Keller understand the relationship between the referent, the signifier, and the signified through signing, making it possible for her to communicate with the world. Keller

---

7 Debs, *Walls and Bars*, 49. 8 Debs, *Walls and Bars*, 67.

was a Swedenborgian Christian, a suffragist, a pacifist, and a disability rights activist; she supported the NAACP and in 1909 joined the Socialist Party of America. In her collection *Out of the Dark: Essays, Letters, and Addresses on Physical and Social Vision* (1907), she writes this extraordinary passage on how interrogating her own blindness led her to feel compassion toward the workers in their plight:

> Step by step my investigation of blindness led me into the industrial world. And what a world it is! How different from the world of my beliefs! I must face unflinchingly a world of facts – a world of misery and degradation, of blindness, crookedness, and sin, a world struggling against the elements, against the unknown, against itself. How to reconcile this world of fact with the bright world of my imagining? My darkness has been filled with the lightness of intelligence, and, behold, the outer day-lit world was stumbling and groping in social blindness![9]

Then Keller goes on to ask a simple question: "'Why is it,' I asked, and turned to the literature of our day for an answer, 'why is it that so many workers live in unspeakable misery?' . . . O pitiful blindness! O folly that men should allow such contradictions – contradictions that violate not only the higher justice but the plainest common sense."[10] In her essay "How I Became a Socialist," she states that reading led her to socialism. The process was an arduous one. She explains:

> My reading has been limited and slow. I take a German bimonthly Socialist periodical printed in braille for the blind. (Our German Comrades are ahead of us in many respects.) . . . The other Socialist literature that I have read has been spelled into my hand by a friend who comes three times a week to read to me whatever I choose to read. . . . It is no easy and rapid thing to absorb through one's fingers a book of fifty-thousand words on economics.[11]

In a perhaps surprising passage, she emphasizes how much she loves the red of the socialists' flag, one of which she had hanging in her study. The red of the flag becomes more than a visible color; in her writing, it is a symbol of the party that can be sensed in other ways than through the eyes and can, consequently, be loved all the more deeply. Much of the rest of the essay is a defense against her antisocialist critics. She closes the piece with a critique of an editor at the Brooklyn *Eagle*, who praised and complimented Keller until she became a socialist: "But now that I have come out for Socialism he

---

9 Helen Keller, *Out of the Dark: Essays, Letters, and Addresses on Physical and Social Vision* (New York: Doubleday, Page, 1920), 10–11.
10 Keller, *Out of the Dark*, 13–14. 11 Keller, *Out of the Dark*, 20–21.

reminds me and the public that I am blind and deaf and especially liable to error."[12] She critiques the *Eagle*, his paper: "Socially blind and deaf, it defends an intolerable system – a system that is the cause of much of the physical blindness and deafness which we are trying to prevent."[13] She closes the essay this way: "If I ever contribute to the Socialist movement the book that I sometimes dream of, I know what I shall name it: 'Industrial Blindness and Social Deafness.'"[14] In another short piece, a letter sent to strikers at Little Falls, New York, in 1912, she offers a closing, rousing paragraph that sums up the social justice spirit:

> Until the spirit of love for our fellowmen, regardless of race, colour or creed, shall fill the world, making real in our lives and our deeds the actuality of human brotherhood – until the great mass of the people shall be filled with the sense of responsibility for each other's welfare, social justice can never be attained.[15]

In her writings, she advocates for the rights of the blind and deaf, of women and of workers. Juxtaposed with Debs's writings, Keller's have a practical and down-to-earth quality and rely more on understatement than hyperbole. She offers guidance on writing, on organizing, and on keeping one's spirits high in the face of adversity. In *Optimism: An Essay* (1903), she writes:

> If I am happy in spite of my deprivations, if my happiness is so deep that it is a faith, so thoughtful that it becomes a philosophy of life, – if, in short, I am an optimist, my testimony to the creed of optimism is worth hearing. As sinners stand up in meeting and testify to the goodness of God, so one who is called afflicted may rise up in gladness of conviction and testify to the goodness of life.[16]

Throughout the essay, she lists signs of "awakened and enlightened public conscience"[17] about everything from improvements in employment and housing conditions for the working poor to the concerted effort to expand their rights. These improvements, she argues, are grounds for optimism, the same optimism that she radiates as a Christian and a believer in the utopia of social progress. A common theme in Keller's writings is that of service to one's fellow man. In her essay "The Message of Swedenborg," on the Swedish theologian and mystic Emanuel Swedenborg (1688–1772), she writes

---

12 Keller, *Out of the Dark*, 28.   13 Keller, *Out of the Dark*, 28.
14 Keller, *Out of the Dark*, 29.   15 Keller, *Out of the Dark*, 35.
16 Helen Keller, *Optimism: An Essay* (New York: Cromwell, 1903), 12–13.
17 Keller, *Optimism*, 40.

that the deaf and the blind are yearning to be of service to humankind and need only be given the means to do so:

> Our service to others is limited. Our thirst for larger activity is unsatisfied. . . . Swedenborg says that "the perfection of man is the love of use," or service to others. Our groping acts are mere stammering suggestions of the service we intend. . . . The dearest of all the consolations which Swedenborg's message brings to me is that in the next world our narrow field of work shall grow limitlessly broad and luminous. There the higher self that we long to be shall find realization.[18]

Helen Keller recognized in Christianity and socialism the common language of service toward those in need and used her writerly talents to bind these discourses in the minds of her readers, who otherwise might never have seen the connection.

Peter Maurin's Easy Essays

The French expatriate Peter Maurin (1877–1949) spent most of his life in New York, advocating for the melding of Catholic and socialist principles in service of the homeless and the working classes. In the *Catholic Worker*, which he cofounded with Dorothy Day, he began to publish what he called "Easy Essays." In his introduction to *The Forgotten Radical Peter Maurin: Easy Essays from* The Catholic Worker, Lincoln Rice describes the curious genre as "short poetic phrases" and "the *modus operandi* for communicating his vision." Rice elaborates: "At first glance, Maurin's Easy Essays appear overly simplistic and preposterous. Further investigation reveals complexity and nuance. The essays are packed with demanding ideas meant to convey dense information and encourage the listener to ponder different ways to understand and interact with reality. Jesus preached parables: Peter Maurin recited Easy Essays."[19] Rice is correct to point out the orality and pedagogical emphasis of these pieces. One feels compelled to read them aloud, like nursery rhymes, short tales, or other verbal forms meant to convey lessons to malleable minds.

Taken as an ensemble, the Easy Essays explore a set of themes one could naturally anticipate finding in a Catholic workers' newspaper. For example, just between 1933 and 1934, Maurin published pieces with titles such as "Ethics

---

18 Keller, *Out of the Dark*, 260.
19 Lincoln Rice, "Introduction," in *The Forgotten Radical Peter Maurin: Easy Essays from* The Catholic Worker, by Peter Maurin, ed. Lincoln Rice (New York: Fordham University Press, 2020), 2–3.

and Economics," "Wealth-Producing Maniacs," "Commercializers of Labor," "Self-Organization," "The Duty of Hospitality," "Houses of Catholic Action," "The Spirit of the Masses," "To Be a Marxian," "Reconstructing the Social Order," "Scholars and Bourgeois," "Catholic Social Philosophy," and "Christianity, Capitalism, and Communism." To give a sense of the structure of his writings, here is his anaphoric essay "Houses of Hospitality" in its entirety:

> We need Houses of Hospitality
> to give to the rich
> the opportunity to serve the poor.
>
> We need Houses of Hospitality
> to bring the Bishops to the people
> and the people to the Bishops.
>
> We need Houses of Hospitality
> to bring back to institutions
> the technique of institutions.
>
> We need Houses of Hospitality
> to show what idealism looks like
> when it is practiced.
>
> We need Houses of Hospitality
> to bring Social Justice
> through Catholic Action
> exercised in Catholic Institutions.[20]

Many of the Easy Essays share this almost incantational quality, often characterized by anaphor and aphorism, short phrases and shrewd observations. When Maurin would respond to personal or open letters, he would also use the Easy Essay style. Maurin was obviously an idealist, and his utopian spirit comes through particularly well in the unpublished essay titled "Near Easton":

> To bring back American people
> back to the Founders of America
> the Catholic Worker
> intends to transform
> the Farming Commune
> near Easton, Pennsylvania
> into a Folk School.

20 Maurin, *Forgotten Radical*, 430.

> In that Folk School,
>> people will learn:
>> Farming
>> Canning
>> Bio-Dynamics
>> Building
>> Furniture making
>> Knitting
>> Weaving
>> Dancing
>> Singing
>> Public speaking.[21]

Maurin's utopianism permeates all of his writings and underscores the extent to which both Catholicism and socialism are utopian thought systems at their core.

Dorothy Day's Attempts for Justice

In the early 1930s, Maurin began to mentor someone who would become a more famous Catholic radical, namely, Dorothy Day (1897–1980). From early on, Day was an avid reader of the Bible and socially conscious fiction such as Upton Sinclair's *The Jungle* (1906). As this consciousness developed, she became politically active and, after quitting college, began to work for several radical periodicals. Maurin put in her hands the writings of many progressive Catholic thinkers, and on 1 May 1933 the pair launched the newspaper the *Catholic Worker*. In an essay collection celebrating the centennial of Day's birth, William J. Thorn wrote:

> Today, tomorrow, next year and throughout this new century Dorothy Day provokes us, pricks our consciences, upsets the comfort of middle class Christianity, and challenges our assimilation in contemporary American life by bearing witness to the possibility of living a life guided solely by the principles Christ proclaimed.[22]

During her lifetime, Day produced countless essays and autobiographical writings focused on the overlap of Catholic and socialist thought. Among her

---

21 Maurin, *Forgotten Radical*, 430.
22 William J. Thorn, "Introduction: Still Provoking Us after All These Years: Dorothy Day of and outside Her Time," in *Dorothy Day and The Catholic Worker Movement: Centenary Essays*, ed. William J. Thorn, Phillip M. Runkel, and Susan Mountin (Milwaukee, WI: Marquette University Press, 2001), 14–27, 14.

more recognized books are *From Union Square to Rome* (1938), *The Long Loneliness* (1952), and *Loaves and Fishes: The Inspiring Story of the Catholic Worker Movement* (1963). Many of her writings were gathered and republished after her death in collections such as *Dorothy Day: In My Own Words* (2002), *Dorothy Day: Writings from* Commonweal (2002), *Dorothy Day: Selected Writings* (2005), and *The Reckless Way of Love: Notes on Following Jesus* (2017). The autobiographical mode features heavily in Day's essays, where she traces how she became a committed Catholic and how she came to understand the compatibility between her spiritual yearnings and her desire to improve the lives of those suffering in her midst. In her book *House of Hospitality* (1939), she mentions that Mary Sheehan, a friend of the family, decided one day to name Day's black cat Social Justice. No better name could have been found for the cat of a woman whose whole life was dedicated to caring for those on the lowest rung of the social ladder. In "Houses of Hospitality," an essay published in 1938 in *Commonweal*,[23] Day argues that the Church should provide hospices for the impoverished:

> Hospices in the shadow of churches would mean a constant recognition of Christ the Worker, Christ our Brother. The priests living in close contact with the poorest of transients and ministering to them, holy Mass, missions, constant indoctrination through Catholic literature, Catholic surroundings – what a change this would make in the outlook of the poor![24]

She continues in a similar vein in *Meditations* (1970), a compilation of her writings:

> I watched that ragged horde and thought to myself, "These are Christ's poor. He was one of them. He was a man like other men, and He chose His friends among ordinary workers. These men feel they have been betrayed by Christianity. Men are not Christian today. If they were, this sight would not be possible. Far dearer in the sight of God perhaps are these hungry ragged ones, than all those smug, well-fed Christians who sit in their homes, cowering in fear of the Communist menace."[25]

Day's remarks here are characteristic of many essays produced under the rubric of spiritual socialism in that they make a distinction between "real" Christianity,

---

23 Founded in 1924, *Commonweal* is an American liberal Catholic opinion journal, similar to the *Nation* (founded in 1865) and the *New Republic* (founded in 1914) but with a Catholic twist.
24 Dorothy Day, *Dorothy Day: Writings from* Commonweal, ed. Patrick Jordan (New York: Commonweal, 2002), 59.
25 Dorothy Day, *Meditations* (New York: Missionary Society of St. Paul the Apostle, 1970), 11.

which puts care for the poor at the heart of its mission, and a fake bourgeois Christianity, which treats the poor with condescension and blame. For example, Martin Luther King Jr. wrote the following in his chapter "How Should a Christian View Communism?": "In spite of the noble affirmations of Christianity, the church has often lagged in its concern for social justice and too often been content to mouth pious irrelevances and sanctimonious trivialities."[26] A key feature of social justice essays (in the spiritual-socialist sense of the term) is that they critique Christianity and lobby for its improvement.

In 2016, Kate Hennessy, the American writer and granddaughter of Dorothy Day, put together a photo essay that pairs excerpts of Day's essays with photographs by Vivian Cherry (1920–2019), the socially conscious American street photographer. In many respects, this remarkable assemblage, titled *Dorothy Day and the Catholic Worker: The Miracle of Our Continuance*, echoes the extraordinary photo essay *Let Us Now Praise Famous Men* (1941) by James Agee and Walker Evans in its highlighting of the ever-present class-based sufferings in the United States. Assigned to document the Catholic worker movement at Day's side, Cherry "began by photographing the soup line meals at the house of hospitality at 223 Chrystie Street, a block away from the Bowery with its gin mills, flophouses, and drunk or sleeping men lying on the sidewalks or in doorways."[27] As Hennessy notes in the introduction, "Vivian's instincts drew her to all the basic elements of the Catholic Worker – hospitality and farming, prayer and protest."[28] As Day wrote in a piece that appears in that collection, "Poverty is a mysterious thing. We need to be always writing and thinking about it."[29] Through the essay form, Day tried to put into the hands of new readers the kind of beautiful, action-seeking prose that had inspired her own political and spiritual engagement.

Cornel West's Prophetic Essayism

Cornel West (1953–), the prominent American academic, activist, and Democratic Socialist, would likely agree with Day's assertion that we should always think and write about poverty. His oeuvre has been laser focused on

---

26 Martin Luther King Jr., *Strength to Love* (New York: Harper and Row, 1963), 97. King himself studied Marx's writings and the histories of Marxism, socialism, and communism and in doing so concluded that he could not endorse the dogmatic elements he saw in these ideologies.
27 Kate Hennessy, "Introduction," in *Dorothy Day and the Catholic Worker: The Miracle of Our Continuance*, by Vivian Cherry and Dorothy Day, ed. Kate Hennessy (New York: Fordham University Press, 2016), 2.
28 Hennessy, *Dorothy Day*, 3.   29 Day, in Hennessy, *Dorothy Day*, 39.

the struggles of working and impoverished people through the lens of Christianity. West is a panoramic thinker and writer, and the capaciousness of his thought can barely be contained by such a diminutive form as the essay. This has not stopped him from marshaling the form to reach audiences across generations. His essays, like Helen Keller's, are marked by an indomitable optimism and a firm belief that, with the right kind of political and spiritual dynamism, the world can be made vastly more hospitable to those who suffer. With its particular blend of commitments to improving the lives of Black Americans, working and poor people, and other groups that have incurred the collateral damage of the capitalist system, his work can be situated in a genealogy of early Black Christian social justice activists leading from Rev. George W. Woodbey, Rev. Martin Luther King Jr. and Rev. James H. Cone to contemporary figures such as Rev. Jesse Jackson and Rev. William Barber.[30] This is likely why so many of West's essays bear the residue of the sermon as literary genre. West has also been a professor at universities including Harvard and Princeton and religious institutions such as the Union Theological Seminary, Harvard Divinity School, and Yale Divinity School, teaching and researching on everything from literature and theology to philosophy and civil rights. At Harvard, he was a W. E. B. Du Bois fellow and has written and thought extensively about Du Bois's contributions to the improvement of Black people's lives. West's essays and interviews have appeared in magazines including *Tikkun, October,* the *American Prospect, Smithsonian,* the *Christian Century, Commonweal,* the *Progressive,* the *Nation, Dissent,* the *Atlantic, New York Times Magazine,* and others. While most of his writings are book-length reflections on topics such as race, religion, and politics, he has also produced a vast number of shorter essays on the overlap of Christianity and the rights of the working class. Among those collected in *Prophetic Fragments* (1988) and *The Cornel West Reader* (1999) are "Religion and the Left," "On Liberation Theology: Segundo and Hinkelammert," "On

---

30 James H. Cone traces part of this rich history in his book-length essay *The Black Church and Marxism: What Do They Have to Say to Each Other?*, published by the Institute for Democratic Socialism in 1980. He closes his essay with these thoughts: "Perhaps what we need today is to return to that 'good old-time religion' of our grandparents and combine with it a Marxist critique of society. Together black religion and Marxist philosophy may show us the way to build a completely new society. With that combination, we may be able to realize in the society the freedom of which we sing and pray for in the black church." James H. Cone, *The Black Church and Marxism: What Do They Have to Say to Each Other?* (New York: Institute of Democratic Socialism, 1980), 10.

Michael Harrington's *The Politics at God's Funeral*," "The New Populism: A Black Socialist Christian Critique," "Prophetic Christian as Organic Intellectual: Martin Luther King, Jr.," "The Black Church and Socialist Politics," and "Subversive Joy and Revolutionary Patience in Black Christianity." In the first of these, originally published in *Monthly Review* in 1984, West writes:

> Notwithstanding the secular sensibilities of most leftist intellectuals and activists, religion permeates and pervades the lives of the majority of the people in the capitalist world. And all signs indicate that the prevailing crisis in the capitalist world is not solely an economic or political one. Recent inquiries into the specificity of racism, patriarchy, homophobia, state repression, bureaucratic domination, ecological subjugation, and nuclear exterminism suggest that we need to understand this crisis as that of capitalist civilization. To extend leftist discourses about political economy and the state to a discourse about capitalist civilization is to accent a sphere rarely scrutinized by Marxist thinkers: the sphere of culture and everyday life. And any serious scrutiny of this sphere sooner or later must come to terms with religious ways of life and religious ways of struggle.[31]

By pointing out this religious blind spot in the Marxist thought of the mid-1980s, West signals the need for a renewal of the productive bond of Christian and socialist thought described throughout this chapter. In *Keeping Faith: Philosophy and Race in America* (1993), he describes the kind of Christian thought that most compels him: "The synoptic vision I accept is a particular kind of prophetic Christian perspective which comprehensively grasps and enables opposition to existential anguish, socioeconomic, cultural and political oppression and dogmatic modes of thought and action."[32] While West recognizes the church's *potential* to act as a furthering force for social justice, given that Jesus is seen by many as its original proponent, he argues that it has not lived up to this promise. In this passage from *Democracy Matters: Winning the Fight against Imperialism* (2004), which bears the aforementioned features of spiritual socialism's persistent self-critique, West argues:

> [I]t is undeniable that the challenge of keeping the prophetic Christian movement vital and vibrant in the age of American empire is largely unmet as of yet. The pervasive sleepwalking in American churches in regard to social justice is frightening. The movement led by Martin Luther King Jr. – the legacy of

---

31 Cornel West, "Religion and the Left," in *Prophetic Fragments: Illuminations of the Crisis in American Religion and Culture* (Grand Rapids, MI: Eerdmans, 1988), 13.
32 Cornel West, *Keeping Faith: Philosophy and Race in America* (New York: Routledge, 2009), 120.

which has been hijacked by imperial Christians – forged the most subtle and significant democratic Christian identity of modern times. And it now lies in ruins. Can prophetic Christians make its dry bones live again?[33]

In West's view, certain powerful American Christians corrupted King's original vision by committing themselves to imperialist interests rather than sustaining his original legacy of service toward the oppressed. In his essay "The Black Church and Socialist Politics," West notes the singular history of the Black church, distinct from the white Protestant tradition in America that leans toward the politically conservative:

> [T]he distinctive feature of Afro-American Christianity has been its capacity to make visible and potent its progressive prophetic pole. Nat Turner, Denmark Vesey, and Gabriel Prosser – Christian preachers who led slave insurrections in the nineteenth century – signify in dramatic fashion the crucial role of the black church in the Afro-American struggle for freedom. . . . This Afro-American Christianity serves as the major resource upon which black people draw strength and sustenance in their encounter with the modern American capitalist order – as urban dwellers, industrial workers, bureaucratic employees, and franchised citizens.[34]

In West's view, it is the church more than any other institution that nourishes Black Americans as they fight for social justice in capitalism's punitive system, which has been disproportionately harsh toward them. In a particularly striking passage from his essay "We Socialists" (1991), West forges his unique understanding of Democratic Socialism, applying to it the language of faith, sacrifice, and love so central to Christian thought:

> Democratic faith is not a romanticizing and idealizing of ordinary persons. It's a recognition of their potential and possibility. And the labor of love has to do with the level of sacrifice needed. We're talking in part about a way of life as much as a struggle; and this is one thing I actually admire deeply in the old Communist comrades. I might have deep intellectual, ideological and moral reservations and disagreements with the old Communist comrades, but what they understood is something that a lot of black church activists understood: that if you are serious about this struggle, there's going to be levels of sacrifice that are unimaginable, but you go ahead anyway. And the only thing I can call it is a labor of love.[35]

---

33 Cornel West, *Democracy Matters: Winning the Fight against Imperialism* (New York: Penguin Press, 2004), 167–68.
34 Cornell West, "The Black Church and Socialist Politics," in *Prophetic Fragments*, 67.
35 Cornel West, "We Socialists," in *Prophetic Reflections: Notes on Race and Power in America*, vol. 2, *Beyond Eurocentrism and Multiculturalism* (Monroe, ME: Common Courage Press, 1993), 243.

In West's work, we find the consistent merging of two thought systems – prophetic Christianity and Democratic Socialism – whose vocabularies and principles overlap far more than many acknowledge. His essays readily blend these traditions, showing their obvious compatibilities and attempting to revive a tradition truncated by two types of skepticism: on the one hand, general American skepticism toward socialism and its adjacent traditions, and, on the other hand, the skepticism of leftist intellectuals toward religion. In a sense, West's writings function as peace accords between two thought systems that have lived uneasily side by side in the United States since the nineteenth century.

As this chapter shows, the term *social justice* has been emptied in our moment of much of its original significance. Most people who use the term are probably unfamiliar with the rich history of American essayists celebrating the earlier camaraderie between Christianity and socialism. Their essays deftly show the obvious affinities between the two and illustrate the delicate and complicated coexistence of religion and politics in the United States since its inception. The essay, itself a hybrid form, allows for the blending of the logics and languages of these doctrines through the subjectivity of the impassioned essayist. Both Christianity and socialism are preoccupied with a better world to come, and the essay, too, announces the possibility of a future, more fully developed iteration of itself.[36] Essays on social justice are where the manifesto and the sermon meet, where political and religious zeal find expression. By recalling the earliest context of the term social justice, this chapter adds another dimension to contemporary debates on the term as it applies to everything from Black struggle to economic inequality, from climate justice to equitable representation at all levels of government. The essay form allowed the writers studied in this chapter to articulate in a variety of styles – from the lyrical to the vociferous, the pedagogical to the morally urgent – the need for a compassionate understanding of human wretchedness in an industrialized world bent on breaking the worker. This important tradition in American writing may find new life again among a generation of young people who are responsive to the language of social justice.

---

36 As György Lukács phrased it in his famous piece "The Nature and Form of the Essay," "The essayist is a Schopenhauer who writes his *Parerga* while waiting for the arrival of his own (or another's) *The World as Will and Idea*, he is a John the Baptist who goes out to preach in the wilderness about another who is still to come, whose shoelace he is not worthy to untie." György Lukács, *Soul and Form*, trans. Anna Bostock, ed. John T. Sanders and Kate Terezakis (New York: Columbia University Press, 2010), 32.

11

"Zones of Contention" in the Genteel Essay

JENNY SPINNER

for Ned Stuckey-French

On 25 August 1911, George Santayana (1863–1952) stood before a gathering of the Philosophical Union of the University of California to deliver a lecture on what he deemed the current defects in American thought and literature. Santayana's depiction of a literary and cultural stagnation at the turn of the century, which he pinned directly on the "genteel tradition," became a call to arms against the writers, thinkers, and educators in this tradition whom Santayana faulted for their egoism and mental laziness, which he felt impeded American progress.[1] The coinage caught on. As Douglas Wilson explains, "The phrase served not only to focus attention on the most vulnerable chink in the Establishment's armor, but it also served the 'literary radicals' as a rallying cry in their insurgent war on intellectual poverty."[2] That war had already begun in the prior century. By the time Santayana produced its label, the genteels were already losing ground, attacked by critics for the tradition's "tea-table gentility," as Sinclair Lewis (1885–1951) put it in his acceptance speech for the 1930 Nobel Prize for Literature.[3] In that speech, Lewis singled out William Dean Howells (1837–1920), a pillar among genteel essayists, for having the "code of a pious old maid" and, along with other writers, for "effusively seeking to guide America into becoming a pale edition of an English cathedral town."[4] If Santayana's lecture was an epilogue

---

[1] See George Santayana, "The Genteel Tradition in American Philosophy," in *The Genteel Tradition: Nine Essays by George Santayana*, ed. Douglas L. Wilson (Cambridge, MA: Harvard University Press, 1967), 37–64.
[2] Santayana, "Introductory," in "Genteel Tradition," 14.
[3] Sinclair Lewis, "The American Fear of Literature," in *Nobel Lectures: Literature, 1901–1967*, ed. Horst Frenz (Amsterdam: Elsevier, 1969), 278–89, 288.
[4] Lewis, "American Fear," 287, 288.

on the tradition, Lewis's speech was its afterword. By the late 1930s, the genteel writers had largely been snuffed into irrelevance, a generation of essayists among them.

While contemporary scholars and historians of the essay frequently don recovery gear in search of forgotten or overlooked contributors, the genteel tradition rarely entices critics to take a closer look around. Most volumes of genteel essays reek of the dust that has settled over their outsize focus on the morals ("Can a Husband Open His Wife's Letters?"), manners ("On Teaching One's Grandmother How to Suck Eggs"), and other life concerns ("The Soul of the Gentleman") of the upper-middle class ("The Discomforts of Luxury: A Speculation").[5] The genteel essayist himself – pronoun intended – presents as a caricature, as Charles S. Brooks (1878–1934) does in the 1922 essay "The Writing of Essays":

> An essayist is not a mighty traveler. He does not run to grapple with a roaring lion. He desires neither typhoon nor tempest. He is content in his harbor to listen to the storm upon the rock, if now and then by a lucky chance he can shelter some one [sic] from the wreck. His hands are not red with revolt against the world. He has glanced upon the thoughts of many men, and as opposite philosophies point upon the truth, he is modest with his own and tolerant of others. He looks at the start and, knowing in what dim immensity we travel, he writes of little things beyond dispute.[6]

However pleasant the fellow behind them may be, the essays that Brooks and other genteel essayists produced can be a slog to read. They are not very teachable. Ned Stuckey-French stopped to take a long look around while a graduate student at the University of Iowa in the 1990s, ultimately publishing in 2011 *The American Essay in the American Century*, a comprehensive scholarly examination of the American essay during this period. Stuckey-French argues that the genteel essay exemplified the culture wars of a changing America, and signified a change in the essay itself: "It was in this zone of contention where older forms of the essay and self, forms that we associate with the Genteel Tradition, were giving way to new ones that

---

5 See Charles Dudley Warner, "Can a Husband Open His Wife's Letters?," in *As We Go* (New York: Harper and Brothers, 1893), 49–53; Louisa Imogen Guiney, "On Teaching One's Grandmother How to Suck Eggs," in *Patrins* (Boston: Copeland and Day, 1897), 223–29; George William Curtis, "The Soul of the Gentleman," in *Ars Recte Vivendi* (New York: Harper and Brothers, 1898), 30–35; and Agnes Repplier, "The Discomforts of Luxury: A Speculation," in *In the Dozy Hours* (Boston: Houghton Mifflin, 1894), 112–22.
6 Charles S. Brooks, "The Writing of Essays," in *Modern Essays and Stories*, ed. Frederick Houk Law (New York: Century, 1922), 219–24, 220.

modern America was written."[7] The "new" essays not only differed in shape – newspaper columns, chief among them – but also in tone. They were edgier, less polite and less erudite, more middle than upper class, and gradually more representative of a wider array of Americans and their experiences. Amid the cultural and political upheavals at the beginning of the twentieth century, the genteel essayists dug in, ultimately reinforcing the notion of the essay as an old-fashioned form written by Anglophiles in tweed jackets, propped in front of their cozy fires, and kept company by their libraries and their thoughts. This image of essayist as doddering white male persisted well into the twentieth century, a relic of the genteel essay tradition that outlasted the genteel essay itself. Eventually, though, the genteel essayist, too, gave up the proverbial ghost, or rather became it. Aside from Stuckey-French's work, the occasional scholarly essay, or a chronological appearance in an anthology charting the history of the essay, the genteel essayists – among them, once popular writers like Brooks, Katharine Fullerton Gerould (1879–1944), Louise Imogen Guiney (1861–1920), Gail Hamilton (1833–1896), Gertrude Bustill Mossell (1855–1948), Agnes Repplier (1855–1950), Benjamin Brawley (1882–1939), George William Curtis (1824–1892), Donald Grant Mitchell (1822–1908), and Charles Dudley Warner (1829–1900) – remain largely where they were shelved in the 1930s.

In some ways, it is hard to make a case for a serious study of these essayists from our own contemporary moment, when we are demanding a diverse genre that celebrates a multiplicity of voices and corresponding scholarship on the essay that also seeks to address those demands. With few exceptions, genteel essays reflect Anglo, upper-middle-class, Christian values. As Ellery Sedgwick III points out, genteel essayists used those values as a protective shield against the enemies of high culture: "industrialism, urbanization, corporate capitalism, class polarization, immigration, and mass culture."[8] In her 1915 essay "The Extirpation of Culture," Gerould blames democratization, immigration – "the influx of a racially and socially inferior population" – science, and materialism on the decline of American culture.[9] While they might have supported abolitionism and suffragism,

---

7 Ned Stuckey-French, *The American Essay in the American Century* (Columbia, MO: University of Missouri Press, 2011), 2.
8 Ellery Sedgwick III, *A History of* The Atlantic Monthly, *1857–1909: Yankee Humanism at High Tide and Ebb* (Amherst, MA: University of Massachusetts Press, 1994), 249.
9 Katharine Fullerton Gerould, "The Extirpation of Culture," in *Modes and Morals* (New York: Scribner's, 1920), 66–93, 68.

essayists like Gerould represented "the older immigration," according to Malcolm Cowley:

> They were English by descent, except for a few whose forbears were Scottish or Knickerbocker or Huguenot, and they looked down in a kindly way on the Irish and the Germans. England for them was "our old home," to be regarded with a mixture of emulative jealousy and pride of kinship. Their literary models were English, with the result that much of their writing seemed less national than colonial.[10]

What they stood to lose in modern society was a softer, romanticized (white, upper-middle class) past that privileged respectability and good manners. And while the genteel essayists counted among themselves numerous women, the men, as is typical in the essay's history, garnered far more critical attention. Thus, the genteel essay tradition itself has been passed down to us as mostly male as well. Yet the genteel essay is rife with what Stuckey-French calls "zones of contention" that make it worthy of our attention. They can be found in the ongoing obituaries for the form, among the "custodians of cultures"[11] who controlled the literary marketplace and university curricula, in the literary and commercial success of women essayists whom historians and critics have largely sidelined, and in the essays of Black writers who contorted a genre rooted in whiteness largely to benefit fellow Black Americans.

Obituary as Essay Criticism

Burton Rascoe's (1892–1957) celebration of American essayists in 1922 reads like fevered nationalism: "For I hold these truths to be self-evident: that in the field of essay writing contemporary Americans are incomparably superior to the modern Englishmen; that our essayists hold their own with the essayists of all other countries; and that it is intimidated deference to assume the contrary."[12] The most positive of essay criticism during the genteel period situated itself in larger discussions about the ability of American writers to produce a distinctly American literature. Fans of the genteel felt they succeeded. But the modern essay's direct lineage to Montaigne (1533–1592),

---

10 Malcolm Cowley, "Foreword: The Revolt against Gentility," in *After the Genteel Tradition: American Writers 1910–1930*, ed. Malcolm Cowley (Carbondale, IL: Southern Illinois University Press, 1964), 3–20, 13.
11 See Henry F. May, "Custodians of Culture," in *The End of American Innocence* (Chicago: Quadrangle Books, 1964), 30–51.
12 Burton Rascoe, "What of Our Essayists?" *Bookman* 55 (1922): 74–75, 74.

William Hazlitt (1778–1830), and Charles Lamb (1775–1834), whom the genteel essayists frequently invoked, made it difficult to untether the form from its European roots, and the genteel essayist's Anglophilia made it all the harder. In a 1917 essay, "Melodious Meditations," Virginia Woolf (1882–1941) panned American essayist Henry Dwight Sedgwick (1861–1957) as yet another example of an American essayist bound to Victorian sensibilities that even the English had abandoned: "We sometimes fancy that these antiquated ghosts merely took shop to America, lodged with the best families, and now walk abroad in those essays which the American writes so frequently upon Old Age, Old Maids, On Being Ill, and Sorrow."[13] But beyond the nationalists, essay critics during the genteel period generally sounded a note of defeat. For the first three decades of the twentieth century, they sat vigil at the essay's deathbed, casting about for something to blame the crisis on. By 1933, when John Waters's oft-cited essay, "A Little Old Lady Passes Away," appeared in *Forum and Century*, the essay appeared to have finally taken its last breath. As Stuckey-French argues, though, the essay itself was never in peril; what the genteel stakeholders were mourning was the familiar essay as perfected by the English in a bygone world where that essay once made sense.[14] Waters, who loved the old essay's "intimacy, reverie, whimsy," is sad to see the familiar essay replaced by "crisp articles, blatant exposés, or statistic-laden surveys" – in other words, articles.[15] This complaint was common. In "Information, Please!," which appeared in December 1934, in the *Saturday Review of Literature*, Gerould too bemoaned the preponderance of articles – all "dope and statistics" – that filled the pages of the period's magazines.[16] Gerould wonders, though, if the dearth of familiar essays stems from the fact that readers want fewer of them or that editors and publishers *think* readers want fewer of them; unable to imagine a world in which readers prefer articles over essays, she suggests polling readers to find out. The next month, the *Saturday Review* published Alfred Dashiell's letter to the editor in response to Gerould's essay. In that letter, Dashiell, managing editor of *Scribner's Magazine*, reports that, in fact, Scribner's *had* polled its readers,

---

13 Virginia Woolf, "Melodious Meditations," in *The Essays of Virginia Woolf*, ed. Andrew McNeillie (San Diego, CA: Harcourt Brace Jovanovich, 1987), 2:80–82, 80.
14 See Ned Stuckey-French, "Why Does the Essay Keep Dying, and What Do Little Lord Fauntleroy and the 'Lavender-Scented Little Old Lady' Have to Do with It?," *CEA Critic* 61, no. 2–3 (1999): 30–36.
15 John P. Waters, "A Little Old Lady Passes Away," *Forum and Century* 90, no. 1 (1933): 27–29, 27.
16 Katharine Fullerton Gerould, "Information, Please!," *Saturday Review of Literature* (29 December 1934): 393, 395, 393.

and the magazine was giving them exactly what they wanted. It is Gerould, he suggests, who is out of touch: "I suspect from other statements in Mrs. Gerould's article that she simply does not care much for the life of the present days and looks back with some regret at the comparative tranquility of the turn of the century."[17] Henry Seidel Canby, editor of the *Saturday Review,* weighed in as well in a February 1935, editorial, contending that the essay is an artifact from a different age, and the current age, in which "time is out of joint," simply cannot sustain it. It is not the essay's fault, he says, that no one wants essays and no one wants to write them: "[N]ot many can read them without a nervous feeling that the writer is taking his time when there is no time to take from a hurrying year in which war or revolution or a dictatorship may be declared in the next headline."[18]

So much of the hand-wringing in essay criticism at the turn of the century alighted upon how ill-suited the essay was for the quick and fragmented pace of the modern world. Essays, they argued, were like cud that needed to be chewed over. It was no accident that Oliver Wendell Holmes (1841–1935) situated so many of his genteel essays at the breakfast table[19]; in Brooks's "The Writing of Essays," the essayist even has time to chew on his own pencil.[20] But it was the First World War that rattled the genteel essayists more than anything else. Paradoxically, at least initially, the war gave purpose to the essayists, who, according to Ellery Sedgwick, were delegated "the task of morally and spiritually justifying the war."[21] Some took that mission to heart, sticking to their light rambles and keeping the catastrophes of war at a figurative distance. In her 1917 volume of essays, *Days Out and Other Papers,* Elisabeth Woodbridge Morris (1870–1964) uses the word *war* (and *a* war rather than *the* war) only once, in the essay "A Meditation Concerning Form," encouraging Americans to embrace outward expressions of patriotism in a show of good manners.[22] In Brooks's essay "1917," images of war appear in a terrible, vivid, unshakeable dream of "cries of anguish," "men

---

17 Alfred Dashiell, "Letter to the Editor," *Saturday Review of Literature* (26 January 1935): 444.
18 Henry Seidel Canby, "The Essay as Barometer," *Saturday Review of Literature* (16 February 1935): 488
19 See Oliver Wendell Holmes, *The Autocrat of the Breakfast-Table* (1858), *The Professor at the Breakfast-Table* (1859), and *The Poet at the Breakfast-Table* (1872).
20 Brooks, "Writing of Essays," 219.
21 Ellery Sedgwick III, "The American Genteel Tradition in the Early Twentieth Century," *American Studies* 25, no. 1 (1984): 49–67, 50.
22 Elisabeth Woodbridge, "A Meditation Concerning Form," in *Days Out and Other Papers* (Boston: Houghton Mifflin, 1917), 133. The word *war* appears in the following sentence: "[T]he young people who are growing up among us ... think of war as something in a textbook, and loyalty as something mentioned in poetry and history ... "

blinded by gases and crazed by suffering," and "children lying dead among their toys."[23] By couching these images in his subconscious, however, Brooks protects himself, and his gentle readers, from the wide-awake consciousness of war's realities. As the war wore on, however, any cheery optimism, once the hallmark of the genteel essay, began to seem almost farcical, desperate, or at the very least, severely out of touch. And given the increasingly cranky, and even bitter, tone of some of their essays, it appears the genteel holdouts of the twentieth century found it difficult to maintain that optimism anyway.

Yet Repplier, in her 1918 piece "The American Essay in War Time," argues that essayists *had* to ignore greater matters of the world because an essay, by its very definition, could not otherwise be an essay. Writing essays in politically turbulent times, she contends, requires a "greater power of detachment than had Montaigne or Lamb,"[24] and she mourns the fact that the familiar essay had "withered in the blasts of war."[25] Gerould, in an "Essay on Essays," wrote similarly that "a state of war produces any literary form more easily than the essay."[26] As Repplier must admit, though, when genteel essayists soldier on, so to speak, when they adhere to what she calls their "birthright" to write of themselves as Montaigne and Lamb did, the essay crumples under the weight of war.[27] Repplier offers no solution, only aggrieved resolve to wait it out. The idea of the essay as "birthright" is itself indicative of a viewpoint enmeshed in a genteel tradition obsessed with its own upper-class ethos. The genteel essayist seemed incapable of interrogating the privilege that the familiar essay embodied. Since the time of Montaigne, the personal essay in particular had been the purview of those with the personal, cultural, and commercial freedom to use the essay as vehicle for self-reflection. White writers with means enjoyed that freedom more than anyone else, and white men most of all. Essayists without such privileges often found work-arounds, and the form morphed to suit the age it was in. What the genteels failed to recognize in their mortuary tributes, in their attempt to cast blame on anyone and anything other than themselves, was that the genteel essayists' own narrow appreciation of the essay, and their refusal to adapt, doomed them to the back shelf of the essay canon.

23 Charles S. Brooks, "1917," in *Chimney-Pot Papers* (New Haven, CT: Yale University Press, 1920), 43–44, 43.
24 Agnes Repplier, "The American Essay in War Time," *Yale Review* 7, no. 10 (January 1917–8): 249–59, 258.
25 Repplier, "American Essay," 253.
26 Katharine Fullerton Gerould, "An Essay on Essays," *North American Review* 240, no. 3 (1935): 409–18, 415.
27 Repplier, "American Essay," 258.

The Custodians of Culture

One of Woolf's complaints in "Melodious Meditations" is that American essayists thought of themselves as a revered "priesthood" who believed that "intellectual traditions of generations of educated men should be taught by them as a special cult."[28] Historian Henry F. May called this priesthood "the custodians of culture"; they were the mostly elderly (white) men who served as the "champions of moralism, progress, and culture" and who "retained a hold on nearly all of the strategic centers of cultural war, on the universities, the publishing houses, the weightier magazines, and most of the other centers of serious opinion."[29] The custodians of culture are significant to the turn-of-the-century essay genre in particular because the essay functioned as the primary communiqué of their cult. In the mid-to-late nineteenth and early twentieth centuries, the "weightier magazines" – the *Century Magazine*, *Scribner's*, *Harper's*, and the *Atlantic* – were important repositories for genteel essays, and both the editors' desires to promote the ideals of the genteel tradition in their magazines and the writers' desires to be published in them were mutually sustaining. Writers chosen for publication in one of these elite publications enjoyed both reputational and monetary benefits. But their writing had to meet the literary and cultural standards set forth by the custodians. No doubt many of them truly believed in the ideals they espoused, but promoting those ideals was nonetheless a requisite for the rewards of publishing in the elite magazines during the height of the genteel period. So it would remain until the rise of a new generation of writers, disaffected by the genteels' ideals and standards, altered marketplace demands. Until that point, many Americans, not just the stakeholders and gatekeepers of the genteel tradition but the general citizenry as well, believed in the interlocking nature of culture and civilization,[30] such that a cultured people, a cultured America, might access a higher form of civilization. For the genteel writers and editors, that access was provided through a "flourishing didactic literature" that reinforced their moral and cultural code.[31] That was a tall order for a periodical, but many editors, and readers, shared a belief in the possibility that literature, that essays, could make a better world. The bookish essays and long-running columns of genteel writers like Holmes, Howells, and James Russell Lowell (1819–1891) seemed intent on doing just that. The unseating of the genteels came about, at least in part, when

---

28 Woolf, "Melodious Meditations," 81.   29 May, "Custodians of Culture," 51.
30 May, "Custodians of Culture," 31.   31 Sedgwick, "American Genteel Tradition," 41.

subscribing readers, reflective of a larger public, no longer wanted or needed, or believed in, what the genteels had to offer.

The college student had less choice in the matter. In English composition classrooms, in particular, students were often assigned a diet of readings from anthologies that contained essays reprinted from the period's elite magazines. As May notes, "For those who intended to fight and win the great battle for culture in democracy, the main battleground was clearly education."[32] In universities, then, the genteel essay served as a vehicle for the study, promotion, and imitation of the code that the custodians of culture (the magazine editors, the anthology editors, the college professors) prescribed and hoped to preserve. Ralph Philip Boas's 1921 *Youth and the New World: Essays from the Atlantic Monthly* is just one of many compilations that the Atlantic Monthly Press published for the education market, a venue that provided additional opportunities for the custodians to exert influence. Boas recognized the challenges that his young readers faced. They were growing up in "a period of violent change and readjustment, born of war and destruction," and without "new standards" to guide them."[33] The genteel essayists embraced the task at hand. Amid all the "crude and sordid elements of modern life," as Samuel McChord Crothers (1857–1927) put it in "The Evolution of the Gentleman," the genteel essayists stood ready to offer guidance, and the occasional reprimand.[34]

Margaret Sherwood (1864–1955) and Cornelia A. P. Comer (1865–1929), two "old-school" *Atlantic* contributors, open *Youth and the New World* with essays sharply critical of younger people: Sherwood with "The Other Side" and Comer with "A Letter to the Rising Generation." Comer's essay, which first appeared in the February 1911 issue of the *Atlantic*, pits the people of Comer's generation – "your seniors" – against those in the next, whom she finds ill mannered, vulgar, selfish, and lacking character and a sense of duty.[35] (She does make exceptions for those young people who read the *Atlantic*.[36]) Comer's essay did not sit well with Randolph Bourne (1886–1918), a young writer who first read Comer's essay not in the *Atlantic* itself but in a philosophy class at Columbia University. Bourne responded with "The

---

32 May, "Custodians of Culture," 39.
33 Ralph Philip Boas, "Introduction," in *Youth and the New World*, ed. Ralph Philip Boas (Boston: Atlantic Monthly Press, 1921), 2–16, 2.
34 Samuel McChord Crothers, "The Evolution of the Gentleman," in *The Gentle Reader* (Boston: Houghton Mifflin, 1903), 201–26, 202.
35 Cornelia A. P. Comer, "A Letter to the Rising Generation," *Atlantic Monthly* 107, no. 2 (February 1911): 145–54, 145.
36 Comer, "Letter to the Rising Generation," 153.

Two Generations,"[37] which his professor, using his connections with then *Atlantic* editor Ellery Sedgwick, helped Bourne publish in May 1911.[38] In *Youth and the New World*, Boas follows Comer's essay with another essay by Bourne on the same subject, "The Older Generation," which had been published in the *Atlantic* in September 1915. Both essays make a similar argument: that the code that guides the older generation is selfish and undemocratic, and young people are set to wage "guerilla warfare" on that code.[39] Young people are onto the older generation's tactics, writes Bourne in "The Older Generation": "In an effort to retain the *status quo* of that world of inequalities and conventions in which they most comfortably and prosperously live, the older generation has stamped, though all its agencies of family, church, and school, upon the younger generation, just those seductive ideals which would preserve its position."[40]

Women and the Genteel Essay

For essay scholars in our own time, anthologies like *Youth and the New World* are important historical artifacts. Their introductions help to historicize and contextualize critical discussions of the form. Tables of contents showcase essays that met commercial publishing demands at any given time. These are the essayists whom editors found worthy of preserving and teaching – because they were successful and known to editors and readers, and because there were a part of a network of like-minded editors, critics, educators, and writers who promoted one another's work, as genteel critics and writers did with zeal. As instructive as they are, however, anthologies also tell an incomplete history, revealing the complex gender dynamics and divisions of the literary marketplace and the value-laden decisions that guided editors' selection criteria. The growth of the periodical landscape after the Civil War provided more opportunities for women to write and publish professionally than ever before, and many did, particularly in fiction, in part because editors believed that fiction was best suited for their growing female readership. But women essayists did not enjoy that same welcome. Even though nonfiction dominated periodicals like the *Atlantic*, only a select few women contributed

---

37 See Randolph S. Bourne, "The Two Generations," *Atlantic Monthly* 107, no. 5 (May 1911): 591–98.
38 Bruce Clayton, *Forgotten Prophet: The Life of Randolph Bourne* (Columbia, MO: University of Missouri Press, 1998), 49.
39 Bourne, "The Older Generation," *Atlantic Monthly* 116, no. 3 (September 1915): 385–91, 389.
40 Bourne, "Older Generation," 389.

essays.[41] The canonization of American literature that began at the end of the nineteenth century, in which genteel writers and editors played a significant role, impacted the essay as well. Because nonfiction was seen as male territory, the canonized essay was also generally male. And yet the genteel essay was often characterized as a feminine or "sissified" form,[42] dominated by sentimental bachelors who, according to Ann Douglas, generally "escaped censure because they did not take themselves seriously. They confessed to indolence. They pleaded implicitly for a special status, that of perpetual child, of the observer licensed only because he is incapable of participation."[43] Mitchell, known by his penname Ik Marvel, certainly capitalized on that portrayal. His *Reveries of a Bachelor* was a best seller for nearly fifty years. In "Smoke – Signifying Doubt," published in that collection, Mitchell dreamily weighs the temptations of taking a wife against the imagined bothers of actually having one.[44] Eventually, though, the genteel essay's feminine sentimentality became an object of criticism, especially as the more aggressive, masculine voice of the newspaper columnist began to dominate periodicals. Stuckey-French posits that this change in tone was not just about literary voice but about "a struggle to make America more manly" itself.[45]

The ultimate success of female genteel essayists like Gerould, Guiney, Hamilton, Morris, and Mossell did not necessarily translate to anthologization and lasting critical attention. For example, of the twenty-eight essayists who appear in Brander Matthews's 1914 *The Oxford Book of American Essays*, none are writers of color; none are women. Instead, the genteel period was, and remains, represented by the same oft-anthologized men – Holmes, Lowell, Thomas Wentworth Higginson (1823–1911), Curtis, Warner, Howells, Crothers – whose essays represent what Matthews believes good (genteel) essays should contain: the "flavor of good talk" and "sprightly conversation that may sparkle in front of a wood fire and that often vanishes

---

41 See Shirley Marchalonis, "Women Writers and the Assumption of Authority: The *Atlantic Monthly*, 1857–1898," in *In Her Own Voice*, ed. Sherry Lee Linkon (New York: Garland, 1997), 3–26.
42 Stuckey-French, *American Essay*, 40. See also my introduction to *Women and the Essay: An Anthology from 1655 to 2000* (Athens, GA: University of Georgia Press, 2018), where I argue that this rendering of male essayists as feminine, generally in negative terms, while also limiting women's access to the form, is a common trope in essay criticism throughout the centuries.
43 Ann Douglas, *The Feminization of American Culture* (New York: Avon, 1978), 285.
44 See Ik Marvel [Donald Grant Mitchell], "Smoke – Signifying Doubt" in *Reveries of a Bachelor* (New York: Baker and Scribner, 1851), 19–28.
45 Stuckey-French, "Why Does the Essay Keep Dying," 31.

with the curling blue smoke."[46] Matthews's omission of Repplier is particularly striking.[47] Repplier was a prolific contributor of genteel essays, publishing two dozen volumes during her lifetime. But as Ann Boyd argues, "the genteel elite, many of whom were ensconced at the *Atlantic*, feared that a diverse culture was set to replace the one in which privileged Anglo-Saxon males had a monopoly on power."[48]

The Black Genteel Tradition

On the whole, Black writers did not have access to the powerhouse periodicals of the white genteel elite. Thus, Black periodicals like the *Crisis* and the *Opportunity*, founded in 1910 and 1923 respectively, provided Black writers with a crucial outlet for their work. Charles Johnson, founder of the *Opportunity*, noted that "other established media" refused to publish the work of Black writers and schools "because it could not be believed to be of standard quality despite the superior quality of much of it."[49] In his introduction to *Ebony and Topaz* (1927), a collection of essays, poetry, and illustrations by Black artists, Johnson observes that Black artists in the early twentieth century are "much less self-conscious, less interested in proving that they are just like white people and . . . seem to care less about what white people think, or are likely to think about race."[50] But the issue was not cut and dried. Some Black writers and editors, perhaps accepting the position on art as racial uplift, understood gentility as a means of access not only to the privileges of white culture but to the higher civilization that genteel ideals promised. The Black essayist writing during the genteel period seemed to have two choices: to write directly from the position of a Black American living in a racist society, or to craft an unraced persona in order to participate in a tradition rooted in whiteness. A handful of essayists chose the latter, not for their entire oeuvre, perhaps, but in essays here and there. Mossell's "A

---

46 Brander Matthews, ed., *The Oxford Book of American Essays* (New York: Oxford University Press, 1914), x.
47 Repplier and Gerould do occasionally appear in other anthologies, as does, less frequently, Louise Imogen Guiney. Repplier and Gerould are the female genteel essayists most likely to be anthologized today.
48 Ann Boyd, "What! Has she got into the 'Atlantic'?": Women Writers, the *Atlantic Monthly*, and the Formation of the American Canon," *American Studies* 39, no. 3 (Fall 1998): 5–36, 30.
49 Patrick J. Gilpin, "Charles S. Johnson: Entrepreneur of the Harlem Renaissance," in *Remembering the Harlem Renaissance*, ed. Cary D. Wintz (New York: Routledge, 1996), 215–24, 222.
50 Charles S. Johnson, "Introduction," in *Ebony and Topaz: A Collectanea*, ed. Charles S. Johnson (1921; repr., Freeport, NY: Books for Libraries Press, 1971), 12.

Lofty Study," which appeared in her 1908 volume *The Work of the Afro-American Women*, is a cheerful, optimistic essay about the need for women to find a space of their own within their homes in order to write. A popular columnist and the highest-paid Black female journalist of her time, Mossell did not avoid writing about race and racism, but as a member of the Black literary elite, moving along the upper echelon of Black society, her hopes for Black Americans, particularly Black women and children, reflected many of the same ideals espoused by white, upper-class genteel writers.[51] Similarly, at the beginning of his essay "A Southern Boyhood," Brawley establishes himself as an urban Black man from a good family who experienced racism growing up but who also was smart and educated, and who used that education to make something of himself. One of the lessons that Brawley says he learned is the "unusual standard of excellence" that a Black man must hold himself to in order to succeed: "Where discount had to be made for prejudice, he had often to do a task even better than anybody else."[52] Brawley later used his prominence as writer and educator to argue for a Black literature that matched the same high (but arguably white) standards the genteel elite subscribed to. He believed, for instance, that Black essayists should mimic the essays of Lamb, and avoid "shrieking" and "hysterics."[53] Interviewed by the *Crisis* in 1926 for a series titled "The Negro in Art," Brawley responded that he regretted how artists "prefer today to portray only what is vulgar. There is beauty in the world as well as ugliness, idealism as well as realism."[54]

The polarizing generational divide that split white genteel essayists and younger white writers was present among Black writers as well. However, as Stuckey-French points out, the debate in Black literary circles was typically connected to racism: "White domination of the educational system, publishing industry, and the cultural context, high, low and middle, places tremendous pressures on black essayists to be political – to speak for their race – but also to be patient and accommodating – to deny their race."[55] The genre

---

51 See Nazera Sadiq Wright, "'Teach Your Daughters': Black Girlhood and Mrs. N. F. Mossell's Advice Column in the *New York Freeman*," in *Black Girlhood in the Nineteenth Century* (Champaign, IL: University of Illinois Press, 2016), 93–117.
52 Benjamin Brawley, "A Southern Boyhood," *Reviewer* 5, no. 3 (July 1925): 1–8, 78–86, 82.
53 Benjamin Brawley, "The Writing of Essays," *Opportunity* 4, no. 45 (September 1926): 284.
54 Benjamin Brawley, quoted in Chidi Ikoneé, *From Du Bois to Van Vechten: The Early New Negro Literature, 1903–1926* (Westport, CT: Greenwood Press, 1981), 101. Brawley's interview originally appeared in the *Crisis* (32, no. 2 [June 1926]: 72).
55 Ned Stuckey-French, "Hitler and Hogs: The Personal Essay and American Culture Between the Two World Wars," PhD diss., University of Iowa (1997), 155.

expectations of the genteel essay seem especially ridiculous for a Black essayist in this context: write cheerful, light fireside chats in the spirit of the white people who enslaved them, avoiding vulgar and difficult subjects that might offend the gentle reader. Indeed, the easygoing persona of the familiar essayist was a particular challenge for Black writers whose observations and lived realities were not topics deemed appropriate for genteel literature. All essay personae are crafted, the narrator becoming the authorial subject whom society and the literary marketplace demand. But, again, Black essayists struggled against a larger backdrop of race and racism. As Henry Louis Gates Jr. argues, in an attempt to demonstrate "the full intellectual potential of the black mind," Black genteel essayists "erased their racial selves, imitating those they least resembled."[56] The genteel tradition seemed purposefully construed to exclude writers of color, and, for the most part, it succeeded.

Conclusion

In "The Black Genteel Tradition," a rare analysis of the impact of the genteel tradition on Black writers, Gordan Beauchamp makes a compelling case for continuing to shine our critical light on a period long gone that many might feel best to ignore. In fact, Beauchamp argues, the genteel tradition is not dead; it has, "Dracula-like, made a comeback of sorts" in the form of demands on minority artists to "accentuate the positive when depicting their own."[57] Examining specifically the criticism of Black women writers like Ntozake Shange, Alice Walker, and Sapphire for their portrayals of Black male violence, Beauchamp is haunted by the ghosts of the "old canard"[58] that insists "black writers conform to some retreaded version of the Genteel Tradition."[59] Beauchamp underscores the point that whether or not we read the essayists of the genteel tradition, the often racial, sexed, classed ideals they espoused linger. And for essay scholars, that point is all the more profound. It was the essay that communicated the messages of these ideals most directly, in the periodicals where the essay form dominated, and in the classrooms where, as the chief pedagogical tool of the academy, they were fed to another generation of writers and thinkers. Too often essay criticism

---

56 Henry Louis Gates Jr., "The Trope of a New Negro and the Reconstruction of the Image of the Black," *Representations*, no. 24 (Autumn 1998): 129–55, 148.
57 Gorman Beauchamp, "The Black Genteel Tradition," *Antioch Review* 74, no. 1 (Winter 2016): 20–28, 21.
58 Beauchamp, "Black Genteel Tradition," 23.
59 Beauchamp, "Black Genteel Tradition," 28.

fails to interrogate what drove essayists to write as they did, or did not; to examine the critical and cultural values that shaped how the essay's history has been passed on to us; to note who is part of that history, and who is not. The zones of contention in the genteel tradition, perhaps more than any other period in the essay's history, provide important opportunities to do just that. It was Santayana himself who famously remarked, "Those who do not remember the past are condemned to repeat it."[60] The period of the genteel essay carries its own compelling call for further study: If we check ourselves against what the genteel tradition offered, and what it demanded of its essayists, perhaps we will not repeat the worst of it.

60 George Santayana, *The Life of Reason*, critical ed., ed. Marianne S. Wokeck and Martin A. Coleman (1905; repr., Boston: MIT Press, 2011), 172.

12
The American Comic Essay

DAVID E. E. SLOANE

From its inception, sociopolitical concerns have dominated the American comic essay. Borrowing from British sources and employing features common to humorous writing more generally, the American comic essay customizes these for an American public using national imagery, local allusions, and distinctly American language. The mix of ethical commentary, exaggeration, and sarcasm has resulted in a varied and sometimes bizarre genre noted by foreign observers for its lawlessness. Earlier humorists vigorously voiced independent religious and political ideologies, even before the formation of the new nation. Later, fictional personae expressed themselves in hyperbolic style and used vernacular and vulgar language, laden with irony and sarcasm, to capture the discontinuities of the industrializing nation and its new urban landscape. Articulating ethical visions of the new democracy, literary comedians like Artemus Ward expanded the naïve, deadpan voice that was brought to international prominence by Mark Twain. Later essayists maintained the rhetoric, persona, exaggeration, irony, and fantasy that caricature Americans' core pragmatism, and further expanded the range of themes to include personal psychology, sexuality, and other once taboo topics.

Nathanial Ward and Early American Wit

The earliest "American" comic essay is Thomas Morton's (1579–1647) *New English Canaan* (1637), with its denigration of "Captain Shrimp" (his nickname for Myles Standish, an English colonist and military officer) and its derision of the rigid Puritans of Plymouth. Morton was an early English colonist who founded the utopian community of Merrymount, located in contemporary Massachusetts, and who used his writing to acknowledge the superiority of the local Algonquin culture over that of the Puritans. Closely following is Nathanial Ward's (1578–1653) *The Simple Cobler of Aggawam in America*, published in 1647. Although a form of "colonial" humor, Ward's cantankerous persona argued for egalitarianism through an aggressive appeal to common sense, still a hallmark of the American medium. His exuberant rhetoric projected both the emotional energy of the author and the harshness of the contrasts he exposed: "When a kingdom is broken just in the neck joynt, in my poore policy, ropes and hatchets are not the kindliest instruments to set it: Next to the spilling of the blood of Christ for sin, the sparing of the blood of sinners, where it may be as well spared as spilt, is the best way of expiation."[1] For Ward, morality then becomes political: "Are you [the king of England] well advised, in trampling your Subjects so under your feet, that they can finde no place to be safe in, but over your head . . . ?"[2] Early federal comic essayists would have no trouble translating this discourse from a colonial context to their own.

Later essayists indeed developed analogous mock speeches, newspaper columns, and letters in order to lecture politicians, wealthy socialites, and royalty on the duties of citizenship. In historical terms, the formula has roots going back to the Greeks and Romans,[3] but the independent-spirited American writers delivered these lectures in colloquial language and often with egregious enthusiasm. Ward's rambunctious "verbal dexterity," as noted by P. M. Zall, freely switches in and out of character, closely following the *Cobler of Canterbury* (1608) and the Martin Marprelate tracts in their "mechanic preaching," combining medium and target.[4] Ward's flamboyant overstatement, along with his irony and social satire, would soon become primary characteristics of American humorous essays in the comic periodicals of the next century.

From Colonial to Federal: Benjamin Franklin, Timothy Dexter, and Washington Irving

Benjamin Franklin (1706–1790), moderating Nathaniel Ward's style, employed irony and implication to advance the libertarian and egalitarian philosophy developing in colonial America. Emphasizing the importance of periodicals in

---

[1] Nathaniel Ward, *The Simple Cobler of Aggawam in America*, ed. P. M. Zall (Lincoln, NE: University of Nebraska Press, 1969), 62.
[2] Ward, *Simple Cobler*, 52.
[3] P. M. Zall traces Nathaniel Ward's lineage through Burton's *Anatomy of Melancholy* (1621) back to the Greek Cynic Democritus, known as "the Laughing Philosopher."
[4] Zall, "Introduction," in Ward, *Simple Cobler*, xiv–xvi.

the comic tradition, Addison and Steele's *Spectator* ranks first in his substantial list of influences,[5] although the reflective sophistication of London's coffee-houses also inspired his writing.[6] Franklin followed Alexander Pope's adage that "want of modesty is want of sense," but concludes with a characteristic ironic recoil: "This however I should submit to better Judgements."[7] Some of his most trenchant comedy can be found in these kinds of extensions. For example, reason number seven in "Old Mistresses Apologue" – which states that affairs with older women cause less compunction (whereas seducing a young girl condemns her to misery, an idea expressed strongly in a letter in the *Spectator*) – is further extended: "8thly and Lastly [Franklin put blank spaces in, denoting a pause] They are *so grateful!!*"[8] Like Twain, a later master of comic extension, Franklin labeled his mockery of argumentation a "Paradox" and advised his correspondent to marry rather than remain "the odd Half of a Pair of Scissors."[9] The rhetorical manipulation of the idea served the ideology, which placed sexual desire of men and women on the same plane, established as reason number five: that since a human being's legs retain their form, covering all that lies above the girdle with a basket makes older and younger women alike, "as in the dark all Cats are grey."[10] The appeal through natural science to sexual chauvinism, capped by a vulgar folk aphorism, creates a symphony of conflicting ironic implications – Franklin at his best. The same can be seen in the single closing line of "A Witch Trial at Mount Holly": After the stupid locals fail to get results in a trial of possible witches, clothed only in muslin shifts for modesty, Franklin sarcastically notes that the women will be tried again, "in the next warm weather, naked."[11]

Using abundant irony, Franklin often developed phrases around a pragmatic core of economic and political philosophy. "The Speech of Miss Polly Baker" (1747) discusses sexual reproduction using patriotic rhetoric, pointing out that the titular figure has served the new country by bringing forth five children at no cost to the state; the resulting advice is that great men should "not turn natural and useful Actions into Crimes."[12] In denying false rumors of Canadians monopolizing fishing in the Great Lakes, Franklin's essay "The Grand Leap of the Whale" exaggerates the marine

---

5 Benjamin Franklin, *Writings: The Autobiography; Poor Richard's Almanack; Bagatelles, Pamphlets, Essays, and Letters*, ed. J. A. Leo Lemay (New York: Library of America, 1987), 1320.
6 Franklin, *Writings*, 1321.   7 Franklin, *Writings*, 1322–23.
8 Franklin, *Writings*, 302–303. Original emphasis.   9 Franklin, *Writings*, 302.
10 Franklin, *Writings*, 303.   11 Franklin, *Writings*, 157.   12 Franklin, *Writings*, 306–307.

mammal's jump up Niagara Falls to chase cod, elaborating on the dangers of credulousness. To undercut the Society of the Cincinnati, he suggests that the eagle on their shield looks like a turkey, a better choice based on character, anyhow.[13] Franklin's comments on the sale of Hessian soldiers and the rules for reducing a great empire to a small one are well known, but often overlooked are other subversive jokes, sarcastic asides, epigrams, and examples of irony that undercut supposedly serious matters. Some comparable soliloquies appeared elsewhere: "The Speech of David Wood" (1801), for example, which was published anonymously in the *Spirit of the Farmer's Museum and Lay Preacher's Gazette*, excoriated disparities between the treatment of the rich and poor. Going forward, a similar style and mood were reflected in pieces published from 1810 to 1815 in comic papers such as the *Corrector* (New York), the *Scourge* (Baltimore), *Satirist* (Boston), and the *Cynick*. Creators of other periodicals often chose names like the *Bee* (the first solely comic periodical, launched in 1765), the *Wasp*, the *Lancet*, and the *Spy* (in 1833 and more recently from 1986 to 1998) to reflect their intent to satirize, correct, and punish economic and social inequality and accompanying moral weakness. Franklin's more elevated essays, like "The Ephemera,"[14] also questioned a society that lacked moral vision and hoarded wealth in the face of inevitable dissolution. Such neoclassical themes carried forward from Franklin in the work of writers such as Washington Irving, Mark Twain, E. B. White, and more contemporary comic essayists.

Lord Timothy Dexter's (1747–1806) *A Pickle for the Knowing Ones* (1802) exaggerated and vulgarized Ward's and Franklin's style in a kind of barnyard homespun tale born of his half-educated status as an autodidact. In his rant on democracy, Dexter's most pungent demand is to be shown a man with a sole (soul) not made out of shoe leather: "I want to know what a sole is I wish to see one Not a gizzard."[15] Unpunctuated, misspelled, and rambling, his work demanded "commanding pease and the greatest brotherly love."[16] Whereas the first edition lacked punctuation altogether, Dexter put all the punctuation at the end of the second edition on a new final page, so that the "knowing ones" could pepper and salt the marks throughout his text as they pleased.[17]

---

13 Franklin, "The Grand Leap of the Whale," in *Writings*, 559–62; and "The Turk'y Is in Comparison a Much More Respectable Bird," in *Writings*, 1084–89.
14 Franklin, *Writings*, 922–24.
15 Lord Timothy Dexter, *A Pickle for the Knowing Ones*, 4th ed. (Newburyport, MA: Blanchard and Sargent, 1848), 14.
16 Dexter, *Pickle for the Knowing Ones*, 15.   17 Dexter, *Pickle for the Knowing Ones*, 32.

Dexter's formal lawlessness exemplified that risks needed to be taken to express the American egalitarian ethic.

A little later in the same decade as Dexter's *Pickle*, Washington Irving (1783–1859) and James Kirke Paulding (1778–1860) employed a more urbane style, still containing democratic idealism, but giving it the literary polish of New York in the periodical *Salmagundi* (1807–08) and the luster of historical narrative in Irving's *A History of New York* (1809). The cultivated correspondents of *Salmagundi* were masked behind various pen names: Launcelot Langstaff, writing from his "Elbow-Chair," Mustapha Rub-A-Dub Keli Kahn, Anthony Evergreen, or Pindar Cockloft. These tongue-in-cheek pseudonyms at the end of the Colonial and Federalist eras would be followed by more folksy identities found in the cheap popular presses. The list of names above hints at new developments in the form: feigned naïvety (green is synonymous with naïvete or countrified innocence throughout the nineteenth century), literary connections and pretensions ("cockloft" suggests a sexual parallel for the egotistical poetaster), roots in literature and history (Pindar is overtly classical, in keeping with many pseudonyms of nineteenth-century satirists in both prose and poetry), and awareness of other writers at home and abroad – a constant characteristic of the literary comedians from Irving throughout the rest of the century. Oliver Goldsmith's (1728–1774) *The Citizen of the World* letters (1762) provided precedent for Irving's Mustapha and, later, for Mark Twain's *Goldsmith's Friend Abroad Again* (1870–71), which recounts the abuse of the Chinese in California for the *Galaxy Magazine*. Writers openly mixed literary allusions and historical references; they sometimes expressed social criticism harshly, made references to contemporary American culture and experience, and used increasingly informal language.

The 7 March 1807 *Salmagundi* column "From My Elbow-Chair" was representative of these tendencies.[18] The perspective of the *naif* was provided by the narrator, Mustapha Rub-A-Dub Keli Kahn, who addresses his friend Snorer, whose name is a typical stylistic choice of Irving's, implying dullness and lack of interest. Mustapha describes a raucous jumble of lower-class workers, involving 600 shoemakers, candlemakers, and other working-class city types in formation to celebrate a feast day. He digresses one step lower to observe that "The Battery" nearby once boasted a wooden stockade later pulled to pieces by frugal – but obviously crass – city fathers to provide heating for the poor, an example of the dominant

---

18 Washington Irving, *History, Tales and Sketches*, ed. James Tuttleton (New York: Library of America, 1983), 112–27.

American ethic: "ECONOMY," the national watchword.[19] The city guard marches through the streets in a shower of cats, old hats, and shoes. This type of unruly crowd was a recurring trope in comedy that sought to portray urban life. Examples include not only two later comic journals, both named *Kaleidoscope* (1819 and 1869), but numerous comic sketches including Joseph C. Neal's "The Prison Van; or, The Black Maria" (1844), George P. Burnham's *The History of the Hen Fever: A Humorous Record* (1855), and even an ending sequence in Mark Twain's "No. 44, The Mysterious Stranger," published after his death in 1916. These and other books and comic periodicals portrayed rowdy throngs, fitting for a disorderly democracy in action.

Various comic histories of the United States also followed in the footsteps of Irving's narrator, Diedrich Knickerbocker, in *A History of New York* (1809), itself a parody, ushered into public attention by a hoax. Irving's account begins with a history of the world, but rapidly narrows to recount the exploits of a handful of stolid Dutch forebears of Gotham, an absurd progression burlesquing the egocentrism inherent in America's, and especially New York's, sense of self-importance. Readers find outrageous, embellished details, such as the description of the "Good Woman," the "Ark" that brought the Dutch pilgrims from Holland to "Gibbet Island," which was named "in complement to the wife of the President of the West India Company, who was allowed by every body (except her husband) to be a singularly sweet tempered lady, when not in liquor."[20] The closing detail, with its false naïvety, is only topped by the closing sentence of the paragraph – a joke still current two hundred years later, reworked in a 1999 "Down East" Maine folk song, "Cappy John's Bride," by Fred Gosbee: "Like the beauteous model, who was declared the belle of Amsterdam, [the ship, but by implication the woman] was full in the bows, with a pair of enormous cat-heads, a copper bottom, and withal, a most prodigious poop!"[21]

Joseph C. Neal, Fanny Fern, and the Literary Comedians

Irving's language was transplanted in the 1830s to the vulgar urban frontier of Philadelphia by Joseph C. Neal (1807–1847), a long-neglected comic essayist, along with Fanny Fern (1811–1872) and Doesticks (Mortimer Neal Thomson

---

19 Irving is also credited with the phrase "the Almighty Dollar," America's spiritual idol throughout the remainder of the century and up to the present time.
20 Irving, *History, Tales and Sketches*, 434–35.
21 Fred Gosbee, *The Ballad of Cappy John and Other Songs of Coastal Maine*, Castlebay Music, 1999, compact disc.

[1832–1875]) a little later on. Neal's *Charcoal Sketches* (1838, enlarged in the T. B. Peterson Brothers edition of 1865) specializes in a modified Theophrastan "character," a form popular in seventeenth-century England. His sketches eventually filled three volumes, the first of which reached eight printings in little more than two years. One volume, pirated by Henry Colburn in London to fill the middle volume of a three-decker credited to Charles Dickens, *The Pic Nic Papers* (1841), cemented Neal's reputation among dismissive critics as the "American Dickins." His "hard cases" from the Philadelphia night court, however, are a unique survey of the down-and-out slum class at the time of America's social transformation into the industrial age. From craven office seekers like "Peter Brush, the Great Used Up" to drunken rowdies like "Orson Dabbs, the Hittite," Neal preserved an American setting as influential on the American character as the Old Southwest's frontier. But his urban settings, lightly ironic Irvingesque elaborations, and caricatures of editorial mannerisms escaped literary historians, who were instead mesmerized by the roughhouse rambunctiousness of the parallel frontier genre described below.

Joseph C. Neal, James Kirke Paulding, and others[22] have received less attention than the humorists of the Old Southwest,[23] largely due to the overdramatized roughness of the "frontier" genre of humor. Characters like Simon Suggs and Sut Lovingood engaged in horse swaps, bear and coon hunts, and drunken battles, and fought with cunning human predators and misfits. However, as with the Northeast pieces, less attention has been paid to these essays, sketches, and related forms as contributions to the essay genre. Augustus Baldwin Longstreet's (1790–1870) *Georgia Scenes* (1835), subtitled "Characters, incidents &C, in the first half century of the republic," and Joseph G. Baldwin's (1815–1864) *Flush Times in Alabama and Mississippi* (1853) are two of the central volumes documenting the fast-vanishing frontier and its regional characteristics. Even volumes appearing as fiction rather than reportage, like *Odd Leaves from the Life of a Louisiana Swamp Doctor* (1843) by Madison Tensas (Henry Clay Lewis [1825–1850]) were intended to create a historical record of local experience, local dialect, and folk customs. Thomas Bangs Thorpe's (1815–1878) "The Big Bear of Arkansas" (1841), a sketch most representative of the genre, is easily distinguished from stories

---

22 For a complete list, see David E. E. Sloane, *The Literary Humor of the Urban Northeast, 1830–1890* (Baton Rouge, LA: Louisiana State University Press, 1983).
23 See Hennig Cohen and William B. Dillingham, eds., *The Humor of the Old Southwest*, 3rd ed. (Boston: Houghton Mifflin, 1964; Athens, GA: University of Georgia Press, 1994). Citations refer to the University of Georgia Press edition.

like Neal's or the urban life recorded by Mortimer Thomson ("Doesticks") in motifs, language, setting, and even ethical motivation. The contrasting cultures, unfortunately, foreshadow the divergent social views buffeting American democracy in the twenty-first century. Many of the authors, like Longstreet, for example, made a point of explicitly disapproving of the experiences they recorded.

A second writer who, like Joseph C. Neal, disappeared from American literary histories is Mortimer Thomson (Q. K. Philander Doesticks, P. B.), represented by two volumes of comic sketches of New York's urban frontier and one epic poem, *Pluri-bus-tah* (1856), a fabulous mock-heroic travesty on Hiawatha that predicts the apocalyptic Civil War to follow, and a serious exposé of baby-murderers (abortionists), *The Witches of New York* (1859). *Doesticks, What He Says* (1855) anticipated Mark Twain's short essays and sketches, uncovering the Barnumization of Niagara Falls,[24] with political brawls, quack faith healers, and other characteristics of the under crust and their fresh urban argot. Doesticks's consciousness of history and literary culture, and unique traits of language, along with urban detailing and social awareness, were hallmarks of the American comic essay in the latter half of the nineteenth century. His sardonic newspaper report "The Great Slave Auction at Savannah, Georgia" (1859) inflamed Northern readers through its pathos, Juvenalian style, and furious satiric refrains; although widely reprinted, it was quickly forgotten along with his other antebellum writings, overshadowed by the work of Artemus Ward and Mark Twain.

Fanny Fern (Sara Payson Willis Parton) is another outstanding satirist of the 1850–1870 period. Attacked in her own time as unfeminine, she skewered the inequality of the sexes with bitter, slang-infused invective. *Fern Leaves from Fanny's Portfolio, Second Series* (1854) provides a representative fusillade. "A Grumble from the (H)altar" includes a husband complaining that he'd rather face one of Colt's revolvers than return to his angry wife empty-handed without the two feet of ribbon he had promised her. "Mistaken Philanthropy" sarcastically notes that the "golden rule" has been changed: "'Taint suited to our meridian."[25] "Insignificant Love," in exasperation, declares that you can't find a man with more "goaheadativeness" than

---

24 The showman and trickster P. T. Barnum (1810–1891) was famous for his pranks. Barnum charged a hefty twenty-five-cent admission for visitors to see his replica of Niagara Falls, but it was only eighteen inches high and activated by a single barrel of New York City water.
25 Fanny Fern, *Fern Leaves from Fanny's Portfolio, Second Series* (Auburn, NY: Miller, Orton, and Mulligan, 1854), 132–39.

a smart, talented, energetic woman.[26] The concentrated mood, confrontational diction, unornamented sentences, and sarcastic slang asserted the "go-ahead" Yankee spirit, all while challenging the degradation of American women. Sentimental essays and short stories included among Fern's social critiques caused some later (male) critics to dismiss her; Nathanial Hawthorne, who was not above writing an occasional sentimental sketch, knew better: "The woman writes as if the devil was in her."[27] Her brother, N. P. Willis (1806–1867), who distanced himself from her, was also a popular writer of light social comedy, but Fern's writings are more forceful and significant than his.

Fanny Fern, along with Petroleum V. Nasby (David Ross Locke [1833–1888]), was notable for giving longevity to the confrontational vulgar vernacular of the early essayists. Fern is best represented in *The Life and Beauties of Fanny Fern* (1855), published for revenge by an angry former editor, William Moulton, whose strategy was to showcase her most offensive (he presumed) essays to discredit her. Her slangy sarcasm in "Horace Mann's Opinion" drops into false ecstasy over Mann's pronouncement that women ought not preach the gospel because *their* part is to practice it. She rolls her eyes, wishing she could hoist a "True Flag" (Moulton's newspaper) and shout "huzza": "He's too much of a curiosity for a *monopoly*. Barnum must have him" for his *"moral courage* in propagating such an unpopular sentiment!"[28] As for Nasby, Abraham Lincoln named him as one of the three Northern assets that won the Civil War (along with the Union Army and Navy). Though he would exceed Fern's caustic style by impersonating a Southern bigot, his work will not be resurrected because of the brutal employment of the N-word. His *Morals of Abou ben Adhem* (1875), supposedly originating from an obviously fake "seer" located in New Jersey, proved that his range reached beyond the Civil War to criticism of general American social, economic, and political misbehavior. Even the sincere dedication to his mother-in-law, with its genuine admiration, was shaded by subtle ironic implications about the norms of American life. Ambrose "Bitter" Bierce, Mark Twain, and H. L. Mencken continued the lawlessly energetic rhetorical style of writers

---

26 Fern, *Fern Leaves*, 137.
27 Nathaniel Hawthorne, "Letter, February 2, 1855," in *The Centenary Edition of the Works of Nathaniel Hawthorne*, ed. Thomas Woodson et al. (Columbus, OH: The Ohio State University Press, 1988), 17:307–308. See also Joel Myerson, "Introduction," in *Selected Letters of Nathaniel Hawthorne* (Columbus, OH: The Ohio State University Press, 2002), ix–xix, xiv.
28 Fanny Fern, *The Life and Beauties of Fanny Fern* (New York: H. Long and Brother, 1855), 111–12.

such as Fern and Nasby, but with more control of tone, which made them acceptable to a wider readership.

From Seba Smith's (1792–1868) Jack Downing letters from Portland, first published in 1830,[29] to James Russell Lowell's (1819–1891) *Biglow Papers*, literary comedians employed varied pseudonyms to denote outsider personae and their dialects. B. P. Shillaber nurtured the careers of several of these writers in *The Carpet-Bag* (1851–53), printing works by Samuel L. Clemens (Mark Twain), George H. Derby (John Phoenix, Squibob), Charles Farrar Browne (Artemus Ward), and Matthew Whittier (Ethan Spike). Judge Haliburton (1792–1865) – a Canadian essayist sharing in the American tradition also known as "Sam Slick, the Clockmaker" – portrays his Yankee clockmaker in an extended series of letters as part peddler-manipulator and part social philosopher who depends on "soft sawder and human natur."[30] *Traits of American Humor* (1852), a collection edited by Haliburton, closely identifies him with the "American" school of humor and offers short pieces from Southwest, Northeast, and Midwest sources written in the style of newspaper letters and stories. John Phoenix (George Derby [1823–1861]) was credited by Ward, and incidentally, Twain, as deeply influencing his uniquely digressive style and naïve pose.[31] Another, usually ignored, branch of the genre, extended comic memoirs, includes P. T. Barnum's *Autobiography* (1855) and his rival George Burnham's *History of the Hen Fever* (1855). Both men were mendacious exploiters of the gullible public through the exaggerated advertising and humbug for which Barnum became famous – and rich. The Yankee sharp traders were not merely cynics, however; Barnum went to jail defending freedom of the press in 1832 and published, in one revision of his *Autobiography*, his speech to the Connecticut legislature, laced with humor, demanding voting rights for Black Connecticut residents, which had been suspended to please the South in 1817.

For higher-brow magazine audiences, Nathaniel Hawthorne (1804–1864) and Herman Melville (1819–1891) produced various humorous sketches, such as Melville's "I and My Chimney," among other short writings. Also notable are Edgar Allan Poe's (1809–1849) newspaper hoaxes and burlesques. Many of these writings pointed toward literary comedy as a genre on its own.

---

29 Major Jack Downing was a fictional character Smith invented to poke fun at the American political class.
30 Thomas Chandler Haliburton, "The Sayings of Sam Slick/The Clockmaker," in *Native American Humor*, ed. Walter Blair (New York: Harper and Row, 1960), 229–31, 229.
31 See Melville D. Landon, "A Biographical Sketch," in *The Complete Works of Artemus Ward*, by Artemus Ward (New York: A. L. Burt, 1898), 13–26, 14.

Other essayists bridging the Civil War period include Donald G. Mitchell (Ik Marvel) with *Reveries of a Bachelor* (1850); Charles Dudley Warner with *Backlog Studies* (1873); G. W. Curtis, whose *Niles Notes of a Howjdi* (1852) was read by Samuel L. Clemens (Mark Twain) to a companion aboard the *Quaker City* on his way to the Holy Land; and Frederick S. Cozzens and Max Adeler (Charles Heber Clark). Orpheus C. Kerr (Robert Henry Newell) failed to develop a successful postwar formula. For common readers, Josh Billings published hundreds of widely popular short essays placing his down-to-earth comic pragmatism in a strictly vernacular voice, as in his "Essay on the Mule" (1865). His comic almanacs were so popular that Mark Twain decided not to compete.

Artemus Ward (Charles Farrar Browne [1834–1867]) elevated (some would say "lowered," if the ignorant lines below are any measure) the status of American humor through the newspaper exchanges that spread his caricature of Barnum nationally. The Old Showman urged: "Albert Edard, ... tho I'm agin Princes as a gineral thing, I must say I like the cut of your Gib. When you git to be King try and be as good a man as yure muther has bin!"[32] The lowbrow character depicted in these writings, where purposeful misspellings (known as cacography) dominate every letter and speech, morphed into a platform lecturer in 1863 without even pretending to combine the Old Showman in print and the sophisticated, rail-thin bohemian speaker. Mark Twain would build on Ward's example by writing comic lectures, widening his market nationally and internationally by eliminating the humor of misspelling and transmuting the hidden ethics into overt social criticism, often in his jokes. Literary allusions balanced backwoods vernacular; historical references travestied the exaggerated political, moral, and intellectual pretensions of the era. These literary comedians advanced multiple viewpoints that twisted the language of spread-eagle patriotism and skewered the self-serving morality of ideologues in religion, temperance, and politics. In the "Trater's Gate," Ward muses that "Traters" "are a onfortnit class of people. . . . They conspire to bust up a country – they fail, and they're traters. They bust her, and they become statesmen and heroes."[33] In his own voice, Ward mused elsewhere that the pen is mightier than the sword but would stand little chance against the "needle gun."[34] Through the many writers who contributed to Ward's humor, the frontier West and the urban Northeast fused into a new

---

32 Ward, *Complete Works*, 82.   33 Ward, *Complete Works*, 332.
34 Ward, *Complete Works*, 326.

national voice, steeped in irony and sarcasm, just as capitalism and the Industrial Age intensified America's clashing images of immense wealth and democratic equality.

Mark Twain and Some Later Literary Comedians

Mark Twain (1835–1910) surfaced in Virginia City, Nevada, in 1863 as a rambunctious reporter for Joe Goodman's *Territorial Enterprise* and continued on to touch sensitive political nerves and ingrained anti-Chinese racism in San Francisco. Twain's early essays vaulted back and forth across the lines between fiction and fact. He could veer into the biblical story of Samson before revealing that he was hoaxing a rival reporter. In response to the new state motto, oriented toward helping out in the Civil War in the East – *Volens et Potens* (willing and able) – he remarked that Nevada was "volens" enough, but not so damn "potens."[35] As his mentor, Joe Goodman of the *Enterprise*, might have taught him: "Get your facts first, and then you can distort them as much as you please,"[36] a statement credited to Twain in an interview with Rudyard Kipling. In fact, Twain was known early on (circa 1863–64) as "The Moralist of the Main," because he brought with him more than facts; he came loaded with humane ideals driving his comic social rhetoric, scathing satire, and suggestive and ironic distortions. He caricatured advice columns to boys and girls, lambasted the police for ignoring the violent persecution of Chinese, and even wrote parodies of the female suffrage movement in St. Louis and of P. T. Barnum running for Congress.[37] As early as the end of the decade, his exposure of the absurdity of social indoctrination eventually elevated Twain, an expat Missourian, to the throne of the New England conscience as the spokesman of his (r)age against racial injustice, religious irrationality, and the worldwide exploitation of the downtrodden.

Twain's San Francisco reporting led him East to write a series on New York from a "Western" perspective for the *Alta California*, which, in turn, was coaxed into including in Twain's itinerary a "first" in American

---

35 Mark Twain, *Collected Tales, Sketches, Speeches, and Essays*, vol. 1, *1852–1890*, ed. Louis J. Budd (New York: Library of America, 1992), 67–68.
36 Rudyard Kipling, *From Sea to Sea: Letters of Travel* (New York: Doubleday and McClure, 1899), 2:180.
37 Mark Twain, *Collected Tales, Sketches, Speeches, and Essays*, vol. 1, *1852–1890*, and vol. 2, *1891–1910*, ed. Louis J. Budd (New York: Library of America, 1992) provide the most comprehensive and authoritative collection of these materials, including indexes and chronological organization. These two volumes contain all the works cited in this discussion.

tourism: the *Quaker City* voyage to Europe and the Holy Land. His letters ripened into the mature style of *The Innocents Abroad* (1869), his most widely sold book through the end of the century, but the voice of Mark Twain is constant from his sarcastic essays in 1864 through his attacks on imperialism during the Philippine War, the overt imperialist expansion of the McKinley-Roosevelt era, and the corrupted humanity manifest in Africa by the Boers and King Leopold.

The Innocents Abroad is the American comic essay in its most extended and brilliant form. Various readers complained that they could not distinguish when the narrative was factual and when it was imaginary. The manufactured identity of reporter/confidence man fit the mode of American travel narratives. The genre's breadth – from memoir to observation, through historical reportage and reflection, and into philosophy and religion – was elastic and pliable. Twain became a confrontational comic spokesman for practical morality. In a single paragraph, he projects the best side of the American professional class when he chastises his fellow travelers for overworking their horses merely to avoid breaking the Sabbath. He was making something new of the comic travelogue that was unapologetically semifiction: half himself and half his persona. Borrowing from *Artemus Ward in London*, he and "the boys" ask about an Egyptian mummy and Christopher Columbus, "Is he dead?"[38] Twain's American readers identified with his voice, which became the mainstay of *Roughing It* (1872), *A Tramp Abroad* (1880), and his novels, enveloping traveling heroes, professional ethics, and humane practicality in humor.

Life on the Mississippi (1883) contains some of the best of Twain's comic essay writing. The "Lightning Pilot" episode, where a group of river pilots expresses amazed admiration for Horace Bixby, who was running one of the most dangerous crossings of the Mississippi River in the dark, captures American professionalism in one of Twain's best portrayals.[39] A few chapters later, the narrative provides a model of the compare-and-contrast essay in describing how the face of the river has changed, with Twain's naïve admiration of its beauty overtaken by his professional knowledge as a pilot steering through the hazards.[40] Both episodes are outstanding achievements in the American comic essay genre. Later essays, including "To the Person Sitting in Darkness" and "King Leopold's Soliloquy," return to

---

38 Ward, *Complete Works*, 319. The joke drifted through chapter 27 of *The Innocents Abroad* and into chapter 28.
39 See chapter 7 in *Life on the Mississippi*.
40 See the second half of chapter 9 in *Life on the Mississippi*.

outraged rhetoric exposing imperialist inhumanity. From "Only a N—r," printed in the *Buffalo Express* in 1869,[41] his antagonism toward racism in America was fixed, continuing in the tradition of Doesticks and Nasby. Twain's earliest newspaper pieces excoriated San Francisco's institutionalized abuse of Chinese immigrants. He later returned to those themes in Chinese Pidgin English letters, following Goldsmith's device, in 1871 in the *Galaxy* magazine, exposing American xenophobia. Twain's major works also revisited these themes, as seen definitively in "The United States of Lyncherdom," written in 1891 but published posthumously, and in outraged articles against the Philippine War in 1898–1900, which ran contrary to popular sentiment. Morality and humor were woven together with the pragmatism and skepticism of a daily reporter; in doing so, Twain demolished many limitations for later essayists. He even took on New England's heritage in "Plymouth Rock and the Pilgrims" (1881), in conformity with Ward's jokes targeting the same group. The fusion of ethics and slangy reportage made his speeches as sought after as his sketches and essays. Mark Twain was on the way to becoming a world icon.

Concurrent with Twain, though overshadowed by him, Marietta Holley (1836–1926) wrote travelogues without traveling and wove comic narratives of local and travel experiences without plots. Her books, like Twain's, were sold by subscription, and her first publisher was also Twain's. Unmarried, refined, and reclusive, Holley wrote on women's rights as "Josiah Allen's Wife," also known as "Samantha Allen," forcefully stating her opinions on women's role in American society and challenging male chauvinist prejudices demeaning women's "sphere." *My Opinions and Betsy Bobbit's* (1872) was presented as a guide to freedom from male stupidity. In *Samantha at Saratoga* (1887), she targets the supercilious fashions of the middle class. Holley's detailed travel narratives touched on every topic pertaining to the personal side of American life: domestic life, international travel, the World's Fair, tourism, religion, temperance, and racism (*Samantha on the Race Problem* [1892]). In her genteel Victorian study, composed in the folksy dialect of a farmer's wife, Holley's twenty or more major works, popular in America and Europe, argued for temperance, protection for children, and the importance and capacity of women in politics.

Other lost humorous essay writers can be found in various anthologies such as *Mark Twain's Library of Humor* (1888). George Ade's (1866–1944)

---

41 This essay is the only one not included in Twain, *Collected Tales*; it can be found in Joseph B. McCullough and Jan McIntire-Strasburg, eds., *Mark Twain at the Buffalo Express* (DeKalb, IL: Northern Illinois University Press, 1999), 22–23.

Fables in Slang (1900) captures "types" so realistically that his traveling salesman was plagiarized by Theodore Dreiser for the naïve seducer, Drouet, in *Sister Carrie* (1900). Edgar Wilson "Bill" Nye (1850–1896), of the *Laramie Boomerang*, published sixteen books, including a comic history of the United States, beginning in 1881 with *Bill Nye and Boomerang*. Boomerang, the name of Nye's mule, was a symbol of his commitment to the stubborn, vulgar voice. Comic little magazines also flourished in the 1900–1930 period alongside prominent national ones; representative is Billy Barlow's *Sagebrush Philosophy* (1904–1910) with its characteristic motto: "Consider the Mummy, he ain't had no fun in 4,000 Years." Barlow reflected the gentler style of Bill Nye, his model, and was less furious than the cynical San Francisco columnist Ambrose Bierce (1842–1914), who lambasted suffrage and sentimentalism in *The Fiend's Delight* (1873), under his pseudonym Dod Grile, and attacked everything else in *The Devil's Dictionary* (1911).

Barlow was a cowboy-styled journalist, but one greater was coming: Will Rogers (1879–1935). Rogers said he never met a man he didn't like, or a politician who could be trusted, or whose behavior rose above buffoonery: "When Congress makes a joke it's a law, and when they make a law, it's a joke."[42] His quips were widely admired, but care was taken to conceal his Native American heritage. Before him came "Fus Fixico," Alexander Posey (1873–1908), who wrote comic letters from the viewpoint of an Oklahoma Creek native on local and national policies. A further glance backward leads to forgotten Indigenous humor mentioned by Washington Irving. *A Tour of the Prairies* (1835) describes young Osage Native Americans lying by their campfire chanting waggish suggestions about sexual matters: "This mode of improvising is common throughout the savage tribes; ... they chant their exploits in war and hunting, and occasionally indulge in a vein of comic humour and dry satire, to which the Indians appear to me much more prone than is generally imagined."[43] Much of their humor is directed at whites, full of "criticism, satire, mimicry, and mirth."[44] Irving's Indigenous people even used grunts and rhythmic belly slapping, just as present drummers use drums and cymbals (the "rimshot": bada boom!), to underscore comic punchlines.

---

42 Many of Will Rogers's most famous remarks, like this one, made on 12 May 1935, originated from his radio essays on the *Good Gulf Show* before appearing in the newspapers. My thanks to Jennifer Holt at the Will Rogers Memorial Museum for this information.
43 Washington Irving, *A Tour on the Prairies* (London: John Murray, 1835), 51–52.
44 Irving, *Tour on the Prairies*, 53.

Transcribed Indian Trickster Tales support Irving's observations, but otherwise the tradition of Native American humor is mostly lost because so much of it was disseminated orally rather than in print.[45]

From Fin-de-Siècle Funny Pages to Manhattan Magazine Writers

The period from 1890 to 1930 was a heyday for common-voice writers and versifiers, with Mr. Dooley (Finley Peter Dunne [1867–1936]) being the greatest representative. His columns were reprinted in eight widely sold collections, mostly between 1899 and 1910. He featured an Irish immigrant bartender who spoke political truths in a vulgar Irish brogue, as in the tour de force "The Chinese Situation," in *Mr. Dooley's Philosophy* (1901), where Dunne adopts the persona of a Chinese man defending himself against accusations of being godless and uncultivated:

> Here am I, Hop Lung Dooley, ar-runnin' me little liquor store an' p'rhaps raisin' a family in th' town iv Koochoo. . . . Along comes a bald-headed man with chin whiskers from Baraboo, Wisconsin, an' says he: "Benighted an' haythen Dooley," says he, "ye have no God," he says. "I have," says I. "I have a lot iv thim," says I. "Ye ar-re an oncultivated an' foul crather," he says. "I have come six thousan' miles f'r to hist ye fr'm th' mire iv ignorance an' irrellijon in which ye live to th' lofty plane iv Baraboo," he says.[46]

A reformer turns up and tells "Hop Lung Dooley" that eating rice and rats is no good and that he must change his diet to eat Armour's "canned roast beef iv merry ol' stock yards or I'll have a file iv sojers in to fill ye full iv ondygistible lead."[47] Twain and Dooley both recognized the ugliness of American commerce as a driver of pious imperialism and readily critiqued it in their pages.

C. L. Edson's (1881–1975) *The Gentle Art of Columning* (1920) dissects the strategies of comic essays of the 1900–1920 period. The chapter on the "News Slant Paragraph" opens with a travesty of Woodrow Wilson's vanity in two lines: "'Wilson Up Early to View Alps,' says a headline. 'The Alps had stayed up all night waiting for him.'"[48] The period extending from the 1920s through World War II was also the age of the Algonquin Round Table and Harold Ross's

---

45 See, for example, Richard Erdoes and Alfonso Ortiz, eds., *American Indian Trickster Tales* (New York: Penguin, 1998).
46 Finley Peter Dunne, *Mr. Dooley's Philosophy* (New York: R. H. Russell, 1900), 78.
47 Dunne, *Mr. Dooley's Philosophy*, 79.
48 C. L. Edson, *The Gentle Art of Columning: A Treatise on Comic Journalism* (New York: Brentano's, 1920), 41. See also the book's introductory essays by Don Marquis, Christopher Morley, Franklin P. Adams, and George Horace Lorimer on pages 9–27.

New Yorker, where the razor wit of Dorothy Parker (1893–1967) and the whimsey of Robert Benchley (1889–1945) reigned. One dramatic Parker review, which appeared under the name "Constant Reader" in the *New Yorker*, simply remarks: "'The House Beautiful' is the play lousy."[49] In destroying A. A. Milne's *The House at Pooh Corner*, Parker identifies the first childish song, called a "Hum," at the moment where Pooh describes it as "more hummy," as "the first place ... at which Tonstant Weader Fwowed up [Constant Reader threw up]."[50] In another instance, she lampoons Professor William Lyon Phelps's self-satisfied treatise *Happiness* (1927) by observing that "[i]t is second only to a rubber duck as the ideal bathroom companion," and scorned its ending in lyric admiration of the "American cow" as a perfect model of contentment.[51]

In the late '40s, Langston Hughes's (1901–1967) humorous Harlem spokesman, Jesse Semple, illuminated the oppressed situation of African Americans – an unhappy alternative reality to Phelps's complacency, as derided by Parker. The scant two-page "Foreword," introducing *The Best of Simple* (1961), simultaneously explains and demonstrates the driving motive behind the offhandedly antiracist sarcasm that distinguished Hughes's essays for over a generation. Both the reality and the philosophy behind Jesse Semple was visible when he asked a young Black man in a neighborhood bar about his job:

> Not knowing much about the young man, I asked where he worked. He said, "In a war plant."
> I said, "What do you make?"
> He said, "Cranks."
> I said, "What kind of cranks?"
> He said, "Oh, man, I don't know what kind of cranks."
> I said, "Well, do they crank cars, tanks, buses, planes or what?"
> He said, "I don't know what them cranks crank."
> Whereupon, his girl friend, a little put out at this ignorance of his job, said, "You've been working there long enough. Looks like by now you ought to know what them cranks crank."
> "Aw, woman," he said, "you know white folks don't tell colored folks what cranks crank."
> And that was the beginning of Simple. ... But out of the mystery as to what the cranks of this world crank, to whom they belong and why, there evolved the character in this book, wondering and laughing at the numerous problems of white folks, colored folks, and just folks – including himself.[52]

49 Louis Botto, "Quotable Critics," *Playbill* (29 May 2008), n.p.
50 Dorothy Parker, *The Portable Dorothy Parker* (New York: Penguin Books, 1976), 513.
51 Parker, *Portable Dorothy Parker*, 498–99.
52 Langston Hughes, *The Best of Simple* (New York: Hill and Wang, 1961), vii–viii.

And out of that beginning was born Jesse Semple, or "Simple," one of the truly unique characters in American fiction, drawn from life but presented as fiction that read as a comic essay, a complexity that applies to many of the essayists in this chapter from Franklin and Irving onward.

H. L. Mencken (1880–1956) detested the Algonquin group as much as Dorothy Parker disliked the complacency of Phelps, and considered their humor trashy. Mencken's six volumes of *Prejudices* (1919–1927) are landmarks in the combination of sarcastic rhetoric with high cultural expectations. Castigating vulgar stupidity, Mencken holds little hope of reforming the American "booboisie," a word he may not have coined but made well known. His essay "The Sahara of the Bozart" (1920) complains of "so vast a vacuity," culturally speaking, as to boggle the imagination; and Yankee New Englanders were no better, for he saw them as "tawdry and tacky fellows."[53] Mencken, like Parker, flourished in an age devoted to the short essay and the savage one-liner. The essays of George S. Schuyler (1895–1977), one of Mencken's favorite commentators in the *American Mercury*, stood out for his independence and acerbic phraseology. Now best known for his novel, *Black No More* (1931), Schuyler's conservative opinions, which he expressed so strongly, alienated many liberals.

E. B. White (1899–1985) and James Thurber (1894–1961), closely associated with the *New Yorker*, were gentler humorists, given more to whimsy than sarcasm. White's "Once More to the Lake," his signature piece, resembles Franklin's "Ephemerae" in its nostalgic vision, and he presents "Death of a Pig" as an age-old farm tragedy "with perfect fidelity to the original script."[54] In White's unique, personal sentimentality, medical language transmutes into sentimental language – the vet's diagnosis, "deep hemorrhagic infarcts," becomes "deep hemorrhagic intears," and White pledges to visit the pig's grave on flagless memorial days in future seasons of reflection and despair.[55] These essays move away from tumultuous political and social affairs toward the internal tumult of emotions triggered by existential change and recollected in moments of tranquility, as in *Here Is New York* (1949), White's nostalgic portrait of changing America, which sold millions of copies.

---

[53] Cited in an excellent article on Mencken's position by Guy Story Brown, "H. L. Mencken and the South," *Abbeville Institute Press* (blog) (10 March 2017), www.abbevilleinstitute.org/h-l-mencken-and-the-south.
[54] E. B. White, "Death of a Pig," *Atlantic Monthly* (January 1948): 30–33, 30.
[55] White, "Death of a Pig," 32–33.

Postwar and Contemporary Comedian-Essayists

The "modern" comic essay takes varying paths. Erma Bombeck (1927–1996) describes the mundane domestic trivialities of motherhood and suburban life with titles like *The Grass Is Always Greener over the Septic Tank* (1976). Editorial political columnists include Russell Baker (1925–2019) and Art Buchwald (1925–2007), first among equals as humorous political commentators, especially in their writing in the period surrounding the Kennedy-Johnson-Nixon era, with passing mention to Mike Royko (1932–1997) in and about Chicago. What better title for a book of Nixon-era columns than Buchwald's *I Am Not a Crook* (1974)? Later comic essayists combined the personal, the cultural, and the political: Nicholas Bakalar's *American Satire: An Anthology of Writings from Colonial Times to the Present* adds Kurt Vonnegut (1922–2007), Gore Vidal (1925–2012), Calvin Trillin (1935–), P. J. O'Rourke (1947–2022), and Molly Ivins (1944–2007), among others, to the list of great comic writers.[56] Jean Shepherd (1921–1999) was a creative and forceful monologist on popular American values primarily through radio. His hour-long rambles on WOR Radio in New York City from 1955 through 1977 survive as "Old Time Radio," or in an eight-performance audio CD, *Jean Shepherd: The Fatal Flaw*, covering popular concepts of heroism, the hunger for "balderdash," and comic strip values. *In God We Trust: All Others Pay Cash* (1991) exhibits his ability to juxtapose epigrams and American catchphrases to score ethical points. Other stand-up comedians have also delivered their essayistic work in oral venues outside the print medium. These include Mort Sahl (1927–2021), Bob Newhart (1929–), Lenny Bruce (1925–1966), Richard Pryor (1940–2005), George Carlin (1937–2008), Phyllis Diller (1917–2012), and Joan Rivers (1933–2014). Woody Allen's (1935–) three slim books are more likely to be classified as fiction than essay, but, in fact they are primarily sketches and burlesques of commencement speeches, autobiographical reflections, and even the Socratic dialogue. The speaker in "My Apology," in *Side Effects* (1979), takes over the Greek philosophical dialogue in Socrates's death scene, although he says his deep thinking is more likely to revolve around a Swedish airline stewardess. In "My Speech to the Graduates," Allen parodies thousands of college commencement speeches. "Yes, but Can the Steam Engine Do This?" in *Getting Even* (1972) is a parody of the brief chronology articles in popular magazines, in this case elaborating fancifully around the invention of the

---

56 Nicholas Bakalar, ed., *American Satire: An Anthology of Writings from Colonial Times to the Present* (New York: Penguin Books, 1997).

sandwich, set in ridiculous perspective by the title reflecting a major technological advance.

Crossing into the twenty-first century, comedians such as Roy Blount (1941–) and Garrison Keillor (1942–) have offered highly personal, philosophical statements that champion local values and experience. Keillor's recent blog writings of the 2010s and '20s are consistently powerful in attacking rising fascist bigotry in the Trump era. Both Blount and Keillor use their kindly and down-to-earth regional style as a hopeful model for a national ethos, one that would remain optimistic in the face of modern angst about a planet teetering on the edge of political and environmental disaster, as differentiated from the personalized angst of Woody Allen.

Finally, many contemporary comic writers have turned to the autobiographical essay to offer reflections on the surreal and absurd aspects of life, family, identity, sex, and relationships. The most well known of these is David Sedaris (1956–) whose essay collections such as *Me Talk Pretty One Day* (2000) and *Let's Explore Diabetes with Owls* (2013) continue to delight readers with whimsy and mimicry of contemporary personal behavior. Other recent notable examples include Chelsea Handler's *Are You There Vodka? It's Me, Chelsea* (2008), Justin Halpern's *Sh*t My Dad Says* (2010), Sarah Silverman's *The Bedwetter: Stories of Courage, Redemption, and Pee* (2010), Jenny Lawson's *Let's Pretend This Never Happened* (2012), Eddie Huang's *Fresh Off the Boat: A Memoir* (2013), Ophira Eisenberg's *Screw Everyone: Sleeping My Way to Monogamy* (2013), Issa Rae's *The Misadventures of Awkward Black Girl* (2015), and Jenny Slate's *Little Weirds* (2019). Without falling into either folksiness or angst, the comic essay now seems to be oriented toward intensely personalized recollections. The flamboyant surrealism of Andy Borowitz's contributions to the *New Yorker*, however, stand by themselves as tightly encapsulated statements on national political and cultural behavior.

In Closing

The comic essay has occupied a central position in American life for 400 years and has maintained its commitment to liberty and freedom of expression, most brilliantly represented by the early comic statements of Ben Franklin. The continuum stretches from Thomas Morton to Andy Borowitz, and can be recognized by various traits: an often exaggerated regional rhetoric or absurdist narration of scenes of daily life, an attachment to individuality, and a focus on the problem of authority, no longer represented by the monarchy but by those presidents and billionaires who still privilege the interests of a few over the interests of the many. The path runs through the urban – and urbane – irony of Ben Franklin and Washington Irving. It then continues through the suffragist exclamations of Fanny Fern into the essays of the comic writers of the 1820–1860 period who labored to identify the traits of the American natural (sometimes called "native") and urban frontiers as villages, then cities, replaced the wilderness, changing American culture radically. Mark Twain's definitions of American ethics – both early and late – set him above all other comic writers, but the patterns remained largely the same through his anti-imperialist tirades at the turn of the nineteenth century, unpopular in his time but widely admired now. The increasingly localized and personalized comic writers of the twentieth century, and now the twenty-first, no longer mask their egalitarian personae in pseudonyms or contrived vulgar dialect and misspellings, but their objectives have remained the same. Modalities changed as we passed from print through radio and television to the Internet, where the record of its various forms and transmutations may be all but impossible to track. If recent developments are any indication, the American comic essay will continue to thrive and change in unexpected ways as we make our way through the twenty-first century.

13

Nineteenth-Century American Travel Essays: Aesthetics, Modernity, and National Identity

BRIGITTE BAILEY

Modernity offered the ideal conditions under which American travel essays could proliferate: developing infrastructures in transportation, communication, and the publication and distribution of books and periodicals; the growing commercial and imperial reach of the United States; rising literacy rates, which ensured a market for these texts; Old World tourism as a marker of elite and then middle-class identity; the status of Europe as a site of professional training; transatlantic networks of reformers; missionary activity in Asia and Africa; and hemispheric travel in the Americas. Travel writings were popular – a sign that they were performing significant cultural work. William Stowe notes the rising number of travel books (over 1,800) and essays in newspapers and magazines (thousands) published before 1900, most recounting European tours.[1] This chapter focuses on travel writing and expatriate nonfiction writing in short form from 1820 to 1910 and on European travel writings, with some reference to essays about other destinations. The tourist's or expatriate's provisional relationship to other peoples and places lent itself to the genre of the essay, a genre influentially defined by Michel de Montaigne at the inception of the post-Columbian modern world as an attempt, an exploratory movement through a series of observations and ideas.[2] This emphasis on the provisional and situational informed many nineteenth- and early twentieth-century travel and expatriate essays. In rendering the interactions between consciousness and place, Americans

---

[1] William W. Stowe, *Going Abroad: European Travel in Nineteenth-Century American Culture* (Princeton, NJ: Princeton University Press, 1994), 3–4. See also Harold F. Smith, *American Travellers Abroad: A Bibliography of Accounts Published before 1900*, 2nd ed. (Lanham, MD: Scarecrow Press, 1999).

[2] For current perspectives on the genre, see Thomas Karshan and Kathryn Murphy, eds., *On Essays: Montaigne to the Present* (Oxford: Oxford University Press, 2021).

pushed the boundaries of the genre, as travel essays blended with journalism, fiction, and autobiography.

Early National and Antebellum Travel Writings: Supervision and Aesthetic Sketches

In the post-Revolutionary period, US elites traveling in Europe modeled their approach to travel on the British Grand Tour, an approach that sought to strengthen the supervisory position of a propertied ruling class by linking visual comprehension with economic management.[3] Thomas Jefferson (1743–1826) advised travelers to collect useful information on agriculture and "mechanical arts" and to get a visual grasp of a place by buying a map and "go[ing] to the top of a steeple to have a view of the town." His own 1787 travel journal in southern France followed this practice, providing an overview of the geographical situation of towns, along with their soil quality, crops, wages, and social conditions.[4]

After the Napoleonic wars, when travel increased, and through the antebellum period, tourists translated this supervisory orientation into an aesthetic stance, adapting the perspective of an eighteenth-century landowning or mercantile elite into a cultural form of supervision suitable for a democratizing society experiencing the market revolution.[5] The training in knowledge and vision that had counted among the acquisitions of the gentleman on tour became what John Urry calls the modern "tourist gaze," a form of visual work that helped to construct not only class but also national identity through the viewing of places, people, and activities defined as other to the United States.[6] Although this gaze was culturally acquired, it was supposedly natural and democratically available.[7] Such visual conventions as the panoramic view – as seen from elevated tourist sites – prompted what Alan Wallach calls the "panoptic sublime," an experience naturalizing the exercise of power through "oversight" and corresponding to ideologies

---

3 Christopher Hibbert, *The Grand Tour* (London: Weidenfeld and Nicolson, 1969), 20.
4 Thomas Jefferson, *The Life and Selected Writings of Thomas Jefferson*, ed. Adrienne Koch and William Peden (New York: Random House, 1972), 135–48.
5 On the shift to a market economy in the United States, see Charles Sellers, *The Market Revolution: Jacksonian America, 1815–1846* (Oxford: Oxford University Press, 1991).
6 John Urry, *The Tourist Gaze: Leisure and Travel in Contemporary Societies* (London: Sage, 1990).
7 Kenneth John Myers, "The Cultural Construction of Landscape Experience: Contact to 1830," in *American Iconology*, ed. David C. Miller (New Haven, CT: Yale University Press, 1993), 73–77.

through which white elites sought to shape the nation.[8] An equally enduring component of the tourist gaze was the picturesque, a visual practice of discerning harmony in a scene rich with contrasts and that corresponded to American attempts to see unity in the diverse scene of nineteenth-century life. As Carrie Tirado Bramen argues, this aesthetic could have liberatory or coercive implications when directed at human subjects, as the "pictorial gaze" could imagine ways to reconcile difference or could become "a mode of social control," of "master[ing] otherness."[9] The popularity of these and similar conventions created a national gaze, which could be trained on domestic and foreign scenes.

American writers incorporated panoramic and picturesque views into their works at home and abroad. Their usual term for short descriptive pieces was the "sketch," a term flagging the centrality of vision in travel and that, as a version of the essay, was provisional in its claims. James Fenimore Cooper (1789–1851), who drew both on the early national persona of the landed gentleman and on the antebellum tourist gaze, featured US panoramic views that modeled the "imperial eye" in such novels as *The Last of the Mohicans* (1826).[10] His five-volume travel series, *Gleanings in Europe* (1836–38), includes such views but to different ends; the series illustrates the American tourist's polarized conceptual map of Europe. While England is the masculine center of empire, representing human domination over nature, and France – especially Paris – is associated with political and economic debates, Italy is associated with the feminine and the heart, and Switzerland represents nature's untamed power. The meanings Americans ascribed to these places correspond to aspects of the observer's identity and thus result in shifts in authorial voice among Cooper's volumes. He discusses England analytically, using the gentleman's supervisory gaze to critique British sociopolitical systems, contrasting them with US republican values. However, the Swiss Alps oust the rational critic for the rhapsodic tourist in "a sublime communion with nature" that leads to "religious awe." Here the panoptic sublime's "bewildering" "sweep of vision" distends the viewer's rational self by "exceed[ing]" his preconceived "pictures"; this destabilization also unleashes regressive energies, awakening anti-Catholic and childish fantasies of dirty monks washed away in a mountain torrent. In

---

8 Alan Wallach, "Making a Picture of the View from Mount Holyoke," in Miller, *American Iconology*, 80–91, 84.
9 Carrie Tirado Bramen, "A Transatlantic History of the Picturesque: An Introductory Essay," *Nineteenth-Century Prose* 29, no. 2 (Fall 2002): 1–19, 7, 15.
10 Mary Louise Pratt, *Imperial Eyes: Travel Writing and Transculturation* (London: Routledge, 1992).

Cooper's Swiss sketches, the natural sublime is both an insight into divine power and a psychological risk.[11]

The aesthetic tourist gaze informed other kinds of travel. Americans in Europe for professional training fused visual responses with professional aspirations. Henry Wadsworth Longfellow's (1807–1882) *Outre Mer: A Pilgrimage beyond the Sea* (1835), a sketchbook of travels in France, Spain, and Italy, is an exercise in the tourist's composition of picturesque views – peasants harvesting grapes, ruined castles, and scenic villages, views supplemented by sentimental stories about the people he sees – but also, along with study at the University of Göttingen, part of his literary and linguistic preparation for becoming the professor of modern languages at Bowdoin College.[12] Longfellow's use of these visual and sentimental conventions and his quotations from the literature of the countries he visits exemplifies the tourist's cultivation of a rich interiority, a form of personal development and cultural capital that also serves as a credential for his future academic work.

This achievement of a cultivated interiority through the tourist gaze is an aspect of professional identity and a political statement in James McCune Smith's (1813–1865) travel journal, published in the *Colored American* (1837–39), describing his sea voyage and sojourn in Liverpool en route to medical school in Glasgow – training he was denied in the United States as a Black man. McCune Smith describes the sea's sublimity in biblical and Byronic terms and, although lauding the American-built ship on which he sails as a symbol of "the great and rising" United States, he contrasts its "baneful" influence in spreading the "canker" of racism with the ocean's "spirit of liberty." His descriptions of Liverpool comment on visual perspectives as tools of sociopolitical insight. Making landfall at night, he delights in a "splendid" view – "myriads of twinkling gas lights" – but the morning reveals a harsher scene: "[W]ind mill shafts, black and smoky, ... seem the scorched remains of the previous night's superb exhibition. The long wall enclosing the docks ... remind[s] you ... of an immense prison house." However, the next entry begins, "'I am free!' ... flashed through my mind, as I trod the strong wharf."[13] This sequence, where an illusion of picturesque harmony yields to a realistic view of an imprisoning industrial scene, which in turn yields to

---

[11] James Fenimore Cooper, *Gleanings in Europe: Switzerland*, ed. Robert E. Spiller, James F. Beard, Kenneth W. Staggs, and James P. Elliott (Albany, NY: State University of New York Press, 1980), 5, 41, 112, 115, 185–87.
[12] Leslie Elizabeth Eckel, *Atlantic Citizens: Nineteenth-Century American Writers at Work in the World* (Edinburgh: Edinburgh University Press, 2013), 21–27.
[13] James McCune Smith, "Dr. Smith's Journal," in *The Works of James McCune Smith*, ed. John Stauffer (Oxford: Oxford University Press, 2006), 8–24, 12–13, 16.

its opposite – the fact of McCune Smith's greater freedom in this British cityscape – both participates in tourism's aesthetics and critiques their truth value.

In spite of its promise of visual power, the tourist gaze contained contradictions. In southern Europe, it allowed tourists to manage impressions of culturally and ethnically different landscapes and peoples but also could make tourists vulnerable to new sights. In a chapter of *Letters from Abroad to Kindred at Home* (1841), Catharine Maria Sedgwick (1789–1867) explores the class and gender dynamics of the cultivated man's aesthetic response by observing her friend, the poet John Kenyon, watching a scene of dancing Neapolitan peasant girls, his face "soul-lit, ... as if by magic he were beholding the elder time." In the elite male tourist's sensibility, viewing the apparently archaic identities performed by "these wild children of the South" opens the "floodgates of poetry" and allows him to recall such aspects of identity and integrate them safely (as "poetry") into the modern self.[14] As the United States signified, for Americans, narrative movement through history and an active transformation of the natural environment, this posture of aesthetic arrest corresponded with the essence of the other, which implied narrative arrest and landscape stasis – an assumption that frames, for example, Washington Irving's (1783–1859) Spanish sketchbook *The Alhambra* (1832). The desire of US tourists for this experience meant that, while sympathetic to European republican movements, they often ignored modernizing political events and insisted on seeing southern Europe as a set of picturesque landscapes left behind by progress. However, aesthetic openness to the other could bring unanticipated insights into the traveler's consciousness and dislodge a secure national self. Hence a repeated theme in travel fiction about the danger of being seduced by the visited country; Sedgwick also wrote a tale about a young male tourist who goes mad "groping" among Italian ruins and gets sidetracked from a "manly career" at home.[15] Nevertheless, in most nonfiction writings on southern Europe the author remained what Ralph Waldo Emerson (1803–1882) called a "protected

---

14 [Catharine Maria Sedgwick], *Letters from Abroad to Kindred at Home* (1841; New York: Harper and Brothers, 1845), 2:267–69.
15 C. M. Sedgwick, "An Incident at Rome," *Graham's Lady's and Gentleman's Magazine* 27 (1845): 104–108. On Italy as a seductive woman in male writings, see James Buzard, *The Beaten Track: European Tourism, Literature, and the Ways to "Culture," 1800–1918* (Oxford: Oxford University Press, 1993), 132–39. On the theme of "enervation" in southern Europe, see Kenneth Churchill, *Italy and English Literature, 1764–1930* (London: MacMillan Press, 1980), 58, 159

witness," an "invisibl[e]" visitor, who sees but who is not the object of a returning gaze.[16]

If US travelers equated southern Europe with aesthetic arrest, their approaches to Britain ranged from picturesque views to analyses of modernity. Given the historical ties between the United States and the United Kingdom, writers saw Britain as emblemizing aspects of the American past, present, or future. Irving's *The Sketch-Book* (1820–21) modelled an "anxious form of masculinity," uprooted from secure forms of property by the emerging market economy;[17] the book was, therefore, popular in both countries. In his English sketches, Irving is nostalgically drawn to social and economic forms that are already superseded in Britain; he thereby conveys the alienation of the "stranger" in "the land of my forefathers" as a generalizable psychological state of early nineteenth-century white male subjects. The sketch "A Sunday in London" describes the pausing of the city – "the gigantic monster" – on this day of rest, when its "fires of forges and manufactories" relent; the day restores a preindustrial world of church attendance, visits to nature, and family reunions of those "separated by the laborious occupations of the week."[18] Sunday neutralizes the modern world in London, the metropolis most saw as the vanguard of modernity. In this Irving echoed the insistence of many US tourists that, in spite of Britain's preeminent modernity, premodern England was, as Christopher Mulvey says, "the real England"; while most Americans landed in industrial Liverpool, they quickly sought out a nearby site of medieval structures and Roman remains: "The antidote to the modern city of Liverpool was the ancient city of Chester."[19]

Abolitionists, Reformers, and Antebellum Travel Writing

If Irving ignored modernity in Britain, Frederick Douglass (1818–1895), Margaret Fuller (1810–1850), and Emerson sought it out. Like Cooper, they used their travels in Britain to work through definitions of both nations; as

16 Ralph Waldo Emerson, *Journals*, ed. Alfred R. Ferguson (Cambridge, MA: Harvard University Press, 1964), 4:78. On travel aesthetics, see Brigitte Bailey, *American Travel Literature, Gendered Aesthetics, and the Italian Tour, 1824–1862* (Edinburgh: Edinburgh University Press, 2018).
17 David Anthony, *Paper Money Men: Commerce, Manhood, and the Sensational Public Sphere in Antebellum America* (Columbus, OH: The Ohio State University Press, 2009), 42.
18 Washington Irving, *The Sketch-Book*, ed. Susan Manning (Oxford: Oxford University Press, 1996), 19, 100–101.
19 Christopher Mulvey, *Anglo-American Landscapes: A Study of Nineteenth-Century Anglo-American Travel Literature* (Cambridge, UK: Cambridge University Press, 1983), 37, 42.

Susan Roberson notes, even as "Emerson is contemplating what makes 'England, England' ... he is also thinking about what makes America, America."[20] In doing so they worked in a different tradition of the essay from the travel sketch: analytical and sociological rather than aesthetic. Traveling in the 1840s, they encountered a nation transformed by technology, imperial power, and global commerce and debating the social consequences of its transformation. During his antislavery lecture tours in Britain and Ireland (1845–47), Douglass traveled by railway, whose expansion gave unprecedented access to the United Kingdom, and embraced revolutions in travel and communication as furthering the abolitionist cause. Arguing that Britain "has an influence on America that no other nation can have," he adds that this influence is heightened by "the power of steam": "denunciations [of slavery], uttered in London this week, may be heard in a fortnight in the streets of Boston."[21] His chapter "Twenty-One Months in Great Britain" in *My Bondage and My Freedom* (1855) reverses associations of Britain with a repressive past and the United States with the progressive present: Publishing his 1845 *Narrative* "endangered my liberty, and led me to seek a refuge from republican slavery in monarchical England." Similarly, Douglass replaces the descriptive travel book he could have written – "I might write a book twice the size of this ... I lectured in nearly all the large towns and cities in the United Kingdom" – with a mention of the abolitionist network of "dear friends" who supported his travels and bought his freedom, that is, by highlighting a progressive community within the nation.[22]

Working as a correspondent for the *New-York Tribune*, Fuller followed Douglass to the United Kingdom in 1846 and, indeed, traveled on the same steamship he had taken. Her first essay for the *Tribune* links two manifestations of modern Britain: the landscape of industrial and commercial modernity and the reform activities growing out of it. She brings together the "miles" of Liverpool Docks and the "magnificent" warehouses of commodities in Manchester – signaling Britain's domination of an integrated world

---

20 Susan L. Roberson, "Emerson's English Traits and the Paradox of Empire," *New England Quarterly* 84, no. 2 (June 2011): 265–85, 267.
21 Hannah-Rose Murray and John R. McKivigan, "'To Remove the Mask from Her Face': 1845–1847," in *Frederick Douglass in Britain and Ireland, 1845–1895*, ed. Hannah-Rose Murray and John R. McKivigan (Edinburgh: Edinburgh University Press, 2021), 18–20. This speech is excerpted in an appendix in Frederick Douglass's *My Bondage and My Freedom*, ed. William L. Andrews (Urbana, IL: University of Illinois Press, 1987); the quotation is on 260–61.
22 Douglass, *My Bondage*, 223, 228. Douglass returned as a tourist in Europe and the Near East (1886–87) and wrote an account in his third autobiography; see David W. Blight, *Frederick Douglass: Prophet of Freedom* (New York: Simon and Schuster, 2018), 667–74.

market – with the "squalid" conditions of mill workers and beggars, and with mechanics' institutes (organizations for working-class education) and working-class newspapers. Fuller asks her readers to connect the often disjointed images tourists saw, to resist denarrativizing the other, and to turn spectacle into a critical account of British capitalist modernity, which prefigures American modernity.[23] Fuller pursued conversations with reform intellectuals and activists in London and Paris and then wrote dispatches on the 1848–49 Roman Revolution that replace the tourist's static and feminized images of Italy with active historical figures and "resolute" revolutionaries, that translate political documents for her readers, and that argue for a modern Italian state.[24]

Emerson's *English Traits*, written after his UK lecture tour (1847–48), is an ambitious exploration of British national identity. Also connecting industrialism, empire, and print culture, he introduces England's "factitious," reconstructed "geography" in a scene where trains and the London *Times* symbolize modern Britain: "Cushioned and comforted ..., the traveller rides as on a cannon-ball, ... over rivers and towns, ... and reads quietly the 'Times' newspaper, which, by its immense correspondence ... ha[s] machinized the rest of the world for his occasion."[25] The essays, on such topics as "Land," "Race," and "Wealth," toggle between deterministic categories (race, geography) and concepts of "will" and achievement in defining the nation. Roberson finds that Emerson's "insistent concern" is with the globalization of commerce and "the paradox of empire," which brings both brutal conquest and British concepts of liberty, while Christopher Hanlon analyzes Emerson's use of British theories of Saxon and Norman "races" to define "English traits": "Race is everywhere" in these essays.[26] Emerson concludes that "London is the epitome of our times" and "England is the best of actual nations," "a poor best," as its pursuit of physical ends lacks an "ideal framework." Given his similar description of the United States in such

---

23 Margaret Fuller, *"These Sad but Glorious Days": Dispatches from Europe, 1846–1850*, ed. Larry J. Reynolds and Susan Belasco Smith (New Haven, CT: Yale University Press, 1991), 39–47. On Fuller's British dispatches, see Brigitte Bailey, "Margaret Fuller's Dispatches from Great Britain," in *Transatlantic Women: Nineteenth-Century American Women Writers and Great Britain*, ed. Beth L. Lueck, Brigitte Bailey, and Lucinda L. Damon-Bach (Durham, NH: University of New Hampshire Press, 2012), 49–70.
24 Fuller, *"These Sad but Glorious Days,"* 304.
25 Ralph Waldo Emerson, *English Traits*, ed. Howard Mumford Jones (Cambridge, MA: Harvard University Press, 1966), 60, 21.
26 Roberson, "Emerson's English Traits," 267–68, 275; Christopher Hanlon, "'The Old Race Are All Gone': Transatlantic Bloodlines and 'English Traits,'" *American Literary History* 19, no. 4 (Winter 2007): 800–23, 804, jstor.org/stable/4497013. Hanlon argues that Emerson starts to critique racial "purity"; see pages 808, 816.

essays as "The American Scholar" (1837), the implied question is whether the United States, which Emerson sees as succeeding the United Kingdom, will transcend the limitations of the "actual."[27]

Concerns about power, liberty, and identity inform travel writings emerging from transatlantic abolition and peace movements, in book chapters by George Copway (1818–1869), William Wells Brown (1814 or 1815–1884), and Harriet Beecher Stowe (1811–1896). Written after attending the 1850 World Peace Congress in Frankfurt, Copway's *Running Sketches of Men and Places in England, France, Germany, Belgium, and Scotland* (1851), Kate Flint argues, reveals his complex "engagement with modernity" and consciousness of his own "hybridity" as an Ojibwa convert to Christianity. Representing Native American converts at the congress, he writes in a "collage" of voices, viewing Europe through shifting lenses.[28] Also in Europe for a peace congress (Paris, 1849), Brown, a fugitive from slavery stranded in Britain by the 1850 Fugitive Slave Act, spent the next four years lecturing against slavery and publishing books. In an aesthetic travel book, *The American Fugitive in Europe: Sketches of Places and People Abroad* (1855), he claims the (white) tourist gaze at such sites as Tintern Abbey, where he quotes British poets and composes a textual picture of the ruins, departing from Douglass's refusal to engage in such travel writing conventions. His London sketches include an empowering panoramic view and its opposite: an episode of visual, financial, and social "darkness" that highlights modern urban isolation but also British imperialism; figures representing problems of labor, power, and slavery in the Atlantic world emerge out of the fog.[29] Stowe's *Sunny Memories of Foreign Lands* (1854) also juxtaposes tourism with antislavery. A collaboration with her husband Calvin Stowe (1802–1886) and brother Charles Beecher, the book records her European tour – including antislavery meetings and tourist sights – in the wake of *Uncle Tom Cabin*'s success.[30] While the antislavery speeches Calvin contributes blend evangelical and abolitionist rhetoric, Stowe's travel sketches employ the rhetoric of the sublime in the Alps, the picturesque at Gothic ruins, and the sentimental in, for example, Luther's home in Wittenberg. Where Calvin contrasts Britain's abolition of slavery with the United States' proslavery

---

27 Emerson, *English Traits*, 194, 23.
28 Kate Flint, *The Transatlantic Indian, 1776–1930* (Princeton, NJ: Princeton University Press, 2009), 216, 219.
29 William Wells Brown, *The American Fugitive in Europe: Sketches of Places and People Abroad* (Boston: John P. Jewett, 1855), 131, 117–21. See William W. Stowe, *Going Abroad*, 70–71.
30 Sarah Ruffing Robbins, "Harriet Beecher Stowe, Starring as Benevolent Celebrity Traveler," in Lueck, *Transatlantic Women*, 71–88.

entrenchment, her sketches work to unite Americans with the British as "kindred" sharing "English life-blood" and the "Anglo-Saxon vigor" that is "spreading our country from Atlantic to Pacific" – to the point where this community of blood seems to erase the enslaved Americans on whose behalf she wrote her novel.[31] As does Emerson, she absorbs British valorizations of Saxon "racial" qualities, now identified with New England.

Reformers' attempts to rethink the national identity and tourists' views shared positions of oversight, even as reform and tourism often worked at cross-purposes, given the reform movement's desire to set communities in motion and tourism's propensity for arrest. However, both reform movements and travel writing offered cultural authority and social mobility to women, African Americans, Native Americans, and nonelite white men, from Bayard Taylor (1825–1878) to Mark Twain (1835–1910), who wrote their way into elite society via travel essays. As a woman, Sedgwick oversees both the "archaic" Italian scene and the male poet's subjectivity. What Christina Zwarg says of Fuller is also true of Sedgwick, Brown, and others: Being both "inside and outside" of the dominant culture offered a position from which to survey and critique that culture.[32] Hence the convergence of travel writing and reform in several texts.

Other Genres, Other Places in the Long Nineteenth Century

While this chapter focuses on the travel essay or sketch and on accounts of European travel, other genres and accounts of other geographies represent a broad field for analysis. As Douglass's autobiography and Fuller's journalism indicate, travel essays appear within these and other nineteenth-century forms, such as scientific reports, fiction, artists' memoirs, and missionary accounts. Missionary texts include, for example, Agnes McAllister's *A Lone Woman in Africa: Six Years on the Kroo Coast* (1896), which Mary Suzanne Schriber discusses as travel writing and which intersperses narrative incidents with essays on Liberian women, customs, and beliefs.[33] Journalists reporting on the 1848 revolution in Paris, such as Charles Dana, wrote descriptive and analytical columns, while forty years later such women journalists as Nelly Bly (Elizabeth Cochrane

---

31 Harriet Beecher Stowe, *Sunny Memories of Foreign Lands* (Boston: Phillips, Sampson, 1854), 1:18, 2:364–65, 379.
32 Christina Zwarg, *Feminist Conversations: Fuller, Emerson, and the Play of Reading* (Ithaca, NY: Cornell University Press, 1995), 125.
33 Mary Suzanne Schriber, *Writing Home: American Women Abroad, 1830–1920* (Charlottesville, VA: University Press of Virginia, 1997), 134.

Seaman), who beat Jules Verne's fictional hero's time in traveling around the world, wrote accounts that drew on both the reporting practices of Joseph Pulitzer's "new journalism" and the "tradition of travel writing," as Karen Roggenkamp notes.[34] The journalist and fiction writer Lafcadio Hearn wrote travel accounts of the Caribbean and Japan.[35] Artists' memoirs contain travel essays, from the sculptor William Wetmore Story's depiction of Rome in *Roba di Roma* (1862) to the painter Henry Ossawa Tanner's account of travels in Palestine in his "Story of an Artist's Life," in the magazine the *World's Work* (1909).[36] And travel sketches appear in fiction throughout the century: For example, Nathaniel Hawthorne drew on his travel journals both for his book of British sketches, *Our Old Home* (1863), and for his Italian romance, *The Marble Faun* (1860). Writings about non-European places, especially Caribbean sites, increasingly receive critical attention. Nancy Prince's writings about postemancipation Jamaica in her *Life and Travels* (1841) as "a freeborn African American Christian" combine missionary, travel, and abolitionist discourses, as Cheryl Fish argues.[37] Ivonne García examines travel accounts of Cuba by Sophia Peabody, William Cullen Bryant, and others as examples of "Gothic geoculture."[38] Travel essays pervaded the nineteenth century and illuminate the ways in which Americans understood themselves and their world.

Travel Essays in the Gilded Age: Class, Fragmented Views, and the Amorous Gaze

Late nineteenth-century essayists moved away from the panoptic gaze toward partial views, parody, and – at times – elite expressions of intimacy with Old World scenes. Although tourism still did – and does – promise to

---

34 On Dana, see Adam-Max Tuchinsky, *Horace Greeley's* New-York Tribune: *Civil War–Era Socialism and the Crisis of Free Labor* (Ithaca, NY: Cornell University Press, 2009), 88–98. Karen Roggenkamp, *Narrating the News: New Journalism and Literary Genre in Late Nineteenth-Century American Newspapers and Fiction* (Kent, OH: Kent State University Press, 2005), 34.
35 Roger Célestin, "Lafcadio Hearn," in *American Travel Writers, 1850–1915*, ed. Donald Ross and James J. Schramer (Detroit, MI: Thomson Gale, 1998), 144–59. Accessed through Gale Literature: *Dictionary of Literary Biography*.
36 On Tanner's travels, see John Davis, *The Landscape of Belief: Encountering the Holy Land in Nineteenth-Century American Art and Culture* (Princeton, NJ: Princeton University Press, 1996), 209.
37 Cheryl J. Fish, *Black and White Women's Travel Narratives: Antebellum Explorations* (Gainesville, FL: University Press of Florida, 2004), 29–30.
38 Ivonne M. García, *Gothic Geoculture: Nineteenth-Century Representations of Cuba in the Transamerican Imaginary* (Columbus, OH: The Ohio State University Press, 2019). See also Caroline Field Levander and Robert S. Levine, eds., *Hemispheric American Studies* (New Brunswick, NJ: Rutgers University Press, 2008).

deliver the panoptic sublime, travel writing paralleled the visual arts as the taste for panoramic landscape views declined by the 1870s.[39] In the late 1860s, three books exemplify these changes: William Dean Howells's (1837–1920) *Venetian Life* (1866), Julia Ward Howe's (1819–1910) *From the Oak to the Olive* (1868), and Twain's (1835–1910) *The Innocents Abroad* (1869).

Serving as US consul in Venice, Howells separates his sketches from earlier travel writing by disabusing his reader of "sentimental errors"; he writes on tourist sights but also on "every-day life," such as "Housekeeping." This Venice has abandoned its carnival and is a "nation in mourning," resenting its Austrian occupiers. His metaphor for his perspective is the "stage-box," from which theatergoers see both "the play and the by-play," the "scene-shifters ... [and] the characters": "The illusion which I had thought essential in the dramatic spectacle, turned out to be ... of small importance." The ensuing essays do not abandon aesthetics but they relocate the "spell" of the city's "beauty" to "narrow ... streets" and hidden corners; Venice remains a "fantastic vision," but the viewer is "startled" by little pockets of beauty as well as by the "proper Objects of Interest."[40] In other essays, Howells responds to yet qualifies picturesque landscapes. In *Italian Journeys* (1867) he delights in the view from the island of Capri – "the sea was flushed with sunset, ... the heights rising from it softened ... into [ghostly] dreams" – then drops into ironic, colloquial language to imagine the emperor Tiberius's brutal enhancement of the aesthetic experience of sunset "by popping a boon companion over the cliff, and thus enjoy[ing] [a] fine poetic contrast ... to that scene of innocence and peace."[41] Howells's sarcasm undercuts the tourist's impulse to harmonize and manage – make picturesque – the landscapes of the past.

In Howe's chapters on Rome, the distance between the remembered enthusiasm of her youthful trips and her sometimes acerbic comments on the present reflects not only personal change but also this cultural shift. While the "pleasures" of visiting "the riches of this Roman world" and the contrast between old Italy and new America remain ("Rome is the true antipodes of America. Our business is to build – her business is to excavate"), Rome is now not the static "eternal city" but the site of new excavations; its

---

39 Angela Miller, *The Empire of the Eye: Landscape Representation and American Cultural Politics, 1825–1875* (Ithaca, NY: Cornell University Press, 1993), 18.
40 William Dean Howells, *Venetian Life*, rev. ed. (Boston: Houghton Mifflin, 1907), 4, 83, 12, 1–2, 22–23, 113, 24. I have not quoted from chapters added in later editions.
41 William Dean Howells, *Italian Journeys*, rev. ed. (Boston: Houghton Mifflin, 1901), 114.

British archeological society is a "modern feature of Rome, especially as it travels by rail." Howe's family's trip to Greece is the heart of the book; they distribute clothing made by Boston women to refugees from the war between Greece and Turkey. A New England reformer, Howe later gave women's rights lectures in Europe.[42] Here, Howe the reformer intervenes in current events, while Howe the tourist visits the ancient Acropolis. Like Howells and Twain, she is often aesthetically moved by what she sees but satirizes the postures of tourists (including herself), the impostures of guides, and the economics of tourism. Her chapter "Sorrento" opens with the conceit that the view will replace the tourist's desire for commodities: "Here our rapture will cost nothing. We will feed our eyes." However, soon local shops have them "coveting wildly"; shopping ensues.[43]

Twain reported in newspaper articles on the first modern "transatlantic cruise," a steamship excursion to Europe and the Holy Land.[44] He engages the motives for this tour – consumption, piety, status seeking – by creating a "protean narrative persona" that shifts among forms of masculinity in encountering the feminine "high culture" of European travel.[45] Just as Howells and Howe resist immersion in romantic landscape vistas, so Twain resists the tour's historical vistas by drawing on nineteenth-century boy culture. Although it is "hard" not to admire the Vatican museum, Twain and his friends – "the boys" – refuse the imperative to admire, an imperative embodied in their guides; one chapter is an essay on "vanquish[ing]" guides by asking, as they are shown an Egyptian mummy or a bust of Columbus, "Is – is he dead?" The question flattens the past, implies that cultural tourism is focused on death, and asserts the function of the "American joke" in reinforcing boy culture's "education in autonomy."[46] Twain's chapters on the Near East target the pious tourist's overvaluation of the Holy Land and illustrators' sentimental exoticism by describing a "blistered" landscape marked by poverty and disease. Arriving at a desert well surrounded by "picturesque Arabs," he says, "Here was a grand Oriental picture which I had worshipped ... [in] steel engravings! But in the engraving there was no

---

42 Mary Suzanne Schriber, ed., *Telling Travels: Selected Writings by Nineteenth-Century American Women Abroad* (DeKalb, IL: Northern Illinois University Press, 1995), 153.
43 Julia Ward Howe, *From the Oak to the Olive: A Plain Record of a Pleasant Journey* (Boston: Lee and Shepard, 1868), 65, 81, 85–88, 120–21.
44 Jeffrey Alan Melton, *Mark Twain, Travel Books, and Tourism: The Tide of a Great Popular Movement* (Tuscaloosa, AL: University of Alabama Press, 2002), 60, ProQuest Ebook Central, ebookcentral.proquest.com/.
45 William W. Stowe, *Going Abroad*, 158, 129.
46 E. Anthony Rotundo, *American Manhood: Transformations in Masculinity from the Revolution to the Modern Era* (New York: Basic Books, 1993), 46.

desolation; ... no rags; no fleas; ... no besotted ignorance; ... no raw places on the donkeys' backs," and Twain fantasizes blowing up the scene with "tons of [gun]powder" – an aggression aimed at both the overwhelming otherness of Palestine and misleading Orientalist aesthetic conventions.[47]

Nevertheless, the post–Civil War period continued to see travel to Europe and the Near East as a marker of elite identity, and the era's "'quality journals'" published literary fiction next to travel writing in support of this identity.[48] As a regionalist writer in the United States and then an expatriate in Europe, Constance Fenimore Woolson (1840–1894) exemplifies this pattern; she contributed both fiction and travel essays to *Harper's Magazine*, which Harper and Brothers then collected into books.[49] She both wrote within the class interests that *Harper's* represented and critiqued them. Her understanding of travel's social contexts – leisure-class behavior, gender norms, the tourist economy – emerges in a hybrid piece, "At Mentone" (1884), a travel essay and story whose plot turns on courtship and sexual competition as motives for sightseeing and that implies that travel is no escape from the gender constraints of home. A two-part travel essay on Cairo exemplifies the late-century rejection of the comprehensive view. As do American paintings of Venice in this period, explains Margaretta Lovell – and as do Howells's essays – Woolson's essay "repudiat[es] ... the monumental" and panoramic, in favor of the "confined prospect[s]" and "partial" views characteristic of the modern spectator, who delights in the "fragmentary" nature of perception. "Cairo in 1890" features this "slide off the monument."[50] Woolson gives short shrift to the pyramids but emphasizes Cairo's mosques ("so embedded in other structures ... that you can see but little of their external form") and bazaars ("maze[s]" of narrow lanes); both create painterly "impressions" of color and light. Her essay argues that to "love Cairo" means to pursue idiosyncratic explorations, be receptive to unexpected sights, and love color – and thereby indicates the mutation of the visual and aesthetic practices central to travel essays.[51]

---

47 Mark Twain [Samuel L. Clemens], *The Innocents Abroad, or The New Pilgrim's Progress* (Hartford, CT: American Publishing, 1869), 288–93, 456, 543–44.
48 Richard H. Brodhead, *Cultures of Letters: Scenes of Reading and Writing in Nineteenth-Century America* (Chicago: University of Chicago Press, 1993), 124–32.
49 On Woolson's contract with Harper and Brothers, see Anne Boyd Rioux, *Constance Fenimore Woolson: Portrait of a Lady Novelist* (New York: W. W. Norton, 2016), 151.
50 Margaretta M. Lovell, *A Visitable Past: Views of Venice by American Artists, 1860–1915* (Chicago: University of Chicago Press, 1989), 39–42, 87.
51 Constance Fenimore Woolson, *Mentone, Cairo and Corfu* (New York: Harper and Brothers, 1896), HathiTrust Digital Library, 163, 183–84, 150.

Henry James (1843–1916) follows the pattern of publishing travel essays in periodicals and collecting them in volumes; he wrote essays for the *Atlantic* and other magazines that he revised and gathered into *A Little Tour in France* (1884), *English Hours* (1905), and *Italian Hours* (1909). The English and Italian essays especially investigate the tourist's aesthetic perception, in what James Buzard calls James's "vacillation between irony and investment."[52] He goes from a critical embrace of the picturesque to the modernist "repudiation of the monumental" and to an urban aesthetic that, in its toleration of opacity, departs from antebellum tourist gazes. His early essays follow in the footsteps of antebellum Americans; disembarking at Liverpool and seeking out Chester, James is the "picturesque" and "sentimental" tourist. However, Chester's medieval architecture, which makes it "the most picturesque city in the world," is also "fatally picturesque," as the economic pressure to keep the town antique for tourists is coercive for its inhabitants. While British industrial and picturesque landscapes seem opposites, James notes that they are determined by the same forces; Chester makes him "hear afresh the steady rumble of that deep keynote of English manners ... the economic struggle for existence."[53] By shifting from pictorial to audial terms, he steps outside the conventions of the tourist gaze. This rhetorical move anticipates his later essay "London," which notes the writer's complicity with this center of empire and capitalism. Conflating the darkness of the city's winter weather with that of the "immense misery" of its social conditions, James says that "the impression of suffering is a part of the general vibration, ... [of] the sound that is supremely dear to the consistent London-lover – the rumble of the tremendous human mill," and this climatic and social darkness is "the best time for writing."[54] If "London" describes modernity, the Italian essays represent "the face of things as it mainly *used* to be." "Venice" urges the elite "sentimental tourist" to outlast the mob of other tourists and recover a "love-affair" with the old "charm[ing]" feminine Venice. Like Woolson, James uses the vocabulary of "love" to indicate a private tourist experience, here one that (as opposed to the "London-lover['s]" experience) bypasses traces of modernity for a visual immersion in details – the "molten color

---

52 Buzard, *Beaten Track*, 225.
53 Henry James, *Transatlantic Sketches* (1875; repr., Boston: Houghton Mifflin, 1903), 12–17.
54 Henry James, *Collected Travel Writings: Great Britain and America* (New York: Library of America, 1993), 35, 37. See Brigitte Bailey, "Travel Writing and the Metropolis: James, London, and *English Hours*," *American Literature* 67, no. 2 (June 1995): 216–21.

that drops from the hollow vaults" – that restores aesthetic looking as "almost a spiritual function – or, at the worst, an amorous one."[55]

Early Twentieth-Century Directions: Professionalism, Gender, and Race

By 1900, notes Schriber, "a wave of professionalism had washed over travel writing," as the "culture of the expert" came to define American culture generally.[56] This professionalism characterizes early twentieth-century travel essays by Edith Wharton (1862–1937) and Henry Adams (1838–1918), especially in Wharton's *Italian Villas and Their Gardens* (1904) and Adams's *Mont Saint Michel and Chartres* (1904), works of erudition written in a conversational style similar to James's and addressed to a similar reader. Adams drew on his knowledge as a historian to explain the art and architecture of medieval France, while Wharton carried out extensive research to explain the early modern fusion of villa and landscape in "the same composition."[57] Both sets of essays depict tours in space and time, in effect traveling abroad to other geographies and eras. Adams's famous essay "The Dynamo and the Virgin" in *The Education of Henry Adams* (1907), which builds on the insights of *Mont Saint Michel and Chartres,* is well understood as a travel essay, as he develops his comparative understanding of the medieval cult of the Virgin and the modern power of technology at the Paris Exposition of 1900. However, newspapers and periodicals continued to produce travel essays, even as, in the era of the New Woman, more women traveled abroad without male companionship; Willa Cather wrote travel articles on sites from Liverpool to Arles in 1902 for the *Nebraska State Journal.*[58]

World War I and its aftermath transformed relationships between American writers and Europe. While such writers as Wharton and Gertrude Stein already lived in Paris, the war and the cultural forces of modernism drew the next generation of writers, from Ernest Hemingway

---

55 Henry James, *Collected Travel Writings: The Continent* (New York: Library of America, 1993), 281, 290, 292–95.
56 Schriber, *Writing Home,* 191, 181. See especially Schriber on Stowe, Woolson, and Wharton, 166–200.
57 Schriber, *Writing Home,* 192. Edith Wharton, *Italian Villas and Their Gardens* (New York: Da Capo Press, 1976), 7.
58 George N. Kates, "Introduction," in Willa Cather, *Willa Cather in Europe; Her Own Story of the First Journey,* ed. George N. Kates (New York: Knopf, 1956), v. See Libby Bischof, "A Summer in England: The Women's Rest Tour Association of Boston and the Encouragement of Independent Transatlantic Travel for American Women," in Bailey, *Transatlantic Women,* 153–71.

to Claude McKay, into France as sojourners. Even as writers such as Hemingway continued to write travel essays about Africa that featured "black primitivism and white ... modernity," the French treatment of African American troops during and after the war offered a release from US racism and, as Michel Fabré documents, brought to Paris more Black writers, who then wrote travel essays; Countee Cullen wrote the column "Letters from Paris" for the periodical that W. E. B. Du Bois edited, the Crisis.[59] The 1920s and '30s saw the further acceleration of travel and a new emphasis on cosmopolitan identities; the travel essay increasingly became the expatriate essay.

59 Edward Whitley, "Race and Modernity in Theodore Roosevelt's and Ernest Hemingway's African Travel Writing," in *Issues in Travel Writing: Empire, Spectacle, and Displacement*, ed. Kristi Siegel (New York: Peter Lang, 2002), 13–28, 13; Michel Fabre, *From Harlem to Paris: Black American Writers in France, 1840–1980* (Urbana, IL: University of Illinois Press, 1991), 81.

14
American Pragmatism: An Essayistic Conception of Truth

JONATHAN LEVIN

Writing in a 1935 letter to the *Amherst Student*, Robert Frost (1874–1963) famously declared his affection for the "lesser" forms we "throw off, like vortex rings of smoke, all our individual enterprise and needing nobody's cooperation; a basket, a letter, a garden, a room, an idea, a picture, a poem."[1] Frost does not specifically mention the essay, but as someone who occasionally turned to the essay to reflect on his poetry and poetics, he would have likely been quick to acknowledge the affinity. His notion of a modest form, posited against what he describes in the letter as a background that is all "hugeness and confusion shading away from where we stand into black and utter chaos," corresponds perfectly with the notion of understanding implicit in what William James (1842–1910) called the pragmatist conception of truth. What Frost elsewhere called "a momentary stay against confusion," such a form is valued not for its insight into permanent and unchanging realities, but rather, in Frost's typically playful defense against modernist anomie, for "how much more it is than nothing."[2]

Frost's sensibility was shaped by many of the intellectual currents of modernity, but no figure was more central to his developing imagination than William James, whose *Psychology: A Briefer Course* (1892) and *Talks to Teachers on Psychology* (1899) he adopted as textbooks when teaching psychology at the Plymouth Normal School as early as 1911. In *The Principles of Psychology* (1890), James famously described an infant's perception of the world as "one great blooming, buzzing confusion," and James's entire intellectual project, including his later pragmatism, was founded on his

---

1 Robert Frost, "Letter to *The Amherst Student*," in *Collected Poems, Prose, and Plays*, ed. Mark Richardson and Richard Poirier (New York: Library of America, 1995), 739–40, 740.
2 Robert Frost, "The Figure a Poem Makes," in *Collected Poems, Prose, and Plays*, 776–78, 777.

understanding of how the mind, through cultivation of intellectual habit, manufactures working models of the world that facilitate development and reinforcement of adaptive traits.[3] These models don't have to be "true," in the sense of corresponding to some preestablished or objective nature of things; they simply have to enable those who adopt them to get on in the world. Those models that confer greater adaptive advantage will thrive, but even these remain provisional and incomplete.[4]

It should be no surprise that James and others whom he influenced felt a special affinity for the essay. The essay proved to be the perfect vehicle not simply to fashion and explore provisional truths, but to drive home the case that truth is inherently provisional. James and other pragmatists saw thinking as a mode of action in the world – quite different from the standard dualism that separates "mind" from "matter." It was Charles Sanders Peirce (1839–1914) who first coined the term *pragmatism* in the 1870s, and in his 1878 *Popular Science* essay "How to Make Our Ideas Clear," he announced the pragmatic maxim that launched James's and John Dewey's (1859–1952) projects: "Consider what effects, that might conceivably have practical bearings, we conceive the object of our conception to have. Then, our conception of these effects is the whole of our conception of the object."[5] In his essay "What Pragmatism Means" (1907), William James traced the root of the word to the Greek word *pragma*, "meaning action, from which our words 'practice' and 'practical' come."[6] Just as the noun *essay* calls to mind the verb form – *to essay*, attempt or try – so pragmatism was for James less a philosophical position or ideology than a method or practice. For James and Dewey in particular, pragmatism helped explain how we use ideas and beliefs to achieve our aims and how we modify and adapt those ideas and beliefs as we test them in the contexts of our daily living and engagement with others.

Though James did produce a massive textbook, *The Principles of Psychology*, he was always most comfortable writing shorter pieces, often first developed as talks and then published in both popular and academic journals. This

---

3 William James, *The Principles of Psychology* (Cambridge, MA: Harvard University Press, 1981), 462. See also chapter 9, "Habit," 109–31.
4 There is a considerable body of commentary on pragmatists' rejection of the "correspondence theory of truth." See especially Richard Rorty, *Philosophy and the Mirror of Nature* (Princeton, NJ: Princeton University Press, 1979) and the many essays Rorty contributed and collected in subsequent volumes on John Dewey, Martin Heidegger, Ludwig Wittgenstein, and other philosophers.
5 Charles Sanders Peirce, "How to Make Our Ideas Clear," in *Peirce on Signs*, ed. James Hoopes (Chapel Hill, NC: University of North Carolina Press, 1991), 160–79, 169.
6 William James, "What Pragmatism Means," in *Writings 1902–1910*, ed. Bruce Kuklick (New York: Library of America, 1987), 505–22, 506.

perhaps explains his development of the two popular volumes that Frost taught at the Plymouth Normal School, the abridged version of the *Briefer Course* (known among students at Harvard as the "Jimmy," as distinct from the "James") and *Talks to Teachers on Psychology*, designed to apply lessons from the *Principles* to the immediate pedagogical needs of teachers. That volume also included three other widely admired essays by James: "The Gospel of Relaxation," "On a Certain Blindness in Human Beings," and "What Makes a Life Significant." Each of these pieces applies James's insights as a psychologist to common human problems, the latter two in particular addressing the difficulty of understanding or appreciating other, especially non-Eurocentric perspectives. These essays highlight James's pluralistic respect for diverse points of view. James's other major unified volume, *The Varieties of Religious Experience* (1902), was originally delivered, to great popular acclaim, as the Gifford lectures at the University of Edinburgh. Though James conceived the talks as a unified series, his emphasis on myriad examples of spiritual, mystical, and paranormal experiences reflects his faith in the ultimate authority of individual experience, however different, strange, or seemingly inexplicable. Every other volume James would publish, including *The Will to Believe* (1897), *Pragmatism* (1908), and *The Meaning of Truth* (1909), would be constituted of loosely related essays.

James biographer Robert Richardson helpfully distinguishes three styles in James's writing: the "labored technical writing of his early papers and parts of *The Principles of Psychology*"; a "middle style" that "he used when addressing college philosophy clubs" (for example, "The Will to Believe" and the other talks collected in the volume bearing that title); and a third style that is "his plainest, clearest, most public style," at once "vivid, personal, comprehensible, and without a shred of condescension" (best exemplified, Richardson suggests, by *Talks to Teachers*).[7] These distinctions are useful, but it should be observed that James could often slide seamlessly from one style to another: He always had a strong instinct to adopt what Richardson identified as his third, most public style as a way of connecting with audiences. The brilliant and entertaining chapter on "The Stream of Consciousness" in *The Principles of Psychology* is a classic example in which all three styles are effectively blended.

James everywhere underscores the relationship between beliefs and ideas and the dynamic situational contexts that frame their relevance and appeal. In

---

7 Robert Richardson, *William James: In the Maelstrom of American Modernism* (Boston: Houghton Mifflin, 2006), 360.

"What Pragmatism Means," one of the many essays where he sets out the leading ideas and attitudes that inform his pragmatism, he famously depicted the pragmatist rejecting the habits of most philosophers:

> A pragmatist turns his back resolutely and once for all upon a lot of inveterate habits dear to professional philosophers. He turns away from abstraction and insufficiency, from verbal solutions, from bad *a priori* reasons, from fixed principles, closed systems, and pretended absolutes and origins. He turns towards concreteness and adequacy, towards facts, towards action and towards power.[8]

For James, philosophers' verbal solutions too often do violence to what we feel and know from experience: Concepts, ideas, and truth achieve their significance in the vivid push and pull of our lives, not as mental representations abstracted from our living.

James's pragmatist conception of truth initially attracted a lot of attention, especially among critics who took him to mean that truth is whatever you want it to be. They held that he viewed truth as untethered to any "reality," a wholly subjective product of pure imagination. But even if his theory of truth is incomplete and raises as many problems as it solves, James did repeatedly address the charge of subjectivism, arguing that what he called "the whole body of funded truths squeezed from the past and the coercions of the world of sense around him" work to ensure that truth is never either a purely subjective affair nor merely that which is most expedient to believe.[9] An overly subjective version of truth would fail to confer adaptive advantage and would therefore put the believer at serious risk. James regarded truth more as a process than as an endpoint. As he put it in "Pragmatism's Conception of Truth," "[t]he truth of an idea is not a stagnant property inherent in it. Truth *happens* to an idea. It *becomes* true, is *made* true by events. Its verity *is* in fact an event, a process: the process namely of its verifying itself, its veri-*fication*. Its validity is the process of its valid-*ation*."[10] As James further notes in the same essay, experience "has ways of *boiling over*, and making us correct our present formulas."[11] The process of making and validating truths is inherently self-correcting: Whenever new information

---

8 James, "What Pragmatism Means," 508–509.
9 William James, "Pragmatism's Conception of Truth," in *Writings 1902–1910*, 572–90, 588. Many scholars have observed the connection between James's pragmatist conception of truth and various Nietzschean and postmodern conceptions of truth. For a useful review of James's treatment of "truth" and the views of his critics, see Hilary Putnam, "James's Theory of Truth," in *The Cambridge Companion to William James*, ed. Ruth Anna Putnam (Cambridge, UK: Cambridge University Press, 1997), 166–85.
10 James, "Pragmatism's Conception," 574.   11 James, "Pragmatism's Conception," 583.

challenges a settled truth, that truth gets adjusted. As the familiar runs into the unfamiliar, our notions of the familiar are put under pressure, and if the evidence is sufficient, they shift. Truth *happens* to an idea in the sense that the idea becomes true as formerly unexplained phenomena are integrated into the standing body of truths (which at one time also *became* true in similar fashion).

Both Peirce and Dewey would adopt roughly the same view, though both stressed the social dimensions of truth more than James usually did. James's thought always remained deeply rooted in individual experience, whereas Peirce and Dewey saw pragmatism as upending not only traditional conceptions of meaning and truth but also the independence and authority of the individual believer. Both Dewey and Peirce also stressed the role of the scientific community in establishing truths. Peirce never leaves his reader with the impression that he might be saying that truth is malleable or irreducibly subjective, as many of James's formulations so evidently did. For Peirce, truth always had a prospective quality, its confirmation always hinging on the convergence of ongoing inquiry: "The opinion which is fated to be ultimately agreed to by all who investigate, is what we mean by the truth, and the object represented in this opinion is the real."[12] Peirce's notion of truth was also informed by his pioneering understanding of statistics: He recognized that while he could not predict any individual result, he could predict the patterns many individual results would reveal. As Peirce points out in "Grounds of Validity of the Laws of Logic" (1869), most of what we know, we know by inference: "We know that, by faithfully adhering to that mode of inference, we shall, on the whole, approximate to the truth."[13] Peirce also developed a rich and complex semiotics that addressed the role of symbolic representations. While in some ways echoing postmodern semiotics, Peirce's "infinite semiosis" ultimately supports his underlying realism, since it is the shared, public nature of signs and symbols that makes communication and understanding possible. While James frequently complained that the world of thought was a pale and incomplete substitute for our rich and pulsating experience of the world, Peirce drew a firm line between the actual world and the symbolic domain and considered it an error to expect the latter to share the qualities of the former.

---

12 Charles Sanders Peirce, "How to Make Our Ideas Clear," in *Peirce on Signs*, 160–79, 177.
13 Charles Sanders Peirce, "Grounds of Validity of the Laws of Logic," in *Peirce on Signs*, 85–115, 113. For a useful overview of the significance of Peirce's understanding of statistics and "the law of errors," see Louis Menand, *The Metaphysical Club* (New York: Farrar, Straus and Giroux, 2001), 177–200.

Peirce tried to capitalize on James's popularization of his pragmatic method, offering a series of lectures on pragmatism at Harvard in 1903 and a further series of essays on pragmatism in the *Monist* in 1905 and 1906, but his densely argued essays found few followers. By contrast, John Dewey took up the task of reimagining pragmatism for a wide modern audience, addressing professional philosophers, other scholars in a wide range of disciplines (largely the social sciences), educators, and the general public. Dewey's project as a philosopher was ultimately carried out on two main fronts: providing a comprehensive critique of the history of Western philosophy – a project neatly summarized in the title of one of his major book-length works, *The Quest for Certainty* (1929) – and engaging with the urgent problems of the day (a project largely carried out in essays and short volumes). Around the same time Peirce was reworking his pragmatism, Dewey published a widely read *Popular Science* essay, "The Influence of Darwinism on Philosophy" (1909). In it, Dewey traces the influence of Darwin's revolutionary shift in focus from essential and unchanging essences that constitute the real – a tradition he traces back to the ancient Greeks – to always evolving adaptations that reframe the real as that which always changes over time. Species are not given, ordained, essential, or unchanging, but rather constitute a stage in an unceasing and largely chance-driven development. As Dewey observes, philosophy in the wake of Darwin "forswears inquiry after absolute origins and absolute finalities in order to explore specific values and the specific conditions that generate them."[14] In some ways, Dewey's occasional essays are more central to his project than his longer, often better-known books because they directly address "the specific conditions" that shape our contingent values.

Beyond addressing topics in philosophy in both popular and formal academic venues, Dewey's many essays, written for popular and specialist audiences alike, address both domestic and international political contexts (e.g., "On Understanding the Mind of Germany," which appeared in *Atlantic Monthly* in 1916); the promise of democracy (e.g., "Creative Democracy: The Task before Us," Dewey's address composed for his eightieth birthday celebration in New York City in October 1939, delivered there on his behalf by Horace Kallen); the role of science and technology in society (e.g., "Science and Society," the only previously unpublished essay to appear in the essay collection *Philosophy and Civilization* in 1931); and perhaps most

---

14 John Dewey, "The Influence of Darwinism on Philosophy," in *America's Public Philosopher: Essays on Social Justice, Economics, Education, and the Future of Democracy*, ed. Eric Thomas Weber (New York: Columbia University Press, 2021), 239–48, 245.

influentially, the role of education in a modern democracy (e.g., "Democracy and Education in the World of Today," published as a pamphlet in 1938 by the New York Society for Ethical Culture). These essays are typically founded on Dewey's conviction that individuals find meaning and purpose not in private interests but rather through their public purposes and shared social commitments; he holds throughout that people's values and beliefs are always evolving as they develop their understanding of the world and work to expand the domain of liberty and justice. Because he held that there is no overarching or unchanging ideal of the true or good, the pursuit of both was always a matter of direct engagement with the endlessly malleable social conditions that shape and condition individual lives. For example, in "Democracy and Education in the World of Today," he suggests that democracy is something that is always coming into being and always at risk; teaching democratic principles therefore is not a matter of "stating merely the ideas of the men who made this country, their hopes and their intentions," but, as Dewey puts it, "of teaching what a democratic society means under existing conditions."[15] Writing in 1938, he suggests that we cannot be content to simply contrast our society with "the tragic racial intolerance of Germany and now of Italy": "Are we entirely free from that racial intolerance, so that we can pride ourselves upon having achieved a complete democracy? Our treatment of the Negroes, anti-Semitism, the growing (at least I fear it is growing) serious opposition to the alien immigrant within our gates is, I think, a sufficient answer to that question."[16] Dewey asks, "[W]hat are our schools doing to cultivate not merely passive toleration that will put up with people of different racial birth or different colored skin, but what are our schools doing positively and aggressively and constructively to cultivate understanding and goodwill which are essential to democratic society?"[17] Dewey's essays on democracy, education, and domestic and global social conditions are designed to act as catalysts in shaping what kind of people, community, nation, or global citizens we will choose to become.

If Peirce and Dewey work to align pragmatism with modern science, George Santayana (1863–1952), who was a student and, eventually, a colleague of William James, viewed science as simply another mythos, by which he did not mean to dismiss it as false and misleading but rather to confer the dignity and power inherent in any compelling mythology.

---

15 John Dewey, "Democracy and Education in the World of Today," in Weber, *America's Public Philosopher*, 162–70, 166.
16 Dewey, "Democracy and Education," 168.
17 Dewey, "Democracy and Education," 168.

Though, like Peirce, he would criticize many specific features of Jamesian pragmatism, he very much shared the underlying naturalism of James's philosophy. A philosopher, poet, essayist, novelist, and memoirist, Santayana considered *The Principles of Psychology* James's great accomplishment, far more than his later essays on pragmatism and radical empiricism. Santayana shared James's sense of the thoroughly naturalistic origins of our values and beliefs, but, as he explained in numerous essays, he felt that our capacity to enjoy those values and beliefs was ultimately more important than their practical "cash value" to us.

Born in Spain to Spanish parents, Santayana immigrated at the age of eight to the United States, where his mother moved with her children from a previous marriage to Bostonian George Sturgis after the death of Santayana's father. Though he spent the next forty years in and around Boston, Santayana always felt like an outsider in New England, and, for all their influence on him, he adopted an outsider's perspective on James, pragmatism, and the intellectual habits of Americans more broadly. Some of his most insightful and enduring essays were those that directly addressed intellectual life in America. "The Genteel Tradition in American Philosophy" was originally delivered as a talk to the Philosophical Union in Berkeley in 1911, not long after Santayana had decided to leave Harvard and the United States permanently and return to Europe. Much of the essay focuses on the timidity of American philosophers, many of whom were drawn to forms of subjective idealism that grew out of Kant and Hegel. Against this background, Santayana cites just two recent exceptions, Walt Whitman and William James. Both remain receptive to the variety and diversity of human types, including marginalized and otherwise stigmatized individuals. More than anything, Santayana admired James's openness, both as a scholar and as a man: "James kept his mind and heart wide open to all that might seem, to polite minds, odd, personal, or visionary in religion and philosophy. He gave a sincerely respectful hearing to sentimentalists, mystics, spiritualists, wizards, cranks, quacks, and impostors – for it is hard to draw the line, and James was not willing to draw it prematurely."[18] If Santayana had one complaint about his teacher and colleague, it was James's relative lack of interest in the reflective and appreciative powers of mind, a point he makes in "William James," which appeared in *Character and Opinion in the United States* (1920):

18 George Santayana, "The Genteel Tradition in American Philosophy," in *The Genteel Tradition in American Philosophy and Character and Opinion in the United States*, ed. James Seaton (New Haven, CT: Yale University Press, 2009), 3–20, 14.

But what is a good life? Had William James, had the people about him, had modern philosophers anywhere, any notion of that? I cannot think so. They had much experience of personal goodness, and love of it; they had standards of character and right conduct; but as to what might render human existence good, excellent, beautiful, happy, and worth having as a whole, their notions were utterly thin and barbarous. They had forgotten the Greeks, or never known them.[19]

Santayana's understanding of what rendered human existence "good, excellent, beautiful, happy" was steeped in Jamesian provisionality. In "William James," he observed that James "believed in improvisation, even in thought; his lectures were not minutely prepared. Know your subject thoroughly, he used to say, and trust to luck for the rest."[20] This reliance on what might be called a loose improvisational practice goes a long way toward explaining James's attraction to the essay, a genre long associated with provisional and open-ended reflection, a vehicle for thinking things through, or thinking them out. The spatial metaphors here are especially apt. In a later essay Santayana traced the origins of animal intelligence to animals' evolved capacity to move about their environment in order to gain access to desired objects or to escape (or destroy) those that cause fear. Such travel must necessarily be improvisational, given the ever-changing setting of all travel:

> Thinking while you walk . . . keeps you alert; your thoughts, though following some single path through the labyrinth, review real things in their real order; you are keen for discovery, ready for novelties, laughing at every little surprise, even if it is a mishap; you are careful to choose the right road, and if you take the wrong one, you are anxious and able to correct your error.[21]

There is wisdom, Santayana suggests, "in turning as often as possible from the familiar to the unfamiliar: it keeps the mind agile, it kills prejudice, and it fosters humor."[22] This balance or tension between the familiar and the unfamiliar is at the heart of the pragmatist understanding of how truth grows and evolves, as our stock of knowledge meets and seeks to explain new and hitherto unexplained phenomena. Santayana's observations in "The Philosophy of Travel" are typical of pragmatists' association of thinking and writing with dynamic, open-ended, and often wildly unpredictable

---

19 George Santayana, "William James," in Seaton, *Genteel Tradition in American Philosophy and Character and Opinion in the United States*, 51–63, 59.
20 Santayana, "William James," 52.
21 George Santayana, "The Philosophy of Travel," *Virginia Quarterly Review* 40, no. 1 (1964): 1–10, 4.
22 Santayana, "Philosophy of Travel," 9.

movement. The mind's excursions are inherently uncertain and full of risk (one can easily be led astray), but the danger of these improvisations is offset by the unlimited potential for discovery.

Just as Santayana's Spanish-Catholic background influenced his response to James, so too W. E. B. Du Bois (1868–1963) responded to James from his position as an African American scholar and activist. Du Bois also acknowledged James's influence on his early intellectual development. He describes his experience at Harvard – where he matriculated as a junior in 1888 and was the first African American to receive the PhD in 1895 – in his 1940 autobiography *Dusk of Dawn*, and he expanded on that description in an autobiographical essay published in 1960 in the *Massachusetts Review*. He took a course on ethics with James in his first semester at Harvard, and also studied philosophy with Santayana. While Du Bois is frank and explicit about the racism he experienced at Harvard, he also writes admiringly about James and several other teachers, noting that James occasionally invited him to his home for dinner. He suggests that his "salvation" at Harvard was "the type of teacher I met rather than the content of the courses" and proceeds to single James out for guiding him "out of the sterilities of scholastic philosophy to realist pragmatism."[23] He also notes that it was James and historian Albert Bushnell Hart "with his research method" who "turned me back from the lovely but sterile land of philosophical speculation to the social sciences as the field for gathering and interpreting the body of fact which would apply to my program for the Negro."[24]

Du Bois had a prolific career as an essayist, shaped in part by his role as editor, from 1910 to 1934, of *The Crisis*, a publication of the National Association for the Advancement of Colored People (NAACP). As one of the leading voices of his era among African American intellectuals, Du Bois also frequently contributed essays to magazines and other publications. Nine of the fourteen chapters that would appear in Du Bois's best-known work, *The Souls of Black Folk* (1903), originally appeared as essays in magazines, four of them, including the widely cited first chapter, "Of Our Spiritual Strivings," in the *Atlantic Monthly*. There, Du Bois introduced the widely influential phrase *double-consciousness*: "[t]his sense of always looking at one's self through the eyes of others, of measuring one's soul by the tape of a world that looks on in amused contempt and pity."[25] He further describes this as

---

23 W. E. B. Du Bois, "A Negro Student at Harvard at the End of the 19th Century," *Massachusetts Review* 1, no. 3 (1960): 439–58, 440.
24 Du Bois, "Negro Student," 453–54.
25 W. E. B. Du Bois, *The Souls of Black Folk*, in *Writings*, ed. Nathan Huggins (New York: Library of America, 1986), 357–547, 364.

a condition of *two-ness*: "[a]n American, a Negro; two souls, two thoughts, two unreconciled strivings; two warring ideals in one dark body, whose dogged strength alone keeps it from being torn asunder."[26] While James shows empathy with marginalized people in essays like "On a Certain Blindness in Human Beings," he does so from a comfortable and protected position of privilege, whereas Du Bois here makes plain the wrenching psychological wounds inflicted by both external conditions and internally felt contradictions. Du Bois wrote repeatedly about the challenges and inhumanity of segregation and Jim Crow laws, even as he insisted, in a 1934 *Crisis* essay, "Segregation in the North," that in order to address segregation, African Americans would have to "associate with ourselves," "[r]un and support our own institutions."[27] Because he wrote so frequently on so many issues and leading figures of the day, Du Bois's essays leave a compelling record of the shifting fortunes of the movement to advance the civil rights of African Americans, especially from the time of Reconstruction to the flowering of the civil rights movement in the 1950s and '60s.

James's influence also extended to a number of poets who either studied with him at Harvard or studied with others there, mostly in the philosophy department, who were variously engaged in an extended conversation with James about his major ideas.[28] While best known for their poetry and other creative works, these pioneering modernists – among them, T. S. Eliot (1888– 1965), Robert Frost, Gertrude Stein (1874–1946), and Wallace Stevens (1879– 1955) – also contributed essays in which they addressed issues in literary history and theory and reflected on their poetry and poetics for a general audience. None of these figures would likely have called him or herself a pragmatist, but each was influenced, in some degree, by James's teaching and writing. Though Eliot explicitly rejected pragmatism in a number of places (he mainly objected to what he regarded as its subjectivism), many commentators have found strong echoes of pragmatism in his completed but never-defended Harvard dissertation on F. H. Bradley.[29] Still, among these

---

26 Du Bois, *Souls of Black Folk*, 364–65.
27 W. E. B. Du Bois, "Segregation in the North," in Du Bois, *Writings*, 1239–48, 1242.
28 Studies of pragmatism and American poetry include Richard Poirier, *Poetry and Pragmatism* (Cambridge, MA: Harvard University Press, 1993); Jonathan Levin, *The Poetics of Transition* (Durham, NC: Duke University Press, 1999); David Kadlec, *Mosaic Modernism* (Baltimore: Johns Hopkins University Press, 2000); and Joan Richardson, *A Natural History of Pragmatism* (Cambridge, UK: Cambridge University Press, 2007).
29 For an excellent review of the issues, see Gregory Brazeal, "The Alleged Pragmatism of T. S. Eliot," in *Philosophy and Literature* 30, no. 1 (2006): 248–64.

figures, Eliot worked hardest to distinguish his brand of modernism from James's. His treatment of the impersonality of the poet in "Tradition and the Individual Talent" (1919) charts a course almost designed to challenge James's strenuous individualism. On the other hand, Eliot highlights the interplay of the familiar and the unfamiliar in his suggestion that the modern artist must first assimilate literary tradition in order to add something new to that tradition. This dynamic is similar to James's notion that past truths provide the relatively stable background against which new truths emerge to explain previously unexplained (or ill-explained) phenomena. In "Ulysses, Order, and Myth" (1923), Eliot makes clear that the modern individual, lacking faith in the traditional authority associated with religion and mythology, may still embrace mythic paradigms as a means of asserting a continuing relationship to the underlying mythic order. The mythos is not "true," in the sense of corresponding to the actual nature of things, but it is true by virtue of how it creates a meaningful sense of order amid what Eliot famously calls the "immense panorama of futility and anarchy which is contemporary history."[30]

Eliot's "order" is in some ways similar to Robert Frost's notion of a "momentary stay against confusion" alluded to at the outset of this chapter, but Frost's "order" is not steeped in history in quite the way Eliot's is. Frost addresses this most directly in "Education by Poetry," first delivered as a talk to the Amherst College Alumni Council in 1930. Frost is not concerned that his audience share a sense of the classics so much as that they understand the working of metaphor in everyday life and the role of the poet in using metaphor to help us believe in larger ideals. "Poetry begins in trivial metaphors, pretty metaphors, 'grace' metaphors," Frost observes, "and goes on to the profoundest thinking that we have."[31] Metaphor, as he points out, is just "saying one thing in terms of another," but, as he also notes, to tell people that is "to set their feet on the first rung of a ladder the top of which sticks through the sky."[32] At its most profound, Frost suggests, metaphor is at the heart of all philosophy and religion: "Greatest of all attempts to say one thing in terms of another is the philosophical attempt to say matter in terms of spirit, or spirit in terms of matter, to make the final unity. That is the greatest attempt that ever failed." This attempt failed because, as Frost points out, metaphor always "breaks down somewhere: "That is the beauty of it. It is

---

30 T. S. Eliot, "Ulysses, Order, and Myth," in *Selected Prose of T. S. Eliot*, ed. Frank Kermode (New York: Harcourt Brace Jovanovich, 1975), 175–78, 177.
31 Robert Frost, "Education by Poetry," in *Collected Poems, Prose, and Plays*, 717–28, 719.
32 Frost, "Education by Poetry," 723.

touch and go with the metaphor, and until you have lived with it long enough you don't know when it is going. You don't know how much you can get out of it and when it will cease to yield. It is a very living thing. It is as life itself."[33] In Frost's strikingly Jamesian formulation, metaphor stimulates belief, but at some point, it also stimulates awareness of the limits and ephemerality of that belief.

Wallace Stevens's essays largely serve to elucidate his poetic method, but they also share many of the defining features of that method, which is to say they are often ambiguous and elusive. Stevens's technique is highly improvisational, taking up fragments from various philosophers, historians, critics, poets, and others and weaving these fragments together with his own running commentary, usually reflecting on the interrelatedness of what he calls "reality" and "imagination." In his 1942 essay "The Noble Rider and the Sound of Words," Stevens highlights the displacement of imagination by the heightened awareness of the real that marks modern sensibilities, but he also insists throughout that imagination and reality must remain mutually interdependent:

> We have been a little insane about the truth. We have had an obsession. In its ultimate extension, the truth about which we have been insane will lead us to look beyond the truth to something in which the imagination will be the dominant complement. It is not only that the imagination adheres to reality, but, also, that reality adheres to the imagination and that the interdependence is essential.[34]

By the end of the essay, Stevens insists, "The mind has added nothing to human nature. It is a violence from within that protects us from a violence without. It is the imagination pressing back against the pressure of reality."[35] Stevens returns again and again in his essays to the still vital role of imagination in a world increasingly understood through the lens of a hardheaded realism. At one point in "Imagination as Value," a paper first delivered at Columbia's English Institute in 1948, Stevens insists that there is no single figure of imagination – or as Stevens puts it in one of his most famous poems, no supreme fiction – that could be considered the chief: "The imagination itself would not remain content with it nor allow us to do so. It is the

---

33 Frost, "Education by Poetry," 723.
34 Wallace Stevens, "The Noble Rider and the Sound of Words," in *Collected Poetry and Prose*, ed. Frank Kermode and Joan Richardson (New York: Library of America, 1997), 643–65, 663.
35 Stevens, "Noble Rider," 665.

irrepressible revolutionist."[36] Stevens's essays display a thoroughly Jamesian confidence in the "will to believe," though he ultimately shares more of the contemplative poise associated with Santayana.

Gertrude Stein, who studied with James while attending the Harvard "Annex" (later, Radcliffe College), takes these attitudes and methods to their furthest imaginable extreme. Stein reimagines the essay as a space to explore what might be called a form of radical, pervasive provisionality. Her essays, which were for the most part initially developed as lectures, are largely taken up with the effort to contextualize and "explain" her own innovations as a writer in the early decades of the twentieth century. In "What Is English Literature," for example, the first of her *Lectures in America* (1934), Stein offers a short history of English literature, leading up to the radical break posed by American literature and, ultimately, by Stein herself. After suggesting that English literature tells about "daily living" in England, she suggests that American literature "tells something because that anything is not connected with what would be daily living if they had it."[37] This sense of disconnection reaches a peak, she notes, with Henry James, whose paragraph, she suggests, thinking perhaps of James's late style, "was detached what it said from what it did, what it was from what it held, and over it all something floated not floated away but just floated, floated up there."[38] Finally, Stein herself came along and "had to do more with the paragraph than ever had been done ..., breaking the paragraph down." She further describes this method as "the American thing the disconnection and I kept breaking the paragraph down, and everything down to commence again with not connecting with the daily anything and yet to really choose something."[39] Characteristically, it is hard to know exactly what Stein means by the "daily living," let alone the "daily anything," or by describing this disconnection as "the American thing." That said, if "daily living" is understood to be some kind of habitual routine, then the "American thing" that Stein associated with Henry James and with her own formal experiments must serve to challenge or defamiliarize routine habits of perception and understanding.

Stein's lectures and essays not only describe Stein's development as a writer within the context of experimental avant-garde and modernist writing of the early twentieth century but also further perform the very dislocation and "disconnection" she is describing. For the most part, those

---

36 Wallace Stevens, "Imagination as Value," in *Collected Poetry and Prose*, 724–39, 736.
37 Gertrude Stein, "What Is English Literature," in *Writings 1932–1946* (New York: Library of America, 1998), 195–223, 220.
38 Stein, "What Is English Literature," 222.   39 Stein, "What Is English Literature," 222.

influenced by James, Dewey, and Peirce remain more interested in the ways in which these inevitable feelings of discontinuity are overcome by the will to fashion new continuities. Many philosophers, literary and cultural critics, and social scientists continue to be engaged with the legacy of pragmatism, and they continue to reflect on and perform this legacy with particular flair in the essay. Whether in the many engagements of Richard Rorty (1931–2007) with modern and postmodern philosophers around questions of truth and meaning; the explorations by Richard Shusterman (1949–) of new modalities of aesthetic experience inspired by Dewey's *Art as Experience*; the reflections of Richard Poirier (1925–2009) on the effects of literary language rooted in his deep reading of Emerson and William James; the blending by Steven Mailloux (1950–) of new, revisionist readings of rhetorical and pragmatist traditions; the reimagination by Cornel West (1953–) of African American culture through the lens of what he calls a "prophetic pragmatism"; or the explorations by Giles Gunn (1938–) of the link between religious and pragmatist impulses, the essay has proven to be a resilient resource for contemporary scholars and cultural critics. If pragmatism today does not command the attention it did at the turn of the twentieth century, when philosophers either bought into the new way of thinking exemplified by Peirce, James, and Dewey or fought it tooth and nail, it has nevertheless continued to exercise a considerable influence over those who are drawn to a style of thinking and writing that challenges many of our most formative beliefs about the nature of thinking and the "mind" that thinks and continues to do so in that mode of expression that highlights the fluid, improvisational genius of all thinking, the essay.

15

The Essay in the Harlem Renaissance

SHAWN ANTHONY CHRISTIAN

Fueled by demands for civil rights and by racial and national pride, the Harlem Renaissance (1919–1940) was a defining period of African Americans' literary and artistic expression. Centered in Harlem, New York, but influencing African American communities across the country and other contexts of the African Diaspora, the Harlem Renaissance was a period of possibility and a testament to the endurance of Black life amid racial violence locally and nationally. The period included the triumphant return of the members of the "Harlem Hellfighters," the all–African American 369th Regiment that fought in World War I, and their "heroes' welcome" parade down New York City's Fifth Avenue in February 1919. Premieres like Paul Robeson's (1898–1976) 1924 Broadway appearance in Eugene O'Neill's play *All God's Chillun Got Wings* and, a year later, Josephine Baker's (1906–1975) Paris debut in *La Revue Nègre* were widely celebrated events. The Harlem Renaissance was especially memorable as a period when the "literary life of the race" energized and helped foster works like novelist Jessie Fauset's (1882–1961) *There Is Confusion* (1924) and poet Countee Cullen's (1903–1946) volume *Color* (1925), awards ranging from Guggenheim Fellowships to the literary prizes that NAACP's *Crisis* and the National Urban League's *Opportunity* offered, and artistic collaborations such as the volume *FIRE!!* (1926).[1] Writer George Schuyler (1895–1977) conveyed some of the excitement about Harlem Renaissance literature, specifically Fauset's *There Is Confusion*, when he noted, "I started reading [*There Is Confusion*] on a Sunday morning and finished its 297 pages before I went to bed." He added, "I trust the thousands of Negro book lovers will *buy* this book. If it is a *financial* success, there will be a widening field of opportunity for our rising group of young

---

1 "The New Negro Is Reading," *Half-Century Magazine* 6, no. 5 (May 1919): 3, 15–16, 3.

writers, struggling to express the yearnings, hopes, and aspirations of the race."[2]

Whether through the visual arts, music, or literature, many African Americans responded to the changing national and international dynamics of the 1920s as an opportunity to leverage their creative arts and redefine their place within the nation. As the wealth of Harlem Renaissance print material exhibits, poetry and fiction were the literary genres African Americans increasingly employed for these efforts. More ubiquitous was their frequent complement: the essay. Writers like Gwendolyn Bennett (1902–1981), Benjamin Brawley (1882–1939), W. E. B. Du Bois (1868–1963), Jessie Fauset (1882–1961), Zora Neale Hurston (1891–1960), James Weldon Johnson (1871–1938), Alain Locke (1885–1954), and Eulalie Spence (1894–1981) infused the essay with this ethos and positioned it as an equally important genre for chronicling the period. Indeed, it was through the essay, for example, that readers in the United States and in other parts of the world encountered rhetorical styles reflecting the racial pride and determination of the "New Negro." The period's documentary history features essays rich with arguments about the importance of literature, music, and the visual and performing arts for racial uplift and African Americans' contribution to American culture. Essays from the period detailing the array of forces and ideas shaping African American life – including migration, racial violence, civil rights, and Pan-Africanism – constitute dynamic narratives combining history, opinion, and critical redress. In these and other ways, the forms, circulation, and functions of the essay in the Harlem Renaissance reflected but also advanced a changing discourse about race within the nation.

World War I and the Early Years of African American Migration

African Americans' writings in the 1920s emerged in the aftermath of World War I and conveyed the energy and promise fueling the waves of the first Great Migration. Military service and mobility during the period forged African Americans' different perspectives about the nation and the prospects for their future within it. They were increasingly vocal about the contradictions of citizenship they endured during the period and argued for legal and political changes. As Hubert Harrison (1883–1927) wrote in 1920, "Things are

---

[2] George Schuyler, review of *There Is Confusion*, by Jessie Fauset, "New Books," *Messenger* 6, no. 5 (May 1924): 145–46, 146.

different now. The New Negro is demanding elective representation in Baltimore, Chicago, and other places. He is demanding it in New York. The pith of the present occasion is that he is no longer begging or asking. He is demanding as a right that which he is in position to enforce."[3] As responses and counters to racial violence, disenfranchisement, and sustained economic precarity, millions left the South for cities such as Philadelphia, Detroit, and Los Angeles. The effort to articulate rationales for such actions propelled the growth of the Black press and interest in Black writing among white publishers. Through daily and weekly newspapers, monthly magazines and journals, and firms such as Knopf as well as Boni and Liveright, African Americans created and secured venues to document and chart the realities of what had been, what was then happening, and what could yet be in their lives. Their embrace of the "new," especially in terms of the New Negro, was as much a manifestation of their efforts to claim full citizenship and make the case for their contributions to the country as it was a commitment to realize a growing body of writing as a tradition. Just like other modernists, African American writers negotiated and claimed the cultural moment as theirs while innovating received narrative forms and producing new ones. The early decades of the twentieth century were a dynamic period in American letters, and African Americans' development of the essay during the Harlem Renaissance furthered it as an appreciable and socially efficacious genre of American writing.

Investing in the essay during the Harlem Renaissance made sense not simply because it was a recognized genre gaining renewed currency and interest among facets of the American reading public. It also made sense because it allowed entry into the public sphere and afforded writers a genre in which to document but also debate progress, setbacks, and possibilities from both inter- and intragroup perspectives. H. L. Mencken (1880–1956), one of the most provocative essayists of the period, suggested this idea in his review of Alain Locke's volume *The New Negro* (1925). "Go read it attentively," he urges readers of *American Mercury*.[4] He adds that the representative writer in the volume discusses "the problems of his people soberly, shrewdly and without heat. He rehearses their achievement in the arts and compares it dispassionately to that of whites. He speculates upon their economic future

---

3 Hubert Harrison, "The New Politics," in *When Africa Awakes: The "Inside Story" of the Stirrings and Strivings of the New Negro in the Western World* (New York: Porro Press, 1920), 39–54, 39.
4 H. L. Mencken, "The Aframerican: New Style," *American Mercury* 7, no. 26 (February 1926): 254–55, 255.

with no more than a passing glance at the special difficulties which beset them."[5] "The whole thing [the anthology]," Mencken argues, "is a masterpiece of self-possession."[6] The inventory of topics Mencken notes in his iconoclastic reading of *The New Negro* refers to the several essays giving the volume its force as a formidable venue for this genre of writing. *The New Negro* contributed usefully to the extensive catalogue of essays that came into print during the Harlem Renaissance, which were as diverse in topic as they were in style. Still, a few shared characteristics help those interested in this genre of writing make better sense of its role during the period. As Cheryl Wall argues in *On Freedom and the Will to Adorn: The Art of the African American Essay* (2018), "Black writers have used the essay for interventions in social and political debates, whether over slavery and abolitionism, civil rights, feminism, or affirmative action. The dialogic form of the essay which strives to produce the effect of the spontaneous, the tentative, and the open-ended lends itself to exploring complex and contentious issues."[7] What Wall contends about this quality of the essay operates pointedly in the writings of the Harlem Renaissance. The forms this characteristic took, the venues in which essays appeared, and the purposes for which writers penned their essays underscored the viability of this body of writing during the Harlem Renaissance and for subsequent generations of readers interested in African American life and culture.

The Essay as Literary Genre

Throughout the Harlem Renaissance, the essay was heralded as a central literary genre in which to consider African American experience seriously and deliberately. In soliciting entrants to the magazine's famed literary prize contests, for example, the editors of the National Urban League's *Opportunity* advanced the Harlem Renaissance as a context for employing the essay – as a familiar form and a process – for this purpose. The description of the genre included in the contest rules published in the September 1924 issue argued this point explicitly: "The object here is simply to bid for a much abused type of literary expression, in the hope of finding some examples of recognizable literary merit," Charles S. Johnson (1893–1956) and his editorial

---

5 Mencken, "Aframerican," 255.   6 Mencken, "Aframerican," 255.
7 Cheryl A. Wall, *On Freedom and the Will to Adorn: The Art of the African American Essay* (Chapel Hill: University of North Carolina Press, 2018), 29.

team wrote.[8] "The contestant will strive for clarity of diction, forcefulness, and originality of ideas, logical structure, deft and effective employment of language, accuracy of data, and economy of words. The subject may be of the contestant's selection but must relate directly or indirectly to Negro life and contacts, or situations in which Negroes have a conspicuous interest."[9]

The essay that won first prize in the 1925 contest, E. Franklin Frazier's (1894–1962) "Social Equality and the Negro," embodies several of these characteristics in its effort to define a concept through the particularity of African American experience. "Social equality is essentially a social ideal," Frazier writes.[10] As he later notes, in "the present social status of the Negro we have found that he is generally denied rights as a person and a member of a democratic commonwealth ... As the Negro struggles to break down these discriminations he is struggling for social equality as other classes have done."[11] Over the course of the four sections of his essay, Frazier explored broad notions of social equality to examine the obstacles African Americans encountered in pursuit of it. His aim was to demonstrate why African Americans' arguments for equal treatment, though distinctive, were not only understandable but were also comparable to similar assertions throughout human history.

Though the contest rules set by *Opportunity*'s editors emphasized what were at the time accepted attributes of the essay to distinguish it from other genres, what appeared in the form of personal, cultural, and social essays during the period not only exhibited those elements but often also drew on other literary genres and engaged with a range of topics. A palpable instance was Marita Bonner's (1899–1971) essay "The Young Blood Hungers" (1928), where Bonner writes, "Voices and Hunger. Searching and Seekings. Stumbling – falling – rising again. – I speak not for myself alone, Lord! The Young Blood Hungers. – Back toward eternity. Facing Eternity. Perhaps that is the way in which Young Blood is to sit – back toward an Eternity – face toward an Eternity – hungering."[12] In addition to the way Bonner's essay draws on the trope of generational change present in much writing during the period, we might note that the alliterative cadence in, and epistolary nature of, this passage reflect the influence of poetry and fiction – genres that

---

8 Charles S. Johnson et al., "*Opportunity*'s Literary Prize Contest," *Opportunity* 2, no. 21 (September 1924): 277–79, 277.
9 Johnson et al., "*Opportunity*'s Literary Prize," 277.
10 E. Franklin Frazier, "Social Equality and the Negro," *Opportunity* 3, no. 30 (June 1925): 165–68, 165.
11 Frazier, "Social Equality," 167.
12 Marita Bonner, "The Young Blood Hungers," *Crisis* 35, no. 5 (May 1928): 151, 172, 172.

African American writers employed to celebrate speech variation and develop complex, introspective characters. In these and other ways, "The Young Blood Hungers" was part of a body of Harlem Renaissance essays – Jessie Fauset's "The Gift of Laughter" (1925), Langston Hughes's (1901–1967) "The Negro Artist and the Racial Mountain" (1926), and Zora Neale Hurston's "Characteristics of Negro Expression" (1934) were representative – demonstrating, again and again, how "form [was] intrinsically connected to the substance" of the writing.[13]

Engaging Harlem Renaissance Readers

A reader during the Harlem Renaissance was just as likely to encounter a range of such substance and form in the pages of a weekly newspaper like the *Chicago Defender* as she was in the monthly issue of the NAACP's the *Crisis*. Whether in long-form editorials, reflections on crucial events in African American life, or rebuttals to ideas penned in an essay from a previous issue or another publication altogether, writers utilized the genre to bring nuance to the general coverage within the Black press, often commenting on the straight (local and national) news, advertising, and literary and social interest features that drove its content. Certain essayists – Gwendolyn Bennett, Sterling Brown (1901–1989), Alice Dunbar Nelson (1875–1935), and George Schuyler among them – were widely known because they had regular columns in a select publication and frequently wrote for others. This dynamic helped produce recognizable styles of the essay and furthered its innovation. Poet Sterling A. Brown's column The Literary Scene: Chronicle and Comment in *Opportunity* magazine was a case in point. Throughout his column, which ran virtually every month from December 1930 to December 1935, Brown wrote with fervor and an intimacy that reflected the long-held practice of direct address in the African American press. Brown displayed a commitment to African American writers and their work, and to speaking truthfully to and for African Americans in general. His characteristic tone exhibited his impassioned refusal to "accept formula[ic] approaches to black literature and stereotyped responses to black people."[14] Brown's fellow writers and many of his readers appreciated his efforts and regarded him as the period's most genuine and thoughtful poet-critic.

---

13 Wall, *On Freedom*, 84.
14 Abby Johnson and Roland Johnson, *Propaganda and Aesthetics: The Literary Politics of Afro-American Magazines in the Twentieth Century* (Amherst, MA: University of Amherst Press, 1979), 101.

The essay also served as a key genre for dialogue and information exchange between Black and white America. This was especially true when African American writers like Langston Hughes were invited to write essays for publications with a predominately white readership such as the *Nation*. Hughes's "The Negro Artist and the Racial Mountain" and George Schuyler's "Negro Art Hokom" brought an already visible debate about the realities and aims of the Harlem Renaissance and artistic autonomy to a wider audience. The poetry and agency of Hughes's statement in "The Negro Artist" – "We build our temples for tomorrow, strong as we know how, and we stand on top of the mountain, free within ourselves" – complemented Schuyler's potent assertion in "Negro Art Hokom":

> Aside from his color, which ranges from very dark brown to pink, your American Negro is just plain American. Negroes and whites from the same localities in this country talk, think, and act about the same. Because a few writers with a paucity of themes have seized upon imbecilities of the Negro rustics and clowns and palmed them off as authentic and characteristic Aframerican behavior, the common notion that the black American is so "different" from his white neighbor has gained wide currency.[15]

Together, Hughes's and Schuyler's features in the *Nation* demonstrated the vitality of the essay in pushing diverse perspectives about African American creative expression into the center of public discourse.

Essayists like Hughes and Schuyler found a consistent home in the newspapers and journals covering but also advancing the Harlem Renaissance. An additional measure, and enduring context, for what their works achieved as a genre of writing during the period was the number of anthologies featuring them. Alain Locke's *The New Negro* was emblematic. This collection not only opened with the lead essay "The New Negro," which was a revision of two essays published earlier in the social work journal *Survey Graphic*. Locke's volume also included important treatments of the period including Arthur Huff Fauset's (1899–1983) "American Negro Folk Literature," W. A. Domingo's (1889–1968) "Gift of the Black Tropics," Melville Herskovits's (1895–1963) "The Negro's Americanism," Elise Johnson McDougald's (1885–1971) "The Task of Negro Womanhood," and Du Bois's "The Negro Mind Reaches Out." In related ways, "The Negro Mind Reaches Out" presents Du Bois as an African American who was a somewhat casual

---

15 Langston Hughes, "The Negro Artist and the Racial Mountain," *Nation* 122 (23 June 1926): 692–94, 693; George Schuyler, "The Negro-Art Hokom," *Nation* 122 (16 June 1926): 662–63, 662.

observer of the conditions in the United States, but more so as a scholar and critic of the political, economic, and social situations facing people of color throughout the world. As Du Bois writes, "One might indeed read the riddle of Europe by making its present plight a matter of colonial shadows, speculating on what might happen if Europe became suddenly shadowless – if Asia and Africa and the islands were cut permanently away. At any rate here is a field of inquiry, of likening and contrasting each land and its far-off shadow."[16] In its entirety, "The Negro Mind" reads as a travelogue wherein Du Bois offers his perspectives on local conditions for Black populations under the control or influence of select European countries. Du Bois positions the racism in United States as an example of structural and cultural oppression and then provides scenarios for challenging such forces. The essays in *The New Negro* usefully enact its subtitle, *An Interpretation*, by probing "the breadth of Negro character and experience."[17]

Beyond those appearing in *The New Negro*, the prefaces and critical essays published in the anthologies of the period told related but different stories about the evolving intersection of public writing and African American experiences. The titles of these volumes, like James Weldon Johnson's *Book of American Negro Poetry* and Nancy Cunard's (1896–1965) *Negro: An Anthology*, and the essays within them, point again to the currency in African American subject matter. These and other anthologies reverberated with Locke's urging that "Whosoever wishes to see the Negro in his essential traits, in the full perspective of his achievement and possibilities, must seek the enlightenment of that self-portraiture which present developments of Negro culture are offering."[18] The essay in the Harlem Renaissance aided anthologies in both announcing this self-portraiture and constituting an instance of it. For example, in her review column As to Books, Jessie Fauset writes to *Crisis* readers in 1922 that *The Book of American Negro Poetry* "has the value of an arrow pointing in the direction of Negro genius, but the author's preface has a more immediate worth. It is not only a graceful piece of expository writing befitting a collection of poetry, but it affords a splendid compendium of the Negro's artistic contributions to America."[19]

Among Johnson's many efforts to make the African American literary tradition visible, *The Book of American Negro Poetry* (1922) was especially influential because of the works it collected and its position as a pioneering

---

16 W. E. B. Du Bois, "The Negro Mind Reaches Out," in *The New Negro: An Interpretation*, ed. Alain Locke (New York: Albert and Charles Boni, 1925), 385–414, 386.
17 Wall, *On Freedom*, 91. 18 Alain Locke, "Foreword," in *New Negro*, ix.
19 Jessie Fauset, As to Books, *Crisis* 24, no. 2 (June 1922): 66–68, 66.

instance of literary criticism. When Fauset described Johnson's preface as a "graceful piece of expository writing," perhaps she had a moment of Johnson's pointed advocacy of African American poetry in mind. Johnson writes compellingly of the genre and especially envisions its development into a form that is able to express "the imagery, the idioms, the peculiar turns of thought, and the distinctive humor and pathos, too, of the Negro, but which will also be capable of voicing the deepest and highest emotions and aspirations, and allow of the widest range of subjects and the widest scope of treatment."[20] Throughout his preface, Johnson makes related arguments about African American artistry that names early and later poets as the crucial foundation for this aesthetic form. For example, when he turns to the work of Phillis Wheatley (ca. 1753–1784), Johnson contends that "the American Negro has accomplished something in pure literature."[21] He adds "the list of those who have done so would be surprising both by its length and the excellence of the achievements."[22] As Johnson writes, "Such a list begins with Phillis Wheatley."[23]

To contextualize Wheatley's primacy, Johnson reprints and provokes his readers to compare her "Imagination" with Anne Bradstreet's (1612–1672) earlier "Contemplation." Rather than follow this opportunity to read excerpts from each poem with what captures his attention as he interprets them, Johnson only informs his readers that Bradstreet "was wealthy, [and a] cultivated Puritan girl" and that Wheatley "was a Negro slave girl born in Africa." In doing so, he suggests and compels his reader to consider if these differences might be reasons why Wheatley, whose excerpt reveals parity with Bradstreet's, "is kept out of most of the books especially text-books on literature used in schools."[24] The poems Johnson selects here and his engaged reading of them respond, albeit implicitly, to the roles that race and racism play in the formation of an American literary canon. For readers of *The Book of American Negro Poetry* who have an interest in the nation's literary history, Johnson models how comparative analysis and close reading reveal it to be a complex field of racial representation and achievement.

As venues for the essay during the Harlem Renaissance, anthologies provided additional access to this genre of writing and, like the periodical

---

20 James Weldon Johnson, *The Book of American Negro Poetry* (New York: Harcourt, Brace, 1922), 41–42.
21 Johnson, *Book of American Negro Poetry*, xxi.
22 Johnson, *Book of American Negro Poetry*, xxi.
23 Johnson, *Book of American Negro Poetry*, xxi.
24 Johnson, *Book of American Negro Poetry*, xxii.

press, afforded readers opportunities for collective review within the same textual space. Though controversial and expansive (in content and size), the bulk of the content in Cunard's *Negro: An Anthology* consists of essays, which give coherence to the "scraps and ephemera of Black expressive life" the anthology gathers.[25] A reader could encounter essays, including Gladis Berry Robinson's (1908–1978?) "Three Great Negro Women," Olga Comma's (1913–1994) "Folklore in Trinidad," and George Padmore's (1903–1959) "Pass Laws in South Africa," as individual reflections or as linked narratives helping Cunard curate her understanding of the African Diaspora. For example, Comma writes, "In recent years our folk have been very much inclined to believe that they [Trinidadian ghosts] may be the creations of the highly nervous minds of timid night travelers, but the likeness of one man's creation to that of another's prevents a total disbelief in this nocturnal apparition and soucouyans still exist in our midst."[26] Throughout her essay, Comma frequently shifts the mode of address from the representative reader of her chapter to the Trinidadian communities whose lives and culture she studies. At such moments, her fellow citizens are both the essay's subject and its implied audience. In doing so, Comma adopts a tone of familiarity with readers and replicates a common convention among essayists during the Harlem Renaissance. "Folklore in Trinidad" and the other essays in *Negro* serve to locate a discursive "panorama" of "150 voices of both races" into a spatial terrain conjoining "the struggles and achievements, the persecutions and the revolts against" Black people in the United States, the Caribbean, Europe, and Africa.[27]

Additional evidence points to how the essay facilitated the transnational reality pervading the Harlem Renaissance. In forms ranging from travel narratives to historical accounts, writers employed the essay to comment on the movement of Black people within the United States and between the other nations and cultures of the African Diaspora. This circulation of the genre, especially translations of pivotal texts, fueled the experience of the period as a dynamic, global phenomenon. As Brent Hayes Edwards argues, "the practice of translation is indispensable to the pursuit of any project of internationalism, any 'correspondence' that would connect

---

25 Laura A. Winkel, "Nancy Cunard's *Negro* and the Transnational Politics of Race," *Modernism/modernity* 13, no. 3 (September 2006): 507–30, 510.
26 In Caribbean folklore, a soucouyant is an evil spirit. Olga Comma, "Folklore in Trinidad," in *Negro: Anthology*, ed. Nancy Cunard (London: Wishart & Company, 1934), 486–88, 486.
27 Nancy Cunard, "Foreword," in *Negro: Anthology*, iii.

intellectuals or populations of African descent around the world."[28] As an often translated text, the essay in the Harlem Renaissance furthered such connection as writers sought to reproduce and exchange nuanced ideas about modern Black subjectivity articulated in several languages, especially English, French, and Spanish. For example, shortly after the publication of *The New Negro*, the Martinican writer and philosopher Jane Nardal wrote to editor Alain Locke requesting permission to translate the volume into French.[29] The essay in the Harlem Renaissance did not function simply as a cultural and social bridge within the United States, but it was also an essential genre of writing in the making of a modern Black world.

Social and Cultural Change

This mediating role of the essay in the Harlem Renaissance compels consideration of its other functions during the second decade of the twentieth century and later. Perhaps its most basic function was to note and offer perspectives on the changing nature of African Americans' racial consciousness, as a group of essays did in announcing the emergence and presence of the New Negro. Writing in 1916, William Pickens (1881–1954) contends, "The 'new Negro' is not really new: he is the same Negro under new conditions and subjected to new demands."[30] For Alain Locke, the register of the New Negro lies in the facts that the "younger generation is vibrant with a new psychology" and "the new spirit is awake in the masses."[31] When it came to literature and other cultural arts, which were often discussed in terms of New Negro ideology, Charlotte Taussig (1876–1963) located the implications of the "new" differently: "In approaching the subject of the new Negro, whether it be in his social or community life, his relations to his own or the white race, or in his artistic endeavors, it is necessary to readjust our minds and bring to its consideration a new point of view."[32]

Through a more pointed, rhetorical effort at educating their readers, Harlem Renaissance writers often employed the essay to compel changes in viewpoint. Take, for example, Allison Davis's (1902–1983) "Our Negro

---

28 Brent Hayes Edwards, *The Practice of Diaspora: Literature, Translation, and the Rise of Black Internationalism* (Cambridge, MA: Harvard University Press, 2003), 20.
29 Edwards, *Practice of Diaspora*, 16.
30 William Pickens, "The New Negro," in *The New Negro: His Political, Civil, and Mental Status, and Related Essays* (New York: Negro Universities Press, 1916), 224–39, 224.
31 Locke, *New Negro*, 3.
32 Charlotte E. Taussig, "The New Negro as Revealed in His Poetry," *Opportunity* 5 (April 1927): 108–11, 108.

'Intellectuals.'" One of several essays advancing intragroup critique as a parallel fixture of Harlem Renaissance public discourse, Davis's essay detailed the problems she found with the literature of the period but also offered solutions. As she argues to *Crisis* readers,

> the qualities of fortitude, irony, and a relative absence of self-pity are the most important influences in the lives of Negroes, and . . . these qualities are the secret strength of that part of us which is one with a universal human nature. Our poets and writers of fiction have failed to interpret this broader human nature in Negroes, and found it relatively easy to disguise their lack of a higher imagination by concentrating upon immediate and crude emotions.[33]

Davis's perspective here was part of the debates over aesthetics and artistic autonomy characterizing the Harlem Renaissance and documented in several essays from the period. Her "Our Negro 'Intellectuals'" complemented this body of writing by also arguing for "genuinely qualified critics of Negro life [who] will fix upon the inner strength of Negro character."[34] Though *Opportunity* editor Charles S. Johnson shared Davis's interest in developing critical frameworks for Harlem Renaissance literature, he employed the essay to compel readers to also recognize, if not accept, African American writers' terms for their artistic freedom. He develops this point in the anthology *Ebony and Topaz* (1926):

> Negro writers, removed by two generations from slavery, are now much less self-conscious, less interested in proving that they are just like white people, and, in their excursions into the fields of letters and art, seem to care less about what black people think, or are likely to think about the race. Relief from the stifling consciousness of being a problem has brought a certain superiority to it.[35]

The wealth of essays articulating problems comprising varied facets of African American life and proposing solutions to them were also indicators of how often Harlem Renaissance writers employed the genre to practice and model racial uplift. Because this cultural work was targeted at and often addressed directly to Black and white readers, collectively and individually, Harlem Renaissance writers employed the essay to characterize and examine what James Weldon Johnson described as the challenge of "double

---

33 Allison Davis, "Our Negro 'Intellectuals,'" *Crisis* 35, no. 8 (August 1928): 268–69, 284, 284.
34 Davis, "Our Negro Intellectuals," 284.
35 Charles S. Johnson, *Ebony and Topaz* (New York: National Urban League, 1927), 12.

audience."[36] In his 1926 *American Mercury* essay, "The Dilemma of the Negro Author," James Weldon Johnson not only detailed a persistent demand for stereotypical images of Black life from a segment of white readers and publishing entities, but he also contended African American writers negotiated a simultaneous demand for positive representations from their Black, especially middle-class, readers. More pragmatic than hopeful about the challenges African American writers faced in meeting the needs of an audience comprising "always both white America and Black America" during the period, Johnson still gestured toward the prospect of a more viable future.[37] "There will come a breaking up and remodeling of most of white America's traditional stereotypes, forced by the advancement of the Negro in various phases of our national life," he writes. Johnson adds that "Black America will abolish many of its taboos" and "become strong enough to render a constantly sensitive and defensive attitude on the part of the race unnecessary and distasteful."[38] As Johnson's essay illustrates, the genre was crucial for writers endeavoring to name and mediate the growing reading public during the Harlem Renaissance, especially within the United States. The genre also furthered an interracial focus, as Locke framed it in *The New Negro*, where he called for "white and black alike" to transform their perceptions of African Americans.[39]

If the effort to acknowledge and navigate readers' expectations is traceable through the essay, then so too are the counternarrative practices of African American writers as they redress and critique racist discourse and representations, white supremacy, and anti-Black ideology and violence during the period. In the early years of the Harlem Renaissance, Du Bois's "Returning Soldiers" employed the first-person plural form to reproach the "America that represents and gloats in lynching, disenfranchisement, caste, brutality and devilish insult," and declare, "*We return. We return from fighting. We return fighting*. Make way for Democracy! We saved it in France, and by the Great Jehovah, we will save it in the United States of America, or know the reason why."[40] In "Returning Soldiers," Du Bois drew on a long tradition in African American writing, particularly in the form the essay, of asserting self-determination while holding the United States accountable for its ideals. The all-too-visible contradictions of American democracy in the early

---

36 James Weldon Johnson, "The Dilemma of the Negro Author," *American Mercury* 15, no. 60 (December 1928): 477–81, 478.
37 Johnson, "Dilemma of the Negro Author," 478.
38 Johnson, "Dilemma of the Negro Author," 480–81.   39 Locke, *New Negro*, 15.
40 W. E. B. Du Bois, "Returning Soldiers," *Crisis* 18 (May 1919): 13–14.

decades of the twentieth century fueled pointed uses of the essay almost as much as the urgency to end racial violence did.

In addition to its function as a site for critical redress and political calls to action, the essay in the Harlem Renaissance was frequently a forum for individual and collective inspiration. In 1925, William Stanley Braithwaite (1878–1962), an acclaimed writer, was excited for African Americans' artistic future because his fellow author "Jean Toomer [was] a bright morning star of a new day of the Race in literature."[41] For Braithwaite, Toomer's (1894–1967) writing, specifically his multigenre text *Cane*, marked the Harlem Renaissance as a moment when one could "write about the Negro without the surrender or compromise of the artist's vision."[42] In "Mr. Garvey as a Poet," T. Thomas Fortune (1856–1928) recast the charismatic orator as a literary artist whose "poetic consciousness ... reaches and moves the masses."[43] Accounts of racial firsts, celebratory reflections on an instance when African Americans received justice, or any moment of individual success – whether local, national, or international – often compelled writers' use of the essay to render a moment of lived experience, in resonant and innovative language, as evocative of African Americans' perseverance and humanity. Jessie Fauset argues this point in "The Gift of Laughter":

> The remarkable thing about this gift of ours is that it has to rise, I am convinced, in the very woes which beset us. Just as a person driven by great sorrow may finally go into an orgy of laughter, just so an oppressed and too hard driven people breaks into compensating laughter and merriment. It is our emotional salvation.[44]

Just like poetry, fiction, and drama during the period, the essay in the Harlem Renaissance served writers' efforts to foster racial pride and engender critical self-reflection.

Perhaps the most characteristic function of the essay in the Harlem Renaissance was in positioning and marking the period itself as a cultural and social assay. Among the many ways that the Harlem Renaissance was experienced, several essays from the period chronicled it as a testable and measurable phenomenon. Questions about its actual existence as a movement, its efficacy, and its longevity were central to the development of the essay contemporaneously and to the wealth of retrospective essays that

---

41 William Stanley Braithwaite, "The Negro in American Literature," in Locke, *New Negro*, 44.
42 Braithwaite, "Negro," 44.
43 T. Thomas Fortune, "Mr. Garvey as a Poet," *Negro World* 23, no. 11 (22 October 1927): 4.
44 Jessie Fauset, "The Gift of Laughter," in Locke, *New Negro*, 161–67, 166.

followed. Whether to assert that a set of novels "mark[ed] an epoch," as Du Bois did in a 1924 review essay or, later, to reflect on the 1929 stock market crash as Claude McKay (1890–1948) did when he wrote, "Looking back to that period today the Negro Renaissance seems to have been no more than a mushroom growth that could send no roots down in the soil of Negro life," several writers employed the essay to respond to an array of social dynamics and currencies for their limitations and possibilities.[45] Across this body of writings are rhetorical and personality-driven narratives further defining the essay in the Harlem Renaissance as a useful tool for conveying just how real but idealistic the period felt. Though many later assessments of the period attend to this duality, Arna Bontemps's (1902–1973) "The Awakening: A Memoir" is especially representative of such essays. Writing as both a participant and an observer, Bontemps notes, "Much that had gone before can now be seen as part of the Awakening, but still another year was to pass before those personally involved could make themselves believe that they were, or had been, a part of something memorable."[46] As a historic moment when reading and writing reflected the complex, often difficult entry into and participation within a dynamic public culture for African Americans generally, the essay in the Harlem Renaissance facilitated this movement and, more importantly, helped solidify their presence. From the early 1920s through the mid-1930s especially, a host of writers employed the essay in ways that made the genre – as a cultural practice and an affirmation of racial identity – central to the Harlem Renaissance.

45 Claude McKay, "For a Negro Magazine," in *Voices from the Harlem Renaissance*, ed. Nathan Irvin Huggins (New York: Oxford University Press, 1976), 402–404, 402.
46 Arna Bontemps, "The Awakening: A Memoir," in *The Harlem Renaissance Remembered: Essays*, ed. Arna Bontemps (New York: Dodd Mead, 1972), 1–26, 1.

16

The Southern Agrarians and the New Criticism

SARAH E. GARDNER

Poet John Crowe Ransom (1888–1974) despaired of many things in the late 1930s, but perhaps none more so than the state of literary criticism. Few of its practitioners could define the art, he claimed in his influential 1937 essay, "Criticism, Inc.," in large measure because "they had not been trained to criticism so much as they have simply undertaken a job for which no specific qualifications were required."[1] No one escaped Ransom's withering critique. The most disappointing of the lot were the professors of English, who had abdicated their responsibility to study literature in favor of studying *about* literature, stressing historical context over literary form. The moralizing New Humanists, whose judgment rested on ethics rather than aesthetics, fared no better in Ransom's estimation. Moral criticism, Ransom asserted, made a poor substitute for literary criticism. There is no reason to assume "that when a moralist is obliged to disapprove a work the literary critic must disapprove of it too."[2] Worst of all, however, were those who wrote for the daily newspapers, the Sunday book supplements, and the intellectual weeklies, who concerned themselves solely with the effect of literature on the reader. "It is hardly criticism," Ransom fumed, "to assert the proper literary work is one that we can read twice; or one that causes in us some remarkable physiological effect, such as ... the flowing of tears."[3] None of these so-called critics appreciated art for art's sake. Ransom found these approaches to literature "odious," for they deny "the autonomy of the artist as one who interests himself in the artistic object in his own right, and likewise the autonomy of the work itself as existing for its own sake."[4] Enough, he

---

1 John Crowe Ransom, "Criticism, Inc.," *Virginia Quarterly Review* 13, no. 4 (Autumn 1937): 586–602, 586.
2 Ransom, "Criticism," 591.   3 Ransom, "Criticism," 597.   4 Ransom, "Criticism," 598.

declared. The time had come for those trained in criticism to remind their readers of the importance of form. More to the point, it was time for them to reclaim their craft.

This chapter surveys the rise of New Criticism in American letters during the interwar years through the 1950s. It pays attention to the influence of two overlapping associations – the Fugitive Poets and the Nashville Agrarians – each of which exercised outsize influence on American letters and politics during the second quarter of the twentieth century. The Fugitives, an ideologically diverse group of Vanderbilt English professors "and other Nashville luminaries," had formed in the years leading up to World War I to discuss current trends in literature and philosophy.[5] The Agrarians, a loosely knit group of southern commentators trained in a variety of disciplines, collaborated on a symposium in the 1930s that decried the deleterious effects of industrial capitalism and promoted those values that purportedly undergirded an agrarian economy. Together the two groups came to shape the tenets of New Criticism at midcentury.

Because some of the Fugitive Poets became Agrarians, though not all, and some Agrarians came to champion New Criticism, though not all, the movements are often conflated. But like most movements, neither the Fugitive Poets, nor the Southern Agrarians, nor the New Critics maintained stable rosters. Nor did their proponents achieve unanimity. For these reasons the three groups did not align neatly. But they shared much. New Critics mourned the turn away from formalist principles that had established the criteria by which one should evaluate literature. Agrarians bemoaned the demise of a set of values that ostensibly emerged from a labor system that championed family farming, property ownership, and small government. Both New Critics and Agrarians, then, engaged in reclamation projects as they sought to salvage what they believed to be all that was good and beautiful in the world. John Crowe Ransom stood at the center of both movements.

The 1920s

By the time Ransom published "Criticism, Inc.," he was well known in literary circles. He had earned his reputation as a member of the Fugitives, for his literary contributions as well as his discerning eye for promising

---

[5] Kieran Quinlan, "Tracking the Fugitive Poets," in *The Cambridge Companion to Modern American Poetry*, ed. Walter Kalaidjian (Cambridge, UK: Cambridge University Press, 2015), 116–27, 116. See also Paul K. Conklin, *The Southern Agrarians* (Knoxville, TN: University of Tennessee Press, 1988), 23.

newcomers. Ransom, who graduated from Vanderbilt in 1903 and had joined the faculty in 1913, for example, recruited undergraduate Donald Davidson (1893–1968) to the group. World War I suspended the Fugitives' meetings, and by the time they reconvened after the war, Davidson had joined Ransom as a member of Vanderbilt's English department. Like Ransom, he left his imprint on the Fugitives' trajectory.

Perhaps most importantly, Davidson invited Allen Tate (1899–1979), then a student at Vanderbilt, to join the Fugitives, a move literary scholar Louis D. Rubin Jr. considered "of incalculable importance to the group's makeup."[6] Rubin's assessment is not necessarily hyperbolic. Tate was the most in tune with modernism, "in language and attitude." As Rubin explained, Tate was the one "who kept the group in touch with what was most challenging and vigorous in literary developments of the early 1920s." And Tate was the one who was "most thoroughly at ease in modernism, however much he deplore-[d] its values."[7]

In a lecture delivered more than three decades after the Fugitives had disbanded, Davidson described a typical meeting: Each poet read their work aloud while members followed along with a typed copy. The poet was often met with stony silence. "Then the discussion began." Woe be to the squeamish, Davidson intimated. Discussions were often "ruthless" in their "exposure of any technical weakness as to rhyme, meter, imagery, metaphor and was often minute in its analysis of details. . . . A poem had to prove itself," Davidson continued, "if possible, its perfection in all its parts."[8] As Davidson's summation makes clear, formalism had a great impact on the Fugitive poets.

In 1922, the Fugitives founded an influential, though short-lived, little magazine that sought to break away from the moonlight and magnolia school of southern literature, perhaps best exemplified by Joel Chandler Harris's "Uncle Remus" stories and Thomas Nelson Page's Reconstruction-era novels that romanticized the plantation South as a place that fostered harmonious relations between the enslaved and the enslaver, that cultivated the literary arts, and that rejected the ethos of the North's industrial order. The magazine's first editorial rather cheekily outlined the group's purpose: "Official exception having been taken by the sovereign people to the mint

---

6 Louis D. Rubin Jr., "The Wary Fugitive John Crowe Ransom," *Sewanee Review* 82, no. 4 (Fall 1974): 583–618, 590.
7 Rubin, "Wary Fugitive," 590–91.
8 Donald Davidson, *Southern Writers in the Modern World* (Athens, GA: University of Georgia Press, 1958), 21.

julep, a literary phase known rather euphemistically as Southern literature has expired, like any other stream whose source is stopped up." The death of one literary tradition, the group explained, allowed the "birth" of another, under more propitious circumstances.[9] Not surprisingly, the Fugitives cast themselves as the vanguard of this new literary tradition.

Despite the group's puckishness, the Fugitives understood themselves to be "somehow within the general Southern tradition in having attachments that could be taken as a matter of course." They were not wholly removed from southern culture, Davidson elaborated in retrospect, "for we could assume that we belonged in an existing, rather stable society as persons, if not poets." What they wanted, Davidson continued, was for their poetry "to be judged on its own merits. We asked for no indulgence for our verses on the ground that we were Southerners – as some of the lady poet laureates of the South at the time seemed to be doing."[10] The declaration's flippancy makes the Fugitives' position clear. Some poets deserved to be read. Others did not. Technical proficiency, not subject matter, determined who was in and who was out.

The Fugitives published their final issue in 1925. Three years later, Harcourt and Brace published *Fugitives: An Anthology of Verse*, signaling "that their poetry" had, according to literary scholar William Pratt, garnered "a national reputation."[11] Capitalizing on their newfound prominence in the world of letters, Davidson, Ransom, Tate, and Robert Penn Warren (1905–1989), who had joined the Fugitives in 1923, suddenly changed tack. Formalism was out and cultural criticism was in. The four poets, three of whom became the nucleus of the Nashville Agrarians, sought to reach a broader audience by weighing in on current cultural influences that they believed threatened "the Southern way of life." Perhaps unsurprisingly, the genre of choice was the essay, which enjoyed popularity with American readers since the nation's founding and remained popular as national periodicals proliferated during the nineteenth and twentieth centuries.

The publication of Vanderbilt English professor Edwin Mims's study of southern progressivism, *The Advancing South* (1926), had provoked Davidson, Ransom, and Tate, with its celebration of recent developments that countered perceptions of the region as "hopelessly captive to outspoken religious

---

9 For the complete text of the Fugitives' opening declaration, see footnote 3 in Davidson, *Southern Writers*, 5–6.
10 Davidson, *Southern Writers*, 5–6.
11 William Pratt, ed., *The Fugitive Poets: Modern Southern Poetry in Perspective*, rev. ed. (Nashville, TN: J. S. Sanders., 1991), xvi.

fundamentalists and belligerent reactionaries."[12] Mims had perceived a reformist impulse at work in every quarter of the South. Indeed, "a veritable war of liberation" was taking place, he declared.[13] That was in 1926.

1926 was not 1929, however. The Great Depression exposed the hollowness of Mims's sunny optimism and called into question the future of industrial capitalism. Davidson, Ransom, and Tate seized the moment to defend their region's purportedly traditional agrarian society, which, they argued, fostered values, modes of thinking, and habits of living that were incompatible with northern liberalism and reformism. "Suddenly we realized to the full what we had long been dimly feeling," Davidson wrote in retrospect, "that the Lost Cause might not be wholly lost after all. In its very backwardness the South had clung to some secret which embodied, it seemed, the elements of its own reconstruction – and possibly, even the reconstruction of America, might be achieved. With American civilization, ugly and bent on ruin, before our eyes," Davidson continued, "why should we not explore this secret?"[14] And explore they did, most pronouncedly in a 1930 manifesto, *I'll Take My Stand: The South and the Agrarian Tradition*, a collection of essays that countered attacks from outsiders who questioned the region's ability to contribute to an increasingly modernizing world.[15]

And just like that, literary scholar Louis D. Rubin suggested, "the Fugitives became Agrarians."[16] Only not quite. Davidson, Ransom, Tate, and Warren became Agrarians. James M. Frank (1886–1944), Sidney Mttron Hirsch (1884–1962), Stanley P. Johnson (1892–1946), Merrill Moore (1903–1957), William Yandell Elliot (1896–1979), among others, did not. Equally to the point, the core group recruited outsiders to the Agrarian project, including historian Frank Lawrence Owsley (1890–1956), political scientist Henry Clarence Nixon (1886–1967), and Stark Young (1886–1963), the *New Republic*'s theater critic and an accomplished Russianist who is perhaps best known for his translations of Anton Chekhov. The conflation makes it possible to imagine that each

---

12 Sarah Gardner, *Reviewing the South: The Literary Marketplace and the Southern Renaissance, 1920–1941* (Cambridge, UK: Cambridge University Press, 2017), 6.
13 Edwin Mims, *The Advancing South* (Garden City, NY: Doubleday, Page, 1926), 311.
14 Donald Davidson, "*I'll Take My Stand*: A History," *American Review* 5, no. 3 (Summer 1935): 301–21, 308.
15 John Crowe Ransom et al. [Twelve Southerners], *I'll Take My Stand: The South and the Agrarian Tradition* (1930; repr., Baton Rouge, LA: Louisiana State University Press, 1990); see also Virginius Dabney, "The Crusade of the Southern Agrarians: Its Excellencies and Its Defects," *Richmond Times-Dispatch* (4 January 1931): 20.
16 Louis D. Rubin, "Introduction," in Ransom et al., *I'll Take My Stand* (1930; repr., New York: Harper Torchbooks, 1962), xxvi. This edition differs from the 1990 Louisiana State University Press edition, referenced in note 15.

movement had more adherents than it did. In reality, a handful of critics directed much of the literary and political conversations during the 1930s.

I'll Take My Stand "rejected the common judgment of the South as a culturally backward wasteland, tragically impaired by poverty and racial violence, and, instead, presented the region as a source of salvation from the barbarity of industrial capitalism."[17] The collection's "Statement of Principles," written by Ransom but purportedly subscribed to by all the contributors, advocated for a "Southern way of life against what might be called the American or prevailing way; and all as much agree that the best term to represent the distinction are contained in the phrase, 'Agrarian *versus* Industrial.'"[18] Importantly, the Agrarians disclaimed any expectation that economic autonomy would somehow lead to political autonomy. "That idea,"[19] Ransom suggested, died in 1865.

They did, however, imagine that the economic devastation wrought by the collapse of industrial capitalism might convince other regions of the nation, particularly the West, to subscribe to the Agrarian Manifesto and align with the South against the industrial East. They also hoped that young southern apostates who had been duped by the phony gospel of industrialism might rejoin the fold. "They must be persuaded to look very critically," Ransom urged, "at the advantages of becoming a 'new South,' which will be only an undistinguished replica of the usual industrial community."[20]

Although Ransom rejected the need to define the constitutive elements of an Agrarian society, he nonetheless observed that in such a society "agriculture is the leading vocation, whether for wealth, for pleasure, or for prestige." Once agrarianism is conceived as "a form of labor that is pursued with intelligence and leisure," he maintained, it "becomes the model" for societies organized along other lines to "approach as well as they may." Even if other regions failed to accept the logic of Agrarianism, Ransom held, "an agrarian regime will be secured readily enough where the superfluous industries are not allowed to rise against it." In 1930, the threat that industrial capitalism would collapse under its own weight was real. But the Agrarians thought there was reason to facilitate its demise. "The theory of agrarianism," they summarized, "is that the culture of the soil is the best and most sensitive of

---

17 Gardner, *Reviewing the South*, 225.
18 Ransom et al., "Introduction: A Statement of Principles," in *I'll Take My Stand: The South and the Agrarian Tradition* (1930; repr., Baton Rouge, LA: Louisiana State University Press, 1990), xxxvii.
19 Ransom et al., "Introduction," xxxviii.
20 Ransom et al., "Introduction," xxxviii–xxxix.

vocations, and that therefore it should have the economic preference and enlist the maximum number of workers."[21]

And here, perhaps, we can see the connection between Ransom's promotion of Agrarianism and his advocating of New Criticism. Only Agrarianism, he maintained, saw labor tied to a vocation rather than a paycheck. Only Agrarianism valued leisure instead of time-clock efficiency. Only Agrarianism allowed for the cultivation of the mind. And only Agrarianism encouraged the writing and reading of poetry. Imagining *I'll Take My Stand* as a rallying cry for revolution, the contributors concluded that any people "groaning under industrialism ... must find the way to throw it off. To think that this cannot be done," they concluded, is pusillanimous. And if the whole community, section, race, or age thinks it cannot be done, then it has simply lost its political genius and doomed itself to impotence."[22]

As literary scholar Robert H. Brinkmeyer observes, the Agrarians' assault on industrialism was "long on idealism and short on pragmatics." Few contributors offered more than a reiteration of the Statement's principles.[23] Not surprisingly, the Agrarians faced rebuke in many of the reviewing outlets. Henry Hazlitt (1894–1993), one of those critics who wrote for the intellectual weeklies, penned a response that was typical. The Agrarians, he wrote in the *Nation*, offered *I'll Take My Stand* as "a rationalization of nostalgia for ancestral ways rather than a rational approach to real problems." Viewing the past through a sentimental haze, he asserted, the Agrarians saw in the Old South "a perfect flowering of art and music and beautiful letters," never acknowledging the region depended on a brutal system of enslaved labor. "Their disingenuous claim that "humanism [was] ... rooted in the agrarian life" was not "that of the man who picked the cotton but that of the man who owned the plantation," Hazlitt reminded his readers.[24]

The general response of northern critics hardly surprised the Agrarians. Indeed, Agrarian Stark Young had warned his fellow contributors that because *I'll Take My Stand* was an attack against prevailing ideas about progress, it would itself be attacked, "especially by outsiders and especially

---

21 Ransom et al., "Introduction," xxxix.
22 Ransom et al., "Introduction," xlviii. See also John Crowe Ransom, "The South – Old or New," *Sewanee Review* 36, no. 2 (April 1928): 139–47; and John Crowe Ransom, "The South Defends Its Heritage," *Harper's* 159 (June 1929): 108–18. For Ransom on the statement's purpose, see John Crowe Ransom to Allen Tate, Nashville, Tenn., 5 January 1930, in *Selected Letters of John Crowe Ransom*, ed. Thomas Daniel Young and George Core (Baton Rouge, LA: Louisiana State University Press, 1985), 189.
23 Robert H. Brinkmeyer Jr., *The Fourth Ghost: White Southern Writers and European Fascism, 1930–1950* (Baton Rouge, LA: Louisiana State University Press, 2009), 29.
24 Henry Hazlitt, "So Did King Canute," *Nation* 132 (14 January 1932): 48–49.

by New York journalism."[25] Yet Ransom intuited in 1927, well before the Symposium's publication, that the Agrarians' battle had "to be waged not so much against the Yankees as against the exponents of the New South."[26] Though Ransom's supposition was correct, the Agrarians' strategy to reach the hearts and minds of southern liberals failed miserably. Southern critics, historian Paul V. Murphy explained, excoriated the Agrarians for their failure to acknowledge "pervasive southern problems, such as rural poverty and disease." Too, they condemned the "Neo-Confederates" for pining for a "return to a burdensome past."[27]

The 1930s

After publication, Ransom acknowledged the multipronged approach of the Agrarians' symposium was ill suited to win converts. It was too diffuse, with essayists commenting on too many topics for the symposium to cohere. "The book consisted in so many overtures to the spirit of man, so many appeals to taste," Ransom regretted. What's more, though each mourned the passing of a putative "southern way of life," none offered a plan for how it could be recovered.[28] The following year, Ransom set out to redress this failing in a proposed book, *Land!*

If "Industrialism" was the bogeyman in *I'll Take My Stand*, in Ransom's new project, the villain was "capitalism," although the two shared the same character. "Capitalism is the economic organization," Ransom explained, and "industrialization is the kind of culture which it supports."[29] Ransom worked on his manuscript while he was on a Guggenheim Fellowship in Great Britain. Although he published two essays, one in *Harper's Monthly Magazine*, the other in the *New Republic*, the full manuscript was not published until after his death.[30] Ransom attributed the failure of *Land!* to win over publishers to his inability to write with "the economist's flair, style,

---

25 Young, quoted in Gardner, *Reviewing the South*, 225.
26 Ransom, quoted in Collier, "Introduction," xix.
27 Paul V. Murphy, *The Rebuke of History: The Southern Agrarians and American Conservative Thought* (Chapel Hill, NC: University of North Carolina Press, 2001), 64. See also Brinkmeyer, *Fourth Ghost*, 32–33.
28 John Crowe Ransom, *Land! The Case for an Agrarian Economy*, ed. Jason Peters, intro. Jay T. Collier (Notre Dame, IN: University of Indiana Press, 2017), 4.
29 Ransom, *Land!*, 4.
30 See John Crowe Ransom, "Land! An Answer to the Unemployment Problem," *Harper's Monthly Magazine* (July 1932): 216–24; and "The State and the Land," *New Republic* (17 February 1932): 8–10.

method, or whatnot." To Tate he confessed, "I'd better stick to poetry and aesthetics."[31]

By the late 1930s, many of the Agrarians, including John Crowe Ransom, had retreated from their earlier positions. Ransom's 1936 essay "What does the South Want?," which appeared in the *Virginia Quarterly Review*, highlights the concessions he and others were willing to make. "The Agrarians have been rather belabored," he quipped, "both in the South and out of it, by persons who have understood them as denying bathtubs to the Southern population. But I believe they are fully prepared to concede the bathtubs."[32] Ransom's remark suggests the degree to which outsiders imagined the Agrarian position as an attack against modernity. Ransom still held little sympathy for those laborers who left the farm for industrial work. "The men who labor," he believed, "are on the whole, those who are backward in economic initiative and intelligence." But, he acknowledged, "they are men, and if they are too helpless or too docile to defend their human dignity they must be assisted."[33] He granted that workers, "as citizens," should "enjoy minimum advantages. It should be possible," he imagined, for "a combination of law, public opinion, and labor union policy" to improve the conditions of labor. Workers' jobs should be secure. If industry fails, "there should be a fresh source of income, . . . a fund to fall back on."[34] In other words, Ransom asserted, the South is wholly in line with federal programs that supported the unemployed. But Ransom still doubted whether industrial labor encouraged dignity. And he continued to reject the primacy of time-clock efficiency. "Here," he claimed, "the Southern temperament discloses a peculiarity which sets the region quite apart from others as a field of industry. Southern labor will not work as fast as other labor."[35] Their refusal was, he said, a matter of pride.

If Agrarianism lost whatever traction it once held, its erstwhile adherents found an outlet for their conservative politics in Seward Collins's new magazine, *American Review*, which began publication in 1933, one month

---

[31] Ransom to Tate, 19 May [1932], in Young and Core, *Selected Letters*, 208. Harcourt, Harper's, and Scribner's each rejected Ransom's second go at a manifesto. See Emily S. Bingham and Thomas A. Underwood, eds., *Southern Agrarians and the New Deal: Essays After I'll Take My Stand* (Charlottesville, VA: University Press of Virginia, 2001), 226.

[32] John Crowe Ransom, "What Does the South Want?," *Virginia Quarterly Review* 12, no. 2 (April 1936): 180–94, 191.

[33] Ransom, "What Does the South Want?," 191.

[34] Ransom, "What Does the South Want?," 192–93.

[35] Ransom, "What Does the South Want?," 193.

after the inauguration of Franklin D. Roosevelt.[36] Collins had cut his teeth in the publishing world first with Condé Nast's *Vanity Fair* and later with the *Bookman*, a literary magazine he and Burton Roscoe purchased in 1918. By the early 1930s, Collins became less interested in belles lettres and increasingly concerned with politics and economics. Already disillusioned with liberalism, Collins credited *I'll Take My Stand* with solidifying ideas he had been toying with for the past few years. As literary scholar Mark Royden Winchell notes, the day after Roosevelt's inauguration, Collins wrote to Donald Davidson, outlining his vision for the new magazine.[37] Although Collins disclaimed any interest in publishing a magazine that pushed only one position, he nonetheless made clear that "'it was the Agrarian view" he wished to "emphasize.'" Collins thus granted the former Agrarians a new platform from which to advance their agenda. "Think of the magazine as being in large measure your own," he advised Davidson, promising that *American Review* was at the Agrarians' "disposal for anything you cared to say."[38]

Although the former Agrarians did not provide all the magazine's content, they nonetheless came to shape *American Review*'s direction, in part, Winchell explained, because of the productivity of former Agrarians and those adjacent to them. Davidson alone published twenty-one essays during the magazine's short run.[39] Notably, though, the former Agrarians did not center their contributions on politics alone. John Crowe Ransom and Robert Penn Warren contributed poetry as well as essays on belles lettres, for example. Equally worth noting, the former Agrarians continued to place their work in other publications, including *American Mercury, Forum, Harper's,* the *Nation*, the *New Republic*, and *Scribner's*, none of which promoted the profascist propaganda espoused in the *American Review*. In the end, literary scholar Albert E. Stone suggests, the "ardently pro-fascist" tenor of the magazine alienated many of the *American Review*'s contributors, including the former Agrarians.[40] Their split with Collins doomed the *American Review*. Without the steady contributions from Davidson, Tate, Warren, and their supporters, including Cleanth Brooks and Herbert Agar, Collins could no longer keep the magazine afloat. Perhaps tellingly, the *American Review*'s demise in October 1937 coincided with the publication of "Criticism, Inc."

---

36 Albert E. Stone Jr., "Seward Collins and the *American Review*: Experiment in Proto-Fascism, 1933–1937," *American Quarterly* 12, no. 1 (Spring 1960): 3–19, 4.
37 Mark Royden Winchell, *Where No Flag Flies: Donald Davidson and the Southern Resistance* (Columbia, MO: University of Missouri Press, 2000), 156.
38 Collins to Davidson, quoted in Winchell, *Where No Flag Flies*, 156.
39 Winchell, *Where No Flag Flies*, 157–58.   40 Stone, "Seward Collins," 12–13.

Ransom returned to his Fugitive roots, arguing that criticism "must become more scientific." Put another way, it must develop and follow its own methodology. And that meant that criticism "must be developed by the collective and sustained effort of learned persons" who teach literature at the university level. In other words, formalism was back in. "Rather than occasional criticism by amateurs," Ransom concluded, "the whole enterprise might be seriously taken in hand by professionals."[41] Ransom's definition of criticism made such an assertion possible. However lay critics understood the function of criticism, Ransom and his fellow New Critics understood it as "the attempt to define and enjoy the aesthetic or characteristic values of literature."[42] The barrier to understanding rested not with the seeming opacity of any given work, New Critics maintained, but with a deficient educational system that failed to train readers in formal criticism and with the proliferation of so-called critics who were similarly untrained and thus ill equipped to assess a literary work according to its aesthetic qualities.

Ransom hardly had the first word on what had already developed into a lively debate about the nature of criticism during the interwar period. Margaret Marshall and Mary McCarthy, for example, wrote a five-part series for the *Nation* in 1935 titled "Our Critics, Right or Wrong," which leveled a similar critique, although they were less concerned with the apparent demise of formalist criticism than they were with the rise of advertising copy passing itself off as criticism.[43] Their series garnered attention among the New York literati but it did not hold the kind of traction that Ransom's essay held with poets, essayists, and professors of literature.

Indeed, Ransom saw literary criticism as "practically a new, underdeveloped field, just waiting for new directions."[44] By the mid-1930s Ransom had already contemplated founding a new literary review. "In the severe field of letters," he explained to Tate, "there is vocation enough for us: in criticism, in poetry, in fiction."[45] He cited the *Southern Review*, a quarterly literary magazine housed at Louisiana State University, by way of example. Although in its infancy – Robert Penn Warren had founded the review only two years earlier – it was, in Tate's estimation, "slipping." The *Southern Review* had benefited from the dearth of reviewing outlets. "They are at their high

---

41 Ransom, "Criticism," 587–88.   42 Ransom, "Criticism," 590.
43 See Margaret Marshall and Mary McCarthy, "Our Critics, Right or Wrong," *Nation* (23 October 1935): 468–71; (6 November 1935): 542–44; (20 November 1935): 595–99; (4 December 1935): 653–55; (18 December 1935): 717–18.
44 Conklin, *Southern Agrarians*, 135.
45 John Crowe Ransom to Allen Tate, 4 November 1937, in Young and Core, *Selected Letters*, 233.

standard by the pure accident that there are now a good number of critics who [have] nowhere to market their wares," he told Tate. Warren's friends could certainly continue to contribute to the *Southern Review*. But, Ransom maintained, a publication of half its size, carrying only literary works, "and all of the highest contemporary excellence would be a distinguished thing." Lambert Davis, then managing editor of the *Virginia Quarterly Review*, encouraged Ransom's plan, noting that "a rather larger number" of literary reviews "might regularize or standardize a form of critical literature and all might help each other."[46] Ransom thus had every reason to be optimistic.

As Thomas Daniel Young and John Hindle suggest in the introduction to a collection of Ransom's selected essays, Ransom had a way of writing to lay readers that invited them into his world. "Rather than projecting the image of a 'learned pedagogue,' issuing proclamations from Mount Olympus intended for others like him," they explain, Ransom positioned himself as an interested and concerned" general reader "discussing matters of importance to all enlightened citizens."[47] Whether he and others of his cohort reached general readers is another matter. Many of Ransom's essays appeared in those literary journals Ransom promoted, such as the *Virginia Quarterly Review*, the *Southern Review*, the *Sewanee Review*, and the *Kenyon Review*, founded by Ransom in 1939. These journals appealed to smaller and more specialized audiences than those published by the commercial press, such as the *New York Times Book Review* or the *New Republic*. But they certainly reached the academy.

The 1940s and 1950s

New Criticism appealed to a particular cohort of academics. In a retrospective essay on the ascendancy of New Criticism, Cleanth Brooks (1906–1994), an Agrarian fellow traveler, told of his difficulties in teaching literature surveys to undergraduates:

> When Robert Penn Warren and I found ourselves teaching 'literary types and genres' ... we discovered that our students, many of whom had good minds, some imagination, and a good deal of lived experience, had very little knowledge of how to read a story or a play, and even less knowledge of how to read a poem. Some had not been taught how to do so at all," he continued,

---

46 Young and Core, *Selected Letters*, 233.
47 Thomas Daniel Young and John Kindle, "Introduction," in John Crowe Ransom, *The Selected Essays of John Crowe Ransom*, ed. Thomas Daniel Young and John Hindle (Baton Rouge, LA: Louisiana State University Press, 1984), 2.

"many had been thoroughly mistaught. Some approached Keats' 'Ode to a Nightingale' in the same spirit and with the same expectations with they approached an editorial in the local county newspaper or an advertisement in the current Sears, Roebuck catalogue.[48]

Allen Tate argued a similar point. "It was – and still is – a situation in which it is virtually impossible for a student to get a critical literary education," he lamented. He had even less faith in graduate programs. If a student attends graduate school, they come out "incapacitated for criticism," Tate charged.[49] Graduates were unable to discuss the "literary object in terms of its specific form." All they can do, he claimed, "is to give you its history or tell you how" they "feel about it," which was Tate's way of saying students were incapable of saying much of anything worth listening to. If only contextual background and feelings were on the table, Tate and his like-minded literary critics had nothing "to judge."[50]

Like Ransom and his fellow Fugitives, Tate turned to the poem, in large measure because "[t]he formal qualities of a poem are the focus of the specifically critical judgment." These qualities, Tate asserted, "partake of an objectivity that the subject matter, abstracted from the form, wholly lacks."[51] But too few literary scholars shared his view. Tate's summation of the problems facing the profession at midcentury was damning: "It would be simpler," Tate observed, "if not easier, to discuss the form if we had a way of discussing it; yet before we can understand a literary problem we must first confess the problem exists. We no longer admit the problem because we no longer believe in the specific quality of the work of literature, the quality that distinguishes it from a work of history or even of science." Worse, he continued, "we no longer believe in literature."[52]

Tate overstated the case. Others took up the cause, questioning logical fallacies that threatened any real attempt to judge a work's merit. A decade or so after Ransom published "Criticism, Inc.," W. K. Wimsatt and M. C. Beardsley published "The Intentional Fallacy," which challenged the assumption that one could assess literature according to the author's intent, something Wimsatt and Beardsley thought unknowable. "The poem ... is detached from the author at birth and goes out in the world beyond his

---

48 Cleanth Brooks, "The State of Letters: The New Criticism," *Sewanee Review* 87, no. 4 (Fall 1979): 592–607, 593.
49 Allen Tate, "Miss Emily and the Bibliographer," *American Scholar* 9, no. 4 (Autumn 1940): 449–60, 455–56.
50 Tate, "Miss Emily," 456–57.   51 Tate, "Miss Emily," 456.
52 Tate, "Miss Emily," 456–57.

power to intend about it or control it. The poem," they concluded, "belongs to the public."⁵³ If Wimsatt and Beardsley argued that a poem does not belong to its creator, they similarly argued that a poem does not belong to its reader. "The report of some readers ... that a poem or story induces in them vivid images, intense feelings, or a heightened consciousness," they explain, "is neither anything which can be refuted nor anything which it is possible for the objective critic to take into account."⁵⁴ As a method of criticism, New Critics held, it is worthless.

By the mid-twentieth century, New Criticism was ascendant. And perhaps in an unexpected way, so too was Agrarianism. A recent study of Cold War–era culture by literary scholar Louis Menand emphasizes what others have observed, namely, that "American New Criticism was founded by writers associated with a reactionary political and religious program."⁵⁵ Here, Menand refers to the former Agrarians and those who wrote for Seward Collins's *American Review*. They might not have shared Mussolini's brand of nationalism, but they were reactionary, nonetheless.

The ascendancy of New Criticism in universities invites scrutiny. "How," Menand wonders, "did the way these writers thought about literature become dominant in the postwar university, an institution that is the incarnation of the values of the modern liberal state? After all, meritocracy is precisely an attempt to counteract the undertow of region, tradition, and 'orthodoxy.'"⁵⁶ Menand points to the former Agrarians' disengagement with politics as part of the answer. Because New Criticism "validated academic criticism itself," literature professors might have found it easy to swallow reactionary views, whether telegraphed or subsumed, as part of the bargain.⁵⁷ With New Criticism came increased status. But that status was continually threatened.

In 1951, the Modern Language Association, a professional organization that advocates the study of literature and languages, added "'criticism' to its constitutional statement of purpose." Summarizing the sentiments of New Criticism's practitioners, Menand reminds his readers that the term "criticism" had been anathema among literary scholars. "'Criticism' meant appreciation, interpretation, and evaluation – subjective responses, not

---

53 W. K. Wimsatt, Jr., and M. C. Beardsley, "The Intentional Fallacy," *Sewanee Review* 54, no. 3 (July–September 1946): 468–88, 470.
54 W. K. Wimsatt Jr., and M. C. Beardsley, "The Affective Fallacy," *Sewanee Review* 57, no. 1 (Winter 1949): 45.
55 Louis Menand, *The Free World: Art and Thought in the Cold War* (New York: Farrar, Strauss and Giroux, 2021), 456–57.
56 Menand, *Free World*, 464.   57 Menand, *Free World*, 465.

scholarship." Appealing to Ransom's initial concern, Menand quips, "Criticism is what magazines were for."[58] Academic criticism needed to suggest it was something other than what was practiced by reviewers. "And it needed to present itself as not just as a method," according to Menand, "but as a discipline, a body of accumulated knowledge."[59] It succeeded. But it did so by hewing closely to the tenets of formalism that Ransom and his compatriots had advocated for decades. They had failed to influence American political economy, but their contributions to literary criticism endure, despite whatever methodological challengers have entered the field.

58 Menand, *Free World*, 457.   59 Menand, *Free World*, 467.

17
Subjective and Objective: Newspaper Columns

WILLIAM E. DOW

Newspaper columns or editorials were some of the most powerful manifestations of the American essay around the turn of the twentieth century. This is a period in which a new kind of personal essay began to emerge that revealed a tension between the genteel and the modern, progressivism and prejudice, and what were thought of as subjective and objective essayistic forms. While essayistic objectivity aspired to provide verifiable evidence, to leave no questions unanswered, and to be "truthful" in its interpretations of the world, essayistic subjectivity attempted to engage the reader by means of the essayist's own subjective discourses in which the essayist exists in the foreground of the text. Significantly, during the 1880–1920 period, the essay increasingly produced specific articulations of subjectivity, be they fictional or nonfictional, that provided the foundations for this new personal essay. Of course, subjectivity has always been essential to the essay, the "literary genre most explicitly focused on subjectivity," as Ned Stuckey-French contends, "the one that claims on the one hand to create the subject and on the other to issue directly from it."[1] And yet, coming into certain prominence in the 1880–1920 period, the subjectivity and objectivity of the essay were not so much opposed as related and interdependent categories. Historical subjectivity and objectivity begin with the essayist's perception of the past and present, and they are sustained through the essayist's desire to make that perception integral to the essay form.

Some of the most important essayists and editorialists of the period included Franklin P. Adams (1881–1960), Don Marquis (1878–1937), Robert Benchley (1889–1945), Stuart Sherman (1881–1926), Henry Seidel Canby (1878–1961),

---

[1] Ned Stuckey-French, *The American Essay in the American Century* (London: University of Missouri Press, 2001), 7.

Burton Rascoe (1892–1957), Heywood Broun (1888–1939), Simeon Strunsky (1879–1948), Robert Cortes Holliday (1880–1947), Christopher Morley (1890–1957), and H. L. Mencken (1880–1956). Beginning with the rise of the columnists – or as they were called, "the colymnists" – a new kind of personal essay began to emerge in the major city newspapers and magazines. These essayists detached themselves from the genteel tradition that largely catered to elite northwestern readers and standard bourgeois values. Instead, more ironic and street smart than the genteel essayists who preceded them, the columnists mainly wrote for a middle-class national readership.[2] Crucially, in this context, many of the new essayists – for example, Sherman, Canby, and Rascoe – saw their roles in the newspapers and magazines they wrote for as those of educators and tastemakers; they aimed their columns at educated generalists, or what Joan Shelley Rubin has called a "middlebrow public."[3]

At the same time, the personal essay was responding to the objective news style dominant in the second half of the nineteenth century: a "form of brief, objective news writing [that] helped newspapers build mass circulation audiences instead of targeting partisan niches."[4] It must be noted that the turn of the century was a period of unparalleled growth for American newspapers: As the US population grew more literate and urban, new technologies such as linotypes, high-speed presses, typewriters, and telephones fueled the publishing industry. It was also a period marked by notions of racial and male supremacy and by foreign expansionism. Perfectly suited for the challenges and pressures of this era, subjective first-person essay forms took their place alongside the objective news style. In fact, such American newspapers and magazines as the *New-York Tribune*, the *World-Telegram*, and *Vanity Fair* soon discovered that storytelling, vivid sketches, and a self-conscious and entertaining narrator had both a commercial and a democratic appeal. Of equal importance, many of these new essayists, adhering to and broadly representing the middle class, assumed the task of explaining the United States to itself. In doing so, they fulfilled the social function of tastemaking in which notions of objectivity and subjectivity, and public and personal arguments, come together. Serving the public-oriented

---

2 Stuckey-French, *American Essay*, 41.
3 Joan Shelley Rubin, "The Genteel Tradition at Large," *Raritan* 25, no. 3 (Winter 2006): 70–91, 73.
4 Lisa A. Phillips, "From Major to Minor: Literary Journalism and the First Person," in *The Routledge Companion to American Literary Journalism*, ed. William E. Dow and Roberta S. Maguire (New York: Routledge, 2020), 385–95, 387.

dimensions of both literature and journalism, the personal essay became the most conducive form for this task.

Although he had much affinity with the new essayists, H. L. Mencken also served as a bridge between these essayists and some of the modernist and nontraditional writers that followed. "A champion of modernism and realism," he participated in the new personal essay, but in his roles as editor, essayist, and journalist, "facilitated the blending of journalism into a modernist milieu."[5] Beginning with his association with the Baltimore *Sunpapers* (1906), Mencken "encourage[ed] originality and discourage[ed] imitations of the English journalistic style (long considered a model) . . . the *Sun* became distinctly American, known for its incisive conversational writing."[6] At the same time, Mencken combined in his essays objective journalism with iconoclastic infusions of subjective commentary, a distinctly American idiom, and a largely progressive cultural criticism. Perhaps more than anyone else during the immediate pre–World War I period, while rescuing "American literature from its former formalism and hollowness,"[7] he hoped to redefine the essay.

But any redefinition of the American essay from this period must also feature alternative and nonmainstream forces such as African American essayists, essayists of color, female essayists, and essayists from radical and marginalized groups. Representing tensions between factual evidence and the writer's imagination that conjures such evidence into a story, their work often took the form of columns or editorials. These essayists include Victoria Earle Matthews (1861–1907), T. Thomas Fortune (1856–1928), Anna Julia Cooper (1858–1964), Mary Church Terrell (1863–1954), James Weldon Johnson (1871–1938), W. E. B. Du Bois (1868–1963), and Ida B. Wells (1862–1931). Writing about their personal experiences, essayists such as Du Bois and Wells adopted the apparent open form and formlessness of the essay to their own purposes and social agendas. As Phyllis Garland explains, "The black Press was never intended to be objective because it didn't see . . . the white press being objective. It often took a position . . . This was a press of advocacy."[8]

---

5 Stacy Spaulding, "Literary Journalism's Historical Lineage: In Defense of Mencken," in *The Routledge Companion to American Literary Journalism*, ed. William E. Dow and Roberta S. Maguire (New York: Routledge, 2020): 288–99, 294.
6 Marion Elizabeth Rodgers, *Mencken: The American Iconoclast* (Oxford: Oxford University Press, 2007), 59.
7 Rodgers, *Mencken: The American Iconoclast*, 59.
8 Phyllis Garland, interviewed in Stanley Nelson, Jr., dir., *The Black Press: Soldiers without Swords* (Arlington, VA: PBS, 1999).

Indeed, "subjectivity," as Roberta S. Maguire asserts, "is at the heart of the African American journalistic tradition ... set[ting] it apart from the history of mainstream US journalism."[9] At the same time, African American columnists and editorialists in the period (and beyond) did bind themselves to their readers by warranting objective statements that could be factually verified. Although most often having different social, cultural, and racial motivations than those of the new essayists, they too created subjective-objective narrative combinations that advanced their communal and collective intentions. By often insisting, in first-person forms, on a verifiable autobiographical self and by simultaneously employing subjective expressiveness that aimed to be as effective as the discourse of a literary text, essayists such as Du Bois (*The Souls of Black Folks*, 1903), Anna Julia Cooper (*A Voice from the South*, 1892), and Ida B. Wells (*The Red Record*, 1895) took the essay in new directions, combining personal experiences with racial, labor, and social advocacy.

Because these essential forces are largely covered elsewhere in this volume, my focus here will be on the social upheaval and innovation in the personal essay form between the turn of the century and the 1920s. While anticipating and ultimately encouraging diverse and adversarial positions to the personal essayists, Mencken's essays and columns will serve as examples of many of these changes. Like the personal essayists, Mencken functioned as a tastemaker – he was, in Walter Lippman's view, "the most powerful personal influence in his whole generation of educated people,"[10] but he was also aware that for Black essayists such as James Weldon Johnson and Walter White (1893–1955) (both of whom Mencken promoted), the essay became a primary tool for social justice and cultural identity. And although Mencken reflected some of the basic racist elements of American social thought of his time, he was, following and amplifying the credo of the personal essayists, a strident individualist and iconoclast. As this chapter will demonstrate, he helped push the essay form into particular ontological, cultural, and practical perspectives that had crucial consequences for late nineteenth-century and early twentieth-century America.

---

9 Roberta S. Maguire, "The 'Black Difference' in African American Literary Journalism," in Dow and Maguire, *Routledge Companion to American Literary Journalism*, 399–415, 400–401.
10 Carl Bode, *Mencken*, 2nd ed. (Baltimore: Johns Hopkins University Press), 4.

A New Kind of Personal Essay: The Rise of the Columnists

WILLIAM E. DOW

Between 1880 and 1920 – a period marked by industrialization, incorporation, immigration, racial divisions, labor grievances, and the first wave of American feminism – the personal essayists, while "resist[ing] the opacity and high literariness of modernist fiction and poetry,"[11] held to the narrative tenets of clarity, accessibility, and familiar language, and to forms best suited for the general readers of magazines and newspapers. As Philip Lopate states, one way the American essay thrived "in the 1910s, '20s, and '30s was to gravitate to the newspaper or magazine column."[12] Alongside humorous sketches, these columns often contained book reviews, light verse, stories about daily existence, political commentary, the idioms of the street, and life in American cities. Many of these columns were also, in the essay tradition of the time, "written not by retired aesthetes, but by practicing journalists," as Christopher Morley notes in his edited anthology, *Modern Essays* (1921), whose intention was to create "a mood rather than a form."[13]

Although unsigned editorials and leading articles were already a feature of US newspapers, beginning in 1814, when Nathan Hale made them a characteristic of the *Boston Daily Advertiser,* signed columns started to be seen at the turn of the nineteenth century and at the beginning of the twentieth in such newspapers as the *Chicago Daily News* and the *Chicago Tribune.* First appearing in the *New-York Tribune* in 1914, one of the most famous newspaper columns of the 1920s was Franklin P. Adams's The Conning Tower, known for occasionally featuring pieces from such writers as Dorothy Parker (1893–1967), Edna St. Vincent Millay (1892–1950), Robert Benchley, James Thurber (1894–1961), Don Marquis, and John O'Hara (1905–1970). In The Conning Tower and other later columns such as The Diary of Our Own Samuel Pepys, written in the style of an English seventeenth-century essay and published on Saturdays, Adams expressed his opinions on topical events, books, plays, artists, and the routines of ordinary people. He made his personality and his writing inseparable from each another. Full of wit and satire, his poems, appearing in many of his columns, were self-

---

11 Nicole B. Wallack, review of *The American Essay in the American Century*, by Ned Stuckey-French, *Fourth Genre: Explorations in Nonfiction* 14, no. 1 (Spring 2012): 213–17, 215.
12 Phillip Lopate, "Introduction," in *The Glorious American Essay: One Hundred Essays from Colonial Times to the Present*, ed. Phillip Lopate (New York: Pantheon Books, 2020), xi–xviii, xiv.
13 Christopher Morley, ed., *Modern Essays* (New York: Harcourt, Brace, 1921), v.

mocking, cleverly constructed, and unpretentious. Here is "Q. H. F's Address to His Book" from Adams's *By and Large* (1920), which first appeared in The Conning Tower:

> Ho, ambitious little book!
> Wan and wistful is your look,
> Think you that a lyricist
> E'er could lead The Bookman's list?
> Get you gone, and, booklet, learn,
> Once away there's no return.
> Verse fashioned for a colyum,
> Who told you you were a volume?[14]

For thirty years, The Conning Tower successively traveled to the op-ed pages of the *New-York Tribune*, the *New York World*, and the *New York Herald Tribune*.

In his Saturday column, The Diary of Our Own Samuel Pepys, Adams provided a more serious analysis and commentary on national and world events. He wrote about the brutal killings of Jews and the nights of terror in Germany in 1938 that became known collectively as the *Kristallnacht* ("Night of Broken Glass"). He argued that in the Berlin of the late 1930s, "human indecency and savagery can go no further, and daily it seems that yesterday all of us were in error."[15] In this column he also wrote literary and theater criticism and was one of the first critics to recognize and praise such talents as D. H. Lawrence (1885–1930), Somerset Maugham (1874–1965), Eugene O'Neill (1888–1953), Sinclair Lewis (1885–1951), Ring Lardner (1885–1933), and others. One of the keys to Adams's popularity, like that of many of the new personal essayists, is that he wrote his criticism and commentary on a wide variety of essayistic subjects in a clearly accessible language, addressed to the widest audience possible.

Like Adams, Don Marquis showed that essays have their rightful place in newspaper columns, and he actively contributed to the essay in a column form. In the traditions of many other columnist-essayists of the period – most notably Adams, Robert Benchley, Heywood Broun, Christopher Morley, and H. L. Mencken – Marquis was a parodist, historian, poet, satirist, playwright, reporter, and humorist – one who, as Sam G. Riley argues, "deserves a place in the front row ... [i]n any selection of important American humor

---

14 Franklin P. Adams, *By and Large* (New York: Doubleday, 1920), 9.
15 Nancy Roberts, "Franklin P. Adams," in *Dictionary of Literary Biography: American Newspaper Journalists, 1901–1925*, vol. 25, ed. Perry J. Ashley (Farmington Hills, MI: Gale, 1984), 23.

columnists."[16] In 1912, fulfilling a lifelong ambition to have his own column, Marquis was hired to write The Sun Dial column for the *New York Evening Sun*. Ten years later, he left the *Sun* to write a column called The Lantern for the *New-York Tribune*. Incorporating the narrative diversity of mainstream essayists of his time, Marquis's columns included philosophical commentaries, parodies, poems, profiles, vignettes, and epigrams, but, like Adams, he is best known as a humor columnist who, as Christopher Morley argues in *Letters Askance* (1939), "reached his best vein in dealing with outcasts, freaks, ham actors, dogs, kings and queens, newspaper men, drunkards, and Shakespeare – in fact anyone on the losing side of society but still alert to the bewildering absurdity of life."[17]

Best known for his contributions as an essayist for the *New Yorker* and *Vanity Fair*, Robert Benchley was an American humorist who blended dialects and a disdain for pretention and intellectualism with a style of humor that relied on puns, wordplay, and the kind of literary allusions suited to the tastes of the readers of the *New Yorker* at the time. Like Adams and Marquis, he often wrote his essays as humorous pieces, made modest claims as a literary artist, and relied on topicality and an absurdist point of view. As Michael Bell argues, "[Benchley's] stock and trade was the gentle, insistent mockery of American culture between the wars ... His weapon was absurdity."[18] Amplifying the narrative diversity and humor of such essayists as Adams and Marquis, Benchley plied this weapon in newspaper columns (e.g., Books and Other Things for the *New York World*), theater reviews, scripts, profiles, sketches, and his acclaimed short films. In his thirty-year career, publishing over 600 essays, sixteen books, and starring in sixty-five film shorts, Benchley had a profound influence on such later essayists as James Thurber, E. B. White (1899–1985), and S. J. Perlman (1904–1979).[19]

One of Benchley's primary contributions to the essay was his creation of the persona "the Little Man," an exaggerated representation of the common man who was often a middle-class suburbanite, educated but not overeducated, befuddled, and out of sync with his family and bureaucratic working environment. In "Coffee, Megg and Ilk, Please," collected in Benchley's *Of All*

---

16 Sam G. Riley, "Don Marquis," in *Dictionary of Literary Biography: American Newspaper Journalists, 1926–1950*, vol. 29, ed. Perry J. Ashley (Farmington Hills, MI: Gale, 1984), 191.
17 Louis Hanley, "Don Marquis: Ambivalent Humorist," *Prairie Schooner* 45, no. 1 (Spring 1971), 59–73, 62.
18 Michael J. Bell, "Robert Benchley's 'Cooper Folk Songs,' 'Typical New Yorkers,' and 'Real Americans'," *Western Folklore* 77, no. 1 (Winter 2018): 57–91, 59.
19 See Norris W. Yates, *Robert Benchley* (New York: Twayne, 1968).

Things (1921), we find a representative example of this immensely popular persona:

> Give me any topic in current sociology, such as "The Working Classes vs. the Working Classes," or "Various Aspects of the Minimum Wage," and I can talk on it with considerable confidence. I have no hesitation in putting the Workingman, as such, in his place among the hewers of wood and drawers of water – a necessary adjunct to our modern life, if you will, but of little real consequence in the big events of the world. But when I am confronted, in the flesh, by the "close up" of a workingman with any vestige of authority, however small, I immediately lose my perspective – and also my poise. I become servile, almost cringing. I feel that my modest demand on his time may, unless tactfully presented, be offensive to him and result in something, I haven't been able to analyze just what, perhaps public humiliation ...
>
> And yet I have no doubt that if one could see him in his family life the Workingman is just an ordinary person like the rest of us ...
>
> And he would probably be the first person to scoff at the idea that he could frighten me.[20]

A parody of the privatized and rational citizen, The Little Man – living in the frenzied world of the early twentieth century – humorously embodied the anxious inadequacies of the new middle class.

In addition to the humor essay, many of the essayists of the period also wrote literary criticism, engaging with "the question of whether attention should take the form of 'news' or 'criticism' [that] had shaped American book reviews since the nineteenth century."[21] As Joan Shelley Rubin observes, "[t]he same factors that enhanced the 'news' treatment of books renewed some individuals' faith in the 'higher' possibility of fostering critical acumen in a wide public as well."[22] Stuart Pratt Sherman, an American literary critic, academic, and journalist, emphasized such a premise in his pleas for "democratic" literary standards; his advocacy, at least initially, of a defense of traditional American narrative modes (as his books on Matthew Arnold and Sinclair Lewis attest); and his tirades against literary naturalism and modernism. In 1924, Sherman began writing a weekly column called Books, the literary supplement to the *New York Herald Tribune*: each issue of Books contained, in addition to Sherman's lead essay, such features as "a children's book page, a column for book collectors, correspondence from

---

20 Robert Benchley, *Of All Things* (New York: Henry Holt, 1925), 10, 17.
21 Joan Shelley Rubin, *The Making of Middlebrow Culture* (Chapel Hill, NC: University of North Carolina Press, 1992), 40–41.
22 Rubin, *Making of Middlebrow*, 45.

readers, news of 'Books Abroad,' a column about reissues of older works, and, together with publishers' advertisements, a full page of classified ads."[23] The Books columns reflected the middlebrow mode of expression that Sherman was searching for in the early 1920s: a definition of selfhood, a middle-class conception of culture, and an accessible and democratic mode of literary criticism. As he told Ellery Sedgwick, the editor of the *Atlantic Monthly*, "I have long felt a desire to develop a somewhat different style than these [weekly organs of opinion] foster – something less journalistic; more, in a certain sense, personal; with more undertones and overtones; utilizing more of one's experience, feeling."[24] Like the New York colymnists, Sherman believed that the essay could lend itself to a more accurate representation of life than the academic or genteel genres of his immediate predecessors, which included such essayists as Samuel McChord Crothers (1857–1927), Brander Matthews (1852–1929), Agnes Repplier (1855–1950), and Henry Van Dyke (1852–1933).[25]

Henry Seidel Canby and Burton Rascoe were also part of the stream of essayist-columnists who held high-profile editorial positions in the domain of literary criticism, wrote books about literature and authors, and became middlebrow cultural authorities. In this regard, Canby was "perhaps the most influential book critic that twentieth-century literary journalism ever produced."[26] As Janice Radway argues, "Canby's authority to pronounce on the stature of newly published books was dually staked on his position as a Yale professor of English and on his previous work as the editor of the generalist quarterly *The Yale Review*."[27] In addition to these responsibilities, Canby was also the editor of the prestigious *Saturday Review of Literature*, which served him for promoting "a literature adequate to the discontinuities and disorientations of the modern age"[28] and in developing a literary tradition that would appeal to middle-class tastes. In his capacity as editor, he championed the New York columnists as the "new essayists" who would "introduc[e] literature to the newspaper and mass magazines and middle-class readers to literature."[29] Likewise, Burton Rascoe, a journalist and

23 Rubin, *Making of Middlebrow*, 69.
24 Jacob Zeitlan and Homer Woodbridge. *Life and Letters of Stuart P. Sherman* (New York: Farrar and Rinehart, 1929), 2: 477.
25 Stuckey-French, *American Essay*, 115–16.
26 Gordon Hutner, "'The Good Reader' and the Bourgeois Critic," *Kenyon Review* 20, no. 1 (1998): 17–32, 18.
27 Janice Radway, *A Feeling for Books: The Book-of-the-Month Club, Literary Taste, and Middle-Class Desire* (Chapel Hill, NC: University of North Carolina Press, 1997), 177.
28 Radway, *Feeling for Books*, 177.   29 Stuckey-French, *American Essay*, 117.

literary editor for the *New York Herald Tribune*, and syndicated columnist from the 1920s to the 1950s (e.g., "A Bookman's Daybook," "The Book of the Week," and "TV First Nighter"), was a cultural critic who identified the New York columnists as the most important essayists of the period. Like Sherman and Canby, he wished for a literary independence of the essay and a national identity for it. In 1922, he wrote in "A Bookman's Daybook," "I hold these truths to be self-evident: that in the field of essay-writing contemporary Americans are incomparably superior to the modern Englishmen; that our essayists hold their own with the essayists of all other countries; and that it is intimated deference to assume the contrary."[30]

In the grain of these personal essayists who wanted to give voice to the rising middle class, Heywood Broun – Algonquin Circle wit, Book-of-the-Month Club judge, founder of the American Newspaper Guild, sportswriter, and newspaper columnist – created a form of advocacy journalism that focused on such topics as social injustice, labor, and class. Broun "wrote for the commercial press but flouted negative framings of labor news and disavowed 'impartiality,' cultivating instead a journalistic ethos of political engagement and bold conveyance of truth as [he] saw it."[31] At the same time, his journalism was literary and imaginative and, as an author of thirteen books, he "was perhaps the most highly respected newspaper essayist of his era."[32] Broun was a sportswriter for the *New Morning Telegraph* and a drama critic for the *New-York Tribune* in the early 1920s before becoming a syndicated columnist and writing the regular feature It Seems to Me for the *World-Telegram* in 1921. He regularly used the column to express his outspoken views on such issues as censorship, racial discrimination, and academic freedom, and even – through a campaign he entitled "Give a Job Till June" – to find jobs for the unemployed. While noting Broun's self-deprecation and humanistic bemusement (hallmark traits of the personal essayists), a 1935 *New York Times* review of Broun's columns emphasizes his wide-ranging interests and subject matter:

> It becomes apparent that anyone who reads this lively and courageous book – taken from the past ten years of his columns in The World-

---

30 Burton Rascoe, "What of Our Essayists?," *Bookman* 55 (1922): 74–75, 74.
31 Christopher Phelps, "Heywood Broun, Benjamin Stolberg, and the Politics of American Labor Journalism in the 1920s and 1930s," *Labor: Studies in Working-Class History of the Americas* 15, no. 1 (March 2018): 25–51, 26.
32 Whitney R. Mundt, "Heywood Broun," *Dictionary of Literary Biography: American Newspaper Journalists, 1901–1925*, vol. 25, ed. Perry J. Ashley (Farmington Hill, MI: Gale, 1984), 41.

Telegram ... that the sun never sets on Brouns. Here you will find Broun the fabulist, Broun the deep-sea sailor, Broun the humanitarian, Broun the gambler, Broun the leader of the Newspaper Guild, Broun the author of a book that was felled by Deems Taylor ... Broun the expert on wooing by wire, Broun the convention goer and Broun the defender of Kipling.[33]

Nonetheless, particularly in his later essays and columns, Broun could be vociferously political and often demanded justice for the politically repressed. For instance, he defended and supported Eugene V. Debs (1855–1926), Margaret Sanger (1879–1966), John T. Scopes (1900–1970), D. H. Lawrence, Sacco (1891–1927) and Vanzetti (1888–1927), and others who were persecuted in the United States for their political allegiances and social opinions.[34] Known as perhaps the most left-liberal columnist in the country at the time, Broun would later run unsuccessfully for Congress in 1930 on the Socialist ticket.[35] Significantly, he considered his founding role in the American Newspaper Guild as his most important contribution to the US press. While faithfully serving as president of the guild until his death in 1939, he never relinquished his role as a champion of the underprivileged and the underdog.

Other personal essayists who served as advocacy journalists, some of whom wrote newspaper columns, include John Jay Chapman (1862–1933), George Creel (1876–1953), Carleton Beals (1893–1979), and, perhaps most importantly, Simeon Strunsky. Strunsky's columns were published in *Harper's Weekly*, *Atlantic Monthly*, *Collier's*, and *Bookman*. After serving as a chief editorial writer for the *New York Evening Post*, for which he wrote a series of columns under the general title of The Patient Observer, Strunsky wrote a weekly column called About Books – More or Less for the *New York Times*, which he began writing in 1924. His most lasting contributions to the *Times* were his editorial essays, Topics of the Times, featuring a blend of his liberal beliefs with culture satire, irony, and large doses of human sympathy. The essay

---

33 C. G. Poore, "As It Sometimes Seemed to Mr. Broun," *New York Times* (8 December 1935): 3.
34 For writings and background information on many of these figures, see *The Radical Reader: A Documentary History of the American Radical Tradition*, ed. Timothy Patrick McCarthy and John McMillian (New York: New Press, 2003).
35 This information is outside of the 1880–1920 period but is included here because it illustrates how Broun's writing became more politicized in the 1930s and '40s, anticipated in such Broun books as *Seeing Things at Night* (1921) and *Pieces of Hate: And Other Enthusiasms* (1922).

"Nocturne," published in Strunsky's collection of essays, *Post-Impressionism* (1914), captures such a combination:

> Sometimes I wonder why people think that life is only what they see and hear, and not what they read of. Take the Night Court. The visitor really sees nothing and hears nothing that he has not read a thousand times in his newspaper and had it described in greater detail and with better-trained powers of observation than he can bring to bear in person. What new phase of life is revealed by seeing in the body, say, a dozen practitioners of a trade of whom we know there are several tens of thousands in New York? They have been described by the human-interest reporters, analysed by the statisticians, defended by the social revolutionaries, and explained way by the optimists ... Can the upper classes really acquire for themselves, through slumming parties and visits to the Night Court, anything like the knowledge that books and newspapers can furnish them? Can the lower classes ever hope to obtain that complete view of the Fifth Avenue set which the Sunday columns offer them? And yet there the case stands: only seeing and hearing for ourselves, however imperfectly, do we get the sense of reality.[36]

Representing an intriguing blend of objectivity and a situated subjective viewpoint, Strunsky freely vaunted a rejection of value-free editorials and essays. As "Nocturne" suggests, he frequently relied on firsthand experiential accounts while prescribing his "sense of reality" to the reader. In this way, departing from the weightier tone of the genteel essay, he developed a more personal and intimate style.

Another dimension of the new essayists as columnists during this period concerns those who published their ideas about the essay as a narrative form: Robert Cortes Holliday, Christopher Morley, and Katherine Fullerton Gerould (1879–1944) are representative examples of conservative theorists who competed with the more progressive forces during the 1880–1920 period. Like many of the newspaper "colymnists," Holliday "display[ed] his considerable learning with a light touch while maintaining the guise of a lazy, slow witted Everyman."[37] He did not distinguish the genre of the essay from that of the article, believing that both – in the tradition of Montaigne – were most effective when they contained many ideas and digressions. Through this nondidacticism, Holliday followed a main current of the nineteenth-century view of the essay, as articulated by Agnes Repplier in "The Passing

---

36 Simeon Strunsky, *Post-Impressionism: An Irresponsible Chronicle* (New York: Dodd, Mead, 1914; Project Gutenberg, 14 July 2012), www.gutenberg.org/files/40232/40232-h/40232-h.htm.
37 Lopate, *Glorious American Essay*, 395.

of the Essay" (1895): "[The essay] offers no instruction, save through the medium of enjoyment, and one saunters lazily along with charming unconsciousness of effort."[38] In a like manner, Christopher Morley argues that "in the essay (of an informal sort) we ask not relevance to plot, but relevance to mood" [and] "that the perfection of the familiar essay is a conscious revelation of self done inadvertently."[39] This position anticipates Fullerton Gerould's "plebiscite" on the essay, in which she argues that "[t]he basis of the essay is meditation, and it must in a measure admit the reader to the meditative process. ... Meditating on facts may bring one to truth; facts alone will not. Nor can there be an essay without a point of view and a personality."[40] Fullerton Gerould saw this development as a takeover of the essay by factual articles and topical polemics; polemical essayists such as Randolph Bourne (e.g., "The Handicapped," 1911) and John Jay Chapman (e.g., "Coatesville," 1912), however, who combined the personal subjective orientation of the essay with the objective factual genre of the article, viewed their writing as an opportunity to provide an alternative to the personal essay.

H. L. Mencken: The Essayist of Contradictions

H. L. Mencken was perhaps the most important columnist of the period, fusing the factual appeal of the article writer "with the personal voice, personal thought, and personal voice of the essayist."[41] As Douglas C. Stevenson contends, Mencken "defied the genteel assumption that American letters must be primarily Anglo-Saxon, optimistic, and morally uplifting. He ridiculed literary commercialism, dramatized the view that an essential function of art is to challenge accepted axioms, and conducted a boisterous onslaught against the 'snouters' who favored literary censorship."[42] A reporter, editor, essayist, literary critic, and columnist, Mencken wrote over twenty-five books and collections of essays, including *George Bernard Shaw: His Plays* (1905); *The Philosophy of Friedrich Nietzche*

---

38 Agnes Repplier, "The Passing of the Essay," in *In The Dozy Hours and Other Papers* (Boston: Houghton Mifflin, 1898), 226–35, 232.
39 Morley, *Modern Essays*, v.
40 Katherine Fullerton Gerould, "From 'An Essay on Essays,'" in *Essayists on the Essay: Montaigne to Our Time*, ed. Carl H. Klaus and Ned Stuckey-French (Iowa City, IA: University of Iowa Press, 2012), 61–65, 61, 63.
41 Carl H. Klaus, "Toward a Collective Poetics of the Essay," in Klaus and Stuckey-French, *Essayists on the Essay*, xv–xxvi, xix.
42 Douglas C. Stevenson, "Menken, Henry Louis," *Dictionary of American Biography: Supplement Six, 1956–1960*, ed. John A. Garraty (New York: Scribner's, 1980), 444.

(1908); a highly regarded philological study, *The American Language* (1919); an autobiographical trilogy of essays, *Happy Days* (1940), *Newspaper Days* (1941), and *Heathen Days* (1943), devoted to his experiences in journalism; and volumes on politics (e.g., *Notes on Democracy*, 1926), literary criticism (the *Prejudices* series, 1919–1927), and religion (e.g., *Treatise on the Gods*, 1930).

When Mencken was twenty-three, he was appointed city editor of the *Herald*, a paper in which his first column, Rhymes and Reason, appeared in 1900. The column was laced with Mencken's humor, political satire of Baltimore politicians, and clunky, stilted poetry. This column would subsequently adopt other titles – Terse and Terrible Texts, Knocks and Jollies, Untold Tales, Baltimore and the Rest of the World – but all were filled with Mencken's invective style and sarcastic social criticism. In effect, the *Herald* played an essential role in establishing Mencken as a social critic and in providing a forum in which he honed his essayistic skills. In this connection, as Marion Elizabeth Rodgers argues, "[s]tandards that Mencken insisted on in his own writing were also imposed on the Herald. Dull padding, stupidity, and verbosity were castigated; dispatches told their stories simply and briefly."[43] The knowledge that Mencken gained in writing such columns, where he "showed his affection for his city and his agitation for reform of laws that impinged on individual freedom,"[44] was decisive for the rest of his career.

In 1906, Mencken was hired as a Sunday editor by the *Baltimore Sun*, for which he wrote editorials and reviewed plays. When the *Baltimore Sun* became the new *Baltimore Evening Sun*, Mencken served as an associate editor and began writing a daily column called "H.L.M." under a free-reign mandate to be blunt, provocative, and controversial while continuing his trenchant cultural condemnations. Mencken expanded his caustic reporting in his Free Lance columns for the *Baltimore Sun*, which first appeared in 1911. For Mencken, in his words, the Free Lance, "was a private editorial column devoted wholly to my personal opinions and prejudices."[45] But it was also, as W. H. A. Williams contends, "Mencken's venture into journalism ... a rebellion against the middle-class insistence on gentility in culture and on respectability in professions." At the same time, however, "[h]is was a halfway rebellion. If he rejected the surface of middle-class life, he was to cling tenaciously to its essentials. Although he would satirize bourgeois

---

43 Rodgers, *Mencken: The American Iconoclast*, 96.
44 Rodgers, *Mencken: The American Iconoclast*, 66.
45 William H. A. Williams, *H. L. Mencken Revisted*, Twayne's United States Authors Series (Farmington Hills, MI: Gale, 1998), 19.

mores, Mencken took with him into his journalism the discipline of his ambition, and the basic values of his class."[46]

And yet Mencken *was* instrumental in resisting "the 'familiar' or 'polite' essay that had been a literary staple of the preceding era."[47] In his columns, he pushed the later twentieth-century essayists' proclivity for expanding the parameters of self-disclosure that went far beyond the workings of the genteel essay. Mencken explained his approach in a memorandum written in 1937 to the publisher Paul Paterson:

> A lot may be accomplished by simply presenting the facts, but not everything. Some effort must be made to show their significance, and to expose the motives and methods of those who seek to sophisticate them. In other words, we must take some appeal in the sense of fair play, and even in the sense of the self-interest of readers. We'll get nowhere so long as we try to counteract a wholesale and highly skillful playing on the emotions with nothing more formidable than a resort to reasoning.[48]

Along with Mencken's plea to problematize the reporter's role as a mere objective conveyor of facts and to underscore the writer's subjectivity as an expression of a journalistic mission, his further advice for the *Sunpapers* – which essentially constituted the political position he held throughout his life – explicitly advocated sustaining a liberal politics, sometimes eliding into libertarian positions:[49]

> I believe that the safe and rational course for the papers themselves is still that of Liberalism, and that we should be watchful of radical propaganda by our own men. We should fight resolutely at all times for the chief Liberal goods, all of them well tested and of the highest value: e.g., the limitation of governmental powers, economy in all the public services, complete publicity, the greatest tolerable degree of free speech, and a press secure against official pressure.[50]

---

46 Williams, *H. L. Mencken Revisited*, 5.
47 Robert Atwan, "Foreword: The Essay in the Twentieth Century," in *The Best American Essays of the Century*, ed. Joyce Carol Oates and Robert Atwan (New York: Houghton Mifflin, 2000), ix–xiv, xi.
48 Richard J. Schrader, ed., "Journalist: The National Stage," in *Dictionary of Literary Biography*, vol. 222, *H. L. Mencken: A Documentary Volume* (Farmington Hills, MI: Gale, 2000), 15–84, 71.
49 For Mencken's libertarianism, see Bill Kaufman, "'My Plan Is to Let People Do Whatever They Please': The Daily Newspaper Columns of H. L. Mencken," *Reason* 49, no. 9 (February 2018): 64–65; and Joanne C. Kao, "The Monday Articles: H. L. Mencken and the American Religious Scene," *Menckeniana*, no. 141 (Spring 1997): 1–10.
50 Schrader, "Journalist," 71.

As expressed in the Free Lance columns, Menken's liberalism went hand in hand with his comic exaggeration, satire, and humor. The coverage of a speech by the chairman, Bertrand H. Snell, at the Republican convention in 1936 illustrates Mencken's satiric style:

> This time the ayes prevailed, and the learned speaker proceeded to quote George Washington and Abraham Lincoln, both of whom he spoke of in the highest terms. He ended with a polite reference to God, who, by orthodox Republican theory, has been an *ex officio member* of the Republican National Committee since the Civil War days ... the speech, intellectually speaking, seldom goes above the level of a high school commencement address.[51]

Mencken's caustic intellect served him well when he assumed coeditorship of *Smart Set* with New York drama critic George Nathan in 1914. In 1923, the two writers cofounded the highly respected *American Mercury*. For the *Smart Set*, Mencken reviewed major works by Upton Sinclair (1878–1968), Theodore Dreiser (1871–1945), Sinclair Lewis (1885–1951), Henry James (1843–1916), and F. Scott Fitzgerald (1896–1940) and, as editor, published such new and emerging writers as Eugene O'Neill, O. Henry (1862–1910), and Dorothy Parker. Under the coeditorship of Mencken and Nathan, the *Smart Set* became a standard of literary rebellion and independence, with Mencken urging American writers to look to contemporary Europe for their modes of literary excellence and to America for their subject matter. Mencken fought against what he saw as conventionally successful writers and worked for the recognition of such poets and writers as Theodore Dreiser, Ezra Pound (1885–1972), W. B. Yeats (1887–1962), Robinson Jeffers (1887–1962), D. H. Lawrence, and Joseph Conrad (1857–1924).

All in all, Mencken was probably the most influential American literary critic in the 1920s, but it should be noted that in his columns he often used his literary criticism as a base for his various cultural judgments and in support of the modernistic literary "rebellion" of the period. Nonetheless, as Williams observes, there were self-imposed constraints on this rebellion:

> The *Smart Set*'s involvement with the rebellion ... had its limits. Neither editor had any interest in experimental writing of any sort, especially in poetry, and they largely ignored the avant-garde prose that followed in the wake of James Joyce's *Ulysses* ... Nor did they have much sympathy for the "bread and rose" radicalism of the Greenwich Village bohemians ... [D]espite the editors' anti-Puritanism, both Menken and Nathan looked askance

---

51 Schrader, "Journalist," 33.

at attempts to take the gates of prudery by a full frontal assault on sexual taboos.[52]

At the same time, however, Mencken was obsessed with condemning those pieties and moral codes that he believed prevented writers from depicting the reality of American life. In this regard, Mencken stated about his own work, "Whether it appears to be burlesque, or serious criticism, or mere casual controversy, it is always directed against one thing: unwarranted pretension."[53]

Another significant Mencken column was called Monday Articles, written for the *Baltimore Sun* from 1920 to 1938. Mencken's subjects included national politics, race, Prohibition, the FDR presidency, celebrities, political conventions, immigration, literature, members of the press, religion, and other provocative issues. Significantly, while "the 'Free Lance' had brought his ideas to the attention of his hometown," the Monday Articles, like the *Smart Set* and the *American Mercury*, reached a national readership.[54] Mencken became a national figure and the Monday column, based on his own editorial latitude, quickly became a standard of American newswriting. "An unprecedented level of freedom enabled Mencken to tackle subjects seldom mentioned in other papers," Rodgers writes. "He pummeled censorship, Prohibition, and hypocritical Puritanism with equal ardor. The defense of individual freedom always brought out the best of his powers, and the suppression of civil liberties became one of his dominant targets."[55] Menken's style in these columns still depended on his eclectic vocabulary (e.g., terms such as "hokum," as well as German and Yiddish words and phrases) and neologisms (e.g., "Bible Belt," "booboisie," "homo boobiens") but was based less on the overdetermined effects of the Free Lance columns and more on "an originality of thought and a genuine distinction of style" that featured a more sophisticated use of hyperbole, overstatement, and paradox.[56] Mencken thought that the Monday columns represented some of his best writing and, toward the end of his career, was puzzled by the lack of critical commentary on them: "The stuff I wrote for the Evening Sun . . .

---

52 Williams, *H. L. Mencken Revisited*, 45–46.
53 H .L. Mencken, *The Letters of H. L. Mencken*, ed. Guy J. Forgue (New York: Alfred A. Knopf, 1961), 188
54 J. James McElveen, "H. L. Mencken," in *Dictionary of Literary Biography*, vol. 29, *American Newspaper Journalists, 1926–1950* (Farmington Hill, MI: Gale, 1984), 234.
55 Rodgers, *Mencken: The American Iconoclast*, 216.
56 Rodgers, *Mencken: The American Iconoclast*, 215.

included [some of] my best [work] yet most of it is buried in [the Sun] files."[57]

A related, undervalued element of Mencken's later essayistic columns is how they fit into a protest-oriented tradition of the essay,[58] beginning most widely with his writings in the 1920s. Mencken had an uncanny ability to claim and critique the promises of US inclusion and democracy, particularly concerning the claims of African Americans. For example, in a 1931 column for the *Sunpapers*, Mencken responded to a lynching on the Eastern Shore of Maryland of an African American, Matthew Williams. Demanding that the perpetrators be arrested and convicted, Mencken criticized the local press coverage of the tragedy:

> It was indeed a demonstration of what civilization can come to in a region wherein there are no competent police, little save a simian self-seeking in public office, no apparent intelligence on the bench, and no courage and decency in the local press. Certainly it would be irrational to ask for enlightenment in communities whose ideas are supplied by such pathetic sheets as the Cambridge Daily Banner and the Salisbury Times.[59]

By participating in a tradition anchored both in the personal essay and in the essayistic spirit of valuing social experience over abstract truths, he wrote about racial injustices and actively promoted African American writers. As Cheryl A. Wall notes, Mencken "befriended numerous black writers, including James Weldon Johnson and Walter White ... [a]s editor, he solicited articles from Rudolph Fisher, E. Franklin Frazier, Eugene Gordon, and J. A. Rogers, as well as Du Bois, White, Hurston, and [George] Schuyler."[60]

But Mencken was also a product of his times. As Richard O'Mara asserts, "[Mencken] absorbed all the standard prejudices extant in the early part of the last century against blacks and Jews and immigrants and added a few of his own."[61] Mencken's *Men versus the Man: A Correspondence between Rives La*

---

57 Joanne C. Kao, "The Monday Articles: H. L. Mencken and the American Religious Scene," *Menckeniana*, no. 141 (Spring 1997): 1–10, 2.
58 For this tradition, see Brian Norman, *The American Protest Essay and National Belonging: Addressing Division* (Albany, NY: State University of New York Press, 2007). Norman argues that the protest essay is a distinct narrative form grounded in the European personal essay and American political oratory informing and informed by social movements.
59 Marion Elizabeth Rodgers, "H. L. Mencken: Courage in a Time of Lynching," *Nieman Reports* (1 June 2006): 74–76, 74.
60 Cheryl Wall, *On Freedom and the Will to Adorn: The Art of the African American Essay* (Chapel Hill, NC: University of North Carolina Press, 2018), 98.
61 Richard O'Mara, "The Intellectual Bully of Baltimore," review of *Mencken: The American Iconoclast*, by Marion Elizabeth Rodgers, *Sewanee Review* 115, no. 1 (Winter 2007): 146–52, 147.

Monte, Socialist, and H. L. Mencken, Individualist (1910), a meditation on Social Darwinism, eugenics, heredity, and race, locates "the American negro" as "low-caste," and the "superior white race" as "fifty generations ahead of him."[62] Following the publication of *Men versus the Man*, however, Mencken, "a man of maddening contradictions,"[63] reversed his views of white superiority and began calling for civil rights for African Americans. "He was relentless in his campaigns against the Ku Klux Klan, and joined forces with the NAACP to testify against lynching before the U.S. Congress."[64] Further, as Rodgers notes, "[d]uring the 1930s, in a departure from popular opinion ... Mencken argued for the admission of Jewish refugees into the country, and personally sponsored a Jewish family's emigration to the United States."[65] By the 1930s, Mencken was "The Most Quoted Man in America," who had garnered a considerable reputation in Europe, South Africa, Japan, Venezuela, and elsewhere abroad.[66] In this connection, notwithstanding his contradictions and inconsistencies, perceptions of his national and international reputation as a journalist were largely based on his (quasi-)rebellion against middle-class gentility and respectability.

Conclusion

The personal mode of discourse championed by the new essayists was driven by a belief in improving middle-class tastes and helping readers see beyond the mundane worlds of American consumerism and commerce. Taken together, these essayists presented an alternative form of cultural capital. And yet Mencken went even further. A recurring theme in his columns and editorials, his position that "the essential weakness of America was to be found in the very essence of Americanism"[67] parallels the views of such essayists and columnists as Du Bois, Ida B. Wells, and Emma Goldman (1869–1940) and resonates with those of such later writers as Richard Wright (1908–1960), James Baldwin (1924–1987), Alice Walker (1944–), Claudia Rankine (1963–), and Ta-Nehesi Coates (1975–). For Mencken and these writers, the political and personal are inseparable and the essay often

---

62 Marion Elizabeth Rodgers, "H. L. Mencken and the Alt-Right," *Menckeniana*, no. 223 (Fall 2018): 10–11, 10.
63 Rodgers, *Mencken: The American Iconoclast*, 552.
64 Rodgers, "H. L. Mencken and the Alt-Right," 11.
65 Rodgers, "H. L. Mencken and the Alt-Right," 11.
66 Rodgers, *Mencken: The American Iconoclast*, 306, 309.
67 Williams, *H. L. Mencken Revisited*, 30.

functions as a form of authorial mediation, of narrative outrage, and a call to social action.

Because the essay both alternates between and conjoins the particular and universal, it draws from the immediate social moment and the meaningfulness of personal experience.[68] In the period under discussion, the essay did not decline but rather developed new modern forms in the context of an increasingly cosmopolitan audience, the immense challenges of racial tensions and immigration, the economic changes brought by industrialism and consumerism, and a reader demand for accessible, entertaining writing. While seeking to educate a wide readership, essayists such as Franklin P. Adams, Don Marquis, Robert Benchley, Stuart Sherman, Heywood Broun, Simeon Strunsky, Christopher Morley, and H. L. Mencken remade the form that "helped spark the 'magazine revolution,' launch radio book shows, and give voice to the new and ascendant middle class."[69] The years 1880–1920 chronicle the passing of preindustrial newspaper practices and the creation of a market-oriented magazine and newspaper industry dominated by the daily press and hard, objective news. Rachel Blau DuPlessis's theory that "the essay ruptures the conventions – especially the scientific ethos of objectivity – of critical writing"[70] can usefully be combined with its practice of unabashed subjectivity, the result of which is particularly apt in describing the essay form between the turn of the century and the 1920s.

---

68 Norman, *American Protest Essay*, 156.   69 Stuckey-French, *American Essay*, 2.
70 Rachel Blau DuPlessis, "*f*-Words: An Essay on the Essay," *American Literature* 1, no. 1 (March 1996): 15–45, 25.

18

The Experience of Art: The Essay in Visual Culture

TOM HUHN

The rise in the prominence of the essay on visual art in the mid-twentieth century neatly corresponds with the ascendancy of abstract over figurative and representational painting and sculpture. It is as if the retreat from figuration opened a breach through which language – in the form of the essay – took up the role of advance guard. The essay begins to aim at enacting the *experience* of visual art rather than continuing merely to describe and to judge it. In parallel with the proliferation of abstraction, writing on art turns away from representing the art object and toward the production of a self-sufficient experience whose possibility was signaled by the new works of visual art, which proceeded by severing any perceived dependency on things beyond themselves. Pointing to nothing outside itself, the autonomous abstract work is matched by the essay attempting to become a wholly independent force of intellectual creation.

If abstraction in painting means the jettisoning of figure and representation, then abstract picture-making is also a strategy for moving the struggle away from the veracity of the representation to its referent, and toward the resources within each painter, and likewise within the boundaries of the medium of painting itself. More broadly, the transition from representation to abstraction in picture-making parallels the twentieth century's long slide away from text and language and toward the image and visual experience. To put bluntly the role played by abstraction in the cultural shift from text to image, we might conjecture that in order for a picture to become at least as significant as a complex piece of writing, the picture as a *representation* had to be surmounted, if not effaced. Granted the growing prowess of the visual regime, the mid-century essay on art is thus also a rearguard action, enthusiastically articulating the case for the primacy of the visual object while riding its coattails.

Clement Greenberg (1909–1994) is central to the transformation of essay writing in the middle of the last century. He accomplished an expansion of the particular force of the essay by employing it to promote the supremacy of the visual experience of art over reading, regardless of the paradox that it was by dint of language that the visual was made out to be supreme. Greenberg led the way by replacing the usual containers of art writing – criticism and history – with the essay, specifically by premising the forward movement of culture upon the legitimacy of individual taste. Greenberg establishes himself in essay writing as the central act of his intellectual project. The brilliance and lucidity of his essays played no small part in how his position came to shift and then to dominate the reception of modern painting and sculpture and their role in contemporary culture. The essay became a tour-de-force demonstration of self-legitimation.

The essay on visual art showcased how assertion and self-justification lay the foundation for establishing the primacy of experience in tandem with the legitimization of one's own taste, which in turn became the barometer of cultural progress. (It is no leap to imagine the great increase in the value of personal style in the 1960s and '70s, the valorization of what came to be considered hip or cool, as founded on the midcentury triumph of ostensibly self-made individual taste.) It is just here where the novel status of the essay on visual art taps deeply into the tradition of American writing on the robustness and centrality of the individual; think of Ralph Waldo Emerson (1803–1882) and Henry David Thoreau (1817–1862), Walt Whitman (1819–1892) and Gertrude Stein (1874–1946), but so too of William James (1842–1910) and John Dewey (1859–1952) and James Baldwin (1924–1987). The essay on visual art sought to install itself as the engine for driving the advance as well as the shape of modern culture. Because the topic of abstraction was often twinned with the question of art's relation to its medium, the *medium* of the essay in turn became the invisible – if not silent – partner bankrolling this phase of the modernist project.

In his essays, abstraction and medium serve as the grounds on which Greenberg at once exercises his taste – and, in exercising his taste, grounds himself – as well as defensively projects himself as a self-made intellect. The suggestion is that medium – which is the key theme for his two most significant academic followers, Rosalind Krauss (1941–) and Michael Fried (1939–) – was the arena in which one might most profoundly struggle with the nature of abstract art and the individual's relationship to it. Likewise, the medium of the essay became the place where Greenberg could erect and enact himself as autonomous individual, within history, but also somehow just above its vicissitudes.[1]

Those writing in the wake of Greenberg – and despite their disagreements – implicitly carried forward the conviction regarding the gravity of serious culture, celebrated and embraced as highbrow culture.[2] Upon the highest brow of that culture rests the individual's *experience* of visual art. Greenberg served as lay minister for the renewed faith in the American church of the transcendent, in the emphatic expectation of some form of secular salvation secured by the dynamic experience of the individual. The instrument of that redemption was the essay on visual art; it was from within its confines that the figure of salvation was to be embodied and articulated. The new status and impact of the essay on visual art, and in particular on modernist abstraction, took effect from the late 1930s through the '50s. Among the most significant contributions in art writing were those made by academics like Meyer Schapiro (1904–1996), journalists like Harold Rosenberg (1906–1978), and artists like Barnett Newman (1905–1970). In the 1960s and '70s, art writing proliferates across all three fields by academics Rosalind Krauss, Michael Fried, Leo Steinberg (1920–2011), and Irving Sandler (1925–2018); by artists Mary Kelly (1941–), Martha Rosler (1943–), Robert Smithson (1938–1973), and Donald Judd (1928–1994); by journalists Hilton Kramer (1928–2012) and Max Kozloff (1933–); and joined by curator Lucy Lippard (1937–).

The Modern Struggle with Medium

The modernist paradox of medium consists of the unavoidable requirement that medium cannot be entirely escaped – art always takes place *in* and *as* something – and medium thereby becomes, in addition to the vehicle, the largest impediment to the forward progress of making art. Modern art's progress would come to be measured by how it increasingly bumped up

---

[1] Another prominent midcentury writer for whom medium was the nub of modern experience is Marshall McLuhan (1911–1980), a Canadian philosopher whose writings had a great influence on American scholars of new media. See Alex Kitnick, *Distant Early Warning: Marshall McLuhan and the Transformation of the Avant-Garde* (Chicago: University of Chicago Press, 2021).

[2] The rise of Pop Art in the late 1950s, including the sensibility affiliated with it, is often mistakenly understood to be a retreat from the seriousness of what was thought to be at stake in midcentury abstract art. Pop Art has more recently been viewed as expressing a variety of strategies to move beyond the single-mindedness that had come to be associated with Abstract Expressionism. See Thomas Crow, *The Rise of the Sixties: American and European Art in the Era of Dissent* (New Haven, CT: Yale University Press, 1996); and Katy Siegel, *Since '45: America and the Making of Contemporary Art* (London: Reaktion Books, 2011).

against medium as an ineluctable partner. This dance of medium and artmaking, in which the desired forward step of art's progress is partnered inevitably with the impediment of a clumsy medium, was taken up in the 1960s by the two most influential art writers of that era, Krauss and Fried, who both trained as art historians. For the subsequent five decades, their legacy was overshadowed by another, that of medium, which had been established as the central conundrum of art. Fried's justly famous essay "Art and Objecthood" (1967) stages the agonistic struggle within medium between individual and artwork: "[W]orks of art must somehow *confront* the beholder – they must, one might almost say, be placed not just in his space but in his *way*."[3] That essay serves to set the course for many of Fried's later writings. If "absorption" and "theatricality" later become the touchstones for Fried, the notion of "presence" – which we might consider a kind of contraction and distillation of the experience of art into a durationless, contentless moment, akin even to a kind of mystical unity or grace – places the individual's experience of the artwork as the telos of art. The famous final sentence of the essay, "Presentness is grace,"[4] nicely encapsulates the centrality of the viewer's experience as well as locating the focus on experience as particularly American, insofar as Fried opens the essay by citing the consummately American preacher Jonathan Edwards's eighteenth-century journals regarding the presence of the divine in each timeless moment. With Krauss, we find the authorizing of experience within the performance of writing itself. Indeed, in her writings Krauss sometimes not only includes her own experiences but addresses herself, and thereby her writing, within the text itself. The vacillation in Krauss's writings between high theory and personal encounter indicates the continuing allegiance to both intellect and experience in art writing, all the while keeping focus on the status of medium, as evidenced, for example, in the subtitle of her 2000 book, *A Voyage on the North Sea: Art in the Age of the Post-Medium Condition*.[5]

Medium is established as the locus for claims about the relation of history to culture in Greenberg's essay "Toward a Newer Laocoön" (1940).[6] That essay likewise serves as the basis for his self-realization, which parallels that of

---

3 Michael Fried, "Art and Objecthood," in *Art and Objecthood: Essays and Reviews* (Chicago: The University of Chicago Press, 1998), 148–72, 154.
4 Fried, "Art and Objecthood," 172.
5 Rosalind Krauss, *A Voyage on the North Sea: Art in the Age of the Post-Medium Condition* (London: Thames and Hudson, 2000).
6 Clement Greenberg, "Toward a Newer Laocoön," in *The Collected Essays and Criticism*, vol. 1, *Perceptions and Judgments, 1939–1944*, ed. John O'Brian (Chicago: University of Chicago Press, 1986), 23–37. Lessing's 1766 book, *Laocoön*, is generally credited with the

the artworks he most prized. Success came to be measured not in relation to prior human accomplishment but only in direct struggle with the medium. Victory, in what many believed was the major struggle of their era, would be the liberation and autonomy of the individual. It is not that the battles within abstract picture-making are a proxy for the ongoing struggle of the individual against all those attempts to administer her; they are rather one and the same. Medium, like history, ought not be understood as merely the container within which some meaningful content or another might be safely housed. It is the sheer otherness of content that disqualifies it from taking up any legitimate place in the modern work of art. The most pronounced forward movements of science and modernism consist in their shared move away from the comfort of past achievement, indeed of the status quo; both orient themselves toward a frontier whose premise is a dissatisfaction with what has been, and with the present.

An unrelenting forward motion, which culture finds best modeled by scientific inquiry, is fueled by the conviction that the past remains *unequal* to the present, which we witness especially in modern art, but only when things made in the present demonstrate their superiority to things of the past.[7] The way forward is not to set a compass toward the new or the unknown, but rather, the rise toward the future occurs by sacrificing the ballast of the past. Modernist art-making is to be a process of purification, the jettisoning of everything extraneous, even while acknowledging that no art could ever achieve complete purity, for that would entail an art without any medium at all, a logical as well as practical impossibility. Abstraction in art-making might well be understood as, among other things, a strategy of asceticism and purification, in pursuit of distilling only those features of each medium without which the medium would cease to exist. The struggle over medium is a proxy for the fight to liberate the individual from whatever constrains her and so too a proxy for the forward movement of culture. The essay on visual art sought not simply to describe this struggle, but to engage and enact it.

Traditional culture persists by nurturing the regressive tendency of endlessly reproducing static images of the status quo. Culture, instead, always

---

introduction of the notion of medium. See Gotthold Ephraim Lessing, *Laocoön: An Essay on the Limits of Painting and Poetry*, trans. Edward Allen McCormick (Baltimore: Johns Hopkins University Press, 1984).

[7] Reversing this formulation, whereby the past remains continuously unapproachable by the present, brings us to the modern condition of art's mournfulness. See Gregg M. Horowitz, *Sustaining Loss: Art and Mournful Life* (Stanford, CA: Stanford University Press, 2001).

advancing and expanding away from what it has been, is the most pragmatic means whereby a collective of the like-minded might make their own history rather than remain mere by-products of it. The guiding conviction is that the most genuinely human emancipatory project is the struggle against the backward and downward pull that threatens to swamp each individual in the very history that produced her. There is no better example of the antagonistic struggle within modern culture than in the title in which Greenberg proclaims kitsch and the avant-garde as adversaries ("Avant-Garde and Kitsch," 1939), and so too in his explanation for the advent of the avant-garde as a defense against the forces of the rear-garde. "Hence it developed that the true and most important function of the avant-garde was not to 'experiment,' but to find a path along which it would be possible to keep culture *moving* in the midst of ideological confusion and violence."[8] In short, the modern origin of the fraught struggle to move culture forward lies in the retarding effects of traditional and mass culture, in what Theodor Adorno (1903–1969) and Max Horkheimer (1895–1973) labeled – in the same decade Greenberg is diagnosing the relation between the avant-garde and kitsch – as the culture industry.[9] At times, Greenberg aligns this project with what he believes is the progress inherent to science; other times he describes this forward movement as modernism, even if he famously describes Immanuel Kant (1724–1804) as the first modernist: "Because he was the first to criticize the means itself of criticism, I conceive of Kant as the first real Modernist."[10] His disdain for conventional learning is most pronounced in his equating of kitsch to everything academic, as if the academy and the precincts of higher learning might indeed prove to be the true source for what is most regressive in culture.

Art Writing and the Academy

Though the experience of art remains paramount for Fried and Krauss, the status of their experience somehow loses its self-sufficient posture. Thus, though the most influential academic writing on art followed the midcentury essay's turn away from mere art-historical revisionism, it substituted,

---

8 Clement Greenberg, "Avant-Garde and Kitsch," in O'Brian, *Collected Essays and Criticism*, vol. 1, *Perceptions and Judgments, 1939–1944*, 5–22, 8.
9 Max Horkheimer and Theodor Adorno, *Dialectic of Enlightenment*, trans. John Cumming (London: Allen Lane, 1973).
10 Clement Greenberg, "Modernist Painting," in *The Collected Essays and Criticism*, vol. 4, *Modernism with a Vengeance, 1957–1969*, ed. John O'Brian (Chicago: The University of Chicago Press, 1993), 85–93, 85.

however, the bulwark of theory for the urgency of individual taste. Academic art writing came to depend on the support of one theoretical orientation or another as foundation for its pronouncements on the status and meaning of visual art. Such writing sought to locate the deep structure of visual art, and with the belief that only theory might provide not so much an interpretation, but rather a revelation regarding whence the art arrived. Hence not mind but structure provides the deepest soundings – if not the meaning – of visual art, at least its origins and genesis. In contrast to the academicism of Krauss and Fried, we might instead take note of other writers on visual art who are defined more by the tenacity of their writings, and their taste, than they are by the theories they propound in defense of their experience, even if they find themselves oriented by feminism, anti-institutionalism, or even poetry. This is to suggest that it might well be the nonacademic writers on visual art who are, even if unbeknownst to themselves, the true followers of the midcentury transformation of art writing, insofar as they take up the essay on visual art as the means both to argue for the authority of a particular orientation as well as to practice a more pure form of self-reliance.

Consider here then the writings in the 1960s and '70s by Lucy Lippard, and then a bit later by Laura Cottingham (1959–).[11] Or note the essays in art criticism by poets, for example, John Yau (1950–) and Peter Schjeldahl (1942–2022), or a generation earlier with John Ashbery (1927–2017) and Frank O'Hara (1926–1966).[12] The poet's assumed facility with language is not what qualifies him to write on modern or contemporary art; it is rather the mimetic affinity between the poet to language and the visual artist to material. The kinship lies, in other words, in the way each relates to their medium. In the decade of the 1960s, the single most consequential publication for writing on art is the widely read "Against Interpretation" by Susan Sontag (1933–2004), first published in the journal *Evergreen Review* in 1963, and then in 1966 as the titular essay of a collection of her writings.[13] Most famously, or infamously, she writes: "Interpretation is the revenge of the intellect upon art. Even more. It is the revenge of the intellect upon the world. To interpret is to impoverish, to deplete the world – in order to set up

---

[11] An especially illuminating opportunity to encounter Lippard and Cottingham together is via the latter's long essay on the former: see Laura Cottingham, "Shifting Ground: On the Critical Practice of Lucy R. Lippard," in *Seeing through the Seventies: Essays on Feminism and Art* (London: Routledge, 2000), 1–45.

[12] See Ellen Levy, *Criminal Ingenuity: Moore, Cornell, Ashbery, and the Struggle Between the Arts* (Oxford: Oxford University Press, 2011).

[13] Susan Sontag, "Against Interpretation," in *Against Interpretation, and Other Essays* (New York: Farrar, Straus and Giroux, 1966), 3–14.

a shadow world of 'meanings.' It is to turn the world into *this* world."[14] One might read this accusation as, strangely, a testament to the success of what the midcentury art essays had in fact accomplished: They did, in effect, create a world bounded by the significance of interpretation. And yet it is important to note a certain ambiguity in Sontag's words, for it is not that Greenberg and company proclaimed the "meaning" of abstract art, or of this or that painting or sculpture. Likewise, it won't quite fit to say that they "interpreted" individual works of art, despite how much ink might have been spilled in that direction. Nonetheless, it is easy enough to acquiesce to Sontag's conclusion that the triumph of interpretation lay in its having erected the primacy of what she calls *"this* world" over the everyday world of sensuous life. We might say that Sontag's criticism is in fact a testament to the new authority and power established by the earlier generation of art writers. Sontag's objection to interpretation is not that it installs an agonistic struggle among competing meanings – even if those meanings are for her hollow, but rather that modern interpretation brings with it, unavoidably, an unearned and misplaced authoritativeness. And she identifies that authority with intellect.

Hardly an anti-intellectual, Sontag instead suggests that the interpretation of art and literature is a case of the misapplication of intellect. Intellect has no business in the experience of art. We might well see this as aligned with the midcentury position that taste is not a matter of intellect, and thus even highbrow art is not defined by its making some greater appeal to the mind than lesser forms of art. High art and culture aim instead at a more refined, and not more intellectual, taste, and thus authority. Sontag, Greenberg, and others concur in what might be called the essentially thoughtless character of the experience of art. The experience of art – echoing Kant here – is not a matter for cognition; taste becomes the premier capacity of the individual to outwit the limiting strictures of intellect, the confinement by means of concepts, and thinking's headlong rush to summary and conclusion. And thus taste – or more simply: one's responsiveness to art, even when abandoning intellect – cultivates itself as the most privileged locale of the individual, and especially her autonomy. Just here we might spy an unexpected affinity between Sontag and modernist abstraction, especially if we recall the latter's long-standing exclusion of figure and representation from genuinely forward-moving visual art. Figurative art provides grist for the mill of interpretation; representations are mere lures to beckon the interpreting intellect. It is as if

---

14 Sontag, "Against Interpretation," 7.

figurative art is akin to what is now known as clickbait, tempting morsels for the consumerist mind. And the intellect, with its penchant for interpretation, distracts from the crucial opportunity presented by modern art for the sake of the individual: to take up the challenge to struggle and realize oneself precisely in the absence of any interpretable clues, content, or meaning. (It is important to note that despite the affinity between Sontag and Kant in regard to the nonintellectual experience of art, Kant locates an alternative path to aesthetic experience rather far removed from Sontag's recommendation of an "erotics" of art.)

Origin Story

Installing Clement Greenberg at the pinnacle of midcentury American art writing is unavoidable. He rests atop that plinth on the basis of three quite solid reasons, the first of which is the role he played in championing the work of Jackson Pollock (1912–1956), and alongside him the movement whose most prominent exemplar Greenberg helped him become.[15] That Greenberg was not the sole instigator of the ascendency of what came to be called Abstract Expressionism is best evidenced by the fact that he preferred another name for that movement. Greenberg preferred the term Painterly Abstraction over Abstract Expressionism.[16] Still, it is no stretch to recognize that Greenberg's writings remain the most compelling account of the significance of abstract art in general. Finally, the indisputable evidence of Greenberg's centrality lies simply in the number of those who followed him, regardless how faithlessly, in his insights, analyses, and reconstructions of the sweep of modernist painting and sculpture.

I want to suggest that there is yet a further way in which Greenberg might best be understood as a public intellectual who cast himself, wittingly or not,

---

15 "Champion" is the word used most often to denote Greenberg's relationship to the art of Jackson Pollock. It rightly indicates the agonistic struggle that characterizes Greenberg's intellectual posture. See, for example: *Encyclopedia Britannica*, s.v. "Clement Greenberg," www.britannica.com/biography/Clement-Greenberg; Henry Adams, "Decoding Jackson Pollock," *Smithsonian Magazine* (November 2009), www.smithsonianmag.com/arts-culture/decoding-jackson-pollock-142492290/; or Adam Gopnik, "The Power Critic," *New Yorker* (8 March 1998), www.newyorker.com/magazine/1998/03/16/the-power-critic. In the same ballpark with championing is triumphalism, a notion used by some to indicate the supremacy of postwar American art. See Irving Sandler, *The Triumph of American Painting: A History of Abstract Expressionism* (New York: Harper and Row, 1970).

16 See Clement Greenberg, "'American-Type' Painting," in *The Collected Essays and Criticism*, vol. 3, *Affirmations and Refusals, 1950–1956*, ed. John O'Brian (Chicago: University of Chicago Press, 1986), 217–36.

as consummately American in how he fashioned himself a thinker and essayist on visual art. It might help to recall here the numerous attempts by Greenberg to define and declare what was particularly American, and hence superior, about the art that he argued was most advanced in Western culture. For example, in 1949, he would write in his column in the *Nation* that in America "our new painting and sculpture constitute the most original and vigorous art in the world today."[17] We might consider him the culmination of particularly American ideas, some of them about art, others about experience and self-fashioning. Greenberg, like many American intellectuals of his generation, shared the novel and influential position of John Dewey (1859–1952) regarding the democratization of taste.[18] Dewey's widely read *Art and Experience* (1934), while retaining the Enlightenment notion of the aesthetic as a special kind of experience, nonetheless valorized the availability of that experience within the course of everyday life, which means that Dewey thereby greatly diminished the importance of any refinements in taste for its successful occurrence.[19] For Greenberg, this came to mean that anyone, regardless and despite their educational attainment or social class, might fully participate in the aesthetic experiences occasioned by the objects of highbrow culture. This Deweyan understanding of the ready availability – and equality – of taste dovetailed nicely not only with Greenberg's early socialist politics but so too with his reading of Kant's aesthetics as prizing the unmediated, and thus unprejudiced, character of taste. If Greenberg's encounters with works of art bear the imprint of Deweyan pragmatism, that imprint in turn contains traces of Emerson's (1803–1882) notions of experience and self-reliance. The Emersonian man of action, the thinker who ought also be an active agent always in process, making and finding experience, is readily apparent in both how Greenberg approaches a work of art as well as in his account of what happens in the

---

17 Clement Greenberg, "The New York Market for American Art," in *The Collected Essays and Criticism*, vol. 2, *Arrogant Purpose, 1945–1949*, ed. John O'Brian (Chicago: University of Chicago Press, 1986), 319–22, 322.
18 John Dewey is often considered to be among the most influential public intellectuals in the first half of the twentieth century in the United States. *The Stanford Encyclopedia of Philosophy* entry describes him as "arguably the most prominent American intellectual" of that period. See David Hildebrand, "John Dewey," in *Stanford Encyclopedia of Philosophy*, ed. Edward N. Zalta (Winter 2021), https://plato.stanford.edu/entries/dewey/.
19 John Dewey, *Art and Experience* (New York: Capricorn Books, 1934).

encounter between painter and canvas, or, more tellingly, between artist and medium.[20]

If we look further back than Emerson, we might locate another vein in the American character that finds ample depth in the midcentury essays on art.[21] That vein in American identity is famously noted early in the nineteenth century by Alexis de Tocqueville (1805–1859) in his diagnosis of the premier value of individualism in the American character.[22] Following Tocqueville, and his insight into what might be called the paradox of equality in the American citizen, namely, that precisely because we Americans believe so fervently in equality we find ourselves saddled with an outsize ambition to prove ourselves first among equals. One hundred years later this reappears in the paradoxical elitism of the midcentury essay in regard to the equality of taste. That is, à la Tocqueville, the very condition that renders all our taste equal is also just that which provides the motivation to distinguish ourselves as individuals, to make our taste superior. Put differently: Our taste ought to at least make itself *equal* to superior things. This paradoxical dynamic of the midcentury essay applies as readily to aesthetic judgments as it does to what the stakes are for each person who paints a picture.[23]

To appreciate the novelty of the midcentury essay establishing the autonomy of the individual as well as of the art critic, recall the embedded tradition of those consummately literary figures such as Diderot (1713–1784) and Baudelaire (1821–1867) who became not only commentators on art but so too theoreticians of it, as if visual art were but a province of the literary mind. As Leo Steinberg notes, in "the mid-1950s, practicing art critics were mostly artists or men of letters."[24] In other words, it was still from within the

20 Still further, the so-called Happenings and Performance Art of the 1960s and '70s might be taken as rather literal interpretations of Greenberg, among others, having given priority to the interactions occasioned by the work of art, over the value of the static work itself.
21 What makes American life so well situated for the cultural "self-cure and self-correction" prompted by abstract art, and accompanied by its demand for a still greater disinterestedness, is precisely the postwar advance of American materialism: "There is no question but that our Western civilization, especially in its American variant, devotes more mental energy than any other to the production of material things and services; and that, more than any other, it puts stress on interested, purposeful activity in general." Clement Greenberg, "The Case for Abstract Art," in *The Collected Essays and Criticism*, vol. 4, *Modernism with a Vengeance, 1957–1969*, ed. John O'Brian (Chicago: University of Chicago Press, 1986), 75–84, 76.
22 Alexis de Tocqueville, *Democracy in America*, ed. Richard D. Heffner (New York: Signet Classics, 2001).
23 Important to recall here that Greenberg was himself for many years a painter.
24 Leo Steinberg, *Other Criteria; Confrontations with Twentieth-Century Art* (Oxford: Oxford University Press, 1972), vii.

province of literature, or as an artist oneself, that the warrant to write about art was acquired. In addition to the self-authorizing individual and her experience, we might also spy in the midcentury essays a still more virulent strain of individualism, a peculiarly American myth of "regeneration through violence," of the necessity of violence in service of the making and remaking of all things most American, and that holds especially for the individual self.[25] This also means that there is not only struggle, but adversarialism in the encounter between viewer and the work of visual art, and by extension in the midst of the variety of competing impulses within each individual.[26] The struggle and even combativeness that were constitutive of midcentury judgments of the value of particular works of visual art, not to mention the often deplored authoritativeness of the pronouncements of critics, are both key pieces of another strain of Americanness. Central to the American myth of generative violence is the image of the frontier, of a boundary that beckons not only with the challenge to be confronted, but so too with the promise of encountering the unknown, the foreign, the as yet unconquered.[27] This overdetermined American urge to overreach – to dominate – swells forward, hoisting the flag emblazoned with an image of new life, the complementary fantasy to that of the ease of leaving the old life behind. It was the art critic and essayist Harold Rosenberg who explicitly revivified the American ideology of self-making by mixing with it the midcentury fashion of European existentialism, and baptizing it with the consummately American name of "Action Painting."[28] Despite how easily some mocked Rosenberg's contention regarding the priority of the artist's active gesture in the picture, it nonetheless expressed a shared conceit regarding the tension between the static timelessness of painting and sculpture with the dynamic processual

---

25 See Richard Slotkin, *Regeneration through Violence: The Mythology of the American Frontier, 1600–1860* (Norman, OK: University of Oklahoma Press, 1973).
26 For a canny update on how the legacy of Abstract Expressionism continues to reverberate through the precincts of individualism, see the recent contribution by one of the most celebrated current abstract painters: Amy Sillman, "AbEx and Disco Balls: In Defense of Abstract Expressionism II," *Artforum* (Summer 2011): 321–25.
27 Greenberg early on links the violence in Pollock's art to a specifically American literary tradition where he likewise finds a call to violence arising from the unknown and foreign: "[T]he feeling it contains is perhaps even more radically American. Faulkner and Melville can be called in as witnesses to the nativeness of such violence, exasperation and stridency." Clement Greenberg, "The Present Prospects of American Painting and Sculpture," in *The Collected Essays and Criticism*, vol. 2, *Arrogant Purpose, 1945–1949*, ed. John O'Brian (Chicago: The University of Chicago Press, 1986), 160–69, 166.
28 Harold Rosenberg, "The American Action Painters," in *The Tradition of the New* (Chicago: University of Chicago Press, 1959), 23–39. Reprinted from *ARTnews*, December 1952.

unfolding of the active life.[29] We might graft the midcentury essay's theory of the purity and self-standing of a work of art to the notion of the individual who creates himself within and by means of the form of the essay.

By extension, then, it is as if each human life is akin to culture: Both are most alive when pragmatically addressing their own conditions of existence. Just as the boundaries of advanced art lie entirely within the confines of art-making itself, so too for the form of the essay. The frontier has migrated to the interior and its boundaries are to be policed by the authority of individual taste – whose exemplary figure is the self-authorizing critic of art, the essayist as mimetic twin to the maker of art. We might acknowledge how the mediumlessness of taste – a notion owed to Kant – the long-standing formulation of it as a certain *je ne sais quoi*, is constitutive of aesthetic judgment.[30] The very ungroundedness and unboundedness of taste and abstract art precisely provide the opportunity for the ongoing struggle toward ever more autonomy, both in the work of abstract visual art as well as in the viewer who beholds it and the essayist who enacts it. In aesthetic experience, it is just the peculiar combination of blankness and conviction together that provides the force as well as the empty ground from which the midcentury essay launches itself into an independent existence. The medium of essay writing is made into a prototype for what ought to take place in the medium of painting: the transcendence of the means in the achievement of an end.[31] And though historically it has long been maintained that there are no grounds on which to dispute taste, midcentury essays and reviews nonetheless demonstrate the personal and professional value of arguing for the legitimacy of one's individual taste, even while acknowledging that all such argumentation might only proceed ad hominem.

Still, the only way to move forward, to transcend the limits of whatever instruments we find in our hands, in either the project of the advancement of

29 In her review of *The Tradition of the New*, Mary McCarthy famously admonished Rosenberg's notion of action painting by writing, "You cannot hang an event on the wall, only a picture." See Harold Rosenberg's "Preface" to the 1960 edition of *The Tradition of the New* (New York: Horizon Press, 1960) for his thoughtful response to her. More damning perhaps were Roy Lichtenstein's 1965–66 series of screen-printed *Brushstroke* paintings. See Roy Lichenstein, *Brushstroke*, 1965, screenprint, Tate Gallery, London, www.tate.org.uk/art/artworks/lichtenstein-brushstroke-p07354.
30 The expression *je ne sais quoi*, used to denote an ungraspable feature of something attractive, first appears in English in the mid-seventeenth century. It prefigures well a key feature of the aesthetics of Kant and Hume, that beauty remains an uncognizable, inexplicable experience.
31 One of the richest philosophical accounts of the nature of aesthetic transcendence in contemporary art-making is to be found in Arthur C. Danto, *The Transfiguration of the Commonplace: A Philosophy of Art* (Cambridge, MA: Harvard University Press, 1983).

painting or that of the establishment of the legitimacy of individual taste, is via a reckoning with the history that delivers us to whatever present moment we find ourselves in. This constraint, or what can also be called a dialectic, according to which the new must be at once both continuous as well as discontinuous with the past, is at the heart of the midcentury essay's reconstruction of modernism. Though the status and nature of medium was the central concern of the midcentury essay, it was not wedded to any notion that proclaims the inherent value of one particular medium or another. It was acknowledged to be mostly a matter of historical accident that brought one medium or another into existence, let alone into prominence. What mattered instead would be to account for what unfolded within any particular medium after the historical accident of the establishment of a set of constraints as a *medium*. The active, ceaseless interrogation of a medium, the stripping away of all elements extraneous to it, is not in pursuit of any particular knowledge about the medium. A medium in fact holds no special knowledge for human beings. Medium is rather the ideal arena in which human struggle might be stripped of the distractions of content, of fighting merely for or against one thing or another. Medium is not an instrument to be used to accomplish or produce something but is rather itself an opportunity for self-interrogation, and only thereby the taking possession of self-making.

19
The Essay in American Music

KYLE GANN

"I don't think myself confined to any Rules of Composition laid down by any that went before me," thundered Boston patriot William Billings (1746–1800) in 1770, in the introduction to his *The New England Psalm-Singer*.[1] It was a declaration of musical independence, and it pointed to what would become the perennial problem of the American composer: that we had started with no national tradition of composed music. The French or German composer could merely absorb the style of his predecessors and move forward, but the American – if he wanted to consider himself American – had to start from scratch. Of course, many American composers imitated European models, but they were branded as epigones, considered inferior to the composers they copied from, and it was easy for orchestras to ignore as a whole an American repertoire that seemed to have nothing American about it.

That dilemma has driven American composers into a particular reliance on writing essays. More than their European counterparts, they felt a pressure to define and defend their achievements, urge listeners not to judge them by European standards, theorize about what would make music American, advocate for their inclusion in the repertoire, all while educating a public for whom cultivated music is not second nature. Though the musicians who settled our early musical centers were of English, Dutch, German, Italian, and other stock, it was considered by many natural, even imperative, that American music would find its own distinct path. Outlining that path required words.

---

1 William Billings, "To All Musical Practitioners," reprinted in *The American Composer Speaks*, ed. Gilbert Chase (Baton Rouge, LA: Louisiana State University Press, 1969), 29–31, 31.

Of course, not all creative musicians write prose; a relative few seemed to be called to do it on behalf of everyone else. In this chapter, American music's essays are divided into four categories, three of them historically determined. Early on, American composers wrote manifestos advocating for a music that would be uniquely and recognizably American. In the 1940s and '50s, American music was better established and beginning to spread via radio, but the audience was starting to drift away from classical music, so composers wrote to educate and explain their music to a larger public. Later, composers wrote to announce and justify new aesthetic positions. And throughout all these decades, some composers have written more to reflect on the nature of music and musical life in general.

The word *essay* is used here in its most colloquial sense, excluding reviews, memoirs, interviews, academic articles, and so on, though many a printed essay began life as a public lecture. The main essays of focus here are by well-known creative musicians. American music has been copiously written about in essays in periodicals such as the *Village Voice*, *Rolling Stone*, *Downbeat*, and other outlets, but to venture into the work of music critics and, later, bloggers, would require more than a book, let alone a chapter.

The Essay as Advocacy

The nineteenth-century struggle toward an identifiably American music was carried out via music reviews, pamphlets, letters to the editor, private letters, and prefaces to music collections, less in the calm of literary endeavor than in the heat of political argument. Anthony Philip Heinrich (1781–1861), William Henry Fry (1813–1864), and George Frederick Bristow (1825–1898) fought for their right to be American composers in a land whose cultured enclaves recognized only German and Italian music as worthwhile.[2] Innovations and deviations from European precedent were interpreted as signs of incompetence; as Henry Cowell (1897–1965) would write in 1955, "Transplanted to the United States, the rules of harmony and composition took on a doctrinaire authority that was the more dogmatic for being second-hand."[3]

The rising advocate of the early twentieth century was composer Arthur Farwell (1875–1952). Although he sometimes based pieces on songs he had transcribed at Native American powwows, he insisted that he did not see

---

2 Douglas W. Shadle, *Orchestrating the Nation* (Oxford: Oxford University Press, 2016), 88ff, 113.
3 Henry Cowell and Sydney Cowell, *Charles Ives and His Music* (Oxford: Oxford University Press, 1955), 8.

folklore as the only source for an American music: "A certain nationalism . . . we cannot avoid," he wrote in 1909. "It is not to be striven for in itself . . . It is not an end, but a quality, a by-product."[4] In 1908, writing for the *Atlantic*, he blamed classical music performing ensembles for the suppression of American composers:

> Society has been so long compelled to import musical art if it wished to have any, that it cannot believe that there is any other source of this art than Europe . . . The managers of musical enterprises care nothing for our national artistic development; their one concern is to keep secure the patronage of society.[5]

And in words that apply all too often to the classical music world today, he observed: "Society has always sanctioned the trivial American work as a foil to the serious European, but never the more significant American work for its own sake."[6]

Similarly, Farwell's ally Henry Gilbert (1868–1928) made the point even more sharply in his 1915 essay "The American Composer."[7] He points out that while we notice differences of atmosphere and emotional tone among the two repertoires of French and German music, an American repertoire capable of displaying identifiable national tendencies did not yet exist – largely because America was such a heterogeneous mixture of people from different parts of the globe. He then notes the wondrous rise of American orchestras, opera companies, and composition prizes, as well as a wealth of available music criticism in the newspapers, but notes that since the institutions are run by Europeans, and the criticism written by experts in European music, they invariably award the palm to the most European-sounding music, and thus retard rather than further the development of a home-grown American music. The charge has not entirely ceased to be relevant even today.

The most important writer for the perceived establishment of an American music was indisputably composer Henry Cowell, partly because rather than simply argue for an American music, he was in a position to champion composers he saw as innovatively American. He was not the most eloquent

---

4 Arthur Farwell, "National Work vs. Nationalism," reprinted in Arthur Farwell, *"Wanderjahre of a Revolutionist" and Other Essays on American Music* (Rochester, NY: University of Rochester Press, 1995), 200.
5 Arthur Farwell, "Society and American Music," reprinted in Farwell, *"Wanderjahre,"* 194.
6 Farwell, "Society and American Music," 196.
7 Henry Gilbert. "The American Composer," reprinted in Chase, *American Composer Speaks*, 95–104.

writer – one rarely feels that the brilliance of his insight is wedded to the words in which he expressed it – but he understood the music he wrote about and was factually accurate. In particular, he initiated and edited a 1933 book of essays titled *American Composers on American Music*, in which not only he but other American composers described the music of their colleagues. For instance, Charles Seeger wrote the essay on his protégés Carl Ruggles (1876–1971) and Ruth Crawford (1901–1953), Nicolas Slonimsky (1894–1995) wrote about Walter Piston (1894–1976), and eight of the essays were by Cowell himself, on Roy Harris (1898–1979), Edgard Varèse (1883–1965), John J. Becker (1886–1961), Henry Brant (1913–2008), and others. "The reason knowledge concerning American composers is confused," Cowell explains in his opening keynote, "is that it comes exclusively from professional critics who are not themselves composers."[8] He starts with a ten-part classification of American composers, in categories such as those who developed Indigenous materials, foreign-born composers who found a new style in America, Americans influenced by "Teutonic" tendencies. composers who follow French neoclassic tendencies (the style to which Cowell was manifestly least sympathetic). and so on.

The book did not shy away from negative assessments. Theodore Chanler's sour article on Copland relates that composer's habit of repeated chords to a kind of "poverty of harmonic resource,"[9] and Cowell himself points to "unbelievable commonplaces of harmony"[10] in Harris's music. Yet in the Harris article, Cowell admits quite perceptively that

> [m]odernism and originality have been so associated with harmony that if one performs for a sophisticated audience a work with new harmonies it is taken for granted as modern; but if one performs for them a work with old types of harmony but with real innovations in rhythm, form, or even melody, it will be called old-fashioned, and the newer elements will pass unnoticed.[11]

The book ends with several brief, more general statements on American musical subjects, including George Gershwin's "The Relation of Jazz to American Music," in which Gershwin discusses jazz as America's folk music, and William Grant Still's "An Afro-American Composer's Point of

---

8 Henry Cowell, ed., *American Composers on American Music* (New York: Ungar, 1962), iii.
9 Theodore Chanler, "Aaron Copland," in Cowell, *American Composers*, 49–56, 52.
10 Henry Cowell, "Roy Harris," in Cowell, *American Composers*, 64–69, 64.
11 Cowell, "Roy Harris," 65.

View." The latter states that the music of Black Americans "possesses exoticism without straining for strangeness."[12]

Having grown up in multicultural San Francisco, Cowell was uniquely sensitive to the wide diversity of national and vernacular musical traditions that contributed to the American melting pot. Thus in "Charles Ives," his essay on the then little-known Charles Ives, Cowell places Ives in a context of American vernacular musics, and insightfully details how he was willing to bend and complicate his notation to match the kinds of nuance common to amateur marching bands, folk fiddlers, and the like. Cowell also ventured abroad, and his most exuberant essays stem from his 1928 tour of Russia, where he documented musical scientists working with eighth-tones, the subharmonic series, and attempts to analyze in detail recordings of non-Western musics. In "Conservative Music in Radical Russia" (*New Republic*, 1929), "Adventures in Soviet Russia" (*San Franciscan*, 1931), and "Playing Concerts in Moscow" (*Musical Courier*, 1931), he wrote vividly about the paradox that the Russian officials condemned anything but the most bourgeois neoromantic music as being out of line with communist ideals, while the music professors and students were fascinated with anything radical and innovative. In "Playing Concerts in Moscow" he wrote:

> The psychology of these Russian students is particularly interesting, on account of being so very different from that of our audiences here. If an encore is demanded of an artist here, and he is forced to play a piece over, it is a sure sign that the auditors were pleased with the music and understood it. Among the Russian students the pieces which were at once understood were taken for granted, while the more abstruse compositions were the ones they wished to hear over the most times; they were unwilling to let a piece go by without understanding it as nearly as they could by repeated hearings.[13]

The content and style of Cowell's essays changed markedly following the tragic event of his life: his incarceration in San Quentin on a sexual morals charge. Thanks to supporting materials from a wide range of artists (including Ives), he was paroled in June 1940 and eventually pardoned by the governor at the end of 1942, allowing him to resume a normal life.[14] No longer the fiery revolutionary, he became New York correspondent for the

---

12 William Grant Still, "An Afro-American Composer's Point of View," in Cowell, *American Composers*, 182–83, 182.

13 Henry Cowell, "Playing Concerts in Moscow," *Musical Courier* (21 May 1931): 6, 30–31, 6, 30; reprinted in *Essential Cowell: Selected Writings on Music by Henry Cowell*, ed. Dick Higgins (Kingston, NY: McPherson, 2001), 41.

14 Joel Sachs, *Henry Cowell: A Man Made of Music* (Oxford: Oxford University Press, 2012), 353, 386.

Musical Quarterly, and benevolently reviewed American works that, in his youth, he might have disdained as conservatively Europhile. Yet he was ever open-minded, and in 1951 wrote a review of a concert of John Cage, Morton Feldman, Pierre Boulez, and Christian Wolff, which was the first major notice given in the United States of the postwar avant-garde and with musical examples.

As well as a composer and writer, Cowell was also the leading theorist of American music. The "Rhythm" section of his book *New Musical Resources* (1930) outlined a theory, still considered radical until fairly recently, that "harmonies of rhythms" could be written and played analogously to harmonies of pitches by having various tempos, or unsynchronized patterns of various beats, played at the same time in arithmetical relationships that the ear could learn to perceive as logical and satisfying. Drawn out at length, his rhythmic ideas influenced generations of American composers, notably Harry Partch (1901–1974) and Conlon Nancarrow (1912–1997; Nancarrow spent his entire career exploring rhythmic complexity from Cowell's templates), and even European avant-gardists such as Karlheinz Stockhausen (1928–2007) and Mauricio Kagel (1931–2008). In a host of underground ways, he was the font from whom a distinctively American music flowed.

The Essay as Education

The post–World War II period into the 1960s was the golden age for the public music essay. Aaron Copland (1900–1990) and his protégé Leonard Bernstein (1918–1990) took on the education of the public as personal crusades; Virgil Thomson (1896–1989) joined the prestigious *New York Herald Tribune* as music critic from 1940 to 1954; and thriving music magazines allowed Edward "Duke" Ellington (1899–1974) to become a frequent spokesperson for the jazz and swing world. Copland took up his pen reluctantly, calling himself "a kind of salesman for contemporary music"[15]; Bernstein's theatrical flair made him a star in television, film, and the lecture circuit as well as on the concert stage; and Thomson's crystalline prose set a high standard for twentieth-century musical criticism. None of them needed any longer to advocate for American music, which was now well established (and in Ellington's case, quite popular), and that Bernstein and Thomson wrote brilliantly about European music as well increased their authority.

---

15 Aaron Copland and Vivian Perlis, *Copland 1900 through 1942* (New York: St. Martins/Marek, 1984), 175.

Copland presented himself in his writings as a spokesperson, the professional composer willing to answer any and all questions from the lay public. His essay collections and Charles Eliot Norton lectures make simple though authoritative reading; for instance, his second Harvard lecture, "The Sonorous Image," traces an insider's view of the history of orchestration from someone who had been involved with its evolution since his student years. Probably Copland's most influential and widely quoted essay, though, was his 1939 autobiographical statement "Composer from Brooklyn." Not only does it provide a vivid and concise picture of the development of American music between 1920 and 1939, but Copland writes the words that have best encapsulated American composers' turn toward simplicity during the Depression:

> During these years I began to feel an increasing dissatisfaction with the relations of the music-loving public and the living composer. The old "special" public of the modern-music concerts had fallen away, and the conventional concert public continued apathetic or indifferent to anything but the established classics. It seemed to me that we composers were in danger of working in a vacuum. Moreover, an entirely new public for music had grown up around the radio and phonograph. It made no sense to ignore them and continue writing as if they did not exist. I felt that it was worth the effort to see if I couldn't say what I had to say in the simplest possible terms.[16]

If Copland is the professional instructing the layman, Bernstein – in his essays, his televised *Young People's Concerts*, and his own Harvard lectures – is, more entertainingly, the music lover sharing the secrets he's collected in his celebrated travels with fellow enthusiasts whom he *knows* will be similarly enchanted by them. His printed essays, dotted with keyboard-reduced score excerpts, conjure up the teacher able to illustrate any music that comes to his mind on the piano. Most of his talks apostrophize the European masterpieces, but he discusses ragtime and Copland with the same sense of awe he does Brahms, and he can praise Gershwin's *Rhapsody* while still being frank about its weakness: "*The Rhapsody in Blue* is so sectional and choppy that you can cut it, interchange the sections, leave out half of it . . . play it on the piano, or organ, or banjo, or kazoo; but whatever you do, it's still *The Rhapsody in Blue*."[17]

---

16 Aaron Copland, "Composer from Brooklyn: An Autobiographical Sketch," in *The New Music, 1900–1960* (New York: W. W. Norton, 1968), 151–68, 158–59.
17 Leonard Bernstein, "Jazz in Serious Music," in *The Infinite Variety of Music* (New York: Simon and Schuster, 1966), 49–64, 64.

Bernstein's 1973–74 Harvard lectures, The Unanswered Question (title taken from Charles Ives's composition of the same name),[18] are based on his amateur enthusiasm for linguist Noam Chomsky's then-current theories about a universal grammar, to which he feels certain he can draw parallels to musical structure and meaning. Doubt has been cast on whether Bernstein's central thesis was correct, but even so these are easily the most educative and enduring Norton Lectures by a composer. Bernstein's applications of poetic terms such as zeugma, chiasmus, antithesis, and auxesis to musical devices are thought-provoking, and his conclusion that the irony of "objective expression" in Stravinsky can be a more profound mode than outright sincerity is an insight that transcends national or even temporal boundaries.[19]

Thomson's considerable virtues are more purely literary: Etching his ideas with the precision of a master glass-cutter, he demonstrated that objectivity is not the absence of conflicts of interest, but a quality of writing. "Nouns are names and can be libelous," he wrote of his critical method; "the verbs, though sometimes picturesque . . . tend toward alleging motivations. It is the specific adjectives that really describe and that do so neither in sorrow nor in anger."[20] One could quote from almost anywhere in his oeuvre, but I'll demonstrate with his 1945 description of Copland's *Appalachian Spring*: "The style is pastoral, the tone, as is appropriate to the pastoral style, blithe and beatific. The material is folklore, some of it vocal, some violinistic. The harmonic treatment . . . evokes our sparse and dissonant rural tradition rather than the thick suavities of our urban manner."[21]

The bulk of Thomson's writing consists of reviews, but few music critics have so blurred the distinction between review and essay by intertwining general aesthetic principles with the event at hand. Writing about music of all countries and all periods, Thomson didn't specifically advocate for American music, yet he was generous in word count with his American colleagues. His educational mode was not as musician to layman, but as professional critic defining the responsibilities of the position, to clarify for the rest of society how things are supposed to work. He wrote with considerable authority of how the various segments of the music world interrelated. For instance, in

---

18 Later published as Leonard Bernstein, *The Unanswered Question* (Cambridge, MA: Harvard University Press, 1976).
19 Bernstein, *Unanswered Question*, 376.
20 Virgil Thomson, "The Paper," reprinted in *Thomson: The State of Music and Other Writings*, ed. Tim Page (New York: Library of America, 2016), 493–506, 498.
21 Virgil Thomson, "Two Ballets," reprinted in *Thomson: Music Chronicles 1940–1954*, ed. Tim Page (New York: Library of America, 2016), 448–50, 448.

1950, he attributed the suppression of new and adventurous music to, basically, capitalism:

> Beneath all of management's dealings with the intellectual group lie two assumptions. One is that intellectuals like novelty and modernity. The other is that the mass public dislikes both. I think the first is true. I doubt the second. I am more inclined to believe, from long acquaintance with all sorts of musical publics, that it is management which dislikes the novelty and everything else that interferes with standardization. I suspect that management's design is toward conditioning the mass public to believe that it dislikes novelty. Some success has already been achieved in this direction.[22]

In one of his best-known essays from *The State of Music*, "Why Composers Write How," Thomson provides a psychologically astute (if perhaps historically limited) schema of how a composer's style is invariably, even if subconsciously, influenced by his primary income source. Composers who are executants (performers) become overly concerned about writing in a way that privileges the performers' pleasure in playing. A composer who teaches full time "must always have an answer for everything. If he doesn't he loses prestige. He must make up a story about music and stick to it. Nothing is more sterilizing."[23] As for the composer who works as a critic:

> It teaches him about audiences. Nobody who has ever tried to explain in writing why some piece got a cold reception that he thought merited better, or why some musical marshmallow wowed them all, has ever failed to rise from his desk a wiser man. And the composer who has written criticism with some regularity – who has faced frequently the deplorable reality that a desired audience-effect cannot be produced by wishful thinking – ... cannot help learning a good deal that is practical to know about clarity, coherence, and emphasis.[24]

Though the essay is not about American music per se, it draws a deeply insightful portrait of the American composing world as a whole. "Why Composers Write How" has remained a favorite article among a wide range of composers.

Jazz musicians were in a separate category when it came to education, for they had to battle against ignorant stereotypes and overcome a certain public distrust, despite having a built-in fan base. Not many important jazz creators

---

22 Virgil Thomson, "The Intellectual Audience (I)" (15 January 1950), reprinted in Page, *Thomson: Music Chronicles*, 746–48, 748.
23 Virgil Thomson, "Why Composers Write How," reprinted in Page, *Thomson: The State of Music*, 57–61, 77.
24 Thomson, "Why Composers Write," 80.

resorted frequently to public prose, but "Duke" Ellington wrote many articles, and became jazz's most important spokesperson in print. He wrote as if explaining jazz to the white (and classical) music world, and if his views diverged at all from those of his jazz colleagues, the reader finds little hint of the fact; he spoke for his art form and for his race. Tiptoeing around categories, he called his own music swing rather than jazz, but in 1944 wrote, in agreement with Gershwin, "because of all the confusion about what swing is and isn't, I prefer to say that I am carrying on the tradition of American folk music, particularly the folk music of my people."[25]

In gruff and occasionally folksy prose, Ellington attested time and again to jazz's serious aspirations: "Because I think that the music of my race is something which is going to live, something which posterity will honour in a higher sense than merely that of the music of the ballroom today, I put my best musical thoughts forward into my tunes ... "[26] He acknowledges the tensions in jazz between commercial viability and artist vision: "[W]hen the artistic point of view gains commercial standing, artistry itself bows out, leaving inspiration to die a slow death."[27] When critics started comparing Ellington's music to Ravel and Stravinsky, he replied, "Even though I appreciate the compliment, no amount of self-examination seems to bear out the contention ... To attempt to elevate the status of the jazz musician by forcing the level of his best work into comparisons with classical music is to deny him his rightful share of originality."[28] In the end, however, he shied away from genre distinctions. "There are simply two kinds of music, good music and the other kind ... the only yardstick by which the result should be judged is simply that of how it sounds. If it sounds good it is successful; if it doesn't it has failed."[29]

Another outlet jazz musicians had available could be found in their record liner notes, and Charles Mingus (1922–1979) (who occasionally wrote for *Downbeat* magazine as well) included an essay with his groundbreaking album *Let My Children Hear Music*, titled "What Is a Jazz Composer?," that

---

25 Duke Ellington, "Swing Is My Beat," reprinted in *The Duke Ellington Reader*, ed. Mark Tucker (Oxford: Oxford University Press, 1993), 248–50, 249.
26 Duke Ellington, "Ellington's First Article: The Duke Steps Out," reprinted in Tucker, *Duke Ellington Reader*, 46–50, 49.
27 Duke Ellington, "Duke Says Swing Is Stagnant" (1939), reprinted as "Ellington in *Down Beat*: On Swing and Its Critics," in Tucker, *Duke Ellington Reader*, 132–40, 134.
28 Duke Ellington, "Certainly It's Music!" (1944), reprinted in Tucker, *Duke Ellington Reader*, 246–48, 246–47.
29 Duke Ellington, "Where Is Jazz Going?" (1962), reprinted in Tucker, *Duke Ellington Reader*, 324–26, 326.

became as well known as the album. In it he dissected the world of different approaches to jazz, praised what he found good, and lamented the bad:

> I always wanted to be a spontaneous composer ... I admire anyone who can come up with something original. But not originality alone, because there can be originality in stupidity, with no musical description of any emotion or any beauty the man has seen, or any kind of life he has lived. For instance, a man says he played with feeling. Now he can play with feeling and have no melodic concept at all. That's often what happens in jazz: I have found very little value left after the average guy takes his first eight bars – not to mention two or three choruses, because then it just becomes repetition, riffs and patterns, instead of spontaneous creativity. I could never get Bird to play over two choruses. Now, kids play fifty thousand if you let them. Who is that good?[30]

The poet and playwright Langston Hughes's (1901–1967) 1956 essay "Jazz as Communication" was an important contribution to discussions of the functions of jazz music. Hughes sees jazz as an ocean into which currents flow and out of which come many forms of expression, his own poetry included. He denies any difference in inspiration level between the southern levees and cotton fields and Tin Pan Alley, and – with a poet's finesse for simile – affirms that rock music, nascent at the time, gathers together the "gut-bucket heartache" of Blind Lemon Jefferson and Leadbelly, the drums of Congo Square, the jubilees and gospel songs: "Rock and Roll puts them all together and makes a music so basic it's like the meat cleaver the butcher uses – before the cook uses the knife – before you use the sterling silver at the table on the meat that by then has been rolled up into a commercial filet mignon."[31] For Hughes, jazz was a spirit not limited to music.

Of course, among noncomposing literary thinkers, the jazz essay has been a lively art. Amiri Baraka (LeRoi Jones) (1934–2014) wrote brilliantly about the jazz world from the inside, outlining its history and geography in detail as it was happening. Political writer and public intellectual Cornel West (1953–) keeps jazz and blues as metaphors for struggle and negotiation central to his philosophy. Among practitioner-essayists, jazz pianist Ethan Iverson (1973–) writes a well-researched, more retrospective blog called *Do the Math*,[32] offering insights into not only the jazz greats, but lesser-known American classical composers as well.

---

30 Charles Mingus, "What Is a Jazz Composer?," liner notes to *Let My Children Hear Music*, Columbia C 31039.
31 Langston Hughes, "Jazz as Communication," Poetry Foundation, www.poetryfoundation.org/articles/69394/jazz-as-communication.
32 Ethan Iverson, *Do the Math*, Ethan Iverson's Home Page, https://ethaniverson.com/.

The Essay as Self-Justification

The aesthetic manifesto increased in importance in the 1960s, when composers began splintering away from the modernist mainstream. Perhaps an earlier example, though, is *Essays before a Sonata* by Charles Ives (1874–1954), the book he wrote in 1919 to accompany his self-publication of the *Concord Sonata* (more formally Piano Sonata no. 2 [*Concord, Mass., 1840–60*]). Unlike his contemporaries, he is suspicious of conscious attempts to sound American: "[T]here is good authority that an African soul under an X-ray looks identically like an American soul. There is a futility in selecting a certain type to represent a 'whole' ... ."[33] The *Essays* are a monument to self-effacement: Ives barely mentions his sonata, never talks about his music, but instead weaves his aesthetic speculations about program music and musical greatness around essays on his understanding of Ralph Waldo Emerson (1803–1882), Nathaniel Hawthorne (1804–1864), Louisa May Alcott (1832–1888) and her father, Bronson Alcott (1799–1888), and Henry David Thoreau (1817–1862), the writers whose work the sonata purports to depict in tones. Expanding on an essay he had written as a Yale student, and quoting Emerson frequently, Ives characterizes what he sees as the heterogeneous complexity of Emerson's prose in terms that really apply somewhat more aptly to his own music:

> Carlyle told Emerson that some of his paragraphs didn't cohere. Emerson wrote by sentences or phrases, rather than by logical sequence. His underlying plan of work seems based on the large unity of a series of particular aspects of a subject, rather than on the continuity of its expression. As thoughts surge to his mind, he fills the heavens with them, crowds them in, if necessary, but seldom arranges them along the ground first.[34]

Ives's essays on Hawthorne and the Alcotts essays are brief; his longer essay on Thoreau offers a valiant defense of that writer against the negative judgments that had made his posthumous reputation slow to catch on, as well as connecting the music programmatically to Thoreau's wanderings around Walden Pond.

It is the epilogue, though, that raises the *Essays* above the standard explication of a composer's preoccupations. Here Ives sorts out for himself the preconditions and qualities that make the music of Bach and Beethoven seem eternally relevant, while composers like Rossini and Wagner go out of

---

33 Charles Ives, *Essays before a Sonata* (New York: W.W. Norton, 1961), 79.
34 Ives, *Essays before a Sonata*, 22.

fashion after a while: the difference, in other words, between immortal music and fashionable music. Echoing John Ruskin's categories of imagination and fancy,[35] he draws an opposition between substance, which springs from a deeply felt moral sense, and manner, which has to do with superficial pleasures and tricks of media. In several places, however, Ives seems to imply that what substance may be contained in music has less to do with what the music communicates to the listener than with what the composer felt while writing it. "Whether [a composer] be accepted or rejected, whether his music is always played, or never played ... it is true or false by his own measure."[36] For Ives, the intensity of the composer's experience in the moment of creation is the important thing, and that intensity will eventually translate to the listener whether the latter consciously understands the work or not. This stirs him to radical conclusions: "That music must be heard, is not essential – what it sounds like may not be what it is." And, "My God! what has sound got to do with music?"[37] There has been a regrettable recent tendency in Ives scholarship to downplay the *Essays*, but insofar as Ives's music does seem to rise above history as not simply a product of its time, his account of the creative process deserves serious scrutiny.

Interestingly, the closest parallel to Ives's *Essays* in one respect are John Cage's (1912–1992) first two books, *Silence* (1961) and *A Year from Monday* (1967). Unlike Ives, Cage is happy to focus on his own music, but both spend much space talking about sympathetic writers and ideas that, if you contemplate them, may make the author's music more sympathetic. However, Cage is also the anti-Ives, for if Ives thinks sound has nothing to do with music, Cage, in his post-1950 period, decided that music was sound and nothing else. By that year he had come in contact with Zen, and it made him a far more prolific writer. In his books, he says little about his famous silent piece *4'33"*, the prepared piano, or percussion (for which latter two media most of his music had been written) but very much about serialism – the new complex style of European music – and magnetic recording tape, the sudden commercial availability of which was changing the way humans related to sound.

The best, most broadly philosophical, and Zen-inspired essays in the book are the "Lecture on Nothing," and "Lecture on Something" (both first published in 1959 though apparently delivered sometime around 1950), "45' for a Speaker" (1954), and "Where Are We Going and What Are We Doing?" (1961). All four pieces are laid out on the page with spaces left for silence and

---

35 See Kyle Gann, *Charles Ives's Concord: Essays after a Sonata* (Urbana, IL: University of Illinois Press, 2017), 276–77.
36 Ives, *Essays before a Sonata*, 81.   37 Ives, *Essays before a Sonata*, 84.

all are intended to be read aloud as performances. Yet they are readable as essays, and the gaps in midsentence, discouraging breezy reading, lead one to pause and take the words in more than one possible sense. "I have nothing to say," Cage famously states, "and I am saying it, and that is poetry as I need it."[38] Over and over he makes the point elliptically (because it can hardly be made directly) that listening can be like Zen meditation, that we can be attentive to sounds without caring what their connections, intentions, or underlying meanings are. "Our poetry now is the realization that we possess nothing. Anything therefore is a delight (since we no longer possess it) and thus need not fear its loss."[39]

The popularity of *Silence* was a watershed in Cage's career; after years of poverty and struggling, he became famous. No other book by a composer has had so much impact outside the field of music, for it proved an inspiration for artists, dancers, poets, and the 1960s counterculture in general. This is despite the pontifical nature of some of the essays of the late 1950s having to do with "experimental music," in which Cage tried to place his ideas on an objective basis in competition with the European serialists with their math-based twelve-tone manipulations. Nevertheless, Cage's genial good humor, played up even more in the sequel *A Year from Monday*, attracted a following and won him a (not completely on-point) reputation as an artist who had stripped away all prohibitions and mandates.

Cage's experimental rival Harry Partch (1901–1974) wrote mostly essays that were practically motivated, necessary to explain to a world accustomed to the standard twelve pitches per octave why he had gone to the trouble of devising a forty-three-tone microtonal scale and inventing his own fantastical instruments to play it on. But his freestanding essays are glorious attacks on the conformity that he found throughout the classical music world. "Thus have twelve equal tones become Mosaic law," he thunders, "and the *Well-Tempered Clavichord* the Arc of the Covenant."[40] Music, Partch argued, is a physical art, yet our young musicians are trained to deny the evidence of their senses and focus instead on hallowed abstractions – to avoid acoustic investigations, or manners of expression (by which he means vernacular and non-Western singing styles, among other things) outside the realm of petrified tradition. "[N]othing could be more futile," Partch the patriarch intones,

---

38 John Cage, *Silence* (Middletown, CT: Wesleyan University Press, 2011), 109.
39 Cage, *Silence*, 110.
40 Harry Partch, "Bach and Temperament" (1941), reprinted in Harry Partch, *Bitter Music: Collected Journals, Essays, Introductions, and Librettos*, ed. Thomas McGeary (Urbana, IL: University of Illinois Press, 1991), 162–64, 163.

"(or downright idiotic) than to *express* this age. The prime obligation of the artist is to transcend his age, therefore to show it in terms of the eternal mysteries. What this age needs more than anything is an effective antidote."[41]

In the 1960s, composer George Rochberg (1918–2005) wrote manifestos of a different sort. He had been America's best twelve-tone composer (as attested by his Second Symphony and *Serenata d'Estate*), but upon the death of his son, a poet, from cancer in 1964, he made a bold apostasy from twelve-tone music on the grounds that it was too expressively limited. In a 1964 article entitled "In Search of Music," he wrote, "Something strange has happened to music ... And this is the strange thing that has happened: by applying the scientific attitude and ideology to the art of music, the composer has transformed music into a unique, if curious, form of applied science."[42] Five years later, in "No Center," he ramped up the rhetoric: "Why do you want to write music nobody can love? Do you hate yourself? Or do you hate them? ... Why do you want to write music that no one can remember? Do you hate music?"[43] And he summed up an entire, antimodernist manifesto in two sentences: "We are not Slaves of History. We can choose and create our own time."[44] Rochberg's subsequent symphonies and string quartets abandoned modernism to indulge at times in polystylistic and quotational collage, earning him much vituperative condemnation from his academic colleagues – until, one by one, many of them succumbed to the same trend.

Pauline Oliveros (1932–2016) also rebelled against the scientification of music, from a different, feminist viewpoint. In "The Contribution of Women Composers" (1984), she outlined two modes of creativity: "(1) active, purposive creativity, resulting from cognitive thought, deliberate acting upon or willful shaping of materials, and (2) receptive creativity, during which the artist is like a channel through which material flows and seems to shape itself."[45] Although she finds evidence for both kinds in quotations from Mozart and Beethoven, she contends that our society valorizes the active kind, associated with a masculine archetype, at the expense of the more feminine passive: "Western society seems to value most highly, not only its results, but the active analytical mode itself. In education, the development of the analytical mode is fostered almost exclusively, often to the detriment of

---

41 Harry Partch, "The Ancient Magic" (1959), reprinted in Partch, *Bitter Music*, 181–87, 185.
42 George Rochberg, *The Aesthetics of Survival* (Ann Arbor, MI: University of Michigan Press, 1984), 151.
43 Rochberg, *Aesthetics of Survival*, 158–59.   44 Rochberg, *Aesthetics of Survival*, 160.
45 Pauline Oliveros, *Software for People* (Baltimore: Smith Publications, 1984), 132.

men and women who would develop more readily using the intuitive mode."[46]

Oliveros goes on to link analytical creativity to serialist (twelve-tone) music of the postwar years, calling this music one-sided, though conceding that entirely intuitive works might be one-sided as well:

> Traditionally, men are encouraged in self-determining, purposive activity, while women are encouraged to be receptive and dependent ... Culturally, woman is the symbolic representation of intuition as man is the symbolic representation of analytical activity. It is my hypothesis that the emergence of women in male dominated fields means the move toward an inclusion of intuition as a complementary mode of activity.[47]

Oliveros's articles tend toward describing new tendencies of music in general, though with emphasis on sonic meditation, which was the focus of her music throughout her life, and in which she includes many characteristics of minimalism. Her most influential points, though, came from her questioning of the male framing of aesthetic principles.

Another woman composer of the next generation, Beth Anderson (1950–), has been widely identified with a 1980 essay called "Beauty Is Revolution." Similarly rejecting the mandates of serialist music and its mandarins, she wrote: "To make something beautiful is revolutionary (not low class, not easy, not a sign of low intelligence)." Anderson continues:

> Beauty got a bad name some time after the first world war. Musical craft (ear training, orchestration, the real reasons for voice leading, etc.) was hardly even taught in the 1960's and 70's, probably because of the revolt against a tradition that could allow the war in Vietnam to happen. Beauty seemed a low value in relation to life itself. But life goes on and ugliness and lack of skills and nihilism are no excuse. The destruction of the world would not improve social conditions, and making painful, ugly music will not redistribute the wealth.[48]

The essays that most specifically justified the new style of minimalism were those of Steve Reich (1936–). The bulk of Reich's public writing has been explanations of his own works – program notes, essentially – but his small 1974 book *Writings about Music* set out to explain the attractions of the new style. In the essay "Music as Gradual Process," he clarifies, "I do not mean the process of composition, but rather pieces of music that are, literally,

---

46 Oliveros, *Software for People*, 134.   47 Oliveros, *Software for People*, 135–36.
48 Beth Anderson, "Beauty Is Revelation," *New Music Box*, https://nmbx.newmusicusa.org/beauty-is-revolution/.

processes."[49] He distinguishes his own gradual processes from both the composing processes of John Cage and twelve-tone technique, since those latter processes are not audible to the listener in the resulting music. A gradual process, he writes, invites close, sustained attention on the listener's part, and stretches their hearing by letting them perceive minute details that might ordinarily be missed. He details his studies in Ghanaian drumming and Indonesian gamelan, which did more to confirm than inspire his intuitions. And toward the end, he places a sentence that shines out from the 1970s like a bright ray of light that has been all too quickly obscured: "Obviously music should put all within listening range into a state of ecstasy."[50]

The Essay as Personal Reflection

If the vast majority of writing composers write to gain some practical end – advocacy, publicity, understanding – there have always been a handful who wrote for the love of writing, who took pleasure in editing their musical musings and opinions for their own entertainment and that of others. One of the most suave and prolific of these is Ned Rorem (1923–2022), the openings of whose essays make it impossible to resist reading further:

> What, you may well ask, is an art song? I myself had composed dozens before ever hearing the term, and suddenly realized – like the Molière character who learns he's been speaking prose all his life – how clever I'd been. Yet then as now I mistrusted the term, found it pompous, never used it.[51]

> Asked how fast a song of his should go, Fauré replied, "When the singer is bad – very fast." The quip sounds glib. But remember, composers do have fewer preconceptions about their songs than about their sonatas.[52]

Along the way he might educate, he might explicate his personal aesthetic, but even a Rorem review is never just a review but a weaving together of cultural references, poignant memories, pointed insights. He is the master of the *aperçu*, the *bon mot*. His frequent themes are his preference for French music over German, his love of the *Lied* or *mélodie* versus his indifference to opera, his dislike for such cold authoritarianism as Pierre Boulez's, his

---

49 Steve Reich, *Writings about Music* (Halifax, Nova Scotia: Press of the Nova Scotia College of Art and Design, 1974), 9.
50 Reich, *Writings about Music*, 44.
51 Ned Rorem, "The American Art Song," in *Setting the Tone: Essays and a Diary* (New York: Limelight Editions, 1984), 225–40, 225.
52 Ned Rorem, "Fauré's Songs," in *Setting the Tone*, 247–50, 247.

antagonism toward clichés of classical music dogma. His insights are small but sharp, in keeping with his affection for the modest statement. He observes, for example, that "[a] nation's music resembles its language in all respects, and since French is the only European tongue with no rhythm (no tonic accent), any metricalization of a French phrase in music can be construed as correct."[53] Perhaps no large ideas flowed into American music from his pen, but he is always entertaining, and his eloquence is an exemplary model.

For many, the most profound essayist in American music is Morton Feldman (1926–1987). Some of his essays explain particular works, others are colorful descriptions of the painting and poetry milieu of 1950s Manhattan, but the most memorable are psychologically nuanced musings on the nature of composing itself. He frequently compares the act of composing to that of painting – "In painting if you hesitate, you become immortal. In music if you hesitate, you are lost"[54] – and defines the freedom of the artist in often paradoxical pronouncements. For him, artists who cultivate a method based on rational principles can only create dead art, because real art requires a leap of faith:

> [T]he real tradition of twentieth-century America, a tradition evolving from the empiricism of Ives, Varèse, and Cage, has been passed over as "iconoclastic" – another word for unprofessional. In music, when you do something new, something original, you're an amateur. Your imitators – *these* are the professionals.
>
> It is these imitators who are interested not in what the artist did, but the means he used to do it ... The imitator is the greatest enemy of originality. The "freedom" of the artist is boring to him, because in freedom he cannot reenact the *role* of the artist.[55]

Feldman's unique rhetorical style blends a quasi-Talmudic authority with deeply personal insights. For example, he pronounces: "For art to succeed, its creator must fail."[56] Or he declares: "[A] modest statement can be totally original, where the 'grand scale' is, more often than not, merely eclectic."[57] Of the academic composers who made twelve-tone music a university lingua franca in the 1970s, he writes, "These men are their own audience. They are

---

53 Ned Rorem, "Notes on a French Bias," in *Setting, the Tone*, 273–77, 275.
54 Morton Feldman, "Some Elementary Questions," in *Give My Regards to Eighth Street* (Cambridge, MA: Exact Change, 2000), 63–66, 65.
55 Morton Feldman, "The Anxiety of Art," in *Give My Regards*, 21–32, 23.
56 Feldman, "Anxiety of Art," 27.
57 Morton Feldman, "Neither/Nor," in *Give My Regards*, 80–82, 81.

their own fame. Yet they have created a climate that has brought the musical activity of an entire nation down to a college level."[58] And of his close friend John Cage, he writes, "What [Cage] has to teach is that just as there is no way to arrive at art, there is also no way not to."[59]

Among the subsequent generation of composers, computer-music composer Laurie Spiegel (1945–) has written essays on the nature of electronic music that are (unusually for the field) readable and thought-provoking for the general public. Her aesthetic has centered around the computer as a new kind of folk instrument, and thus in "Music: Who Makes It? Who Just Takes It?," she writes: "Once upon a time almost everyone made music. Households were self-sufficient, making their own food and clothing too. People were generalists, doing their personal best at each thing. People sang or played at whatever their level of skill, adapting a constantly evolving grassroots repertoire to their expressive needs and personal techniques."[60] In "Should Music-Making Be Reserved for an Elite?," she rejects the "socio-musical model in which music is assumed to consist of individual complete unique works actively created and performed by a small number of elite experts for a large passive listening audience," and extols the fact that the creation of music is no longer restricted to a select few:

> [A] greatly expanded variety of technologies for sound capture, manipulation, and dissemination are cheaply available to all. This is not new. It is a return. Long before concert halls, famous virtuosi, classic instrumental scores, publishers, recordings, and broadcasts – globally and for our entire human past – music was almost certainly something that most people did actively. In many cultures it still is ... [61]

Spiegel's "Thoughts on Microsoft's Algorithmic Composition Patent" would seem to address a very contemporary technical issue, but she opens with an eighteenth-century musing:

> To hypothesize an instance, what if someone had patented the replaying of a musical theme at a time delay to itself early in the era of Bach? By what scenario might the result still give us the most important imitative contrapuntal repertoire of all time, the canons, fugues, et cetera that inspired so

---

58 Morton Feldman, "Boola Boola," in *Give My Regards*, 45–49, 48.
59 Feldman, "Anxiety of Art," 29.
60 Laurie Spiegel, "Music: Who Makes It? Who Just Takes It?," *Electronic Musician* 8, no. 1 (January 1992): 114.
61 Laurie Spiegel, "Should Music-Making Be Reserved for an Elite?," *Computer Music Journal* 22, no. 1 (Spring 1998): 6–7, 7, http://retiary.org/ls/writings/cmj_not_for_a n_elite.html.

many lives and so much later work? If that patent had existed in Bach's time, could that music still have been written?[62]

As Spiegel continues, she explores all the pros and cons of patents and commercialization with a truly philosophical spirit of questioning, admitting multiple and contradictory perspectives. Although her essays have appeared mostly in specialist journals, they were at one point collected on her website,[63] and constitute an ambitious set of guidelines for considering where electronic music and its makers fit in contemporary culture.

John Luther Adams (1953–) is the first composer of the late twentieth century to publish collections of essays. Many of these are memoirs of his life in Alaska, first as an environmental activist and then as a composer, but some of the best draw metaphors between music as a practice and his life in the wilderness. "Just as global climate change threatens the health of the biosphere," he writes, "commercial monoculture threatens the integrity of the cultural sphere, from Greenland to Australia, from Papua New Guinea to Siberia."[64] He draws folk wisdom from his nonmusician neighbors, and details how, as he was building his cabin northwest of Fairbanks, he found his musical principles echoed in the work of carpenters, plumbers, electricians, and other tradespeople: "The best of these workers don't force things. They don't call attention to themselves. They simply reveal the essence of the design and the character of their materials." And in words that he felt applied to music composition, a carpenter (and poet) he worked with told him: "Wholeness is better than perfection."[65]

The trajectory of this survey of writings, from Revolutionary Boston to twenty-first-century Zen Fairbanks, is an instructive one. We can trace in words the unique dilemma our early composers tackled: how to create a national music without models, or at least by carefully negotiating such models as are available. Two and a half centuries later, the dialogue follows a smooth arc as our composers gradually prove themselves and come to take the national identity of their music as assumed. Today, American music as a repertoire is well established in tones as well as words: a secure starting point that composers are free to transcend as they ponder, rather than their mere right to exist, the eternal mysteries.

---

62 Laurie Spiegel, "Thoughts on Microsoft's Algorithmic Composition Patent," *Computer Music Journal* 22, no. 4 (Winter 1998): 4–5.
63 Laurie Spiegel, *Retiary Ramblings*, http://retiary.org/ls/writings.html.
64 John Luther Adams, "Global Warming and Art," in *Winter Music: Composing the North* (Middletown, CT: Wesleyan University Press, 2004), 177–83, 181.
65 Adams, "Global Warming," 171.

PART III

★

POSTWAR ESSAYS AND ESSAYISM (1945–2000)

20

The Essay and the Twentieth-Century Literary Magazine

ELENI THEODOROPOULOS

The first American literary magazine originated in 1741. But across the following century the literary magazine in America would still face the enormous task of negotiating the terms of a national identity, before it could acquire a consistent readership or editorial program. The literary magazine would not acquire the character, following, or influence of its modern model until the late nineteenth and early twentieth centuries, with the appearance of the "little magazine." Motivated by the contrarian personalities of their founding editors against commercial tastes, these small-circulation periodicals prioritized aesthetic experimentation and quickly established themselves as an avant-garde force in the arts. Without the burden of gross fiscal responsibility or the pressure of abiding by conservative in-house standards, magazine editors let themselves be driven by passion and idealism, earning their distinction as literary tastemakers by keeping a perpetual "open-mindedness," as Ezra Pound (1885–1972) said, "toward the possible and the plausible."[1] A famous editor himself, Pound viewed "small magazines" as catalysts for aesthetic change, going so far as to claim that "[t]he history of contemporary letters has, to a very manifest extent, been written in such magazines."[2] In other words, the little magazine, posted on the outskirts of publishing, came to act as the editorial and aesthetic umpire of American literature. Nevertheless, its impact, scope, and quality would fluctuate throughout the twentieth century. Literary magazines would become institutionalized and relinquish their financial and intellectual independence. The revolutionary ones would fold while the conservative ones would live long, healthy lives. Its avant-garde status, once represented

---

1 Ezra Pound, "Small Magazines," *English Journal* 19, no.9 (1930): 689–704, 704.
2 Pound, "Small Magazines," 702.

by a collectively upheld editorial persona, would become overshadowed by individual cults of personality around popular writers. Magazines' social programs would become watered down, but instead, writers would make themselves into social actors. Print forms would give way to digital media. What magazines would lose in materiality, they would gain in generic hybridity and global access. In championing the art and social causes of its time, the literary magazine has preserved a significant record of the past, and so tracing its history will also reveal pivotal moments of cultural change.

Since the protean nature of the literary magazine precludes it from being historicized according to just one predominant feature, and its innumerable iterations resist a single evolutionary narrative, this chapter will present the American literary magazine's milestones across the twentieth century and highlight its crossings with major developments in the literary essay. Three sections follow. The first section charts the gradual formation of the magazine model throughout the eighteenth and nineteenth centuries before moving on to highlight the magazine's golden age at the turn of the twentieth century with the emergence of the little magazine, when literary modernism, the Harlem Renaissance, and the style of free verse arguably began. The second section follows the changes experienced by the literary magazine during a period of radical transformation when, institutionally, it became increasingly integrated into university campuses, and culturally, it renegotiated its political role in the wake of New Journalism's social-realist experiments in long-form narrative nonfiction. Joan Didion (1934–2021), here, will serve as an exemplary figure, given that her keen critical eye and singular essayistic style represent for many the golden standard of periodical feature writing. Lastly, the third section addresses New Journalism's legacy by contextualizing it against an increasingly hybrid era both in writing – in terms of blurred generic boundaries – *and* media, as evidenced by the literary magazine's entrance into a digital age.

The American Literary Magazine before 1940

Only 15 magazines existed before the American Revolution, 70 by 1800, and 700 came into circulation after the Civil War, though growth here did not necessarily denote prosperity since "magazines [then] had been scraggly sheets, usually living short unhappy lives," most of them folding within a year.[3] According to Frank Mott, the great historian of the American periodical, the race to print the first magazine occurred in Philadelphia between Benjamin Franklin (1706–90)

---

3 George H. Douglas, *The Smart Magazines* (Hamden, CT: Archon Books, 1991), 12.

and Andrew Bradford (1686–1742), with Bradford making off with Franklin's idea and editor to publish the *American Magazine* (1741) just three days ahead of Franklin's publication of the *General Magazine* (1741).[4] This secured Philadelphia its status as "the birthplace of magazines,"[5] even if the city actually tied with Boston as a publishing center.[6] New York City's destiny as a publishing hub would not manifest until after the 1900s.

Half of the century's periodicals arrived after the American Revolution. They aspired to promote a more appealing image and to encourage original contributions that would separate American interests from British colonial influence. Readership moved beyond a tight-knit, educated elite of lawyers, ministers, and politicians, among them Thomas Paine (1737–1809), Noah Webster (1758–1843), and Isaiah Thomas (1749–1831). Regular columns written in the style of "Mr. Spectator" by supreme English essayist Joseph Addison (1672–1719) drew in a steady readership, especially in Boston, where the genre of the periodical essay became a staple. American copycats abounded. Especially Addisonian, for instance, was Mather Byles's (1706–1788) "Proteus Echo" persona, an old bachelor who issued moralistic reflections about his studies and foreign travels. A slight American departure from Addison's apolitical ironist was Benjamin Franklin's "Mrs. Silence Dogood," a widow who, contrary to the suggestiveness of her penned name, dared not hold her tongue where infringements of personal liberty or "arbitrary Government"[7] were concerned. Despite great strides foreshadowing what the magazine might accomplish, deficient production methods, low readership, and short life spans should have very well dissuaded new ventures, but, in the words of Noah Webster, "The expectation of failure is connected with the very name of a Magazine."[8] This dogged spirit paid off in the nineteenth century when the magazine experienced two golden ages. Golden not for its earnings but for the "variety, exuberance, and abundance" of its magazines, the first golden age took place roughly between 1800 and 1860, a period during which *Graham's Magazine* (1840–58) proved an indispensable predecessor to modern magazine standards. Its founder and editor, George Graham

---

4 Frank Luther Mott, *A History of American Magazines*, vol. 1, *1741–1850* (Cambridge, MA: Harvard University Press, 1957), 24.
5 John William Tebbel, *The American Magazine: A Compact History* (New York: Hawthorn Books, 1969), 8.
6 Mott, *History of American Magazines*, 31.
7 Benjamin Franklin, *The Writings of Benjamin Franklin*, vol. 2, *1722–1750*, ed. Albert Henry Smith (New York: Macmillan, 1905), 7.
8 Noah Webster, cited in Dorothy A. Dondore, *Mississippi Valley Historical Review* 17, no. 4 (1931): 617–18, 618.

(1813–1894), embraced advertising, restricted reprintings by instituting copyrights, and incentivized writers to contribute to his publication by paying them more and featuring their names on the cover.

Writers' impact increased accordingly. Harriet Beecher Stowe (1811–1896), frequent magazine contributor (e.g., to *Godey's*), and an editor herself, enhanced antislavery talks in the years leading up to the Civil War by serializing *Uncle Tom's Cabin* (1851–52), albeit in a newspaper. Washington Irving saw the essay through from its "genteel" to its nineteenth-century "familiar" phase – going from writing the periodical-essay series *The Letters of Jonathan Oldstyle, Gent.*, to satirizing the form with his brother William (1766–1821) and James Kirke Paulding (1778–1860) in their periodical *Salmagundi* (1807–1808). Taking after British masters Charles Lamb (1775–1834) and William Hazlitt (1778–1830), Irving's familiar essay replaced moral didacticism with the intimate first-person narrator; more importantly, Irving cast the essay in more colloquial American language and explored subjects specific to the culture of the United States, making him for some the first American essayist.

During its second golden age, the magazine made itself into an American enterprise. In the aftermath of the Civil War, postal rates for media-class mail substantially decreased, print technologies advanced, and society's habits and class structure changed. Urbanization gave rise to a leisure class, which rivaled the elite in purchasing power and cosmopolitan tastes, as shown by the number of mass-circulation general-interest magazines flourishing, including the *Ladies' Home Journal* (1883–2016), the *Saturday Evening Post* (1821–), *McClure's* (1893–1929), *Cosmopolitan* (1886–), and *Collier's* (1888–1957). These made good on advertising's glamor and flashiness, unlike the first golden age's highbrow periodicals, represented by the *Atlantic* (1857–) and *Harper's Monthly* (1850–), which clung to haut-monde pretensions. For example, the *Ladies' Home Journal* reached a circulation of 700,000 at ten cents an issue by 1893. Publishers spared little expense to put out and fund their own magazines, as in the case of *Lippincott's* (1868–1915) or *Scribner's* (1887–1939); in one instance, *Scribner's* allotted thousands of dollars to the photograph travel series called "The Great South," while later, as *Century Magazine*, it ran an extensive series on the Civil War written by generals and Mark Twain,[9] which *Scribner's* turned into a best-selling book, *Battles and Leaders of the Civil War*.[10]

---

9 An aside: Twain shined in the *Galaxy's* "Memoranda," a sharp satire of Americans' racial and class biases, in the humor tradition of *Puck* and *Judge*, which foregrounded the lasting twentieth-century editorial style of so-called smart magazines.
10 Tebbel, *American Magazine*, 128.

Most formidable in the literary magazine's history proved the 1890s, when catchy, targeted advertising, sharp business acumen, and rampant if shoddy commercialism ushered in new castes of literary writers and editors with big personalities. One of the more somber, politically inclined was S. S. McClure (1857–1949), whose titular magazine is credited with having started muckraking journalism. Of the more stylish and eccentric was the *Smart Set* (1900–30), progenitor of the "smart magazine," whose middlebrow taste drew the newly leisured, well-to-do (but hardly affluent) upper-middle class who loved to indulge in travel adventures and gossip implicating "men-about-town." Some of the more literary little magazines were sometimes called "bibelots" after their French models;[11] these consisted of small-circulation periodicals dedicated to literary works, criticism, and aesthetic ideas most often created by writers for writers.

In publishing's increasingly commercializing and homogenizing environment, the little magazine manifested itself as a counterexample, a revolutionary force. The discipline-shaping book written by Frederick J. Hoffman, Charles Albert Allen, and Carolyn F. Ulrich, *The Little Magazine: A History and Bibliography* (1946), defined the little magazine as a literary, noncommercial, experimental kind of periodical devoted to "conscientious revolt against the guardians of public taste."[12] Over time, the little magazine would rightfully earn its place as the advance guard of the literary world. For one, its track record for discovering writers who would later become canonical, such as William Faulkner (1897–1962), Ernest Hemingway (1899–1961), and Jean Toomer (1894–1967), made it an invaluable risk-taker among publishing's generally conservative big players. For another, what it lacked in resources – editors usually funded their issues out of pocket, or out of a friend's pocket – it made up for in taste, having nurtured many an aesthetic movement from the grassroots. Big publishers might have had capital and control of the market, but little magazines had the nerve to champion novelty at its earliest, rawest stage. They were the literary tastemakers always on the lookout for the next big talent, captains of the literary avant-garde who jostled the publishing world out of stasis.

---

11 For an extended study of the influence of bibelots on American modernism, see Brad Evans, *Ephemeral Bibelots: How an International Fad Buried American Modernism* (Baltimore, MD: Johns Hopkins University Press, 2019).

12 Frederick J. Hoffman, Charles Albert Allen, and Carolyn F. Ulrich, *The Little Magazine: A History and a Bibliography* (Princeton, NJ: Princeton University Press, 1946), 4.

According to Hoffman, as well as Ezra Pound's survey of "small magazines,"[13] the first little magazine was Harriet Monroe's Chicago-born *Poetry* (1912–) – not because none had preceded it; a notable few had, including Henry Clapp's *Saturday Press* (1858–66), or in the 1890s, the Chicago *Chap Book*, *Lark*, *M'lle New York*, and the early installments of the *Dial*. In terms of historical significance, however, timing mattered less than influence, because even though *Poetry* had not been the first, its arrival heralded a little-magazine "renaissance."[14] Soon enough, its company grew and the inaugural twentieth-century set of little magazines came to encompass the *Masses* (1911), *Blast* (1914), the *Little Review* (1914), the *Midland* (1915), the *Glebe* (1913–14), and *Others* (1915–19). To better grasp the little magazines' diversity and range as they multiplied by the hundreds, Hoffman, Allen, and Ulrich grouped them as experimental, regional, leftist, poetic, eclectic, or critical, acknowledging frequent overlap between categories. Today, largely due to the digital humanities, and fueled by ventures like the Modernist Studies Project, the little magazine has made a comeback in the academy, giving rise to the study of periodicals not "merely as containers of discrete bits of information" but as "autonomous objects of study."[15] New debates have consequently arisen, targeting Hoffman, Allen, and Ulrich's definition and dating of the little magazine;[16] modernism's narrow definition, which excludes late nineteenth-century and Harlem Renaissance magazines and authors;[17] and the little magazine's relation to the umbrella category of "literary magazine,"[18] post-1990s digital-only magazines, and reproductions of defunct "digittle magazines."[19]

But in principle, historically, one thing remained the same across the most successful little magazines. This was the communication of their programs

---

13 See Pound, "Small Magazines."   14 Hoffman, Allen, and Ulrich, *Little Magazine*, 7.
15 Sean Latham and Robert Scholes, "The Rise of Periodical Studies," *PMLA* 121, no.2 (March 2006): 517–18.
16 See, for example, Kirsten MacLeod, who turns her attention to the 1880s and '90s for the intersectional emergence of the little magazine and modernism, in "The Fine Art of Cheap Print: Turn-of-the-Century American Little Magazines," in *Transatlantic Print Culture, 1880–1940: Emerging Media, Emerging Modernisms*, ed. Ann L. Ardis and Patrick Collier (New York: Palgrave Macmillan, 2008), 182–98; and Paul Bixler, who asks why the history of little magazines shouldn't begin with the leftist magazine the *Masses*, created in 1911. Paul Bixler, "Little Magazine, What Now?," *Antioch Review* 50, no. 1/2 (Winter–Spring 1992): 75–88.
17 See, for example, Adrienne Johnson Gosselin, "Beyond the Harlem Renaissance: The Case for Black Modernist Writers," *Modern Language Studies* 26, no. 4 (1996): 37–45.
18 Donal Harris, "Chapter 249: Literary Magazines," in *The Encyclopedia of Contemporary American Fiction 1980–2020*, ed. Patrick O'Donnell, Stephen J. Burn, and Lesley Larkin (Hoboken, NJ: John Wiley and Sons, 2022), 1–8.
19 Eric Bulson, *Little Magazine, World Form* (New York: Columbia University Press, 2017), 268.

(or manifestos) in a carefully crafted editorial voice whose tone tended toward the iconoclastic, offbeat, and idealistic. For scholars, personality would ultimately become the chief marker of the little magazine genre – a way to articulate its mission and set aesthetic standards – which would lead historian John Tebbel to claim, "The history of little magazines is essentially a history of personality, whether of the editors or contributors."[20] Editors developed their magazine's persona as an act of individuation, attempting to attract readers the way one does friends.[21] While the myth of the great artist had him working (and suffering) alone, small magazines, often self-funded passion projects, were always the fruit of relationships, sprouting invariably from either friendships or feuds (or sometimes, friendships-turned-feuds). *Poetry*, coedited in its formative years by Harriet Monroe (1860–1936) and Alice Corbin Henderson (1881–1949), and Margaret C. Anderson (1886–1973) and Jane Heap's (1883–1964) the *Little Review* (1914–29) exemplify two such cases.

In the twentieth century's first decade, when American magazines gradually broke with muckraking journalism and focused instead on Europe's aesthetic movements, a true vanguard was rising in *Poetry*. Monroe conceived of the monthly as a "home" to poetic experimentation and its practitioners; gradually, it would be credited with no less than the formation of modernism, the spread of vers libre and imagism (rivaled only by the *Globe*). Not only did *Poetry* catalyze the development of American modern poetry, but the collaborative spirit of its team of women challenged the individualism so rampant in both art and culture. Monroe elevated women's voices, discovered unknown talents like Wallace Stevens (1879–1955), and navigated "big men," "the egos and ambitions of Chicago's culture-conscious business class."[22] She butted heads with Pound, *Poetry*'s foreign correspondent from 1912 to 1917, often, famously, and to her detriment, with him painting her as "forbidding" and intimidating.[23] Unfazed by social hierarchies, she reserved

---

20 Tebbel, *American Magazine*, 215.
21 Ned Stuckey-French allied such an editorial inclination with Warren Susman's (1927–1985) historical claim that America's progression from the nineteenth to the twentieth century reflected a "shift from a culture of character to one of personality," moving from "self-control, duty, and restraint" to "self-expression and the cultivation of a personality designed to make friends." Ned Stuckey-French, *The American Essay in the American Century* (Columbia, MO: University of Missouri Press, 2011), 11.
22 Liesl Olson, "100 Years of Poetry: 'In the Middle of Major Men,'" *Poetry Foundation* (16 October 2012), www.poetryfoundation.org/articles/69867/100-years-of-poetry-in-the-middle-of-major-men.
23 Jayne E. Marek, *Women Editing Modernism: "Little" Magazines and Literary History* (Lexington, KY: University Press of Kentucky, 1995), 27.

her energy for defending aesthetic freedom with *Poetry*'s staple open-door policy, which promised to publish "the best English verse ... regardless of where, by whom, or under what theory of art it is written."[24] Monroe was not alone in this effort. As coeditor, Henderson pushed for "middle-western regionalism"[25] – including Native American and Hispanic American oral histories and native songs, to which she attributed the formation of American poetry.[26] This inclination resulted, partly, from the fact that regional magazines, invested in a tactile realism via representation of the quotidian, were developing the form of the modern American short story, most notably in the *Midland*, *Southwest Review* (1924–?), the *Prairie Schooner* (1927–?), the *New Mexico Quarterly Review* (1931–?), the *Frontier* (1920–39), and in more eclectic magazines like *Story* (1931–?), and University of Illinois' *Accent* (1940–?), one of the first to publish Flannery O'Connor (1925–1964), William Gass (1924–2017), and Grace Paley (1922–2007).

But *Poetry* had its share of competitors, too. Among its poetic contemporaries were Nashville's *Fugitive* (1922–25), *Measure* (1921–2?), African American *Palms* (1923–40), and notably, *Others* (1915–19), which helped establish the careers of modernist titans like William Carlos Williams (1883–1963) and Marianne Moore (1887–1972). It also contended with multigenre experimental journals like New Orleans' the *Double Dealer*, reputed for discovering both Hemingway and Faulkner; *Secession* (1922–24), which brought the famous American expatriate experience of the 1920s and '30s (especially of Paris) to home soil; the Harlem Renaissance's most politically radical journal, the *Messenger* (1917–28); and the notable *Dial*, begun as a Transcendentalist journal (1840–44) publishing Ralph Waldo Emerson (1803–1882), Henry David Thoreau (1817–1862), and Margaret Fuller (1810–1850) and later transformed into a modernist hub after being the first to publish T. S. Eliot's (1888–1965) *The Waste Land* (1922). Last but not least, influential in developing modernism's talent, and openly antagonistic to *Poetry*'s tastes, was the *Little Review*, a journal Pound thought to have accomplished more in its first two years than *Dial* did in ten.[27]

Anderson and Heap made *Little Review* into an arts and culture phenomenon. For one, they proved peerless arbiters of literary merit, serializing

24 Harriet Monroe, "The Open Door," *Poetry: A Magazine of Verse* 1, no.2 (November 1912), Poetry Foundation, www.poetryfoundation.org/poetrymagazine/articles/58891/the-open-door.
25 Marek, *Women Editing Modernism*, 27.
26 Marek, however, qualifies this by saying that this arguably led to white co-optation of primitive art. Marek, *Women Editing Modernism*, 27.
27 Pound, "Small Magazines," 697.

European modernists like James Joyce (1882–1941) and Dorothy Richardson (1873–1957) alongside American modernists Gertrude Stein (1874–1946) and Pound, with Heap representing one of the first American art proponents of Dadaism, Constructivism, and Surrealism – even before Paris's first Surrealist exhibition (1925). They kept their standards unapologetically high, to the extent that, once, on 16 September 1916, they left sixteen pages in their issue blank on account of having found no submission worthwhile. For another, they prized dialogic exchange and often provoked engagement. Namely, Heap and Anderson did not hide behind their magazine's persona; they were confrontational editors who relished every opportunity to arouse heated discussion, often starting fires themselves simply by juxtaposing sources (e.g., reviews and articles) and leaning into controversy, as shown by their insistence on publishing *Ulysses* despite its court-ordered censorship. In Jayne Marek's view, and in proper modernist fashion, the *Little Review's* unusual, mercurial tactics of critical exchange approximated Cubist thought, in that Heap and Anderson aimed to undermine objective authority by presenting a dizzying multiplicity of voices and viewpoints.[28] To this end, they also established a forum for dialogue between editor and reader called "Reader Critic," an innovative column in which the magazine's unflinching, blasé persona responded to a selection of readers' comments. Though it did not claim itself to be a critical review in the style of *Hound and Horn* (1927–34), the *Dial*, *Symposium* (1930–33), and *S4 N* (1919–25), *Little Review* wanted to produce criticism "from the point of view of the artist," "a blend of philosophy and poetry."[29] In this spirit, they would publish conversations between themselves and their contributors on the nature and value of art, producing what appears to be a predecessor of the modern craft interview, in which writers reflect on their writing life and their relationship to their art.

In general, as Churchill and McKible have argued, "Little magazines acted as open, heterogeneous social settings in which writers of various races, nationalities, and classes read and responded to each other's work,"[30] making it the case that as the century wore on, magazines' social programs became just as revolutionary as their artistic manifestos. For *Little Review*, that meant supporting feminist, semianarchist, and openly queer texts, including Stein's "Bundles for Them," Bryher's (1894–1983) "Chance Encounter," and Heap's "I Cannot Sleep" in an effort to supplant gender norms by configuring a "vision of social

28 Marek, *Women Editing Modernism*, 63.
29 Margaret Anderson, "Announcement," *Little Review* 1, no.1 (March 1914): 2.
30 Suzanne W. Churchill and Adam McKible, "Little Magazines and Modernism: An Introduction," *American Periodicals* 15, no. 1 (2005): 1–5, 2.

reform articulated through the interactions of artist, critic, and audience."[31] Separately, the progenitors of the Harlem Renaissance built their social programs around Black aesthetics, culture, and art, none of which were otherwise represented in mainstream periodicals, an exclusion that made it seem as if the Harlem Renaissance "happened outside 'the magazines'" as compared to modernism, which happened "in the magazines."[32] Some Renaissance writers became known in the 1920s and '30s for publishing in journals focused solely on Black communities and Black aesthetics, like the NAACP's the *Crisis* (1910–); *Opportunity* (1923–49); *Fire!!* (1926) cofounded by Zora Neale Hurston (1891–1960) and Gwendolyn Bennett (1902–81); and Chicago-based *Negro Story* (1944–53). Others made their names by publishing in typically white magazines whose broader, interracial audiences sometimes offered them more freedom to experiment. Jean Toomer's *Cane* (1932), for example, appeared in the European modernist magazine *Broom* (1921–24), while H. L. Mencken's (1880–1956) *American Mercury* (1924–81) published James Weldon Johnson's (1871–1938) "The Dilemma of the Negro Author" and repeatedly sought contributions from George Schuyler (1895–1977), Countee Cullen (1903–46), and W. E. B. Du Bois (1868–1963). In the volatile postwar years of the Depression, leftist magazines, too, gathered speed, influenced by the Bolshevik Revolution and Marxist thought. These made their reputations in various politicized ways: by allegedly catalyzing the (literary) proletarian movement, as in the case of the *Masses* or *New Masses*; publishing major cultural critics, as did the *Liberator* (1918–24) and *Partisan Review* (1934–2003); or pronouncing little-known aesthetic movements, as did Wyndham Lewis (1882–1957) and Pound's *Blast* (1914–15) with Vorticism. No matter the aesthetic, formal, or personal variations the little magazine took – or how long a given little magazine lasted, for that matter – it came to represent a bulwark of the arts, avidly protective of public discourse, self-expression, and estranged young talent.

New Journalism and the American Magazine between 1940 and 1970

As the magazine continued to soar past its early-century prime with a diversification of funding and publishing venues, incentives for emerging writers increased. Pioneering academic programs like Middlebury's Bread

---

31 Marek, *Women Editing Modernism*, 75.
32 John K. Young, "The Renaissance Happened in (Some of) the Magazines," in *Editing the Harlem Renaissance*, ed. Joshua M. Murray and Ross K. Tangedal (Clemson, SC: Clemson University Press, 2021), 15–45, 15.

Loaf Writers' Conference (1926–), the University of Iowa's model Writers' Workshop (1936–) and Nobel Prize–nominated International Writing Program (1967–), along with artist residencies like Yaddo (1926–), professionalized the writer's career path by institutionalizing a model of apprenticeship whereby the writer progressed through successive stages of mentorship. Through education, writers became part of a literary community, learned to demystify the act of writing, and gained access to a lateral pipeline to publication. The idea was that writers who were trained and credentialed could more easily catch the eye of literary magazines; in turn, their inaugural publications would attract attention from literary scouts, agents, or editors, at which point the circle of magazine-to-press publication would be complete. To compete with the demand by and for emerging writers, big presses resolved to put out magazines themselves, lest they appear antiquated, as in the case of the New American Library's founding of *New World Writing* (1951–64) and *American Review* (1967–77). Magazine purists, however, responded with insistence that the magazine should remain independent from mainstream publishing; so, to resist acquisition, the small press, soon to become publishing's underdog, was invented. The most emblematic became New Directions Press (1936–), an experimental press founded by James Laughlin (1914–1997), a mentee of Pound's, offering a self-publishing business model later to be followed by the successful little magazine *Kayak* (1964–84) that ran imagistic, "dreamlike"[33] poetry, and was put out singlehandedly by "the pre-eminent maverick independent magazine publisher"[34] and poet George Hitchcock (1914–2010).

Institutional support for the humanities bolstered writerly activity around the nation and on campuses. Magazines were tendered sponsorships from newly established organizations such as the National Endowment for the Arts (1965–), the Community of Literary Magazines and Presses (CLMP, 1967–), and the since defunct Committee of Small Magazines, Editors, and Publishers of the 1970s, making magazine publications all the more prestigious for writers. The college campus became the nucleus of modern literary criticism at midcentury, following the example of John Crowe Ransom (1888–1974), whose book of essays *The New Criticism* (1941) ultimately put a name to the impartial, scientific practice of literary interpretation. Among the most prominent academically housed periodicals were several journals that astoundingly continue to this day: the *Kenyon Review* (1939–); the *Virginia*

---

33 William Grimes, "George Hitchcock, Kayak Magazine Founder, Dies at 96," *New York Times* (4 September 2010), www.nytimes.com/2010/09/04/arts/04hitchcock.html.
34 Grimes, "George Hitchcock," n.p.

Quarterly Review (1925–); the *Southern Review* (1935–); and the record-breaking *Sewanee Review* (1892–) as the oldest continuously published American quarterly, and the *Yale Review* (1892–) as the oldest literary magazine. Beyond the academy, critical journals like the *Hudson Review* (1948–) and *Symposium* privileged aesthetics and form over context, purporting methods of close reading, which confined meaning to what was found strictly within the text. The 1950s and '60s also saw an uptick in specialized magazines, motivated by the increased professionalization of the humanities, which drew as a result smaller and smaller crowds around niche topics. At the same time, eyes turned to the literature of Asia, Africa, and Latin America in an effort to systemically unsettle the Western canon and the chronic whiteness of academic institutions. New types of magazines turned up, some devoted almost exclusively to translations,[35] like the *Journal of Translations* and the poetry journal *Mundus Artium* (1967–?), while others, like *American Scholar* (1932) and *Carleton Miscellany* (1960–80), dedicated entire issues to printing talks from symposia.

In hindsight, for magazine historian Charles Allen, the American magazine's greatest contribution between 1945 and 1970 was its active role in "social protest."[36] This meant that many magazines opposed American politics by leaning left, though their socialist commitments differed in degree between periodicals and according to their place of publication. For example, a regional magazine like the *Midland* left its greatest legacy by tending to the American social realist short story, a short narrative form that sought "to impress the reader with prevailing political and economic conditions; to arouse him to indignant action against these conditions."[37] Among milestone leftist magazines were Missouri's proletarian *Anvil* (1933–35) and, more importantly, New York City's Marxist little magazine the *Partisan Review* (which afterwards moved to two different college campuses, first to Rutgers and then to Boston University). In its midcentury heyday, the *Partisan Review* published the powerhouse group of women intellectuals Hannah Arendt (1906–1975), Susan Sontag (1933–2004), Mary McCarthy (1912–1989), and Elizabeth Hardwick (1916–2007), but gradually became more conservative, as evidenced by its covert funding from the Central Intelligence Agency (CIA) during the Cold War. At the time, publications experienced a number of free speech violations, as they were censored from publishing literary works

---

35 Dennis A. Hill, "Little Magazines and Translations," *Serials Review* 6, no.1 (1980): 35–37.
36 Charles Allen, "The Little Magazine in America: 1945–70," *American Libraries* 3, no. 9 (1972): 964–71, 970.
37 Hoffman, Allen, and Ulrich, *Little Magazine*, 158.

deemed obscene, as happened with the *Chicago Review*'s (1946–) publication of Allen Ginsberg (1926–1997) and other Beats in 1959. As Karl Shapiro (1913–2000), former editor of *Poetry* (1950–56) and *Prairie Schooner* (1956–66), stated, censorship did not stop – or start, for that matter – at the academy's aesthetic tastes but could "go as high as the governors of states and involve the suppression of historical fact itself."[38] In view of the suppression of the freedom of speech and historical facts – a political climate familiar to us in the so-called posttruth era of politics – the magazine's resistance could prove formidable. For Lawrence Grauman Jr., former editor of the *Antioch Review*, a plurality of radical magazines imagined the best precaution against spreading censorship because of how they could "mirror, refute, propose countercultures, provide ways of perceiving reality, and generally force a culture to consult itself."[39]

As far as journalists were concerned, no one forced America to confront itself more than Joan Didion (1934–2021). Having reported extensively on the losses incurred during the tectonic social shifts of the 1960s, Didion has been critically received as "perhaps our keenest observer of the chaos,"[40] the voice of her generation, a journalist and personal essayist whose meticulous attention to the actions, beliefs, and desires of representative pockets of American society have preserved for us a clear image of the 1960s and '70s. She displayed a vigilant sensitivity toward the "mythologies" touted by political leaders and showed great concern about America's break with the past, which she saw especially reflected in California's suppression of its history (one cause of the apparent symptom of American disorder). She often profiled places, from California and New York City to Hawai'i and El Salvador, and dissected prevalent social identities, looking to deconstruct any public or personal narrative.[41] She was skeptical of narratives because of their dependence on rhetoric, ideals, and abstractions. Looking at the counterculture, for instance, she saw "the desperate attempt of a handful of pathetically unequipped children to create a community in a social vacuum."[42] She lamented its

---

38 Karl Shapiro, quoted in Allen, "Little Magazine in America," 968.
39 Lawrence Grauman Jr., quoted in Allen, "Little Magazine in America," 970.
40 Tracy Daugherty, *The Last Love Song: A Biography of Joan Didion* (New York: St. Martin's Press, 2015), xii.
41 Kathleen M. Vandenberg, *Joan Didion: Substance and Style* (Albany, NY:State University of New York Press, 2021), 16. Didion became especially known for her bleak and noir portraits of California, an aesthetic style that has been described by critics as "California Gothic." See, for example, Bernice M. Murphy, *The California Gothic in Fiction and Film* (Edinburgh: Edinburgh University Press, 2022).
42 Joan Didion, *Slouching Towards Bethlehem* (New York: Farrar, Straus and Giroux, 2008), 122.

youth-following whose "only proficient vocabulary is in the society's platitudes" and whose impoverished language, life experience, and absence of community ties turned them into "an army of children waiting to be given the words."[43] Doubt was a mainstay of Didion's incisive style of writing. Meanwhile, her spare prose made her sentiments of disillusionment and skepticism stand out, as evidenced in her famous opening line from the titular story of *The White Album* (1979), "We tell ourselves stories in order to live," a statement she undercuts just a paragraph later, disclosing in an elegiac tone her experience at the near turn of the 1960s: "I began to doubt the premises of all the stories I had ever told myself."[44] As her use of the personal voice here indicates, Didion understood better than arguably any journalist of her generation that the best kind of reporting involved just as much a confrontation with facts as it did with oneself.

Placing oneself in a reported story, either as an impartial observer or a character, was not a practice exclusive to Didion but common to the cluster of writers with whom she was grouped, the New Journalists. New Journalism came to signify a journalism based in fact but written, narratively, as fiction. Reporters would present their data with techniques imported from fiction, making use of dialogue, sensory specificity, dramatic structure, and the construction of scene, character, and atmosphere. Just how and when this practice began remained a mystery even to its oft-credited founder, Tom Wolfe (1930–2018). One reason for this was that its alleged forerunners occupied a dizzying historic and generic range. Among the more apparent forerunners to New Journalism are counted John Hersey's multiperspective article "Hiroshima" (*New Yorker*, 1946) and Lilian Ross's "Come In, Lassie" (*New Yorker*, 1948), an exposé on how McCarthyism took over Hollywood. But to this list could also be added Upton Sinclair's (1878–1968) meticulously reported muckraker novel *The Jungle* (1906), in addition to, in a very different vein, Charles Dickens's (1812–1870) self-published peripatetic personal essay "Night Walks" (1860), inspired by his evening strolls around London. Another reason was that New Journalism sprouted all of a sudden, in the same places, in the big ranks of *Esquire* (1933–), *Rolling Stone* (1967–), Vox Media's *New York* (1968–), and the *Saturday Evening Post* (1897–). As it was surfacing, New Journalism generated a lot of chatter from critics and editors inspired to put a name to the phenomenon: the *New York Review of Books* called it "parajournalism," while essays in the *Atlantic* and *Harper's* by Dan

---

43 Didion, *Slouching Towards Bethlehem*, 123.
44 Joan Didion, *The White Album* (New York: Farrar, Straus and Giroux, 2009), 11.

Wakefield (1932–) and Norman Podhoretz (1930), respectively, argued that nonfiction was finally being treated "as a serious artistic form," in reference to the "discursive prose" found in the essays of James Baldwin (1924–1987) and Isaac Rosenfeld (1918–1956), and in Truman Capote's (1924–84) "non-fiction novel," *In Cold Blood*, serialized in the *New Yorker* (1965).[45] Just as the critics had said of modernism, New Journalism seemed to have started *in the magazines*, albeit not the little ones. New Journalism's critics contended that it was a nonmovement galvanized (mostly) by Tom Wolfe and (also) Gay Talese into a seismic cultural event when reporters had always, to varying degrees, used such methods. Regardless, it became clear from its amassing practitioners – most importantly, Wolfe, Didion, Jimmy Breslin (1928–2017), Gay Talese (1932–), Norman Mailer (1923–2007), Nora Ephron (1941–2012), Doon Arbus (1945–), and Gail Sheehy (1936–2020) – that "the traditional tools of reporting [had been] inadequate to chronicle the tremendous cultural and social changes of the era."[46] In veering away from traditional journalistic conventions, New Journalism left an enduring legacy by greatly increasing the tools at the disposal of nonfiction writers.

The Digital Era of Literary Magazines since 1970

In retrospect, New Journalism was neither the revolution Wolfe hailed it to be nor the commonplace, pedestrian form its critics sometimes portrayed it as[47]; regardless, it gathered significant momentum for magazine writing by expanding the variety and appeal of journalism's subjects. The profile piece, in particular, rose to formidable prominence as a magazine feature with the New Journalists. The allure of the profile hinged on an irresistible formula: to pry into the private life and thoughts of a celebrity or public figure. Even her subjects seemed to forget, as Didion once said, "that my presence runs counter to their best interest."[48] It was not just the choice of personality, however, that enticed readers to read profiles, but how their figures were being written about, as if they were characters belonging to a paperback novel. The standard for the profile was set in the early issues of the

---

45 Tom Wolfe, "Why They Aren't Writing the Great American Novel Anymore," *Esquire* (December 1972), www.esquire.com/lifestyle/money/a20703846/tom-wolfe-new-journalism-american-novel-essay/.
46 Marc Weingarten, *The Gang That Couldn't Write Straight: Wolfe, Thompson, Didion, and the New Journalism Revolution* (New York: Crown, 2006), 6.
47 John Hollowell, *Fact and Fiction: The New Journalism and the Nonfiction Novel* (Chapel Hill, NC: University of North Carolina Press, 1977), 44–47.
48 Didion, *Slouching Towards Bethlehem*, xiv.

New Yorker, its artistry and descriptive nuance honed in the midcentury by A. J. Liebling (1904–1963) and Joseph Mitchell (1908–1996), only to reach the perfect "eavesdropping" pitch by Lillian Ross's and Truman Capote's uniquely gifted "sensitive ear for the incongruous."[49] Ross's famous profile of Ernest Hemingway, "How Do You Like It Now, Gentlemen?" (*New Yorker*, 1950), for example, made ample use of dialogue with little attribution, letting her subject speak freely and at length.[50] According to Gay Talese, the "art of listening"[51] lay at the heart of a great profile, with listening, here, implying a whole range of observational skills. These he exemplified in his timeless piece "Frank Sinatra Has a Cold" (*Esquire* 1966). Not having been granted an interview with Sinatra, Talese wrote the profile based solely on interviews with Sinatra's acquaintances and his observation of an impromptu, tense encounter between Sinatra and Harlan Ellison (1934–2018) in a bar.[52] In essence, the truly great profiles came to read like short stories. The narrative technique of "composite characterization" allowed New Journalists to synthesize details gathered from interviews, research, and observation into "composites," individual characters made up from the aggregate details of many to represent a whole class of subjects.[53] This technique was used in features, too, like Gail Sheehy's series of articles on prostitution in *New York* (1968–), later gathered in her book *Hustling* (1970). The technique sought to bring journalistic subjects to life in the manner of characters one would find in a work of fiction.

After the late 1970s, however, the aesthetic contours of the profile gave way to the once reviled publicity puff piece. Thus came a transition in magazine culture, as Weingarten argues, highlighting the example of *Rolling Stone*, whose rapid increase of movie stars featured on its covers in just two years, between 1977 and 1979, seemed to symbolize how magazines were now to become merely "press organs for movie stars."[54] Celebrity culture was not only spreading among musicians and across Hollywood, but in intellectual circles as well, aided by the glamor and heyday of

---

49 Hollowell, *Fact and Fiction*, 66.
50 Lillian Ross, "How Do You Like It Now, Gentlemen?," *New Yorker* (6 May 1950), www.newyorker.com/magazine/1950/05/13/how-do-you-like-it-now-gentlemen.
51 Christopher Silvester, Gay Talese, and Robert A. Wilson, *The Norton Book of Interviews: An Anthology from 1859 to the Present Day* (New York: W. W. Norton, 1996), xxi.
52 Gay Talese, "Frank Sinatra Has a Cold," *Esquire* (April 1966), www.esquire.com/news-politics/a638/frank-sinatra-has-a-cold-gay-talese.
53 Hollowell, *Fact and Fiction*, 30.
54 Weingarten, *Gang That Couldn't*, 292. Specifically, Weingarten writes, "From 1967 to 1977, *Rolling Stone* features movie stars on seventeen covers. From 1977 to 1979, it had twenty-two such cover stories" (292).

photojournalism depicted in *Life* (1883–1972) and *Look* (1937–71). Especially in New York City and the historic literary hub of Greenwich Village – owing its revival as a revolutionary arts scene in the 1960s to figures of the Roaring Twenties like Edna St. Vincent Millay (1892–1950) – magazines manifested cults of personality around certain authors predisposed to them. A short list might include Joan Didion, immortalized in a black-and-white photo in which she is leaning on the hood of her Corvette holding a cigarette (presumably in California), Tom Wolfe dressed in pristine white suits, or figurehead of the Beats Jack Kerouac (1922–1969), who valorized a nomadic, hedonistic lifestyle. In addition, there resulted a proliferation of a certain kind of editorial column – writing on writers writing, alongside increasing author profiles and interviews in publications such as *Contemporary Literature* (1960–) and the *Paris Review,* whose iconic interview series had reached sixty installments by 1970, and is still thriving today, boasting a great many copycats.[55] Readers became wrapped up in the appearances of the writing life as represented by their favorite authors, sometimes getting inspired to become writers themselves, fancying a life dedicated to one's art to signify not merely an aesthetic life choice but a political stance.

The fact that the personalities of writers loomed large in pockets of American culture helped stimulate the personal essay's popularity across periodicals. For one, cults of personality had made readers more curious to learn intimate details about authors. For another, New Journalism had expanded the possibilities for essay writing under new generic categories such as "creative nonfiction" or "literary nonfiction." In the words of Elizabeth Hardwick, New Journalism had blurred the boundaries of nonfiction to such a degree that, as she put it, "If we cannot be sure we are reading journalism according to the rules of the professional schools, we are even less certain that we are reading the elevated essay."[56] Of course, the essay had already been elevated before New Journalism in the pages of the *New Yorker,* thanks to its early chief writer, E .B. White, who developed there from columnist to essayist, infusing the allegedly dead familiar essay – as the magazines had speculated since the 1930s – with new life. Since his arrival at the magazine, White brought to the first-page column Notes and Comment, a "mild-mannered, somewhat genteel, wellread [sic] man-on-the-street

---

55 Allen, "Little Magazine in America," 968.
56 Elizabeth Hardwick, "Its Only Defense: Intelligence and Sparkle," *New York Times* (18 September 1986), www.nytimes.com/1986/09/14/books/its-only-defense-intelligence-and-sparkle.html.

persona,"[57] a weekly routine he grew tired of, leading him, in 1938, to leave New York for Maine and the *New Yorker* for a series in *Harper's* called "One Man's Meat," in which he was finally free to broach heated political topics such as segregation and America's intervention in the war. In "One Man's Meat," White struck a rarefied balance for the personal essay between intimacy and social concern, restoring the genre not simply to a past glory but making it relevant to its time by expanding its possible topics and dignifying it as a literary form. When White was coaxed back to his *New Yorker* column in 1943, he "[was] no longer the amused spectator"[58] but filled with convictions, like the need for a world government, which he explored across multiple installments of Notes and Comment.[59] White's style or essayism, more broadly, denotes the magazine essay's arc throughout the twentieth century, progressing at the start from an outdated genteel form to the tightly wound editorial column, to arrive finally at a socially aware, highly stylized modern personal essay that determined for itself what it needed to say and how. In some ways, it seemed as if the scope and influence of the essay had grown by such a degree that the singular personality of writers could well override in readerly appeal the magazine's broader editorial character, thus making writers more autonomous social actors. Aside from White, other writers who had an unmistakable social impact nationwide included Baldwin on issues of race, Didion on California's mythology, and Susan Sontag on illness, to name just a few of the twentieth century's most important essayists.

As a result of the writer's increased influence and choice of platforms, some essays of the 1970s had explosive receptions within their network. Norman Mailer's "The Prisoner of Sex" (1971) in *Harper's* exemplifies one such instance. With a speculative essay written in the style of New Journalism, Mailer meant to provoke radical feminists, which he did, helped by *Harper's* editorial introduction, which read, "[N]o writer in America could have illuminated as Norman Mailer has the deep underlying issues raised"[60] by women's liberation movements. The publication detonated a series of essay responses, including Germaine Greer's (1939–) in *Esquire*,[61] a multiauthor

---

57 Ned Stuckey-French, "American Essay. 7. The 1940s: The Example of E. B. White," in *Encyclopedia of the Essay*, ed. Tracy Chevalier (London: Routledge, 1997). EBSCO Host.
58 Morris Bishop, "Introduction," in E. B. White, *One Man's Meat* (New York: Harper, 1950), v–xii, ix.
59 Bishop, "Introduction," ix.
60 Annette Barnes, "Norman Mailer: A Prisoner of Sex," *Massachusetts Review* 13, no. 1/2 (1972): 269–74, 269.
61 Germaine Greer, "My Mailer Problem," *Esquire* (1 September 1971), https://classic.esquire.com/article/1971/9/1/my-mailer-problem.

spread in the *Atlantic*,[62] a review in the *New York Times*,[63] a scholarly analysis in the *Massachusetts Review*[64] and then still evoked the fury and heckling of New York City's Town Hall Theater as Mailer debated, and (controversially) moderated, panelists Jacqueline Ceballos (1925–), Greer, Jill Johnston (1929–2010), and Diana Trilling (1905–96), with Susan Sontag, Betty Friedan (1921–2006), Elizabeth Hardwick, and Cynthia Ozick (1928–) saying their piece from the crowd. Released as a documentary, *Town Bloody Hall* (1979), the event captured a social crisis blown into a media circus by the volatile, enmeshed New York network of intellectuals, writers, and magazinists, prefiguring today's mercurial opinion-giving encouraged by social networking platforms and the performative transparency of reality television.

Commercial magazines caught on to the ways in which provocative literary content could boost both their sales and their social presence in topical conversations. In contrast to passion-project periodicals, whose means were unlikely to attract a great deal of attention (like inciting Mailer's scale of response to make hosting such a panel possible), commercial magazines would run literary work only incidentally. Peripheral magazines, for example, tried their hand at gaining literary attention, with *Playboy* (1953–2020; 2020–) presenting the most unlikely contender. Inside Hugh Hefner's (1926–2017) magazine, "entertainment for men"[65] lay alongside fiction and poetry by critically acclaimed authors such as Ray Bradbury (1920–2012), Doris Lessing (1919–2013), John Cheever (1912–1982), and Anne Sexton (1928–1974). On the surface, Hefner's magazine-for-men conceit sought to offer an alternative to the postwar domestic ideology held by women's homemaking magazines at the time, *Good Housekeeping* (1885–), *Woman's Day* (1931–), *Mademoiselle* (1935–2001) (once famously guest edited by confessional poet Sylvia Plath [1932–1963]), and most importantly, *McCall's* (1873–2003), and the *Ladies' Home Journal*. Beneath the surface, Hefner's ambition might have arisen from his early days as a copywriter at "smart magazine" *Esquire* or, alternately, the awareness that his bachelor "man-about-town" character went as far back as the well-traveled, leisure-loving "Mr. Spectator."

---

62 The multipart spread was entitled "With Norman Mailer at the Sex Circus," *Atlantic* (July 1971), www.theatlantic.com/magazine/archive/1971/07/ii-out-of-the-machine/664726/.
63 Brigid Brophy, "Meditations on Norman Mailer, by Norman Mailer, against the Day a Norman Mailest Comes Along," review of *The Prisoner of Sex*, by Norman Mailer, *New York Times* (23 May 1971), https://www.nytimes.com/1971/05/23/archives/the-prisoner-of-sex-240-pp-boston-little-brown-co-595-prisoner-of.html.
64 Barnes, "Norman Mailer," 269–74.
65 Elizabeth Fraterrigo, *Playboy and the Making of the Good Life in Modern America* (New York: Oxford University Press, 2009), 1.

Playboy's progressive pretenses came under attack, notably, from Gloria Steinem (1934–), the future founder of radical feminist and activist *Ms.* (1971–), who would depict the magazine as little short of a gimmick in the exposé that made her famous, "A Bunny's Tale" (1963), in which, in diary format, she details her brief undercover stint as a "playmate."

For Andrei Codrescu (1946–), the watered-down counterculture sentiments championed by general-interest magazines hinted at an underlying disappointment that even the true avant-garde had lost its nerve.[66] As an exception to this plight, Codrescu created the Surrealist-inspired *Exquisite Corpse* (1983–), meant to ignite political discussions that do "the kind of harm that promotes health."[67] In the same vein, he pointed out the legacy of *Black Mountain Review* (1954–57), having inspired first the Black Mountain projectivist poets and then the Language Poets, who went on to create *L=A=N=G=U=A=G=E* (1978–81) and *This* (1978–81).[68] Nowadays, journals opposing the status quo will challenge existing norms by deconstructing the terms of popular discourse that perpetuate false and problematic notions of gender, race, or political commitments. Examples include the leftist *Baffler* (1988–), feminist *Rumpus* (2009–), and *Bitch: A Feminist Response to Pop Culture* (1996–2022). Moreover, magazines are increasingly incorporating into the avant-garde mission historically underrepresented communities, a cause central to (regionalist) magazines like Charles Henry Rowell's *Callaloo* (1976–), focused on the African Diaspora or the innovative writing of the Black South; the *Americas Review* (1980–), dedicated to Latinx and Chicanx writers; and San Francisco's *Zyzzyva* (1985), which has managed to rile up competition with New York's literary scene from the West Coast. The importance of cultural exchange and challenging the hegemony of English goes part and parcel with this mission and has led to more international online websites dedicated to publishing works in translation, like *Words without Borders* and *Asymptote*, along with initiatives that increase the visibility of works in translation like the Thousand Languages Project, launched by *Hayden's Ferry Review* (1986–) and the yearly Unsung Masters Series partnership between three university-set journals: *Pleiades* (1981–), *Copper Nickel* (2002–), and *Gulf Coast* (1982–).

---

66 Ian Morris and Joanne Diaz, eds., *The Little Magazine in Contemporary America* (Chicago: University of Chicago Press, 2015), ix.
67 Andrei Codrescu, "Exquisite Corpse," in Morris and Diaz, *Little Magazine*, 97–106, 97.
68 Codrescu, "Exquisite Corpse," 104.

In general, since the steady expansion of higher education after World War II,[69] a literary magazine's affiliation with a university did not necessarily compromise its avant-garde aesthetic or mission. Given that the percentage of college-educated Americans rose to around 50 percent in the 1970s (from under roughly 10 percent before World War II), universities experienced comprehensive growth, including an expansion in creative writing programs. It followed that the students of creative writing would run or even start their own literary magazines to feature the kind of writing they thought was missing from the literary landscape in order to stoke conversation beyond campus and excite the urge for renewed experimentation. Not only did such activity reorient literary publishing, but it has since organized American writers into the academic establishment, a phenomenon described by Mark McGurl as "the program era" of American writing.[70] Several of today's best-ranked magazines came from this campus sprawl, among them *Ploughshares* (1971–), started at Emerson College, Boston University's *AGNI* (1972–), Bard College's *Conjunctions* (1981–), New York University's *Washington Square Review* (1996–), Middlebury College's *New England Review* (1978–), and Gettysburg College's *Gettysburg Review* (1988–), along with Western Michigan's lesser-known *Third Coast* (1995–) and fabulist-favorite *Fairy Tale Review* (2005–), published by Wayne State University Press. The continuing spike of MFA programs – having gone from 79 degree-granting programs in 1975 to 854 in 2010[71] – has fueled the drawn-out "MFA vs NYC" debate, as *n+1* cofounder Chad Harbach coined it,[72] which bifurcates the literary scene into New York publishing and university writing, pitting the two worlds against each other. Certainly, there exist independently published magazines like *n+1* (2004–) and *A Public Space* (2005–) that can boast of growing subscribers and steady revenue. But as the majority of the longest-lasting and best-ranking literary magazines demonstrate, – (e.g., *Virginia Quarterly Review*, the *Southern Review*, *Kenyon Review*, and *Sewanee Review*) universities can provide an enduring source of support for working writers and provide the training ground for emerging editors.

---

69 At the time, the number of university degree seekers rose, in part, because of the original 1944 G.I. Bill, which provided veterans with several wide-ranging incentives, among them the financial assistance to seek high school, university, or vocational degrees.
70 Mark McGurl, *The Program Era: Postwar Fiction and the Rise of Creative Writing* (Cambridge, MA: Harvard University Press, 2009).
71 Chad Harbach, "MFA vs. NYC," *n+1* (Fall 2010), www.nplusonemag.com/issue-10/the-intellectual-situation/mfa-vs-nyc/.
72 Harbach, "MFA vs. NYC," n.p.

When it comes to the magazine's development over the last thirty years, the replacement of print forms with online platforms has effected potentially "the most radical paradigm shift since the invention of movable type,"[73] according to Morris and Diaz. Exploiting the low production costs of the Internet, some magazines exist entirely online, like *Electric Literature* (2009–), *Guernica* (2004–), *Diagram* (1999–), *At Length* (2003–), *Narrative* (2003–), and *Memorious* (2004–), or travel-writing adjacent *Off Assignment* (2016–).[74] In contrast, Dave Eggers's cult-favorite quarterly *McSweeney's* (1998–) honors the physicality of print and elevates the art object by designing printed issues in the likeness of arcane objects like a bundle of "mis-delivered mail"[75] or a book of 1930s pulp.[76] In general, the majority of these magazines sustain a hybrid model with an online mirrored layout of the print issue whereby the reader can consume the contents online as opposed to through a printed subscription, as is the case with the *Believer* (2003–), sister publication to *McSweeney's*; environmentally focused *Ecotone* (2005–); and zines such as *Lady Churchill's Rosebud Wristlet* (1996–), published under Kelly Link's Small Beer Press, or the feminist, nonconforming *Ginger* (2015–). As a matter of survival, certain properly staffed magazines like *Poetry*, the *Paris Review*, and *Ploughshares* have also instituted ways to supplement their regular print issues with web-catching content that is published more frequently. This comes in the form of online dailies, blogs, or columns on themes that entice a large part of the readership, like emerging writers, especially when it comes to talk of craft, process, teaching writing methods, or the writing life. Literary websites like Literary Hub, Electric Literature, and Catapult have acted as hybrids between journals and daily publications, launching email newsletters and essay columns dedicated purely to intimate feature essays on craft by famous writers. In the same vein, each of the *Sewanee Review*'s print issues includes a "Craft Lecture," while the *Paris Review* has launched several types of podcast to promote its published authors and preserve its legacy. Arguably, no periodical has developed a more successful or nuanced interview paradigm than the *Paris Review*, whose exchanges with authors have now become a ritualized part of almost every arts and culture magazine. (At the public's request, the *Paris Review* now archives and collects its esteemed interviews in a book series called "Writers at Work.")

73 Morris and Diaz, *Little Magazine in Contemporary America*, vii.
74 "About," *Off Assignment*, www.offassignment.com/about/team.
75 Jeffrey Lependorf, "A Decade or So of Little Magazines: One Reader's Perspective," in Morris and Diaz, *Little Magazine*, 1–19, 2.
76 Harris, "Chapter 249," 4.

To keep up with the enormous output of digital literary content, many magazines have aligned themselves with the quasi-intellectual mission of encouraging public (but rigorous) engagement in the public humanities. Critical reviews like the *Los Angeles Review of Books* and the long-standing *New York Review of Books* now both operate active websites and promote themselves to a wider-than-scholarly audience, all the while gravitating toward a style and subject preference that necessitates an interest in ideas. Many online magazines, in fact, have developed out of the perceived gap between the world of ideas and the quotidian life of individuals; in response, they have tried to pay more mind to the intersection between culturally relevant topics (e.g., film and television, celebrity culture) and academic scholarship, rendering conversations usually reserved for university classrooms or peer-reviewed academic journals into ordinary language. *The Point* (2008–) serves as a salient example. Created by then doctoral students of the University of Chicago's Committee on Social Thought, the founding editors of *The Point* sought to incorporate more critical depth and philosophical analysis into the discussion of general interest topics or profile pieces. Central to *The Point*'s ethos, one finds the idea that "humanistic thinking has relevance for contemporary life."[77] Thus it strives beyond mere "intellectual tourism,"[78] treating ideas more seriously and showing their relevance to one's daily life. Other examples of digital periodicals committed to expanding the disciplinary boundaries of a literary magazine include *Aeon*, film-focused *Bright Wall/Dark Room*, the academically minded but publicly facing *Public Books*, the *Critical Flame* (2008–), and the *Drift*. The public humanities trend evidenced in magazines of the digital era suggests the public's greater desire for intelligent exchange between private institutions like universities and common culture. Looking ahead, one can imagine that the accessibility and adaptability of digital platforms in addition to the increasing number of academics in non-academic careers could substantially alter the intellectual gravity of media in general, including television, radio, or newspapers. To this end, the online literary magazine could serve as a valuable model.

At the close of 2021, the Community of Literary Magazines and Presses in New York registered 589 literary magazines operating in the United States alone, although its required minimum of three issues for inclusion has surely left out numerous smaller ventures in addition to exclusively digital

---

77 "About," *The Point*, accessed 5 March 2023, https://thepointmag.com/about/.
78 Michael Miner, "The Point – Something New to Read in Chicago," *Chicago Reader* (2 June 2009), https://chicagoreader.com/blogs/the-point-something-new-to-read-in-chicago/.

magazines that have not yet been assigned a proper category. As its history has shown, the literary periodical can emerge from individual personalities bent on iconoclasm and idiosyncrasy, but what sustains it is an active network of fellow magazinists, writers, and readers unafraid to challenge and improve upon its ideas. If there is anything the literary magazine has proven it can tolerate, it is change; nothing drives it more than healthy competition, formal innovation, and its editors' sincere conceit that the future of good literature has fallen onto their shoulders. "Essays end up in books," wrote Susan Sontag, "but they start their lives in magazines."[79] Magazines, she suggests, give writers their first break; they are a guild in the hard world of publishing not merely of fellowship but of necessity.

---

79 Susan Sontag, cited in Joyce Carol Oates and Robert Atwan, eds., *The Best American Essays of the Century* (Boston: Houghton Mifflin, 2000), xiii.

21

Germans in Amerika: Written Possibility, Uninhabitable Reality

FLORIAN FUCHS

By necessity, immigrants must think, act, and live experimentally when they arrive at their new destination. Given that the essay also possesses an experimental quality, using data collected through the senses and lived experience to conduct various trials in that laboratory called the world, it is unsurprising to find that in the United States – often called the land of immigration – the canon of American essays includes a vast corpus of essayistic writing by immigrants. Indeed, the dual or multiple identity of an immigrant-essayist is one of the most common in American writing. This chapter is concerned with a particular group of such immigrant-essayists: those who arrived in the United States as a result of exile from Germany. Among others, it focuses particularly on German-speaking essayists who – like countless other artists, scholars, authors, directors, and other intellectuals – fled to the United States from war, persecution, and precarity in war-torn and fascism-ridden Europe during the 1930s and '40s.[1]

The history of German speakers contributing to a history of the American essay of course begins much earlier, spanning at least from the essay "Paradise" (published around 1740) imagining an egalitarian society in the American Southeast by the German utopist Christian Gottlieb Priber (1697–1744) to Alexander von Humboldt's (1769–1859) mid-nineteenth-century writings on abolitionism and Hugo Münsterberg's (1863–1916) essays on interdisciplinary psychology around 1900. The

---

[1] For selective overviews, see Martin Jay, *Permanent Exiles. Essays on the Intellectual Migration from Germany to America* (New York: Columbia University Press, 1985); Sabine Eckmann and Lutz Koepnick, eds., *Caught by Politics: Hitler Exiles and American Visual Culture* (New York: Palgrave Macmillan, 2007); Eckart Goebel and Sigrid Weigel, eds., *"Escape to Life": German Intellectuals in New York: A Compendium on Exile after 1933* (Berlin: De Gruyter, 2012).

scope of this chapter is more narrow, however, focusing on the central role that the essay played in the writing of several twentieth-century authors, including Hans Richter (1888–1976), Hannah Arendt (1906–1975), Theodor W. Adorno (1903–1969), Herbert Marcuse (1898–1979), Bertolt Brecht (1898–1956), Ernst Kantorowicz (1895–1963), Thomas Mann (1875–1955), and Christa Wolf (1929–2011).

These exiles and refugees wrote essays dreaming of America before they arrived and analyzing America once they reached its shores. In order to come to terms with the chaotic, often overwhelming experience of migration, they were forced to test out a new life, first in writing, then in action. Many went directly to the United States soon after Hitler took power, such as the director Fritz Lang, the philosopher Herbert Marcuse, and the sociologist Leo Löwenthal. Others, like the author and director Bertolt Brecht in Sweden, the literary scholar Erich Auerbach in Istanbul, and the film critic Siegfried Kracauer in Paris, first tried living in other, non-Nazi-controlled European countries before the terror came closer and made fleeing across the Atlantic the only option. Others, like Karl Löwith in Kyoto, took greater detours before they arrived in the United States. And others still, like the political theorist Hannah Arendt, were incarcerated by the Nazis and their allies across Europe before they escaped to America. This chapter explores the range of moods and modes through which these essayists tried out their new home. Optimism, resistance, critique, nostalgia: The essay accommodated the many ways they attempted to come to terms with the United States. Some stayed only a few months, some the rest of their lives, but for all of these essayists, America remained only a written possibility, never an inhabitable reality. Their essays, in other words, were both possibilitarian attempts to understand America as a livable reality for an author, while measuring at the same time how impossible it was to overcome their foreignness.

Richter against Pessimism

One of the first of these German speakers' many significant essays to reach the shores of America was an essay about the essay itself – in fact about a whole new essayistic medium, the essay film. A year before emigrating to the United States, living in Switzerland and in danger of being deported back to Germany, the Berlin film artist Hans Richter (1888 –1976) published a long-overlooked text, "The Film Essay: A New Type of Documentary Film." Writing in 1940, "when it was clear that he would have to go into exile from Europe,"[2] Richter presents no finished scholarly article, nor an avant-garde manifesto, but an attempt to understand a particular object: the nongenre, or not-yet-genre, of essay film. Richter does so by sketching the uncharted territory between the established feature film and the newly emerged documentary film. "The essay film," Richter explains,

> in its attempt to make the invisible world of imagination, thoughts, and ideas visible, can draw from an incomparably larger reservoir of expressive means than can the pure documentary film. Since in the essay film the filmmaker is not bound by the depiction of external phenomena and the constraints of chronological sequences, but, on the contrary, has to enlist material from everywhere, the filmmaker can bounce around freely in space and time.[3]

The aim all essay films have in common is thus to visualize thoughts on screen. Notice the suggestions of a conjectural quality – "the essay film draws from a large reservoir of means" – and an investigative quality – "the essay film in its attempt" – that mark the two aspects of the essay written in exile. Richter argues that essay films are both conjectural and investigative. They are conjectural in that they attempt to chart a possible, not-yet-charted subject of pressing necessity – here, a radically new use of film. They are investigative in that they inquire into their subjects by thought alone – here, approaching film's nonpropagandist use (as opposed to the propagandist films spreading at the time, particularly in totalitarian states such as Germany, Italy, or the Soviet Union).

Richter affirms this investigative nature of the essay film (and thereby of the essay more generally) when he proposes an idea for an essay film, namely, the "treatment of a subject such as 'The United States of Europe.'" Conversely, this also affirms how the very idea of a United States of America is by definition an essayistic one and how, as Richter illustrates, it can incite from its very nature more essayistic writing and further essayistic projects. This acknowledges the utopian and optimistic political role of this essay for the soon-to-be-exiled Richter and, consequently, injects the essay film with the utopian potential of the essay. Richter classifies two of his own earlier works as examples of essay films, namely *Inflation* (1928) and *Stock Exchange* (1939). While *Inflation* borrows its essayistic mode from Richter's earlier work within the Dada movement's critique of supposed sense-making, *Stock*

---

2 Nora M. Alter, "Hans Richter in Exile," in Eckmann and Koepnick, *Caught by Politics*, 223–43, 239.
3 Hans Richter, "The Essay Film," in *Essays on the Essay Film*, ed. Nora M. Alter and Timothy Corrigan, trans. Maria P. Alter (New York: Columbia University Press, 2017), 89–92, 91.

Exchange has turned the nonsensical into an open-ended way of addressing the political aspects of the stock market.

Richter arrived in New York in 1941 with the help of the German artist and patron Hilla von Rebay (1890–1967), who also put him in touch with Solomon Guggenheim's Museum of Non-Objective Painting, which would later become the Guggenheim Museum. Richter's expertise and his connections allowed him to start teaching at the Institute of Film Techniques of the City College of New York (CCNY). There, he made his first essay film in exile, *Dreams That Money Can Buy* (1944–47), featuring seven episodes by other exiled artists such as Max Ernst (1891–1976) and Marcel Duchamp (1887–1968), as well as by Man Ray (1890–1976) and himself. At CCNY, Richter also taught to his students what he first sketched in his 1940 essay. Many of these students would become the initiators of the American avant-garde of experimental film on the East Coast: Stan Brakhage (1933–2003), Shirley Clarke (1919–1997), Maya Deren (1917–1961), and Jonas Mekas (1922–2019).[4] The fact that the latter two had themselves fled Europe before they became experimental filmmakers only reaffirms the exile-conditioned foundation of Richter's essay on the essay film.

It was no surprise that Mekas invited Richter to spearhead the inaugural issue of the journal *Film Culture* in 1955, which Mekas founded with his brother and which remained the central publication venue for essays on American experimental film for decades. In Richter's seminal text for *Film Culture*, "The Film as an Original Art Form," he strategically updated his earlier 1940 essay with newer artists, directors, and films, but retained his fundamental interest in fusing the documentarian's authenticity-focused methods with the artist's fictional storytelling. Notably, Richter no longer speaks of "essay film" (as in the 1940 German text) but the term "essay" is now replaced by the English "experimental," which paradoxically strengthens his original notion, albeit under a different name. Given that in American English, "essay" and "article" are often used synonymously and not with the definition Richter gave in his 1940 text – "the word 'essay' is used for treatment of difficult subjects and themes to render them into a generally comprehensible form"[5] – it is only logical to name what Europeans title "essay film" as "experimental film"[6] in American English. (Note that the

---

4 See Timothy O. Benson, "Hans Richter: Encounters," in *Hans Richter: Encounters*, ed. Timothy O. Benson (Los Angeles: Los Angeles County Museum of Art, 2013).
5 Richter, "Essay Film," 91.
6 Hans Richter, "The Film as an Original Art Form" (1955), in *Film Culture Reader*, ed. P. Adams Sitney (New York: Cooper Square Press, 2000), 15–20, 18.

omnipresence of "essay" in American English likely presents sociolinguistic evidence for the essential American role of the genre.) Richter's 1940 essay on the essay film, whose ideas envisage his precarious emigrant situation, thus amplify the experimental aspects of American daily life when they are adopted by Richter's students.

Richter's *Dreams That Money Can Buy* tells perhaps the most clichéd American story of all: A poor everyman named Joe turns his life around by becoming a self-made man. To do so, he adapts psychoanalytic practices and comes up with the perfect product to sell to his fellow Americans: personalized dreams for the neurotic customer. As the title's play on the central phrase of American capitalism already suggests ("there's nothing money can't buy"), the film mediates, optimistically but quite literally, between the European and the American mind: Freudian analysis versus materialist dreams, destructive idealism versus constructive pragmatism. The Dada spirit of Richter's famous film *Ghosts before Breakfast* (1928) had finally taken shape in the United States and turned into an essayistic mode of addressing older European problems with American reality by using the new medium of film. Already the film's opening frame announced "a story of dreams mixed with reality," that is, the essay's qualities of conjecture and investigation forcibly fused into an immigrant way of life.

Arendt against Optimism

Hannah Arendt (1906–1975) reached New York the same year as Richter. Unlike him, she had been incarcerated by the Vichy regime in the Gurs camp in occupied France, where Jews, political prisoners, and other persecuted people were held by order of the Nazis. In the summer of 1940, she was able to flee the camp and later escaped France, eventually reaching a ship in Lisbon. Informed by this refugee experience of internment and near deportation, she started her life in the United States as a different kind of essayist and writer than Richter and employed the conjectural and investigative nature of the essay to different ends. Her essay "We Refugees," for example, published in January 1943 in the leading Jewish American *Menorah Journal*, offers a concise analysis of the figure of the refugee from her own perspective and experience as a Jew. In that sense, whereas Richter's essay conjectured the future of (his) artistic work to figure out at the same time how he could continue his life, Arendt's essay was almost forensic, trying sentence by sentence to capture the recent experience of refugees because she knew exactly what had been necessary to survive. Arendt thus focused on coming to terms with a catastrophe that had hardly ended instead of diluting its effects through an essayistic spirit that looked forward beyond current insecurities. She used the investigative nature of the essay to excavate what lies underneath the blind optimism of texts like Richter's and the open-endedness such approaches entail. In fact, Arendt's article can be read as an attempt to understand what she calls the "insane optimism"[7] of refugees. Throughout, the essay provides scenes showing where and how this false projection follows the initial logic of the refugee, which Arendt presents on the first page as simply a necessity for survival: "In order to rebuild one's life one has to be strong and an optimist. So we are very optimistic."[8] The most open-ended, pensive, and hence most essayistic passages thus expose the losses that optimism tries to cover up by unraveling slowly what could be called a phenomenology of refugee optimism, narrated in the voice of a collective confessional:

> Our optimism, indeed, is admirable, even if we say so ourselves. The story of our struggle has finally become known. We lost our home, which means the familiarity of daily life. We lost our occupation, which means the confidence that we are of some use in this world. We lost our language, which means the naturalness of reactions, the simplicity of gestures, the unaffected expression of feelings. We left our relatives in the Polish ghettos and our best friends have been killed in concentration camps, and that means the rupture of our private lives.
>
> Nevertheless, as soon as we were saved – and most of us had to be saved several times – we started our new lives and tried to follow as closely as possible all the good advice our saviors passed on to us. We were told to forget; and we forgot quicker than anybody ever could imagine. In a friendly way we were reminded that the new country would become a new home; and after four weeks in France or six weeks in America, we pretended to be Frenchmen or Americans. The more optimistic among us would even add that their whole former life had been passed in a kind of unconscious exile and only their new country now taught them what a home really looks like.[9]

In trying to detach these formulations of self-assurance and self-persuasion – "even if we say so ourselves" – from herself as speaker, Arendt collects a repository of speech gestures that, while directed at the new "saved" existence of the refugee who uses them, are revealed as directed primarily at the other members of the refugee community. Against their fear of never arriving and of losing all hope, the self-persuading gestures falsely suggest to the refugee herself

---

7 Hannah Arendt, "We Refugees" (1943), in *The Jewish Writings*, ed. Jerome Kohn and Ron H. Feldman (New York: Schocken, 2007), 264–74, 268.
8 Arendt, "We Refugees," 264.   9 Arendt, "We Refugees," 264–65.

that hope can continue. The next coming change of identity may be the "right" one, so it is worth trying and performing it. By isolating these gestures from the individual who lives through them, Arendt can exhibit them as what they are: collective experimental practices of make-believe and then later routines of projecting a change of citizen identity, from German to French to Japanese, American to New Yorker to Californian and so on. "If patriotism were a matter of routine or practice," Arendt continues her analysis, "we [refugees] should be the most patriotic people in the world."[10] Yet patriotism is determined by belonging to a nation-state legally and is hence unattainable by cultural performance.

After this essayistic phenomenology of refugee speech acts, the last two pages of the essay lead to a final fundamental insight that ascribes the failure of projection to the nation-state itself. It is not simply the case, Arendt argues, that nationality can no longer be attained through practices that allow legally binding citizenship but rather that the idea of the nation-state itself has proven an empty performance and ineffective routine of collectives. The refugee is not a person caught in an infinite essayistic loop of remaking herself; the refugee is evidence that the nation-state has failed to protect the liberty of its citizens. If trying to attain citizenship becomes a hopeless performance of optimism because allegedly more "native" citizens remain suspicious, then this presents not a sociological or anthropological problem but a shortcoming of the idea of a nation, and at the same time the insufficient performativity of patriotism. "The comity of European peoples went to pieces," concludes Arendt, "when, and because it allowed its weakest member to be excluded and persecuted." In other words, "the outlawing of the Jewish people in Europe has been followed closely by the outlawing of most European nations."[11] The utopia of a post-Nazi "United States of Europe," which Richter thought could be best presented in the timely utopian and optimistic medium of an essay film, had become nothing more than a dangerous specter for Arendt. Her essay shows that the refugee's essayistic mode of life had been necessitated by the corrupted nation-state, not the other way around. Because it failed to allow the Jewish refugees to stop needing to perform national identities by fully accepting them as citizens, any system of nation-states is effectively doomed to fail. Arendt's essayistic mode of writing political theory, which she would develop further for the next decades while remaining in the United States, already here redrew the line between the essay as the intellectually most persuasive genre of text and the essayistic as an uninhabitable mode of life.

10 Arendt, "We Refugees," 272.   11 Arendt, "We Refugees," 274.

Adorno against German Systems

Richter's capturing of a new form of film timely to the European American experience and Arendt's capturing of the European American refugee as the timely marker of the nation-state's failure were synthesized by Theodor W. Adorno (1903–1969). In his book-length essay collection *Minima Moralia* (1951), he tried to combine the two, writing a new form of essay that guided readers toward a new form of essayistic experience. Composed while in exile in California in the years 1944–1947, just after Richter's and Arendt's essays, the text attempts to capture what the subtitle of the book calls "reflections from damaged life." From the minutest, epiphanic, and hence "minimal" observations of his American lifeworld, Adorno draws moralistic contemplations about the condition of life in general and the "damaged" exiled existence in particular. Longer than aphorisms but too short to be stand-alone articles, the 153 numbered sections constitute microessays based on literary, philosophical, and especially cultural meditations. In a way, these reflections are the moral philosophical sister project to the more systematic work *Dialectic of Enlightenment*, which Adorno wrote in the same years with his Los Angeles neighbor Max Horkheimer (1895–1973), who was head of the then exiled Frankfurt Institute for Social Research. This suggests that there would be no Frankfurt School without the United States, as at least one research conference has proposed,[12] and that, consequentially, the (unessayistic) method of "critical theory" that Adorno, Horkheimer, Jackson Pollock (1912–1956), and others developed from the 1930s to the '60s could have not come into being.

The microessays of *Minima Moralia* are hybrids of cultural theory and critical moral philosophy. Adorno focuses particularly on the decay of the bourgeois existence under the condition of what the Frankfurt School began to call "late Capitalism." The following piece, number 125, entitled *Olet* (reversing the maxim *Pecunia non olet* ["Money doesn't smell"] into the positive), discusses the relation of the European versus the American to money, less in sociological terms than in compressed, essayistic, or even aphoristic terms:

> Every child of the European upper classes blushed at a monetary gift made by relations, and even if the greater force of bourgeois utility overcame and overcompensated such reactions, the doubt nevertheless remained whether

---

12 Detlev Claussen, Oskar Negt, and Michael Werz, eds., *Keine Kritische Theorie ohne Amerika* (Frankfurt am Main: Neue Kritik, 1999).

man was made merely to exchange. The remnants of the old were, in the European consciousness, ferments of the new. In America, on the other hand, no child of even well-off parents has inhibitions about earning a few cents by newspaper rounds, and this nonchalance has found its way into the demeanour of adults. This is why, to the uninformed European, Americans in their entirety can so easily appear as people without dignity, predisposed to paid services, just as, conversely, they are inclined to take him for a vagabond and aper of princes. The self-evidence of the maxim that work is no disgrace, the guileless absence of all snobbery concerning the ignominy, in the feudal sense, of market relationships, the democracy of the earnings-principle, contribute to the persistence of what is utterly antidemocratic, economic injustice, human degradation. It occurs to nobody that there might be services that are not expressible in terms of exchange value.[13]

Adorno's style transforms any more strictly scholarly language or observational attitudes into bursts of condensed aphoristic twists, acuities, and brief digressions. What is particularly noteworthy is that each microessay or even each sentence often originates from negative observations, that is, from a lack, a disappearance, an oblivion. Adorno would develop this attitude of philosophizing via the negative further in the following decades. In piece 21, entitled "Articles May Not Be Exchanged," we find his take on a similar economic subject as above, namely, exchange, but one now drawn from cultural-anthropological notions: "We are forgetting how to give presents. Violation of the exchange principle has something nonsensical and implausible about it; here and there even children eye the giver suspiciously, as if the gift were merely a trick to sell them brushes or soap. Instead we have charity, administered beneficence, the planned plastering-over of society's visible sores."[14] Thinking and writing from the negative, *Minima Moralia* builds itself in this matter, eventually amassing a multitude of other observations about communicative and social aspects of American life, such as marriage, racism, or work relations, as well others about music, objects, or architecture, that is, the "culture industry" of late capitalism that is central to Adorno's focus in *The Dialectic of Enlightenment*. It is thus no surprise that two sentences most cited from Adorno's whole oeuvre are negations and originate from these microessays: "The whole is the untrue"[15] and "There's no right living in false life."[16] They illustrate what could be called Adorno's negative essayism, namely, working through an object essayistically until it can be negated

---

13 Theodor W. Adorno, *Minima Moralia* (New York: Verso, 2005), 195.
14 Adorno, *Minima Moralia*, 42.   15 Adorno, *Minima Moralia*, 80–81.
16 Adorno, *Minima Moralia*, 63–64.

philosophically and vice versa. The approach – or, perhaps better, the style – that Adorno would later define as "Negative Dialectics" originated from his earliest American works, especially his 1938 essay "On the Fetish Character of Jazz." Perhaps due to the institutional requirements of the discipline of philosophy, Adorno did not publish other such microessays. He kept writing them in his diaries, though, including after his return to Germany in 1951, likely as the basis for other larger works and articles, and possibly even for a second edition of microessays that he sought to call "Graeculus: Experiences after the Return."[17]

Shortly after publishing Minima Moralia back in Germany in 1951, Adorno indirectly acknowledged that his method of dialectical critique is indebted to essayistic thinking, and especially to a non-German experience. In his article "The Essay as Form," an influential attempt to define the form of the essay, Adorno ascribes to the essay the autonomy of thought necessary to develop a mode of critique between philosophy and literature that is "condemned as a hybrid"[18] in Germany, especially by its respective disciplines. While Adorno hence places the emergence of the essay in the French Enlightenment tradition, he also sees his American experience as the essayistic counterpoint to German culture's "resistance" to essays. "The way the essay appropriates concepts," he writes, in what reads like a schematic recollection of writing Minima Moralia while in the United States, "can best be compared to the behavior of someone in a foreign country who is forced to speak its language instead of piecing it together out of its elements according to rules learned in school."[19] One of the core definitions that Adorno gives for the essay is therefore one that sketches the blueprint of Minima Moralia, namely, the ability to take cultural objects at face value, as true items of an unfamiliar lifeworld that need to be conceptualized through writing:

> Instead of "reducing" cultural phenomena, the essay immerses itself in them as though in a second nature, a second immediacy, in order to negate and transcend the illusion of immediacy through its perseverance. It has no more illusions about the difference between culture and what lies beneath it than does the philosophy of origin. But for it culture is not an epiphenomenon

---

17 Theodor W. Adorno, "Graeculus (II). Notizen zu Philosophie und Gesellschaft 1943–1969," *Frankfurter Adorno Blätter* 8, no. 21 (my translation). See also Stefan Müller-Doohm, *Adorno. A Biography* (Cambridge, UK: Polity, 2005), 483.
18 Theodor W. Adorno, "The Essay as Form," in Alter and Corrigan, *Essays on the Essay Film* (New York: Columbia University Press, 2017), 60–82, 60.
19 Adorno, "Essay as Form," 70–71.

that covers Being and should be destroyed; instead, what lies beneath culture is itself *thesis*, something constructed, the false society.[20]

Adorno's experience in America demanded that he be an essayist, which clearly did more than shape his ability to analyze the logic of capitalism as the generative principle behind new social and cultural phenomena in Western societies; more importantly, it also equipped him with the non-German mode of analytic writing necessary to develop critical theory. From this perspective, it is not surprising that Adorno's mode of writing fell back to stricter philosophical monographs when he returned to Germany. Later works such as *The Jargon of Authenticity* (1964) or *Aesthetic Theory* (1970) are known for their almost incomprehensible style, which offered antisystematic and partly aphoristic writing, that, for some part, must be ascribed to the "hybrid" experience of exile and the adoption of the "hybrid" essayism in *Minima Moralia* and the Graeculus project, respectively. At the level of syntax, Adorno's German would continue to carry the hybrid but highly cryptic signature of the systematic German philosopher who had once been forced to write essays by his exile in America.

Davis and Marcuse against Oppression

When Angela Davis (1944–) traveled to Frankfurt in 1965 to study with Adorno for her postgraduate work, she was disappointed. "During the first few weeks," she writes in her autobiography of 1974, "I didn't understand a word of what Adorno was saying. Not only were the concepts difficult to grasp, but he spoke his own special aphoristic variety of German. It was a consolation to discover that most German students attending his lectures for the first time were having almost as much trouble understanding Adorno as I."[21] Staying in Frankfurt for two years, studying in the context of the Institute for Social Research and experiencing the growing New Left and the German student movement, Davis made her decision to return to the United States not simply because of Adorno's complicated style. Instead, as she writes later, it was because "Adorno discouraged me from seeking to discover ways of linking my seemingly discrepant interests in philosophy and social activism."[22] During her undergraduate years at Brandeis University, Davis

---

20 Adorno, "Essay as Form," 77.
21 Angela Davis, *Angela Davis: An Autobiography* (New York: Random House, 1974), 139.
22 Angela Davis, "Marcuse's Legacies," in Herbert Marcuse, *Collected Papers of Herbert Marcuse*, ed. Douglas Kellner, vol. 3, *The New Left and the 1960s* (London: Routledge, 2005), xi.

had studied with Herbert Marcuse (1898–1979), a former colleague of Adorno's at the Institute for Social Research (while it was housed in Germany as well as during its US residence), and it was Marcuse who had originally sent her to Frankfurt to study continental philosophy. When Davis left Germany for the United States, she stopped at the famous activist Dialectics of Liberation conference in London in July 1967, where Marcuse spoke next to civil rights activists such as Stokely Carmichael (1941–1998). She reconnected with Marcuse, and he welcomed her back as his student in the following years to work on her doctoral degree at UC San Diego. While studying Marx and Hegel and writing her dissertation in the critical theory tradition, Davis at the same time followed through with her activist plans and became member of the Black Panther Party. Still a graduate student, she also started to teach philosophy at UCLA in 1969, beginning with a course that became known as "Lectures on Liberation."[23]

As she later explained, it was Marcuse who demonstrated to her "that it was possible to be an academic, an activist, a scholar, and a revolutionary."[24] Unlike Adorno and Horkheimer, Marcuse remained in the United States for the rest of his life, teaching, publishing, and speaking publicly until his death in 1979. After returning to the United States, Angela Davis's activist work became as important for the Black liberation movement as her scholarly work was for the emergence of the field of Black studies and intersectionality. Her successful combination of theory and practice is thus also a direct effect of the same combination that the Frankfurt School critical theory demanded. Marcuse's *An Essay on Liberation* was published at the height of the New Left's activism in 1969 and attempted to show that societies across the globe were in a phase in which liberation from capitalism, neocolonialism, and race and gender inequality were finally becoming a possibility. "What is denounced as 'utopian,'" summarized Marcuse in his introduction of utopian speculation into critical theory, "is no longer that which has 'no place,'"[25] but that "revolution" can be taken "out of the continuum of repression and placed into its authentic dimension: that of liberation."[26] Even more than in his earlier more strictly philosophical works, Marcuse had now turned the critical theory of society that Adorno and Horkheimer used for analysis

---

23 Angela Davis, *Lectures on Liberation* (New York: NY Committee to Free Angela Davis, 1971).
24 Angela Davis, quoted in Barbarella Fokos, "The Bourgeois Marxist," *San Diego Reader* (23 August 2007), www.sandiegoreader.com/news/2007/aug/23/bourgeois-marxist/.
25 Herbert Marcuse, *An Essay on Liberation* (Boston: Beacon Press, 1959), 3.
26 Marcuse, *Essay on Liberation*, x.

into an attempt to teach a practice. His *Essay* signaled this possibilitarian mode by its overabundance of conditional constructions and future perfect: "the new society could then reach...,"[27] "the construction of a free society would create...,"[28] "features of a classless society must have become...."[29]

In the same year, Davis went in the same direction as Marcuse when she titled the first course she taught at UCLA "Lectures on Liberation." This was before her membership in the Communist Party and her use of "inflammatory language" got her fired from the faculty, and before she was imprisoned in 1970 for an alleged involvement in the Marin County Civic Center attacks. In prison, she wrote some of her most influential essays, especially *Political Prisoners, Prisons, and Black Liberation* (1971) and *Reflections on the Black Woman's Role in the Community of Slaves* (1970), which radically and sharply analyze the deep social foundations of the ongoing inequality and cruelty against Black people in the United States and elsewhere. Davis thus pursued the utopian potential of liberation that Marcuse had outlined in the essay form and wrote later that she and many others were "encourag[ed] ... to attempt to further develop the emancipatory promise of the German philosophical tradition."[30]

Brecht, Kantorowicz, and Mann against the American Essay

Herbert Marcuse had encouraged a direct continuation of the Frankfurt School tradition by US authors, scholars, and activists, especially among his students in California. In a way, this success stood in opposition to the many German émigrés in California who returned to Germany immediately after the war, and hence also returned to more academic and scholarly – and thus less essayistic – production. Expats like Bertolt Brecht (1898–1956) and the historian Ernst Kantorowicz (1895–1963) had instead become suspected of communist and hence anti-American influence during McCarthyism. One day after being interrogated by the House on Un-American Activities Committee in 1947, Bertolt Brecht decided to leave the United States for Switzerland, and eventually arrived home in Germany, that is, in the newly founded German Democratic Republic. He never returned to the United States, and the five years he spent in Santa Monica can by no means be called a productive phase. Kantorowicz, who arrived in the United States in 1938 and became a full professor at Berkeley in 1945, was also asked to position himself

---

27 Marcuse, *Essay on Liberation*, 86.
28 Marcuse, *Essay on Liberation*, 91.
29 Marcuse, *Essay on Liberation*, 89.
30 Davis, "Marcuse's Legacies," ix.

against communism. In 1949, the regents of the University of California system demanded from every faculty member the signing of a so-called loyalty oath, vowing that they had no connection to "any party or organization that believes in, advocates or teaches the overthrow of the United States Government by any illegal, unconstitutional means."[31] Kantorowicz declined to sign, stating that his experience with history in Germany forbade him any cooperation with "political inquisition, which paralyzes scholarly production."[32] He was fired from his position the next year and moved to the Princeton Institute for Advanced Study, where he conducted research until his death in 1963. In contrast to Marcuse, Kantorowicz remained rather withdrawn and dedicated most of his time not to teaching students or discovering new essayistic genres but to his extremely specialized studies on medieval history and theology.

Thomas Mann (1875–1955) was perhaps the most famous German author of the time and like Kantorowicz also lived in Princeton. He was equally irritated by McCarthyism and had to defend himself before the committee, but decided to stay in the United States and vowed never to return to Germany. Unlike Adorno's, Arendt's, and Marcuse's work in the United States, Mann's writing, like Kantorowicz's, did not adapt to the new conditions of the United States. These and other exiled scholars continued to live in Europhilic microcommunities and thus evaded any notable influence by the American essay, not producing any work that bears the features of American essayism. For a history of the German essayists in America, these émigré authors who avoided all essayism paradoxically still provide helpful insight. The forcefulness with which they refused essayism underscores its overwhelming power among others of their compatriots who found it a necessary tool of expression. In addition, such a rejection of American essayism also points to the condition mentioned at the very beginning of this chapter, namely, that an essayistic element of the American way of life might indeed exist (or had existed) that Brecht, Kantorowicz, and Mann felt but did not want seeping into their thinking and writing. With Adorno's proessayistic work in mind, Mann's famous sentence "Where I am, there is Germany," recorded by the *New York Times* upon his arrival in exile in 1938, can in retrospect hence be reframed from a statement about the immunity of German culture against fascism to a declaration of expat defiance against the American lifeworld in later age.

---

31 Ernst H. Kantorowicz, *The Fundamental Issue: Documents and Marginal Notes on the University of California Loyalty Oath* (San Francisco: Parker, 1950), 4.
32 Ernst H. Kantorowicz, "Letter to President Robert G. Sproul, October 4, 1949," in *Fundamental Issue*, 7.

Wolf against Socialism

Given the fact that many of the exiled Germans were indeed rather left leaning and influenced other progressive and anticonservative writers, artists, and activists, it is surprising to be confronted with the fact that perhaps the most famous author of the German Democratic Republic, Christa Wolf (1929–2011), took a year of respite from (post)socialism in California in 1992. As an intellectual accepted by the regime but also renowned outside of the German Democratic Republic, Wolf was already allowed to visit the United States during the Cold War by invitation of Oberlin College in 1974 and Ohio State University in 1983. During the fall of 1989, she had publicly demanded progressive changes to the socialist system of the German Democratic Republic and in 1990 published the autofictional novella *What Remains*, about living under the surveillance of the Stasi, the East German secret service. The fact that she claimed the novella had been written ten years prior, in 1979, led to a fierce controversy between the former East and West German intellectuals about her allegedly fraudulent self-fashioning as an intellectual critical of the regime. When in the spring of 1992 Wolf was granted access to her own Stasi surveillance file, she also found the reports about her brief activity as an unofficial spy against fellow authors in 1959. She publicly acknowledged her short involvement with the state apparatus, but when the records of her spying were published by the media, the controversy about the authenticity of her person and her writing flared up a second time. At that point, she had already accepted an invitation to the Getty Center in Santa Monica and thus left East Berlin burdened with the double weight of her own complicated involvement in the even more complicated history of East and West Germany after World War II. She stayed almost a year in the United States, ending with a visit to Dartmouth College in July 1993. Seventeen years later, she compressed that year into a book entitled *City of Angels, or: The Overcoat of Dr. Freud*, a winding attempt to come to terms with her own memories, involvement, and remaining agency vis-à-vis her history and her own work as it was shaped by living in East Germany. Wolf called this essayistic work a "novel,"[33] though it appears largely to be a cryptic autobiography. A much shorter text on the same complex exists, however, that more accurately fits the genre of the essay, compressing nearly the whole novel into fourteen pages. This essay is Wolf's entry for the year 1992 in her

---

33 Christa Wolf, *City of Angels, or: The Overcoat of Dr. Freud* (New York: Farrar, Straus and Giroux, 2013).

work *One Day a Year*, consisting of annual autobiographical essays written on or around each 27th of September since 1960 (a day she picked haphazardly).

The short essay about the last days of September 1992 consists of multiple layers woven into a cloth of memory: her arrival at the "paradise" of Santa Monica; her confrontation with new electronic machines and foreign everyday tools; rules of behavior in the United States; the history of California, especially the colonization of the Native Americans living in the area by the Spanish and later the Anglo-Americans; the disintegration of the former German Democratic Republic and the role of the West Germans in this process; and the role of the intellectuals in this situation, and, as she put it, "how much integration she should demand from herself without losing her integrity."[34] Historical layers of US history up to the present become interspersed with layers of German history, all concerning personal experiences and personal memories. At the same time, however, Wolf is not merely writing a diary entry, nor simply a description or memoir; she weaves these factual and personal observations into an essay that seeks to understand both: the objective through the subjective and vice versa. Here, conjecture and investigation of the United States are once again brought to convergence by a German essayist, and Wolf does so to arrive at a place where, hopefully, her own self and the course of history can be related or at least brought into harmony. Trying to expand this effort, the *City of Angels* project demonstrates how strenuous and draining the work of the exiled essayist is and how it still may not yield any of the desired results, especially not when extended over seventeen years. The fact that Wolf writes most of her last major work, *Medea*, during this very year in California and then practically ceases to work on new projects until her death in 2011 only confirms that the Californian year is decisive for her. An essayism situated in "Paradise" – looking back from a Californian perspective toward postsocialist Germany – is the only writerly mode in which Wolf is capable of processing the entanglement of history and self. In a way, Wolf could thus only bring this American essayism with her back to Berlin, where it took much of the rest of her life to finish the essayistic reinvestigation of her Californian avatar as she had encountered her in 1992–93.

Wolf's ambiguous relationship with "Paradise" thus echoes the 1740s "Paradise" essay by Christian Gottlieb Priber, discussed at the beginning of this chapter, which briefly tried to make manifest a utopian state in the

---

34 Christa Wolf, "Sonntag, 27. September 1992," in *Ein Tag im Jahr. 1960–2000* (Munich: Luchterhand, 2003), 491–507, 506 (my translation).

Carolinas, comprised of Indigenous people and foreigners with equal rights, before it was shut down by the French and British colonists.[35] It is, however, no accident that German authors writing over two centuries apart have stuck to such ambivalent ciphers as "Paradise" for America. As Wolf's work illustrates, authors and artists like Harun Farocki (1944–2014) and Kathrin Röggla (1971–) have more recently found similar and new ciphers to create essayistic works to bring out the essayism in American life. This country demanded and still demands, particularly from European émigrés, a continuous negotiation between idealized projection and hard-fought pragmatism, which, on the level of genre, simply describes one of the very core operations of an essay.

---

35 John Jeremiah Sullivan, "Ein Durchbruch in der Priber-Forschung: Die Entdeckung der Variante der Kapitelüberschriften," in *Priber Sommer Zittau 2016*, ed. Peter Knüvener (Görlitz: Gunter Oettel, 2017), 42–46.

22

The Essay and the American Left

ANDREA CAPRA

The politicization of the personal alters the status of the essay. Beginning from the 1960s, "the personal is political" became the rallying cry of student and feminist movements, which sought to affirm that personal experiences cannot be separated from sociopolitical structures, and that the former are conditioned by the latter. A few years earlier, in 1958, Theodor Adorno (1903–1969) argued in "The Essay as Form" that the essay shows how personal experiences are mediated "by the all-encompassing experience of historical humanity": In so doing, according to Adorno, the genre challenges the "self-delusion of an individualistic society and ideology," which resists acknowledging that the individual is to a large extent a product of social and historical configurations.[1] If the personal is political, the authority of the essayist – an authority based more on personal traits such as style, character, and lived experiences than institutional credentials – is strengthened, and her role vitalized.

The political nature of the personal was nothing new, per se: It was simply not commonly accepted, in particular for nonwhite, nonmale persons. African American writers of the first half of the century such as W. E. B. Du Bois (1868–1963) or Zora Neale Hurston (1891–1960) knew all too well the political nature of their personal struggles, which they thematized in autobiographical essays on racial segregation. Similarly, the political essence of, for instance, Randolph Bourne's (1886–1918) disability or Jane Addams's (1860–1935) womanhood are defining characteristics of their essayistic production. However, it was only in the second half of the century,

---

[1] Theodor W. Adorno, "The Essay as Form," *New German Critique*, 32 (Spring–Summer 1984): 151–71, 158.

under different social and political circumstances, that the personal became a shared paradigm for a series of political campaigns.

In keeping with a broad understanding of "the Left" as a political position that at a minimum supports social equality and progressivism,[2] this chapter, though by no means exhaustive, gives an account of several generations' worth of contributions to the American Left via the essay form. Simultaneously, it also explores why and how the essay became such a powerful and widespread platform for leftist voices. The politicization of the personal, as it became a foundational idea for the Left in the second half of the twentieth century, is a landmark that will assist navigating this sprawling archipelago.

The New York Intellectuals and the Postwar Left

The years after World War II and the beginnings of the Cold War were marked by profound difficulties for the American Left. The triumphalism of the United States coalesced with McCarthyism in creating an atmosphere of suspicion toward leftist positions, as organized labor, Socialist and Communist Parties – the base that made the 1930s New Deal possible – were under constant scrutiny, when not directly persecuted. A number of American leftists reacted by softening their political proclamations, and drew closer to the dominating ideology. Against this trend of complicity between intellectuals and ruling power, the socialist-democrat literary and social critic Irving Howe (1920–1993) published his 1954 essay "This Age of Conformity," in which he attacked the "undignified prostrations before 'wealth'" of his contemporaries, whose radical edge had been dulled by the promise of prestige and official recognition.[3] Howe's essay was a call for intellectual independence against the institutions holding the reins of power, in the political world and in the academic as well. According to Howe, the political

---

2 To provide a definition of "the Left" is no easy task given the heterogeneity of movements it loosely refers to, spanning revolutionary agents and others instead fully embedded in a capitalist framework. A more modest proposal is to define a lowest common denominator for what the Left is, one that leaves space for the various historical conjugations of the term. On the American Left and its history, see John Patrick Diggings, *The Rise and Fall of the American Left* (New York: W. W. Norton, 1992); and Seymour Martin Lipset, *It Didn't Happen Here* (New York: W. W. Norton, 2000). More recently, see James Gregory, "Remapping the American Left: A History of Radical Discontinuity," *Labor: Studies in Working-Class History of Americas* 17, no.2 (2020), 11–45; on the issues of defining what the Left is, see 14–15.
3 Irving Howe, *A Voice Still Heard: Selected Essays of Irving Howe* (New Haven, CT: Yale University Press, 2014), 7.

age of conformity was being replicated in literature departments by academics – the New Critics in particular – who promoted "a gradual bureaucratization of opinion and taste," which flattened out the complexities of literature to "schemes of structure and symbols."[4] Howe's piece read as a passionate defense of the intellectual humanist as "a mind committed yet dispassionate, ready to stand alone, curious, eager, skeptical," a species he considered at risk of being assimilated by the ideology of the age of conformity.[5]

Howe's explicit target was the essayist Lionel Trilling (1905–1975), who belonged, like Howe, to the ranks of the so-called New York Intellectuals, a community of writers and critics, for the most part Jewish, centered in New York in the mid-twentieth century, and outspoken supporters of an anti-Stalinist left.[6] The magazines *Partisan Review* and *Dissent* were the two main venues of the group, as they both embraced socialist views while rejecting the Soviet model. Their writings were characterized by an engagement with politics and the arts from a perspective outside academia, which resulted in an erudite yet witty and biting style. This was predominantly carried forth through the essayistic form, which allowed these writers to retain and leverage the tensions between political engagement, literary production, activism, and aesthetics. The group was almost entirely white and male, with the notable exception of Mary McCarthy (1912–1989), whose production intertwined sociopolitical matters with artistic ones – a typical trait of the New York Intellectuals indeed – as represented by the division of her 1961 essay collection *On the Contrary: Articles of Belief 1946–1961* into three sections titled "Politics and the Social Scene," "Woman," and "Literature and the Arts." McCarthy's interest in bringing together these three prongs of critical engagement made her a disruptive figure in the otherwise more compartmentalized and self-celebratory American culture of the 1950s, not only through her own essays but also through her perspicacity as a promoter of European female essayists: McCarthy had been an intimate friend of Hannah Arendt (1906–1975) since the 1940s, and in 1945 she translated for the magazine *politics* Simone Weil's (1909–1943) essay "The Iliad or the Poem of Force," written in the wake of Germany's assault of Paris in 1940, at a time when Weil was still practically unknown both in Europe and in the States.

Ideologically, the New York Intellectuals were rooted in a sociodemocratic activism connected with well-organized political forces such as labor unions

---

4 Howe, *Voice Still Heard*, 20. 5 Howe, *Voice Still Heard*, 25.
6 On the group, see Alan Maynard Wald, *The New York Intellectuals: The Rise and Decline of the Anti-Stalinist Left from the 1930s to the 1980s* (Chapel Hill, NC: University of North Carolina Press, 2017).

and the Socialist Party of America. A canonical distinction, to which we will return, counterpoises this Old Left to a New Left that arose in the 1960s and focused on topics such as sexual liberation, race and gender, libertarianism, and more participatory forms of democracy.[7] Among the main figures of the New York group, Howe remained one of the most consistent and authoritative voices on the sociodemocratic left, whereas some other essayists, such as Trilling, dissatisfied with the novel shifts in political discourse in the progressive field, drifted toward more moderate stances. Some others, such as Irving Kristol (1920–2009), moved on to lay the ideological foundations of the neoconservative movement.

Howe himself gave an account, in some part retrospective, of the tensions within the Left in his 1969 essay "The New York Intellectuals." There, he argued that the New Left's revolutionary enthusiasm abandoned "the ethical nail-biting of those writers of the left who suffered defeat and could never again accept the narcotic of certainty."[8] A novel political sensibility was gaining momentum, particularly among younger generations, and Howe acutely sensed the difficulties of the New York group in sustaining a confrontation with such new forces: The politicization of the personal and the revolutionary communitarianism of the New Left collided with the more class-based, traditional sociodemocratic credo of the New York Intellectuals.

In the same essay, Howe indeed explicitly separated the personal from the political: While he traced the roots of the group to the immigrant Jews fleeing Europe in the 1930s, he resolutely affirmed that Jewishness did not play any relevant role in the development of their common political sensibility. McCarthy's 1953 essay "Artists in Uniform" is also symptomatic of this tendency. The text describes McCarthy's encounter with a colonel and her refusal to share a meal with him after hearing his anti-Semitic remarks. The colonel is convinced that her strong reaction must be connected to some personal reason, and, in fact, the reader is made aware of McCarthy's Jewish ancestry. The colonel, on the contrary, remains oblivious to this detail, and the piece evolves into an intellectual skirmish between the two, with McCarthy fending off the colonel's insinuations about the personal motivation of her beliefs. Anything personal could be read by the colonel as a reason for McCarthy's political positions: Her green dress, she worries,

---

7 On the similarities, differences, and continuities between the Old and New Left, see Maurice Isserman, *If I Had a Hammer . . . The Death of the Old Left and the Birth of the New Left* (New York: Basic Books, 1987).
8 Howe, *Voice Still Heard*, 116.

may be taken as a symbol of bohemianism, which would in turn undermine her efforts at providing a depersonalized explanation for her political attitude.[9]

The complex interplay between the New York Intellectuals' personal backgrounds and their activism offers, in hindsight, a better understanding of their struggles in embracing the emerging political sensibilities of the 1960s. Their efforts to keep the personal and the political separated also demonstrate the rising public relevance of the interconnectedness of the two – something that became explicit once thousands of African American veterans were repatriated after the end of World War II to a country that treated them as second-class citizens. Starting with the mass protests of the 1950s, the politicization of the personal had become a political agenda for the civil rights movement, and the essay was about to become a weapon for change.

Essaying the Civil Rights Movement

Few writers have been as influential as James Baldwin (1924–1987) for the racial and sexual liberation movements. Born and raised in Harlem during the period of intellectual, social, and artistic effervescence of the local Black community known as the Harlem Renaissance, Baldwin grew increasingly frustrated with the racism and puritanism ingrained in American society, which profoundly affected his life as a Black homosexual. In 1948, he moved to France, where he would spend the rest of his life, mostly between Paris and the southern village Saint-Paul-de-Vence, while frequently traveling back to the United States, in particular during the 1960s, as a spokesperson for civil rights.

Baldwin's 1955 autobiographical essay anthology *Notes of a Native Son* paved the way for the evolution of the genre in the postwar period by explicitly reading his lived experiences as a Black man against the backdrop of society's political framework and ideological underpinnings. The collection comprised pieces that had already appeared in magazines such as *Harper's*, but also included works first published in more radical venues such as the *Partisan Review*. Its content spanned from art criticism to more overtly autobiographical essays about Baldwin's youth, and his experiences as an African American expatriate in Europe. "Notes of a Native Son" – the essay that gives the anthology its title – recounts Baldwin's experience with racial segregation in

---

9 Mary McCarthy, "Artists in Uniform," in *On the Contrary* (New York: Octagon, 1976), 55–74.

New York and New Jersey, and the death of his father on the day of the 1943 Harlem Riot, which took place after the shooting of an African American soldier by a white police officer. Through a fiery narration of his past, Baldwin sketches a personal genealogy of his tormented relation with the feeling of hatred kindled by racial discrimination, a feeling he describes as a disease that is both contagious and chronic: "[O]nce [one has] contracted [it]," Baldwin says, "one can never be really carefree again." The racialized nature of this contagion meant that "[t]here is not a Negro alive who does not have this rage in his blood,"[10] given the inherently political nature of the Black individual's personal struggle – a struggle more tied to structural forms of discrimination than specific, individualized ones. Hatred, however, "becomes an exhausting and self-destructive pose" – one that, according to Baldwin, must not go unchecked and should instead be leveraged to fight a just battle against one's own despair and society's injustices.[11]

Baldwin considered the essay to be a weapon for change, which allowed him to reach the consciences of his readers through the exorcism of his own demons rather than via depersonalized calls for action. His fire-and-brimstone style, deeply influenced by exposure to charismatic preachers such as his own father, found an ideal venue of expression in a genre characterized by an open, self-seeking, digressive, and even contradictory nature. For Baldwin, however, realizing the perils of hatred and trying to exorcise them does not pave the way for a smooth transition to love: "This does not mean, on the other hand, that loves comes easily: The white world is too powerful, too complacent, too ready with gratuitous humiliation, and above all, too ignorant and too innocent for that."[12] The path ahead remained a complicated and unresolved business – both personally for Baldwin and politically for society as a whole, as he wrote with disappointment in his new preface to *Notes of a Native Son* in 1984.[13]

In many ways, the personal yet political journey through hatred and love sketched by Baldwin's essays characterizes the American Left of the 1960s. Massive peaceful mobilizations and experiments in alternative lifestyles went hand in hand with clashes involving different demographics of the same nation and acts of violent insubordination against the ruling powers. Within the movement for racial liberation, the complex coexistence of different rhetorical positions is exemplified by Malcolm X (1925–1965) and Martin Luther King Jr. (1929–1968). Baldwin knew them both, and took issue with

---

10 James Baldwin, *Collected Essays* (New York: Library of America, 1988), 70.
11 Baldwin, *Collected Essays*, 83.   12 Baldwin, *Collected Essays*, 83.
13 Baldwin, *Collected Essays*, 808–15.

both: He was often impatient with King's nonviolent optimism but, at the same time, could not wholeheartedly embrace Malcolm X's belligerent and at times openly violent tone. Yet the two ministers – King was Christian, Malcolm X Muslim – both carried forth in their writings a personal struggle that was explicitly political. Two of the most influential documents of the fights of the 1960s are King's "Letter from Birmingham Jail" and *The Autobiography of Malcolm X*,[14] both of which are inherently essayistic both in form and content. The individual experiences they depict emerge from, and refer to, an instantiation of the "historical humanity" that Adorno sees as distinctive of the genre – and thus in both the personal becomes indistinguishable from the political. King's text, composed during his incarceration, is an indictment against his fellow clergymen, who, wanting to keep the personal and the political separate, advocated for carrying forth the battle against segregation only in the courts. Malcolm X's autobiography describes how his life and personal experiences formed the political persona who would go on to become a leading human rights activist.

Within the civil rights movement as well as the Left more broadly, the essay was also a means for internal debate. A notorious confrontation in the 1960s opposed Howe and African American writer Ralph Ellison (1913–1994), a former Communist. Ellison's essay "The World and the Jug" criticized Howe's "Black Boys and Native Sons," which appeared in 1963 in *Dissent*.[15] The dispute concerned the delicate balance of personal experiences and political militancy in African American literature: Howe saw militant protest as the foundational raison d'être of Black authors; Ellison, in response, indicted the New York writer for flattening out Black artistic expression. The essay also was at times a weapon for much more virulent attacks, such as in the case of Eldridge Cleaver (1935–1998). Cleaver was an early member of the Black Panther Party, which, founded in 1966 in Oakland, quickly became one of the most charismatic and controversial far-left Black revolutionary movements. While imprisoned for charges of sexual assault, he composed his essay collection *Soul on Ice*, published in 1968 after his release. Cleaver's essays present both a blunt portrait of life in segregated Black communities and a series of commentaries on the main topics and figures of the political

---

14 Martin Luther King Jr., "Letter from Birmingham Jail," in *Why We Can't Wait* (Boston: Beacon Press, 2010), 85–109; Malcolm X and Alex Harley, *The Autobiography of Malcolm X* (New York: Grove Press, 1965).
15 Ralph Ellison, "The World and the Jug," in *Shadow and Act* (New York: Random House, 1972), 107–43; Irving Howe, "Black Boys and Native Sons," *Dissent* (Fall 1963): 353–68.

landscape of the 1960s. His admiration for Malcolm X[16] clashes with the contempt he expresses in "Notes on a Native Son" for King's "self-effacing love for his oppressors,"[17] or for Baldwin's alleged "hatred for blacks" and sexual orientation – Cleaver considered Baldwin's homosexuality to be "a sickness, just as baby-rape or wanting to become the head of General Motors."[18]

The 1960s also witnessed intense political activism against the Vietnam War. That mobilization brought together preexisting social movements, such as the fight for civil rights, with new forces such as the student movement. The Students for a Democratic Society (SDS) quickly became one of the most important voices against the American involvement in Vietnam: Resolutely antiwar, the SDS advanced an agenda of participative democracy with an emphasis on self-organization and liberation of personal mores tied to sexuality and alternative lifestyles, and sided with the up-and-coming feminist movement. These movements laid the foundations of the New Left, which saw in the essay a formidable medium to wage its societal battles and express its novel political sensibility.

The New Left and the Essay against America

The New Left put at the forefront a broad range of social issues closely tied to personal rights and antiauthoritarian instances. It also abandoned for the most part the anti-Communism that defined the New York Intellectuals, and looked with increased interest at communist experiments taking place in countries such as China, Cuba, or Vietnam.

The linguist and intellectual Noam Chomsky (1928–) emerged in these years as one of the most important figures of the movement, and to this day he remains one of the leading voices in the progressive field. Chomsky rose to national popularity with his 1967 essay "The Responsibility of Intellectuals," first published in the *New York Review of Books*. Chomsky here argued that intellectuals have a moral responsibility to be active and informed participants in public life: "It is the responsibility of intellectuals to speak the truth and to expose lies. This, at least, may seem enough of a truism to pass over without comment. Not so, however. For the modern intellectual, it is not at all obvious,"[19] wrote Chomsky in a tone that echoes Howe's call to react

---

16 Eldridge Cleaver, "Initial Reactions on the Assassination of Malcolm X," in *Soul on Ice* (New York: Delta, 1999), 72–84.
17 Cleaver, "Initial Reactions," 132.   18 Cleaver, "Initial Reactions," 136.
19 Noam Chomsky, *The Responsibility of Intellectuals* (New York: New Press, 2017), 17–18.

against the age of conformity. Chomsky argued that the politicization of the personal does not only occur in face of oppression, but may also be triggered by privilege: The intellectuals' personal responsibility derives from their own political liberty and the free access to information and expression they enjoy. In the 1960s, according to Chomsky, this responsibility involved speaking up against the technocratic and political establishment that sought to justify the crimes perpetrated by American forces on foreign soil, with particular emphasis on the armed conflict in Vietnam. Chomsky's essay marked a new direction that became characteristic of the New Left also insofar as it explicitly attacked American foreign policies and the authoritative role that the United States played on a geopolitical level.

With Chomsky, the other most prominent voice of the New Left was Susan Sontag (1933–2004), whose public recognition soared after the publication in *Partisan Review* of her 1964 essay "Notes on 'Camp.'"[20] This piece exemplified an ongoing shift in cultural sensibility, moving from a preoccupation with high art to more "pop" forms of cultural consumption. However, the text in which Sontag best addressed the emerging political forces of the decade is her "What's Happening in America." The essay was written in 1966 as a response to a questionnaire from *Partisan Review* about the moral and political state of the nation, and offers a harsh critique of the United States, which Sontag considered to be a conservative country "founded on a genocide" and still haunted by the ghosts of slavery.[21] While attacking the premises and the contemporary development of the United States' foreign and internal politics, Sontag praised the youth movement of counterculture for their "renewed interest in politics (as protest and as community action, rather than as theory) and the way they dance, dress, wear their hair, riot, make love,"[22] with specific emphasis on the intertwinement of the political with personal praxis. For Sontag, herself involved in political militancy (in particular against the Vietnam war), the revolutionary potential of the current young generation stemmed from a radicalism that was "as much an experience as an idea": It was their personal experiences with drugs, nonnormative forms of sexuality, and alternative lifestyles that played the most fundamental role in shaping the political belief that "[t]he white race is the cancer of human history," and that it is "it alone – its

---

20 Susan Sontag, "Notes on 'Camp'" in *Against Interpretation* (New York: Farrar, Straus and Giroux, 1966), 275–92.
21 Susan Sontag, "What's Happening in America," in *Styles of Radical Will* (New York: Farrar, Straus and Giroux, 1969), 193–204, 195.
22 Sontag, "What's Happening in America," 199.

ideologies and inventions – which eradicates autonomous civilizations wherever it spreads, which has upset the ecological balance of the planet, which now threatens the very existence of life itself."[23]

For Adorno the essay was "the critical form *par excellence*,"[24] and the New Left certainly leveraged the critical potential of this genre. But, as the following section shows, the essay also allowed marginalized voices to express themselves freely and effectively, and thus substantially contribute to the emancipatory season of the 1970s.

Identity Politics and Marginalized Essayists

Internal tensions and differences notwithstanding, the battles fought by the Left led to considerable advances both in jurisprudence and in society at large. The novel attitudes of the New Left triggered significant changes in activism, particularly concerning the structure of political movements and the scope of their goals: As a result, in the 1970s, and continuing into the 1980s, the rising awareness of the politicized self gave visibility to marginalized racial, ethnic, and sexual groups in American society. Identity politics remains to this day one of the most relevant developments of the period, with its emphasis, shared with the New Left, on communitarianism. The term was coined in 1977 by the Black feminist organization Combahee River Collective,[25] and is generally understood as a political approach relying on the creation of limited-scale alliances between members of the same identifying group (e.g., racial or sexual) to carry forth a political agenda aimed at the recognition and betterment of the conditions of that specific group.[26] Against the backdrop of this political context, the essay, in bringing together the sociohistorical with the immediate life of the individual, was a privileged form of expression for voices that thus far had gone unheard or been silenced. In return, these voices brought forth their own political sensibilities, such as environmental awareness or a critique of heteronormativity, and in so doing further challenged the dogmas of the age of conformity lamented by Howe. A necessarily incomplete overview of some of these new figures offers

---

23 Sontag, "What's Happening in America," 203.   24 Adorno, "Essay as Form," 166.
25 Combahee River Collective, "A Black Feminist Statement (1977)," in Joy James and Denean Sharpley-Whiting, eds., *The Black Feminist Reader* (Hoboken, NJ: Wiley-Blackwell, 2000), 261–70.
26 For a general overview of the topic in the twentieth century, see James Tully, "Identity Politics," in *The Cambridge History of Twentieth-Century Political Thought*, ed. Terence Ball and Richard Bellamy (Cambridge, UK: Cambridge University Press, 2003), 517–33.

a glimpse at this emerging landscape, and shows the singular relevance of the essay as a platform of public outreach for marginalized identities.

The first Native American to be awarded the Pulitzer Prize, Navarre Scott Momaday (1934–) centered most of his production around his Kiowa heritage and achieved national popularity with his 1968 novel *House Made of Dawn*. In the introductory essay to his 1969 poetic memoir *The Way to Rainy Mountain*, Momaday encapsulates recurring themes of uprootedness and displacement via a lyric *nostos* to the Kiowa lands in Oklahoma, where he journeyed to visit the tomb of his late grandmother.[27] The personal engagement with his Kiowa heritage informs Momaday's sensibility in relation to environmental issues, which are prominent in his essayistic production. It was during those years, indeed, that the environmental movement started gaining traction in the general population, as the public progressively gained awareness of environmental concerns spanning from air and water pollution to the perils of nuclear energy and weapons. Momaday's 1970 essay "An American Land Ethic," first published in *Ecotactics: The Sierra Club Handbook for Environmental Activists*, insisted on the political necessity of embracing an ecological attitude in relation to the environment and its preservation: "We Americans must come again to a moral comprehension of the earth and air. We must live according to the principle of a land ethic. The alternative is that we shall not live at all."[28]

Parallel to Momaday, Asian American author Maxine Hong Kingston (1940–) plays with the malleability of short literary prose pieces of essayistic nature in her 1976 book *The Woman Warrior* to explore her personal past against the backdrop of both her Chinese ethnicity and broader societal issues. The mixture of lyric fiction, folklore, and autobiography that characterizes the collection is immediately at the forefront in the first piece of the collection, "No Name Woman," which centers on gendered topics such as pregnancy in a patriarchal society, and ethnic ones such as migration and community-building.[29] Although controversial to some due to her allegedly stereotypical representation of her ethnicity,[30] the importance of Kingston for

---

27 Navarre Scott Momaday, *The Way to Rainy Mountain* (Albuquerque, NM: University of New Mexico Press, 2019), 1–11.
28 Navarre Scott Momaday, "An American Land Ethic," in *The Man Made of Words* (New York: St. Martin's Press, 1997), 42–49, 49.
29 Maxine Hong Kingston, "No Name Woman," in *The Woman Warrior* (New York: Random House, 1977), 1–19.
30 See in particular Frank Chin, "Come All Ye Asian Americans Writers of the Real and the Fake," in *The Big Aiiieeeee! An Anthology of Chinese American and Japanese American Literature*, ed. Jeffery Paul Chan, Frank Chin, Lawson Fusao Inada, and Shawn Wong (New York: Meridian, 1999), 1–92.

the visibility of Asian minorities in the Unites States is unquestionable, and her work offers a nuanced, pained representation of their experiences as individuals and as a group. Similarly, in a later decade, Judith Ortiz Cofer's (1952–2016) autobiographical writings wrestle with the gendered experience of immigrant women. In her 1993 essay "The Myth of the Latin Woman," she discusses her own personal struggle with stereotypes that portray "the Hispanic woman as the 'Hot Tamale' or sexual firebrand," which she connects to a one-dimensional view intentionally promoted by the media.[31]

The examples of Kingston and Ortiz Cofer show how the encounter between the civil rights movement and the women's movement constituted a platform for new voices focusing on the intersection between structural racism and sexism. A critique leveled at the feminist movement of the 1960s and '70s was precisely that it overrepresented white women, while leaving underrepresented minorities in secondary positions. Audre Lorde (1934–1992) and Alice Walker (1944–) are two of the main figures in the African American community to have discussed this topic in their literary production. Both were engaged in social and political activism, and Walker theorized "womanism" in her essays as a current of feminism that places particular emphasis on the racialized experiences and concerns of women of color.[32] Their works, in particular essay collections such as Walker's 1983 *In Search of Our Mothers' Gardens* and Lorde's 1984 *Sister Outsider*, affirm the necessity of self-education regarding the oppressions of others, rather than expecting the oppressed minority to ascend to the role of educators, in order to trigger true change in society.[33] From this standpoint, the side of Walker's work aimed at rediscovering early Black writers not only assumes genealogical value, but also becomes a necessary requisite to dismantle racist and patriarchal thought.

Both Lorde, as a lesbian, and Walker, as a bisexual, explored the intersection of race, gender, and sexuality in their works. They also shared a friendship with the poet Adrienne Rich (1929–2012), whose writings played a decisive role in contemporary discussions about lesbianism and lesbian visibility. Rich's 1980 essay "Compulsory Heterosexuality and Lesbian Experience" attempted to demonstrate the socially and ideologically constructed nature of heterosexuality as a tool to preserve patriarchy by placing

---

31 Judith Ortiz Cofer, "The Myth of the Latin Woman," in *The Latin Deli* (New York: W. W. Norton, 1995), 148–54, 150.
32 Alice Walker, *In Search of Our Mothers' Gardens: Womanist Prose* (San Diego, CA: Harcourt, 1983), xi–xii.
33 Audre Lorde, *Sister Outsider* (Trumansburg, NY: Crossing Press, 1984).

women in a subordinate position.[34] Lesbianism, according to Rich, is not only a sexual orientation, but also a form of rebellion, and an extension of the struggle of feminism, focusing on the political nature of one's own sexuality.

These essays, in reading individualized experiences against the backdrop of broader societal issues, all react to an increasing awareness of the political nature of the personal. And fittingly, the formulation "the personal is political" itself originates from an essay, although it permeated the atmosphere of those years well before it became the title of a 1970 piece by the feminist Carol Hanisch (1942–), in which she refuted the alleged apolitical nature of women's discussion groups concerning gendered issues such as childcare or the division of household labor.[35]

West Coast Resistances

In the wake of the political movements of the period, academia sought to give formal recognition to, and expand upon, sociopolitical topics of pressing relevance. A number of the students whose political consciousness arose in the context of the New Left transitioned to university teaching positions, and produced works, for a considerable part of essayistic nature, whose relevance for the Left extends far beyond academic discourse. Where the essay allowed the authors of the previous section to express themselves and make their unique voices heard, academia made of the essay an analytical form of militant prose, which brought together theoretical sharpness and a strong, unabashed political tone. From this perspective as well, the personal – one's profession, in this case – became explicitly political.

If New York was the undisputed center of intellectual production in the years following the end of World War II, the West Coast became the locus of resistance against the ruling forms of conformity in the last third of the century. In particular, the Department of History of Consciousness at the University of California, Santa Cruz, housed some of the most relevant figures of recent decades for the progressive field, such as Angela Davis (1944–) and Donna Haraway (1944–). Their writings, although different in their aims and methodologies, both contributed to the evolution of the Left

---

[34] Adrienne Rich, "Compulsory Heterosexuality and Lesbian Experience," *Signs: Journal of Women in Culture and Society* 5, no. 4 (Summer 1980): 631–60.
[35] Carol Hanisch, "The Personal Is Political," in *Notes from the Second Year: Women's Liberation. Major Writings of the Radical Feminists*, ed. Shulamith Firestone and Anne Koedt (New York: Radical Feminism, 1970), 76–78.

at large by broadening the historical and speculative horizons of the feminist movement.

Davis's primary focus has been the study of the history and praxis of gendered and racial structural oppression, including slavery, violence against women, and the juridical and penitentiary system. Her production takes an approach explicitly focused on the role of race in the United States as an unavoidable point of departure for understanding historically situated forms of subjugation. The result of this work, starting from her early essays such as "Woman and Capitalism: Dialectics of Oppression and Liberation," written in jail and first published in 1977,[36] is an output that takes a Marxist standpoint in connecting female oppression to issues of class exploitation, colonial expansion, and national, patriarchal, and racial domination.[37]

While Davis's approach is historiographic in its nature, Haraway's production focuses more on the subversive role of science and technology in the feminist cause. In 1985, Haraway published in the magazine *Socialist Review* her essay "A Manifesto for Cyborgs: Science, Technology, and Socialist Feminism in the 1980s," which sought to disrupt standard dualisms, such as male/female, self/other, culture/nature, and their domineering roles in Western civilization through the novel opportunities offered by technoscientific development. In Haraway's words, the manifesto is "an effort to build an ironic political myth faithful to feminism, socialism, and materialism,"[38] and the cyborg symbolizes the possibility of reconfiguring identities according to different tenets: Irony, contradiction, instability, and hybridity become salient features of this novel entity, one that constantly traffics in an area of crossed boundaries rather than prefixed dualisms. In so doing, the cyborg refuses to abide by the separation of the personal and the political: "The cyborg is a kind of disassembled and reassembled, post-modern collective and personal self. This is the self feminists must code."[39]

---

36 In August 1970, Davis was charged with kidnapping, murder, and criminal conspiracy when some weapons she had purchased were used in an armed takeover of a courtroom in California. Proclaiming herself innocent, Davis fled. She was arrested in October in New York City, and spent sixteen months in jail before being released on bail. In 1972, after a trial that gathered substantial national and international attention, Davis was acquitted of all charges.
37 Angela Davis, "Woman and Capitalism: Dialectics of Oppression and Liberation," in James and Sharpley-Whiting, *Black Feminist Reader*, 146–82.
38 Donna Haraway, "A Cyborg Manifesto: Science, Technology, and Socialist-Feminism in the Late Twentieth Century," in *Simians, Cyborgs, and Woman. The Reinvention of Nature* (New York: Routledge, 1991), 149–82, 149.
39 Haraway, "Cyborg Manifesto," 163.

Similarly, the importance of Judith Butler's (1956–) critique of gender essentialism had echoes well outside academia. Butler's theories of gender performativity found first exposition in her 1988 essay "Performative Acts and Gender Constitution: An Essay in Phenomenology and Feminist Theory," written just a few years before Butler moved to the University of California, Berkeley, in 1993. In the essay, as she then articulated at greater length in her 1990 book *Gender Trouble*, Butler questions the appearance/substance dualism in relation to gender, arguing that "gender identity is a performative accomplishment compelled by social sanction and taboo."[40] For Butler, gender is an identity socially produced through a repetition of conventional acts, rather than something stable and possessing a preexisting nature. What preexists, on the contrary, are ideological and political discourses that enforce normative gender structures in society. The personal acts of performing one's gender are thus quintessentially political, and Butler reclaims the feminist slogan in her essay: "There is, latent in the personal is political formulation of feminist theory, a supposition that the life-world of gender relations is constituted, at least partially, through the concrete and historically mediated acts of individuals."[41]

Over the course of a handful of decades, as we've seen, the essay became one of the most important tools for leftist voices across the demographic and geographical spectrum of the States: The personalization of the political allowed academics and activists alike to leverage this form to reach broader audiences, thus expanding the realm of the politically possible. Yet the electoral landscape of the country gave the Left substantial reasons for concern; the essay, as was the case almost fifty years before, remained a privileged venue for assessing the direction and contradictions of the progressive movement.

Unachieved Genre, Unachieved Country

The vitality of the left on a literary and critical level did not translate to electoral successes on a national scale. After Lyndon Johnson concluded his mandate in 1969, the Republican Party won five out of the six of the presidential elections that followed. While much of the progressive intellectual discourse was increasingly critical of the United States' societal structures

---

40 Judith Butler, "Performative Acts and Gender Constitution: An Essay in Phenomenology and Feminist Theory," *Theater Journal* 40, no. 4 (December 1988): 519–31, 520.
41 Butler, "Performative Acts," 523.

and geopolitical influences, Ronald Reagan's conservatism ruled the 1980s undisputed, and at the end of his second term successfully passed the baton to his vice president, George Bush. The end of the Cold War did not recreate an age of conformism similar to the one that Howe lamented in the 1950s, yet it still triggered reflections about the political nature of the Left and its position in society. Supported by a Democratic Party increasingly pushed to the center, the Clinton presidency seemed to certify a split occurring at the heart of the public discourse: On the one hand was the political hegemony of the Right, exemplified by the New Democrats' embrace of fiscal conservatism; on the other hand the cultural hegemony of the Left, particularly in academia and in spheres of high culture. The nonsystematic nature of the essay remained a privileged field of debate for such issues on the Left, which to this day are still mostly unsolved.

The philosopher Richard Rorty (1931–2007) dedicated an important part of his work to the increasing distantiation between the intellectual Left and the rest of the society. Rorty believed that valid criticism against the United States and its history had mutated into unpatriotic feelings, which he considered detrimental to the leftist agenda. In his essays "The Unpatriotic Academy" and "Back to Class Politics," Rorty celebrated labor unions and the civil rights activists as bottom-up movements that built broad and effective political coalitions, which in turn allowed palpable progress in American society. Starting from the late 1960s, however, Rorty argued that the preconditions of this alliance ceased to exist due to the New Left's rejection of a baseline national pride, which thus resulted in the alienation of the working class and part of the middle class from the progressive movement. For Rorty, on the contrary, American patriotism and respect for cultural differences could and should coexist. This shift on the Left also effectively stripped the intellectual class of their role as cultural and political mediators, insofar as they "concentrated their energies on academic politics rather than on national politics."[42] Rorty was adamant that this greatly improved the morality of academia, and made university campuses better, more welcoming places for, in particular, nonmale, nonheterosexual, nonwhite persons. However, this turn inward also meant that the progressive intelligentsia invested fewer energies fighting the unchecked globalization of the markets in capital and labor, as had been promoted by the Right in particular during the 1980s. In light of the increasing economic inequalities caused by the development of a world-scale economy, Rorty argued that the priority for leftist academic politics should be to

---

42 Richard Rorty, *Philosophy and Social Hope* (New York: Penguin Books, 1999), 260.

reestablish bonds with the unions and the nation as a whole by centering itself "on the struggle to prevent the rich from ripping off the rest of the country."[43]

Rorty's political writings culminated in the last years of the 1990s, when he too began teaching in California, at Stanford University. There, he published the 1998 work *Achieving Our Country: Leftist Thought in Twentieth-Century American*, an amended collection of three lectures and two essays on the past and present condition of the Left in the United States, and the 1999 essay collection *Philosophy and Social Hope*, which reprinted the two texts discussed above after they had appeared, respectively, in the *New York Times* and *Dissent*.[44] Writing on the verge of the new century, Rorty dedicates *Achieving Our Country* to the memory of the essayist Irving Howe, who, like Rorty, did not ascribe any sense of inevitability or irrevocability to the victories of the Left. Rorty's retrospective analysis of a century of progressive movements did not shy away from its achievements: The outcome was unquestionably positive, spanning from increased wages and better working conditions to societal improvements for women and minorities. Yet, Rorty continues, the leftist project, in being the project of hope and progress, remains by definition unachieved and precarious, with its conquests threatened by rising inequality and the increasing distance between the working class on the one hand and society's institutionalized organs of sensemaking on the other hand. In raising these issues, Rorty foresaw some of the unresolved questions that the Left has dealt with since the turn of the millennium.

The personalization of the political and the debates around the topic accompanied the struggles of the progressive field for the second half of the twentieth century. And, as shown here, some of the main protagonists of this story found in the essay a privileged medium of expression – a genre that allowed them to turn themselves, to quote Adorno, into "an arena of intellectual experience, without simplifying it."[45] No matter how sprawling and contradictory, the history of the essay and the American Left is one of intense intellectual production, expressed through one's own signature style of writing and engaging directly in the political disputes of the moment.

---

43 Rorty, *Philosophy and Social Hope*, 261.
44 Richard Rorty, *Achieving Our Country: Leftist Thought in Twentieth-Century America* (Cambridge, MA: Harvard University Press, 1998); Rorty, *Philosophy and Social Hope*.
45 Adorno, "Essay as Form," 161.

23

The Native American Essay

HERTHA D. SWEET WONG

> *For Native writers, who have long operated within a literary sphere in which most depictions of Native lives are created by non-Natives, nonfiction allows for a revision of the dominant cultural narratives that romanticize Native lives and immobilize Native emotional responses: the essay is the work of feeling and thinking. It is the flux of character, not a frozen image of one.*
>
> *– Elissa Washuta and Theresa Warburton*[1]

Whether it is defined as a short piece of subjective writing on a specific topic or in the more experimental mode proposed by Michel de Montaigne as a "trial" or a process of self-reflection, the essay form arose from literate Western societies. It goes without saying that the essay is not indigenous to what is now the United States. And yet, as with many other literary genres, Indigenous writers, surviving settler colonialism in its various stages, have made it their own.

The Western essay assumes alphabetic literacy and the individual autonomous subject. In contrast, story is a key Indigenous form that arises in orality but shifts into writing as well, all the while assuming a communal subjectivity. Similarly, Montaigne's emphasis on the essay as a process of self-discovery is based upon individualism and a certain class status. Unlike the self-centered focus of Western forms of essay, Indigenous forms insist on community. But, of course, there are variations after so many years of settler colonial domination. So what do essays by Native American writers look like?

It is feasible to argue that Indigenous essays appear embedded in the forms of stories, sermons, appeals, ethnographies, autobiographies, journals, and

---

1 Elissa Washuta and Theresa Warburton, "Introduction: Exquisite Vessels," in *Shapes of Native Nonfiction: Collected Essays by Contemporary Writers*, ed. Elissa Washuta and Theresa Warburton (Seattle, WA: University of Washington Press, 2019), 3–20, 10.

periodicals, as well as in scholarship. For a long time, Indigenous essays in the United States tended to be less inner directed and more outer directed, less explorative and more educational and argumentative. Historically, they have performed the work of bearing witness to individual and collective loss and injustice. Again and again, Indigenous writers have told the history of murder, dispossession, forced reeducation, exploitation, and mistreatment. Again and again, Indigenous people have proclaimed their existence and continuance and argued for sovereignty.

Early Nonfiction

It is fitting to start with the writings of Samson Occom (Mohegan, 1723–1792), an ordained Presbyterian minister and author of sermons, journals, letters, ethnographies, petitions, and an autobiography. An "intertribal political figure acutely engaged in the day-to-day business of survival" in a world being disfigured by settler colonialism, Occom was conversant with the "intersecting tribal, intertribal, and colonial situations and their respective rhetorical demands."[2] His works offer rare insight into Indigenous life and thinking in the eighteenth century. My focus here is on his petitions and his short, remarkably incisive essay comparing Indigenous people and African Americans to Europeans and European American settlers.

Throughout his thirteen petitions and legal documents, Occom composes argumentative essays that make the case for the collective rights of Indigenous people: the right to exist in peace, to self-govern, to keep their land and its resources, and to educate their own children. With an early "intersectional" awareness,[3] Occom begins "The Most Remarkable and Strange State Situation and Appearance of Indian Tribes in the Great Continent" (1783) by lamenting the material poverty of Indigenous and Black people. He quickly expands his vision, however, from the local to the global: "[W]hen I Come to Consider and See the Conduct of the Most Learned, Polite, and Rich Nations of the World, I find them to be the Most Tyranacal, Cruel, and inhuman oppressors of their Fellow Creatures in the

---

2 Joanna Brooks, "Prose," in *The Collected Writings of Samson Occom, Mohegan: Literature and Leadership in Eighteenth-Century Native America*, ed. Joanna Brooks (New York: Oxford University Press, 2006), 41–44, 41.

3 Occom's awareness of the linked oppressions of Native and African American peoples is revealed also in his correspondence with Phillis Wheatley. This awareness continues in essays by many Native writers such as William Apess, Charles A. Eastman (who corresponded with W. E. B. Du Bois), and Vine Deloria Jr.

World."[4] With intentional irony, he invokes Europe's self-perception as "the Most Learned, Polite and Rich Nations," but turns it on its head, unmasking the benign façade of colonial horrors: wealth that is obtained through atrocity and tyranny and at the expense of Indigenous and Black people.[5]

Nineteenth-Century Nonfiction

There are many nineteenth-century autobiographical works, histories, stories, ethnographies, newspaper and magazine articles, and boarding school writings, some of which contain what may be considered short essays within them. A Methodist preacher, writer, and Native rights activist who was jailed for his participation in the Mashpee Revolt, William Apess (Pequot, 1798–1839) wrote autobiographies, essays, and sermons that circulated as pamphlets to reach a white audience. In "An Indian's Looking-Glass for the White Man" (1833), he offers an early scathing critique of white supremacy, what Jace Weaver refers to as "resistance literature."[6] Using biblical language and stories, Apess links prejudice against Indigenous people to that against Black people. It is neither skin color nor race, he argues, but "principles" that matter. If God believed that "black or red skins" were inferior, he concludes, "it appears he has disgraced himself a great deal – for he has made fifteen colored people to one white."[7]

Sarah Winnemucca Hopkins (Paiute, 1844–1891) advocated for Indigenous rights as a writer, interpreter, and performer. In chapter 2 ("Domestic and Social Moralities") of *Life Among the Piutes* [sic]: *Their Wrongs and Claims* (1883), she folds a brief ethnographic essay into her account. She describes the role of stories, peaceful life before the settlers came, and many cultural customs. Throughout, she contrasts then and now: Before, life was beneficent, but now "[m]y people have been so unhappy for a long time they wish now to *disincrease*, instead of multiply."[8] Mothers are afraid to bring children, especially daughters, into such a violent world.

---

4 Samson Occom, "The Most Remarkable and Strange State Situation and Appearance of Indian Tribes in the Great Continent," in *The Collected Writings of Samson Occom, Mohegan: Literature and Leadership in Eighteenth-Century Native America*, ed. Joanna Brooks (New York: Oxford University Press, 2006), 58–59, 58.
5 Occom, "Most Remarkable," 58.
6 Jace Weaver, *That the People Might Live* (New York: Oxford University Press, 1996), 55.
7 William Apess, "An Indian's Looking-Glass for the White Man," in *On Our Own Ground: The Complete Writings of William Apess, a Pequot*, ed. Barry O'Connell (Amherst, MA: University of Massachusetts Press, 1992), 155–61, 157.
8 Sarah Winnemucca Hopkins, "Domestic and Social Moralities," in *Life Among the Piutes: Their Wrongs and Claims*, ed. Mrs. Horace Mann (Bishop, CA: Chalfant Press, 1969), 45–57, 48.

Celebrated spokesman and writer Simon Pokagan (Potawatomi, 1830–1899) composed numerous birchbark books. Chief among these is *The Red Man's Rebuke* (1893), in which he addresses "the pale-faced race that has usurped our lands and homes." His people, he explains, do not feel like celebrating the "great Columbian Fair" occurring in Chicago.[9] Rather than laud the grand achievements of the conquerors, he advises that white people "not forget that this success has been at the sacrifice of *our* homes and a once happy race."[10] He makes an eloquent plea for whites to rid themselves of their prejudice against Indians. He concludes with a vision that righteous people (Indian and non-Indian) will rise and "the remaining shame-faced multitude" will be judged by the Great Spirit who will declare: "[Y]ou are guilty of having tyrannized" Indigenous people; "I find you guilty of having made wanton wholesale butchery of their game and fish"; "I find you guilty of using tobacco" in unhealthy ways;[11] "I find you guilty of ... cheating and robbing." "I also find you guilty," he concludes, of introducing alcohol.[12] The series of parallel repetitions generates mounting intensity for his denunciation.

Early Twentieth-Century Nonfiction

Zitkála-Šá (Gertrude Simmons Bonnin, Yankton Dakota, 1876–1938) served as secretary of the Society of the American Indian and president of the National Council of American Indians. She also edited the *American Indian Magazine* from Carlisle Indian School. Her own essays criticizing the Carlisle agenda to "kill the Indian, save the man" were controversial among some white readers. Her account of her Quaker boarding school experience in *The School Days of an Indian Girl* (1900) documents her cultural disorientation and loneliness. In *Impressions of an Indian Childhood* (1921), she recuperates memories of her family prior to boarding school. Perhaps best remembered for her 1902 essay, "Why I Am a Pagan" (published in the *Atlantic Monthly*), she describes her connection to the natural world and the stories of her people animating it.

In his autobiography *Indian Boyhood* (1902), Charles Alexander Eastman (Dakota, 1858–1939) tells the story of his early life. It is filled with descriptions of childhood training, family traditions, dances, and feasts as well as accounts of brutal encounters with the *Wasichu* (white man). In the penultimate chapter of *Indian Boyhood*, "The Laughing Philosopher," Eastman produces

---

9 Simon Pokagan, *The Red Man's Rebuke* (Hartford, MI: C. H. Engle, 1893), 1.
10 Pokagan, *Red Man's Rebuke*, 2. Pokagan's emphasis.
11 Pokagan, *Red Man's Rebuke*, 14.   12 Pokagan, *Red Man's Rebuke*, 15.

a meditative essay, combining description, narration, and argument. Eastman challenges "the idea that the natives of this country have no sense of humor and no faculty for mirth."[13] Claiming that Indian humor is abundant and hearty, consisting "as much in the gestures and inflections of voice as in words," Eastman declares Indian humor "untranslatable."[14] Even so, he attempts to translate it by sharing three humorous stories told by men smoking pipes around a fire. Eastman enlivens the stories with character, dialogue, and listener response. After asserting his main point that Indians have a vibrant sense of humor, he illustrates it with narrative examples, incorporating storytelling into his essay.

Indian Boyhood was followed by *The Soul of the Indian* (1911), a sketch of "the religious life of the typical American Indian as it was before he knew the white man."[15] Five years later, in the midst of Native advocacy for citizenship rights, Eastman published another autobiography, *From the Deep Woods to Civilization* (1916). Fluctuating between Eurocentric and Indigenous perspectives, Eastman carefully mediates between them, most notably in his pronoun shifts as he refers to Indians sometimes as "we" and sometimes as "they." Irony is a powerful tool for Eastman. He uses the language often used by whites to describe Indians, but reverses it, illustrating the "savagery of civilization."[16]

E. Pauline Johnson (Mohawk, 1861–1913), a poet and stage performer (known as the "Mohawk Princess") in Canada, made several trips to England to advocate for Indigenous rights. Johnson published a well-known essay, "A Pagan in St. Paul's Cathedral," in her book of stories, *The Moccasin Maker* (1913). Johnson describes traveling to London, the "camping-ground of the paleface."[17] Upon entering St. Paul's Cathedral, she is transported home to her people and "the camp fires of the Onondaga 'long-house,' and the resinous scent of the burning pine across the fetid London air."[18] Like Eastman, she sets up a series of binary oppositions – Indian/white – and insists on an equality between Christianity and her Indigenous religious practices.[19]

---

13 Charles A. Eastman, "The Laughing Philosopher," in *Indian Boyhood* (New York: Doubleday, Page, 1911), 267–76, 267.
14 Eastman, "Laughing Philosopher," 267.
15 Charles A. Eastman, "Foreword," in *The Soul of the Indian: An Interpretation* (Lincoln, NE: University of Nebraska Press, 1980), ix–xiv, ix–x.
16 Charles A. Eastman, *From the Deep Woods to Civilization: Chapters in the Autobiography of an Indian* (Boston: Little, Brown, 1916), 139.
17 E. Pauline Johnson, "A Pagan in St. Paul's Cathedral," in *The Moccasin Maker* (Toronto: Ryerson Press, 1913), 139–43, 139.
18 Johnson, "Pagan in St. Paul's," 142.
19 Johnson published other essays on this topic: E. Pauline Johnson, "The Iroquois of the Grand River," *Harper's Weekly* (23 June 1894): 587–89; and "The Great New Year White Dog: Sacrifice of the Onondagas," *Daily Province Magazine* (14 January 1911): 16.

These early essayists wrote for primarily European American audiences (and future Indigenous ones), and they had to employ rhetorical dexterity to simultaneously criticize and engage with their readers.

Newspapers and Periodicals, Nineteenth Century to the Present

Indian newspapers and periodicals have been an important resource for Indigenous essays. Oliver Scheiding notes that Native "newspapers and journals contributed to a larger Native American intellectual tradition."[20] Following in the footsteps of Joshua Nelson,[21] Scheiding argues that newspapers (and periodicals) like the *Cherokee Phoenix* (1828–34) edited by Elias Boudinot (Cherokee, 1802–1822) and *Copway's American Indian* (1851) edited by George Copway (Kah-Ge-Ga-Gah-Bowh, Anishinaabe, 1818–1869) are not examples of assimilated Indians who sold out, but of nuanced "progressive work" with "a distinct Indigenous perspective."[22] John Rollin Ridge (Yellow Bird, Cherokee, 1827–1867), the first Native American novelist, worked as a newspaper editor and writer for the *Sacramento Bee* and the *San Francisco Herald*. Under the name Fus Fixico, Alexander Posey (Creek, 1873–1908) published newspaper columns in the form of letters satirizing federal Indian policy as well as local and national politics.[23] Native writing in newspapers and periodicals helped to establish what Scott Richard Lyons has termed "rhetorical sovereignty."[24]

A special category of newspaper and periodical publications arose in the boarding schools in which Indian students wrote essays at the prompts of their teachers for consumption by the school and supporters of Indian

---

20 Oliver Scheiding, "Nineteenth-Century American Indian Newspapers and the Construction of Sovereignty," in *The Cambridge History of Native American Literature*, ed. Melanie Benson Taylor (Cambridge, UK: Cambridge University Press, 2020), 89–112, 91; see also Robert Warrior, *The People and the Word: Reading Native Nonfiction* (Minneapolis: University of Minnesota Press, 2005), xvii.

21 Joshua B. Nelson, *Progressive Traditions: Identity in Cherokee Literature and Culture* (Norman, OK: University of Oklahoma Press, 2014).

22 Scheiding, *Nineteenth-Century American Indian*, 92. For an anthology of early Indigenous writing, see Daniel F. Littlefield Jr. and James W. Parins, eds., *American Indian and Alaska Native Newspapers and Periodicals, 1826–1924* (New York: Greenwood Press, 1984); and Bernd C. Peyer, ed., *American Indian Nonfiction: An Anthology of Writings, 1760–1930* (Norman, OK: University of Oklahoma Press, 2007).

23 See Daniel F. Littlefield and Carol A. Petty Hunter, "Introduction," in Alexander Posey, *The Fus Fixico Letters: A Creek Humorist in Early Oklahoma*, ed. Daniel F. Littlefield and Carol A. Petty Hunter (Norman, OK: University of Oklahoma Press, 1993), 1–48, 8.

24 Scott Richard Lyons, "Rhetorical Sovereignty: What Do American Indians Want from Writing?" *College Composition and Communication* 51, no. 3 (2000): 447–68, 449.

education. Student work was used as evidence of educational "success" and included in fundraising efforts.[25]

Essays published today in newspapers such as *Indian Country Today* (formerly the *Lakota Times*), *Akwesasne Notes* (Mohawk Nation), the *Native American Times* (Tahlequah, Oklahoma), and the *Circle: Native American News and Art* (Minnesota), as well as others, deserve systematic study as a rich source of Indigenous thought in essay form. These are important voices that while reaching a local community may not be reaching a national or global readership. In addition, sustained attention to essays by Indigenous writers that have been published in magazines (Native-focused publications such as *News from Native California*, special topic magazines such as *Sierra*, or general magazines) would make audible voices that are now scattered throughout various regions.[26] All of these types of nonfiction publications have been present in the nineteenth century and into the twentieth and twenty-first centuries.

Mid-Twentieth- to Twenty-First-Century Nonfiction: Political Essayists[27]

Like Sarah Winnemucca Hopkins, in her *A Salishan Autobiography* (written in the 1930s, published 1990), Mourning Dove (Christine Quintasket, Colville Confederated Tribes, ca. 1885–1936) interweaves ethnographic essays and critiques of US Indian policies into her personal narrative. She includes chapters on "female activities, seasonal activities, and incidents from recent history."[28]

---

25 See Jacqueline Emery, *Recovering Native American Writings in the Boarding School Press* (Lincoln, NE: University of Nebraska Press, 2017); and Arnold Krupat, *Changed Forever: American Indian Boarding-School Literature*, 2 vols. (Albany, NY: State University of New York Press, 2018–2020).
26 For example, see the essay published by Indigenous rights lawyer Sherri Mitchell (Weh'na Ha'mu Kwasset), "Theory of Natural Connection," *Year in Search: The Search for Why, Pop-Up Magazine* (December 2020): 42–43. See also the essay by Native ecologist and professor Melissa K. Nelson (Anishinaabe/Métis), "Time to Indigenize Conservation," *Sierra* (January–February 2021): 42–43. These types of essays are often overlooked.
27 While I divide these essays into "political" and "literary" categories, I am well aware that the distinction is dubious. Of course, all of the "literary" (and by this I mean written by writers of fiction and poetry, etc.) essays are political, and many of the "political" essays are literary.
28 Jay Miller, "Introduction," in *Mourning Dove: A Salishan Autobiography*, by Mourning Dove (Christine Quintasket), ed. Jay Miller (Lincoln, NE: University of Nebraska Press, 1990), xi–xxxix, xxxiii.

No Indigenous writer has written more, and more influential, essays than Vine Deloria Jr. (Standing Rock Lakota, 1933–2005). Embedded in his Standing Rock community and with an MA in theology and a JD, Deloria was in a powerful position to offer insights about religion, law, and history. He published more than twenty books (many of which were collections of essays), but I will focus on two to illustrate his key critiques of not only US Indian policies, but Western culture more generally. Like Apess, he denounces settler colonialism. In his famous *Custer Died for Your Sins: An Indian Manifesto* (1969), Deloria presents a concise overview of American Indian history – broken treaties, boarding schools, and termination policy as well as critiques of missionaries, anthropologists, and the Bureau of Indian Affairs (BIA). He discusses Native humor and compares "Red and Black" oppressions.[29] This volume of essays greatly influenced the Red Power movement of the 1970s.

In *God Is Red: A Native View of Religion* (1973), Deloria continues Eastman's work, revealing the core differences between Christianity and Indigenous religions. In "Thinking in Time and Space," he explains that European Americans and Native Americans ground their religions in two fundamentally distinct ways: "American Indians hold their lands – places – as having the highest possible meaning … . Immigrants review the movement of their ancestors across the continent as a steady progression …, thereby placing history – time – in the best possible light."[30] The European focus on individual revelation and the need to preach extracts "the deity of a particular local situation"[31] and leads to a claim about its "universal" relevance.[32] In contrast, most Native religions have "a sacred center at a particular place";[33] revelation focuses on survival of the community or nation rather than on the individual. Rather than preaching, for Indigenous peoples, "[e]thics flow from the ongoing life of the community and are virtually indistinguishable from the tribal or communal customs."[34] Boldly unapologetic, Deloria offers a searing critique of settler colonialism and its epistemological underpinnings.[35]

---

29 Vine Deloria Jr., *Custer Died for Your Sins: An Indian Manifesto* (New York: Macmillan, 1969).
30 Vine Deloria Jr., "Thinking in Time and Space," in *God Is Red: A Native View of Religion* (Golden, CO: Fulcrum, 2003), 61–76, 61.
31 Deloria, "Thinking in Time," 65.   32 Deloria, "Thinking in Time," 64.
33 Deloria, "Thinking in Time," 66.
34 Deloria, "Thinking in Time," 67. Deloria expands upon this difference in another essay in the volume – "The Spatial Problem of History," in *God Is Red*, 113–33 – in which he outlines an Indigenous "sacred geography" (121).
35 Deloria also wrote *We Talk, You Listen: New Tribes, New Turf* (New York: Macmillan, 1970) in which he criticizes individualist capitalism and argues for the inclusion of

Like many others, environmental and Indigenous rights activist Winona LaDuke (Anishinaabe, 1959–) continues the call for Americans to acknowledge Indigenous people and the original and continuing wrongs committed against them in order to imagine ways to heal. In *Recovering the Sacred: The Power of Naming* (2005, 2015), she asks: "*How does a community heal itself from the ravages of the past*,"[36] especially when those ravages are not only not apologized for, but unacknowledged? Her answer is in "the multifaceted process of recovering that which is 'sacred.'"[37] Like Deloria, she discusses settler colonial history, Christianity, and Native epistemologies. Vividly, she documents the grassroots efforts of Native Americans from many nations as they design recovery programs: recovery of people from substance abuse, recovery of "traditional agriculture" and Indigenous diets and medicines that nurture the people, recovery of land (both working to gain its return or to heal it from abuses of pesticides or overuse), recovery of animals, recovery of ancestral remains and cultural artifacts from museums, recovery from over 500 years of colonization. Like others, she offers hope that "[t]hrough it all the people and the land remain."[38]

In *Everything You Know about Indians Is Wrong* (2009), Paul Chaat Smith (Comanche), like Vine Deloria Jr., eviscerates – with dry wit, irony, and the humor of a stand-up comic – the entire historical-present scenario for Indigenous people. As an activist turned art curator at the National Museum of the American Indian, he critiques historic injustices as well as perpetual stereotyping of Indigenous people. Smith discusses the distortions of Hollywood Western films, the contributions of Native conceptual artists, and the complex formulations of Native identity.

Native epistemologies as part of a corrective reckoning. In *Red Earth, White Lies: Native Americans and the Myth of Scientific Fact* (Golden, CO: Fulcrum, 1997), Deloria inspired many Indigenous people to speak up, resulting in collections of essays such as M. Annette Jaimes's edited collection of essays, *The State of Native America: Genocide, Colonization, and Resistance* (Boston: South End Press, 1992); Elizabeth Cook-Lynn's (Crow Creek Dakota, 1930) *Why I Can't Read Wallace Stegner* (Madison, WI: University of Wisconsin Press, 1996); William S. Penn's (mixed-blood Nez Perce, 1949–) *All My Sins Are Relatives* (Lincoln, NE: University of Nebraska Press, 1995), and *As We Are Now: Mixblood Essays on Race and Identity* (Berkeley, CA: University of California Press, 1997). See also MariJo Moore, ed., *Genocide of the Mind: New Native American Writing* (New York: Thunder's Mouth Press/Nation Books, 2003); fiction writer Thomas King's (Cherokee, German, Greek) *The Truth about Stories: A Native Narrative* (Toronto, ON: House of Anansi Press, 2003); and *The Inconvenient Indian: A Curious Account of Native People in North America* (Minneapolis, MN: University of Minnesota Press, 2013).

36 Winona LaDuke, *Recovering the Sacred: The Power of Naming* (Chicago: Haymarket Books, 2015), 20. Italics in original.
37 LaDuke, *Recovering the Sacred*, 20.   38 LaDuke, *Recovering the Sacred*, 176.

Indigenous essays also address specific disciplines as Native scholars work to indigenize them. See, for example, the philosophical essays in *American Indian Thought: Philosophical Essays* (2004) edited by Anne Waters (Seminole) and the environmental essays in Professor of Environmental and Forest Biology Robin W. Kimmerer's (Potawatomi, 1953–) *Braiding Sweetgrass: Indigenous Wisdom, Scientific Knowledge, and the Teachings of Plants* (2013).

Mid-Twentieth to Twenty-First-Century Nonfiction: Literary Essayists

Talking to the Moon (1945) by John Joseph Mathews (Osage, 1895–1979) is a collection of lyric essays based on Mathews's ten years living in solitude in Osage country (northeast Oklahoma). After obtaining an Oxford education and serving as a pilot in World War I, he returned to his home. "I wanted to become a part of the flow in so far as I was able," he explains, "to learn something of the moods of the little corner of the earth which had given me being; to learn something of the biological progression and the mysterious urge which inspired it."[39] His wife, Elizabeth Mathews, describes *Talking to the Moon* as "John Joseph Mathews' *Walden*."[40] In the collection, organized by seasons, Mathews meditates upon the land, plants, and animals, incorporating stories, ethnographic information, and humor.

N. Scott Momaday (Kiowa, 1934–), novelist, poet, essayist, and artist, is best known for his novel *House Made of Dawn* (1968), which was awarded the Pulitzer Prize for Literature in 1969.[41] Momaday's most famous essay, "The Man Made of Words," articulates his personal and literary philosophy and sets the key themes for all of his other essays. He discusses his Kiowa heritage, the power of language and imagination, the Indigenous relationship with the land, and the interplay among these. For Momaday, "we are all made of words," because language is "the element in which we think and dream and act, in which we live our daily lives."[42] In 1997 he published a book entitled

---

[39] John Joseph Mathews, *Talking to the Moon: Wildlife Adventures on the Plains and Prairies of Osage Country* (Chicago: University of Chicago Press, 1981), 2.
[40] Elizabeth Mathews, "Foreword [1980]," in Mathews, *Talking to the Moon*, n.p.
[41] This event was credited with launching what Kenneth Lincoln called the Native American Renaissance. Kenneth Lincoln, *Native American Renaissance* (Berkeley, CA: University of California Press, 1983).
[42] N. Scott Momaday, "The Man Made of Words," in *The Remembered Earth: An Anthology of Contemporary Native American Literature*, ed. Geary Hobson (Albuquerque, NM: University of New Mexico Press, 1979), 162–73, 162.

The Man Made of Words: Essays, Stories, Passages, which includes essays and short writings from his long career, from the 1960s to the 1990s, as well as his own illustrations.

Many essays speculate about the power of words. Others focus on the dire need for an "American Land Ethic" that rejects the European American history of seeing land as property in favor of a notion of the earth and humans in a complex interrelationship. "We Americans need now more than ever before," he writes, "to imagine who and what we are with respect to the earth and sky. I am talking about an act of imagination, essentially, and the concept of an American land ethic."[43] Like so many before him, Momaday insists on the sacred and intimate relationship to land shared by Indigenous people who have lived upon it for centuries or millennia. What links all of these essays is Momaday's concern for a loss of the sacred – of land, of language, of culture. It is language, he concludes, that can help to heal such persistent material and psychic diminishment.

Leslie Marmon Silko (Laguna Pueblo, 1948–), novelist, poet, and artist, covers a broad array of topics in her essays: Indigenous history, literature, religion, culture, land, and photography. In *Yellow Woman and a Beauty of the Spirit: Essays on Native American Life Today* (1996), "structured like a spider's web" with the land at the center,[44] Silko reiterates what so many others have said: "The Pueblo people and the land and the stories are inseparable."[45] I will focus on three essays, not only because they have been influential, but because they most comprehensively articulate Silko's central concerns. In "Interior and Exterior Landscapes: The Pueblo Migration Stories," Silko explains the Pueblo understanding of human relationship to the land. She critiques the word "landscape" because it "assumes the viewer is somehow *outside* or *separate from* the territory she or he surveys. Viewers are as much a part of the landscape as the boulders they stand on."[46] She describes how Pueblo artists abstracted the essence of an object, connecting it "with a complex system of relationships that the ancient Pueblo people maintained with each other and with the populous natural world they lived in."[47] The land, sky, all the creatures, including humans, are part of a "a complex and

---

43 N. Scott Momaday, "An American Land Ethic," in *The Man Made of Words: Essays, Stories, Passages* (New York: St. Martin's Press, 1997), 42–49, 47.
44 Leslie Marmon Silko, "Introduction," in *Yellow Woman and a Beauty of the Spirit: Essays on Native American Life Today* (New York: Simon and Schuster, 1996), 13–24, 21.
45 Silko, "Introduction," 14.
46 Leslie Marmon Silko, "Interior and Exterior Landscapes: The Pueblo Migration Stories," in *Yellow Woman*, 25–47, 27. Silko's emphasis.
47 Silko, "Interior and Exterior," 28.

fragile" Pueblo landscape.[48] "The oral narrative, or story, became the medium through which the complex of Pueblo knowledge and belief was maintained," Silko notes. "Whatever the event or the subject, the ancient people perceived the world and themselves within that world as part of an ancient, continuous story composed of innumerable bundles of other stories."[49]

In "Language and Literature from a Pueblo Indian Perspective," Silko explains a Pueblo perspective as "one that embraces the whole of creation and the whole of history and time."[50] For Pueblo people, says Silko, "language is story."[51] Individual words may have their own stories, and there are stories within those. Pueblo narrative, in short, consists of "story within story, the idea that one story is only the beginning of many stories and the sense that stories never truly end."[52] Importantly, stories link humans across time and space.

Silko illustrates these points – about land, language, and interwoven stories – in her memoir, *The Turquoise Ledge* (2010), a collection of personal essays. Filled with detailed descriptions of the plants, animals, and meteorology of the land around her Tucson ranch, her essays are natural history infused with cultural history. She does something similar in *Sacred Water: Narratives and Pictures* (1993), describing the natural world near her home. In *Sacred Water*, however, she is interested in mingling photographic images and text to create a photo-essay with words.

Best known for her novels and poetry, Louise Erdrich (Anishinaabe, 1952–) has also written essays. Most influential among them was "Where I Ought to Be: A Writer's Sense of Place" (1985), in which she emphasizes her identity as a writer, especially as a writer in a specific place: North Dakota. She discusses the long history of Indigenous residence on this land and the stories embedded in it. Native American writers, she concludes, "must tell the stories of contemporary survivors while protecting and celebrating the cores of cultures left in the wake of catastrophe."[53]

Ten years later, she published *The Blue Jay's Dance: A Birth Year* (1995). "This book," she explains, "is a set of thoughts from one self to the other – writer to parent, artist to mother."[54] Addressing Montaigne's notion of *essai*, she

---

48 Silko, "Interior and Exterior," 29.   49 Silko, "Interior and Exterior," 30–31.
50 Leslie Marmon Silko, "Language and Literature from a Pueblo Indian Perspective," in *Yellow Woman*, 48–59, 49.
51 Silko, "Language and Literature," 50.   52 Silko, "Language and Literature," 50.
53 Louise Erdrich, "Where I Ought to Be: A Writer's Sense of Place," *New York Times Book Review* (28 July 1985): 24.
54 Louise Erdrich, *The Blue Jay's Dance: A Birth Year* (New York: HarperCollins, 1995), 5.

writes: "These pages are a personal stretch and an extended wondering at life's complexity."[55] Organized according to the four seasons, in *The Blue Jay's Dance* Erdrich weaves together descriptions of the animals and plants she encounters on her daily walks, interspersed with recipes, memories of her Ojibwa [sic] relatives,[56] and reflections on her artist-mother struggle. Erdrich is embedded in place: in her own body, her family, her New Hampshire woods.

In *Dwellings: A Spiritual History of the Living World* (1995), Linda Hogan (Chickasaw, 1947–), a novelist, poet, and environmental writer, focuses on the wonders of the natural world, the particular Indigenous relationship with the earth, and the necessity of an environmental/spiritual awakening. Hogan's essays arose out of "wondering what makes us human, out of a lifelong love for the living world and all its inhabitants" and out of her "native understanding that there is a terrestrial intelligence that lies beyond our human knowing."[57]

The essay "Dwellings" focuses on where we dwell, how and from what we build homes, how the earth is our home within the universe. She plays with the word "dwell," which can mean to linger or think long about something, actions she illustrates in her extended musings on the natural world and human embeddedness in it. She concludes her chapter with a reflection on finding a bird's nest, realizing that it is composed not only of twigs and leaves, but also of a blue thread of one of her skirts and a black hair from one of her daughters. She is fascinated by "how the remnants of our lives are carried up the hill ... and turned into shelter,"[58] by the evidence of how humans are part of, not separate from, the natural world.

Many of Hogan's essays focus on interiorities: caves with their mazes and healing waters; vessels that hold water or grain or light; the human body with its many chambers, especially the womb. She descends with sacred intention into caves: "a feminine world, a womb of earth, a germinal place of brooding."[59] She writes with reverence about creatures that for many others are the stuff of nightmares: Bats and snakes, she insists, have their own special medicines. Bats serve as the "intermediaries between our world and the

---

55 Erdrich, *Blue Jay's Dance*, 5.
56 There are various spellings of Ojibwe, including Ojibwa and Ojibway. More recently, Anishinaabe is the term of choice.
57 Linda Hogan, "Preface," in *Dwellings: A Spiritual History of the Living World* (New York: Touchstone, 1995), 11–14, 11.
58 Linda Hogan, "Dwellings," in *Dwellings: A Spiritual History*, 117–24, 124.
59 Linda Hogan, "The Caves," in *Dwellings: A Spiritual History*, 29–35, 31.

next,"[60] while snakes are beings of "holy inner earth."[61] Repeatedly, Hogan calls for a new self-awareness that is also a new collective awareness that is also an ecological awareness. But, of course, what she is identifying is not "new," but a return to Indigenous understandings of interrelatedness. Like Momaday, she affirms the power of language, calling for "a language that heals the relationship [between humans and the natural world], one that takes the side of the amazing and fragile life on our life-giving earth."[62]

Gerald Vizenor (Anishinaabe, 1934–), writer of literary and cultural criticism, poetry, short fiction, novels, plays, and essays, was also a journalist for the *Minneapolis Tribune*. Throughout his many works, he introduced important concepts for Native American Studies: "postindian," "Native transmotion" (which he defines as "an original union in the stories of emergence and migration that relate humans to an environment and to the spiritual and political significance of animals and other creations";[63] a refusal of Indigenous "victimry" in favor of Native "survivance," a word that joins survival and continuance, and that Vizenor defines as "renunciations of dominance, tragedy and victimry."[64] Another important contribution is a reclamation of playful and powerful trickster resistance.[65]

The recent publication *Shapes of Native Nonfiction: Collected Essays by Contemporary Writers* (2019), edited by Elissa Washuta and Theresa Warburton, includes an eclectic assortment of essays. Some are primarily political, but many are highly literary. I will note only one out of the many excellent essays. Stephen Graham Jones (Blackfeet, 1972–), known for his science/horror/experimental fiction, wrote an essay entitled "Letter to a Just-Starting-Out Writer – and Maybe to Myself." Jones's essay is a fitting conclusion to this overview of Indigenous essays because in his irreverent tone, he points to a new generation of Indigenous writers and a new set of

---

60 Hogan, "Caves," 27.
61 Linda Hogan, "The Snake People," in *Dwellings: A Spiritual History*, 135–43, 140.
62 Linda Hogan, "A Different Yield," in *Dwellings: A Spiritual History*, 47–62, 59.
63 Gerald Vizenor, *Fugitive Poses: Native American Indian Scenes of Absence and Presence* (Lincoln, NE: University of Nebraska Press, 1998), 183.
64 Gerald Vizenor, *Manifest Manners: Narratives on Postindian Survivance* (Lincoln, NE: University of Nebraska Press, 1999), vii.
65 It is not possible to discuss all Indigenous essayists in this short overview. In her *Off the Reservation: Reflections on Boundary-Busting, Border-Crossing, Loose Canons* (Boston: Beacon Press, 1998), Paula Gunn Allen (Laguna Pueblo, 1939–2008), a scholar and poet, continues the feminist and LGBTQ critique of settler colonialism that she began in *The Sacred Hoop: Recovering the Feminine in American Indian Traditions* (Boston: Beacon Press, 1986). Other notable essayists include Simon Ortiz (Acoma Pueblo, 1941–), who has written about growing up during the era of enforced assimilation, and Tiffany Midge (Hunkpapa Lakota, 1965–).

possibilities. Organized as a list of advice to aspiring writers, Jones begins: "This isn't the Native American Renaissance. That was a great and essential and transformative movement without even meaning to be a movement, but it was a different generation, with different issues."[66] Rather than arguing against stereotypes and invisibility, he says, Indigenous people today have to deflect "commodification."[67] Most emphatically, he advises his Indigenous readers to be unafraid to write in any genre, to resist categorization as Native American writers (only), and to not succumb to being defined by literary critics or "the process of legitimization" as Indian.[68] Jones insists that Native writing be considered as art first, not as an access point into another culture. *Shapes of Native Nonfiction*, overall, is an important contribution to understanding the wide range, diverse content, and many shapes of Indigenous essays. More importantly, the collection suggests new possible directions for Native nonfiction.

From Samson Occom's eighteenth-century essays through the nineteenth-century essays found in Indigenous ethnographies, autobiographies, newspapers, student writings, and periodicals to twentieth- and twenty-first-century political and literary essays, Native people have persistently and eloquently described Indigenous epistemologies and cultural practices, documented settler-colonial murders, thefts, and abuses, argued for Indigenous rights to their land and its resources, made the case for the sacredness of land, language, and all of life, illustrated the power of stories, and insisted on sovereignty and healing. Across Indigenous nations, a remarkably consistent message resounds: We are (still) here; our cultures, languages, and epistemologies are sophisticated and relevant; we are sovereign. Future scholarship needs to be done on the long history of Indigenous essays published in Indian newspapers and in periodicals more generally. Finally, more work needs to be done on the more recent outpouring of Indigenous blogs and digital literature that has begun to expand awareness of ways to indigenize the Internet.[69]

---

66 Stephen Graham Jones, "Letter to a Just-Starting-Out Indian Writer – and Maybe to Myself," in Washuta and Warburton, *Shapes of Native Nonfiction*, 31–38, 31.
67 Jones, "Letter," 31.
68 Jones, "Letter," 37. In the 1980s, Louise Erdrich voiced similar concerns about not wishing to be labeled a "Native American writer," but simply "a writer."
69 See Deborah Madsen, "Indigenizing the Internet," in *The Cambridge History of Native American Literature*, ed. Melanie Benson Taylor (New York: Cambridge University Press, 2020), 481–500.

24

Conservatism and the Essay

JEFFREY R. DUDAS

It has become conventional to note that the ethos of modern American conservatism is reactionary provocation.[1] But isn't it odd to identify a performative tone, a prevailing attitude toward public expression, as the animating impulse of a specifically political movement? Wouldn't we expect such a movement, one that is indisputably consumed with both the maintenance and the use of power, to have a more substantive vision? Shouldn't scholars be able to identify in modern American conservatism a set of governing ambitions that amounts to something more than revanchist posturing and uncritical genuflection to conventional sources of authority?

Indeed, these types of questions haunt movement exiles. Prominent thinkers such as George Will, Tom Nichols, and David Brooks recurringly lament the reactionary, apparently principle-free politics of their onetime colleagues, even as they lionize the "intellectually serious" American conservatism that apparently once infused the Republican Party – which formerly characterized itself a "party of ideas."[2] Their collective

---

[1] See, for example, Kevin Mattson, *Rebels All! A Short History of the Conservative Mind in Postwar America* (New Brunswick, NJ: Rutgers University Press, 2008); and Corey Robin, *The Reactionary Mind: Conservatism from Edmund Burke to Donald Trump*, 2nd ed. (New York: Oxford University Press, 2017).

[2] Nichols made the point. Insisting that "American conservatism once meant something definite and tangible," Nichols lamented that "[a]ll of that is gone ... [t]he GOP now stands for nothing." Tom Nichols, "The GOP Now Stands for Nothing," *Atlantic* (28 May 2021), www.theatlantic.com/ideas/archive/2021/05/republicans-stand-for-nothing-january-6-co mmission/619036/. See also Zack Stanton, "Does 'Conservatism' Actually Mean Anything Anymore?," *Politico* (17 September 2021), www.politico.com/news/magazine/2021/09/17/ future-politics-conservatism-george-will-512308; and David Brooks, "What Happened to Conservatism?," *Atlantic* (January–February 2022), www.theatlantic.com/magazine/arch ive/2022/01/brooks-true-conservatism-dead-fox-news-voter-suppression/620853/.

410

nostalgia[3] points in two directions at once. On one hand, they pine for the conservative thinkers of the mid-late twentieth century, with special attention lavished upon such figures as Russell Kirk (1918–1994), Irving Kristol (1920–2009), and, above all, William F. Buckley Jr.[4] (1925–2008) – the latter of whom did indeed regularly proclaim that the transformation of American conservatism into an intellectually respectable creed was his lifelong goal.[5] On the other hand, today's exiles are nostalgic for an American conservatism that was communicated primarily through the written word, especially the essay. Buckley, in particular, is the essential object of a contemporary *double nostalgia*: As the founder and editor in-chief of, and regular contributor to, the signal publication of modern American conservatism, *National Review* (a biweekly publication made up exclusively of essays), Buckley towers in the imaginations of today's "serious conservatives" both for the apparently heightened substance of his political vision and for the primary form (the essay) in which it was communicated.

But this contemporary nostalgia is double also in its misreading and misappropriation of the actual history of modern American conservatism, and especially in its lionization of William F. Buckley Jr. and the essays that made up *National Review*. For Buckley was himself an arch provocateur, a propagandist whose reactionary opposition to the New Deal governing coalition, and later to its transformation into a civil rights–based alliance, was so essential to his political vision that he proclaimed it the literal starting point

---

3 The ancient Greek etymology of *nostalgia* ("home-pain") captures the emotional duress felt and expressed by these writers. Thomas Dumm, *Home in America: On Loss and Retrieval* (Cambridge, MA: Belknap Press of Harvard University Press, 2019).

4 Kirk's *The Conservative Mind* (originally published in 1953 and subsequently issued in seven revised editions) remains a touchstone work of political theory for contemporary American conservative thinkers. Similarly, Kristol's essay *Neo-Conservatism: The Autobiography of an Idea* (1995) is frequently lauded. Neither, however, approach the widespread reverence in which Buckley's essays are held. For this reason, and because of significant space constraints, this essay deals nearly exclusively with Buckley's works. For more on other conservative essayists, see Russell Kirk, *The Conservative Mind: From Burke to Eliot, with an Introduction by Henry Regnery* (Washington, DC: Regnery Gateway, 2001); and Irving Kristol, *Neo-Conservatism: The Autobiography of an Idea, Selected Essays 1949–1995* (New York: Free Press, 1995).

5 Jeffrey R. Dudas, *Raised Right: Fatherhood in Modern American Conservatism* (Stanford, CA: Stanford University Press, 2017), 1–3; Rick Perlstein, *Before the Storm: Barry Goldwater and the Unmaking of the American Consensus* (New York: Hill and Wang, 2001), 70–76; Jeffrey Hart, *The Making of the American Conservative Mind: National Review and Its Times* (Wilmington, DE: Intercollegiate Studies Institute, 2005), xi–xii; and David Farber, *The Rise and Fall of Modern American Conservatism: A Short History* (Princeton, NJ: Princeton University Press, 2010), 59–65.

(the "ancient mooring") of modern American conservatism.[6] The animating purpose of the American conservatism that Buckley championed was, according to *National Review*'s 1955 founding mission statement, to "stand athwart [liberal] history, yelling Stop."[7] On this vision and purpose, Buckley was consistent. First in 1963, and then again in 1970, he defined American conservatism not according to any substantive understanding of the proper relationships between citizens and government (the classic stuff of political theory), but rather as the embodiment of a "spirit of defiance," as a set of postures that "challenge[d] root and branch the presumptions of the twentieth century."[8] In 1988, Buckley published an expanded version of the collection in which this reactionary definition of American conservatism was contained.[9] Relevant also in this regard was Buckley's long-running television show *Firing Line* and his infamous televised debates with Gore Vidal at the 1968 Republican National Convention – both of which were known primarily for pioneering the sort of rapid-fire verbal jousts that characterize our contemporary, frequently anti-intellectual era of political media.[10]

A great many of Buckley's contemporaries, as well as his contemporary acolytes in conservative media who so thrill to "owning the libs," recognized the primarily reactionary and oppositional character of his political vision. Indeed, lifelong friend Ronald Reagan hailed Buckley as a "shining knight" whose fights on behalf of American conservatism "changed our country." The late conservative provocateur Rush Limbaugh affirmed that Buckley was the "founding father" of the very conservative movement that elevated him (and similar conservative media personalities) to political prominence.[11] Buckley and his *National Review* compatriots thus offered, in Mattson's words, "a new anti-intellectualism of the intellectuals."[12]

Misplaced also is the contemporary nostalgia for the conservative essay as a principled and intellectually robust form of political communication. It is, as

---

6 Dudas, *Raised Right*, 2–3. See also Michael J. Lee, "WFB: The Gladiatorial Style and the Politics of Provocation," *Rhetoric and Public Affairs* 13, no. 2 (2010): 43–76.
7 William F. Buckley Jr., "Our Mission Statement," *National Review* (19 November 1955): 1.
8 William F. Buckley Jr., "Did You Ever See a Dream Walking?," in *American Conservative Thought in the Twentieth Century*, ed. William F. Buckley Jr. (Indianapolis, IN: Bobbs-Merrill, 1970), xv–xl, xxxviii–xxxix.
9 William F. Buckley Jr. and Charles R. Kessler, eds., *Keeping the Tablets: Modern American Conservative Thought* (New York: Harper and Row, 1988).
10 Robert Gordon and Morgan Neville, dirs., *Best of Enemies: Buckley v. Vidal* (Los Angeles, CA: Tremolo Productions, 2015). The Hoover Institute hosts a large tranche of video and written transcripts of *Firing Line*. See https://digitalcollections.hoover.org/searc h/%22buckley%2C%20william%20f.%2C%20jr.%22.
11 Dudas, *Raised Right*, 40.   12 Mattson, *Rebels All!*, 45.

we will see, unsurprising that the voluminous essays (written over the course of nearly sixty years) with which Buckley articulated his reactionary and oppositional political vision were revanchist in character. He employed the essay, as did many midcentury authors, as a vehicle for elevating his conservatism into the realm of a newly developing "middle-brow" of American culture.[13] Indeed, the essay was an appropriate form for realizing Buckley's ambitions of making American conservatism middlebrow respectable (i.e., "intellectually serious"), not because it excised the fantasies that characterized conservatism's opposition to New Deal politics, but rather because the essay's veneer of intellectualism helped to entrench those fantasies into mainstream public discourse.

A Dream Walking

The great majority of William F. Buckley Jr.'s writings appeared in essay form, but the total volume of his output makes any sort of comprehensive analysis daunting. Biographer Carl Bogus estimates that Buckley published 5,600 columns (filled with a staggering 3.75 million words), 56 books (many of which were compilations of essays), and "countless other articles."[14] And there are an additional 982 boxes of Buckley's personal papers (correspondence, written notes, and additional written material) that are stored at the Yale University archives.[15] Daunting enough is this written record that most Buckley scholars have foregone comprehensive textual analysis and pursued instead a biographical approach. Accordingly, there are multiple, excellent accounts of Buckley's life that focus upon signal moments: his childhood in Sharon, Connecticut; his early intellectual development at Yale and immediately thereafter; and, especially, his conservative movement–building activities – the founding of *National Review*, Buckley's use of *National Review* to

---

13 I refer here to Warren Susman's discussion of the rise of "personal identity" as the modal American personality in the immediate postwar period – the exact era in which Buckley and many of his colleagues were coming of age. As Ned Stuckey-French further notes, the essay "was one of the central organs through which [Americans] told [their] stor[ies]," even as those stories were themselves influential in the development of American "middlebrow institutions," such as American conservative politics. Warren Susman, *Culture as History: The Transformation of American Society in the Twentieth Century* (Washington, DC: Smithsonian Institution, 2003), 284–85; Ned Stuckey-French, *The American Essay in the American Century* (Columbia, MO: University of Missouri Press, 2011), 7–8.

14 Carl T. Bogus, *Buckley: William F. Buckley Jr. and the Rise of American Conservatism* (New York: Bloomsbury Press, 2011), 349.

15 William F. Buckley, Jr., Papers, MS 576, https://archives.yale.edu/repositories/12/resources/4822.

shape what counted as "conservative" ideas and personalities, and his engineering of the conservative takeover of the Republican Party through the simultaneous championing of insurgent candidates (such as Barry Goldwater and Ronald Reagan) and attacks on "establishment" party figures (such as Nelson Rockefeller and George Romney).[16] Some of these scholarly accounts also dwell on Buckley's intentionally shambolic 1965 New York City mayoral campaign or his development of the TV program *Firing Line*.[17]

By and large, then, Buckley scholars tend to offer fine-grained analyses of only a few of Buckley's most prominent writings, such as God and Man at Yale (1951), his coauthored book-length defense of Joseph McCarthy (*McCarthy and His Enemies* [1954]), and his infamous *National Review* defenses of southern segregation. An alternative approach, taken by a few scholars, has been to focus upon crystallizing moments in Buckley's career, either singular events (such as Buccola's 2019 analysis of the 1965 Cambridge debate between Buckley and James Baldwin) or highly specific threads of Buckley's writing (such as my own 2017 account of his best-selling Blackford Oakes spy novels).[18] Each approach has benefits and drawbacks; but together they illustrate both the felt need for, and the virtual impossibility of, exhaustive analysis of Buckley's oeuvre. Yet if never quite scaling such heights, the collected Buckley scholarship does effectively plot the most important coordinates of his political vision.

Indeed, although he had various interests, Buckley gathered his abiding political concerns under two topical umbrellas that were themselves related to one another: the definition of modern American conservatism, on the one hand; and attacks on the logics and practices of the American New Deal, on the other hand. His attacks on the American New Deal, moreover, were animated by existential, Cold War–era anxieties that touched multiple policy areas – including US-Soviet relations abroad and civil rights at home.[19] These

---

16 See, generally, Bogus, *Buckley*; Farber, *Rise and Fall of Modern American Conservatism*, 39–76; Perlstein, *Before the Storm*, 153–56; and Alvin S. Felzenberg, *A Man and His Presidents: The Political Odyssey of William F. Buckley Jr.* (New Haven, CT: Yale University Press, 2017).
17 Bogus, *Buckley*, 257–89; Heather Hendershot, *Open to Debate: How William F. Buckley Put Liberal America on the Firing Line* (New York: Broadside Books, 2016), generally.
18 Nicholas Buccola, *The Fire Is upon Us: James Baldwin, William F. Buckley, Jr., and the Debate over Race in America* (Princeton, NJ: Princeton University Press, 2019); Dudas, *Raised Right*, 40–66.
19 I have previously argued that Buckley's account of civil rights – or, more specifically, his account of the logic of individual rights broadly – can be usefully treated as a signifier of his overall political vision. In particular, I have argued that Buckley's anxieties over how historically marginalized Americans increasingly engaged in rights-based activism intersected with his articulate desires for, and repressed trauma over, the exercise of stern paternal authority; this intersection of rights and paternal

two broad concerns, at once definitional and substantive, endured throughout Buckley's nearly sixty-year career. And his treatment of them left little doubt as to the accuracy of the collected scholarly wisdom: Buckley's writings registered largely in the domain of reactionary provocation rather than principled intellectualism.

Consider, for example, the first of these political concerns: Buckley's attempts to offer a coherent, positive definition of modern American conservatism. As I suggested earlier, Buckley's goal of establishing an "intellectually serious" modern American conservatism was at the center of *National Review*'s mission. Indeed, the periodical's 1955 founding was necessary, Buckley thought, because the then-current state of American conservatism was bereft. Its standard bearer, President Dwight Eisenhower, was characteristic of the Republican Party's postwar acquiescence to New Deal governing sensibilities. And while Buckley appreciated Eisenhower's clear-eyed view of the Soviet Union's geopolitical ambitions, he was appalled by establishment Republican capitulation to both the practices and the principles of the American social welfare state. This was surrender, Buckley believed, to a socialistic subversion of the conventional relations of authority that rightly governed and organized American life; it pointed to a troubling "beatification" and "integration" of the state "as a member of the American household" that upturned the proper state of things – a state of things that was, according to Buckley, protected by right in the "enabling documents of our Republic." Thus was *National Review* born of a "spirit of defiance"; it would, as its famous mission statement indicated, "stand athwart history, yelling Stop." Understand: Buckley sought to establish a modern American conservatism that was fundamentally oppositional and negative – a source of resistance to a New Deal politics and governing coalition that threatened America's conventional power relations, including those relations that articulated in the domains of race, class, gender, and religion.[20]

Multiple scholars have explored the early years of *National Review*, focusing especially upon the travails of the diverse group of writers Buckley enlisted in his anti–New Deal crusade. Hart's (2005) history, which exhaustively documents the routinely conflictual interpersonal and intellectual relationships

---

authority is, in fact, characteristic of modern American conservatism writ large. See Dudas, *Raised Right*, 40–66.
20 Robin, *Reactionary Mind*, 3–39.

among these figures, is the standard account of this era.[21] While writers such as James Burnham, Willmoore Kendall, Frank Meyer, and Russell Kirk more or less shared Buckley's hostility to American New Deal politics, they varied considerably in their personalities, intellectual styles, and commitments to Buckley's insurrectionist movement politics.[22] But in spite of the instability caused by Buckley's choices of senior writers and editors, *National Review*'s influence in postwar America grew apace. Indeed, in both critical and popular appeal *National Review* easily outstripped rival conservative publications such as Irving Kristol and Daniel Bell's urbane but boutique *Public Interest* and the scholarly but technical *Intercollegiate Review*.[23]

Central to *National Review*'s growth was its revanchist politics, about which Buckley was not coy. It is true that he pursued them with the help of an extravagant vocabulary. It is also true that he rarely admitted to the base authoritarian impulses that fired his opposition to American New Deal politics, preferring instead to deflect from scrutiny with sarcasm and obfuscation.[24] But Buckley nearly always followed his reactionary instincts and the insurrectionary movement politics to which they pointed. With respect to the building of an "intellectual serious" conservatism, these instincts led Buckley to "processes of exclusion" whereby he cast out ideas and people that he deemed either not conservative enough (read: insufficiently oppositional to contemporary

---

21 Hart, *Making of the American Conservative Mind*, generally; see also Farber, *Rise and Fall of Modern American Conservatism*, 59–75.
22 Kirk and Meyer, for example, "despised each other," with Meyer's libertarian impulses grating harshly against Kirk's detached traditionalism. Meanwhile, everyone except Buckley hated Kendall, whom Hart generously describes as "weird," thereby glossing over Kendall's long history of unprofessional and abusive behavior at and beyond *National Review* – a history that eventually led to Yale's enthusiastic acceptance of his resignation from its faculty in 1961. Hart, *Making of the American Conservative Mind*, 39–43.
23 On the history of the *Public Interest*, see Irving Kristol, *The Neoconservative Persuasion: Selected Essays, 1942–2009* (New York: Basic Books, 2011), 338–58. Henrie details the history of the *Intercollegiate Review* in Mark C. Henrie, ed., *Arguing Conservatism: Four Decades of the Intercollegiate Review* (Wilmington, DE: ISI Books, 2008), xv–xxi.
24 His opposition to the Equal Rights Amendment is illustrative. Ignoring the evidence of decades' worth of his own essays, Buckley proclaimed that he had "never even flirted with the notion that women are inferior." No: The problem with the proposed ERA, he insisted, was that its "rhetoric of equality" pointed to unforeseen consequences, such as the possibility that it would become illegal to marry a pretty woman because such a marriage would "permit discrimination against non-pretty people." The point is not that this slippery slope logic was offered to readers in good faith; Buckley admitted that his rhetorical strategy amounted to "ad absurdum to be sure." The point, rather, is that Buckley's ludicrous analogy here (and in literally countless others of his essays) was offered instead of a transparent and honest depiction of his actual, deeply held beliefs in entrenched hierarchies. William F. Buckley Jr., "Women's Lib," in *Inveighing We Will Go* (New York: G. P. Putnam's Sons, 1972), 287, 289.

liberalism, such as onetime confidant Garry Wills or firebrand author Ayn Rand) or "kooky" (read: intellectually or otherwise embarrassing, such as the paranoid conspiracists of the John Birch Society or, later, unapologetic anti-Semites such as Pat Buchanan). Buckley's self-professed stewardship of modern American conservatism amounted to a gatekeeping operation – or, as he put it, a "keeping of the tablets" that ensured that his reactionary brand of conservatism was both militant and, consistent with the expectations of the twentieth-century American essay, aesthetically high-minded.[25] Bogus makes the point: "By clothing his arguments with formal syntax and elegant writing, Buckley could make the outlandish seem dignified."[26]

Accordingly, it is unsurprising that Buckley was never able to articulate a positive and coherent definition of modern American conservatism. His failure was not for a lack of trying. Buckley's 1963 "Notes toward an Empirical Definition of Conservatism" first articulated his "processes of exclusion" definitional method. Noting that he knew "who is a conservative less surely than I know who is [not]," Buckley's excisions from modern American conservatism were many. Those who were cast out included the already mentioned Rand, Wills, and John Birch Society founder Robert Welch; anarchist economist Murray Rothband; and former confidant and *National Review* contributor (but committed atheist) Max Eastman. Impressively robust, Buckley's exclusions nonetheless left the reader little closer to understanding Buckley's own question, "[W]hat is conservatism?"[27] On this point, Buckley concluded only, and without elaboration, that an intellectually serious American conservatism consisted of a "general consensus on the proper balance between freedom, order, and tradition."[28]

Buckley revisited the matter in "Did You Ever See a Dream Walking?" (1970) – the lead text in a book-length collection, *American Conservative Thought in the Twentieth Century*, that reprinted the 1963 essay with an additional series of ruminations. Disappointingly, however, Buckley's new prose tread the same ground already covered by *National Review*'s 1955 mission statement – the one that linked conservative purpose to resistance to the American welfare state. The "spirit of defiance" that he first identified in 1955 now was said to issue "from distinctively American patterns of

---

25 Stuckey-French, *American Essay*, 6–8.
26 Bogus, *Buckley*, 76. See also Mattson, *Rebels All!*, 45–48.
27 William F. Buckley Jr., "Notes toward an Empirical Definition of Conservatism," in *The Jeweler's Eye* (New York: G. P. Putnam's Sons, 1968), 15–31.
28 Buckley, *Jeweler's Eye*, 30.

thought, from the essence of the American spirit" – a spirit that was reflected in "certitudes" and the "faith of our fathers."[29] Yet Buckley was silent on precisely which certitudes, or which desires harbored by famous dead American fathers, were embodied in modern American conservatism. He had been barely more specific in 1955, when he wrote that conservative opposition to the American welfare state was based in the "fixed postulates having to do with the meaning of existence, with the relationship of the state to the individual, of the individual to the neighbor, so clearly enunciated in the enabling documents of the Republic."[30]

I have previously argued that Buckley was referring here in nonspecific ways to the doctrines of individual rights and limited government that appear in the Declaration of Independence and the US Constitution.[31] But given Buckley's checkered record on race relations and his abiding elitism, a skeptical analyst could justifiably conclude instead that Buckley had top of mind some of the more antidemocratic elements of those documents, such as the Constitution's relegation of enslaved Americans to three-fifths of a person for representational purposes or its refusal to allow direct election of US senators.[32] In any event, Buckley's *third* reprinting of his 1963 essay in 1988's *Keeping the Tablets* offered no further clarity on "what conservatism is." In that coedited overview of twentieth-century American conservative thought, Buckley appended a few introductory remarks in which he admitted, ultimately, that "there [was] no final authority on the matter" of what makes one an American conservative. Washing his hands of the matter, Buckley insisted that the term *conservative* was both "elusive and glamorous" and that the best that could be done definitionally was to state modern

---

29 William F. Buckley Jr., "Did You Ever See a Dream Walking?," in Buckley, *American Conservative Thought*, 34–35.
30 Buckley, "Our Mission Statement," 1. 31 Dudas, *Raised Right*, 2–3.
32 This is not hyperbole. Consider, for example, Buckley's 1964 attack on the US Constitution's Twenty-Fourth Amendment (which prohibited the use of the poll tax): "I do not believe that everyone should vote. I do not even believe that everyone should have the right to vote." And, while he valued certain of the American founders' political commitments, Buckley consistently rejected their occasional dalliances with democratic politics – halting embraces that were the efforts of "a little cult of democratist ideologues, grown in our time into a raging universal obsession." William F. Buckley Jr., "The Twenty-Fourth Amendment," in *Jeweler's Eye*, 73; William F. Buckley Jr., "We Want Our Politicians to Be Hypocrites," in *Jeweler's Eye*, 68. See also Buckley's 1986 essay on the Philippines: "[T]he notion that ... anyone eighteen years old, whether literate or illiterate, instructed or dumb, should participate in political decision-making ... is a Western superstition." William F. Buckley Jr., "Overtaxing Democracy," in *Happy Days Were Here Again: Reflections of a Libertarian Journalist* (Holbrook, MA: Adams, 1993), 227.

American conservatism's distinctive "attitudes" and "tones."[33] Those attitudes and tones, of course, consisted predominantly of resistance to, and defiance of, American New Deal politics. And, so, after thirty-five years of trying to define its positive attributes, of employing the essay form to relay the intellectual creed that supposedly made up modern American conservatism, Buckley concluded that he had been right all along: What made one conservative was not a commitment to distinctive, high-minded principles but instead a commitment to performative injunction. Conservatives were people who stood athwart twentieth-century American liberalism, with its more inclusive vision of American democracy, "yelling Stop."

So much, then, for Buckley's lifelong goal of making American conservatism intellectually, definitionally robust. What about his attacks on American New Deal politics – attacks that expressed existential Cold War–era anxieties over such interconnected matters of US-Soviet relations abroad and civil rights at home?[34] It is, to begin, difficult to overstate just how comprehensively and viscerally repulsed Buckley was by communism in general and by the Soviet Union in particular. Buckley reviled the atheism, the centralized planning, and, especially, the anticapitalist, antielitist ethos that characterized the Soviet Union and Soviet-bloc polities. Indeed, those traits produced "gruesome data" that revealed "the nature of the enemy we face."[35] Communist rule, Buckley insisted, was "the worse abuse of freedom in history"[36]; it amounted to government-sponsored acts of brutality and unfreedom – acts that also upended "natural" relations of authority both in public and private spheres of life. Accordingly, Buckley judged nearly every aspect of modern American life according to whether, and how much, it advanced the communist-inspired nightmare of implanting the state as a favored "member of the American household." And, according to

---

33 William F. Buckley Jr., "Did You Ever See a Dream Walking?," in Buckley and Kessler, *Keeping the Tablets*, 19. This version of the essay varies from the one printed in *American Conservative Thought in the Twentieth Century*.
34 Many historians have analyzed the contemporaneous, linked development of mid-twentieth-century American Cold War politics abroad and civil rights activism and reform at home. Representative examples include Mary L. Dudziak, *Cold War Civil Rights: Race and the Image of American Democracy* (Princeton, NJ: Princeton University Press, 2011); and Jason Sokol, *There Goes My Everything: White Southerners in the Age of Civil Rights, 1945–1975* (New York: Alfred A. Knopf, 2006).
35 William F. Buckley Jr., "Harvey Schechter on Liberal Anti-Communism," in *Jeweler's Eye*, 47.
36 William F. Buckley Jr., "Instructing Norman Mailer on the True Meaning of the American Right Wing," in *Rumbles Left and Right* (New York: Macfadden Books, 1964), 66.

Buckley, American New Deal politics was alarmingly welcoming, if in frequently unintentional ways,[37] to this catastrophe.

American liberal foreign policy, for example, revealed a "creeping softness toward communism."[38] On the one hand, the fashionable doctrines of containment and, later, détente displayed insufficient "enthusiasm for liberating the slaves of communism"; on the other hand, American struggles in Vietnam and Cambodia, coupled with untoward fealty to the United Nations,[39] made it clear that liberals could not be counted on to "fight, fight hard, at every front, with courage to oppose Soviet advances by the threat of the use of force."[40] Instead, the "American Liberal" assumed that "nothing [was] more important than peace, and that the way to have peace [was] to compromise with the enemy."[41] Deeply deluded on foreign policy matters, American liberals "[did] not understand reality" and thus lacked the "will to victory."[42]

Things were no better, and perhaps even worse, on matters of domestic policy. For here American liberals were not simply ignorant of the communist menace; they were actively courting a socialistic, big government ethos that did violence to the American political tradition itself. Indeed, New Deal and Great Society programs smacked of socialist coercion and centralized planning; together they violated the desires of the "men who forged this country" and who "thought the federal government should have enough power to maintain order, but no more."[43] In a dubious, but characteristic, conflation of a variety of founding figures who in reality seldom agreed with one another, Buckley insisted that "the insights of men like Hamilton and Jefferson and Madison and Marshall" were trampled upon by liberals who didn't understand, as had these founders, that "government, unless it is kept in hand, grows tyrannical."[44]

---

37 American liberals had an "accidental blindness" to the nature of communism – an occlusion borne of a "deep psychological problem" that "caused ... paralysis of the liberal will." Buckley, "Harvey Schechter," 49.
38 William F. Buckley Jr., "No More Comrades," in *Jeweler's Eye*, 54.
39 Buckley consistently assailed the United Nations. His 1980 pronouncement that the organization was a "moral mess" that acted as "primarily an anti-Israel lobby" is representative. William F. Buckley Jr., "What to Do?," in *Right Reason* (New York: Doubleday, 1985), 150.
40 William F. Buckley Jr., "Barry Goldwater and the Thunder on the Right," in *Rumbles Left and Right*, 29.
41 William F. Buckley Jr., "Will Formosa Liberate the United States?," in *Rumbles Left and Right*, 41.
42 Buckley, "Will Formosa Liberate," 41–42.   43 Buckley, "Barry Goldwater," 28.
44 Buckley, "Barry Goldwater," 28.

Buckley also cast his consistent opposition to civil rights reforms of all sorts in this light. Aggressive strategies taken to dismantle Jim Crow social and political structures (such as those pursued in the 1964 Civil Rights Act and the 1965 Voting Rights Acts), for example, were tyrannical "assaults" upon southern communities that were conducted by a communist-like "superstate." Mixing his characteristic phobia of "big government" with a long-held belief in African American inferiority, Buckley held that it was much better to wait for the "right kind of integration" to occur organically, after there no longer existed the "biological, intellectual, cultural, and psychic" differences between the races and "the Negroes have finally realized their long dream of attaining to the status of the white man."[45] Such a take on race relations was typical for Buckley. His infamous 1957 *National Review* editorial "Why the South Must Prevail" held that, because it was made up of "the advanced race," the "White community in the South [was] entitled to take such measures as [were] necessary to prevail, politically and culturally, in areas in which it does not predominate numerically."[46]

Buckley's essays on women's rights were similarly retrograde. Consider, for example, a 1990 *National Review* column ("Are You 'Responsible'?") on whether women who seek abortions should be viewed as responsible, rights-bearing subjects. Conflating abortion with out-of-wedlock birth, Buckley insisted that "illegitimate birth is ... an act of irresponsibility. Children are supposed to have legal fathers and mothers. If they do not, their parents can be said to be behaving irresponsibly ... [Thus] women who go to an abortionist, or who procreate illegitimate births, are not the best judges of right and wrong."[47] Buckley summarized his position on gender relations in a 1991 *National Review* essay that argued against the propriety of women serving as jet fighter pilots. Women serving in such a combat role, Buckley

---

45 William F. Buckley Jr., "Can We Desegregate, Hesto Presto?," in *Rumbles Left and Right*, 96–97.
46 William F. Buckley Jr., "Why the South Must Prevail." *National Review* 4, no. 7 (24 August 1957), 148–49 . The record of Buckley's racism is long, consistent, and ignominious, even though he typically disclaimed it – disclaimers that credulous sympathizers (including otherwise discerning observers such as his biographer, Alvin Felzenberg) continue to tout. Alvin Felzenberg, "How William F. Buckley, Jr., Changed His Mind on Civil Rights," *Politico* (13 May 2017). On Buckley's abiding racism, see Bogus, *Buckley*, 149–73; and Buccola, *Fire Is upon Us*, 363–64. On how that racism shaped the *National Review*'s commentary on anticolonial politics and its defenses of "Western Civilization," see Jesse Curtis, "'Will the Jungle Take Over?' *National Review* and the Defense of Western Civilization in the Era of Civil Rights and African Decolonization," *Journal of American Studies*, no.4 (November 2019): 997–1023. Among contemporary sympathizers, Brooks is unusual in his acknowledgment and condemnation of Buckley's racism. Brooks, "I Remember Conservatism," n.p.
47 William F. Buckley Jr., "Are You 'Responsible'?," in *Happy Days Were Here Again*, 114.

claimed, violated the "tropism" of a "civilized order" that "assigns to the woman primary responsibility for the care of the child, and to the man, primary responsibility for the care of the woman."[48]

Buckley's essays on the various rights movements of the late twentieth century thus emphasized, on the one hand, that white male supremacy was the natural condition of American civilization. And they fretted, on the other hand, about how the nation was under subversive, communistic assault from those who sought to employ rights to upend the conventional relations of authority to which white male supremacy gave rise. An exasperated Buckley made the point in 1988: "[S]omebody, somewhere, somehow, has got to stop the civil rights thing."[49]

Accordingly, it was clear to Buckley that American liberalism threatened the nation's interests both at home and abroad. Yet he was equally alarmed that liberalism's softness toward communism had fostered a false intellectual equivalence between American and Soviet forms of empire. "Self-denigration," especially prominent among American intellectuals and opinion leaders in the post-Vietnam era, gave rise to cynicism about American purpose and, according to Buckley, widespread suspicion that American anticommunist practices were the immoral equivalent of Soviet acts of aggression and domination. Such national self-flagellation amounted to a "radical ideological egalitarianism . . . [a] criticism whose base was, in effect, 'who says [we] are better off than [them]?'"[50] The problem became even more acute, Buckley wrote, upon exposure of the dubious workings of the American security state (the FBI and CIA in particular) in the mid-1970s. A former (short-lived) CIA officer himself, Buckley was appalled that so few American liberals understood the difference between American espionage (no matter how brutal or contemptible) in the name of freedom and similar acts committed by Soviet security forces in the name of oppression.[51] The difference between American and Soviet espionage, in Buckley's oft-repeated analogy, was just the difference between pushing an elderly woman on the street in order to save her from, or to condemn her to, oncoming traffic: one

---

48 William F. Buckley Jr., "Combat Duty for Women?," in *Happy Days Were Here Again*, 221.
49 William F. Buckley Jr., "Terminological Right of Way," in *Happy Days Were Here Again*, 50.
50 William F. Buckley Jr., "Human Rights and Foreign Policy: A Proposal," in *Right Reason*, 164–65.
51 William F. Buckley Jr., "The Stigma of Having Been One," in *A Hymnal: The Controversial Arts* (New York: G. P. Putnam's Son, 1978), 63–65.

shouldn't in general be pushing elderly women on the street, but intent makes all the difference.[52]

Here, then, are the lasting imprints of Buckley's efforts. Collectively his essays gave to modern American conservatism both a distinctive style (uncompromising defiance) and a distinctive substance (reactionary defenses of conventional hierarchies). And this style and substance were offered righteously, contained in an oeuvre that insisted that conservatives need not denigrate themselves or seek penance for defending American power in all of its forms. After all, such countersubversive defenses were nothing more than self-evidently right and proper defenses of the American nation from its many foreign and domestic enemies.[53]

It is tempting to wonder, in spite of the singular influence outlined here, if modern American conservatism hasn't left William F. Buckley Jr. behind. A great many conservative exiles and nostalgists, including those noted earlier, believe it to be so. George Will is hardly alone among contemporary pundits in his assessment that modern American conservatism "is an affront to anyone devoted to the project William F. Buckley began ... in 1955 ... [of] making conservatism intellectually respectable and politically palatable."[54] Such claims notwithstanding, however, William F. Buckley Jr. remains very much the "intellectual godfather" of modern American conservatism.[55] As this essay's analysis makes clear, there is a straight line that connects Buckley's catalogue to the reactionary authoritarianism that informs contemporary conservative politics.

Perhaps, then, it is not the style and substance of Buckley's political vision but rather the form in which that vision appeared (the essay) that today feels alien. It is, after all, undeniably true that the twenty-first century's most prominent American conservative voices communicate through the spoken word, whether visual or aural in medium. Indeed, the two most important events in recent conservative media history are the national syndication of

---

52 William F. Buckley Jr., "Blackford Oakes," in *Miles Gone By: A Literary Autobiography* (Washington, DC: Regnery, 2004), 345–46. Buckley was so offended by the equivalence that he was inspired to write a series of spy novels that featured the ongoing heroics of a dashing CIA agent (Blackford Oakes). I analyze these novels, which were explicitly intended to redeem the American security state for popular audiences, in Dudas, *Raised Right*, 40–66.
53 Jeffrey R. Dudas, *The Cultivation of Resentment: Treaty Rights and the New Right* (Stanford, CA: Stanford University Press, 2008), 137–53.
54 George F. Will, "Donald Trump Is a Counterfeit Republican," *Washington Post* (12 August 2015).
55 Edwin J. Feulner, "The Legacy of William F. Buckley Jr.," Heritage Foundation (28 February 2018), www.heritage.org/conservatism/commentary/the-legacy-william-f-buckley-jr.

Rush Limbaugh's daily radio program in the early 1990s and the founding of Rupert Murdoch's *Fox News* in 1994. Together these events have been just as influential for the history of modern American conservatism as was Buckley's 1955 founding of *National Review*. In addition to the television and radio/ podcast stars that these ventures have produced over the previous generation, each has also inspired the establishment of a host of similar media projects. Nothing comparable has emerged in conservative print media. In fact, the print circulation of *National Review* itself has declined precipitously over the last decade, from 170,000 in 2011 to just 75,000 in 2021.[56]

There are, of course, some who remain dedicated to the old ways. Those commentators whom I have referred to here as conservative exiles and nostalgists, for example, communicate predominantly as Buckley did, through the written word and the essay form. Indeed, in addition to those previously mentioned, other nostalgists – such as the *Washington Post*'s Jennifer Rubin, the *Atlantic*'s David Frum, and the writers formerly associated with William Kristol's defunct the *Weekly Standard*, which has rebranded as the online publication the *Bulwark* – retain meaningful platforms. Employing the essay form to bemoan rather than to promote the state of modern American conservatism, these writers imagine that they are Buckley's true heirs. But in confusing his form with his style and substance, it turns out that it is the exiles themselves who have minimized Buckley's contemporary relevance. For although the essay form in which William F. Buckley Jr. typically expressed his political vision has been eclipsed in popular conservative media, that political vision – in both oppositional style and reactionary substance – is itself the beating heart of modern American conservatism.

---

56 Pew Research Center, "State of the News Media 2015" (19 April 2015); National Review, 2021 Media Kit.

25

Opinions and Decisions: Legal Essays

PETER GOODRICH

It is easy to think that the essay is a quintessentially legal form. Derived from *assayer*, to try, and *essai*, or trial, the etymology of the word connotes action, endeavor, and experiment aimed at proof leading to judgment. The juridical character of the term is further bolstered by the history of two jurists, Michel de Montaigne (1533–1592) and Francis Bacon (1561–1626), as early and exemplary practitioners of the art. Greater familiarity with the morphology of the form, however, leads to an opposite conclusion in which the essay is a collective noun for multiplicity, denoting a plurality of genres, most often marked by levity, incompletion, indigestion, distraction, and exploratory attempts. The essay is in principle unfinished, a sketch, a trial run. The British lawyer Thomas Blount (1618–1679), in his *Glossographia* (1656), indeed associates the form with theatrical rehearsals: "Among Comœdians the tryal or proof of their action, which they make before they come forth publiquely upon the Stage, is their *Essay*."[1] The further connotation of such a definition is of a divagating literary excursion as a pastime, an entertainment, simulation and fictive sally, an occasional and leisured imaginative endeavor, quite antithetical to what, since the mid-nineteenth century, has been deemed the science of precedent and the professional exposition of doctrine, dogma, and law.

The apparently antithetical senses of the essay, as comedic and judicial, frivolous and veridical, theatrical and juristic, popular and esoteric are key to understanding its later development and certain specifically distinctive features of the "American" genre of legal exploratory discourse.[2] The term *essay*

---

[1] Thomas Blount, *Glossographia* (London: Newcomb, 1656), s.v. "essay" (Fr.).
[2] It is impossible to ignore the exceptionalist use of the soubriquet "American," not even "North American," to refer to the United States. The paradoxical root of the term is the reference to the British American colonies, but in more recent history the cause of the

may be new, but the practice is antique, epistolary, and poetic. It comprehends dispersed meditations, conceits, brief notes, unfinished recreations, or, in Montaigne's case, the substance of the self that finds its way into letters familiar or missives to family and friends. Bacon, in the 1612 edition of the *Essays*, references Seneca's epistles to Lucilius.[3] Amicable, unguarded, and unfinished, the essay takes the rhetorical modality of correspondence, is dialogic or conversational in form, and at its best or most formal, it is preparatory to the longer and more studied forms of syntagm, dissertation, tractate, treatise, and, in contemporary terms, article, monograph, textbook, and scientific manual.

If the essay form is prior to law, extralegal, a nonprofessional endeavor *strictu sensu*, or quasi-judicial mode of contemplation and elaboration, an incidental and marginal form of expression, then it is also the most indicative and symptomatic of the lawyer's desire, of juristic jouissance or of the jurisliterary as the portal into legality.[4] The essay form in its early modern heyday, that of the Augustan age of Joseph Addison (1672–1719), Richard Steele (1671–1729), and the bricolage of the *Spectator*, of Jonathan Swift (1677–1745) and Alexander Pope (1688–1744), Samuel Johnson (1709–1784), and even Laurence Sterne (1713–1768), is marked by the comedy of satire and the fripperies of fiction. Francis Lenton's (fl. 1629–1653) *Characterismi: Expressed in Essayes and Characters never before written on* provides a rogue's gallery modeled on Juvenal, and Sterne (1713–1768) digresses exquisitely upon the necessary confluence of wit and judgment, the comedic and the legal.[5] It is this conjunction, in its multiple and oblique forms, that David Hume (1711–1776), in "Of Essay Writing," takes up by way of arguing that the task of the scholar essayist is that of joining the learned and the conversable: "I cannot but consider myself as a kind of resident or ambassador from the dominions of learning to those of conversation" with a view to promoting correspondence between the twain.[6] It is precisely to that flirtatious relation between erudition and the everyday, to the codependency of principle and populism, protocol and policy that the "American" legal essay most properly

> catachresis is in significant measure juristic and jurisdictional, signifying a strong and jealous sense of proprietorship, as in "ours." To be annoying, I will follow convention and use "United States," "US," and "American" interchangeably.

3 Francis Bacon, *The Essaies* (London: Beale, 1612), n.p.
4 Anne Teissier-Ensminger, *Fabuleuse juridicité: sur la littérarisation des genres juridiques* (Paris: Garnier, 2015).
5 Francis Lenton, *Characterismi or Lenton's Leasures* (London: Newcomb, 1631), with the epigraph: *Dum vivo, video / Errorem in humanis / Terrorem in libris.*
6 David Hume, "Of Essay Writing," in *"Essays* [1741–42] (Oxford: Oxford University Press, 1963), 570.

and distinctively belongs. It is the exemplary moment of the juris-literary, the opening of law to a wider audience and to political reform. The beyond of law, viewed from the interior of the juridical, is what the essay at its best portends. It is the proleptic mark of imagination, ever threatening a heretical impugning of doxa, critical escapades that aspire to what common law as precedent cannot give, which is novelty, imaginal escape, and intellective experimentation in the mode of an aesthetic sensibility freed of the burden of prior norms.

Pedagogy

The trajectory of the legal essay, in conformity with other academic specialisms, has been from the experimental and exploratory occasional excursus to the imperial and judgmental. The genres of legal writing are jurisdictional. Belonging to a territory and the imagined community of the new nation, the American legal system is both a transplant and withal a relatively recent disciplinary adventure. Rooted jurisdictionally and linguistically in English common law, citing to Magna Carta, Sir Edward Coke, William Blackstone, and the infinite particulars of Anglican precedent, the legitimacy of nineteenth-century US common law was predicated ideologically upon the European legal tradition. Until the latter portions of the nineteenth century, there were few university law schools, and while predecessor private law tutoring colleges existed, their approach was primarily that of training for the profession in the mode of practice and took the form of being articled to, or being a clerk for a practitioner. What substantive literature there was came from and was modeled on its English forebears.

An anonymously published enchiridion, *Advice on the Study of Law*, from 1811, subtitled *With Directions for the choice of books, addressed to attornies' clerks: with additional notes for the American student*, exhibits all of the Anglophilia of US law when it came to the substance of their practice. Authored by an English barrister, published in Maryland, and running to three editions over the next two decades, the work begins with a hortatory epigraph taken from Bacon's essay "Of Studies."[7] It proceeds to recommend recourse to the classic

---

7 The epigraph from Bacon is on the title page of the first edition but is replaced by a moralizing quotation from Bishop Richard Hurd in the third edition, perhaps because of Bacon's somewhat checkered legal career. I have used the third, expanded edition, William Wright, *Advice on the Study and Practice of the Law* (London: C. Hunter, 1824). As for the epigraph, see *Bacon's Essays with Annotations by Richard Whately, D.D.* (London: Parker, 1858): "Read not to contradict and confute, nor to believe and take for granted, nor to find talk and discourse, but to weigh and consider" (474).

preparatives and directives on the study of law, authored in the early modern era by William Fulbeck (1599), John Doderidge (1620), and William Phillips (1667), suggesting a fairly timeless literature of dogma and method. Wright continues to suggest supplementing the didactic works with epistolary and familiar advice from "Letters on the Study and Practice of the Law." To this is added reference to the similarly essayistic "observations on the study of the law [that] may be found in Sir Matthew Hale's Preface to Rolle's Abridgment" and "two letters on the same subject" written by Justice Reeve and by Lord Ashburton, and concluding with "Mr Watkins, in his *Principles*, and Mr Barton, in his *Elements* of Conveyancing."[8] The prefatory essay, dating back at least to Sir Edward Coke (1552–1634) and Sir John Davies (1569–1626), who provided prolegomenal discourses of a didactic and eulogistic character to their *Reports* or *Annales* of the law, is bound to and explicative of the inscription of judgments and rules that follow. It is a prelude (*prae-ludium*), an exploration or play upon the greater themes that the author desires to promote or believes to be implicit, if obliquely, in the records of practice and acts of justice that their substantive work relays.

That the early literature of US law, in common with the English tradition, is concerned primarily with introducing law reports, and less often with comments on legislation, is hardly surprising. It leaves an indelible mark on the scholarship that follows. Reportage, the essentially journalistic accounting of contemporary juridical developments, the pronouncements of judges and legislatures, were the principal object of and constraint on the genre.[9] When, in the latter half of the nineteenth century, the universities began founding law schools, it was practitioners who, understandably enough, were recruited to the professorial positions, and whose work was expected to stand astride the two cultures, professional and pedagogic, so as to train the student for the practice of the trade. The model of substantive legal literature was taken from England, in the form of commentaries on law and on equity and in treatises for practitioners, together with the invention of the casebook as a didactic tool, yet here again the cases were primarily from England. As Joseph Story (1779–1845) puts it in his treatise on *Equity*, one must

---

8 William Wright, *Advice on the Study of Law, with directions for the choice of books, addressed to attornies' clerks: with additional notes for the American student* (Baltimore: Croake, 1811), vi–vii.
9 A point well made in relation to the English bar, in Neil Duxbury, "When We Were Young: Notes in the Law Quarterly Review, 1885–1925," *Law Quarterly Review* 116 (2000): 474–503, 474.

begin with "a brief review of its origin and progress in England, from which country America has derived its own principles and practice on the same subject."[10]

Pragmatism

The distinctively American juristic perspective emerges in the second half of the nineteenth century, with the law school, the nascent law reviews, and the Metaphysical Club.[11] A Harvard Law School professor, now also a named building, and a justice of the Supreme Court of Massachusetts, Oliver Wendell Holmes Jr. (1841–1935), son of Oliver Wendell Holmes Sr., poet, renowned essayist, and author of several volumes of *Table Talk*, rebelled against the reverential strictures of European legal formalism and the abstraction of a German-inspired dogmatic method that dominated and would continue to dominate the casebooks and treatises of substantive legal systematics. While the law school in Cambridge *ultra mare* was busy establishing the Socratic method of law teaching, the hothouse library science of precedential casuistry associated most often with Christopher Columbus Langdell (1826–1906), J. B. Ames (1846–1910), and Samuel Williston (1861–1963), Holmes inaugurated the grand style of legal essay, the philosopher law professor at the podium pithily invoking the metaphysical contingency of a venal and distinctively tellurian vocation.

One of three "long-headed youths," together with Charles Sanders Peirce (1839–1914) and William James (1842–1910), embroiled in a post–Civil War, post-Darwinian search for an agnostic philosophy, Holmes committed his intellectual life to the pursuit and promulgation of a pragmatist theory and practice of law. Contingency was the sign that governed thought, and moral skepticism was the pragmatist's shield against the ideal. A survivor of the Civil War and committed to rebuilding and legitimating the union, Holmes grew up alongside the new law school, and the bulk of his work lay in systematizing the burgeoning case law of the new jurisdiction. Already famous for his book *The Common Law*, his first articles in *Harvard Law Review* were podium talk, the transcription of lectures that attempted to make pragmatic sense of the precedents, English and American, on agency. The seemingly technical topic of vicarious acts and liabilities was the oblique

---

10 Joseph Story, *Commentaries on Equity Jurisprudence* (Boston: Little, Brown, 1857), 42.
11 See Louis Menand, *The Metaphysical Club* (London: Flamingo, 2002). For an overview of Holmes's legal career, see Edward G. White, "Introduction," in *The Common Law*, by Oliver Wendell Holmes Jr. (Cambridge, MA: Harvard University Press, 2009), vii–xxxiii.

yet powerful avenue into a highly erudite critique of legal dogma, and specifically the elaboration of juristic fictions for the purposes of symmetry – *elegantia iuris* – as opposed to decisions according to justice and common sense. Although the referent may appear obscure, the article, divided into two parts to keep it essay length, is in many respects exemplary.

Bacon positions the essay form between rationalism and empiricism, and as Duxbury notes, the protorealist Holmes both revolts against formalism and at other times on other issues remains resolutely formalist.[12] This may in part reflect the bifurcated role of judge and scholar, professional and academic, but is better conceived as the nascent form of an independent and distinctly American legal genre. The exercise is a search for truth: to study the theory of agency "to the end that it may be understood upon evidence, and not merely by conjecture."[13] This means a critical tracing of the genealogy of the juristic concept of agency, the debunking of antique legal fictions that have lost their reason for being – that suffer desuetude – and produce manifest injustice. The conflict of logic and common sense is resolved consistently in the interests of the latter and against a blind obedience, familiar to English judges, "of striving to carry fictions out to consistent results" and concluding that "common sense is opposed to the fundamental theory of agency."[14] The legal fiction that one person be responsible for the crime, negligence, possession, or contract of another is frequently exposed in the development of English common law, from Bracton and Glanvill to Blackstone and Mansfield, to defy rational explanation. Baron Parke's (1782–1868) attempt to extend the maxim *qui facit per alium, facit per se*, which derives from a direct act – *vi et armis* – in trespass, to the careless acts of a servant in employment law, which is a vicarious act and an action on the case, is dismissed in pithy Holmesian style: "Considered as reasoning, it would be hard to unite more errors in as many words."[15] The unity of the principle of agency may be pleasing to lawyers, but is shown to be a survival

---

12 On the essay and method, the key analysis remains that of Theodor W. Adorno, "The Essay as Form," in *Notes to Literature*, ed. Rolf Tiedeman, trans. Shierry Weber Nicholsen (New York: Columbia University Press, 1991), 1:3–23, 9. On Holmes and company, see Neil Duxbury, *Patterns of American Jurisprudence* (Oxford: Oxford University Press, 1997), 10.
13 Oliver Wendell Holmes Jr., "Agency," *Harvard Law Review* 4, no. 8 (March 1891): 345–364, 345.
14 Oliver Wendell Holmes Jr., "Agency II," *Harvard Law Review* 5, no. 1 (April 1891): 1–23, 14.
15 Holmes, "Agency II," 20. On the checkered career of the concept, see Raymond Westbrook, "Vitae necisque potestas," *Historia* 48, no. 2 (1999): 203–23, 203.

of antique traditions and classical fictions whose "ancient meaning" has gradually been forgotten, and which should now disappear.

Much though the two-part article might appear technical, Holmes the essayist has a greater philosophical cause in mind. The law of agency reviewed goes to the heart of the legal and political aspirations of the newly founded and even more recently reunited, postbellum, state. The concept of agency, of acting for oneself or for another, raises fundamental ontological questions of identity and responsibility, as well as epistemological dissections of predestination versus free will. The law of vicarious responsibility pitches servitude against independence, but it is clearly the latter, the moral responsibility and liberation of the colony and then most proximately of master and servant, that had been the cause of the war and the aspiration of those who, like Holmes, had lived through it and could reformulate the tale in the argute terms of law. What matters are the historical reasons for the discordance of opinions in the cases and the injustices that they generate. The root of the concept lies in Roman patriarchy, the power of the father who owned and had the right to kill his chattels, his servants and children: "[T]he law undoubtedly started from slavery and *patria potestas*."[16] With its roots in the sovereignty of the paternal figure and the servitude of the agent – slave, child, thing – the legal fictions that expand this principle unconsciously also extend a law of domination of one person over others. Holmes notes that "Justinian's Institutes tell us that the right of a slave to receive a binding promise is derived *ex persona domini*."[17] That the agent disappears into the persona of the principal is a legal subsumption that is increasingly no more than a surreptitious residue of history, and with it a negation of the self-determining and free subject of law: "But a fiction is not a satisfactory reason for changing men's rights or liabilities."[18]

Polemic

That agency and questions of identity and free will should be a founding theme of the nascent legal system in a society marked most indelibly by the wound of racial division and the desire for freedom as equals is hardly surprising. That students at the law school were responsible for eliciting and publishing the piece is more remarkable and is one of the most enduringly distinctive features of the American law essay. The forum of the form is predominately the law review, and it is one that expands alongside the

---

[16] Holmes, "Agency," 350.   [17] Holmes, "Agency," 351.   [18] Holmes, "Agency II," 18.

growth of legal education. Its trajectory can be discerned *in nuce*, in Holmes's critique of agency, and it gains further and more explicit projection in an even more famous early entry in the *Harvard Law Review*, from 1897, "The Path of the Law."[19] It falls within the top ten law review articles ever cited according to an econometric study from the year 2000, but it is less quantity than style that merits focus for what it indicates of legal essayism in the United States.[20] The piece is a ceremonial address for a celebratory occasion, "the dedication of a new hall at Boston University School of Law, on January 8, 1897." So the students' footnote informs us, and it is indeed the architecture, the atmosphere, and building blocks of law, rather than the Via Appia of legal knowledge, that is the principal focus of this epideictic digression. The essay is the text of a vocational address, a paradoxically critical eulogy and pragmatic dissection of the practices of lawyers. Holmes, as he puts it in a letter to Harold J. Laski, was not much inclined to the speeches that "loose-fibred and coarse-grained men drool," and so the pabulum of academic pontification and the prolixity of scholarship are disdained.[21] The path of the essay is short. From the building to the battlefield of social conflict and warring morals is but a brief step.

The law, as the later realists, Karl Llewellyn (1893–1962) in particular, were prone to pointing out, is a job, a task with consequences for others, and it is in its actions, in court decisions, in law application, and not in law books or theoretical rhodomontade that its importance lies.[22] Thus the exhortation is to clear the building, sweep the path of fallacious moralisms, misleading abstractions, rules in books. Away too with Roman law, archaisms, and other esoteric antiquities, in favor of straightforward, clear-eyed, and candid, not candied, predictions. The critique is of tradition, and most particularly of the sclerosis of the English legal tradition, of which Holmes opines, "I look

---

19 Oliver Wendell Holmes Jr., "The Path of the Law," *Harvard Law Review* 10, no. 8 (March 1897): 457–78, 457.
20 Ranked third in Fred R. Shapiro, "The Most-Cited Legal Scholars," *Journal of Legal Studies* 29 (2000): 409–26, 424.
21 Oliver Wendell Holmes Jr. to Harold J. Laski (1 June 1922), in *Holmes-Laski Letters: The Correspondence of Mr. Justice Holmes and Harold J. Laski [1916–1935]*, ed. Mark DeWolfe Howe (Cambridge, MA: Harvard University Press, 1953), 430, cited in David Lubban, "The Bad Man and the Good Lawyer: A Centennial Essay on Holmes's The Path of the Law," *NYU Law Review* 72 (1997): 1547–83, 1547.
22 Karl N. Llewellyn, "Some Realism about Realism: Responding to Dean Pound," *Harvard Law Review* 44, no. 8 (June 1931): 1222–64, provides a later, realist, and self-consciously literary version of the same arguments: "The law of the schools threatened at the close of the century to turn into words – placid, clear-seeming, lifeless like some old canal. Practice rolled on, muddy, turbulent, vigorous. It is now spilling, flooding, into the canal. It brings ferment and trouble" (1222).

forward to a time when the part played by history in the explanation of dogma shall be very small, and instead of ingenious research we shall spend our energy on a study of the ends sought to be attained and the reasons for desiring them."[23] The path to be hewn is away from fustian or more properly dogmatic constraint toward a consequentialist universe, a *tao* of law, that consists of predictions, of advice to the "bad man," Holmes to Moriarty, and calculations of what it will cost, the likely length of a prison sentence, the amount that will be mulcted in damages.[24]

It is pragmatism, too, that places the vehicle of the legal essay in the hands of law students. Selecting, editing, and disseminating the reportage and commentary on legal novelties, as also advocacy and scholarship in doctrine and discipline, rest in the hands of acolytes and novices. This is in part because the students in the late nineteenth century wanted periodicals with news, and began with journals in the French meaning of the word. The other ground for student editing was the consequentialist view that this was a perfect paper training for the prophet-to-be, a second order of law reporting, an exercise in the cut and thrust of dialogue and debate within the profession. All of this juristic Sturm und Drang was to be coordinated by the students because faculty would neither have the time nor the inclination for such distraction from their lofty pedagogic and professional pursuits, their onerously bifurcated role as practitioners as well as pedants.

The student-edited law review is a conduit rather than a judge of essays. The twentieth century thus saw a radical diversity of topoi, styles, and forms of juristic writing, an exponentially expanding length of essay and of law review, as well as a multiplication of the number of journals. Each law school is home to anywhere from three to thirteen student-edited journals. Plurality reigns, and since the increase in the number of law schools since the 1970s, a significant portion of the content of the law reviews is taken up with the publication of essays by students. That provides a sense of the Wild West of legal essays, and as early as 1936 led the legal realist Fred Rodell (1907–1980), author, among other things, of a book titled *Woe unto You, Lawyers* (1939), to begin what he termed "probably my last law review article" with a cutting observation: "There are two things wrong with almost all legal writing. One

---

23 Holmes, "Path of the Law," 474.
24 On Holmes and tao, see Laurent de Sutter, "Défense et illustration du réalisme juridique," in *La voie du droit* ["The Path of the Law," 1897], by Oliver Wendell Holmes, Jr., trans. Laurent de Sutter (Paris: Dalloz, 2014), 1–32, 26–28.

is its style. The other is its content. That, I think, about covers the ground."[25] He goes on to opine: "The average law review writer is peculiarly able to say nothing with an air of great importance." The issue is that the student editing does not control but rather expands into lengthy explanatory text and limitless footnotes proving the textual resting place of any given statement, whatever its insignificance, making the article with its myriad superscripted numbers look something like a crossword puzzle, and leaving the product resembling "a cross between a nineteenth century sermon and a treatise on higher mathematics."[26] As Rodell's two excurses show, long before any postmodern marshaling of "anything goes," it was possible to say pretty much anything and at any length in the law review forums. Status came to override content, and in its disciplinary manifestations the insecure search for legitimacy sacrificed style to the reification of tangible sources and the student's sense of evidence.[27]

There is another sense in which the essay returned to the prototype, which was that to have effect and to be meaningful, it needed to find forums and styles that challenged the law review. So the radicals took to the podium, to interdisciplinary and other academically edited forums of publication, which diversity of venues came to mark the scholarly contributions of the realistically and critically inclined, while the status-oriented, citation-counting, increasingly graded and ranked lottery of the law review remained an open space of adversarial and advocacy-oriented expositions of increasing length and wild diversity. Pierre Schlag's (1954–) article "Normative and Nowhere to Go" opens with these lines: "Last I remember, it was 1979 and I was beginning my career. I had these incredible utopian visions and these absolutely uncontrollable yearnings to prescribe these normative visions to large numbers of strangers."[28] Roberto Unger's (1947–) "The Critical Legal Studies Movement," the rallying cry for the Left in the law school, an article that launched a thousand radicals, ran to 115 pages.[29] It was in origin a very lengthy

---

25 Fred Rodell, "Goodbye to Law Reviews," *Virginia Law Review* 23, no. 1 (November 1936): 38–45, 38. He later published a reprise: Fred Rodell, "Goodbye to Law Reviews – Revisited," *Virginia Law Review* 48, no. 2 (March 1962): 279–90, 279.
26 Rodell, "Goodbye to Law Reviews" (1936), 41.
27 The best account of the peculiarities of the US law review is that of an Australian literature graduate turned law professor who moved to the American legal academy: Penelope Pether, "Discipline and Punish: Despatches from the Citation Manual Wars and Other (Literally) Unspeakable Stories," *Griffith Law Review* 10, no. 2 (2001): 101–35, 101.
28 Pierre Schlag, "Normative and Nowhere to Go," *Stanford Law Review* 43, no. 1 (November 1990): 167–91, 167.
29 Roberto Unger, "The Critical Legal Studies Movement," *Harvard Law Review* 96, no. 3 (January 1983): 561–675, 563; the article was released as a book in 1986 and reissued in

after-dinner speech, and it ends an extremely abstract and equally expansive critique of formalism and objectivism with the claim to undermining "the central ideas of modern legal thought." These are to be replaced by another conception of law, even though the last line enigmatically claims to turn away from the cold altars of the legal priesthood and find "the mind's opportunity in the heart's revenge."[30]

Neorealism in the form of critical legal studies finally inserted the rallying cries of the culture wars, the academic and often dilettante jargons of interdisciplinarity and politics of practice, into the juristic forum of the law essay. The legal academy itself came under critical attack, and in the foment and fulmination of radical politicization momentarily appeared to falter. Duncan Kennedy (1942–) at Harvard Law self-published a samizdat, book-length essay, in the form of a scathing attack on the legal academy, titled "Legal Education as Training for Hierarchy." The critique aims to expose the corporatization of the law school culture and curriculum, the elite character of its clientele, the tacit codes, status assurances, and backroom deals that governed reproduction of lawyering in the classroom and latterly in synchronized form in the public sphere.[31] His argument was that a composite ideology dominated the syllabus and that "what teachers teach along with basic skills is wrong, is nonsense about what law is and how it works ... nonsense with a tilt; it is biased and motivated nonsense rather than random error."[32] The law essay became a battleground, a polemical force and political rallying cry for Left lawyering as well as a vehicle for advocacy of radical restructuring of curriculum and institution. The mood was again that of revolt or what Sartre termed rebellion rather than revolution. The conservative movement in law, spearheaded by the school of law and economics, quickly quelled the institutional ambitions of the critical movement. The profusion of critical styles and an accentuated awareness of the limits of legality as a structurally white male operation was predicated as much as anything else upon the political will of a dominant class, which marginalized

---

2015. Roberto Unger, *The Critical Legal Studies Movement: Another Time, A Greater Task* (London: Verso, 2015), reproduces the original essay and provides a retrospective.
30 Unger, "Critical Legal Studies Movement," 675.
31 Self-published as a booklet in 1983, a truncated version (cited here) was later printed as Duncan Kennedy, "Legal Education as Training for Hierarchy," in *The Politics of Law: A Progressive Critique*, ed. David Kairys (New York: Pantheon, 1982), 54–75; and reproduced again in book form, with commentaries, as *Legal Education and the Reproduction of Hierarchy: A Polemic against the System* (New York: NYU Press, 2004).
32 Kennedy, "Legal Education," 54.

its influence in internecine institutional conflicts, as opposed to launching any radically new modes of thinking diversity in law.

It may seem idiosyncratic to view the short-lived critical legal essay as a founding moment in the pluralization of legal forms of juris-literary advocacy and expression, but the crucible of critique brought together and helped to launch an expanded awareness of civil rights, sexual politics, and critical race theory within and beyond the legal academy.[33] The classical paradigm of legal thought, as a positive and autonomous technical rubric of governance, died a second death, captured adroitly in an essay both brilliant and paradoxical by Stanley Fish (1938–). In "The Law Wishes to Have a Formal Existence," the contrarian iconoclast and one of the only law professors in the United States not to have a law degree, managed both to irrefutably demonstrate that the bedrocks of legal textualism, literalism, and plain meaning were epistemologically bankrupt, and that formalism, meaning certainty, and decision are what society wants from law.[34] His version of pessimism of the intellect and optimism of the will could be viewed and was perceived as nihilistic but also, as with Jacques Derrida's call for an incalculable justice in his famous lecture in 1989, opened the door to a move beyond juridical technicalities to advocacy of civil and political causes.[35] It was not case law but legislation that would change the world.

Feminist jurisprudence and critical race theory introduced intimate experience and affect into the conceptualization and polemical advocacy of legal change. What further characterizes the postcritical legal essay is not simply a search for effect, an engagement with the question of an audience, but also the endeavor to leave the law review forum for sites that fitted the focus and political drive of the work. Catharine MacKinnon (1946–) published her most important analysis of juristic method in the feminist journal *Signs*, where she spelled out a sexual division of labor structuring intimate relations and, most famously, translated juristic objectivity into sexual objectification.[36] The

---

33 The brief life and times of critical legal studies, as a movement, can be followed in Richard Michael Fischl, "The Question That Killed Critical Legal Studies," *Law and Social Inquiry* 17, no. 4 (1992): 779–820, 779; and from a distinct perspective in Steven Teles, *The Rise of the Conservative Legal Movement: The Battle for Control of the Law* (Princeton, NJ: Princeton University Press, 2008).
34 Stanley Fish, "The Law Wishes to Have a Formal Existence," in *The Fate of Law*, ed. Austin Sarat and Thomas R. Kearns (Ann Arbor, MI: Michigan University Press, 1991), 159–208.
35 Jacques Derrida, "Force of Law: The 'Mystical Foundation of Authority'," *Cardozo Law Review* 11, no. 5–6 (1990): 919–1046, 919; originally delivered at the Deconstruction and the Possibility of Justice colloquium at Cardozo Law School in 1989.
36 Catharine MacKinnon, "Feminism, Marxism, Method, and the State: An Agenda for Theory," *Signs* 7, no. 3 (1982): 515–44, 541.

forum of the essay and subsequent elaboration of a feminist jurisprudence had radical political effects and played a major part in the development of domestic violence and harassment laws.[37] The shift in forum marked a change in style, from legalism to affective experience, rage at structural inequality, and fury at the limpness of law that was to be countered by consciousness-raising. The phenomenological theater of the body was finally levitated into a juristic arena accused of epistemicide and an ontography of violence. The indeterminacy of law that was the sign of the times and the spool upon which critique had been woven gave way to a more literary imagination and visceral political causes whose vulnerability required legal protections.

Sex was one division. Race was another.[38] Their combination compounded inequalities.[39] The most formally innovative of proponents of an autobiographical style and of a more popular audience for the legal essay was and is Patricia J. Williams (1951–), whose *Alchemy of Race and Rights* (1991) collected a series of existential vignettes in the form of political and legal analyses of quotidian encounters. Where Holmes had defined a contract as a promise to perform or pay damages, without any moral or political dimension, Williams explained how, when moving to New York, color and femininity necessitated that she fight for a signed contract, a lease that would protect her tenancy and give her rights that her white male colleague Peter Gabel viewed as otiose. A handshake was all that he needed.[40] She relayed the story of learning from her mother, on the day Patricia was to leave for a place at Harvard Law, that her great-great-grandmother had been an enslaved woman raped by a white attorney owner, and so she had law in her blood. It was a story that set her soul aflame and found its vivid path into her work.[41]

---

37 Catharine MacKinnon, "Feminism, Marxism, Method, and the State: Toward Feminist Jurisprudence," *Signs* 8, no. 4 (1983): 635–58.
38 Critical race theory, of course, has longer tendrils and roots. Derrick Bell, *Race, Racism and American Law* (Boston: Little, Brown, 1973), was the first casebook on the topic of racism and law, and was followed by Derrick Bell, "Serving Two Masters: Integration Ideals and Client Interests in School Desegregation Litigation," *Yale Law Journal* 85, no. 4 (March 1976): 470–516, 470. A valuable history and conspectus is provided in Richard Delgado and Jean Stefancic, "Critical Race Theory: Past, Present and Future," *Current Legal Problems* 51, no. 1 (1998): 467–91.
39 The concept of intersectionality as a tool for legal critique is elaborated by Kimberlee Crenshaw, "Mapping the Margins: Intersectionality, Identity Politics, and Violence against Women of Color," *Stanford Law Review* 43, no. 6 (July 1991): 1241–99.
40 Patricia J. Williams, *The Alchemy of Race and Rights: Diary of a Law Professor* (Cambridge, MA: Harvard University Press, 1984).
41 Patricia J. Williams, "On Being the Object of Property," *Signs* 14, no. 1 (1988): 5–24, 5.

The locus of radical legal thought in a *corpus iuris* conceived in corporeal terms, as the materiality of the body, as color, sex, performativity, living text, and testimony, the vestige and embodiment of histories of oppression and of privilege, almost sidelined legal doctrine in the rush to confront the site of its intersection with other disciplines and their heterotopic spaces. The vast embrace of the student-edited law reviews could accommodate almost anything and frequently did so, as a plethora of new political causes, from sex and race to the environment and climate, affective dispute resolution, legal semiotics, food and law, theatrical jurisprudence, psychoanalytic legal studies, and synaesthetics, found their way back into the omnium gatherum of the school publications. Disciplinary copula, law and economics, law and literature, aesthetics and law, movement and law, law and religion, washed over the previously rigid juridical boundaries. In contemporary contexts, the new materialism leads to earth jurisprudence and Anthropocene legal thought, which in its scope and imagination comes close to reviving the Renaissance explorations of juris-astrology. The propensity of the legal essay in the postcritical era is thus to seek to escape law so as to change it, by finding an audience and rallying to a cause.

A brief survey of the topoi of law essays does scant justice to the diversity and inventiveness of themes and styles, but does allow for the extraction of certain distinctive characteristics and styles that mark the genre. The United States is a youthful jurisdiction in the context of the *longue durée* of common law. There is certainly a sense of enthusiasm and desire, a positive affect that anything is possible, that structures can be restructured, which accompanies a lack of antique institutional traditions and inculcated offices, patterns of method, and normative constraint. That the essay can change the law is more fundamental and operative in the United States than in most other common law systems. If pragmatism is the founding principle of jurisprudence and the immediacy of consequences governs cognitive and normative elaborations, then law will change more easily according to juristic and judicial points of view. As early as 1890, an essay created a new tort of privacy. Where tradition and precedent dictate that new laws are a matter for the legislature – judges are supposed simply to declare and apply extant rules – the essayists prefer to recognize a more intangible principle: "Political, social, and economic changes entail the recognition of new rights, and the common law, in its eternal youth, grows to meet the demands of society."[42] These demands are

---

42 Samuel Warren and Louis Brandeis, "The Right to Privacy," *Harvard Law Review* 4, no.5 (December 1890): 193–220, 193.

then listed on the basis of the author's most fortunate access to the inner workings of "the advance of civilization" and, in analogous cases to those of invasion of privacy, remedies have been fashioned by "the beautiful capacity for growth which characterizes the common law and enabled the judges to afford the requisite protection, without the intervention of the legislature."[43] Samuel Warren (1852–1910) and Louis Brandeis (1856–1941), two attorneys, both graduates of Harvard Law School, successfully make the plea for such invention in the form of an essay that is conventionally viewed as adding a chapter to American law.

Much has changed since the founding assertions of the Socratic method and the law school laboratory, but it would be wrong to end without an appreciation of the multicolored anarchy of the academic law essay that currently still lingers in the hands of law student editors. Untutored wit, wild inventiveness, and a propensity to optimism are the predominant distinguishing marks of the legal essay in the United States. The sheer size of the law review output means that pretty much any contribution can find a site of publication somewhere. Student essays pile up, eager for change, while profession and professoriate plunder other disciplines in endless search of what law lacks, from linguistics to aesthetics, economics to sociology, spatial awareness, emotional intelligence, historical depth, psychoanalytic acumen, race consciousness, trans-sensibility, algorithms, atmospherics, and the Anthropocene. The clash of ideas has always sounded at some distance from the agonistic practice and pursuit of warring parties' interests in court, and yet the distinct potential of US law lies precisely in the willingness of judges and other practitioners to pluck an argument, an idea, a policy goal, good or bad according to one's point of view, and put it to use.

The importance of the essay form is to clear a space, to act out in ideas what practice has not yet tested, and so to become the theater that stages in advance the future of law. The techniques of such proleptic prognostication are drawn from across the unrestrained kaleidoscope of academic copulas and allow a conclusion that can draw together the themes of this essay as a juris-literary excursus. The referent is not to legal belles lettres, but to the prolegomenal, introductory, theoretical, and interdisciplinary attempts that lawyers, jurists, and practitioners make to engage with the public sphere, to open law to quotidian intellection, to political dialogue, to the republic of letters, and to the aspirations for liberty and equality that the Constitution inscribes. The legal essay as an exemplary exhibition of juris-literary values

---

43 Warren and Brandeis, "Right to Privacy," 195.

gains its most expansive expression in the United States because a pragmatic founding philosophy and egalitarian realism placed neither constraint nor control on the literary production of the law schools. The essay as a form was free to experiment, to advocate, satirize, invent, and excoriate as mood and trend inspired.

26

World War Two to #MeToo: The Personal and the Political in the American Feminist Essay

ELLENA SAVAGE

Contemporary writings on the essay have tended to underplay its significance in the radical political movements of the twentieth century and beyond. Instead, they have situated it as an apolitical and ahistorical literary genre independent of technologies of publishing and selfhood. The genre's history, writes Ruth-Ellen Boetcher Joeres, is an elitist one that "has almost always been a tool of the privileged classes"[1] and as a product of leisure, the essay is an activity not "generally undertaken in the midst of great and distracting external activity."[2] With a first peak in the Enlightenment period – philosophically radical, yes, but whose philosophies are largely constitutive of Western European, bourgeois, male neutrality and centrality – the essay is also a hybrid, boundary form, one of the most "flexible and adaptable of all literary forms,"[3] and therefore adaptable to multiple and multiplying contexts. As if to insist on the essay's legibility as a literary form, its belles-lettres affiliations are sometimes privileged over its application in radical political contexts. For example, Cynthia Ozick (1928–) is not alone in claiming that a "genuine essay has no educational, polemical, or sociopolitical use; it is the movement of a free mind at play."[4] To the contrary, a great number of the essays published over the past eighty years that are still in circulation are animated by radical political desires that deploy the individual speaker, the "free mind," as a performative stand-in for broader political assemblages.

---

1 Ruth-Ellen Boetcher Joeres, "The Passionate Essay," in *The Politics of the Essay: Feminist Perspectives*, ed. Boetcher Joeres and Elizabeth Mittman (Bloomington, IN: Indiana University Press, 1993), 151–71, 151.
2 Boetcher Joeres, "Passionate Essay," 151.
3 J. A. Cuddon, *Dictionary of Literary Terms and Literary Theory* (London: Penguin, 1999), 286.
4 Cynthia Ozick, "SHE: Portrait of the Essay as a Warm Body," *Atlantic Monthly* 282, no. 3 (September 1998): 114–18, 114.

As Rachel DuPlessis has written, "Sociality and textuality meet in the essay. It is not aesthetic only, not political only, but aesthetico-political."[5] Feminist scholarship teaches us to look closely at what is being counted; what is included, what is excluded, and why.

The post–World War II period in the United States offers a rich bibliography of feminist essays to reread within their own context, as well as a retrospective tradition of volumes and anthologies seeking to critically "re-vision"[6] and recirculate, memorialize and critique feminisms' recent past. This chapter will chart the postwar feminist essay in three directions: first, as a site of consciousness-raising during feminism's second wave[7] ("Consciousness"); second, as a space for feminist critiques of feminisms during the so-called third wave ("Difference"); and third, in its contemporary iteration in a revived consciousness-raising context: the #MeToo essay ("Re-Raising Consciousness"). In historicizing a set of texts under the critical term "feminist essay," I draw together a number of formally and contextually various texts into a longer conversation about how the essay can be read as a politicized and politicizing literary form. The essays that appear in this chapter include multiple nonfiction subgenres often thought to be subordinate to the essay: an article, "A Bunny's Tale" by journalist Gloria Steinem; a collectively authored set of papers, "Study Papers of 1968" by the Mount Vernon/New Rochelle Group; a prose poem, "I Don't Understand Those Who Have Turned Away from Me" by the Menominee poet Chrystos; a short memoir, "Ambivalence about Feminism" by Barbara Epstein; and a victim impact statement published online, "Here's the Powerful Letter the Stanford Victim Read to her Attacker by Chanel Miller. I will argue that what makes these texts "feminist" *and* "essays" – despite significant formal differences – is their shared engagement with critical, documentary, and experiential literary modes and their stakes in connecting the individual to politically invested collectives, past and future. These five essays explicitly address gender and contingent forces of oppression that both bond and trouble emancipatory collectives.

---

5 Rachel Blau DuPlessis, *Blue Studios: Poetry and Its Cultural Work* (Tuscaloosa, AL: University of Alabama Press, 2006), 37.
6 I refer here to Adrienne Rich's "re-vision" in "When We Dead Awaken: Writing as Re-Vision": "Re-vision – the act of looking back, of seeing with fresh eyes, of entering an old text from a new critical direction – is for us more than a chapter in cultural history: it is an act of survival," *College English* 34, no. 1 (October 1972): 18–30, 18.
7 The "waves" metaphor is contested; it privileges certain North American and European historiographies of gender struggle. I use it in this chapter due to its utility in describing contemporaneous US concepts of feminist history.

Feminism, writes Joeres, has traditionally been ambivalent "toward matters of form (if form implies schools, canons, separations, hierarchies)."[8] The formal variation across the feminist essays I study in this chapter attests to this. What we now read under the moniker "essay" is often first circulated in paraliterary spaces. For example, Eleanor Flexner's (1908–1995) *Century of Struggle* (1959), a history of the United States' first wave of feminism, was initially self-published as a pamphlet essay in 1954, just as Kate Millett's (1934–2017) *Sexual Politics* was expanded from a pamphlet she self-published in 1968. These early women's movement essays contain the nuclei of feminist ideas that are still in passionate discussion today. Notable instances include the Pat Robinson Group's "Study Papers" included in this chapter; the newspapers published by the New York City–based radical feminist collective, the Redstockings ("Notes from the First [/Second/Third] Year," published 1968, 1969, and 1970), which included work by Shulamith Firestone (1945–2012), Jo Freeman (1945–), Elaine Showalter (1941–), Ann Snitow (1943–2019), Rosalyn Baxandall (1939–2015), the author of the famed "The Personal Is Political" essay Carol Hanisch (1942–), and many more feminists who went on to contribute some of the feminist movement's most influential essays well into the 1990s and beyond; and countless self-published pamphlets, like Kate Millet's. These early, radical postwar feminist essays have a provisional quality to them: Titles like "Notes" and "Study papers" suggest they are points of entry into radical ideas, open to response, rather than conclusive findings.

Later in the postwar history of the feminism in the United States, when feminist viewpoints found a foothold in the university, media, and publishing, feminist essays took the form of a kind of public scholarship. These essays often combine the rigor of academic training with the lucidity and style of literary essays. A small sample of essays of note here include Linda Nochlin's "Why Have There Been No Great Women Artists?" (1971); Jo Freeman's "The Tyranny of Structurelessness" (1971); Adrienne Rich's many contributions, including "When We Dead Awaken: Writing as Re-Vision Author(s)" (1972), "Emily E. Dickinson" (1976), and "Compulsory Heterosexuality and Lesbian Existence" (1980); Susan Sontag's "The Double Standard of Aging" (1972); Andrea Dworkin's canon of essays published from around 1974; Alice Walker's "Saving the Life That Is Your Own: The Importance of Models in the Artist's Life" (1976) and "Beauty: When the Other Dancer Is the Self" (1983); Audre Lorde's "Poetry Is Not a Luxury" (1977), "Uses of the Erotic: The Erotic as Power" (1978), and "The Master's Tools Will Never Dismantle

---

8 Boetcher Joeres, "Passionate Essay," 155.

the Master's House" (1979); "The Combahee River Collective Statement" (1977); bell hooks's canon of essays, published from 1978; Tille Olsen's collection *Silences* (1978); Angela Y. Davis's collection *Women, Race and Class* (1981); Elaine Showalter's "Feminist Criticism in the Wilderness" (1981); Iris Marion Young's "Throwing like a Girl: A Phenomenology of Feminine Body Comportment Motility and Spatiality" (1981); Susan Gubar's "'The Blank Page' and Issues of Female Creativity" (1981); June Jordan's "Report from the Bahamas" (1982); Minnie Bruce Pratt's "Identity: Skin Blood Heart" (1984); Donna Harraway's "A Cyborg Manifesto" (1985); Judith Butler's five essays on gender published between 1985 and 1989; Kimberlé Williams Crenshaw's "Demarginalizing the Intersection of Race and Sex: A Black Feminist Critique of Antidiscrimination Doctrine, Feminist Theory and Antiracist Politics" (1989) and "Race, Gender, and Sexual Harassment" (1992); Patricia J. Williams's essay collection *The Alchemy of Race and Rights* (1991); "Riot Grrrl Manifesto" (1991); Jack Halberstam's "Telling Tales" (2000); and Gender Violence and the Prison Industrial Complex's manifesto "Incite! Women, Gender Non-conforming, and trans People of Color against Violence" (2001).

During the 1990s and early 2000s, the feminist essay appears to have retreated. Much US feminist activity during this period was concentrated on women's representation within public and corporate industrial sectors and the Democratic Party; women and girl-led subcultural spaces; the development of queer and trans feminisms; and globalist feminist projects more broadly, which tended to focus on issues of migration, peacekeeping, economic injustice, and gender-based violence. Yet the dawn of the Internet saw the emergence of the feminist blog, notable authors of which include Jackie Wang, Bhanu Kapil,[9] Ariana Reines, and Kate Zambreno. The resurgence of feminist essayistic activity picks up again around 2008, when the technologies of user-generated and participatory online cultures are mobilized by feminist writers, editors, and publishers. Rebecca Solnit's 2008 essay "Men Explain Things to Me" marks a shift. The new, online feminist essay is, like previous iterations of the subgenre, a form of public scholarship; unlike in previous epochs, the modalities of social media create a real-time feedback loop. Online, this period saw a resurgence of a post-Saidian stance, arguing that reporters, writers, and commentators from hegemonic groups necessarily project on and distort the experiences and interests of any subjugated groups

---

9 Bhanu Kapil is British but worked at Naropa University in Boulder, Colorado, from 2000 to 2020 and wrote from there.

they write about. The online essay, in response, becomes a form wherein the challenge of self-representation can be uniquely met; nonprofessionalized writers may publish essays alongside "professionals," as has always been true of the essay. Some examples of the feminist-identified blogs this period include *Feministing, The Hairpin,* and *The Toast,* and some of the websites include *xoJane, Jezebel,* and *Rookie.* Notable feminist essays of this period include Emily Gould's "Exposed" (2008); Eileen Myles's "Being Female" (2011); Molly Lambert's "Can't Be Tamed: A Manifesto" (2011); Roxane Gay "Bad Feminist" (2012); Daniel Mallory Ortberg's "My Female Students Don't Seem as Impressed with Me as They Used To" (2013); Leslie Jamison's *The Empathy Exams* (2014); Jenny Zhang's "They Pretend to Be Us While Pretending We Don't Exist" (2015); Carmen Maria Machado's "A Girl's Guide to Sexual Purity" (2015) and "The Trash Heap Has Spoken" (2017); Jia Tolentino's media commentary "No Offense" (2015), "The Personal-Essay Boom Is Over" (2017), and "The Rising Pressure of the #MeToo Backlash" (2018); and Andrea Long Chu's "On Liking Women" (2018). This new feminist essay tends to veer more closely to self-conscious "literariness," perhaps due in part to the professionalization and institutionalization of postgraduate academic training and creative writing programs that many North American feminists are conditioned to today.

Consciousness

In 1963, a twenty-eight-year-old journalist, Gloria Steinem (1934–), went undercover at a Playboy Club as a "bunny" and documented the experience for *Show Magazine.* In print, the editorial layout betrays the spirit of its time: two full-body portraits of Steinem appear: the first, "Gloria before," dressed in a knee-length skirt and cardigan, captioned "Who says a Smith girl . . . ";[10] and the second, "Marie after," in her bunny outfit, captioned " . . . has to be dull?,"[11] yet the content of the article is politicized and politicizing. In detailing the degraded work conditions at the Playboy Club, Steinem makes connections to broader gender struggles at work and in society at large. For example, to get the Playboy Club job, Steinem is subjected to a full physical exam, including an internal exam. She calls the Board of Health to inquire what physical exams waitresses are required to undergo in the state. "'None at all,' they said."[12] She and her colleagues bind themselves into satin corsets, pad

10 Gloria Steinem, "A Bunny's Tale," in *Show: The Magazine of the Arts* (May 1963): 90–93, 114–115, 90.
11 Steinem, "Bunny's Tale," 91.   12 Steinem, "Bunny's Tale," 93.

their busts with plastic laundry bags, and perform their jobs with professionalism; meanwhile, they are subjected by management to a demerit points system ("Messy hair, bad nails and bad makeup cost five demerits each"),[13] their meager wages are withheld, and their tips stolen ("We get tips, but the Club takes 50% of the first $30").[14] This example of undercover labor journalism hit a nerve in the culture. While Steinem has said that she did not yet understand herself as a feminist in 1963,[15] the article went a long way in describing gendered and sexualized labor exploitation in the club industry, the weak position of a female workforce that had become progressively less educated and mobile since the end of World War II,[16] and charted some of the problems of a "sexual revolution" that privileged heterosexual men's libidinal autonomy over all else. "A Bunny's Tale" also anticipates what would become *the* methodology of so-called second wave feminism: the deployment of first-person narrative to substantiate collectivist political analyses. The journalistic style here is obviously deployed under the influence of New Journalism,[17] albeit with a feminist bent. "Feminist" because in gender-marking the first-person speaker, Steinem connects her individual experience – working at a club – to a wider political strategy – documenting women workers' degraded status in society at large – which goes some way toward describing a sex class, that is, a political assemblage with defined shared interests around which mass mobilization is not only possible, but desirable.

As we will see later in this chapter, this "personal-as-political" methodology has more recently come under scrutiny for collaborating in neoliberalizing, atomizing discourses that shatter the collective identifications required in the maintenance of a political class. For now, the analysis rests at the nexus of the personal and political; Steinem documents the lived,

---

13 Steinem, "Bunny's Tale," 114.   14 Steinem, "Bunny's Tale," 114.
15 Malin Lidström Brock, *Writing Feminist Lives: The Biographical Battles over Betty Friedan, Germaine Greer, Gloria Steinem, and Simone de Beauvoir* (London: Palgrave Macmillan, 2016), 113.
16 This period was famously documented by Betty Friedan in *The Feminine Mystique*: "By the end of the nineteen-fifties, the average marriage age of women in America dropped to 20, and was still dropping, into the teens. Fourteen million girls were engaged by 17. The proportion of women attending college in comparison with men dropped from 47 per cent in 1920 to 35 per cent in 1958. . . . By the mid-fifties, 60 per cent dropped out of college to marry, or because they were afraid too much education would be a marriage bar. Colleges built dormitories for 'married students,' but the students were almost always the husbands. A new degree was instituted for the wives – 'Ph. T.' (Putting Husband Through)." Betty Friedan, *The Feminine Mystique* (New York: Dell, 1977), 12.
17 Brock, *Writing Feminist Lives*, 113.

dynamic effects of unjust power distributions. For example, when she speaks to her colleagues in the changing room, one tells her she took the job to pick up extra money, "because she wasn't trained for anything."[18] Another says: "'One time we all got together and said we'd quit if they didn't pay us more, but they said to go right ahead, they'd just hire more girls.'"[19] On a shift, Steinem counts "a few customers, a very few, either men or women (I counted ten), who looked at us not as objects but smiled and nodded calmly as if we might be human beings."[20] Together, these accounts describe a highly exploitative workplace capitalizing on a deficit of better employment options for women. In a 1995 edition of Steinem's 1983 essay collection *Outrageous Acts and Everyday Rebellions*, the author reflects on the insights she gained writing the article, among them understanding that "all women are Bunnies":

> After feminism arrived in my life, I stopped regretting that I had written this article. Thanks to the television version, I also began to take pleasure in the connections it made with women who might not have picked up a feminist book or magazine, but who responded to the rare sight of realistic working conditions and a group of women who supported each other.[21]

If for white working- and middle-class women the postwar period was one of a social regression so acute they might as well have been living in the nineteenth century, for Black, Indigenous, and non-European migrant women, the challenges of the postwar period were rather a continuation of a longer struggle for basic civic, economic, and legal entitlements the nation largely denied them. "Among the jobs open to women of all colors," writes Kay Lindsey in the 1970 anthology *The Black Woman*, "it does not take long to realize that Black women are expected to be primarily mothers, domestics and prostitutes. Teaching, social work, clerk-typing, and other office work are possibilities only if one has managed to finish high school or college."[22] Having been excluded from the advances some white women inherited from earlier feminist struggles, and having grown up in contact with civil rights movement strategies, many Black American women arrived at postwar feminism with a more theoretically nuanced appreciation of the multiply

---

18 Steinem, "Bunny's Tale," 110.   19 Steinem, "Bunny's Tale," 114.
20 Gloria Steinem, "A Bunny's Tale, Part II," *Show: The Magazine of the Arts* (May 1963): 66–69, 110–13, 67.
21 Gloria Steinem, *Outrageous Acts and Everyday Rebellions* (New York: Henry Holt, 1995), 75.
22 Kay Lindsey, "The Black Woman as a Woman," in *The Black Woman: An Anthology*, ed. Toni Cade Bambara and Eleanor W. Traylor (New York: Washington Square Press, 2005), 103–108, 107.

intersecting oppressions that naturalized exploitative power relations. Lindsey writes that the family "has been used by the white agency to perpetuate the state, and Blacks have been used as extensions of the white family, as the prisoners of war enslaved, to do the dirty work of the family, i.e. the state."[23] Black feminists, writes Valerie Smith, are "among the first theorists and activists to recognize that gender and race are mutually constitutive and interlocking modes of experience and social construction."[24] The history of liberal feminism has been widely accounted for in the literature: After all, writes Rosalyn Baxandall, "the participants were professional women who left a trail of minutes and published writings"[25] – in other words, women who were likely to wield other forms of cultural and institutional power. Black feminists of this period remain underhistoricized as the architects of contemporary feminism.

While predominantly white consciousness-raising groups began meeting in the major cities around 1967,[26] Black feminists had already been meeting in similar formations for some time. Many of these women had grown up in politicized households and were no strangers to the strategies the women's liberation movement was learning, in part, from the civil rights movement playbook. For these women, notions of gendered (and racialized) class struggles were already apparent. Some of these women were already leading lives shaped by radical forms of feminist care by being neither consigned nor economically protected by the "domestic prison" of the nuclear family. From 1960, seven years before consciousness-raising groups were becoming a mainstay of feminist praxis in the major cities, a proto-consciousness-raising group met to read, think, write, and act together in their class interests as poor Black women. This was the Mount Vernon/New Rochelle women's group, also referred to as the Pat Robinson Group or "the Damned."[27]

Their 1968 essays, "Poor Black Women's Study Papers by Poor Black Women of Mount Vernon, New York," were published in Bambara's 1970 anthology *The Black Woman*. These papers illuminate a set of strategies possible for the emergent radical feminist essay: They are collectively authored; in their direct address they give "the impression of speaking-to,

---

23 Lindsey, "Black Woman," 105.
24 Valerie Smith, "Abundant Evidence: Black Women Artists of the 1960s and 1970s," in *Entering the Picture: Judy Chicago, The Fresno Feminist Art Program, and the Collective Visions of Women Artists*, ed. Jill Fields (New York: Routledge, 2011), 119–31, 120.
25 Rosalyn Baxandall, "Re-Visioning the Women's Liberation Movement's Narrative: Early Second Wave African American Feminists," *Feminist Studies* 27, no. 1 (Spring 2001): 225.
26 Baxandall, "Re-Visioning," 229.   27 Baxandall, "Re-Visioning," 234.

communicating-with, stimulating response";[28] they employ strategies of intercollective (in this case cross-racial) identification; they collapse distinctions between abstract, dialectical thinking and embodied analysis; and the titular "study" of the study papers suggests provisionality and an openness to unknown, radically transformed futures. The first paper, "Letter to a North Vietnamese Sister from an Afro-American Woman – Sept. 1968," begins: "Dear sister. We know full well that the power structure of our country is so threatened now by you, the great vanguard of this historical period."[29] It goes on to describe a genealogy of American imperialism rooted in a racialized, gendered class hierarchy. "The poor Black woman," the authors write, "is the lowest in this capitalist social and economic hierarchy,"[30] with white women and Black men above them, and white men at the top. "Letter" uses a shifting collective pronoun as a frame of address: The "we" at times refers to the imperialist United States and at others to the oppressed position of its authors. This multivalent use of "we" in telling the story of a nation from the position of its dispossessed embodies another of the letter's key engagements, and that is with the Marxist dialectic. In "On the Position of Poor Black Women in This Country," the Group writes:

> If it is granted that it takes two to oppress, those who neurotically need to oppress and those who neurotically need to be oppressed, then what happens when the female in a capitalist society awakens to this reality? She can either identify with the male and opportunistically imitate him, appearing to share his power and giving him the surplus product of her body, the child to use and exploit. Or she can rebel and remove the children from exploitive and oppressive male authority.[31]

Like many revolutionary traditions, much feminist thought challenges the hegemony of institutionalized knowledge production; it looks to theoretical engagements with collective experience as a legitimate and legitimizing knowledge base. One theoretical observation made in these papers is that subject categories like "Black" and "woman" are not stable forms but are forms produced by material entanglements. The Group writes of a stratified Black community, wherein elite members collude in capitalist exploitation

---

28 Boetcher Joeres, "Passionate Essay," 157.
29 Pat Robinson and Group, "Poor Black Women's Study Papers by Poor Black Women of Mount Vernon, New York," in *The Black Woman: An Anthology*, ed. Toni Cade Bambara and Eleanor W. Traylor (New York: Washington Square Press, 2005), 239–50, 240.
30 Pat Robinson and Group, "Poor Black Women's Study Papers," 245.
31 Pat Robinson and Group, "Poor Black Women's Study Papers," 249.

and where poorer members are caught between fantasies of individual empowerment and realities of disenfranchisement. They write of stratifications within the gender hierarchy, whereby white women's relative power in the class society is contingent on the subjugation of poor Black women working in domestic service. "With the help of the Black woman," they write, "the white woman had free time from mother and housewife responsibilities and could escape her domestic prison overseen by the white male."[32] To bring the "Study Papers" into discourse with a literary understanding of the essay is to acknowledge the essay's use in radical and revolutionary movements, and this claim argues for the politicization of the essay. The essay has long been in conversation with social movements engaged with reorganizing power arrangements. These essays, in particular, correlate to concrete, collective political processes with material outcomes. The Pat Robinson Group ran a freedom school for Black children and supported safe and affordable birth control and reproductive justice, "despite Black movement concerns that the pill was a tool of genocide."[33] The feminist essay of this period is a literary form inextricably tied to grassroots, material activism. It is a given that different social histories produce different theoretical frameworks; according to a Marxist understanding of consciousness, it "is not the consciousness of men that determines their being, but, on the contrary, their social being that determines their consciousness."[34] This is an important insight to bear in mind as we move on to the next moment in the feminist essay, which considers the sometimes insurmountable interpersonal conflicts that emerged within US feminist politics.

Critique

The first utterances of the postwar feminist essay often involved documenting women's oppression and synthesizing radical political programs with the purpose of raising consciousness to establish a sex class. While this work contributed to what was a colossal shift in the arrangement of social and political power, it also laid the foundations for another kind of feminist essay, one that takes into account the disappointments – political *and* personal – that

---

32 Pat Robinson and Group, "Poor Black Women's Study Papers," 247.
33 M. Rivka Polatnick, "Diversity in Women's Liberation Ideology: How a Black and a White Group of the 1960s Viewed Motherhood," *Signs* 21, no. 3 (Spring 1996): 679–706, 681.
34 Karl Marx, *A Contribution to the Critique of Political Colonial Economy*, trans. Nahum Isaac Stone (Chicago: Charles H. Kerr, 2014), 12.

followed this period of intense idealism. The reality for human beings engaged in processes of radical social transformation is that "difference" is not an abstraction. Difference can betray; difference can abandon. The 1981 anthology *This Bridge Called My Back*, edited by Cherríe Moraga (1952–) and Gloria Anzaldúa (1942–2004), was a landmark volume in this new feminist utterance. The anthology collected works – importantly not differentiated by genre, but by theme, such as "Theory in the Flesh" and "Racism in the Women's Movement" – by women of color on their feminism as well as their experiences *with* feminism. Toni Cade Bambara (1939–1995) writes in the foreword to the 1983 edition:

> How I cherish this collection of cables, esoesses, conjurations and fusile missiles. Its motive force. Its gathering-us-in-ness. Its midwifery of mutually wise understandings.
> ... and letters testimonials poems interviews essays journal entries sharing."[35]

One arresting entry in the anthology is "I Don't Understand Those Who Have Turned away from Me" by the Menominee poet Chrystos (1946–). While we can read this work as a prose poem, the feminist dedifferentiation suggested by the codex invites readers to undiscipline their reading from the rigors of genre. The editors have intentionally mingled the personal with the scholarly and the poem with the polemic in a rejection of institutionalized and institutionalizing hierarchies of form. It is in this spirit of inclusion that I bring this piece of writing into discourse with the essay, and that I draw attention to it as a riveting example of feminist essaying a negative critique of the women's movement. The opening passage is both an affront and an open door:

> 5:23 am – May 1980 I am afraid of white people Never admitted that before
>   deep secret[36]

The affront is only to the white reader, who might presume ease of entry; its door is instead open to readers of color. In one line, any notion of a sex class independent of racial hegemony is unsettled. Chrystos goes on to describe the personal pains of the hypocrisies within the women's movement:

> I think about all the white women I knew in San Francisco

---

35 Toni Cade Bambara, "Foreword," in *This Bridge Called My Back: Writings by Radical Women of Color*, ed. Cherríe Moraga and Gloria Anzaldúa (Latham, NY: Kitchen Table: Women of Color Press, 1983), vi. The original used this spacing.
36 Chrystos, "I Don't Understand Those Who Have Turned Away from Me," in Moraga and Anzaldúa, *This Bridge Called My Back*, 68–70, 68. The original used this spacing.

> Women with Master's degrees from Stanford University & cars that daddy bought, [...]
> They chose to be poor   They were quite convincing in the role of oppressed victim[37]

The essay addresses worldly issues such as class difference, racial injustice, colonization, educational institutionalization, lesbianism, and women's self-hatred within patriarchy, through the lens of the individual – vulnerable, contradictory, and with a grim and necessary humor. Foucault writes that philosophical activity is "entitled to explore what might be changed, in its own thought, through the practice of knowledge that is foreign to it." There are times, he says, "in life when the question of knowing if one can think differently than one thinks, and perceive differently than one sees, is absolutely necessary if one is to go on looking and reflecting at all."[38] This description aptly describes Chrystos's method of critique here. This summons to mind the work of Sara Ahmed on the complaint, another feminist form of critique. Ahmed writes, "Although complaint can be a shattering – yes, I am picking up many sharp pieces – to make a complaint is often to fight for something. To refuse what has come to be is to fight to be."[39]

If the women's movement found life-giving energy in the personal narratives of injustice wrought on women by a dominant and dominating class (men), Chrystos shows how patterns of domination are reproduced within feminist spaces. By the late 1970s, the ideology of the world beyond has saturated feminist spaces. Chrystos states: "Certainly I won't obey that lesbian mafia nonsense that one must dress in a certain way or cut off one's hair to be real Those are all the most superficial rules silly I no longer believe that feminism is a tool which can eliminate racism – or even promote better understanding between different races & kinds of women."[40] "I Don't Understand" demonstrates how a personally framed negative critique can serve an individual expressive function ("that lesbian mafia nonsense") while also gesturing toward more radical futures; "I no longer believe" suggests new thinking beyond the limitations of the sex class established during the second wave. Chrystos's account of racism and classism within the women's movement employs the register of one aspect of feminist

---

37 Chrystos, "I Don't Understand," 68. The original used this spacing.
38 Michel Foucault, *The Uses of Pleasure: The History of Sexuality* (London: Penguin, 1985), 2:9, 8.
39 Sara Ahmed, *Complaint!* (Durham, NC: Duke University Press, 2021), 26.
40 Chrystos, "I Don't Understand," 69.

philosophy – that without constant attention, hierarchies will produce domination – and it likewise addresses the tensions between individuals vis-à-vis the theoretical positions they imaginatively inhabit. "I Don't Understand" shows us the real pain and alienation caused by attempts at coalition and political collaboration within deeply unjust social conditions: The speaker has been betrayed and abandoned by comrades who, unlike Chrystos, have built-in escape routes: parentage, race, class, and educational privileges. This essay's form incorporates a particular poetics;[41] the address is digressive, and its logic associative, perceptive, and intuitive, as per a worldliness structured by marginality. The nexus of "personal" and "political" remains unbroken. Both feminist and antifeminist, "I Don't Understand" offers a radical politics via the personal address by embracing the drama of particularity and difference while critically undermining abuses of interpersonal power in radical spaces; these methodologies are still deployed in contemporary feminist analysis and essaying today.

Fifteen years after the publication of *This Bridge Called My Back*, another feminist anthology set out "to create a record" of the early days of the contemporary US feminist movement "and speculate about that record":[42] *The Feminist Memoir Project* (1998). Among the first-person accounts of those early years is an essay in the school of negative critique by Barbara Epstein (1928–2006) titled "Ambivalence about Feminism." Prior to the emergence of the New Left of the late 1960s, Epstein was a committed communist, and "Ambivalence" documents the clash between the "Old Left" and the "politicos" and the emergence of the women's movement amid it all. Epstein describes noticing that newer feminist members of the Communist Party to which she belonged began raising the issue of women "being treated as sex objects"[43] in the party, and were not being taken seriously as comrades. "I thought," she writes, "I wish I had their problem." As a woman belonging to the "other" category of woman, as she describes it – a sexual nonbeing – Epstein *was* taken seriously as a comrade, and this, she writes, seemed "as much of a problem as being regarded as a sexual object. But it did not seem

---

41 I deploy "poetics" here to infer an ethics of worldliness as described by Lyn Hejinian: "[T]he term poetics names not just a theory of techniques but also attentiveness to the political and ethical dimensions of language[;] worldliness is essential to a poetics." Lyn Hejinian, *The Language of Inquiry* (Berkeley, CA: University of California Press, 2000), 31.
42 Rachel Blau DuPlessis and Ann Snitow, in *The Feminist Memoir Project* (New Brunswick, NJ: Rutgers University Press, 2007), 3.
43 Barbara Epstein, "Ambivalence about Feminism," in DuPlessis and Snitow, *Feminist Memoir Project*, 124.

possible to talk about this."[44] Here begins Epstein's difficulty in relating to the feminists in her political community at Berkeley. Their focus at the time seemed to be, she writes, (a) the sexual objectification of women, and (b) their subjugation within the nuclear family, which were both necessary responses to the "extreme sexism of the New Left/antiwar movement, and on a deeper level ... a response to the role of women in the middle-class nuclear family of the fifties ..." Yet Epstein writes that "neither of these assertions fitted my experience";[45] she was neither raised nor sexualized by men. She goes on: "It did not seem to me that feminism had managed to create an arena in which one could count on being able to speak honestly."[46] Furthermore, women's identification with one another, it seemed to Epstein, was grounded in a shared rejection of men – who were seen as the source of domination – which jarred with Epstein's political training in the Communist Party, where women held leadership positions and where there were formal avenues for complaints and grievances. The New Left, on the other hand, obliterated such processes in favor of "spontaneity," she writes, "which was likely to mean women being disregarded."[47] If these conflicts were felt by white, middle-class women like Epstein, they were amplified for heterosexual women of color, writes Shirley Geok-lin Lim (1944–), for whom "intimacy with the (male) other was possible," because within intimate connections with men existed "a space for relationship and struggle."[48] In short, by narrowing feminism's focus to a few experiences shared by many but by no means all women, the period of consciousness-raising was for certain already politicized women an imaginative leap too far from their extant political commitments. However, the theoretical insights developed during this period have resonances today: Epstein writes of the emergent feminist thought framework that it entailed "suspicion of abstract principles (so often used by men to legitimize their power), [and] a return to personal experience and perceptions as a legitimate basis for political analysis."[49] These bases for political analysis, the *personal* and *perceptive* styles, ground the essay as a key tool for feminist argument, recruitment, discourse, complaint, and synthesis. While the "critique of gender-as-monocause and sisterhood-as-monocure came

---

44 Epstein, "Ambivalence about Feminism," 124.
45 Epstein, "Ambivalence about Feminism," 128.
46 Epstein, "Ambivalence about Feminism," 145.
47 Epstein, "Ambivalence about Feminism," 135.
48 Shirley Geok-lin Lim, "Ain't I a Feminist? Re-Forming the Circle," in DuPlessis and Snitow, *Feminist Memoir Project*, 450–66, 453.
49 Epstein, "Ambivalence about Feminism," 144.

immediately and from many locations,"[50] feminism's methodological legacy of bringing the particular into discourse with the collective is lasting. Epstein writes that a positive influence here is that there is "now a very wide arena in which feminist rhetoric is not only accepted but expected."[51]

Like the positive influence of feminism Epstein identifies, the essay is personal and perceptive, but it is not only that. Or rather, "personal" and "perceptive" are not terms that necessarily refer only to an author's atomized being. Just as feminists read the personal, private, and experiential as inextricable from the political, social, and historical, so too does the essay mediate among individuals – author, reader, narrator, addressee – and their social context. Tension between theory and experience is at the heart of the essay's lasting powers of persuasion. Instead of reading these two texts, "I Don't Understand" and "Ambivalence," as documents of feminist failure, I argue that negative critique in the feminist essay is evidence of the feminist essay's inherent ambiguity, in that its vitality is born of its capacity to contain productive contradictions. The publication and archiving of the feminist essay in anthologies has allowed contemporary feminists to continue to build on an expansive – and historical – view of the myriad struggles as they arise in social movements.

Re-Raising Consciousness

Difference is now axiomatic to feminist discourse, and coalition and collaboration remain fundamental strategies for feminist thinkers and organizers, particularly influenced by the intersectional model of Kimberlé Williams Crenshaw (1959–), a model that dismantles the "single-axis framework . . . dominant in anti-discrimination law"[52] – and feminist theory – and "embrac[es] the complexity of compoundedness."[53] Furthermore, there remains no consensus on what constitutes a "female subject"; Judith Butler (1956–) has famously argued in their work on gender in the 1980s:

> The incorporation of the cultural world is a task performed incessantly and actively, a project enacted so easily and constantly it seems a natural fact.

---

50 DuPlessis and Snitow, *Feminist Memoir*, 8.
51 Epstein, "Ambivalence about Feminism," 147.
52 Kimberlé Crenshaw, "Demarginalizing the Intersection of Race and Sex: A Black Feminist Critique of Antidiscrimination Doctrine, Feminist Theory and Antiracist Politics," *University of Chicago Legal Forum* 1, article 8 (1989): 139–67, 139, https://chicagounbound.uchicago.edu/uclf/vol1989/iss1/8.
53 Crenshaw, "Demarginalizing the Intersection," 166.

Revealing the natural body as already clothed, and nature's surface as cultural invention, Simone de Beauvoir gives us a potential radical understanding of gender. Her vision of the body as a field of cultural possibilities makes some of the work of refashioning culture as mundane as our bodily selves.[54]

Gender's shifting relationship to power requires ongoing and active attention. Where Epstein's Berkeley feminists imagined common ground in their experiences of male oppression at home and in the student movement – experiences explicitly *not* universally female – today's feminists, armed with the lessons from the recent past, find themselves less secure in their declarative belonging to a class with members whose experiences of gender might involve other class antagonisms. And yet finding sources of commonality among women remains a popular component of feminist discourse. Here, the #MeToo movement can be read as a re-raising-consciousness project, one that draws into a common space the experiences of women and non-binary people (who might otherwise occupy antagonistic economic positions, for example) around their common vulnerability to sexual violence and humiliation. This distillation of a renewed class consciousness appears to have been somewhat successful. However, compelling as it is, today's consciousness-raising initiatives take place within a media and economic framework that is radically different from what the feminists of the 1960s were contending with. Neoliberalization has transformed those formerly politically powerful personal narratives into consumer objects ripe for fetishization and commodification. Feminists, when they choose to participate in what they might deem the essential work of communicating widespread gender-based violence, must grapple with the possibility that their words, their *essays,* can feed mass media's financially enriching fixation on women's trauma and the immiseration of historically (and often still) powerless people. This is a result of the emergent contemporary subject formation in the United States, which is that, regardless of status or positionality, contemporary subjects are in large part constituted by their neoliberalization and their relation to consumerism. A person's differentiation and particularity is surveilled and commodified online; and in this disciplinary arena, subjects reproduce their own capitalization.[55]

---

54 Judith Butler, "Sex and Gender in Simone de Beauvoir's Second Sex," *Yale French Studies*, no. 72, *Simone de Beauvoir: Witness to a Century* (1986): 35–49, 49.

55 By capitalization, I refer to the disciplinary regime required of contemporary workers as described by Maurizio Lazzarato: "personally responsible for the education and development, growth, accumulation, improvement and valorization of the 'self' in its

For contemporary feminists, these two facts – that one source of imaginative gender identification occurs at the site of male violence or humiliation; and that the contemporary subject is, above all other identities or allegiances, a consumer subject – align to create a profound discursive problem. If the feminist strategy of consciousness-raising occurs within digital spaces (the technological givens), and the neoliberal order seeks to bring "all human action into the domain of the market,"[56] is it possible for the feminist essay to meaningfully challenge the capitalization – commodification, fetishization, self-exploitation – of the already alienating effects of subjectification? This very conflict has been the object of media discourse over the past decade. In "The First-Person Industrial Complex," Laura Bennet writes:

> First-person essays have become the easiest way for editors to stake out some small corner of a news story and assert an on-the-ground primacy without paying for reporting. And first-person essays have also become the easiest way to jolt an increasingly jaded Internet to attention, as the bar for provocation has risen higher and higher. For writers looking to break in, offering up grim, personal dispatches may be the surest ways to get your pitches read.[57]

Feminism, like other liberation frameworks, must continually adapt to and resist the emergence of new regimes of oppression. The feminist essay, likewise, is adapting and attempting to resist such forms. It draws attention not only to the specific harm caused by historical male sexual violence against women but the scale of it: its vast and endless repetitions across various sites of intimacy. The feminist essay, when expressed in the spirit of collectivity and solidarity, depersonalizes the injury of sexual assault and urges us to recognize it as a political structure that informs almost every social institution in the culture – as a matter of primary urgency. As the focus on sexual abuse became central to post-2017 feminist activity, the feminist essay has taken on a vital role in demonstrating the flawed legal practices around gender-based violence. One particular contribution of the peri-#MeToo feminist essay is its repudiation of the alarmist position that

capacity as 'capital.' This is achieved by managing all its relationships, choices, behaviors according to the logic of a costs/investment ratio and in line with the law of supply and demand." Maurizio Lazzarato, "The Misfortunes of the 'Artistic Critique' and of Cultural Employment," trans. Mary O'Neill, in *Critique of Creativity: Precarity, Subjectivity and Resistance in the "Creative Industries"*, ed. Gerald Raunig, Gene Ray, and Ulf Wuggenig (London: MayFlyBooks, 2011), 41–56, 47.

56 David Harvey, *A Brief History of Neoliberalism* (Oxford: Oxford University Press, 2005), 3.
57 Laura Bennet, "The First-Person Industrial Complex," *Slate* (14 September 2015), www.slate.com/articles/life/technology/2015/09/the_first_person_industrial_complex_how_the_harrowing_personal_essay_took.html.

public descriptions of abuse are tantamount to violations of the legal principal of "assumption of innocence." As Amia Srinivasan writes, "The presumption of innocence does not tell us what to believe. It tells us how guilt is to be established by the law: that is, by a process that deliberately stacks the deck in favour of the accused."[58]

While #MeToo is largely a social media phenomenon, it is the feminist essay that acts as a key stage for expanding on the specific experiences of oppression, which are in turn made collective. In 2016, BuzzFeed published the victim impact statement of Chanel Miller (1992–) in the high-profile sexual assault trial of Brock Turner as "Here's the Powerful Letter the Stanford Victim Read to Her Attacker." In it, Miller details the profound harm caused not only by the assault itself but by the legal institution's built-in processes of retraumatizing victims and witnesses of sexually violent crimes. This letter, which I am bringing into discourse with the feminist essay, is at once intensely personal and expansive in its political strategies. Miller describes the yearlong legal proceedings for a case she had not expected to go to trial as utterly brutal for her and her family. While the accused, Brock Turner, was found guilty of three felonies, his own statement deflects responsibility for his crimes, aside from the mistake of drinking too much.[59] Turner was sentenced to three months in prison. Miller writes, "I was not only told that I was assaulted, I was told that because I couldn't remember, I technically could not prove it was unwanted. And that distorted me, damaged me, almost broke me." She writes about the greater injustices of the legal system, which privileges defendants who can afford aggressive counsel: "The fact that Brock was an athlete at a private university should not be seen as an entitlement to leniency, but as an opportunity to send a message that sexual assault is against the law regardless of social class." Crucially, Miller relinquishes the seductions of personal achievement and individual resilience in the face of harm, and instead aligns herself with those harmed by the appalling diminishment of women that occurs in sexual assault legal proceedings. Addressing Brock directly, she describes what it was like "[t]o listen to your attorney attempt to paint a picture of me, the face of girls gone wild, as if somehow that would make it so that I had this coming for me." Miller closes her address with a message to others like her: "To girls everywhere, I am with you." Just as the Pat Robinson

---

58 Amia Srinivasan, *The Right to Sex* (London: Bloomsbury, 2021), 10.
59 Emily Doe [Chanel Miller], "Here's the Powerful Letter the Stanford Victim Read to Her Attacker," Buzzfeed (3 June 2016), www.buzzfeednews.com/article/katiejmbaker/heres-the-powerful-letter-the-stanford-victim-read-to-her-ra. Later republished as the concluding chapter in Miller's National Book Critics Circle Award–winning memoir *Know My Name* under the title "Emily Doe's Victim Impact Statement" (New York: Viking, 2019).

Group's Study Papers employ depersonalization and deindividuation as political strategy, Miller deindividualizes the harm done to her by collectivizing it. "In court," reflects Miller in 2019, on the publication of the initial statement, "they'll try to make you believe you are unlike the others, you are different, an exception. You are dirtier, more stupid, more promiscuous. But it's a trick. The assault is never personal, the blaming is."[60]

As DuPlessis warns, "The essay can seem to be a genre of sensibility, expressing the fetishized individual, in various postures of apparent self-revelation"[61] – yet it also disrupts the supposedly integrated, highly individualized self and places her instead within a history of struggle. The Enlightenment "human" subject that the essay historically emerges from, becomes, in its feminist instantiation, a textual performance that tests the limits of that conceptualization of selfhood. In her daily life, Miller wanted her therapist to know of her as Chanel, who "in all [her] fumblings, [her] confusion, managing everyday life," was an incomplete and fragmented person and not her authorial pseudonym, the "defiant and courageous" Emily, "who seemed to have all the answers."[62] In other words, Miller offers the possibility of simultaneous identification and disidentification. The feminist essay is therefore a form wherein liberation ideas are developed, tested, and critiqued. It is a literary form in which the declarative "I" – or "we" – invites itself into a critical relation with its own biases and the limits of self-representation. In the three distinct moments I have identified in the postwar American feminist essay, we see a range of addresses and political claims. All describe certain political desires, which imply an unfolding futurity, whether it be in an imaginative identification with women living in other times and different places; the articulation of strategic political historical interpretations and activist platforms and projects; the desire inherent in negative critique – that is, to reach across the threshold of the other to be recognized; or the struggle against atomization and subjugation by developing bonds of collective recognition and care. As this chapter has shown, to write a genealogy of the feminist essay is to break with the dominant story of the essay. Though many feminist essays can be found among the canonized literatures of the essay, we need an expansive view of activist literatures to capture just how mobile and flexible the essay is. Just as the essay's inherent variety allows it to be constantly renewed, so too does feminism's relationship to individual women – a continuously contradictory and unfolding collective project.

60 Chanel Miller, "Chanel Miller on What Happened after Her Victim Statement Went Viral," BuzzFeed (2 October 2019), www.buzzfeednews.com/article/chanelmiller/chanel-miller-know-my-name-book-stanford-victim?bfsource=relatedmanual.
61 DuPlessis, *Blue Studios*, 40.   62 Miller, "Chanel Miller."

27

Self-Portraits in a Convex Mirror: The Essay in American Poetry

LUCY ALFORD

Writing on poetry's relationships to other genres, Jahan Ramazani asks: "What is poetry?" – a question he sees as both impossible and unavoidable:

> impossible because poetry and its readers redefine it from one time to another, one place to another, perhaps even one work to another; unavoidable because every time we draw up a syllabus, submit a work to a poetry journal or workshop, or choose a poem to read at a wedding or funeral, we act on ideas about what a poem is and isn't.[1]

Moreover, what we designate as poetry incorporates a heterogeneous and evolving array of discursive modalities, including those of nonpoetic genres; this in turn stretches and reshapes the boundaries of poetry.[2] To examine the relationship between two things (x and y, essay and poem), one must first (even loosely) define x and y. Poem and essay are porous, evolving, defined differently by readers and writers at different times. There are poems on what poetry is, essays on what essays are,[3] and, in each form, richly contested

---

[1] Jahan Ramazani, *Poetry and Its Others: News, Prayer, Song, and the Dialogue of Genres* (Chicago: University of Chicago Press, 2014), 1.
[2] On generic analogies, see David Fichelow, *Metaphors of Genre: The Role of Analogies in Genre Theory* (University Park, PA: Penn State University Press, 1993). On dialogism, see M. M. Bakhtin, *The Dialogic Imagination: Four Essays*, ed. Michael Holquist, trans. Caryl Emerson and Holquist (Austin, TX: University of Texas Press, 1981), 285, 298, 286. On dialogism in poetry, see Jahan Ramazani, "A Dialogic Poetics: Poetry and the Novel, Theory, and the Law," in *Poetry and Its Others*, 1–62; see esp. 7–8; Mara Scanlan, "Ethics and Lyric: Form, Dialogue, Answerability," *College Literature* 34, no. 1 (Winter 2007): 1–22; David Richter, "Dialogism and Poetry," *Studies in the Literary Imagination* 23, no. 1 (Spring 1990): 9–27; and Jonathan Monroe, *A Poverty of Objects: The Prose Poem and the Politics of Genre* (Ithaca, NY: Cornell University Press, 1987).
[3] On the challenge of defining the essay, see Kara Wittman and Evan Kindley, "Introduction," in *The Cambridge Companion to the Essay* (Cambridge, UK: Cambridge University Press, 2022), 1–6; and Brian Dillon, *Essayism: On Form, Feeling, and Nonfiction* (New York: New York Review Books, 2017), 11. On the impact of definitional instability

sub-genres.[4] These transhistorical genres have been in dialogue throughout their histories. If we include works of philosophy and criticism that predate the naming of the essay as a literary genre, such as Aristotle's *Poetics*, Plato's *Republic*, and Pseudo-Longinus's *On the Sublime*, this ancient (sometimes quarrelsome) conversation takes us from the origins of art, religion, and philosophy into the present day.

Over the course of the modern and contemporary periods, particularly as genre itself was deconstructed, unmade, and hybridized in the postmodern era, these two "horizons of expectation," to use Jauss's term, begin to occupy increasingly proximal and overlapping spaces.[5] This increased interest in generic boundary-crossing is attributable to a range of economic, political, and environmental changes: the Depression, two World Wars, and a subsequent state of ongoing war; political and aesthetic antipathies toward convention; technological developments; and an escalating ecological crisis. As the poem becomes a place to "essay" in contemporary politics, the essay likewise tests new modes of attending to (and addressing) history as well as the present. Over the course of the twentieth and twenty-first centuries, poems begin to *say* more, and essays to *do* more.

This chapter tracks some of the ways in which poetry and the essay approach and overlap in modern and postmodern American writing, with special attention to how their interaction manifests in poetic form. Beginning by examining the proliferation of essays *on* poetry accompanying the rise of the modern poet-critic, I then consider several examples of formal and procedural essaying *in*

    on canon inclusivity, see Jenny Spinner, "Introduction," to *Of Women and the Essay: An Anthology from 1655 to 2000*, ed. Jenny Spinner (Athens, GA: University of Georgia Press, 2018).

4 Examples of essayistic subgenres include philosophical meditation, article, treatise, sermon, satire, and lyric essay; poetic subgenres include epic, lyric, doggerel, concrete, found, slam, flarf, and transmedia poetries. Recent debates on the lyric play out in Yopie Prins, *Victorian Sappho* (Princeton, NJ: Princeton University Press, 1999); Virginia Jackson, *Dickinson's Misery: A Theory of Lyric Reading* (Princeton, NJ: Princeton University Press, 2005); Virginia Jackson, "Lyric," in *The Princeton Encyclopedia of Poetry and Poetics*, 4th ed., ed. Roland Greene, Stephen Cushman, Clare Cavanagh, Jahan Ramazani, and Paul Rouzer (Princeton, NJ: Princeton University Press, 2021), 826–34; Stephen Owen, "Poetry," in *Princeton Encyclopedia*, 1065–68; "The New Lyric Studies," special cluster, *PMLA* 123, no. 1 (January 2008): 181–234; and Jonathan Culler, "Lyric as Genre," in *Theory of the Lyric* (Cambridge, MA: Harvard University Press, 2015), 39–90, esp. 83–85. Stephanie Burt offers a concise account and insightful response to these debates in "What Is This Thing Called Lyric?" *Modern Philology* 113, no. 3 (February 2016): 422–40. Andrew Welsh traces the heterogenous roots of lyric (riddle, ideogram, charm, chant, etc.) in *Roots of Lyric: Primitive Poetry and Modern Poetics* (Princeton, NJ: Princeton University Press, 1978).

5 Hans Robert Jauss, *Toward an Aesthetics of Reception*, trans. Timothy Bahti (Minneapolis: University of Minnesota Press, 1982), 8; cf. Ramazani, *Poetry and Its Others*, 4.

postmodern and contemporary poetry: construction and deconstruction of a speaker-subject, theoretical experimentation, translation, documentary, and social critique. The poets highlighted here represent not a trajectory but illustrative exemplars within a vast, variegated landscape of poessayistic difference.

Modernism, Manifestos, and Poet-Critics

The modern period brought an emergence of new forms of poetry as well as an increase in criticism on poetry. If modernism can be broadly characterized by an increasing sense of fragmentation, dislocation, and alienation, and an increasing interest across the arts in producing forms and processes of making that reflect these conditions, it makes sense that the break from generic conventions would profoundly affect the relationship between genres as well. In modernism's experimentations in montage, fragmentation, and depersonalization, we see an increase in essays by poets, essays *on* poetry, formal and political manifestos on the politics of poetic form, and poetry behaving increasingly essayistically. In its break with inherited verse forms, modern poetry became less conventionally legible and required more explication. Manifestos called for new kinds of poems, while new kinds of poems called for new manifestos, modes of reading, and hermeneutics. Given poetry's limited readership, more poets also began to write literary essays, which were more publishable in the emergently influential little magazines.

The modern period also saw, in figures such as Matthew Arnold (1822–1888), T. S. Eliot (1888–1965), and Ezra Pound (1885–1972), the rise of the poet-critic, or poet-scholar. Major examples of the increased output of critical prose by poets in the first half of the twentieth century include Eliot's *The Sacred Wood* (1920), Pound's *ABC of Reading* (1934), and Wallace Stevens's (1879–1955) *The Necessary Angel* (1951), as well as essays by Gertrude Stein (1874–1946), Langston Hughes (1901–1967), and Marianne Moore (1887–1972). Situating the modern poet-critic in the context of a longer history of exchange between poetry and criticism, Evan Kindley points out that while "there is a long and august tradition of poets who have written critical prose on literary and cultural subjects, including Philip Sidney, John Dryden, John Milton, Samuel Johnson, Samuel Taylor Coleridge, Percy Bysshe Shelley, Ralph Waldo Emerson, and Matthew Arnold, to list only the obvious and prestigious Anglo-American names,"[6] the modern period witnessed a marked increase in writers engaged professionally in this dual occupation as "poet-critics," a term that

---

6 Evan Kindley, *Poet-Critics and the Administration of Culture* (Cambridge, MA: Harvard University Press, 2017), 3.

gains currency in the mid-twentieth century. Kindley attributes this to a dramatic shift in the institutional funding model supporting aesthetic and literary output: The 1929 market crash and resulting Depression dissolved the aristocratic patronage model that had long supported the arts, including poetry, forcing poets to turn to institutional sources for their livelihood, namely, the federal government, philanthropic institutions, and institutions of higher education. Kindley writes, "All three served a similar role of protecting modernism and modernists from an unregulated free market that was assumed to be uninterested in, if not actively hostile to, the survival of the arts, and in particular poetry – the least remunerative and, in the popular imagination anyway, least materialistic of art forms."[7]

The shift in funding structures also entailed a changing relationship between poets and national culture. In addition to the many environmental, political, industrial, and philosophical upheavals shaping and reflected in modernist art and writing, modernist poets were also responding (in prose) to new pressures to explain their work in order to gain access to institutional grants and salaried positions. The introduction of public funding for the arts meant that poets were writing on the state's dime, and academic positions meant that they were, as professors, both administering institutional curricula and boosting institutional visibility through publishing. Since positions as English professors far outnumbered opportunities to teach creative writing (particularly before the rise of creative writing departments in the second half of the twentieth century), poets with academic posts had to write *about* literature, in addition to producing the thing itself. Meanwhile, the increase in possibilities for literary distribution, as well as the circulation of writers and teachers within and among university and college settings, meant new readership, more poetry, and new schools and scenes. The proliferation of creative writing MFA and PhD programs over the course of the twentieth century and into the twenty-first has meant more poetry, more poetry criticism, more poet-critics, and more market consciousness.[8]

The rise of literary academia and the increasing embeddedness of poetic production within literature departments not only offered an institutional

---

7 Kindley, *Poet-Critics*, 5.
8 Some contemporary writers inhabiting and reinventing poet-scholarship: Stephanie Burt, Nathaniel Mackey, Fred Moten, Christopher Nealon, Juliana Spahr, Daniel Tiffany, and Edgar Garcia. On the "program era" and its impact on poetry, see Marc McGurl, *The Program Era: Postwar Fiction and the Rise of Creative Writing* (Cambridge, MA: Harvard University Press, 2011); and Kimberly Andrews, "A House Divided: On the Future of Creative Writing," in "Creative Writing in the Twenty-First Century," special topic, *College English* 71, no. 3 (January 2009): 242–55.

shelter and security to modern poets; it also encouraged poetry's participation in a more critical and theoretical conversation. As the conversation between poetry and criticism shifted from exclusive salons to the domain of the literary profession, poetry as a formal genre became both institutionally and discursively bound to explanatory and evaluative prose. Hence the apparent paradox between modernist poetry's insistence on the unexplainable, unparaphrasable nature of art (Archibald MacLeish's claim that poetry should "not mean but be," for example[9]) and the growing number of poets explaining their work in prose. As Kindley points out, "Despite modernism's theoretical commitment to authorial impersonality and formal autonomy, imagining the great works of twentieth-century literature without their authorized paratexts – manifestos, personal statements, exegeses, footnotes, and justifications – is next to impossible."[10] This trend remains strong into the present, evident in the long-standard practice of accompanying new work with explanatory forewords and "poetics statements," and in the continued proliferation of essay collections such as Nathaniel Mackey's *Discrepant Engagement* (1993), Ellen Bryant Voigt's *The Flexible Lyric* (1999), Robert Hass's *What Light Can Do* (2012), Carl Philips's *The Art of Daring* (2014), and Molly McCully Brown's *Places I've Taken My Body* (2020), to name only a few. Poets and artists are now expected not only to create but also to explicate, theorize, and/or narrate their own work as well as the work of others.

Essaying in Poetry, Poiesis in Prose

In addition to a rise in poets writing critical essays, wearing both artistic and academic hats, the course of the twentieth century also finds poetry and the essay moving closer to (or borrowing more from) one another in terms of form and affective style, so that their already loose, porous, and contested boundaries overlap more frequently – the definitional Venn diagrams of "poem" and "essay" occupying more of the same terrain.

---

9 Also, Roman Jakobson's "poetic function": "Linguistics and Poetics," in *Language in Literature*, ed. Krystyna Pomorska and Stephan Rudy (Cambridge, MA: Harvard University Press, 1987), 62–94; originally published as "Concluding Statement: Linguistics and Poetics," in *Style in Language*, ed. Thomas A. Sebeok (Cambridge, MA: MIT Press, 1960), 350–77. Along similar lines, in a 1965 conversation with Kenneth Koch, John Ashbery quipped, "It's rather hard to be a good artist and also be able to explain intelligently what your art is about. In fact, the worse your art is the easier it is to talk about it" (John Ashbery, "A Conversation with Kenneth Koch," *This Recording* [20 January 2011], http://thisrecording.com/today/2011/1/20/in-which-john-ashbery-and-kenneth-koch-start-making-sense.html).
10 Kindley, *Poet-Critics*, 2–3.

The subjective "I" can be seen as an originating impulse for both poem and essay. Both the essay and the poem – in the lyric tradition *or* read as lyric – can be said to share an originating interest in making legible (or audible) the working of the mind as it perceives, evaluates, and performs its position in relation to the world. This is particularly true in the case of the essay, since the genre has so few other defining characteristics besides the writing of the individual mind – its experiences, memories, judgment, questions, and tastes. The essay is historically tied to notions of individualism just as the lyric tradition has been associated with a singular voice. In both genres, language is a medium of sharing and transmitting experience and judgment, rendering the subjective translatable, at least in part, to a collective.

In the modern period and its various after- or through-lives, both genres can be seen to test the limits of self-disclosure. In poetry, we see this in the vein of confessionalism and hermeticism; in the essay we see this already at play in Montaigne but emphasized and exaggerated in the emergence of the personal essay and, later, the lyric essay, defined by John D'Agata and Deborah Tall in 1997 as a form that "partakes of the poem in its density and shapeliness, its distillation of ideas and musicality of language."[11] On the lyric essay's emergence, D'Agata and Tall ask:

> What has pushed the essay so close to poetry? Perhaps we're drawn to the lyric now because it seems less possible (and rewarding) to approach the world through the front door, through the myth of objectivity. The life span of a fact is shrinking; similitude often seems more revealing than verisimilitude. We turn to the artist to reconcoct meaning from the bombardments of experience, to shock, thrill, still the racket, and tether our attention.[12]

Interestingly, while the essay moves toward the lyrical (incorporating more vocative, sonic, imagistic, and figurative elements), poetry takes up argumentation, theory, documentation, and deconstructive/disruptive procedures while divesting from conventions central to lyricism: individual subjectivity, experience, and emotion. Major texts of the American modernist canon, such as T. S. Eliot's *The Waste Land*, Ezra Pound's *Cantos*, Gertrude Stein's *Tender Buttons*, and William Carlos Williams's (1912–1963) *Paterson*, readily exemplify poetry's movement toward polyvocality, fragmentation, montage, and intertextual citation.

---

11 John D'Agata and Deborah Tall, "New Terrain: The Lyric Essay," *Seneca Review* 27, no.2 (Fall 1997): 7–8, 7. See also Eula Biss, "It Is What It Is," in *Bending Genre: Essays on Creative Nonfiction*, ed. Margot Singer and Nicole Walker (London: Bloomsbury, 2013), 195–200.

12 D'Agata and Tall, "New Terrain," 8.

Taking up the "speaking subject" already problematized in modernism's first decades, a diverse assembly of midcentury poets can be seen to dilate and deconcentrate an antilyrical subject space through self-reflexivity and discursivity, drawing on the essay's spirit of process and the excursions of conversation. In different but inherently conversant ways, the works of Frank O'Hara (1926–1966) and John Ashbery (1927–2017) unmake and remake the tradition of confessional poetry by opening confessionalism's closed box through conversation's lively interruptions, intimacies, and swerves. O'Hara's often unrevised, on-the-wing "I do this, I do that" poems capture the quality of banter and conversation. Ashbery's poems, while both demanding and emerging from a more concentrated attentional labor, nonetheless evoke the dynamism, movement, and interruptions of a mind in conversation with itself, with others, and with objects in the world. Bits and pieces of memory and perception move through these poems, sometimes held in eddying attention and sometimes glinting in passing, like chips of colored glass swept along in the current of mind. The "subject," or the space of a "speaker," is not an intact "I" so much as a passage of thought through language.

We see the essayistic impulse at play in Ashbery's work beginning with his first published volume, *Some Trees,* and coursing throughout his oeuvre. Ashbery's poetry can be seen to extend, more experimentally, Wallace Stevens's mode of ongoing philosophical inquiries into the strange position of being "in" a mind "in" a world and "in" language. Both poets seem pulled between the movement of the attention into infinite reaches (like those prompted by works of art), and by the continual return of the same attention back to the "plain sense" of an utterly nontranscendent world. In Ashbery, this line of inquiry often takes ekphrastic form. We see this in early poems such as "The Skaters" (*Rivers and Mountains*, 1966); in the later book-length poem *Girls on the Run* (1999), inspired by the work of Chicago outsider artist Henry Darger; and, most famously perhaps, in "Self-Portrait in a Convex Mirror,"[13] a 502-line essay-poem on the eponymous painting by Francesco Mazzola, or Parmigianino.

In "Self Portrait," the poet's attention travels around the painted image, finding motion in static visual composition and in perspectival tricks of the eye; finding temporal puzzles of duration, presence, mortality, and the moment-to-moment experience of being, revealed by and before a work of art. The poem discovers, in conversation with the painting,

13 John Ashbery, "Self-Portrait in a Convex Mirror," in *Collected Poems 1956–1987* (New York: Library of America, 2008), 474–87; originally published in *Poetry* (August 1974).

> ... that the soul is not a soul,
> Has no secret, is small, and it fits
> Its hollow perfectly: its room, our moment of attention.

Mirroring the movement of the not-soul moving in its attentional hollow, moment to moment, the poem's line of thought unfolds in long passages, flowing from thing to thing. There is no way outside of the room in which the mind essays itself and its world:

> it is life englobed.
> One would like to stick one's hand
> Out of the globe, but its dimension,
> What carries it, will not allow it.[14]

In this poem, the thinking "I" enters late – on line 104. The "you," Francesco, is addressed, implying a speaking or essaying subject from which the poem issues. Ashbery's first-person subject places itself in the second section, turning to face the movement of attention itself, in the poem-room in which the contemplation of the painting is taking place:

> The balloon pops, the attention
> Turns dully away. Clouds
> In the puddle stir up into sawtoothed fragments.
> I think of friends
> Who came to see me, of what yesterday
> Was like.[15]

The notion that "no part / Remains that is surely you"[16] in which "you" and "I" become colloquially interchangeable as "one" reflects the dilation and porosity of the poetic speaker as it essays in attention. Thought mixes with perception; object merges with subject; memory stirs around in the present:

> desk, papers, books,
> Photographs of friends, the window and the trees
> Merging in one neutral band that surrounds
> Me on all sides, everywhere I look[17]
> ....
> [in the] concentric growing up of days
> Around a life.[18]

---

14 Ashbery, "Self-Portrait," 475. 15 Ashbery, "Self-Portrait," 475.
16 Ashbery, "Self-Portrait," 476. 17 Ashbery, "Self-Portrait," 477.
18 Ashbery, "Self-Portrait," 481.

The dissolution of the subject and the turn to surfaces and materials rather than depths and ultimate forms are by no means uniquely Ashberian signatures. Nor is the entrance of reference, argumentation, quotation, and deconstructive theory into the realm of "the poem." These essaying elements tie into broader ontological, political, and aesthetic questions being worked out, midcentury, in postmodern arts and thought. The very notion of genre begins to break down in these decades, in favor of process-oriented and generically anti-categorical *writing* aimed at deconstructing, surprising, and undoing prior categorically bounded structures of thought, language, and social systems.[19] These emerge, of course, out of earlier modernist experimentation and the movement of arts into the academy. In the Black Mountain College context of the 1950s, Charles Olson (1910–1970) put forward (in fragmentary essay form) a notion of "projective verse"[20] that is dynamic, kinetic, a projection of breath and energy into a likewise energetic field of the world. Likewise, Olson's serial masterpiece, *The Maximus Poems* (1953–1975) both builds up and breaks down the striving speaker as well as the heroic protagonist. Coming on the heels of Black Mountain and the New York School, experimental groups such as Oulipo, the Cambridge School, and, in the United States, Language Poetry, were created. Originating around the publication of the magazine *L=A=N=G=U=A=G=E* in the 1960s and '70s, this movement is associated centrally with the conceptual writings of poets such as Larry Eigner (1927–1996), Lyn Hejinian (1941–), Leslie Scalapino (1944–2010), Joan Retallack (1941–), Ron Silliman (1946–), Bob Perelman (1947–), and Charles Bernstein (1950–), among others. Gaining influence amid the 1980s and '90s, in step with the rise of deconstruction, critical theory, and continental philosophy in the American academy, Language Poetry sought to break down the notion of poetic composition as a process of "craft," using procedural constraints and play to disrupt individual authorial intent. Processes like John Cage's (1912–1992) "chance operations" aim at enabling the unexpected – what Joan Retallack describes as "swerves" in language and thinking.[21] The lasting conceptual, procedural, and disruptively playful influence of

---

19 On the mainstream/experimental and lyric/language divides, as well as alternative/circumventing approaches, see Lynn Keller, *Thinking Poetry* (Iowa City, IA: University of Iowa Press, 2010); and Linda A. Kinnahan, *Lyric Interventions: Feminism, Experimental Poetry, and Contemporary Discourse* (Iowa City, IA: University of Iowa Press, 2005).
20 Charles Olson, "Projective Verse," in *Charles Olson: Collected Prose*, ed. Donald Allen and Benjamin Friedlander (Berkeley, CA: University of California Press, 1997), 239–49.
21 Joan Retallack, *The Poethical Wager* (Berkeley, CA: University of California Press, 2003), 4.

Language poetry can be traced in the work of Myung Mi Kim (1957–), Juliana Spahr (1966–), Lisa Robertson (1961–), Harryette Mullen (1953–), and Fred Moten (1962–).

Central to the Language canon and its legacy, Lyn Hejinian's book-length prose-poetic sequence, *My Life* (1980), can be seen, like Ashbery's ekphrastic essay-poem, to essay the writing subject, dilating it to stretch and problematize the formal, conceptual, and experiential reaches of "a poem" "a subject," "a life."[22] While the "I" is central in *My Life*, and the entries do cohere around a perceiving-recalling subject, the book works on and works against self-narration, essaying the relationship between the material of language, the stuff of memory, and the one who thinks, remembers, makes.

My Life resists classification – an impulse that runs through Hejinian's work, articulated in her 1983 talk-turned-essay, "The Rejection of Closure."[23] The "I" is neither the "speaker of a poem" nor the "narrator" of an essay. Rather, the work casts the writing-subject as a space of investigation. The speaker of an essay is also neither narrator nor "speaker," since essays are tied to writing, and less to voicing or song. Yet Hejinian's language is undeniably poetic in its use of rhythm, repetition, and juxtaposition. Consider the sonic density of these snatches, which appear on a single page: "Greenery, insects – the rain as well. After C, I before, E except. Obbligato"; "The bareback rider in her boots leaping from muddy horse to buddy horse"; "A further folk among the rocks"; "For you, forsythia. The grass in my glass."[24] Hejinian turns over this relationship between voicing and writing early in the work: It is "[a]n 'oral history' on paper,"[25] but "[t]he very word 'diary' depresses me."[26]

My Life unpacks the space of a life rather than packing it into a book: "Considering the immediate, considering the same, small. All many details needed for seeing, they are like a walking stick. Spin it, then weave it, and wear it out, out. The synchronous keeps its reversible logic, and in this it resembles psychology, or the logic of a person."[27] Instead of the personal essay's "self" or the poem's speaker-singer, we find a raveling/unraveling of the interwoven acts of recalling, perceiving, and writing: "As if words could

---

22 Lyn Hejinian, *My Life and My Life in the Nineties* (Middletown, CT: Wesleyan University Press, 2013 [1980]).
23 Lyn Hejinian, "The Rejection of Closure," in *The Language of Inquiry* (Berkeley, CA: University of California Press, 2000), 40–58. See also her investigation of subjectivity in "Who Is Speaking?," in *The Language of Inquiry*, 30–39.
24 Hejinian, "Rejection of Closure," 57.   25 Hejinian, "Rejection of Closure," 4.
26 Hejinian, "Rejection of Closure," 37.   27 Hejinian, *My Life*, 35.

unite an ardent intellect with the external material world. Listen to the drips. The limits of personality ... Break them up into uncounted and voluminous digressions."[28]

Essaying Eros: The Reach of Translation

In a related but distinct mode of generic interweaving, Anne Carson's (1950–) work combines processes of interpretation, composition, and translation – poessaying in the reach across languages and millennia. In a section of *Eros the Bittersweet* (1986) entitled "Symbolon," Carson writes, "When we try to think about our own thinking, as when we try to feel our own desire, we find ourselves located at a blind point. ... We are no one in particular and we are standing at a blind point."[29] Noting Foucault's reading of the blind point as "that essential hiding place into which our gaze disappears from ourselves at the moment of actual looking," Carson suggests that "we cannot see that point, as we cannot think thought or desire desire, except by a subterfuge"[30] – a triangulation of perception. The aim of such triangulation is freeing the subject from its auto-contemplative bind, allowing it to get out of its own way by directing the gaze toward another. It requires, for Carson, a *reach*.

Carson's work enacts this triangulating reach at several levels: in the reach inherent to both reading and translation, in the reach of genres toward one another, and in the archival reach backward in time that also illuminates the present. By directing a sustained and unsentimental gaze toward fragmentary objects of the past, she allows their presence *and ours* to become visible. By *doing poetry* in essay form and *essaying* in poetic form, she shows how the two modes of writing and thinking can illuminate one another, just as the act of translation can cast both history and the present in new light.

Eros the Bittersweet poses its own genre as a formal question to think with and against. Originally published in 1986 with the subtitle "An Essay," the book proceeds as a sequence of microessays, turning over the "sweetbitter" (Sappho's *glukupikron*) of erotic love through brief, crystalline engagements with the language of a chorus of ancient others: centrally Sappho but also Aeschylus, Aristophanes, Homer, Pindar, Sophocles, Aristotle, and Plato. Yet despite their focus on the language of others and on the

---

28 Hejinian, *My Life*, 37.
29 Anne Carson, *Eros the Bittersweet* (Princeton, NJ: Princeton University Press, 1998), 71. Originally published as *Eros: The Bittersweet: An Essay* (Princeton, NJ: Princeton University Press, 1986).
30 Carson, *Eros the Bittersweet*, 72.

generative (and themselves erotic) intricacies of translation, the lyricism of Carson's own language makes each section read as a "primary text," an aesthetic object in itself (neither prose poetry nor lyric essay) enacting critical translation, philosophy, theory, and poetic making at once, in a way reminiscent of Walter Benjamin (1892–1940), Franz Kafka (1883–1924), and Jorge Luis Borges (1899–1986).

In a section entitled "The Reach," Carson reads Sappho's three-line fragment 105a, which she translates as follows:

> As a sweet apple turns red on a high branch,
> high on the highest branch and the applepickers forgot –
> well, no they didn't forget – were not able to reach[31]

"The poem is incomplete, perfectly,"[32] writes Carson: "It is a poem about desire. Both its content and its form consist in an act of reaching."[33] The three lines form part of a sentence from which both principal verb and principal subject are missing. Also missing is the *comparandum* of the simile opened by the first line ("*As* a sweet apple") but never closed. The poem may be from an epithalamium (a song or poem celebrating a marriage), in which case perhaps the bride is "the point," but we cannot know this. "If there is a bride," writes Carson,

> she stays inaccessible. It is her inaccessibility that is present. As the object of comparison suspended in line 1, it exerts a powerful attraction, both grammatical and erotic, on all that follows; but completion is not achieved – grammatical or erotic. Desiring hands close on empty air in the final infinitive, while the apple of their eye dangles perpetually inviolate two lines above.[34]

Essaying this three-line fragment further, Carson's reading reveals the way in which an essaying "reach" also plays out *within* the fragment, not only in its incompletion:

> As the poet's eye reaches up to locate the apple ("on a high branch"), that location is made more exact ("high on the highest branch") and more remote. As the poet's interpretation reaches to explain the apple ("and the applepickers forgot"), that explanation is emended in stride ("well, no they didn't forget – were unable to reach").[35]

---

31 Carson, *Eros the Bittersweet*, 26.   32 Carson, *Eros the Bittersweet*, 27.
33 Carson, *Eros the Bittersweet*, 26.   34 Carson, *Eros the Bittersweet*, 27.
35 Carson, *Eros the Bittersweet*, 27.

In this reading, "Sappho begins with a sweet apple and ends in infinite hunger." Following, "we learn several things about eros: The reach of desire is defined in action: beautiful (in its object), foiled (in its attempt), endless (in time)."[36]

Carson's work does not fit easily within a school, movement, or group, yet it is difficult to think of a single poet of the late twentieth and early twenty-first centuries in whose work the dual mobilization of poem and essay has been such a defining aspect, formally and methodologically. Additionally, while many of Carson's books employ both poetry and essay (*Eros the Bittersweet: An Essay*; *Glass, Irony and God* [1995]; *Plainwater: Essays and Poetry* [1995]; *Decreation: Poetry + Essays + Opera* [2005]), none of them fit the mold of essays-by-poets or essays-on-poetry in the poet-critic tradition, nor do they fuse or break down the binary between the genres in the way that some veins of Language Poetry and other conceptual or procedural approaches have done. Rather, poem and essay are brought proximal enough to desire but not collapse into one another. Working sweetbitterly with and against, they function for Carson as dialogic tools of translation: reaching into the past and illuminating the present at the same time.[37]

Essaying History in the Present: Documentary, Witness, Critique

Reaching into the past and illuminating the present are also central in the poetics of political protest and social critique, which have undergone a profound renewal in twenty-first-century poetry. The galvanization of poetry toward social change participates in wider public movements to address systemic racism, police brutality, gender and sexual violence, the colonization and marginalization of Indigenous groups, and environmental inequality. Introducing the anthology *American Poets in the 21st Century: Poetics of Social Engagement* (2018),[38] coedited with Claudia Rankine, Michael Dowdy writes, "When poets reinvent the roles of historians, ethnographers, and,

---

36 Carson, *Eros the Bittersweet*, 29.
37 Theodor Adorno: "The desire of the essay is not to seek and filter the eternal out of the transitory; it wants, rather, to make the transitory eternal." Theodor Adorno, "The Essay as Form," trans. Bob Hullot-Kentor and Frederic Will, *New German Critique* 32 (Spring–Summer, 1984): 151–71, 159.
38 Michael Dowdy, "Introduction," in *American Poets in the 21st Century*, vol. 4, *Poetics of Social Engagement*, ed. Claudia Rankine and Michael Dowdy (Middletown, CT: Wesleyan University Press, 2018), 1. It should be noted that the five-book series of which this volume is a part exemplifies the contemporary entwinement of poetry and essays: Each poet's section includes a sampling of poems, a "Poetics Statement" by the poet, and a scholarly essay on the work.

most broadly, activists, ... they create alternative conceptions of the processes that produce the cultures and subjectivities of the United States."[39]

Contemporary protest poetics are marked by a dynamic methodological fusion of documentary research, testimony, and critical argumentation. While these elements can be found in earlier projects, such as Muriel Rukeyser's (1913–1980) documentation of the Hawk's Nest Tunnel disaster of 1931 in *The Book of the Dead* (1938), Charles Reznikoff's (1894–1976) court poems in the *Testimony* volumes (1965, 1968, 1978–79) and *Holocaust* (1975), and Theresa Hak Kyung Cha's (1951–1982) documentary memoir *Dictee* (1982), the first two decades of this century have seen a more encompassing movement to combine sociopolitical, archival, and documentary capacities of poetry in essaying. Central poets in this movement include M. NourbeSe Philip, Layli Long Soldier, Rosa Alcalá, Daniel Borzutzky, Carmen Giménez Smith, Cathy Park Hong, Bhanu Kapil, Fred Moten, Edwin Torres, Tyehimba Jess, and Claudia Rankine. While these poets share a commitment to social critique, their works also critique the complicity of "poetry business" itself for promoting and maintaining a functionally racist, "post-identity" pseudo-neutrality – what Juliana Spahr and Stephanie Young describe as "program-era" poetry business's "mainly white room."[40] Their divergent formal, aesthetic, and procedural approaches resist categorization, demonstrating a parallel rejection of dated formal/methodological boundaries.

Claudia Rankine's (1963–) work exemplifies the integration of poetry and the essay (among other genres) into a distinctly new form of expansive, complex, and multifaceted writing. As evidenced in their subtitles alone, the volumes *Don't Let Me Be Lonely: An American Lyric* (2004), *Citizen: An American Lyric* (2014), and *Just Us: An American Conversation* (2020) demonstrate a profound essaying of the boundaries and possibilities of genres to engage collective discourse. *Citizen* documents and critiques the insidious, often invisible forms systemic racism takes in American life.[41] The book places an addressed/ indicted "you" in the position of victim and perpetrator of the manifold microaggressions through which contemporary systemic racism plays out in the grocery store, on sidewalks, on the livestreamed tennis court, and in the

---

39 Dowdy, "Introduction," 1. See also Lytle Shaw, *Fieldworks: From Place to Site in Postwar Poetics* (Tuscaloosa, AL: University of Alabama Press, 2012).
40 Juliana Spahr and Stephanie Young, "The Program Era and Mainly White Room," *Los Angeles Review of Books* (20 September 2015), https://lareviewofbooks.org/article/the-program-era-and-the-mainly-white-room/. "Program-era" here refers to McGurl, *Program Era: Postwar Fiction and the Rise of Creative Writing*, 2011 (see note 10, above).
41 Claudia Rankine, *Citizen: An American Lyric*, 3rd ed. (Minneapolis: Graywolf Press, 2014).

literary academy. Short prose accounts are placed alongside a full-length essay on Serena Williams, a collaborative script with John Lucas, and contemporary artworks by David Hammons, Michael David Murphy, Kate Clark, Hennessy Youngman, Nick Cave, Mel Chin, and many others. The book closes with two images of Joseph Mallord William Turner's *The Slave Ship* (ca. 1840): The full painting faces a detail therefrom, showing a chained leg entering or thrusting up from the waves, surrounded by thrashing fish.[42]

Because *Citizen* rejects the formal conventions of lyric poetry, one could easily read the subtitle "An American Lyric" ironically, as a straightforward rejection of the lyric tradition. Yet the book resists such a reading, as do Rankine's own remarks on the matter. Rather, Rankine undoes and transforms lyric individualism toward a collectively embodied witness encounter that is systemic, intimate, othering, and internally vexed.[43] *Citizen*'s "you" is communitized as a populational subject relation bound up, without exception, in systemic racism's countless daily double-binds. Speaking about the book in an interview with Saskia Hamilton, Rankine noted that "'You' can be singular or plural, intimate or accusative."[44] In the same conversation, she described *Citizen* as "a book about intimacy" as well as a "community document." The stories therein draw from many individuals' archives of experience: friends, colleagues, fellow artists, and public figures such as Serena Williams.

The lived experiences collected in the book played out first at the level of an individual body, and were then channeled by the poet's writing body, to be heard/felt by many individual reading bodies. The sounds given to this ache in Rankine's work are nonverbal, tied to the body and breath: "The sigh is the pathway to breath; it allows breathing. That's just self-preservation. No one fabricates that. You sit down, you sigh. You stand up, you sigh. The sighing is a worrying exhale of ache."[45] This ache, these sighs, connect to what Rankine has spoken of as the "constant state of grief"[46] in and for Black

---

42 Rankine, *Citizen*, 160–61.
43 Marjorie Perloff has defined as "post-lyric" poems that demonstrate awareness of the lyric even as they push against, explode, expand, or reinvent it. Marjorie Perloff, "Poetry on the Brink: Reinventing the Lyric," *Boston Review* (18 May 2012), https://bostonreview.net/forum/poetry-brink/. Hadara Bar-Nadav considers this term in relationship to her own work in "The Post-Lyric Impulse: Appropriation and Elegy," *Evening Will Come* 47 (November 2014), https://thevolta.org/ewc47-hbar-nadav-p1.html.
44 Claudia Rankine and Saskia Hamilton, "Claudia Rankine, Conversation, 6 May 2015," Lannan Foundation (8 May 2015), https://www.youtube.com/watch?v=ZYa25y4EGec.
45 Rankine, *Citizen*, 60.   46 Rankine and Hamilton, "Claudia Rankine, Conversation."

life. In the third revised edition, Rankine added a page containing a list of names belonging to victims of lynching and police brutality:

> In Memory of Jordan Russell Davis
> In Memory of Eric Garner
> In Memory of John Crawford . . .[47]

And these names run down the length of the page in fading ink: Michael Brown, Laquan McDonald, Akai Gurley, Tamir Rice, Walter Scott, Freddy Gray, Sharonda Coleman-Singleton, Cynthia Hurd, Susie Jackson, Ethel Lee Lance, DePayne Middleton Doctor, Clementa Pinckney, Tywanza Sanders, Daniel L. Simmons Sr., Myra Thompson, Sandra Bland, Jamar Clark, Alton Sterling, Philando Castile, Jordan Edwards. The facing page reads:

> because white men can't
> police their imagination
> black people are dying.[48]

In subsequent reprintings of *Citizen* (while keeping the 2014 copyright), Rankine has added to the growing list of names, and the list continues in fading ink down the page with spaces for future names:

In Memory of Ahmaud Arbery
In Memory of Breonna Taylor
In Memory of George Floyd
In Memory of Rayshard Brooks
In Memory
In Memory
In Memory . . .

Rankine's work shows poessaying as activist and elegiac, urgent and ongoing: opening and holding open a vital conversation and refusing the easier, everyday silence.

Making and Trying: Form and Process

That the lines between the poem and the essay begin, in the twentieth century, to blur, should not be surprising. Many boundaries are problematized or undone in this period: personal/political, high/low, fiction/nonfiction, secular/sacred. Postwar American poets have stretched generic reaches

---

[47] Rankine, *Citizen*, 134. [48] Rankine, *Citizen*, 135.

by essaying the speaker/subject, employing nonlineated prose, judgment and counter-judgment, intertextual reference, translation, documentation, and polemic.

One could say that poetry has done many of these things all along – just as prose has employed poetic modes of signification.[49] The essay can be seen as definitionally underway, as a process of "trying."[50] This underscores the changing meanings of "making" involved in *poiesis*: Is a poem the *product* or *process* of making? The poem as the *product* of making stands in formal finality like the Grecian urn, while the poem as poietical *process* is an ongoing act of essaying-in-making. It may be that poetry and the essay are bound together by more essential entwinements between making and trying, sense and sense-making, form and formation.

49 See Tzvetan Todorov, *The Poetics of Prose*, trans. Richard Howard (Ithaca, NY: Cornell University Press, 1977).
50 Adorno quoting Lukács: "The essay form has not yet, today, travelled the road to independence which its sister, poetry, covered long ago; the road of development from a primitive, undifferentiated unity with science, ethics, and art." Adorno, "Essay as Form," 151. cf. György Lukács, *Soul and Form*, trans. Anna Bostock (Cambridge, MA: MIT Press, 1974), 13. G. Douglas Atkins calls the essay a "formless form" in *Tracing the Essay: Through Experience to Truth* (Athens, GA: University of Georgia Press, 2005), 1. See also Dillon, *Essayism*, 11; and Jeff Porter, "A History and Poetics of the Essay," in *Understanding the Essay*, ed. Patricia Foster and Jeff Porter (Peterborough, Ontario: Broadview Press, 2012), excerpted online at the *Essay Review*, http://theessayreview.org/from-a-history-and-poetics-of-the-essay/.

28
The American Essay and (Social) Science

TED ANTON

This chapter chronologically follows the development of the American science essay beginning in the eighteenth century, through the foundation of government, corporate and university research institutes, and ending with contemporary critics of research practices. Throughout the history of science writing, essayists have brought knowledge of new discoveries to the general public by writing in accessible, unexpected, and lyrical prose. They fill a gap between the specialist's research and the public's hunger for science news. Beyond communicating research to a mass audience, the science essay offers a space for moral reflection and debate about the implications of scientific knowledge and technological advancements. Science essayists share the common goal of situating research within both a personal perspective and a broad worldview. The science essay acknowledges humanity's place within nature, embracing scientific insight while questioning the instrumentalism from which it springs.

The essay as a form enables the writer freedom to interpret research, Theodor Adorno argues in his article "The Essay as Form" (1991). As a "rebellion against repressive order," the essay "defies the ... absolute certainty"[1] of science and technology, Adorno observes. Science essayists write in open-ended, diverse styles rather than in the often abstract and authoritative voice of most peer-reviewed scholarly publications. In so doing, science writers make their work available to a much wider readership. To understand how these essayists achieve this goal, this chapter traces the science essay from its origins to its present diverse forms.

---

1 Theodor Adorno, "The Essay as Form," trans. Bob Hullot-Kentor and Frederic Will, *New German Critique*, no.32 (Spring–Summer 1984): 151–71, 161.

Science Writing before the Twentieth Century

In the American colonies' push for independence, science was a main driver behind the Enlightenment argument for freedom. Several shapers of the American Revolution's core documents, like Benjamin Franklin (1705–1790) and Thomas Jefferson (1743–1826), were obsessed with science, reporting on the latest developments in electricity, meteorology, zoology and geology. New social sciences, like anthropology, psychology, sociology, or political science, in turn helped other later thinkers explore a new democracy's vexing unruliness and emphasis on short-term advances, making its government understandable as a social *experiment*. The Constitution was an imperfect instrument, its critics observed. It would need constant amendment, much as science theories required continual refinement.

The nineteenth century produced a wave of nature essayists, including Henry David Thoreau (1817–1862), who practiced natural philosophy (the term *scientist* was first used in 1834). Thoreau recognized the empirical tendency of the essay and argued that observation was essential for any self-respecting essayist or scientist. His book *Walden* (1854) explored Transcendentalist themes by condensing two years of life in a cabin into a one-year diary, motivated by faith in nature's restorative quality, encouraging self-reliance and attentiveness to the world. He also spoke to a growing audience of middle-class readers. The increase in audience size paralleled a growth in colonial exploration and discovery that revolutionized scientific theories of evolution and natural selection. Thoreau's writing, in turn, inspired numerous essayists to follow his lead.

Popular magazines proved to be an effective venue for communicating new scientific ideas to the public. In fact, before the advent of the scientific journal directed toward an academic audience, the dominant mode of scientific communication was the popular essay or letter to a scientific society. The American astronomer Maria Mitchell (1818–1889), for instance, wrote a riveting account of a solar eclipse seen from Burlington, Iowa, for the October 1869 issue of *Hours at Home,* a Scribner's general-interest magazine. Other key publishers of science essays included *Scientific American*, founded in 1845; *Harper's*, founded in 1850; and the *Atlantic Monthly*, founded in 1857.

Soon, however, academic journals like the British journal *Nature*, started in 1869, and *Science*, published by the American Association for the Advancement of Science and started in 1880, offered professional forums for "real" scientists to report discoveries. This new mode of reporting, with its formalized format and sequence of title, abstract, literature review, methods, results, and conclusion, became the accepted method for communicating specialized knowledge. That shift left general-interest magazines as the venues for freer, looser, and more impassioned study of the world and human society in it.

Early Twentieth-Century Activism

The twentieth-century combination of innovation and unbridled capitalism gave rise to monopolies in industries like petroleum, meatpacking, and auto building, and the accompanying exploitation of workers. Entering the escalating protest against exploitation came the muckraking journalists and activists who applied the rigors of science-based, investigative reporting to unfair business practices and civil rights violations. Journalistic essayists such as Ida B. Wells (1862–1931), in a wide range of articles (collected in *The Light of Truth: Writings of an Anti-Lynching Crusader* [2014]), and Ida Tarbell (1857–1944) in her book on John D. Rockefeller, *The History of the Standard Oil Company* (1904), wrote social science–based long-form essays that helped to lay the groundwork for the civil rights, labor, and women's movements to come.

At the same time, popular science essayists reconceptualized the tradition of the romantic English nature walk into passionate support for conservation. The writings on California by naturalist John Muir (1838–1914) refocused the essay's aim outward, moving from interior feeling to external political action. Muir, who was born in Scotland but immigrated to the United States as a boy, was a leading advocate in journals like the *Atlantic*, the *Century Magazine*, and *Harper's* for the establishment of Sequoia and Yosemite National Parks in California. A founder of the Sierra Club and inspired by Thoreau, he collected his essays in books such as *The Mountains of California* (1894); these books reached both popular readers and policymakers, setting the tone for the environmental movement of the 1960s.

Another essayist protesting the vanishing of the American wilderness was Iowa-born Aldo Leopold (1887–1948). With an advanced degree in forestry, Leopold developed his ideas while on government postings to Arizona and New Mexico. After crafting the original federal Grand Canyon master plan, he moved to a professorship at the University of Wisconsin, where he purchased eighty acres of deforested land to test his theories of wilderness recovery. "That land is to be respected is a question of ethics,"[2] he wrote in his popular book, *A Sand County Almanac*, published by Oxford University

---

2 Aldo Leopold, *A Sand County Almanac* (Oxford: Oxford University Press, 1949), 21.

Press in 1949, shortly after his death. Leopold became an influential proponent of widening environmental protections, setting the stage for the science writer as idealist.

Mid-to-Late Twentieth-Century Idealists

As World War II produced advanced weapons, investigative journalists exposed their horrors in works like reporter John Hersey's (1914–1993) brilliant four-part *New Yorker* series, "Hiroshima" (1946). Born in China to Protestant missionary parents, Hersey coupled a spiritual awe at fate's randomness with new journalistic techniques that provided novelistic detail. In those articles, six people described, minute by minute, their separate experiences of the bomb in a rotating narrative based on the style of Thornton Wilder's novel *The Bridge of San Luis Rey* (1927). Essayist and author Richard Rhodes (1944–) used character analysis to similar advantage in his tale of the bomb's manufacturing, *The Making of the Atomic Bomb* (1961), which featured dramatic backroom scenes of feuding researchers. Despite the apparent triumph of the military-industrial complex, such writers revealed the cracks in its moral foundation.

No science idealist was more influential than Rachel Carson (1907–1964). As a witness to the beauty of tidal breakwaters in the 1950s and '60s, she did as much as any writer to spark the environmental movement. Carson grew up on her family's land north of Pittsburgh and began her career studying the wetlands of the mid-Atlantic coast. Her talented scientific explications of coastal wetlands moved from articles in the *Baltimore Sun* to lyrical essays in the *New Yorker*. As a researcher in marine biology, Carson joined the scientific staff of the US Fish and Wildlife Service where, from 1947 to 1952, she served as editor in chief of its publications. She followed this assignment with a career as an important and popular writer. It would be hard to overestimate the impact of Carson's book *Silent Spring* (1962), which described the harmful effects of the pesticide DDT on birds' eggs and the resulting near extinction of the American bald eagle. On a political level, the book led to the creation of the Environmental Protection Agency. On a social level, it helped spark the Whole Earth movement of the 1960s. On a literary level, it was appreciated as a beautiful series of laments on the damage humans inflict on nature. For all this, Carson was attacked by government officials and pesticide industry executives. In addition to *Silent Spring*, Carson also wrote eloquently on the mysteries of the deep sea. She combined personal profiles with reporting on the newest oceanographic discoveries. Her style, as demonstrated in

"The Marginal World," a chapter from *The Edge of the Sea* (1955), contrasted her knowledge of shore life with the sometimes lonely lives of the researchers who studied it.

A leading 1960s nature advocate was researcher Loren Eiseley (1907–1977), who wrote sweeping, lyrical considerations of civilization through the ages, gaining hundreds of thousands of readers. The Nebraska-raised Eiseley switched from studying English and editing the literary magazine *Prairie Schooner*, founded in 1926, to becoming a paleontologist and writer. He covered the human experience in essays collected in books like *The Immense Journey* (1957) and *The Firmament of Time* (1960). Referred to as "the modern Thoreau" in *Publishers Weekly*, Eiseley emphasized the need for spending time with nature "to observe, to speculate, and to dream."[3]

A medical-doctor-essayist of the idealist school was Lewis Thomas (1913–1993), a Yale Medical School dean and president of New York's Memorial Sloan-Kettering Institute. His collections of explanatory, interdisciplinary essays on medicine, biology, and other topics, in anthologies like *The Lives of the Cell* (1973) and *The Medusa and the Snail* (1975), channeled his knowledge of cell organelles like mitochondria toward lyrical metaphors and contrarian observations about the ways human and animal lives are intertwined. Writers like Thomas, Eiseley, and Carson helped inspire a next type of science essayist, the explainer.

The Postwar Explainers

With the 1957 launch of the Soviet satellite Sputnik, American science experienced a boom in government funding and an opening in popular culture to explain discoveries. Few researchers were more popular as explainers in the 1960s and '70s than astronomer Carl Sagan (1934–1996). Writing essays and books and appearing on Johnny Carson's talk show, Sagan was famous for his lines – his reference to "billions and billions" of Earth-like planets is his most well known[4] – or his musings on extraterrestrial life in his book and public television series *Cosmos* (1980). In one of his renowned essays, "Can We Know the Universe? Reflections on a Grain of Salt" (1979), Sagan mused on the way two toxic elements, sodium and chloride, combine to produce table salt, but also how scientific "understanding is a kind of

---

3 Loren Eiseley, quoted in Howard Blum, "Loren Eiseley, Anthropologist, 69, Writer on Man and Nature," *New York Times* (11 July 1977): 22.
4 Carl Sagan, *Billions and Billions: Thoughts on Life and Death at the Brink of the Millennium* (New York: Ballantine Books, 1998).

ecstasy."[5] Sagan detailed the benefits of marijuana in a pseudonymous extended passage (he called himself "Mr. X") in a 1971 volume edited by Lester Grinspoon, *Marihuana Reconsidered*. Smoking marijuana improved his appreciation for music, Sagan noted, enabling him to "hear the separate parts of three-part harmony and the richness of counterpoint."[6]

Sagan wasn't the only scientist turned writer in the postwar period. Among them was Harvard's Edward O. Wilson (1929–), a winner of two Pulitzer Prizes who united close observation and a sometimes problematic interdisciplinary vision. His early books, such as *The Insect Society* (1971), focused on somewhat narrow, technical topics, while his later ones, including *On Human Nature* (1978) and *Genes, Mind, and Culture* (1981) explored broader subjects. He was most known for the controversial concept of sociobiology, the idea that many social customs are determined by biology. The controversy stemmed from his argument that nature shapes human behavior in a kind of determinism that today's reader could still find problematic. Wilson considered himself a humanist crusader and wrote pieces such as the *New York Times Magazine* trend essay, "Is Humanity Suicidal?" (1993), which warned that the human impact on Earth was threatening the planet's survival.

Writing in a similar lyrical explanatory vein, but concentrating on paleontology and evolutionary biology, was Harvard professor Stephen Jay Gould (1941–2002). In *Scientific American* magazine columns collected in books like *Bully for Brontosaurus: Reflections on Natural History* (1991), Gould eloquently explained the workings of natural selection and his theory of "punctuated equilibrium," in which epochs of stasis are interrupted by brief, rapid, convulsive periods of change and adaptation, often caused by a climate or geologic cataclysm. Gould was also one of the most visible researchers to protest the Vietnam War and to address science's schism with religion. He maintained in his writings on the schism, one unfinished at the time of his death, that religion and science are two separate but "nonoverlapping magisteria,"[7] or domains of pedagogical authority. They are fully imagined but separate thought systems explaining the world, Gould suggested, one based on faith, the other on doubt.

---

5 Carl Sagan, "Can We Know the Universe? Reflections on a Grain of Salt," in *Broca's Brain: Reflections on the Romance of Science* (New York: Random House, 1979), 15–21, 17.
6 Mr. X [Carl Sagan], "Acute Intoxication. Literally Reports: Mr. X," in *Marihuana Reconsidered*, ed. Lester Grinspoon (New York: Counterpoint, 1991), 112.
7 Stephen Jay Gould, *Rocks of Ages: Science and Religion in the Fullness of Life* (New York: Ballantine Books, 2002), 7.

A final essayist of the explainer school was microbiologist Lynn Margulis (1938–2011), a University of Massachusetts microbiologist and ex-wife of Carl Sagan, who explored the fundamental power of symbiosis, or mutualistic biological relationships, to drive evolution in ways unimagined by Darwin. Often writing with her son Dorion Sagan (1959–), Margulis espoused the idea that human identity was not a fixed entity but a process shaped in part by neurochemical changes caused by our gut microbes. Her book *Microcosmos: Four Billion Years of Evolution from Our Microbial Ancestors* (1997) played on the title of the TV series hosted by her ex-husband. Cowritten with Dorion and featuring an introduction by Lewis Thomas, it argued that we are microcosms of trillions of bacteria that shaped our planet and the life on it. Margulis coined the term "microbiome," years before it became a popular concept, to describe the critical role one-celled organisms play in the health of the Earth and ourselves.

The New Science Journalists

The next innovation of the American science essay was a stylistic one, as some science writers began to engage in forms of New Journalism, a term coined by Tom Wolfe in his 1973 anthology *The New Journalism*. In the 1980s and '90s, writers like Dennis Overbye (1944–), a trained astrophysicist turned *New York Times* reporter, applied the literary and investigative innovations of creative nonfiction to science topics such as cosmology. In books like *Lonely Hearts of the Cosmos* (1991), vivid settings, poetic style, scenes, dialogue, and character development were combined to engage an audience hungry for narrative immersion in research. Some followers of this approach displayed an attitude of childlike wonder in exploring the complexities of our universe. A list of such writers might include Dava Sobel (1947–), also a *New York Times* science essayist, who reached a wide audience with her lyrical historical books *Longitude* (1995) and *Galileo's Daughter* (1999). Another quality of the new science journalism was relentless investigation to expose the inside stories of research, both positive and negative, as in the work of Pulitzer Prize–winner Deborah Blum (1954–), who wrote about topics like primate research and food adulteration in books such as *The Monkey Wars* (1995) and *The Poisoner's Handbook* (2010) and in essays for the *Sacramento Bee*, the *Los Angeles Times*, and the online journal *Undark*.

These essayists made complex topics accessible, entertaining, and sometimes personal. One classic example of the personal style was Annie Dillard's cabin idyll, the Pulitzer Prize–winning *Pilgrim at Tinker Creek* (1974), which echoed Thoreau's *Walden* and was inspired by spiritual autobiographies such as St. Augustine's *Confessions*. Dillard's widely anthologized *Harper's* essay "Total Eclipse" recounted the solar eclipse of 1979 in imagistic writing that began with a description of a clown portrait in her cheap motel room. Dillard is a master of metaphor, likening the giant Crab Nebula to a smoke ring and the eclipse experience to prehistoric anguish. Her work employed rich symbolism and a literary style, yet many of her essays appeared in conventional mass market magazines ranging from *Sports Illustrated* to *Cosmopolitan*. She was highly influential on a new generation of creative science essayists, many of them women.

In the 1990s, *New York Times* science writer Natalie Angier (1958–) forged a similarly lyrical and personal voice, starting with her book-length, true-life account of a cancer team, *Natural Obsessions: Striving to Unlock the Deepest Secrets of the Cancer Cell* (1988), and following with a series of award-winning humorous and well-researched essays in the Tuesday Science Times section of the *New York Times*. That weekly section remains a showcase of the best in journalistic science writing to this day. Angier relished the inherent beauty in nature, reflected in the alliterative title of her third book, *The Beauty of the Beastly* (1995), and in her articles exploring topics like the life of a dung beetle or the prevalence of laziness in the animal kingdom in "Busy as a Bee? Then Who's Doing the Work?" (1991). A former French literature graduate student, Angier wrote in an ironic and alliterative style, often on topics about women, as in her book *Woman: An Intimate Geography* (1999).

Two other essayists outpaced the others in popularity and their ability to make complex topics seem easy to grasp. Michael Lewis (1960–) achieved a rare simplicity in his coverage of global economics and sports sciences (*The Big Short* [1999] and *Moneyball* [2003]), as Malcolm Gladwell (1963–) did with explanations of conceptual breakthroughs in psychology (*The Tipping Point* [2000] and *Blink* [2005]). These writers adapted the magazine feature's form – narrative opening, concept statement, background, and alternation of scenes and summary – and slowed it into an expansive discourse with humorous metaphors, catchy concepts, and self-deprecating asides and acronyms.

During roughly the same years, a group of science essayists used the new hybrid essay form, approaching a single topic from multiple angles, to address looming crises in the world and in ourselves.

The Hybrid Science Essay

Two of the most highly regarded science journalists tackling the climate and extinction crises are Bill McKibben (1960–) and Elizabeth Kolbert (1961–). McKibben's international best-selling book *The End of Nature* (1989) was the first work to sound the alarm on rising global temperatures. A Middlebury College Schumann Distinguished Scholar in Environmental Studies, McKibben has authored some twenty titles on subjects ranging from climate change to social inequality. In contrast, Elizabeth Kolbert, reporting from around the world for the *New Yorker*, has written articles on coral reefs and habitat and species extinction, often fashioned as profiles of researchers, coupled with her personal misadventures in her journeys to interview them. These articles have been transformed into books, one of which – *The Sixth Extinction: An Unnatural History* (2014) – won a Pulitzer Prize for popularizing the concept that we are living in an extinction crisis caused by humans. Both McKibben and Kolbert mix data analysis, narrative storytelling, and dire predictions to tell vivid and damning stories of Earth's present and future.

Another brilliant artist of the hybrid essay was neurologist Oliver Sacks (1933–2015), who wrote influential psychological and medical mysteries with a self-critical eye trained on the science profession. Sacks was best known for his fascinating case histories presented in his *New Yorker* essays and in books such as *The Man Who Mistook His Wife for a Hat* (1985), which tells the stories of patients struggling with neurological disorders. The theme of Sacks's writing, seen in his poetic style, was that the human brain was wondrous even in its deepest dysfunction.

As challenges to the social structures of science concerning gender and race began to surface, the stage was set for even more creative, daring, and introspective science essays in the late 1990s and early 2000s. New science essayists applied the innovations of the contemporary memoir, using techniques such as stream of consciousness, collage, jump cuts, and lyrical line breaks to explore the subjectivity of human experience. This nonlinear style came to the forefront of science writing in a *New Yorker* article by JoAnn Beard (1955–). Her memoir of a campus shooting at the University of Iowa astronomy building, "The Fourth State of Matter" (1996), expanded the range of the American science essay. The work coupled personal experiences – Beard's divorce, her care for a dying pet dog – with the shocking campus shooting of two particle physicists and two staff members and the suicide of the shooter, a disgruntled graduate student from China. One of the particle physicists was Beard's close friend and employer. The title referred to her murdered friend's research into the "plasmasphere" located outside Pluto's orbit.

In her ambitious essay "The Pain Scale," published in the *Seneca Review* and later republished in a shortened version in *Harper's* (2005), Eula Biss (1977–) wove personal pain into deep musings on the inadequacies of measurement. The essay chronicled Biss's chronic pain following the format of pain-scale questionnaires that patients complete when they enter a doctor's office. Divided into ten numbered sections, the essay became a philosophical exploration of the limits of knowledge. It opened with the concept of zero; referred often to Christ, mathematics, and Biss's doctor father; and used various scales such as Fahrenheit and Celsius for temperature and Beaufort for wind to measure how little we understand about human emotions. Biss wrote, "Assigning a value to my own pain has never ceased to feel like a political act."[8] Drawing on literature, mathematics, and art, Biss's essay launched her into a career that has included a widely respected volume on antivaccine parents, *On Immunity: An Inoculation* (2015), and pieces in the *Believer*, *Gulf Coast*, *Denver Quarterly*, and *Third Coast*. Writing in a similar collage-like style, another major writer of the braided personal science essay is Leslie Jamison (1983–). In the title essay of her 2014 collection, *The Empathy Exams*, she explored her heart surgery, abortion, aborted love affair, and her job as an actor grading medical students for their demonstrated responses of empathy, and offered a meditation on the impossibility of telling a story objectively. In the essay, Jamison quoted from her medical records, recalled personal conversations, and inserted scripts used in her job as a medical school actor, all in a quest to discover whether human beings can ever share others' pain. The stylistic touchstones of these essays included self-deprecating humor, random lists, ironic use of subheads, and argument by juxtaposition. Their antisystemic impulses challenged the expertise of the professional researcher or medical doctor. Leslie Jamison even incorporated line cross-outs to question her conflicting emotions as she overheard her doctor speaking into a tape recorder her notes on Jamison's case.

Many of the aforementioned essays were collected in the annual anthologies, *The Best American Science Writing*, appearing the years in 2000–2012, and *Best American Science and Nature Writing* (2002–). The collections highlight essays judged the most important of the year, as well as notable essays listed in the back pages that bring innovations to the science essay form and in turn

---

8 Eula Biss, "The Pain Scale," *Seneca Review* 35, no. 1 (Spring 2005): 5–24, 12.

inspire new essayists to experiment in writing for publication. The anthologies are frequently assigned in new graduate programs in science and medical writing at institutions like MIT, the University of California Santa Cruz, and Columbia University, where many of the next generation of science essayists are learning their craft.

The Investigators

The freer and longer formats offered by online publications and digital versions of magazines have provided outlets for important writers like Brooke Borel and Jacqueline Detwiler-George to expand on vital subjects. Borel investigated a global onslaught of bedbug infestations with in-depth reporting and creative writing in her book *Infested: How the Bed Bug Infiltrated Our Bedrooms and Took Over the World* (2018). In the mainstream publication *Popular Mechanics*, editor Jacqueline Detwiler-George wrote an extended lyrical essay titled "It'll Take an Army to Kill the Emperor" (2017), which explores the cancer research complex through interviews with doctors, patients, drivers, food vendors, homeless people, and even airport rental car agency employees, who interact with those battling the disease.

One of the most important contemporary science essayists is Pulitzer-winner Ed Yong (1970–), who got his start writing in the *Atlantic* and expanded into books and the print media. Yong won a Pulitzer for his coverage of the Covid pandemic, and his writing on the microbiome in *I Contain Multitudes: The Microbes within Us* (2016) and *A Grander View of Life* (2020) is a lively mixture of science explanation, personal opinion, literary references, and eloquent observations of the difficulties of lives spent in research.

The consolidation of print outlets in the 2010s and 2020s unleashed a wave of new, inexpensive, and more democratic electronic venues for the science essay. Science essays could be accessed in publications suitable to internet media like podcasts, YouTube videos, and documentaries for Netflix and Apple. The documentaries and podcasts are reaching more younger people than the traditional magazine essay, inspiring them with creative insider stories of science. Some of the notable science podcasts include *This Podcast Will Kill You, Hidden Brain, Weird Things I Learned This Week, The Sway, Kurzgesagt, StarTalk Radio,* and *Ologies,* among others. Netflix documentaries like *Unnatural Selection* (2019) confronted pressing ethical issues in science such as inequitable vaccine distribution and embryonic human gene editing.

The New Nature Essay

By the 2020s, as species were vanishing and global development was making unspoiled nature harder to find, the walk-on-a-wilderness-trail essay was somewhat out of step with contemporary science writing. Some aspiring science writers, lacking the means to access remote wilderness sites, began writing about nearby rural and urban lots or industrial wastelands. Science's social and class barriers were exposed by LGBTQ, female, white lower-class, Latinx, and Black essayists. Organizations such as Society for Access for Colored and Native American Scientists (SACNAS) sought to bring research opportunities to new communities. Writers like Seattle poet Jourdan Imani Keith explored the dangers of camping alone for a Black woman, as well as a lack of access to nature for city children in essays like "Desegregating Wilderness" and "At Risk" (*Orion* [2014]). Others wrote about overgrown community gardens or rural junkyards in an effort to achieve deeper understandings of neglected regions. In her book of essays *World of Wonders: In Praise of Fireflies, Whale Sharks, and Other Astonishments* (2020), Aimee Nezhukumatathil imbued her nature topics with mythological powers, such as a catalpa tree that could hide the author's shy identity.

Other new voices include Kimberly Garza, novelist and assistant professor of English at University of Texas San Antonio, interested in the power of climate change and regional landscape in shaping lives. Garza published, for example, "The Seedy Corner" (2019), an essay in the journal *Diagram*, about her family in multiethnic, working-class Galveston Island. Another Texas writer, Clinton Crockett Peters, author of *Pandora's Garden* (2017), discussed snake farms and some of the ignored territories of rural Texas and Oklahoma, with an eye for grotesque beauty. Such voices reignited science essay forms by reminding readers that issues of class and race permeate the perception of the world around us, and even of some scientists. They send the message that overlooked places and points of view are relevant, important, and beautiful.

Today, the American science essayist struggles to keep up with the challenges of pandemics, climate change, crises in waste recycling and clean energy, and a growing number of voices calling for economic justice in distributing the benefits of discoveries. The new science essayists evoke some of the best traditions of older forms while adapting them to more complex material and to a bigger, smarter audience than ever before. The multiple mistakes and triumphs of the Covid vaccine effort alone have produced a treasure trove of essays and lyrical memoirs.

The American Essay and (Social) Science

From its dawn in the early days of the American republic, through its development alongside rapid technological change in the nineteenth, twentieth, and twenty-first centuries, to its current fluidity in blog, podcast, documentary, and print forms, the American science essay offers a collection of rich and flexible approaches to the world. Gifted new writers of different economic classes, genders, and races are turning their talents to writing about research. Contemporary essayists enrich science by sharing its strengths and exposing its flaws. Eloquent and inventive, investigative and personal, these science essayists draw on a rich tradition to help readers see the world anew.

29

Philosophy as a Kind of Writing

PAUL JENNER

In some intricate remarks about the French Renaissance philosopher and essayist Michel de Montaigne, the American philosopher Stanley Cavell set out a distinctive take on the genesis and nature of the essay form within philosophical writing. In "inventing the essay," Cavell contends, Montaigne thereby invented

> an intimate discourse for addressing strangers. He calls those whom he addresses his "relatives and friends," and so they are, after his discourse has made them so (which it does in part by showing its strangeness to them, hence their strangeness to him, so that they may understand that there is something yet for them to become familiar with).[1]

Cavell's purposive sketch here brings together questions of philosophical format and questions of audience. It might also elicit a raised eyebrow. If the essay form established by Montaigne in the sixteenth century is to be understood as, in Cavell's words, "an intimate discourse for addressing strangers," readers might determine this characterization to be fundamentally retrospective in nature. They might struggle, in other words, to recognize this hospitable discourse in the kinds of writing produced within the increasingly professionalized form of life of academic philosophy as it came to be practiced in the United States in the twentieth century. The kind of philosophical writing dominant by the end of the twentieth century might well appear not as an "intimate discourse" but as decidedly impersonal (and not accidentally impersonal, but *methodologically* so): closer in spirit to the scientific article than to the essayistic. As a highly specialized kind of writing, moreover, this dominant discourse might be understood as being addressed

---

[1] Stanley Cavell, "A Cover Letter to Molière's *Misanthrope*," in *Themes Out of School: Effects and Causes* (San Francisco: North Point Press, 1984), 97–105, 104.

not to strangers but, closer to home, exclusively to fellow academic philosophers, or at least to those working within the relevant professionalized specialisms and subspecialisms.

Focusing on the work of Cavell, Richard Rorty, and Cora Diamond, this chapter will recount how twentieth-century academic philosophy in the United States can be characterized in part by an ongoing interest in and by explorations of the possibilities of the essay as a philosophical form. In a pluralist spirit, these explorations approach the essay form as a place to rethink and to remodel what philosophical argumentation might look like. Related to this work of reimagining, such writing addresses the proximity of philosophy to literature in two senses. First, it is open about and attentive to the potentially literary, written character of philosophy. Second, such writing tends to be characterized by an interest in taking up works of literature philosophically, as a continuation of philosophical analysis and as a means of immanent criticism precipitating questions about philosophical analysis itself.

Stanley Cavell: Philosophical Writing and the Human Voice

The subtitle of Stanley Cavell's (1926–2018) first book, *Must We Mean What We Say?* (1969), identifies the collection quite precisely as "A Book of Essays." This categorization is deliberate and can be connected to the intense methodological questioning as to the nature of philosophical writing underway throughout the collection. The foreword notes that "the isolated analytical article is the common form of philosophical expression now, in the English speaking world of philosophy; something reflected in the fact that the common, and best, form of philosophy textbook is the assemblage of articles around individual topics."[2] Cavell's drift here is not to critique the isolated analytical article (although styling it as a form of philosophical "expression" suggests his own hopes for philosophical writing). Nevertheless, the essays collected in *Must We Mean What We Say?* conform to this form only partially and restively. This restlessness is more than a temperamental characteristic of Cavell's writing. His essays make the *philosophical* case for keeping questions of philosophical format and "expression" productively open rather than seeing these parameters as needing to be delimited before philosophy can take place or make progress.

---

2 Stanley Cavell, *Must We Mean What We Say?* (Cambridge, UK: Cambridge University Press, 1976), xxxiv.

The acknowledgment of the written character of philosophy that emerges and endures in Cavell's work certainly reflects his considerable personal investment and delight in writing. The foreword to his first collection ends with the reflection that "[t]here is the audience of philosophy; but there also, while it lasts, is the performance."[3] The performance of philosophy for Cavell can be understood in terms of the performance or act of writing. This acknowledgment and its attendant performance are unique but not wholly idiosyncratic, arising out of and responding to a broader disciplinary moment of self-awareness and immanent critique. As Cavell puts this in one of the essays, "What I have written, and I suppose the way I have written, grows from a sense that philosophy is in one of its periodic crises of method."[4] Within this crisis, Cavell undertook to defend and articulate what was then the new philosophical method of ordinary language philosophy, a method that he portrays as at once radically new and as recognizably, even "traditionally," philosophical when seen in its broader contours. If methodological crisis provides a disciplinary context for understanding the "way" Cavell writes, a further, still broader "explanation of the way I have written, or the way I would wish to write" involves his perception and contention that philosophy can be understood and pursued as existing in a condition of modernism.[5]

Cavell's account of modernism is influenced by Clement Greenberg's art criticism in essays such as "Modernist Painting" (1960) and by Greenberg's emphasis on difficulty and autonomy. His understanding of philosophy's modernist condition involves, first of all, a sense of difficulty, whereby the modernist philosopher is not giddily liberated from philosophical tradition but is rather somewhat loyal to it, driven to find new ways to satisfy what are understood to be or presented as traditional ambitions. This sense of trying to express newly something antecedent and given articulates a premise of disciplinary autonomy in Cavell's work. His philosopher resembles Greenberg's modernist painter, a figure concerned with identifying what is *unique* to their practice (in the case of the painter, the flatness of the canvas). Such disciplinary autonomy provides an anchor in Cavell's work, whereby a newness of writerly experimentation understands itself not as postdisciplinary but as responsive to traditional disciplinary aspirations. Absolutely fundamental to this posit and premise of philosophical autonomy, of course, is Cavell's care to remember the disciplinary autonomy of philosophy from science, such that the teaching,

---

3 Cavell, *Must We Mean*, xlii.   4 Cavell, *Must We Mean*, 74.
5 Cavell, *Must We Mean*, xxxiii.

history, and writing of philosophy need not be deemed unscientific or unprofessional for not conforming to scientific templates.

Cavell's understanding of what the differences between science and philosophy might involve, along with his attendant resistance of scientism within philosophy, are informed by Thomas Kuhn's *The Structure of Scientific Revolutions* (1962) – a work itself much influenced by Kuhn's intellectual companionship with Cavell. The very idea of philosophy as undergoing periodic crises of method, for instance, nods to Kuhn's notion of paradigm-led normal science as marked by methodological consensus over fundamentals. The comparative absence of consensus in philosophy, which might be taken negatively as a lack of disciplinary progress and maturity, comes to be stylized by Cavell as a characteristic rather than as a shortcoming. Such absence is understood to be reflective of the lived uncertainties and unsettledness that Cavell would have philosophy incorporate. Philosophy for Cavell, after all, is a "major form of expression," and Cavell understands ordinary language philosophy as "an attempt to return the human being to the language of philosophy."[6]

Another consequence of Cavell's account in *Must We Mean What We Say?* of philosophy as encountering modernist predicaments is that, raising the stakes, it creates something of a drama of the present moment. The drama relates to the question of whether philosophy will continue to be something live, or, by contrast, something repetitiously curated and no longer "expressive" of voice. This returns us to Cavell's remarks about the performance of philosophy being there, "while it lasts," which is to say while the performance lasts but also while philosophy itself survives. This drama and performance are inseparable in Cavell's work from the thematization of writing. (In fact, the thematization of writing in his work becomes so intense that properties he ascribes to philosophical writing end up characterizing for him writing as such, or "serious" writing at least.) Cavell's first essay on Ludwig Wittgenstein (1889–1951) pays careful attention to the *written* character of Wittgenstein's *Philosophical Investigations*:

> Why does he write that way? Why doesn't he just say what he means, and draw instead of insinuate conclusions? ... The first thing to be said in accounting for his style is that he *writes*: he does not report, he does not write up results. Nobody would forge a style so personal who had not wanted and needed to find the right expression for his thought. The

6 Cavell, *Must We Mean*, xxxiv; Stanley Cavell, "An Emerson Mood," in *Emerson's Transcendental Etudes* (Stanford, CA: Stanford University Press, 2003), 20–32, 23.

German dissertation and the British essay – our most common modern options for writing philosophy – would not work; his is not a system and he is not a spectator.[7]

A privileged term, *writing* here is methodologically fundamental, but invested and personal rather than detached and totalizing. Cavell takes Wittgenstein's writing to be shaped by his "method of self-knowledge."[8] If "there is virtually nothing in the *Investigations* which we should ordinarily call reasoning," this is because Wittgenstein exhorts his readers instead to "self-scrutiny." What readers will find in Wittgenstein's text are not arguments in support of settled beliefs but "questions, jokes, parables, and propositions so striking (the way lines are in poetry) that they stun mere belief."[9]

The elaborations and explanations of ways of writing underway in *Must We Mean What We Say?* are further developed and deepened in Cavell's subsequent turn to American Transcendentalism, first to Henry David Thoreau's (1817–1862) *Walden* in *The Senses of Walden* (1972) and then, from the late 1970s onward, to a selection of essays by Ralph Waldo Emerson (1803–1882), including "Self-Reliance," "Fate," "The American Scholar," and "Experience." This turn to Transcendentalism continues Cavell's methodological defense and broad thematization of ordinary language philosophy, proposing deep affinities between Thoreau's and Emerson's meditations on the ordinary and the alienated intimacies between words and world disclosed in ordinary language philosophy. Transcendentalists and ordinary language philosophers both perceive our words (and therefore, as Cavell sees it, our lives) as somehow away. Close readings of Thoreau and Emerson help Cavell to articulate the sense in which his mode of ordinary language philosophy engages with philosophical skepticism. In the distinctive reading of Wittgenstein developed in his doctoral dissertation and eventually published in *The Claim of Reason* (1979), Cavell argues that, rather than setting out either to refute or to promulgate skepticism, Wittgenstein would have us appreciate the truth of skepticism: that our relationship to the world and to others is not best understood as one of belief or of certainty. In Cavell's hands, skepticism emerges as something other than a static philosophical problem permitting of a stable solution. Rather, skepticism is stylized as a permanent threat and ineliminable fact of human life in language, to be met by ceaseless, detailed returns to the ordinary, returns that avoid disfiguring the ordinary as foundational or given precisely by preserving its vulnerability to skeptical

7 Cavell, *Must We Mean*, 70.   8 Cavell, *Must We Mean*, 70.   9 Cavell, *Must We Mean*, 71.

suspension and disappointment. The philosophical response to skepticism is therefore an ongoing, lived dynamic, and Cavell stages this dynamic in processes of writing, such that Thoreau's, Emerson's, and Wittgenstein's writings model ongoing recoveries from skepticism.

An obvious objection to Cavell's suggestion that contemporary philosophers take Thoreau and Emerson seriously is that Emerson's essays, for example, depart from perhaps the central disciplinary norm of professional philosophy in their apparent lack of argumentation. His response is pluralist, contending that other forms of philosophical rigor are also conceivable: "[S]uppose that what is meant by argumentation in philosophy is one way of accepting full responsibility for one's own discourse. Then the hearing I require depends upon the thought that there is another way, another philosophical way (for poetry will have its way, and therapy will have its way) of accepting that responsibility."[10] In addition to refining his signature thematic of skepticism, then, Cavell's interest in Thoreau's and Emerson's writing intensifies the questions about philosophical authority and expression posed in *Must We Mean What We Say?* Such questions are of course precipitated and provoked by the very idea that Thoreau's *Walden* or Emerson's essays might have something to contribute to the conversation of professionalized, academic philosophy. Cavell's meticulous readings of Emerson and Thoreau further develop his own philosophical method, whereby questions of philosophical authority are a burden taken on by the writing itself, as opposed to such questions being settled at an institutional level, conferred through the adoption of disciplinary conventions. The contrast here, again, is with science, and by extension a scientific model of philosophy, within which the "standards of performance are institutionalized" and thereby less unsettled.[11] Thoreau and Emerson become increasingly important to Cavell as exemplars of what a differently inspired type of philosophical writing might look like, writing in which "philosophical authority is non-transferable, [such] that each claim to speak for philosophy has to earn the authority for itself, say account for it."[12] It is hard for Cavell's readers to miss how his characterizations of Transcendentalist writing tend to describe his own work and aspirations for philosophy rather exactly. This reflects a favored methodological premise of his, whereby an object of interpretation (such as an Emersonian essay) is at the same time a means of interpretation – something not just to think about but to think with.

---

10 Stanley Cavell, "The Philosopher in American Life (toward Thoreau and Emerson)," in *Emerson's Transcendental Etudes*, 33–58, 45.
11 Cavell, *Must We Mean*, xli.   12 Cavell, "Philosopher," 51.

A further dimension of Cavell's turn to Thoreau and Emerson is the occasion their work provides for reflecting upon the United States as a context for philosophy. Amid his early reflections on philosophical writing as encountering modernist difficulties, Cavell considered the pertinence of national identity to these perplexities: "Am I talking only about a condition in America? If so, it is said in the spirit in which a certain kind of American has usually spoken of his country's release from the past: out of a sense of disappointment in struggle with vistas of peculiar promise."[13] Although such considerations of national identity are extracurricular to academic philosophy (officially, at least), they may be seen as in keeping with a central procedure of ordinary language philosophy, which considers philosophers' words not in the abstract but in specific experiential contexts. The conviction that considerations of national identity must be extracurricular, moreover, gets some of its force from the impersonal and scientific model of philosophy that Cavell seeks to win distance from, whereby philosophy is not a national expression but is to resemble science as *"the* cosmopolitan, anyway international, means of communication."[14] "When I ask whether we may not understand Emerson and Thoreau as part of our philosophical inheritance as philosophers," Cavell writes,

> I am suggesting that our foreignness as philosophers to these writers (and it is hard to imagine any writers more foreign to our currently established philosophical sensibility) may itself be a sign of an impoverished idea of philosophy, of remoteness from philosophy's origins, from what is native to it, as if a certain constitution of the cosmopolitan might merely consist in a kind of universal provincialism, a worldwide shrinking of the spirit.[15]

If understanding Emerson and Thoreau as part of an American philosophical inheritance will help to redress an impoverished idea of philosophy, at stake here is a question as to the relationship between philosophy and literature. Although a good portion of his first book was dedicated to discussion of literary works such as Beckett's *Endgame* and Shakespeare's *King Lear*, Cavell was careful to resist the idea that these essays represented "pieces of literary criticism, or at best applications of philosophy" as opposed to "straight philosophy."[16] This resistance is not informed by stable categorizations but rather by a sense that "notions of philosophy and of literature and of criticism ... are themselves unexamined:"[17] Cavell elaborates: "In wishing to

---

13 Cavell, *Must We Mean*, xxxvii. 14 Cavell, "Emerson Mood," 23.
15 Cavell, "Emerson Mood," 25. 16 Cavell, *Must We Mean*, xxxii.
17 Cavell, *Must We Mean*, xxxii.

deny that some of these essays are philosophical and others not, I do not deny that ... there are differences between philosophy and literature or between philosophy and literary criticism; I am suggesting that we do not understand these differences."[18] The emphasis on differences here speaks to the premise of philosophical autonomy in Cavell's writing, which works against the free conflation of philosophy, literature, and criticism under an expansive umbrella term such as "discourse" or, indeed, "literature." The way that an understanding of these differences will emerge, for Cavell, is precisely through close reading or criticism. Sufficient attentiveness to an object of criticism will reveal how it discloses, first of all, the terms and framework of interpretation within which the object is to be read and thereby impart how these trouble and challenge given disciplinary terms and frameworks.

Cavell's rediscovery of Thoreau and Emerson, then, along with his contention as to their "philosophicality,"[19] is inseparable from his pursuit of a kind of philosophical writing responsive to the literary and to its own literariness. This leads, in *This New Yet Unapproachable America* (1989), to consideration of how his reading of the American Romantics relates to Phillipe Lacoue-Labarthe and Jean-Luc Nancy's claims for German Romanticism in *The Literary Absolute: The Theory of Literature in German Romanticism* (1988). Lacoue-Labarthe and Nancy identify German Romanticism as, in Cavell's words, "calling for a new relation, a kind of union or completion of work between philosophy and literature."[20] Cavell's conviction is that "measured against, say, Friedrich Schlegel's aphoristic, or rather fragmentary, call for or vision of the union of poetry and philosophy, Emerson's work presents itself as the realization of that vision."[21] This claim might seem unresponsive to the very dialectic between the fragment and the system explored in *The Literary Absolute* (since the point about fragments is that they remain *unrealized*), but Emerson's essays realize romanticism, Cavell suggests, precisely by "maintaining fragmentariness."[22] Emerson's essays and Thoreau's *Walden*, for Cavell, model writing in which philosophy and literature are expressed together. As such, they represent for him a philosophical moment prior to a felt division within what he describes as the "philosophical mind," articulated in disciplinary-institutional terms as the distinction between analytic and continental philosophy. In *The Claim of Reason*

---

18 Cavell, *Must We Mean*, xxxii.
19 Cavell, "Introduction," in *Emerson's Transcendental Etudes*, 1–9, 2.
20 Stanley Cavell, *This New Yet Unapproachable America: Lectures after Emerson after Wittgenstein* (Albuquerque, NM: Living Batch Press, 1989), 4.
21 Cavell, *This New Yet Unapproachable*, 20–21.
22 Cavell, *This New Yet Unapproachable*, 20.

(1979), Cavell discloses his own aspiration "to realign these traditions, after their long mutual shunning, or at any rate to write witnessing the loss in that separation."[23] Although he is sometimes presented as an outlier and exception within postanalytic philosophy given the range of his interests (writing not just on Transcendentalism but on Hollywood cinema), he might also be understood as representing that tradition's richness.

Richard Rorty: Postdisciplinary Conversations

Richard Rorty (1931–2007) possessed a radically different philosophical sensibility from that of Cavell. A broad commonality between these two American philosophers, however, is that they would both place philosophy within the humanities rather than trying to model it on the natural sciences, a position setting them somewhat at odds with the dominant intellectual sensibility of their profession. This metaphilosophical stance means that for Rorty, as for Cavell, the writing of philosophy takes on a particular significance and importance, closer to the essayistic than to a scientific report or article. In substance and in tone, though, the kind of philosophical writing Rorty produced reflects a very different set of philosophical premises and goals. Cavell's writing enacts a performance of sorts in which the philosophizing self seeks perspicacity. This philosophizing or thinking is pictured as taking steps, a picture lending itself to the essayistic since the goal is to be found at each step or stage of the journey (at the close of each Emersonian sentence for instance) rather than postponed to an arrival at some ultimate destination (the completion of a philosophical system or narrative). Rorty's work, although undeniably distinctive and similarly uninterested in system building, feels much less personal by comparison. The perspectives of his writing are in a sense broader – more historicist and sociological than psychological – offering a sweeping narrative overview of the rise and fall of intellectual endeavors and shifting philosophical fashions.

Like Cavell, Rorty can be seen as a philosopher of philosophy. Where Cavell finds it fruitful to keep metaphilosophical questions open, however, Rorty reaches a more explicit position. Rorty's writings are animated by his call, set out in *Philosophy and the Mirror of Nature* (1979) and refined across his career in key works such as *Consequences of Pragmatism* (1982), *Contingency,*

---

23 Stanley Cavell, *The Claim of Reason: Wittgenstein, Skepticism, Morality, and Tragedy* (Oxford: Oxford University Press, 1979), xiii.

Irony, and Solidarity (1989), and numerous volumes of collected *Philosophical Papers*, for philosophy to move away from a correspondence theory of capital "T" truth. Philosophers should cease thinking of their work in metaphysical terms, as aiming to somehow hook words or thoughts onto a nonhuman reality as it is "in itself." Antagonizing his philosophical interlocutors still further, Rorty proposes that this recommendation is not to be understood as a novel move within a reassuringly familiar philosophical game – not be assimilated to a thesis asserting that there is no capital "T" truth to which human thoughts and utterances might correspond. Rorty's proposal is not so much that the correspondence theory of truth gets something wrong, and more that it be regarded as a picture or paradigm that has outlived its usefulness, bequeathing stale puzzles and anomalies. It should give way to imaginative new pictures and paradigms that will lead to fresher, more interesting puzzles. Although philosophical argumentation informs and has a role within Rorty's position, it is regarded as one discursive tool among others. His favored discursive mode is less argumentation and more conversation and redescription. Philosophy is to be understood as involving solidarity rather than objectivity: not as getting subjects closer to objects or a nonhuman reality as it is in itself but as getting subjects closer to other subjects in ever-wider and more tolerant communities enabled by and further productive of novel imaginative vocabularies.

Rorty's philosophy can be understood, like Cavell's, as a bold and original response to a moment of methodological crisis within analytical philosophy. In Cavell's case, this methodological crisis is reflected tonally in the fervor of his writing, in the ways it wrestles with and internalizes the crisis in somewhat existential and experiential terms. The tone Rorty aspires to, by contrast, is one of insouciance, modeling the task, as he sees it, of shrugging off traditional philosophical aspirations rather than wrestling to recapture them expressively. If analytic philosophy might be said to be in crisis for Rorty, this is a disciplinary matter reflective of a broader cultural shift but not usefully staged in personal or existential terms. Both philosophers respond in different ways to Wittgenstein's counsel that philosophy should not issue theses, with Cavell aiming to locate orienting experiential truths underlying philosophical disputes and Rorty contending that philosophical problems are not so much to be solved as to be forgotten. The forgetting of philosophical problems is more than a description of the way philosophy tends to proceed looked at from an intellectual historical perspective, as philosophical problems wax and wane over time. It is also an explicit proposal on Rorty's part for a shift from "Philosophy" and "Truth" to "philosophy" and "truths," from philosophy understood as a foundational discipline to philosophy as one more or less useful voice amid others in the cultural conversation, good at showing how new and old paradigms or pictures might hang together:

> The urge to make philosophy into Philosophy is to make it the search for some final vocabulary, which can somehow be known in advance to be the common core, the truth of, all the other vocabularies which might be advanced in its place. This is the urge which the pragmatist thinks should be repressed, and which a post-Philosophical culture would have succeeded in repressing.[24]

A distinctive component of Rorty's narrative of analytic philosophy is that he understands the movement to have become, as it were, self-consuming through a process of characteristically rigorous auto-critique, whereby its most gifted practitioners upended the discipline-defining tenets of their predecessors: "[A]nalytic philosophy culminates in Quine, the later Wittgenstein, Sellars, and Davidson – which is to say that it transcends and cancels itself."[25] Where Cavell turns to American Transcendentalism to help unfold his own mode of postanalytic philosophy, Rorty by contrast finds the tradition of American pragmatism pioneered by William James (1842–1910) and John Dewey (1859–1952) to be exemplary for a post-Philosophical, anti-foundationalist culture. Less "foreign" than Transcendentalism, versions of pragmatism – or at least pragmatist motifs – still remained in the texture of professional philosophy. Turning the dialectical tables against the idea that the currents of pragmatism within logical positivism and analytic philosophy represented the absorption of pragmatism and disclosed its underlying positivist character, Rorty presented pragmatism as catalyzing an unraveling of the internal rationale of analytic philosophy:

> [T]he pragmaticization of analytic philosophy ... did not find a way for Philosophy to become "scientific," but rather found a way of setting Philosophy to one side. This postpositivistic kind of analytic philosophy thus comes to resemble the Nietzsche-Heidegger-Derrida tradition in beginning with criticism of Platonism and ending in criticism of Philosophy as such. Both traditions are now in a period of doubt about their own status. Both are living between a repudiated past and a dimly seen post-Philosophical future.[26]

---

24 Richard Rorty, *Consequences of Pragmatism: Essays 1972–1980* (Minneapolis: University of Minnesota Press, 1982), xlii.
25 Rorty, *Consequences of Pragmatism*, xviii.   26 Rorty, *Consequences of Pragmatism*, xxi.

Where Transcendentalism provides Cavell with sufficient distance from contemporary philosophy to begin to consider commonalities between seemingly divergent, mutually intolerant analytic and continental traditions, Rorty's narrative about the resurgence of pragmatism offers a way of seeing these traditions as traveling, after all, in a shared direction: "On my view, James and Dewey were not only waiting at the end of the dialectical road which analytic philosophy traveled, but are waiting at the end of the road which, for example, Foucault and Deleuze are currently travelling."[27]

Rorty's postdisciplinary sensibility and critique of truth placed him in close alignment (closer than most of his peers in the analytic tradition would have found tolerable) with contemporaneous debates, widespread within the humanities, concerning "theory," "postmodernism," and "poststructuralism." His postdisciplinarity in particular is comparable with the absorption of philosophy by an emergent "theoretical discourse" that Fredric Jameson (1934–) identified as a sign of postmodernism:

> A generation ago there was still a technical discourse of professional philosophy – the great systems of Sartre or the phenomenologists, the work of Wittgenstein or analytic or common language philosophy – alongside which one could still distinguish that quite different discourse of the other academic disciplines – of political science, for example, or sociology, or literary criticism. Today, increasingly, we have a kind of writing simply called "theory" which is all or none of these things at once. This new kind of discourse, generally associated with France and so-called French theory, is becoming widespread and marks the end of philosophy as such. Is the work of Michel Foucault, for example, to be called philosophy, history, social theory or political science? It's undecidable, as they say nowadays.[28]

Jameson overstates things here in that the technical discourse of professional philosophy did not disappear with the rise of "theory." It is the case, however, that although the humanities during this period were in a sense awash with philosophy, this philosophy was not drawn from or even recognized by the analytic tradition. The heterogeneous kind of writing called "theory" did not give much attention to analytic philosophy. Rorty came to find "postmodernism" too broad to be credible, with Jameson's sifting of variegated cultural forms for an underlying cultural dominant going against Rorty's pragmatist, antimetaphysical grain. Jameson's sketch of "theory" as a hybrid, postdisciplinary form is still consonant, however, with Rorty's own conception of

---

27 Rorty, *Consequences of Pragmatism*, xviii.
28 Fredric Jameson, "Postmodernism and Consumer Society," in *The Cultural Turn: Selected Writings on the Postmodern, 1983–1998* (London: Verso, 1998), 1–20, 3.

philosophy as a kind of writing. Rorty's post-Philosophical culture repackages philosophy as

> a study of the comparative advantages and disadvantages of the various ways of talking which our race has invented. It looks, in short, much like what is sometimes called "culture criticism" ... The modern Western "culture critic" feels free to comment on anything at all. He is a pre-figuration of the all-purpose intellectual of a post-Philosophical culture, the philosopher who has abandoned pretensions to Philosophy. He goes rapidly from Hemingway to Proust to Hitler to Marx to Foucault to Mary Douglas to the present situation in Southeast Asia to Ghandi [sic] to Sophocles. He is a name-dropper, who uses names such as these to refer to sets of descriptions, symbol-systems, ways of seeing.[29]

As Rorty articulates this in a later essay, philosophy should be seen not only as a genre but as a *transitional* genre, a stepping stone on the intellectual historical path from a religious to a literary culture, such that "a fully self-conscious literary culture would think of both religion and philosophy as largely obsolete, yet glorious, literary genres."[30]

Does thinking with Rorty of philosophy as a mostly obsolete literary genre represent what Jameson identified as "the end of philosophy as such" in the wake of theory? Rorty's reassurance here is not especially reassuring and somewhat arch: If he is not an end-of-philosophy thinker, this is because he does not regard philosophy in essentialist terms (philosophy "as such") as a distinct *Fach* capable of possessing a beginning, middle, or end. Rorty's thinking of philosophy as a genre or kind of writing entails the subsumption of philosophy within a broader literary culture, such that to see philosophy as a genre for Rorty is to see it as a kind of *writing*. The contrast with Cavell here is instructive. When Cavell considers the significance of the written character of Wittgenstein's *Philosophical Investigations*, he turns to Northop Frye's *Anatomy of Criticism* (1957) for an appreciation "of the fact that writing of all kinds (not just 'literature') is dependent, in structure and tone and effect, on a quite definite (though extensive) set of literary forms or genres."[31] Cavell's consideration of genre in relation to philosophy departs from Rorty's deployment of the term in that his goal is to better understand what is distinctively philosophical about Wittgenstein's writing. Cavell acknowledges the written character of philosophy – that philosophy is a kind of writing – but resists the

---

29 Rorty, *Consequences of Pragmatism*, xl.
30 Richard Rorty, "Philosophy as a Transitional Genre," in *Philosophy as Cultural Politics: Philosophical Papers* (Cambridge, UK: Cambridge University Press, 2007), 4:89–104, 95.
31 Cavell, *Must We Mean*, 7n14.

idea that this has postdisciplinary implications. Philosophy for Cavell is therefore not so much a kind of *writing* as a *kind* of writing. The extracurricular character of the texts Cavell considers – from Thoreau to Emerson to Hollywood movies – inscribes a version of disciplinary autonomy for philosophy rather than representing a postdisciplinary dissolution of boundaries, since the point for him is not so much "which texts get on a list but rather how a text is to be discovered and taken up."[32] Where Cavell works outward, showing how the close reading of a given text necessitates the suspension or rethinking of the intellectual assumptions and ontologies condensed in disciplinary divisions as they stand, Rorty has a more explicit prior position when it comes to disciplinary dispensations.

Cora Diamond: Fantasies of Realism and the Realistic Spirit

Cora Diamond's (1937–) work is no less distinctive than that of Cavell and Rorty and no less impatient with certain elements of academic philosophy. For all their originality, each philosopher reflects a broader tendency within the analytic tradition of eschewing the production of weighty tomes adumbrating comprehensive philosophical systems. One way in which they depart from this tradition, however, is by radicalizing the tendency and approaching the essay form as a place to reconsider the nature of philosophical argumentation, to acknowledge the written character of philosophy, and to put philosophy in dialogue with literature.

An overarching concern of the essays collected in Diamond's *The Realistic Spirit: Wittgenstein, Philosophy, and the Mind* (1991) is with the ways that Wittgenstein's work aims to liberate philosophy from the laying down of philosophical requirements: liberation from requirements as to what philosophical explanations should look like and where such explanations should be looked for, and, more fundamentally, liberation from the very requirement that philosophy should consist in the laying down of requirements. In "Realism and the Realistic Spirit," the hard lesson of Diamond's Wittgenstein is that the "best answer we can give ourselves" to philosophical tangles is oftentimes "one we cannot imagine is an answer at all," such that overcoming this failure of imagination represents "the real difficulty ... in philosophy."[33] Diamond's reception of Wittgenstein is consonant with that of

---

32 Cavell, *This New Yet Unapproachable*, 4.
33 Cora Diamond, "Realism and the Realistic Spirit," in *The Realistic Spirit: Wittgenstein, Philosophy, and the Mind* (Cambridge, MA: MIT Press, 1991), 39–70, 68.

Cavell, foregrounding as it does the ways in which philosophy comes to alienate and exile itself from human words, needs, and interests through the imposition of impossible metaphysical demands that displace and obscure real needs. Although philosophical questions "are in fact verbal elaborations of ordinary questions," philosophers are apt to "reject, as inadequate, ordinary answers, in the belief that we are asking something that passes those answers by."[34] In this disposition, philosophical elucidations will only satisfy if philosophers understand them, or feel they understand them, to be "in some sense ... not dependent on what goes on in our lives."[35] Diamond's argument is that realism in philosophy, rather than granting this metaphysical wish, involves "open-eyedly giving up the quest" it represents: "that is, not just stopping, but with an understanding of the quest as dependent on fantasy."[36] In the case of realism, Diamond characterizes the fantasy as one in which our ordinary practices seem too weak or too threadbare to serve as the site of philosophical explanations:

> The demands we make for philosophical explanations come, seem to come, from a position in which we are as it were looking down onto the relation between ourselves and some reality, some kind of fact or possibility. We think that we mean something by our questions about it. Our questions are formed from notions of ordinary life, but the ways we usually ask and answer questions, our practices, our interests, the forms our reasoning and inquiries take, look from such a position to be the "rags." Our own linguistic constructions, cut free from the constraints of their ordinary functioning, take us in: the characteristic form of the illusion is precisely philosophy as an area of inquiry, in the sense in which we are familiar with it.[37]

Fundamental to Diamond's argument is that open-eyedly giving up a fantasy or myth is distinct from ceding whatever the fantasy happens to be *of*. Asking philosophers to relinquish a *fantasy* of realism, for example, might feel like asking them to give up on realism itself (asking them to make do with rags). Giving up a *fantasy* of argument, further, will be apt to feel like giving up on argument altogether and having to make do with mere persuasion. A fantasy of necessity imagines necessity "as fact," whereas Wittgenstein aims to free us up to "see necessity where it does lie, in the use of ordinary sentences."[38]

"Anything but Argument?," a response to Onora O'Neill's review of Stephen Clark's *The Moral Status of Animals* (1977), asks questions about the nature and scope of philosophical argument. Diamond foregrounds and critiques what she identifies as a premise of O'Neill's assessment, that

---

34 Diamond, "Realism and the Realistic," 69.
35 Diamond, "Realism and the Realistic," 69.
36 Diamond, "Realism and the Realistic," 69.
37 Diamond, "Realism and the Realistic," 69.
38 Diamond, *Realistic Spirit*, 195.

"when someone is *reasonably* convinced of something, the convincing will have to have proceeded by arguments (or what could, at any rate, be set out as arguments), and the capacities of his head and not of his heart will be all that is involved."[39] On this assumption, to become convinced of the moral status of animals by any means other than argument would be "merely a matter of the operation of *causes*," an alteration of the heart and therefore a mere persuading rather than a reasonable convincing. In "Eating Meat and Eating People," Diamond critiques the idea that the "awful and unshakeable callousness and unrelentingness with which we most often confront the non-human world" can only be condemned with "reasons which are reasons for anyone, no matter how devoid of all human imagination or sympathy."[40] Aside from unworking a fantasy of argument, according to which argumentation could somehow compel those with closed hearts to change their minds about our treatment of nonhuman animals, Diamond's contention here is that a philosophical text, no less than a novel, can set out to "widen the imagination" and still count as a work of philosophy.[41] The appeal of such a work would be "to the intelligence," but not "via arguments – however hard *that* may be to fit into our philosophical schemes."[42]

Questions about philosophical argument and the relationships between philosophy and literature intertwine in Diamond's "The Difficulty of Reality and the Difficulty of Philosophy" (2003). The title phrase ("the difficulty of reality") is itself drawn not from the work of a professional philosopher but from the novelist John Updike (1932–2009), and Diamond's essay analyzes a poem by Ted Hughes (1930–1998) and J. M. Coetzee's (1940–) *The Lives of Animals* (1999), placing these in dialogue with Cavell's interpretations of philosophical skepticism. *The Lives of Animals* is a short story delivered by Coetzee across two lectures. Diamond's analysis focuses on the life of the *human* animal at the story's center, the author Elizabeth Costello: her woundedness at the way society treats nonhuman animals and her attendant sense of affective and discursive isolation in finding this norm to be obscene in the midst of a society that has normalized the industrial production and consumption of nonhuman animal flesh. Diamond notes a shortcoming of critical and philosophical responses to Coetzee's lectures, which tend to understand Coetzee as using a fictional frame to articulate philosophical arguments about animal rights, "pulling out ideas and arguments as if they had been simply clothed in fictional form as a way of

---

39 Diamond, *Realistic Spirit*, 293. 40 Diamond, *Realistic Spirit*, 334.
41 Diamond, *Realistic Spirit*, 294. 42 Diamond, *Realistic Spirit*, 301.

putting them before us."[43] Such responses bypass Costello and her experiences altogether, despite their raw urgency, and overlook the explicit *critique* of philosophical argumentation Costello builds in her own intradiegetic lectures, lectures that enmesh philosophical and family arguments. This critical neglect of experience and overemphasis on argumentation are of a piece since, as Diamond notes, Costello "sees our reliance on argumentation as a way we may make unavailable to ourselves our own sense of what it is to be a living animal."[44]

Rushing past the fictional dimension of Coetzee's lecture story and foregrounding its supposed argumentative kernel betrays, of course, a particular understanding of the relationship between philosophy and literature, one that Diamond rejects. What would a better approach look like? Refining her own position, Diamond keeps the question of relationships between philosophy and literature productively open: "I am not sure how helpful it is to say 'Coetzee's lectures have to be read first of all as literature,' because it is not clear what is meant by reading them as literature."[45] The remark recalls Cavell's premise that differences among philosophy, literature, and criticism are yet to be understood, but differentiates Diamond and Cavell from Rorty's more determinate, developmental picture of philosophy as a transitional genre on the way from a religious to a literary culture. Indeed, Diamond's essay closes by questioning the good of a philosophical position recognizable as Rorty's neopragmatism. The examples that Diamond provides as to the "difficulty of reality" are experiences "of the mind's not being able to encompass something which it encounters."[46] Although such experiences of thought and reality coming apart are thematic to Cavell's interpretations and explorations of philosophical skepticism (seen there as constitutively human rather than as intellectual puzzles to be outthought or outgrown), they are hard to do justice to from within Rorty's pragmatism:

> That our thought and reality might fail to meet is itself the content of a family of forms of skepticism, to which one response is that the very idea of such a failure is confused, that what I have spoken of as the content of such forms of skepticism is not a content at all. A language, a form of thought, cannot (we may be told) get things right or wrong, fit or fail to fit reality; it can only be more or less useful. What I want to end with is not exactly

---

43 Cora Diamond, "The Difficulty of Reality and the Difficulty of Philosophy," in *Philosophy and Animal Life* (New York: Columbia University Press, 2008), 43–90, 53.
44 Diamond, "Difficulty of Reality," 53. 45 Diamond, "Difficulty of Reality," 53.
46 Diamond, "Difficulty of Reality," 54.

a response to that: it is to note how much that coming apart of thought and reality belongs to flesh and blood. I take that, then, to be itself a thought joining Hughes, Coetzee, and Cavell.[47]

Not exactly a response, but a substantive divergence, since Rorty's pragmatism shoulders out[48] or occludes the very experience of thought being shouldered out by reality that Diamond takes as her subject and as signature of the human (although "flesh and blood" holds open the possibility that nonhuman animals might not be shouldered out from such moments either).

Returning to Cavell's sketch of the essay form as an intimate discourse for addressing strangers, with which this overview began, it might now be said that Cavell, Rorty, and Diamond, in the aftermath of Wittgenstein but in different ways, use the essay form to explore quite radical philosophical possibilities projecting new constellations of friends, relatives, and strangers. Their turn to literature, for example, speaks to literary scholars, but in different accents from those of literary theory. Their reflections on professional philosophy certainly disclose its strangeness to them (with philosophy stifling human voices for Cavell, persisting in puzzles without purpose for Rorty, and misplacing ordinariness for fantasy or myth for Diamond). Their own work in turn is in a sense strange by comparison with disciplinary norms, although their departures from philosophical orthodoxy (such as their willingness to reconsider the shape and nature of philosophical argument) can also be seen as underscoring and extending the richness of analytic or postanalytic philosophy. That the essay became a salient form for these philosophers reflects their methodological

---

47 Diamond, "Difficulty of Reality," 78.
48 In her essay "The Difficulty of Reality and the Difficulty of Philosophy," Diamond borrows the expression "shoulders out" from Ted Hughes's poem "Six Young Men." She cites the final stanza:

That man's not more alive whom you confront / And shake by the hand, see hale, hear speak loud, / Than any of these six celluloid smiles are, / Nor prehistoric or fabulous beast more dead; / Nor thought so vivid as their smoking blood: / To regard this photograph might well dement, / Such contradictory permanent horrors here / Smile from the single exposure and shoulder out / One's own body from its instant and heat.

(Ted Hughes, "Six Young Men," quoted in Diamond, "Difficulty of Reality," 43. Originally published in Ted Hughes, "Six Young Men," in *The Hawk in the Rain* [London: Faber and Faber, 1957], 54–55, 55.)

radicalism. Each asks questions about philosophy as a kind of writing and, as Rorty noted, writing tends to come to the foreground in periods of disciplinary crisis or radicalism, when the implicit "stage-setting" of a discipline comes under question.[49]

---

[49] Rorty, *Consequences of Pragmatism*, 106.

30

The Essay and Literary Postmodernism: Seriousness and Exhaustion

STEFANO ERCOLINO

Since the late 1960s, the essay has been a highly popular form of intellectual expression among major US postmodernist writers such as William H. Gass (1924–2017), Raymond Federman (1928–2009), John Barth (1930–), and Ronald Sukenick (1932–2004). More recently, it has also enjoyed the same success in the work of authors from the United States and abroad such as Kathy Acker (1947–1997), William T. Vollmann (1959–), Carole Maso (1956–), Jonathan Franzen (1959–), David Foster Wallace (1962–2008), Richard Powers (1957–), and Zadie Smith (1975–), who have often been considered in some aspects to be among the heirs of those (and other) great postmodernist masters. For all these writers, the essay has been an essential discursive and cognitive resource for formulating the scope and significance of their fiction writing. On the one hand, by separating essay from fiction, such writers saw the essay as an alluring tool for unburdening their intensely self-reflexive narrative works from essayistic excesses; on the other, through the essay, they managed to open up new rhetorical spaces for refined aesthetic reflections about the state and task of fiction in their days, especially in the context of what we generally refer to today as postmodernism.

Throughout the 1960s and '70s, important essays by US postmodernist writers featured a recurring theme, namely, the perceived seriousness of the toil of being an innovative and intellectually aware author. In "The Literature of Exhaustion," while commenting upon Jorge Luis Borges's (1899–1986) short story "Tlön, Uqbar, Orbis Tertius," Barth states that what makes Borges a great artist is the "combination of that intellectually serious vision with great human insight, poetic power, and consummate mastery of his means."[1] Further on, writing about imitation as one of the foundational acts

---

[1] John Barth, "The Literature of Exhaustion" (1967), in *The Friday Book: Essays and Other Non-Fiction* (Baltimore: Johns Hopkins University Press, 1997), 62–76, 70.

in the history of the modern novel and taking Miguel de Cervantes and Henry Fielding as examples, Barth highlights the fact that imitation was taken very seriously by the writers of his time: "[I]mitation ... is something new and may be quite serious and passionate."[2] A few years later, in several essayistic interventions, Sukenick assumes an explicitly polemical stance toward the unseriousness of contemporary US fiction,[3] the tastes of the reading public,[4] and national cultural politics.[5] On a similar militant note, in "Surfiction: A Postmodern Position," while advocating for his idea of surfiction and its importance for a renewal of US narrative, Federman expresses his worry about the future of fiction thus: "[L]ike most of my fellow-surfictionalists, I think this is the path that must be followed and explored if fiction is to have a chance to survive as a serious genre in our complex postmodern world."[6] Twenty years later, when the last sparks of the golden age of US literary postmodernism were fading into the darkness, in a famous interview with Larry McCaffery accompanying the publication of his essay "E Unibus Pluram: Television and U.S. Fiction," Wallace would still appeal to the concept of "seriousness" to point the way forward for fiction of the 1990s: "I guess a big part of serious fiction's purpose is to give the reader, who like all of us is sort of marooned in her own skull, to give her imaginative access to other selves."[7] And further on, in the same vein, he states: "The classic Realist form is soothing, familiar, and anesthetic; it drops us right into spectation. It doesn't set up the sort of expectations serious 1990s fiction ought to be setting up in readers."[8]

---

2 Barth, "Literature of Exhaustion," 72. In "The Literature of Replenishment," Barth returns to the "seriousness" of being a postmodernist writer in a more self-conscious way. See John Barth, "The Literature of Replenishment" (1980), in *Friday Book*, 193–206, 194.
3 "[W]e can't tolerate anything serious in fiction unless it's dull or comes from Europe." Ronald Sukenick, "The New Tradition" (1972), in *In Form: Digressions on the Act of Fiction* (Carbondale, IL: Southern Illinois University Press, 1985), 211.
4 "If we are going to have a wide and serious audience for fiction again we are going to have to re-examine the source of the novel's power beyond the particular forms of fiction that have become so dull to so many." Ronald Sukenick, "Innovative Fiction/ Innovative Criteria" (1974), in *In Form*, 241–43, 242.
5 "Perhaps it is time also for the National Endowment for the Humanities to recognize the educational function of serious contemporary writing." Ronald Sukenick, "Eight Digressions on the Politics of Language" (1979), in *In Form*, 49–65, 63.
6 Raymond Federman, "Surfiction: A Postmodern Position" (1973), in *Critifiction: Postmodern Essays* (Albany, NY: State University of New York Press, 1993), 47.
7 Larry McCaffery, "An Expanded Interview with David Foster Wallace" (1993), in *Conversations with David Foster Wallace*, ed. Stephen J. Burn (Jackson, MI: University Press of Mississippi, 2012), 21–52, 21–22.
8 McCaffery, "Expanded Interview," 33–34.

In all of Barth's, Sukenick's, Federman's, and Wallace's essayistic declarations on fiction – and particularly novel writing as a serious undertaking – the word "serious" lacks the bourgeois and aesthetic inflections it generally has in the scholarly discourse on novelistic form.[9] Here, "serious" mostly indicates experimental fiction, namely, fiction that is "not intended simply to amuse, please, or entertain."[10] From the 1960s through the '90s, Barth, Sukenick, Federman, and Wallace use "experimental fiction" to mean something similar in several aspects, which are generally traceable to the question of the seeming exhaustion of literary language and the pursuit of the new in American literature, as first formulated by Barth in the 1960s. Nevertheless, these four writers' positions and use of the essay differ in a number of respects, which makes them especially relevant to the task of debating essay writing on fiction by US postmodernist authors during the 1960s–1990s.

The Literature of Exhaustion

Barth's essay "The Literature of Exhaustion," published in the *Atlantic Monthly* in August 1967, started a heated debate on experimental fiction in the United States. At that time, Barth was teaching at the State University of New York at Buffalo, and his novel *Giles Goat-Boy* (1966) had recently been released. While working on his iconic collection of short stories, *Lost in the Funhouse* (1968), which would appear the following year, he originally delivered "The Literature of Exhaustion" as a Peters Rushton Seminars Lecture at the University of Virginia. "The Literature of Exhaustion" is a piece on Anglophone experimental fiction in the late 1960s, disguised as an essay on Borges's narrative. Barth uses Borges as a prism through which to reflect upon what he labels the "literature of exhausted possibility," or better, the "literature of exhaustion."[11] By the term "exhaustion," Barth means the "used-upness of certain forms or the felt exhaustion of certain possibilities."[12]

With a crystal-clear and compelling essayistic style, Barth does not aim to describe the actual state of things. Rather, he bases his argument on doxastic ground, namely, the widespread perception of the exhaustion of literary language. In this way, Barth shapes his essay around a sly understatement, which makes the text's argument apparently less radical yet more suggestive at the same time. Barth places in the most exalted category of "technically up-to-date"

---

9 See Franco Moretti, *The Bourgeois: Between History and Literature* (London: Verso, 2013), 67–74.
10 *Oxford English Dictionary*, 2nd ed. (2007), s.v. "serious."
11 Barth, "Literature of Exhaustion," 64.   12 Barth, "Literature of Exhaustion," 64.

artists authors such as Borges, Samuel Beckett (1906–1989), Vladimir Nabokov (1899–1977), and himself, "whose artistic thinking is *au courant* ... but who manage nonetheless to speak eloquently and memorably to our human hearts and conditions, as the great artists have always done."[13] Barth takes his cue from Borges's short story "Tlön, Uqbar, Orbis Tertius," in which the Argentinian writer concocts a secret society of scholars who have assembled a fictitious encyclopedia of the imaginary world of Tlön: an encyclopedia meant to differ entirely – "from its algebra to its fire"[14] – from the one describing their own reality. "Algebra" and "fire" are regarded by Barth as metaphors to describe the work of the technically up-to-date and "intellectually serious" artist who, just like Kafka in the past, is capable of a deep philosophical vision and technical mastery but also of "great human insight."[15] In other words, for Barth, what serious contemporary writers should eagerly pursue is a "passionate virtuosity."[16]

According to Barth, in the late 1960s, technically up-to-date artists inhabited an "age of ultimacies and 'final solutions' – at least *felt* ultimacies, in everything from weaponry to theology, the celebrated dehumanization of society, and the history of the novel."[17] This is why the work of writers like Borges (*Labyrinths*), Beckett (*Molloy, Malone Dies,* and *The Unnamable*), Nabokov (*Pale Fire*), and Barth himself (*The Sot-Weed Factor* and *Giles Goat-Boy*) revolves around ultimacy, both thematically and morphologically. Borges's short story "Pierre Menard, Author of the *Quixote*" gives Barth the occasion to introduce a number of "ultimacies" in his discourse on the literature of exhaustion, mainly through the themes of repetition, self-consciousness, and irony. With the French symbolist poet Pierre Menard, whose *Don Quixote* literally recomposes sections of Cervantes's novel word by word, Barth believes that the revival of old forms or obsolete ideas and conventions is unacceptable unless it is made with a certain amount of irony by a mindful writer.[18] From this perspective, the newness and originality of Menard's version of *Don Quixote*, namely, the newness and originality of rewriting and the literature of exhaustion, reside in their very existence: Thematizing the impossibility or, unnecessity, of new literature is itself new and original, and represents an artistically valuable venture. By recalling Borges's understanding of the Baroque as a style that intrinsically tends to exhaust its formal and thematic options while verging on self-parody, Barth regards

---

13 Barth, "Literature of Exhaustion," 66–67.　14 Barth, "Literature of Exhaustion," 70.
15 Barth, "Literature of Exhaustion," 70.
16 Ian Carruthers and Alan Prince, "An Interview with John Barth," *Prism* (Spring 1968): 42–62, 62.
17 Barth, "Literature of Exhaustion," 67.　18 Barth, "Literature of Exhaustion," 69.

Borges's work and the literature of exhaustion in general as an intellectual Baroque,[19] a labyrinth exemplified by the image of the Library of Babel from Borges's short story of the same name. The writer of exhaustion – the "chosen remnant, the virtuoso, the Thesean *hero*"[20] – has to act, then, like Theseus in Minos's labyrinth. Highly aware of the Baroque saturation of reality and literary history and guided by the unfolding and folding of the red thread of irony, such a writer "need *not* rehearse [literature's] possibilities to exhaustion, any more than Borges needs actually to *write* the *Encyclopedia of Tlön* or the books in the Library of Babel. He need only be aware of their existence or possibility, acknowledge them, and with the aid of very special gifts . . . go straight through the maze to the accomplishment of his work."[21] This leads, for Barth, to the paradoxical creation of authentically new literature out of the feeling of the impossibility or undesirability of such an enterprise.

In 1980, thirteen years after the publication of "The Literature of Exhaustion," when the term *postmodernism* had become common coin within the debate on contemporary US fiction, in the essay "The Literature of Replenishment" (1980), Barth returned to his idea of the literature of exhaustion. "The Literature of Replenishment" was meant as a complement to and emendation of his 1967 contribution. This time, however, Barth deals explicitly with (as he himself labels it) postmodernist fiction while trying to downplay the apocalyptic and nihilistic feel of his former piece, offer a few clarifications, and restate some of the core ideas of his earlier essay. Having highlighted both the continuity and discontinuity between modernism and postmodernism, Barth affirms in hindsight that what "The Literature of Exhaustion" was really about is not the exhaustion of all literary possibilities but only the exhaustion of the high-modernist aesthetic.[22] In this sense, postmodernist literature should be regarded as a progressive phenomenon, a "literature of replenishment";[23] a literature attempting to recharge and renew the exhausted high-modernist art. Unlike the modernist writer, the postmodernist one (someone like Italo Calvino [1923–1985] or Gabriel García Márquez [1927–2014]) shows, according to Barth, a more democratic vocation toward literature and the reading public. Never oblivious of the fact that, in literature, the feeling of exhaustion is a quite ancient one and not just a discussion topic for US authors from the 1960s to the 1980s, Barth deems his "ideal postmodernist" to be someone who "neither merely repudiates nor

19 Barth, "Literature of Exhaustion," 73–74.   20 Barth, "Literature of Exhaustion," 75.
21 Barth, "Literature of Exhaustion," 75–76.
22 Barth, "Literature of Replenishment," 206.
23 Barth, "Literature of Replenishment," 206.

merely imitates either his twentieth-century modernist parents or his nineteenth-century premodernist grandparents."[24] Such an ideal postmodernist writer may not succeed in speaking to popular art admirers but *"should* hope to reach and delight, at least part of the time, beyond the circle of ... professional devotees of high art."[25] Compared to the proud intellectual Baroque and high sophistication of Borges, Nabokov, and Beckett's literature of exhaustion – which Barth glorified in his 1967 essay – this might rightly be held as an about-face. Barth's new understanding of postmodernist fiction as something somehow timidly situated between high and popular literature, winking at a wider reading public, is indeed a product of the early 1980s, when the heroic phase of the debate on experimental fiction had lost much of its momentum.

Bossa Nova, Surfiction, Critifiction

In 1972, a few years after the release of his first novel, *Up* (1968), and the collection *The Death of the Novel and Other Stories* (1969), Sukenick published "The New Tradition" in the *Partisan Review*. In this essay, he defines the features of a new style of fiction writing that, in his view, is establishing itself as the vanguard of US narrative in the early 1970s. He labels it "Bossa Nova," and describes it as the style of a type of fiction that has "no plot, no story, no character, no chronological sequence, no verisimilitude, no imitation, no allegory, no symbolism, no subject matter, no 'meaning.'"[26] Bossa Nova is "non-representational – it represents itself. Its main qualities are abstraction, improvisation, and opacity."[27] Among its champions, Sukenick includes Donald Barthelme (1931–1989), Douglas Woolf (1922–1992), and Steve Katz (1935–2019). Often mistaken by critics as yet another instance of "'writing on writing'"[28] or of metafiction, Bossa Nova fiction approaches, according to Sukenick, the structure of the contemporary experience of the world more closely than any other style related to realist fiction.

Sukenick superimposes his notion of Bossa Nova onto Sharon Spencer's idea of "architectonic novel," one that "embod[ies] approximations of timespace fusions achieved by various structural procedures"[29] and is

---

24 Barth, "Literature of Replenishment," 203.
25 Barth, "Literature of Replenishment," 203. Original emphasis.
26 Sukenick, "New Tradition," 211.   27 Sukenick, "New Tradition," 211.
28 Sukenick, "New Tradition," 207.
29 Sharon Spencer, *Space, Time and Structure in the Modern Novel* (New York: New York University Press, 1971), xx.

"characterized by the spatialization of its form."[30] Thinking of John Cage's prose, Barth's *Lost in the Funhouse*, and Federman's *Double or Nothing* (1971), Sukenick claims that the inventive handling of the layout and of narrative space plays an antimimetic role in Bossa Nova fiction.[31] Chronological sequentiality and linearity in the unfolding of the plot, in particular, are among the hallmarks of the old tradition of fiction writing against which the "new tradition" of American narrative – whose roots can be traced to a multilingual and transnational set of writers such as François Rabelais, Cervantes, and Laurence Sterne, and to which Bossa Nova authors also belongs – has launched an attack. As "things don't appear to happen according to Aristotle anymore,"[32] contemporary fiction has the task, in Sukenick's view, of exploring this change in the perception of reality, while turning to models of novelistic writing that, in the past, sprang from an analogous sense of perceived disjointedness and disorder of the real: *Gargantua and Pantagruel*, *Don Quixote*, and *The Life and Opinions of Tristram Shandy, Gentleman*.

Sukenick's defense of Bossa Nova fiction is not uniquely related, however, to a renewed need to describe the world as a chaotic maze of experiences and meanings. It is also a positive response to the ambivalently dysphoric feeling of exhaustion of literary language posited by Barth in his 1967 essay. In "Thirteen Digressions," which appeared in the *Partisan Review* in 1976, Sukenick recognizes that the literature of his time may have its reasons to no longer "believe in its own reality" and make a "constant recourse to irony and self-parody," being often a literature that "has lost confidence in itself: Barth's 'literature of exhaustion.'"[33] The following year, in one of his most articulate interventions in the debate on contemporary American narrative, "Fiction in the Seventies: Ten Digressions on Ten Digressions" (1977) – first published in *Studies in American Fiction* – Sukenick returns to the problem that "The Literature of Exhaustion" had posed for US writers. Influenced by Jerome Klinkowitz's derogatory definition of Barth and Thomas Pynchon (1937–) as "regressive parodists,"[34] Sukenick maintains – in the first of the ten digressions of which the essay is made, the "Parodic Digression" – that in America in the 1960s, "[t]here were novels by novelists who no longer believed in THE novel but felt compelled for one reason or another to

---

30 Sukenick, "New Tradition," 204.   31 Sukenick, "New Tradition," 204.
32 Sukenick, "New Tradition," 204.
33 Ronald Sukenick, "Thirteen Digressions" (1976), in *In Form*, 16–33, 23.
34 Jerome Klinkowitz, *Literary Disruptions: The Making of a Post-Contemporary American Fiction* (Urbana, IL: University of Illinois Press, 1975), ix, 4–22.

write it."³⁵ As if whole geological eras had passed since the appearance of major works by regressive parodists Barth and Pynchon, Sukenick uses (like Klinkowitz again) the label "post-contemporary"³⁶ to characterize the many authors who emerged in the 1970s, among whom he counts George Chambers, Federman, Ishmael Reed (1938–), Katz, Jonathan Baumbach (1933–2019), Russell Banks (1940–2023), and Robert Coover (1932–). In Sukenick's view, what differentiates US postcontemporary authors from those regressive parodists of the 1960s are the following characteristics: the stern refusal of any residual form of mimetic pretension;³⁷ the belief in the necessity to "extend, reorder, and vitalize" the domain of human experience, not by means of an imitation of reality but through a "generat[ion]" of it;³⁸ the attempt to move away from the mediated character of the traditional novel toward a sort of open, "unpremeditated,"³⁹ and "unpredictable text";⁴⁰ a heightened consciousness of the potentialities of the written medium;⁴¹ and the constant tendency, in both the literary practice and criticism, to "defamiliarize the novel, to de-define fiction, as fiction simultaneously creates and decreates itself."⁴² No matter how well detailed or substantial the differences might be between the American writers who established themselves in the 1960s and those who did so in the 1970s, no matter how varied the latter group is, and no matter how problematic the chronology looks, three things can be noticed while reading "Fiction in the Seventies" and Sukenick's essays on US experimental fiction in general. These exhibit (1) a militant trust in the vitality of literature opposing, in a somewhat polemical way, Barth's argument in "The Literature of Exhaustion"; (2) the effort to distinguish between what he and his fellow postcontemporary writers were doing in the 1970s and what (other) postmodernist writers did in the 1960s; and (3) the frequent references to Federman as one of the most representative writers of the 1970s and to his idea of surfiction.⁴³

In the 1973 summer issue of the *Partisan Review*, Federman – by then working at the State University of New York at Buffalo and the author of the novel *Double or Nothing* (1971) – published "Surfiction: A [Postmodern]

---

35 Ronald Sukenick, "Fiction in the Seventies: Ten Digressions on Ten Digressions" (1977), in *In Form*, 34–48, 36.
36 Sukenick, *In Form*, 35; Klinkowitz, *Literary Disruptions*, ix–x.
37 Ronald Sukenick, "Twelve Digressions toward a Study of Composition" (1974), in *In Form*, 3–15, 3.
38 Sukenick, "Thirteen Digressions," 31.   39 Sukenick, "Twelve Digressions," 8.
40 Sukenick, "Thirteen Digressions," 33.   41 Sukenick, "Fiction in the Seventies," 44, 47.
42 Sukenick, "Fiction in the Seventies," 48.
43 See Sukenick, "Twelve Digressions," 8; Sukenick, "Thirteen Digressions," 31–32, 33; and Sukenick, "Fiction in the Seventies," 45.

Position."[44] Graphically creative and written in the form of dogmatic statements arranged in interconnected fragments, the essay is a manifesto for what Federman labels "surfiction," a kind of experimental fiction that exhibits the constructed character of narrative and the fictionality of the real.[45] Resonating in some aspects with later works – such as David Shields's *Reality Hunger: A Manifesto* and John D'Agata and Jim Fingal's *The Lifespan of a Fact*, key texts in the 2010s renaissance of the essay form – Federman deems surfiction as a synonym of postmodern fiction[46] as well as of "New Fiction, Antifiction, [and] Metafiction,"[47] but compared to Sukenick's Bossa Nova, it aspires to be a more oblique but still progressive answer to the literature of exhaustion theorized by Barth.[48] Influenced by the French theory of the 1960s and early '70s, especially that of Roland Barthes (1915–1980) and Michel Foucault (1926–1984), Federman believes that language creates meaning and that the latter creates the world. As often happens in Barth's and Sukenick's essays on postmodernist literature, the target in "Surfiction" is mimesis: the idea according to which fiction should represent a preexisting reality and meaning, instead of producing them. For Federman, the mission of serious fiction in the 1970s is, then, to "create a **DIFFERENCE**, and not to pretend that fiction is the same thing as reality."[49] Surfiction's task is the "presentation of difference – a liberation of what is different."[50]

As Federman makes clear, surfiction should revise traditionally accepted views on (1) how we read fiction, (2) narrative form, (3) its material, and (4) meaning. In particular, it breaks with the convention of sequential reading, and rethinks "**paginal** . . . [and] **grammatical syntax**" in order to give readers more freedom during the act of reading.[51] Linear and chronological narratives are no longer accepted since they have been used up by obsolete and deceitful (supposedly realist) forms of fiction. In so doing, surfiction qualifies itself as a self-reflexive type of fiction,[52] in a sort of ambivalent, self-destructive "denunciation of [its] own fraudulence, of what **IT** really **IS**: an illusion (a fiction), just as life is an illusion (a fiction)."[53] The imagination of the writer should have no restrictions. Characters should stop being conceived as coherent, plausible aggregates of psychological and social features,

---

44 Federman added the word "postmodern" later to the title, when the essay was reprinted in his 1993 collection *Critifiction: Postmodern Essays*.
45 Federman, "Surfiction," 37–38.   46 Federman, "Surfiction," 46.
47 Raymond Federman, "Fiction Today or the Pursuit of Non-Knowledge" (1978), in *Critifiction*, 1–16, 3.
48 Federman, "Surfiction," 35.   49 Federman, "Surfiction," 38. Boldface in original.
50 Federman, "Surfiction," 38.   51 Federman, "Surfiction," 41. Boldface in original.
52 Federman, "Surfiction," 43.   53 Federman, "Surfiction," 43. Boldface in original.

and instead be "as changeable, as volatile, as irrational, as nameless, as unnamable, as playful, as unpredictable, as fraudulent and frivolous as the discourse that makes them."[54] No empathy or identification is possible with such characters.[55] Ultimately, with a nod to reader-response criticism, it is the reader who invents the meaning of the text; the idea of the author as an "omnipresent, omniscient, omnipotent creator" should be definitively discarded.[56]

Despite the success of "Surfiction" and its ambition of having a long-term programmatic reach, three years after the publication of his 1973 contribution (when his novel *Take It or Leave It* was released, too), in "Critifiction: Imagination and Plagiarism (... an Unfinished Endless Discourse ...),"[57] Federman's position on the current state and future of American experimental narrative changes in a number of relevant ways. "Critifiction" is one of the most formally self-conscious and sophisticated essays written by US writers contributing to the debate on the exhaustion of the literary language and postmodernism. Presented as a digressive and fragmented "**montage/collage** of thoughts, reflections, meditations, quotations, pieces of [Federman's] (previous) discourses ... as well as pieces of discourses by others,"[58] the essay relies on a defamiliarizing, whirlwind succession of various materials as well as single words, sentences, or sections written in different case styles (italics, bold, lowercase or uppercase). This is made in a surfictional – or, better, "[s]uressayistic" – spirit that aims to expose the fabricated, "critifictional" nature of a discourse that wants to be "critical as well as fictitious."[59]

With French theory still solidly serving as the background for Federman's musings, "Critifiction" is an essay on a "kind of narrative that contains its own theory and even its own criticism."[60] Strictly speaking, however, "Critifiction" is a piece on literary imagination, which, in Federman's view, is always based on plagiarism, on what has already been said by others.[61] The moment

---

54 Federman, "Surfiction," 44.   55 Federman, "Surfiction," 45.
56 Federman, "Surfiction," 46.
57 In 1976, this essay originally appeared under a slightly different title in *New Literary History*.
58 Raymond Federman, "Critifiction: Imagination as Plagiarism" (1976), in *Critifiction*, 48–64, 51. Boldface in original.
59 Federman, "Critifiction," 49.
60 Raymond Federman, "Self-Reflexive Fiction or How to Get Rid of It" (1988), in *Critifiction*, 17–34, 31. For more on French theory, see François Cusset, *French Theory: How Foucault, Derrida, Deleuze, and Co. Transformed the Intellectual Life of the United States*, trans. Jeff Fort (Minneapolis: University of Minnesota Press, 2008).
61 Federman, "Critifiction," 52.

postmodernist literature started reflecting upon itself, Federman argues, and "turned inward ... in order to question, examine, challenge, even mock itself, and at times negated or cancelled its purpose, its intentionality, its own means of production and communication," the two myths of originality and the author as the "sacred source" of the work collapsed.[62] The consequence is that postmodernist literature can no longer produce masterpieces or great writers, but only narratives that all "resemble one another, and artists who imitate or plagiarize each other's work."[63] Entrapped in the web of writing, of *écriture*, the postmodernist or surfictional writer cannot reach a reality outside language anymore, because there is no such extralinguistic reality to be found.[64]

Regardless of his faint, indirect appeal to critifiction to create a "new perception" of the world and his declared faith in the power of the (inevitably plagiaristic) imagination of surfictional (or critifictional) writers,[65] Federman takes a step back from his previous positive outlook on US experimental fiction as formulated in "Surfiction," and plunges the debate over postmodernist American narrative once more into the stifling atmosphere of Barth's literature of exhaustion. Two quotations from Beckett's *Murphy* and *The Unnamable*, placed in crucial positions in the text – one immediately after "**insertion number two**": "*The sun shone, having no alternative, on the nothing new;*"[66] the other, at the very end of the essay: "*But the discourse must go on. So one invents obscurities. Rhetoric*"[67] – authoritatively register this somber shift.

Two years later, in "Fiction Today or the Pursuit of Non-Knowledge," first published in *Humanities in Society* in 1978, Federman would return to this shift. While extensively and explicitly investigating the Barthian feeling of the "impossibility of literature" in the postmodern world,[68] he ends up suggesting that much of the transnational landscape of contemporary experimental literature might be gathered under the label of the literature of exhaustion – including surfiction and critifiction.[69] Notwithstanding Federman's early anxiety over differentiating his work from that of former postmodernist writers (an anxiety shared with Sukenick), the debate on experimental fiction in his essayistic production from the mid-1970s folds back on itself. The avantgarde, utopian impulse that had sustained "Surfiction" – as well as Sukenick's

---

62 Federman, "Critifiction," 56.   63 Federman, "Critifiction," 56.
64 Federman, "Critifiction," 59–60.   65 Federman, "Critifiction," 63.
66 Federman, "Critifiction," 60; Samuel Beckett, *Murphy* (New York: Grove Press, [1938] 1957), 1. Boldface in original.
67 Federman, "Critifiction," 64; Samuel Beckett, "The Unnamable" (1953), in *Three Novels: Molloy, Malone Dies, The Unnamable* (New York: Grove Press, 1959), 399–577, 405.
68 Federman, "Fiction Today," 8.   69 Federman, "Fiction Today," 11.

"The New Tradition" and "Fiction in the Seventies" – is reabsorbed into the powerful, persisting negative aesthetic of exhaustion, half-nihilistically and half-playfully articulated by Barth over ten years before.

The Prison House of Postmodern Irony

In the early 1990s, over two and a half decades after the appearance of "The Literature of Exhaustion," a long, wide-ranging, and densely argumentative essay by David Foster Wallace shows that the heritage of Barth's aesthetic of exhaustion remained burdensome. In "E Unibus Pluram: Television and U.S. Fiction," written in 1990 and published in the *Review of Contemporary Fiction* in 1993, Wallace selects two of the many issues raised by Barth in relation to the literature of exhaustion – irony and self-consciousness – and analyzes them in order to reflect on the impact that television had on US narrative, take stock of a certain kind of American fiction since the 1960s, and attempt to forge a path for serious, experimental literature in the 1990s.[70]

Wallace's thesis is that "irony, poker-faced silence, and fear of ridicule are distinctive of those features of contemporary US culture (of which cutting-edge fiction is a part) that enjoy any significant relation to the television whose weird pretty hand has [my] generation by the throat."[71] An entertaining and effective instrument for the previous generation of postmodernist "fathers," to which Barth, Pynchon, William Gaddis (1922– 1998), Don DeLillo (1936–), Coover, and a few others belong, irony loses its debunking power once its language has been digested by television and commercial advertising – two intrinsically ironic devices.[72] To react against such an assimilation, a new "subgenre of pop-conscious postmodern fiction,"[73] which Wallace calls post-postmodernist, hyperrealist or "Image-Fiction,"[74] has emerged. Practiced mostly by young American writers in the early 1990s, Image-Fiction has "made an attempt to transfigure a world of and for appearance, mass appeal, and television";

---

70 For another temporally close perspective on these topics, which is partly similar, even though narrower, and partly different from the one adopted in "E Unibus Pluram," see Wallace's essay "Fictional Futures and the Conspicuously Young," first published in the *Review of Contemporary Fiction* in 1988. David Foster Wallace, "Fictional Futures and the Conspicuously Young" (1988) in David Foster Wallace, *Both Flesh and Not: Essays* (London: Penguin, 2013), 37–68.
71 David Foster Wallace, "E Unibus Pluram: Television and U.S. Fiction" (1990), in *A Supposedly Fun Thing I'll Never Do Again: Essays and Arguments* (New York: Back Bay Books / Little, Brown, 1998), 21–82, 49.
72 Wallace, "E Unibus Pluram," 35.   73 Wallace, "E Unibus Pluram," 49.
74 Wallace, "E Unibus Pluram," 50.

nevertheless, "televisual culture has somehow evolved to a point where it seems invulnerable to any such transfiguring assault."[75] Wallace argues that, in the face of the transformation and distortion of the very idea of what reality (and consequently literary realism) is for a generation of writers who grew up with television as an integral component of their lives, Image-Fiction represents an "involution of the relations between lit and pop that blossomed with the '60s postmodernists."[76] An alternative form of realism mediated by televisual culture, Image-Fiction took its first steps in the 1970s, with such works as DeLillo's *Great Jones Street* (1973) and Max Apple's "The Oranging of America" (1974), and in the 1980s, with Coover's *A Night at the Movies, or You Must Remember This* (1987) and Vollman's *You Bright and Risen Angels* (1987). It was only in the late 1980s and early '90s, though, that it established itself as a more widespread and relevant literary phenomenon in works such as Vollman's *The Rainbow Stories* (1989), A. M. Homes's *The Safety of Objects* (1990), Michael Martone's *Fort Wayne Is Seventh on Hitler's List* (1990), and Mark Leyner's *My Cousin, My Gastroenterologist* (1990). Highly self-conscious and rich in defamiliarizing devices, Image-Fiction cannot really shun, in Wallace's view, the "televisual aura" from which it is born and that it is supposed to break while remaining "reverently ironic" toward it.[77] How could it ever happen that a writer could develop any form of avant-garde, revolutionary approach to fiction writing – Wallace wondered in the wake of Fredric Jameson's reflection on postmodernism – if avant-garde and revolution had themselves become empty rhetoric, "pop-cultural institution[s],"[78] following their commodification by the late capitalist entertainment industry? Put otherwise: How could a fiction writer, or an artist in general, possibly be a true iconoclast in the 1990s, if "Burger King sells onion rings with 'Sometimes You Gotta Break the Rules'"[79]? Wallace's answer is simply that such a fiction writer can't.

Whereas the irony of the early postmodernists had an idealistic and utopian dimension that made it an often powerful tool to unmask the insincerity and chaos of US public life in the 1960s and '70s, the fact that irony "is *still around*, bigger than ever after 30 long years as the dominant form of hip expression,"[80] is cause for great cultural anxiety. For, as Wallace writes by quoting Lewis Hyde's essay *Alcohol and Poetry: John Berryman and the Booze Talking* (1979), "[i]rony has only emergency use. Carried over time, it is the

75 Wallace, "E Unibus Pluram," 49–50.   76 Wallace, "E Unibus Pluram," 50.
77 Wallace, "E Unibus Pluram," 76.   78 Wallace, "E Unibus Pluram," 68.
79 Wallace, "E Unibus Pluram," 68.   80 Wallace, "E Unibus Pluram," 67.

voice of the trapped who have come to enjoy their cage."[81] Irony is a negative figure of speech,[82] a potent one when it comes to demystifying reality, but also a weak ally when it comes to "constructing anything to replace the hypocrisies it debunks."[83] Wallace speculates, then, that postmodern irony took on a poisonous character in the 1990s, and winded up "tyranniz[ing]" American writers.[84] Once – in Barth's "The Literature of Exhaustion" – the Ariadne's thread to be rewound in order to reach the heart of the maze of literary history and the complexity of the postmodern world, Wallace deems irony and its persistence as the principal communicative form in US experimental narrative, the epitome of the difficulty or impossibility for American fiction to say something new. A helpful tool by the time of the early postmodernists, irony is now felt as a mark of epigonality. Exhausted by its widespread mediatization and crystallization in sterile intellectual poses, it is a road leading nowhere other than creative paralysis.

The occurrence, in the first sentence of the last paragraph of "E Unibus Pluram," of the words "impossibility" and "exhaustion" forcefully brings us back to the very beginning of the debate on the literature of exhaustion initiated by Barth in 1967: "It's entirely possible that my plangent noises about the impossibility of rebelling against an aura that promotes and vitiates all rebellion say more about my residency inside that aura, my own lack of vision, than they do about any exhaustion of U.S. fiction's possibilities."[85] As had already happened with Federman's "Critifiction," Barth's aesthetic of exhaustion proves once more to be able to cast its shadow far forward in time, giving a direction to the debate over the future of American experimental narrative while also making it collapse in on itself. For nothing escapes exhaustion; nothing escapes the prison house of self-conscious writing, the trap of metafiction, Bossa Nova, surfiction, critifiction or, more simply, postmodernist fiction; nothing – no manifestos, no voluntaristic stances – escapes the terminality of art reflecting upon itself.[86] This is why Wallace maintains that he and his young, committed fellow writers have reached "some kind of line's end's end,"[87] and that the only way to dispose of

---

81 Wallace, "E Unibus Pluram," 67; Lewis Hyde, *Alcohol and Poetry: John Berryman and the Booze Talking* (Dallas, TX: Dallas Institute of Humanities and Culture, 1986), 16.
82 See Stefano Ercolino, "'End of the End of the Line': The Broken Temporality of David Foster Wallace's *Infinite Jest*," in *A Question of Time: American Literature from Colonial Encounter to Contemporary Fiction*, ed. Cindy Weinstein (Cambridge, UK: Cambridge University Press, 2019), 293–311.
83 Wallace, "E Unibus Pluram," 67.   84 Wallace, "E Unibus Pluram," 67–68.
85 Wallace, "E Unibus Pluram," 81.   86 McCaffery, "Expanded Interview," 30, 40.
87 Wallace, "E Unibus Pluram," 82.

what, over the years, has become a nightmare for US fiction (namely, the responsibility to create something new, notwithstanding the ultimately unbearable legacy of the aesthetic of exhaustion) might be that of ceasing to be a postmodernist writer altogether. Wallace imagines, indeed, that "the next real literary 'rebels' in [the] country might well emerge as some weird bunch of anti-rebels, born oglers who dare somehow to back away from ironic watching, who have the childish gall actually to endorse and instantiate single-entendre principles."[88] These "anti-rebels" will run the risk of being sincere and taking emotions seriously, while eschewing postmodernist "self-consciousness and hip fatigue."[89] Whether Wallace succeeded or not in the task of becoming such an "anti-rebel" in his production as a fiction writer, especially in his masterpiece, the 1996 novel *Infinite Jest*, is controversial and a matter for another occasion. Therefore, all we will say in conclusion is that, from the late 1960s on through the early '90s, in major and stylistically diversified essayistic pronouncements by some of the most representative postmodernist (and supposedly post-postmodernist) American writers, the debate over serious experimental fiction and the exhaustion of literary language took an inescapably circular shape. Its terrain was akin to a patch of quicksand to be crossed cautiously, lest one be ensnared by it – a quicksand one can only imagine jumping over in order to conceive of a future for US narrative.

---

88 Wallace, "E Unibus Pluram," 81.   89 Wallace, "E Unibus Pluram," 81.

PART IV

★

TOWARD THE CONTEMPORARY AMERICAN ESSAY (2000–2020)

31
The American Essay Film: A Neglected Genre

NORA M. ALTER

If Descartes were to write his *Discours* today, argued French film theorist and filmmaker Alexandre Astruc (1923–2016) in 1948, it would be "written" as a 16mm essay film.[1] Early articulations of the essay film have been around for at least a hundred years. For example, in 1928, Sergei Eisenstein (1898–1948) referred to his unrealized plan to film Marx's *Capital* as an essay film.[2] Over the decades, the essay film has developed as a form of audiovisual social commentary or filmed philosophy. In film history, the essay film readdresses and troubles questions raised by the earliest forms of cinema, such as the distinction between verisimilitude and fabrication. In 1940, German avant-garde filmmaker Hans Richter (1888–1976) called for a type of nonfiction film production that, by making "problems, thoughts, even ideas" perceptible, would render visible what is not visible. Richter dubbed the result "essay," since it deals with "difficult subjects and themes to render them into a generally comprehensible form."[3] The essay film has developed into a new form of cinema that, with its dual audio and visual dimensions, progressively transforms the nature of traditional philosophical discourse, just as that discourse, when filmed, transforms the nature of cinema. Astruc promoted the notion of a *caméra-stylo* (camera-stylus) that would "become a means of writing, just as flexible and subtle as written language, ... [rendering] more or less literal 'inscriptions' on images as 'essays.'"[4] Some

---

1 Alexandre Astruc, "The Birth of a New Avant-Garde: La Caméra Stylo," in *Film and Literature: An Introduction and Reader*, ed. Timothy Corrigan (Upper Saddle River, NJ: Prentice Hall, 1999), 158–62, 159.
2 Sergei Eisenstein, "Notes for a Film of 'Capital,'" *October* 2 (Summer 1976): 3–26.
3 Hans Richter, "The Film Essay: A New Form of Documentary Film" (1940), in *Essays on the Essay Film*, ed. Nora M. Alter and Timothy Corrigan (New York: Columbia University Press, 2017), 89–92, 91.
4 Astruc, "Birth of a New," 159.

essay films have literally included textual or graphic inscription on the celluloid, though most only do this figuratively. The result is a multilayered product: an image track, a sound track, and then a written track, often accompanied by a voiceover. The properly textual track or layer sometimes directly contradicts the image track, creating within the total filmic text a jarring collision of opposites and complex levels of meaning that the audience must coproduce. Technological innovations over the years have affected the form of the essay film from video to digital, from theatrical release to internet platforms.

In the twenty-first century, the genre of essay film is accepted as a practice of moving image production, distribution, and reception.[5] Beginning in the aughts, numerous publications, institutional labels, designations, and systems of classification have come together to solidify the genre.[6] Essay films tend to be transnational as well as transdisciplinary – as likely to be produced by independent filmmakers as by documentarians and artists. There are essay film festivals and academic conferences; definitions and filmographies may be found in such diverse venues as Oxford bibliographies, BFI, IMDb, and YouTube. However, this has not always been the case, and the genre and its reception have had an uneven development across the globe. The European avant-garde embraced the form early on, and it continued to flourish during the postwar period in France, spreading quickly to Germany, Italy, the Netherlands, and the United Kingdom during the 1970s and '80s. This is not to say that essay films did not exist in other national cinemas but that at the time of their production, they were not identified as such.

This is nowhere truer than in the United States, where an acceptance of the genre and a circulation of the term in intellectual and popular discourse did not occur until the new millennium. Such a blind spot is striking when one considers the international status of the United States as the global standard-bearer in film production. But it is precisely because of the predominance of Hollywood that the essay film was occluded.

---

5 Throughout this essay, I will use the term "essay film" to include film, video, and digital works.

6 See, for example, Ursula Biemann, *Stuff It: The Video Essay in the Digital Age* (Zurich: Voldemeer, 2003); Laura Rascaroli, *The Personal Camera: Subjective Cinema and the Essay Film* (London: Wallflower Press, 2009); Timothy Corrigan, *The Essay Film: From Montaigne to Marker* (Oxford: Oxford University Press, 2013); Caroline Eades and Irene Papaziam, *The Essay Film: Politics, Dialogue, Utopia* (London: Wallflower Press, 2016); Nora M. Alter and Timothy Corrigan, *Essays on the Essay Film* (New York: Columbia University Press, 2017); Nora M. Alter, *The Essay Film after Fact and Fiction* (New York: Columbia University Press, 2018); and Brenda Hollweg and Igor Krstic, *World Cinema and the Essay Film* (Edinburgh: Edinburgh University Press, 2021).

Hollywood does not bear sole responsibility, I argue; it was also the regulating force of the disciplinary boundaries of documentary film, as well as the predominance of aesthetic formalism in artistic practice that repressed the essay film from being acknowledged as a genre in North America. Indeed, as I will show, the essay film exists from the earliest years throughout the twentieth century in the US cinematic landscape, even if many refuse to see it.

Documentary

One of the earliest examples of an essay film is D. W. Griffith's (1875–1948) *A Corner in Wheat* (1909), which translates abstract economic concepts of free-market capitalism into film. While often characterized as a narrative film, *A Corner in Wheat* is a cornerstone of the essay film tradition in the United States. It was made in an era marked by muckraking novelists like Upton Sinclair (1878–1968) and photographers such as Lewis W. Hines (1874–1940) who used their pens and cameras to expose society's ills and advocate reform. In this fourteen-minute short, which mixes fact and fiction, Griffith demonstrates the process whereby locally sourced wheat becomes a commodity that is traded, bought, and sold on international markets. After its initial cultivation, the grain takes on a financial life of its own that makes it unattainable as a food staple to those who planted and harvested it. Instead, the profits go to wealthy entrepreneurs who cleverly manipulate the market. Through careful staging and parallel editing, Griffith underscores the chasm between the classes, the employment of police to keep the poor under control, and the unstoppable abstract machinations of capital.

In the 1930s, two interventions affected the development of the essay film. The first was sound technology that provided an additional layer of meaning to written text and images. The second was the identification and consecration of the documentary genre by John Grierson (1898–1972). Grierson, a Scot, studied in the United States in the 1920s and was acquainted with filmmaker Robert Flaherty (1884–1951). Grierson coined the term *documentary* to describe Flaherty's *Nanook of the North* (1921) and *Moana* (1926). Grierson's theory of nonfiction filmmaking came to be the standard-bearer of documentary film with its rigid rules and conventions that strictly adhered to facts. However, a close reading of Grierson's early writings, with his stress on "creative" manipulations of reality and an analysis of film productions under his supervision, reveals that they were much closer to today's essay films than documentaries.[7] However, for myriad reasons including those of World War II propaganda efforts, the playful, contradictory essays films that were composed of multiple intertwined threads of meaning and mixtures of fact and fiction gave way to newsreels and "objective" reports based on the facts.

In the United States, the founding of the Works Progress Administration (WPA) in the mid-1930s provided work for numerous artists, including writers, photographers, and theater troupes. Although there was no specific film division, the WPA supported projects such as Pare Lorentz's (1905–1992) *The Plow That Broke the Plains* (1936), an essay film on the devasting consequence of overfarming and industrial agriculture. That same year, photographer Paul Strand (1890–1976), who was involved in Lorentz's film, worked with Fred Zinnemann (1907–1997) on *Redes* (1936), a docufiction on life in a fishing village in Mexico. *Redes* began as a documentary but metamorphosed into a fictional work, resulting in its hybrid status. A few years later, Strand collaborated with Leo Hurwitz (1909–1991) and Paul Robeson (1898–1976) on *Native Land* (1942). *Native Land* intertwines documentary footage with fictional reenactments and stories to produce a scathing critique of antiunion tactics by corporations. Documentary footage of a violent Ku Klux Klan rally, scenes of Black and white sharecroppers, and shots from racist demonstrations, along with Robeson's voiceover commentary, introduce the importance of conjoining race and labor activism. At the time, critics noted the strategic employment of Robeson's vocalization. Essay films such as these imparted a radical critique of society that was quickly labeled as socialist with communist sympathies. At the end of the war came the rise of McCarthyism and the House of Un-American Activities Committee trials, which managed to shut down progressive voices of the American Left for decades to come.

As a result, in the 1950s, documentaries pushed for a style that stressed "objectivity" instead of subjective partisan views. Voiceovers and commentaries were abandoned, and the subjects of the films were left to speak for themselves. What came to be called American Direct Cinema dominated the documentary mode of production in the United States from the 1950s well

---

7 In "The First Principles of Documentary" (1932), Grierson differentiated *Nanook* from earlier forms of nonfiction films such as actualities, newsreels, and travelogues, because it initiated a change "from the plain (or fancy) descriptions of natural material, to arrangements, rearrangements, and creative shapings of it." John Grierson "The First Principles of Documentary" (1932), *The Documentary Film Movement: An Anthology*, ed. Ian Aitken (Edinburgh: Edinburgh University Press, 1998), 81–93, 83.

into the 1980s.[8] One of the basic tenets of American Direct Cinema was its allegedly unmediated representation of objective reality, which was equated to truth. Essayistic qualities like personal subjectivity, creative manipulations, a surfeit of aesthetic framing and composition, or poetic and meditative contemplation had no place in the genre. At the same time as the genre of documentary underwent streamlining and strict codification, a medium of production and dissemination emerged that further affected its shape and form: television. Not only did television have rigid temporal parameters, but the three major networks in the United States, in contrast to Europe, were private commercial enterprises. From television's beginnings, programs were designed to sell products and were part of an infrastructure that produced, supported, and transmitted the tenets of a consumer-based society. Unlike their European counterparts, public broadcasting channels offered few opportunities for alternative voices, viewpoints, and formats to be aired.

The result in the field of nonfiction filmmaking was a pause in the development of the essay film in North America. It wasn't until the 1980s that increased pressure and challenges to the institution of documentary started to emerge from filmmakers and critics. Essay films such as Ross McElwee's (1947–) *Sherman's March* (1986), Michael Moore's (1954–) *Roger and Me* (1989), and Trinh T. Minh-ha's (1952–) *SurName Viet: Given Name Nam* (1989) confronted the medium, with Trinh provocatively asserting: "There is no such thing as documentary – whether the term designates a category of material, a genre, an approach, or a set of techniques."[9] Concomitant with the shift from analog to digital production in the 1990s, the essay film as an alternative to documentary reemerged.

Art

Although the essay film may have been in hibernation in the field of documentary filmmaking, it was making an appearance within the field of art. The first US production of Hans Richter (1888–1976), a recent émigré

---

8 As late as 1989, Michael Moore's *Roger and Me* was prevented from being considered in the documentary category for the Academy Awards because it violated certain rules of the genre, such as overt personal subjectivity of the director and metafilmic strategies that drew attention to the cinematic apparatus. Documentarians were expected to let the facts speak for themselves and not to interpret, engage with, and manipulate material. The documentary genre was extremely doctrinaire, and if nonfiction filmmakers didn't adhere strictly to the established protocols, they had a difficult time finding sponsorship, exhibition, and distribution venues for their work.
9 Trinh T. Minh-ha, "The Totalizing Quest of Meaning," in *When the Moon Waxes Red: Representation, Gender, and Cultural Politics* (New York: Routledge, 1991) 29–50, 29.

from Europe, was the essay film *Dreams That Money Can Buy* (1947). The collaborative film brought together members of the European avant-garde who had sought refuge in the United States during the war. The film is a meditative analysis and restaging of the movement, showcasing the work of members of the group including Marcel Duchamp (1887–1968), Max Ernst (1891–1976), Fernand Leger (1881–1955), and others. *Dreams That Money Can Buy* is composed of loosely connected segments devoted to a range of contemporary artworks, with Richter serving less in the role of director than as the editor of a volume or curator of an exhibition. The film is comprised of seven parts, each scripted by a different artist. Richter was responsible for bringing together the contributors, creating the overarching narrative structure, and framing the story. Each episode is not only a personal essay about the individual artist's oeuvre but also a commentary on the film as a medium for artistic expression. The overarching structure provides a historical narrative or archive of the avant-garde and its migration.

In *Dreams That Money Can Buy*, Richter sought not only to provide a record of an artistic movement but also to develop a new mode of aesthetic production. Each film attempts to chart the dreamworld of the unconscious as it is conditioned by the exilic condition. In organizing a historical account of the aims and aspirations of Dada and Surrealism, Richter transformed the notion of the historical document or archive from its written or graphic form to the audiovisual register. His essay film involves not only a geopolitical move from Europe to America but also a transmedial shift from painting and sculpture to film.

Richter's intervention was significant in part because it helped to establish the viability of film as an artistic medium alongside painting, sculpture, and drawing. However, Richter's choice of the essay as a form that includes narrative countered the abstract film experiments that were being produced in North America at the time. These films from the 1960s focused almost exclusively on the materiality of the celluloid medium, championing formal innovation over narrative invention. This was due in no small part to the influence of art critic Clement Greenberg (1909–1994), who argued for purity of medium self-reflexivity in the visual arts. Underscoring this tendency, P. Adams Sitney (1944–) introduced the phrase "structural film" in 1969 to account for this new movement.[10] Structural or materialist film, as it was also known, emphasized the formal (material) qualities of the medium at the expense of content or subject matter.

---

10 P. Adams Sitney, "Structural Film," *Film Culture* 47 (Summer 1969): 1–10.

As Abstract Expressionism dominated the North American art world, the growing wave of protest, political activism, and antiestablishment rebellions that were sweeping the nation seeped into the arts. In the 1960s, new art movements, such as Conceptual Art, challenged formalism. In addition to new lightweight sync cameras, the technology of video – a medium without the burden of a genealogy – entered the scene. The film or video essay as it emerged out of conceptualism was an unrecognized genre and when practiced in video, an unrecognized medium. Video cameras were lightweight, affordable, and easy to use. Years of advanced training and skill were not required, and they were designed for single-person use. The combination of these factors meant video was taken up by those individuals who traditionally had been excluded from art schools, including women, people of color, and others on the margins who were politically engaged and saw artistic practice as part of their social message. This meant that artists began to embed narrative into their films and video – a feature that ran against the tenets of formalism. Their works developed as self-reflexive filmic essays that addressed several topics ranging from the role of art and the artist to the inclusion of poetic or literary texts to explorations of the boundaries of the medium. For example, Robert Smithson's (1938–1973) *Spiral Jetty* (1970) connects the scientific theory of entropy to history and art; Richard Serra (1938–) and Carlota Fay Schoolman's (1950–) *Television Delivers* (1973) offers a scathing critique of the medium of commercial television; Vito Acconci's (1940–2017) *The Red Tapes* (1976) turns inward to examine the "narcissistic" medium of video within the larger context of the artist's subject formation in the changing social, political, and geographic landscape of the 1960s; and Dan Graham's (1942–2022) *Rock My Religion* (1982–84) links contemporary rock music to early American Shaker revivals and rebellion. At the same time, video was embraced by artists and media collectives, such as Videofreex and Paper Tiger, who saw its potential as an alternative medium to create a counter-public sphere.

During the 1970s, numerous female artists, including Joan Jonas (1936–), Dara Birnbaum (1946–), Carolee Schneeman (1939–2019), and Linda Benglis (1941–), began working in video. Veering away from the pure formalism of structuralist film, they introduced elements of narrative. This presence of narrative content, compounded by the secondary status of video as well as the gender of the artists, led to the initial exclusion of these filmmakers from the canon of experimental film. As Jackie Hatfield argues, "the majority of women's practice of the '70s and '80s was marginalized as being narrative and therefore not art (i.e., not coming from the abstract or formal film) and not part of the purism debate."[11] The narratives that structure these video productions are related to a larger political practice that exceeds purely formal concerns and should be considered in concert with feminist filmmakers such as Chantal Akerman (1950–2015), Michelle Citron (1948–), and Sue Friedrich (1954–). Their work ruptures the patriarchal order of the art world, just as their authors' recourse to artistic and experimental forms of film constitutes a break from the male-dominated world of cinema and television documentary production. The artists linked video as a medium with the essay as a form that breaks the rules of the father's house to produce powerful feminist critiques.

For example, dancer and choreographer Yvonne Rainer (1934–), one of the founding members of the Judson Dance Theater, shifted from dance to film in the 1970s as a result of her recognition of the limitations of her own aging body and her growing involvement in feminism. Her first film, *Lives of Performers* (1972), is a documentary that records experimental dance and choreography. She began to practice essayistic filmmaking to address her cognizance of gender issues. In early films such as *Kristina Talking Pictures* (1976), she employed a disjunctive soundtrack in which sounds and images (for example, of men and women) are mismatched to produce a feminist critique. Art school–trained painter and photographer Martha Rosler (1943–) turned to video as a new technology to address her frustration with commercial television's collusion in maintaining patriarchal bourgeois norms and expectations. Her video trilogy, *A Budding Gourmet* (1974), *Semiotics of the Kitchen* (1975), and *The East Is Red and the West Is Bending* (1977), adopted the structure of a cooking show to critique the stultifying power of television as a mass medium. Yet at the time none of these works were recognized as essay films.

Similarly, in the 1980s, African American artist Tony Cokes (1956–), who was trained in sculpture, had difficulty in attaching well-worn categories and labels to his artistic practice. He referred to himself as a "post-conceptual" artist, a term that did not restrict him to norms. Later, as the term *essay film* entered into the art world vocabulary, Cokes called his works video essays. In his montage videos, Cokes assembles text, music, and images to produce politically charged works that address political violence, popular culture, racism, and "evil."[12] Cokes refers to himself as a DJ, and his bites come

---

11 Jackie Hatfield, "Expanded Cinema and Narrative: Some Reasons for a Review of the Avant-Garde Debates around Narrativity," *Millennium Film Journal*, no. 39–40 (Winter 2003): 50–65, 61.

12 Tony Cokes. "Tony Cokes in Dialogue." Artist lecture presented as part of Illuminations: Black Cinematic Artists and Scholars Speaker Series, Temple University and Moore College of Art and Design, Philadelphia, PA, 11 April 2022.

from a vast televisual archive of found footage, quotations from writings, and popular music. One example, *Fade to Black* (1990), is a dense compound mixture that brings together myriad sources circulating in contemporary popular culture to form a critical essay on structural racism in the United States. In *Confession* (1992), words by Catherine Clément and Jacques Attali are interwoven by Kaja Silverman into a text that runs across the screen on which plays a diversity of clips including extracts from Dreyer's *The Passion of Joan of Arc* and *The Ed Sullivan Show*. All the while these images and text are displayed, contemporary rock music is heard on the soundtrack.

As a contemporary essayist, Cokes reacts to immediate events. From 2009 to 2011, he made *Evil.16 (Torture.Musik)* on the use of sound in US torture strategies. For this work, he assembled the musical tracks used by the United States in their sonic torture of prisoners held in Abu Ghraib and elsewhere. And in 2021, in response to the deaths of Black Americans by police, he paired the language of social media and texting to deliver his messages. Cokes's *His Last Words* (2021) comes from the transcription of police bodycam audio of the dying words of Elijah McClain.[13] The repetition of McClain's "I am sorry" matched with the music of Joy Division from the 1980s underscores the tragic repetition of violent acts of racism over the decades. Whether it be textual, mediatic, or musical, true to the written essay quotation is the source of Cokes's essayistic strategy and as such evokes Walter Benjamin's pronouncement: "Quotations in my work are like wayside robbers who leap out, armed, and relieve the idle stroller of his conviction."[14] This strategy recalls recourse to citation as a fundamental practice of the written essay since Montaigne. For his part, Cokes cites an aphorism attributed to Lautréamont: "Plagiarism is necessary. Progress demands it."

Film

Emerging out of the filmmaking world, essay films followed a different trajectory. Some early practitioners of the North American essay film were recent émigrés from Europe, like Jonas Mekas (1922–2019) and Maya Deren (1917–1961). Mekas's film *Lost, Lost, Lost* (1976) is a poetic, diaristic contemplation on the perpetual feeling of unmooredness and dislocation due to the trauma of migration. Mekas was based in New York and traveled in similar

---

13 Elijah McClain was a twenty-three-year-old African American who died due to the violent use of a chokehold by police in August 2019.
14 Walter Benjamin, "Hardware," in *One Way Street* (1928), ed. Michael Jennings (Cambridge, MA: Harvard University Press, 2016), 84.

circles as Richter. Like Richter, he was actively involved in promoting an avant-garde film scene and regularly programmed and curated film series of alternative works and European art cinema. For her part, Deren relocated from Ukraine to the West Coast. Deren's *Meshes in the Afternoon* (1943) is a meditation on rhythm, repetition, and replay through the lens of psychoanalytic concepts of trauma and compulsion. In both *A Study in Choreography for the Camera* (1945) and *Ritual in Transfigured Time* (1946), Deren explores the boundaries of filming the human body in movement and compares the time-based media of film and dance. Other essay filmmakers from that era, including Kenneth Anger (1927–), who was raised in Hollywood, highlight homoeroticism and homosexuality in the filmic milieu of Hollywood in contrast to the artificial heteronormative images presented to mainstream audiences. Anger's works critique the hypocrisy of censorship, and his first film, *Fireworks* (1947), draws parallels between the military and the dream factory, suggesting that both seek to repress desire. *Puce Moment* (1949) is an ode to the desire for clothes and costuming and performance. In the 1960s, Anger was part of gay American subculture, and films like *Scorpio Rising* (1963) and *Kustom Kar Kommandos* (1965) address queer culture and the machismo fetish culture attached to motorcycles and cars. Like Cokes, Anger is particularly attuned to how pop songs such as "Dream Lover," when matched against certain images, can transform both the song and the image. Moving in the same circles as Anger, Jack Smith (1932–1989) explored the world of extravagant performers such as Mario Montez. Smith's *Flaming Creatures* (1963) is a hybrid essay that brings together a theater of the burlesque, film, dance, and music to celebrate kitsch celebrity and underground film sexuality and gender. Against this backdrop, Andy Warhol's (1928–1987) film experiments may be taken as meditative essays that contemplate the borders of the medium. The employment of the essay film to explore sexuality and gender continued throughout the twentieth century with added layers complicated by race, such as in Marlon Riggs's (1957–1994) *Tongues Untied* (1989), as well as by the AIDS crisis, as in the collaborative omnibus film *Silence=Death* (1990) and Gregg Bordowitz's (1964–) *Fast Trip, Long Drop* (1993). The essay film as a genre thus addresses difficult topics that are outside of convention and tradition.

As in Europe, the American essay film was also taken up by mainstream directors, such as Orson Welles (1915–1985). Welles's *F for Fake* (1973) plays with the audience's belief in the veracity of the filmic medium to deliver an indexical truth. Welles delivers a quasi-mockumentary that unsettles preestablished codes and conventions that determine how we receive images: as true or fake. A few years later, in *Filming Othello* (1978), Welles continued along this vein and deconstructed the process of filmmaking, revealing hidden secrets and tricks of the trade that are used to produce the grand illusions for the silver screen. However, unlike a documentary, in the essay film unstable elements, uncertainty, and questioning are sometimes put forth. Welles is one of many directors who used the essay form as a mode of investigation and experimentation into the filmic medium. What is striking is the delay in critical reception and identification of these practices. For example, it was not until 2009 that Robert Gardner's (1925–2014) *Dead Birds* (1963) was recognized as an essay film.[15] US scholars and critics only began to use the term in the early 1990s. One early mention was Jonathan Rosenbaum's 1991 review of Welles's *Filming Othello*, which begins with a provocative discussion of the film's essayistic qualities:

> Two propositions:
> 1. One of the most progressive forms of cinema is the film in which fiction and nonfiction merge, trade places, become interchangeable.
> 2. One of the most reactionary forms of cinema is the film in which fiction and nonfiction merge, trade places, become interchangeable.[16]

Rosenbaum's characterization of the essay film as potentially both progressive and reactionary is particularly relevant today, when the essay film has become a prevalent genre employed by many filmmakers and artists regardless of their political commitments. Piggybacking on Rosenbaum's review, film critic Phillip Lopate sought, in "In Search of the Centaur: The Essay Film" (1992), "to define, describe, survey and celebrate a cinematic genre that barely exists."[17] Unlike Rosenbaum, whose review does not provide a definition of the essay film, rigid Lopate insists on specific qualities and characteristics that the genre must include: "[I]t must have words"; "the text must represent a single voice"; it "must have a strong personal point of view"; and finally, it "should be as eloquent, well-written and interesting as

---

[15] See Charles Musser's "First Encounters: An Essay on *Dead Birds* and Robert Garner," in *Looking with Robert Garner*, ed. Rebecca Meyers, William Rothman, and Charles Warren (Albany, NY: State University of New York Press, 2016), 143–70.

[16] Jonathan Rosenbaum, "Orson Welles's Essay Films and Documentary Fictions: A Two-Part Speculation," *Cinematograph* 4 (1991), reprinted in *Placing Movies: The Practice of Film Criticism* (Berkeley: University of California Press, 1995), 171–83, 173–74.

[17] Phillip Lopate, "In Search of the Centaur: The Essay Film," in Alter and Corrigan, *Essays on the Essay Film*, 109.

possible."[18] Lopate focuses on European film essayists such as Jean-Luc Godard (1930–2022), Chris Marker (1921–2012), and Alain Resnais (1922–2014) and asserts that North American filmmakers did not take up the genre with any regularity until the 1980s. In addition to Welles and Rainer, Lopate singles out Ralph Arlyck's (1940–) *An Acquired Taste* (1981), Su Friedrich's (1954–) *The Ties That Bind* (1984), Ross McElwee's *Sherman's March* (1986), and Michael Moore's *Roger and Me* (1989). At the same time, academic film scholars such as Michael Renov and Timothy Corrigan started to address the genre at academic conferences. Noteworthy, though, is their uniform lack of awareness not only of artists and underground cinema practitioners of the essay film but also their blind spot to another community of essay filmmakers.

At roughly the same time that Rosenbaum and Lopate were penning their remarks on the American essay film, Manthia Diawara published *Black American Cinema* (1993). Beginning in the 1970s, Diawara identifies the emergence of a new Black independent cinema. In part to explain its significance and "its influence on the mainstream cinema," he remarks that "the French appropriately refer to independent cinema as *cinema d'art et essai*." Diawara states that the *cinema d'art et essai*'s "main emphasis [is] towards artistic development, documenting an area of research, and delineating a certain philosophy of the world."[19] He locates the beginning of this genre with Melvin van Peebles's (1932–2021) *Sweet Sweetback's Baadasssss Song* (1971) and traces its uneven development to a group of Black filmmakers who studied at UCLA's Department of Theater, Film, and Television in the 1970s and '80s. Known as the LA Rebellion, they included Camille Billops (1933–2019), Charles Burnett (1944–), Larry Clark (1943–), Julie Dash (1952–), Haile Gerima (1946–), Billy Woodberry (1950–), and others. Their films are marked not only by radical politics that openly questioned dominant historical narratives but also by a new form of aesthetic expression that challenged the hegemony of Hollywood-style filmmaking.[20] LA Rebellion filmmakers produced a rich and varied corpus of films that challenged racism from both thematic and formal perspectives. This included mixing fact and fiction,

---

18 Lopate, "In Search," 111–13.
19 Manthia Diawara, "Black American Cinema: The New Realism," in *Critical Visions in Film Theory*, ed. Timothy Corrigan, Patricia White, and Meta Mazaj (Boston: Bedford / St. Martins, 2011), 594–609, 597.
20 For an analysis of the aesthetic component of LA Rebellion films, see Franklin Cason, "The Souls of Black Film: Art and Politics" (PhD diss., University of Florida, 2010). For an institutional history of the formation of Black filmmaking at UCLA, see Zeinabu Irene Davis's documentary *Spirits of Rebellion: Black Film at UCLA* (2015).

disjunctive and contradictory soundtracks, odd camera angles and focus, film speed, and self-reflexive addresses to the audience. Burnett's *Killer of Sheep* (1978), Gerima's *Bush Mama* (1979), Dash's *Daughters of the Dust* (1991), and later Billops and Jim Hatch's *The KKK Boutique Ain't Just Rednecks* (1994) are all essay films that use the genre to address and provide counterimages and representations of Black life to those provided by white media.

The style of LA rebellion films has been likened to a mixture of Italian neorealism and Third Cinema, both of which have been acknowledged as essayistic.[21] Ethiopian-born American scholar Teshome H. Gabriel's (1939–2010) 1979 doctoral dissertation, "Third Cinema in the Third World: The Aesthetics of Liberation," was the first comprehensive English-language history of Third Cinema. Published in book form in 1982, it circulated widely in North America, Great Britain, and parts of Africa.[22] One of the propositions of the founders of Third Cinema was that practitioners disregard Hollywood genre conventions and instead adopt new cinematic forms, including that of the essay and manifesto. In his study, Gabriel did more than chronicle the formation of Third Cinema as it developed in Latin America; he extended its principles and theories to include diverse practices of emergent cinema around the globe, including in Africa and the United States. As a professor of film studies at UCLA, Gabriel mentored the generation of filmmakers who formed the core of Black independent cinema.

Gabriel further reflected on Third Cinema in "Third Cinema as Guardian of Popular Memory" (1989). There he stressed the significance of popular memory as an invaluable counter-narrative to official history. Echoing Benjamin's "Theses on the Philosophy of History," Gabriel views history as a phenomenon based primarily on the written accounts of the powerful. Dominant historical accounts, he argues, "claim a 'centre' which continuously marginalises others .... [Their] ideology inhibits people from constructing their own history or histories."[23] By contrast, "for popular memory, there are no longer any 'centres' or 'margins,' since the very designations imply that something has been conveniently left out .... Popular memory ... is a 'look

---

21 See Jaques Rivette, "Letter on Rosellini," in *Cahiers du Cinéma: The 1950s: Neo-Realism, Hollywood, New Wave*, ed. Jim Hillier (Cambridge, MA: Harvard University Press, 1985), 192–204; and Nora M. Alter, *The Essay Film after Fact and Fiction*, especially chapter 6, "New Migrations: Third Cinema and The Essay Film," 239–88.
22 Teshome H. Gabriel, *Third Cinema in the Third World: The Aesthetics of Liberation* (Ann Arbor, MI: UMI, 1982), xi.
23 Teshome H. Gabriel, "Third Cinema as Guardian of Popular Memory: Towards a Third Aesthetics," in *Questions of Third Cinema*, ed. Jim Pines and Paul Willemen (London: BFI, 1989), 53–64, 53.

back to the future,' necessarily dissident and partisan, wedded to constant change."[24] Gabriel asserted that Third Cinema emerged from popular memory, whereas "cinemas of the system" represent official history.[25] Whereas "official history" is expressed formally in the documentary genre, popular memory, which is not necessarily rooted in fact, may include fictional moments and interludes. Because it often confronts or is in dialogue with "official history," the result is often a hybrid essay that freely mixes fact and fiction, objective records, and subjective interpretations.

Under the mentorship of Gabriel, the filmmakers who attended UCLA were encouraged to experiment both formally and thematically. The result was a new aesthetic that called into question conventions in filmmaking – white norms and values made for a white public – that dominated the film industry. In particular, the filmmakers reconfigured Classic Hollywood configurations of time and space, which corresponded to a different understanding of personal and public history. As noted by Diawara, "[t]hese films are concerned with the specific of identity, the empowerment of Black people through mise-en-scène and the rewriting of American history. Their narrative contains rhythmic and repetitious shots, going back and forth between the past and the present."[26] Like the essay that does not follow a clear linear development but instead meanders freely and often circles back on itself, the narratives produced in these films defy conventional logic. For example, *Bush Mama* is constructed both through a series of flashbacks and flashforwards. The film's remarkable opening sequence begins in medias res with a jumble of seemingly disconnected sequences whose chronology is only apparent after viewing the entire film. Adding further to the confusion is the disjunctive soundtrack that seems to be disconnected from the images. The story unfolds partially from the interior dialogue and memories of the protagonist, Dorothy, but also externally from those around her. *Bush Mama* is about being Black and poor in Los Angeles in the 1970s; it is about welfare and administrative bureaucracies, unplanned pregnancies, Black-on-Black crime, police harassment, PTSD, and the legacy of the Vietnam War. Documentary footage (both images and audial) is interwoven with fictional creations. In one sequence, police attempt to arrest some members of Gerima's filmmaking crew (for the trespass of being Black while filming), an event that is filmed by other members of the crew from the set's apartment window. *Bush Mama* is elliptical; sequences and individual shots recur, rhythmically organized

---

24 Gabriel, "Third Cinema," 53–54.   25 Gabriel, "Third Cinema," 55.
26 Diawara, "Black American Cinema," 601.

according to a musical score. In the beginning, the camera tracks Dorothy's long barefoot trek after she has had her purse snatched by a youth. She walks along the sidewalk, weaving through passersby, passing storefronts as her high-heeled shoes – the focus of the camera – dangle in her hand. The camera cuts away at brief instances but is drawn back and returns to that image of swinging shoes. The soundtrack is a jumble of different voices going through Dorothy's mind, soundbites from her encounters over the past twenty-four hours in the welfare office, conversations with her daughter, incidents at a bank, police sirens, and memories from the past. The swinging of the shoes in rhythm with her stride produces an almost metronymic beat that paces the film according to its own time. The effect underscores Dorothy's isolation and alienation. A parallel sequence occurs later in the film when Dorothy's partner, T. C., is incarcerated. Through an extended tracking shot, Gerima depicts his journey from the outside world as he advances through a long cell-lined corridor. The almost abstract pattern of bars reinforces his physical and mental separation from his family and community. Gerima produces a cinematic effect of *ostranenie* – a new perspective or way of seeing – that is a characteristic of the essay film.

An extraterritorial space is the main location for Billops and Hatch's *The KKK Boutique*, in which the filmmakers imagine a crude funhouse set containing a series of chambers in which various acts of racism unfold. Reminiscent of Jean Genet's *The Balcony* (1954), the self-reflexive film foregrounds the performative nature of racism – its learned and acquired patterns of repetition. Billops and Hatch directly address the camera and foreground their collaborations as an interracial couple. *The KKK Boutique* discloses and provides insights into desires and fantasies motivating racism, which discomfortingly are not relegated only to white players but manifest in Black protagonists as well. The viewer is positioned as both spectator and participant. The staged quality continuously draws attention to its constructed nature, recalling the structure of Bertolt Brecht's learning plays, which have served as models for a variety of essay films.

A different strategy affecting time and space is at play in Dash's *Daughters of the Dust*. In this instance, manipulations of Aristotelian codes unifying time, action, and place are distorted and discarded. However, unlike *Bush Mama*, the tactic in *Daughters of the Dust* aims to amplify and enhance community and build strong connections between individuals and their environment. Shot in color, stunning imagery celebrates the beauty of the Black subjects and the natural landscape of Ibo Landing, located on a barrier island off the coast of Georgia (St. Simons today). During the eighteenth and nineteenth centuries, the island was populated by formerly enslaved peoples who lived there in relative isolation. Close-knit communities were formed that retained their Creole language, Gullah, a mixture of several West African dialects. Through meticulous archival research, Dash has her characters communicate both in Gullah and English, thereby adding a further layer of creolization to the soundtrack. *Daughters of Dust* centers on a final family feast and celebration in 1902, commemorating the departure of most members of the diasporic community who will migrate north. Dash reimagines what such a scene of parting would have been like, replete with the anxiety forecast by a second rupture and severing of connections to Africa that were still present on the island. There are three generations of the Peazants family, and a fourth is imagined as the voice of an unborn child who narrates from an as yet unrealized future space. Dash's narrative strategy recalls Saidaya Hartman's theory of fabulation. Hartman explains that in fabulation, she plays with and rearranges "the basic elements of the story, by representing the sequence of events in divergent stories and from contested points of view." In so doing she jeopardizes "the status of the event, to displace the received or authorized account, and to imagine what might have happened or might have been said or might have been done."[27] As Tina Campt asserts in her discussion of Black photography, fabulation extends beyond the narrative and may be rendered through the Black body, in what she refers to as *"Black countergravity"*: "Black countergravity defies the physics of anti-blackness that has historically exerted a negating force aimed at expunging Black life."[28] The visual representation of the characters in *Daughters of the Dust* is stunning. The effect is not just to make this peripheral community beautiful, but also to conceive of a future marked by possibility. Toni Cade Bambara observes, "The camera moves through, maintaining crisp focus, and approaches the children, except that the frame rate has slowed, just enough for us to register that the children are the future. For a split second, we seem to go beyond time to a realm where children are eternally valid, are eternally the reason for right action."[29] Like the essay, *Daughters of the Dust* is a formal and thematic creolization of multiple genres, of fact and fiction.

Arthur Jafa (1960–), the cinematographer for *Daughters of the Dust*, produced this extraordinary effect in part by altering time and defying the industry norm that dictated film speed at twenty-four frames per second to

---

27 Saidiya Hartman, "Venus in Two Acts," *Small Axe* 26 (2008): 1–14, 11.
28 Tina Campt, *A Black Gaze* (Cambridge, MA: MIT Press, 2021), 47. Original emphasis.
29 Toni Cade Bambara, "Reading the Signs: Empowering the Eye: Daughters of Dust and the Black Independent Cinema Movement," in Corrigan, White, and Mazaj, *Critical Visions in Film Theory*, 871–86, 883.

produce the optimum illusion of reality.[30] Jafa explains: "Irregular, non-tempered, non-metronomic camera rates and frames ... prompt filmic movement to function in a manner that approximates Black vocal intonation. Utilizing what I term alignment patterns, which are simply a series of fixed frame replication patterns ... the visual equivalent of vibrato, rhythmic patterns slurred or bent notes, and other musical effects are possible in film."[31] Jafa is drawing on a tradition in Black music that seeks to unsettle and disrupt centuries of prescribed white beats and rhythms. Bambara underscores this point: "In the early forties, when Dizzy Gillespie announced that 3/4 and 4/4 time signatures were not adequate for rendering the Black experience, Bebop was ushered in.... It came to overhaul the tenets of Black improvisational music-making and music listening."[32] By translating structures of musical innovations and tactics of improvisation to a visual regime, Jafa and Dash provide a different way of seeing; a counter-cinema that opens up alternative histories and futures. More recently, Jafa's media essays, including *Love Is the Message, The Message Is Death* (2016) and *The White Album* (2019), use sound, noise, and music as architectural structures upon which layers of racism and violence are hung. As observed by Richard Wright, "jazz music has been called time and again by many critics the greatest surrealistic music ever heard in human history ... jazz music proceeds on the basis of a steady beat in the bass and then there is an endless series of improvised, tone-colored melodies carried on in terms of rhythm."[33] The connection between surrealism and jazz is fruitful when one recalls that essay filmmakers such as Alberto Cavalcanti (1897–1992), Chris Marker, and Humphrey Jennings (1907–1950) were close to the surrealists. In addition to jazz, the sonic provides alternative perceptions and allows for a different sort of thinking. Sound opens onto an elsewhere. Recall Robeson's voiceover commentary in *Native Son*, his signature baritone, the grain of his voice, added an invisible layer of critique and meaning that could only be heard and not seen. And an integral feature of the essay film from the beginning has been its aural component. Even before sound sync recording, musical structures and rhythms were mobilized to supplement meaning.

30 *Daughters of Dust* won Sundance's best cinematography award. After his role in filming *Daughters of Dust*, Arthur Jafa Fiedler dropped Fiedler from his name and is now known as Arthur Jafa or "AJ."
31 Arthur Jafa, "69," in *Black Popular Culture: A Project by Michelle Wallace*, ed. Gina Dent (Seattle: Bay Press, 1992), 254.
32 Bambara, "Reading the Signs," 881.
33 Richard Wright, "Memories of My Grandmother," in *The Man Who Lived Underground* (New York: Penguin Random House, 2021), 163–201, 187.

The impact of LA Rebellion filmmakers in transforming the shape of Black Cinema and in adopting the genre of the essay into their practice cannot be understated. Not only do artist filmmakers Cokes and Jafa continue to make works today, but a second generation, as represented by figures like Khalil Joseph, continues the project. Joseph's *BLKNWS* (2019), which he refers to as "conceptual journalism," is an intermix of current events accessed from the Internet. Whereas the essay film in the United States developed in three separate fields of production (art, documentary, and film), contemporary essay films such as *I Am Not Your Negro* (2016) constitute hybrid practices that do not differentiate or distinguish their genealogical roots. In the new millennium, such disciplinary boundaries and borders are porous, as documentarians such as Laura Poitras (1964–) make essay films alongside filmmakers like Raoul Peck (1953–) and artists like Kevin B. Lee (1975–). Additionally, changes in media and exhibition platforms have had a significant impact on the essay film. "Desktop cinema," which is also referred to as "computer screen film," begins with the premise that increasingly the world is experienced and accessed through computer screens and networked interfaces. In the words of Lee, the computer screen functions as "both a camera lens and a canvas." For Lee, video essays become a "means of thinking about media, through media."[34] Sounds, images, and texts are generated, gathered, assembled, and distributed through the home computer. All production is now postproduction. Today, the essay film constitutes an established practice, one that in its most progressive form provides, in the words of Bambara, "a space of contestation, a liberated zone in which to build a cinema for social change."[35] The increased presence of the essay film results in a revisioning of cinematic history that draws attention to its omissions and blind spots.

---

34 See Lee's website, *alsolikelife*, on both "desktop cinema" and "video essays": *alsolikelife*, www.alsolikelife.com/home/video-essays. It is interesting to note that recently, Lee, like other practitioners including Hito Steyerl, has moved away from the term *essay* and has resuscitated the term *documentary*. As he explains, "[a]t its best, desktop cinema not only depicts screen-based experience, but critically reflects on it. To date, this potential has been most fully realized through the form of **desktop documentary**. If the documentary genre is meant to capture life's reality, then desktop recording acknowledges that computer screens are now a primary mode of daily experience through an always-on network of audiovisual data. Desktop documentary seeks to both depict and question the ways we explore the world through the computer screen." Kevin B. Lee, "Desktop Films," *alsolikelife*, www.alsolikelife.com/home/desktop-films. Italics and boldface in original.

35 Bambara, "Reading the Signs," 883.

32

Literary Theory, Criticism, and the Essay

CAROLINA IRIBARREN

Poised at the intersection of more than one formal antinomy – between the scientific and the poetic, the conventional and the experimental, the scholarly and the amateurish, the belletristic and the militant, the object-oriented and the self-reflexive, the linear and the perspectivist, and so on and so forth – the essay has justly been the subject of much discussion among American theorists and critics since the consolidation of literary studies in the postwar period. Ever within the purview of literary theory and criticism, the essay has not always elicited consensus or acclaim in the United States, however; far from it. In tandem with the institutional twists and theoretical turns of literary studies itself, the essay has seen a cycle of booms and busts (or "supposed deaths and rebirths," according to Mario Aquilina) over the past century which has rendered its definition and value as a cultural artifact uncertain.[1] As Claire de Obaldia explains, "the essay's potential contribution to literature is dependent upon the arbitrary criteria of value that determine canons . . ., so that like other forms of its kind, the essay is likely to appear on one or the other side of the literary margin according to the period."[2] Thus, in their epochal *Theory of Literature* (1949), New Critics René Wellek and Austin Warren recognize the importance of the essay in the history of literature – especially where such writers as Montaigne, Pascal, Emerson, and Nietzsche are concerned – but not without expressing strong reservations about the genre's "intellectualist" impulse: that is, its patent (and apparently extraliterary) concern with ideas

---

[1] Mario Aquilina, ed., *The Essay at the Limits: Poetics, Politics and Form* (London: Bloomsbury, 2021), 11. In this vein, Alastair Fowler remarks on the unique "ambiguity of literary status" that the essay boasts as a genre. Alastair Fowler, *Kinds of Literature: An Introduction to the Theory of Genres and Modes* (Oxford: Clarendon, 1982), 11.
[2] Claire de Obaldia, *The Essayistic Spirit: Literature, Modern Criticism and the Essay* (Oxford: Clarendon, 1996), 4–5.

and "ideology."[3] Meanwhile, in his poststructuralist classic *The Barthes Effect: The Essay as Reflective Text* (1987), Réda Bensmaïa (quoting Blanchot) underscores the essay's built-in "fragmentary exigency," as well as its tendency to "proliferat[e] the 'centers' of enunciation and ... their fundamental heterogeneity," before unabashedly declaring the genre "literature in its own right."[4] This chapter takes stock of the various definitions and valuations the essay has accrued over the course of the history of American literary theory and criticism. Starting with the historical-materialist criticism of the Great Depression era and moving on to the New Criticism of the 1940s and '50s, then delving into the myriad structuralisms and poststructuralisms of the Cold War and postcommunist eras, before concluding with contemporary critical trends, it tracks the discipline's trajectory in the American context, all the while zeroing in on the essay's shifting position therein. Though necessarily reductive and inexhaustive, the present chapter fulfills at least two aims: First, it throws into relief the fundamental dialectic between hermetic formalism and committed social criticism that has shaped literary studies in the United States since its rise early in the twentieth century; and second, it teases out the way this perennial vacillation has rendered more or less appealing, more or less useful the essay as a form and object of analysis. What follows, then, is a historical sketch of an inadvertently dialectical tradition and its relation to an inherently dialectical form.

The Red Dawn

That socialism, if not full-blooded communism, should lie at the origin of any important institution in the United States is bound to sound unlikely. As Michael Denning points out, the country possesses an "uniquely un-marxist character," which has long influenced not only its economic policies (against corporate regulation, workers' unionization, progressive taxation, universal health care, etc.) but also its orientation, consumptive as well as analytic, to culture: what Fredric Jameson has referred to as the "old American tradition of anti-intellectualism or know-nothingism, which [has] simply replicated the general attitude of a business society to culture generally."[5] Yet, abnormal

---

3 René Wellek and Austin Warren, *Theory of Literature* (New York: Harcourt, Brace, 1949), 112.
4 Réda Bensmaïa, *The Barthes Effect: The Essay as Reflective Text*, trans. Pat Fedkiew (Minneapolis: University of Minnesota Press, 1987), xxiii, 53, 36.
5 Michael Denning, "'The Special American Conditions': Marxism and American Studies," *American Quarterly* 38, no. 3 (1986): 356–80, 362; Fredric Jameson, *Jameson on Jameson: Conversations on Cultural Marxism*, ed. Ian Buchanan (Durham, NC: Duke University Press, 2007), 14.

though it may be, that precisely is the case of American criticism and theory, whose beginnings happen to be inseparable from a distinctly revolutionary fervor. "[T]he central fact in American life is the class struggle," writes self-proclaimed Marxian analyst Granville Hicks (1901–1982) in his enormously influential *The Great Tradition: An Interpretation of American Literature since the Civil War* (1933). He elaborates:

> Not every writer can make the choice that his ideals demand, but many can and will break the ties that bind them to the bourgeoisie, and give their support to the class that is able to overthrow capitalism. ... For they will know that what is struggling for utterance on their pages is the spirit, not of an isolated individual, not of some literary clique, not of some decadent tradition, but the spirit of that class with which the future rests.[6]

How much of this zeal, this twofold commitment to the proletariat and to the revolution to come, was homegrown and how much of it was imported wholesale from Europe remains a matter of contentious debate among specialists. What is certain is that such pioneering critics as Hicks, V. F. Calverton (1900–1940), James T. Farrell (1904–1979), Bernard Smith (1907–1999), and *Partisan Review* founders William Phillips (1907–2002) and Philip Rahv (1908–1973), all based in cities along the East Coast and working outside academic institutions, practiced what in hindsight can only be described as a historical materialist analysis of literature built on the orthodox Marxist model.

What this means first of all is that, for these early literary critics, the notion that aesthetic forms not only have a bearing on but are fully determined by the social and economic forces operating around them was paramount. "I believe that aesthetic criticism is fundamentally social in character, and can only be significant when derived from a sound social philosophy," writes Calverton in his pathbreaking *The Liberation of American Literature* (1932). Without an understanding of "the development of American literature in relationship with those [socioeconomic] forces, expressed in the form of class content," he adds, "all analysis of the aesthetic element can amount to nothing more than subjective caprice."[7] The belief that literary works are if not reducible at least essentially bound to the material conditions of their production led pioneering American critics to experiment with historically

---

6 Granville Hicks, *The Great Tradition: An Interpretation of American Literature since the Civil War* (New York: Macmillan, 1933), 304, 306.
7 V. F. Calverton, *The Liberation of American Literature* (New York: Charles Scribner's Sons, 1932), xii–xiii.

and sociologically charged forms of committed – that is, politically conscious – criticism. Soon to be disparaged as "extrinsic" and "ideological" by the apolitical (when not archconservative) New Critics, this original method of interpretation concentrated on contextualizing through historical research and demystifying by dint of class analysis works of literature already deemed canonical or "classic." The idea, as Farrell explains, was to "uncover points of the social and economic origin of aesthetic standards," to "understand ... the uneven and irregular ... development of ideology" as it manifests in aesthetic production and experience.[8] Such a strong preoccupation with the literary work's social character, its embeddedness in and indebtedness to the conflicts and contradictions of everyday life, drove Marxist critics to overemphasize at times the "functional" side of literature at the expense of formal consideration. Interested in how literary works acted both as indices of present social configurations and as "weapons" in the class struggle for an equitable society – in other words, interested in the incommensurability or asymmetry that seems to preside over the relationship between art and politics – they often neglected to take into account such "esthetic principles" as atmosphere, tone, and style in their analyses. The result, as Smith himself regretted, was that "[w]hile [Marxian literary theory] could throw light on the nature of whole and movements, it could rarely illuminate the distinctive quality of a single work," disposed as it was toward "the mechanical linking of literary ideas to economic phenomena."[9]

Insofar as the essay as a genre is concerned, "the red decade," as Daniel Aaron dubbed in retrospect this era of unprecedented leftist literary critical activity in the United States, was also for the most part patchy, if less tendentiously so.[10] The fact is that the essay as such is not discussed in any of the major works of the period. The most form-attuned remark that Calverton makes apropos of Emerson qua essayist in his *Liberation of American Literature* is, for instance, that he "fashion[ed] his sentences in the manner of an American Carlyle," and this despite devoting a number of pages to discussing the writer's essays (at least in terms of their content and context).[11] Hicks's *Great Tradition* boasts an even greater lacuna in this regard, privileging as it does postbellum works of fiction as objects of analysis.

---

8 James T. Farrell, *A Note on Literary Criticism* (New York: Vanguard Press, 1936), 38, 63.
9 Bernard Smith, *Forces in American Criticism: A Study in the History of American Literary Thought* (New York: Harcourt, Brace, 1939), 288.
10 See Daniel Aaron, *Writers on the Left: Episodes in American Literary Communism* (New York: Columbia University Press, 1992).
11 Calverton, *Liberation of American Literature*, 284.

Though an overt book-length argument against the reduction of form to content, Smith's *Forces in American Criticism* likewise neglects the genre, save where it is a matter of identifying specific instantiations thereof ("In the essay on the 'Celebration of Intellect' [Emerson] was marvelously eloquent in defending immediate realities as poetic themes . . . ").[12] Were 1930s critics, with their "theocratic" adherence to communism, their "clear, logical, and cold" style of writing, their disinclination toward "independent speculation" and "original thinking," then as profoundly unessayistic as Malcolm Cowley suggests in his proleptic insider's account of the decade *And I Worked at the Writer's Trade* (1978)?[13] Glaring though the absence of discussions of the essay as form may be, it would be a mistake to conclude from this that American criticism was at its inception indifferent to the genre. As the two most salient magazines of the time – Phillips and Rahv's *Partisan Review* (founded in New York in 1934) and Max Eastman (1883–1969), Mike Gold (1894–1967), and Hicks's *New Masses* (launched in New York in 1926) – put in evidence issue after issue through their emphasis on the "scheme of lived experience" as well as "the *process* of judging" ("value-determining" characteristics of the essayist according to contemporaneous Hungarian Marxist literary theorist Georg Lukács), early American critics were actually partisans of the essay.[14] Theirs, however, was not a theoretical endorsement, but rather a practical one, a lived commitment to the form.

Criticism, Inc.

From the historical materialist perspective, the rise of New Criticism as the dominant school of literary thought in the United States from the late 1930s to the 1950s represents a regressive, if not aberrant, chapter in the history of the discipline. This is not surprising. The New Critics were in nearly every respect the antithesis of early Marxist critics. Indeed, under the aegis of elite higher education institutions such as Vanderbilt, Yale, and Kenyon, these self-styled "reactionary" scholars explicitly eschewed historically situated, socially oriented, and politically committed criticism in favor of immanent modes of analysis centered exclusively on poetic form and textual

---

12 Smith, *Forces in American Criticism*, 110.
13 Malcolm Cowley, *And I Worked at the Writer's Trade: Chapters of Literary History, 1918–1978* (New York: Viking, 1978), 145–47.
14 Georg Lukács, "On the Nature and Form of the Essay," in *Essays on the Essay Film*, ed. Nora M. Alter and Timothy Corrigan (New York: Columbia University Press, 2017), 21–40, 29, 40. My emphasis.

structure.[15] Theirs, in other words, was a hermeneutic program carried out, not in the public-facing pages of the literary magazine, but behind the departmental office's shut doors and designed to exalt the autonomy and quasi-sacred nature of the poetic artifact, all the while insisting on the privileged status of the critic, now reimagined as a business executive. "Rather than occasional criticism by amateurs," John Crowe Ransom (1888–1974), one of the movement's founding figures, proposes in a pivotal article, "I should think the whole enterprise might be seriously taken in hand by professionals. ... I have the idea that what need is Criticism, Inc., or Criticism, Ltd."[16] In the end, it was through the geographically dispersed but ideologically concordant efforts of literary experts like Ransom, Austin Warren (1899–1986), Allen Tate (1899–1979), René Wellek (1903–1995), R. P. Blackmur (1904–1965), Cleanth Brooks (1906–1994), and W. K. Wimsatt (1907–1975) that this decidedly anti-Marxist vision of literary studies took hold of the American academy in the years following the Great Depression, thereby definitively displacing the discipline's red pioneers.

Methodologically speaking, the New Critics' hermeneutic program consisted in an especially close and totalizing kind of close reading. Their objective, as Blackmur explains, was to stick as tightly as possible to the text and nothing but the text: "[T]he literary critic aesthetics comprises the study of superficial and mechanical executive techniques, partly in themselves, but also and mainly in relation to the ulterior techniques of conceptual form and of symbolic form."[17] In other words, the scrutiny of form "on the plane of words and ... linguistics ..., on the plane of intellectual and emotional patterns" – form, that is, divorced from its historical, material, social conditions of production – constituted the warp and woof of the "critic's job of work."[18] Buttressed by a fundamentalist belief in "the principle of unity," that is, the structural "equilibrium" based on "the working out of the various tensions – set up by

---

15 cf. Allen Tate, *Reactionary Essays on Poetry and Ideas* (Freeport, NY: Books for Libraries Press, 1968).
16 John Crowe Ransom, "Criticism, Inc.," *Virginia Quarterly Review* 13, no. 4 (Autumn 1937), www.vqronline.org/essay/criticism-inc.
17 R. P. Blackmur, "A Burden for Critics," *Hudson Review* 1, no. 2 (Summer 1948): 170–85, 182.
18 R. P. Blackmur, "A Critic's Job of Work," in *Language as Gesture: Essays in Poetry* (New York: Harcourt, Brace, 1952), 396. In its tendency toward ahistorical formalism as well as its aspiration to institutional entrenchment, New Criticism overlapped with another movement active – though to far less success – at the same time: the Chicago School of Criticism, as represented by the likes of R. S. Crane (1886–1967), Richard McKeon (1900–1985), and Elder Olson (1909–1992). See Vincent B. Leitch, "The Chicago School," in *American Literary Criticism since the 1930s* (London: Routledge, 2010), 52–69.

whatever means – by propositions, metaphors, symbols" inherent to all "great literature," New Criticism's formalist poetics not surprisingly led its proponents to prioritize poetry, especially the self-consciously complex poetry of high modernists such as T. S. Eliot and W. B. Yeats, in their analyses.[19] This generic bias is readily discernible from the movement's leading publications: consider Brooks's *Modern Poetry and the Tradition* (1939), his *Well Wrought Urn: Studies in the Structure of Poetry* (1947), Tate's *On the Limits of Poetry* (1948), Blackmur's *Form and Value in Modern Poetry* (1952) as well as his *Language as Gesture: Essays in Poetry* (1952), Wimsatt's *The Verbal Icon: Studies in the Meaning of Poetry* (1954), and Murray Krieger's *The New Apologists for Poetry* (1956), to name but a few of the manifold studies and theories of poetry produced in the name of New Criticism.

Thus concerned with the "unification of attitudes into a hierarchy subordinated to a total and governing attitude," with "life at the remove of form and meaning; not life lived but life framed and identified" (Brooks's and Blackmur's definitions of poetry, respectively), the New Critics naturally did not much value loose prosaic forms such as the essay in theory or in practice.[20] The most dedicated treatment the genre receives is to be found in Wellek and Warren's magisterial *Theory of Literature* (1948), where together with biography and "much rhetorical literature" it is deemed a "transitional form" and where an essayistic ("as distinct from lyric") narrative mode is identified and, sure enough, coolly dismissed.[21] Though startling in its bluntness, this snubbing of the essay, and really of any literary form resistant to structural and ideological closure, is perfectly consistent with the New Critical program. Terry Eagleton summarizes this approach:

> The literary text, for American New Criticism ..., was ... grasped in what might be called "functionalist" terms: just as American functionalist sociology developed a "conflict-free" model of society, in which every element "adapted" to every other, so the poem abolished all friction, irregularity and contradiction in the symmetrical cooperation of its various features. "Coherence" and "integration" were the keynotes.[22]

Little wonder, then, that the essay did not flourish in the hands of the New Critics.

---

19 Cleanth Brooks, "The Heresy of Paraphrase," in *The Well Wrought Urn: Studies in the Structure of Poetry* (New York: Harcourt, Brace, 1947), 176–96, 189.
20 Cleanth Brooks, *The Well Wrought Urn: Studies in the Structure of Poetry* (London: Dennis Dobson, 1949), 189; Blackmur, "Critic's Job of Work," 372.
21 Wellek and Warren, *Theory of Literature*, 14, 223.
22 Terry Eagleton, *Literary Theory: An Introduction* (Malden, MA: Blackwell, 2008), 41.

CAROLINA IRIBARREN

Continental Drift

Even though New Critics remained active well into the latter half of the twentieth century – as Brooks's enlarged edition of the *Princeton Encyclopedia of Poetry and Poetics*, published in 1974, attests – by the middle of the twentieth century, New Criticism's sway over literary studies had begun decidedly to wane and a multiplicity of alternative approaches to criticism to crop up both within and outside the academy. Cultural criticism, semiotics, reader-response theory, narratology, hermeneutics – these are just the most noteworthy of the plethora of literary studies movements that burgeoned and spread between the early 1950s and the late 1970s in the wake of New Criticism. Now, though widely divergent in aim and method, these new formations shared a basic tendency: They all drew more or less directly from currents of thought of European extraction. From the Frankfurt School and French structuralism to the Geneva School and Slavic formalism, European frameworks had a major impact on the development of American literary criticism and theory from the midcentury onward. This derivativity, though arguably already present in the Marxist criticism of the 1930s, was in fact unprecedented in both scale and directness, and as such bespoke an important shift in literary culture in the United States: a shift away from the nativist poetics of the New Critics (many of whom, it must be remembered, launched their literary careers as members of blood-and-soil groups like the Southern Agrarians and the Fugitives) toward ideological heterogeneity and its various methodological possibilities.

Following a loose chronology – loose because the majority of these midcentury movements formed and evolved concurrently, if not as a rule dialogically – the first of them that warrants attention is the so-called School of New York Intellectuals. To designate an eclectic assemblage of anti-institutional, free-thinking writers such as Lionel Trilling (1905–1975) and Diana Trilling (1905–1996), Philip Rahv (initially associated, as we saw, with 1930s Marxist criticism), Lionel Abel (1910–2001), Mary McCarthy (1912–1989), Alfred Kazin (1915–1998), Elizabeth Hardwick (1916–2007), Irving Howe (1920–1993), and Susan Sontag (1933–2004) a "school" is, of course, an act of retroactive reification. These critics had many things in common: a deep-seated suspicion of academic thought and expression, a predilection for post-Enlightenment European culture in general and modernist literature in particular, a penchant for democratic socialism with a tinge of liberalism, an affinity for journalistic writing and modes of collaboration, an aversion to theoretical orthodoxy, and, most important of all, a firm commitment to an expansive socially situated understanding of culture. Furthermore, the better part of them had a Jewish background and hailed from New York, an identarian configuration to which Kazin's *New York Jew* (1978) is testament. Yet none of these critics – save perhaps for William Barrett (1913–1992), editor of *Partisan Review* and advocate of a hardline type of social-moral criticism – could be said to have aspired to the theoretical consistency and institutional organization necessary for the formation of a "school"; their association was essentially nonprogrammatic, their similarities and collaborations the product of a shared intellectual disposition with little regard for institutionalized backing or longevity. "We have to ask ourselves whether in our day too much does not come within the purview of the academy," Trilling urged in the article "On the Teaching of Modern Literature," originally published in *Partisan Review* in 1961. And in a piece pertinently titled "The Function of Criticism Today" (1962), Kazin similarly insisted that "[c]riticism should never be so professional that only professionals can read it": the critic "writes for the public, not to a few imagined cospecialists; he writes to convince, to argue, to establish his argument; he writes dramatically, marshaling his evidence in a way that pure logic would never approve and pure scholarship would never understand."[23]

In the context of the present discussion, the most consequential aspect of this basic anti-institutional, free-thinking ethos is the way it manifested in a blatant proclivity for the essay: not only was "essayism" – that is, that general (and *generalist's*) attraction to everything that lies "between religion and knowledge, between example and doctrine, between *amor intellectualis* and poetry," as Musil first outlined it – a defining characteristic of the New York Intellectualist project, but New York Intellectuals were also deeply, explicitly invested in the craft of essay writing itself.[24] This was in large part as a measure against the ossification typical of scholarly criticism at the time. Witness the vehemence with which Kazin denounces "the attempt of university 'New Critics' to divorce literature from life ... with their pseudo-moral imbecilities" ("[t]he scholarly journal," he adds, "in this sense, is no more an organ of criticism than is the *Saturday Review*"). Now witness the praises he sings of the essay form, which, as the examples of

---

23 Lionel Trilling, "On the Teaching of Modern Literature," in *Beyond Culture: Essays on Literature and Learning* (New York: Viking, 1968), 10; Alfred Kazin, "The Function of Criticism Today," in *Contemporaries: From the 19th Century to the Present* (Boston: Little, Brown, 1962), 502, 501.
24 Robert Musil, *The Man without Qualities*, trans. Sophie Wilkins (London: Picador, 1995), 273.

Hazlitt and Emerson, Arnold and Eliot, Woolf and Wilde demonstrate, singularly enables the critic not only to "know his argument in full ... by writing it, by coming to grips with this own mind," but also to cultivate a "personal and even idiosyncratic ... style ... thus reversing the usual academic recipe of the trivial point and the heavy style."[25] It is, in effect, with the New York Intellectuals that our contemporary conception of the essay as an inherently capacious, experimental, hybrid form first finds full expression in the American scene. Hardwick, editor of the first (1986) volume of *The Best American Essays* and one of the group's most celebrated essayists, captures this point of view well:

> [The essay] is nothing less than the reflection of all there is; art, personal experience, places, literature, portraiture, politics, science, music, education – and just thought itself in orbit. . . . Expressiveness is an addition to statement, and hidden in its clases [sic] is an intelligence uncomfortable with dogmations [sic] wanting to make allowance for the otherwise case, the emendation. . . . Conviction itself is partial and the case is never decided. The essay is not the ground of verdicts. It rests on singularity rather than consensus. . . . Expertise, an acquisition promoted by usefulness, is less cogent to the essay than passion, less to the point than is the soloist's personal signature flowing through the text.[26]

Ambulatory, tentative, and eccentric – thus conceived, the essay became this renegade coterie's favorite genre, which they wielded and adapted to produce their signature (though by no means uniform or formulaic; their aim, after all, was to "express the individual's wholly undetermined and freely discovered point of view," which is precisely why is the essay, "that peculiarly modern ... form," as Kazin characterized it, suit them so well) public-facing politically attuned cultural analyses.[27] Sontag, one of the "school's" most enduring figures, pushed the connection between critic and essay even more in the introduction to her own edited volume of *The Best American Essays*: "Sometimes 'essayist' seems no more or less than a sneaky euphemism for 'critic.' And, indeed, some of the best essayists of the twentieth century have been critics"; for instance, Sontag added, "[l]iterary studies has produced

---

25 Kazin, *Contemporaries*, 482, 502, 503–504.
26 Elizabeth Hardwick, "Its Only Defense: Intelligence and Sparkle," *New York Times* (14 September 1986), www.nytimes.com/1986/09/14/books/its-only-defense-intelligence-and-sparkle.html.
27 Alfred Kazin, "The Essay as a Modern Form," in *The Open Form: Essays for Our Time* (New York: Harcourt, Brace, 1961), x.

a vast constellation of major essayists – and still does, despite the engulfment of literary studies by academia."[28]

Not every midcentury literary movement was as essayistic, anti-institutional, or for that matter as welcoming of women and those "too singular for polite society" as the New York Intellectuals were.[29] In effect, the era's next prominent contingent of critics – the Structuralists – was largely a male-dominated bourgeois affair in both its semiotic and its narratological iterations. Its most important practitioners included Roman Jakobson (1896–1982), Michael Riffaterre (1924–2006), Claudio Guillén (1924–2007), Robert Scholes (1929–2016), Gerald Prince (1942–), and Jonathan Culler (1944–). Profoundly influenced on the one hand by the Slavic tradition of linguistic analysis stemming from the Bakhtin and Prague Linguistic circles and culminating with the Tartu-Moscow School, and on the other by the more recent phenomenon of French structuralism associated with Ferdinand de Saussure (1857–1913), Jacques Lacan (1901–1981), Claude Lévi-Strauss (1908–2009), Roland Barthes (1915–1980), Gérard Genette (1930–2018), Tzvetan Todorov (1939–2017), and Julia Kristeva (1941–), American structuralist critics harbored a perspective on literature that was at once narrow and far-reaching. Far-reaching because their aim, as Prince lays it out in his movement-delineating *Narratology: The Form and Functioning of Narrative* (1982), was not only to "account for and define the specificity of any given narrative" by painstakingly studying its structural, narratorial, and logical elements and mechanisms, but also to "account for the infinite variety of possible narratives": "to account for their form and functioning, to examine how and why it is that we can construct them, paraphrase them, summarize them and expand them, or organize them in terms of such categories as plot, narrator, narratee, and character," thus "help[ing] us understand what human beings are."[30] Yet, despite (or perhaps owing to) these aspirations to totality, structuralism as a method of literary analysis ultimately proved narrow, for whether focused on "hypograms" (Riffaterre's semiological name for units of intertextuality) or on "grammars of narrative" (per Prince's narratology), it tended – in Guillén's own words – to suppress literature's "referential function": that is, it tended to treat literature as an autonomous closed system, thereby

---

28 Susan Sontag, "Introduction," in *The Best American Essays, 1992*, ed. Susan Sontag and Robert Atwan (New York: Ticknor and Fields, 1992), xvi.
29 Phillip Lopate, "How Do You End an Essay?" *Salmagundi*, no. 168–169 (Fall 2010–Winter 2011): 135–49, 140.
30 Gerald Prince, *Narratology: The Form and Functioning of Narrative* (Berlin: Mouton, 1982), 60, 164.

insulating it from material reality.[31] The result, as Culler later recognized, was "a powerful tropological model ..., a logical or epistemological system whose momentum is its own, not the movement of history."[32]

Technical and thus preoccupied with literature strictly qua narrative or poetic discourse, the structuralist program in the United States for the most part took no heed of marginally literary forms such as the essay. Often operating at such a high level of abstraction as to forgo examples altogether, structuralists otherwise gravitated toward traditional European novels – mostly nineteenth-century French bildungsromans in the model of Balzac, Hugo, and Flaubert – and toward modernist or protomodernist poetry by Baudelaire, Verlaine, Éluard, and the like. These, not the messy or homegrown meditations and experiments of the essayistic tradition, furnished them with the source material needed to build their total sign-systems and grammars. Nor did American structuralists avail themselves of the essay as form: More interested in mathematical formalizations, graphs, and visual schemas than in "diversity of level, subject, tone, diction," they generally embraced their French antecedents' metalinguistic manner of writing.[33] Reflecting on the way "this peculiar regressive structure of the concept of metalanguage [may] account in particular for the stylistic characteristics of the Structuralists," Fredric Jameson puts his finger on what renders the structuralist project inimical, on a formal and intellectual level, to essayification:

> [W]hether hermetic or white, whether the high style and classical pastiche of Lévi-Strauss or the bristling neologisms of Barthes, whether the self-conscious and over-elaborate preparatory coquetterie of Lacan or the grim and terroristic hectoring of Althusser – there is in all these styles a kind of distance from self, what one would like to call an unhappy consciousness on the stylistic level [whose] ideological effect is ... to prevent the ultimate return of the specialized intellectual discipline to that concrete social and historical situation in which it is of necessity grounded.[34]

Committed to an ideology of separate spheres wherein literature not only could but had to be grasped as a system operating *in vacuo* according to its own logics and mechanisms, structuralism turned its back on the range of facts and possibilities on which history and the essayistic live.

---

31 Claudio Guillén, *Literature as System: Essays toward the Theory of Literary History* (Princeton, NJ: Princeton University Press, 1971), 10.
32 Jonathan Culler, *The Pursuit of Signs: Semiotics, Literature, Deconstruction* (London: Routledge, 2001), 71–72.
33 Sontag, "Introduction," xvi.
34 Fredric Jameson, *The Prison-House of Language: A Critical Account of Structuralism and Russian Formalism* (Princeton, NJ: Princeton University Press, 1972), 209, 211.

Tear It Down

With the advent of the 1980s, the scope of literary theory began to widen for good. While white male-dominated circles of self-serious experts did not cease overnight to be in force – the enormous influence of the Yale School, to be discussed below, is testament to their longevity – starting in the mid-1970s, a slew of alternative voices and visions of what literature and its study may be gained unprecedented traction across the United States. Especially in the academy, where structuralism disintegrated into a number of different analytical frameworks (deconstructive, feminist, decolonial, psychoanalytic, etc.), literary theory came to be associated in this period not only with the scrutiny of those elements and mechanisms particular to literary works or even a given culture, but also with the empirical interrogation of the racial, gendered, geopolitical, as well as more properly economic dimensions of what Gayatri Spivak (1942–), building on Derridean theories of language from a Marxist decolonial feminist perspective, referred to as textuality.[35] Often classed collectively under the rubric of "poststructuralism" in order to signal both their methodological and periodical distance from the semiological and narratological analyses of the previous decades, these novel approaches were in fact quite different from one another, were organized around rather distinct histories, subject positions, and aims, and therefore merit separate consideration.

To begin with, the 1980s saw the consolidation – really the explosion – of a phenomenon already in the works in Europe throughout the previous decade: Derridean deconstruction. Informed by Husserlian and Heideggerian phenomenology as well as by Freudian and Nietzschean critiques of humanistic idealism, Derridean deconstruction originated, as its names indicates, in the iconoclastic work of French philosopher Jacques Derrida (1930–2004). Bent on combating the excessive and frequently blind metaphysical ratiocinations of so much Western philosophy, Derrida's most original and long-lasting contribution to literary theory was to formulate a concept of writing so expansive that the classical claims of identity, closure, and even coherence characteristic of all philosophical systems could be replaced, or at least complemented by, alternate dynamics at the level of signification. In Derrida's account of writing, meaning was always fundamentally unstable, indeterminate, based on difference and free play. Rather than try to pin

---

[35] See Gayatri Chakravorty Spivak, "The Politics of Interpretations," 118–33; as well as "Feminism and Critical Theory," 77–92, in *In Other Worlds: Essays in Cultural Politics* (New York: Routledge, 1988).

signifiers down on the lines of structuralism, what the critic (or "reader") therefore needed to do was to unearth this essential undecidability by paying punctilious attention to the way texts tend formally and conceptually to reflect and "conserve," but also subvert and "annul," "inherited conceptual oppositions" of the order of speech/writing, self/other, object/sign, signifier/signified, reality/representation, and male/female, to name but the most recurrent.[36] The point of this for the most part immanent analysis was, as Derrida explained, to bring "equivocality ... into play" in order to "open [the] field [of writing]" and in this way perhaps "resolve [some of its] epistemological obstacles."[37]

Throughout his career, Derrida fostered a strong link with American universities, which not only hosted him with regularity but also came to function themselves as major engines in the propagation of Derridean philosophy across the United States. This was the case at Yale, where Derrida held a prestigious visiting professorship in the mid-1970s and which thereafter became arguably the most important center for deconstructive criticism in the nation. The Yale School, as this new literary formation came to be called, operated primarily under the auspices of Yale's English, French, and Comparative literature programs and was spearheaded by Paul de Man (1919–1983), J. Hillis Miller (1928–2021), Geoffrey Hartman (1929–2016), and, to a much lesser extent, Harold Bloom (1930–2019). These critics all had different takes on the deconstructive project. De Man emphasized semantic undecidability in tandem with rhetoricity, that is, recurrent and self-referential figurative language; Miller, following de Man, focused on rhetorical play and repetition as well as on attendant problematics of reading; Hartman, coming from a robust phenomenological-critical background in the vein of Belgian critic Georges Poulet (1902–1991), interrogated logocentric claims and engaged in destabilizing etymological forays as these related to issues of consciousness, intentionality, and experience; and lastly, Bloom, always the outlier, pursued questions of influence, reception, and intertextuality from the comparatively conservative perspectives of literary history and psychology.[38] Despite their differences – differences which even the

---

36 Jacques Derrida, *Of Grammatology*, trans. Gayatri Chakravorty Spivak (Baltimore: Johns Hopkins University Press, 1997), 105.
37 Jacques Derrida, *Positions*, trans. Alan Bass (Chicago: University of Chicago Press, 1981), 11, 13.
38 See Paul de Man, *Allegories of Reading: Figural Language in Rousseau, Nietzsche, Rilke, and Proust* (New Haven, CT: Yale University Press, 1979); Paul de Man, *Blindness and Insight: Essays in the Rhetoric of Contemporary Criticism* (Minneapolis: University of Minnesota Press, 1983); J. Hillis Miller, *Fiction and Repetition: Seven English Novels* (Cambridge, MA:

School's "manifesto," the enormously influential 1979 coedited collection of essays *Deconstruction and Criticism*, throws into relief – collectively de Man, Miller, Hartman, and Bloom were responsible for ensconcing Derridean deconstruction deep in the American academy, shaping generations of scholars and critics to come.[39]

Now, if Derrida's first American acolytes were male, stuffy, and white, their students – which is to say, their PhD advisees and seminar participants but also their more distant readers – represented a surprisingly diverse and politically oriented group of voices and perspectives. Invested in feminism, Marxism, antiimperialism, and antiracism in a way that their predecessors were markedly not, this new wave of critics was eager not only to cross-examine deep-rooted ideological assumptions through painstaking immanent analyses, but also to push poststructuralist procedures beyond androcentric Western problematics and canonical objects toward more radical possibilities. Henry Louis Gates Jr. (1950–) poignantly described this theoretical shift in his introduction to *Critical Inquiry*'s 1985 special issue on "'Race,' Writing, and Difference":

> Scores of people are killed every day in the name of differences ascribed only to race. This slaughter demands the gesture in which the contributors to this special issue ... are collectively engaged: to deconstruct, if you will, the ideas of difference inscribed in the trope of race, to explicate discourse itself in order to reveal the hidden relations of power and knowledge inherent in popular and academic usages of "race."[40]

To be sure, second-generation deconstructionists like Gates, Spivak, Houston A. Baker Jr. (1943–), Barbara Johnson (1947–2009), Mary Louise Pratt (1948–), Homi K. Bhabha (1949–), Drucilla Cornell (1950–), Eve Kosofsky Sedgwick (1950–2009), Deborah McDowell (1951–), John Guillory (1952), Chandra Mohanty (1955–), and Judith Butler (1956–), among others, were informed by and in conversation with other critical traditions besides poststructuralism. The Black aesthetics of Addison Gayle Jr. (1932–1991), Amiri Baraka (1934–2014), and Larry Neal (1937–1981); the cultural criticism of Talal Asad

---

Harvard University Press, 1982); Geoffrey Hartman, *Criticism in the Wilderness: The Study of Literature Today* (New Haven, CT: Yale University Press, 1980), Geoffrey Hartman, *Saving the Text: Literature/Derrida/Philosophy* (Baltimore: Johns Hopkins University Press, 1981); Harold Bloom, *Poetry and Repression: Revisionism from Blake to Stevens* (New Haven, CT: Yale University Press, 1976), and Harold Bloom, *The Breaking of the Vessels* (Chicago: University of Chicago Press, 1982).

39 See Harold Bloom, Paul de Man, Jacques Derrida, Geoffrey Hartman, and J. Hillis Miller, *Deconstruction and Criticism* (New York: Seabury, 1979).

40 Henry Louis Gates Jr., "Editor's Introduction: Writing 'Race' and the Difference It Makes," in "'Race,' Writing, and Difference," special issue, *Critical Inquiry* 12, no. 1 (1985): 1–20, 6.

(1932–) and Edward Said (1935–2003); the militant feminism of Audre Lorde (1934–1992), Kate Millett (1934–2017), Toni Cade Bambara (1939–1995), and Lillian Robinson (1941–1941); the "new" leftism of Jameson, Gerald Graff (1937–) and Frank Lentricchia (1940–) – all these different, and at times incommensurable, currents of thought had a major impact on literary theorists and critics born in the postwar era. Sandra Gilbert (1936–) captures the motley nature of literary studies at this time when, in a widely read article titled "What Do Feminist Critics Want?" (1980), she claims of herself and her feminist comrades in the discipline, "[W]e are Marxists, Freudians, deconstructionists, Yale rhetoricians, and Harvard historians."[41] It was in fact largely out of such a mix of deconstructive methods and homegrown needs and ideas that critical movements like postcolonial theory, psychoanalytic theory, queer theory, neo- and post-Marxist theories, Black studies, and race theory – all still active in one form or another today – took shape in the context of literary studies during the final decades of the twentieth century.

Perhaps as a consequence of Derrida's and de Man's own genre-bending (albeit dense and at times overly fussy and technical) styles or perhaps as a kind of knee-jerk response to poststructuralism's general investment in ambivalence, liminality, and indeterminacy, starting in the late 1980s, literary critics and theorists began to give unparalleled attention to the essay. Indeed, for the first time in the history of American literary criticism, entire studies – a whole lot of them – were being written about the form. Consider: Bensmaïa's *The Barthes Effect: The Essay as Reflective Text* (1987), Hartman's *Minor Prophecies: The Literary Essay in the Culture Wars* (1991), Lydia Fakundiny's *The Art of the Essay* (1991), G. Douglas Atkins's *Estranging the Familiar: Toward a Revitalized Critical Writing* (1992), Thomas Harrison's *Essayism: Conrad, Musil, and Pirandello* (1992), Paul Heilker's *The Essay: Theory and Pedagogy for an Active Form* (1996), de Obaldia's *The Essayistic Spirit* (1996), and Graham Good's *The Observing Self: Rediscovering the Essay* (1998), not to mention countless stand-alone articles and papers (such as Timothy Corrigan's groundbreaking "The Cinematic Essay: Genre on the Margins" [1995]). Another noteworthy piece from the epoch, Rachel Blau DuPlessis's "f-Words: An Essay on the Essay" (1996), provides a revealingly long inventory of contemporaneous adherents of the form:

> There has been a good deal of such intransigent, willful [i.e., essayistic] writing recently – from David Antin and Gloria Anzaldúa, Charles

---

41 Sandra Gilbert, "What Do Feminist Critics Want? or a Postcard from the Volcano," *ADE Bulletin* 66 (1980): 16–24, 21.

Bernstein and Etel Adnan, Nancy Miller and Gerald Vizenor, Susan Howe and Diane Glancy, Bruce Andrews and Eve Sedgwick, Adrienne Rich and Eliot Weinberger, Trinh T. Minh-ha and bell hooks, Alice Walker and Robert Hass, and – many others.[42]

Besides magnitude, DuPlessis's list also illuminates how diversified essay writing had become by the 1990s: Poets, journalists, academics, and activists of a variety of race, gender, and class backgrounds actively turned to the genre as a means of formulating and broadcasting their projects. "The essay ... is and has been a form open to the articulation of estrangements and contra-dictions, a place for expressing the strains, differences, rejections as well as connections experienced by those who feel or have felt particularly marginalized by the discourses which have composed the social text," Rebecca Blevins Faery argued in "On the Possibilities of the Essay" (1990).[43] It was at this time, too, that a nonfiction books market in which the essay figured center stage shot up in the United States. G. Douglas Atkins, in an oft-cited article titled "The Return of/to the Essay" (1990), summed up the situation: "[W]hether we are returning to the essay, whether the essay as a form possesses some power of survival and renewal, or whether certain material and cultural conditions have coalesced to effect that return, there can be little doubt concerning both general readers' growing interest in, and writers' new commitment to, this venerable genre."[44]

The Essayification of Everything

Can there be too much of a good thing? Or, more precisely, is volume antithetical to value such that too much of something (however "venerable") makes that thing bad? "The attempt to evade convention eventually becomes conventional. ... The current liberties of the essay will doubtless look mannered in thirty years' time; its vaunted self-consciousness will look naïve, the fractured forms quaint rather than radical."[45] It has been only a little over a decade since James Wood made that pronouncement in a New Yorker piece on essayist John Jeremiah Sullivan; yet signs of essay fatigue are already perceptible in the cultural sphere. For if during the

---

42 Rachel Blau DuPlessis, "f-Words: An Essay on the Essay," *American Literature* 68, no. 1 (1996): 15–45, 16–17.
43 Rebecca Blevins Faery, "On the Possibilities of the Essay: A Meditation," *Iowa Review* 20, no. 2 (1990): 19–27, 22.
44 G. Douglas Atkins, "The Return of/to the Essay," *ADE Bulletin* 96 (1990): 11–18, 11.
45 James Wood, "Reality Effects: John Jeremiah Sullivan's Essays," *New Yorker* (11 December 2011), www.newyorker.com/magazine/2011/12/19/reality-effects.

poststructuralist years the essay garnered a record level of critical and theoretical consideration, that attention has only mounted since; the transition – difficult to pin down periodically – from Derridean deconstruction to current modes of literary analysis has been accompanied by an acceleration, a truly unprecedented surge, in essay writing in the United States. Almost as if Christy Wampole's invitation to "deploy . . . the essay's spirit in all aspects of life" had been heeded to the letter, the nonfiction essay has become one of the most popular, and lucrative, genres of the twenty-first century, as well as a preeminent object of critical theorizing.[46] To cite just four studies from the past few years that illustrate the genre's theoretical proliferation, consider Brian Dillon's *Essayism: On Form, Feeling, and Nonfiction* (2017), Erin Plunkett's *A Philosophy of the Essay: Scepticism, Experience, and Style* (2018), Nora Alter's *The Essay Film after Fact and Fiction* (2018), and Cheryl Wall's *On Freedom and the Will to Adorn: The African American Essay* (2019). Today the essay as form and target of analysis arouses the interest of queer and affect theorists, film theorists, philosophers of art and literature, critical race theorists – in short, of all corners of the literary milieu. While this massive essayism has helped revitalize writing, especially academic writing, turning it into "a technology for original thought and deep engagement with texts, with the self, and with the world," as Nicole Wallack has argued, it has also potentially disabled some of the genre's most compelling features (e.g., curiosity, ambivalence, tentativeness, experimentation, divagation) by calcifying them into a predictive and incessant pattern.[47] "If there is 'novelization' and its clanking machinery, then there will also be 'essayism' and *its* clanking machinery," Wood conjectured in 2011.[48]

Published in *The New York Times*'s defunct philosophical forum "The Stone" under the prescient title "The Essayification of Everything," Wampole's call to approach every speck of life essayistically – "what we eat, things upon which we stumble, things that Pinterest us," to say nothing of "the Big Questions: What are the implications of the human experience? What is the meaning of life? Why something rather than nothing?" – was meant to serve as an antidote to, "a resistance against the zealous closed-endedness of the rigid mind," which according to Wampole typified so much

---

46 Christy Wampole, "The Essayification of Everything," *New York Times* (26 May 2013), https://archive.nytimes.com/opinionator.blogs.nytimes.com/2013/05/26/the-essayification-of-everything/.
47 Nicole B. Wallack, *Crafting Presence: The American Essay and the Future of Writing Studies* (Logan, UT: Utah State University Press, 2017), 4.
48 Wood, "Reality Effects," n.p.

of the American life in 2013. The essay, Wampole expounded, "is a form for trying out the heretofore untried. Its spirit resists closed-ended, hierarchical thinking and encourages both writer and reader to postpone their verdict on life. It is an invitation to maintain the elasticity of mind and to get comfortable with the world's inherent ambivalence."[49] In a recent piece published in the *Yale Review*, Vivian Gornick has advanced an equally optimistic view of the genre: Drawing on her own experience of writing about nineteenth-century suffragist Elizabeth Cady Stanton, Gornick commends "essayistic presentations," "essayistic forms" as especially well equipped to capture and reflect on "the existential in women's condition": "not only ... how it was but how it felt to be a person who was a woman."[50]

Still, in spite of its record of formal and intellectual amplitude, some critics worry that the essay – above all the personal essay – has so expanded its reach that essayistic "elasticity" has degenerated into essayistic overkill. Jackson Arn writes in a review of Phillip Lopate's latest anthology, *The Contemporary American Essay* (2021):

> Since 2011 ... essays have outsold mainstream fiction and outranked it on best-of-the-year lists. Essays have actually *become* mainstream fiction .... Nowadays when someone comes out with a long, plotless piece of prose that's, say, 50 percent memoir, 30 percent travel diary, and 20 percent book reviews already published as standalone magazine articles, it hardly bears pointing out.[51]

The problem, Arn continues, is not the sheer volume of essays currently in circulation; the problem is rather the "studied ambivalence," the "mess of *maybes* and *perhapses* and hot, urgent rhetorical questions," the "countless smart-sounding pronouncements that turn out to be trivially correct," the relentless "fingering [of] the knot of first-personhood." "When ambivalence becomes the rule instead of the exception," Arn concludes, "the result is a 'valid truth,' to borrow Lopate's tactful phrase [from the volume's introduction], but it's also a trivial, tautological truth."[52] Thus prone to pointless equivocation, gimmicky stylistic ticks, as well as a "conceptual production of personhood as a salable commodity," as Merve Emre puts it in a provocative

---

49 Wampole, "Essayification of Everything," n.p.
50 Vivian Gornick, "The Power of Testimony: Why Personal Narrative Has Displaced Fiction," *Yale Review* (1 December 2021), https://yalereview.org/article/the-power-of-testimony.
51 Jackson Arn, "Dot Dot Dot Dot Dot: Against the Contemporary American Essay," *Drift* (31 January 2022), www.thedriftmag.com/dot-dot-dot-dot-dot-dot/.
52 Arn, "Dot Dot Dot Dot Dot," n.p.

article published in the *New York Review of Books*, today's personal essays leave much to be desired by most critics' account.[53]

Fortunately, the personal essay is not the contemporary essay. Beyond the abusive ellipses and gratuitous *I*'s, even Arn concedes that a whole range of public critical essays is being written at this moment. Driven by the growing precarization of academic labor on the one hand and the growing obsolescence of intellectual culture on the other, millennial writers in particular have drifted toward impersonal essayistic modes as a means to open up otherwise hermetic scholarly debates, all the while taking stock of the present. Featured in academia-adjacent journalistic venues such as *n+1*, the *Point*, the *Drift*, and the *Baffler*, essays like Andrea Long Chu's "On Liking Women" (2018), Frank Guan's "Useful Idiots" (2018), Christian Lorentzen's "Like This or Die: The Fate of the Book Review in the Age of the Algorithm" (2019), Danielle Carr's "The Bad Feature" (2020), James Pogue's "They Made a Movie Out of It: The Decline of Nonfiction in the IP Era" (2020), Tobi Haslett's "Magic Actions: Looking Back on the George Floyd Rebellion" (2021), Apoorva Tadepalli's "Careerism: The Writing Life and Its Discontents" (2021), Maggie Doherty's "The Abortion Stories We Tell" (2022), and Malcolm Harris's "Just Beans: What Was Ethical Consumption under Capitalism?" (2022) manage to mete out original reflections on the crucibles of capitalist society with a stylistic and intellectual acuity reminiscent of the New York Intellectuals. If the history of American literary studies traced here shows anything, it is that the fortunes of the essay are never secure; robust essayism may well give place to scholastic quietism or wishy-washy speculation in a generation or two. Yet, judging from the strength of many – if not always the best-selling – essays being written today, the genre's millenarian momentum is still pushing on.

---

53 Merve Emre, "The Illusion of the First Person," *New York Review of Books* (3 November 2022), www.nybooks.com/articles/2022/11/03/the-illusion-of-the-first-person-merve-emre/.

33
Gender, Queerness, and the American Essay

DAVID LAZAR

In "What Is Reading? It's Eating on the Sly," Hélène Cixous (1937–) writes, "Montaigne, with whom I am, in a certain intimate and actually enlightening way, a relative more than with anybody else."[1] Reading this, other women writers who see themselves as kindred spirits of Montaigne (1533–1592) come to mind, such as Marie Jars de Gournay (1565–1645), his amanuensis and arguably the first female and protofeminist essayist, having written *The Equality of Men and Women* (1622), or, more recently, Nancy Mairs (1943–2016) and Rachel Blau DuPlessis (1941–), both of whom saw in Montaigne a kind of queered or feminized paterfamilias. DuPlessis, in "f-Words: An Essay on the Essay," writes that the openness and transgressive nature of the essay are reasons "why the essay has been summed up by the term *feminine*."[2] Mairs, in "Essaying the Feminine: From Montaigne to Kristeva," says that "intentionally or not, Montaigne invented, or perhaps renewed, a mode open and flexible enough to enable the feminine inscription of human experience as no other does."[3] One wants to read a queer Montaigne because, like Cixous, one loves his writerly transgressions, his thematic strangeness, and his focus on the self as an object that might fall between fixed categories. In the *Essais*, he imagined a plastic sense of self, resisting the currencies and commonplaces of strict gender definitions.

Issues of identity and difference have had a profound effect on the writing of our age, and certainly on the essay, the most elusive of genres. Therefore,

---

1 Hélène Cixous, *Three Steps on the Ladder of Writing*, trans. Sarah Cornell and Susan Sellers (New York: Columbia University Press, 1994), 23.
2 Rachel Blau DuPlessis, "f-Words: An Essay on the Essay," *American Literature* 68, no. 1 (March 1996): 15–45, 33.
3 Nancy Mairs, "Essaying the Feminine: From Montaigne to Kristeva," in *Voice Lessons: On Becoming a (Woman) Writer* (Boston: Beacon Press, 1994), 71–87, 76.

it is worth considering the intersections of essay, gender, and queer studies/ consciousness over the last few decades, perhaps first in a general sense, and then through the lens of specific essayists who seem to have had the most significant impact on the direction of the essay since 1970 in the United States. Beginning with second-wave feminism, this chapter discusses the work of those essayists in feminist and LGBTQ+ communities whose foundational writing on gender still resonates today.

On the Second-Wave Feminist Essay

Before considering the work of these influential and remarkable women essayists individually, we should note that what binds, most strikingly, all their work, with different emphases and stylistic variations, are the following thematic considerations: the role of the female body in patriarchal society, the connection between one's personal and political lives, and how misconceptions about gender should be addressed.

Though sometimes critiqued for its cisgendered academic whiteness, the writing of Adrienne Rich (1929–2012), perhaps the most influential second-wave feminist essayist, was critical of the very movement to which she belonged. In addition to her critiques of feminism, she covered a wide range of topics. In *On Lies, Secrets, and Silence: Selected Prose 1966–1978* (1979), Rich wrote on literary subjects with political implications ("Jane Eyre: The Temptations of a Motherless Woman"), gender matters as they related to national violence ("Vietnam and Sexual Violence"), and autobiographical excursions ("It Is the Lesbian in Us"). In an accessible, rueful, semiacademic style, Rich was able to share her experience – as a poet and as a lesbian exploring her identity after living a heteronormative existence for years – with a large audience of mostly white, middle-class readers. In the foreword to *On Lies, Secrets, and Silence*, titled "On History, Illiteracy, Passivity, Violence, and Women's Culture," she writes:

> In a world dominated by violent and passive-aggressive men, and by male institutions dispensing violence, it is extraordinary to note how often women are represented as the perpetrators of violence, most of all when we are simply fighting in self-defense or for our children, or when we collectively attempt to change the institutions that are making war on us and our children.[4]

---

4 Adrienne Rich, *On Lies, Secrets, and Silence: Selected Prose 1966–1978* (New York: W. W. Norton, 1995), 16.

This is just one example of her attention to the paradoxes and snares of navigating a highly gendered world. Here, Rich is attuned to the rhythms of the political-personal essay and committed, as she is in other essays, to exploring power dynamics and structural complacencies. Her essays were templates for politically engaged literary prose for decades. In *Of Woman Born: Motherhood as Experience and Institution* (1976), Rich broke new ground in articulating painful, difficult, even at times ugly truths about women's experience and her own background, including negative feelings about motherhood that had, perhaps, never been articulated in American prose before. In essays such as "Violence: The Heart of Maternal Darkness," Rich confronts the underside of the maternal experience. Her analysis of these forbidden themes was electrifying and liberating for many of her readers. In "Split at the Root: An Essay on Jewish Identity" (*Blood, Bread and Poetry* [1979]), certainly one of the most widely read American essays of the last fifty years, Rich writes about buried and repressed identity. Although she writes specifically about the confusions that arise in her life from belonging to multiple cultures – in her case, with a Jewish father with Ashkenazi and Sephardi roots and a white Episcopalian mother, both from the South – the message and sentiments continue to resonate for contemporary readers of increasingly diverse heritage. Drawing parallels between the early 1980s in the United States and Europe under the shadow of National Socialism, she writes:

> Yet we can't wait for the undamaged to make our connection for us; we can't wait to speak until we are wholly clear and righteous. There is no purity, and, in our lifetimes, no end to this process.
> This essay, then, has no conclusions; it is another beginning, for me. Not just a way of saying, in 1982 Right-wing American, *I too will wear the yellow star*. It's a moving into accountability, enlarging the range of accountability.[5]

Carolyn Heilbrun (1926–2003), also a second-wave feminist writer, published several influential books in the 1970s and '80s that expanded the intellectual universe of the biographical-critical essay and our sense of how to read and interpret women's experience. The two most influential of these books were *Toward a Recognition of Androgyny* (1973) and *Writing a Woman's Life* (1988), essay collections in which the universe of women in literature is expanded in significant ways. *Androgyny*, written in elegant prose and following thematically in the footsteps of Virginia Woolf's (1882–1941) *Orlando* (1928), advances

---

5 Adrienne Rich, "Split at the Root," in *Blood, Bread and Poetry* (New York: W. W. Norton 1986), 100–23, 123.

a case for a pyschosexual reading that displaces sexual binaries. The thrilling conclusion to *Androgyny*, built on a discussion of Woolf's novel, points toward transcendent future possibilities: "For the mind too, Woolf thought, after being divided, can be reunited in just so natural a fusion. There was always the possibility of so natural a fusion, of a force in things overlooked, which might lead 'elsewhere.'"[6] This summons to mind the conceptual slippages between gender and genre and the generic in-betweenness of the essay form, which can accommodate uncertainties about all fixed categories, including gender. Heilbrun's *Writing a Woman's Life* (1988), dedicated to another second-wave feminist, Nancy K. Miller, was a casually radical book of essayistic criticism devoted to women's friendship, the ways a woman's autobiographical impulse was sometimes redirected into fiction, and the stylistic and thematic innovations women have crafted to narrate their experience. In addition to bringing feminist theory to a mainstream audience, *Writing a Woman's Life* opened up suggested avenues of scholarship for a future generation of women writers and presented a way of doing so in a fully essayistic form.

Nancy K. Miller (1941–) cofounded the Gender and Culture series at Columbia University Press with Carolyn Heilbrun and has been a significant voice in both feminist theory and essay scholarship for the last forty years. What distinguished Miller's work early on was a three-strand focus, the emphasis of which has varied over the years, but whose essential elements have remained consistent: scholarship on French literature; a sometimes formal, sometimes informal feminist theory; and autobiography. These strands merged into a new kind of autobiographical feminist essay/memoir, one that is personal, experiential, scholarly, self-aware, ironic, and theoretically deft. In *Bequest and Betrayal* (1996), writing about Susan Cheever and herself, Miller writes:

> Home before dark. Our parents want us home before dark. They want us home so that we will be safe. In some ways the memoir is the revenge of a poor reader: having failed to read the signs in her life, she makes a work of art out of her reinterpretation. [. . .] It's not safe when the darkness is at home.[7]

As an avid reader of Simone de Beauvoir (1908–1986), the role of the daughter is frequently on Miller's mind, conflicted and far from always dutiful.[8] "I'm

---

6 Carolyn Heilbrun, *Toward a Recognition of Androgyny* (New York: Alfred A. Knopf, 1973), 48.
7 Nancy K. Miller, *Bequest and Betrayal* (Bloomington, IN: Indiana University Press, 2000), 147.
8 Simone de Beauvoir wrote about the figure of the daughter both autobiographically (*Memoirs of a Dutiful Daughter*, 1958) and as a subject of social science (*The Second Sex*, 1949).

keeping myself alive as a child,"[9] she writes, sounding a note not at all unlike Charles Lamb self-administrating to his childhood self in "New Year's Eve" (1821).[10] Miller continues, writing, "I'm still asking myself the questions I can't answer," the essential impulse of every essayist.[11]

Nancy K. Miller's most influential book of essays was undoubtedly *Getting Personal: Feminist Occasions and Other Autobiographical Acts* (1991). In the eponymous essay, "Getting Personal: Autobiography as Cultural Criticism," Miller approaches head-on the questions surrounding the merging of feminist (or queer, or any) theory and the essay:

> Why personal criticism now? Is it another form of "Anti-Theory"? Is it a new stage of theory? Is it gendered? Only for women and gay men? Is it bourgeois? Postmodern? A product of Late Capitalism? Reaganomics? Post-feminism? It might be possible, and the reflexes of my structuralist training make me contemplate the project, to construct a typology, a poetics of the "egodocuments" that constitute personal criticism: confessional, locational, academic, political, narrative, anecdotal, biographic, etc. But is it really a good idea?[12]

In the last essay, "My Father's Penis," Miller invokes Jane Gallop's (1952–) well-known essay, "Phallus/Penis: Same Difference" (1981),[13] in a tender, melancholy consideration of her father and herself through a focus on glimpses of his penis as his death approached. There can be no doubt that Miller's exclamation in the middle of the essay – "What do I know?"[14] quoting the great Montaignian motto (*Que sais-je?*) – is fully self-aware.

Late Second-Wave Feminist Essayists and the Third Wave

As we move from second-wave to third-wave feminism, a new vocabulary begins to coalesce around gender, namely, that of performativity and masquerade. Following Simone de Beauvoir's notion of a socially constructed femininity (embodied in the famous sentence from *The Second Sex* (1949),

---

9 Miller, *Bequest and Betrayal*, 154.
10 Lamb writes of his childhood self, "[F]or the child Elia – that 'other me,' there, in the back-ground – I must take leave to cherish the remembrance of that young master." Charles Lamb, "New Year's Eve," in *Essays of Elia* (Paris: Baudry's European Library, 1835), 29–34, 30.
11 Miller, *Bequest and Betrayal*, 171.
12 Nancy K. Miller, "Getting Personal: Autobiography as Cultural Criticism," in *Getting Personal: Feminist Occasions and Other Autobiographical Acts* (Oxford: Routledge, 1991), 5.
13 Jane Gallop, "Phallus/Penis: Same Difference," in "Men by Women," ed. Janet Todd, *Women and Literature* 2 (1981): 243–51.
14 Nancy K. Miller, "My Father's Penis," in *Getting Personal*, 144.

"One is not born but rather becomes a woman"), Judith Butler (1956–) showed the many ways in which gender is a form of social theater in "Performative Acts and Gender Constitution" (1988), *Gender Trouble* (1990), and *Bodies That Matter* (1993). In these groundbreaking texts, Butler challenged binary categories – sex/gender, male/female – and focused insistently on the dynamics of power as they relate to performances of gender. Along with Eve Sedgwick's (1950–2009) *Epistemology of the Closet* (1990), these are works that cleared a new discursive space for queer/feminist self-consideration in the essay, in critical-creative forms such as Sedgwick's *Tendencies* (1993) and *A Dialogue on Love* (2000) or Butler's *Antigone's Claim* (2000). Both Butler and Sedgwick – along with many other queer theorists – were influenced by Michel Foucault (1926–1984), especially his multivolume study, *The History of Sexuality* (1976–2018). There, Foucault advanced questions about modern sexual construction and the emergence of the "homosexual" as a self-aware and culturally distinct entity in the late nineteenth century. Queerness, according to Foucault – and certainly to Sedgwick and Butler – is destabilizing, and so, we might argue, is the essay, the most unstable genre, if, in fact, it is a genre at all.

The following passage by Butler from *Gender Trouble* echoes the references at the beginning of this chapter to the inherent femininity or in-betweenness of the genre coined by Montaigne: "Precisely because 'female' no longer appears to be a stable notion, its meaning is as troubled and unfixed as 'woman,' and because both terms gain their troubled significations only as relational terms, this inquiry takes as its focus gender and the relational analysis it suggests."[15] Similar to early essay theorists like György Lukács (1885–1971), both Sedgwick and Butler are critical-theoretical writers who enlarge the boundaries of what this special kind of prose can express as the self tries to negotiate a place in the social world. Neither has written explicitly about the formal qualities of the essay or how to push the genre in new creative directions, but their theoretical inventions, discoveries, and expansions model how a scholar might combine theory and an identifiable personal style to explore the problems of selfhood and identity. Without Sedgwick's and Butler's introduction of the notion of performativity into gender discourses – which has been applied to great effect by literary, journalistic, and scholarly essayists such as Mary Cappello, Maggie Nelson, Jennifer Finney Boylan, and many others – it is hard to imagine that the sense we have today of the "queer essay" could have emerged.

---

15 Judith Butler, *Gender Trouble: Feminism and the Subversion of Identity* (New York: Routledge, 1990), ix.

Unlike Sedgwick and Butler, whose contributions are more theoretical, bell hooks (1952–2021) is a major essayist whose politically charged works – autobiographical, focusing on gender, race, pedagogy, the body, and ways to resist reified thinking – are rendered in a lucid, ironic, accessible prose that combines colloquial and intellectual discourse seamlessly. One of her earliest books, *Ain't I a Woman: Black Women and Feminism* (1981), received vast critical acclaim and is still a fixture on American university syllabi in courses on race and gender. However, two of her other major books, *Talking Back: Thinking Feminist, Thinking Black* (1989) and *Teaching to Transgress: Education as the Practice of Freedom* (1994), perhaps best illustrate her advancement of the essay form.

In *Talking Back*, hooks accomplishes again and again the difficult combination of self-exploration and the expression of political outrage, creating a space for pointed commentary and new ways to consider the lives and experiences of queer, Black women. In "'Whose Pussy Is This': A Feminist Comment," hooks writes:

> A passionate viewer of films, especially the work of independent filmmakers, I found much to appreciate in the technique, style, and overall production of *She's Gotta Have It*. It was especially refreshing to see images of black people on screen that were not grotesque caricatures, images that were familiar, images that imaginatively captured the essence, dignity and spirit of that elusive quality known as "soul." It was a very soulful film.
>
> Thinking about the film from a feminist perspective, considering its political implications, I find it much more problematic.[16]

Her ability to cut to the heart of both the problematic representation and treatment of women in Spike Lee's film(s) in disarming prose is characteristic of hooks's work, which nevertheless is frequently sharp and unsparing. The opening paragraph of "Homophobia in Black Communities" begins with a domestic scene disrupted by familial conflict:

> Recently I was at my parents' home and heard teenage nieces and nephews expressing their hatred for homosexuals, saying that they could never like anybody who was homosexual. In response I told them, "There are already people who you love and care about who are gay, so just come off it!" They wanted to know who. I said, "The who is not important. If they wanted you to know, they would tell you. But you need to think about the shit you've been saying and ask yourself where it's coming from."[17]

16 bell hooks, "'Whose Pussy Is This': A Feminist Comment," in *Talking Back: Thinking Feminist, Thinking Black* (Boston: South End Press, 1989), 134.
17 bell hooks, "Homophobia in Black Communities," in *Talking Back*, 120.

In *Teaching to Transgress* (1994) – part essay, part pedagogical manifesto – hooks explores multiculturalism, the work of Brazilian educator Paolo Freire (1921–1997), and problems regarding feminism, homonormativity, and linguistics. This rich set of essays reflects on how educators can change the nature of education, the classroom space, their praxis, or their sense of mission. In the formal and rhetorical force and variety of her work, bell hooks has contributed to the expansion of the essay's possibilities in the United States.

Another important voice during the transition from second- to third-wave feminism is that of Vivian Gornick (1935–), who in 1978 published *Essays in Feminism*, an influential series of personal, social, and literary essays told from a feminist perspective. Her voice is literary, spirited, full of occasional asperity, and, in contrast to more provocative feminist essays by Germaine Greer (1939–), Andrea Dworkin (1946–2005), and others, is geared to a middle-class, white audience. Essays such as "Feminist Writers: Hanging Ourselves on a Party Line" would inspire later feminist essayists such as Roxanne Gay (1974–), whose *Bad Feminist* (2014) has had a broad and enthusiastic readership. In the literary essays, Gornick picks apart misogyny unsparingly and shows her brilliance and boldness as a reader, sometimes with a surplus of self-confidence. Like Adrienne Rich, Gornick at times used her voice to critique the women's movement so that feminism – a more abstract notion – would expand and thrive at a faster pace. She writes, "It seems to me this growth of doctrinaire opinion in the women's movement can do nothing but retard the progress of modern feminism."[18] Elsewhere in the collection, Gornick broaches the topic of women and work – in essays such as "Why Women Fear Success," "The Conflict between Love and Work," and "The Price of Paying Your Own Way" – which, while not new, is enlivened by her spirited prose and her updating of these themes to address working women at the end of the twentieth century. While some of the essays in *Essays in Feminism* might feel dated for contemporary readers, others may seem so only by virtue of the fact that Gornick's insights were so prescient and that the themes have since been explored in great detail.

Andrea Dworkin's brilliant, provocative essays have too often been dismissed or attacked because of political objections to her antiobscenity project with Catherine MacKinnon (1946–). Dworkin (while teaching for the Women's Studies Program at the University of Minnesota) and MacKinnon drafted the antipornography civil rights legislation that was twice passed by

---

18 Vivian Gornick, *Essays in Feminism* (New York: Harper and Row, 1978), 116.

the Minneapolis City Council but vetoed by the mayor. For many readers, Dworkin's antipornography actions, which put her in temporary alignment with the interests of "right-wing women" and which were opposed by many mainstream feminist and civil liberty groups, became the definition of her work. This is unfortunate, because she created a major body of important essayistic work, starting with *Woman Hating* (1974), not to mention her extraordinary *Right-Wing Women* (1983), which includes the essay "The Coming Gynocide." In it, she writes:

> The United States, a young, virile imperialist power compared to its European precursors, has pioneered this kind of reproductive imperialism. The United States was the perfect nation to do so, since the programs depend so much on science and technology (the nation's pride) and also on a most distinctive recognition of precisely how expendable women are as women, simply because they are women. Obsessed with sex as a nation, the United States knows the strategic importance of the uterus, abroad and at home.[19]

She ends the essay by writing, "We know what men can do."[20] This cryptic and sinister closing signal consolidates the "battle of the sexes" ethos that dominated much second- and third-wave feminist writing. Perhaps the imagined line that "all heterosexual sex is rape," misconstrued from Dworkin's most brilliant book of essays, *Intercourse* (1987), and for which she is, ironically, most famous, partially explains why her work is not more celebrated. Dworkin writes in the essay "Occupation/Collaboration" that "intercourse is the pure, sterile, formal expression of men's contempt for women," especially in the patriarchal expressions of sex so often represented as violent, dominating, controlling, demeaning, and so forth.[21] In this cultural context, Dworkin asks how sex, how intercourse can *not* be debased, how heteronormativity can *not* be undermined, unless we radically challenge and purge certain practices, images, and atavistic laws. There was a reason Christopher Hitchens (1949–2011) admired Andrea Dworkin. She, like English essayist William Hazlitt (1778–1830), did not fully belong to any group; she made almost everyone a little uncomfortable. And she was a superb prose writer. She is an undervalued master of the American political essay in the latter twentieth century, and as a queer feminist managed to craft essays that, in the white-hot fury of her prose style, have not seemed to age in

---

19 Andrea Dworkin, "The Coming Gynocide," in *Right-Wing Women* (New York: G. P. Putnam, 1983), 151.
20 Dworkin, *Right-Wing Women*, 194.
21 Andrea Dworkin, "Occupation/Collaboration," in *Intercourse* (New York: Free Press, 1987), 138.

the ways that the work of some others has. In *Letters from a War Zone* (1988), Dworkin writes in the essay "Look, Dick, Look. See Jane Blow It":

> We have to be brave enough to confront in ourselves the desire to be reassimilated back into the male world, to know that we might lie to ourselves – especially about the righteousness of male political imperatives – to get back in. We always think it is safer there. But, if we dare to keep facing it, we know that there lies madness, there lies rape, there lies battery, there lies forced pregnancy and forced prostitution and forced mutilation, there lies murder. If we go back, we cannot go forward. If we do not go forward, we will disappear.[22]

Dworkin's vociferous and graphic depictions of the relationships between men and women might strike contemporary readers as too blunt and distressing, but it is for this very reason that the images and scenes she depicts have not easily dissipated in the consciousness of her readers.

Nancy Mairs's first book of essays, *Plaintext* (1986), displays her expertise in feminist theory but deploys it subtly. These are not theoretical or polemical essays; they are personal ones. The titles – such as "On Having Adventures," "On Not Liking Sex," "On Living behind Bars" – gesture toward Montaigne or Francis Bacon (1561–1626), who also used such titles.[23] In her writing, Mairs introduces a very specific and intense consideration of her relationship to her body, a body that is both disabled and sexual, a topic generally unbroached in nonfiction writing of the time. In "On Being a Cripple," Mairs writes:

> Like many women I know, I have always had an uneasy relationship with my body: I was not a popular child, largely, I think now, because I was peculiar: intelligent, intense, moody, shy, given to unexpected actions and inexplicable notions and emotions. But as I entered adolescence, I believed myself unpopular because I was homely: my breasts too flat, my mouth too wide, my hips too narrow, my clothing never quite right in fit or style. I was not, in fact, particularly ugly, old photographs inform me, though I was well off the ideal; but I carried this sense of self-alienation with me into adulthood, where it regenerated in response to the depredations of MS.[24]

---

22 Andrea Dworkin, "Look, Dick, Look. See Jane Blow It," in *Letters from a War Zone* (Brooklyn, NY: Lawrence Hill Books, 1993), 132.
23 Such titles include Montaigne's "On the Inconstancy of Our Actions," "On Drunkenness," or "On Vanity"; or Bacon's "Of Marriage and Single Life," "Of Seeming Wise," or "Of Deformity."
24 Nancy Mairs, "On Being a Cripple," in *Plaintext* (New York: Harper and Row, 1986), 17.

In 1994, Mairs published a book of essays titled *Voice Lessons: On Becoming a (Woman) Writer*. The book includes essays about Mairs's sentimental education as a feminist and the influence of women writers such as Virginia Woolf, Alice Walker, and Doris Lessing. Other important essays from the collection are "The Literature of Personal Disaster," a groundbreaking piece considering the literature of disability, and "Essaying the Feminine: From Montaigne to Kristeva." In this piece, Mairs finds qualities in the "Montaignesque" essay that break or escape phallocentric discourse, an essentially feminine quality in the heart of the essay that makes the very form, in its openness, a site for *écriture féminine*[25] that transgresses traditional ideas of gender:

> I want a prose that is allusive and translucent, that eases you into me and embraces you [...] choosing each word for its capacity, its ambiguity, the space it provides for me to live my life within it, relating rather than opposing each word to the next, each sentence to the next, "starting on all sides at once ... twenty times, thirty times, over": the stuttering adventure of the essay.[26]

In subsequent books, such as *Ordinary Time: Cycles in Marriage, Faith, and Renewal* (1993) and *Waist-High in the World: A Life among the Nondisabled* (1996), Mairs continued to explore her central subjects: the body, disability, the tensions between her feminism and Catholicism, and the essay itself. In "Introit: A Wanton Gospeller," from *Ordinary Time*, she writes:

> I was raised, in classical ladylike fashion, never to discuss religion, politics, or sex, and I'm still more comfortable with the weather than any other topic of conversation. When someone asks me with born-again fervor whether I've accepted Jesus Christ as my personal savior, I cringe; the question seems so intimate as to be slightly indecent. Religious belief is something like masturbation: You may do it – and it won't even make you crazy or give you warts if you do – but it's the sort of thing you keep to yourself.[27]

Mairs's body of work in the personal essay in the period she was active (between 1993 and 2016) was a model for the ways in which feminist theory could be incorporated and personalized in the essay.

Rachel Blau DuPlessis's "f-words: An Essay on the Essay," first published in *American Literature* in 1996 and then reprinted in *Blue Studios: Poetry and Its Cultural Work* (2006), is one of the most important feminist essays on the

---

25 Cixous's well-known essay on *écriture féminine* ("Le rire de la Méduse") explores some of the essay's in-between qualities as well. See Hélène Cixous, "The Laugh of the Medusa," trans. Keith Cohen and Paula Cohen, *Signs* 1, no. 4 (Summer 1976): 875–93.
26 Mairs, "Essaying the Feminine," 4.
27 Nancy Mairs, "Introit: A Wanton Gospeller," in *Ordinary Time: Cycles in Marriage, Faith, and Renewal* (Boston: Beacon Press, 1993), 4.

essay because it challenges assumptions about the nature of the form. DuPlessis's essay is perhaps closer in spirit to the essays on the essay by Adorno (1903–1969) and Lukács (1885–1971)[28] than most American essays on the genre. In it, she expresses less interest in the essay's autobiographical or lyrical modes and focuses instead on its veiled systems, its skepticism, and its transgressive nature. As previously mentioned, she reflects on the reasons "why the essay has been summed up by the term *feminine*."[29] The brilliance of DuPlessis's essay stems from her way of incorporating dialectical resistance to her own oppositions. She writes:

> This is an essay (my essay) about the essay. Essay is always opposite. Well, often opposite. Oppositional. How does the essay function? What is it taxonomically? The adjective *autobiographical*, often used for this manner of work, flails and grasps – it is an inadequate descriptor, even though some people may take the stance denominated "I." These are works of "reading" – for essays are acts of writing-as-reading. Acts of trying out, as the French root *essayer* says.[30]

DuPlessis's essay – a fitting companion to Nancy Mairs's essay on the essay and *écriture féminine*, but more radical in spirit – returns again to the transgenred and transgendered spirit of Montaigne mentioned in this chapter's opening pages.

A final note on Gloria Anzaldúa's (1942–2004) *Borderlands/La Frontera* (1987), an important work that combines several forms, including poetry, essay, and experimental prose. The hybrid form mimics the book's theme: intersectionality, the blending of identities and categories, *mestizaje*. Anzaldúa shows that these concepts, emergent in American consciousness in the late 1980s, were best explored through a hybrid literary form. Her focus is the divided identity and consciousness of Mexican American women. She writes:

> I am a border woman. I grew up between two cultures, the Mexican (with a heavy Indian influence) and the Anglo (as a member of a colonized people in our own territory). I have been straddling that *tejas*-Mexican border, and others, all my life. It's not a comfortable territory to live in, this place of contradictions. Hatred, anger and exploitation are the prominent features of this landscape.[31]

---

28 See Theodor W. Adorno, "The Essay as Form," *New German Critique* 32 (Spring 1984): 151–71; and György Lukács, "On the Nature and Form of the Essay," in *Soul and Form*, trans. Anna Bostock, ed. John T. Sanders and Katie Terezakis (New York: Columbia University Press, 2010), 16–34.
29 Du Plessis, "f-Words," 36.   30 Du Plessis, "f-Words," 16.
31 Gloria Anzaldúa, "Preface," in *Borderlands/La Frontera: The New Mestiza* (San Francisco: Aunt Lute Books, 1987), n.p.

As second-wave feminism yielded to third-wave feminism, a new language was emerging for people whose experiences could not be neatly described in a binary language. Anzaldúa was one of the earliest feminist essayists to describe what it meant to straddle categories and to exist at the intersection of identities that were sometimes at odds.

On Queer Male and Transgender Essays

As noted earlier, there is an androgynous quality to Montaigne's voice and to the genre he inaugurated, a sense that the subject is indeed embodied but only playfully and with self-deprecation. The remoteness of the essayistic voice from the stable, certain, and entitled self so often associated with masculinity represents a challenge to the Cartesian cogito. In "On Repentance," Montaigne celebrates the fluidity of identity:

> I must suit my story to the hour, for soon I may change, not only by chance but also by intention. It is a record of various and variable occurrences, an account of thoughts that are unsettled and, as chance will have it, at times contradictory, either because I am then another self, or because I approach my subject under different circumstances and with other considerations. Hence it is that I may well contradict myself, but the truth, as Demades said, I do not contradict. Could my mind find a firm footing, I should not be making essays, but coming to conclusions; it is, however, always in its apprenticeship and on trial.[32]

Montaigne told us over 400 years ago that an unstable self is perhaps more exciting than a stable one. Many essayists who wrote after Montaigne have played with the variable persona of the essayist, and feminist and queer writers in particular have harvested some of the implications of the Montaignian essayistic project, which, in terms of identity, privileges ambivalence.

Until now, this chapter has focused on the writing of women. Here, I turn to queer male essayists, whose work seems somewhat distinct in its philosophy and poetics from the writing presented thus far. While the essay has generally been a favored outlet for straight men to offer their opinions, observations, and feelings about the world, there is also a rich essay tradition among gay and queer men. Many queer male American essayists owe a debt, consciously or not, to both Karl Heinrich Ulrichs (1825–1895), the late nineteenth-century German writer generally acknowledged as the

---

32 Michel de Montaigne, *Essays*, trans. J. M. Cohen (Baltimore: Penguin Books, 1971), 235.

first uncloseted Western writer, and Oscar Wilde (1854–1900), the Anglo-Irish poet, playwright, and essayist whose suggestive and overt self-revelations offered a model for queer male writing that followed. Ulrichs published *Forschungen über das Rätsel der mannmännlichen Liebe* (Studies on the riddle of male-male love) in 1898, and was thoroughly vilified at the time, but since the 1980s, his legacy has been revived. Wilde mostly offered aesthetic reflections, witticisms, and polemics in his essays, but his letters written from prison during his incarceration on charges of sodomy and indecency reveal important and intimate details on how he thought about his homosexuality. Alongside these important forerunners of gay and queer male writing, the French writer Jean Genet (1910–1986) is also an important model. His *Thief's Journal* (1949) used memoir and narrative essay to speak fully and unapologetically about queer male experience, and its boldness would be imitated in the decades that followed. Queer and gay male essay writing tends to explore constructed sexual identities as well as the very real personal and political experience of queerness in America. There are countless coming out memoirs and essays that date from late 1970s on. Beginning in the late 1980s, AIDS becomes a central theme in many works of nonfiction from American and non-American writers, including books by Paul Monette, Alain Emmanuel Dreuilhe (1949–1988), Andrew Holleran (1944–), David Wojnarowicz (1954–1992), Hervé Guibert (1955–1991), Edmund White (1940–), and others. Queer essays often deliver unflinching descriptions of sexual intimacy in a context in which one's sexuality must be hidden, denied, or repressed. For example, in his trying out of the possibilities of a Black, queer essayist in a country hostile to Blackness and queerness, James Baldwin (1924–1987) writes the following in his essay "Freaks and the American Ideal of Manhood":

> One afternoon, the young boy I was standing behind put his hand behind him and grabbed my cock at the very same moment that a young boy came up behind me and put his cock against my hand: Ignobly enough, I fled, though I doubt that I was missed. The men in the men's room frightened me, so I moved in and out as quickly as possible, and I also dimly felt, I remember, that I didn't want to "fool around" and so risk hurting the feelings of my uptown friend.[33]

---

33 James Baldwin, "Freaks and the American Ideal of Manhood," *Playboy* (January 1985) 150–57. Reprinted as "Here Be Dragons," in *The Price of the Ticket* (New York: St. Martin's / Marek, 1985), 677–90, 682–83. Citations refer to the "Here Be Dragons" reprint.

Published in *Playboy* in 1985, Baldwin's essay was one of the first to speak publicly and with authority about male American homoerotic experience and about the tribulations of gay men in the United States. "On every street corner, I was called a faggot," he writes.[34] Baldwin's essays transcend any single subject or set of rhetorical maneuvers, despite the oft-noted lyrical rhythms of his prose and his sensitivity to the most oppressive themes in the American cultural and political discourse: race, gender, and the complexities of personal identity within these frameworks. For many critics and readers, it is this richness of prose in the service of inescapably complex ideas that marks Baldwin as the most important American essayist of the twentieth century.

Baldwin's groundbreaking work on race, gender, and sexuality and the theoretical work on gender by scholars like Butler, Sedgwick, and Toril Moi (1953–)[35] are important precursors to the more recent essays of Wayne Koestenbaum (1958–). Since the 1990s, Koestenbaum has used the essay form to explore questions of gender, sexuality, and identity. His first book of note, *The Queen's Throat: Opera, Homosexuality, and the Mystery of Desire* (1993), was followed, over the next two decades, by a series of books that pay homage to his intellectual influences (Julia Kristeva [1941–], Jean Genet [1910–1986], Michel Foucault [1926–1984], Roland Barthes [1915–1980], and the aforementioned gender theorists) through a creative blend of queer theory and poetic imagination. Through these essay collections – such as *Hotel Theory* (2007), *Humiliation* (2011), and *Figure It Out* (2020) – Koestenbaum has staked out a significant territory in the homoerotics of the essay. In *Humiliation*, he writes:

> I'm not sure Freud is correct about abreaction: Genet, for example, didn't dilute the strength of his early humiliation; he simply performed an act of alchemy on it. Abreaction neutralizes value; alchemy adds value. Alchemy is imagination and moral transformation – or, as Nietzsche put it, transvaluation. Genet turns moral values inside out by repeatedly eroticizing the humiliated position – spit, stink, sperm.[36]

Here, characteristically, Koestenbaum mixes theoretical and visceral language, adding a note of whimsy. These characteristics apply more broadly to his work. He also tends to share highly personal information but presents it in an almost dissociated voice. In "My 1980s" from *My 1980s and Other Essays*

---

34 Baldwin, "Here Be Dragons," 684.
35 See Toril Moi's books *Sexual/Textual Politics: Feminist Literary Theory* (1985) and *What Is a Woman? And Other Essays* (1999), and her anthology *French Feminist Thought: A Reader* (1987).
36 Wayne Koestenbaum, *Humiliation* (New York: Picador, 2011), 102.

(2013), he writes, "A stranger smooched me during a 'Read My Lips' kiss-in near the Jefferson Market Public Library: festive politics. 1985? I stumbled on the ceremony. Traffic stopped."[37]

In the United States in the 1980s, essays by gay and queer men truly flourished. Here we can point to books like Cary Alan Johnson's *Other Countries: Black Gay Voices* (1988), a mixed-genre anthology in which gay Black men use literature to articulate the specificities of their experience. The HIV and AIDS epidemic occasioned a host of nonfiction narratives, both AIDS-specific and more general coming out stories. Since this era, many historical studies of queerness and more general personal reflections have been published and widely read, including essays and memoirs by such writers as Martin Duberman (1930–), Paul Monette (1945–1995), Mark Doty (1953–), Reinaldo Arenas (1943–1990), Edmund White (1940–), Samuel R. Delaney (1942–), John Francisco Rechy (1931–), Larry Kramer (1935–2020), Bruce Benderson (1946–), Assotto Saint (1957–1994), Hilton Als (1960), David Sedaris (1956–), and Alexander Chee (1994–), just to name a few. I would like to single out the work of David Wojnarowicz, whose *Close to the Knives* was published in 1991, followed by *Memories That Smell like Gasoline* (1992), and posthumously, *The Waterfront Journals* (1997). In Wojnarowicz's work, especially *Close to the Knives*, the knife edge of gender and genre combine in radical essayistic forms, tones, and self-expositions. Wojnarowicz died of AIDS in 1992, but his legacy of essays, essay films, and other experimental forms should be acknowledged as essential contributions to the innovation of the essay form.

If the essay is today enjoying another "golden age," it is due in part to an efflorescence of queer writing, including, in the last ten years, works by transgender essayists such as Thomas Page McBee, Ryka Aoki, Daniel M. Lavery, Grace Lavery, T. Fleischmann, Julia Serrano, Jennifer Finney Boylan, Lucy Sante, and others. The work of transgender writers has, as one might expect, an a serious and sustained interest in the body in all of its facets: the visceral body, the body as construct, and the ways that gender and sexuality are politically and culturally fraught. T. Fleischman and Lucy Sante, for example, resist conventional genres – *transcend* genres – in books that combine essay, memoir, lyric poetry, and history.[38] The LGBTQ+ essay has come out of the literary closet, offering some of the most daring and

---

37 Wayne Koestenbaum, "My 1980s," in *My 1980s and Other Essays* (New York: Farrar, Straus and Giroux, 2013), 3–14, 5.
38 See, for example, T. Fleischman, *Syzgy, Beauty: An Essay* (Louisville, KY: Sarabande Books, 2012); and Lucy Sante, *The Factory of Facts* (New York: Knopf Doubleday, 1999).

innovative essayistic prose of the contemporary era. That we have voices as varied as Piper Daniels, in *Ladies Lazarus* (2018), Matilda Bernstein Sycamore, in *The Freezer Door* (2020), and Wayne Koestenbaum, in *Humiliation*, is a testament to the overdue democratization of the essay in America and the essay's ability to continually renew and revise its boundaries as a form, as a genre, as a vehicle for intimate, public, and politically and personally necessary expression.

34
Disability and the American Essay

ANNE FINGER

Say the name Helen Keller (1880–1968), and the image that in all likelihood will come to mind will be that of a Victorian girl in a starched white pinafore, her hand held beneath gushing cold water as Annie Sullivan saws away at a pump handle, finger spelling "W-A-T-E-R, W-A-T-E-R" into the child's outstretched hand. That moment of Keller's entry into the English language was no doubt a turning point in her life, but it was just that – one of many turning points in a long life. Keller was a remarkable writer, the author not only of *The Story of My Life* (1902), in which that scene at the water pump was first told, but of works that delved into her experience of disability – notably *The World I Live In* (1908) – and of essays that link disability to her radical politics, collected in both *Helen Keller: Her Socialist Years* (1967) and in *Helen Keller: Selected Writings* (2005).[1]

In "How I Became a Socialist," Keller countered the argument that she had been hoodwinked into socialism by Annie Sullivan's husband, John Macy, pointing out that she had read widely in socialist literature – everything from H. G. Wells's *New Worlds for Old* (1908) to Karl Kautsky's writings on the Erfurt program,[2] available in Braille in German. Other texts were finger spelled into her hand. "It is no easy and rapid thing to absorb through one's fingers a book of 50,000 words on economics. But it is a pleasure," she declared, "and one which I shall enjoy repeatedly until I have made myself acquainted with all the classic socialist authors."[3] In the beautifully

---

[1] Helen Keller, *Helen Keller: Her Socialist Years*, ed. Philip Sheldon Foner (New York: International, 1967); and Helen Keller, *Helen Keller: Selected Writings*, ed. Kim E. Nielsen (New York: New York University Press, 2005).
[2] Karl Kautsky, *Das Erfurter Programm in seinem grundsätzlichen Teil erläutert* [The class struggle (Erfurt Program)] (Stuttgart: Social Democratic Party, 1892).
[3] Keller, *Helen Keller: Her Socialist Years*, 22.

written "The Hand of the World," she returns to the hand, which figures so prominently in nearly all of her work. Noting the safe and comfortable life that she leads, writes: "Through these generous surroundings I feel the touch of a hand, invisible but potent, all-sustaining – the hand that wove my garments, the hand that stretched the roof over my head, the hand which printed the pages that I read."[4] While many her essays are timeless, there are pieces in *Her Socialist Years* that have not aged well, particularly those that celebrate the since fallen Soviet Republic. In "Onward, Comrades!" she writes: "The hour has struck for the Grand March! Onward, comrades, all together! ... All the powers of darkness could not still the shout of joy in faraway Moscow! Meteor-like through the heavens flashed the golden words of light, 'Soviet Republic of Russia.'"[5]

Unlike *The Story of My Life*, which reveals Keller's entry into a world centered on nondisability, *The World I Live In* asks the reader to enter into Keller's world and become familiar with her ways of knowing through touch and smell and taste. "The blind," she dryly notes, "are not supposed to be the best of guides,"[6] but she assures readers that she will not lead them into fire, water, or a deep pit. How does one know the world through those senses assumed to be lesser? Keller speaks of the sulfuric smell of a match being lit, of the scent of a far-off storm, of the feel of a rose, of a peach. The book is sensuous, in all meanings of that word. Unfortunately, it was not a financial success; the book-buying public was drawn to the sentimentalized child rather than to the complicated adult woman. Keller may seem to be a saintly creature who had ascended into an ethereal realm far removed from petty financial considerations, but this was far from the case: She had to scrape together enough money to support not just herself but Annie Sullivan. Money – or, more accurately, the lack thereof – is a theme that runs through many essays about disability.[7]

It certainly runs through Randolph Bourne's essay "The Handicapped – By One of Them." First published anonymously in 1911 in the *Atlantic Monthly*, it was later revised and reprinted in Bourne's 1913 collection, *Youth and Life.*

4 Keller, *Helen Keller: Her Socialist Years*, 38.   5 Keller, *Helen Keller: Her Socialist Years*, 107.
6 Helen Keller, *The World I Live In* (New York: Century, 1908), 4.
7 The title essay in Paul Longmore's *Why I Burned My Book*, discussed later in this chapter, details the grinding poverty in which Longmore lived while receiving Social Security disability benefits. In her memoir, *Sick*, Porochista Khakpour writes that living with Lyme disease has cost her more than $140,000. The poverty rate is more than twice as high for the disabled population as for the nondisabled, with poverty both causing disability and disability causing poverty. Rebecca Vallas and Shawn Fremstad, "Disability Is a Cause and Consequence of Poverty," *Talk Poverty* (19 September 2014), https://talkpoverty.org/2014/09/19/disability-cause-consequence-poverty/.

Bourne (1860–1918) was a journalist, an opponent of militarism, an advocate of women's suffrage, and a radical about town in Greenwich Village. John Dos Passos wrote about Bourne in his sprawling – and now sadly overlooked – novel *Nineteen Nineteen*, describing him as follows:

> This little sparrowlike man,
> tiny twisted bit of flesh in a black cape,
> always in pain and ailing,
> put a pebble in his sling
> and hit Goliath square in the forehead with it.[8]

In his aforementioned essay, Bourne didn't neglect the psychological impact of being disabled, but he did argue that his experience of disability was largely shaped by the social experience of disability discrimination. He described the years during which he had "besieged . . . firm after firm" seeking employment, meeting with the attitude, "'How could it enter your head that we should find any use for a man like you?'"[9] One of the essay's techniques is a series of shifts between the first and third person, as sometimes Bourne speaks of his experiences as his own, and at other times speaks as a handicapped Everyman. Bourne was, of course, a product of his time – how could it be otherwise? – and despite his political sympathies with feminism, the handicapped are always male in his writing. Bourne saw disability as a path to a broader understanding of the world:

> He [the handicapped man] will be filled with a profound sympathy for all who are despised and ignored in the world. When he has been through the neglect and struggles of a handicapped and ill-favored man himself, he will begin to understand the feelings of all the horde of the unpresentable and the unemployable, the incompetent and the ugly, the queer and crotchety people who make up so large a proportion of human folk.[10]

Bourne died when he was just thirty-two years old. His writing often prefigures the concerns of the social movements that grew in the later part of the century. His admirers can only imagine the work he might have produced had his life not been cut short by the 1918 flu pandemic.

While we know the essays of writers such as Keller and Bourne, who had access to mainstream publications and a broad audience, other lesser-known essayists' work might be uncovered in the archives of publications such as the *Polio Chronicle*, published at the rehabilitation center in Warm Springs,

---

8 John Dos Passos, *Nineteen Nineteen* (New York: Harcourt Brace, 1930), 140.
9 Randolph Bourne, *Youth and Life* (Boston: Houghton Mifflin, 1913), 147.
10 Bourne, *Youth and Life*, 350.

Georgia, or the *Bedpan Gazette*, published at the rehabilitation center Rancho Los Amigos in Southern California. Before the advent of the disability movement at the end of the twentieth century, writings about disability were rarely able to find a mainstream audience. While both Bourne and Keller speak of their personal experiences in their essays, their focus is always on the broader social experience of disability. Bourne's work in particular begins to imagine a disabled community by linking him to others who have been scorned by society. Elsewhere, Bourne made central to his work the notion of the "beloved community," envisioning a world of mutual care and productive social tension.

The polio epidemics of the first half of the twentieth century produced a raft of memoirs and essays. Publishers seemed more inclined to give a voice to polio survivors like President Franklin Delano Roosevelt, whose prominence brought attention to the affliction, rather than to those who dealt with diseases that still lived in the shadows, such as muscular dystrophy, spina bifida, and psychiatric impairments. Most of these memoirs follow a predictable arc: One day the narrator is playing baseball or hopscotch, and the next they wake up with a fever and aching legs. Before the day is out, they find themselves catapulted out of the world of the well, their limbs paralyzed, perhaps even in iron lungs. These works chart their path back into the "normal" world, albeit on its fringes. Leonard Kriegel (1933–2022), disabled by polio at the age of eleven, is one of the most skilled writers of this genre, detailing with rage and depth the losses he experienced, and how he strove, in the face of what he saw as a wound to his masculinity, to recreate himself as a man. He defiantly claimed the word "cripple," liking its roughness, its lack of euphemism, its in-your-face quality. *The Long Walk Home* (1964) delved into his experiences with hospitalization and rehabilitation. Two later books, *Falling into Life* (1991) and *Flying Solo: Reimagining Manhood, Courage, and Loss* (1998), continued this exploration of his lifelong project of remaking himself. Lorenzo Milam's *The Cripple Liberation Front Marching Band Blues* (1992), Jim Marugg's *Beyond Endurance* (1954), and Mark O'Brien's *How I Became a Human Being* (2012) are three among the many memoirs in this genre.

While the essayists who wrote about their experiences with polio did not think of themselves as part of a disability movement, they did have a sense of community. In *Black Bird Fly Away: Disabled in an Able-Bodied World* (1998), Hugh Gregory Gallagher (1932–2004) wrote of the links formed between patients at Warm Springs, the Georgia rehabilitation center for people with polio founded by Franklin Delano Roosevelt. Those who had had polio, raised with the belief that they could achieve anything – after all, a polio survivor had been president – and finding themselves confronted with discrimination and inaccessibility – formed the core of the early disability rights movement.

A Book Burning

Like Kriegel, Milam, Marugg, and O'Brien, Paul K. Longmore (1946–2010) was disabled by polio. His collection of essays, *Why I Burned My Book and Other Essays on Disability* (2003) is a sharp break with such memoirs, rooted in the social and economic conditions resulting from disability rather than in his personal experiences.

The book Longmore set on fire in front of the Los Angeles Federal Building on an October day in 1988 was his own, *The Invention of George Washington* (1988). It was a book he'd spent nearly ten years writing and was proud of: It had begun as his doctoral dissertation in history, and then been expanded into the text that had been accepted by one of the nation's most prestigious academic publishers, the University of California Press. But as about forty or so supporters of disability rights and members of the press looked on, Longmore ignited wads of newspaper in a grill meant for roasting hamburgers and hot dogs, and then watched a copy his book be consumed by flames.

While Randolph Bourne had written both of "the beloved community" and of how his experiences of disability had given him a sense of kinship with those who were thrust out of the mainstream of society, he did not seem to have imagined a disability community, inspired by the civil rights struggles of Black Americans during the 1950s and '60s, organizing politically for social change. By the time that Longmore burned his book, a disabled community had come into being, albeit one that was marked by the world in which it had been born: While a foundation of the movement was an analogy between disability oppression and racism – Longmore speaks of "a minority group"[11] model as central to the disability rights movement – the movement rarely interrogated its own overwhelming whiteness and its relegation of disabled people of color to the sidelines.

Longmore's *Why I Burned My Book and Other Essays on Disability* exemplifies work that grew out of the disability rights movement, which came to national prominence with the 1977 sit-in at San Francisco's Federal Building.

---

[11] Paul K. Longmore, *Why I Burned My Book and Other Essays on Disability* (Philadelphia: Temple University Press), 205.

Section 504 of the Rehabilitation Act of 1973 forbade discrimination against disabled people by any entity receiving federal financial assistance. After years of seeing the law largely ignored, activists in Atlanta, Boston, Chicago, Denver, Los Angeles, New York City, Philadelphia, San Francisco, and Seattle staged demonstrations at federal office buildings, demanding enforcement of the law. At the San Francisco Federal Building the sit-in lasted close to a month, with over 100 disabled people and their supporters occupying the building. The demonstrators were not only successful in getting the federal government to begin implementing the law, but more importantly in establishing the disability rights movement as a powerful force for change.

Longmore introduces the title essay with a memory of sitting in a wood-paneled seminar room at Stanford, taking part in a discussion about welfare policy. He looks around the room and wonders if anyone else in the room has ever been "on welfare," known the system's petty humiliations and endless strictures, strictures that "severely constricted [his] life and work."[12] Detailing how his life was shaped by bureaucratic policies does not come easily to him: He would prefer, he notes, to write biography rather than autobiography, but his struggle to get an education needed to be told. The trajectory of his life was profoundly shaped by "pervasive social prejudice, systematic segregation, and institutionalized discrimination."[13] His impairment involved the need for intermittent respiratory support from a ventilator and daily assistance from aides, which meant that he needed to structure his finances so that these services, provided by the State of California, would be continual. Without them, he would have died. In order to continue to receive those benefits, he had to continue to receive Supplemental Security Income (SSI), the federal income program for poor people with disabilities – so that along with it, his attendants could be paid and MediCal (California's version of Medicaid) would continue to pay for his ventilator. His life was spent in a bureaucratic maze. He received $135 a month from SSI, and somehow, out of that pittance, he managed to pay tuition for a single course each year. He had been turned down for a fellowship because the grad school committee administering the award was convinced that, because of his disability, no one would ever hire him to teach. The committee nonetheless assured him that they found his courage admirable. His plan to get a doctorate was then nearly thwarted by Claremont Graduate School's regulations, which required doctoral students to complete their course work within a specified time. For those who have never wrestled with these Kafkaesque systems, Longmore's

---

12 Longmore, *Why I Burned*, 230.   13 Longmore, *Why I Burned*, 231.

story may seem shocking; to those who have lived with the constraints and irrationalities of the disability system, it will be all too familiar. He was repeatedly turned down for fellowships. He tried – unsuccessfully – to get help from disability-related charities and even wrote to then president Ronald Reagan in hopes that something could be done. Perseverance, resilience, determination: Longmore had all of these in spades, but his essays make clear that the forces arrayed against him were and are part of deeply embedded structures, not personal problems that could be willed away. Healing, adjustment, and peace are not on the menu in such a pernicious system.

Longmore's publication of a book was an important step in furthering his academic career. However, research fellowships and book royalties are considered "unearned" income and thus jeopardized his benefit payments. He doesn't fail to note the irony of receiving royalties for a book he spent ten years writing being considered "unearned income." In his writing, he also criticizes the fact that students have had to turn down scholarships in order not to lose medical coverage and personal assistance services. Longmore's protest was part of a push that finally required that the Social Security Administration consider book royalties as earned income, although grants and fellowships are still considered unearned income. Other essays in the book are less personal, but no less passionate: He writes of the League of the Physically Handicapped, a Depression-era group that lobbied for the right to be included in New Deal programs; of the dangers to disabled people posed by physician-assisted suicide; of Princeton University's appointment of philosopher Peter Singer – who advocates the killing of some disabled newborns – to an endowed chair. Longmore's essays are straightforward, and, as one would expect from a historian of his caliber, rigorously researched. Writing against the then prevailing attitude that disabilities are individual tragedies, he emphasizes the broader forces that have shaped disability history.

Things Fall Apart

In her essay "On Being Ill" (1926), published nearly one hundred years ago, Virginia Woolf wrote, "Considering how common illness is ... it becomes strange indeed that illness has not taken its place with love, battle, and jealousy among the prime themes of literature."[14] The last few decades have seen an upsurge in writings about illness and disability, primarily memoirs. The feminist movement's insistence that the personal is political

---

14 Virginia Woolf, "On Being Ill," *New Criterion* 4, no. 1 (January 1926): 32–45, 32.

certainly played a role in this, as did the disability movement's increasing cultural visibility. Some memoirs from the past and today tend to focus on overcoming one's disability and returning to normalcy, such as Clifford Beers's (1876–1943) *A Mind That Found Itself* (1908) or Charles Mee's (1938–) *A Nearly Normal Life* (1999). More recent memoirs often reject the expected narrative arc of a descent from the ordinary world into the shadow world of sickness, and a return to some form of health – whether that is a physical recovery or to a self that has been burnished by suffering. Instead, these works emphasize the richness of disability experience and interrogate the assumption that disability makes one a lesser human being who must strive to achieve or imitate a nondisabled experience. Nancy Mairs's (1943–2016) series of book-length essays about her life with multiple sclerosis – including *Plaintext* (1986), *Waist High in the World* (1996), *Carnal Acts* (1990), *Remembering the Bone House* (1989) – explore religious belief, sexuality, and family relations in a body that will never be cured. Kenny Fries's (1960–) *Body, Remember* (1997) uses his experience of being born with shortened lower limbs to explore the intersections of masculinity and queerness with disability. His more recent works mix his personal experiences with broader questions: *A History of My Shoes and the Evolution of Darwin's Theory* (2007) asks what disability brings to our understanding of evolution; *In the Province of the Gods* (2017) explores being a disabled outsider in Japan; *Staring Back: The Disability Experience from the Inside Out* (1997), a collection that Fries edited, gathers a number of essays along with poetry, fiction, and plays. The book's title asserts the necessity for disabled people to narrate their own experiences rather than being defined by others.

John Hockenberry's (1956–) essay in that collection, "Walking with the Kurds," describes his journey with Kurds made refugees by the wars in Iraq, shifting between a description of the Kurdish people with whom he is traveling, that people's long and tragic history, and the strange sensation that riding a donkey gives him – as if he is walking again after fifteen years as a wheelchair user. His body is seen as a metaphor by some of the Kurds traveling with him: "'Bush is speaking of freedom and here we are free? You see us. They send you to us. You, who cannot stand?'" Hockenberry concludes, "To him my presence was an unsightly metaphor of America itself: able to arrive but unable to stand."[15] What is rich in this essay, and what marks a break from much previous disability writing, is not just the unashamed presence of the disabled body; it is that this body, though in

---

15 John Hockenberry, "Walking with the Kurds," in *Staring Back: The Disability Experience from the Inside Out*, ed. Kenny Fries (New York: Plume, 1997), 22–36, 28.

pain much of the time, is not defined by that pain. Hockenberry details how it feels to ride a donkey along a rutted trail going uphill in his paraplegic body, and the radically different way it feels to ride that donkey downhill. Life goes on in this body, which is not a blank, closed, devastated space, not a landscape after battle. It still brings a rich variety of experiences and nurtures the spirit through unexpected sources of amazement.

G. Thomas Couser devotes the last chapter of *Signifying Bodies: Disability in Contemporary Life Writing* (2009) to what he terms "new disability memoirs," works that "are characterized ... as their authors' lives have come to be, by a sharp awareness of how disability is socially and culturally constructed,"[16] seeing Stephen Kuusisto's *Planet of the Blind* (1997), Georgina Kleege's *Sight Unseen* (1998), Anne Finger's *Elegy for a Disease: A Personal and Cultural History of Polio* (2006), Harriet McBryde Johnson's *Too Late to Die Young* (2006), and Simi Linton's *My Body Politic* (2005) as exemplars of this new tendency.

The writers of these memoirs, in addition to all being white, are all also either blind or have mobility impairments. In contrast, *The Collected Schizophrenias: Essays* (2019) by Taiwanese American writer Esmé Weijun Wang plunges us into her life with schizoaffective disorder. Her disability causes her real suffering: She dodges invisible demons, and she watches a locomotive hurl toward her and then disappear. The radical decentering she experiences,[17] the way that her life does not cohere into a single, neat narrative, is echoed in the structure of the book. In Wang's account of her life with schizoaffective disorder, there is no center to hold. Wang writes:

> Schizophrenia terrifies ... Craziness scares us because we are creatures who long for structure and sense; we divide the interminable days into years, months, and weeks. We hope for ways to corral and control bad fortune, illness, unhappiness, discomfort, and death – all inevitable outcomes that we pretend are anything but. And still, the fight against entropy seems wildly futile in the face of schizophrenia, which shirks reality in favor of its own internal logic.[18]

The structure of her book conveys the fragmentation she experiences. Wang's writing about her life comes at her readers in shards. Charles Mee, a playwright disabled as a teenager by polio, describes a similar approach to

---

16 G. Thomas Couser, *Signifying Bodies: Disability in Contemporary Life Writing* (Ann Arbor, MI: University of Michigan Press, 2009), 165.
17 The metaphor of decentering can be found earlier in Elyn Saks's memoir of dealing with schizophrenia, titled *The Center Cannot Hold* (2007).
18 Esmé Weijun Wang, "Diagnosis," in *The Collected Schizophrenias: Essays* (Minneapolis: Graywolf Press, 2019), 3.

his writing: "I like plays that are not too neat, too finished, too presentable. My plays are broken, jagged, filled with sharp edges, filled with things that take sudden turns, careen into each other, smash up, veer off in sickening turns. That feels good to me. It feels like my life. It feels like the world."[19] Alice Wong's *Year of the Tiger: An Activist's Life* (2022) goes even further in rejecting the traditional structures of a memoir, mixing narrative with photographs, drawings, recipes, and tweets.

Wang notes the resistance to diagnosis, common in the disability movement, which sees diagnosis as reinscribing the medical model. The distinction between impairment and disability is not so neatly drawn here. She (sometimes) finds comfort in her diagnosis of schizoaffective disorder, bipolar type, linking her to a long history of others who have been similarly affected. *The Diagnostic and Statistical Manual of Mental Disorders* even assigned a number – 295.70 – to the diagnosis that affects her and so many others: "A diagnosis is comforting because it provides a framework – a community, a lineage ... A diagnosis says that I am crazy, but in a particular way: one that has been experienced and recorded not just in modern times, but also by the ancient Egyptians."[20] This need to break with some of the certainties of what have become orthodoxies within the disabled community is crucial to Wang's expansion of disability: the easy division between impairment and disability. Wang also upends another expectation of mental illness memoirs: that they be written from a perspective of sanity, looking back at one's period of madness.[21] In the words of Anne Sexton, one is to have traveled at least partway back from bedlam.[22] Wang, however, begins one of her essays, "Perdition Days," with the line: "I write this while experiencing a strain of psychosis known as Cotard's delusion, in which the patient believes that they are dead."[23] That sentence captures some of the shifting sands on which she stands. She is both convinced of the fact that she is dead and is, at the same time, writing an essay. She is aware of the terror induced by the diagnosis of what she terms "the schizophrenias," schizophrenia and its associated disorders. She quotes a psychoanalyst who says that

---

19 Charles Mee, "What I Like," *Charles See: The (Re)making Project*, www.charlesmee.org /charles-mee.shtml.
20 Wang, "Diagnosis," 5.
21 All of these terms, I should note, are fraught and contested, with some who have psychiatric disabilities claiming terms such as "madness" or "mental illness" while others find them pejorative. I will simply acknowledge that there is a lively discussion among those with psychiatric impairments/biopsychosocial disabilities/madness/ mental illness about these terms.
22 Anne Sexton entitled her book of poems about her stay in a psychiatric ward *To Bedlam and Partway Back* (Boston: Houghton Mifflin, 1960).
23 Esmé Weijun Wang, "Perdition Days," in *Collected Schizophrenias*, 145.

schizophrenics seem to have "'crossed over from the human world to the non-human environment.'" "People speak of schizophrenics as if they were dead without being dead,"[24] Wang writes.

While the book opens with a firm rooting in diagnosis – indeed, "Diagnosis" is the title of her first essay – Wang also allows for the possibility of other ways of seeing her condition, within limits. She firmly rejects the views of the many who ask her if she has ever considered that her condition might be a spiritual characteristic, or that in another culture – one purer, surely than the one in which we reside – she might have been a shaman or a healer. Perhaps, but this dismissal of the very real suffering she experiences strikes her as too easy, although she allows for certain other, less glib, ways of looking at her condition. Referred for a complementary and alternative medicine consult, she is told that the root of her ailment is her Fire Qi; a genetic analysis reveals a mutation that gives her "slightly higher odds" of schizophrenia; an astrological chart reveals a fragile energetic field due to the placement of Neptune, Saturn, and Pluto in her chart.

Wang rejects the normalizing impulse that insists, We are just like you, we happen to be disabled, but it is a small matter, a part of who you are. As part of her training to be a speaker who will seek to remove the stigma around mental illness, she is taught to use "person first" language, to say, "a person with schizophrenia," rather than "a schizophrenic." "Our conditions," she dryly notes, "lie over us like smallpox blankets: we are one thing and the illness is another."[25] But this is not her experience: She does not have a sense of herself apart from her illness.

None of this suggests that there isn't a profound social dimension to what she experiences. Her second essay, "Toward a Pathology of the Possessed," tells us about the death of Malcoum Tate, a thirty-four-year-old schizophrenic man shot thirteen times by his younger sister. The newspaper headlines reporting on the death are in some ways more chilling than the murder itself: "Family's Nightmare Ends with Slaying of Problem Child," "Death Ends Family's Nightmare," and "NC Family's Final Solution Was Murder." That last headline is both horrific and revealing with its echoes of the Nazis' "Final Solution" of the killing of the Jews, which was preceded by the killing of people with disabilities, most often people with psychiatric diagnoses. In this case a family's "problem" was resolved by thirteen blasts

---

24 Wang, "Diagnosis," 3.
25 Esmé Weijun Wang, "Toward a Pathology of the Possessed," in *Collected Schizophrenias*. 145.

from a gun, with the person firing the weapon saying, "'Malcom, I love you, and I'm sorry'" as she lets loose another round.

Wang also details how she needs to stage-manage her presentation of self. A former fashion blogger, Wang would most likely dress in designer clothes with tasteful make-up no matter what, but she makes it clear how much she needs to differentiate herself from the assumptions about those with schizophrenia: She doesn't live in a tent under the freeway, her body doesn't reek, she's well dressed, she's attended prestigious universities – although at one point, hospitalized in rural Louisiana, her statements about having attended Yale and Stanford are assumed to be delusions of grandeur. Speaking of Yale: As a high school senior, Wang opened the mailbox to see a large envelope from Yale, and stood at the mailbox shrieking with joy – although she was not the type of girl to shriek. The presence of disabled student service offices, ramps, curb cuts, Braille signage and the sight of students and professors in wheelchairs or using canes might have given the impression that the problem of disability had been solved on college campuses, but Wang makes it clear that this was not the situation for students with her kind of disability. She was warned by other students in the Asian American performance art group she'd joined to be wary of the Mental Hygiene Department, part of student health services: Watch out for that place. Never let them know if you're thinking about killing yourself. The advice turns out to be good: The university's first solution to Wang's mental health crisis was to allow her to stay if she moved off campus and her mother came to live with her. Wang also writes against the widespread assumption that medications are the solution to mental illness: She does use medications, but they are hardly the miracle drugs they are touted to be. They have frightening "side" effects. In her work, she writes against the simple certainties of much of the disability rights movement, insisting on the complexities of her life with her disability.

Roxane Gay's (1974–) memoir *Hunger* does not immediately identify itself as a disability memoir. Toward the end of the book, Gay states, "I don't know if fat is a disability,"[26] and then goes on to detail some of the questions she asks herself before entering a new space: "Is there an elevator? Are there stairs to the stage? How many? Is there a handrail?"[27] To my mind, Gay makes it clear that fat *is* a disability, not only in terms of her physical needs for navigation of space, but also in the way that her body limits job opportunities: At one point her father says to her, "[A]ll those degrees you are getting

---

26 Roxane Gay, *Hunger* (New York: HarperCollins, 2017), 297.   27 Gay, *Hunger*, 298.

aren't going to do you any good because no one is going to hire you at your size."[28] Her body is a lightning rod for social anxieties. While fat people face discrimination regardless of their gender, women and others who are not firmly ensconced in maleness are seen as presenting an added affront to the world. Gay's body becomes emblematic of women who take what they need – and then take even more, who indulge themselves, who give themselves pleasure, who take up space, who refuse to please the male gaze.

Gay traces her fatness to the fact that she was gang-raped at the age of twelve. In language that is spare, riveting, almost hypnotic, Gay recounts her ordeal: Something terrible happened. She says those words over and over again. A chorus, a chant, an incantation. Something terrible happened. Something terrible happened. And then she takes us into the abandoned cabin in the woods where the boy she loved and his friends raped her. After the gang rape, Gay eats. She eats because it seems to be the only way she can brings herself comfort; she eats because she wants to turn her body into a fortress. She eats because a body like hers – defined by doctors as super morbidly obese – thwarts male desire.

Like many of the other disability essays I have focused on here, Gay's story is not one of overcoming, of victory. "This story of my body is not a story of triumph. This is not a weight-loss memoir."[29] There won't be a picture of a thin Gay on the cover, perhaps standing in the single leg of the trousers she had worn before. Gay is clear that her body is often regarded as transgressive to the point of seeming criminal. The crime of daring to fill herself up. The crime of having a body that bears the marks of what it has endured. The crime of taking up space. She is also sharply observant of what it means to be fat within a capitalist system, which encourages overconsumption and then sells solutions to that overconsumption – weight-loss camps, diet foods, bariatric surgery. She is not entirely comfortable with the designation "survivor": "Victim" is an alternative word she claims. Her writing on victimhood resonates with that of Leah Lakshmi Piepzna-Samarasinha, who wrote in "Not over It, Not Fixed, and Living a Life Worth Living"[30] about how ableist notions of recovery, like the necessity to heal or find closure speedily, are often forced upon those who have been through trauma. Similarly, Porochista Khakpour's *Sick: A Memoir* (2018) recounts not the smooth

---

28 Gay, *Hunger*, 118.   29 Gay, *Hunger*, 4.
30 Leah Lakshmi Piepzna-Samarasinha, "Not over It, Not Fixed, and Living a Life Worth Living: A Disability Justice Vision of Survivorhood," in *Whatever Gets You Through: Twelve Survivors on Life after Sexual Assault*, ed. Stacey May Fowles and Jen Sookfong Lee (Vancouver: Greystone Books, 2019), 373–413.

narrative of life interrupted when a white-coated doctor stands by the patient's bed and delivers a grim diagnosis. Her experience of chronic illness is that of a disease that fluctuates, confounding physicians. She offers us neither a triumphant recovery nor a wounded self who has grown inwardly whole through her suffering.[31] In Gay's account, her body does not tell a tale of triumph over adversity either. Her essays, like many newer writings in this genre, opt for ambivalence over certitude, openness over closure, and blurred categories over hard-edged ones.

Conclusion

Bourne and Keller, the two disabled essayists who inaugurated the contemporary disability essay, stand as lone individuals, voices crying out in the wilderness. While Bourne speaks of the handicapped man understanding "the feelings of all the horde of the unpresentable and the unemployable,"[32] he cannot yet imagine a world where such a horde might find common cause. By the time Longmore burned his book in front of the Los Angeles Federal Building, a movement of disabled people had come into being, seeking access and integration into existing structures. It is not surprising that the works from this period do not yet contest the traditional forms of the essay and memoir; their priority was first to expand what could be articulated about disability before turning to the form these articulations might take. As Couser points out, the genre he terms "new disability memoirs" grew out of the field of disability studies, linking personal experience to broader social circumstances and engaging in formal experimentation. More recently, authors like Gay have expanded the notion of disability and contested the boundaries between the disabled and nondisabled worlds. At the same time, writers such as Wang and Wong have rejected linear narratives and received structures of memoir and essay. Their works reflect in their form the roughness and jaggedness, the surprises and unsteadiness, that are part of so many disabled lives.

Indeed, disability is part of human life; it affects all of us, from the moment we are first seen by the world. Sometimes, that is when we emerge from another human body or first appear on a sonogram: From that early moment, we are already slotted into the categories of abled or disabled. "Everything looks fine," those attending the birth may say, or perhaps they

---

31 Porochista Khakpour, *Sick: A Memoir* (New York: HarperCollins, 2018).
32 Bourne, *Youth and Life*, 350.

will utter a worried, solemn, "There seems to be a problem." Disability is often random (a virus, a genetic roll of the dice, an autoimmune disorder) or sometimes it is not at all random (a bullet, a bomb, trauma). The polio memoirs of the 1950s and '60s generally told the tale of a white person – usually, although not always, male – with a certain amount of privilege – a suburban home, a university education, a stable home life – suddenly finding life's trajectory interrupted by a bout of illness and subsequent paralysis, and chart a return, in Charles Mee's words, to "a nearly normal life." Newer memoirs, such as Wang's and Gay's, detail more complicated lives, where race and class and trauma intersect with disability. With essays on disability being published and anthologized with ever-greater frequency and the field of disability studies quickly expanding,[33] the American essay will surely benefit from this growing record of experience, told in original, moving, and powerful ways.

---

33 For example, see Peter Catapano and Rosemarie Garland-Thomson, eds., *About Us: Essays from the Disability Series of the New York Times* (New York: Liverlight, 2019); and Lennard J. Davis, *The Disability Studies Reader*, 6th ed. (Milton Park, UK: Taylor and Francis, 2021).

35

The Radical Hybridity of the Lyric Essay

MICHAEL ASKEW

Classrooms and Carnivals

The strength and joy of the lyric essay – a term that has emerged in the last quarter century to describe the genre-fluid, formally experimental work of writers like Annie Dillard (1945–), Anne Carson (1950–), Claudia Rankine (1963–), Maggie Nelson (1973–), Judith Kitchen (1941–2014), Eliot Weinberger (1949–), Wayne Koestenbaum (1958–), Lia Purpura (1964–), Sarah Manguso (1974–), Eula Biss (1977–), Ander Monson (1975–), Kate Zambreno (1977–), and Jenny Boully (1976–) – lies in its resistance to fixity. Its component parts, sitting there in juxtaposition like two apparent strangers on a park bench, are not secure in their relation to each other. Lyric essay: Either word might be adjective and either noun. The term is used equally for the essayistic poetry of Rankine's *Citizen* (2014) as it is for the poetic essays in Dillard's *For the Time Being* (1999), or the twin-noun hybridity of Carson's *Plainwater* (1995), where essays and poems jostle and collide. It is applied, too, to experimental writing that does not obviously fit either of its component categories, like the disembodied footnotes of Boully's *The Body* (2002), or the aphoristic fragments in Nelson's *Bluets* (2009) and Koestenbaum's *Humiliation* (2011). Such broad application suggests that perhaps the most appropriate reading of the term is the least obvious: "lyric (adj.) essay (adj.)," a nounless conjunction of adjectives, a way of reading both essayistically and lyrically without needing to make definite the object of said reading or to concretize it as either essay or lyric. Unmoored from nouns, the lyric essay skates over boundaries, dissolves dichotomies, and makes radical again a form that is at times stuck in the stodginess of its tradition.

Those well versed in the essay's history might find such claims rather inflammatory and myopic – for what could be more radical than the essay in its original, Montaignean incarnation? Yet such a claim must be understood within the context of the lyric essay's emergence within the North American writing program, an environment in which the radical potential of the essay has been buried under a crust of associations with the very things it was originally antithetical to: rote learning, methodology, the classroom. For the contemporary American writing student, the essay is not unlike the *dispositio*, the form of oration Montaigne himself reacted to in his *Essais*: a form of regurgitated learning, fixed in structure and scope, introducing, arguing coherently, and concluding.[1] Paraphrasing its own meaning, its limits are not the productive, fertile edges that Mario Aquilina recently described as the essential quality of the essay as form, but merely reflections of its center.[2]

The lyric essay, at least initially, was an attempt to revivify the essay for such students, for whom this once fluid form had become a fixed, static noun. It was born out of conversations between Deborah Tall, a teacher at Hobart and William Smith Colleges, with her then student John D'Agata, who has gone on to become the term's figurehead, promoting it through works such as his three-volume *A New History of the Essay* (2003, 2009, 2016) and his controversial *Lifespan of a Fact* (2012), as well as in his subsequent teaching. Together, Tall and D'Agata edited the 1997 special edition of *Seneca Review* that announced their term to the world, claiming it as "a fresh way to make music of the world" and, indeed, to find "new worlds."[3] Their manifesto was an attempt to reclaim for the essay its original, transgressive, exploratory spirit. To do so, they would take it somewhere new: to the poetry classroom.

1 O. B. Hardison Jr., "Binding Proteus: An Essay on the Essay," *Sewanee Review* 96, no. 4 (Fall 1988): 610–32, 613.
2 Mario Aquilina, ed., *The Essay at the Limits: Poetics, Politics and Form* (London: Bloomsbury, 2021), 1–4, 12–13.
3 Deborah Tall and John D'Agata, "New Terrain: The Lyric Essay," *Seneca Review* 27, no. 2 (Fall 1997): 7–8, 7–8. D'Agata and Tall were not the first to use the term "lyric essay." In English, it dates back to at least the eighteenth century, to "The Prospect: A Lyric Essay" (1769), a satirical work attributed to Martinus Scriblerus, the persona used by Alexander Pope and Jonathan Swift's Scriblerus Club. The term has an even older history in French, dating back to Frey des Landres's "Essai lyrique sur la religion" (1753), and found attached (sometimes in the plural form "essais lyriques") to later works by Théodore Desorgues, Pierre Colau, Eugène Senoble, and Albert Camus. However, D'Agata and Tall were the first to use the term in the sense of describing a new subgenre, rather than in reference to a specific essay or essays, and the first to suggest that a distinctively "lyric" form of the essay was emerging in North American writing. Moreover, the importance of the 1997 *Seneca Review* manifesto in defining the term for American readers cannot be overstated; it is found referenced in almost every subsequent article, essay, and blog post on "the lyric essay" since. For more on the French lyric essay, see Pierre Glaudes's *L'Essai: métamorphoses d'un genre* (Toulouse: Presses Universitaires du Mirail,2002), which includes a section on the "essai lyrique."

Such an argument might suggest that the lyric essay was merely a new name for the essay, a trendy rebrand. Yet it is notable that the term reimagines the essay *by bringing it into contact with another genre*. Unlike "creative nonfiction" – another term that emerged during the booming interest in nonfiction programs in the 1990s – the lyric essay is not a new subcategory of an existing term, but a term that smashes categories together, that brings the techniques taught in an Introduction to Poetry seminar crashing into a class on the nonfiction narrative, and vice versa. One specific idea the term conveyed at the University of Iowa – where D'Agata went on to study and disseminate his coinage, and where he currently works as director of the nonfiction writing program – was that nonfiction was not its own separate thing, sequestered off from poetry. D'Agata comments that it is the "dirty little secret" at Iowa that the "genres are segregated," something he became increasingly uncomfortable with as he moved from his first MFA in poetry to his second in nonfiction.[4] The lyric essay, as something close to a portmanteau, resists the compartmentalization of genres under what Gerald Graff calls the "field coverage" model of education, in which knowledge is treated as a "set of discrete bricks of information," covered by separate schools, subjects, and modules.[5] Such a model allows departments to be "virtually self-regulating" by providing "enormous flexibility in assimilating new ideas, subjects, and methods";[6] whenever a new idea arises – whether feminism or Marxism, New Journalism or the new nature writing – it can simply be given its own module, its own instructor, added as a new category to the whole. Whatever radical potential the idea may have had is stripped away by the defanging process of modularization. Modules let English departments do what Rebecca Solnit says all categories also do: "let people tidy up the complicated world into something simpler."[7] By choosing a phrase that moves *across* two existing categories, Tall and D'Agata resist the neatness and safety of such modular thinking, and deliberately invite transgression. Unlike "creative nonfiction" – which positions itself as just another easily subsumed subgenre – the term "lyric essay" suggests that there are kinds of learning that can only take place outside of categories, in the spaces that exist between them.[8]

---

4 Sandra Allen, "John D'Agata," *Wag's Revue*, no. 3 (Fall 2009): 31–44, 32.
5 Gerald Graff, *Professing Literature: An Institutional History* (Chicago: University of Chicago Press, 2007), 9.
6 Graff, *Professing Literature*, 7.
7 Rebecca Solnit, "Mysteries of Thoreau, Unsolved," *Orion* 32, no. 3 (June 2013): 18–23, 19.
8 This is one way the lyric essay is distinguishable from other preexisting subcategories of both the essay and the lyric: for example, the tradition of the verse essay, best typified by

Setting the lyric essay in this context reveals something else about how genres work: that the act of creating a space for something can neutralize and thus diminish the very thing space is being made for. Genres teach us the expected standards of behavior within them, licensing certain kinds of thinking. A miscellaneous or ill-defined genre like the essay initially seems to counter this, providing a space in which there are no rules, a space for unlimited play, in which any question can be asked, any idea challenged. Yet it may be that such a category is necessary in order to uphold the conservative standards of the genre system, in the same way that Bakhtin theorizes about the space of carnival: a "temporary liberation from the prevailing truth and from the established order," one that works to release tension and thus reinforce the status quo, rather than letting that tension accumulate and bubble over into revolution.[9] The essay's miscellaneous play, we might say, arises *because of* the rigidity of the norms and rules of classical rhetorical composition, in the same way that carnival is an inevitable side-product of the rigidity of social norms, one that actually enables it. In some sense, delineating such writing as "essay" or "miscellany" reinforces, by creating a space in which all this loose, unrigorous stuff is allowed to spill out, the strict boundaries and rules of the conventional forms that the essay is being pitted against. The formulation of the essay as a genre thus becomes a conservative move, rather than a radical one.

It is only by allowing essayism into other forms that it becomes subversive. By its nature as a hybrid form, the lyric essay places things where they are not meant to go; though its two component genres might be "safe" in their own right, in their combination they become potentially dangerous, like a Harvard men's club colliding with a biker-gang bar. The lyric essay thus unleashes the power of the essayistic mode – that is, the radical potential of *essaying* – which is constrained when it is held within the essay genre. The essay is freest outside "the essay." The rise of the lyric essay and its growth beyond the classrooms in which it was born reveal how important it is to the

Alexander Pope's "An Essay on Criticism" (1711) and "An Essay on Man" (1732–34), but with a lineage that stretches from the ancient verse of Lucretius through John Dryden's "Religio Laici" (1682), Robert Nugent's "An Essay on Happiness" (1737), and Samuel Johnson's "The Vanity of Human Wishes" (1748–49), to more modern examples such as Charles Bernstein's "The Artifice of Absorption" (1988). Such a tradition can be comfortably seen as a subcategory of verse in a way that formally experimental work by writers like Carson and Rankine cannot. See also Judith Kitchen's "Mending Wall," *Seneca Review* 37, no. 2 (Fall 2007): 45–49, which makes a distinction between the "lyric essay" as a genuinely hybrid form and the "lyrical essay" as a subcategory of the essay.

9 Mikhail Bakhtin, *Rabelais and His World*, trans. Hélène Iswolsky (Bloomington, IN: Indiana University Press, 1984), 10.

essay's own nature that it never remain static. It must keep being made anew, given new names and brought into contact with new forms, if it is to retain its essayistic spirit.

Anne Carson's Illusory Towns

The radical potential of the lyric essay as a hybrid genre is felt most strongly in the work of Anne Carson (1950–), the only writer explicitly mentioned in Tall and D'Agata's manifesto, and a crucial figure in the lyric essay's development. Carson's work moves with enormous freedom from form to form, subject to subject, and moment to moment, taking in everything from television to Telemachus, while showing an "imperious disregard for even the laxest of forms," writing poems that read like essays, and essays that read like poems.[10] She seems to choose genres as much for how they fail as how they succeed, as captured by Adam Phillips's comments that, in Carson's work, "all the rituals of form are first and foremost an expression of their own limitations, the sign of what leaks out of them."[11] Like the towns she describes in *Plainwater* as epitomizing the "illusion that things hang together somehow, my pear, your winter," genres in Carson are a convenient organizing fiction, but they are also an "illusion."[12] The analogy is a rich one. Though there might, for practical and political purposes, be a town border, a "Welcome to [Here]" sign, there is no obvious material edge to towns, which usually become sparser at their edges, gradually merging into the surrounding countryside; it is, analogously, in such border regions that Carson resides, where there is "leakage" from one thing into another. There is also no strict taxonomical principle governing when a group of settlements gains enough volume and solidity to be considered a town; it is a matter to be decided by culture, whether a group of houses, shops, public buildings, and roads "hang together" enough – that is, have enough integrity, unity, and cohesion – that we consider them a town. That decision process – analogous to the conversations we have around genres – is something Carson continually prompts us to investigate.

Towns, too, are abstract nouns made up of concrete nouns: They do not themselves exist, but neither are they purely abstract. So it is with genres, and

---

[10] Daphne Merkin, "Last Tango," *New York Times Book Review* (30 September 2001): 12–13, 13.
[11] Adam Phillips, "Fickle Contracts: The Poetry of Anne Carson," *Raritan* 16, no. 2 (Fall 1996): 112–19, 117.
[12] Anne Carson, *Plainwater: Essays and Poetry* (New York: Vintage, 2000), 93.

their relation to the individual texts that they both do and do not consist of; as noted by Jacques Derrida, every text contains a mark of its genre, yet this mark itself "does not belong" to the genre, or rather, "belongs without belonging."[13] Similarly, forms in Carson do not "live" in the towns they belong in; we do not find all of her essays in a neat book of "Essays," but instead encounter them scattered among poems, fictionalized interviews, journal entries, fully referenced pieces of academic prose, numbered lists, scripts for TV shows and operas, and a variety of appendices, epigraphs, and quotations. Many of her works carry subtitles that seem to gently mock the impossibility of labeling or containing what lies therein: "A Fictional Essay in 29 Tangos," for *The Beauty of the Husband* (2001); "Poetry, Essays, Opera" for *Decreation* (2005). Carson is alive to the possibility of the title as a feint, or sleight of hand, as in the impossible promise of an *Autobiography of Red* (1998), the subtitle of which offers two further, contrasting generic entry points: "A Novel in Verse." The title of *Short Talks* (1992), meanwhile, carries the essayist's gesture of modesty, as captured in Abraham Cowley's ironically titled "Of Greatness," in which he wrote that the essay is marked by a taste for "littleness."[14] It suggests that these are neither long, sustained pieces of scholarship nor fully developed theses or arguments; rather, they are "short" and they are "talks" – mere fireside chats, or conversational openings. By not explicitly calling the pieces essays, Carson only enhances their essayistic freedom; one might go further and say, by not actually *writing* essays – for the pieces are too short, their ideas too condensed, to really be seen as examples of the essay *form* – but instead engaging, within these fragments of poetic prose, in the essayistic *mode*, she maximizes the essay's freedom, recalling again the idea that the essay is most fully realized when it takes place inside other genres.

Or rather, for Carson, when it takes place *between* other genres. Carson is at her most essayistic when she is combining different forms. We see this in the poem "Sumptuous Destitution," whose oxymoron title gestures at Carson's love of wrangling with various oppositions (ancient and modern; scholarly and amateur) through the conflation of different forms, held apart but together. Two contrasting elements – short lines of heavily enjambed lyric, and a collage of quotations taken from Emily Dickinson's letters – dance around each other, the relation between them at once both lyrical and essayistic:

---

13 Jacques Derrida, "The Law of Genre," in *Modern Genre Theory*, ed. David Duff (London: Routledge, 2014), 220–31, 230.
14 Abraham Cowley, "Of Greatness," in *Essays, Plays and Sundry Verses*, ed. A. R. Waller (Cambridge, UK: Cambridge University Press, 2014), 429.

"Sumptuous destitution"
Your opinion gives me a serious feeling: I would like to be what you deem me.
(Emily Dickinson letter 319 to Thomas Higginson)

is a phrase
You see my position is benighted.
(Emily Dickinson letter 268 to Thomas Higginson)

scholars use
She was much too enigmatical a being for me to solve in an hour's interview.
(Thomas Higginson letter 342a to Emily Dickinson)[15]

Carson here uses poetic juxtapositions to create essayistic movement. The quotations interrupt the movement of the sentence of the poem, recalling her claim in *Short Talks* that one can "never impede movement harshly enough";[16] the poem thus enters into a kind of dialectic relationship with the quotations, mirroring the contradiction of the title. Across the jumps from the end of a quotation to the start of the next line of the poem, we move from "benighted" to "scholars" and later from "silence" to "rushing" and from "female" to "God," "Sir," and "master," the new line, in each case, picking up an opposite idea, a Socratic countering that propels the poem forward (though note, too, how it is never a *direct* reversal, never a one-eighty bounce-back to where we started, but always a contrasting idea that takes us somewhere new – not "benighted" to "enlightened" but to "scholars"; not "female" to "male" but to "God" – something emphasized by the shift in word type in each case, from adjective to noun, or noun to verb). The gathering of the quotations together is also essayistic, recalling the collage of the commonplace book, and the idea of the essay showing its working; there is a sense of gathering up loose threads, without necessarily tying them together, one that we find throughout *Men in the Off Hours* (2000): Note how it is the "little dropped comments" people made after George Eliot's death that are "saddest of all" in the poem "A Station."[17]

Yet, though there is something tangibly essayistic about the poem, it remains nonetheless unclear which part of it is the essay and which the lyric; the two categories are kept in an unresolved tension. For the quotes, as much as they act as oblique comments on each line of the poem, are also

---

15 Anne Carson, *Men in the Off Hours* (London: Jonathan Cape, 2000), 13.
16 Anne Carson, *Short Talks* (London: Brick Books, 2017), 23.
17 Carson, *Men in the Off Hours*, 23.

commented on, as a whole, by the poem itself, which runs like a thread or rope down the left margin:

> 'Sumptuous destitution'
> is a phrase
> scholars use
> of female
> silence.
> Save what you can, Emily.
> Save every bit of thread.
> One of them may be
> the way out of here.[18]

Each part, then, essays on the other. There is no noun, here: only the verb, *essaying*. In her conglomerate town, the essayistic spirit is free again to move about and roam.

Annie Dillard's Abundant Fecundity

Alongside Carson, perhaps the most important early lyric essayist is Annie Dillard (1945–), whose work, though less hybrid in form than Carson, nonetheless further reveals how even the most capacious and flexible forms can be inadequate, on their own, for writing about certain subjects. Dillard's writing exists in a constant tension between the sacred and the profane, or, to use her terms, the abundant and the fecund. The former is best depicted by a passage from the much-anthologized "Living like Weasels" (1982) where Dillard expresses her admiration for a weasel she encounters in the wild:

> And I suspect that for me the way is like the weasel's: open to time and death painlessly, noticing everything, remembering nothing .... [I] could live under the wild rose wild as weasels, mute and uncomprehending ... muteness as a prolonged and giddy fast, where every moment is a feast of utterance received. Time and events are merely poured, unremarked and ingested directly, like blood pulsed into my gut through a jugular vein ... yielding at every moment to the perfect freedom of single necessity.[19]

The weasel here (and thus the writer who is "living like" it) absorbs the world's abundance unreservedly. Its instinctive, omnivorous way of living aligns it with the immediacy and multitudinousness of the American lyric in

---

18 Carson, *Men in the Off Hours*, 13.
19 Annie Dillard, *Teaching a Stone to Talk: Expeditions and Encounters* (New York: Harper Perennial, 1992), 33–34.

the tradition of Whitman: "I am large ... I contain multitudes."[20] It is a desire for fresh, unfiltered experience traceable back to Emerson, who wrote of how we are "[e]mbosomed for a season in nature, whose floods of life stream around and through us," calling in "Nature" for a literature that would meet this life-flood head-on and behold "God and nature face to face."[21] Either the Emersonian essay or the Whitmanesque lyric would, such parallels suggest, be capacious enough to capture such a consciousness: abundant forms for the world's abundance. The openness of both essay and lyric make them ideal forms for Dillard to explore her admiration for the open, exploratory ways of the weasel, taking in the world's "extravagance of minutiae."[22]

Yet such abundance is later recast, in the chapter "Fecundity" from *Pilgrim at Tinker Creek* (1974), as something abject, disgusting, and cruel:

> Creatures extrude or vent eggs; larvae fatten, split their shells, and eat them; spores dissolve or explode; root hairs multiply, corn puffs on the stalk, grass yields seed, shoots erupt from the earth turgid and sheathed; wet muskrats, rabbits, and squirrels slide into the sunlight, mewling and blind; and everywhere watery cells divide and swell, swell and divide. I can like it and call it birth and regeneration, or I can play the devil's advocate and call it rank fecundity – and say that it's hell that's a-poppin'.[23]

We might read this passage as a kind of fallen, or postlapsarian, reimagining of abundance. There is something nauseating in Dillard's choice of verbs ("extrude," "slide," "puffs") and adjectives ("turgid and sheathed," "wet," "mewling"), for these are all words that seem to apply equally to birth and death. It thus reminds us that the former – in the fallen world – depends on the latter. The abundance of the world curdles here, becomes fetid; life may proliferate, but it does so only by treating individual lives themselves cheaply, like the rock barnacle that releases "a million million larvae" into the sea, only a handful of which will ever find something hard to clasp onto and survive.[24] The world's abundance depends on this mass death: "[I]t is death that is spinning the globe."[25]

It is because of this tension between abundance and fecundity that Dillard can neither live like the weasel she so admires, nor write in a singular,

---

20 Walt Whitman, *Leaves of Grass*, ed. David S. Reynolds (New York: Oxford University Press, 2005), 43.
21 Ralph Waldo Emerson, "Nature," in *The Collected Works of Ralph Waldo Emerson*, vol. 1, *Nature, Addresses, and Lectures*, ed. Robert Ernest Spiller and Alfred R. Ferguson (Cambridge, MA: Belknap Press of Harvard University Press, 2010), 7–45, 7.
22 Annie Dillard, *Pilgrim at Tinker Creek* (New York: Harper Perennial, 1988), 129.
23 Dillard, *Pilgrim at Tinker*, 161.   24 Dillard, *Pilgrim at Tinker*, 166.
25 Dillard, *Pilgrim at Tinker*, 180.

abundant, capacious form. In a world of pure abundance – that is, the bounty of Eden – such writing might be plausible. Adam can babble all he wants – what could he say that would possibly be untrue, if his language is in perfect union with the world, creating it as he speaks? Such is the pure, abundant babble of the idealized lyric, an idea that recalls Northrop Frye's theory that childish "babble" and language play are at the root of the lyric's musicality, what he calls its *melos*.[26] But, *Pilgrim* suggests, the world is not just abundant; it is fecund. Its abundance contains violence – animals survive by eating and destroying other animals, and meanings survive by eating and destroying other meanings. Thoughts, in this world, can only progress by negating or modifying prior thoughts, as in a Socratic dialogue. That is, to push the analogy further, they develop parasitically, feeding on prior knowledge and thus destroying it; or, to push it further still, cannibalistically, a kind of prose that eats itself.

In such a world, a multiplicity of forms or modes is necessary. Though Dillard might not be as explicitly a "hybrid writer" as other lyric essayists like Carson or Rankine, we find in her work this idea that an irresolvable tension or dichotomy leads to the necessity of combining different genres or generic traits – the defining quality of the lyric essay. Dillard tempers her flighty, rhapsodic, lyrical prose with a more self-conscious, critical, essayistic voice, and it is in this combination of registers that her unique style is found. In fact, we find this happening even as the aesthetic of the weasel is first offered to us: Its unconscious, instinctive behavior, captured so potently in Dillard's mixture of electrical and bodily language ("live spot," "plug," "pulse"), is presented not just alongside but *through* the conscious, speculative register of the essayist, observing and pondering ("I suspect that ...," " "I could live under ... "). The key word in "Living like Weasels" is that middle preposition, "like." The weasel is only ever a simile, a *like*: a rhetorical figure that is itself only possible in a conscious, processing mind, one that makes connections between the things it absorbs. The weasel cannot live like anything else, because that "like" is unavailable to it – it does not make connections between anything, but absorbs everything equally, "mute and uncomprehending." Dillard, by contrast, can make her life like the weasel's, and make her essay like the lyric. She can reach from one context into another, can reach from the essay to the lyric; indeed, can *only* do this, never escaping the context from which she reaches entirely.

---

26 Northrop Frye, *Anatomy of Criticism: Four Essays* (Princeton, NJ: Princeton University Press, 2020), 296–97.

Maggie Nelson's Slippery Coherence

While Carson and Dillard's experiments predate the lyric essay's American christening in 1997 by Tall and D'Agata, Maggie Nelson (1973–), who published her first book, *Shiner*, in 2001, is an example of a writer whose work has been shaped by the emergence of the term as a new genre category. Taught at Wesleyan University by Dillard, whom she describes as her "mentor" and her "first writing teacher, whose influence on me abides," she takes from Dillard a desire to avoid the active pursuit of meaning, instead allowing it to accrue as though on its own terms, a Dillardesque principle she translates into her own Nelsonese as "you can't fuck up the space for God."[27] She admires Carson, meanwhile, for her "spectacular melding of literary criticism, scholarship, poetry, and prose," something that has given her "an enormous liberated space from which to work."[28] That mention of "space," in her descriptions of both authors' work, gives a sense of how these writers opened up a territory for Nelson to inhabit, a sense of finding one's space that chimes with many other writers' comments on their attraction to the lyric essay term: Mary Heather Noble, for example, describes how discovering the lyric essay was like "opening the door to the Secret Garden … a place that provided permission and space for me to play and explore," with that word "permission" also picked up on by Eula Biss, who writes that "[n]aming something is a way of giving it permission to exist."[29] Writers like Nelson and Biss, along with contemporaries like Sarah Manguso and Lia Purpura, can be thought of as inhabiting this now identified space of "the lyric essay," writing in the gap wrenched open by figures like D'Agata, Dillard, and Carson.

---

27 Maggie Nelson, "What's Queer Form Anyway? An Interview with Maggie Nelson," interview by Annie DeWitt, *Paris Review* (14 June 2018), www.theparisreview.org/blog/2018/06/14/an-interview-with-maggie-nelson; Maggie Nelson, "The Rumpus Interview with Maggie Nelson," interview by Darcey Steinke, *Rumpus* (6 May 2015), https://therumpus.net/2015/05/the-rumpus-interview-with-maggie-nelson.

28 Maggie Nelson, "Q&A: Sasha Frere-Jones and Maggie Nelson Discuss Writing and Form," *Los Angeles Times* (8 March 2016), www.latimes.com/books/jacketcopy/la-et-jc-sasha-frere-jones-maggie-nelson-q-a-20160307-story.html; Maggie Nelson, "All That Is the Case: Some Thoughts on Fact in Nonfiction and Documentary Poetry," in *Lit from Within: Contemporary Masters on the Art and Craft of Writing*, ed. Kevin Haworth and Dinty W. Moore (Athens, OH: Ohio University Press, 2011), 160; Maggie Nelson, *Women, the New York School, and Other True Abstractions* (Iowa City, IA: University of Iowa Press, 2007), 215–16.

29 Mary Heather Noble, "On the Lyric Essay," *Mary Heather Noble* (blog) (5 January 2014), www.maryheathernoble.com/on-the-lyric-essay; Eula Biss, "It Is What It Is," *Seneca Review* 37, no. 2 (Fall 2007): 55–60, 55.

Yet Nelson herself would surely balk at being positioned as a site of cohesion, as emblematic of or central to a particular category – for her writing is defiantly and deliberately *anti*categorical. Declaring for herself, in *The Argonauts* (2015), the totem animal of the otter (in what may be a subtle nod to her mentor Dillard's love of fellow mustelid the weasel), Nelson writes in a way that is continually slippery, that extends the essay's own anticategorical impulse by combining it with lyric's impulse toward the slippage of language.[30] *Bluets* (2009), for example, finds her attempting to capture the feeling of "blue" through a series of numbered short paragraphs – a technique we also find in David Shields's influential manifesto *Reality Hunger* (2010), which did much to popularize the term "lyric essay" itself. In both books, the apparent order bestowed by the numbering of the paragraphs recalls more rigid forms – museum catalogues, lists of dictionary definitions, scientific or philosophical arguments – while the content of these paragraphs – slippery, elusive – undermines them. The diffuse meanings of each book's titular concern ("reality," "blue") bleed like dye into different contexts. That the sequential, seemingly controlled structure of *Bluets* is ultimately an ironic ruse to be bent out of shape is gestured to in the hopelessness with which other attempts at counting or measuring are described in the book, as with Bénédict de Saussure's futile attempt to measure the blue of the sky with his "cyanometer," something that Nelson writes "brings me great pleasure, but really it takes us no further – either into knowledge, or into beauty."[31] It is a feeling carried over from her previous *The Red Parts* (2007), in which she tries to make a numbered list of the facts of a court case but finds that they "explain virtually nothing," and in which the numbering of "pieces of evidence" cannot stop them from taking on "allegorical proportions."[32] Though lists and numbers may appear to wrangle the world into order, to contain it and make it legible – like the neatness of separate genre categories, or university modules – they in fact take us nowhere, says Nelson: to "nothing," to the point of "no further." They are not stepping stones to meaning; rather, they are a dead end.

Nelson, then, is not interested in already delineated space, but in the very act of space *being created* by walls and boundaries moving, breaking, dissolving: It is the act itself that concerns her. *The Argonauts* continues this interest in moving across the boundaries of categories: in the "like" of Dillard's "Living like Weasels." It is a book that is always aware of the pressure and

30 Maggie Nelson, *The Argonauts* (Minneapolis: Graywolf Press, 2016), 112.
31 Maggie Nelson, *Bluets* (Seattle: Wave Books, 2009), 40.
32 Maggie Nelson, *The Red Parts: Autobiography of a Trial* (London: Vintage, 2017), 47, 120.

presence of boundaries, even as it tries to resist them. Nelson quotes William James: "We ought to say a feeling of *and*, a feeling of *if*, a feeling of *but*, a feeling of *by*, just as readily as we say a feeling of *blue*."[33] If *Bluets* is about the feeling of blue, then *The Argonauts* is about the feeling of these conjunctions and prepositions. That is, it is a book keenly aware of the complexity of the shifts and relations in which it tries to dwell, and the ways in which a preposition is both a shift and a boundary. Take this sentence, in which Nelson considers her need to resist the arrangement of thought into discrete categories:

> On the one hand, the Aristotelian, perhaps evolutionary need to put everything into categories – *predator, twilight, edible* – on the other, the need to pay homage to the transitive, the flight, the great soup of being in which we actually live.[34]

Initially *The Argonauts* seems to be concerned primarily with the latter half of this construction: with the "need to pay homage to the transitive," to that which slips between categories. The sentence itself seems to privilege this drive by placing it second, and thus creating a sense of the thought *arriving* at it. Yet the lyric force of the sentence in fact dwells in those italicized words in the middle: "*predator, twilight, edible.*" The strangeness of the word choices (which seem to have no obvious meaning within the sentence), as well as the delicate dance of dental consonants between two bilabial plosives, brings attention to them as pure sound. At the same time, they are also words with strong evolutionary connotations (hunting/being hunted, night, food), emphasizing what Nelson herself describes as their "evolutionary need" to fit into discrete, understandable categories: that is, firstly, that words cannot function without being discrete from each other and so retain this discreteness even as the lyric drive of the sentence attempts to blur and make "soup" of them; secondly, that the need to put things into categories might itself be read as an evolutionary need to work out what we can eat, suggesting that "taste" is a matter of survival. The separation of the three words from the rest of the sentence by both em dashes and italics plays into these contradictory traits: On the one hand, it further emphasizes the words as discrete signifiers; on the other, it isolates them as a source of reading pleasure, seeming to linger and take care over them, until their meanings start to spread and leak, as when a child, delighting in speech, repeats a word ad nauseam and, thus, ad absurdum.

[33] Nelson, *Argonauts*, 54. [34] Nelson, *Argonauts*, 53.

It is, more than anything, this keen interest in categories themselves, their uses and their failures, that makes Nelson the prototypical lyric essayist. The irony is this: that the category of lyric essay, as a modern mode of writing, is most detectable in one of its most anticategorical practitioners; that it coheres, as an idea, in a writer who herself refuses to cohere. Nelson's writing refuses to keep things separate that either taste, tradition, or form would keep separate: sex and motherhood, art and theory, violence and love. This continual refusal is what connects her otherwise disparate, nonrepetitive works, and it is the ability of the lyric essay to make manifest this refusal that continually attracts her to different permutations of the form. To read her as a lyric essayist, then, is not to put her in a category, but to highlight how she uses the interplay of lyric and essay to resist categories – the "woman," the "mother," the "theorist," the "depressed person" – across her work. Or rather, it is, paradoxically, to do both. Like Roland Barthes, from whom she borrows her metaphor of the Argo, she is interested in the processes of forgetting and unlearning, "yielding to the unforeseeable change which forgetting imposes on the sedimentation of knowledges, cultures, and beliefs."[35] We can perhaps view Nelson's simultaneous embrace of and resistance to the lyric essay as a Barthesian attempt to "unlearn" the form, even as she inherits it. As one of the first writers to receive this newly gifted form, Nelson nonetheless feels the need to unravel it, recognizing, perhaps, that the moment a genre hardens into shape it may cease to be useful.

From Carson's playfulness with both the markers of genre and the combination of different textual elements, to Dillard's continually unsettled negotiations between abundance and fecundity through the combination of rapturous lyric with postlapsarian essay, to Nelson's queering of the essay through the slipperiness of lyric language that threatens to carry us into danger, what unites the lyric essayists is their resistance to staying put, their refusal to write within singular, defined spaces. In their work we find, reawakened, that restless, transgressive spirit that so animated Theodor Adorno when he praised the essay's "anti-systematic impulse" and "childlike freedom."[36] In this sense, the lyric essay is both something new in the essay, in that it expands what the essay can do by combining elements from it with

---

35 Roland Barthes, "Lecture: In Inauguration of the Chair of Literary Semiology, Collège de France, January 7, 1977," trans. Richard Howard, *Oxford Literary Review* 4, no.1 (1979): 31–44, 43–44. Notably, this is also the lecture in which Barthes claimed to have "produced only essays," describing himself as a "fellow of doubtful nature, whose every attribute is somehow challenged by its opposite (31)."

36 Theodor Adorno, "The Essay as Form," trans. Bob Hullot-Kentor and Frederic Will, *New German Critique*, no. 32 (1984): 151–71, 160, 152.

elements from the lyric poem, and, at the same time, is merely a continuation of the essay's already radical spirit, a reminder that this is a genre that must continually make itself new if it is to retain its core identity. Let us not, then, be too hasty to fix the lyric essay down – for its strength, as an idea, is in its mobility.

36

Writing Migration: Multiculturalism, Democracy, and the Essay Form

CYRUS R. K. PATELL

The personal essay has proven to be a powerful tool for US writers seeking to explore what it means to be a migrant or a descendant of migrants. Social scientists tend to look at the big picture when it comes to migration, theorizing and investigating migration as the large-scale movement of people from one place to another. But every mass migration is an aggregation of individual experiences, fraught with hardship, sacrifice, and the full gamut of human emotions, from hope to despair. Personal essays about migration and its effects chart the transformations that occur when people leave one place for another, often leaving behind a homeland in the hope of finding a new place to live. Leaving home is inevitably wrenching, and many essays about migration register a nostalgia for the place – and the life – left behind. For the epigraph to the "Arrivals" section of *The Penguin Book of Migration Literature* (2019), the volume's editor Dohra Ahmad chose the final lines from Claude McKay's (1890–1948) poem "The Tropics in New York" (1920), in which the speaker is overcome by a visceral feeling of nostalgia as he passes a shop window filled with tropical fruits: "And, hungry for the old, familiar ways, / I turned aside and bowed my head and wept."[1]

Ahmad reminds us that "'migration' denotes any long-term movement; 'emigration' is the act of leaving a place; and 'immigration' refers to arrival. All migrants may be classified as emigrants or immigrants, depending on perspective, but more realistically all migrants feel themselves to be both emigrants and immigrants at once."[2] James Baldwin (1924–1987) wrote in "Many Thousands Gone" (1955):

---

1 Claude McKay, "The Tropics in New York," quoted in Dohra Ahmad, ed., *The Penguin Book of Migration Literature* (New York: Penguin, 2019), 103.
2 Ahmad, *Penguin Book*, xv–xvi.

> The making of an American begins at that point where he himself rejects all other ties, any other history, and himself adopts the vesture of his adopted land. This problem has been faced by all Americans throughout our history – in a way it *is* our history – and it baffles the immigrant and sets on edge the second generation until today.[3]

What we find in essay after essay about the subject of US migration, however, is that "adopt[ing] the vesture" of the adopted land is never easy and rarely complete.

The personal essay offers an opportunity for writers to come to terms with the experiences that arise as a result of migration, while presenting these experiences as exemplary and therefore instructive. In "The Writing Life" (2018), Alexander Chee (1967–) recounts what he learned from Annie Dillard (1945–) in a creative writing seminar on nonfiction: The personal essay is "a moral exercise that involved direct engagement with the unknown, whether it was a foreign civilization or your mind, and what mattered in this was you."[4] According to Philip Lopate, this underlying confidence in the exemplarity of personal experience means that "the personal essay has an implicitly democratic bent, in the value that it places on experience rather than status distinctions."[5] The personal essay is thus a form suited to capturing the motivations, achievements, and disappointments of migrants who have often come to the United States because of the promise of the nation's democratic principles.

Migration and Cosmopolitanism

By the early twenty-first century, these principles had fractured into two competing visions of the nature of the United States: For some, the United States is a nation grounded in the white Anglo-Saxon Protestantism of its so-called Founding Fathers and should reflect those roots; for others, it is a nation of immigrants, who have transformed the United States into a multicultural society that may yet evolve into a cosmopolitan nation in which difference is embraced rather than feared. The irony, of course, is that of the two views, it is the second that is literally true: Those "Founding Fathers" were themselves the descendants of migrants who came to North

---

3 James Baldwin, *Notes of a Native Son*, in *Collected Essays*, ed. Toni Morrison (New York: Library of America, 1998), 1–129, 23.
4 Alexander Chee, *How to Write an Autobiographical Novel: Essays* (New York: Houghton Mifflin, 2018), 50.
5 Philip Lopate, ed., *The Art of the Personal Essay* (New York: Anchor, 1994), xxiii.

America from Europe. These alternative visions map in sociological terms onto the distinction between the melting-pot model of assimilation and the multicultural model of US cultural diversity; philosophically, they map onto the distinction between universalism and pluralism.

Personal essays about US migration and its legacies are inevitably marked by the conflicts among these competing visions, but as a genre, the personal essay of migration presents a cosmopolitan approach to the idea of transnational movement: In dramatizing encounters between "natives" and migrants, between different groups of migrants, and between first- and subsequent-generation immigrants, the genre promotes conversations across boundaries of difference, especially between authors and their readers. In his essay "On Becoming an American Writer" (2018), Chee puts it this way:

> To write is to sell a ticket to escape, not from the truth, but into it. . . . Something new is made from my memories and yours as you read this. It is not my memory, not yours, and it is born and walks the bridges and roads of your mind, as long as it can. After it has left mine.[6]

What Chee is describing is a cosmopolitan reading practice based on the idea of conversation across boundaries of difference. For twenty-first-century theorists of cosmopolitanism like Kwame Anthony Appiah (1954–) and Martha Nussbaum (1947–), cosmopolitanism remains rooted in the idea of being a citizen of the world, but it has migrated away from its origins as an alternative to nationalism toward being a way of approaching the idea of difference. "The world is getting more crowded," writes Appiah, noting that "in the next half a century the population of our once foraging species will approach nine billion. Depending on the circumstances, conversations across boundaries can be delightful, or just vexing: what they mainly are, though, is inevitable."[7] In her essay "Patriotism and Cosmopolitanism" (1994), Nussbaum reminds us of the genesis of the idea of cosmopolitanism:

> When Diogenes the Cynic replied, "I am a citizen of the world," he meant, apparently, that he refused to be defined by his local origins and group memberships, so central to the self-image of the conventional Greek male; instead, he defined himself in terms of more universal aspirations and concerns. The Stoics, who followed his lead, further developed his image of the *kosmou politês* (world citizen) arguing that each of us dwells, in effect,

---

6 Chee, *How to Write*, 255.
7 Kwame Anthony Appiah, *Cosmopolitanism: Ethics in a World of Strangers* (New York: W. W. Norton, 1990), xxi.

in two communities – the local community of our birth, and the community of human argument and aspiration.[8]

Nussbaum reminds us that, for the Stoics, conceiving of oneself as a citizen of the world did not mean giving up local attachments. "They suggest," she writes, "that we think of ourselves not as devoid of local affiliations, but as surrounded by a series of concentric circles. The first one encircles the self, the next takes in the immediate family, then follows the extended family, then, in order, neighbors or local groups, fellow city-dwellers, and fellow countrymen." Extending the concept to account for twentieth-century perspectives, she notes that "we can easily add to this list groupings based on ethnic, linguistic, historical, professional, gender, or sexual identities."[9] At the same time, if cosmopolitanism originally represented a migration in thought away from the city – the locus of personal and political identity in classical Greece – and toward the world, it has migrated in its journey to the twenty-first century back to the city: Cosmopolitanism is customarily associated with urban identities, with cities like New York, London, or Abu Dhabi, to which people migrate from all over the world.

With the rise of the nation-state in Europe in the seventeenth century, cosmopolitanism became a universalist alternative to the particularism of nationalism. Because of the early association between the idea of nation and homogeneity of citizenry in Europe, nationalism became linked to ethnocentrism. Commenting on the Indian novelist Rabindranath Tagore's dramatization of the failure of cosmopolitanism in *The Home and the World* (1916), Nussbaum writes that Tagore recognizes that "nationalism and ethnocentric particularism are not alien to one another, but akin – that to give support to nationalist sentiments ... substitutes a colorful idol for the substantive universal values of justice and right," with the ironic result that nationalism thus "subverts, ultimately, even the values that hold a nation together."[10] If, however, cosmopolitan thinking draws on universalism in its opposition to particularisms of nationalism and ethnocentricity, it also understands that universalism can become stifling when its emphasis on sameness becomes an overemphasis that wrongly discounts the significance of human diversity. As the intellectual historian David Hollinger puts it, "Cosmopolitanism urges each individual and collective unit to absorb as much varied experience as it

---

8 Martha C. Nussbaum, "Patriotism and Cosmopolitanism," in *For Love of Country*, ed. Joshua Cohen (Boston: Beacon Press, 1996), 2–17, 6–7. Originally published in *Boston Review* (October–November 1994): 3–6.
9 Nussbaum, "Patriotism and Cosmopolitanism," 9.
10 Nussbaum, "Patriotism and Cosmopolitanism," 5.

can while retaining its capacity to advance its aims effectively. For cosmopolitans, the diversity of humankind is a fact. For universalists, it's a potential problem."[11]

In the United States, multiculturalism arose as a response to the disjunction between the ostensible universalism of the nation's founding democratic principles and the discriminatory ways in which US democracy was actually practiced. Universalism was linked ideologically to an ethnocentric nationalism that favored the descendants of Anglo-European immigrants. Multiculturalism called attention both to the importance of the idea of human difference, which universalist thinkers tend to de-emphasize as they seek common denominators among people, and to the historical injustices suffered by women and non-white immigrants and their descendants throughout US history. Over time, however, US multiculturalism itself began to migrate toward ethnocentricity, in what the educational theorist Diane Ravitch described as a shift away from "pluralistic multiculturalism" to a "new, particularistic multiculturalism." In Ravitch's view, pluralist multiculturalists "seek a richer common culture," while "the particularists insist that no common culture is possible or desirable."[12]

The idea of a common culture lies at the heart of twenty-first-century theories of cosmopolitanism, in which cosmopolitanism is less as an alternative to nationalism than an approach to difference, a way of adjudicating among the competing claims of universalism and multiculturalism. Cosmopolitanism thus emerges as a structure of thought, a perspective that embraces difference and promotes the bridging of cultural gaps. Appiah's influential account of cosmopolitanism is based on the belief that it is the natural tendency of cultures to reinvent themselves. Cultures, in his account, never tend toward purity: They tend toward change, toward mixing and miscegenation, toward an "endless process of imitation and revision."[13] This idea of a US culture that is constantly changing, reinventing itself within the broad confines of democratic principles, animates the second view of US history that I described above, while the first view, which I identified with certain descendants of the first Anglo-European immigrants, is rooted in an atavistic aversion to the kinds of cultural change that result from waves of

---

11 David A. Hollinger, *Postethnic America: Beyond Multiculturalism* (New York: Basic Books, 1995), 84.
12 Diane Ravitch, "Multiculturalism: E Pluribus Plures," *American Scholar* 59, no. 3 (Summer 1990): 337–54, 340.
13 Kwame Anthony Appiah, "The Case for Contamination," *New York Times Magazine* (1 January 2006): 30–37, 52, 52.

migrations. More than a century ago, Horace Kallen (1882–1974) wrote about the beginnings of this atavism in his essay "Democracy versus the Melting Pot" (1915):

> Today the descendants of the colonists are reformulating a declaration of independence. Again, as in 1776, Americans of British ancestry find that certain possessions of theirs, which may be lumped under the word "Americanism," are in jeopardy. ... The danger comes, once more, from a force across the water, but the force is this time regarded not as superior, but as inferior. The relationships of 1776 are, consequently, reversed. To conserve the inalienable rights of the colonists of 1776, it was necessary to declare all men equal; to conserve the inalienable rights of their descendants in 1914, it becomes necessary to declare all men unequal.[14]

Kallen concluded with a vision and a question. The vision was hopeful, offering the possibility that "'American civilization' may come to mean the perfection of the cooperative harmonies of 'European civilization,' the waste, the squalor, and the distress of Europe being eliminated – a multiplicity in a unity, an orchestration of mankind." The question, however, was less hopeful: "Do the dominant classes in America want such a society?"[15]

What we now think of as personal essays became an important part of the voluminous writings produced by the European invaders and settlers who arrived in North America from the late fifteenth through the early seventeenth centuries.[16] "The literature of American colonization," writes Myra

---

14 Horace M. Kallen, "Democracy versus the Melting Pot: A Study of American Nationality," part one, Nation 100, no. 2590 (18 February 1915): 190–94, 190.
15 Horace M. Kallen, "Democracy versus the Melting Pot: A Study of American Nationality," part two, Nation 100, no. 2591 (25 February 1915): 217–20, 220.
16 The Anglo-European migrations that began with Columbus were by no means the first movement of peoples into North America: Without migration, there would have been no "America" because the continent was devoid of human inhabitants during the Ice Age. Approximately 25,000 years ago, during what archeologists call the Late Glacial Maximum, ice covered most of Asia, Northern Europe, and North America. The receding of the ice some 10,000 years later enabled a small population of humans to migrate from Siberia into North America via the land bridge that existed across what is now the Bering Strait, perhaps following the herds of the Ice Age big game that they hunted. According to the archeologists Brian M. Fagan and Nadia Durrani, the first great radiation of humans was the result of migration from Africa into temperate Europe and tropical Asia; the settlement of the Americas marked the end of the second great radiation, "the climactic development of world prehistory," which resulted in "the great biological and cultural diversity of modern humankind." By 10,000 BC, they write, "Stone Age foragers occupied every corner of the Americas. The overall human population probably numbered no more than a few tens of thousands, but they had adapted to every form of local environment imaginable," leading "ultimately, to the brilliant array of Native American societies that Europeans encountered in the late fifteenth century AD." Brian M. Fagan and Nadia Durrani, World Prehistory: A Brief Introduction, 9th ed. (New York: Routledge, 2017), 91, 147.

Jehlen in the first volume of *The Cambridge History of American Literature* (1994), is "characterized by its writers' conviction that writing could wield material power in shaping history. Only some thirty years separate the first printing of the Gutenberg Bible from Columbus's departure for the Canary Islands."[17] Writing, however, not only accompanied the conquest of the so-called New World, but was also one of the aspects of European civilization that was used to justify it: According to Jehlen, "the observation that the Indians do not have their own system of writing seems to these prolific writers to be a definitive sign that the American natives do not have a right to the land."[18]

In his "Letter to Luis de Santangel regarding the First Voyage," which was written at sea in 1493 and might be considered one of the first personal essays about European migration to the Americas, Christopher Columbus (1451–1506) describes his arrival at "the Indies," where he "found very many islands thickly peopled, of all which I took possession without resistance for their Highnesses [the King and Queen of Spain] by proclamation made and the royal standard unfurled."[19] When he reaches the island that he names *La Española* (Hispaniola), Columbus sends two men ashore "to ascertain if there were a king or large cities in that part," but they report after three days' journey that they "found countless of small hamlets with numberless inhabitants, but with nothing like order."[20] The letter includes descriptions of the wonderful resources that he has discovered, which include "seaports with which none that I know in Christendom can bear comparison," lush vegetation, "many mines of metals," and a "population innumerable" that is intelligent but awed by European technology.[21] Seeking funding for his next voyage, Columbus promises Spain's rulers in return "all the gold they require" and "slaves, as many of these idolators as their Highnesses command to be shipped," while expressing his belief that "the men I have left behind me" will find "a thousand other valuable things."[22] Columbus had planted the first permanent European colony in the Americas, beginning a wave of migration that would see approximately one and a half million Europeans come to the New World from 1500 to 1800. European migration would

---

[17] Myra Jehlen, "The Literature of Colonization," in *The Cambridge History of American Literature*, vol. 1, *1590–1820*, ed. Sacvan Bercovitch and Cyrus R. K. Patell (Cambridge, UK: Cambridge University Press, 1994), 11–168, 13.

[18] Jehlen, "Literature of Colonization," 13–14.

[19] Christopher Columbus, *Select Letters of Christopher Columbus, with Other Original Documents*, ed. R. H. Major (London: Ashgate, 2010), 1–2.

[20] Columbus, *Select Letters*, 3.   [21] Columbus, *Select Letters*, 4–5.

[22] Columbus, *Select Letters*, 15.

explode during the nineteenth century, with approximately fifty million people emigrating from Europe to the United States.[23]

Twenty-first century scholars who think about the ways in which the United States was shaped by waves of migration have recognized the necessity of revising traditional accounts of US immigration to include the history of the transatlantic slave trade. A full account of the personal essay of migration must consider two centuries' worth of writing about US slavery and anti-Black racism in texts like Frederick Douglass's (ca. 1817–1895) "What, to the Slave, Is the Fourth of July?" (1852), James Baldwin's *Notes of a Native Son* (1955), Audre Lorde's (1934–1992) *Sister Outsider* (2007), Ta-Nehisi Coates's (1975–) *Between the World and Me* (2015), and Toni Morrison's (1931–2019) *Mouth Full of Blood* (2019), written by the descendants of slaves who were involuntary migrants from Africa to North America. In the twentieth century, the personal essay has also become a form through which Indigenous writers like Linda Hogan (1947–) can address the forced migration of Indigenous people, while also drawing attention to the destruction of the landscape that accompanies colonization. For example, in "Ways of the Cranes" (2013), Hogan writes:

> Many tribes have watched these elegant birds, many tribes, even those in the north, and for many years. In Mississippi, where we are from, the cranes have gathered in the deep green of water, the blue of it, the sand of it, and remained, never leaving, as if they are The Ones Who Hid and Remained, while the rest of us, my people, were forced to leave our country and walk to Indian Territory.[24]

Hogan's essay vividly dramatizes what Ahmad describes as "an essential element to note about migration": that "it exists in a continuum of involuntary to voluntary. Forced migrations – enslavement, 'transport' (i.e., deportation to an overseas prison), trafficking, political or religious persecution, exile, expatriation – formed the world that we know."[25] In the wake of Columbus's voyages, approximately ten million slaves in North America arrived from Africa from the sixteenth to the late nineteenth century,

---

23 Roger Daniels, *Coming to America*, 2nd ed. (New York: HarperPerennial, 2002), 15; Ida Altman and James Horn, eds. *"To Make America": European Emigration in the Early Modern Period* (Berkeley, CA: University of California Press, 1991), 3; Philip D. Curtin, *The Atlantic Slave Trade: A Census* (Madison, WI: University of Wisconsin Press, 1969), 137, table 39; John Higham, *Send These to Me: Immigrants in Urban America*, rev. ed. (Baltimore: Johns Hopkins University Press, 1984), 13–15.
24 Linda Hogan, "Ways of Cranes," *Image Journal* 79 (2013), https://imagejournal.org/article/ways-of-the-cranes.
25 Ahmad, *Penguin Book*, xv–xvi.

migrants whose immigration to the United States was forced rather than voluntary. The history of US immigration must now also account for the arrival of refugees, migrants forced to flee their home countries because of war, political or religious persecution, life-threatening economic deprivation, or the climate crisis – though one might argue that the "Pilgrims" who came to North American in 1620 are more accurately described as refugees rather than immigrants. The history of migration to the United States is as much a history of conquest, imperialism, colonialism, and refugees as it is a story of immigrants seeking to take advantage of the so-called American Dream of upward mobility.

Individualism and the American Dream

Personal essays about migration to the United States are full of meditations about the allure of that American Dream. In her contribution to the anthology *The Good Immigrant* (2019), Nicole Dennis-Benn (1982–) describes her first conversations with new friends at a US college, "most of whom were Caribbean and African immigrants with aspirations as big as mine":

> It did not take me long to discover that we were all absolutely and mercilessly united by our ambitions to stay afloat on our parents' dreams – the American Dream. We were, after all, the good immigrants. I lowered my head and continued to study, the memory of the ocean rising in my gut. I threw up in the restroom after lunch.[26]

Dennis-Benn realizes that for the immigrant, the American Dream was about "independence," which in the United States means financial independence. "I learned very early," she writes, "that to be an immigrant in this country meant I didn't have the luxury of choosing what I wanted, only what was necessary." Observing her fellow immigrant students at the community college that she first attends, Dennis-Benn comes to realize that they knew that "they couldn't afford for their ambitions to be bigger than their pockets unless their ambitions would prove to be lucrative; and they knew their American Dream was really about independence. And so," she tells us, "I chose medicine."[27] The materialism of the American Dream often manifests

---

[26] Nicole Dennis-Benn, "Swimmer," in *The Good Immigrant: 26 Writers Reflect on America*, ed. Nikesh Shukla and Chimene Suleyman (New York: Little, Brown, 2019), 16–27, 21–22.
[27] Dennis-Benn, "Swimmer," 18.

itself in smaller details of the immigrant's new everyday life. For example, in "How Not to Be" (2019), Priya Minhas writes:

> My two pairs of denim cutoffs, one pink and one blue, are perhaps a seemingly insignificant detail, but wearing those shorts became just as much a part of our new American Dream as the yellow school buses, the Pledge of Allegiance each morning, and Chinese food that arrived in little white boxes on Friday nights. Before this, my sisters and I had worn shorts only on vacation.[28]

The American Dream emerges as an emblem for various manifestations of the idea of "independence," inflected by the ideology of liberal individualism and its materialistic manifestations. Minhas's anecdote serves as an emblem of the power of what the political theorist C. B. Macpherson describes as "possessive individualism,"[29] which boils down to the idea that you are what you have.

In addition to its affinity with a democratic principle of equality, the personal essay seems at first to be a natural fit with the idea of individualism because the genre emphasizes the exemplarity of personal experience. If individualism is a social theory that regards the individual as a priori and society as a second-order construct designed to preserve individual liberty, the narrative strategy of the personal essay generally follows a conceptual trajectory that gives priority to individual experience. In the United States, the personal essay became a hallmark of the transition from a pre-Enlightenment emphasis on community and religious experience to a post-Enlightenment emphasis on individual consciousness and personal experience. The historian John Demos argues that for those first European refugees – the Pilgrims – and their immediate descendants, "self was decidedly *off* center; instead, their center – as writers – was all the unusual things they had witnessed and endured, the 'providences' that revealed the will of God."[30] In *Tiger Writing: Art, Culture, and the Interdependent Self* (2013), a set of personal essays first delivered in lecture form at Harvard University, the novelist Gish Jen (1955–) cites Demos's work as she meditates on two competing conceptions of self: "the independent, individualistic self that dominates in the West, especially America, and the interdependent, collectivist self that dominates in the East, including China, from whence [her] parents emigrated in the 1940s."[31]

---

28 Priya Minhas, "How Not to Be," in Shukla and Suleyman, *Good Immigrant*, 52–56, 59.
29 C. B. Macpherson, *The Political Theory of Possessive Individualism: Hobbes to Locke* (Oxford: Oxford University Press, 1962), v.
30 John Demos, *Circles and Lines: The Shape of Life in Early America* (Cambridge, MA: Harvard University Press, 2004), 64.
31 Gish Jen, *Tiger Writing: Art, Culture, and the Interdependent Self* (Cambridge, MA: Harvard University Press, 2013), 3.

Ironically, from the standpoint of understandings of the self, the Pilgrims had more in common with the "Eastern" point of view that Jen describes than they did with their post-Enlightenment, nineteenth-century descendants, who were the subjects of Alexis de Tocqueville's (1805–1859) study *Democracy in America* (1835–1840). In his second volume (1840), Tocqueville felt compelled to use the unfamiliar term "individualism" to describe what he believed to be a particular characteristic of democracy in the United States. According to Tocqueville, "Individualism" was "a word recently coined to express a new idea. Our fathers only knew about egoism." The term was unusual enough to lead Tocqueville's American translator, Henry Reeve, to comment in a footnote, "I adopt the expression of the original, however strange it may seem to the English ear, . . . because I know of no English word exactly equivalent to the expression."[32] Tocqueville argued that individualism, unlike egoism, "is based on misguided judgment rather than depraved feeling," but he worried that this distinction would ultimately become irrelevant: "Egoism sterilizes the seeds of every virtue; individualism at first only dams the spring of public virtues, but in the long run it attacks and destroys all the others too and finally merges in egoism." Calling egoism "a vice as old as the world," Tocqueville argued that individualism is a new phenomenon "of democratic origin" that "threatens to grow as conditions get more equal."[33] Nearly half a century later, another commentator from across the Atlantic, the British historian James Bryce (1838–1922), would write in *The American Commonwealth* (1888) that "individualism, the love of enterprise, and the pride in personal freedom, have been deemed by Americans not only their choicest, but their peculiar and exclusive possessions."[34]

The Constraints of Genre and Expectation

This cultural mythology serves as the backdrop against which personal essays about migration to the United States set themselves, usually with some mixture of inspiration and antagonism. In *Tiger Writing*, Jen recounts the experience of reading her father's thirty-two-page memoir, written in 2005 when he was eighty-five years old. Noting that cultural commentators would use the personal narratives written by nineteenth-century Americans

---

32 Alexis de Tocqueville, *Democracy in America*, trans. Henry Reeve (New York: Schocken, 1961), 2:1.
33 Alexis de Tocqueville, *Democracy in America*, ed. J. P. Mayer, trans. George Lawrence (Garden City, NY: Doubleday-Anchor, 1969), 507.
34 James Bryce, *The American Commonwealth*, rev. ed. (New York: Macmillan, 1910), 591.

as evidence of a "special synergy between American-ness and autobiography," Jen sees in her father's memoir a different way of making use of the personal, which severs the link between democracy and individualism. Jen marvels at "how much more emphasis in general [her] father placed on his context than on what we in the West might think the proper focus of an autobiography, namely himself," a strategy that she comes to understand through the work of the psychologist Qi Wang: "[W]hile contemporary European Americans, brought up to treasure their uniqueness as individuals, tend to tell long narratives about themselves that help illuminate, explain, and celebrate what is special about them, Asians and Asian Americans typically do not."[35]

Although in Jen's account, her father's personal essay resists the strictures of US liberal individualism, in many ways, Norman Jen's story is a prime example of the kind of biography that led Asian Americans to be dubbed the model minority in the 1960s: He arrived in the United States in the 1940s as a hydraulics engineer, went on to become a university professor, and worked on the atomic bomb program known as Starfish. For many Asian American essayists, however, the label "model minority" became not a badge of honor but a form of suffocating constraint. In her collection of personal essays, *Minor Feelings: An Asian American Reckoning* (2020), the poet Cathy Park Hong (1976–) recounts her father's rather different immigrant story. "On paper, my father is the so-called model immigrant. Upon meeting him, strangers have called my father a gentleman for his quiet charisma and kindness, a personality he cultivated from years of selling life insurance and dry-cleaning supplies to Americans of all manner of race and class. But like many model immigrants, he can be angry." Hong tells us why:

> When the 1965 immigration ban was lifted by the United States, my father saw an opportunity. Back then, only select professionals from Asia were granted visas to the United States: doctors, engineers, and mechanics. This screening process, by the way, is how the whole model minority quackery began: the U.S. government only allowed the most educated and highly trained Asians in and then took all the credit for their success. *See! Anyone can live the American Dream!* they'd say about a doctor who came into the country already a doctor.
> My father lied. He wrote down he had training as a mechanic. He, along with my young mother, was sent to the hinterlands of Erie, Pennsylvania, where he worked as an assistant mechanic for Ryder trucks. Despite lack of training, he got by, until a cracked stone in an air grinder came loose and

---

35 Jen, *Tiger Writing*, 59.

shattered his leg so badly he was in a cast for six months. Ryder fired him instead of giving him workman's comp because they knew he couldn't do anything about it.[36]

In Hong's hands, the personal essay becomes a way of confronting the constraints placed on immigrants by the expectations of mainstream US culture. Hong suggests that for the immigrant, particularly one who has not mastered the English tongue, writing prose can be hard. "Poetry," she argues, "is a forgiving medium for anyone who's had a strained relationship with English. Like the stutterer who pronounces their words flawlessly through song, the immigrant writes their English beautifully through poetry." Hong reveals that she has "relied on those silences, maybe too much, leaving a blank space for the sorrows that would otherwise be reduced by words." Hong turned to prose – and to the essay form – as a way of "cluttering that silence," in order, she explains, "to try to anatomize my feelings about a racial identity that I still can't examine as a writer without fretting that I have caved to my containment."[37]

In the late twentieth-century United States, multiculturalism opened the door to the flourishing of personal essays by immigrants and their descendants. In *Tiger Writing*, Jen recalls, "I once wrote a talk called 'Rewriting the Context' describing how, as multiculturalism developed, books that were impossible one year became possible the next, and how I both seized the new possibilities as they cropped up and sought to speed this process along."[38] The personal essay became a way for the immigrant to avoid the kind of cultural invisibility that Ralph Ellison (1913–1994) so vividly dramatized in his novel *Invisible Man* (1952). As Edwidge Danticat (1969–) reminds us,

> [o]ne of the most distressing aspects of migration, for both adults and children, is how invisible the migrant can become, even when being detained, or imprisoned, in our proverbial backyards. When vulnerable populations are kept hidden, or are forced into hiding – which is the daily reality of so many undocumented migrants, immigrants, and refugees – they not only live in the shadows; they become slowly erased and their voices become muffled or go unheard.[39]

---

36 Cathy Park Hong, *Minor Feelings: An Asian American Reckoning* (New York: One World, 2020), 13–14.
37 Hong, *Minor Feelings*, 197.   38 Jen, *Tiger Writing*, 115.
39 Edwidge Danticat, "Foreword," in Ahmad, *Penguin Book*, xii.

At the same time, however, the expectations of readers and publishers can lead the personal essay to become another form of containment. In "How to Center Your Own Story," Jade Chang argues:

> There's a form of currency from immigrants and people of color that publishers, producers, and audiences have long recognized: pain. Whether it's the larger pain of being a refugee or an enslaved person, or the smaller-scale pain of not fitting in, for a long time these were the only stories that got told. Or, rather, the only stories that got sold."[40]

Written in the ironic voice that often accompanies the essayistic use of the second-person imperative, Porochista Khakpour's (1978–) "How to Write Iranian-America, or The Last Essay" vividly charts the ways in which the essay can become a form of confinement:

> Know you're an essayist and know you can't back out now. During an interview someone asks you why essays, and you remind them you write fiction, and they ask again why essays, and you joke about them finding you, and they ask again why essays, and you stumble on another answer: Service. That somehow your people are not visible, these three decades of being in the US, and people have needed you, and while you can't speak for everyone, you can speak some part of this truth. Service? Service. Afterward, bum the few cigarettes the interviewer offers and smoke through a silence you did your best to create.[41]

As the twenty-first century progresses, the challenge for the essayists who use the personal essay to represent the experience of migration will be to find ways to free the genre from this horizon of expectations. Perhaps the thought experiment that Baldwin undertakes in his 1955 essay "Stranger in the Village" suggests a way forward by reversing the historical process of migration to which Africans were subjected: In contrast to the involuntary migrations of Africans into North American slavery, Baldwin voluntarily relocates himself to a "tiny Swiss village" where, "from all available evidence no black man had ever set foot."[42] Baldwin uses his experience there to remind his reader:

> The ideas on which American beliefs are based are not, though Americans often seem to think so, ideas which originated in America. They came out of

---

40 Jade Chang, "How to Center Your Own Story," in Shukla and Suleyman, *Good Immigrant*, 301–13, 312.
41 Porochista Khakpour, "How to Write Iranian-America, or The Last Essay," *Brown Album: Essays on Exile and Identity* (New York: Vintage, 2020), 186–99, 192.
42 Baldwin, *Notes of a Native Son*, 117.

Europe. And the establishment of democracy on the American continent was scarcely as radical a break with the past as was the necessity, which Americans faced, of broadening this concept to include black men.[43]

More than half a century later, we might broaden Baldwin's concept by substituting "nonwhite immigrants and their descendants" and take heart from Baldwin's suggestion that, despite the terrible racist history of the United States, African Americans have won the battle, as Baldwin frames it, "to establish an identity":

> [The African American] is not a visitor to the West, but a citizen there, an American; as American as the Americans who despise him, the Americans who fear him, the Americans who love him – the Americans who became less than themselves, or rose to be greater than themselves by virtue of the fact that the challenge he represented was inescapable.[44]

Perhaps essayists writing about migration in the years to come will be able to assert, without hesitation, the migrant's right to claim the identity "American" and to shift the genre of the essay of migration away from a fixation on the costs of migration to an emphasis on its potential for positive transformation. As Jade Chang puts it, "Things are slowly changing. We're creating new forms of currency in which our joy is as valuable as our suffering."[45]

---

43 Baldwin, *Notes of a Native Son*, 126.   44 Baldwin, *Notes of a Native Son*, 127.
45 Chang, "How to Center," 312.

37
Latinx Culture and the Essay

YOLANDA PADILLA

Latinx writers have long recognized the power of the essay for personal and polemical expression, despite the genre's relative neglect in the literary marketplace and among literary and cultural critics. By "Latinx," I refer to US-based writers who have migrated or are descended from Latin America and/or the Caribbean. "Latinx" is a relatively new term, with the "x" conveying gender inclusivity and a space for nonbinary forms of sexual and gender presentation. While I will use "Latinx" throughout this chapter, the term has not been universally adopted by any means, with many continuing to favor "Latina/o" to mark the continuing significance of a male/female gender binary, including for queer constituencies. Moreover, terms such as "Hispanic" and the more specific "Chicana/o/x," "Nuyorican," "Afro Latino," and "Central American" – to give only a partial list – continue to be prominent. The range of labels indicates the heterogeneity of the group, one characterized by many differences as commonalities, including those of nationality, history, culture, and racial identity. Keeping these tensions in mind, this chapter understands "Latinx" as naming an identity based on a shared history of oppression and exclusion of peoples of Latin American and Caribbean descent in the United States. The usefulness of the term is gained as much from its potential as an analytic term as a descriptive one, enabling examinations of histories of racism and imperialism, and the development of alternative visions of the future.

The Latinx essay reflects this heterogeneity, as authors have used the form for everything from personal recollection and spiritual reflection to cultural affirmation and aesthetic evaluation. However, given that Latinx communities find themselves in a perpetual state of crisis, whether because of immigration policies, racial conflicts, or other structural inequities, Latinx writers often use even their most personal essays to engage pressing social and political debates, even if obliquely. At the same time, these authors take advantage of the essay's dialogic nature in their explorations of contentious issues, so that the process they go through in reaching their conclusions and the dialogue the process opens with the reader are as important as the conclusions themselves. While Latinx authors blur and blend the boundaries among different types of essays, I identify three broad strands of the Latinx essay that have been significant: the Latinx *crónica*, the personal essay, and the radical feminist essay.

The Latinx *Crónica*

The Latin American *crónica* is an important touchstone for considerations of the Latinx essay. It is a hybrid genre that emerged in newspapers in the 1870s and '80s, combining "literary with journalistic elements ... resulting in brief texts that often focus on contemporary topics and issues addressed in a self-consciously literary style."[1] As Monica Hanna explains, contemporary Latinx *crónicas* lay claim to the legitimacy granted to journalistic writings while using narrative techniques to "give flesh to numbers" and "humanize the stakes" of the topics they explore,[2] including border crossings and the politics of migration, Latin American political concerns such as narcopolitics and corruption, and examinations of the "cultures arising from Latin@ migrations, often considering Latinidad as it is constituted within the United States and in relation to Latin America."[3]

Born in Los Angeles to a Salvadoran mother and Mexican American father, Rubén Martínez (1962–) has made a name for himself through his *crónica*-style essays. In his collection *The Other Side: Notes from the New L.A., Mexico City, and Beyond* (1992), he established his enduring concern with exploring issues of globalization, immigration, and Central American and Mexican politics and culture, anchoring his explorations in Los Angeles, which he characterizes as "the eye of the hurricane."[4] In his analysis of Latinx Los Angeles creative nonfiction writers, Victor Valle asserts that these authors work in a mode of "radical cosmopolitanism" through which they necessarily "think

---

1 Anibal González-Pérez, *A Companion to Spanish American Modernismo* (Woodbridge, UK: Tamesis, 2007), 24.
2 Monica Hanna, "Chronicling Contemporary Latinidad," *American Literature* 88, no. 2 (2016): 361–89, 362.
3 Hanna, "Chronicling Contemporary," 366. @ sign in original.
4 Rubén Martínez, *The Other Side: Notes from the New L.A., Mexico City, and Beyond* (London: Verso, 1992), 4.

and act around, under, and beyond the nation-state's categories and spatial imaginary," representing multiple homelands that are at once "parallel" and deeply, ambivalently interconnected.[5] This radical cosmopolitanism animates Martínez's writings, as one sees in his description of the many realities in which he lives at once:

> I give thanks that ... I can be in San Salvador in Los Angeles by hanging out in Little Central America, and in Los Angeles in Mexico City by dancing to the rhythms of its underground rock 'n' roll ... but the fires of nationalism still rage, and in the cities of the United States, blacks and Koreans and Latinos and Anglos live in anything but a multicultural paradise.[6]

In referencing the "fires of nationalism," Martínez shows that his cosmopolitanism is neither naïve nor unmoored, nor does it discount the continued force of the nation. Whether he is considering the legacies of the 1992 Los Angeles uprisings ("Ecology of a Riot: The Deserts of Rodney King and Mike Davis") or the devastating consequences of gentrification for communities of color ("My Father's House"), he trains his critical eye as much on racism and interethnic conflict within the United States as on transnational possibilities.[7] Even more, and in keeping with the larger Latinx *crónica* tradition in which he writes, he foregrounds the fact that the transnational and multinational social formations he examines are due to past and ongoing US imperial designs, and that their beauty and promise are inextricable from the violence and oppression that bring them into being. He illustrates this simultaneity in his pieces on the arts, such as when he discusses the US-Mexico border as a place constructed by the "global economy, by surplus value and the bodies of laborers, by the interlacing of race and class that was born of colonialism."[8] He considers the transborder artists who challenge such walls through their work, "dream[ing] them and tear[ing] them down, reconfigur[ing] them ... transform[ing] them into dark matter ... mak[ing] them vibrate, levitat[ing] them."[9]

---

5 Victor Valle, "LA's Latina/o Phantom Nonfiction and the Technologies of Literary Secrecy," in *Latinx Writing Los Angeles: Nonfiction Dispatches from a Decolonial Rebellion*, ed. Ignacio López-Calvo and Victor Valle (Lincoln, NE: University of Nebraska Press, 2018), 1–32, 7.
6 Martínez, *Other Side*, 4.
7 See Rubén Martínez, "Ecology of a Riot: The Deserts of Rodney King and Mike Davis," *KCET Artbound* (1 May 2017), www.kcet.org/news-analysis/ecology-of-a-riot-the-deserts-of-rodney-king-and-mike-davis; and "My Father's House," *Huizache: The Magazine of Latino Literature* 4 (Fall 2014), http://huizachemag.org/read/prose/my-fathers-house/.
8 Rubén Martínez, "What Wall? We've Already Brought Down the Border," *KCET Artbound* (19 January 2017), www.kcet.org/news-analysis/what-wall-weve-already-brought-down-the-border.
9 Martínez, "What Wall?," n.p.

The work of Francisco Goldman (1954–) similarly spans countries, languages, and genres, with a focus on the legacies of war and political corruption in the context of US interventions in Central America and Mexico. Born in Boston to a Catholic Guatemalan mother and a Jewish American father, he was drawn to writing from an early age, and after college moved to his uncle's house in Guatemala City in the hope of writing stories that he could use to apply to MFA programs.[10] He had no plans to go into journalism, but found himself in Guatemala at the height of the civil wars in Central America, and felt compelled to report on them and on the role played by the United States in the conflicts. As he put it, "I was in my twenties, and the two parts of the world I am from – the United States and Central America – were essentially at war with each other. I wasn't going to miss that."[11] Thus, while he has established himself as a highly acclaimed novelist, he first made his mark through his long-form journalism pieces, which have many of the qualities that are the hallmark of the *crónica*. He makes the influence of the *crónica* tradition explicit when he cites one of the genre's great practitioners, commenting that "[Gabriel] García Márquez is always saying that journalism – he means narrative journalism – is just another branch of literature, and he's completely right of course."[12]

Goldman interweaves quotidian experiences with traditional journalistic subjects in order to, as he puts it, bring to life "how the lives of ordinary [Central Americans] intersect with, and are affected by, the larger political issues that people get so worked up over in Washington."[13] He also writes with a heightened level of self-reflexivity, emphasizing his "multiple positionings somewhere between 'insiders' and 'outsiders' in a variety of national and situational contexts."[14] One sees both of these qualities in his piece on attending a Guatemalan folklore festival. He juxtaposes the mundane happenings of the festival – one imposed upon the Indians by the ladino (non-Indian) government and composed of a "'folklore' detached from Indian life"[15] – with the terror experienced by Indigenous peoples on a daily basis

---

10 Ariana E. Vigil and Linda Wagner-Martin, *Understanding Francisco Goldman* (Columbia, SC: University of South Carolina Press, 2018), 1–2.
11 Vigil and Wagner-Martin, *Understanding Francisco Goldman*, 2.
12 Vigil and Wagner-Martin, *Understanding Francisco Goldman*, 4.
13 Francisco Goldman, "Lost in Another Honduras: Of Bordellos and Bad Scenes," *Harper's Magazine* 273, no. 1673 (1 October 1986): 49–57, 52.
14 Monica Hanna and Jennifer Harford Vargas, "'Transnational Forms,'" *Latino/a Literature in the Classroom: 21st Century Approaches to Teaching*, ed. Frederick Luis Aldama (New York: Routledge, 2015), 64–77, 66.
15 Francisco Goldman, "Guatemalan Death Mask: Pomp and Terror in a Dark Country," *Harper's Magazine* 272, no. 1628 (1 January 1986): 56–63, 57.

due to the country's civil war. He comes across three Indigenous girls, sisters whose parents were killed by the military, and feels the inadequacy of his response, his powerlessness to do anything to help them and the countless others like them. One tells him that her parents were murdered on April 26:

> "April 26," I repeated. I wanted to let her know I'd memorized the date. But there was little I could do but listen, for I wasn't in Guatemala as a newspaper reporter or human-rights activist – perhaps she'd mistaken me for one of those. And so helplessness took its usual form, silence between us, punctuated by the usual helpless exhortations.[16]

By going beyond the basic facts typical of conventional journalism, Goldman adds narrative depth to his accounts, and raises ethical questions and consciousness-raising imperatives that implicate his readers, while entering those narratives – little known or ignored in the United States – into the historical record.[17] These narrative strategies continue in his more recent work for the *New Yorker*, including the series of articles he wrote from 2014 to 2016 on the ongoing search for justice for forty-three students disappeared from Iguala, Guerrero, Mexico, in September 2014.

Karla Cornejo Villavicencio (1989–) has been writing professionally since she was a teenager, reviewing jazz albums for a New York City magazine. She first garnered national attention during her senior year at Harvard, when she penned an anonymous essay for the *Daily Beast* titled "DREAM Act: I'm an Illegal Immigrant at Harvard."[18] Appearing during a period of increasing awareness about the plight of undocumented students, the essay revealed that the author was born in South America (in Ecuador), was undocumented, and had no idea what she would do after graduation due to her citizenship status. She also established her acerbic writing style, her rejection of liberal immigrant narratives touting the "American Dream," and her profound ambivalence at the sympathy for "hardworking kids who 'hadn't done anything wrong' while their parents and grandparents were being deported in record numbers."[19] The article eventually led to the publication of *The*

---

16 Goldman, "Guatemalan Death Mask," 60.
17 See, for example, Francisco Goldman, "What Price Panama: A Visit to a Barrio Destroyed by U.S. Forces," *Harper's Magazine* 281, no. 1684 (September 1990): 71–78.
18 Karla Cornejo Villavicencio, "DREAM Act: I'm an Illegal Immigrant at Harvard," *Daily Beast* (27 November 2010), www.thedailybeast.com/dream-act-im-an-illegal-immigrant-at-harvard?ref=scroll.
19 Lucas Iberico Lozada, "Karla Cornejo Villavicencio: DREAMer Narratives Have Their Purpose. But That's Not What I Set Out to Write," *Guernica* (10 June 2020), www.guernicamag.com/karla-cornejo-villavicencio-dreamer-memoirs-have-their-purpose-but-thats-not-what-i-set-out-to-write/.

Undocumented Americans (2020), a highly acclaimed collection of essays that was a finalist for the National Book Award, a first for an undocumented author.

The book has been aptly characterized as "dispatches from what we might call undocumented America: a country within a country."[20] The foundation for its six essays is the set of interviews that Cornejo Villavicencio conducted with undocumented Latinx individuals in five states. The essays include "profiles [of] Staten Island day laborers who cleaned up New York City after Hurricane Sandy ... families poisoned by lead pipes and negligent politicians in Flint, Michigan ... and the intimate fallout of the deportation machine."[21] But these are not conventional journalistic pieces, as Cornejo Villavicencio points out: "This book is a work of creative nonfiction, rooted in careful reporting, translated as poetry, shared by chosen family, and sometimes hard to read."[22] She imbues the essays with the self-reflexivity typical of the *crónica*, as she interweaves her own story throughout, "reflecting on her parents' sacrifices and her daily battles with trauma and mental illness."[23] Moreover, she employs the strategy of fictionalization to conjure those stories and lives that were never recorded, and for which we have no archive from which to draw. Consequently, she compels her readers to consider the limitations of strict genre categories by asking if the blurring of fact and fiction is how, "in the face of so much sacrilege and slander, we reclaim our dead."[24] Ultimately, she insists on honoring the humanity of the "day laborers, housekeepers, construction workers ... people who don't inspire hashtags ... Randoms. People,"[25] and compels her readers to "consider their own positionality and investment in inequitable systems of power" while "refus[ing]," as Stacy Alex words it, "to rely on white-washed caricatures for the sake of shoring up support."[26]

The Latinx Personal Essay

The personal essay has been characterized as a tool of the privileged classes – that is, as a genre ideally suited for the expression and reinforcement of liberal humanist values of individualism elevated to the domain of universality.

---

20 Iberico Lozada, "Karla Cornejo Villavicencio," n.p.
21 Iberico Lozada, "Karla Cornejo Villavicencio," n.p.
22 Karla Cornejo Villavicencio, *The Undocumented Americans* (New York: Random House, 2020), xvi.
23 Iberico Lozada, "Karla Cornejo Villavicencio," n.p.
24 Cornejo Villavicencio, *Undocumented Americans*, 30.
25 Cornejo Villavicencio, *Undocumented Americans*, xvi–ii.
26 Stacy Alex, "Undocumented Latinx Life-Writing: Refusing Worth and Meritocracy," *Prose Studies* 41, no. 2 (2020): 108–28, 121.

Within this Western worldview, the writings of those deemed "other" are delegitimized as too particular, subjective, and irrational. It is against this contextual backdrop that we can understand Mexican American author Richard Rodriguez (1944–) as a figure unique among Latinx writers both in the elite stature he has achieved as a practitioner of the personal essay, and in his defiant embrace of liberal ideals of individualism in opposition to ethnic affiliation and collective identity. His level of renown as an essayist and as a champion of liberal humanism makes him an important point of comparison to other Latinx practitioners of the form, many of whom have identified the radical possibility inherent in the genre to express minoritized identities and to validate the collective over the individualistic.[27] Accordingly, Latinx essayists such as Jennine Capó Crucet use the personal essay to question liberal humanist ideals, emphasizing difference and resistance over exclusionary imperatives of unity and commonality.

Rodriguez is most well known as a prose stylist and has used the personal essay form extensively throughout his career. While his essays often have a fragmentary and conversational quality, they advance what he intends as conclusive lines of argument. His controversial first collection, *Hunger of Memory: The Education of Richard Rodriguez, An Autobiography* (1982) – which he describes as a collection of six "fuguelike" essays "impersonating an autobiography"[28] – tracks his journey of linguistic assimilation, from a predominantly Spanish-speaking boy to an English-speaking citizen "in a crowded city of words."[29] In his telling, his achievement of the identity of "citizen" required him to turn his back on his Mexican culture and the private, familial language of Spanish, and to embrace the public language of English that was foundational to his education. The binary of "public" versus "private" – central for the formation of the liberal humanist political subject – underwrites his staunch arguments against bilingual education and affirmative action, political positions that made him a darling of conservative media and organizations while putting him at odds with activists and scholars in ethnic studies.

Over the next twenty years, Rodriguez published two more collections, completing what he calls "a trilogy on American public life and [his] private life".[30] *Days of Obligation: Arguments with My Mexican Father* (1992) and *Brown:*

---

27 Ellena Savage, "The Emancipatory Personal Essay?," in "The Essay," special issue, *TEXT* 39 (April 2017): 1–11, 3, www.textjournal.com.au/speciss/issue39/content.htm.
28 Richard Rodriguez, *Hunger of Memory: The Education of Richard Rodriguez, An Autobiography* (New York: Bantam Books, 1982), 7.
29 Rodriguez, *Hunger of Memory*, 32.
30 Richard Rodriguez, *Brown: The Last Discovery of America* (New York: Viking, 2002), xiv.

The Last Discovery of America (2002). Despite his continued rejection of bilingual education and affirmative action, the latter two volumes conduct more nuanced explorations of race, ethnicity, and culture in the United States. In *Brown*, he challenges the insistence in the United States on a black/white racial binary, using the color as a metaphor for mixture, hybridity, contradiction, and, ultimately, for "America" itself. The metaphor is grounded in but exceeds ideas of race and racial mixture, encompassing ethnic, aesthetic, sexual, and religious fusions, among countless others. He is his own best example of what he strives for when he speaks of "brown." He writes, "My mestizo boast: as a queer Catholic Spaniard Indian, at home in a temperate Chinese city [San Francisco] in a fading blond state in a post-Protestant nation, I live up to my 16th-century birth."[31] Through his conceptualization of "brown," Rodriguez intends to promote freedom of being and doing. However, as Jeehyun Lim argues, he "treats [these] freedoms as primarily a matter of individual choice," ignoring the "structural inequities and social injustices that often apply a differentiated notion of freedom to people of color,"[32] and ultimately promotes a neoliberal form of multiculturalism that ignores asymmetrical relations of power.

Cuban American author Jennine Capó Crucet (1981–) is a novelist, short-story writer, and prolific essayist, and is currently a contributing opinion writer for the *New York Times*. Her first essay collection, titled *My Time among the Whites: Notes from an Unfinished Education*, appeared in 2019. Like Rodriguez in *Hunger of Memory*, Capó Crucet frames her essays as a consideration of an educational journey. The two collections diverge in their subtitles, however, intimating important points of contrast. If *The Education of Richard Rodriguez* suggests a totalizing experience culminating in educational assimilation, *Notes from an Unfinished Education* indicates a process that is ongoing and contested, one averse to liberal humanism's transcendental truths based in binaries or other essentialized categories. Thus, while the conflict that animates Rodriguez's narrative – his growing alienation from his family as the price of admission into the public realm – is present in Capó Crucet as well, it does not become an irrevocable moment of identity formation in opposition to family and culture. Capó Crucet writes that her university education "moved [her] into a different class of people – out of the class that had forged [her] – and this shift would remain a painful

---

31 Rodriguez, *Brown: The Last Discovery*, 35.
32 Jeehyun Lim, *Bilingual Brokers: Race, Literature, and Language as Human Capital* (New York: Fordham University Press, 2017), 139.

source of tension from that moment on."[33] Yet later she foregrounds the indispensability of collectives past and present for her survival:

> [W]e have ancestors who have survived much worse. Not just ancestors: I'm talking about our grandmothers, our mothers, women who've held us and seen us for the dreams we are, even as they wanted so much more for and from us. . . . They've left behind – some by choice and some by force and some through a combination of both – more than we have yet to leave behind. That blood: It runs through us. There is so much power in that, and so in us.[34]

Capó Crucet, then, understands relationships, ontologies, and conditions to be fluid and contingent, interrelated and ever shifting. She does not draw a hard line between the individual and the collective; in fact, she never posits the achievement of sovereign individuality as her goal.

This kind of complexity informs her approach to her collection's primary topic of exploration, the relationship among Latinx culture, the American Dream, and the whiteness that undergirds it. In essays on family trips to Disney World and the Miss USA pageant and on her time as a tourist working on a midwestern cattle ranch, among others, she brings to light the unmarked nature of whiteness and the power dynamics embedded in that invisibility:

> Many white people I've met often think of themselves as culture-less, as vanilla: plain, boring, American white. What they are revealing when they say this . . . is how little race impacts their lives, how whiteness is ubiquitous to them, and they mistake that ubiquitousness as a kind of neutrality or regularness that renders their race and culture invisible to themselves.[35]

But this is not a "white versus Latinx," "us versus them" interrogation. She is just as interested in Latinx aspirations to whiteness, and how some Latinxs have had at least a partial access to whiteness, or off-whiteness, not available to others. She writes, "To be Cuban in Miami was to be a kind of white, with all the privileges and sense of cultural neutrality whiteness affords."[36] That sense of privilege is illusory, however, as she notes in her reflections on the ideology of the American Dream:

> The American Dream commonly told: You can accomplish anything if you work hard enough for it. All you have to do is work hard. My parents really believed this, and I believed it long enough to get me to college, where I learned

---

33 Jennine Capó Crucet, *My Time among the Whites: Notes from an Unfinished Education* (New York: Picador MacMillan, 2019), 18.
34 Capó Crucet, *My Time*, 42.   35 Capó Crucet, *My Time*, 80.
36 Capó Crucet, *My Time*, 82.

to see this idea for the dangerous lie it is, one that doesn't take into account many things, like, for instance, history.[37]

Renee Hudson sees Capó Crucet's essay collection as part of a larger literary trend, which she calls "post-Trump Latinx literature," by which she means literature that highlights, on the one hand, the specific complicity between some Latinxs and white supremacy and, on the other hand, how Latinx authors are building a resistance canon, or "a counter-archive to the white supremacy that dominates the news."[38] In the process, Capó Crucet also resists the personal essay's history as a tool for expressing liberal humanist imperatives, tapping into the form's potential instead for the "disrupt[ion] of hegemonic thinking."[39]

Radical Latina Feminists and the Intersectional Essay

The Latina essayists I identify as "radical feminist" were part of a larger group of US woman-of-color feminists who found themselves excluded both by feminist organizations dominated by white women and race-based liberation movements dominated by men. While Capó Crucet's resistance to the essay's elite history manifests itself primarily in the content of her essays, radical feminists additionally draw attention to the mutually constituting relationship between form and content, and this is especially true of those who began publishing in the 1980s. Their interest in formal innovation aligns with Ruth-Ellen Boetcher Joeres's contention that radical feminists embrace the essay's resistance to definition, its position "somewhere on the boundary of traditional ideas about genre."[40] Accordingly, these essayists appropriated and revised the form itself, making it their own in ways that were constitutive of the intersectional theoretical framework animating all of their writings, a framework that theorized the interlocking nature of oppressions, meaning the way that gender intersects with domination along the lines of sexuality, class, race, religion, nationality, and language to create new categories of oppression.

Among Latina feminists, Chicanas Cherríe Moraga (1952–) and Gloria Anzaldúa (1942–2004) were among the most influential in creating a hybridized

---

37 Capó Crucet, My Time, 28.
38 Renee Hudson, "Jennine Capó Crucet and Post-Trump Latinx Literature," Los Angeles Review of Books (3 September 2019), https://lareviewofbooks.org/article/jennine-capo-crucet-and-post-trump-latinx-literature/.
39 Savage, "Emancipatory Personal Essay," 3.
40 Ruth-Ellen Boetcher Joeres, "The Passionate Essay: Radical Feminist Essayists," in The Politics of the Essay: Feminist Perspectives, ed. Ruth-Ellen Boetcher Joeres and Elizabeth Mittman (Bloomington, IN: Indiana University Press, 1993), 150–71, 152–53.

essay form, first doing so in the now classic volume they coedited in 1981, *This Bridge Called My Back: Writings by Radical Women of Color*. The volume is anchored by numerous essays that elucidate its political commitments and organizing theoretical method, and which are themselves collages of dreams, journal entries, poems, letters, critical analysis, and autobiographical reflection. Fittingly, Amy Kaminsky uses the "borderlands" metaphor, which Anzaldúa developed in her 1987 essay and poetry collection *Borderlands / La Frontera*, to understand this "indeterminate area of prose writing that is no longer normative essay but not yet narrative, life story, poetry, or journalism" as promoting the feminist project of "decentering."[41] For Moraga and Anzaldúa, this includes the decentering of the individual in favor of the collective, but, even more, it emphasizes a decentering of Western notions of subject formation propped up by the essay as traditionally understood. If the ideal Western subject is the individual (white, male) thinker, sovereign, self-determining, and self-authorizing, then Moraga and Anzaldúa use form in alignment with theme to foreground fragmentation, particularity, and plurality, expressing consciousness "as a site of multiple voicings" against which "the subject must struggle with constantly."[42] In essays such as Moraga's "La Güera" and Anzaldúa's "La Prieta," these writers interweave poetry, letters, and journal entries with exposition to introduce other voices into their narratives. At times they "split" or multiply their own subjectivities, as when Moraga quotes a letter that expresses an earlier version of herself, or when Anzaldúa mixes in her own poems without elaboration. At others they cite the words of other woman-of-color feminists, doing so in ways that contrast with traditional uses of quotation in the essay. Boetcher Joeres offers Montaigne's observation that he "only quote[d] others to make [himself] more explicit."[43] In contrast, radical feminists allow quotations to "take over [their] own words," temporarily ceding their authority as "essayist" by foregrounding the "other" as much as the "self."[44]

The intersectional framework at the heart of Moraga and Anzaldúa's thinking allows them to analyze the woman of color's fragmented consciousness as one that "emerges from a subjectivity structured by multiple determinants – gender,

---

41 Amy Kaminsky, "Essay, Gender, and Mestizaje: Victoria Ocampo and Gabriela Mistral," in Boetcher Joeres and Mittman, *Politics of the Essay*, 113–30, 123.
42 Norma Alarcón, "The Theoretical Subject(s) of *This Bridge Called My Back* and Anglo American Feminism," in *Making Face, Making Soul: Haciendo Caras*, ed. Gloria Anzaldúa (San Francisco: Aunt Lute, 1990), 28–40, 368.
43 Boetcher Joeres and Mittman, *Politics*, 152.
44 Boetcher Joeres and Mittman, *Politics*, 156–57.

class, sexuality, and contradictory membership in competing cultures and racial identities."[45] Following from this, and in opposition to the liberal humanist ideal of the "unmarked" and "universal" subject, they validate their fragmented subjectivities as a site for theorization, rejecting the universal in favor of, in Anzaldúa's words, "the particular and the feminine and the specific historical moment."[46] Consequently, they conceptualize a "theory in the flesh," which Moraga describes as one where "the physical realities of our lives – our skin color, the land or concrete we grew up on, our sexual longings – all fuse to create a politic born out of necessity."[47] Such a theory describes "the ways in which Third World women of color derive a feminist political theory specifically from our racial/cultural background and experience."[48] The "collage essay" would remain an important form for both writers throughout their careers. While they emphasized different issues, they both continued to organize their writings around an intersectional framework and the theory of the flesh.

Latina feminists using the essay form in the twenty-first century do not employ formal innovation in the mode of earlier radical feminists of color, but they do continue to build on the theory of the flesh, and on the language and politics of intersectionality passed on to them by Moraga and Anzaldúa. Daisy Hernández (1975–), a Cubana-Colombiana raised in New Jersey and former executive editor of *ColorLines Magazine*, coedited *Colonize This! Young Women of Color on Today's Feminism* (2002), a major anthology of essays that follows in *This Bridge*'s footsteps by bringing together women representing a range of racial, ethnic, gender, and sexual identities.[49] Hernández and her coeditor, Bushra Rehman, are explicit about their volume's indebtedness to *This Bridge* and other writings by radical feminists of color from the 1970s and '80s, particularly to their centering of race and sexuality alongside gender and their insistence on the interlocking nature of oppression. In her introduction to the volume, Hernández writes:

> These young women of color are leveraging social media to their advantage. They are using it to organize and to break silences and also to learn about feminism and to redefine it. They have grown up in a more multiracial

---

45 Yvonne Yarbro-Bejarano, "Gloria Anzaldúa's *Borderlands / La frontera*: Cultural Studies, 'Difference,' and the Non-Unitary Subject," *Cultural Critique* 28 (1994): 5–28, 11.
46 Gloria Anzaldúa, "Speaking in Tongues: A Letter to 3rd World Women Writers," in *This Bridge Called My Back: Writings by Radical Women of Color*, ed. Cherríe Moraga and Gloria Anzaldúa (New York: Kitchen Table: Women of Color Press, 1983), 165–73, 170.
47 Moraga, *This Bridge*, 23.
48 Cherríe Moraga and Gloria Anzaldúa, "Introduction," in *This Bridge*, xxiii–xxvi, xxiv.
49 Fittingly, Moraga contributed the preface to the anthology.

United States with faster access to the work of feminists of color, and as a result they are articulating an intersectional feminism that is rooted in the work of the women who have come before us.[50]

Hernández exemplifies a general move on the part of "next generation" feminists to "stress their connection to the feminisms of the past even as they s[eek] to posit themselves as new."[51] The "newness" Hernández identifies among young feminists of color includes their role at the forefront of key social justice movements, "from Black Lives Matter and trans visibility to organizing undocumented families and protesting at Standing Rock."[52]

While she has published a memoir and occasional pieces of short fiction, Hernández's form of choice is the essay. She engages an impressive array of issues in her essays, ranging from her inventive and beautifully wrought meditation on grammatical conventions and the fluidity of gender identity ("Grammatical Disquisitions"),[53] to her exploration of the relationship among language, colonization, and the grief of cultural loss ("Before Loss, Memory"),[54] along with her persistent concern with religious and spiritual syncretism and the significance of such belief systems in the contexts of political exile and state and intrafamilial violence ("The Noble Abode of Equanimity" and "The Buddha Loves Boundaries").[55] No matter her topic, all of her writings are anchored in her identity as a bisexual Latina feminist and in an intersectional framework, one that places a special emphasis on sexuality as a key node of analysis. As Vanessa Pérez-Rosario observes, if for Moraga lesbianism was the "supreme trope in the quest for newer gender identities" and for the valorization of difference "in the face of hetero gender norms," Hernández "explores bisexuality and transgender identity as a way to interrogate the idea of 'normal' and a future that is impossible to predict."[56]

---

50 Daisy Hernández, "Introduction to the Second Edition," in *Colonize This! Young Women of Color on Today's Feminism*, ed. Daisy Hernández and Bushra Rehman, 2nd ed. (New York: Seal, 2019), xvii.
51 Astrid Henry, *Not My Mother's Sister: Generational Conflict and Third-Wave Feminism* (Bloomington, IN: Indiana University Press, 2004), 30.
52 Hernández, "Introduction," xvi–xvii.
53 Daisy Hernández, "Grammatical Disquisitions," *Iowa Review* 48, no. 2 (2018): 155–66.
54 Daisy Hernández, "Before Loss, Memory," *Fourth Genre: Explorations in Nonfiction* 14, no. 2 (2012): 1–15.
55 Daisy Hernández, "The Noble Abode of Equanimity: On Not Getting Swept Up in the Political Storm," *Tricycle: The Buddhist Review* (2019), https://tricycle.org/magazine/daisy-hernandez-immigration/; and Daisy Hernández, "The Buddha Loves Boundaries," *Killing the Buddha* (26 February 2015), https://killingthebuddha.com/mag/confession/the-buddha-loves-boundaries/.
56 Vanessa Pérez-Rosario, "Latina Feminist Theory and Writing," in *The Cambridge History of Latina/o American Literature*, ed. John Morán González and Laura Lomas (Cambridge, UK: Cambridge University Press, 2018), 488–509, 506–507.

Chicana author and artist Myriam Gurba has made a name for herself as a provocative writer whose work is marked by her dark and biting humor and her irreverent engagement with hot-button topics typically treated solemnly if at all. As Gurba herself puts it, "I've always been kind of an aggressive person. Someone who likes to roughhouse not only physically but intellectually."[57] While she works in numerous genres, she has gained most renown for her "true crime" memoir, *Mean* (2017), and for her essays. Two of these, both engaging Jeanine Cummins's novel *American Dirt* (2020), brought her national attention, as she directed her sharp critical eye and take-no-prisoners style to bludgeoning what essentially had been marketed as the book of the year.[58] While Cummins says that she wrote the novel in order to humanize migrants – it is about a middle-class Mexican bookseller who flees to the United States with her son to escape cartel violence – Gurba argues that it "reeks of patriarchal white saviorism" and is a form of "trauma porn that wears a social justice fig leaf."[59] Gurba goes beyond simply criticizing Cummins, however, as she views *American Dirt* as symptomatic of the larger problem of institutional racism pervading the publishing industry. True to the impulse of the radical feminist essay, Gurba's is a call to action. In response, numerous high-profile writers of color have spoken out about "the erasure of Brown people in the publishing industry."[60] Moreover, a social movement emerged under the hashtag #DignidadLiteraria, which aims to promote racial dignity within the publishing industry by pushing for systemic change through grassroots organizing.

Gurba's review of *American Dirt* hastened racist and misogynist responses, including death threats. In fact, one of Gurba's major criticisms of *American Dirt* is that it misrepresents the United States as a safe harbor for women fleeing violence, when in reality "[f]emicide is a public health crisis on both sides of the U.S.-Mexico border."[61] In her response to one such anonymous

---

57 Steve Weiberg, "*Mean* Author Wields a Potent Weapon against Trauma: Humor," *Kansas City Star* (12 February 2018), www.kansascity.com/entertainment/books/article199649684.html.
58 Cummins garnered a seven-figure advance for *American Dirt*, which received glowing blurbs from literary luminaries and a large amount of attention from major publishing venues such as the *New York Times*. Moreover, the book was selected as an Oprah Book Club pick.
59 Myriam Gurba, "Pendeja, You Ain't Steinbeck: My Bronca with Fake-Ass Social Justice Literature," *Tropics of Meta* (12 December 2019), https://tropicsofmeta.com/2019/12/12/pendeja-you-aint-steinbeck-my-bronca-with-fake-ass-social-justice-literature/.
60 Myriam Gurba, "I Called Out *American Dirt's* Racism. I Won't Be Silenced," *Vox* (12 March 2020), www.vox.com/first-person/2020/3/12/21168012/racism-american-dirt-myriam-gurba-jeanine-cummins.
61 Gurba, "I Called Out," n.p.

threat, in which the author hopes that Gurba will confront the police with her "ethnic ire" and that they will "relive [sic] [her] of the burden of a life spent in feckless fury,"[62] Gurba writes another essay, one focused on the issue of violence against women of color. As a victim of sexual assault herself, this is personal for Gurba, and she writes about her experience along with those of other women of color frequently, doing so by situating specific cases within a larger system of misogyny that controls and punishes women who challenge male dominance. In doing so, her analysis always insists on an intersectional approach that understands misogyny in the context of race and sexual identity, as she makes clear:

> Albert Memmi wrote that "[r]acism is a pleasure within everyone's reach," and this thesis is golden. We can also exchange the word racism for gender or sexuality and still have the statement ring true. I, however, would prefer for us to layer these nouns on top of each other and then mash them up because I'm a queer as fuck Chicana with European, Indigenous, and Black ancestry. My body is a product of Spanish colonialism and as such, it resides at a dangerous crossroads, one which often exposes me to a very specific type of racist misogyny.[63]

Gurba proceeds to hit back at her anonymous threatener with her trademark humor and irreverence. In a separate essay she observes that stories of sexual assault are saturated "with piety, banishing irreverence from the narrative" and creating a stasis that does not allow survivors "to really be alive." Humor, on the other hand, disrupts stasis, and is a "form of action."[64] With her commitment to using intersectional frameworks in her writings and attending to questions of sexuality and the body, Gurba positions herself within a Latina radical feminist essay tradition.

The Latinx essay has a long, rich, and varied history. The outline I have provided is suggestive rather than definitive, in that at least some of the essayists I include could fit into more than one strand, and the strands themselves have some overlap. One might discuss "humor" essayists such as José Antonio Burciaga (1940–1996) and Michelle Serros (1966–2015), or sketch a tradition of the Latinx environmental essay that could include

---

62 Myriam Gurba, "My Taco Laughs at You: At Death Threats Aimed at Women of Color Who Don't Fellate White Supremacy," *Los Angeles Review of Books* (23 January 2020), https://lareviewofbooks.org/article/my-taco-laughs-at-you-on-death-threats-aimed-at-women-of-color-who-dont-fellate-white-supremacy/.
63 Gurba, "My Taco," n.p.
64 Myriam Gurba, "Why I Use Humor When Talking about My Sexual Assault," *Time* (30 March 2018), https://time.com/5221206/myriam-gurba-sexual-assault-humor-power/.

Fabiola Cabeza de Baca Gilbert (1894–1991) as a precursor to Moraga, Anzaldúa, and Ana Castillo (1953–). John Phillip Santos (1957–) has written a significant body of essays exploring Tejano politics and culture, and Erika L. Sánchez (1984–) and Angela Morales (1966–) are emerging voices in the genre. We are in the midst of a renewed interest in the essay among Latinx writers, one that promises to build on the writings that have come before, while also staking out new ground, reshaping and remaking our sense of what the Latinx and, more broadly, the US essay can look like.

38
Black Experience through the Essay

WALTON MUYUMBA

When Ta-Nehisi Coates (1975–) published his book-length essay, *Between the World and Me* (2015), he became, for many, the embodiment of Black intellectual thought, a tradition that many reviewers and pundits sometimes reduced to James Baldwin's essays, such as those found in *Notes of a Native Son* (1955) or *The Fire Next Time* (1963). That Baldwin's writing has marked Coates's analyses and prose is unmistakable. However, as Baldwin writes in his essay "The Price May Be Too High" (1969), white Americans haven't been able to "conceive that their version of reality, which they want me to accept, is an insult to my history and a parody of theirs and an intolerable violation of myself."[1] We ought to read Baldwin's critique for both its political and literary dimensions. That is, outside of Black cultural and critical discourse, African American experience is often described as, firstly, dysfunctional and, secondly, as a confrontation with anti-Black racism and its vagaries, including those social practices and government policies that have curtailed the educational, financial, and health outcomes for members of that group. Over time, those narrative tracks have become so entrenched, so pervasive, so dominant that even in the twenty-first century, many Americans are unprepared to recognize Black life as human experience rather than a cord of ahistorical pathologies.

This has also been true in American literary culture. During the nineteenth and twentieth centuries, critics, scholars, writers, and readers often structured American literature's boundaries in order to deny Black American artists entry. Black writers have countered that exclusion by producing works designed to describe, narrate, and affirm Black humanity. Those efforts were meant to advance artistic practices, dismantle literary

[1] James Baldwin, *The Cross of Redemption* (New York: Random House, 2010), 106.

segregation, and support the larger, unscripted, multilateral initiative to win political, sociocultural, and economic equality for all African American citizens. With all that in mind, Black writers, critics, and scholars began theorizing the aesthetic practices and critical techniques that have generated the African American literary tradition and, in the process, broadened the American literary canon.

Though Coates would like to emulate Baldwin's ability to generate in readers "the reflex to strip away illusion, to break away from dreams,"[2] he knows that he is the progeny of a broader literary ancestry. As a member of "a tradition stretching back to a time when reading and writing were, for black people, the marks of rebellion,"[3] Coates is part of an extensive and powerful cousinage of impressive, innovative essayists, including writers such as Darryl Pinckney (1953–), Hilton Als (1960–), Jerald Walker (1964–), Kiese Laymon (1974–), Jesmyn Ward (1977–), Sharifa Rhodes-Pitts (1978–), Nawali Serpell (1980–), Harmony Holiday (1982–), and Jesse McCarthy (1984–), just to name a few.

And yet, in much of mainstream American literary criticism, as in much of all arts criticism, writers who have been unwilling to learn from the full range of Black life and Black aesthetics continue producing responses that exclude the great range of and unique practices of African American essayists. Take, for example, Philip Lopate's narrative of the midcentury essay, *The Golden Age of the American Essay, 1945–1970*. Writing in the introduction about the essayistic style that dominated the immediate postwar moment, Lopate notes that the "prevalence of a formal intellectual tone" encompassed a generation of writers who, "regardless of how their positions may have differed or how much they lambasted each other, ... were all writing to show off their intelligence and learning."[4] Lopate argues that American writers who defined the essay in the era leading up to World War II based their aesthetic sensibilities on the critical mold T. S. Eliot had offered in his essay "Tradition and the Individual Talent." In it, Eliot argues that "[t]he emotion of art is impersonal. And the [literary artist] cannot reach this impersonality without surrendering himself wholly to the work to be done. And he is not likely to know what is to be done unless he lives in what is not merely the present, but the present

---

[2] Ta-Nehisi Coates, *We Were Eight Years in Power* (New York: One World, 2017), 216.
[3] Coates, *We Were Eight*, 6.
[4] Philip Lopate, *The Golden Age of the American Essay, 1945–1970* (New York: Anchor, 2021), xviii.

moment of the past, unless he is conscious, not of what is dead, but of what is already living."[5] Essayists such as Edmund Wilson, Lionel Trilling, and Mary McCarthy diminished their personal sensibilities in order to fashion personas on the page that spoke in the "high formal tone ... that had signified quality in American nonfiction prose."[6] By the 1960s, Lopate explains, the New Journalists shifted the form away from "the impersonal ... all-knowing authority of the public intellectual," toward a "more subjective autobiographical" mode, a flashier, "no-holds-barred, jazzy, sometimes stream-of-consciousness style."[7] But Lopate's story of the transition from the critical, intellectual essay to the personal essay during the form's golden era is framed and animated by a cast of white writers such as Gore Vidal (1925–2012), Tom Wolfe (1930–2018), Hunter S. Thompson (1937–2005), Joan Didion (1934–2021), and Norman Mailer (1923–2007).

Though Lopate has placed selections from Baldwin, N. Scott Momaday (1934–), and Albert Murray (1916–2013) in his collection, these Native and Black American essayists are merely bit players in his narrative about white writing; in this volume, the artists of color seem to be present in order to offer racial representation rather than to demonstrate innovation central to the essay's history.[8] Where are the selections from, say, Ralph Ellison (1913–1994), Amiri Baraka (1934–2014), June Jordan (1936–2001), James Alan McPherson (1943–2016), or Alice Walker (1944–) – an array of Black authors who invented modes of essay unseen before their emergence in print? As Jesse McCarthy points out in his own essay collection, *Who Will Pay Reparations on My Soul?* (2021), in the African American literary tradition, the essay holds "a special place, as a space not only for argument but for experimental writings that mix and chop the old ways into new ones."[9] Arguably, Black essayists innovated the improvisatory, autocritical modes that Lopate ascribes to the white, Cold War–era Americans dominating his anthology.

Cheryl A. Wall's literary history, *On Freedom and the Will to Adorn: The Art of the African American Essay* (2019), offers a counternarrative to Lopate's

---

[5] T. S. Eliot, "Tradition and the Individual Talent," in *The Sacred Wood* (New York: Knopf, 1921), 53.
[6] Lopate, *Golden Age*, xviii. [7] Lopate, *Golden Age*, xviii.
[8] With an understanding that anthology editors must contend with manuscript word count limitations and exclusive copyright controls, it is stunning nonetheless that so many titanic figures are absent from the table of contents.
[9] Jesse McCarthy, *Who Will Pay Reparations on My Soul? Essays* (New York: Liveright, 2021), xix.

story. Wall suggests that African American writers have departed from the essay's Montaignean origins in order to refashion the form for their multipurpose needs. Michel de Montaigne (1533–1592), she argues, was concerned primarily with his own mental process, rather than the activism that has come to characterize the work of Black essayists:

> For Montaigne the challenge of the essay was not so much to express his ideas as to convey the experience of thinking itself, to convey the flow, the wanderings of his thoughts. He believed in the integrity of his experience and boasted of his putative lack of erudition. He did not expect his words to produce actions; he hoped only to communicate his thoughts and the process that produced them.[10]

Black American essayists have turned away from Montaigne's approach because their pieces have frequently emerged as explicit efforts to marry artistic innovation with calls to political action or intellectual renewal. And yet, as Wall puts it, even as many Black writers "reject Montaigne's sense of the essential privacy of the essay, its limitations to the mind of the writer, they retain a desire to make the process of their thinking transparent."[11] Focused on innovative acts of transparency in the essay, Wall explains that Black writers have "worked new variations on the genre of the essay itself. The open-endedness of the form provided its practitioners an artistic freedom. The essay allowed them to stamp the apparent formlessness of the essay with their own artistic signature."[12] African American writers have always been committed artistically to exercising the elegant flexibility of the essay form while analyzing the conditions of and arguing for Black freedom. Unfortunately, this chapter cannot support an encyclopedic, exhaustive survey of African American essayists from the last 150 years. Instead, it offers a sampler of Black writers working in the essay. Here, I will trace some of the aesthetic choices these writers have employed in order to demonstrate the essay's capacious formal dimensions for imagining and practicing freedom.

Rather than think of freedom as a destination, African American essayists have revised and restructured the form in ways that allow them to document how freedom is practiced continually. Here, Michel Foucault's "distinction between liberation (conceived of as a momentary act) and practices of

---

[10] Cheryl A. Wall, *On Freedom and the Will to Adorn: The Art of the African American Essay* (Chapel Hill, NC: University of North Carolina Press, 2019), 2.
[11] Wall, *On Freedom*, 2.   [12] Wall, *On Freedom*, 10.

freedom (conceived of as ongoing)" offers useful context.[13] In his late interviews, "On the Genealogy of Ethics" (1983) and "The Ethics of the Concern for Self as a Practice of Freedom" (1984), Foucault argues that philosophers and theorists ought to question "domination at every level and in every form in which it exists."[14] The critical function of philosophy, Foucault explains, "derives from the Socratic injunction to 'Take care of yourself,' in other words, 'Make freedom your foundation, through the mastery of yourself'."[15] Foucault named human experience as art and recognized the technologies of the self as enabling the art of living: "[C]ouldn't everyone's life become a work of art?"[16]

Well before Foucault articulated these positions, African American writers were advancing their own arguments about freedom, self-care, and life as art. And the essay, given its formal indeterminacy and malleability, has been the apt vehicle for writers to interrogate Black experience as art, to think about language, narrative, and criticism, and to exhibit practices of freedom. As Andrew J. Angyal has argued, in order to "achieve more than journalism or mere expository prose," Black writers seeking to meet the demands of the personal essay must articulate individual styles that convey their distinctive voices and personalities.[17] He writes:

> The personal (or familiar) essay may also use anecdotes or events from the writer's life as emblematic or illustrative of larger issues. Thus the writer's experiences and his or her responses to them become a paradigm for the audience. Often the African-American essay writer has served as an interpreter for his culture and as a spokesperson for its concerns to a more general audience.[18]

---

[13] Maggie Nelson, *On Freedom* (Minneapolis: Graywolf Press, 2021), 6. In *On Freedom*, in essays on "freedom, care, and constraint," Nelson adapts Foucault's "distinction" in order to illustrate how practices of freedom allow us to grapple with the new power relationships that emerge following acts of liberation. Because freedom, care, and unfreedom are bound together in barbed relation, Nelson argues, we ought to pay close attention to the sometimes ecstatic, sometimes catastrophic knotted points of "sovereignty and self-abandon, subjectivity and subjection, autonomy and dependency, recreation and need, obligation and refusal, the supranatural and the sublunary" (9). These knots might teach us, she claims, how to dwell in complexity and develop a "greater tolerance for indeterminacy" (17).

[14] Michel Foucault, *The Essential Works of Michel Foucault*, vol. 1, *Ethics, Subjectivity, and Truth*, ed. Paul Rabinow, trans. Robert Hurley (New York: New Press, 1997), 300.

[15] Foucault, *Essential Works*, 301.   [16] Foucault, *Essential Works*, 261.

[17] Andrew J. Angyal, "The 'Complex Fate' of Being an American: The African-American Essayist and the Quest for Identity," *CLA Journal* 37, no. 1 (September 1993): 64–80, 66.

[18] Angyal, "'Complex Fate,'" 66.

As interpreters and spokespeople, Black essayists must analyze the systems and structures limiting African American freedom while also offering practices that might liberate the group to enter new political or social contexts. We can find writers attempting to balance these desires beginning in the years following the end of Reconstruction in the southern United States.

The Essay: A Form of Resistance

In the latter part of the nineteenth century, Black writers brought formal and intellectual newness to the essay to "reflect the changing situation and concerns of African American people."[19] Anna Julia Cooper (1858–1964) and W. E. B. Du Bois (1868–1963) used cultural criticism to model forms of resistance against marginalization, insisting instead that Black people are central to the American democratic experiment. As Cooper's *A Voice from the South* (1892) suggests, Black women writers were especially pivotal during this period as they published essays that "focused solidly and more stridently, not just on the social, educational, and political needs of the newly freed communities of formerly enslaved people, but also on the particular needs of women."[20] Marilyn Sanders-Mobley suggests that Cooper's essay collection is the first book-length Black feminist text.

Late in "Womanhood: A Vital Element in the Regeneration and Progress of the Race," the collection's opening piece, Cooper contends that "[o]nly the BLACK WOMAN can say 'when and where I enter, in the quiet, undisputed dignity of my womanhood, without violence and without suing or special patronage, then and there the whole *Negro race enters with me.*'"[21] As Sanders-Mobley explains, *A Voice from the South* represents Cooper's recognition that "the women's movement needed the voice of black women who 'confronted ... both [the] woman question and [the] race problem.'"[22] She was thus "an articulate spokesperson" for both the women's and the racial uplift movements.

In a move that predates Du Bois's use of musical quotation from Negro spirituals as epigraphs for the essays in *Souls of Black Folk* (1903), Cooper divided her book into two sections: "Part First: *Soprano Obbligato*" and "Part

---

[19] Marilyn Sanders-Mobley, "African American Women Essayists," in *The Cambridge Companion to African American Women's Literature*, ed. Angelyn Mitchell and Danille K. Taylor (New York: Cambridge University Press, 2009), 228–30.
[20] Sanders-Mobley, "African American Women," 228.
[21] Anna Julia Cooper, *A Voice from the South* (Xenia, OH: Aldine, 1892), 31.
[22] Sanders-Mobley, "African American Women," 134.

Second: *Tutti Ad Libitum*." In the opening section, where Cooper "gives voice to an ethic of care and social uplift,"[23] her unique analysis of America's domestic reality represents a vocal line indispensable to performing the social composition, if you will. Here, then, Cooper's Black feminist critique rises above the national clamor to elaborate specific melodic lines within the arrangement.

Interestingly, the musical concept framing the second section suggests that all (*tutti*) the voices of the national discourse sing together. But as an instruction in this context, *tutti ad libitum* might indicate that the group is improvising freely together. This is a fascinating notion given that Cooper spends the second half of the book taking on American imperialism, and the treatment of and response to Native Americans, and issues of race and representation in the literary works of writers such as Harriet Beecher Stowe (1811–1896), George Washington Cable (1844–1925), and William Dean Howells (1837–1920). White writers, Cooper claims, having not "focused closely enough to obtain a clear-cut view," explain that "all colored people look alike" and then note "every chance contortion or idiosyncrasy as a race characteristic."[24] Ultimately, because white artists have only "slight" knowledge of Black life, they "cannot even discern diversities of individuality."[25]

The Negro's two-ness, his "double consciousness," as Du Bois described it in the August 1897 issue of the *Atlantic Monthly*, is exactly what white writers, such as, say, Howells, couldn't imagine about African American experience.[26] When Du Bois collected "Strivings of the Negro People" as "Of Our Spiritual Striving" in *The Souls of Black Folk*, he offered a preceding "Forethought" in which he claimed that "the color line" would be the central problem of the twentieth century. The color line, he argues, both produces and maintains a social order and a political hierarchy based on white supremacy. Du Bois's interpretation of the line separating the races points to the inexorable relationship between the definitions of Blackness and whiteness.

And yet, Du Bois writes, white Americans seem continually predisposed to ask Black people: "How does it feel to be a problem?" Du Bois uses this question to assess the seemingly antithetical relationship between Blackness and Americanness:

> [T]he Negro is a sort of seventh son, born with a veil, and gifted with second-sight in this American world, – a world which yields him no true

---

[23] Sanders-Mobley, "African American Women," 229.
[24] Cooper, *Voice from the South*, 186–87.   [25] Cooper, *Voice from the South*, 206.
[26] For a decade (1871–1881), Howells was editor in chief of the *Atlantic Monthly*.

self-consciousness, but only lets him see himself through the revelation of the other world. It is a peculiar sensation, this double-consciousness, this sense of always looking at one's self through the eyes of others ... in amused contempt and pity. One ever feels this two-ness, an American, a Negro ... two warring ideals in one dark body, whose dogged strength alone keeps it from being torn asunder.[27]

Du Bois's description is also an attempt at understanding and overcoming the racial dilemmas embedded in the American sociopolitical circumstances. But understanding and overcoming can only arrive, Du Bois argues throughout *Souls*, when Americans confront the political problems born at the abrupt ending of Reconstruction in the postbellum South, the Black Codes/Jim Crow laws negating African American equal citizenship (in the South and urban North), and the rampant vigilante lynchings of Black people. Without willing address of the history of Negro dehumanization and the address of democracy thus withheld, Americans, Black and white, cannot fulfill the social hope for more freedoms.

The advent of the twentieth century saw national Black leaders and intellectuals shifting away from Booker T. Washington's accommodationist policies toward progressive practices of resistance, including the cultural critiques put forth in Cooper's and Du Bois's essays. During this period, Black people "became racially conscious and self-assertive, affirmed their humanity, and demanded respect;" they began calling themselves "New Negroes."[28] The New Negro crafted the Black self creatively, through the expressive arts, and used the critical essay to study and analyze those representations. Race magazines became the cultural spaces where expression and critique sat in discourse together, especially *Opportunity: A Journal of Negro Life*, the *Crisis*, and the *Messenger* – respectively, the organizational magazines of the National Urban League, the NAACP, and the independent Socialist periodical periodical founded by Chandler Owen and A. Philip Randolph in 1917.[29] All three magazines became venues for writers in the 1910s and '20s to essay on the political and cultural conditions of Black life.

There were also Black radical platforms such as William Monroe Trotter's (1872–1934) weekly activist newspaper the *Guardian* (founded in Boston in 1901), and Hubert Harrison's (1883–1927) the *Voice* (founded in New York City

---

[27] W. E. B. Du Bois, *The Souls of Black Folk* (Chicago: A. C. McClurg, 1903), 3.
[28] Angelyn Mitchell, ed., *Within the Circle: An Anthology of African American Literary Criticism from the Harlem Renaissance to the Present* (Durham, NC: Duke University Press, 1994), 3.
[29] For further context on the essay and the Harlem Renaissance, see Shawn Anthony Christian's chapter in this volume, "The Essay in the Harlem Renaissance."

in 1917), a Socialist paper connected to Marcus Garvey's Universal Negro Improvement Association and African Communities League (UNIA). Just as Du Bois did with his progressive editorial columns in the *Crisis*, Trotter and Harrison (known as "the Father of Harlem Radicalism") used their respective opinion columns to shape African American radical-leftist resistance to racist America. Both activists also wrote essays in order to offer deep, serious analyses of Black leadership and leaders, including pieces that raised concerns about Du Bois himself.[30]

Possibly the most significant publication placing the arts and literary/critical essays in conversation was the Alain Locke–edited *The New Negro: An Anthology* (1925). With fiction, poetry, and nonfiction from writers such as Rudolph Fisher (1897–1934), Jean Toomer (1894–1967), Claude McKay (1890–1948), Countee Cullen (1903–1946), Georgia Douglas Johnson (1880–1966), Angelina Weld Grimké (1880–1958), James Weldon Johnson (1871–1938), and Eric Walrond (1898–1966), and designs and artwork by Miguel Covarrubias (1904–1957) and Winold Reiss (1886–1953), *The New Negro* remains a signature collective representation of African American art and thought between the wars. In William Stanley Braithwaite's "The Negro in American Literature," Jessie Fauset's "The Gift of Laughter" (1925), and Locke's own introduction, "The New Negro" (1925), the essayists practice literary and cultural criticism in order to "establish the presence and continuities of varying traditionals – folklore, group customs, beliefs, values, styles – in African American cultural expressions."[31]

Though Locke's volume demonstrates that New Negro literary artists were not a monolithic cohort, it could also be read as an example of the kind of extra-artistic work that Du Bois argues for in his essay "Criteria for Negro Art" (1926): Black art, as aesthetically shaped propaganda, ought to advance African American political ends. While writers like Zora Neale Hurston (1891–1960) and Langston Hughes (1901–1967), both contributors to Locke's anthology, would neither disagree with Cooper's and Du Bois's political critiques nor reject Trotter's and Harrison's radicalism, they did find fault with politically or ideologically driven artmaking. Hurston and Hughes resisted making agitprop, emphasizing instead their personally

---

[30] See Chad L. Williams, *The Wounded World: W. E. B. Du Bois and the First World War* (New York: Farrar, Straus and Giroux, 2023); Kerri Greenidge, *Black Radical: The Life and Times of William Monroe Trotter* (New York: W. W. Norton, 2021); and Jeffrey Perry's biographies, *Hubert Harrison: The Voice of Harlem Radicalism, 1883–1918* (New York: Columbia University Press, 2008) and *Hubert Harrison: The Struggle for Equality, 1918–1927* (New York: Columbia University Press, 2020).
[31] Mitchell, *Within the Circle*, 5.

developed aesthetic standards and individual intellectual desires as opposed to those determined by white critics or Black leaders. Both Hurston and Hughes used the essay to declare their individual sensibilities.

Hughes made his statement of escape from the edicts established by Harlem Renaissance/New Negro leaders in the manifesto "The Negro Artist and the Racial Mountain" (1926). Not only does Hughes lay claim to his artistic independence, but he outlines his own aesthetic principles:

> [T]here is, for the American Negro artist who can escape the restrictions the more advanced among his own group would put upon him, a great field of unused material ready for his art. Without going outside his race and even among the better classes with their "white" culture and conscious American manners, but still Negro enough to be different, there is sufficient matter to furnish a black artist with a lifetime of creative work.[32]

Hurston's most significant essays from that period read as rich articulations of the possibilities that Hughes announces in his essay. For example, in her meditation on freedom and racial identity, "How It Feels to Be Colored Me" (1928), Hurston fashions her persona through colloquial diction and a humorous tone. Speaking only as herself with "nothing to prove," she escapes from the conception of Black experience as a "problem" and the criterion that Black art ought to uplift the race or act as political weaponry. And yet, as she records in her anthropologically driven essay "Characteristics of Negro Expression" (1934), Hurston believed that attending deeply to "the wealth of metaphor and simile [and] the angularity, asymmetry, and originality"[33] emanating from Black culture, as Wall describes it, liberated the artist to be, in Hughes's words, "Negro enough to be different."

The Great Depression effectively ended white patronage for Black artists associated with the Harlem Renaissance. Worse yet, the great mass of Black America suffered terrible damage from the global economic decline. Black essayists reckoned with these new political and cultural circumstances by attempting to balance their intellectual critiques of American life with their individually shaped aesthetic approaches. One burgeoning young writer from this period, Richard Wright (1908–1960), argued that individual literary desires alone could not break down the injustices of capitalism, nor could they quell the seemingly endless hardships devastating the African American

---

[32] Langston Hughes, "The Negro Artist and the Racial Mountain," in Mitchell, *Within the Circle*, 55–59, 56.
[33] Wall, *On Freedom*, 108.

masses. Countering Hughes and Hurston, Wright presented a plan for wedding literary expression with political action in his essay "Blueprint for Negro Writing" (1937).

Essaying Escape from the Margin

As Lawrence P. Jackson describes in *The Indignant Generation: A Narrative History of African American Writers and Critics, 1934–1960*, Wright was not "clumsily ideological." Rather, "[h]e presented himself as a politically committed artist in pursuit of a nuanced understanding of the cultural, social, and psychological conditions that shaped the ground of radical political action."[34] "Blueprint for Negro Writing" became Wright's first articulation of his radical aesthetic politics. Though he drafted the essay in New York during the summer of 1937, Wright collaborated with members of the South Side Writers' Club, a Black literary collective in Chicago, later that year to push the essay toward its final formation.

According to Jackson, "Blueprint" argues that Black writers must "reject the ethic of racial celebration for which the Harlem Renaissance group had been known."[35] Wright himself rejected the New Negro notion that Black art must convince white patrons that Negroes were fully human or that Black artists must be unideological individualists:

> Negro writers must accept the nationalist implications of their lives, not in order to encourage them, but in order to change and transcend them. They must accept the concept of nationalism in order to transcend it. They must possess and understand it. ... For purposes of creative expression it means that the Negro writer must realize within the area of his own personal experience those impulses which, when prefigured in terms of broad social movements, constitute the stuff of nationalism.[36]

"Instead of celebrating the beauty of the race as a kind of primping necessary to enter the white mainstream," Wright argued, Negro writers ought to embrace their "superior" folkloric tradition as both the source of Black nationalist thought and the source a "commanding literature."[37]

---

[34] Lawrence P. Jackson, *The Indignant Generation: A Narrative History of African American Writers and Critics, 1934–1960* (Princeton, NJ: Princeton University Press, 2011), 75.
[35] Jackson, *Indignant Generation*, 76.
[36] Richard Wright, "Blueprint for Negro Writing," in Mitchell, *Within the Circle*, 97–106, 101.
[37] Jackson, *Indignant Generation*, 76.

By the end of the 1930s, both Wright and Ralph Ellison had settled in New York City. The two writers began their long, close, complex friendship, with the older novelist serving as mentor to the younger writer. Wright's editorial direction and encouragement gave Ellison license to advance his plans to build a life in the arts and letters. In the early 1940s, Ellison, already engaged in the radical quarters of Black Manhattan and the New York arts world, began publishing short stories and book reviews in magazines like the Marxist *New Masses* and the Black nationalist *New Challenge* (where Wright was an associate editor), and became the managing editor at *Negro Quarterly: A Review of Negro Arts and Culture*.

Ellison's intellectual and literary pursuits during the 1940s led to his producing two towering works of American literature in the 1950s and '60s: his novel *Invisible Man* (1952) and his collection of critical, personal, and social essays, *Shadow and Act* (1964). Though Ellison's novel articulates a complex, satirical interrogation of both African American accommodationism and Black radicalism, *Shadow and Act* – which could be read as a portrait of the intellectual as a young man – does not include many of the critical or editorial essays he penned during his years as a fellow traveler among Marxists and Black Nationalists. Though he'd given up those ideologies, Ellison still burrowed to the center of the national circumstance in order to locate Black experience at the core of its symbolic discourse. Ellison's postwar essays – "Richard Wright's Blues" (1945), "Harlem Is Nowhere" (1948), "Twentieth Century Fiction and the Black Mask of Humanity" (1953), "Society, Morality, and the Novel" (1956),[38] "The Golden Age, Time Past" (1958), "The Charlie Christian Story" (1958), "The World and the Jug" (1963), and "Blues People" (1963) – display his well-honed ability to weave together ribbons of literary, musical, and political analysis into brilliant forms.

Throughout *Shadow and Act*, Ellison argues that the Black body is central to any definition of American identity, democracy, or culture. American literary ideas and the problems of American nationhood are yoked together. Though white American novelists are at their best when diagnosing problems of identity, they've helped corrupt the spirit of democracy, Ellison explains, by trucking in stereotypes of Black people. Because of the pervasive stereotypes of Black life in white writing, the national discourse about the definitions of "American" and "America" remains a perpetual debate. African American writers enter this fray, in a mode of "antagonistic co-operation,"

---

[38] Though "Society, Morality, and the Novel" was written and published during Ellison's postwar period, he did not collect and republish the essay until his second book of essays, *Going to the Territory* (1986), was released.

a phrase Ellison first used in his essay "The World and the Jug."[39] In that practice, Ellison argues, African American writers accept the tenets of the national literature and constitutional principles of the national discourse but offer in exchange humane representations of Black experience, characters modeling more rounded, multiethnic definitions of American identities, and African American musical and vernacular aesthetics.

Ellison employs that critical approach in "Richard Wright's Blues," one of the few pieces from the 1940s in *Shadow and Act*. Though he was a young writer when he reviewed Wright's *Black Boy* (1945), in this extended essay, Ellison articulated a definition of the blues idiom sensibility that married pragmatist philosophy, African American vernacular theory, and narrative analyses into a deft criticism:

> The blues is an impulse to keep the painful details and episodes of a brutal experience alive in one's aching consciousness, to finger its jagged grain, and to transcend it, not by the consolation of philosophy but by squeezing from it a near tragic, near comic lyricism. As a form, the blues is an autobiographical chronicle of personal catastrophe expressed lyrically.[40]

Here, like jazz musicians in cutting/jam sessions, Black artists write "within and against" the American political context and the national literary tradition. Each of the Black writer's works – be it essay, poem, story, memoir, or novel – springs "from a contest in which each artist challenges all the rest; each solo flight, or improvisation, represents (like the successive canvases of a painter) a definition of his identity: as individual, as member of the collectivity and as a link in the chain of tradition."[41] Ellison's model of the improvising artist – be it jazz musician or African American literary writer – is charged with revising and extending the tradition, overriding, with one hand, dehumanizing characterizations of Black life while simultaneously, with the other hand, demonstrating how Black people best embody the ideals of the democratic arrangement.

On an intellectual track parallel to Ellison's, James Baldwin (1924–1987) developed his talent in the essay through his thoroughgoing political, historical, and moral examination of African American unfreedom. As with Ellison, Hughes, and Hurston before him, Baldwin was suspicious of edicts about political and aesthetic criteria for Negro artistic expression. While Baldwin's moral vision is drawn, in part, from the Gospels, his diction and philosophies

---

[39] Ralph Ellison, *The Collected Essays of Ralph Ellison* (New York: Modern Library, 1995), 188.
[40] Ellison, *Collected Essays*, 129.   [41] Ellison, *Collected Essays*, 267.

suggest literary-genetic kinship to writers like Frederick Douglass (ca. 1818–1895), Fyodor Dostoevsky (1821–1881), Ralph Waldo Emerson (1803–1882), and Henry James (1843–1916). For instance, Baldwin believes, like Douglass, that once we free ourselves from racial thinking, specifically white supremacy, our political principles will be realized finally. After Emerson, he considers the poet a "representative man": "[P]oets (by which I mean all artists) are finally the only people who know the truth about us. . . . Art is here to prove, and to help one bear, the fact that all safety is an illusion. In this sense, all artists are divorced from and even necessarily opposed to any system whatever."[42]

Baldwin amplifies his resistance to thought or writing governed systemically in a lesser known piece "Mass Culture and the Creative Artist: Some Personal Notes" (1959). Arguing against Americans' penchant for blind liberalism and belligerent conservatism, he notes that both ideologies have failed "to make people happier or to make them better."[43] Rather than adhering to the guideposts of the political status quo, Baldwin implored Black Americans to evade marginalization, modeling a new form of citizenship for others. If we "don't now move," writes Baldwin, "literally move, sit down, stand, walk, don't go to work, don't pay rent, if we don't now do everything in our power to change this country, this country will turn out to be . . . so immobilized by its interior dissension that it can't do anything else."[44] Black movement will illustrate, Baldwin suggests, that "[w]e can change the government, and we will."[45]

While *The Fire Next Time* (1963) recycles some of the critical positions he tested in his earlier essay collections *Notes of a Native Son* (1955) and *Nobody Knows My Name* (1961), no other Baldwin book exemplifies his layered literary skill and forceful intelligence. Few works in Anglophone writing can measure up to Baldwin's merging of personal writing and cultural critique. Here, pulling together two public letters, each published previously and separately, Baldwin turns his personal statement of psychological torment into a critique of the American sociopolitical dilemma, the crippled attempt to "achieve our country."[46]

The author addresses the opening section, "My Dungeon Shook," to his nephew and namesake in celebration of the young James's fifteenth birthday

---

[42] James Baldwin, *The Cross of Redemption: Uncollected Writings* (New York: Knopf Doubleday, 2010), 42.
[43] Baldwin, *Cross of Redemption*, 5.   [44] Baldwin, *Cross of Redemption*, 52.
[45] Baldwin, *Cross of Redemption*, 52.
[46] James Baldwin, *Collected Essays* (New York: Library of America, 1998), 347.

and the one-hundredth anniversary of the Emancipation Proclamation. At the conclusion of this brief overture, Baldwin establishes one of the main arguments of the lengthier second essay: American racism is a prison house in which white jailers and Black inmates are both incarcerated: "We [Black people] cannot be free until they [white Americans] are free."[47] Writing in early 1962, Baldwin argues that the African American life force may be the one thing able to bring American freedom to fruition: "[W]e, with love, shall force our [white] brothers to see themselves as they are, to cease fleeing from reality, and begin to change it. ... [W]e can make America what America must become."[48] Implicit in Baldwin's remark is an idea that his early benefactor, Richard Wright, eloquently described as a battle between white and Black Americans over the nature of American social reality.

"Down at the Cross: Letter from a Region in My Mind," the formally dynamic second section of *The Fire Next Time*,[49] refracts the national racial history into its multiple layers through the prism of Baldwin's personal story of growing up in Harlem. This is one of the hallmarks of Baldwin's writing: Whether in his frequently superb, ambitious, sometimes unwieldy fiction or his earlier, exemplary personal essays – "Notes of a Native Son," "Fifth Avenue, Uptown" – Baldwin's accounts of Harlem life allow him to offer close study of the nation's democratic failures. Recalling 1938, his fourteenth year, Baldwin describes realizing that the evil he saw on Harlem streets was generating an evil within him. Noticing that crime was offering him the surest financial prospect, Baldwin recognized that his destiny would change only when others began to fear his power to retaliate. In a fascinating pivot, Baldwin's refusal to accept "Harlem, the ghetto" as his only "place," a cage to be trapped in, becomes his most potent form of retaliation.

In *Harlem Is Nowhere* (2011), with some disappointment and disdain, Sharifa Rhodes-Pitts calls this Baldwinian rhetorical move "the Jimmy." Desirous of making Harlem and his personal experience there resonate universally, Baldwin employs the writerly version of a cinematic technique wherein the camera's perspective begins in a tight shot and then zooms out to a "wide view while the lens remains focused on a point in the distance."[50] He seems unable to balance his social critique with affirmative aspects of Harlem life, claims Rhodes-Pitts. However, it's possible to read Baldwin's

---

[47] Baldwin, *Collected Essays*, 295.   [48] Baldwin, *Collected Essays*, 294.
[49] The essay was originally published as "Letter from a Region in My Mind" in the 17 November 1962 issue of the *New Yorker*.
[50] Sharifa Rhodes-Pitts, *Harlem Is Nowhere: A Journey to the Mecca of Black America* (New York: Little, Brown, 2011), 119.

Harlem as a synecdoche for the larger critiques that surface in the essay; Harlem is not a measure of African American depravity but rather the exact measure of equality, full citizenship, and access to American democracy denied them.

Near the essay's ending, explaining the difficulty of discussing "any conundrum – that is, any reality" with white American men and women because they are not equipped "to renew themselves at the fountain of their own lives," Baldwin states: "[W]hatever white people do not know about Negroes reveals, precisely and inexorably, what they do not know about themselves."[51] Without knowledge (or the acknowledgment) of Black citizenship, it is impossible to achieve American democracy in actuality. Here, Baldwin amplifies the problems that arise from the misrepresentation or misrecognition of Black life that Cooper and Du Bois diagnosed at the end of the nineteenth century.

Baldwin doesn't simply chastise in his critique; he argues that any failure to recognize the human condition in Black experience means that white Americans can never realize their own full humanity. He asserts this claim in methodical, lyrical American English sentences that bear his ambivalences, measure consequences with devastating accuracy, and raise his vision of the world in relief:

> The glorification of one race and the consequent debasement of another – or others – always has been and always will be a recipe for murder.... But I am also concerned for their dignity, for the health of their souls, and must oppose any attempt that Negroes may make to do to others what has been done to them. I think I know – we see it around us every day – the spiritual wasteland to which that road leads. It is so simple a fact and one that is so hard, apparently, to grasp: *Whoever debases others is debasing himself.*[52]

By the mid-1960s, younger writers, like Amiri Baraka (born Everett LeRoi Jones, 1934–2014), had begun to forgo Ellisonian cultural or Baldwinian moral appeals for political rearrangement. Driven by his barely bridled indignation and fierce intelligence, Baraka's 1965 essay collection *Home: Social Essays* announces the arrival of a vital, new form of righteous criticism. Though the lead essay in that collection, "Cuba Libre" (1960), predates Baraka's turn toward Third World Marxism by fourteen years, it presents the author's initial attempts at situating the African American freedom movement within an international Black context of decolonization and revolution. Blending

---

[51] Baldwin, *Collected Essays*, 312.   [52] Baldwin, *Collected Essays*, 334.

memoir, travel writing, political theory, and cultural critique, Baraka details his participation in a junket to Cuba following the Fidel Castro–led revolution and coup. Baraka's essay connects the Cuban revolution, the other Caribbean islands, and African regions in the processes of decolonizing to the civil rights movement in an early, dramatic expression of the postwar, anti-imperialist, avant-gardist posture that would emerge in full flower as the Black Power/Black Arts movement.[53]

Though *Home* presents Baraka's literary and cultural criticism alongside his political essays, the author's analytical muscles were best exercised through his music criticism. In the late 1960s, having become a crucial Black Cultural Nationalist theorist, Baraka's *Black Music* (1968) presents a record of his intellectual and political becoming through his jazz criticism. The collection's anchor essay, "The Changing Same," is a tour-de-force theorization of Blackness. Mining the multiple styles and genres of Black popular music, Baraka describes a phenomenological aesthetic of music making, and thus, an essentialist formation of Black identity.[54]

For Baraka, the long-standing African sensibilities that survived the Middle Passage, slavery, and Reconstruction have held Black music together in its various forms, from gospel and the blues to free jazz and soul. Even as Black music evolved into its separate genres and its differing performance ideals, Baraka noted that improvisation was the central aesthetic principle of every variety. Throughout his music writing, Baraka argues that improvisation changes the music while maintaining itself as the core of African American aesthetics. Thus, we might imagine, what is essential about Blackness is a need to evolve continually while remaining wedded to the foundational tenets of African cultural expression.[55]

Ellison, Baldwin, and Baraka used the essay to render their claims about the cultural, moral, and phenomenological stakes of the civil rights and Black Arts movements. Each essayist revised the form's possibilities, improvising new rhetorical structures that made their essays into portals for delivering Black experience from the margin to the center of midcentury American life. The ingenuity of their formal renovations and arguments is also borne out through the influence they have had on their acolytes,

---

[53] Amiri Baraka, "Cuba Libre," in *Home: Social Essays* (New York: Akashi Classics, 2009), 23–78.
[54] LeRoi Jones [Amiri Baraka], "The Changing Same," in *Black Music* (New York: William Morrow, 1967), 180–212.
[55] Walton Muyumba, *The Shadow and the Act: Black Intellectual Practice, Jazz Improvisation, and Philosophical Pragmatism* (Chicago: University of Chicago Press, 2009), 131–32.

agemates, and literary juniors: writers such as Audre Lorde (1934–1992), Jordan, Ishmael Reed (1938–), John Edgar Wideman (1941–), Walker, Stanley Crouch (1945–2020), McPherson, Gerald Early (1952–), bell hooks (1952–2021), and Greg Tate (1957–2021).

The male writers in this group have been among the most significant writers of last half-century: Reed's *Writin' Is Fightin': Thirty-Seven Years of Boxing on Paper* (1988) set the table for a combative style of political and cultural critique that emerged during the Black Power/Black Arts period. Crouch, who began his career as a poet and drummer in the Black Power/Black Arts milieu, fashioned his contrarian persona and iconoclastic reputation through his battle-forged titles: *Notes of a Hanging Judge* (1989), *The All-American Skin Game* (1994), *Always in Pursuit* (1998), *The Artificial White Man: Essays on Authenticity* (2005), and *Considering Genius: Writings on Jazz* (2006). Sparring in print with Baldwin, Baraka, Walker, Miles Davis (1925–1991), Toni Morrison (1931–2020), and Spike Lee (1956–), Crouch's streetwise, muscular, fistic prose style belied his substantial intellectual acumen. Crouch championed *Tuxedo Junction* (1989) and *The Culture of Bruising* (1994), Early's elegant and award-winning first collections. But, rather than initiating fights on the page, Early examined the ironies of Black masculinity in musical and athletic performance, especially the boxing game. Like Crouch, Early's nuanced approach to the study of jazz, baseball, boxing, and literature bears the influence of Baraka's early social and music criticism.

Coming to prominence as poets and fiction writers during the Black Power/Black Arts movement, Lorde, Jordan, and Walker took up the work of redefining the constitutional conception of "we the people" in ways that revolutionized the Black freedom movement, feminist thought and practice, and the essay form. For example, in their major collections from the early 1980s, Jordan's *Civil Wars: Observations from the Front Lines of America* (1981), Walker's *In Search of Our Mothers' Gardens: Womanist Prose* (1983), and Lorde's *Sister Outsider: Essays and Speeches* (1984), these essayists pursued and expanded "the implications of the redefinition of national belonging" and protested "against the often unreported violence against women and children" in order to include "people left out of the social compact for reasons of gender, class, ethnicity, and sexual preference."[56] These collections contain modes of literary essaying that are now touchstones for the most innovative twenty-first-century Black essayists.

---

[56] Wall, *On Freedom*, 179.

The Gold Standard: The Black Lesbian Feminist Essayist

Lorde's major, masterful essays – "Uses of the Erotic," "The Master's Tools Will Never Dismantle the Master's House," "Poetry Is Not a Luxury" – seem to emanate from the claim embedded in that final line of Baldwin's thought in the quotation above – that *"[w]hoever debases others is debasing himself."* The literary voice, political vision, and philosophical attitude that Lorde expresses and communicates in her 1970s and '80s essays belongs to a Black feminist tradition that suggests she is a writerly kin to Anna Julia Cooper. Because of that intellectual and artistic link, Lorde's essays are fundamental imaginative and intellectual equipment for participation in twenty-first-century movements for prison and police abolition, economic and political justice, and LGBTQI rights, and against misogynoir and white supremacy.

In "Poetry Is Not a Luxury," for example, Lorde explains her prowess and powers when she writes that it is the Black lesbian feminist mother, "the poet" inside all of us, who "whispers in our dreams: I feel, therefore I can be free. Poetry coins the language to express and charter this revolutionary demand, the implementation of that freedom."[57] Poetry is not simply the compression of experience into lyric forms; it's also, as Lorde describes in the title of another piece, "The Transformation of Silence into Language and Action," a practice that allows the elucidation of despair and the resistance to despair to occur simultaneously. Reckoning with a mastectomy meant to mitigate the cancer then ravaging her body, Lorde uses the essay form to model how silence becomes linguistic action:

> Battling despair does not mean closing my eyes to the enormity of the tasks of effecting change, nor ignoring the strength and the barbarity of the forces aligned against us. It means teaching, surviving and fighting with the most important resource I have, myself, and taking joy in that battle. It means, for me, recognizing the enemy outside and the enemy within, and knowing that my work is part of a continuum of women's work, of reclaiming this earth and our power, and knowing that this work did not begin with my birth nor will it end with my death. And it means knowing that within this continuum, my life and my love and my work has particular power and meaning relative to others.[58]

For Lorde, "breast cancer, with its mortal awareness and the removal which it entails, can still be a gateway, however cruelly won, into the tapping and

---

[57] Audre Lorde, *The Selected Works of Audre Lorde* (New York: W. W. Norton, 2020), 70.
[58] Audre Lorde, *The Cancer Journals* (New York: Penguin, 2020), 10.

expansion of her own power and knowing."[59] That accounting anchors us, Lorde argues, in the present tense while allowing us to imagine and construct futures as communities: "We must learn to count the living with the same particular attention with which we number the dead."[60]

At the end of "The Transformation," Lorde notes that our collective advancement depends on our speaking loudly about our mutuality, our significant and unremittable indebtedness to each other, the natural world, and our technologies: "The fact that we are here and that I speak these words is an attempt to break that silence and bridge some of those differences between us, for it is not difference which immobilizes us, but silence. And there are so many silences to be broken."[61] In Lorde's essays, speaking thoughts, political truths, and desires aloud is a form of amplified action. Perhaps what her essays illustrate most powerfully is that our bodies, demanding of use and care, must speak and enact thoughts lyrically and artistically.

While Lorde used the form to unpack her identity as a "black, lesbian, mother, warrior, poet," her self-fashioned intersectionality *avant la lettre*, the essay enabled Alice Walker to give "voice to sentiments and concerns long unarticulated": The form offered her capacious space for queries and claims about gender that her poems and fiction could not contain.[62] In her 1983 collection *In Search of Our Mothers' Gardens: Womanist Prose*, Walker developed a five-stage definition of "womanist," her own intersectional construct. Though Walker initially defines the term as "a black feminist or feminist of color,"[63] she subsequently "grounds the term in southern African American female language and intergenerational relations; in women's love, culture, agency, and commitment to the well-being of all the people, male and female; in the ludic (the joyful, the celebratory), the natural, the Spirit, and the Self; and in relationship to feminism."[64]

Walker uses the collection's eponymous essay to consider previous generations of Black women and their artistic practices:

> What did it mean for a black woman to be an artist in our grandmothers' time? ... How was the creativity of the Black woman kept alive, year

---

[59] Lorde, *Cancer Journals*, 50. [60] Lorde, *Cancer Journals*, 46.
[61] Lorde, *Selected Works*, 14.
[62] Sanders-Mobley, "African American Women," 240.
[63] Alice Walker, *In Search of Our Mothers' Gardens: Womanist Prose* (New York: Harcourt Brace Jovanovich, 1983), xi.
[64] Rachel Elizabeth Harding, "Authority, History, and Everyday Mysticism in the Poetry of Lucille Clifton: A Womanist View," *Meridians* 12, no. 1 (2014): 36–57, 37.

after year and century after century, when for most of the years Black people have been in America, it was a punishable crime for a Black person to read or write? And the freedom to paint, to sculpt, to expand the mind with action, did not exist.[65]

Behind these questions is "the grotesque historical scene of raped and beaten and abused women," the material experiences that inform Walker's "spiritual art."[66] Though her essays express a revolutionary critique, Walker is, according to Cheryl Butler, an "artist first and a change-agent second."[67] Coming through slaughter, so to speak, the Black womanist essayist's most revolutionary act is modeling the self in its spiritual openness and in the midst of its evolution. Like Walker, June Jordan used the essay to work through her political positions, to define herself as a Black woman, and to "formulate aesthetic principles" that serve her practices across the literary genres. According to Cheryl Wall, Jordan's writing "exemplifies the importance of the essay as a medium for black women's intellectual production."[68] Scott MacPhail argues that the essays in Jordan's *Civil Wars* "evidence the ways that she alternately adopts aspects of both Baldwin's and Baraka's notions of the black intellectual as they suit her strategic purposes."[69] Indeed, Jordan's collection could have been called *Notes of a Native Daughter* or *Home: Community Essays*.

However, as a queer Black feminist, Jordan could not simply adorn herself in the performative robes of the Black Nationalist or those of the Black humanist intellectual; instead, she had to transform "the bounds of self and society with a revolutionary vision."[70] Take, for example, Jordan transforming personal correspondence into public speech in her 1964 essays "Letter to Michael" and "Letter to R. Buckminster Fuller." Placed consecutively in the opening section of *Civil Wars*, the pieces read as a pastiche of Baldwin's use of letters in *The Fire Next Time*. In "Letter to Michael," Jordan employs the techniques of Baldwinian "witnessing" and first-person reportage to describe her experience of the 1964 Harlem Uprising following the police killing of James Powell, a fifteen-year-old African

---

[65] Walker, *In Search*, 233–34.
[66] Cheryl B. Butler, *The Art of the Black Essay: From Meditation to Transcendence* (New York: Routledge, 2003), 17, 82.
[67] Butler, *Art of the Black Essay*, 97. [68] Wall, *On Freedom*, 169.
[69] Scott MacPhail, "June Jordan and the New Black Intellectuals," *African American Review* 33, no. 1 (Spring 1999): 57–71, 63.
[70] Cheryl J. Fish, "Place, Emotion, and Environmental Justice in Harlem: June Jordan and Buckminster Fuller's 1965 'Architextual' Collaboration," *Discourse* 29, nos. 2–3 (Spring–Fall 2007): 330–45, 331.

American child.[71] Jordan responded to her time on the uprising's front line and in its rear guard offering aid by closely examining the architectural/urban design enclosing and dehumanizing Harlemites. "Letter to R. Buckminster Fuller" is a record of Jordan's research in urban planning and her plan for redesigning housing and green space for a new Harlem, one meant to enhance Black life in that village. Writing about design and planning, she presents herself as a "poet-philosopher of the urban environmental justice movement,"[72] Cheryl Fish argues. Jordan maps the geographical dimensions of racial psychology, political economy, and social discourse textually and visually. Rather than a situation in which "[s]erious improvement of a physical community where Black people lived almost always meant the literal eviction of Black families," Jordan made affordable housing and Black being central to her redevelopment plan. The letters define the emotional, psychological, and political terrain Jordan navigates throughout the collection, which assembles an array of essayistic forms, including op-eds, personal narratives, lectures, political and pedagogical theorizing, and literary criticism.

Unlike some of his generational brethren, John Edgar Wideman (1941–) took up many of the emotional concerns and aesthetic techniques of Black women essayists in his nonfiction. Though Wideman has not produced an essay collection in the vein of Baldwin or Jordan, his individual occasional essays are frequently daring artistic exercises. Wideman's essay "In Praise of Silence" (1998) is an argument for recognizing in silence "a measure of resistance and tension. A drastic expression of difference that maintains the distinction between using a language and allowing it to use you."[73] While Lorde breaks silences in order to transform collectivity into action and resistance, Wideman desires silence as a way of maintaining difference or escape from or refusal of the racial status quo. Silence, then, is "a way of thinking about how it might feel to be both creature and creator ... Nice work if we could get it, and even though we can't, we have the power to see ourselves other than we are. Silence is proof that the decision to listen or not is ours. Proof that we are called to pay attention."[74]

That call to watch, listen, or read closely animates Wideman's essay "Whose War: The Color of Terror" (2002). Paying attention to linguistic

---

[71] Off-duty New York Police Department lieutenant Thomas Gilligan shot and killed Powell.
[72] Fish, "Place, Emotion," 331.
[73] John Edgar Wideman, "In Praise of Silence," *Callaloo* 22, no. 3 (1999): 547–49, 548. Originally published in the *Washington Post*, 29 November 1998.
[74] Wideman, "In Praise," 549.

deconstruction as a pathway to escape, Wideman interrogates the words "terror" and "terrorism" in the aftermath of the September 11, 2001, attacks on New York and Washington, DC. The author argues that both terms have been removed from the lexical field used for describing specific tyrannical governing practices or specialized wartime tactics, leaving us to understand both terms as markers of "pure evil." This conceptualization, Wideman argues, is born from the power imbalances among different racial and ethnic groups: "[T]o label an enemy a terrorist confers the same invisibility a colonist's gaze confers upon the native. ... Once a slave or colonized native is imagined as invisible, the business of owning him, occupying and exploiting his land, becomes more efficient, pleasant."[75]

Warring against terror can only induce more terror, Wideman warns. Worse yet, such a cycle causes an inability to *imagine* or *see* terror as central to the human experience: "We can't off-load [terror] onto the back of some hooded, barbaric, shadowy other. Someone we can root out of his cave and annihilate. However, we continue to be seduced by the idea that we might be able to cleanse ourselves of terror, accomplish a final resolution of our indeterminate nature."[76] Labeling our others "terrorists," rendering them invisible, is an attempt to disguise the terror we all own and can inflict (or that can be inflicted in our names). When he asks, near the essay's end, what "radical reconfiguration"[77] of human experience and freedom will arrive with terror's defeat and eradication, Wideman is also asking us to retract our gazes, retrace our sightlines and imaginations, in order to *see* ourselves within and without our political and social machinations simultaneously.

The Beautiful Struggle Continues

In his 2008 memoir, Ta-Nahesi Coates describes the labor of imagining Black experience both within and without the dehumanizing contexts of racially segregated urban spaces, historical disenfranchisement, and radiating forms of violence as "the beautiful struggle."[78] In *We Were Eight Years in Power* (2017), he borrows from several disciplines in order to gain both insider knowledge of the systems he investigates and the outsider's broad, far-reaching perspective on the implications of his studies. He is a master synthesizer, drawing together investigative and reported journalism,

---

[75] John Edgar Wideman, "Whose War: The Color of Terror," *Harper's Magazine* (1 March 2002): 33–38, 36.
[76] Wideman, "Whose War," 38.   [77] Wideman, "Whose War," 38.
[78] See Ta-Nehisi Coates, *The Beautiful Struggle: A Memoir* (New York: One World, 2008).

African American studies, political science, sociology, literary criticism, and American history, blending deep research with his personal writing into artful essays.

In "The Case for Reparations" and "The Black Family in the Age of Mass Incarceration," his most significant individual efforts, Coates explains how oppressive systems whittle down individual Black lives and families. However, in keeping with the essay's formal rejection of conclusions or resolutions, Coates often refuses to present concepts for dismantling the machinations that produce injustice, structural racism, and inequality. Both pieces hark back to works by Wideman, Jordan, Baldwin, and Ellison. Coates, however, veers from earlier Black essayists in his (seeming) disbelief in hope as a powerful intellectual and spiritual tool. As far as Coates is concerned, neither religious hope for the future, heavenly redemption, nor political hope for equity or equality will erase the belief that whiteness is the American ideal. Unwilling to offer a hopeful front while confronting white supremacy, some critics and readers have deemed Coates's work pessimistic. Rejecting hope, Coates seems Hughesian or even Hurstonian, as he might be asserting his individual talent and artistic independence through acts of resistance against or attempted escape from the boundaries of the African American literary tradition.

One could counterpoint what Darryl Pinckney has called the Afro-pessimist temptation in Coates's essays with Ross Gay's (1975–) essay "Some Thoughts on Mercy" (2013).[79] Steeping ourselves in delight, Gay argues, can lead us toward building stronger communities and enriched imaginations. He wonders throughout the piece what might happen if "we acknowledged this country's terrible and ongoing history of imagining its own citizens – indigenous, Black, Japanese American, Arab American, Latino – as monsters? What if we acknowledged the drug war, and the resulting mass incarceration of African Americans, and the myriad intermediate crimes against citizens and communities as a product of our fears?"[80] Here, Gay employs supposition to challenge readers to assess themselves honestly and confront our collective "corrupt imagination." Readers must acknowledge the nation's historical terror, its violence, and its inequalities.

---

[79] Darryl Pinckney, "The Afro-Pessimist Temptation," *New York Review of Books* (8 June 2018), www.nybooks.com/articles/2018/06/07/ta-nehisicoates-afro-pessimist-temptation/.

[80] Ross Gay, "Some Thoughts on Mercy," *Sun Magazine* 151 (July 2013): 24–28, https://www.thesunmagazine.org/issues/451/some-thoughts-on-mercy-issue-451. In the decade following the essay's publication, Gay devoted himself more fully to essay writing, producing two collections: *The Book of Delights* (2020) and *Inciting Joy* (2022).

When they embrace these reckonings – and this may be the greatest form of fugitivity – with generosity, forgiveness, and mercy, writes Gay, "deep and abiding change might happen."[81]

Interestingly, Gay's study of joy's enmeshment with historical reckoning illuminates a broad, rich constellation of contemporary Black essayists usually obscured in the cultural discourses that mistakenly place Coates at the center of Black writing. A wider scope reveals a matrix that includes Clifford Thompson (1963–) whose strong debut collection *Love for Sale* (2013) carries traits inherited from Early and McPherson; Emily Bernard (1967–), whose superb essay "Teaching the N-Word" (2005)[82] describes the powder keg–like experience of teaching Carl Van Vechten's novel *Nigger Heaven* to her white students at the University of Vermont; Wendy Walters (1970–), whose finely attuned collection *Multiply/Divide* (2015) melds cultural criticism, life writing, and lyric essayism to stunning effect; Roxane Gay (1974–), whose *Bad Feminist* (2014) chronicles the nation's recent upheavals and continued injustices, while also detailing, along multiple routes, the contradictory desires that have propelled the nation into strange, incredible contortions; and Hanif Abdurraqib (1983–), whose *They Can't Kill Us Until They Kill Us* (2017) overlays musical exploration with personal narrative, orchestrating a novel brand of affect-criticism.

Like Coates, these writers are ethically aligned with Baldwin's fundamental claim: "[O]ur dehumanization of the Negro then is indivisible from our dehumanization of ourselves: the loss of our own identity is the price we pay for our annulment of his."[83] Like Ross Gay, these essayists employ the essay as a means of joyfully reveling in delight, mercy, gratitude, and beauty. And after Jordan, these essayists examine Black life for beautiful, imaginative, and paradigmatic constructs to aid those struggling "for radical change in this country."[84]

---

[81] Gay, "Some Thoughts on Mercy," n.p.
[82] Emily Bernard, "Teaching the N-Word," *American Scholar* 74, no. 4 (Autumn 2005): 46–59. Also see Bernard's award-winning memoir-in-essays, *Black Is the Body: Stories from My Grandmother's Time, My Mother's Time, and Mine* (New York: Knopf, 2019).
[83] James Baldwin, *The Price of the Ticket* (New York: Henry Holt, 1987), 66.
[84] Jordan, *Some of Us*, 198. June Jordan, *Some of Us Did Not Die: New and Selected Essays* (New York: Basic/Civitas Books, 2002).

39
The Essay and the Anthropocene

DAVID CARLIN

Beginnings

Beginnings, writes the poet Mary Ruefle, are origins, and "origins ... have consequences."[1] The Anthropocene is the contested, speculative story of the beginning of a new geological era, shaped by *anthropos*. Anthropos, for a long time translated as "mankind," has latterly, in response to the pressure of feminism, been relabeled "humankind." If "relabeled" suggests a superficial shift, it is because, as the phonetics suggest, "humankind" was an enlargement of the existing idea of "mankind" to include women rather than a more fundamental rethinking of the term. Inside both concepts persist the traces of an exclusionary concept of whiteness.[2] Looking into the history of the trans-Atlantic slave trade, alongside multiple other instances of the appropriation of land, extraction of resources, and policies of dispossession and genocide, Kathryn Yusoff concludes: "Black and brown death is the precondition of every Anthropocene origin story."[3] She calls for "a billion Black Anthropocenes or none."[4] To talk of the Anthropocene is to speak of an existential crisis of planetary dimensions powered by the ongoing history of a racialized, globally distributed mosaic of injustices.[5]

---

1 Mary Ruefle, *Madness, Rack, and Honey: Collected Lectures* (Minneapolis: Wave Books, 2012), 7.
2 Ibram X. Kendi, *Stamped from the Beginning: The Definitive History of Racist Ideas in America* (New York: Bold Type Books, 2016).
3 Kathryn Yusoff, *A Billion Black Anthropocenes or None* (Minneapolis: University of Minnesota Press, 2018), 66. Kindle.
4 Yusoff, *Billion Black Anthropocenes*, xx.
5 See also Zoe Todd, "Indigenizing the Anthropocene," in *Art in the Anthropocene: Encounters among Aesthetics, Politics, Environments and Epistemologies*, ed. Etienne Turpin and Heather Davis (London: Open Humanities Press, 2015), 241–54.

"The Anthropocene" marks a renewed push, too, for the denaturalizing of all things commonly seen as natural in the Cartesian binaries of Western reason – the supposedly objective divisions, scientifically proven and philosophically defended, between nature and culture, human and nonhuman, man and woman, Black and white, the "civilized" and the "primitive," and so on. The previous geological era, the Holocene, was a time of refuge for many life-forms on Earth. The Anthropocene is a time of the widespread destruction of refuge.[6] This includes, too, any refuge taken by the beneficiaries of the "advance of Western civilization" in the illusions of the Enlightenment narrative of progress.

In the midst of which: the essay. What does the essay make of beginnings, not to mention middles and ends? The essay has long been thought of as a kind of antistory, famously plotless. No matter its subject matter, the essay tends to wander and digress.[7] But arguably, its wanderings can be something other than a means to settle down and colonize new territories. An essay can operate through "wayfaring"[8] treading softly and carefully, following traces as well as leaving them behind. Lauret E. Savoy's book-length essay *Trace: Memory, History, Race, and the American Landscape* activates this metaphor, defining it thus: "*Trace*. Active search. Path taken. Track or vestige of what once was."[9] Savoy's work is an apt marker for a rising current in American writing that challenges the setting apart of writing about the natural environment and natural history from writing about the cultural and social histories that infuse, create, and grow out of place. Hence, what Savoy has said, in relation to her book, is also shorthand for the most fundamental shift, for the essay in America, occasioned by the time of the Anthropocene: "Imagine "environment" broadly – not just as surroundings; not just as the air, water, and land on which we depend, or that we pollute; not just as global warming – but as sets of circumstances, conditions, and contexts in which we live and die – in which each of us is intimately part."[10] The American essay in the Anthropocene is, in fact, the site of many beginnings. Among them is the composting (as Donna Haraway [1944–] would have it) and decomposition of

---

6 Donna Haraway, *Staying with the Trouble* (Durham, NC: Duke University Press, 2016).
7 For discussion, see, for instance, Phillip Lopate, ed., *The Art of the Personal Essay: An Anthology from the Classical Era to the Present* (New York: Anchor, 1995); and Brian Dillon, *Essayism: On Form, Feeling, and Nonfiction* (New York: New York Review Books, 2018).
8 Tim Ingold, *The Life of Lines* (London: Routledge, 2015).
9 Lauret Savoy, *Trace: Memory, History, Race, and the American Landscape* (Berkeley, CA: Counterpoint, 2015), 225.
10 Lauret Savoy, quoted in Catherine Buni, "Toward a Wider View of 'Nature Writing,'" *Los Angeles Review of Books* (10 January 2016), https://lareviewofbooks.org/article/toward-a-wider-view-of-nature-writing/.

the tradition of (Anglocentric) American nature writing into new experiments in essaying the relations between human and nonhuman beings. Hitherto marginalized voices are claiming a growing space of attending to these relations and in so doing, redefining modes and loci of attention. Further, to find ways to describe the scale and complexity of entanglements in what is going on, knowledge disciplines, from botany to anthropology, have recognized the need for the essay's affective and poetic tendencies, its personal investments and reflexive refusals, to bend and push their normative writing practices.

The Anthropocene began, as a concept, in geology,[11] or as Yusoff calls it, "White Geology," to mark an institution inflected with European concerns and interests, including the possession of whiteness,[12] rather than the neutral, universal knowledge system it claims to be. *When* the Anthropocene began, as a geological epoch, is a cause for much debate. The three most popular dates are 1610, 1800, and 1950. The year 1610 marks the time of initial "exchange in flora and fauna" between "Old" and "New World,"[13] which is a way of making an invasion and a genocide sound like something more reciprocal. The year 1800 marks the beginning of the Industrial Revolution, when the use of coal to power steam engines for factories and railways led to an explosion in pollution, and slave plantation cotton, sugar, and tobacco fueled European colonial expansion across the globe. Finally, 1950 marks the era of the first atomic bomb tests, after which time traces of radioactive isotopes can be found in the bodies of humans and nonhumans all across the planet. It also marks the "Great Acceleration" of industrial activity and associated pollution through the petrochemical production of plastics, fertilizers, and other neomaterials. Yusoff argues that within each of these stories of origination lie other stories – and the lived experience of countless lives – not commonly spoken of in White Geology: "Origins draw borders that define inclusion and exclusion, and their focus is narrow, narrating a line of purpose (read Progress) and purposefulness (read Civilization), while overlooking accident, misdirection, or the shadow geology of disposable lives, waste, toxicity, contamination, extinction, and exhaustion."[14]

---

11 The geological debates around the Anthropocene began to get widespread notice with the publication of Paul Crutzen, "Geology of Mankind: The Anthropocene," *Nature* 415 (3 January 2002).
12 Cheryl Harris, "Whiteness as Property," *Harvard Law Review* 106, no. 8 (June 1993): 1707–91.
13 Simon L. Lewis and Mark A. Maslin, "Defining the Anthropocene," *Nature* 519, no. 7542 (12 March 2015): 171–80.
14 Yusoff, *Billion Black Anthropocenes*, 24.

With all of this in mind, an account of the American essay in the time of the Anthropocene might best begin with a project of affirmation, enticement, and refusal. Robin Wall Kimmerer's (1953–) acclaimed essays include "Learning the Grammar of Animacy" (2017) and "Returning the Gift" (2014), and the book-length *Braiding Sweetgrass* (2013). They follow after classic essays of place from the late twentieth century by Native American writers including N. Scott Momaday's "An American Land Ethic" (1970) and Leslie Marmon Silko's "Interior and Exterior Landscapes: The Pueblo Migration Stories" (1986). Kimmerer writes: "I don't believe that we are entering the Anthropocene, but that we are living in a transient period of profoundly painful error and correction on our way to a humbler consideration of ourselves."[15] In artfully fluid personal narratives, Kimmerer, a biologist who has devoted much of her life to the "lexicon of science,"[16] reflects on how she has increasingly come to see its limitations. She learns to pay more attention to the language, storyworlds, and knowledge systems of her Potawatomi ancestors. In *Braiding Sweetgrass*, she invites readers into First Nations ways of being and knowing, to experience the wonder – and in the Anthropocene, the urgent necessity – of a transformed relationship with "the meaning of land." "In the settler mind," she writes, "land was property, real estate, capital, or natural resources. But to our people, it was everything: identity, the connection to our ancestors, the home of our nonhuman kinfolk, our pharmacy, our library, the source of all that sustained us."[17] She draws out the implications: "For all of us, becoming indigenous to a place means living as if your children's future mattered, to take care of the land as if our lives, both material and spiritual, depended on it."[18]

Kimmerer's essays feel at times familiar in timbre to those of the tradition of American nature writing through Henry David Thoreau (1817–1862), Aldo Leopold (1887–1948), and Annie Dillard (1945–). There is the gentle warmth of their attention to ecologies of detail, their spiritual overtones. But what sets Kimmerer apart is her explicit call to rediscover "the grammar of animacy."[19] Humans are not alone in having agency; our exceptionalism leads us to disregard what plants and animals can teach us – to treat them as soulless "natural resources" rather than as our nonhuman friends and neighbors.

15 Robin Wall Kimmerer, "Returning the Gift," *Minding Nature* 7, no. 2 (May 2014): 18–24, 23.
16 Robin Wall Kimmerer, "Learning the Grammar of Animacy 1," *Anthropology of Consciousness* 28, no. 2 (Fall 2017): 128–34, 132.
17 Robin Wall Kimmerer, *Braiding Sweetgrass: Indigenous Wisdom, Scientific Knowledge and the Teachings of Plants* (Minneapolis: Milkweed Editions, 2013).
18 Kimmerer, *Braiding Sweetgrass*, 194.   19 Kimmerer, "Learning the Grammar," 131.

To learn the grammar of animacy means, for Kimmerer, to practice extra-species reciprocity. Recounting her attempts to learn the Potawatomi language for the first time, as part of a tribal project of language revitalization, Kimmerer describes her frustration with the strange grammar: not enough verbs, too many nouns. Words which *should* be nouns *are* verbs. *Wiikegama* means not "bay" (noun) but "to be a bay" (verb). She then shows how her English-thinking confusion flips: "A bay is a noun only if water is dead. ... But the verb *wiikegama* – to be a bay – releases the water from bondage and lets it live. [It] holds the wonder that, for this moment, the living water has decided to shelter itself between these shores, conversing with cedar roots and a flock of baby mergansers."[20]

Kimmerer's work is akin to that of other scientist-writers, like Savoy, who are turning to the personal essay to give a fuller, more nuanced picture of their preoccupations. Likewise, many Native American essayists are experimenting in different essay forms, or "exquisite vessels," as Elissa Washuta (1985–) and Theresa Warburton put it in the introduction to the groundbreaking anthology *Shapes of Native Nonfiction* (2019).[21] Washuta's essay "Apocalypse Logic,"[22] punctuated into fragments by ambiguous "X" marks, which might be signatures on dishonored treaties, signs of refusal, or multipliers, deploys Indigenous language as a subversive logic of resistance. Toni Jensen's "Women in the Fracklands: On Water, Land, Bodies, and Standing Rock"[23] adopts second-person address to both displace and intensify the registers of violence against bodies and lands in the Dakota fracklands, in a voice that is at the same time incendiary and acutely observant.

Endings

The Anthropocene often figures as an Ending. The concept landed amid a turn-of-the millennium moment in which it appeared as if (Western) civilization as it had known itself was over. Modernism was over, structuralism too. Marxism, history, colonialism, industrialism, everything was *post-* and *after*. Amid all of these endings, the catastrophic implications of the

---

20 Kimmerer, "Learning the Grammar," 131.
21 Elissa Washuta and Theresa Warburton, "Introduction," in *Shapes of Native Nonfiction: Collected Essays by Contemporary Writers*, ed. Elissa Washuta and Theresa Warburton (Seattle, WA:University of Washington Press, 2019), 10.
22 Elissa Washuta, "Apocalypse Logic," *Offing* (21 November 2016), https://theoffingmag.com/insight/apocalypse-logic/.
23 See Toni Jensen, "Women in the Fracklands: On Water, Land, Bodies, and Standing Rock," *Orion* 36, no. 4 (2017): 57.

accelerating pollution of the land, air, and sea, for humans and nonhumans alike, loomed even larger. The early warning signs were evident as early as the publication of Rachel Carson's *Silent Spring*, with its "elixirs of death."[24] As Bill McKibben put it in his eponymous book, we were looking at the end of nature.[25] This was reinforced by a slew of American nonfiction including Elizabeth Kolbert's *The Sixth Extinction*,[26] Roy Scranton's *Learning to Die in the Anthropocene*[27] and Jedediah Purdy's *After Nature*.[28] Nothing less than life on Earth *tout court* was/is on a rapid flight toward an apocalyptic ending. Scientific modeling[29] showed that this was neither metaphor nor hyperbole, but the best approximation of cold, hard fact.

For the essay, the end of nature also meant the end of nature writing, although the name lingers on, either out of nostalgia or because writers and publishers have not been able to settle on a new name for writing about human and nonhuman enmeshments and encounters. If one word were to characterize the Romantic tradition of Nature writing,[30] it might be *immersion*. One gets away from humans, away from "normal" life. One loses oneself "out there" and in so doing discovers meaning. As Deming (1946–) and Savoy write in the introduction to their excellent anthology of essays, *The Colors of Nature: Culture, Identity and the Natural World*, "[m]any of the early, Euro-American luminaries of the genre wrote about solitary explorations of wild places from a poetic, philosophical, or scientific perspective; seeing nature as a place apart, where wisdom and inspiration could be harvested for day-to-day life in the 'real' world of cities."[31]

A dominant strand in nature writing, which continues in this vein, has been the voice of the white male philosopher/adventurer, of which some of the most revered have been Barry Lopez (1945–2020), Edward

---

24 Rachel Carson, *Silent Spring* (Boston: Houghton Mifflin Harcourt, 2002), 17.
25 Bill McKibben, *The End of Nature* (New York: Random House, 2006).
26 Elizabeth Kolbert, *The Sixth Extinction: An Unnatural History* (New York: Henry Holt, 2014).
27 Roy Scranton, *Learning to Die in the Anthropocene: Reflections on the End of a Civilization* (San Francisco: City Lights, 2015).
28 Jedediah Purdy, *After Nature: A Politics for the Anthropocene* (Cambridge, MA: Harvard University Press, 2015).
29 See, for example, Intergovernmental Panel on Climate Change (IPCC), *Climate Change 2014: Synthesis Report. Contribution of Working Groups I, II and III to the Fifth Assessment Report of the Intergovernmental Panel on Climate Change*, ed. Rajendra K. Pachauri and Leo Meyer (Geneva, Switzerland: IPCC, 2014).
30 See Alison Hawthorne Deming and Lauret E. Savoy, eds., *The Colors of Nature: Culture, Identity, and the Natural World* (Minneapolis: Milkweed Editions, 2011).
31 Alison Hawthorne Deming and Lauret E. Savoy, "Widening the Frame," in Deming and Savoy, *Colors of Nature*, 3–12, 5.

Abbey (1927–1989), Gary Snyder (1930–), and Rick Bass (1958–).[32] They have taken rich advantage of the unparalleled opportunities for travel and freedom from immediate responsibilities open to them, courtesy of their gender and ethnicity. Reflecting near the end of his life on one of his many trips into wild places, Lopez wrote: "During those days we all resided at the heart of incomprehensible privilege."[33] To see how much the ground has shifted beneath the assumptions of the nature essay, we can take one brief reading of a late essay by Lopez, published shortly before he died in 2020, entitled "Love in a Time of Terror." His tone is mournful, elegiac: It begins with an abrupt non sequitur in a minor chord – "Some years before things went bad" – and the accompanying sense that it is unnecessary to explain to the reader what those things and that badness were. We all know what he is talking about. He speaks of "us" being "up against reefs of darkness and walls of despair ... in a time of extinction, ethnic cleansing and rising seas."[34] These, indeed, are the end-times.

Lopez recounts the story of an epiphany occasioned by a conjunction of circumstances: a lone walk in Warlpiri country, in central Australia, and his reading of a book written by a white man, William John Peasley, entitled *The Last of the Nomads* (1983). All too conscious of his cultural position, Lopez's essay is studded with qualifiers, attempting to signal limits on his own pronouncements: "to my cultural eyes," "it has always seemed to me," "but, again, perhaps this is only me." A single sentence opens with "To my way of thinking" and ends with a hesitant tag: "in my experience." As with so many nature writers before him, Lopez decries the stupidity and violence of his own modern/settler culture that, unlike the Indigenous cultures he admires, has, as he sees it, abandoned "wisdom's oldest tool, metaphor." However, the narrator, who in his own mind has traveled to a strange, uncanny place on the other side of the world, shows little or no interest in the local people, for whom this place is their familiar, ancient, but also modern home, living in a community in which Lopez is "dropped off" by an anthropologist friend and then, paradoxically, "on [his] own." Arriving at the emotional climax that is the essay's destination, at the end of his solo walk

---

32 Scott Hess, "Imagining an Everyday Nature," *Interdisciplinary Studies in Literature and Environment* 17, no. 1 (Winter 2010): 85–112.
33 Barry Lopez, "Love in a Time of Terror: On Natural Landscapes, Metaphorical Living, and Warlpiri Identity," *Literary Hub* (7 August 2020), https://lithub.com/barry-lopez-love-in-a-time-of-terror/.
34 Lopez, "Love in a Time," n.p.

into the "desert," Lopez yearns for "intimacy" – not with his hosts, but with "an unknown world like this spinifex plain."[35]

Amid the riches of the world's oldest living culture, Lopez is alone, immersed in his own thoughts while struggling to break free of their restrictions. In Jamaica Kincaid's (1949–) essay "In History" (1997), she reflects on the narrative of Columbus's "discovery" of the Americas, including the land now called Antigua, where she was born. Kincaid writes of Columbus: "[A]nd then finding in these new lands people and their things, and these people and their things, he had never heard of them before, and he empties the land of these people, *and then he empties the people, he just empties the people*."[36] Barry Lopez is no Columbus, but he is a white man wandering and wondering in a place he doesn't belong, and yet claims, if only through metaphor. And empties the people.

It is unfair and even absurd to attend to one particular piece of work and have it stand in for an entire (decorated) oeuvre. But such individual "random" instances can be read as symptomatic of wider cultural flows and energetics. This raises the question: Where does the essay situate itself in the Anthropocene, if not on self-absorbed walks carrying the torch of humanity, as inherited by an exclusive few? Anthropologists Mario Blaser (1966–) and Marisol de la Cadena's work suggests one answer might be to invoke the concept of "the uncommons." The uncommons is a place acknowledging "a world of many worlds" rather than "resting on colonial world-making," a site of "constant negotiation with worlding practices that might not – or might not only – reflect [our own]."[37]

Middles

What if, with the Anthropocene, we are neither at a hubristic or tragic beginning, nor close to an apocalyptic end, but in the middle of something? As affect theorists and writers Lauren Berlant (1957–2021) and Kathleen Stewart (1951–) note phlegmatically in their collaboratively written book of constrained essay fragments, *The Hundreds*, "[m]ost people seem to be in the middle of something they somehow ended up in."[38] *This* something

---

35 Lopez, "Love in a Time," n.p.
36 Jamaica Kincaid, "In History," *Callaloo* 20, no. 1 (Winter 1997): 1–7, 4. Emphasis added.
37 Mario Blaser and Marisol de la Cadena, "Pluriverse: Proposals for a World of Many Worlds," in *A World of Many Worlds*, ed. Mario Blaser and Marisol de la Cadena (Durham, NC: Duke University Press, 2018), 1–22, 18.
38 Lauren Berlant and Kathleen Stewart, *The Hundreds* (Durham, NC: Duke University Press, 2019), 41.

called the Anthropocene is difficult to parse. It is too big, too strange, too fearful. Too difficult and threatening. Perhaps all this makes it a problem for which the essay, with its fidelity to wonder, doubt, and felt realities, is ideally suited. As Adorno notes, "In opposition to the cliché of the understandable ... the essay insists that a matter be considered from the very first, in its whole complexity."[39]

By the eve of the 2020s, we had come, as Robert McFarlane puts it,

> very far from "nature writing," whatever that once was, and into a mutated cultural terrain that includes the weird and the punk as well as the attentive and the devotional. ... In much of this work, suppressed forces pulse and flicker beneath the ground and within the air (capital, oil, energy, violence, state power, surveillance), waiting to erupt or to condense.[40]

Deming and Savoy ask, "[W]hat if one's primary experience of land and place is not a place apart but rather indigenous? What if it is urban or indentured or exiled or (im)migrant or toxic?"[41] In her essay "The Pall of Our Unrest" (2020), Terry Tempest Williams (1955–) writes of a time in which wildfires raged across her beloved American West and racialized violence stalked the nation's cities and countryside alike. The situation lent a new horror to the feeling of being home alone: "We are witness to ghostly horizons lit with the scalding colors of red, orange, purple, black .... We are sitting in rooms watching screens alone, waiting, as if this is a pause instead of a place, the place where we find ourselves now. ... We cannot breathe. This is our mantra in America now."[42]

Camille Dungy (1972–), in her essay "Tales from a Black Girl on Fire, or Why I Hate to Walk Outside and See Things Burning," examines how her love for hiking in the woods of Virginia is complicated, in a way not experienced by her white friends, by her certain knowledge that these places had been not uncommonly the site for lynching parties – scenes of ritualized, racialized, murderous celebration lit by bonfires: "Because I was afraid of what humans had done to other humans in those woods and on

---

39 Theodor Adorno, "The Essay as Form," *New German Critique* 32 (Spring-Summer 1984): 151–71, 162.
40 Robert Macfarlane, "The Eeriness of the English Countryside," *Guardian* (10 April 2015), www.theguardian.com/books/2015/apr/10/eeriness-english-countryside-robert-macfarlane.
41 Deming and Savoy, "Widening the Frame," 6.
42 Terry Tempest Williams, "The Pall of Our Unrest," *Mountain Journal* (19 September 2020), https://mountainjournal.org/terry-tempest-williams-says-it-time-to-rally-for-nature-and-country.

those tree-provided fires, I'd come to fear the forests and the trees."[43] Even at a party at an artists' colony in Maine, where there are dense forests in which she can walk without the sense of haunting, when a bonfire is lit one evening, around which her white companion artists are laughing and joking, she has to tell herself: "Calm down, it's safe out here, I had to repeat this to myself many times."[44] In a rush of feeling conveyed in a staccato of second-person fragments, like a chorus of nightmarish voices, Dungy realizes the further origins of her fear of fire, dating from her childhood "in the semi-arid hillsides of Southern California." Now, the terror is that she herself was to blame for what she might have done: "Now look what you've done. The whole family's in danger now. The whole neighborhood, Acres of wild country, All the beasts and all the birds. You had to look. You wouldn't look away. A child with a magnifying glass."[45] Historical fears of violence passed down through her family had coalesced with a more immediate terror of the catastrophe she herself might be somehow responsible for unleashing.

Essayists such as Ray Gonzalez (1952–), Lesley Stern (1950–2021), Valeria Luiselli (1983–), and Francisco Cantu (1985–) have all written, in different ways, of the United States' fraught southern borderlands. Gonzalez's essay "Hazardous Cargo"[46] tells the story of the toxic waste dump located in Sunland Park, New Mexico, just outside his hometown of El Paso, and of the daily flow of dangerous materials coursing through the veins of his city, hidden in plain sight. Curious about the waste facility, he takes the public road leading through the forest in which it is tucked away and stops to look at the trucks lined up at the entrance. He is told to turn around and leave. As he begins to pay attention, he notices a stream of unmarked trucks carrying hazardous waste – 300 vehicles a day, 250 of them from the maquiladoras, US-owned factories across the border in post-NAFTA Mexico – converging on this dumping site. The Southwest is America's epicenter of hazardous dumping and nuclear test sites. Regulations put in place have meant HC – for "hazardous cargo" – markers have to be put up on the roads on which these trucks can drive: "ut, as I count the HC markers, I realize the only freeway in El Paso is a legal route and so is every major street in town!"[47] He starts seeing HC markers everywhere, "large diesel trucks carrying their secret

---

43 Camille Dungy, "Tales from a Black Girl on Fire, or Why I Hate to Walk Outside and See Things Burning," in Deming and Savoy, *Colors of Nature*, 28–32, 30.
44 Dungy, "Tales from a Black Girl," 31.   45 Dungy, "Tales from a Black Girl," 31.
46 Ray Gonzalez, "Hazardous Cargo," in Deming and Savoy, *Colors of Nature*, 134–40.
47 Gonzalez, "Hazardous Cargo," 138.

cargoes" everywhere. The signs are required by law but designed to be invisible. He watches as his home is silently overrun with the dangerous but profitable by-products of "a thriving border industrial revolution."[48] What is actually thriving here, his essay asks, and where and when will this particular revolution come to its conclusion?

In a different register, writers like Nicole Walker (1971–), in her books including *Sustainability: A Love Story* (2018) and *Egg* (2017),[49] and Christina Nichol, in her essays "An Account of My Hut" (2018) and "The Earth Dreams in Ritual" (2020),[50] are attempting to document the messy and confusing in-the-middleness – the paradoxical liminality – of living, self-consciously, in the Anthropocene as an atmospheric disturbance, both internal and external. They use irony and deadpan humor to career between different registers of feeling and thinking. Nichol, in her essay "The Earth Dreams in Ritual," is searching for an exit strategy for those of us "in recovery from Western Civilization," and she is coming to think that this means a regrounding in ritual and "communitas" (a concept from anthropologists Victor and Edith Turner): "a mass of connection and belonging."[51] The essay is populated with befuddled questions that cascade it from scene to scene.

Nichol, like Haraway, lives in California; this means her essayistic enquiries deviate via Zoom Zendos (virtual meditation halls), permaculture courses, local climate summits, and community grieving rituals led by therapist Francis Weller (of the last: "It helped a little."). One of the essay's most telling threads is its attention to how non-Indigenous people, such as she, have a habit of turning toward Native Americans, in a quasi-innocent but racially inflected way, to demand from them the answers to their own eco-spiritual dilemmas. She describes a scene from one of the climate summits she attended:

> Whenever one of the Native Americans spoke the room went silent. . . .
> A Native woman from Canada said, "We have a sacred connection to the earth, so we will defend her, for she is our mother." Another audience member asked, "How can *we* develop that connection?" "I can't answer that for you," she said, "because I don't know what it's like to live without that connection.

---

48 Gonzalez, "Hazardous Cargo," 138.
49 Nicole Walker, *Egg* (New York: Bloomsbury, 2017); and *Sustainability: A Love Story* (Columbus, OH: Mad Creek Books, 2018).
50 Christina Nichol, "An Account of My Hut," *n+1*, no. 31 (Spring 2018), https://nplusonemag.com/issue-31/essays/an-account-of-my-hut/; and "The Earth Dreams in Ritual," *n+1*, no. 38 (Fall 2020), https://nplusonemag.com/issue-38/essays/the-earth-dreams-in-ritual/.
51 Nichol, "Earth Dreams," n.p.

When we are born our mothers bury our umbilical cords in the earth. But don't take our ceremonies. Ask your own ancestors. They will bring you back."

Straight after this, with a cut into a new section, comes the self-deprecating, wisecracking undercut that exemplifies the zigzag path the essay navigates as the narrator enacts her own stumbling quest: "The next time I saw my boyfriend, Bongjun, I said, 'I think I have to learn how to talk to my ancestors. Their wisdom contains medicine that we need for our time.' 'Christina?' he said, 'Instead of learning to talk to your ancestors, I think it's more important to learn how to talk to swing voters.'"[52]

Since the "posthuman turn" in the humanities, scholars and theorists, including Yusoff, Haraway, Anna Tsing (1952–), Jane Bennett (1957–), Karen Barad (1956–), Ian Bogost (1957–), Timothy Morton (1968–), and Kathleen Stewart (1951–), have been seeking to define and speculate on new ways to exercise "response-ability"[53] – the ability to respond ethically to the magnitude and complexity of the planetary-scale situation and multiple microscale situations we, variously, are in.[54] New research in disciplines as disparate as anthropology, physics, environmental humanities, media studies, cultural geography, and extinction studies have highlighted previous Western biases. Nonhuman matter, which had been seen as inert and lacking its own agency, is instead "vibrant"[55] and "intra-active."[56] Evolution, previously conceived as a process of progress, ascendancy, and competition (the Tree of Life), involves the development of increasingly complex, rhizomic, networked communities. These are sometimes subterranean or subcutaneous.[57]

These theorists have been calling for, and experimenting with, methods of textual production, accounting and documentation – that is, nonfiction writing – that could be fit for purpose in this epoch. Bruno Latour outlines

---

52 Nichol, "Earth Dreams," n.p.
53 Donna Haraway, "Anthropocene, Capitalocene, Plantationocene, Chthulucene: Making Kin," *Environmental Humanities* 6, no. 1 (2015): 159–65.
54 David Carlin, "The Essay in the Anthropocene," *Journal of Writing and Writing Courses* 39, no. 1, special issue (April 2017): 1–13.
55 Jane Bennett, *Vibrant Matter: A Political Ecology of Things* (Durham, NC: Duke University Press, 2010).
56 Karen Barad, *Meeting the Universe Halfway: Quantum Physics and the Entanglement of Matter and Meaning* (Durham, NC: Duke University Press, 2007).
57 For discussion on the interdependence of mycorrhizal fungi and trees, see Anna Lowenhaupt Tsing, *The Mushroom at the End of the World: On the Possibility of Life in Capitalist Ruins* (Princeton, NJ: Princeton University Press, 2015). For discussion on symbiogenesis and holobionts, see Anna Lowenhaupt Tsing, Nils Bubandt, Elaine Gan, and Heather Anne Swanson, *Arts of Living on a Damaged Planet: Ghosts and Monsters of the Anthropocene* (Minneapolis: University of Minnesota Press, 2017).

a "compositionist manifesto,"[58] arguing that the action of critique – taking things apart so as to reveal how they work and interpret what they mean – is no longer a sufficient strategy. Haraway calls for an ethics of "multispecies storytelling,"[59] Morton, in the face of "hyperobjects"[60] such as global warming, suggests writing that allows for thinking of things as weird. Stewart, an anthropologist by training who says all the classes she teaches are now creative writing classes, asks: "What might we do with the proliferation of little worlds of all kinds that form up around conditions, practices, manias, pacings, scenes of absorption, styles of living, forms of attachment (or detachment), identities, and imaginaries, or some publicly circulating strategy for self-transformation?"[61]

One obvious answer would seem to be: write essays. Diverse works such as Morton's *Being Ecological* (2018); the collection *Arts of Living on a Damaged Planet* (2017), edited by Anna Tsing, Heather Anne Swanson, Elaine Gan, and Nils Bubandt; and Haraway's *Staying with the Trouble* deploy resources from the toolkit of the essay to disrupt orthodox academic genres of critical writing. These affectively charged resources include self-reflexivity, contradiction, digression and nonlinearity, speculation, ambiguity and ambivalence, lyricism and humor.

The "great derangement," as Amitav Ghosh dubs the Anthropocene,[62] sees the improvisation of new modes of ethical response. An alliance of kindred ensembles brings to bear multiple embodied histories, archives, and repertoires to unsettle Western practices of knowledge production and storytelling. They challenge business as usual in our unsustainable economies of extraction and allied structures of unfeeling and thoughtlessness – the radical disconnection of humans from each other and from our nonhuman kin and neighbors – and demand a radical humility, an openness to listening. The essay is an artifact of the Enlightenment, with all that entails, for better and worse. Always hybrid, it is overlapping more and more with poetry and the lyric. For example, see Claudia Rankine's (1963–) groundbreaking works, including *Citizen: An American Lyric*,[63] pertaining to environmental risks and justice.[64] Composition

---

58 Bruno Latour, "An Attempt at a 'Compositionist Manifesto,'" *New Literary History* 41, no. 3 (Summer 2010): 471–90, 473.
59 Haraway, *Staying with the Trouble*, 9.
60 Timothy Morton, *Being Ecological* (London: Penguin, 2018), 22.
61 Kathleen Stewart, "Atmospheric Attunements," *Environment and Planning D: Society and Space* 29, no. 3 (June 2011): 445–53, 446.
62 Amitav Ghosh, *The Great Derangement: Climate Change and the Unthinkable* (Chicago: University of Chicago Press, 2016), 11.
63 Claudia Rankine, *Citizen: An American Lyric* (Minneapolis: Graywolf Press, 2014).
64 Angela Hume, "Toward an Antiracist Ecopoetics: Waste and Wasting in the Poetry of Claudia Rankine," *Contemporary Literature* 57, no. 1 (Spring 2016): 79–110.

is cross-hatching with improvisation, the written with the oral, individual writing practices with methods collective and collaborative.[65]

Poet, critic, and theorist Fred Moten's (1962–) writing expands, challenges, and ignores the essay in equal measure. His performance poem/essay, "come on, get it!"[66] is subtitled "with Thom Donovan, Malik Gaines, Ethan Philbrick, Wikipedia and the Online Etymology Dictionary" to acknowledge the other textual players featured in his essayistic band. The piece riffs from verse to prose, jazzing with quotation and allusion. At one point, Moten arrives at a notion that can be read aslant as a fundamental challenge to the essay form. It might invite us to ask how the figure of the essayist, offering the reader a "theater of [their] brain," as David Shields describes it,[67] either resists or perpetuates the settler dynamics that have propelled us into the Anthropocene:

> [The] idea that thinking, which is to say the thinker, comes first and everything (else . . .) revolves around it, is a problem of settlement, of the settler *who brings the center with them, as them, everywhere they go*; and today the question is whether the idea→state→activity of "bewilderment" does anything to ameliorate it.[68]

Bewilderment: a not knowing that is also a becoming wild. But is this still a settler fantasy? Elsewhere, Moten (this time with Stefano Harney [1962–]) conjures the notion of the space of the "fugitive enlightenment . . . the life stolen by enlightenment and stolen back, where the commons give refuge, where the refuge gives commons."[69] Harking back to Blaser and de la Cadena's notion of "the uncommons," this points toward a radical space of possibility to which the resources of the essay can contribute.

One of the most beguiling essays in poet Aimee Nezhukumatathil's (1974–) debut lyrical-essay collection, *World of Wonders* (2020),[70] is made up entirely, as its title suggests, of "[q]uestions while searching for birds with my half-white

---

65 See Berlant and Stewart, *Hundreds*; and David Carlin and Nicole Walker, *The After-Normal: Brief, Alphabetical Essays on a Changing Planet* (Brookline, MA: Rose Metal Press, 2019).
66 Fred Moten, "come on, get it!" *New Inquiry* (19 February 2018), https://thenewinquiry.com/come_on_get_it/.
67 David Shields, *Reality Hunger: A Manifesto* (New York: Knopf, 2010), 131.
68 Moten, "come on." Emphasis added.
69 Stefano Harney and Fred Moten, *The Undercommons: Fugitive Planning and Black Study* (Wivenhoe, UK: Minor Compositions, 2013), 36.
70 Aimee Nezhukumatathil, *World of Wonders: In Praise of Fireflies, Whale Sharks, and Other Astonishments* (Minneapolis: Milkweed Editions, 2020).

sons aged six and nine, National Audubon Bird Count Day, Oxford, MS." One son asks:

> What happens if there is a bird count when I'm forty and we don't find any birds?
> Will you be missing when I'm forty?
> Will you be missing when I'm sixty?[71]

Just when we get the feeling of a classically elegiac, Anthropocene subtext, the boy continues:

> Mommy! What if there were a hundred more green birds in the forest right now, and we just didn't know it? And they were all camouflaged and watching us with our notepads, and we couldn't see them, and they were giggling and telling each other our bird count is all wrong?
>
> Birds don't giggle.
> What if they were winking at each other, then?[72]

---

71 Nezhukumatathil, *World of Wonders*, 131.   72 Nezhukumatathil, *World of Wonders*, 131.

Recommendations for Further Reading

Books

Adams, Thomas R. *American Independence: The Growth of an Idea: A Bibliographical Study of the American Political Pamphlets Printed between 1764 and 1776.* Providence, RI: Brown University Press, 1965.

Alter, Nora M. *The Essay Film after Fact and Fiction.* New York: Columbia University Press, 2018.

Anderson, Chris. *Style as Argument: Contemporary American Nonfiction.* Carbondale, IL: Southern Illinois University Press, 1987.

Atkins, G. Douglas. *Estranging the Familiar: Toward a Revitalized Critical Writing.* Athens, GA: University of Georgia Press, 1992.

On the Familiar Essay: Challenging Academic Orthodoxies. New York: Palgrave Macmillan, 2009.

Reading Essays: An Invitation. Athens, GA: University of Georgia Press, 2008.

Tracing the Essay: Through Experience to Truth. Athens, GA: University of Georgia Press, 2005.

Baker, Sheridan. *The Essayist.* New York: Harper and Row, 1981.

Barsam, Richard M. *Non-Fiction Film: A Critical History.* Bloomington, IN: Indiana University Press, 1992.

Bensmaïa, Réda. *The Barthes Effect: The Essay as Reflective Text.* Minneapolis: University of Minnesota Press, 1987.

Brodbeck, May. *American Non-Fiction, 1900–1950.* Chicago: Regnery, 1952.

Butler, Cheryl. *The Art of the Black Essay: From Meditation to Transcendence.* New York: Routledge, 2003.

Chevalier, Tracy. *Encyclopedia of the Essay.* London: Fitzroy Dearborn, 1997.

Corrigan, Timothy. *The Essay Film: From Montaigne, after Marker.* New York: Oxford University Press, 2011.

Davis, Hallam Walker. *The Column.* New York: Knopf, 1926.

Dillon, Brian. *Essayism: On Form, Feeling, and Nonfiction.* New York: New York Review Books, 2017.

Edson, C. L. *The Gentle Art of Columning: A Treatise on Comic Journalism.* New York: Brentano, 1920.

Eleanore, Sister Mary. *The Literary Essay in English.* Boston: Ginn, 1923.

Ercolino, Stefano. *The Novel-Essay, 1884–1947*. New York: Palgrave Macmillan, 2014.
Good, Graham. *The Observing Self: Rediscovering the Essay*. New York: Routledge, 1998.
Granger, Bruce. *American Essay Serials from Franklin to Irving*. Knoxville, TN: University of Tennessee Press, 1978.
Guynn, William. *A Cinema of Nonfiction*. Rutherford, NJ: Fairleigh Dickinson University Press, 1990.
Harrison, Thomas. *Essayism: Conrad, Musil, and Pirandello*. Baltimore: Johns Hopkins University Press, 1992.
Hartman, Geoffrey. *Minor Prophecies: The Literary Essay in the Culture Wars*. Cambridge, MA: Harvard University Press, 1991.
Heilker, Paul. *The Essay: Theory and Pedagogy for an Active Form*. Urbana, IL: National Council of Teachers of English, 1996.
Hellmann, John. *Fables of Fact: The New Journalism as New Fiction*. Urbana, IL: University of Illinois Press, 1981.
Hollowell, John. *Fact and Fiction: The New Journalism and the Nonfiction Novel*. Chapel Hill, NC: University of North Carolina Press, 1977.
Hollweg, Brenda, and Igor Krstić. *World Cinema and the Essay Film: Transnational Perspectives on a Global Practice*. Edinburgh, Scotland: Edinburgh University Press, 2019.
Johnson, Michael L. *The New Journalism: The Underground Press, the Artists of Nonfiction, and Changes in the Established Mode*. Lawrence, KS: University Press of Kansas, 1971.
Junker, Carsten. *Frames of Friction: Black Genealogies, White Hegemony and the Essay as Critical Intervention*. Frankfurt, Germany: Campus, 2010.
Kirklighter, Cristina. *Traversing the Democratic Border of the Essay*. Albany, NY: State University of New York Press, 2002.
Klaus, Carl H. *The Made-Up Self: Impersonation and the Personal Essay*. Iowa City, IA: University of Iowa Press, 2010.
Klingensmith, Kelly. *In Appropriate Distance: The Ethics of the Photographic Essay*. Albuquerque, NM: University of New Mexico Press, 2016.
Korhonen, Kuisma. *Textual Friendship: The Essay as Impossible Encounter, from Plato to Montaigne to Levinas and Derrida*. Amherst, NY: Humanity Books, 2006.
Kostelanetz, Richard. *Skeptical Essays in the 21st Century: Individuals, Institutions, Errors, Issues*. Brooklyn: Autonomedia, 2010.
Lounsberry, Barbara. *The Art of Fact: Contemporary Artists of Nonfiction*. Westport, CT: Greenwood Press, 1990.
Marr, George S. *The Periodical Essayists of the Eighteenth Century*. London: Clarke, 1923; New York: Appleton, 1924.
Milnes, Tim. *The Testimony of Sense: Empiricism and the Essay from Hume to Hazlitt*. New York: Oxford University Press, 2019.
Montero, David. *Thinking Images: The Essay Film as a Dialogic Form in European Cinema*. Oxford: Peter Lang, 2012.
Mott, Frank Luther. *A History of American Magazines*. 5 vols. Cambridge, MA: Harvard University Press, 1930–57.
Murphy, James E. *The New Journalism: A Critical Perspective*. Lexington, KY: Association for Education in Journalism, 1974.
Norman, Brian. *The American Protest Essay and National Belonging: Addressing Division*. Albany, NY: State University of New York Press, 2007.

Recommendations for Further Reading

Obaldia, Claire de. *The Essayistic Spirit: Literature, Modern Criticism, and the Essay.* New York: Oxford University Press, 1995.

Piercy, Josephine K. *Studies in Literary Types in Seventeenth Century America, 1607–1710.* New Haven, CT: Yale University Press, 1939.

Plantinga, Carl. *Rhetoric and Representation in Nonfiction Film.* Cambridge, UK: Cambridge University Press, 1997.

Plunkett, Erin. *A Philosophy of the Essay: Scepticism, Experience, and Style.* London: Bloomsbury Academic, 2018.

Rascaroli, Laura. *How the Essay Film Thinks.* New York: Oxford University Press, 2017.

―――. *The Personal Camera: Subjective Cinema and the Essay Film.* New York: Wallflower Press, 2009.

Root, Robert K., Jr. *The Nonfictionist's Guide: On Reading and Writing Creative Nonfiction.* Lanham, MD: Rowman and Littlefield, 2008.

Scholes, Robert, and Carl H. Klaus. *Elements of the Essay.* New York: Oxford University Press, 1970.

Sims, Normal. *The Literary Journalists.* New York: Ballantine, 1984.

Smart, Robert Augustin. *The Nonfiction Novel.* Lanham, MD: University Press of America, 1985.

Snow, Zachary. *The Cinematic Essay: Argumentative Essay and Documentary Film.* Saarbrücken, Germany: Lambert Academic Publishing, 2012.

Snyder, John. *Prospects of Power: Tragedy, Satire, the Essay, and the Theory of Genre.* Lexington: University Press of Kentucky, 1991.

Sorescu, Roxana, and Florin Bican. *The Essay: A Space Governed by Freedom.* Bucharest, Romania: Romanian Cultural Foundation, 1998.

Stuckey-French, Ned. *The American Essay in the American Century.* Columbia, MO: University of Missouri Press, 2014.

Tanner, William M. *Essays and Essay-Writing.* Boston: Atlantic Monthly Press, 1918.

Wall, Cheryl A. *On Freedom and the Will to Adorn: The African American Essay.* Chapel Hill, NC: University of North Carolina Press, 2019.

Watson, Melvin R. *Magazine Serials and the Essay Tradition, 1746–1820.* Baton Rouge, LA: Louisiana State University Press, 1956.

Weber, Ronald. *The Literature of Fact: Literary Nonfiction in American Writing.* Athens, OH: Ohio University Press, 1980.

―――. *The Reporter as Artist: A Look at the New Journalism Controversy.* New York: Hastings House, 1974.

Williams, Orlo. *The Essay.* New York: G. H. Doran, 1914.

Zavarzadeh, Mas'ud. *The Mythopoeic Reality: The Postwar American Nonfiction Novel.* Urbana, IL: University of Illinois Press, 1976.

Edited Volumes and Book Chapters

Anderson, Chris, ed. "Life and the Essay Compared to a Forest." In *Edge Effects: Notes from an Oregon Forest*, 155–85. Iowa City: University of Iowa Press, 1993.

―――. *Literary Nonfiction: Theory, Practice, Pedagogy.* Carbondale, IL: Southern Illinois University Press, 1989.

Arthur, Paul. "The Resurgence of History and the Avant-Garde Essay Film." In *A Line of Sight: American Avant-Garde Film since 1965*, 61–73. Minneapolis: University of Minnesota Press, 2005.

Aquilina, Mario, ed. *The Essay at the Limits: Poetics, Politics and Form*. London: Bloomsbury Academic, 2021.

Belloc, Hilaire. "By Way of Preface: An Essay upon Essays upon Essays." In *One Thing and Another: A Miscellany from His Uncollected Essays*, edited by Patrick Cahill, 11–14. London: Hollis and Carter, 1955.

Benson, Arthur. "The Art of the Essayist." In *Modern English Essays*, edited by Ernest Rhys. vol. 5, 150–63. New York: E. P. Dutton, 1922.

Biemann, Ursula, ed. *Stuff It: The Video Essay in the Digital Age*. Zurich, Switzerland: Voldemeer, 2003.

Blair, Walter. "The Essay: A Standard Form Takes on New Qualities." In *American Literature: A Brief History*, edited by Walter Blair, Theodore Hornberger, and Randal Stewart, 95–101. Chicago: Scott, Foresman, 1964.

Brooks, Charles S. "The Writing of Essays." In *Hints to Pilgrims*, 59–76. New Haven, CT: Yale University Press, 1921.

Bulwer-Lytton, Edward George Earle. "On Essay-Writing in General, and These Essays in Particular." In *Caxtoniana: A Series of Essays on Life, Literature, and Manners*, 143–56. New York: Harper and Brothers, 1864.

Burton, Richard. "The Essay as Mood and Form." In *Forces in Fiction*, 85–99. Indianapolis, IN: Bowen-Merrill, 1902.

Butrym, Alexander J., ed. *Essays on the Essay: Redefining the Genre*. Athens, GA: University of Georgia Press, 1989.

Chesterton, G. K. "The Essay." In *Essays of the Year, 1931–1932*, xi–xviii. London: Argonaut, 1932.

——. "On Essays." In *Come to Think of It*, 1–5. London: Methuen, 1930.

Corrigan, Timothy. "The Essay Film as a Cinema of Ideas." In *Global Art Cinema: New Theories and Histories*, edited by Rosalind Galt and Karl Schoonover, 218–37. New York: Oxford University Press, 2010.

——. "The Forgotten between Two Shots: Photos, Photograms, and the Essayistic." In *Still Moving: Between Cinema and Photography*, edited by Karen Beckman and Jean Ma, 41–61. Durham, NC: Duke University Press, 2008.

Culler, Jonathan, ed. *Just Being Difficult? Academic Writing in the Public Arena*. Stanford, CA: Stanford University Press, 2003.

DeMaria, Robert, Jr. "The Eighteenth-Century Periodical Essay." In *The Cambridge History of English Literature 1660–1780*, edited by John Richetti, 525–48. New York: Cambridge University Press, 2005.

Dillard, Annie. "Introduction." In *The Best American Essays, 1988*, edited by Annie Dillard and Robert Atwan, xiii–xxii. Boston: Ticknor and Fields, 1988.

Early, Gerald, ed. *Speech and Power: The African-American Essay and Its Cultural Content from Polemics to Pulpit*, 2 vols. New York: Ecco Press, 1992–93.

Eases, Caroline, and Elizabeth Papazian, eds. *The Essay Film: Dialogue, Politics, Utopia*. London: Wallflower Press, 2017.

Epstein, John. "Piece Work: Writing the Essay." In *Plausible Prejudices: Essays on American Writing*, 397–411. New York: W. W. Norton, 1985.

Epstein, Mikhail. "The Ecology of Thinking." In *Russian Postmodernism: New Perspectives on Post-Soviet Literature*, edited by Mikhail Epstein, Alexander Genis, and Slobodanka Vladiv-Glover, 222–26. New York: Berghahn Books, 2016.

"Essayism: An Essay on the Essay." In *Russian Postmodernism: New Perspectives on Post-Soviet Literature*, edited by Mikhail Epstein, Alexander Genis, and Slobodanka Vladiv-Glover, 216–21. New York: Berghahn Books, 2016.

Fadiman, Clifton. "A Gentle Dirge for the Familiar Essay." In *Party of One*, 349–53. Cleveland: World, 1955.

Fakundiny, Lydia, ed. *The Art of the Essay*. Boston: Houghton Mifflin, 1991.

Fielder, Leslie, ed. *The Art of the Essay*. 2nd ed. New York: Thomas Y. Crowell, 1969.

Flothow, Dorothea, Markus Oppolzer, and Sabine Coelsch-Foisner, eds. *The Essay: Forms and Transformations*. Heidelberg, Germany: Universitätsverlag Winter, 2017.

Forman, Janis, ed. *What Do I Know? Reading, Writing, and Teaching the Essay*. Portsmouth, NH: Heinemann-Boynton/Cook, 1996.

Foster, Patricia, and Jeff Porter, eds. *Understanding the Essay*. Ontario, Canada: Broadview Press, 2012.

Gass, William H. "Emerson and the Essay." In *Habitations of the Word*, 9–49. New York: Simon and Schuster, 1985.

Hamburger, Michael. "An Essay on the Essay." In *Art as Second Nature: Occasional Pieces, 1950–74*, 3–5. Manchester, England: Carcanet, 1975.

Hazlitt, William. "On Familiar Style." In *Table-Talk, or Original Essays on Men and Manners*. vol. 2, 183–99. London: Henry Colburn, 1822.

"On the Periodical Essayists." In *The Selected Writings of William Hazlitt*, edited by Duncan Wu. vol. 5, 84–96. Brookfield, VT: Pickering and Chatto, 1998.

Henley, William E. "Essays and Essayists." In *Views and Reviews: Essays in Appreciation*, 188–93. New York: Charles Scribner's Sons, 1890.

Holdheim, W. Wolfgang. "Introduction: The Essay as Knowledge in Progress." In *The Hermeneutic Mode: Essays on Time in Literature and Literary Theory*, 19–33. Ithaca, NY: Cornell University Press, 1984.

Hume, David. "Of Essay Writing." In *Essays: Moral and Political*. vol. 2, 1–8. Edinburgh, Scotland: A. Kincaid, 1742.

Hurley, Michael, and Marcus Waithe, eds. *Thinking through Style: Non-Fiction Prose of the Long Nineteenth Century*. Oxford: Oxford University Press, 2018.

Huxley, Aldous. "Preface." In *Collected Essays*, v–ix. New York: Harper and Row, 1959.

Joeres, Ruth-Ellen Boetcher, and Elizabeth Mittman, eds. *The Politics of the Essay: Feminist Perspectives*. Bloomington, IN: Indiana University Press, 1993.

Jones, W. Alfred. "Essay Writing – The Champion." In *Essays upon Authors and Books*, 14–21. New York: Stanford and Swords, 1849.

Karshan, Thomas, and Kathryn Murphy, eds. *On Essays: Montaigne to the Present*. Oxford: Oxford University Press, 2020.

Kazin, Alfred. "The Essay as a Modern Form." In *The Open Form: Essays for Our Time*, edited by Alfred Kazin, vii–xi. New York: Harcourt, 1961.

Kirkland, Winifred M. "Foreword: The Ego in the Essay." In *Joys of Being a Woman, and Other Papers*, v–ix. Boston: Houghton Mifflin, 1918.

Kostelanetz, Richard, ed. *Essaying Essays: Alternative Forms of Exposition*. New York: Out of London Press, 1975.

Lazar, David. "Occasional Desire: On the Essay and the Memoir" and "Queering the Essay." In *Occasional Desire: Essays*, 39–67. Lincoln, NE: University of Nebraska Press, 2013.

———, ed. *Truth in Nonfiction: Essays*. Iowa City, IA: University of Iowa Press, 2008.

Lukács, György. "On the Nature and Form of the Essay." In *Soul and Form*, edited by John T. Sanders and Katie Terezakis, translated by Anna Bostock, 16–34. New York: Columbia University Press, 2010.

Lyon, Thomas J. "The Nature Essay in the West" and "The Western Nature Essay since 1970." In *A Literary History of the American West*, edited by Max Westbrook and James H. Maguire, 221–65 and 1246–53. Fort Worth, TX: Texas Christian University Press, 1987.

Macy, John Albert. "The Reading of Essays." In *A Guide to Reading for Young and Old*, 179–92. Garden City, NY: Doubleday, Page, 1913.

Mairs, Nancy. "Essaying the Feminine: From Montaigne to Kristeva." In *Voice Lessons: On Becoming a (Woman) Writer*, 71–87. Boston: Beacon Press, 1994.

Monson, Ander. "Essay as Hack." In *The Far Edges of the Fourth Genre: An Anthology of Explorations in Creative Nonfiction*, edited by Sean Prentiss and Joe Wilkins, 9–22. East Lansing, MI: Michigan State University Press, 2014.

Morley, Christopher. "Preface." In *Modern Essays*, iii–x. New York: Harcourt, Brace, 1921.

Murdoch, Walter. "The Essay." In *Collected Essays*, 284–87. Sydney, Australia: Angus and Robertson, 1945.

———. "Preface." In *Collected Essays*, 3–5. Sydney, Australia: Angus and Robertson, 1945.

Musil, Robert. "[On the Essay]." In *Precision and Soul*, 48–51. Chicago: University of Chicago Press, 1990.

Repplier, Agnes. "The Passing of the Essay." In *In the Dozy Hours*, 226–35. Boston: Houghton Mifflin, 1894.

Retallack, Joan. "Introduction: Essay as Wager." In *The Poethical Wager*, 1–19. Berkeley, CA: University of California Press, 2003.

———. "Wager as Essay." In *The Poethical Wager*, 47–62. Berkeley, CA: University of California Press, 2003.

Sampson, George. "Introduction." In *Nineteenth Century Essays*, vii–xi. Cambridge, UK: Cambridge University Press, 1917.

Schelling, F. E. "The Familiar Essay." In *Appraisements and Asperities as to Some Contemporary Writers*, 9–14. Philadelphia: Lippincott, 1922.

Sherman, Stuart. "An Apology for Essayists of the Press." In *Points of View*, 173–85. New York: Scribner, 1924.

Sims, Normal, ed. *Literary Journalism in the Twentieth Century*. Oxford: Oxford University Press, 1990.

Singer, Margot, and Nicole Walker, eds. *Bending Genre: Essays on Creative Nonfiction*. New York: Bloomsbury Academic, 2013.

Smith, Alexander. "On the Writing of Essays." In *Dreamthorp: A Book of Essays Written in the Country*, 21–45. London: Strahan, 186.

Sontag, Susan. "Introduction." In *The Best American Essays, 1992*, edited by Robert Atwan and Susan Sontag, xiii–xix. New York: Ticknor and Fields, 1992.

Squire, J. C., "The Essay." In *Flowers of Speech*, 108–115. New York: Books for Libraries Press, 1967.

"An Essay on Essays." In *Essays of the Year, 1929-1930*, ix–xviii. London: Argonaut, 1930.
Stephen, Leslie. "The Essayists." In *Men, Books, and Mountains: A Collection of Essays*, edited by S. O. A. Ullmann, 45–73. London: Hogarth Press, 1956.
Talese, Gay. "Introduction." In *The Best American Essays, 1987*, edited by Gay Talese, xiii–xxii. New York: Ticknor and Fields, 1987.
"Origins of a Nonfiction Writer." In *Writing Creative Nonfiction: The Literature of Reality*, edited by Gay Talese and Barbara Lounsberry, 1–25. New York: HarperCollins, 1996.
Thomas, Lewis. "Essays and Gaia." In *The Youngest Science*, 239–48. New York: Viking Penguin, 1983.
Van Doren, Carl. "A Note on the Essay." In *Essays of Our Time*, edited by Sharon Brown, 396–98. Chicago: Scott, Foresman, 1928.
Vassilieva, Julia, and Deane Williams, eds. *Beyond the Essay Film: Subjectivity, Textuality and Technology*. Amsterdam, The Netherlands: Amsterdam University Press, 2020.
Warren, Charles, ed. *Beyond Documents: Essays on Nonfiction Film*. Hanover, NH: University Press of New England/Wesleyan University Press, 1996.
Nonfiction film. Middletown, CT: Wesleyan University Press, 1998.
Wells, H. G. "The Writing of Essays." In *Certain Personal Matters: A Collection of Material, Mainly Autobiographical*, 180–84. London: Lawrence and Bullen, 1898.
Williams, William Emrys. "The Essay." In *The Craft of Literature*, 140–47. New York: International, 1925.
Wittman, Kara, and Evan Kindley, eds. *The Cambridge Companion to the Essay*. Cambridge, UK: Cambridge University Press, 2022.
Wolfe, Tom, and E. W. Johnson, eds. *The New Journalism*. New York: Harper and Row, 1973.
Woolf, Virginia. "The Decay of Essay-Writing" and "The Modern Essay." In *A Woman's Essays*, edited by Rachel Bowlby, 5–7 and 40–49. London: Penguin Books, 1992.
Zeiger, William. "The Personal Essay and Egalitarian Rhetoric." In *Literary Nonfiction: Theory, Criticism, Pedagogy*, edited by Chris Anderson, 301–14. Carbondale, IL: Southern Illinois University Press, 1989.

Articles

Adorno, Theodor W. "The Essay as Form." *New German Critique* 32 (Spring–Summer 1984): 151–71.
Ahrens, Rudiger. "The Political Pamphlet: 1660–1714: Pre- and Post-Revolutionary Aspects." *Anglia* 109, nos. 1–2 (1991): 21–43.
Alter, Nora M. "The Political Im/perceptible in the Essay Film." *New German Critique* 68 (Spring–Summer 1996): 165–92.
"Translating the Essay into Film and Installation." *Journal of Visual Culture* 6, no. 1 (April 2007): 44–53.
Arn, Jackson. "Dot Dot Dot Dot Dot: Against the Contemporary American Essay." *Drift* 6 (31 January 2022), www.thedriftmag.com/dot-dot-dot-dot-dot/.
Arthur, Paul. "Essay Questions: From Alain Resnais to Michael Moore." *Film Comment* 39, no. 1 (January 2003): 53–62.

Atkins, G. Douglas. "In Other Words: Gardening for Love – The Work of the Essayist." *Kenyon Review* 13, no. 1 (Winter 1991): 56–69.
———. "The Return of/to the Essay." *ADE Bulletin* 96 (Fall 1990): 11–18.
Atwan, Robert. "Essayism." *Iowa Review* 25, no. 2 (Spring–Summer 1995): 6–14.
———. "Notes towards the Definition of an Essay." *River Teeth: A Journal of Nonfiction Narrative* 14, no. 1 (Fall 2012): 109–17.
Bazerman, Charles. "The Writing of Scientific Non-Fiction." *Pre-Text: A Journal of Rhetorical Theory* 5, no. 1 (1984): 39–74.
Bennett, James R. "The Essay in Recent Anthologies of Literary Criticism." *Substance*, vol. 18, no. 3, iss. 60 (1990): 55–67.
Benson, Arthur C. "On Essays at Large." *Living Age* vol. 46, no. 3423 (12 February 1910): 408–15.
Bixler, Paul. "The Essay-Fiction Complex." *Antioch Review* 36, no. 1 (Winter 1978): 5–8.
Black, Joel Dana. "The Scientific Essay and Encyclopedic Science." *Stanford Literature Review* 1, no. 1 (Spring 1984): 119–48.
Bloom, Lynn Z. "The Essay Canon." *College English* 61, no. 4 (1999): 401–30.
———. "Essay Hunger: Devouring Essays in the 21st Century." *American Book Review* 33, no. 2 (January–February 2012): 3–4.
Bourne, Randolph. "The Light Essay." *Dial* 65, no. 777 (16 November 1918): 419–20.
Braley, Berton. "On Being an Essayist." *Bookman: A Review of Books and Life* 51 (August 1920): 646–48.
Bresland, John. "On the Origin of the Video Essay" and "Video Suite." *Blackbird* 9, no. 1 (Spring 2010), http://www.blackbird.vcu.edu/v9n1/gallery/ve-intro/intro_page.shtml.
Burgard, Peter J. "Adorno, Goethe, and the Politics of the Essay." *Deutsche Vierteljahr Schrift für Literaturwissenschaft* 66 (1992): 160–91.
Burgess, Glenn. "Protestant Polemics: The Leveller Pamphlets." *Parergon* 11, no. 2 (December 1993): 45–67.
Burton, Richard. "The Essay: A Famous Literary Form and Its Conquests." *New York Times*, 5 April 1924.
Canby, Henry Seidel. "The Essay as Barometer." *Saturday Review of Literature* (16 February 1935): 488.
Cason, Jacqueline Johnson. "Nature Writer as Storyteller: The Nature Essay as a Literary Genre." *CEA Critic* 54, no. 1 (Fall 1991): 12–18.
Chadbourne, Richard. "A Puzzling Literary Genre: Comparative Views of the Essays." *Comparative Literature Studies* 20, no. 2 (Summer 1983): 133–53.
Clarke, H. A. "The Survival of the Essay." *Poet-lore* 9 (1897): 431–36.
Corrigan, Timothy. "The Cinematic Essay: Genre on the Margins." *Iris: A Journal of Theory on Image and Sound* 19 (Spring 1995): 85–91.
Crothers, Samuel McChord. "Making Friends with the Essay." *World Review* 4 (1927): 190.
Cunningham, Vinson. "What Makes an Essay American?," *New Yorker*, 13 May 2016.
D'Agata, John, and Deborah Tall, "New Terrain: The Lyric Essay." *Seneca Review* 72, no. 1 (Fall 1997): 7–8.
Delbecke, Jasper. "The Essay in Times of Crisis." *Performance Philosophy* 4, no. 1 (2018): 106–22.
———. "The Essay, the Maligned." *Performance Research* 25, no. 4 (18 May 2020): 136–44.

"Exploring the Essay in the New Documentary Turn: Mining Stories by Hannes Dereere and Silke Huysmans and Syden by Hedvig Biong, Pablo Castilla, and Niko Hafkenscheid." *Documenta* 36, no. 1 (2018): 8–32.

"Tracing the Essay in Contemporary Performing Arts." *Performance Research* 23, no. 2 (2018): 5–12.

Delbecke, Jasper, and Sébastien Hendrick. "Thinking Out Loud: Essayistic Figures on Stage." *Etcetera* 154 (2018): 46–52.

Dennis, John. "The Art of Essay Writing." *National Review* 1, no. 5 (July 1883): 744–57.

Depp, Michael. "On Essays: Literature's Most Misunderstood Form." *Poets and Writers* (July–August 2002): 14–17.

Dickson, Edith. "Women and the Essay." *Dial* 31, no. 369 (November 1901): 297–310.

Didion, Joan. "Why I Write." *New York Times Book Review*, 5 December 1976.

Drew, Elizabeth. "The Lost Art of the Essay." *Saturday Review of Literature* (16 February 1935): 485–88.

DuPlessis, Rachel Blau. "f-Words: An Essay on the Essay." *American Literature* 68, no. 1 (March 1996): 15–45.

Earl, Peter G. "On the Contemporary Displacement of the Hispanic American Essay." *Hispanic Review* 46, no. 3 (Summer 1978): 329–41.

Eaton, Walter Pritchard. "On Burying the Essay." *Virginia Quarterly Review* 24, no. 4 (Autumn 1948): 574–83.

Erdman, Irwin. "The Art of the Unhurried Essay in a Hurry-Up World." *New York Times Book Review* (18 January 1953): BR3.

Faery, Rebecca Blevins. "On The Possibilities of the Essay: A Meditation." *Iowa Review* 20, no. 2 (Spring–Summer 1990): 19–27.

Flanagan, John T. "A Word for the American Essay." *American Scholar* 13, no. 4 (Autumn 1944): 459–66.

Fort, Keith. "Form, Authority, and the Critical Essay." *College English* 32, no. 6 (March 1971): 629–39.

Freeman, Marilyn. "On the Form of the Video Essay." *Triquarterly* 141 (Winter 2012), www.triquarterly.org/essay/on-the-form-of-video-essay.

Gerould, Katherine Fullerton. "An Essay on Essays." *North American Review* 240, no. 3 (December 1935): 409–18.

Gigante, Denise. "Sometimes a Stick Is Just a Stick: The Essay as (Organic) Form." *European Romantic Review* 21, no. 5 (2010): 553–65.

Gillett, Eric. "A Word for the Essay." *Fortnightly* 156 (July 1941): 82–90.

Gould, Gerald. "The Happy Essayist." *Saturday Review of Literature* 139 (1925): 549.

Graham, Paul. "The Age of the Essay," paulgraham.com (September 2004), http://paulgraham.com/essay.html.

Haefner, Joel. "Unfathering the Essay: Resistance and Intergeniality in the Essay Genre." *Prose Studies* 12, no. 3 (1989): 259–73.

Hall, James Norman. "A Word for the Essayist." *Yale Review* 32, no. 1 (September 1942): 50–58.

Hardison Jr., O. B. "Binding Proteus: An Essay on the Essay." *Sewanee Review* 96, no. 4 (Fall 1988): 610–32.

"In Praise of the Essay." *Wilson Quarterly* 14, no. 4 (Autumn 1990): 54–66.

Hazlitt, William. "A Farewell to Essay-Writing." *London Weekly Review*, 29 March 1828.

Hewett, Heather. "In Search of an 'I': Embodied Voice and the Personal Essay." *Women's Studies* 33, no. 6 (2004): 719–41.

Hoagland, Edward. "To the Point: Truths Only Essays Can Tell." *Harper's* (March 1993): 31–40.

Howells, William Dean. "The Old-Fashioned Essay." *Harper's* (October 1902): 802–803.

Jenks, Tudor. "The Essay." *Outlook* 48, no. 5 (1893): 212–13.

Kauffmann, R. Lane. "The Skewed Path: Essaying as Un-methodical Method." *Diogenes* 36, no. 143 (1988), 66–92.

Kitchen, Judith. "Grounding the Lyric Essay." *Fourth Genre: Explorations in Nonfiction* 13, no. 2 (Fall 2011): 115–21.

Klaus, Carl H. "Embodying the Self: Malady and the Personal Essay." *Iowa Review* 25, no. 2 (Spring–Summer 1995): 177–92.

—— "The Put-Ons of Personal Essayists." *Chronicle Review* (19 November 2010): B14–B15.

Kostelanetz, Richard. "Essaying the Essay." *Book Forum* 1, no. 3 (May 1975): 417–23.

Krutch, Joseph Wood. "No Essays, Please!" *Saturday Review of Literature* (10 March 1951): 18–19.

Laughlin, Clara E. "Concerning Essays." *Book Buyer* 14, no. 4 (May 1897): 349–52.

Lennon, Brian. "The Essay, in Theory." *Diacritics* 38, no. 3 (Fall 2008): 71–92.

Levine, Sara. "What in the Wide Wide World Is the Essay For?" *River Teeth: A Journal of Nonfiction Narrative* 1, no. 2 (2000): 106–22.

Lindberg, Stanley, and Edward Corey. "Focus on Autobiographical Essays." *Georgia Review* 41, no. 2 (Summer 1987): 247–48.

Lopate, Phillip. "The Essay Lives – in Disguise." *New York Times Book Review*, 18 November 1984.

—— "In Search of the Centaur: The Essay Film." *Threepenny Review* 48 (Winter 1992): 19–22.

Lordi, Emily. "Why Is Academic Writing So Beautiful? Notes on Black Feminist Scholarship." *Feminist Wire* (4 March 2014), www.thefeministwire.com/2014/03/academic-writing-black-feminism-krisof/.

Mabie, Hamilton Wright. "The Essay and Some Essayists, Part I." *Bookman* 9 (August 1899): 504–11.

—— "The Essay and Some Essayists, Part II." *Bookman* 9 (September 1899): 49–54.

—— "Essays." *Outlook* (3 December 1904): 879–82.

—— "The Prosperity of the Essay." *Outlook* (25 November 1905): 697–99.

—— "Why the Essay Is Valuable as Reading." *Ladies' Home Journal* (April 1908): 36.

Mack, Peter. "Rhetoric and the Essay." *Rhetoric Society Quarterly* 23, no. 2 (Spring 1993): 41–49.

Matthews, Brander. "Modern Essays." *Munsey's Magazine* 49 (1913): 268–72.

—— "A Note on the Essay." *Book Buyer* 16, no. 3 (April 1898): 201–204.

Mowitt, John. "The Essay as Instance of the Social Character of Private Experience." *Prose Studies* 12, no. 3 (1989): 274–84.

Nehring, Cristina. "What's Wrong with the American Essay." *Truthdig* (29 November 2007).

Nicolson, Harold. "On Writing an Essay." *Observer*, 18 October 1952.

Ozick, Cynthia. "She: Portrait of the Essay as a Warm Body." *Atlantic Monthly* (September 1998): 114–18.

Paul, Arthur. "Essay Questions: From Alain Resnais to Michael Moore." *Film Comment* 39, no. 1 (January 2003): 58–62.

Recommendations for Further Reading

Percy, H. R. "The Essay: An Art in Eclipse." *Queen's Quarterly* (Winter 1959): 642–49.
Perry, Jeannette Barbour. "The Romantic Essay." *Critic* 40, no. 4 (April 1902): 358–60.
Peterson, Linda. "Gender and the Autobiographical Essay: Research Perspectives, Pedagogical Practices." *College Composition and Communication* 42, no. 2 (May 1991): 171–93.
Plimpton, George. "The Story behind a Nonfiction Novel." *New York Times Book Review*, 16 January 1966.
Porter, Jeff. "From a History and Poetics of the Essay." *Essay Review* 1, no. 1 (Spring 2013), http://theessayreview.org/category/2013/1.
Rascaroli, Laura. "The Essay Film: Problems, Definitions, Textual Commitments." *Framework* 49, no. 2 (Fall 2008): 24–47.
Rascoe, Burton. "What of Our Essayists?" *Bookman* 55 (1922): 74–75.
Renov, Michael. "History and/as Autobiography: The Essayistic in Film and Video." *Frame/Work* 2–3 (1989): 6–13.
Repplier, Agnes. "The American Essay in War Time." *Yale Review* 7, no. 2 (January 1918): 249–59.
Rucker, Mary. "The Literary Essay and the Modern Temper." *Papers on Language and Literature* 11, no. 3 (Summer 1975): 317–35.
Routh, H. V. "The Origins of the Essay Compared in English and French Literatures." *Modern Language Review* 15, no. 1 (January 1920): 28–40, 143–51.
Spellmeyer, Kurt. "Common Ground: The Essay in the Academy." *College English* 51, no. 3 (March 1989): 262–76.
Strunsky, Simeon. "The Essay of Today." *English Journal* 17, no. 1 (January 1928): 8–16.
Stuckey-French, Ned. "Why Does the Essay Keep Dying, and What Do Little Lord Fauntleroy and the Lavender-Scented Little Old Lady Have to Do with It?" *CEA Critic* 61, no. 2–3 (Winter and Spring-Summer 1999): 30–36.
Sutherland, Patrick. "The Photo Essay." *Visual Anthropology* 32, no. 2 (2016): 115–21.
Terrill, Mary. "About Essays, and Three." *Bookman* (1 April 1920): 192–95.
Trimbur, John. "Essayist Literacy and the Rhetoric of Deproduction." *Rhetoric Review* 9, no. 1 (Autumn 1990): 72–86.
Wampole, Christy. "The Essayification of Everything." *New York Times*, 26 May 2013, https://archive.nytimes.com/opinionator.blogs.nytimes.com/2013/05/26/the-essayification-of-everything/.
Warner, R. "The Cinematic Essay as Adaptive Process." *Adaptation. The Journal of Literature on Screen Studies* 6, no. 1 (February 2013): 1–24.
Watson, E. H. Lacon. "The Essay Considered from an Artistic Point of View." *Eclectic Magazine* 123 (1894): 50–54.
Watson, Melvin Roy. "The *Spectator* Tradition and the Development of the Familiar Essay." *English Literary History* 13, no. 3 (1946): 189–215.
Wells, Benjamin A. "Contemporary American Essayists." *Forum* 23 (June 1897): 487–96.
Whitmore, Charles. "The Field of the Essay." *PMLA* 36, no. 4 (December 1921): 551–64.
Wiegand, William. "The 'Non-Fiction Novel.'" *New Mexico Quarterly* 37, no. 3 (1967): 243–57.
Woolf, Virginia. "Modern Essays." *Times Literary Supplement*, 30 November 1922.
Zabriskie, Francis N. "The Essay as Literary Form and Quality." *New Princeton Review* 4, no. 5 (September 1887): 227–45.

Anthologies

Aciman, André, and Robert Atwan, eds. *The Best American Essays 2020*. Boston: Houghton Mifflin Harcourt, 2020.

Alden, Raymond Macdonald, ed. *Essays, English and American*. Chicago: Scott, Foresman, 1918.

Alter, Nora M., and Timothy Corrigan, eds. *Essays on the Essay Film*. New York: Columbia University Press, 2017.

Atwan, Robert, and Kathryn Schulz, eds. *The Best American Essays 2021*. Boston: Houghton Mifflin Harcourt, 2021.

Brooks, David, and Robert Atwan, eds. *The Best American Essays 2012*. Boston: Houghton Mifflin Harcourt, 2012.

Chee, Alexander, and Robert Atwan, eds. *The Best American Essays 2022*. New York: Mariner Books, 2022.

D'Agata, John, ed. *The Lost Origins of the Essay*. Minneapolis: Graywolf Press, 2009.
The Making of the American Essay. Minneapolis: Graywolf Press, 2016.
The Next American Essay. Minneapolis: Graywolf Press, 2003.

Daiches, David. *A Century of the Essay: British and American*. New York: Harcourt, Brace, 1951.

Danticat, Edwige, and Robert Atwan, eds. *The Best American Essays 2011*. Boston: Houghton Mifflin Harcourt, 2011.

Dillard, Annie, and Robert Atwan, eds. *The Best American Essays 1988*. Boston: Houghton Mifflin Harcourt, 1988.

Early, Gerald, ed. *Speech and Power: The African-American Essay and Its Cultural Contents from Polemics to Pulpit*. 2 vols. Hopewell, NJ: Ecco Press, 1990–1993.

Epstein, Joseph, ed. *The Norton Book of Personal Essays*. New York: Norton, 1997.

Epstein, Joseph, and Robert Atwan, eds. *The Best American Essays 1993*. Boston: Houghton Mifflin Harcourt, 1993.

Fadiman, Anne, and Robert Atwan, eds. *The Best American Essays 2003*. Boston: Houghton Mifflin Harcourt, 2003.

Franzen, Jonathan, and Robert Atwan, eds. *The Best American Essays 2016*. Boston: Houghton Mifflin Harcourt, 2016.

Frazier, Ian, Geoffrey C. Ward, and Robert Atwan, eds. *The Best American Essays 1997*. Boston: Houghton Mifflin Harcourt, 1997.

Gigante, Denise, ed. *The Great Age of the English Essay: An Anthology*. New Haven, CT: Yale University Press, 2008.

Gopnik, Adam, and Robert Atwan, eds. *The Best American Essays 2008*. Boston: Houghton Mifflin Harcourt, 2008.

Gornick, Vivian, and Robert Atwan, eds. *The Best American Essays 2023*. New York: Mariner Books, 2023.

Gould, Stephen Jay, and Robert Atwan, eds. *The Best American Essays 2002*. Boston: Houghton Mifflin Harcourt, 2002.

Gross, John, ed. *The Oxford Book of Essays*. New York: Oxford University Press, 1991.

Hardwich, Elizabeth, and Robert Atwan, eds. *The Best American Essays 1986*. Boston: Houghton Mifflin Harcourt, 1986.

Hilton, Als, and Robert Atwan, eds. *The Best American Essays 2018*. Boston: Houghton Mifflin Harcourt, 2018.
Hitchens, Christopher, and Robert Atwan, eds. *The Best American Essays 2010*. Boston: Houghton Mifflin Harcourt, 2010.
Hoagland, Edward, and Robert Atwan, eds. *The Best American Essays 1999*. Boston: Houghton Mifflin Harcourt, 1999.
Hongo, Garrett Kaoru, ed. *Under Western Eyes: Personal Essays from Asian America*. New York: Anchor Books, 1995.
Howard, Maureen, ed. *The Penguin Book of Contemporary American Essays*. New York: Penguin, 1985.
Jamison, Leslie, and Robert Atwan, eds. *The Best American Essays 2017*. Boston: Houghton Mifflin Harcourt, 2017.
Kaplan, Justin, and Robert Atwan, eds. *The Best American Essays 1990*. Boston: Houghton Mifflin Harcourt, 1990.
Kidder, Tracy, and Robert Atwan, eds. *The Best American Essays 1994*. Boston: Houghton Mifflin Harcourt, 1994.
Kincaid, Jamaica, and Robert Atwan, eds. *The Best American Essays*. Boston: Houghton Mifflin Harcourt, 1995.
Klaus, Carl H., and Ned Stuckey-French, eds. *Essayists on the Essay: Montaigne to Our Time*. Iowa City, IA: University of Iowa Press, 2012.
Levy, Ariel, and Robert Atwan, eds. *The Best American Essays 2015*. Boston: Houghton Mifflin Harcourt, 2015.
Lightman, Alan, and Robert Atwan, eds. *The Best American Essays 2000*. Boston: Houghton Mifflin Harcourt, 2000.
Lopate, Philip, ed. *The Art of the Personal Essay: An Anthology from the Classical Era to the Present*. New York: Anchor Books, 1995.
   The Contemporary American Essay. New York: Anchor Books, 2021.
   The Glorious American Essay: One Hundred Essays from Colonial Times to the Present. New York: Knopf Doubleday, 2020.
Matthews, Brander. *The Oxford Book of American Essays*. New York: Oxford University Press, 1914.
Menand, Louis, and Robert Atwan, eds. *The Best American Essays 2004*. Boston: Houghton Mifflin Harcourt, 2004.
Meyer, Karl E., ed. *Pundits, Poets, and Wits: An Omnibus of American Newspaper Columnists*. New York: Oxford University Press, 1990.
Norris, Kathleen, and Robert Atwan, eds. *The Best American Essays 2001*. Boston: Houghton Mifflin Harcourt, 2001.
Oates, Joyce Carol, and Robert Atwan, eds. *The Best American Essays 1991*. Boston: Houghton Mifflin Harcourt, 1991.
   The Best American Essays of the Century. Boston: Houghton Mifflin, 2000.
Oliver, Mary, and Robert Atwan, eds. *The Best American Essays 2009*. Boston: Houghton Mifflin Harcourt, 2009.
Orlean, Susan, and Robert Atwan, eds. *The Best American Essays 2005*. Boston: Houghton Mifflin Harcourt, 2005.
Ozick, Cynthia, and Robert Atwan, eds. *The Best American Essays 1998*. Boston: Houghton Mifflin Harcourt, 1998.

Pack, Robert, and Jay Parini, eds. *The Bread Loaf Anthology of Contemporary American Essays.* Hanover, NH: University Press of New England, 1989.

Prentiss, Sean, and Joe Wilkins, eds. *The Far Edges of the Fourth Genre: An Anthology of Explorations in Creative Nonfiction.* East Lansing, MI: Michigan State University Press, 2014.

Sims, Normal, ed. *Literary Journalism: A New Collection of the Best American Nonfiction.* New York: Ballantine, 1995.

———. *The Literary Journalists.* New York: Ballantine, 1984.

Slater, Lauren, and Robert Atwan, eds. *The Best American Essays 2006.* Boston: Houghton Mifflin Harcourt, 2006.

Solnit, Rebecca, and Robert Atwan, eds. *The Best American Essays 2019.* Boston: Houghton Mifflin Harcourt, 2019.

Sontag, Susan, and Robert Atwan, eds. *The Best American Essays 1992.* Boston: Houghton Mifflin Harcourt, 1992.

Spinner, Jenny, ed. *Of Women and the Essay: An Anthology from 1655 to 2000.* Athens, GA: University of Georgia Press, 2018.

Strayed, Cheryl, and Robert Atwan, eds. *The Best American Essays 2013.* Boston: Houghton Mifflin Harcourt, 2013.

Sullivan, John Jeremiah, and Robert Atwan, eds. *The Best American Essays 2014.* Boston: Houghton Mifflin Harcourt, 2014.

Talese, Gay, and Robert Atwan, eds. *The Best American Essays 1987.* Boston: Houghton Mifflin Harcourt, 1987.

Wallace, David Foster, and Robert Atwan, eds. *The Best American Essays 2007.* Boston: Houghton Mifflin Harcourt, 2007.

Ward, Geoffrey C., and Robert Atwan, eds. *The Best American Essays 1996.* Boston: Houghton Mifflin Harcourt, 1996.

Wolff, Geoffrey, and Robert Atwan, eds. *The Best American Essays 1989.* Boston: Houghton Mifflin Harcourt, 1989.

Index

Abdurraqib, Hanif, 667
abolitionist cause/movement, 109
   Colored American, 154
   Freedom's Journal, 152
abolitionist press, women writers, 135
abstract art, and the visual art essay,
   300–301, 307
Abstract Expressionism, 308, 533
academic art writing, 302, 305–306
Adams, Franklin P.
   "Conning Tower," 284–285
   "Diary of Our Own Samuel Pepys,"
   284, 285
Adams, Henry
   "Dynamo and the Virgin," 233
   Mont Saint Michel and Chartres, 233
Adams, John Luther, 333
Addison, Joseph, 20, 339
Ade, George, 210–211
Adorno, Theodor W., 305, 368–371, 394, 676
   Dialectic of Enlightenment, 368–369
   "The Essay as Form," 370–371, 378, 477
   "On the Fetish Character of Jazz," 370
   Minima Moralia, 368–370
Advice on the Study of Law (1811), 427–428
African American essayists. *see* Black
   essayists/writers
African Diaspora
   Harlem Renaissance. *See* Harlem
   Renaissance
Agee, James, *Let Us Now Praise Famous Men*
   (1941), 3, 177
agency
   concept of, 431
   English and American precedents on,
   429–430
   juristic concept of, 430
Agrarianism/Agrarians, 266, 269–272
   Manifesto, 270

Menand on, 278
and New Criticism, 266
and northern critics, 271–272
Ahmad, Dohra, *Penguin Book of Migration*
   Literature, 612, 619
AIDS, 536, 578, 580
Akerman, Chantal, 534
Alcott, Bronson, 84, 85, 88
Alcott, Louisa May, 86
Algonquin Group, 212, 214
Allen, Charles, 348
Allen, Woody, 215–216
Alter, Nora, 562
ambivalence, 577, 595
A.M.E. Church Review, 161
American Anti-Slavery Society, 155
American Commonwealth, 622
American Direct Cinema, 530–531
American Dream, 620–622
American Indian Magazine, 398
American Indians. *See* Indigenous essays;
   Native Americans
American Left, 530
   See also leftist magazines
American Magazine and Monthly Chronicle
   (1757–58), "The Prattler," 37–38
American Mercury, 261–262, 295
American Newspaper Guild, 289
American Review, 273–275, 347
Americas Review (1980–), 356
Amherst Student, The, 235
analytic philosophy, crisis in, 499, 500
Anderson, Beth, 329
Anderson, Jane, *Little Review*, 344–345
Anger, Kenneth, 536
Angier, Natalie, 484
Anglophilia, 186, 427
Angyal, Andrew J., 647
animal rights, 505–506

697

Index

Anthropocene, 668
  concept, 670
  origin story, 668
Anti-Federalist essay, 52–53, 58
anti-intellectualism, 546
Anzaldúa, Gloria
  Borderlands/La Frontera, 3, 576–577, 637
  This Bridge Called My Back, 451–452, 636–638
Apess, William, 79–80, 397
aporia, 69
Appiah, Kwame Anthony, 614, 616
Arendt, Hannah, 348, 365–368, 380
  "We Refugees," 365–367
Aristotle, 461
Arn, Jackson, 563
art/artists, essay films, 531–535
artist residencies, 347
artists' memoirs, travel essays, 228
Ashbery, John, 466–468
Ashurst, William, 19
Asian American writers, 622–624
Astruc, Alexandre, 527
Atkins, G. Douglas, 561
Atlanta Compromise, 162
Atlantic, 189
  Bourne's essay, 190–191
  Comer's essay, 190–191
  conservative writers, 424
  Farwell's essay, 316
  nature writing, 80
  Repplier's "Americanism," 111
  science essays, 487
  women writers, 191–192
Atlantic Monthly, 190, 290, 398, 648
  Du Bois's essays, 165
  writings about disability, 583
atomic bomb, 480, 670
Audubon, John James, 67
  Birds of America, 71, 72
  early life, 71
  Ornithological Biography, 71–72
Auld family, 154, 155–156
autobiography
  contemporary comic essays, 216
  See also Apess, William; Barnum, P. T.; Franklin, Benjamin
avant-garde
  essay films, 528, 532
  experimental film, 364–365
  and kitsch, 305
  music, 318–319

Bacon, Francis, 86–87, 425, 426, 427
  Advancement of Learning (1605), 21
  Essayes or Counsels, Civill and Morall (1597), 21
Baffler, 564
Bakalar, Nicholas, 215
Baker, Josephine, 250
Baker, Russell, 215
Bakhtin, Mikhail, 600
Baldwin, James, 113, 351, 354, 382–384, 578–579, 655–658, 659, 667
  Cleaver on, 385
  "Many Thousands Gone," 612–613
  Notes of a Native Son, 382–383, 643
  "The Price May Be Too High," 643
  "Stranger in the Village," 625–626
Baldwin, Joseph G., 203
Baltimore Sun, 296–297, 480–481
Bambara, Toni Cade, 451, 543, 544, 560
Baraka, Amiri (LeRoi Jones), 324, 658–659
Barlow, Billy, 211
Barnum, P. T., *Autobiography*, 206
Baroque, 512–513, 514
Barrett, William, 553
Barth, John, 509, 511–514
  and irony, 520
  "Literature of Exhaustion," 511–513, 515, 520
  "Literature of Replenishment," 513–514
Barthes, Roland, 517, 610
Bartram, John, 67
Bartram, William, 67–69
Baxandall, Rosalyn, 448
Baxter, Richard, 21
Beard, JoAnn, 485–486
Beardsley, M. C., 277–278
Beauchamp, Gordan, 195
Beauvoir, Simone de, 569–570
Bebop, 543
Beccaria, Cesare, *Essay on Crimes and Punishments* (1774), 46, 48
Beckett, Samuel, 512, 514, 519
Bedpan Gazette, 585
Beers, Clifford, 589
Bell, Daniel, 416
Bell, Philip Alexander, 153
Benchley, Robert, 213
  "Little Man," 286–287
  in *New Yorker*, 286
Bender, Thomas, 116–117
Benjamin, Walter, 539
Bennet, Laura, 457
Bennett, Gwendolyn, 255

Index

Berlant, Lauren, 675
Bernard, Emily, 667
Bernstein, Leonard, 319
  public music essays, 320
  Unanswered Question, lectures, 321
Best American Science and Nature Writing (2002–), 486–487
Best American Science Writing, 486
Bierce, Ambrose "Bitter," 205–206, 211
Billings, Josh, 207
Billings, William, 314
Biss, Eula, 486, 607
Black civil and natural rights, 153–154
Black Codes/Jim Crow laws, 650
Black essayists/writers, 643–644, 647
  and freedom, 149–150
  genteel essay tradition, 193–195
  Harlem Renaissance, 252
  and Paris, WWI, 234
  See also New Negro ideology; *specific names of Black essayists*
Black Independent Cinema, 539, 540–543
  See also Third Cinema
Black liberation movement, 372, 373
  See also civil rights movement
Black Mountain College, 468
Black Mountain Review, 356
Black music, 543, 659
  See also jazz and blues
Black nationalism, 654
Black Power/Black Arts movement, 659, 660
Black press
  columnists, 282–283
  growth in, after WWI, 252
  periodicals, 193
  See also specific names of newspapers and periodicals
Black sharecroppers, 158
Black studies, 372, 560
Black women/feminists, 447–448
  See also Pat Robinson Group ("the Damned"); *specific names of individual women writers*
Blackwood's Magazine, 125
Blaser, Mario, 675
blogs, feminist, 444, 445
Bloom, Harold, 558–559
Blount, Roy, 216
Blum, Deborah, 483
Bly, Nelly (Elizabeth Cochrane Seaman), 227–228
Boas, Ralph Philip, *Youth and the New World*, 190

Boetcher Joeres, Ruth-Ellen, 636, 637
Bombeck, Erma, 215
Bonner, Marita, "Young Blood Hungers," 254–255
Bontemps, Arna, 264
Bookman, 290
Borel, Brooke, 487
Borges, Jorge Luis, 509, 512–513, 514
Borowitz, Andy, 216
Boully, Jenny, 597
Bourne, Randolph, 292, 583–584
  "The Handicapped," 583
  "The Older Generation," 190–191
Boyd, Ann, 193
Boyle, Robert, 18
Bradford, Andrew, *American Magazine*, 339
Bradford, William, 37
Braithwaite, William Stanley, 263, 651
Bramen, Carrie Tirado, 220
Brandeis, Louis, 439
Brawley, Benjamin, 194
  "A Southern Boyhood," 194
Brecht, Bertolt, 373
British imperialism, Brown's London sketches, 226
Broadway Journal, 118
Brockden Brown, Charles, "The Rhapsodist," 40
Brommel, Bernard J., 168
Brook Farm (Utopian community), 85
Brooks, Charles S.
  "1917," 187–188
  "The Writing of Essays," 183, 187
Brooks, Cleanth, 276–277
Brooks, David, 410–411
Broun, Heywood, 289–290
Brown, Sterling, 255
Brown, William Wells, 226
  American Fugitive in Europe, 226
Browne, Thomas, 21–22
Brownson, Orestes, 85
Brownson's Quarterly Review, 85
Bryce, James, 622
Buchwald, Art, 215
  I Am Not a Crook (1974), 215
Buckley, William F., Jr., 411–424
  on American liberals, 420, 422
  anti-intellectualism, 412
  on civil rights and racial injustice, 421
  "Did You Ever See a Dream Walking?" 417–418
  God and Man at Yale, 414
  Keeping the Tablets (reprint), 418–419

699

Buckley, William F., Jr. (cont.)
  McCarthy and His Enemies, 414
  at *National Review*, 411, 412, 413–414, 421–422, 424
  and New Deal politics. *See* New Deal politics
  reactionary instincts and processes of exclusion, 416–417, 418
  and the Republican Party, 414
  scholars' biographies of, 413–414
  on women's rights, 421–422
Buell, Lawrence, 82, 84, 94
Bulwark, 424
Burder, George, 16, 31
Burnham, George, 206
Burroughs, John, nature writing, 77
  influences on, 76, 77
  on Mammoth Cave, Kentucky, 77
  philosophy, 77
  style, 77
Butler, Judith, 455–456, 570
  Gender Trouble, 392
  "Performative Acts," 392
BuzzFeed, 458–459
Byles, Mather, 339

Cage, John, 326–327, 330, 468
  Feldman on, 332
  Silence and *A Year from Monday*, 326–327
Calverton, V. F., 547
  Liberation of American Literature, 547, 548
Cambridge School, 468
Campt, Tina, 542
Canby, Henry Seidel, 187, 281, 288
capitalism, free-market, documentaries, 529
Capó Crucet, Jennine, 633, 634–636
Capote, Truman, 351, 352
Carson, Anne, 472, 601–604, 607
  Eros the Bittersweet, 470–472
Carson, Rachel, 480–481
  Edge of the Sea, 480–481
  Silent Spring, 480, 673
casebook, invention of, 428
Cather, Willa, 233
Catholic Worker, The, 173–174, 175
Catholicism, social/distributive justice, 167–168
Cavell, Stanley, 490, 491–498
  Claim of Reason, 497–498
  Must We Mean What We Say? 491–494, 495
  philosophy and national identity, 496
  and Rorty, 502–503
  and Transcendentalism, 494, 495–496, 497

Cazneau, Jane McManus Storm, 137–138
celebrity culture, and photojournalism, 352–353
Censor, The (1715–17), 34
censorship, 345, 348–349
Century Magazine, 189
Chaat Smith, Paul, 403
Chamberlain, Betsey, 133
Chang, Jade, 625, 626
Channing, William Ellery, 84–85, 90
  circle of Transcendentalists, 85
  Fuller on, 91–92
  at Harvard College, 83
  "Likeness to God," 83–84, 85
  "Self-Culture," 84
Channing, William Tyrell, 82
Chapman, John Jay, 292
Character and Opinion in the United States (1920), 242–243
Chee, Alexander, 613, 614
Cherokee Phoenix, 400
Cherry, Vivian, 177
Chicago Defender, 255
Chicago Review, 348–349
Child, Lydia Maria, 126, 139–140
  abolitionist cause, 139
  Appeal in Favor of That Class of Americans Called Africans, 139
  Letters from New-York, 139
Chomsky, Noam, 385–386
choreography, 534
Christian discourses
  social justice, 169
  See also Catholicism, social/distributive justice
Christian Enlightenment, 18
Christianity
  Black church, 180
  prophetic, Democratic Socialism, 180–181
  social justice essayists' critique, 177
  See also Catholicism
Chrystos (1946–), "I Don't Understand," 451–453
Chubbuck, Emily. *See* Forester, Fanny
City College of New York (CCNY), 364
civil rights movement, 245, 372, 382, 384, 659
  and the women's movement/feminism, 389
  See also Baldwin, James; Black liberation movement
civil rights violations. *See* lynching
Civil War, American, 157, 429
Cixous, Hélène, 565

Index

Clark, William, 62, 69–71
Cleaver, Eldridge, 384–385
Coates, Ta-Nehisi, 643, 644, 665–666
Codrescu, Andrei, 356
Coetzee, J. M., 505–506
coffeehouse essays, 22
Coke, Edward, 427, 428
Cokes, Tony, 534–535
Coleridge, Samuel Taylor, 90, 117, 124
Collier's, 290
Collins, Seward, 273–274
colonization, and writing, 617–618
colonization of former slaves. *See* Liberia
Colored American, 153–154
Columbia University Press, Gender and Culture series, 568
Columbian Magazine, or Monthly Miscellany, 39
Columbus, Christopher, 618
Comer, Cornelia A. P., 190–191
comic essay tradition, 197–217
  newspaper columns, 286–287
comic memoirs, 206
comic papers/journals, 202
  1810 to 1815, 200
Comma, Olga, 259
Commentaries, 428
commercial magazines, 355–356
common law, 427
common law, English, 430
communism, and Soviet Union, 419–420
Communist Party, 453–454
communitarianism, 387
Community of Literary Magazines and Presses, 359–360
confessional poetry, 466
conservation, popular science essays, 479–480
conservatism, 410–424
Constitution, US, 418
  Reconstruction (1865–1877), 157
Constructivism, 345
consumerism, and contemporary feminism, 457
Cook, Vanessa, 167
Cooper, Anna Julia, 283, 648–649
Cooper, James Fenimore, 65, 70
  Gleanings in Europe, 220–221
  Last of the Mohicans, 220
Cooper, Susan Fenimore
  on "Indians," 135
  Rural Hours, 65, 66, 134–135
    influence of naturalists, 66
Coover, Robert, 516, 520, 521
Copland, Aaron, 319

"Composer from Brooklyn," 320
  essay collections and lectures, 320
Copway, George, 400
  Running Sketches (1851), 226
  Traditional History and Characteristic Sketches of the Ojibway Nation, 80
Copway's American Indian, 400
Cornish, Samuel, 151–152, 153–154
Corrector, The, 200
Corrigan, Timothy, 538
Cosmopolitan, 340
cosmopolitanism, 613, 614–616
  and common culture, 616
  radical, 628–629
Cosmos (TV series), 481
Cottingham, Laura, 306
Couser, G. Thomas, 590
Cowell, Henry, 315
  1928 tour of Russia, and essays, 318
  American Composers on American Music, 316–318
  "Charles Ives," 318
  incarceration in San Quentin, 318
  at the *Musical Quarterly*, 318–319
  "Rhythm" in *New Musical Resources*, 319
Cowley, Abraham, 602
Cowley, Malcolm, 185, 549
creative writing programs, 445, 463
Crenshaw, Kimberlé Williams, 455
Crèvecœur, Hector St. John de, 63
  Letters from an American Farmer, 63–65
  life dates and early career, 63
Crisis (periodical), 193, 194, 255, 650
  Du Bois at, 234
  Harlem Renaissance, 260–261
  literary prizes, 250
Critical Inquiry, 559
critical legal studies, 435–436
critical race theory, 436, 437
critical theory, 368, 371
criticism, 496–497, 506
  See also literary theory and criticism
crónicas, Latinx, 628–632
Cronon, William, 79
Crouch, Stanley, 660
Cullen, Countee, 234, 250
Culler, Jonathan, 555, 556
cultural criticism, 552
culture industry, 305
culture wars, and the genteel essay tradition, 183–184
Cunard, Nancy, 257

701

Index

Dadaism, 345, 365
D'Agata, John, 465, 517, 598, 599
Daily Beast, 631
Dana, Charles, 227
dance/choreography, 534
Danticat, Edwidge, 624
Davidson, Donald, 267
   and the *American Review*, 273–274
   I'll Take My Stand, 269–272
Davies, John, 428
Davis, Allison, 260–261
Davis, Angela, 371–373, 390–391
   and Adorno, 371
   "Woman and Capitalism," 391
Davis, Paulina Wright, 144–145
Day, Dorothy, 175–177
   The Catholic Worker, 175
   essays and autobiographical writings, 175
   House of Hospitality, 176
   "Houses of Hospitality," *Commonweal*, 176
   Meditations, 176–177
de la Cadena, Marisol, 675
de Man, Paul, 558, 559
de Obaldia, Claire, 545
Debs, Eugene V., 168–170
   in *Cry for Justice: An Anthology of Social Protest*, 169
   "How I Became a Socialist," 169
   Walls and Bars, 170
   writings for labor publications, 168–169
decolonization, 659
deconstruction, 557–559
Defoe, Daniel, 23
DeLillo, Don, 520, 521
Deloria, Vine, Jr., 402
   Custer Died for Your Sins, 402
   "Thinking in Time and Space," 402
Deming, Alison Hawthorne, 673, 676
democracy
   comic essay tradition, 200–201, 202, 204
   Dewey on, 241
Democratic Party, 392–393
Democratic Socialism, and prophetic Christianity, 180–181
Demos, John, 621
Dennie, Joseph, 130
Dennis-Benn, Nicole, 620
Department of Agriculture, 73
Deren, Maya, 535, 536
Derrida, Jacques, 436, 557–558
   See also deconstruction
Detwiler-George, Jacqueline, 487
Dewey, John, 500

Art and Experience, 309
"Democracy and Education in the World of Today," 241
"Influence of Darwinism on Philosophy," 240
other works, 240–241
pragmatism, 236, 239
on truth, 239
Dexter, Timothy, *A Pickle for the Knowing Ones*, 200–201
Diagram, 488
Dial, The, 85, 88–89, 92, 134, 344
"Dialectics of Liberation" conference, London, 372
Diamond, Cora, 503–508
diary form, nature writing, 65
Diawara, Manthia, *Black American Cinema*, 538, 540
Dickens, Charles, 350
Diderot, Denis, 123, 310
Didion, Joan, 349–350, 351, 353, 354
Dillard, Annie, 483–484, 597, 604–606
   "Living Like Weasels," 604–605
   Pilgrim at Tinker Creek, 605, 606
Dillon, Brian, 562
disability rights movement, 585–587
Dissent, 380, 384, 394
distributive justice, 167–168
   See also social justice
documentaries
   disciplinary boundaries of, 529
   essay films, 529–531
   science essays, 487
Dooley, Mr. (Finley Peter Dunne), 212
Double Dealer, 344
double-consciousness, 165
Douglas, Ann, 192
Douglass, Frederick, 150, 154–158, 619
   antislavery lecture tours in Britain and Ireland, 224
   call to arms, and support for the Union, 157
   European travels, and essays, 109–110
   Frederick Douglass' Paper, 156–157
   letter to Auld, 155–156
   in *My Bondage and My Freedom*, 224
   Narrative of the Life (1845), 109, 155, 224
   New National Era, 157–158
   newspaper writings, 155–156
   North Star, 155, 156
   as orator, 150
   starts periodicals, 155
Douglass' Monthly, 157

Dowdy, Michael, *American Poets in the 21st Century*, 472
"Dreamer, The" (1789), 41
Drift, 564
Du Bois, W. E. B., 163–165, 648
  Atlantic Monthly, 163, 165, 244
  columns, 282
  at *Crisis*, 234, 244
  "Criteria for Negro Art," 651
  double-consciousness, 165, 244–245
  influences on, 244
  "Negro Mind Reaches Out," 256–257
  "Of Our Spiritual Strivings," 165
  "Returning Soldiers," 262–263
  on segregation and "Jim Crow," 245
  Souls of Black Folk, 165, 283, 649–650
  "Strivings of the Negro People," 163–164
Duchamp, Marcel, 364
Dudley, Paul, project-essays, 23
Dungy, Camille, 676–677
Dunne, Finley Peter, *Mr. Dooley's Philosophy*, 212
DuPlessis, Rachel Blau, 459
  Feminist Memoir Project, 453
  "f-words," 560–561, 565, 575–576
Dworkin, Andrea, 572–574
  antipornography actions, 572–573
  Intercourse, 573–574
  Letters from a War Zone, 574
  Right-Wing Women, 573
  Woman Hating, 573

Early, Gerald, 660
Eastman, Charles Alexander
  From the Deep Woods, 399
  Indian Boyhood, 398–399
  Soul of the Indian, 399
Eastman, Max, 549
Ebony and Topaz, 193
Ecotactics, 388
editorials
  on writers writing, 353
  See also newspaper columns
Edsin, C. L., *Gentle Art of Columning*, 212
education, progressive, Transcendentalism, 85, 86
Edwards, Jonathan
  Discourse on the Trinity, 15
  "Personal Narrative," 81–82
  Treatise on Grace, 15
Eisenhower, Dwight, 415
Eisenstein, Sergei, 527
Eisley, Loren, 481

electronic music, 332–333
Eliot, T. S., 113, 245–246, 465
  The Sacred Wood, 462
  "Tradition and the Individual Talent," 644–645
Ellington, Edward "Duke," 319, 323
Ellison, Ralph, 384, 624, 654–655, 659
Emancipation Proclamation (1863), 149, 158
Emerson, Ralph Waldo, 81, 90–91, 309–310, 605
  "American Scholar," 104, 106, 150, 225–226
  and Cavell, 494, 495–496, 497
  and Channing, 82, 83, 86
  The Dial, 88–89
  English Traits, 225
  Essays, 107
  "Experience," 87
  influence on Burroughs and Muir, 76–77
  as lecturer and essayist, 86–88
  on "likeness to God," 83–84
  "Montaigne," 91, 106
  Nature, 62, 76, 89–90, 106
  on poetry and prose, 103–104
  Representative Men, 106
  "Self-Reliance," 106
  sermons, 86
  Snyder on, 91
  Transcendentalism, 82
  of travel writings on southern Europe, 222–223
  travels in Britain, and national identity, 224
Emre, Merve, 563–564
Engels, Friedrich, 99
Enlightenment, 669, 680
Environmental Protection Agency, 480
Epstein, Barbara, "Ambivalence," 453–455
Erdrich, Louise, 406–407
Ernst, Max, 364
Esquire, 352, 354, 355
essay
  christened by Montaigne, 2
  definition/origins, 425–426
essay films, 527–544
European migration to US, 618–619
Evangelical Magazine, 31
Evans, Walker, *Let Us Now Praise Famous Men* (1941), 3, 177
experimental fiction, 511
experimental film, 364–365

fabulation, 542
Faery, Rebecca Blevins, 561
Fagan, Benjamin, 151, 154

Index

Farley, Harriet, 133
   essays in *Godey's*, 133
   Lowell Offering, 133
Farrell, James T., 547, 548
Farwell, Arthur, 315–316
Fauset, Jessie, 250–251, 651
   in *Crisis*, 257
   "Gift of Laughter," 263
Federalist, The, 53–60
Federman, Raymond
   "Critifiction," 518–519
   "Fiction Today," 519–520
   "Surfiction," 516–518
Feldman, Morton, 331–332
female artists
   video essays, 533–534
   See also feminism/feminist essays
Female Tatler, The, 36
feminism/feminist essays, 356, 385, 390, 442–459, 559
   Black, 387
   contemporary/#MeToo, 456–459
   first wave, 443
   and lesbianism, 389–390
   Mailer and, 354–355
   militant, 560
   online, 444–445
   second wave (Consciousness), 445–450, 566–569
   third wave (Difference), 450–455, 577
   video essays, 534
   See also radical feminists, Latina; women's movement; *specific names of individual feminist essayists*
feminist jurisprudence, 436–437
feminist theory, 568
Fern, Fanny, 143–144
   column at *Musical World*, 143
   Fern Leaves, 143
   Fern Leaves, Second Series, 204–205
   Hawthorne on, 205
   "Horace Mann's Opinion," 205
   at *New York Ledger*, 143
   social critiques, 205
fiction, 513–514
   Bossa Nova, 514–515
   experimental, 511
   See also postmodernism, literary; *specific names of fiction writers*
figurative art, 307–308
Film Culture, 364–365
Fingal, Jim, 517
Firing Line (TV show), 412, 414

first-person narrator, 340, 446
Fish, Stanley, 436
Fleischman, T., 580
Flexner, Eleanor, 443
"Forc'd Alliance, The," 48–50
Forester, Fanny, 141–142
   popular essay, introduction of, 141
   popular periodical collections, 141–142
formalism, aesthetic, 529
formalism, legal, 430
formalism, Slavic, 552
Foucault, Michel, 470, 517, 570, 646–647
Founding Fathers, 613–614
Fox News, 423–424
Francke, August Hermann, 18, 19
Francke Foundation, Halle, 19
Frankfurt School, 368, 371, 552
Franklin, Benjamin, 478
   Autobiography
      and Mather's *Bonifacius*, 16–17
      on *The Spectator*, 32
   "The Busy Body," 37
   comic essay tradition, influences on, 198–199
   "The Ephemera," 112–113, 200
   General Magazine, 339
   "The Grand Leap of the Whale," 199–200
   "Old Mistresses Apologue," 199
   shapeshifting narratives, 82
   "Silence Dogood," 36–37, 82, 339
   "The Speech of David Wood," 200
   "The Speech of Miss Polly Baker," 199
   "Witch Trial at Mount Holly," 199
Frazier, E. Franklin, 254
Frederick Douglass' Paper, 156–157
Free Speech and Headlight, 159
Freedom's Journal, 151–153
French theory, 517, 518
Fried, Michael, 301, 303, 305–306
   "Art and Objecthood," 303
Friedan, Betty, 355
Friedrich, Sue, 534
"Friend, The," 34
Fries, Kenny, 589
Frost, Robert, 235–236, 246–247
Fugitive Poets, 266
   Agrarians, 269
   little magazine, 267–268
   and New Criticism, 266
Fugitive Slave Act (1850), 156, 226
Fuller, Margaret, 81, 108, 126
   and Alcott, Temple School, 85
   "American Literature," *Papers on Literature and Art*, 107–108

on Child, 140
death of, 93
The Dial, 85, 88, 92, 140
on Douglass's writings, 109
and Emerson, 92
"Great Lawsuit," 89, 91–92, 140
journalism/travel dispatches, 93, 107, 108–109, 141
New-York Tribune reviewer, 116
Papers on Literature and Art (1846), 140
review of Emerson's *Essays*, 107
Summer on the Lakes, 92–93, 98–99
and Thoreau, 93
at the *Tribune*, 140–141, 224–225
Woman in the Nineteenth Century, 140
on women, 92

Gabriel, Teshome H., 539–540
Galaxy Magazine, 201
Gallagher, Hugh Gregory, 585
García, Ivonne, 228
Gardner, Robert, 537
Garland, Phyllis, 282
Garrison, William Lloyd, 153, 155
Garvey, Marcus, 650–651
Garza, Kimberly, 488
Gates, Henry Louis, Jr., 559
Gay, Ross, 666–667
Gay, Roxane, 593–594, 595, 667
gender
  inclusivity. *See* Latinx writers
  performativity and masquerade, 569–570
  and sexuality, essay films, 536
general interest magazines, 340
  new science essays, 484
Genet, Jean, 578
Geneva School, 552
genre
  essay as, 600
  and philosophy, 502, 506
genteel essay tradition, 182–185
  Black essayists, 193–195
  custodians of culture, 189–191
  essay critics mourn, 185–188
  women writers, 191–193
Geological Survey *See* King, Clarence; Powell, John Wesley
German immigrants/essayists, 361–377
German Romanticism, 497
Gerould, Katharine Fullerton, 184–185, 186–187, 188, 292
  narrative form of essay, 291
  success of, 192

Gershwin, George, 317
Gilbert, Henry, 316
Gilbert, Sandra, 560
Ginsberg, Allen, 348–349
Gladwell, Malcolm, 484
"Gleaner, The," 42–43
Godey's Lady's Book, 132, 133
Gold, Mike, 549
Goldman, Francisco, 630–631
Goldsmith, Oliver, *The Citizen of the World*, 201
Gonzalez, Ray, 677
Gornick, Vivian, 563, 572
Gothic, the, 125
Gould, Stephen Jay, 482
Gournay, Marie Le Jars de, 129
Graham, Dan, 533
Graham, George, "Graham's Magazine," 339–340
Grant Still, William, 317–318
Grauman, Lawrence, Jr., 349
Great Depression, 269, 463, 652–653
Greenberg, Clement, 301–302, 303–304, 305, 308, 492, 532
  on America, and the democratization of taste, 308–310
  "Avant-Garde and Kitsch," 305
  and Pollock, 308
Greenwood, Grace, 141, 142–143
  Haps and Mishaps of a Tour in Europe, 143
Greer, Germaine, 354
Grierson, John, 529–530
Griffith, D. W., *Corner in Wheat*, 529
Grimké, Angelina, 136
Grimké, Sarah, 136–137
  Letters on the Equality of the Sexes, 136–137
Guardian (Black activist newspaper), 650
Guardian (British newspaper), 34
Guatemala, civil war, 630–631
Guiney, Louise Imogen, 192
Gurba, Myriam, 640–641
Guttzeit, Gero, 115

Hak Kyung Cha, Theresa, 473
Hale, Edward Everett, 112
Hale, Sarah Josepha, 132–133
Haliburton, Thomas Chandler, *Traits of American Humor*, 206
Hall, Sarah Ewing, 130–131
  "Defence of American Women," 131
  "On the Extent of Female Influence," 130–131
  Port Folio essays, 130

Hamilton, Alexander, 51–52
  The Federalist, 53–60
Hanisch, Carol, 390
Hanna, Monica, 628
Haraway, Donna, 680
  "Manifesto for Cyborgs," 391
Hardwick, Elizabeth, 348, 355, 552, 554
  on New Journalism, 353
Harlem Renaissance, 250–264, 346, 652
  essay as literary form, 253–255
  and the readers, 255–260
  social and cultural change, 260–264
  WWI and African American migration, 251–253
Harlem Uprising, 1964, 663–664
Harper's Magazine
  science essays, 478
  travel essays and fiction, 231
Harper's Weekly, 290
Harrison, Hubert, 251–252, 650–651
Hart, Jeffrey, 415–416
Hartman, Geoffrey, 558, 559
Hartman, Saidaya, 542
Harvard Law Review, 429–430, 432
Harvard Law School, 439
Hatfield, Jackie, 533–534
Hawthorne, Nathaniel, 97–98, 103
  on Fern, 205
  humorous sketches, 206
  Mosses, Poe on, 127
  travel sketches in fiction, 228
  Twice-Told Tales, Poe on, 127
Hazlitt, Henry, 271
Hazlitt, William (1778–1830), 340, 573
Heap, Margaret, 344–346
Hearn, Lafcadio, 228
Hedge, Frederic Henry, 90
Hefner, Hugh, 355–356
Heilbrun, Carolyn, 567–568
Hejinian, Lyn, 469–470
Hemingway, Ernest, 113, 233–234, 352
Henderson, Alice Corbin, 344
Hennessy, Kate, *Dorothy Day and the Catholic Worker*, 177
hermeneutics, 552
Hernández, Daisy, 638–639
Hersey, John, 350
  "Hiroshima," 480
Hicks, Granville, 547–548, 549
Higginson, Thomas Wentworth,
  "Americanism in Literature," 111–112
Hindle, John, 276
Hitchens, Christopher, 573

HIV/AIDS. *See* AIDS
Hockenberry, John, 589–590
Hogan, Linda, 407–408
  Dwellings, 407
  "Ways of the Cranes," 619
Holley, Marietta
  My Opinions and Betsy Bobbit's, 210
  Samantha at Saratoga, 210
  travelogues and comic narratives, 210
  on women's rights, 210
Holliday, Robert Cortes, 291–292
Hollinger, David, 615–616
Hollywood, 528–529
Holmes, Oliver Wendell, Jr., 187–188, 429–431
  Common Law, 429
  in *Harvard Law Review*, 429–430, 432
homosexuality
  essay films, 536
  See also lesbianism
Hong, Cathy Park, *Minor Feelings*, 623–624
hooks, bell, 571–572
  Ain't I a Woman, 571
  Talking Back, 571
  Teaching to Transgress, 572
Hopkins, Sarah Winnemucca, 397, 401
Horkheimer, Max, 305, 368
Hours at Home, 478
Howe, Irving, 381
  "Age of Conformity," 379–380
  and Ellison, 384
Howe, Julia Ward
  From the Oak to the Olive, 229–230
  as reformer, 230
Howells, William Dean, 182
  Italian Journeys, 229
  Venetian Life, 229
Hughes, Hugh, "Interrogator," 58
Hughes, Langston, 651–652
  Best of Simple, 213–214
  "Jazz as Communication," 324
  in *The Nation*, 256
humanities, institutional support for, 347, 348
Humanities in Society, 519
humankind, 668
Hume, David, 426
humor essays. *See* comic essay tradition
Hurston, Zora Neale, 651–652
Hurwitz, Leo, 530

identity politics, 387
Image-Fiction, 520–521
improvisational practice, 247, 655
  See also jazz and blues

Index

Indian newspapers/periodicals, 400–401
Indigenous essays, 388, 395–409, 619
  See also Native Americans
individualism, 465, 620–622
  and Americanness, 311
  and the personal essay, 621
  Tocqueville on, 622
industrial agriculture, 530
Industrial Revolution, 670
industrial wastelands, new nature essays, 488
interpretation of art, 306–307
intersectionality, 389, 455, 636–638
investigative journalism, new science, 483
irony, 520, 521–522
Irving, Washington, 70
  Alhambra, The, 222
  essays on European identity, 100
  A History of New York, 100, 201, 202
    Knickerbocker (narrator), 202
  on influence of *The Spectator,* 32–33
  "Letters of Jonathan Oldstyle," 32–33, 43–44, 100, 340
  Salmagundi (1807–08), 32–33, 44–45, 201–202, 340
  Sketch-Book, 96–97, 99, 100, 101
  on Britain, 223
  Tour of the Prairies, 211–212
Irving, William (1766–1821), 340
Iverson, Ethan, 324
Ives, Charles, 318
  Essays before a Sonata, 325–326

Jafa, Arthur, 542–543
Jakobson, Roman, 555
James, Henry, 110–111, 112
  English essays, 232
  essay on Hawthorne, 97–98
  Italian essays, 232–233
  "The Théâtre Francais," 110
  travel essays in *Atlantic,* 232–233
James, William, 235–236, 500
  on improvisational practice, 243
  influences on other writers, 244, 245
  other works, 237
  pedagogical volumes for teachers, 237
  pragmatism, 235, 236, 237–238
  Principles, 236, 237, 242
  styles in writings, 237
  on truth, 238–239
  Varieties of Religious Experience, 237
  See also Santayana, George
Jameson, Fredric, 501–502, 546, 556
Jamison, Leslie, 486

Jauss, Hans Robert, 461
Jay, John, *The Federalist,* 53–60
jazz and blues, 322–324, 543, 659
  See also improvisational practice
Jefferson, Thomas, 69, 478
  advice to travelers, 219
  travel journal in France, 219
Jehlen, Myra, 617–618
Jen, Gish, *Tiger Writing,* 621–623, 624
Jensen, Toni, 672
Johnson, Cary Alan, 580
Johnson, Charles
  in *Ebony and Topaz* (1927), 193, 261
  The Opportunity, 193
Johnson, James Weldon, 257
  American Mercury essay, 261–262
  Book of American Negro Poetry, 257–258
Johnson, Pauline ("Mohawk Princess"), 399
Johnson, Samuel, *The Rambler,* 34, 38
Jones, Stephen Graham, 408–409
Jordan, June, 660, 663–664
  Civil Wars, 660, 663–664
Joseph, Khalil, 544
Journals of Lewis and Clark. See Clark, William; Lewis, Meriwether
Joyce, James, 344–345
jurists, 425

Kallen, Horace, 617
Kant, Immanuel, 90, 305, 307
Kantorowicz, Ernst, 373–374
Katz, Steve, 514
Kayak, 347
Kazin, Alfred, 553–554
Keillor, Garrison, 216
Keller, Helen, 170–173
  critique of the *Eagle,* 172
  essay collections, 582
  "The Hand of the World," 582–583
  Her Socialist Years, 583
  "How I Became a Socialist," 171–172, 582
  letter to strikers, 172
  "The Message of Swedenborg," 172–173
  Optimism: An Essay, 172
  Out of the Dark, collection, 171
  World I Live In, The, 582, 583
Kennedy, Duncan, 435
Kennedy, J. Gerald, 116
Kenyon Review, 357
Khakpour, Porochista, 594–595, 625
Kimmerer, Robin W., 404, 671–672
Kincaid, Jamaica, 675
Kindley, Evan, 462–463, 464

King, Clarence, 62, 70
  education and early career, 73
  Geological Survey, 1879–1881, 73
  Mountaineering in the Sierra Nevada (1872), 73–75
King, Martin Luther, Jr., 177, 383, 384
Kingston, Maxine Hong, 388–389
kitsch, and the avant-garde, 305
Klinkowitz, Jerome, 515
Koestenbaum, Wayne, 579–580, 597
Kolbert, Elizabeth, 485
  New Yorker articles, 485
  Sixth Extinction, 485
Krauss, Rosalind, 301, 303, 305–306
Kriegel, Leonard, 585
Kristallnacht ("Night of Broken Glass"), 285
Kristol, Irving, 416
Ku Klux Klan, 160, 530
  See also lynching
Kuhn, Thomas, 493

LA Rebellion, 538–539, 544
  See also Black Independent Cinema
labor activism, 530
Lacoue-Labarthe, Philippe, 497
LaCroix, Allison, 55
Ladies' Home Journal, 340, 355
LaDuke, Winona, 403
Lamb, Charles, 186, 340
Lamb, John, 48
Language Poets, 356, 468–470
Latham, John, 67
Latinx writers, 627–642
Latour, Bruno, 679
Laughlin, James, 347
Law, William, 21
law reports, 428
law reviews, 433, 434
law schools, 428
  Cambridge, 429
  critical legal studies, 435
  law reviews, 433, 434
  legal essays, 431, 433, 439–440
League of the Physically Handicapped, 588
Lee, Kevin B., 544
Left, the. *See* American Left; Marx/Marxism; New Left
leftist literary criticism. *See* Marxist critics
leftist magazines, 346, 348, 356
legal essays, 426–440
  pedagogy, 427–429
  polemic, 431–439
  pragmatism, 429–431, 438

Lenton, Francis, 426
Leo XIII, Pope, distributive justice, 167–168
Leopold, Aldo, 479–480
LeRoi Jones, Everett *See* Baraka, Amiri (LeRoi Jones)
lesbianism, 389–390
  See also radical feminists, Latina
Lewis, Meriwether, expedition with Clark, 62, 67, 69–71
Lewis, Michael, 484
Lewis, Sinclair, 182–183
LGBTQ+ essays, 577–581
Liberia
  colonization/migration of former slaves, 152
  Russwurm migrates to, 153
Liebling, A. J., 352
Life, 353
Lim, Jeehyun, 634
Limbaugh, Rush, 412
Lindsey, Kay, *Black Woman*, 447
linguistic analysis, Slavic tradition, 555
Linnaeus, Carl, 67
Lippard, Lucy, 302, 306
Lippincott, Sara Jane Clarke. *See* Greenwood, Grace
literary comedy, Civil War period, 206–207
literary criticism
  academic periodicals, 347–348
  and New Criticism. *See* New Criticism
  newspaper columns, 287–289
literary magazines, 359–360
  before 1940, 338–346
  1940–70, 346–351
  digital era (since 1970), 351–360
  hybrid model, 358
  online, 359
  and universities, 357
literary postmodernism. *See* postmodernism, literary
literary theory and criticism, and the essay, 545–546
literary websites, 358
literature, and philosophy, 496–497, 505–506
little magazines, 211, 267–268, 337, 341–343
  See also small press
Little Review, 344–345
Llewellyn, Karl, 432
Locke, Alain, *New Negro*, 252–253, 256, 257, 259, 260, 651
London, Jack, 169
London Gazette, 33–34

Longfellow, Henry Wadsworth, 117–118
  Outre Mer, 221
Longmore, Paul K., 586–588
  Why I Burned My Book, 586, 587–588
Longstreet, Augustus Baldwin, 203
Look, 353
Lopate, Philip, 537–538, 613
  The Golden Age, 644–645
Lopez, Barry, 673–675
Lorde, Audre, 389, 619, 660, 661–662
Lorentz, Pare, 530
Los Angeles Review of Books, 359
Louisiana Purchase (1803), 69
Lowell, James Russell, 122, 206
Lowell Offering, 133
lynching, 159–160, 297, 479, 650
lyric essays, 465, 597–611

MacKinnon, Catharine, 436–437, 572–573
Madison, James, *The Federalist*, 53–60
magazines, popular, 114, 116
Magna Carta, 427
Mailer, Norman
  "Prisoner of Sex," 354–355
  Town Bloody Hall (1979), 355
Mailloux, Steven, 249
Mairs, Nancy, 565, 574–575, 589
Malcolm X, 383, 384
Man Ray, 364
Manifest Destiny, 71, 138
Mann, Horace, 86
Mann, Thomas, 374
Marcuse, Herbert, 372
  Essay on Liberation, 372–373
Marek, Jayne, 345
Margulis, Lynn, 483
Mark Twain's Library of Humor, 210
Marquis, Don, 285–286
  Lantern, 286
  Sun Dial column, 286
Marshall, Margaret, 275
Martínez, Rubén, 628–629
Marugg, Jim, 585
Marvel, Ike, 192
Marxist critics, 547–549
  See also neo- and post-Marxist theories
Marx/Marxism, 99, 450
Massachusetts Magazine, 35–36, 41–43
Massachusetts Review, 355
Mather, Cotton
  Account of the Method and Success of Inoculating the Small-Pox in Boston in New England, 22
  baroque style, 20
  Bonifacius: An Essay upon the Good (1710), 16–31
    Burder edition, 16
    influences on, 21
    style, 20–21
  on charity and religious societies, 28
  Christian Enlightenment and pan-Protestantism, 18–19, 24–25
  The Christian Philosopher (1720/21), 18, 22
  on evangelization, 28
  and Francke, 18, 19
  Magnalia, 21
  and millennialism, 30
  publications with "essay" in title, 21
  and "Reforming Societies," 29
  Royal Society fellow, 18
  as a scholar theologian, 18
  and the SPCK, 19
  on style, 20
  Thoughts for the Day of Rain, 22
  and universal relatedness, 26
Mather, Increase, 16
Mathews, John Joseph, *Talking to the Moon*, 404
Matthews, Brander, *Oxford Book of American Essays*, 110, 112–113, 192–193
Maurin, Peter, 173–175
  and Day, 175
  Easy Essays, *The Catholic Worker*, 173–174
  "Near Easton," 174–175
May, Henry F., 189, 190
McAllister, Agnes, 227
McCall's, 355
McCarthy, Jesse, 645
McCarthy, Mary, 275, 348, 380, 645
  "Artists in Uniform," 381–382
McCarthyism, 373–374, 414, 530
McClain, Elijah, 535
McClure, S.S, 341
McCord, Louisa, 138–139
McCune Smith, James, 221–222
McGill, Meredith L., 118
McKay, Claude, 264, 612
McKibben, Bill, 485
  "End of Nature," 485, 673
McSweeney's, 358
medium, and modern art, 301–304, 313
Mee, Charles, 589, 590–591
Mekas, Jonas, 364, 535–536
Melville, Herman
  "Hawthorne and His Mosses," 103
  humorous sketches, 206
  Moby-Dick, 124

memoirs, on illness and disability, 587–595
Menand, Louis, 278–279
Mencken, H. L., 282, 283, 298
  at the *Baltimore Sun*, 293–294, 296–297
  on civil rights and racial injustice, 297–298
  at the *Herald*, 293
  liberalism/libertarianism, 294–295
  literary criticism, 295–296
  on Locke's *New Negro*, 252–253
  Men versus the Man, 297–298
  Prejudices, 214
  works and career, overview of, 292–293
Menorah Journal, 365
mental illness memoirs, 590–593
Messenger, The, 115, 344, 650
metaphor, 246–247
#MeToo movement, 456–459
Midland, 348
migration, 612–626
Milam, Lorenzo, 585
millennialism, 30
Miller, Chanel, 458–459
Miller, J. Hillis, 558, 559
Miller, Nancy K., 568–569
  Bequest and Betrayal, 568–569
  Getting Personal, 569
Miller, Perry, 17
Millett, Kate, 443
Mims, Edwin, 268–269
Mingus, Charles, 323–324
Minhas, Priya, 621
minimalism, and music, 329
missionary texts, 227
Mist's Journal, 34
Mitchell, Donald Grant, 192
Mitchell, Maria, 478
Modern Language Association, 278
modernism, 462, 492
  See also poets, modern
modernist abstraction. *See* abstract art
Momaday, N. Scott, 404–405, 645, 671
Momaday, Navarre Scott, 388
Monroe, Harriet, 343–344
Monroe, James, 50–51
Montaigne, Michel de, 1, 129, 218, 395, 425, 426
  androgynous quality to voice, 577
  and Black American essayists, 646
  and the *dispositio*, 598
  Emerson and, 90
  Essais, 2
  genteel essayists and, 185–186
  women writers and, 565
  See also Emerson, Ralph Waldo

Moore, Marianne, 344
Moore, Michael, 531
Moraga, Cherríe, *This Bridge Called My Back*, 451–452, 636–638
Morley, Christopher, 284, 286, 291, 292
Morrison, Toni, 619
Morton, Thomas, *New English Canaan* (1637), 197–198
Morton, Timothy, 680
Mossell, Gertrude Bustill, 193–194
  "A Lofty Study," *Work of the Afro-American Women*, 193–194
Moten, Fred, 681
Moulton, William, 205
Mount Vernon/New Rochelle women's group. *See* Pat Robinson Group ("the Damned")
Mourning Dove, 401
Muir, John, 479
  on Emerson, 76
  Mountains of California, 479
  on Native Americans, 79
  nature writing
    contemporary critics on, 78–79
    environmental ethic, 77–78
    influences on, 76
    philosophy, 76–77
    Northern California, 62
multiculturalism, 616
Mulvey, Christopher, 223
Murdoch, Rupert, 423–424
Murray, Albert, 645
Murray, Anna, 154–155
Murray, Judith Sargent, "The Gleaner," 42–43
music, 314–333
  Black, 543, 659
  See also jazz and blues
Musil, Robert, 553
Myung Mi Kim, 468–469

Nabokov, Vladimir, 512
Nancarrow, Conlon, 319
Nancy, Jean-Luc, 497
Nardal, Jane, 260
narrative form, essay as, 291–292
narratology, 552, 555
Nasby, Petroleum V., 205
Nash, Roderick, *Wilderness and the American Mind*, 67
Nashville Agrarians. *See* Agrarianism/Agrarians
Nathan, George, 295
Nation, 275

on Agrarians, 271
Black essayists, 256
Greenberg writings in, 309
National Anti-Slavery Standard, 139
National Association for the Advancement of Colored People (NAACP), 244, 250, 650
national gaze, 220
National Park System, 78
National Review, 424
   See also Buckley, William F., Jr.,
National Urban League, 650
nationalism, Poe's resistance to, 117–118
nation-states, 367
Native Americans
  essays of place, 671
  experimental essay forms, 672
  humor, 211–212
  Muir and, 79
  nature writing, 66–67, 79–80
  newspapers/periodicals, 400–401
  Trickster Tales, 212
  See also Indigenous essays
nature writing, 61–80, 669–670, 671
  19th cent., 478
  hybrid form, 62–63
  and immersion, 673
  See also conservation; Kimmerer, Robin W.
Neal, Joseph C., *Charcoal Sketches*, 203
Negro Quarterly, 654
Nelson, Maggie, 597, 607–610
  Argonauts, 608–609
  Bluets, 608
  Red Parts, 608
neo- and post-Marxist theories, 560
neoliberalization, 456
neorealism, 435
neurology, 485
New Criticism, 266, 271, 275, 278–279, 545–546, 548, 552
New Deal politics, Buckley on, 414, 415, 416, 419–420
New England Company, 19, 29
New Journalism, 350–351, 645
  critics, 351
  feminism, 446
  Mailer and, 354–355
  new generic categories, 353
  profile piece, 351–352
  science essays, 483
New Left, 385–387
  activism, 372, 381, 387
  and gender issues, 453–454
  and the New York Intellectuals, 381

New Masses, 549, 654
New Mexico Quarterly Review, 344
New National Era, 157–158
New Negro ideology, 251–252, 260, 650
new science journalism, 483–484
New World Writing, 347
New York Age, 159
New York Evening Post, 290
New York Herald Tribune, 285, 319
New York Intellectuals, 380, 382, 552–555
  and sociodemocratic activism, 380–381
New York Review, 350, 359, 385, 563–564
New York Times, 289–290, 394
  columnists, 290–291
  Latinx writers, 634
  "The Stone," 562–563
New York Tribune, 116, 281, 284–285, 286, 289
New Yorker, 138
  columnists, 286
  comic essay tradition, 212–213, 214, 216
  hybrid science essays, 485
  Latinx writers, 631
  New Journalism, 351–352
  science essays, 480
  White at, 353–354
newspaper columns, 280–299
  Black press, 282–283
  See also editorials
newsreels, 530
Newton, Isaac, 18
Nezhukumatathil, Aimee, 488, 681–682
Nichols, Tom, 410–411
Nicol, Christina, 678–679
Nixon, Richard, 215
North Star, 155, 156
Norton, Mary Beth, 36
Nussbaum, Martha, 614–615
Nye, Edgar Wilson "Bill," 211

O'Brien, Mark, 585
Occom, Samson, 396–397
O'Hara, Frank, 466
"Old Bachelor, The," 38–39
Oliveros, Pauline, "Contribution of Women Composers," 328–329
Olson, Charles, 468
online documentaries and podcasts, science essays, 487
online feminist essays, 444–445
online magazines, 358, 359, 487
Opportunity, 193, 261, 650
  literary prize contests, 253–254
ordinary language philosophy, 494–495

Index

Orientalism, 231
Ortiz Cofer, Judith, 389
Overbye, Dennis, 483
Owen, Chandler, 650

Pagden, Anthony, 96
Paine, Thomas, 83, 339
pamphlet essays, feminist, 443
Paper Tiger, 533
Paris
   1848 revolution, journalism, 227
   Black writers, 234
Paris Review, 358
Parker, Dorothy, 213
Partch, Harry, 327–328
Partisan Review, 348, 380, 386, 548–549
   founders, 547
   postmodernist writers in, 515, 516–517
   Sontag in, 386
Parton, Sara Payson Willis. *See* Fern, Fanny
Passos, John Dos, 584
Pat Robinson Group ("the Damned"), 448–450
Paulding, James Kirke, 203
   Salmagundi (1807–08), 44, 201, 340
Peabody, Elizabeth, 134
   and Alcott, Temple School, 85
   Christian Examiner, 134
   The Dial, 89, 134
   "The Dorian Measure," 134
   kindergarten movement, 86, 134
   Record of a School, 85
peace movements, and travel essays, 226
Peirce, Charles Sanders
   "How to Make Our Ideas Clear," 236
   pragmatism, 236, 239, 240
   statistics, and semiotics, 239
   on truth, 239
Pennsylvania Gazette, "A Receipt for an Antifederalist Essay," 51
Pennsylvania Magazine, 38
Pérez-Rosario, Vanessa, 639
performativity and masquerade, 570
performativity and masquerade, gender, 569–570
periodical essay
   definition, 33
   vs. newspapers, 33
   See also specific names of periodicals
periodicals, American music, 315
personal essays, 188, 465
   and American colonization, 617–618
   and individualism, 621
   Latinx, 632–636

   on migration, 612–613, 614
   See also newspaper columns
pesticide industry, 480
Phelp, William Lyon, 213
Philadelphia
   colonial-era essay serials, 37
   essayists, 37
   and magazines, 339
Phillips, Adam, 601
Phillips, William, 547
philosophy essays, 490–508
photojournalism, 353
Pickens, William, 260
Pinckney, Darryl, 666
Plato, 461
Plato, Ann
   Essays, 131–132
   other works, 132
Playboy, 355–356, 579
Ploughshares (1971–), 357, 358
Plunkett, Erin, 562
Plutarch, and Mather, 21
podcasts, 487
Poe, Edgar Allan, 70, 114–128
   and Coleridge, 117, 124
   critical responses to work of Hawthorne, 102–103, 127
   editor of *Grahams Magazine*, 127
   essay as performance, 121–124
   essay fiction, 116, 124–126
   "How to Write a Blackwood Article," 125
   "Letter to B—," 102
   literary comedy, 206
   literary critic, 118–121, 126–128
   "The Literati of New York City," 120, 127
   and nationalism, 117–118
   "The Philosophy of Composition," 102, 120, 121–123
   "Poetic Principle," 102
   "The Purloined Letter," 120, 124
   "The Raven," 124
   Tales of the Grotesque and Arabesque, 102, 125
poet-critic, rise of modern, 461, 462–463
Poetry, 342, 343–344, 349
   hybrid model, 358
poetry, and the essay, 460–476
poets, art criticism, 306
poets, modern, shift in funding structures, 463
Point, The, 359, 564
Pokagan, Simon, *Red Man's Rebuke*, 398
polemical essayists, 292
polio, 585–586
Polio Chronicle, 584–585

politicization of the personal, 378–379, 390
Pollock, Jackson, 308
Pope, Alexander, 199
popular magazines, science essays, 478
Popular Mechanics, 487
Port Folio, 130
Posey, Alexander, 211, 400
possessive individualism, 621
postcolonial theory, 560
postmodernism, 501–502
postmodernism, literary, 509–523
Pound, Ezra, 337, 344, 462, 465
Powell, John Wesley, 62
   early career, 75
   expeditions of 1869 and 1871, 75
   Exploration of the Colorado River and Its Canyons (1895), 75–76
   family background and enlistment in Civil War, 75
   Geological Survey 1881–1894, 73
pragmatism, 249
   legal essays, 429–431
   Rorty and, 500–501, 506
pragmatists, 235, 236
Prairie Schooner, 481
"Prattler, The," 37–38
Prince, Gerald, *Narratology*, 555
Prince, Nancy, 228
prisons, 170
privacy, rights to, 438–439
professionalization of authorship, 115, 133, 346–347
   feminist essays, 445
   travel essays, 233
profile piece, 351–352
project essays, 23–24
protest poetics, 473
Protestantism, Anglo-Saxon, 613
pseudonyms, literary comedians, 206
psychoanalytic theory, 560
public music essays, 319–324
publicity puff piece, 352
Pynchon, Thomas, 515, 520

queer culture, essay films, 536
queer male writers, 577–581, 589
queer texts, 345–346
queer theory, 560, 570

race and racism. *See* Black essayists/writers; slavery
racism, disability oppression and, 586
   See also disability rights movement

racist theory, 138
radical feminists, Latina, 636–641
radical magazines, and censorship, 349
radical press, women writers, 135
Rahv, Philip, 547
Rainer, Yvonne, 534
Ramazani, Jahan, 460
Randolph, A. Philip, 650
Rankine, Claudia
   American Poets in the 21st Century, 472
   Citizen (2014), 3, 473–475, 597
   Don't Let Me Be Lonely, 473
   Just Us, 473
Ransom, John Crowe, 273, 275–276
   "Criticism, Inc," 265–266
   I'll Take My Stand, 269–272
   Land! 272–273
   New Criticism, 347
   and New Critics, 275
   in *Virginia Quarterly Review*, 273
Rascoe, Burton, 185, 281, 288–289
Ravitch, Diane, 616
Ray, Charles Bennett, 153
reader-response theory, 552
Reagan, Ronald, 393, 412, 414, 588
realism, in philosophy, 504
"Receipt." *See Pennsylvania Gazette*
Reconstruction (1865–1877), 157, 158, 650
Red Power movement, 402
Reed, Ishmael, 660
Reeve, Justice, 428
refugees, 620
   Arendt on, 365–367
   Pilgrims (first European), 621
regional magazines, 344
Rehabilitation Act, 1973, 586–587
Reich, Steve, 329–330
Renehan, Edward, 77–78
reportage, on juridical developments, 428
Repplier, Agnes, 188
   "Americanism," 111
   genteel essays, 193
   "Passing of the Essay," 291–292
Republican Party, 392–393, 410, 414
   See also conservatism
"Retailer, The," 39–40
Retallack, Joan, 468
Review of Contemporary Fiction, 520
Revolution, American, and science essayists, 478
Reznikoff, Charles, 473
"Rhapsodist, The," 39, 40
Rhodes, Richard, 480

Rhodes-Pitts, Sharifa, 657–658
Rice, Lincoln, *The Forgotten Radical Peter Maurin*, 173
Rich, Adrienne, 389–390, 566–567
   On Lies, 566–567
   "Split at the Root," 567
   Of Woman Born, 567
Richardson, Robert, 237
Richter, Hans, 362–365, 527, 531–532
   at CCNY, 364
   Dreams That Money Can Buy, 364, 365
   in *Film Culture*, 364–365
   "Film Essay: A New Type of Documentary Film," 362–363
   Ghosts before Breakfast (1928), 365
Rights of All, 153
Ripley, George and Sarah, 85
Robeson, Paul, 250, 530, 543
Rochberg, George, 328
Rodell, Fred, 433–434
Rodriguez, Richard, 633
   Brown, 633–634
   Days of Obligation, 633
   Hunger of Memory, 633
Rogers, Samuel, 45
Rogers, Will, 211
Rolling Stone, 352
Roosevelt, Franklin Delano, 585
Rorem, Ned, 330–331
Rorty, Richard, 393–394, 496–497, 498–503, 506
   Achieving Our Country, 394
   and Cavell, 502–503
   Philosophy and Social Hope, 394
   postdisciplinarity, 501
   and pragmatism, 500–501, 506
Rosenbaum, Jonathan, 537
Rosenberg, Harold, 311–312
Rosler, Martha, 534
Ross, Lilian, 350, 352
Royal Society of London
   Philosophical Transactions, 22
   publications, 22
Rubin, Joan Shelley, 281, 287
Rubin, Louis D., 269
Rukeyser, Muriel, 473
Russwurm, John Brown, 151–153

Sacks, Oliver, 485
Sagan, Carl, 481–482
   "Can We Know the Universe?" 481–482
   on marijuana, 482
Sagan, Dorion, 483
San Francisco, 356

Sanders, Elizabeth Elkins, 137
   Remarks on the "Tour around Hawaii," 137
   Tract on Missions, 137
Sanders-Mobley, Marilyn, 648
Santayana, George, 182, 242–244
   "Genteel Tradition in American Philosophy," 242
   on improvisational practice, 243
   "Philosophy of Travel," 243–244
   "Williams James," 242–243
Sante, Lucy, 580
Saturday Evening Post, 350
Saturday Review, 187, 288
   Deshiell on Gerould, 186–187
   Gerould on articles, 186
Saussure, Ferdinand de, 555
Savoy, Lauret E., 669, 673, 676
Scheiding, Oliver, 400
Schlag, Pierre, 434
Schlutz, Alexander, 117
School of New York Intellectuals. *See* New York Intellectuals
Schriber, Mary Suzanne, 227
Schuyler, George S., 214, 255, 256
   in *The American Mercury*, 214
   Black No More, 214
   on Fauset's novel, 250–251
Schweninger, Lee, 79
Science, 478
science essays, 477–489
   before the 20th cent., 478–479
   early 20th cent. activism, 479–480
   hybrid forms, 485–487
   mid-to-late 20th cent. idealists, 480–481
   new nature, 488
   new science journalism, 483–484
   postwar explainers, 481–483
Scientific American, 478, 482
Scribner's, 189, 274, 340
Secession, 344
Sedaris, David, 216
Sedgwick, Catharine Maria, 227
   Letters from Abroad, 222
   travel fiction, 222
Sedgwick, Eve, 570
Sedgwick, Ellery, III, 184, 187
self-culture. *See* Channing, William Ellery
semiotics, 552
Seneca Review, 486
Sewanee Review, 348, 357, 358
Sexton, Anne, 591
sexual assault. *See* #MeToo movement
sexuality, and gender, essay films, 536

Index

Shapiro, Karl, 349
Sheehy, Gail, 352
Shepherd, Jean, 215
Sherman, Stuart Pratt, 287–288
Sherwood, Margaret, 190
Shields, David, 517, 608
short stories, regional magazines, 344, 348
Show Magazine, 445
Shusterman, Richard, 249
Sigourney, Lydia Huntley, 131
   "On Domestic Employments," 131
   Girl's Reading Book (1837) and *Boy's Reading Book* (1839), 131
   Letters to Young Ladies, 131
   Moral Pieces, 131
Silko, Leslie Marmon, 405–406, 671
Sinclair, Upton, 529
   Cry for Justice: An Anthology of Social Protest, 169
   The Jungle, 175, 350
Sitney, P. Adams, 532
skepticism, 494–495, 506
slaveholders, and the Fugitive Slave Act, 156
slavery, 138, 431
   Fugitive Slave Act (1850), 226
   McCord on, 138–139
   slaveholders, 138
   transatlantic, 619–620
   See also abolitionist cause/movement; Douglass, Frederick; Emancipation Proclamation (1863)
Slavic formalism, 552
small press, 347
   See also little magazines
Smart Set, 295–296, 341
Smith, Bernard, 547, 548–549
Smith, Jack, 536
Smith, Melancton, 46, 47–48, 52
Smith, Seba, 206
Smith, Sydney, 100–101
Smith, Valerie, 448
Snitow, Ann, *Feminist Memoir Project*, 453
Snyder, John, 91
Sobel, Dava, 483
social and class barriers, science essays, 488
social justice, 166–170
social realism, 348
social sciences, 478
socialism, American, 379
   New York Intellectuals, 380
Socialist Party of America, 171, 381
Socialist Review, 391
Society for Promoting Christian Knowledge (SPCK), 19

Society for the Reformation of Manners, 19
Solnit, Rebecca, 444, 599
Sontag, Susan, 113, 348, 354
   Best American Essays, 554–555
   "Against Interpretation," 306–307
   "What's Happening in America?" 386–387
Southern Review, 275–276, 357
Soviet Union, and communism, 419–420
Spahr, Juliana, 473
specialized magazines, 348
Spectator, 22, 32, 198–199, 426
Spencer, Sharon, 514–515
Spiegel, Laurie, 332–333
Spirit of the Farmer's Museum and Lay Preacher's Gazette, The, 200
spiritual socialists, 167
Srinivasan, Amia, 458
stand-up comedians, 215–216
Stasi (East German secret service), 375
Steele, Richard, 20, 33–34
Stegner, Wallace, 72
Stein, Gertrude, 233, 245, 248, 345–346, 465
Steinbeck, John, 1–2
Steinem, Gloria, 355–356
   "Bunny's Tale," 445–447
   Outrageous Acts and Everyday Rebellions, 447
Sterne, Laurence, 426
Stevens, Wallace, 245, 247–248, 343, 466
Stevenson, Douglas C., 292
Stewart, Kathleen, 675, 680
Stewart, Maria, 135–136
Story, Joseph, 428–429
Stowe, Calvin, 226–227
Stowe, Harriet Beecher
   Sunny Memories of Foreign Lands, 226–227
   Uncle Tom's Cabin, 340
Stowe, William, 218
Strand, Paul, 530
structural film, 532
structuralism, 552, 555–556
Strunsky, Simeon, 290–291
Stuckey-French, Ned, 192, 194, 280
   American Essay in the American Century, 183–184, 185, 186
Students for a Democratic Society (SDS), 385
Sukenick, Ronald
   Bossa Nova fiction, 514–515
   "Fiction in the Seventies," 515–516
   "Thirteen Digressions," 515
Sullivan, Anne, 170, 582
Sun (New York newspaper), 138
Sunpapers, 282, 294–295, 297
Supreme Court, "Supremacy Clause," 55

Surrealism, 345, 543
Swedenborg, Emanuel, 172–173
Swift, Jonathan
  Letter to a Young Gentleman Lately Entered into Holy Orders (1721), 20
  A Project for the Advancement of Religion (1709), 23–24

Tagore, Rabindrinath, 615
Talese, Gay, "Frank Sinatra Has a Cold," in *Esquire*, 352
Tall, Deborah, 465, 598, 599
Tanner, Henry Ossawa, 228
Tarbell, Ida, 479
taste, individual, 310
  and visual art, 301, 307, 308–309, 312
Tate, Allen, 267, 277
  I'll Take My Stand, 269–272
Tate, Malcoum, 592–593
Tatler, The
  female personae, 36
  format, 34
  Steele and, 33
Taussig, Charlotte, 260
television, 520–521, 531
  See also Image-Fiction
Temple School, 85
Tensas, Madison, 203
Third Cinema, 539–540
Thomas, Isaiah, 339
Thomas, Lewis, 481
Thompson, Clifford, 667
Thomson, Mortimer, "Doesticks," 204
Thomson, Virgil, 319, 321–322
  "Why Composers Write How," 322
Thoreau, Henry David, 81, 82, 94, 478
  "Autumnal Tints," 104–105
  and Cavell, 495–496, 497
  The Dial, 88–89
  and Emerson, 88, 104
  and Fuller, 88, 93
  influences on, 65
  "The Natural History of Massachusetts," 89
  nature writing, 84
  Walden, 65, 93–94, 478, 494
Thorn, William J., 175
Thurber, James, 214
Tocqueville, Alexis de, 310, 622
Toomer, Jean, 263, 346
tourist gaze, 219–220
  aesthetic stance, 221
  Brown on, 226
  contradictions of, 222

Town Bloody Hall (1979), 355
Transcendentalism, 81–95, 494, 495–496, 497
transgender essayists, 580
translations, international websites, 356
translations, magazines, 348
travel essays, 218–227
travel fiction, 222
travel journals, nature writing, 66–72
Trent, William Peterfield, "On Translating the Odes of Horace," 113
Tribune, New York, 140–141
Trilling, Lionel, 380, 381, 552, 553, 645
Trinh T. Minh-ha, 531
Trotter, William Monroe, 650, 651
Tuskegee Institute, 161, 163
Twain, Mark, 200, 205–206
  antagonism toward racism in America, 210
  comic lectures, 207
  early essays and humor, 208
  on first modern transatlantic cruise, 230
  in *Galaxy* magazine, 210
  Goldsmith's Friend Abroad Again, 201
  Innocents Abroad, 209, 229, 230–231
  as "The Moralist of the Main," 208
  "Only a N—r," in *Buffalo Express*, 210
  "Plymouth Rock and the Pilgrims," 210
  Roughing It, 209
  series for the *Alta California*, 208–209
  at *Territorial Enterprise*, 208
  Tramp Abroad, A, 209
  "United States of Lyncherdom," 210

Ulrichs, Karl Heinrich, 577–578
Unger, Roberto, 434–435
Unitarian literary society, new idea of "woman," 140
United States Fish Commission, 73
United States Geological Survey, 73
United States (US), Constitution, "the People," 46–47
Universal Negro Improvement Association and African Communities League (UNIA), 650–651
universalism, 615–616
universities
  genteel essay tradition, 190
  and law schools, 428
  literary departments, and poetry, 463–464
  and literary magazines, 357
University of California, 390–391
urbanization, and rise of the leisure class, 340
Urry, John, 219
utopianism, 174, 175

Valle, Victor, 628–629
Vanity Fair, 281
Vidal, Gore, 412, 645
video essays, 533–534
Videofreex, 533
Vietnam War, 385, 482
Villavicencio, Karla Cornejo, 631–632
   Undocumented Americans, 631–632
Virginia Quarterly Review, 273, 276, 347–348, 357
Vizenor, Gerald, 408
Voice, 650–651

Wadsworth, Benjamin, 24
Wadsworth, James, 48
Walker, Alice, 389, 660
   In Search of Our Mothers' Gardens, 662–663
Walker, Nicole, 678
Wall, Cheryl A., 149, 150, 253, 297, 562
   On Freedom, 645–646
   on Jordan, 663
Wallace, David Foster, 520–523
Wallach, Alan, 219–220
Wallack, Nicole, 562
Walters, Wendy, 667
Wampole, Christy, 562–563
Wang, Esmé Weijun, 590–593
Warburton, Theresa, *Shapes of Native Nonfiction*, 408–409, 672
Ward, Artemus, comic essay tradition, 207
Ward, Nathanial, 207
   The Simple Cobler of Aggawam in America, 198
   "Trater's Gate," 207
Warhol, Andy, 536
Warren, Austin, 545–546
Warren, Robert Penn, 268, 274, 275–276
Warren, Samuel, 439
Washington, Booker T., 160–163, 650
   Atlanta Compromise, 162
   "Awakening of the Negro," 162–163
   "Taking Advantage of Our Disadvantages," 161
   Tuskegee Institute, 161, 163
   Up from Slavery, 162
Washington Post, 424
Washuta, Elissa, 672
   Shapes of Native Nonfiction, 408–409, 672
Waters, Anne, 404
Waters, John, "A Little Old Lady Passes Away," 186
websites, translations, 356
Webster, Noah, 339

Weekly Advocate, 153
   See also Colored American
Weil, Simone, 380
Wellek, René, 545–546
Welles, Orson, 3, 536–537
Wells, Ida B., 158–160, 479
   Free Speech, 159
   newspaper columns, 282
   Red Record, 283
   Southern Horrors, 159–160
West, Cornel, 177–181, 249
   "The Black Church and Socialist Politics," 180
   Cornel West Reader (1999), 178–179
   Democracy Matters, 179–180
   on Du Bois, 178
   essays and interviews in magazines, 178
   jazz and blues, 324
   Keeping Faith: Philosophy and Race in America, 179
   Prophetic Fragments (1988), 178–179
   "We Socialists," 180
Wharton, Edith, 233
Wheatley, Phillis, 258
White, E. B., 354
   "Death of a Pig," 214
   at *Harper's*, 354
   Here Is New York, 214
   at *New Yorker*, 353–354
   "Once More to the Lake," 214
White, Gilbert, 66
Whitman, Walt, 77, 91, 242
   "Europe," 97
   Leaves of Grass, "Preface," 103, 106
Wideman, John Edgar, 664–665
Wilde, Oscar, 578
Will, George, 410–411, 423
Willard, Samuel, 15
William, W. H. A., 295, 296
Williams, Patricia, 437
Williams, Raymond, *The Country and the City*, 66
Williams, Terry Tempest, 676
Williams, William Carlos, 465
Willis, Nathaniel P., 141, 143
Willis, N. P., 205
Wilson, Douglas, 182
Wilson, Edmund, 645
Wilson, Edward O., 482
Wimsatt, W. K., 277–278
Winchell, Mark Royden, 274
Winnemucca, Sarah, 80
Wittgenstein, Ludwig, 493–494, 503–504

Wojnarowicz, David, 580
Wolf, Christa, 375–377
   City of Angels, 375, 376
   Medea, 376
   One Day a Year, 375–376
   What Remains, 375
Wolfe, Tom, 350, 353, 483
Woman's Record, 132
women
   artists. *See* female artists
   Fuller on, 92, 140
   New Woman era, 233
   See also feminism/feminist essays
women writers
   Black. *See also specific names of Black women writers*
      on male violence, 195
   The Dial, 89
   genteel essay tradition, 191–193
women's home-making magazines, 355
women's movement
   and civil rights movement, 389
   Davis on, 144–145
   Mailer and, 354–355
   McCord on, 139
   Una, 144
   See also feminism/feminist essays
Wong, Alice, 591
Woodbridge, Elisabeth, 187
Woodward, John, 22
Woodward, Josiah, *Account of the Rise and Progress of the Religious Societies in the City of London* (1698), 23
Woolf, Virginia, 567–568
   "On Being Ill," 588
   "Melodious Meditations," 186, 189
Woolson, Constance Fenimore, travel essays and fiction in *Harper's*, 231
working class
   readership, Eugene V. Debs, 170
   See also social justice
Works Progress Administration (WPA), 530
World War I
   and genteel essayists, 187–188
   Harlem Hellfighters, 250
   travel essays as expatriate essays, 233–234
World War II, science idealists and, 480
World-Telegram, 281, 289
Worster, Donald, 76
Wright, Francis, 135
Wright, Richard, 543, 653, 654, 657
   "Blueprint," 652–653
Wright, William, 427
writers' workshops and apprenticeships, 346–347
writing, and colonization, 618
writing, philosophy as kind of, 508

Yale Review, 288, 563
Yale School, 558–559
Yong, Ed, 487
Young, Stark, 268
Young, Stephanie, 473
Young, Thomas Daniel, 276
Yusoff, Kathryn, 668, 670

Zinneman, Fred, 530
Zitkála-Šá, 80, 398
   "Why I Am a Pagan," 398
Zwarg, Christina, 227
Zyzzyva (1985), 356